TEACHING LANGUAGE AND LITERATURE

SECOND EDITION

TEACHING

LANGUAGE

AND

LITERATURE

GRADES SEVEN–TWELVE

SECOND EDITION

WALTER LOBAN

MARGARET RYAN

JAMES R. SQUIRE

87187

HARCOURT, BRACE & WORLD, INC.
New York / Chicago / San Francisco / Atlanta

COPYRIGHTS AND ACKNOWLEDGMENTS

ELIZABETH COATSWORTH BESTON: for "To Think" by Elizabeth Coatsworth.

DOUBLEDAY & COMPANY, INC.: for "The Sloth," copyright 1950 by Theodore Roethke, from *The Collected Poems of Theodore Roethke*. Reprinted by permission of Doubleday & Company, Inc.

CONSTANCE GARLAND DOYLE and ISABEL GARLAND LORD: for "Do You Fear the Wind" by Hamlin Garland.

FABER & FABER, LTD.: for "Macavity: The Mystery Cat" by T. S. Eliot. From *Old Possum's Book of Practical Cats* by T. S. Eliot. Copyright 1939 by T. S. Eliot; renewed, 1967, by Esme Valerie Eliot.

HARCOURT, BRACE & WORLD, INC.: for "Macavity: The Mystery Cat" by T. S. Eliot. From *Old Possum's Book of Practical Cats*, copyright, 1939, by T. S. Eliot; renewed, 1967, by Esme Valerie Eliot. Reprinted by permission of Harcourt, Brace & World, Inc. For "Primer Lesson" by Carl Sandburg, from *Slabs of the Sunburnt West* by Carl Sandburg, copyright, 1920, by Harcourt, Brace & World, Inc.; renewed, 1948, by Carl Sandburg. Reprinted by permission of the publisher.

HARVARD UNIVERSITY PRESS: for "Blazing in Gold and Quenching in Purple" by Emily Dickinson. Reprinted by permission of the publishers and the Trustees of Amherst College from Thomas H. Johnson, Editor, *The Poems of Emily Dickinson*, Cambridge, Mass.: The Belknap Press of Harvard University Press, Copyright, 1951, 1955, by The President and Fellows of Harvard College.

DAVID HIGHAM ASSOCIATES, LTD.: for "The Tide in the River" by Eleanor Farjeon.

HILL AND WANG, INC.: for "The Story-Teller" and "Former Barn Lot" by Mark Van Doren, from *Collected and New Poems 1924–1963* by Mark Van Doren. Copyright © 1963 by Mark Van Doren. Reprinted by permission of Hill and Wang, Inc.

THE AUTHORS

Walter Loban is Professor of Education and Supervisor of the Teaching of English at the University of California, Berkeley. He has taught junior and senior high school English in Minnesota and Illinois; college English, humanities, and education at Northwestern University, the University of Minnesota, and the University of California at Berkeley. He is engaged in research on the study of language development in children from kindergarten through grade 12, a study sponsored by the United States Office of Education. In 1967 he was awarded the David Russell Award for Distinguished Research by the National Council of Teachers of English.

Margaret Ryan is now retired from the University of California at Berkeley, where she had been supervisor of the teaching of English since 1936. Before that she had been a teacher in the demonstration school at the University and in charge of the speech improvement program for student teachers in all departments there. She is author of *Teaching the Novel in Paperback, Macmillan, 1963.*

James R. Squire, now a book publishing executive, was Executive Secretary of the National Council of Teachers of English from 1960 to 1967, and Professor of English at the University of Illinois from 1959 to 1968. He has taught English at every level from sixth grade through graduate school, and has served as supervisor of student teachers, and associate editor of a teacher education program. From 1963 to 1967 he directed the National Study of High School English Programs, sponsored by the National Council of Teachers of English and the University of Illinois, and supported by the United States Office of Education. In 1967 he received the first Executive Committee Award given by the National Council for distinguished national and international contributions to the teaching of English.

FOREWORD

Recent and continuing efforts to improve the teaching of English have helped to establish priorities of instruction appropriate for the student of today. Central to these developments has been an awareness that ours is both a content and a skills subject; that the internal relationship between these two dimensions of English has been made more explicit by new understandings about the imaginative and linguistic growth of young people and about the nature of their thinking processes.

Such developments have reinforced our belief, stated in the opening sentences of the first edition of this text: at the heart of the problem of teaching English lies the need for integrating purpose, content, and method. The *why* of English must be related to the *what* and the *how*; furthermore, neither *what's-to-be-done* nor *how-it's-to-be-done* can be determined independently; integrity of purpose, content, and method should guide the planning of the English curriculum.

Our organization now, as before, is designed to clarify the relationship among these three aspects of teaching English. We have modified the arrangement slightly for this revision; we believe the new four-part organization is clearer and simpler:

Language, Thought, and Feeling introduces basic concepts about the nature and process of language, about the place of usage and sentence structure, and about the importance of logical and imaginative thinking in the English program.

Understanding and Communication directs attention to the problems of the student as listener and viewer, speaker, writer, and reader.

Appreciation first presents the basic approaches to all literature, then discusses specific ways to stimulate student response to drama, poetry, and the popular arts.

Values considers the examined life as the ultimate purpose of studying language and literature.

Each of these sections ends with suggestions for evaluating achievement in the areas discussed, and with one or more illustrative Units.

The individual chapters also relate purpose, content, and method. Each is divided into two parts; "Perspective" presents a discussion with a point of view about the content to be taught—the essential subject matter, the insights needed by the teacher, the philosophical and psychological problems involved. "The

Teaching Problem" discusses strategies of instruction and gives directions for many "Suggested Learning Experiences."

As before, the prologue, "Teacher and Learner," considers the English teacher in relation to students in a rapidly changing culture, and the epilogue, "Program and Plan," gives specific ways of organizing lessons, units, and curricula.

Readers familiar with the original *Teaching Language and Literature* will recognize this revision as marked not by abrupt change but by amendment, extension, and elaboration of ideas in the first edition:

> The study of language is reinforced by a new chapter describing the English language and the factors that influenced its development. The presentation includes a discussion of the new grammars and their application in the classroom.
>
> The inductive method of teaching poetry is discussed, with specific poems used to illustrate the method.
>
> A new section on television as a medium gives special attention to its influence on our environment.
>
> A new Unit, "Humanities for the Seventies," suggests ways to increase the appeal of the curriculum to nonacademic pupils.
>
> Increased attention is given to applying the insights of modern rhetorical studies to the teaching of composition.
>
> Ideas for educating the disadvantaged pupil are presented in many chapters—suggestions for teaching speakers of nonstandard dialects, for introducing appropriate literary selections written by black as well as white American writers, and for using source material helpful in a variety of classrooms.
>
> "Program and Plan" now includes descriptions of experimental programs being developed by pilot curriculum centers.
>
> The influence and use of dramatics, television, films, and recordings as part of the modern English program are emphasized throughout the text.

Teaching Language and Literature is flexible; it need not be read in the order of its presentation, even though the inner logic of our subject has determined the organization of the book. Depending upon the reader's purpose, he may begin at any point of interest—perhaps with the analysis of planning and curriculum, perhaps with written expression or poetry. Nor is the book intended only for use in college classes on methods and curriculum in English. Other uses are readily apparent:

> as a help to curriculum committees charged with reassessing their programs in English
>
> as a guide to study groups interested in a particular aspect of English, such as grammar, unit planning, inductive teaching, or the teaching of poetry

as a tool for the continuing education of teachers of English in a particular school

as a ready desk reference for the experienced teacher

The index, the table of contents, and the locational aids within each chapter have been planned to encourage flexibility of use. We have endeavored to write a book helpful to the beginning teacher yet of interest to the experienced teacher as well.

In the final analysis, of course, no book on curriculum or method is so important in determining the caliber of instruction as is the teacher's personal philosophy, a philosophy that never remains static but grows as the teacher grows. The choices open to a teacher of English are many; each will teach what he thinks important. Thus it is essential that every teacher know *what* he teaches, *how* he can best teach it, and *why* it must be taught. In no other way can he foresee and utilize the teachable moments that occur daily in the classroom.

W. L.
M. R.
J. R. S.

CONTENTS

ONE:
LANGUAGE, THOUGHT, AND FEELING

Language is a highly personal and extremely flexible method of reacting to environment. In the individuality and the flexibility of language lie both its power and its complexity. This chapter presents a classroom emphasis on understanding language as a dynamic process—an understanding basic to precise thought and controlled feeling.

Basic to using a language with discrimination is a reasonable understanding of its history and structure, as well as its regional and social variations. This chapter outlines the content that seems essential for the secondary curriculum today.

Effectiveness in oral and written expression depends upon ability to relate the forms of language to the idea and the communication situation. This chapter calls for a balanced program based on research in methodology, the studies of modern linguists, and the experience of successful teachers.

Each individual's success in perceiving relationships, making judgments, or solving problems is largely dependent on his ability to reason objectively. Young people need to detect the fallacies in their own thinking as they try to develop sound habits of thinking. The chapter stresses the need for disciplined control of irrational impulses that interfere with objective thinking.

Education based solely on logic fails because of the nature of man. Reason and imagination are not two different kinds of thinking but complementary elements of a single dimension; both are necessary to power over language and appreciation of literature. A balance between the two is the aim of instruction, and this chapter speaks for a classroom emphasis on imagination without discounting the importance of sound conclusions and intellectual achievement.

TWO:
UNDERSTANDING
AND COMMUNICATION

Listening is the principal way of receiving language in our personal and business lives; listening plus viewing is the way the majority of the public receive news. This chapter stresses the importance of objectivity and logic in deciding what to accept as factual, the influence of television on the entire society, and the right and responsibility of the public to demand the best in journalistic tradition.

The spoken word is the main bridge between the individual and his fellow man. This chapter describes a program based on realistic small-group settings for short oral talks and class discussion as a major speech activity.

Growth in power over written expression depends upon the improvement of clear, orderly thinking about matters within the writer's experience. To improve his skill, the pupil must grapple with the expression of his own ideas. He must have ideas to express, a genuine reason for expressing them, and a desire to communicate them effectively. Granted such conditions, the teacher can help pupils with organizing and presenting feeling and thought, as well as with the necessary conventions of punctuation, capitalization, spelling, and handwriting.

No simple formula will ever be discovered for improving reading comprehension. This chapter presents ways to help junior and senior high school students in a complex task, comprehending the printed word. These ways include diagnosis, techniques to improve specific difficulties, and the strategies of classroom instruction.

THREE: APPRECIATION

Ability to comprehend fact and narrative is not enough. Appreciation can develop only when the reader learns to respond emotionally as well as intellectually to many kinds of literature. Permanent taste can be developed only as the result of carefully guided sequences of reading experiences over a period of time. Ways of organizing class, group, and individual instruction are discussed in this chapter as are methods of developing attitudes and abilities.

Appreciating drama and poetry depends upon special reading skills to an extent not true of prose, so much more familiar to young readers. Poetry uses language in exceptional ways. Drama, too, exacts new reading skills. Since both literary forms are written to be heard, both require attention to the development of skills in oral interpretation.

Appreciating the popular arts requires an understanding of the media as well as of the individual presentations themselves. Bombarded by the extravagant outpourings of the mass media, today's youth needs planned guidance in developing standards for judging and responding. This chapter identifies ways of using the media in the classroom, of teaching the essential facts about the media, and of deepening students' interests and tastes in these popular arts.

FOUR: VALUES

Discriminating among values is the architectural capstone toward which this book has been building. Just as it is impossible to separate effective thinking

from strength of character, so is it impossible to establish durable values
without discriminating choice. Good taste and a zest for living depend ultimately upon some degree of coherence in the total style of living.

The art of living depends finally upon the values by which decisions are
made, values that have been thoughtfully examined and judged. The English
program rests, ultimately, upon a program for examining and judging values.

TEACHING LANGUAGE AND LITERATURE

SECOND EDITION

TEACHER AND LEARNER

THE TEACHER VIEWS HIS TASK

Each of us brings to the classroom an image of himself as a teacher of English. Whether one has taught for many years or is just beginning, his conception of his role governs his expectations and determines his actions in any school situation.

What is the source of these conceptions? Primarily, personal experience. Many of us select English as a career because of youthful contacts with teachers we admired and respected. Such direct experiences—whether in one's family, in secondary school, or in college—provide us with a certain image of teaching. Our impressions are supplemented and reinforced by observing teachers in the community, by personal friendships, by reading, and by comments in conversation. Ultimately, of course, experience, first as a student teacher and later as faculty member, forces us to test our images and to modify and expand our conceptions of the role. In the beginning, however, when a new teacher attempts to approximate the theoretical model he has created, he must eliminate many inadequacies in his understanding of the nature of education and the role of the teacher.

Preconceptions are not inherently bad provided they are subject to amelioration and change with practical experience. Some conception of role is inevitable. How else can teachers establish standards against which to measure their effectiveness? A mind that reaches a professional teaching career as a *tabula rasa* lacks purpose and dedication. But a mind that fails to change when faced with the realities of fact is one that does not grow. The role of the teacher appears quite different from the front of the classroom than it does from the rear.

Perhaps no greater challenge faces the beginner than the task of testing and modifying his theoretical model of the English teacher's role. Personal memories of "good" teachers are not always reliable guides. Such images become cloudy over the years, particularly when reconstructed by a student whose very sensitivity to language and literature distinguished his observations from those of his classmates. Beginning teachers usually find difficulty, too, in distinguishing their responsibilities as undergraduate students from those as teachers in secondary schools. Whereas a college student places stress on certain elements of content, valuable and delightful purely as a part of knowledge, the secondary-school teacher must consider how content can be

1

learned and how pupils are to be prepared. Thus the shifts in perception that occur as one enters the profession have a vital influence on each individual's outlook. Few serious students of the educative process pass through this period without considerable soul searching, relying often on the wisdom of experienced associates when uncertain of their own perceptions.

The ideal teacher of English is one whose liberal education has freed him to lead a harmonious, well-balanced life. He has been liberated from those accidental restrictions—the circumstances of birth and environment—that narrow personal vision. The liberally educated teacher of English is one whose feelings, imagination, and intellect have been fused into the stable poise that enables him to grapple with essential and ultimate questions of experience. He sees more clearly than most how ends and means are related, how outer symbols shadow forth the inner truths of existence, and how choices reflect the values—conscious or unconscious—an individual accepts.

Such a teacher clarifies in his own mind and in the minds of his students the values to be gained from studying language and literature. This requires a complex equilibrium of many qualities and skills, but four characteristic outlooks may be identified. In the sections immediately following, the authors present their own viewpoint, the matrix that gives shape to the concepts of teaching in this book.[1]

The English teacher has clarified his viewpoint about human nature. He may be orthodox in his religious beliefs and explain man's imperfections by a fall from grace. He may be a humanist and view the evils of human behavior as partly the result of adverse environment and partly of man's heredity as a creature of the natural world. But whatever his religious or philosophical stand, the English teacher does not, like Machiavelli, accept the deceitful, cowardly, and greedy aspects of man as the essence of his nature. Nor does he, like some of Rousseau's disciples, veer to the opposite extreme and view man as innately good, lacking only the freedom to dispel obstacles to wisdom and virtue. Somewhere between these extremes, teachers of English create their own over-all design and their daily strategies for guiding those they teach. Like Thomas Jefferson, they swear hostility against all forms of tyranny over the mind of man, but like T. H. Huxley, they see their work as that of a gardener in perpetual warfare with weeds and wildness, an effort never intended to bring perfection.

But if the English teacher does not presume to promise utopias, he does expect to help pupils think clearly, communicate effectively, and feel keenly. To the extent that these goals are accomplished, he believes other desirable ends of education will inevitably follow. And this view—neither sentimental

---

[1] The four points of view presented here as characteristic of the ideal teacher of English might be applied to other teachers as well. However, it is our contention that in science and mathematics, the social studies, and the fine or useful arts, additional considerations alter the relationships among these points and extend them in various directions of emphasis. These four represent a crucial quartet that must be kept in balance by the teacher of English.

nor pessimistic—influences both curriculum and methods of instruction in English.

The English teacher has clarified his point of view about thinking. The cruciality of clear thinking in achieving the goals of the English program requires each teacher to sharpen his perception of the relationships among thinking, language, and literature.

What is thinking? We know it is an activity of the nervous system, particularly of the higher brain centers, but this is not very helpful. We may get further, perhaps, by asking why human beings think. Although not the whole explanation, adjustment of the individual for the sake of survival must be considered one dominant function of thought. By thinking, an individual adjusts to his environment, both external and internal; thinking is, at its foundations, essential to human life. Jerome S. Bruner and others have pointed out that thinking enables man to classify objects and to reduce the complexity of his environment.[2] Thinking alleviates the necessity of constant relearning—presumably to conserve energy needed for higher levels of existing—and enables the thinker to estimate in advance appropriate and inappropriate actions. This future-oriented aspect of thinking allows the individual an opportunity for prior adjustment. Thinking helps him know what things are worth his attention and, lest he break down in confusion, what things may safely be ignored. Thus thinking becomes a means of maintaining equilibrium. Yet this cannot be a static equilibrium: growth and change are also part of existence, and curiosity, inseparable from thinking, prevents us from adjusting too well.

Language is not essential to thought. Thinking can be done without verbal symbols—witness Helen Keller before she learned to use words. But language makes possible infinitely more precise and rapid thinking. One way to see the relationship between thinking and language is to study man's capacity for making distinctions. Poison oak differs from maple leaves; proteins offer some advantages over animal fats. Making and using classifications is an important aspect of thinking, and language enables man to maintain his classifications against the confusion and flux of living.

According to John Dewey,[3] language, although it is not thought, is necessary for any high development of thought and communication. Dewey sees words as *fences* that select and detach meanings from what would otherwise be a vague blur, as *labels* that retain and store meanings, and as *vehicles* for transfer and reapplication to new situations. But words have another important aspect; they are organizational instruments as well. Not just indicative of a single meaning, words "also form sentences in which meanings are organized in relation to one another."

But thinking is more than the means by which individuals adjust in

---

[2] Jerome S. Bruner, Jacqueline J. Goodnow, and George B. Austin, *A Study of Thinking* (New York: Wiley, 1957).

[3] John Dewey, *How We Think* (Boston: Heath, 1909; rev. 1933), p. 232.

order to survive. The speed and competence of language make possible such a fine state of equilibrium that human energies need not be entirely consumed in charting a mid-passage between breakdown and stagnation. It is this freedom from animal struggle for survival, this extra dividend of release, that counts most heavily in teaching children and adolescents to use language with power. Thinking becomes reason, to which Alfred North Whitehead assigns a function: the art of life—to live, to live well, and to live better.[4] Through the arts of language—all based upon effective reasoning that transcends the need to outwit the adverse forces of nature—pupils assume their heritage as human beings. They can make choices among ethical and esthetic values; they can weigh and consider, sifting truth from falseness; they can help to organize society on a foundation of wisdom rather than on one of blind authority, class, and raw power.

The English teacher has clarified his point of view on the nature of his task. The secondary-school teacher of English is in the classroom to help pupils shape and order their thoughts and experiences. The more clearly he understands his commitment to the principle of lucidity and coherence, the more skillfully he will play his role as protagonist. But the English classroom involves exceptionally complex forces and tensions in the drama of chaos versus structure.

The attempt to give a perfect order to English, to make it a discipline, has lured many earnest and able teachers. Yet the real need in English is "to shift from a closed body of content to open inquiry, to enable young people to address themselves to cogent questions and thus to the quest for meaning."[5] To help pupils shape and order their thoughts a teacher needs to be concerned with dynamic development rather than pre-organized information, with process fully as much as with content. The discipline needs to be in the teacher's mind; the discipline is a territory to be explored but the exact paths to be covered—and the order in which they are to be covered—**vary** with different pupils from day to day and year to year.

A dead order can be as perilous as vitality without order. To avoid either extreme, the teacher of English must live dangerously, in the sense that all instruction is a dynamic equilibrium, a delicate harmony of many complex elements. But just as one is most aware of life when he is most in danger, so is teaching most exhilarating when it requires an alert accommodation of many unexpected and new elements. Each new discovery opens unforeseen possibilities; each new idea leads to many more. Actually there can be no one ideal English teacher; the paths of language and literature are so varied and numerous. What each can attempt is a dynamic sense of order applied to the study of a rich and complex subject.

Composers order the dissonance of sound and bring forth melodies and

---

[4] Alfred North Whitehead, *The Function of Reason* (Boston: Beacon, 1958), p. 8.
[5] Charles Weingartner, "English for What?" in *English and the Disadvantaged,* ed. by Edward R. Fagan (Scranton, Pa.: International Textbook, 1967), p. 18.

harmonies to express what cannot be put into words; scientists search for order in the universe and find structures to reduce the abrupt and the obscure; teachers of English seek to create in pupils the harmonies of clear, orderly thinking, the controlled resonances of emotional response and lucid expression, that give meaning to life. Both chaos and sterile order may be combated, so the English teacher feels, by helping pupils free themselves from crooked thinking, blurred communication, and dull, sodden feeling-tone.

The English teacher has clarified his point of view on how to relate human nature and his task. In so doing, the secondary-school teacher considers adolescents and how they learn. Because of his familiarity with literature and his understanding of its insights into human behavior, he is unlikely to accept overly simple generalizations about learning or to expect infallible recipes. Nevertheless, the formulation of broad instructional principles, complex though they may be, requires a place in the thinking of every teacher. Indeed, it is essential to realize the importance of selecting classroom procedures consistent with what is known about learning, if one is to rise above the limitations imposed by specific techniques and is to continue to grow as a teacher. The teacher must strive for an intellectualization about method—an intellectualization placing theoretical concerns central in his viewpoint. Such an achievement safeguards the teacher against blindly accepting specific techniques and "definitive" answers to instructional problems and invests him with the personal resources needed for creating procedures consistent with his own philosophy and theory of learning.

The principles of learning summarized in the next few pages suggest the concept of method in English from which the procedures described in this book have grown. Each teacher must develop his own point of view if he is to assess procedures recommended by others and to create appropriate procedures of his own; such a point of view will come to the English teacher only as he learns to relate what he knows about learning to what he knows about language and literature.

THE WAYS OF LEARNING

Certainly the whole domain of educational psychology cannot be summarized here, nor would the rest of this volume suffice for that growing subject. What is possible, however, is a statement of the basic principles influencing the choice of methods recommended in this book. This matrix of learning theory may be summarized under five headings:

> motivation and involvement
> organization and relationships
> process as distinguished from product
> sound evaluation
> individual differences

What has seemed to us of crucial importance in each of these aspects of instruction is presented below, together with a few illustrations of how we have used them in this book.

MOTIVATION AND INVOLVEMENT   Often in this book we speak of *will* or *volition,* terms we use interchangeably. Will power is energy through which an individual chooses and carries out plans of action toward some goal. When strong desire to learn is part of an instructional situation, learning almost certainly occurs; when indifference or perfunctory efforts predominate, learning is always meager. Without persistent, purposeful, and selective effort, learning cannot be efficient. To be purposeful, the learner must accept the goal as his own; otherwise his motivation will be weak or sporadic. To be selective, the learner must have help in identifying those details or major features of the situation that hold the key to understanding. Thus there is an important relation between purpose and selection, a matter of economy in learning.

The first step in economical learning is to establish a goal. The pupil will select and learn the responses that lead to the goal as he perceives it. Then, after each attempt, the learner should gauge his success by references to the goal, adapting his responses in the light of this evaluation. The word *adapt* is of crucial significance because the reason for learning is transfer: learning equips a pupil with broad patterns of behavior, not just with one-to-one relationships. For example, the identical situation—*doesn't* for *don't* in "The calf don't want his milk" or the Mississippi as freedom symbol in *Huckleberry Finn* —may never, in a pupil's entire lifetime, recur in exactly the same context. What is transferred, whether grammatical accuracy or alertness to literary symbolism, will radiate to new situations—provided the teacher arranges for the same skills and concepts to reappear in various ways, embedded in numerous interest-compelling contexts. Students need to see the new in the old and the universal in the particular, organizing and reorganizing them. The contexts for such transfer of learning may be wide-ranging; creative dramatics, a succession of literary selections, home-made classroom films, and motivated discussions or compositions.

Goals and purposes must be clearly understood, not only with respect to the broad pattern of response but also with regard to significant details of performance. Because time spent in drilling perfunctorily on exercises is wasted, teachers should convert some of this time to creating an interest in improvement. There can be no real development of language power except through the general quickening, maturing, and energizing of the mind in all its aspects: interest, emotion, thought, and volition. Goals must be possible; pupils need to feel that they have a chance of success. Repeated failure to reach the goals set by teachers damages the self-confidence and affects the achievement, not to mention the mental health, of any pupil—bright, average, or dull; advantaged or disadvantaged.

Who is to set the goals, teacher or pupil? If the teacher sets the goals, will the pupils be apathetic in their learning? Are pupils wise enough to chart their own courses and persevere in them? In some schools these questions have often proved dilemmas, and in others teachers have taken extreme positions. Some school people have acted as if there were no alternatives between teacher domination and pupil leadership.

Resourceful teachers avoid wasting their time on such futile arguments. They realize they must make the goals of English important and worthwhile to their pupils, and to do this, they are prepared to range quite freely among possible solutions. Depending upon the maturity of their students and the particular content of their courses, they vary their own role. Research, summarized by Lee J. Cronbach, suggests that there is no single method of class organization to be followed in all situations.[6] Whether a class should be group controlled, teacher controlled, or organized in some other way will depend on the purposes to be achieved. Integrity prevents most teachers from pretending that the fundamental questions of what is to be learned and how it is to be learned can be decided by pupils. Most of the time, they rely upon their own ability to help students see the value of what they teach and to choose the best ways to make this clear to pupils. But often, and as ingeniously as possible, teachers draw pupils into the act of charting directions, of selecting among the various means of learning, and of gauging progress.

Teaching is an art, and only the teacher is prepared to practice the art. Pupils cannot possibly be expected to harmonize the delicate strategies and sensitive pacing of instruction, but they can be drawn into the dynamics through expressing their perplexities, sharing their reactions, and taking responsibilities commensurate with their vision. Through questions and inductive procedures they can be led to create their own generalizations. Throughout this book, we draw upon procedures exemplifying the relations among purpose, economy, and volition. For instance: in teaching drama and poetry, oral participation is featured as a means of pupil involvement. An inductive approach to poetry is presented. In the units on "Humanities for the Seventies" and "The Consequences of Character," pupils participate in choosing goals and content. In the program for guiding individual reading, books are chosen for their relevance to the abilities, interests, and purposes of the reader.

ORGANIZATION AND RELATIONSHIPS The main factor responsible for durability in learning always proves to be organization. Pupils—not only the teacher—must relate what is to be learned to some coherent structure; the individual parts must be easily summoned up and sustained by some intrinsic pattern or principle of organization. What one really must learn is a pattern, a generalization with applications, rather than a miscellany of specific reactions.

The danger is that teachers, like their pupils, will be satisfied with placing items in proper classifications, as in naming parts of speech or in listing ten qualities of the lyric poem. But learning is infinitely more than classification; it is seeing relationships, and the ability to see relationships does not occur

---

[6] Lee J. Cronbach, *Educational Psychology*, 2nd ed. (New York: Harcourt, Brace & World, 1963), p. 459.

through mere accumulation. Detail poured upon detail ultimately results in a surfeit that drives pupils to boredom if not rebellion. In order to relate and organize their experiences, students must practice thinking about key qualities and important characteristics—whether of poetry, usage, or paragraphing—in settings other than those in which they were originally perceived.

Learning takes place within an organizing framework. Classification, so satisfying to tidy and limited minds, often proves to be dead order. No one denies the importance of classification as a first step toward bringing order out of chaos. The danger is in stopping there.

> How great is the number of readers who think, for example, that a defective rime—bough's house, bush thrush, blood good—is sufficient ground for condemning a poem in the neglect of all other considerations. Such sticklers, like those with a scansion obsession, . . . have little understanding of poetry. We pay attention to externals when we do not know what else to do with a poem.[7]

And we might add, when we do not know what else to do with any significant learning problem. It is always easier to recite rules of grammar than to apply them and to report on an author's life than to grapple with his intention in a literary selection.

In teaching a subject as complex as English, one temptation is to classify the content by logical analysis of the subject and then allot to each classification a block of time. Presumably even the purist among classifiers does not intend that relationships should never occur between literature on Mondays and grammar on Thursdays or between composition in the fall semester and literature in the spring. Nevertheless, human behavior has not changed since Aristotle noted that the classifications into which things are arranged influence what is done with them. In teaching English, separate emphases on aspects like composition, spelling, and oral communication never prove as effective as their advocates envision. No matter how good a teacher's intentions, classifications tend to be self-contained, diminishing valuable relationships and support from other aspects of English. Furthermore, classifications, although unquestionably determined by the nature of the discipline, lack vitality for most of the learners, who have not themselves made the analysis. Psychology has shown us that the learning process in adolescents, as in all human beings, starts from interest and motive and progresses toward a comprehensiveness enabling them to perceive the logic of a discipline. This may seem perverse, but it is human.

By an integrated program, the reader should understand learning situations that fuse several aspects of English: composition and discussion related to the values and concepts illuminated by the study of literature; reading and library skills taught in preparation for a panel discussion; grammar, spelling, the principles of rhetoric or logic used as means to the effective expression of rational and imaginative thinking. Central to the entire conception of this

---

[7] I. A. Richards, *Principles of Literary Criticism* (New York: Harcourt, Brace & World, 1924), p. 24.

book, then, is a firm rejection of segregated aspects of English arranged separately throughout the week or semester. Integration within the English program is more exacting, for both teacher and student—and also more interesting, more rewarding—than logical categories taught separately, so alluring in their neat simplicity, so deceptive in their promise of efficient order, so disappointing in their results with young learners.

Units are included in this volume to illustrate ways in which procedures discussed separately may be integrated in the classroom. For example, the twelfth-grade study of *Macbeth* shows how language skills may be directed toward the study of a single classic; the tenth-grade plan "Meeting a Crisis" reveals the unity that may be developed out of the study of diverse literary selections. Each unit, however, is planned around basic conceptual goals that supply an underlying organizational framework. In each also are presented the various learning experiences, the materials used, and the methods of evaluation.

Throughout this book we describe procedures that exemplify and exalt organization and the relationships that the pupils perceive—for instance: in "Oral Language," which stresses discussion as a means of integrating various learnings; in "Program and Plan," which shows how teaching a thinking skill may be incorporated within a unit; in the humanities unit, which starts with adolescents' interests and progresses toward comprehensiveness and organization of concepts.

PROCESS AS DISTINGUISHED FROM PRODUCT The English teacher concentrates his attention on the process of his students' learning as well as on the product. Sometimes pupils shrewdly guess at the answer a teacher wants or derive the proper results by uneconomical means. Sometimes pupils come to wrong conclusions but neither teacher nor pupil sees value in determining why. To the extent that a teacher can penetrate beneath the surface of answers and outward behavior to the processes of thought, he can reduce wasteful learning. By emphasizing occasions for the pupil to analyze, synthesize, discriminate, compare, and generalize, he can decrease the amount of meaningless repetition and rote learning. Process, discovery, and problem solving are not always easy to arrange in classroom situations, but they are to rote learning what jet planes are to covered wagons drawn by oxen. The reader is urged to note in this book the procedure of teaching the short story described in "Literature: Basic Approaches." Here the teacher divides a story into its inherent segments and stops to discuss each segment, building a cumulative sureness of response at the same time that he observes the pupils' responses during the process of reading. The reader should also note "Oral Language," which stresses the teacher's role in guiding the process of discussion and in making students aware of process as well as product, and the thesis of the first chapter that understanding language *as process* is basic to acquiring power over language.

The ideal teacher of English avoids the situation in which the teacher does most of the learning attended by a group of docile spectators whose parents pay the bill. The pupils must be encouraged to discover and report processes by which they gain control of problems. There must be silences for reflection, long silences of which neither teacher nor pupil is fearful. There must be time for mistakes and for muddling through and time for evaluation of confusion in order to distill principles for streamlining the next similar situation. There must be repetition of the same skill or concept in a variety of situations wherein the pupil concentrates on the essential features that recur, transferring the key elements to new situations. Over and over again in this book, procedures for teaching composition, literature, listening, and speaking will reflect this concern for process.

SOUND EVALUATION   The teacher of English recognizes that sound evaluation produces sound learning. The experiences of many pupils lead them to think of *test* and *evaluation* as synonymous. The two words, with their contrast in emotional overtone, provide a lesson in language process as well as a means of understanding the purpose of evaluation in the English class. A test is a trial that may or may not result in critical appraisal. For many pupils tests are dreaded experiences tinged with emotional crisis, preceded by cramming, and followed by final and irrevocable judgments concerning personal merit. If the student learns to see tests as indicating degree of progress and giving direction for future learnings, he can develop a healthy attitude toward evaluation. Belief that appraisal must be continual, varied, and inclusive underlies the treatment of evaluation throughout this textbook.

If evaluation is continual, the student realizes its constructive purpose. Brief, frequent appraisals give him a chance to see what he has accomplished and what remains to be learned; they allow time for him to recoup his losses before final assessment must be made. Thus, they serve for evidence of improvement, for diagnosis, and for motivation. Since the scope of each test is narrow, the results are not so dire as to cause discouragement. Continual evaluation should dissipate much of the tension occasional over-all testing seems to generate.

If various methods of estimating progress are used, the pupil learns not to overestimate the importance of written examinations that determine only whether the desired response is available at a given time. He learns the significance of self-evaluation and that made by his peers; he learns ways of gauging progress in oral work; he learns the difference in import of tests that call for remembering facts, that require application of principles, that demand demonstrations of skillful performance. All these necessary learnings can receive impetus if various methods of evaluating are used.

If evaluation is inclusive, all goals set for learning receive proper emphasis. The procedures used for evaluation influence learning in subtle ways. Although lip service may be paid to aims never evaluated, the pupil soon learns to disregard those that do not count in his final grade. For example, a situation like this often arises. One of the goals for learning may be to increase skill in making pertinent contributions to a discussion. Peter writes skillfully, and he hands in all written assignments on time. However, his discussion techniques do not improve; he may maintain complete silence, he may monopolize, he may insist upon acceptance of his statements without support. If frequent evaluations do not call his attention to these deficiencies, he rightly decides that the oral goals mean no more to the teacher than they do to him.

Continual, varied, and inclusive evaluation of learning, an essential part of teaching, is illustrated in this book in many ways:

> in the suggestions for evaluating group interaction in "Oral Language"
> in the procedure of establishing folders of written work discussed in "Written Expression"
> in the use of cumulative reading records to evaluate growth in taste, as described in "Literature: Basic Approaches"

INDIVIDUAL DIFFERENCES   In the Greek myth, the giant robber Procrustes lay in wait for unwary travelers, who were dragged into his cave and stretched or shortened to fit his bed. Sometimes the English curriculum has been like Procrustes' technique, whittling down the brilliant and wracking those whose native abilities were limited. Unlike the citizens of Aldous Huxley's *Brave New World*,[8] human beings are not decanted from bottles according to a standard formula. They vary in many ways—in talent, in energy, in aspiration, in cultural background. This is a fact, and facts are stubborn things. In a nation where almost the entire population of junior and senior high school age is in school, this variation in the human family overshadows almost all other educational problems. In the English class it means great ranges in ability to read, to handle verbal symbols, to see relationships, and to generalize from principles to applications. Virtually every method in this book has been written from the authors' experiences among such pupils in schools ranging from Virginia to Illinois to California. Perhaps, among all the procedures offered, the following may be cited as notable for their evolution as part of the American public schools' adaptation to mass education:

> the unit method of instruction, described on pages 221–23 and illustrated by a series of resource units throughout the book
> guided individual reading to supplement class instruction on a single text
> permitting pupils whenever possible a choice among alternative ways to learn
> methods of evaluation providing for differing levels and for varying rates of speed in understanding
> enrichment for able pupils; simplification and a slower pace of learning for pupils who find it difficult to deal with verbal symbols, as in the lesson described on page 387

Certainly the sequences of human development affect the variations among students found in every classroom. Before a pupil can write a long paper, he must learn how to control the paragraph; before he can summarize a panel discussion, he must learn to generalize from a relatively simple discussion.

---

[8] Titles of literary works and visual aids mentioned throughout the book are listed in special bibliographies at the end of the text.

All the stages of difficulty need to be related to the levels of human development through which pupils are passing. Adolescents ought neither to be forced like hothouse plants, nor left to grow without guidance. It is the teacher's responsibility to see that young people mature as rapidly as is consistent with sound learning. Yet Rousseau had an important insight when he said, "Look at the child and see what he is like. He is not a miniature adult, and your efforts will go to waste if you begin where you, the teacher, stand instead of at the point which the child has reached." Every teacher of adolescents should bear in mind the motto, *Festina lente:* Too swift will arrive as tardy as too slow.

These, then, are crucial aspects of learning that every teacher of English must consider. Only as the content of learning and the form of learning become closely related does teaching really become an art.

DIRECTING ENGLISH LEARNING IN TODAY'S SCHOOLS

Because schools are social institutions, the teaching of any subject is affected by cultural demands and conditions. The teaching of English is strongly influenced by the surrounding world. The impact of environmental factors on language development, the influence of cultural values presented in literature, the importance placed on language proficiency in certain strata of society— these require the teacher to consider the social context in relation to the content of language and literature. Thus the teacher of English needs to be aware of both the general role of the school in American culture and the special ways in which society influences learning in his classroom.

EFFECT OF NONRESPONSIBILITY   When an American teacher stands aside and tries to view his pupils from a historical perspective, he sees one strange and disturbing feature—the long false dawn between childhood and maturity. In no other era of history and in few cultures have adolescents been consigned to such a long period of nonresponsibility. In most times and places, young people mature through fulfilling obligations important to the community. If an Afghan boy fails to guard the sheep, if a Bolivian girl does not know how to weave clothing, the community and the family suffer. Freed—or, more accurately, deprived—of such responsibilities, our own adolescents inevitably experience considerable drift that delays maturity. Nihilism, confusion, and a cynical dependence upon luck and ruthlessness characterize the values of numbers of our high school students at an age when, in other times and places, they would be functioning workers preparing for marriage and molded by the mores of their communities. We might well ask ourselves how much this lack of responsibility contributes to the adolescent's attempt to attain security and status by conforming to the standards of his peers. The impact of a technological culture with its danger of dehumanization shows quite clearly in the alienation of many young people.

IMPACT OF URBANIZATION AND POVERTY   Another notable feature of our technological culture is the detrimental impact of urbanization on the primary social institutions. As the large cities grow larger and the rural population declines, the dominion of home, community, and church diminishes. In many homes both parents work, and the children are in school all day; in the evening various organizations and interests frequently disperse the family again. The vastness of the city, inducing feelings of isolation and anonymity, blunts the feeling of community cohesiveness and weakens traditional ties. In the earlier rural communities the family not only was a necessary economic unit but served also to transmit values from one generation to the next. Boys, as they farmed with their fathers and uncles, absorbed the principles guiding the men in a settled, slowly changing culture; girls, as they sewed and baked with their mothers or older married sisters, talked about men and families and religion, assimilating the values by which the women lived. Most of these adults—unlike many of those today—had not the slightest doubt that their values were absolute and free from inconsistency. Birth, death, marriage, sorrow, and joy were occasions of moment to the entire community. We gain some realization of how different American life is now if we turn from *Our Town* or *Huckleberry Finn* to *The American Dream* or *Manchild in the Promised Land.*

In the United States urbanization has also increased the problems of poverty, both in the ghetto areas of the cities and in the rural areas where the migrations originate. Large numbers of Americans have not been drawn into the main culture. Although many Americans—including educators—are reluctant to admit it, our population has developed a bi-modal structure of affluence and poverty. This polarization of American life has become the major problem in education as well as in national policy planning. Its ramifications are vast, and English teachers are deeply involved because they must deal humanely and intelligently with

the feelings, self-image, and aspirations of pupils who are the victims of poverty, prejudice, and injustice

the limited vision of pupils who are the victims of affluence

social class dialects as well as non-English language backgrounds

a wider spectrum of values and experiences than the educational horizon has ever included

evaluation that is appropriate and free from cultural bias

Revision of the curriculum is necessary. A few isolated literary selections injected into the course of study will be no more effective than preschool Headstarts in a segregated setting or school-parent human relations programs devoted mainly to fine talk. Because the major cause of our problem lies in the prejudice of the white man,[9] the major curriculum efforts in English need to be directed at white pupils as much as toward the black pupils or those from various ethnic groups. In a changing, shrinking world where they are

[9] *Report of the National Advisory Commission on Civil Disorders* (New York: Bantam Books, 1968). This report clearly points to white racism as the prime contributor to the nation's agony; it is, the report asserts, America's number one problem.

the true minority group, cultural isolation and separation are dangerous for the white pupils. Not propaganda but a liberal education in values and wisdom is the direction we must take with all pupils.

Although the problem is by no means limited to the education of the Negro, it is in this area that the major test must be made. McGeorge Bundy, president of the Ford Foundation, makes this clear in his prediction of the direction we will take:

> The white man will outgrow his prejudices and the Negro will strengthen both his sense of identity and his membership in the whole of society. This is the only possible final outcome. All the rest is temporary. It is a colossal task, of course, because the inheritance of neglect and injustice is enormous. But it will happen. . . . The young today, both white and black, are learning to regard as natural the equality which many of the rest of us see only as logical. What we see as a legal right they tend to see as a human reality. They have begun to live on the far side of prejudice, and they will decide.[10]

In our own work, we have found genuinely helpful in curriculum planning the handbook for educators, *Afro-Americans* by Jack D. Forbes.[11] This handbook deals with every complication and contains recent, skillfully annotated lists of resources and literary materials. Of the multitude of books on the problem, we have also found help in the curriculum development of the Project English staff at Hunter College. Their literature and language arts program for grades 7, 8, and 9 is now available as the Gateway English Series.[12] Inasmuch as we participated in the conference that produced *Language Programs for the Disadvantaged*,[13] we are in agreement with the recommendations spelled out in that volume. For guidance in choosing literature, for the junior high school level we have used *We Build Together* and *Negro Literature for High School Students*, and for both junior and senior high school levels "The Soul of Learning." [14]

DEMANDS UPON THE SCHOOL   Is a new and different society emerging, one in which families, churches, and communities will meet further difficulties under the impact of technological changes? Probably. But during periods of adjustment to the unsettling transformations of cultural change, schools will be unable to avoid responsibility for concern with values as well as with basic skills and information. Acquisition of wisdom has always been one of the aims

---

[10] McGeorge Bundy, "The Corrosiveness of Prejudice," *CTA Journal*, Vol. 64, No. 3 (May 1968), p. 8.

[11] Jack D. Forbes, *Afro-Americans* (Berkeley, Calif.: Far West Laboratory for Educational Research and Development, 1968).

[12] Published by Macmillan, New York (1966).

[13] Published by NCTE, Champaign, Illinois (1967).

[14] Charlemae Rollins (ed.), *We Build Together, A Reader's Guide to Negro Life and Literature for Elementary and High School Use* (Champaign, Ill.: NCTE, 1968). Barbara Dodds, *Negro Literature for High School Students* (Champaign, Ill.: NCTE, 1968). Dorothy Sterling, "The Soul of Learning," *English Journal*, Vol. 57, No. 2 (February 1968), pp. 166–80; this was also published as a separate pamphlet by NCTE.

of education; in a time when many of our pupils are receiving fewer of their values from the family and an increasing number from television, comics, and their peers, the school must inevitably examine value choices.

VALUES AND THE TEACHING OF ENGLISH If anyone in the secondary school is concerned with discriminating among values, that person is the teacher of English. Yet he knows that helping individuals find their values is one of the most delicate of all enterprises. Cloying repetition of moral precepts has collapsed as surely as the recent total rejection by the schools of all responsibility. The direction the schools may now take serves as a conclusion to the Rockefeller Report:

> We would not wish to impose upon students a rigidly defined set of values. Each student is free to vary the nature of his commitment. But their freedom must be understood in its true light. We believe that the individual should be free and morally responsible: the two are inseparable. The fact that we tolerate differing values must not be confused with moral neutrality. Such tolerance must be built upon a base of moral commitment; otherwise it degenerates into a flaccid indifference, purged of all belief and devotion.
>
> In short, we wish to allow wide latitude in the choice of values but we must assume that education is a process that should be infused with meaning and purpose; that everyone will have deeply held beliefs; that every young American will wish to serve the values which have nurtured him and made possible his education and his freedom as an individual.[15]

This textbook is very much concerned with values. The final chapter is a statement of conviction about the role of the English teacher: one human being sharing with younger human beings the ethical and esthetic values that animate the teaching of English and give meaning to life.

[15] Rockefeller Brothers Fund, Inc., *The Pursuit of Excellence: Education and the Future of America* (Garden City, N.Y.: Doubleday, 1958).

PART ONE

LANGUAGE, THOUGHT, AND FEELING

ONE

LANGUAGE AS DYNAMIC PROCESS

How beautiful that first slow word
To him who found it,
To those who heard,
Back in the shadowy dawn of Time.
AUTHOR UNKNOWN

PERSPECTIVE

"Give me the right word and the right accent, and I will move the world." [1]
Thus Joseph Conrad pays tribute to the power of language to influence thought,
feeling, and action. Language is indeed the Archimedian lever that allows
each of us to exercise some degree of control over his individual world. By
means of language we enrich and sharpen our thinking, share our experience
with others, receive and transmit the great ideals of our civilization. Therefore,
the fulfillment of our roles as individuals, as participants in an organized society, as members of the human race, depends significantly upon the extent of
our mastery of the linguistic process.

Language, thought, and feeling are interrelated. Problems concerning all
three are complex because their roots are deeply embedded in the intricate
problems of individual and social behavior. For language does not "stand
apart from or run parallel to direct experience but completely interpenetrates
with it." [2] The development of language is man's most important accomplishment; learning to use language effectively is the most complicated task confronting an individual, because language embraces most of life.

Two areas of language-study concern the teacher of English: our students
need to know how their language operates in use and how it has become what
it is today. Basic to both is the understanding that language is not an inert
and static thing entombed in dictionaries but a growing organism created by
man, changing when his demands upon it change.

[1] Joseph Conrad, "A Familiar Preface," *Personal Record* (Garden City, N.Y.: Doubleday,
1923), p. 14.
[2] Edward Sapir, *Culture, Language, and Personality,* ed. by David G. Mandelbaum (Berkeley and Los Angeles: Univ. of California Press, 1957), p. 8.

This chapter deals with semantics, the study of language in relation to its meaning in the communication context.

Chapter Two describes the English language, noting historical events and sociological conditions that have influenced its development.

Man and his language cannot be separated. With Whitman, the student should come to realize that his own language is "not a construction of the learned and of dictionary makers, but something arising out of the work, needs, ties, joys, affections, tastes, of long generations of humanity, and has its bases broad and low, close to the ground."

Basic Characteristics of Language

Three basic characteristics of language account, in large measure, for both its power and its complexity. Language is a symbolism—but only a symbolism—of experience; it is highly individual, its meaning differing from person to person; it is growing and changing, never static.

LANGUAGE AS SYMBOLISM

In theory, language as symbolism is a concept easily understood; yet in practice, language, perhaps because as children we learned it unconsciously, takes on a more substantial quality, seeming almost to have a life of its own. Language is a two-fold symbol of experience. Speech is the primary symbol. For both the individual and the human race, it represents the first attempts to communicate. Writing, the secondary symbol, derives from speech. No language can survive unless rooted in the speech of a people, nor could civilization exist if a way had not been found for one generation to transmit to the next its most complex discoveries.

Study of language is based on speech. Without insight into the nature of speech our knowledge of the human mind would remain perfunctory and inadequate. Psychologists interpret the delight every normal child shows in learning and repeating names as his attempt to understand and control the objective world. Using the name as a focus of thought, he begins to bring some meaning and order to his hitherto vague perceptions and uncertain feelings. Language is the instrument for interpreting and organizing experience. It is the means used to control environment or, control failing, to make appropriate adjustments.

Students need help in understanding the significance of language as symbolism; they need help in ridding themselves of the notion that the word is the thing. Certainly children cannot distinguish between the symbol and the thing symbolized. First words, so closely integrated into the context of the total experience, seem to be not merely descriptive names but the thing itself. To the child, *mama* stands not for the mother alone, but for anyone who takes care of his needs; it stands also for his satisfaction in feeling comforted and protected. These feelings create an aura of magic around some words that persists throughout life. Thus, although the word as mere representation of the thing wins easy intellectual acceptance, actions often belie this understanding. Only intensive study of the characteristics of language in use helps underline this knowledge so that it works for the student in his daily life.

PERSONAL QUALITY OF LANGUAGE

Language differs with each individual. Each responds differently to what might seem to be the same environment; each attempts to exercise control in his own particular way. Guided by his past experience and his immediate needs, he uses language to interpret and integrate present stimuli and thus forge new experiences, never quite the same for any two persons. This all-pervasive, highly individualized quality of language is a source of its power but does create problems.

Since the word is not the thing for which it stands, there is no necessary connection between its sound and its sense. In the normal process a word derives meaning through the force of custom and convention; it gains currency because human beings have agreed, for the most part unconsciously and over a long period of time, to allow certain words to represent certain actions, feelings, things. This agreement results in an area of general meaning, common property of all those who have made the word their own. The personal meaning, however, is an individual matter, arrived at by individual routes; it gathers significance as we encounter language in different situations. Quite literally, the meaning is not in the word; it is not in the dictionary; it is in us.

It is easy to ignore the uniqueness of each person's experience and, consequently, the individual quality of his language. A person is likely to assume that everyone's meaning of a word coincides with his own, that the language he uses means the same to his listener as it does to him. While this assumption is false, the variation in any particular instance is not necessarily extensive; it cannot be, if intelligent communication is ever to take place. Accurate communication between two persons is in direct ratio to the degree to which their experience overlaps: the greater the area of coincidence, the greater the chance for effective interchange of ideas. The first diagram helps visualize this principle; the second shows why precise communication is difficult.

MUTUAL EXPERIENCE AND COMMUNICATION

The circle represents the general meaning of any concept; segment AEB in each case represents the meaning the sender attaches to it; segment CED represents the meaning it has for the receiver.

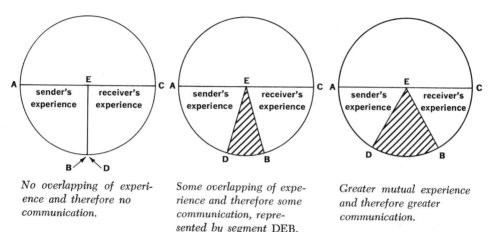

No overlapping of experi-
ence and therefore no
communication.

Some overlapping of expe-
rience and therefore some
communication, repre-
sented by segment DEB.

Greater mutual experience
and therefore greater
communication.

THE COMMUNICATIVE PROCESS

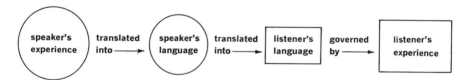

It is impossible to communicate an experience exactly. The speaker must translate his experience into word symbols, which are never capable of transmitting the whole; in turn, the listener must understand the message in terms of his own word symbols, which differ from the speaker's in some degree because the experience and needs of any two people are different.

LANGUAGE CHANGE

Basically, communication is difficult because each individual is different, and the meaning he gives to his language differs from the meaning others may give it. A child knows this long before he is aware of knowing he knows. Very early, without thinking it particularly significant, he learns that different words may be used for the same person—papa, daddy, father, George. He may never have heard *mongrel* used, but he recognizes it as a "bad" word if applied to his dog. And that is significant. Long before he is introduced to his first dictionary, longer still before he is ready to consider language in broad perspective, he knows more than he thinks he knows about language. Fortunately, the aspect of language change most likely to catch and hold his attention is the story to be found in words. Acquaintance with the dictionary and awareness of the way words change in meaning can be fostered at the same time.

Direct the student to an unabridged dictionary. There he will discover that many words arise, gain temporary popularity, and then either become an accepted part of the language or fall into disuse. Words considered appropriate on only certain levels of communication are labeled either informal (*phone, quitter*) or slang (*beat it* for *leave*); the bulk of words are those sanctioned by present usage; a third group includes the archaic, words rarely used (*quoth* for *said*), and the obsolete, those no longer conveying a meaning previously granted (*abandon* for *banish*). Some of the first group will undoubtedly die; others, if they gain general acceptance, will join the living language in later dictionaries.[3]

Who is responsible for creating new words or for charging old ones with new meaning? Normally it is an anonymous process, whether the words appear first in the literary language or in the vernacular. Originators are motivated by the desire for novelty or economy of expression. Someone coins a word that gains tentative acceptance; it may flourish for only a short time, or it may live for centuries. Why do some words quickly die, while others prosper? It is not that one is of more lowly origin than the other. Many words, standard today, began life as slang before finally achieving a secure place in the language. Every word has its chance for survival, but it must win its own way. Usage is the only criterion. Nothing can force a new term into the language if people will not use it, nor can anyone keep it out. If it satisfies a semantic need, it remains. The people are the final arbiters.

When does a word enter a language? Students can learn from the unabridged dictionary that for the vast majority the time can only be approximated. There is a close analogy between the vocabulary of an individual and that of a people. We cannot tell with any certainty when we acquired the greater part of our personal word store, but looking back, we realize that each different area of experience contributed its quota. Occasionally we remember when we first met certain colorful words and added them to our possession, but for most we cannot be exact about the time. This much only do we know definitely: when the experience of existence changes, either for an individual or for a people, so too does the language.

Although little is definitely known about the origins of language, certainly in the beginning words were few. The number is still relatively small, yet we can talk about a multimillion things. How did the first word take on new

---

[3] In the 1961 edition of this book, we used *American College Dictionary* (New York: Random House, 1947). Here, in using the unabridged *Random House Dictionary of the English Language* (1966), these examples of change are worth noting: as symbol of status, *colloquial* has been changed to *informal*, reflecting the current attitude toward language, with none of the derogatory connotations *colloquial* had for some readers; *howbeit* for *although*, archaic in 1947 but now standard, representing a reversal of the usual process of language change. For discussion of dictionaries, see pages 43–45, 70–72, and 91–93.

meanings? That the chief way was metaphorical seems logical. The process goes something like this. Encountering a new phenomenon and having no precise way to describe it, the speaker seizes upon a word denoting something similar and uses it figuratively, the context making the sense apparent. As the process repeats itself, the concept of the word gradually grows to include more and more meanings. An unabridged dictionary furnishes specific examples.

Our own observation further substantiates the theory. Writers presenting new scientific concepts inevitably draw upon analogy to make phenomena comprehensible to the general reader. Thus, the number and kinds of atoms in a molecule are compared to the make-up of a baseball team; the minuteness of the atom is made somewhat more understandable when we are told that those in a drop of water the size of the earth would be only about as big as a basketball. One writer [4] compares scientists trying to smash atoms with boys throwing rocks at a coal pile: the atoms are pieces of coal; the protons and deuterons, rocks; the electric voltage, the arms of the boys. The cyclotron provides a merry-go-round to energize particles on the same principle that David's whirling of the stone gave sufficient force to strike down Goliath. Pictures are the mind's stock in trade; the unknown must be reached through the known.

Students are likely to think of metaphor as embroidery for poetic ideas; they must learn to consider it as an intrinsic part of all language. They need to recognize extension of meaning through metaphor as a fundamental principle of language development—in all probability, one of the most important means by which language has grown and adapted itself to fit our changing needs.

The language of a people and that of an individual grow and change with experience. All education, whether in the classroom or not, takes place by extending the experience of the learner; in each extension, language plays a significant role. In helping the young child acquire language power, teachers are aware of the necessity, first, of providing opportunities for him to enlarge his experience, and then of helping him find appropriate words to clarify and organize it. The same holds true whatever the age or degree of advancement of the learner; understanding comes from dealing not with words alone but rather with the things for which the words stand. Each extension of experience creates new language needs and forces the acquisition of new language power. The vocabulary and concepts of geometry differ from those of algebra, those of the automobile mechanic from those of the television engineer. The person whose associates represent a wide range of backgrounds is likely to have a greater facility with language because he has been forced to use it in widely varying situations.

Wendell Johnson, exploring the relation between the mastery of the linguistic process and the development of the productive personality, places on the lowest level of development the unreflective individual who learns by

[4] Robert D. Potter, *Young Peoples' Book of Atomic Energy* (New York: McBride, 1946).

rote, believes what he is told, and attempts to regulate his life by slogans and formulas; at the other extreme is the person who, possessing a richly developed language for talking about his language, is effective in thinking about his thinking, in judging his judgments, and in evaluating his evaluations.[5] Understanding language as dynamic process offers a basis upon which such mastery can be built.

Concepts for the Student

For intelligent practice in mastering language, the student needs to understand five basic principles—principles he sees illustrated daily. Offering concrete examples of the symbolic, personal, and changing quality of language, they furnish a background for understanding how language functions in thinking and in communication: motivation determines language; language is used for a purpose; factors of context affect meaning; the statement conveys diverse meanings; language approaches accuracy only as it approaches conformity to reality.[6]

MOTIVATION DETERMINES LANGUAGE

Language is an integral part of human behavior. To use language effectively demands awareness of the qualities in human beings that influence thinking, feeling, and action. What are man's probable interests, his possible motives? The answer can never be reduced to a formula, but we know it lies in basic human needs—basic because they are either inherent in our nature or have been built up by our culture. Because we are human, within us are constructive forces urging us to strive for self-realization: because we are individual, these strivings lead to diverse values and to different goals.[7]

HUMAN DRIVES   Three powerful drives common to all men exist side by side: mastery, love, freedom. Never mutually exclusive, each reacts on the others,

---

[5] Wendell Johnson, "Symbolic Processes in Personality Development," *ETC: A Review of General Semantics*, Vol. 8, No. 1 (Autumn 1951). This paper was prepared at the request of the Fact-Finding Committee of the Midcentury White House Conference on Children and Youth.

[6] Throughout this book, *reality* refers to the essence of anything in all its aspects as it would be perceived by an all-wise observer. Since human senses are limited, perceptions are often inaccurate. The way an individual defines his situation constitutes for him its reality. This interpretation of events upon which the individual acts is sometimes called "functional reality," its key contained in the unique background of each participant in any situation. Thus functional reality not only differs with each person, but being partial and incomplete, differs in some degree from reality. See Earl C. Kelley, *Education for What Is Real* (New York: Harper & Row, 1947).

[7] For amplification of ideas expressed here, consult the following: Gordon W. Allport, *Becoming* (New Haven: Yale Univ. Press, 1955); Erich Fromm, *Man for Himself* (New York: Holt, Rinehart & Winston, 1947), *The Art of Loving* (New York: Harper & Row, 1956); Karen Horney, *Neurosis and Human Growth* (New York: Norton, 1955).

reinforcing or restricting. We are endowed by nature with a desire for mastery, with the impulses of self-assertion, and with the emotions of self-satisfaction and pride. Upon these, realistic self-respect and self-confidence can be built. Normally, this drive shows itself in healthy strivings for competencies to meet the challenges of life; gone awry, it may expend its force in attempts to use others for selfish purposes. In achieving mastery, each must choose among the values in his culture; he has to decide which are worth fighting for and which merit compromise or rejection.

Love is a profound urge to preserve and extend life in all its manifestations —a reaching out for union with all living forces that protect, comfort, and sustain. The capacity to give and take is its keynote; its roots lie in realistic self-reliance and genuine self-respect. It includes love of mate, of family, of friends, of work, of humanity, of God—all the qualities of mind and spirit. It is acceptance and affirmation of life.

Everyone needs the freedom to develop his potential at his own rate. He needs the right to experiment, to make his own mistakes, to reach his own decisions, to find his own answers. Freedom, of course, has limitations and carries its own responsibilities: my freedom must not interfere with yours. A selfish desire to be completely free may deprive us of the healthy friction of experience. Wisely, we refrain from involvement with the nonessentials in our environment, but commitment to nothing takes its toll. Rightly used, the drive for freedom can be an invigorating stimulus to personal growth.

INDIVIDUAL DRIVES   It is difficult to generalize about personal motivation; we can, however, isolate certain incentives to behavior that operate in our culture. Students, with teacher guidance, made the classification suggested here. Usually an hour spent with magazines or television will yield enough examples to form the basis for organization. In analyzing appeals, students should remember categories are made to serve the user's purpose; labels are only a matter of convenience. Yet they must realize further that some motivation— however complex and difficult to classify—underlies all human action. Six divisions follow, but students do better to devise their own classification and terminology.

APPEALS TO HUMAN BEHAVIOR

protection   Use of every means within our power to protect all that is peculiarly ours—life, health, comfort, opinions—and to avoid embarrassment and worry.
Young Harcourt, confused in his sense of values, in "The Snob"; Macbeth's later murders, actuated by a desire "to be safely thus."

possessions   Saving money, securing property, collecting—among adolescents, such things as match covers, sweaters, records, etc.; the acquisitive instinct apparent even in small children—*mine* is a word learned early.
Tom Sawyer's propensity for trading; distorting and debasing of the drive in the madness of the sea captain and his son in *Where the Cross*

Is Made and in the warped natures of the principal characters in *The Little Foxes.*

power Desire to accomplish our aims, to maintain our freedom and independence; the pursuit of knowledge, research in science;[8] belief that we have the capacity to do a creditable job, to build a satisfying way of living.

Necessity for confidence in the power to surmount obstacles, the theme of "The Fifty-first Dragon"; the mother's efforts to control the life of her son, in *The Silver Cord;* the symbolic presentation of everyman's story of aspiration and frustration, in *The Great God Brown.*

prestige Desire for approval of our characters, actions, abilities, opinions, even our possessions.

The family in *Confessional,* each member reluctant to admit his willingness to accept a bribe because he thinks he would be repudiating standards the others hold inviolable; the French peasant destroyed by the unjust contempt of his fellow citizens in "The Piece of String"; the couple in *Sham,* afraid they will lose face with their friends if the burglar finds nothing worth taking from their home.

stimulation Need for physical, mental, emotional stimulation: traveling, participating in sports, cultivating hobbies, attending lectures and plays, reading books, visiting art galleries, listening to music.

Undoubtedly, this drive supplies partial motivation for persons involved in feats requiring daring and stamina—the young scientist in *Kon-Tiki,* the mountain climbers in *Annapurna.* Assuredly too, the drive is necessary for sustained learning; the English classroom offers a chance for varied intellectual and emotional stimulation as we share the excitement of the characters in *Treasure Island,* follow the devious thinking of Fortunato in "The Cask of Amontillado," relive the tragic experiences of the pilot in *Night Flight,* enjoy the humor of Ogden Nash, contemplate the wonders of life with the poets.

spiritual security Need for a belief in something greater than self; the quality in man that is dissatisfied with the material only, that gropes toward the ideal; need for developing a satisfying philosophy of living, one that will recognize man's moral and altruistic aspirations.

The man and his wife in *Dust of the Road,* choosing peace of mind in preference to ill-gotten wealth; the motivating force of Cordelia in *King Lear* and of Banquo in *Macbeth.*

Drives to action are intrinsically neither good nor bad; they are forces to be reckoned with. They are good in that attempts to satisfy fundamental wants have resulted in benefits for both the individual and the race. They have evil consequences only when misguided: in *The Scarlet Letter,* Dimmesdale's efforts to maintain his good reputation whatever the cost to others; Macbeth's ruthlessness in his drive for power. The problem is one of recognition and control.

[8] See Bertrand Russell, "The Springs of Human Action," *Atlantic,* Vol. 192, No. 3 (March 1952).

It is easy to understand motivation in principle; it is comparatively easy to understand it in reference to fictional characters, where the author has given the necessary information and we are able to be somewhat objective; in life, where we seldom have all the facts and where personal feelings intrude, it is difficult to assess accurately the forces determining our own behavior and that of others.

Understanding how his motives affect his language makes the student more aware of the personal element in thinking and communicating. The intellect does not function apart from the rest of the personality; in making choices and reaching decisions, one must learn to take emotional tendencies into account.

LANGUAGE IS USED FOR A PURPOSE

Language is always used for a purpose; it is intended to do specific things either for the user or to the recipient. The boy on the playground who says "I can lick you" may be trying to bolster his own confidence or to intimidate his opponent; he may be attempting to do both. The person who upon a chance encounter exclaims "Isn't it a beautiful day!" may be expressing his own feeling of well-being, or he may be trying to cement the bonds of fellowship important to all men. In short, we may use language either to clarify our own thinking and express our own feelings and ideas, or we may use it to accomplish some purpose with others.

Although it is the specific purpose of language at any particular time that must be determined, we can help students with the problem of determining that specific purpose by considering several general purposes: to secure rapport, to inform, to convince, to persuade, to present experience in esthetic form.[9] The fifth purpose pertains to literature.

Purpose—discussed here in reference to those using language with integrity —plays a significant role in thought, communication, and expression. Awareness of the influence personal needs have on language purpose is nowhere more important than in thinking, for our thinking supplies the basis for our language and action.

TO MAINTAIN RAPPORT   In its simplest form, securing rapport is exemplified by the conversation upon chance encounters with strangers and casual acquaintances when convention demands we speak to avoid seeming rude.

---

[9] The terminology and classification given here represent a choice among many. Students of language, although in general agreement about its uses, have selected different labels and categories. For example, Joshua Whatmough, *Language: A Modern Synthesis* (London: Secker & Warburg, 1956), pp. 88 ff., divides language into four categories: informative, dynamic, emotive, and esthetic. Many speech textbooks divide the purposes of language into five categories: to inform, to convince, to move to action, to entertain, to impress. For some classifications two purposes are often sufficient: to give information and to influence feeling. The teacher must decide what classification will make the nature of language most comprehensible to his students.

We introduce subjects that immediately establish a common meeting ground —inconsequential remarks upon unimportant topics. These seem trivial only if we mistake the purpose to be informative. The writer or speaker whose sole aim is to entertain, to arouse interest for the moment, illustrates an extension of this purpose. He may deal in humor, anecdotes—whatever he thinks will please. If he gives information, it is incidental.

But this aim has wider implications; maintaining rapport is basic to achieving all other purposes. If one is irritated or distracted by insincerity, tactlessness, or ineptness, on the part of speaker or writer, communication may be blocked; likewise, a disparaging or hostile attitude on the part of the listener or reader creates an obstacle the communicator may not be able to overcome. Students need help in acquiring respect for the large segment of language used for the legitimate purpose of oiling the machinery of social intercourse.

TO INFORM The aim in giving information is to increase knowledge. If the facts are vital to the recipient, the speaker's only problem is to explain clearly: he uses simple language, includes necessary details in the most comprehensible order. Writers of manuals telling us how to get the most from our car or television set strive only for clarity. Even with an interested audience, the accomplishment of this purpose is not easy.

The task becomes increasingly difficult if the information does not seem pertinent to the listener. Then the speaker must try to spark curiosity. He moves from the known to the unknown; he pictures events vividly and uses concrete examples to illuminate salient points; he makes judicious use of repetition and summary. In short, he tries to make the facts so impressive that they will be remembered.

TO CONVINCE One who seeks to convince appeals to the understanding; he wants only to secure agreement. Any attempt to change a mind uses facts. But the reasoning as to what the facts mean and the language presenting the argument assume great importance. The speaker proceeds cautiously, starting with noncontroversial ideas; he examines opposing viewpoints fairly and dispassionately; he takes care to present a complete and logical picture; if possible, he reinforces his ideas with testimony from competent and acceptable authorities. Often attempts to convince are but a part of attempts to persuade. At times, however, conviction is an end in itself: many post-mortems after games have no other purpose than to show how the losers might have won had their strategy been different.

TO PERSUADE To move to action is the most difficult purpose to achieve because the final appeal is to volition, and most men are reluctant to change. At times a speaker is trying to inspire those who are already convinced but fail to live up to their convictions; he attempts to strengthen their will power so that the desired action will follow. Sermons, pep talks, writings intended to be inspirational fall within this category. When faced with minds made up to the contrary the speaker has a different problem: he must secure and maintain rapport and inform and convince in attempting to persuade—for example, an adult trying to alter the conduct of an adolescent, a writer marshaling facts and arguments for a persuasive editorial.

TO PRESENT EXPERIENCE IN ESTHETIC FORM   The purpose of the literary artist is to present a segment of experience in the most perfect form he can devise. His style is cultivated. His aim is revelation. Although at times he may inform or convince or move to action, that is not his real purpose. Moved by the significance of some aspect of life, he seeks to share his insights concerning human values and human conduct. The student builds his understanding of artistic purpose through continued study of individual literary works, the whole range of literature offering varied and particular examples.[10]

FACTORS OF CONTEXT AFFECT MEANING

The total context of any language situation is a fabric of many interwoven strands, each making its contribution to the texture of the whole. Although the various aspects are treated here as if they were distinct, in practice such arbitrary division is not possible, since all aspects interact to make a closely integrated unit. The personal element is the unifying force.

VERBAL DENOTATION   Understanding the literal meaning of the verbal context is basic to exact interpretation. An isolated word is rarely significant; it must be considered in its verbal context, for words, chameleon-like, take on color from their surroundings. The number of things in existence so far exceeds the number of words in the language that most words must assume various shades of meaning. We may, for example, listen to a musical *round,* give a *round* of applause, watch a *round* of a prize fight, take a *round* trip, climb a *round* of a ladder, fire a *round* of ammunition, speak of the national debt in *round* numbers, and so on and on. Always we consult the verbal context to ascertain the meaning intended. If the clues given there leave us in doubt, if our knowledge of etymology fails us, we then, but not until then, turn to the dictionary. It will serve as a guide, but only as a guide, to interpretation; it will not give infallible answers. The information found there requires critical appraisal. The historian of language has recorded what various words have meant in the past; he has directed attention to areas of meaning, since all situations in which words have been used cannot be listed. He has compiled the available data, but the final decision as to a particular meaning rests with us. To discover which definition seems most fitting, we turn again to the verbal context, because it alone contains the answer.

[10] Although the basic principles of language underlie all five purposes, this chapter is concerned primarily with the first four; later chapters dealing with imaginative thinking and literary appreciation are pertinent to the fifth.

DEGREE OF ABSTRACTNESS The degree of abstractness of language also influences meaning. The less concrete the words, the more difficult it is to determine the extent they conform to reality. Two aspects of abstractness should be noted. Some words are termed abstract (*dread*) in contrast with the more concrete (*chair*); others are called general (*food*) in contrast to the more specific (*custard*). Abstract words have no referents in the objective world; they do have a psychological core of meaning. Because they do not stand for things perceptible to the senses, no universally accepted standard exists for determining their meaning exactly. Such words are used in expressing feelings (joy, anger, happiness) and judgments (just, good, beautiful). We try to pinpoint meaning by giving examples, comparing with similar phenomena, describing ways of behavior. Thus, we attempt to convey what we mean by *justice* in any particular circumstance by citing actions that exemplify our idea of what is just. General words represent groups of items having something in common. The individual units making up each group may be either abstractions (*fear*) or items with concrete referents (*table*). Therefore, group names may have either a psychological core of meaning (*emotion*) or an objective one (*furniture*). Study of both aspects of abstraction will prepare students for some of the difficulties of thinking clearly and communicating accurately.

The process of abstraction, if demonstrated by general words representing groups of items having concrete referents, is readily comprehended in principle. Even young children can understand that by abstracting we arrive at a word that emphasizes the similarities and disregards the differences, that *boys* is an abstraction that includes all the male members of the class, yet the various boys remain individuals. They can see, at least in theory, the significance of the system of indexing recommended by semanticists to remind us that boy$_1$, John, differs from boy$_2$, George, and that both differ from boy$_3$, Peter. Older students can recognize the danger, prevalent in fields where prejudice is more likely to enter, that the use of such a system (Jew$_1$, Jew$_2$, Jew$_3$) attempts to avoid.

Variance in the degree of abstractness can be illustrated on a continuum ranging from the highly abstract to the specifically concrete. Let us take a very simple example.

FOOD	FRUIT	APPLE	WINESAP	THIS WINESAP
most abstract	more abstract	rather abstract *or* rather concrete	more concrete	most concrete

Start in the middle with *apple;* beginning in the middle makes it easy for students to see that we can move back and forth across the scale, that the degree of abstraction varies with the word. Let students decide how apple should be classified. Since the thing for which the word stands remains the same whatever the decision, the terminology is immaterial. What is essential is that students realize the significance of the fact that either term, concrete or abstract, pertains to the same reality, that classifications are seldom rigid but change to suit the convenience of the one making them.

Levels of abstraction constantly shift when language is used effectively; ideas are made concrete by specific examples; details are drawn together by significant generalizations. Consider two illustrations, both from the classroom. If we allow discussions to consist only of a succession of concrete items, no matter how interesting and informative each is, we remain on a low level of abstraction, and a generalization at the end does not remedy matters. Where thinking is purposeful, play between different levels is constant. There is a shuttle-like action, first loosely throwing out threads of different colors (the more concrete), then drawing them taut to construct a meaningful pattern (abstract). Only in this way do we explore the potential of any question. Conversely, "talking over the heads of pupils" usually means that we are speaking on a high level of abstraction; as far as communication goes we are vague, indefinite, and ambiguous; we have failed to make our language, however concrete it may seem to us, conform to a reality the students recognize.

The literature we study is filled with illustrations of the clarification of meaning through interplay of different levels. Cassius' speech to Brutus in Act I, scene 2, of *Julius Caesar* is an excellent example of statements descending the abstraction scale gradually; each idea, stated in more concrete terms, clarifies the one that has immediately preceded. Cassius begins, "Well, honor is the subject of my story"; highly abstract, without amplification it means almost nothing. The next remark explains, but only in a general way: Cassius feels lacking in honor because he must live in awe of a man. What man? What does he mean by awe? He immediately names Caesar, saying that by circumstances of birth, background, and stamina Caesar is in no way superior to Brutus or to himself. He continues with two specific examples intended to show that Caesar not only is not superior but is in reality much weaker than Cassius himself. Finally he concludes,

> Ye gods! it doth amaze me
> A man of such a feeble temper should
> So get the start of the majestic world
> And bear the palm alone.

There is no doubt now what *honor* and *awe* mean to him in this instance; the communication is explicit.

Understanding the process of abstraction, then, is not so simple as recognizing the differences between words or statements at opposite extremes. It is a complicated phase of experience, far-reaching in its implications, requiring discrimination in its use.

AFFECTIVE OVERTONES   Many words, besides having an impersonal meaning, have also affective connotations that arouse in the listener an extremely subtle, almost unconscious, response; this arises not because of any quality inherent in the word itself but because of the association, pleasant or otherwise, that the word has for us. This association is in part traditional, closely allied to the most intense experiences of humanity; it is in part personal, linked with ideas, persons, events that have evoked either our sympathy or our aversion.

The traditional atmosphere clinging to *mother* and *home* conveys pleasant feelings to most of us. Teachers, however, at times meet children whose reaction, due to personal experiences, is the opposite. Probably to most Americans *flight* suggests air travel, the connotation pleasant if they enjoy flying; but to the displaced segments of humanity, their word representing flight undoubtedly means something totally different, arousing feelings akin to panic.

The affective power of words is a readily accepted part of poetry, for we expect the poet to be concerned with emotion, with sensory experience, and with intellectual concepts vitalized by feeling. In prose, spoken or written, formal or informal, these factors are no less important. We do not find them maintained at the same high level of intensity, but they are there. If we want to interest and move the listener, if we wish him to feel toward the ideas expressed as we do ourselves, we must use affective language; when we are the recipients, the problem is one of recognition and evaluation. Furthermore, not only do the chosen words set the tone of any discourse; the way they are combined and used may heighten it. Prose, like poetry, has its rhythm, its alliteration, its repetition of words and phrases, its comparisons, its contrasts, its variously patterned sentences—all forming part of its affectiveness. Moreover, in oral communication the nuances of the voice carry their own connotations, harmonizing with the context or striking a discordant note. This aura of feeling, then, is not a characteristic exclusively of literature. It is a part of the living tissue of everyday thought and language—yet another complexity that must be taken into account in considering language operation.

THE STATEMENT CONVEYS DIVERSE MEANINGS

Just as it is impossible to assign only one meaning to each word, it is also impossible to assign only one meaning to a statement. Students learn that the declarative sentence is used to make an assertion, but when they try to understand how language functions, this information is of only slight significance. There are many kinds of statements, their use depending upon the intention of the speaker. Why has he chosen to express his ideas in this particular way? What is he actually saying? Here, as with the word, a knowledge of the total context is requisite for accurate evaluation. The statement, bearing as it does the crucial part of the load in thinking and communication, deserves intensive study.

Because language, complex though it undeniably is, is more limited than the situations with which it deals, statements will not fit neatly into rigid categories; therefore, any discussion of types of statements tends to be somewhat arbitrary. However, comprehending the diverse roles that the assertion may assume proves difficult for some students; it should be examined from various points of view. Understanding the significance of four types of statement—factual, judgmental, normative, and metaphorical—heightens awareness of the intricacies of language.

STATEMENT OF FACT   A statement of fact is concerned with something outside the speaker; it gives no indication of his feelings, expresses no attitude toward the object, person, or event. The truth or falsity of such a statement can be established by observation (The Times Building is on the corner of First and Franklin), by experimentation (The Midget Car has a maximum speed of 150 miles per hour), or by reference to the record (John Abel in the June 1955 issue of *Harper's* magazine, writes, ". . . . ."). Any combination of the three methods may be used. The assertation may not be true. Nevertheless, because its falsity can be demonstrated by objective means, it is a statement of fact.

An example will clarify. Not long ago an auto supply firm conducted a contest in which participants were to estimate the number of spark plugs in a display window, the dimensions of which were given. Although thousands of estimates were made, no two were identical. Using the same information, each contestant arrived at a different number; all statements described life-facts, and all of them were false, even that of the winner. In most instances, however, absolute proof is not so readily forthcoming. In such cases, if the weight of the evidence seems to indicate probability, the statement is tentatively accepted as true.

JUDGMENT   *Judgment,* as used in this book, refers to statements that cannot be validated by objective means: they have no reference to anything in the external world; they refer to something existing in the mind of the author. Therefore, in attempting to validate judgments, we necessarily concentrate on the person making the statement. Who is he? Why does he say what he does? Why in this particular place and at this particular time? How does he know what he claims to know? Because the answers to such questions are hard to come by, deciding whether to agree with judgments is difficult, at times impossible.

Basically, awareness of the distinction between statement of fact and judgment underlies all cogent thinking. Students will find it comparatively simple to distinguish between the two if they center attention on the referent of the key word or words in the statement. Do they refer to something in the objective world? If so, the statement is factual (Sarah Jones is a *teacher at Redfield High*); truth or falsity can be established by objective means. Does the key word refer to something existing only in the mind of the speaker? If so, the statement is judgmental (Sarah Jones is a *liar*); after considering the reliability of the sources, one can agree, disagree, or decide that more information is necessary before either agreement or rejection is possible. The clear thinker forms the habit of quickly distinguishing between factual assertions and judgments.

NORMATIVE STATEMENT   In a normative statement, the speaker suggests that a norm—a model or pattern—that individuals try to emulate has been established. (Some students of semantics use *directive* to describe this kind of language, because the speaker seems to be directing his listeners to think as he does.) If *should* or *ought* are used, the meaning is immediately apparent; however, if the injunction is obscured in what seems to be a statement of fact, confusion may arise. Because there is no doubt that the purpose is to persuade, normatives used in advertising, in political campaigns, in any recognized propaganda, are easily detected. If our automatic response is not one of suspended judgment, we have only ourselves to blame. "ABC Loan Company relieves you of your money worries" would deceive only the most gullible. "Our candidate has only your interests at heart" deserves at least a grain of skepticism.

Normative statements in reference to personal and social aims may not be so obvious. Like the advertiser, the user here is trying, from either selfish or altruistic motives, to influence future action. At times adults, in an attempt to impose socially accepted patterns of conduct on the young, resort to the reiteration of directives, more or less subtle: "Little boys don't cry" and "Little girls don't climb trees."

Normative statements are an indispensable part of language. Man, committed to life in an organized society, must have some way of impressing individual members with their obligation to the group. Physical coercion, even if it were desirable, is impossible; only words remain as a weapon for social cohesion. One of the most interesting manipulations of language is its use by society as a whole and by groups within the society to enlist individual loyalty and support, to insure that each person has the "right" reaction built in. Mottoes, slogans, songs, written in affective language and repeated with almost ritualistic significance, serve to fortify ideals of behavior. Words, their persuasive overtones embedded in the memory, come back in times of tension and serve to mold action. Who knows what deeds of valor have been inspired by the Marine's idea of his destiny facetiously expressed in the official hymn?

> If the Army and the Navy
> Ever look on Heaven's scenes,
> They will find the streets are guarded
> By United States Marines.

Who can say how many alumni have opened wide their wallets as lines from an almost forgotten college song challenge them from the masthead of official stationery?

> Loyal and true we are always to you,
> Dear old Alma Mater.

The important thing to remember about a normative or a directive is that its purpose is not to inform but to influence action. The important questions to ask are: Is the implied goal worthwhile? Will the suggested action help me attain it?

METAPHORICAL STATEMENT The conscious use of metaphorical language— used here in its comprehensive sense to include all expressed or implied comparisons of the essentially dissimilar—is an act of imaginative identification. Its purpose is to shock us into attending sharply, to force our surrender to the feelings evoked. If it is to increase and intensify the connotative force of the literal, it must be both apt and fresh. Since its intention is to illuminate meaning, it cannot be so strained that the reader stops to marvel at the writer's ingenuity, nor so trite that it irritates. Each extreme diverts attention from the context and fails its purpose. Whether the metaphorical language helps or hinders understanding depends upon the taste and sensitivity of both user and recipient.

Each must decide for himself whether the intended effect is produced by such expressions as "cheese-cake," "a pretty woman whose seventy years had worn her thin like an old coin," "fractured English," "tattered confidence," "her laundry-bag figure," "fever of despair," "wrath exuding like an unpleasant perfume," "a crooner's voice pushing against the ear like a soft, dry sponge."

The student should be helped to see that since metaphorical language is embedded in the pattern of language development and since its purpose is to heighten meaning and feeling, it will be found on all levels from the vernacular to the literary.

For the purpose of studying language as it operates in use, we have isolated words and statements, but both, when divorced from the pressure of context, are lifeless things, yielding no deep secrets. Like bits of mosaic, they reveal their significance only in relation to the whole.

LANGUAGE APPROACHES ACCURACY
AS IT APPROACHES CONFORMITY TO REALITY

One who wishes to use language with integrity must make it conform as closely as possible to the reality it represents. He is aware his reality may differ from that of others, for he knows the dangers inherent in the way we acquire knowledge. What we accept as fact constitutes the basis of knowledge. We gain facts through perception—our own and that of those we accept as authorities. We add to this through inference: we go beyond what seem to be established facts, interpreting and correlating them to reach a satisfying conclusion. Our perceptions may be inaccurate; even if they are accurate, the inferential structure we build on them may not be. The same holds true for those whose testimony we must rely on. Thus, while it may be easy to validate a single fact, validation of a complex belief is almost impossible. We should help students understand and face these difficulties.

PERCEPTION VS. INFERENCE Necessarily, inference bulks larger in acquiring knowledge than does perception: the senses can encompass just so much, while the power of the mind is limitless. Determining whether we are dealing with facts or judgments is a basic problem in clear thinking. The process of inferring begins so quickly after the stimulus and moves so rapidly that we may be unable to distinguish later between what we think we saw or heard and the inferences we have drawn from it. Since literature reflects life, examples of this flaw abound in drama and fiction: Macbeth, accepting the prophecies of the witches literally, rushes to his own destruction; Pip bases his great expectations on a false premise.

Visit any court or view a trial on television. Here, in capsule form we see the problem dramatized: experts in the pertinent fields are the only witnesses who may draw conclusions from the facts presented; all others are restricted to descriptions of firsthand experience. Lawyers say the greatest hazard of the courtroom is the inability of the untrained to differentiate between their perceptions and their inferences. Opposing attorneys, with the judge as arbiter, stand by to see that this distinction is observed. In the ordinary circumstances of life, we must rely on our own powers of discernment.

EVALUATING EVIDENCE   In evaluating experience, we resemble the jurors who must determine what the evidence is worth. Descriptive statements of perceptions from different witnesses may be contradictory; inferences of experts sometimes disagree. Rarely does the evidence point only one way. A juror must give to all statements whatever weight he thinks they deserve; he must ignore those rejected. From the cumulative evidence thus accepted, he makes up his mind as to the verdict. Ideally, when we must decide what to accept, we adopt the same procedure as the jurors in the courtroom. Admittedly, we cannot submit each detail to the same minute scrutiny, but awareness of the desirability of doing so is a basic discipline in precise thinking and discriminating communication.

Language may be compared to a mirror. The image the mirror reflects, the event the words describe, both assume the semblance of reality. Mirrors may create illusions; so too may language. They may flatter, distort, magnify, minimize; language may do the same. When we buy a mirror for general use, we want one that shows things as they appear to be; for most purposes we demand the same of language. In carnival spirit we may enjoy an occasional trip through a crazy mirror house; we can laugh at the grotesque and ludicrous shapes that leer at us from every angle, for we know the purpose is to entertain. We are not tricked. Language, too, recognized as an expression of fantasy, beguiles us but does not deceive. Only when taken as a literal transcription of fact, either in life or in literature, does it mock and delude.

As English teachers we are concerned with language in the world of fact and in the world of imagination. With both logical and imaginative thinking, the role of language looms large; with both we are concerned with the degree to which language conforms to the reality it represents. How trustworthy is the perception? How accurate the memory? How relevant the inferences? How precise the words that describe the experience? How valid the judgments and insights? The two worlds have much in common: they are never completely separated; language is an integral part of both. Ability to cope with both is essential.

Recognition of the many purposes for which language is used, of the various factors that may affect meaning, of language as a symbolism only approximating the reality it represents, will give the student an understanding of his language as dynamic process. Continual evaluation of this process as it manifests itself in the areas of fact and of imagination will reveal to him the wonders and complexities of his language. He will see it as a living thing, changing with experience, its many facets reflecting life in all its aspects.

THE TEACHING PROBLEM

Whatever area of English the teacher is concentrating upon, he must be thoroughly familiar with the particular concepts, attitudes, and skills that instruction within the area can most appropriately foster. He must also, since the durable factor in learning consists of generalizations with applications rather than a miscellany of specific reactions, be aware of the relationships existing among the desired learnings in all areas. Instruction in all aspects of English is continuous and cumulative. The teacher is simultaneously making a three-pronged attack: preparing for concepts, attitudes, and skills to be taught later; teaching those of the moment; re-emphasizing those previously taught. Understanding the relation learning in one area bears to that in another and his own conviction as to what is important for students to learn are the only governing principles he can trust. Without this grounding, he cannot plan learning experiences economical of time; he cannot help students see the study of English as an integrated whole.

ORGANIZING INSTRUCTION

Since language is the major instrument for both teaching and learning, practice in its use goes on continually. The teacher does not need to search for occasions to introduce pertinent experiences; his problem is rather one of wise choice. With any class he must decide when to focus on language as language, what that focus will be, and how the learning can be best accomplished. Although these questions have no categorical answers, the problem of introducing the study, of continuing its emphasis, and of selecting a time for the introduction of various concepts will be considered.

INTRODUCING THE STUDY   Two methods have been used in planning the strategy for teaching language as process: plans concerned with certain aspects of the nature of language (see pages 86–91); series of lessons interspersed through-out the semester or year—for example,

> a lesson on language as symbolism and the importance of context in determining the meaning of symbols, pages 40–42.
>
> a sequence of experiences suitable for teaching understanding of motivation of behavior, pages 45–48.

Either method or a combination of the two provides intervals when the learning experiences may focus on language as dynamic process.

CONTINUING THE EMPHASIS   Two ways of emphasizing concepts previously introduced are effective: incidental teaching, as illustrations of basic principles occur in language used in the classroom; and bulletin board displays. With the first, the teaching is only what might well be done in any case; however, if examples fulfilling the more immediate aim can be tied to a concept concerning the nature of language, a twofold purpose is served. For instance, if a class has studied the sources of words, three minutes spent examining the several elements of a word found in the textbook and allowing students to suggest other words formed on the same pattern will serve as a reminder of one aspect of language process. Ten minutes spent trying to determine why a fictional character draws an inference the reader knows is invalid can emphasize the personal quality of language. Opportunities for such incidental teaching occur almost daily. It is neither necessary nor desirable to use all.

A second plan encouraging regular attention to language as process employs bulletin board displays, frequently changed. All pupils are encouraged to contribute. The examples, given to student clearing committees for selection, are mounted under appropriate headings on large sheets of art paper. After each has served its immediate purpose as a poster, it is inserted as a page in a looseleaf scrapbook. Each contribution bears the name of the donor, his grade level, and the date.

Many teachers, in planning the year's work, use units as well as several series of lessons; both are reinforced with incidental teaching and visual displays, which complement each other. Such a plan is productive of more lasting results than one that concentrates on a few periods of intensive instruction separated by long intervals of neglect.

SELECTING WHAT AND WHEN   Advice concerning concepts to be introduced at any particular grade level cannot be offered unequivocally. So much depends upon the particular situation. In general, the more immature—chronologically and intellectually—the pupil, the more concrete the level of instruction. Certainly it would be unwise to spend time teaching even a brilliant seventh-grade class the general purposes for which language is used—not because it would be difficult for the pupil, but because the time can be more wisely spent in other ways, for instance, in directing his reading. The same holds true for those with less than average ability at all grade levels; other experiences will un-doubtedly prove more profitable. However, even young children use language for specific purposes; therefore, understanding the particular purpose in the language he uses himself and in that used by others should be a part of the learning of all pupils. In this way the stress remains on the concrete.

Another idea—that language only stands for experience—must be empha-sized on all levels. The teacher can combine use of a graphic device (p. 21) with specific examples to help pupils see the individuality of language. Such a simple statement as "I *did* the assignment" means different things to differ-ent students. How much does the meaning of the verb depend upon the con-scientiousness of the individual? How much on his understanding of the problem? How much on his work habits? Stories too can illuminate the per-sonal quality of language. What does "hundred dresses," in Eleanor Estes' story *The Hundred Dresses,* mean to Wanda, who longs for beautiful clothes? What does it mean to her classmates, who interpret as impossible pretense Wanda's reference to having the dresses?

When the teacher introduces the study of language as process, he uses the material the curriculum provides; he starts with examples of language used in a particular situation rather than with the major concepts of language dynamics. For example, selections assigned to seventh and eighth grades can serve to illustrate various aspects of language operation: importance of con-text in determining meaning; effect of personal motives on language; reasons for different inferences by participants of the same event; expressions of opinions incapable of adequate support.

Ninth- and tenth-graders should begin to see relationships among the examples; they can be helped to devise statements of the subordinate ideas that support the major concepts. This will be as much as many young people, even those on higher grade levels, can assimilate. However, if a six-year pro-gram in the study of language dynamics is made part of the curriculum, many advanced classes can take the final step: they can devise a scheme of organiza-tion showing the relation of the ideas to each other and to the general prin-ciples they exemplify.

The control of language is a lifetime job; it cannot be hurried. One quickly learns to recognize single aspects of language dynamics; the difficulty, as any-one can testify, comes in so integrating these understandings that they will function in use. The student should think of language mastery not as some-thing to be gained in one semester or even in many years, but as a problem that will be with him always. The methods presented here are intended to serve as a basis for a six-year program. They are intended to promote under-standings and to initiate habits on which the student can continue to build after he has left the classroom. Committed to such a program, the teacher of English can aid the student in acquiring a healthy respect for the power, the complexity, and the uniqueness of his own language.

SUGGESTED LEARNING EXPERIENCES

The learning experiences given throughout this textbook suggest specific procedures that teachers can use to help students understand and apply the principles discussed. These illustrations are concerned with the particular aspect of teaching English that has just been considered; however, they are not intended to be used solely in the context in which they appear, nor is it implied that they be used in isolation. The teaching of English is an integrated process; teaching one segment as an entity without relation to others or to the whole contradicts the nature of language and of life. What one really learns in English is a pattern—generalizations, skills, attitudes—applicable to many specifics of thinking, feeling, communicating. Thus, in adapting for a certain class any learning experiences suggested, one should be aware of certain principles of learning: relatedness—the importance of an organizational design that helps students see the bearing present learnings have on others; readiness—the teacher's obligation to prepare students for the learnings they need to acquire. Used with this precaution, the experiences can provide not only focus on the particular subject under discussion but ways of supplementing instruction in other areas of English.

TO LEARN TO THINK OF LANGUAGE AS SYMBOLISM

▶ *Learn the nature of symbols*

As the initial venture in arousing interest in the way language works, the teacher of a class of seventh-graders used nonverbal symbols.[11] One day after the pupils had returned from an assembly, he started a discussion by asking, "Why do we salute the flag? . . . Yes, it's ours, but do we salute everything that's ours? . . . Where have you seen the flag flying?" (schools, post office, ships, parades . . .)

"If you were in France and saw our flag flying over a building, what would it tell you? . . . Then our flag stands for what? . . ."

He wrote on the chalkboard, *Our flag stands for the U.S.A.*

"The flag is what we call a *symbol*. That's a new word for us. We use symbols every day. In the light of what we've been saying about the flag, let's see if we can make up a definition of *symbol*. If we cross out some words in this sentence and make a substitution, we have *A symbol stands for* . . . How shall we finish? . . . Yes, U.S.A. would still make sense, but it wouldn't help us with a definition, would it? We're trying to make a statement that will apply to all symbols. . . ." (A symbol stands for something else.)

"Good. Now let's change this statement into a definition. A symbol is . . . ?" (A symbol is something that stands for something else.) "Now we'll try to think of other symbols. . . . Why is there a picture of a cub on your book covers? . . ." (school emblem, policeman's badge and uniform, insignia for cars, for boy scouts . . .)

"All of these symbols are things we can see. Can you think of any we can't see? . . . No? Haven't you been in classes where you haven't smelled smoke, you haven't

[11] An abbreviated transcript of an actual lesson.

seen flames and yet . . ." (fire siren, signal for fire drill, emergency alert, Morse code)

"So in addition to symbols we can see, we have those we can hear. We've seen that some symbols mean only one thing to us—the flag with the stars and stripes in a certain arrangement always stands for the U.S.A.; in this school three blasts on the horn, repeated over and over, mean an emergency. . . .

"Let's look at some other symbols. What does '+' mean? . . ." (plus, addition) "Yes, when we see 3 + 3 it does mean that."

Then he sketched on the board different contexts for "+".

"What does '+' stand for now?" (a church) "And now?" (the Red Cross) And now? . . .

Next he used the same procedure with "×". (crossing, signature, multiplication)

"So we've found symbols that stand for one thing and symbols that may stand for several according to their surroundings. We call such surroundings the *context*. Do you know that word? Let's define it. . . ."

▶ *Study words as symbols*

The same teacher carried the lesson further the next day.

"Let's explore the idea of symbol a little further."

He pointed to his desk.

"What's this?"

He wrote *desk* on the chalkboard.

"Is this *desk*, the one that I've written, the same as that, the one you can see? . . . Why not? . . ."

Through questioning and securing additional examples, he led pupils to see that a word stands for something in the same way as the flag does.

"What, then, can we call these words on the board? . . . What did we say the flag was? . . . A symbol, yes . . . . Language is made up of thousands of symbols. So now we see we have symbols we can write . . . and? . . ." (read, speak, hear)

"You'll remember we found symbols that meant only one thing and symbols that might mean different things. In what class shall we place words?" (Disagreement arose, one pupil insisting that *desk* would always mean desk.)

"You are partially right; *desk* is more specific in meaning than many other words. If I asked you now to come to the desk, you'd know exactly what I meant, wouldn't you? Why?" (The physical and verbal contexts were explored.)

"Suppose we were on the playground and I said, 'Go to the desk.' Would you know where to go?" (The class supplied modifiers to clarify the direction.)

"Let's take a look at some other words. What does *rich* mean?" (*Having a lot of money* met with universal approval.) "Does it mean that in the slogan, 'The richest ice-cream money can buy'? What does it mean when applied to ice-cream? . . ." (good-tasting) "What does rich color in a painting mean? . . ." (vivid) "A rich voice? . . ." (full, pleasant) "A rich joke? . . ." (very funny) "Do you remember what we called the surroundings that changed the meanings of '+' and '×'? . . ." (context)

"*Text* comes from a Latin word meaning *weave;* the *con* means *with*. Therefore, when we speak of the *context* in which we find a word, we mean the words surrounding it—words woven with it to give it a particular meaning.

"Let's take another word and see how the meaning changes as we place it in different contexts. *Fair* is a word you often use; give some examples of different things to which we might apply the word *fair*." (fair as a mark on a report card, fair skin, fair weather, fair decision . . .)

Assignment: "All this week pay particular attention to the words you use and those you hear and read. See how many you can find that have different meanings in different circumstances. Don't take words like *desk* where by the addition of other words you can point out a particular desk; take words like *rich* and *fair* where the meaning of the word itself changes according to the way it is used. Perhaps we can find enough examples to start a bulletin board on one of the ways of language."

TO STUDY THE NEED FOR DISTINGUISHING SYMBOLS FROM REALITY

▶ *Consider examples from literature*

1. Read to junior high school students Ernest Hemingway's short short story, "A Day's Wait." It is the story of a boy of nine who, paralyzed with fear, waits all day in frozen silence expecting to die. He has overheard the doctor say his fever is 102. In France he had learned that a fever of 44 meant certain death. After the difference in thermometers has been explained, death seems less imminent. Discuss with students the way words are sometimes considered to have absolute meaning.

2. Read to senior high school students an excerpt from Ignazio Silone's *Bread and Wine.* Two young men, mistaking the symbol for the reality, engage in an argument.[12]

▶ *Consider examples from life*

Discuss questions such as the following:

Does calling a man a coward make him one?

Does characterizing acquaintances as squares, drips, grinds (whatever the current adolescent slang is) make them fit the category?

Does omission of the number 13 from the floor of an office building make that floor other than the thirteenth?

Is receiving a diploma from high school a guarantee of a high school education?

Is winning a "popularity" contest decided by paid votes an index of the winner's popularity?

In the discussion, lead students to see what confusion may arise when we mistake the symbol for the thing symbolized. Let them supply further examples from their own experience.

▶ *Realize that many words lack a concrete referent*

Ask students to write a paragraph explaining *school spirit* for someone who has never heard the expression.

Read a few examples to the class—the best and the poorest; let students decide which ones give the clearest idea of the meaning. Decision usually goes to those using the most appropriate concrete examples. In the discussion, lead students to

[12] Pages 118–21 of the Penguin edition.

see that examples are necessary because the concept does not refer to anything concrete, but to a manner of acting or way of behavior: we say a student who does so and so has school spirit; a student body shows school spirit when the majority of its members act in such a manner. We are comparing the result of action with a norm we have accepted as desirable. Thus, the word is not only not the thing, but often there is no *thing* to which the word refers.[13]

TO REALIZE THE SIGNIFICANCE OF THE PERSONAL QUALITY OF LANGUAGE

▶ *Recognize evidence of confusion in meaning*

1. Show the film "Do Words Ever Fool You?" Suitable for junior high school, this short film shows the confusion arising from the fact that the meaning of words is seldom absolute but is determined by our associations.

2. Try a further experiment using abstract words, such as *honor, justice, sportsmanship*. Limit the topics to four; number around the class by fours; give those with the same number the same topic. Have the student write in class a short paragraph telling what the word means to him. The results of this assignment should emphasize the fact that when dealing with abstractions, we have to clarify the meaning by giving examples. Compare the examples given by different students in explaining the same concept. Discover reasons for similarities and contrasts. How did the writer happen to pick those particular examples? Discussion should reinforce the idea that we arrive at meaning through experience. The class should examine the implications of this fact for communication.

3. Ask students to interpret, from the viewpoint of different participants, words used in specific situations. Do the italicized words mean the same to the two persons concerned? Why or why not?

> This is an *important* assignment.   (teacher, pupil)
> Be home *early*.   (mother, daughter)
> It is a *bargain*.   (buyer, seller)
> He receives a *generous* wage.   (employer, employee)
> Drive *slowly*.   (father, son)
> It is a *beautiful* car.   (John, Mary)

Pupils prepare original examples; working in pairs, each interprets the other's sentences; class discussion of selected illustrations underlines the need for awareness of the personal quality of language.

TO STUDY CHANGE IN LANGUAGE

▶ *Find evidence that language changes*

1. Ask several members of the class individually and at random to select a page from an unabridged dictionary and to estimate the percentage of words recorded that belong in each of the three time categories: obsolete or archaic, standard, and slang or informal. Have them pool their findings. Before they report, ask the class to estimate what the percentages will be. Exactness is unimportant; the exercise will, however, emphasize both the stable and the slowly changing aspects of the language.

---

[13] See "To explore the difficulties of accurate communication," pages 57–58.

2. Study words that in the course of their history have changed their meanings:

	FROM	THROUGH	TO
silly	blessed	blessed fool	foolish
brave	crooked	scoundrelly	courageous
nice	ignorant	silly	pleasing, exact
villain	serf	one of lowly birth	scoundrel
constable	stable companion	officer of high rank	policeman

Ask volunteers to consult books dealing with language (see titles listed at the end of this chapter) to report similar examples to the class or to prepare examples for the bulletin board.

▶ *Learn how words are made by combining elements in the language*

1. Ask students to consult a dictionary to discover the status and meaning of the following words—all the result of word combinations:

horselaugh	milksop	roughneck
clodhopper	applesauce	windbag
killjoy	crackup	greenhorn
tipoff	grapevine	boom-and-bust
shoplifter	gumshoe	rock-and-roll

2. Help students build words using different combinations of roots, prefixes, and suffixes. A pictorial device, representing families of words as trees, is effective if the concept of word building is new to children; they may enjoy making graphic examples for the bulletin board.

> *root*   postscript, description, conscript, nondescript
>   transport, deportation, portable
>   aqueduct, conduct, introduction
> *prefix* egocentric, egomaniac, egotism
>   antibiotic, anticlimax, antifreeze
>   anteroom, antedate, antecedent
> *suffix* militate, obviate, equivocate
>   specialist, oculist, conformist
>   rectify, vivify, fortify

▶ *Recognize other languages as a source of words*

Ask a committee of students to mark on a map of the world the geographical source of such words. Here are a few to start with; as others occur, indicate their source on the map:

blitz	*Ger.*	corral	*Sp.*
garage	*F.*	kibitzer	*Yiddish and Gk.*
hoi poloi	*Gk.*	ski	*Norw.*
ghoul	*Arabic*	solo	*L.*
ravioli	*Ital.*	typhoon	*Chinese*
taboo	*South Pacific*	banshee	*Irish*
goulash	*Hung.*	viking	*Icelandic*
boomerang	*Australian*	bungalow	*Hind.*

► *Learn three common ways of coining words*

1. These words derive from proper names. Let students work in groups, consulting the dictionary to discover the source, ascertaining if possible the approximate time the word entered the language.

quisling	macadam	derrick	titanic
ampere	pasteurize	sandwich	bedlam
derringer	watt	quixotic	hamburger
martinet	babbittry	vandalism	stentorian

2. With telescoped words, one can focus on word coinage and language change. The lesson also emphasizes that a dictionary's purpose is to reflect the way language is being currently used, that it indicates the choice of those who try to communicate effectively. Use two dictionaries: a recent one and one published some time ago. Our suggestions are based on the *American College Dictionary* (1947) and *Random House Dictionary of the English Language* (1966).

radar, smog   Both are listed in the 1947 edition; the first remains in its original category (standard); the other moves from slang to standard. In either case, what makes lack of change or change logical? These words illustrate two usual ways of telescoping. What are they?

brunch, motel, UNESCO   These are not listed in the 1947 dictionary but are in the recent dictionary; they are considered appropriate on all levels. What circumstances made it possible for all three on their first listings to be given a place in the living language?

cinemaddict, slurbs (suburban slums)   These are in neither dictionary. The first occurred in print and speech before 1960; the second, in print in 1967, always with explanation added. That the first is unlisted does not necessarily mean it is no longer used. What does it mean? Why do users of the second think it needs explanation? Should this make it easier or more difficult for the word to gain a foothold in the language? Why? Why did the word appear when it did?

The purpose of the above lesson is to increase awareness of the nature of language and of dictionaries. Help students make the necessary summaries.

3. The first time we meet words coined by imitating other words, the meaning is instantly clear if we recognize the prototype. The following are examples. Let students supply prototypes.

racketeer	aquacade	majorette
booketeria	beautician	scoopmobile
iffy	realtor	peacenik

Encourage students to make a collection of words coined in this way.

TO REALIZE THE IMPORTANCE OF MOTIVATION

► *Recognize specific human wants*

1. Ask students to select two advertisements in which the advertiser tries to sell his product by implying that everyone wants it, have them show the advertisement and analyze the appeal.

In giving the assignment, the teacher can illustrate by pointing out similarities in the appeals of advertisements for different types of products—for example, appeals to our love of comfort in advertisements for shaving cream, vacuum cleaners, mattresses.

In discussing the appeals in the advertisements collected, the class tentatively agrees on some specific wants that seem widely emphasized. The teacher may add appeals that students miss—for example, nonmaterialistic needs; perhaps he may ask for identification of the appeal in "Do you care enough? Help CARE take care of others," or "The Good Guy Gives." The class secretary should keep a list of the needs featured.

2. Next, post advertisements around the room, taking care that each category is amply illustrated, for example:

GENERAL WANTS	ADVERTISEMENTS FOR	APPEALS
protection	pain reliever	speedy relief
	tires	safety
possessions	book	save with coupon
	gasoline	more miles to the gallon
power	school	prepare for executive job
	dancing lessons	increase popularity
prestige	sterling silver	add to your prestige as a hostess
	car	the right car proclaims your success
stimulation	television set	high fidelity tone
	travel poster	the land of your dreams
spiritual security	March of Dimes	give this child a chance
	blood bank	someone needs your blood today

Ask students to identify the wants to which appeals are made. Add these to the list already compiled.

▶ *Decide upon a classification and validate it*

1. Let students group into tentative categories the specific wants discussed in preceding assignments; through class discussion, teacher and students arrive at an experimental scheme of organization acceptable to both.

2. To cover a large amount of material in a short time, the teacher divides the class into three groups, each to investigate the advertisements in a different type magazine—pulp, slick, elite. They are to consider appeals made to the basic wants and to determine whether the advertisers seem to be appealing to the same wants previously discussed by the class. They prepare a report on their findings. The class, with the teacher's guidance, after discussing the reports made by the groups, either decides that the classification is valid or agrees upon modifications.

▶ *Discover how advertisers tailor their appeals to fit probable readers*

Using the same material brought in by students for the previous assignment, again divide the class into three groups, each containing representatives of the three different types of magazine. Ask students to compare advertisements that appeal to the same want in at least two different types, noting similarities and contrasts in the logical and emotional aspects of the appeals and in the language in which they are couched. Compare, for example, the glamor advertisements in *Vogue* and *Ebony*. Do the findings tell anything concerning the advertiser's estimate of the readers? What effect, if any, would this estimate have on the editor in selecting stories or articles to be published?

▶ *Recognize in the behavior of fictional characters*
   motives for action rooted in the basic human needs

1. Ask students to select from a recent motion picture or television program a specific action of a particular character. Explain the motives. Do they seem based on any of the fundamental drives? Discuss.

2. Plan a series of lessons using short stories and plays.[14] After the literature has been studied, ask students to review the actions of the characters to find illustrations of impelling motives based on the fundamental needs. For example, we recognize the desire for power predominant in "The Secret Life of Walter Mitty," where the hero, figuratively donning the mantle of Superman, encounters in his daydreams experiences that reality denies him.

3. Ask a student to analyze the behavior of one character from the book he has selected as part of the guided reading program.[15] For the discussion of this assignment the class may be divided into groups. Each group discusses motivation for action, determines the main and contributing drives, and selects examples to be reported to the class.

▶ *Determine motives for behavior in life situations*

1. Ask students to identify the desires acknowledged in news items in which individuals give reasons for their behavior. For example:

> It seemed a fool-proof way to make money. (possessions)
> I did it for a thrill. (stimulation)
> He embarrassed me before my friends. (protection)
> They wouldn't let me out in the evenings. (power)
> I'm out of a job and have a family to support. (protection)
> I thought I could sell it. (possessions)
> I wanted to help him. (spiritual security)
> I wanted to see the Giants in action. (stimulation)
> I wanted to impress the neighbors. (prestige)
> I never could do what I wanted to do. (power)
> I didn't want the other kids to know. (prestige)
> My first responsibility was to the passengers. (spiritual security)

The value in such an exercise lies in the discussion it entails. Agreement concerning classification is less important than that students understand the difficulty of correctly assessing motivation.

2. Discuss the possible motives behind these activities:

cheating in an examination	winning a game
owning a hot rod	playing football
running for student-body president	entering an art contest
disturbing a class	belonging to a club
attending a dance	winning a scholarship

---

[14] See the unit "Meeting a Crisis" for a list.
[15] The guided reading program is discussed on pages 454–58.

3. Use a short written exercise, such as the following:

> Analyze a recent action of your own. Are your motives clear to you? Are they based on the fundamental wants? Write a paragraph of explanation. (If these papers are to be discussed, better results will be obtained if the anonymity of the writers is preserved.)

In the above learning experiences, the series of activities suggests a sequence moving from the simple to the more difficult. Offered as an illustration of the study of motivation as it pertains to understanding language as process, this order is logical, but it may not be applicable to any particular class. In many classes, students will have studied motivation in reference to fictional characters before studying it as influencing the use of language. If so, the teacher would start with familiar examples taken from literature or from the students' experience before attempting to lead the class to see that the universality of certain drives permits a classification. The suggested learning experiences elsewhere in the text do not necessarily suggest an order for teaching. In any particular instance the teacher must decide what experiences and what order will be likely to produce the desired learning most economically. The order suggested above is built upon the following rationale:

> Study of the repetitive and forthright appeals found in advertisements will give even the slow student a crude and broad basis for understanding human motives.
>
> Study of the ordered experiences offered by literature will help him refine and interpret his knowledge.
>
> Analysis of life situations will lead him to see the difficulties of accurately determining specific motives for specific behavior.

TO UNDERSTAND PURPOSE IN THE USE OF LANGUAGE

▶ *Realize that all language is used for a purpose*

Ask students to notice the specific purpose of particular language they use and hear and to prepare to report on five examples. In the discussion following, pupils may need help in seeing that:

> A large area of language is aimed at facilitating social intercourse.
>
> To convince may be an ultimate purpose as well as a preliminary to persuasion.

If examples of all the general purposes to be taught are not volunteered by pupils, appropriate questions will elicit those omitted: Did anyone tell a joke, something interesting which had happened to him, something unusual he had observed? Did anyone try to convince a friend that rock-and-roll is real music, that a certain movie is better than another? Did anyone use language without a purpose?

> The discussion should clinch the idea that all language, whether we are aware of it at the time or not, has a specific purpose.

▶ *Classify the purposes for use of language*

The teacher, using the specific purposes given above, leads pupils to discern similarities. After purposes have been placed in groups, the class can agree on names for the categories—not necessarily the ones given here.

After classification has been agreed upon, give the students a list of statements suitable for central ideas for either written or oral work, for example:

The Leaping Leopards should have won the pennant.   (convince)
Give to the United Crusade   (persuade)
A recent survey gives the following facts about the city's industry.   (inform)
Join the rooters at the game.   (persuade)
It was the most exciting incident of a long exciting career.   (interest)
More competent leadership of both industry and labor would have averted the
   strike.   (convince)
There are three steps in making a kite.   (inform)
This is the funniest story I've ever heard.   (interest)

Ask students to place each in a category. Discuss. Disagreement and doubt will be salutary. Discussion should point up the complexity of language and the need for precision in its use.

▶ *Recognize general purposes in one's own language*

1. Ask students to select from their own use of language a specific example to illustrate each of the general categories, for example:

I tried to get my father to increase my allowance.   (persuade)
I explained an assignment for a friend.   (inform)

2. Ask students to compose four sentences, each one possible as a controlling statement for written or oral work and each illustrating a different general purpose.

GENERAL PURPOSE	RESPONSE DESIRED	CONTROLLING SENTENCE
to interest, to entertain, to maintain rapport	I enjoyed myself. (*or*) It held my interest.	Getting up in the morning is the hardest job of the day.
to inform	I understand.	The equipment needed for building a high fidelity set is . . .
to convince	I agree.	If John had obeyed instructions, the accident could have been avoided.
to persuade	I will do it.	Buy a ticket for the class play.

Connecting specific purpose with the response of the listener or reader will help students see that not only the purpose of the speaker or writer must be considered but also that of the recipient.

▶ *Identify the purpose of language used by others*

1. Ask students to clip from a newspaper or magazine examples of the four purposes. Are they used singly or is one used to reinforce the other?

features, stories (to interest, to inform)
news items (to inform)
editorials (to convince, to move to action)
cartoons, comic strips (to interest, to inform, to move to action)

Select the controlling sentence, or if it is only implied, compose one. Prepare to read the sentence, to state both the general and the specific purpose.

This exercise may launch several assignments; it can be carried further with the student analyzing the item to determine its effectiveness and the reasons for success or failure in the accomplishment of its purpose. It can be used as an assignment for all students, or the class may be divided into four groups, each to find illustrations of a different general purpose.

2. Ask students to select a television program that has a combination of purposes, to decide upon the ultimate purpose, and to show how the other purposes contribute to it.

▶ *Use the knowledge gained about purpose in the use of language*

Let students draw names of other class members; each is to write a short composition for the person whose name he has drawn, selecting a specific purpose he wishes to accomplish. The composition is given to the one for whom it has been written; he decides on the writer's general and specific purpose, his degree of success in achieving it, and reasons for his success or lack of it; he makes these comments on the paper and returns it to the owner.

Use class discussion to review principles and to explore ways successful writers have used in trying to accomplish their purpose. How many considered the interests of the reader? In what ways?

TO STUDY CONTEXTUAL FACTORS THAT MAY AFFECT MEANING

▶ *Determine first-level meaning from verbal context*

1. Ask the students to investigate in an unabridged dictionary the meaning of common words applicable to different objects or different areas of experience and to determine why the general meaning is appropriate for the various specifics. One method is to divide the class into groups, giving each a noun that names a part of the human body—arm, eye, face, foot, hand, head, heart, leg, neck, nose. Students are to discover other areas of meaning. For example, *arm* may be used in reference to a chair, a ship, the sea, the government, and so on.

2. Give students the italicized parts of these statements—fictitious quotations—to interpret.

> Senator Doe　*"The report of this committee is remarkable;* never have I seen so many errors in a single document."
>
> Critic A　"Although *the author had access to an abundance of reliable sources,* he apparently did not use them."
>
> Representative X　"If the witness has told the truth, then it would appear that *Mr. B. is engaged in subversive activities;* however, the witness has given no evidence to support his accusations."
>
> Critic Y　*"Dressed in a fashionable gown, Singer C, charming and gracious, captivated her audience* until she began to sing."

Afterward, give students the complete statements; then let them write their own, meeting with a partner to select effective examples for a bulletin board display.

3. Use the same procedure with sentences out of context. Remove from a paragraph a sentence having several interpretations; ask students to think of possible meanings; then read the paragraph. The following sentences show how lacking in precise meaning even the simplest sentence becomes when removed from its context.

Moving was an ordeal.
One or two whiffs was all he could stand.
They had scraped and pinched.

After students have given as many meanings as they can think of, read the sentence in its context.

► *Study the effect of abstractions on meaning*

1. Discuss with students the meanings in fictional names:

If we were to speak of someone as one of the following persons of fact and fiction, saying "He is a regular _____," to what quality would we refer? What would we disregard?

Peter Pan	Babbitt	Beau Brummel
Job	Munchausen	Uncle Tom
Micawber	Frankenstein	Hitler

Let students add to the list.

2. Have students construct abstraction scales with words:

human being, American, man, doctor, pediatrician

3. Do the same with statements:

I like to travel.
I enjoyed my trip to Europe.
France is the European country I prefer to visit.
Paris has much worth seeing.
The Louvre contains many art treasures.
One of the most famous paintings in the Louvre is the *Mona Lisa*.

4. Ask students to examine advertisements to determine the connection, if any, between pairs of statements like the following and the reason for shifts from the more abstract to the more concrete statements:

More doctors recommend it . . . Zylox is safe for you.
Make your children happy . . . Give them Tastie Toasties for breakfast.

5. Re-emphasize the concept whenever possible by using the literature being studied to point out examples and by asking students to select from the books they are reading passages where shifts in the levels of abstraction illuminate meaning. Prepare for the bulletin board or for oral presentation.

► *Consider the emotional effect of language*

1. Have the students collect a list of pairs of words (near synonyms) that have different affective connotations—for example: plump, fat; kind, soft; courageous, brazen; frank, tactless.

2. Discuss the differences in emotional overtones of pairs of statements similar to the following:

LKS scuttles farm aid. President vetoes farm bill.
The Senator persists in his fanatical sniping. The Senator continues his earnest criticism.
The Tigers clobber Bears 5 to 4. The Tigers nose out Bears 5 to 4.

We can now exert positive leadership. We now have the whip hand.
I failed the test. "She" flunked me.

3. Divide students into groups. Let each group select a school problem suitable for an editorial. Then write a pair of lead statements—one in the style of reporting, the other using emotionally toned words. Compare the effects.

4. Play the game introduced by Bertrand Russell on the B.B.C. called "Conjugation of Irregular Verbs." Examples:

I am firm, you are obstinate, he is a pig-headed fool.
I am slender, you are thin, she is skinny.
I am beautiful, you are pretty, she'll get by if anyone likes the type.

5. Discuss the emotional effect of such purely factual statements as:

With the holiday week end only half over, the number of deaths on the highway already exceeds the number of casualties predicted by the National Safety Council for the three-day period.
A gas station attendant died this morning, shot to death by a bandit who got away with less than ten dollars.

Ask the students to find in a newspaper a factual statement that has emotional impact.

▶ *Investigate the effect of history and environment on language*

1. Help students account for such historical changes as

Changing the name of St. Petersburg, Russia, first to Petrograd and later to Leningrad; changing Idlewild to John Fitzgerald Kennedy International Airport
Renaming Stern Park Gardens, Illinois, to Lidice
Approximate time of changing established place names in the United States to Roosevelt Drive, MacArthur Boulevard, Pershing Square, Eisenhower Plaza, and so on
Prevalence of *Los* or *Las* and of *San* in names of towns in California and other parts of the West
Appropriateness of *minne* as a prefix for Minnesota place names

2. Investigate with students the source of place names in your community and state. Have any been changed? What ones can be explained by local events? By national happenings? By historical background?

3. Read to the class "Mother Tongue," by Richard Armour. These verses, prompted by a travel advertisement stating that no language barriers exist between the British Isles and the United States, give examples of differences in terminology.

TO DISCRIMINATE AMONG KINDS OF STATEMENTS

▶ *Compare factual and judgmental statements*

1. Ask the students to decide whether statements similar to these are factual or judgmental and to pick out the elements in each that substantiate their conclusion.

Mary talks incessantly in order to gain attention.
The school dance will be a flop; they've hired Hal's orchestra.

Senator Doe championed desegregation in order to win the Negro vote.

To promote its own selfish ends, the Central Medical Association is opposing socialized medicine.

John is so shy that he avoids school dances.

My mother won't let me go to the party because she doesn't want me to have any fun.

2. Ask the students to examine an editorial from the daily press, to underline the facts, to enclose the judgments in parentheses, and to decide whether the facts are sufficient to support the judgments.

3. Ask the students to supply facts that would be needed to furnish support for the following statements:

Our team is the best in the league.

He's a good sport.

Senator X is against foreign aid.

She's a wonderful girl.

Our candidate would make a good president.

He is an expert driver.

► *Compare factual and normative (or directive) statements*

1. Use a short written exercise such as the following:

Are any of the following factual? Remember that a statement of fact may be false and that a normative or directive may be accepted by the unwary as factual or as giving the whole truth.

The courts insure justice for all.

This magazine will keep you well informed.

"Man shall not live by bread alone."

Our candidate typifies the ideal American.

A rolling stone gathers no moss.

Let me compliment you students on the neatness of your school.

"Absent yourself from felicity a while."

This movie will give you a lift.

Frank Patterson, one of the Senators from Florida, recently left for Asia.

"Let us here highly resolve that these dead shall not have died in vain."

Analyze the ones you have selected as normative statements or as directives. Do they contain any factual parts? What is the aim of each?

2. In discriminating between informative and normative or directive statements, consider the verb "to be," more widely used than any other in the language. When we use *is* as a synonym for *exists* or *takes place,* the intention to inform is clear— for example, "The boy is on the playground," "The dance is tonight." However, three other meanings give the verb the force of a normative or a directive, since the speaker seems to be suggesting that the listener should think as he himself does.

Since these uses of *is* are often found in contexts characterized by strong emotional overtones, the need for pinpointing the exact meaning is great.

    should be, ought to be

        "The right to work is every man's privilege." This is clearly not a statement of fact but a reference to a goal.

in my opinion, appears to me to be

"He is a bully." Such statements are at times accepted by both speaker and listener as fact rather than judgment.

can be classified as

"He is an ex-convict." This is a factual statement. The danger lies in accepting it as telling all about a person rather than just one fact. The verb often has this implication in disparaging remarks about national and ethnological groups.

Ask the students to recast the following sentences so as not to invite misinterpretation.

Blood is thicker than water.   (goal)
Mary is a wonderful friend.   (opinion)
After all, he's a foreigner.   (classification)
Robert is a Communist.   (classification)
A mother is solicitous for the welfare of her children.   (goal)
Isn't that just like a man?   (classification)
Oh well, you know how women are.   (classification)
A doctor is guided by a strict ethical code.   (goal)
He's nothing but a politician.   (classification)
He is generous to a fault.   (opinion)

3. Let the students make up sentences using the verb "to be" with one of the three meanings. Call upon classmates for the exact meaning. Work for accuracy, then speed. Spend a few minutes a day until the idea seems to have become rooted.

▶ *Study metaphor as an intrinsic part of language*

1. A local ice cream parlor displays the sign, "Teen-Age Spoken Here." Discuss the significance of the sign with the class. Let the class compile a list of slang terms in current use with students; see how many are based on metaphor.

2. *Time* magazine is a prolific source of metaphorical language. Most of the articles make use of it; in almost every issue at least one or two items are built on extended metaphor. Remove pages from an old copy, giving one to each student with instructions to underline the metaphorical elements in red. Post examples.

3. Ask students to glance through the indexes of current magazines to find article and story titles based on metaphor. Encourage volunteers to write metaphorical titles for articles suitable for the school or local paper and to explain the content briefly.

4. To emphasize the aptness of metaphor, collect brief examples of metaphorical language. Out of context, such examples sharply point up the need for imaginative cooperation on the part of the reader. Type each example on a separate card. Ask the students to imagine circumstances where it might be appropriate. Examples:

It was Sound itself, a great screeching bow drawn across the strings of the universe.
He received the news with his eyebrows.
The room seemed to empty like a washbowl.
The darkness was piled up in the corners like dust.
The kind of lie the bruised ego feeds upon, course after course, never sickening.
Her blue cape faded haughtily in the distance.

She was no more than a name on a Christmas card, not much of a patch to mend six years with.

His antennae were already out, feeling over this new world.

The kind of room that seemed more interested in people than in things.

She reminded him of a coil of barbed wire.

He chipped away at her self-esteem with the cruel pick of his words.

5. Ask each student to make a copy of one interesting example of metaphorical language found in his reading. Students working in pairs exchange examples, imagine the situation, check with the original. Have volunteers report unusual examples to the class.

6. Divide the class into groups, giving each the name of something that could be described about a person—face, head, hands, posture, walk, voice, smile, and so on. Ask each student to devise metaphorical expressions that could be used in making different kinds of faces, smiles, and so on, vivid for the reader.

The next day have the students meet in groups and make a composite list. Duplicate the list and give one to each student. Ask him to combine terms from the various categories that might be used by a writer in making a character consistent. For example, would a writer be likely to describe "a smile rippling like sunlight" across a "hatchet-face" or would he endow it with a "vulpine" grin? Would he give a "moon face" to an arrogant individual? If so, what might be his purpose?

TO CULTIVATE AWARENESS OF PROBLEMS CONCERNED WITH ACCURACY

▶ *Recognize difficulties involved in drawing valid inferences*

1. Clip explanatory matter from pictures taken from magazines. Let the students study the pictures and write captions. Compare with the original captions. Re-examine the pictures to account for correct or faulty inference. Were sufficient details given? Do they support the students' captions as well as they do the originals?

2. Ask the students to select a cartoon and to clip and preserve the legend. Students working in pairs exchange cartoons and write suitable legends. Choose some for a bulletin board display.

3. Prepare a file of series cartoons that present without commentary the steps in a story or situation. Let the students work in groups preparing legends.

▶ *Develop awareness of the prevalence of inference in our daily use of language*

1. Ask the students to examine an issue of a magazine that uses jokes for fillers in order to determine the percentage of those in which the humor depends on faulty inference. (In those examined by students in various secondary classrooms, the range was from 25 to 50 per cent.) The inference may be made ignorantly because facts have been misinterpreted, or deliberately to cause discomfiture to one who relates facts to establish another conclusion.

2. Encourage groups of students to prepare a file of captioned cartoons where the humor depends upon inference. For example, a man comforting a small boy: "Your mother didn't mean to run over your wagon, and what was it doing in the flower bed in the first place?" Four bridge players: "Reputations conferred in absentia."

3. Most advertisements illustrate inference in two ways. First, the writer from his knowledge of human nature has inferred that the reader wants certain things.

Second, he presents what purport to be facts from which he hopes the reader will draw the desired inference. Discuss with students inferences that could be drawn from sets of facts similar to the following in advertisements:

"The All-News Weekly is designed for people like *you*." List of well-known persons who subscribe.

"Everyone wants a beautiful skin." "Use Glamor Cream like Lita Lovely."

"Knowledge brings success." Picture of a boy with a set of encyclopedias.

An investment firm's claim to knowledge of stocks with high growth potential. Examples of correct predictions made in the past.

"Opportunity no longer knocks." "It telephones."

"That smiling confidence." Picture of a woman and child waving to a man entering a plane.

Encourage students to find other examples.

4. Ask each student to analyze one simple event in which he has participated within the last twenty-four hours and to list the distinct perceptions he was aware of and the inferences drawn from each.

5. In the middle of a class period, allow fifteen minutes for each student to list the perceptions he has made since the class started, stating one inference arising from each. Is there any instance in which a second inference arose from the first? Discussion of such activities should bring out the difficulties in distinguishing between perceptions and the inferences based on them—the almost automatic way an inference occurs.

▶ *Investigate basis for beliefs*

1. Ask a student to make two lists of things he thinks he knows. The first list should contain information gained by observations and by reasoning based on those observations; the second, information gained from the testimony of others. Which list is longer? Which contains the more complex items? Such an investigation shows students that most individual information comes from testimony; that the more complex the testimony, the more it is based not on one fact, or alleged fact, but on a group of facts combined with interpretations of what the facts mean.

2. Ask a student to select two beliefs he holds—one that, if proved incorrect, would not matter to him; the other, that would. Ask him to account for the difference. Discussion should emphasize the significance of personal interest in determining beliefs; a wish to believe sometimes influences what is believed.

3. Ask a student to examine the sources of one of his complex beliefs and to consider the amount of investigation necessary to establish their approximate accuracy. Does any individual have the time, energy, and means to check all his beliefs? What does such inability signify? Discussion should highlight the significance of the preponderance of verbal learning in what the individual looks upon as his store of knowledge, as well as the need for awareness of the inability of language to describe experience completely and accurately.

▶ *Consider factors involved in validating beliefs*

1. Divide the class into three groups; each student is to select a simple fact, or alleged fact, that can be easily checked; those in the first group, a fact that can be validated or disproved by observation; those in the second, by experimentation;

those in the third, by reference to a record. Such an assignment should show it is comparatively easy, if resources are available, to check the authenticity of isolated facts.

2. Allow each student to choose a term from a list similar to the following: football coach, teacher of science, farmer, physicist, member of Congress, newspaper reporter, labor leader, historian, president of a large corporation, movie star. The student, instead of using the general term, substitutes the name of a person he knows, at least by reputation. Then the student is to determine under what circumstances the individual might be considered an expert witness—that is, in what areas his training and experience might make him competent to testify—and under what circumstances he might be considered biased.

For instance, Mr. Z., a prominent motion picture producer, might be competent to testify on the problems involved in producing motion pictures; he might be biased in his belief that certain motion pictures give audiences in India an appreciation of American culture.

Besides pointing up the necessity of considering both competency and the possibility of bias in determining the reliability of witnesses, these assignments emphasize the difficulty of validating complex information based on judgments.

3. Ask each student to select circumstances in which he might be a competent and unbiased witness and others in which he would be competent but might be biased. In the discussion stress the importance in forming conclusions of considering not only the competency and bias of others but also one's own.

TO EXPLORE THE DIFFICULTIES OF ACCURATE COMMUNICATION

▶ *Realize the degree to which experience cannot be communicated*

Give the students a jumbled list of statements containing words with referents.

> *present and concrete*
>> This is my desk. These apples came from our orchard.
>
> *absent and concrete*
>> My grandfather left me his desk. The caves show unusual natural formations.
>
> *abstract, referring to a way of acting, a manner of behavior, a process*
>> My grandfather was a tyrant. Democracy has many advantages.
>
> *abstract, referring to feelings*
>> Terror gripped me. The pain mounted.

Ask the students to number the items in the probable order of increasing difficulty for the communication to have maximum meaning for the recipient. Which require amplification? What form might that amplification take? Which would present the most difficulty in conveying the speaker's experience? Why? These points deserve consideration:

> The user of language should be aware that many words have no concrete referent, but refer to a manner of behaving, a process.
>
> The more abstract the language of the total communication, the less effective it is likely to be.
>
> Differences of experience of sender and recipient make support of abstractions by concrete examples necessary.
>
> No matter how great one's control of language, there are areas of experience

that are incommunicable; especially is this true of feelings—we can tell the results of our own anger; we can see the effect of pain on others; the feelings themselves can never be satisfactorily communicated.

▶ *Through practice cultivate awareness of the problems of communication*

Let the students draw slips, each containing a word without concrete referent: hate, love, beauty, pride, wit, cruelty, justice, hunger, odor, cold, courage, cowardice. Use the same word on more than one slip, to allow for comparisons later. Each student is to write a paragraph or two in which he tries to communicate as many facets of the meaning as possible to one unfamiliar with the concept.

The next day place students in groups to listen to the paragraphs and to determine the characteristics of those that communicate most effectively. If sensations or feelings were aroused in the listener, to what extent did his previous experience contribute to them? What stimulus from the writer initiated them?

Follow with class discussion to synthesize the findings of the groups and to point up some of the major difficulties involved in communication. How many stem directly from the characteristics that make language complex?

The teacher should be aware of the interchangeability of the Suggested Learning Experiences among the various areas of English instruction. For instance, *purpose of language,* offered in this chapter as suitable for inclusion in a unit on language as dynamic process, might also be used in other ways: in analyzing and evaluating assembly and television programs, in the study of newspapers and magazines, in analysis of propaganda techniques, in teaching principles of organization for speaking and writing, in evaluating speeches of characters in stories and plays, in teaching appreciation of an author's writing technique. Such interchange allows students to see the learning in the English class not as a collection of unrelated segments but as an integrated process.

SELECTED READINGS

BOOKS

ANSHEN, RUTH NANDA (ed.). *Language: An Enquiry into Its Meaning and Function.* Science of Culture Series. New York: Harper & Row, 1957. This book, each chapter written by a specialist in his field, develops understanding significant for the English teacher.

BARBER, CHARLES. *Linguistic Change in Present-Day English.* University, Ala.: Univ. of Alabama Press, 1966. This book presents the main changes that have taken place in spoken English during the last few decades. The author thinks it important to listen to the spoken language and note changes as they occur.

BROWN, ROGER. *Words and Things.* New York: Free Press, 1958. A discussion relating language and the psychological principles of human behavior.

CASSIRER, ERNST. *An Essay on Man.* New Haven: Yale Univ. Press, 1944; paperback, Garden City, N.Y.: Doubleday Anchor, 1953. An introduction to the philosophy of culture—its thesis: myth, religion, art, language, science, are all variations on a common theme.

CIARDI, JOHN. *How Does a Poem Mean?* Boston: Houghton Mifflin, 1958. Invaluable for the teacher of poetry, this book is mentioned here for what it has to say about language. See especially the section called "The Words of Poetry."

FUNK, WILFRED. *Word Origins and Their Romantic Stories.* New York: Grosset & Dunlap, 1954. Interesting examples suitable for classroom use.

GAREY, DORIS B. *Putting Words in Their Places.* Chicago: Scott, Foresman, 1957. An explanation of the way language works, with exercises designed for use with first-year college classes.

HALL, EDWARD T. *The Silent Language.* Greenwich, Conn.: Fawcett, 1968. Silent language, often more eloquent than words, is a product of culture. Tradition, taboo, environment—all differ among peoples, fostering different habits and customs that result in different modes of behavior. Manner and action convey their own message. For effective communication both silent and verbal language must be taken into account.

MINTEER, CATHERINE. *Words and What They Do to You.* Evanston, Ill.: Row, Peterson, 1953. Specific lessons for teaching basic understandings concerning general semantics to junior and senior high school students.

SAPIR, EDWARD. *Culture, Language, and Personality.* Ed. by David G. Mandelbaum. Berkeley, Calif.: Univ. of California Press, 1958. A scholarly presentation stressing the implications of language as a cultural and social product.

TWO

THE NATURE
OF LANGUAGE

*The proper study of mankind is man, and there is
nothing so basic to our humanity as our language.*
JAMES SLEDD [1]

PERSPECTIVE

Language is man's greatest achievement. With it he communicates his ideas
and feelings and generates infinite varieties of thought. Language mirrors
man's culture, showing his interests at any time and place, revealing his relations with his fellow men. No one doubts this. Yet the full study of language—
its history, structure, esthetics; its regional and social variations; the way it
operates in practice—has been neglected in the classroom. To be sure, we touch
upon some aspects of language as we struggle to improve speaking and writing, but the uses of language have received primary attention. Understanding
language in its own right and appreciation of its human significance have been
neglected. Like the study of history and biology, the study of language deserves a place in the curriculum because of what it reveals about the nature
of man and about man's linguistic behavior.

Today English has become a world language, spoken or read by some 300
million people, and learning the English language has become a part of the
educational program in countries throughout the world. How did our language become so influential? How did it develop the varieties that become
so apparent when we listen to speakers from diverse countries and regional
groups? How and why did English change from one generation to the next?
How is it structured and ordered within its parts? How is it used to express
and explore ideas and feelings? To develop school programs that concentrate
on the uses of language—on speaking and writing, listening and reading, even
on improving English usage—fundamental as such purposes may be, is not
enough. A soundly designed program of instruction must also introduce young
people to basic understanding of their native tongue as subject matter important in itself. Such study in turn will help pupils understand their own

[1] James Sledd, "Grammar or Grammarye?" *English Journal*, Vol. 49 (May 1960), p. 297.

linguistic processes and will free them from misconceptions about the uses of language by others.

No brief treatment can possibly prepare teachers in all the aspects of language they need to deal with in their classrooms. However, it can identify some of the concepts requiring priority by introducing the history, sociology, geography, structure, and philosophy of language. For further study, teachers should consult the selected references presented throughout the text and at the end of this chapter.

The History of Language

The history of language is a history of change—in pronunciation, in writing systems, in vocabulary, in style, in meaning, in spelling. Even methods of transmitting language change, and each innovation in turn affects the language. Despite the seemingly endless diversity of these changes, an essential unity persists. Man continues to use language to communicate his aspirations, ideas, and feelings; and the essential relationships within the language, such as that of subject-verb, remain largely unchanged.

Attention to the history of language began in the eighteenth century when scholars observed similarities between such languages as Sanskrit, English, Greek, and Latin. Study of written records led to the recognition of certain parent languages. Indo-European, itself a branch of an unknown tongue of yet earlier origin, is presumed to be the forerunner of many language families; it was the source of most northern European languages, including the Germanic dialects from which English evolved. Some 5,000 years ago, Indo-European was the speech of north central Europe, but the separation and geographical isolation of regional groups of men eventually produced separate languages divergent in grammar, sound, and vocabulary. Some languages died as the societies that created them disappeared; others evolved into those we today know as Greek, Latin, Russian, German, French, and English.

WRITING SYSTEMS   The emergence of writing systems, following the development of spoken languages, demonstrates clearly man's efforts to preserve his thoughts and impressions. From the early pictography of the Africans, Chinese, and American Indians, from the development of syllabic writing, and from the invention of the alphabetic system around 2000 B.C. in the Middle East, we see how man has struggled to find written symbols to represent his spoken words and sounds. We can follow the story of the transmission of the alphabet from Phoenicians to Greeks and then to Rome, from where it was spread by the early Christians. The runic inscriptions of early Germanic tribes illustrate the writing system replaced by the Roman alphabet. Tales of deciphering a primitive writing system—the use of the Rosetta Stone, for example —are also part of the story, as is development of the international phonetic alphabet during the nineteenth century and the experiments with a modified alphabet for reading and spelling instruction during our own. Consideration of carefully selected examples will illuminate for young people how through history man has sought more accurate representations of his spoken language.

The history and future of English can be presented as one of the most fascinating parts of the school year in an English class. The language itself is only about 1,500 years old, but already it has become one of the major languages of the world and has an expanding future. At one time it was considered a vulgar, lower-class dialect, incapable of expressing refined and complex ideas and sentiments. Yet today its literature is one of the jewels of civilization and is studied in all nations. English vies with Russian and Spanish for the possibility of becoming *the* world language.

Most pupils respond quickly to lore about their language, yet few of them realize that language changes, that recordings revealing its past will seem almost to be in a foreign tongue. Seldom do they consider that their way of speaking may in years to come sound strange to their descendants. They will be interested in the "advantages" of English:

> its natural gender, so one need not memorize whether *rhubarb, furnace, mug,* and *ghost* are masculine, feminine, or neuter
> the simplicity of certain aspects of its grammar, relatively free from inflections adhering to the ends of nouns, verbs, adjectives
> its cosmopolitan vocabulary, a result of its long hospitality to other languages, new ideas, and new experiences

The "liabilities" of English will also intrigue them:

> its chaotic spelling (How well they know this!)
> its irregular verbs (*come, see, go,* . . .); and its annoying habit of adding *s* to the present-tense verb in only one person (I fall, you fall, he fall*s*)

They can become absorbed in noting how influences such as science, city living, and increase in junior-college attendance are changing our language. From this they can look back with understanding and interest to earlier powerful formative influences on our mother tongue: the victory of the Norman French in 1066; the triumph of the industrial middle class over the aristocratic upper class from 1789 to the American Civil War; the geographical and social mobility that accounts for the amazing unity of American speech across an enormous continent. The miracle of language appeals to students when such lively excursions are made into its history and its future.

TWO INFLUENCES   Consideration of two kinds of language change is important: change forced upon English by external circumstances and change inherent in language growth. The former includes events that have had a profound influence on the culture of the English-speaking people, such as the settlement of Britain and America by particular dialect groups. The key events recorded on the chart on pages 64–65 give students an idea of the continuity of their language and of the many speakers and writers whose contributions have made it what it is today.

Internal change, inevitable in all living languages, affects such aspects as pronunciation, grammar, vocabulary, meaning, and usage. Although these changes can be dramatized by comparing examples from Old, Middle, and Modern English texts, they are probably best understood by considering four significant changes since the Old English period:

1. English has changed from a language relying on full inflection to designate case, number, gender, person, tense, and mood to a language that relies largely on word order, on auxiliary verbs, and on the use of prepositions and special structural words to designate such distinctions.

2. The pronunciation of English has shifted substantially from Old to Middle to Modern English, with the major shift in the pronunciation of vowels occurring from c. 1600 to 1800.

3. The vocabulary of English has been expanded and changed, particularly during three great periods: the impact of Norman French during the thirteenth and fourteenth centuries; the Latin influence of the English Renaissance during the sixteenth and seventeenth centuries; and the impact of new scientific and technological knowledge of modern times.

4. The nature of English spelling has altered, partially as a result of changes in pronunciation but more particularly the result of widespread standardization accompanying the fifteenth-century introduction of the printing press, which regularized the use of certain written symbols to reproduce sound at a time when English pronunciation was still changing.

Samuel Johnson's arbitrary judgments on spelling and Noah Webster's prescriptions for simplifying spelling should also be noted.

If study of the history of language were to be complete, young people would need to become familiar with other aspects of change—style, usage, and so on. Such changes are most clearly seen in reference to particular literary texts or other specific examples. For most of our students, however, direct study of language history might better concentrate on the sweep of external events. From this students will become aware of how and why a language changes. They will realize that the language they speak and write dates back to much earlier times and has been affected by the accumulated experience of English-speaking people.

The Geography of Language

Every language is the product of people living in a specific geographical area; in regions of considerable size, several or many dialects may evolve. Dialects are habitual systems of language set off from each other by differences in grammar, pronunciation, and vocabulary. Such differences occur when communities become isolated by regional or social barriers. Just as the Celtic tribes in Britain established separate communities that developed today's Gaelic (Irish), Welsh, and Cornish, so the Saxon settlement of England established regional dialects influencing the subsequent history of our language. The East

KEY EVENTS INFLUENCING THE DEVELOPMENT OF ENGLISH

Historical event	*Impact on the language*
EARLY ORIGINS (before 449 A.D.)	
Settlement of Britain by Celtic tribes.	Celtic place names: Dover, Wye, Bryn Mawr, Avon; words associated with rural life: valley, badger, shamrock, cradle.
Roman occupation (55 B.C.–410 A.D.), first period of Latin influence.	Introduction of Roman alphabet; Roman place names: *castra* (camp) Winchester.
Isolation of Welsh, Scottish, Cornish settlements.	Development of communities with separate dialects.
OLD ENGLISH (449–1100)	
Landing of Hengist and Horsa in England (449); separate settlements of Angles, Saxons, and Jutes.	Establishment of separate English dialects; English based on two-tense Germanic system rather than six-tense Latin; basic, often monosyllabic, Germanic words: nose, mouth, ears, eyes, kitchen, cup, kettle, chew, think.
Danish invasion and unification of separate Anglo-Saxon groups under Alfred the Great (871–901).	Place names: *by* (town) in Rugby, Derby; g and k sounds in words like egg, kid; reinforcement of words in both languages.
Beginning of written English: *Anglo-Saxon Chronicle;* poetry recorded by West Saxon scribes; *Beowulf.*	Establishment of West Saxon dialect as beginning of written English.
Norman Conquest (1066); Norman French replacing Old English as official language of court; Old English continuing as spoken language of people.	New words in learning and arts: romance, cathedral, physician; French words, especially those associated with food: appetite, pastry, roast, beef, pork; social life: embroidery, apparel, tournament, chess; religion: faith, Cardinal; government: parliament, revenue, squire, libel; introduction of some French spellings.
Lack of successful linguistic invasion in Britain after Norman Conquest.	Development of Anglo-Saxon language, modified by Norman French, into Modern English.
MIDDLE ENGLISH (1100–1500)	
Development of bilingual nation with French spoken in government; English in village and town; Latin confined largely to the Church.	Words expressing distinctions in class or dialect: bold (OE), valiant (Fr.), audacious (Lat.), work (OE), labor (Fr.), town (OE), city (Fr.), ox (OE), beef (Fr.), kind (OE), gentle (Fr.).
Emergence of nationalism: English gradually replacing French and Latin as national language.	Persistence of diversity of English dialects first established in Old English.
Major writers establishing English as a literary language: John Gower, William Langland, Geoffrey Chaucer. John Wyclif's translation of the Bible.	Establishment of English as a major written language.
William Caxton's introduction of first printing press.	Standardization of written English, spelling, even though pronunciation shifts continued.

EARLY MODERN ENGLISH (1500–1700)

Impact of Latin and Greek on English through the humanistic revival of the English Renaissance.

Affixes and root words in new terms express new ideas; words associated with rebirth of learning: Latin—industry, meditate, emancipate, allegory, prosody; Greek—catastrophe, anonymous.

Expansion of English through exploration and trade and the impact of Eastern and Indian tongues on English vocabulary.

Introduction of words from other languages: Dutch and German—freighter, dock, dollar, easel; Italian—balcony, volcano, carnival, dome, violin, opera, novel; Spanish—potato, sombrero, armada; Eastern and Oriental: orange, cotton, turban, cypher, zenith, alcohol.

Continuing development reflecting increasingly complex political, scholarly, and literary interests of Englishmen.

Emergence of major writers in English and their development of literary language: Spenser, Shakespeare, Milton, King James' Bible.

Increasing flexibility and richness of English as a major literary language.

Establishment of a middle-class dialect based on the East Anglic of the Anglo-Saxons as the language of trade and the mercantile class.

Use of middle-class English dialect in colonization throughout world; new words reflecting exploration: South America—pampas, cayenne; East Indies—cashmere, jungle, calico; Africa—voodoo, zebra, chimpanzee; Australia—boomerang, kangaroo.

MODERN ENGLISH: (1700–present)

Spread of English to North American colonies, with middle-class dialects established in New England and language of London aristocracy introduced on Southern plantations.

Beginning of regional variation in United States.

Rise of American English with the American nation, influenced by diverse dialects and languages.

Spread of English through the United States; French place names in Louisiana; Spanish influence in Southwest; Indian words—papoose, tomahawk, wigwam, maize, totem; Indian place names—Illinois, Minnesota, Arizona.

Emergence of scholarly study of the English language, first in early dictionaries, later by grammarians.

Recording the nature of language changes.

Development of mass education and spread of literacy.

Prevalence of writing and reading.

Emergence largely in twentieth century of new literatures in English by writers of Africa and various national groups: Canada, Australia, India.

Emergence of other varieties of literary English: Nigerian, Canadian, Australian, West Indian.

Continued expansion reflecting mercantile, industrial, scientific, technological, and political developments.

New scientific and technological terms: radiator, automobile, clutch, radio, television, telegraph, satellite, superhighway.

Anglic of the West Saxons, modified by continual change, became the London dialect of the middle class and was carried to the New England colonies. The dialect of the London aristocracy was spoken on the plantations of the South. From the beginning of our history, regional variation in language has been characteristic of the United States.

However, American dialects have always possessed greater uniformity than those of Europe. (There are more dialects spoken in the British county of Yorkshire than in the entire United States!) The geographical and social mobility of our population, aided by other social forces, has promoted considerable agreement on the varieties of standard English. Yet what is accepted as standard in Boston is quite different from standard English in Charleston and diverges also from that spoken in Texas or Iowa. Few young television viewers need to be reminded of the regional speech patterns of America.

The study of American regional dialects can help students understand how varieties of language emerged and why they continue to exist. An understanding is essential for those who live in our great cities with their varied mixtures of dialects. The study begins with the settlement of the Atlantic coast, with the linguistic background of the colonies and with the combinations and compromises in local language habits that inevitably took place. The expansion westward, influenced more by some speech communities than others, played a role, as did contacts with French, Indian, and Spanish speakers in various regions. The emergence of key cultural centers, first in Boston, Charleston, and New York, later in Chicago, San Francisco, and other western cities, established influences emulated by speakers in every area. The movement to urban centers broke down the isolation of some dialect groups, but the class structure of the cities promoted certain social distinctions. The impact of foreign-speaking immigrants remained an important influence well into the twentieth century. Even more significant were the rise of mass education, the spread of mass media, and the widespread acceptance of flexible forms of colloquial speech.

Despite the uniformity of much American language, many regional differences remain. For the past forty years, linguistic geographers have studied the differences in pronunciation, vocabulary, and grammar throughout the United States; their findings demonstrate that no single, standard language exists. Perhaps their most interesting discovery reveals three dialect bands extending westward from the east coast (see the map on page 68). Called Northern, Midland, and Southern, these dialects differ somewhat in their system of sounds (phonemes), in the grammatical systems to which words and phrases conform, and in vocabulary. Detailed information concerning the nature of these variations is contained in the Linguistic Atlas of the United States, being compiled in several areas of the country.[2]

___

[2] Several reports on the Linguistic Atlas are presently available: E. Bagby Atwood, *A Survey of Verb Forms in the Eastern United States* (Ann Arbor: Univ. of Michigan Press, 1953); E. Bagby Atwood, *The Regional Vocabulary of Texas* (Austin: Univ. of Texas Press, 1962); Hans Kurath *et al., Handbook of the Linguistic Geography of New England*

Study of regional dialects will inform young people about the flexibility and variety of our language. They need to learn those features of cultivated usage that have national currency, those peculiar to the region in which they live, and something of the divergent language habits of Americans in other regions. These understandings will help them see language as a human creation, relative to change, purpose, and geographical location.

The Sociology of Language

Individuals learn their language in the surroundings in which they grow up. The most significant influences are the most immediate—the speech of parents and family group, the language of the neighborhood, the patterns of communication used by associates. By the time a child is six, he has largely mastered the essential machinery of spoken language: he has acquired a considerable vocabulary; he uses the established idioms and sentence patterns; he selects the grammatical forms corresponding to those he hears; in short, he has learned to speak the local vernacular. As he matures, the social circumstances in which he must use language help him discriminate between the language he will use in the family group and that appropriate for casual or formal circumstances.

MOTIVATION FOR LEARNING LANGUAGE   Motivation influences not only the language one uses in particular instances but the kind of language one learns. Clearly the most powerful motivation for learning language is the desire to identify oneself with another. Thus young children emulate the speech habits of their parents; adolescents, their peers; adults, the prestige figures with whom they wish to associate. To the extent an individual's social experiences are limited, so also are his opportunities to learn language. Only as his experience expands is he able to achieve continuing contact with a wide variety of dialects; and only as social pressures compel him to acknowledge the need will he begin to modify language habits that have persisted since childhood.

Our educational programs have become deeply committed to developing in each student sufficient command of a standard idiom to enable him to fulfill his economic and intellectual potential. Widespread progress is unlikely to be fast, for language habits of long duration are not easily changed. They can be modified slowly as one advances through various levels of education or becomes associated with new social groups; they alter rapidly only when one is convinced he wants them to change.

Television personalities serve as examples. We have long known that one who speaks standard English can, for the purpose of entertainment, acquire

(Washington D.C.: American Council of Learned Societies, 1939); Hans Kurath, *A Word Geography of the Eastern United States* (Ann Arbor: Univ. of Michigan Press, 1949); Hans Kurath and Raven I. McDavid, Jr., *The Pronunciation of English in the Atlantic States* (Ann Arbor: Univ. of Michigan Press, 1961).

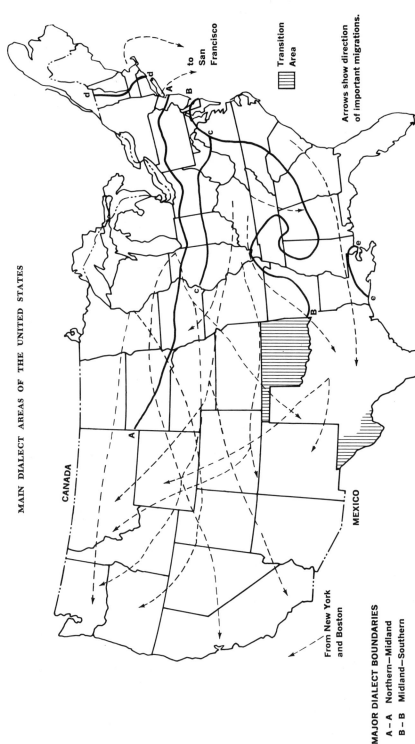

MAIN DIALECT AREAS OF THE UNITED STATES

CANADA

MEXICO

to San Francisco

Transition Area

Arrows show direction of important migrations.

From New York and Boston

MAJOR DIALECT BOUNDARIES

A – A   Northern—Midland
B – B   Midland—Southern

Minor Dialect Boundaries

c – c   North Midland—South Midland
d – d   Coastal New England—Northern
e – e   New Orleans Focal Area—Southern

several dialects. The many conversational programs now popular emphasize a more important development: many persons originally speaking dialects reflecting different ethnic groups have acquired a standard variety of English and can change back and forth at will, neither language betraying a trace of the other. Their accomplishments show what can be done when the incentive is strong.

LINGUISTIC BARRIERS   Scholars have fully appreciated the role of language in maintaining sharp lines of social-class distinction. In the closed societies of the past, each class spoke differently; language was one of the most effective means of preserving the stability, the unchanging nature, of those societies. Illuminating this role of language is a tart Danish comment: "In the old days our aristocrats spoke French to one another, German to their merchants, and Danish to their dogs." In closed societies, class mobility was almost impossible, and language was an effective wall keeping everyone in his place. As long as societies remained closed, the differences in social class speech caused little difficulty. In the upwardly mobile societies of today, class dialects become a social problem and an educational problem. Even in a society like our own, where individual worth and aspiration are intended to count more than circumstances of birth, language preserves class distinctions and remains one of the major barriers to crossing social and economic lines. The picture William Labov gives of the effect of the linguistic barriers on Puerto Rican communities in New York City applies as well to other groups throughout the United States.[3]

Too many Americans think of language in judgmental terms: "good" language is used by prestigious groups; "bad" language is used by any other group. Many Americans, in striving to achieve "correctness," develop a stilted use of language and self-conscious insecurity that blocks clear communication. Language and social position are linked, and people who belong to the more favored economic groups are often inclined to criticize without trying to understand the language of the poor. We need to remind ourselves of the sociological relationship between poverty and language.

Helping students acquire a standard idiom is only part of the picture. No pupil will respond to such help—let alone genuinely welcome it—unless he realizes its value and shares his teacher's purpose. Therefore both pupil and teacher must be aware of what is at stake: freedom. Inability to use informal, standard English will limit the pupil's ability to move in some social and economic directions. When the pupil has learned the standard idiom, he may ultimately decline to use it and to enter into ways of living where its use is

[3] William Labov, *Social Stratification of English in New York City* (Washington, D.C.: Center for Applied Linguistics, 1966).

From Jean Malmstrom and Annabel Ashley, *Dialects U.S.A.* (Champaign, Ill.: NCTE, 1963). Reprinted with the permission of the National Council of Teachers of English and Jean Malmstrom.

customary. The central concern he must share with his teacher is developing a basis for making such a decision.

We must keep in mind that each dialect possesses its own grammar, sound system, and lexicon. A dialect is not merely slovenly speech or an uneducated departure from a variety of standard English. It is a system of English fully capable of communicating in certain social groups; it reflects the nature of the speaker's experience, rather than his carelessness or his stupidity.

Understanding the nature of social dialects and how they are acquired will help eradicate misconceptions of young people about the language behavior of many people they meet. Such study may help eliminate the linguistic snobbery too often associated with attitudes toward social, racial, and ethnic groups—a snobbery that works both ways; it may also incline young people to expend greater effort to understand speakers of English dialects other than their own. The Scottish linguist David Abercrombie asserts that 95 percent of the difficulties in communicating between two dialect groups results from the listener's unwillingness to try to understand the speaker. The study of regional dialects can make students aware that standard English has many acceptable varieties. Teachers who have introduced such study find that adolescents are deeply interested. The subject matter is alive and available.

The Dictionaries of English

Much information on the history, geography, and sociology of the language is recorded in English dictionaries, yet as controversy after the publication of Webster's *Third New International* made clear, many Americans do not understand the nature and purpose of dictionaries. Because understanding is essential to intelligent use, some study of the nature of lexicography is basic to any English program.

DESCRIPTIVE MODERN DICTIONARIES Fundamentally, students must learn that most modern dictionaries are descriptive rather than prescriptive. They do not advocate a standard English usage. Rather, the lexicographers compiling dictionaries attempt to describe the use, pronunciation, and spelling of words used by a selected body of writers and speakers. Therefore, the body of language on which dictionary citations are based will determine the nature of the annotations within the volume. Webster's *New International Dictionary of the English Language* (second edition, 1959) used citations of spoken and written English, many of them from documents of past centuries, obtained prior to publication date. Webster's *Third New International Dictionary of the English Language* (1961) and the *Random House Dictionary of the English Language* (1966) are based on a corpus of material including much written and spoken language of the past few decades. That they are particularly useful in describing the scientific and technical words used in our time is not surprising. (So rapid is language change that the G. W. Merriam

Company, publishers of the *International Dictionary*, have regularly prepared new editions every twenty-five years.) Since the function of lexicographers is to describe, readers who object to the descriptions are in a sense objecting to the inevitable changes in our language.

So that students can understand the basis of any dictionary, they should be urged to examine carefully the prefatory material. Here they will find a discussion of the editorial principles on which the dictionary is based, as well as explanations for the symbols and abbreviations used to designate etymology, pronunciation, and status labels (standard, nonstandard, substandard). When dictionaries present words in actual citations of usage, the pupil should be urged to study the use in context. Where variant spellings and usages appear, he needs to determine whether the editors have attempted to indicate any preferred or "most frequent" variation. Above all he needs to compare the citations and variations in several dictionaries so that the differences will become apparent and he will understand that dictionaries do differ, that no particular one is an authority, and that they vary in purpose.

EVOLUTION OF DICTIONARIES   In studying how dictionaries are compiled and in learning how to use them intelligently, young people will profit from an overview of how dictionaries have evolved. For most classes study need not be detailed, but it should include some consideration of key events in lexicography:

> the early sixteenth-century dictionaries, which attempted to list Latin words and English equivalents
> the development of interest in words and their origins and the publication of the first true English dictionary, compiled by Edward Phillips in 1658
> *Dictionary of the English Language* (1755), in which Samuel Johnson tried to "fix" pronunciation and preserve the "purity" of the language
> *An American Dictionary of the English Language* (1828), in which Noah Webster attempted to record American English and to simplify its spellings
> the publication between 1884 and 1924 of the ten-volume *Oxford English Dictionary*, the first great descriptive dictionary, which established methods of lexicography used to compile most dictionaries today
> modern developments in lexicography, including the publication of major American dictionaries (Webster's *International*, Webster's *New World, Random House*, the *Century, Funk and Wagnall's, New American College*)

SPECIAL-PURPOSE DICTIONARIES AND MANUALS   Students also need to learn about dictionaries designed for special purposes, such as dictionaries abridged for convenient desk use, special editions for schools, those describing usages in particular occupations and areas of scholarly interest. Some, like the *Dictionary of Americanisms* or the *Dictionary of American Slang*, provide information on particular aspects of language and are useful reference works. Particularly helpful to writers are the dictionaries of synonyms and the thesaurus.

Several manuals are available as guides to English usage. Unlike most dictionaries, these make no scientific attempt to describe words as they are used; instead they present the judicious opinions of the editors and offer individuals helpful, informed advice. Fowler's traditional *Modern English Usage* has been revised by Marjorie Nicholson to embrace *Modern American Usage;* Horwell's *Dictionary of Modern American Usage* is also available as is the more liberal *Dictionary of Contemporary American Usage* by Bergen and Cornelia Evans. Conservative and literary attitudes are reflected in *Wilson Follett's Modern American Usage,* edited by Jacques Barzun. Margaret Bryant's *Current American English* is a carefully prepared description of the uses of some 240 items of disputed American usage. All these are valuable to the student and should be made available for both comparison and study. Indeed, the continuing use of a considerable variety of dictionaries and books on usage will reinforce the student's awareness of two related truths: people make the language; the function of the lexicographer is to describe.

The Structure of English

Every language has an orderly structure, and the grammars of English are attempts to describe this system. Some grammars emphasize the phonological structure; others concentrate on syntactical relationships; a complete grammar would describe both spoken and written English as well as the relationships among phonological, morphological, and syntactical patterns.

At the present time no single grammar accounts for the rich diversity of our spoken and written tongue, but each new one provides important insights. In this sense, each grammar of English, whether traditional or modern, provides a different way of looking at language, and each has contributed to our total knowledge. Teachers of English thus profit enormously by keeping informed about modern linguistic scholarship. They need especially to be familiar with two or three different English grammars, if only to avoid being dependent upon a single one. Whether or not they choose to present these grammars to their students, they will find their own understanding of linguistic processes greatly enhanced by such study.

Most individuals have intuitively learned the basic grammar of their language by the time they have reached school age; they have internalized the systematic principles governing the production of spoken sentences in their dialect. Later they may or may not learn to articulate the principles that determine grammaticality. Certainly, many have been able to improve their speech or writing without formal study of structure; everything known about language acquisition suggests that facility in using language is most effectively acquired through active communication in social situations and through the emulation of speakers and writers one admires.

The findings of research have largely invalidated many arguments advanced perennially for studying grammar. Such study has on occasion been justified for its contribution to the discipline of the mind, for its assistance in learning a second language, for showing students how to avoid ungrammatical usages in speech and writing, for providing a vocabulary to make possible discussion of language problems with teachers.[4] The findings of research on the teaching of schoolroom grammar clearly fail to sustain any of these claims. Indeed, after a comprehensive review of all research on the impact of grammatical study on composition, Richard Braddock and others recently wrote, "In view of the widespread agreement of research studies based upon many types of students and teachers, the conclusion can be stated in strong and unqualified terms: The teaching of formal grammar has a negligible or, because it usually displaces some instruction in practice in actual composition, even a harmful effect on the improvement of writing." [5] Advocates of modern grammars argue that the theories of grammar on which earlier studies were based are now outmoded, that the more powerful grammars of today are more likely to contribute to the student's ability to write and speak. Perhaps so, but we do not yet know this is true. Too little controlled experimentation has been made.[6]

One unwisely supports the teaching of grammar on the grounds that it will improve speaking and writing. Substantial evidence demonstrates the superiority of methods that base instruction on the student's own communications. Motivation is greater when it is his own use of language that is under scrutiny. Indeed usage and grammar, far too long intertwined in most secondary schools, involve different considerations and need to be carefully separated in the classroom.[7]

The primary purpose of studying English grammar is to learn the systematic ways in which man produces language. Too, because grammatical description is largely a system of classification, students can learn much about inductive definition in making a grammar from the evidence acquired through their own experience with language. Grammar is knowledge valuable in its own right, and its study should be justified largely on this basis. Such understanding may help some individuals analyze and revise their own sentences; it can scarcely help to produce sentences. In any event, the study of grammar does not require practical justification any more than does the study of biology. One does not study the human anatomy to learn how to walk, nor should he study the structure of language to learn how to talk and write.

---

[4] A valuable summary of arguments for and against the teaching of grammar is presented by the Commission on English in *Freedom and Discipline in English* (New York: College Entrance Examination Board, 1961), pp. 26–31.

[5] Richard Braddock *et al.*, *Research in Written Composition* (Champaign, Ill.: NCTE, 1963), pp. 37–38.

[6] Donald Bateman and Frank Zidonis, *The Effect of a Study of Transformational Grammar on the Writing of Ninth and Tenth Graders* (Champaign, Ill.: NCTE, 1966). This study describes the teaching of modern grammar to forty better-than-average students at a university high school; it suggests this approach may improve sentence structure in one aspect.

[7] For this reason, the improvement of usage and sentence structure is treated separately from grammar in this book. See Chapter Three.

Yet to admit that study of the structure of English is valuable in itself is not to say that such study is for all students or that all aspects of grammar must be presented in any secondary-school program. Teachers must be selective in determining what is to be taught. By its very nature, grammar is abstract and general. Young people who have difficulty learning generalizations are highly unlikely to profit from such study. Programs for students of lower ability should concentrate on more practical aspects of language study, just as instruction in mathematics for such pupils concentrates on basic arithmetical skills and not on algebra and more complex thought processes. Even for the most able pupils, grammatical content must be selected with a scholar-teacher's discrimination.

At least four grammars of English are widely discussed today. Teachers need some understanding of each if only to help them evaluate new textbook materials. Although careful description of any grammar and the countless variations in each point of view require extensive study, a few useful distinctions may be made.

TRADITIONAL SCHOOLROOM GRAMMAR   Until recently the grammar used in our schools derived from the studies of eighteenth-century grammarians and popular grammarians of the nineteenth century. The textbooks presented a description of the English language (called "traditional" grammar by many teachers) based on literary or Latinate models. Such grammars characteristically emphasized written English, stressed inflectional endings, used logic or semantic rules to define eight parts of speech and the relations within the English sentence. Such textbooks tended to stress prescriptive rules for determining grammatical correctness, even in the face of the many exceptions to be found in the usage of distinguished writers. Moreover, they concentrated on the errors that individuals frequently committed rather than on building systematic understanding of the structure of the language. The grammar contributed an important terminology, however, and—in the hands of good teachers—a useful method of syntactic analysis. But the textbooks tended to be fragmentary in approach, strongly deductive, devoting little attention to phonology; they relied heavily on confusing definitions resulting in large measure from attempts to combine semantic explanations and Latinate definitions capable of application to the noninflectional patterns of English.

SCHOLARLY TRADITIONAL GRAMMAR   The work of highly respected linguists like Otto Jespersen and Henry Sweet during the late nineteenth and early twentieth centuries is frequently referred to as "scholarly traditional" grammar. More influential on subsequent linguists than on the school tradition, the grammars of these linguists attempted to describe the English language as English (not Latin). Influenced by the work of philologists, they were concerned with the analysis of speech as well as of writing and devoted attention to the formal characteristics of literary usage; however, as they began to study regional and social variations, they took a more enlightened view of English usage than did schoolbook grammarians. *The Sentence and Its Parts* by Ralph Long is a major contemporary American text continuing this tradition.

STRUCTURAL GRAMMAR   Structural grammar arose from the descriptive studies of American linguists during the 1930's and 1940's. It is an attempt to describe the sound patterns and syntactical patterns of English as they are actually used. The first level of analysis is phonological, beginning with the basic unit of sound (phoneme) and the use of stress, pitch, and juncture (supra-segmental phonemes) to convey additional spoken distinctions. The morpheme, the basic unit of meaning, provides the next level of analysis; the final level is syntax, the arrangement of words within the sentence. In many such approaches the two main parts of the sentence are considered its immediate constituents, and the method of dividing and subdividing until the morpheme units are reached is called immediate constituent analysis. Structural grammarians stress the pattern of English structures; they have provided valuable insights into English phonology and have directed much attention to the spoken varieties of English. Distinctions made among form-words and function-words in analyzing sentences; concern with word order; study of word-function within the sentence context—all these have had considerable impact on pedagogy. These aspects contrast sharply with the independent classification of words in traditional schoolroom grammars. Important teaching methods derived from structural grammar include pattern practice and the use of test frames to determine parts of speech.

American *English Grammar* and *The Structure of English* by Charles C. Fries and *An Outline of English Structures* by Henry Lee Smith, Jr., and George L. Trager are probably the most influential scholarly works. Among the useful structural grammars for teachers are *The Structure of American English* by W. Nelson Francis, *A Short Introduction to English Grammar* by James Sledd, *A Structural View of English* by Morris Finder, and *Structural Grammar in the Classroom* by Verna Newsome.

TRANSFORMATIONAL-GENERATIVE GRAMMAR   Grammarians of this persuasion attempt to explain the underlying series of rules that govern how all sentences in the language can be formed. Unlike structural grammar, transformational-generative grammar is a grammar of process concerned with explaining the rule-governed behavior through which individuals can both understand and generate infinite varieties of the English sentence. Basic to understanding this grammar are the concepts of deep structure and surface structure meanings. Deep structure is the underlying idea in the mind that determines the meaning of a sentence but is only implied in spoken and written sentences. Surface structure is the organization of sentences into phrases, words, and sounds. Semantic rules thus apply to deep structure; phonetic rules to surface structure; and the interplay of the two determines some of the orderly ways in which meaning is conveyed and understood.

Transformational-generative grammars consist of two kinds of rules. Phrase-structure rules explain the construction of a small set of basic sentences (sometimes called "kernel sentences"), which are combined in various ways to build more complicated structures. Transformational rules explain how basic kernel sentences are transformed into more complex ones.

No orientation in linguistics today has recently influenced other disciplines more than transformational-generative grammar. Because of its concern with the production of language and its emphasis on syntax, it offers unusual promise for the teaching of English. Much of the still developing theoretical work in transformational-generative grammar has been reported by such linguists as Noam Chomsky, Robert Lees, and Paul Postal. Teachers will find less arduous the introductions to this theory provided by Owen Thomas, Jr., in *Transformational Grammar and the Teacher of English;* H. A. Gleason, Jr., in *Linguistics and English Grammar;* Syrell Rogovin in *Modern English Sentence Structure;* and Roderick Jacobs and Peter Rosenbaum in *English Transformational Grammar.*

OTHER GRAMMARS   Although varieties of the grammars described above most commonly appear today in textbooks and school curricula, linguists continue to advance other descriptions of language structure. Tagmemics, a grammar relating structural description to the context in which communication occurs, is advanced by Kenneth Pike. Stratificational grammar, advocated by Sidney Lamb in this country and Michael Halliday in England, offers the promise of providing new insights into syntax. The sector analysis developed by Robert L. Allen seems to offer certain refinements on "slot and filler" approaches used by other structuralists. The essential point for teachers of English is that as linguists continue to expand their studies of the structure of English, we can expect new theories and new points of view, each adding substantially to our knowledge.

Faced with a plethora of grammatical theories, the teacher will readily see that no single "linguistic approach" commends itself to attention. If grammar is seen as the theory of English structure, the teacher should teach from the grammar that seems to him to offer the truest and most accurate description of the language. He need not confine himself to one theory. The teacher may choose to present several different grammars to his students, stressing at one point structural description and at another a transformational-generative approach. And in modern metropolitan schools where many students speak nonstandard varieties of English with unique but systematic grammars, the teacher will wish to devote some attention to the grammar of the pupils' language. H. A. Gleason argues for an "eclectic synthesis" and strives to identify those approaches that seem most significant to him.[8] A similar approach is taken by the Center for Curriculum Development in Eng-

[8] H. A. Gleason, Jr., *Linguistics and English Grammar* (New York: Holt, Rinehart & Winston, 1965), pp. 86–87.

lish at the University of Minnesota, which suggests that the following principles form the basis for grammatical study in the secondary school: [9]

rules, principles, or criteria for arranging meaningful elements in words, phrases, and sentences

definition and survey of meaningful elements

identification of four parts of speech

five basic sentence patterns

basic sentence patterns expanded by transformations

syntactic structures of predication, complementation, modification, and coordination

Some, particularly those steeped in transformational-generative theory, would argue that the coherent presentation of a single grammar can more readily be understood by young people. Practically, the decision in each school must be determined by the preparation of teachers and the availability of materials. Whatever the approach, however, the study of English grammar must be seen by students as the study of a system of language.

The study of language cannot be confined to the study of its history, geography, sociology, and structure. The living operation of the limits and possibilities of the language must be studied as well. The many ways of studying language need to be a part of education for every child. Thinking with language includes a concern with how we think: classifying into categories, comparing and contrasting, making subtle distinctions. We deduce and induce. We generalize. We seek relationships and we reason by analogy, using all forms of figurative language. We also dream and imagine and make intuitive leaps in the dark. We unify our thoughts by imposing either a rational or an imaginative design upon the content of our thought. The language of the uneducated man is distinguished from that of the educated man by the greater disjunction and separation in the component parts of whatever he wishes to communicate. In the language of the uneducated, there is a lack of that "prospectiveness of mind, that *surview*, which enables a man to foresee the whole of what he is to convey, appertaining to any one point; and by this means so to subordinate and arrange the different parts according to their relative importance, as to convey it at once, and as an organized whole." [10]

Another aspect of language that education can use more fully may be called the two countenances of language. Language can be shaped toward objective, dispassionate referential use, as in science and mathematics. Or it can be bent toward subjective, vivid emotive use, as in literature. Through scientific language we *understand;* through literary language we *realize.* Both forms—and their mixtures in everyday discourse—reveal much about how

---

[9] "Extended Notes for Minnesota Project English Units," University of Minnesota Center for Curriculum Development in English, Stanley B. Kegler, Director (multilithed), p. 43.
[10] Samuel Taylor Coleridge, *Biographia Literaria,* Chapter XVIII.

language is related to thinking and feeling. Both forms are important to man and need to be taught as a part of education. Such uses of language are discussed in Chapters Four and Five.

LANGUAGE: CONCEPTS FOR EMPHASIS

To classify the wide range of language concepts, seven areas of language have been defined: History of English Language, Dialectology, Lexicography, Semantics, Phonology, Grammar, Usage. A generalized concept of each area is given in italics with more specific concepts ordered sequentially from simple to complex below it. (The semantics section deviates slightly by ordering sequentially within four specific areas.)

A cross-reference device makes use of five specific symbols to designate history, dialect study, lexicography, semantics, and phonology. The use of a specific symbol in the margin of a language area indicates its relationship with the "symbol" area.

LEGEND: △ History of English Language
     ○ Dialectology
     * Lexicography
     □ Semantics
     ☆ Phonology

△ *History of English Language*

GENERAL CONCEPT   Fundamentally Germanic in origin, the English language has a background history of borrowing from many other languages. This process has been accompanied not only by adjustment and deletion but also by use of self-explaining compounds and root words.

SPECIFIC CONCEPTS   Spoken language is exclusively a human activity.

The necessity for written communication forced even primitive man to □set up *a code of symbols.*

 ☆*In order to communicate and preserve ideals, aspirations, and achievements man sought an alphabet by which the sounds of his language could be expressed in more effective symbols.*

 English is becoming increasingly more important and more widely used. Its origin is Indo-European and Germanic. English has been modified and enriched by practically every known language.

 ○*American English is rooted in British English, but has developed its own characteristics, profiting by and absorbing the languages of the many peoples settling in the U.S.*

 Both American and British English have shown continuous development and enrichment because of advance in technology, science, commerce, and all other fields of human endeavor.

FROM *Sequential Programs in English* (Grades 7–12), Educational Research Council of Greater Cleveland, Supplementary Report (December 1966), pp. 40–41.

O Dialectology

GENERAL
CONCEPT

Because language includes the spoken medium of communication, natural differences in vocabulary, grammar, pronunciation, and diction delineate groups within a large language division. The basis for differentiation may be geographic location, cultural conditions, or social structure of a specific group. Local or regional dialects differ from the standard language—the *book words* usable in any region of the country.

SPECIFIC
CONCEPTS

Dialect is the particular variety of language of a specific speech community: peer group, family, the school, the local community, and professions.

□*Even within one's personal environment, dialectal differences are apparent particularly in vocabulary:* peer group, family, school, local community.

□Within the U.S.A., dialectal differences in *vocabulary, pronunciation,* and ☆*grammar* delineate the principal linguistic regions: North, Midland, and South.

△*American dialects differ in origin, development, and distribution.*

Factors influencing origin and development of specific dialect areas are the following: early settlement history, population migration, and physical geography.

Distributive forces of dialect include: communication or lack of it among early settlers; the westward movement; later immigration; such social forces as industrialization, urbanization, education, and travel.

American literature both reveals and preserves dialectal differences in □vocabulary and grammar.

Though basically similar, American English is distinguished from British □☆English by differences in vocabulary, pronunciation, and spelling.

△*The world spread of English has contributed to the development of world regional dialects each with its own distinctive pattern of vocabulary, pronunciation, and grammar.*

△*Dialectal differences in vocabulary, choice of diction, grammar, and word order place a work of literature chronologically and geographically.*

* Lexicography

GENERAL
CONCEPT

The lexicographer attempts to record all the words of a language at a given point in the history of the language. The type of dictionary he produces depends upon whether his purpose is historical: to trace the etymological and semantic history of words; or descriptive: to indicate contemporary meanings, spellings, and pronunciations of words.

SPECIFIC
CONCEPTS

A dictionary entry gives all or some of the following information about a word: spellings, pronunciations, grammatical usage, etymology, special labels, and meanings including synonyms and antonyms.

Depending upon the purpose of the respective dictionary, these items of information may be curtailed or expanded (pocket, abridged, un-△abridged; *O.E.D.*).

A dictionary entry is not meant to be a prescriptive statement but rather a description of a word at a given point in the history of the language; consequently, a single dictionary should not be considered as a sole arbiter in language disputes.

□*Since entries are isolated words, no dictionary can give the metaphorical richness of words in a specific context.*

A lexicographer works with objective evidence in the compilation of a dictionary.

Prime consideration in the selection of words to be included is given to contemporary written citations collected from every possible source. Mere inclusion of a word does not indicate its general acceptance. The inclusion rather means that the word is used by a sufficient number of people to make it an item in the language. Since there is no real consensus about pronunciation even among educated speakers, a dictionary attempts to incorporate all acceptable pronunciations. The dictionary does not arrange pronunciations in order of preference.

□*The lexicographer makes no attempt to exhaust the possible meanings for any word; he merely suggests areas of meanings.*

To provide detailed information of a specific nature, lexicographers compile specialized dictionaries treating terms connected with particular subjects.

□   Semantics

GENERAL CONCEPT   Language is a dynamic, living thing; language changes. Language is not synonymous with thought but a vehicle of thought. Language imposes order upon experience. Meaning in language is determined by communicator, audience or readers, occasion, intention. Accuracy and effectiveness of communication depend upon precision in the use of language.

SYMBOLS

SPECIFIC CONCEPTS   Language is a set of symbols having a meaning by common agreement. There are sets and subsets of words for specific referents.

Subsets of words range from denotative to highly connotative meanings.

Word is symbol; it is meaningless without the referent for which it stands. The symbol is not the referent; the map is not the territory.

Words may show bias.

Words aid in recreating an experience, but they also impose a limitation upon our communication (experience is simultaneous; language, linear).

CHANGE IN MEANING

*Words change in meaning.

△*Historical and comparative word study gives us insights into cultures past and present.*

DETERMINING MEANING

Meanings of words are partially determined by communicator, audience or readers, occasion, and intention.

Meanings of words in context vary from meanings of words out of context; the meaning of a word is more fully understood in context.

Meanings are determined by total context which is both verbal and nonverbal.

Context includes: physical aspect—referent; symbolic aspect—representation of referent; psychological aspect—the individual's personal thought
△about physical and symbolic aspect. *A study of words in context provides clues to literature in evolution (syntax, usage, etc.).*

PRECISION IN USE

Accuracy of communication involves choosing words that best express the precise shade of meaning intended.

Effectiveness of communication is dependent upon precision in use of language: fact, inference, judgment and in the ability to grasp abstractions.

FIGURATIVE LANGUAGE

Comparison enriches language: simple metaphor.

Metaphor is multidimensional.

☆ *Phonology*

GENERAL CONCEPT   Though language is fundamentally composed of phonemes (basic units of sound), for purposes of written communication these phonemes must be represented by symbols (graphemes). In English, there is not always a direct correspondence between phonemes and graphemes.

SPECIFIC △*Speech is the primary symbolic process.*

CONCEPTS   Speech can be analyzed for the number of its phonemes or basic sound units: English has over forty phonemes but only twenty-six letters in the alphabet.

Phonemes are graphically represented by the letters of the alphabet.

There is not always a direct correspondence between phonemes and graphemes (letters of the alphabet).

English has many more sounds than letters of the alphabet; on the other hand, a single sound may be represented by a multiplicity of graphemes. In spite of the discrepancy between the phonemes and graphemes, English pronunciation and spelling do remain basically alphabetic: an examination of sound patterns points to a number of basically phonological rules for spelling (bit . . . bite; dine . . . dinner).

An acceptance of the fact that phonemes and graphemes do not coincide in many English words is an aid to spelling proficiency: these words can be mastered only through practice (e.g., colonel).

△*An understanding of the historical background of the English language explains some of the oddities of English spelling.*

English pronunciation has changed a great deal.

A shift in English vowel sounds in the fifteenth–sixteenth centuries makes it the only language that does not follow the continental pronunciation and is responsible for the many variations in the transcription of vowels (I.P.A.).

Many foreign words have been taken into the English language; some pronunciations have been anglicized; others have not. Consequently, English phonemes are not applicable.

In addition to the segmental phonemes (consonants and vowels) linguists point out that English has a set of suprasegmental phonemes: stress, pitch, juncture. This concept would find its development and primary application in oral communication. Linguists also associate the suprasegmental phonemes with punctuation skills.

Grammar

GENERAL CONCEPT Language is systematic. The study of grammar is concerned principally with describing the way that words and groups of words are put together to establish communication. The English language can be described in more ways than one. (There are many grammars of English.)

GRAMMAR OF THE SENTENCE

SPECIFIC CONCEPTS English is English; there is no universal grammar.

Meaning in the English language is fundamentally dependent on word order.

Bound morphemes operate to project meaning (study of morphology).

The English language contains a finite number of basic sentence patterns.

Sentences can be generated from kernel sentences by applying certain transformational rules.

RHETORIC OF THE SENTENCE

Composition is essentially a process of choice of possibilities. Style is based on the controlled choice of possibilities.

The great complexity of English sentences is created through expansion.

One of the marks of effective style is variety in texture.

Attention to grammatical structure imposes relative importance on ideas:

—value of varying grammatical sentences.

—value of varying rhetorical devices.

☐*Language is a vehicle for clear thinking in the deductive reasoning process.*

Usage

GENERAL CONCEPT Usage changes. The study of usage involves study and practices in making choices. Usage varies according to speaker, audience, purpose, occasion. "Good English is that form of speech which is appropriate to the purpose of the speaker, true to the language as it is, and comfortable to speaker and listener. It is the product of custom, neither cramped by rule nor freed from all restraint: it is never fixed, but changes with the organic life of the language."—R. C. Pooley

SPECIFIC ○Social level, method, situation, and regional dialects determine variations
CONCEPTS   in usage.

> ○*Social dialect defines the use of standard or nonstandard English. Standard English is the language of educated people, the people most skilled in language. A person speaks the language he has heard spoken. The learning of more than one dialect will help to increase social and intellectual mobility.* Method refers to speech or writing. Both speech and writing are governed by usage, but usage in speech is much more arbitrary. Situation demands either formal or informal usage.

> ○*Regional dialects of isolated rural areas, urban centers of culture, north, midland, and southern dialect areas cause variations in usage.*

> △*Usage changes through the years.*

> Functional variety of usage may be any of the following: formal, informal, colloquial, slang.

> There are four doctrines of usage: rules, general usage, appropriateness, linguistic norm; the linguistic norm dictates choice against indiscriminate use of any standard. Social level (cultural level) should not be confused with functional variety. Functional variety is possible on either standard or nonstandard level.

> □*The level of diction determines tone and attitude of speaker or writer.*

> An individual who has established mature habits in speech and writing is able to adapt his dialect and functional variety in usage to the occasion, the audience, and the purpose of communication. For such an individual the skill in adapting language enhances his ability to communicate widely and well.

THE TEACHING PROBLEM

The language content of a secondary-school English program may be taught indirectly in relation to the writing and reading of pupils or directly in a series of special units introduced at appropriate times throughout the six secondary years. Most modern programs combine the two approaches. Incidental opportunities for discussing aspects of language are many. Yet if the total program is to build toward achieving a coherent understanding of the nature of language, a controlling pattern or framework is necessary.

ORGANIZING INSTRUCTION

The first task in organizing language instruction is to identify priorities. The identification of key concepts will establish guidelines and assist teachers in seeing opportunities for relating the study of linguistic concepts to other classroom work. For example, the English Curriculum Committee of the Education Research Council of Greater Cleveland developed a program around language concepts in seven related areas, ranking each list in approximate order of difficulty. (See the chart on pages 78–83.) The concepts appearing at the beginning of each list are normally stressed during grades 7–9; the more mature ideas are introduced in grades 10–12. With such guidelines for instruction, teachers have a basis for seeking pertinent opportunities to develop concepts in class.

Language units

Some direct study of the nature of language is best organized in particular units of instruction. Most of the experimental curriculum centers developing pilot programs during recent years find that separate units in the four following areas are particularly well received.

INTRODUCTION TO LANGUAGE   An initial study of the nature and use of language in communication is frequently presented in the early junior high school years. The suggested unit in this text, "Power Over Language" (pages 223–40) is one example.

THE NATURE OF THE DICTIONARY   An introduction to lexicography and dictionary-building is frequently the basis for a two-week unit in grades 9 or 10.

THE DIALECTS OF ENGLISH   Study of the regional and social variation of English is not uncommonly introduced during grade 11 when students frequently study American literature and American history. A few programs provide for the study of regional variations, particularly in vocabulary, as early as the seventh or eighth grade; they reinforce such study during the later years with a consideration of "the nature of correctness" and the study of varying standard and nonstandard dialects.

THE HISTORY OF ENGLISH   Formal study of the external history of the English language is becoming common in grades 11 or 12. It is delayed until the later years so that it may draw upon pupils' study of European history and frequently so that it may be related to the study of English literature.

Although by no means uniform in length, coverage, or content, units of this kind are becoming rather common in a large number of American schools. Among other language units less frequently introduced are studies of the writing system, English phonology, the history of English spelling, language and persuasion, and similar topics. Depending upon the detail of development, such units may form the basis of three or four weeks of classwork. Some teachers will prefer more frequent, shorter units. Thus curriculum specialists at the University of Minnesota curriculum center have developed more than thirty short units in language to be introduced throughout the six-year program. Some require only a few days of study and are often taught within some larger unit context relating the study of languages to the study of literature and composition.

Teaching grammar

The teaching of English grammar poses particular problems. To be taught effectively as system, grammar cannot be presented piecemeal even though certain applications of it can frequently be introduced in relation to the students' speaking and writing. (See Chapter Three for discussion of such approaches.) The grammatical content to be taught should be carefully selected and ordered for presentation so young people may gain with each subsequent study some over-all sense of the structure of English.

Some teachers prefer to concentrate on different aspects of English grammar at different times—for example, phrase-structure rules or basic patterns in grade 7, the nature of deep structure and surface structure in grade 8, major transformations in grade 9. Such study could be limited to not more than two weeks at each grade level. Others see merit in concentrating on usage and the pupils' own sentences early in junior high school and deferring any concentration on grammar until grade 9. Subsequently, a brief review of basic structure might be provided in the later senior high school years. Whatever the approach, the study is best limited to those crucial principles that yield genuine understanding. The study of grammar is only one aspect of a total program in language. Time must be found both to strengthen the students' own usage and to present aspects of linguistic study discussed elsewhere in this book. By providing carefully for both knowledge about language and the uses of language, teachers can plan balanced programs.

Whatever approach or combination of approaches is used, certain principles seem important in planning instruction in grammar:

> Select the grammar that seems to offer your students the most understandable insights into the structure of English.
> Teach grammar as system.
> Limit the study, teaching only the essentials: many specialists believe sufficient understanding may be developed by limiting study to not more than 10 per cent of English time (two or three weeks per year) in grades 7–10 and even less thereafter.
> Concentrate primarily on syntax and semantics.
> Base instruction on sentences familiar to students, ideally from their own speech and writing.
> Utilize inductive approaches: begin with several concrete illustrations; let students analyze and generalize; introduce the theoretical explanation as a way of summarizing and clarifying the mental operation in which the class has been engaged.
> Use short, meaningful drills (see Chapter Three).
> Emphasize the sentence rather than words or phrases, studying all elements and principles within the context that gives them meaning.
> Use textbooks carefully, critically, selectively.

Ideally each teacher should understand the grammars of English so deeply that he needs only his own plan and the language of his students in organizing classroom instruction. For some time to come, however, teachers learning new grammers on their own will find the textbook a valuable aid. Even so, teachers should examine books with considerable care, selecting for presentation only those items and those illustrations that seem to advance understanding in their particular class.

SUGGESTED LEARNING EXPERIENCES

The exercises that follow illustrate classroom approaches that can be used to develop concepts discussed in this chapter. They should be used flexibly, often within larger units of instruction, frequently in relation to the study of literature and composition. Always the teacher will need to consider the context in which learning occurs. Isolated drills and exercises on language are unlikely to contribute to the broad and basic understanding the teacher of English is seeking.

TO DEVELOP GENERAL UNDERSTANDING OF THE HISTORY OF LANGUAGE

▶ *Use common readings as the basis for class study*

Two or three concise but readable essays on liguistic history can serve as the common study prior to individual research projects. *The History of English* has been used in many high school classes.[11]

▶ *Ask committees of students to report on special problems*

1. Ask committees to engage in library research to determine the dominant characteristics of our language during particular epochs. Such a checklist as the following might serve to guide groups considering the nature of Old English, Middle English, Early Modern English, Early American English:

> What groups of people influenced the language?
> What separate speech communities can be identified?
> What influence did the language have on subsequent history?
> What differences in pronunciation can be noted?
> What words are typical of those entering the language at this time?

2. Assign articles on linguistic history for individual and group reports. Sections may be from important longer works like Albert H. Marckwardt's *American English* or from one or more of the introductory readers dealing with language.[12]

---

[11] W. Nelson Francis, *The History of English* (New York: Norton, 1963).

[12] Albert H. Marckwardt, *American English* (New York: Oxford Univ. Press, 1958). Among the better readers: Wallace L. Anderson and Norman C. Stageberg, *Introductory Readings on Language*, rev. ed. (New York: Holt, Rinehart and Winston, 1966); Richard Braddock (ed.), *Introductory Readings on the English Language* (Englewood Cliffs, N.J.: Prentice-Hall, 1962); Leonard Dean and Kenneth Wilson (eds.), *Essays on Language and Usage,* rev. ed. (New York: Oxford Univ. Press, 1963).

► *Study similarities in languages*

Prepare a series of transparencies indicating how selected words are treated in various related languages. For example, the Texas Education Agency included the following in a series developed for use in schools in that state: [13]

AND THEY ALL MEAN "THREE"

Tre (Alb.) Treis (Grk.) Three (Eng.) Tre (Ital.) Tri (Irish) **Tre** (Toch A.) Tres (Lat.) Tri (Hitt.) Tri (Welsh) Trei (Rum.) Trois (Fr.) Thrir (Old Norse) Tres (Sp.) Tris (Let.) Thri (O.E.) Threis (Goth.) Tre (Swed.) Tri (Czech.) Tri (Russ.) Tri (Norw.) Tre (Dan.) Trys (Lith.) Trayas (Skt.) Thre (M.E.) Orayo (Avest.) **Drei** (Ger.) Trzy (Pol.) Drie (Du.) Trije (Ch. Slavic) Thri (Zend.)

► *Study the writing system*

1. Encourage students to prepare a bulletin board display by searching through the Readers' Guide to Periodic Literature to find references to *Life, Look,* and similar pictorial reviews for illustrations of pictography, different alphabetic systems, and so on.

2. Use *The Art of Writing* as basis for a classroom display.[14] This book contains reproductions of significant writing systems used through the ages.

3. Devote several days in a unit on "The Nature of Language" to a study of the writing system. Use the monograph *Writing Systems* to provide common material for study.[15]

TO COMPARE THE LANGUAGE OF DIFFERENT HISTORICAL PERIODS

► *Study selected texts*

1. "Leaflets on Historical Linguistics," a portfolio of articles, provides annotated leaflets with reproductions of pages from *Beowulf, The Peterborough Chronicle, Canterbury Tales,* Caxton's "Prologue to the Boke of Eneydos," Pope's "Epistle to Bathurst." [16]

2. Compare the following translations of the Lord's Prayer (Matthew 6 : 9–13) in Old, Middle, and Early Modern English as suggested by the Minnesota Curriculum Study Center: [17]

OLD ENGLISH

Fæder ure þu þe eart on heofonum, si þin nama gehalgod.
Father our thou that art on heaven[s], may-be thy name hallowed.

MIDDLE ENGLISH

Fader oure þat art in hevene, i-halwed bee þi name.
Father our that art in heaven, hallowed be thy name.

---

[13] Masters of the transparency series on linguistics developed by the Texas Education Agency are available from Ridgeway Publishing Company, Caroline Street, Houston, Texas.

[14] UNESCO, *The Art of Writing* (Paris, 1965).

[15] Gerd Fraenkel, *Writing Systems* (Boston: Ginn, 1965).

[16] Published by NCTE, Champaign, Ill., 1967.

[17] Morton W. Bloomfield and Leonard Newmark, *A Linguistic Introduction to the History of English* (New York: Knopf, 1963), pp. 228–29.

EARLY MODERN ENGLISH

Our father which art in heaven, hallowed be thy name.
Thy kingdom come. Thy will be done in earth, as it is in heaven.

▶ *Listen to language characteristic of historical periods*

1. Read aloud passages from Old English or Middle English as students follow with duplicated texts. Teachers who have not studied the pronunciation of historical tongues might invite a colleague to provide an interpretive reading.

2. Use one of the excellent recordings of Chaucer, *Beowulf*, or other early literary works. Among the more useful are *The Sounds of Chaucer's English* and *The Harry Morgan Ayers Readings from Chaucer and The Beowulf* (both available from NCTE).

TO DEVELOP A BASIC UNDERSTANDING OF REGIONAL AND SOCIAL DIALECTS

▶ *Use a common book of readings*

Discovering American Dialects, by Roger Shuy, and *Dialects U.S.A.*, by Jean Malmstrom and Annabel Ashley, were especially developed by NCTE for use with secondary students.[18] They provide clear descriptions of major dialect areas and some insight into methods of linguistic geographers. If not used for common reading, have several copies available for student reference. *Language and Society*, by Jean Malmstrom, designed for students, treats language in its social context.[19]

TO BECOME AWARE OF REGIONAL AMERICAN SPOKEN DIALECTS

▶ *Exchange tape recordings*

Arrange with a teacher of a class similar to yours but located in another dialect region to exchange recordings of student speech. Discuss with your students the kinds of questions about local adolescent customs that might reveal differences in vocabulary, grammar, and pronunciation. Record the questions by your students and mail to the other school to be answered.

▶ *Use various sources*

Record on tape samples of dialects obtained from television, radio, or personal visits to regional areas. Over the years build a personal library of tape recordings of English spoken in the United States and in other English-speaking countries.

TO RELATE THE DEVELOPMENT OF THE ENGLISH LANGUAGE TO CULTURAL AND SOCIAL HISTORY

▶ *Integrate the study of language*
  with the study of American cultural history

In integrated or block time courses when American history and geography are taught together with English (by either a team or an individual teacher), provide for some study of our changing language in each cultural period. Louis A. Muinzer's article "Geography and the American Language" suggests many relationships between language and history, home life, folk songs, literature, and American

---

[18] Both available from NCTE, Champaign, Ill. 61820.
[19] Jean Malmstrom, *Language and Society* (New York: Hayden, 1965).

heroes.[20] For example, Muinzer mentions place names suggestive of natural and human resources (Chestnut Hill, Cowpens, Ironworks), names of flora, fauna, and food (catfish, TV-dinner), modern terms for frustration or "chaotic motion" (Blackboard Jungle, isolationism, bottleneck), all in relation to the region or historical period in which they entered popular lexicon.

▶ *Study literary selections from emerging English literatures*

Occasionally introduce a poem, story, or passage by a new English writer from Africa, Canada, Australia, the West Indies, the Philippines, or India. Because of the difficulty of obtaining texts, teachers may need to read such selections aloud to the class. Discuss with students not only the ideas expressed by the writer but what the emergence of such literature suggests concerning the development of the culture in this century.[21]

▶ *Use one of the good commercial recordings*

Americans Speaking not only presents samples of four regional dialects but is accompanied by notes prepared by the dialectologist Ravin I. McDavid, Jr.[22] Also illustrating regional speech patterns are *Our Changing Language* (McGraw-Hill) and *Spoken Language* (Scott, Foresman). Also useful are many of the excellent recordings of folk songs sung in their native dialect. Recordings of John F. Kennedy and Robert Frost will illustrate New England speech characteristics; Carl Sandburg is an example of the Midwest, Eudora Welty of the South.

▶ *Compare regional pronunciations*

To focus student attention on the problem, use transparencies such as the following.[23] Present the words themselves on the first transparency and elicit student response. Place northern and southern pronunciations on an overlay to be presented only after students identify their own habitual pronunciation.

DIALECTS. PRONUNCIATION AND GEOGRAPHY

How do you say it?	*Northern, north midland*	*South midland, southern*
greasy	/griysiy/	/griysiy/
creek	/krik/	/kriyk/
new	/nuw/	/nyuw/
with	/wið/	/wiθ/
Massachusetts	/-xuw-/;/-tuw-/	/-tyuw-/

TO EXAMINE THE DIALECTS OF PARTICULAR REGIONS OR SOCIAL CLASSES

▶ *Discuss the use of dialect in literature*

In reading a literary selection in which dialect is used to suggest a particular regional or social characteristic, examine with students the nature of the dialect and

---

[20] In Janet A. Emig *et al.*, *Language and Learning* (New York: Harcourt, Brace & World, 1966), pp. 130–52.

[21] For assistance in selection, see Priscilla Tyler, *Writers the Other Side of the Horizon* (Champaign, Ill.: NCTE, 1964).

[22] Available from NCTE, Champaign, Ill. 61820.

[23] One in a series of transparencies for grades 8 and 11 developed by the Texas Education Agency, Austin, Texas. Masters are available from the Ridgeway Publishing Company, Caroline Street, Houston, Texas.

the author's purpose in reproducing it. *Huckleberry Finn* probably is the foremost American work involving the use of dialect. However, illustrations of dialect can be easily found in the writing of most local color authors (Sarah Orne Jewett, Hamlin Garland, Jesse Stuart) and in such frequently taught works as Marjorie Kinnan Rawling's *The Yearling*, Willa Cather's *My Antonia*, Mark Twain's "The Celebrated Jumping Frog of Calaveras County," and Robert Frost's "The Death of the Hired Man."

► *Compare dialect terms used by students*

1. Ask students to write down the word or words they use in referring to such actions as the following. Then compare what they have listed:

> *to absent oneself from school* bag school, bolt, cut, cook jack, ditch, lay out, play hookey, play truant, run out of school, skip class, skip school, slip off from school

2. Provide a list of common words associated with two of the three major regional dialects, omitting the words common in the general dialect area in which students reside. Ask students to complete the column with the words familiar to them. For example, one of the following three columns would be left blank and completed by students:

NORTHERN	MIDLAND	SOUTHERN
wishbone, lucky bone	wishbone, pull bone, lucky bone	pull bone, pully bone
cornbread	corn pone, pone bread	corn pone, pone bread
curtains	blinds	roller shades
skunk	pole cat	pole cat
comfortable, comforter tied quilt, tie	comfort	comfort
teeter	totter, seesaw	seesaw, riding horse

► *Compare variations of dialect in United States and Great Britain*

Present students with the following comparison of road signs. Ask them to write a brief description of an imagined motor trip in Great Britain, using the British terms.

UNITED STATES	GREAT BRITAIN
detour	diversion
divided highway	dual carriageway
roadside parking	lay by
traffic circle	roundabout
sharp curves	bends
sand	grit
merging traffic left	left coming
low gears only	dead slow
no parking on shoulder	no stopping on verge
comfort stations	public conveniences
no passing	no overtaking

TO STUDY THE DIALECTS IN THE LOCAL COMMUNITY

▶ *Plan a dialect survey*

After students have read about the methods of the linguistic geographers, conduct an informal survey of dialectal terms spoken in the school or in the local area. Plan with pupils a simplified list of items which may reveal dialectal differences, particularly differences in vocabulary. Ask each student to interview two or three different members of the school community (teachers, administrators, students) or local community (old people, new arrivals, long-time residents). Examine references on dialect study to determine the critical items. For the most part, words associated with everyday events and objects will be the most revealing. Following are some of the critical items identified by specialists in such interviewing:

household	chest of drawers
	metal container carrying lunch
	cloth for drying dishes
	vehicle to push baby
	garbage container
	attractive daytime cover for bed
outdoor life	insect with transparent wings seen hovering over water
	hopping insect that destroys crops
	flying bug that glows at night
	male horse
	male cow
	black and white striped animal with a bad odor
foods	fresh corn served on the cob
	large flat beans
	hard center of peach
	milk that is beginning to sour
	milk that has soured and thickened
	chicken bone that children pull apart
	beans cooked and served in the pod
human activities	a stingy person
	easily offended
	courting (He is courting her.)
	woman whose husband is dead
	pejorative racial and national terms: Italian, Irishman, Negro, Mexican, Frenchman, Jew

TO UNDERSTAND HOW TO USE DICTIONARIES

▶ *Use study aids available from publishers*

Several publishers of dictionaries used in the school distribute complimentary copies of leaflets designed to assist students. Such leaflets may be studied by the entire class or used for individual students who seem to lack basic understandings. Among the pamphlets presently available are *A New Outline for Dictionary Study* (Springfield, Mass.: Merriam, 1963); *A Completely New Dictionary of American English* (New York: Harcourt, Brace & World, 1964).

▶ *Study introductory chapters in available dictionaries*

Provide a check sheet for students to use in studying the explanatory notes that precede annotations. Ask each student to write one sentence summarizing how the dictionary treats the following matters: selection of words, spelling, etymologies, meanings, capitalization, syllabication, pronunciation, grammatical information, usage status labels, synonyms, common English phrases.

▶ *Contrast different views of the dictionary*

Ask a panel of students to read selected essays on the purposes of the dictionary. The controversy over the publication of *Webster's New Third International* in 1961 sparked particularly provocative discussion. Several of the more lively reviews are reprinted in *The Dictionary and That Dictionary* and *Words, Words, and Words About Dictionaries.*[24] Ask students to organize a panel to discuss various ways in which individuals look at dictionaries.

TO UNDERSTAND HOW DICTIONARIES ARE COMPILED

▶ *Compile a dictionary of adolescent language*

After studying methods used by lexicographers, engage the class in developing a dictionary of popular teen-age usage. Determine which words will be included (slang, popular expressions, terms associated with popular music, and so on); then determine how citations for each word will be obtained (study of student newspaper, literary magazine, speech recorded at club meetings). Ask each class member to obtain twenty citations, then compile the class dictionary together. After the project is completed, discuss problems encountered in the compilation, such as variation in the lists, differences in the use of terms, how final citations for each word were determined, determination of whether a particular usage is idiosyncratic or widespread.

▶ *Compare annotations in dictionaries of different periods*

Copy selected annotations from early dictionaries—Johnson's dictionary of 1755 or Noah Webster's of 1826. Ask students to copy and compare annotations from a modern dictionary. Discussion of the entries should develop insights into changes in the attitudes of lexicographers to words, shifts in meaning, changes in the kind of information the dictionary contains. For example, a unit developed by the Curriculum Study Center, University of Minnesota, offers the following comparisons:

ENGLISH DICTIONARY, 1755	THORNDIKE-BARNHART COMPREHENSIVE DESK DICTIONARY, 1953
a dder. A serpent, a viper, a poisonous reptile; perhaps of any species. In common language, *adders* and *snakes* are not the same.	**ad der** (ad r) *n.* 1. a small poisonous snake of Europe. 2. a small, harmless snake of North America. 3. puff adder. (OE *n dre;* in ME *a nadder* was taken as *an adder.*

[24] James Sledd and Wilma R. Ebbitt, *The Dictionary and That Dictionary* (Chicago: Scott, Foresman, 1962); Jack C. Gray, *Words, Words, and Words About Dictionaries* (San Francisco: Chandler, 1963).

antho logy.   ( ) A collection of flowers.

This sense not listed. Note etymology: (L G., *anthos* flower + *legein* gather)

to he ctor.   To threaten; to treat with insolent authoritative terms.

hec tor (hek t r) *n.* a bragging, bullying fellow. *—v.* 1. bluster; bully. 2. tease.

Even these examples will suggest how after examining about a dozen entries students can see signs of change both in the language and in the nature of dictionaries.

TO EXAMINE DIFFERENCES IN ENGLISH DICTIONARIES

► *Refer to several different dictionaries*

1. Keep five or six different dictionaries for student reference in the classroom. When questions arise about particular words, compare the annotations, noting variations in spelling, pronunciation, and usage.

2. Use *Variant Spellings in English Dictionaries,* by Don Emery, to identify a selected list of words. Distribute various dictionaries to the class and ask students to check the spelling of words. As questions arise about which dictionary presented the "correct" or "preferred" spelling, ask students to study the introductory material in each dictionary and to refer to library resources to prepare a brief written explanation of the differences.

► *Compare status labels*

Assist students in compiling a list of various words in the student idiom, words they believe might be considered unstandard or substandard—for example: camp, far out, kook, aint, hot dog, turned on, pop art. See if the words are included in different dictionaries and if they are what status labels have been assigned to each (dialectal, nonstandard, slang, informal, colloquial).

► *Compare entries in general dictionaries and specialized dictionaries*

After studying the differences in words used in general standard English and in the technical vocabulary of various professions, ask students to list words used in the specialized vocations in which they are interested (medicine, auto repair, education, theater, cattle raising, journalism, psychology) and then to compare the annotation of these words in a general-purpose dictionary and a specialized dictionary.

TO LEARN ESSENTIAL ELEMENTS OF THE SENTENCE

► *Recognize signal words within the sentence*

1. Teach students to perceive articles as signals to help in locating words used as nouns. "The sign checks perfectly" differs in meaning from "Sign checks perfectly." Point up the importance of becoming aware of these distinctions by asking students to shift the article to various positions in the following sentences and note the changes in meaning:

> Plan approaches slowly.
> Union demands increase.
> Witness moves carefully.
> Spear flounders in flight.

Then ask students to rewrite the sentences using possessive pronouns as signal words, for example, *my, our, their, his.*

2. Study elements that exist primarily to tie together different parts of the sentence or to point up the function of other words, for example, not only articles like *the, a,* and *an,* but intensifiers like *too* and *very* as well as prepositions and participles like *on* and *coming,* which signal phrases and auxiliaries.

► *Study the clues in word order*

1. Use a flannel board to permit quick changes in word order. Mount on individual strips of tagboard, backed with small pieces of flocking paper, such words as the following:

RUNS PLANS THE HE

Ask individuals or groups of students to rearrange these words in different patterns on the flannel board, for example,

HE RUNS THE PLANS
HE PLANS THE RUNS

Follow the activity by asking students to draw conclusions about the importance of a word's position in the English sentence. Help students see that their inevitable conclusion—changed meaning or no meaning resulting from shifts in word order—applies to all words and groups of words in the sentence.

2. In analyzing sentences, encourage students to rely on natural clues within the sentence, such as a group of words—nouns and their modifiers, phrases, clauses—as well as specific signal words. The importance of such clues within each sentence may be emphasized by asking students to identify the predicates and subjects in such nonsense statements as the following:

The tringes tributhed on the flust.
Thus arthusta was emfressed by the bibblement.

Few will have difficulty in selecting "tributhed" and "was emfressed" as predicates, "tringes" and "arthusta" as subjects. Why? Can they tell? Encourage them to substitute familiar words for each of the nonsense words.

3. Ask students to unscramble sentences like:

peacock jumped she when the screamed

Then let them unscramble parts of sentences like:

funny a very fellow
complain may irrespective of you how

Later students may be asked to add the missing elements in scrambled sentences like the following:

out the green groundhog has of grass onto the

Or they may eliminate the extra word in a scrambled sentence

swooped Quantrill's the overhead down raiders on town

► *Identify similarities and differences in structure*

1. Write pairs of sentences on the chalkboard. Underline one element in the first sentence. Underline and number several elements in the second, for example:

Precious Pansybelle hit the timid boy with a stick.

Ed Snopes carved the carcass with an old hatchet from his woodshed.
      1   2   3   4

Ask students to determine which word in the second sentence corresponds in structure to the underlined word in the first sentence.[25]

2. Follow this exercise by asking students to write sentences of their own containing words parallel in structure.

▶ *Use sentence patterns to test understanding*

Ask students to maintain lists of words that may be substituted in each of the following kinds of sentence.

VERB	NOUN
They _____ if they can.	The _____ was interesting.
Please _____.	I saw the _____.
Please _____ it.	He has no _____.
They _____.	Was he happy with the _____?
They will _____ next week.	Her _____ is here.
She _____s occasionally.	_____s are scarce.

Similar patterns may be introduced as other elements are taught. Examples of substitution tests may be found in many modern grammars.[26]

▶ *Develop awareness of basic phrase structure*

Begin by discussing with students the natural groupings into which words fall in the sentence. Ask which one of the following seems to indicate natural groupings: "A plump robin eyed the shifty cat."

A plump   robin eyed the shifty cat.
A plump robin   eyed the shifty cat.
A plump robin eyed   the shifty cat.
A plump robin eyed the shifty   cat.

Students will readily see that the second example gives the natural groupings in the sentence. Then depict groupings graphically in a single tree diagram:

SENTENCE

A plump robin   eyed the shifty cat.

Discuss how the second phrasing can be broken down into two subsequent groups of words, whereas the first group of words reduces only to three separate words. At this point call attention to the grammatical oral strategy, the pauses that occur after "robin" in the vocal signaling of meaning when such a sentence is uttered by any

---

[25] John B. Carroll discusses how he uses this method in testing in "Psycholinguistics and the Teaching of English Composition," in Harold B. Allen (ed.), *Readings in Applied English Linguistics* (New York: Appleton-Century-Crofts, 1958), pp. 319–26.

[26] See Paul Roberts, *Patterns of English* (New York: Harcourt, Brace & World, 1956), pp. 13–14; James Sledd, *A Short Introduction to English Grammar* (Chicago: Scott, Foresman, 1959), pp. 81–91; W. Nelson Francis, *The Structure of American English* (New York: Ronald Press, 1958), pp. 235–36.

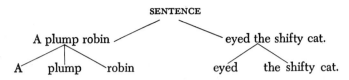

competent speaker. In discussing the word groups (constituents), note how "the shifty cat" could be substituted for "a plump robin" and still produce a grammatical sentence. Continue then to break down "the shifty cat" into its basic constituents and number the constituents of the sentence to indicate those of the same type.

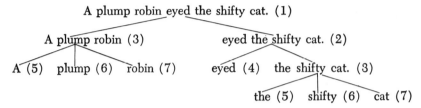

Use the same approach to show relationships between sentence constituents with more complex sentences. For example, show how the passive transformation creates the following modification in the relationships:

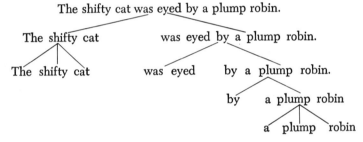

Students can see that the passive transformation not only caused a shift in the order of the constituent "a plump robin" and "the shifty cat" but also the addition of the words "was" and "by." Similar tree diagrams will illuminate the structural changes produced by other transformations. Suggestions for introducing more advanced tree diagrams to illustrate the difference between the surface structure (the structures that we speak and write) and deep structure (the basic structural meaning) are found in several of the transformational-generative grammars developed for school use.[27]

TO UNDERSTAND AND USE METHODS OF EXPANDING THE BASIC SENTENCE

▶ *Use the inductive approach recommended by Robert Pooley* [28]

Have students construct sentences lacking the element to be taught.

EXAMPLE   The boys ran. The friends met.

[27] Paul Roberts, *English Syntax* (New York: Harcourt, Brace & World, 1964); Roderick Jacobs and Peter Rosenbaum, *English Grammar I and II* (Boston: Ginn, 1966); also, see units on phrase structure developed by the Curriculum Study Center in English, University of Oregon, Eugene, Oregon.

[28] Robert Pooley, *Teaching English Grammar* (New York: Appleton-Century-Crofts, 1957), p. 140. Used by special permission. Examples are added for illustrative purposes.

To these sentences add the new element in such a way as to make very clear what has been added.

EXAMPLE   The happy boys ran. The olds friends met.

Lead students to recognize what has happened to the meaning or structure of the sentence as a result of the addition. Have students construct many sentences making use of the new element in its normal applications. At this point watch for confusions and help the students correct them. When the use of the element is familiar, when it can be recognized unmistakably in written sentences, and when the students can create sentences using the element accurately, teach its name and give sufficient practice in the use of the element thereafter to attach the name to the function it performs.

To test the student's grasp of the concept call upon him to write sentences employing the named element in the various sentence patterns to which it applies.

► *Substitute modifiers in basic sentences*

1. Present basic sentences and ask student to supply modifiers:

The boy who was ——————— was sick.

Supply modifier to indicate what the boy was doing (sleeping, sitting on the fence, finishing his lunch).

This approach offers a useful way of developing the understanding that words, phrases, and clauses can function in the same way in a sentence:

———————, Tom was startled.

Supply a modifier to show when this happened to Tom (after reading, having closed the book, running to the door, awakened).

and of understanding increasingly complicated sentences:

The boy who ——————— and who ——————— is likely to receive an "A" grade.

Supply words that tell what the boy has done.

2. Present basic sentences in which noun modifiers and verb modifiers are used and ask the student to select the appropriate forms of several from an accompanying list:

The girl is ———————.	sad	beauty
The girl sings ———————.	sadness	beautiful
	sadly	beautify
	saddens	beautifully

3. Lead students to see structure signals within words that indicate how the words may be used within the sentence. List words that take different forms depending on their use—for example, joy, beauty, sadness. Ask students to note changes that must be made in supplying words in the following sentences:

The girl's (joy) (beauty) (sadness) surprised me.
The girl (saddens) her friends; the girl (enjoyed) (beautified) it.
The girl accomplished it (joyfully) (beautifully) (sadly).
The (joyful) (beautiful) (sad) girl appeared.

▶ *Study basic techniques of transformation*

1. Begin with basic or kernel sentences. Ask students to identify changes in basic pattern resulting from the following transformations:

> *Question transformation*
> Kitty is reading.   Is Kitty reading?
> *Negative transformation*
> Kitty is reading.   Kitty is not reading.
> *Passive transformation*
> Kitty read the book.   The book was read by Kitty.

After establishing each principle, provide students with a number of kernel sentences and ask them to make the required transformation.

2. Use exercises such as the following in introducing the relative clause transformation:

> *Directions*   Combine the following main idea and subordinate idea in a single sentence:
>
> MAIN   Johnny parked the car.
> SUBORDINATE   The car was jet black.
>
> MAIN   The record was deafening.
> SUBORDINATE   The record was playing.

Students will easily create such sentences as:

> Johnny parked the car which was jet black.
> The record that was playing was deafening.

Then examine structural changes created by the transformation and establish the understanding of the adjective clause as a basic sentence with the word *who, whom, whose, which* or *that* substituted for the noun.

3. Use transparencies such as the following [29] to illustrate the internal processes involved in making basic transformations.

INPUT	OPERATION		OUTPUT
		→	*which has a blue cover*
The book has a blue cover. --→	Dep Trans	→	because the book (it) has a blue cover
		→	that the book has a blue cover
The book is mine. --→		→	The book which has a blue cover is mine.
You will recognize the book (it).	Trans	→	You will recognize the book because it has a blue cover.
He knows it.		→	He knows *that the book has a blue cover.*

[29] Developed by the Texas Educational Agency, Austin, Texas.

TO ACHIEVE VARIETY IN SENTENCE PATTERNS

▶ *Study the concepts of subordination and coordination*

1. Pose two statements that may be related: "John saved my life" and "He shot the unicorn." Show that in this case the linking word *and,* frequently used as a connector, acts as a weak tie. Ask students to suggest a better connector—one that more clearly shows the relationship between the two statements. Let them suggest words that may be used to point clearly to possible relationships between two statements: *since, if, although, when, whenever, while, before, after, unless, as if, as though, provided, except that.* Ask students to try various connectors between the two statements: "John saved my life" and "He shot the unicorn." Discuss the effect the choice has upon the meaning.

2. Now present the students with the following list of statements. Ask them to point out the connector and tell what kind of relationship it points to.

1. When the game starts, the crowd roars.   (time)
2. Groundhogs grow where the sun is bright.   (place)
3. She combs her hair as if she were a model.   (manner)
4. Most football players are tall, yet not as tall as most basketball players.   (degree)
5. The bull charged so that it hit the cape.   (result)
6. Girls study harder than boys, so that they can get better grades.   (purpose)
7. Because I jumped from the thirteenth floor, I was almost certain to break a leg.   (cause)
8. The rocket will hit the moon if it has sufficient thrust.   (condition)
9. Although the singer is tired, he will try to entertain.   (concession)

3. Ask students to divide each sentence into two statements and to arrange the statements in two lists:

STATEMENTS THAT CAN STAND ALONE	STATEMENTS THAT DEPEND ON ANOTHER
1. The crowd roars.	1. When the game starts
2. Groundhogs grow.	2. Where the sun is bright
3. She combs her hair.	3. As if she were a model

▶ *Study uses of basic patterns*

1. After students identify a basic pattern, give them an opportunity to substitute different words and phrases for the essential elements; then ask each to write five or six examples of the pattern. Explain that the exercise will require each writer to achieve considerable variety within the pattern framework:

SUBJECT—LINKING PREDICATE—PREDICATE NOMINATIVE

When speaking before the class, John becomes a real orator.
He is a speaker who is a spellbinder.
To students he is both leader and friend.
To teachers he seems to be more a future politician than a teen-ager.
John is a remarkable boy.

2. Study the patterns the students actually use in speech and writing. Ask each student to classify the sentences in one of his compositions according to the basic patterns studied; then summarize the findings for the entire class. Individuals may also compare the results of their personal surveys with patterns used by the entire class or outside groups. One recent survey of American writing, selected from fifty publications, reports the following percentages as indicating the use of basic patterns either as the sole sentence pattern or as the pattern of an independent clause: [30]

Pattern	I	(Subject-Predicate)	30.4%
Pattern	II	(S-P-O)	38.8
Pattern	III	(S-LP-PN)	13.2
Pattern	IV	(S-LP-PA)	13.8
			96.2%

3. Transcribe from a tape recording some selected sentences used by class members in discussion. Ask students to identify the basic patterns of each sentence.

Presenting the English language in broad perspective—its history, its geography, its sociology—will apprise students of its flexibility, variety, and power.

SELECTED READINGS

GENERAL

ALLEN, HAROLD B. (ed.). *Readings in Applied English Linguistics.* 2d ed. New York: Appleton-Century-Crofts, 1964. This introduction to the field presents many useful articles.

GOLDSTEIN, MIRIAM B. *The Teaching of Language in Our Schools.* New York: Macmillan, 1966. This discussion of modern trends is intended for parents but makes valuable reading for teachers as well.

MARCKWARDT, ALBERT H. *Linguistics and the Teaching of English.* Bloomington, Ind.: Indiana Univ. Press, 1966. A comprehensive view of language in relation to different aspects of the school curriculum.

POSTMAN, NEIL, and WEINGARTNER, CHARLES. *Linguistics: A Revolution in Teaching.* New York: Delacorte Press, 1966. This introductory textbook covers many dimensions of language but is most helpful in its treatment of semantics.

HISTORY OF LANGUAGE

BRYANT, MARGARET. *Modern English and Its Heritage.* 2d ed. New York: Macmillan, 1962. A readable introductory textbook containing especially useful discussion of English words.

FRANCIS, W. NELSON. *The English Language: An Introduction.* New York: Norton, 1965. Chapter 3 provides a clear outline of the history of English and has been reprinted for use with student groups.

[30] J. N. Hook and E. G. Mathews, *Modern American Grammar and Usage* (New York: Ronald Press, 1956), pp. 76–94.

PYLES, THOMAS. *The Origins and Development of the English Language.* New York: Harcourt, Brace & World, 1964. An introductory history of internal and external developments.

GEOGRAPHY AND SOCIOLOGY OF ENGLISH

MC DAVID, RAVEN I., JR. "The Dialects of American English." In W. Nelson Francis, *The Structure of American English.* New York: Ronald Press, 1958. A summary of research on regional dialects.

REED, CARROLL E. *Dialects of American English.* Cleveland: World, 1967. A useful introduction to regional variation.

SHUY, ROGER. *Social Dialects and Language Learning.* Champaign, Ill.: NCTE, 1965. A stimulating report on a conference involving linguistic geographers, sociologists, and educators.

THREE

USAGE AND SENTENCE STRUCTURE

There is no language apart from a
speaker active in expression.

CHARLES C. FRIES [1]

PERSPECTIVE

The study of usage and sentence structure, as distinct from the study of English grammar, has as its chief end the development of power over language. Only as students learn to express their ideas clearly and to understand the expression of others is any language-study program worthwhile. Therefore, instruction in improving sentences and usage must be continually applied to the processes of communication, and the teacher's essential task is to relate instruction to use.

Language exists as a vehicle to transmit thought. Speakers and writers active in expression strive for effective communication of ideas; thus, they study ways of conveying precise meaning. Yet, instruction in language must be limited to necessary learnings—to generalizations about the nature of English that help young people understand their native tongue (Chapter Two) and to classroom experiences that help them construct and improve their communications. Research indicates that use of principles in practice occurs most frequently when theoretical knowledge is learned in relation to the student's own writing and speaking rather than when it is studied independently as a set of logical principles.[2] Thus, a sound program for improving usage and sentence structure will stress the pupils' uses of language and will be seen as distinct from instruction designed to increase knowledge about language.[3]

---

[1] Charles C. Fries, *The Teaching of English* (Ann Arbor, Mich.: Wahr, 1949), p. 107.

[2] See Richard Braddock *et al., Research in Written Composition* (Champaign, Ill.: NCTE, 1963), pp. 37–38; Henry C. Meckel, "Research in Teaching Composition and Literature," in N. L. Gage (ed.), *Handbook for Research in Teaching* (Chicago: Rand McNally, 1963).

[3] For this reason teaching "The Nature of Language," including the study of English grammar, is discussed separately in Chapter Two.

Basic Understandings

A grasp of the nature of English usage is necessary before the teacher can select content and teaching procedures appropriate for secondary students. Since the ineffectiveness of some instructional programs stems largely from attempts to teach too much, teachers need to identify the learnings that are basic and then to set up for each level of instruction certain priorities. Often a curriculum guide will provide such leadership. The discussion of important concepts in this section is followed by a consideration of those learnings about structure and usage that are really needed by young people.

The preceding chapters stress change as a quality of language. In teaching usage, one remembers that change occurs continually in speech and more slowly in writing.[4] The teacher of English is neither a harbinger of these changes nor a rigorous defender of outmoded forms. Rather he steers a steady course, recognizing that change cannot be controlled by arbitrary pronouncements. Usually he helps pupils most if he is somewhat conservative. He can develop awareness of fundamental differences in standards for speech and for writing; he can clarify reasons for these differences; he can explain why some speech forms are not acceptable in writing.[5] He can also explain why language appropriate in one dialect may be inappropriate in another. Acceptance of the fact that language changes does not necessarily mean approval or disapproval of specific changes.

To the student of language, the spoken language is of primary importance; writing depends on the prior existence of speech. The studies of many linguists are based on spoken language largely because researchers find in speech a complete signal system of the meanings conveyed in verbal communication—for example, the employment of pitch, stress, and pause. The signal system man uses to convey meaning in spoken language is only imperfectly approximated in writing; moreover, the linear nature of the written language system results in an emphasis on sentence patterns and logical presentation of ideas different from the spoken language system. This does not mean that speech is more important than writing. But from the point of view of the learner of language, speech is where he must begin. Understanding the distinction between the two forms of communication is basic to language study.[6]

Studies of spoken language reveal that secondary students have for many years used in their speech the basic structures and patterns of the English sentence. No matter how poorly educated, one who speaks English knows, at

---

[4] Charles C. Fries, "Linguistic Science and the Teaching of English," in Robert C. Pooley (ed.), *Perspectives on English* (New York: Appleton-Century-Crofts, 1960), pp. 144, 145.

[5] Teachers searching for a guide to specific changes will find useful help in A. H. Marckwardt and Fred Walcott, *Facts About Current English Usage* (New York: Appleton-Century-Crofts, 1938); Albert H. Marckwardt, *Linguistics and the Teaching of English* (Bloomington, Ind.: Indiana Univ. Press, 1966).

[6] An excellent discussion of this point is presented in William G. Moulton, *A Linguistic Guide to Language Learning* (New York: MLA, 1966), pp. 13–16.

the level of use, the inflections, sound structure, and syntactical arrangements that govern the dialect of the English he speaks. The secondary teacher's role is less to reveal new patterns and structures than to make the student conscious of the ones he has been controlling.

Because the structures and patterns of the English sentence are employed in somewhat different ways in speech and in writing, teachers and students need to bear in mind the following distinctions:

> Spoken language contains a wide range of nonverbal signals for conveying meaning; written language does not. Speakers indicate meaning and intent through stress and pitch and through juncture—the pauses that interrupt the sequence of speech sounds. Writers approximate these grammatical signals in other ways, usually by punctuation and capitalization, at best imperfect representations.
>
> Spoken language frequently conveys meaning through phrases, clauses, and other fragments of sentences, because the completeness of the idea can be communicated from sender to receiver in nonverbal ways. Thus, one deer hunter murmurs "on the hill" to another, points in a certain direction, and communicates perfectly that he has spotted game. A speaker conveys meaning through gesture, facial expression, and tone. Written language requires more attention to precision and completeness, hence greater dependence on modification, subordination, and word choice.
>
> Written language, since it must stand alone in conveying meaning, demands greater clarity than does oral language.
>
> Written language requires more attention to the conventions of language. Many colloquial terms and stylistic considerations used in speech are inappropriate in writing. Spoken language cannot, therefore, be the sole determinant of appropriate written usage; no linguist argues that teachers accept in the writing of students all forms accepted in speech.

In developing awareness of unfamiliar written structures, the teacher will draw on the student's oral language habits but will find in each form unique problems demanding separate consideration. Because speech is the primary language, teachers of grammar will search especially for methods to relate what they teach to spoken communication.

But the question remains, what standard should teachers adopt as a guide? What criteria should govern the choice of constructions? Most teachers recognize the complexity of English usage, agreeing that language is neither "correct" nor "incorrect" but rather "appropriate" or "inappropriate" depending upon the situation in which it is used. At one time teachers were inclined to view usage in hierarchial levels descending from formal or literary English through colloquial to slang and substandard speech. Such an oversimplified view tended to neglect the distinctions between speech and writing, the style of the speaker, the nature of the communication situation, and the number of individuals engaged in the communication. Each affects the language appropriate for use on any occasion.

John Kenyon and Martin Joos, two linguists who studied the varieties of English usage, stress that appropriate usage depends upon the function of language in any communication situation.[7] Joos identifies five different styles differing in degree of formality: frozen (used in publication and declamation), formal (used in speaking to large groups), consultative (used in small groups where the speaker has to present much information), casual (used in small groups when speaker need not present full information to communicate ideas), and intimate (used in close personal exchanges). Such work by linguists helps teachers understand the complexity of language in a complex culture.

Teachers of English are careful not to perpetuate false or snobbish dogmas about language. They realize that human worth cannot be measured by the speech patterns a man uses, and they know usage varies from one locality to another and from one historical period to another. But they know, also, that in the American world to which their pupils go, language is a mark of social and educational status. The faculty of any school hopes its students will never, because of language, be denied access to opportunities or entrance to the social groups they desire. But the stubborn fact is that leaders of many communities are sensitive to deviations from the flexible informal English accepted today in many social situations. Thus the teacher must be clear about two points—why he recommends changes and which changes are important enough to merit attention.

The National Council of Teachers of English recommends that teachers accept as good English language "appropriate to the purpose of the speaker, true to the language as it is, and comfortable to the speaker and listener." The Council sees such language as "the product of custom, neither cramped by rule nor freed from all restraint . . . never fixed, but [changing] with the organic life of the language." Bad English, on the other hand, is seen as language that is "unclear, ineffective, and inappropriate to the linguistic occasion, no matter how traditional, 'correct,' or elegant."[8]

Acceptance of this touchstone means recognition of a responsibility to prepare students to evaluate the circumstances under which they are writing and speaking and the factors influencing appropriateness: time, social situation, and other features of the environment. Many students, particularly in our inner cities, come from homes in which the English spoken differs from that of the classroom. Such dialects possess an internal consistency of their own in grammar, vocabulary, and pronunciation; they are frequently rich in their ability to communicate meaning in situations where they are appropriate. In teaching students who command such dialects to suit language to the occasion, teachers need run no risk of seeming to belittle the language of the students' parents and peers. Indeed the very rejection of arbitrary standards of correctness offers teachers an opportunity to explain why usages differ, why a student may use a variety of language in school or at work different from that of the speaker in his neighborhood. Carefully

---

[7] Martin Joos, *The Five Clocks* (New York: Harcourt, Brace & World, 1967); John S. Kenyon, "Cultural Levels and Functional Varieties of English," *College English*, Vol. 10, No. 1 (October 1948), pp. 31–36.

[8] Commission on the English Curriculum, *The English Language Arts*, NCTE Curriculum Series, Vol. 1 (New York: Appleton-Century-Crofts, 1952), p. 277.

avoiding judgments that may offend individuals accustomed to usages quite different from those encouraged in the classroom, the teacher can try to develop understanding of the criterion of appropriateness.[9]

The Usage of English

Once teachers accept appropriateness as the criterion for judging language, the major problems in teaching usage are those of determining the field of coverage and applying tested instructional procedures. This section is particularly concerned with ways of identifying specific usages to be taught and basic principles to observe in teaching them.

SELECTING ITEMS FOR EMPHASIS

How do we identify items to be taught? Establish priorities in order to cover a few items thoroughly and successfully? A survey of informed opinion toward language usage made by L. J. O'Rourke some years ago suggested that instruction in English usage of a standard variety may be divided into three phases:

> the essential elements of usage, for example, avoiding confusion between verb and noun modifiers—He does his work *well* (not *good*)
> elements of secondary importance, for example, distinguishing *who* and *which* in referring to persons and animals
> least important phases, for example, using *so* or *as* in negative comparisons: This is not so useful as that.[10]

O'Rourke's research concerned those who normally speak an informal standard English, but his method is appropriate for other types of learner as well. His findings demonstrated that in attempting to present an overly comprehensive program, schools were actually slighting essential learnings. As his summary on the following page shows, graduating seniors failed to achieve even a 75 per cent mastery of the essentials. Certainly such results point to the need for a selective program concentrating on a few new items in every grade and on a continual attempt to eliminate the more crucial nonstandard usages.

Robert C. Pooley, in a book describing research and practice in teaching usage,[11] suggests certain forms to be emphasized and others to receive no instruction at the elementary, junior, and senior high school levels. Pooley's widely used lists offer a basis for establishing priorities in usage instruction and are particularly helpful for teachers who feel the need for guidance in

---

[9] Teachers will find helpful discussion in Robert Pooley, *Teaching English Usage* (New York: Appleton-Century-Crofts, 1946), pp. 16–24.
[10] L. J. O'Rourke, *Rebuilding the English Curriculum to Insure Greater Mastery of Essentials* (Washington, D.C., Psychological Institute, 1934).
[11] *Teaching English Usage*, pp. 180–81, 194–98, 218–23.

DEGREE OF MASTERY OF ENGLISH USAGE IN GRADES 7 AND 12

	Percentage of correct answers	
	GRADE 7	GRADE 12
Essentials such as	35	74
He invited John and *me.* (not *I*)		
There *are* two apples on the table. (not *is*)		
Secondary elements such as	23	56
John *may* do it if his mother agrees. (permission)		
John *can* do it if he tries. (ability)		
Least important phases such as	12	38
He said that the world *is* round. (not *was*)		
One should be loyal to *one's* country. (not *his*)		

selecting items for emphasis. Using his recommendations and other findings reported in research, committees of teachers in many school districts have attempted to construct guides for sequential language instruction.

Teachers need to consider several factors in identifying items for emphasis at any level. Prevailing language habits in the social environment may create particular problems for a school. At times social conditions may create a need for instruction; at other times they may make such emphasis almost fruitless. Teachers will also need to consider research. A few of the important findings and their implications are summarized in the chart on page 108.[12] Whatever guide for instruction is established in any school, the teacher will concentrate only on necessary forms and then will insist that these be used in the writing and speaking of students.

ADAPTING INSTRUCTION TO LEARNERS

The initial problem in improving usage is to determine the kind of help young people need. In our classes three types of speaker may be identified. Although the research already discussed is concerned with the first type, it has implications for all three.

The student who speaks a variety of standard English generally accepted in his community has essentially mastered the grammar, basic vocabulary, and pronunciation of the language he speaks. Some students—in many classes, all—will need help in eliminating specific errors and inconsistencies in speech and writing. An attempt to accomplish this requires diagnosis, selection of items to emphasize, consideration of the order of study. Such an approach, coupled with extensive practice in communicating ideas in speech and writing, is likely to be successful.

[12] Based on research reported in Walter Loban, "Studies of Language Which Assist the Teacher," *English Journal*, Vol. 36, No. 10 (December 1947); Orville Nordberg, "Research and the Teaching of Written Expression," *California Journal of Educational Research*, Vol. 2, No. 7 (March 1951); Pooley, *Teaching English Usage;* Martin J. Stromzand and M. V. O'Shea, *How Much English Grammar?* (Baltimore: Warwick and York, 1924).

IMPLICATIONS OF RESEARCH FOR INSTRUCTION IN USAGE AND LANGUAGE CONVENTIONS

Finding	*Implications for instruction*
	VERB FORMS
Verb errors account for between 40 and 60 per cent of all errors in usage.	Since confusion in past tense and past participle causes many errors, plan appropriate oral practice in expressing past time.
	Direct special attention to selecting forms of *to be* when used as an auxiliary.
A majority of all verb errors may be traced to usages of *see, do, come,* and *go.*	Provide much practice in using appropriate forms of irregular verbs.
	PRONOUN FORM
Errors in pronoun reference and agreement with antecedent are second in frequency to inappropriate verb forms.	Teach specific forms as well as the underlying rationale.
	SUBJECT-PREDICATE AGREEMENT
Errors in subject-predicate agreement are a widespread source of difficulty.	Concentrate on eliminating the following specific problems:
	1. Confusion in third person singular present tense: He *don't.*
	2. Failure to use plural verb with compound subject: The dog and cat *is* playing.
	3. Confusion when subject and predicate are separated by an element with a different number: The events of the year *is* explained.
	CONVENTIONS OF LANGUAGE
Errors in capitalization of proper nouns account for a large percentage of mechanical problems. Frequent capitalization errors at the beginning of sentences result from a lack of sentence sense rather than misunderstanding of the need for initial capitalization.	Stress distinctions between common and proper nouns throughout secondary school. Avoid repetitive instruction and drill on beginning capitalization; concentrate instead on exercises that promote students' understanding of sentence completeness.

Speakers of dialects pose a different problem. Having mastered the system of their own English dialect, they are now asked to learn a new system that may differ radically from their own. Their speech and writing are not likely to be changed materially by drill on the isolated items needed by those who speak a variety of standard English. Rather, teachers must recognize that such students have already acquired a valid language system capable of generating sentences that communicate in the social context where the dialect is appropriate. Rather than attempting to eradicate or change the language of such pupils, teachers must help them extend their linguistic repertoire to include a standard variety of English and thus become bi-dialectal.

Such attempts require time; they must be supported by continued opportunities to communicate ideas. Thus, providing situations that permit such young people to discuss ideas informally—particularly with speakers using a standard variety of English—is basic in sound program planning. So is systematic and productive drill on the significant features of the dialect differing from those in standard varieties of English.

Contrastive studies of varieties of English dialects, particularly the social dialects spoken in the inner cities, are just a beginning. As the profession devotes more attention to the language problems of disadvantaged youth, more specific teaching aids should become available. In the meantime the following checklist of significant features in social dialects has been prepared by Raven I. McDavid, Jr., as a systematic and significant list based on currently available research.[13] McDavid stresses features recurring frequently and therefore amenable to pattern drills. He cautions that not all features will occur in every situation where differences in social dialects are important, that other systematic features will be found in most local dialects. In using this checklist as a guide for instruction, most teachers will wish to stress inflectional items rather than pronunciation. Differences in pronunciation tend to create far fewer difficulties for pupils than do problems involving inflection.

A CHECKLIST OF SIGNIFICANT FEATURES FOR DISCRIMINATING SOCIAL DIALECTS

Pronunciation

1. The distinction between /θ/ as in *thin* and /t/ in *tin*, /f/ in *fin*, /s/ in *sin*.
2. The similar distinction between /ð/ in *then* and /d/, /v/, /z/.
3. The distinction between the vowels of *bird* and *Boyd*, *curl* and *coil*.

A generation ago this contrast was most significant among older speakers of the New York metropolitan area; uneducated older speakers regularly lacked it. It has become less important, since few of the younger speakers lack this distinction. But it should still be noted, not only for New York City but for New Orleans as well.

---

[13] Reproduced with the permission of Raven I. McDavid, Jr., from a revision of "A Checklist of Significant Features for Discriminating Social Dialects," in *Dimensions of Dialect*, ed. by Eldonna L. Evertts (Champaign, Ill.: NCTE, 1967), pp. 9–11. This list will be incorporated in *A Manual of Social Dialects* being compiled by Alva L. Davis, Illinois Institute of Technology, under a grant from the U.S. Office of Education.

4. The omission, in substandard speech, of a weak-stressed syllable preceding the primary stress, so that *professor* may become *fessor, reporter* may become *porter,* and *insurance* may become *shoo-ance* or *sho-ance.*

5. In substandard speech, a statistically disproportionate front-shifting of the primary stress, giving such forms as *po*-lice, *in*-surance, *ee*-ficiency, *gui*-tar, etc.

Front-shifting is characteristic of English borrowings from other languages; in *bal*cony it is completely accepted; in *ho*tel and *Ju*ly acceptability is conditioned by position in the sentence.

6. In substandard speech, heavy stress on what in standard English is a weak-stressed final syllable, giving acc*ident,* ele*ment,* presid*ent,* evi*dence,* etc.

Inflection

NOUN

7. Lack of the noun plural: Two *boy* came to see me.
8. Lack of the noun genitive: This is *Mr. Brown* hat.

PRONOUN

9. Analogizing of the /-n/ of mine to other absolute genitives, yielding *ourn, yourn, hisn, hern, theirn.*
10. Analogizing of the compound reflexives yielding *hisself, theirself, theirselves.*

DEMONSTRATIVE

11. Substitution of *them* for *those,* as *them* books.
12. Compound demonstratives: *these-here* dogs, *that-(th)ere* house, *them-(th)ere* cats.

ADJECTIVE

13. Analogizing of inflected comparisons: the *wonderfullest* time, a *lovinger* child.
14. Double comparisons: a *more prettier* dress, the *most ugliest* man.

VERB

15. Unorthodox person-number concord of the present of *to be*. This may be manifest in generalizing of *am* or *is* or *are,* or in the use of *be* with all persons, singular and plural.
16. Unorthodox person-number concord of the past of *be: I were, he were; we was, they was.*
17. Failure to maintain person-number concord of the present indicative of other verbs: *I does, he do* (this is perhaps the most widely recognized diagnostic feature).

Note that three third-person singular forms of common verbs are irregular, *has, does* /dʌz/, *says* /sez/. In the last two the spelling conceals the irregularity, but many speakers who are learning this inflection will produce /duz/ and /sez/. The form *bees* is also derived from this kind of analogy.

18. Omission of the /-ŋ/ of the present participle: He was *open* a can of beer.
19. Omission of /-t, -d, -ed/ of the past tense: I burn a hole in my pants yesterday.

Note that before a word beginning with a consonant the /-d/ may be omitted in speech in *I burned my pants.* Those who normally have this contextual loss of the sound may need to learn the special conventions of writing.

Note also that the loss of the inflection extends to those verbs that form the past tense and past participle irregularly.

20. Omission of /-t, -d, -əd/ of the past participle.

21. Omission of the verb *to be* in statements before a predicate nominative: *He a good boy.*

22. Omission of *to be* in statements before adjectives: *They ready.*

23. Omission of *to be* in statements before present participles: *I going with you.*

24. Omission of *to be* in statements before past participles: *The window broken.*

Note that in questions related to features 21–24 the verb *to be* may be omitted in standard oral English, though it would never be omitted in formal expository prose.

25. Omission of the /-s, -z, -əz/ reflex of *has* before *been* in statements: *He been drinking.*

Note that this omission may occur in questions in standard oral English, and also that in standard oral English many educated speakers may omit the /-v/ reflex of *have: I been thinking about it; we been telling you this.* Needless to say, this omission would not occur in standard expository prose.

26. Substitution of *been, done,* or *done been* for *have,* especially with a third singular subject: *He done been finished.* In other person-number situations *done,* at least, often occurs in standard oral English, as *I done told you that three times.*

For reasons similar to those applying to speakers of dialects, people who are learning English as a second language are not likely to profit from the "error-approach" method. Like the speakers of nonstandard dialects, they are learning a new language system, and they will need special help in mastering the features of standard English that differ most significantly from those of their own language. Results of contrastive studies of English and other languages, conducted by qualified linguists, will help teachers plan intelligent programs.[14] To develop fluency in using a standard variety of English, such students will also need frequent opportunities to converse with others for whom standard English is the mother tongue.

PLANNING EFFECTIVE PRACTICE

Sound practice results from observing sound principles of learning. Purposeful drill in usage can be planned only in relation to the readiness of the learner, his interest in learning, and the range of individual differences among students in the classroom. Both research and experience help to identify certain characteristics of effective approaches.

[14] Assistance in teaching English to speakers of other languages is available in the publications of TESOL, Center for Applied Linguistics, 1717 Massachusetts Avenue, N.W., Washington, D.C. 20036.

Practice of any kind takes root best in the human mind when that practice is pleasurable and meaningful. Often when an adult has suffered a stroke and is recovering the use of an arm, friends urge him to hold a rubber ball in his hand and to keep squeezing it. Wise doctors urge the patient to find something functional that he likes to do, whether it be knitting, dusting, or digging around potted plants. One of the awesome qualities of the human mind is its propensity to learn most efficiently when practice is linked to interest, volition, and a sense of significance. This is true whether the learning is physical or mental.

RELATE PRACTICE TO THE COMMUNICATION SETTING   Instruction in usage cannot be presented independently of the writing and speaking of students. Only as the learner sees his classroom study of usage related to his expression of ideas will instruction be effective. By basing practice on errors in the writing and speaking of students, some teachers attempt to relate instruction to thinking. Included in "Program and Plan" is an example showing how usage skills may be taught within a unit of instruction (see pages 703–11). One of the most effective ways to improve the usage of nonstandard speakers is to provide continuing opportunities for such boys and girls to engage in meaningful communication with speakers of a flexible standard English.[15]

PLAN ORAL PRACTICE   Many studies reveal oral practice to be an effective method of improving the usage habits of students.[16] Our basic command of English is established through the spoken word; habits perpetuated in conversation and speech are often continued in writing, and forms eliminated in oral usage most certainly will disappear from written expression. For example, tape recorded practice of appropriate forms, similar to programs developed in language laboratories, have been successfully introduced, even in inner city classrooms.

Such oral practice need not be presented through drill alone. Classroom activities in which students have an opportunity to record, listen to, and analyze their own speech and the speech of their classmates have been used to improve usage. In one study, written drills and formal exercises were abandoned and nearly all language lessons were devoted to recording and analyzing the effectiveness of the communication in the stories and reports of the learners. The results indicated that students instructed in this way did as well as others on tests of competence in the use of written language and significantly better in oral composition and oral usage.[17] Many kinds of oral practice are presented among the Suggested Learning Experiences later in this chapter.

[15] See especially the program described by John Dixon in *Growth Through English* (London: National Association for the Teaching of English, 1967). Available from NCTE.
[16] See Prudence Cutright, "A Comparison of Methods of Securing Correct Language Usage," *Elementary School Journal*, Vol. 39, No. 9 (May 1934); Percival Symonds, "Practice Versus Grammar in the Learning of Correct Usage," *Journal of Educational Psychology*, Vol. 22, No. 2 (February 1931).
[17] Haverly O. Moyer, "Can Ear Training Improve English Usage?" *Elementary English*, Vol. 33, No. 4 (April 1956).

UTILIZE MANY BRIEF AND VARIED DRILLS   Practice—important and necessary if we are to change patterns of language usage—is most effective when it is varied and least effective when it is repetitive. A ten-sentence drill may offer a good exercise; a twenty-five-sentence drill will not necessarily be better. The experience of many teachers, supported by research, points to the value of frequent brief drills and exercises, especially when the need for each drill and relation of the drill to writing and speaking problems are clear to each student.

One tested approach to the teaching of language involves eight steps: (1) pretesting; (2) explaining the problem—for example, an appropriate pronoun form; (3) using mimeographed drill sheets on correct forms; (4) repeating orally each sentence five times in concert with a pupil leader; (5) writing original sentences illustrating the usage; (6) discussing the sentences; (7) reviewing the drill sheets; and (8) final testing.[18] Such a multiple attack is more effective than an equal amount of time spent on a single kind of activity. The teacher plans the work so that no one exercise need take longer than ten or fifteen minutes. Occasionally, varied activities of this type may be introduced within a single class hour, but more frequently teachers will wish to spend only a few minutes in one day on intensive usage drill. Some find the beginning of the period offers a convenient time for such instruction.

Fundamentally, then, effective instruction in usage may be described by four characteristics: emphasis on essential items; relation of their practice to the communication setting; attention to oral practice; and reliance on many brief, varied drills.

In developing a program, a teacher cannot depend solely on the textbook he finds in the school book room. The language needs of students will vary from community to community, influenced to a considerable degree by cultural and social factors.[19] Usages that create teaching problems in one region are not found in others; the standard English of one region is not quite the standard of another. Textbooks written from a national perspective cannot offer sufficient guidance to meet local problems. In addition, teachers must be wary, especially during the early junior high school years, lest they introduce so much in any grade that they defeat their own purpose.[20] For

---

[18] The effectiveness of these procedures is demonstrated by C. C. Crawford and Madie Royer, "Oral Drill Versus Grammar Study," *Elementary School Journal*, Vol. 35 (October 1935).

[19] A practical discussion of ways of teaching usage to children of impoverished backgrounds can be found in Ruth Golden, *Improving Patterns of Usage* (Detroit: Wayne State Univ. Press, 1960).

[20] For an analysis of some of the deficiencies in language textbooks, see Pooley, *Teaching English Grammar*, pp. 45–48. Pooley's belief that heavy grammatical loading in grades 7 and 8 is introduced at the expense of extensive reading experiences, despite the knowledge that most students will read more during these years than at any other time of their lives, is quoted in Mildred Dawson, "Summary of Research Concerning English Usage," *Elementary English*, Vol. 28, No. 3 (March 1951). Also, see James Lynch and Bertrand Evans, *High School English Textbooks* (Boston: Little, Brown, 1963); and Julia W. Thomas, "An Analysis of the Relationship Between Grammar and Writing in Eleventh

these reasons they must be discriminating in their choice of what to teach, selecting at any level a few important items for emphasis. Any attempts to present all elements of language structure and language usage will lead only to failure.

THE TEACHING PROBLEM

ORGANIZING INSTRUCTION

Teachers sometimes refer to *incidental* learning of language, which may occur during the exchange of ideas in social studies and science classes, but certainly students learn language best when definite time is reserved for study and practice. This is not to say that language periods can be divorced from actual experiences in communication nor that several learnings cannot occur in the classroom at the same time; but there is a need for systematic direction and organization. What is embraced by sound incidental learning is instruction in which learning experiences occur in meaningful context, with planned instruction in usage and sentence structure introduced as incidental to, but in essential support of, the student's quest for ideas. Certainly no important learning can be left to chance.

A Basic Method

Relating systematic instruction in usage and sentence structure to the communication setting in the classroom is a major problem. Most successful teaching includes the following steps:

Establishing areas of emphasis for each grade or instructional level
> EXAMPLE   Teaching uses of introductory phrases and clauses in varying sentence patterns may be assigned to the tenth grade.

Planning learning activities requiring students to use the particular skill or usage to be emphasized in instruction
> EXAMPLE   The teacher delays instruction on ways of varying sentences until students are engaged in writing several long papers so need for variation is more readily apparent.

Diagnosing the needs of particular students with reference to the items to be emphasized or reviewed
> EXAMPLE   The teacher asks students to review three previous papers to deter-

and Twelfth Grade English Textbooks," masters thesis, University of Kansas, 1964. Lynch and Evans found no evidence of sequence and selection in the books they examined. Thomas found a similar lack of agreement in emphasis and a tendency to ignore sentence building by the students.

mine the percentage of sentences with the simple subject-predicate pattern or the number beginning with a phrase or dependent clause.

Providing needed instruction and practice for class, groups, and individuals

EXAMPLE   The class discusses the importance of variety in sentence construction. Students then review their papers. Those whose writing already shows an awareness of the principle continue with other activities. Students who need help are assigned special practice in rewriting sentences taken from their own papers, exchanging their revisions with fellow students for analysis and correction.

Maintaining the skill or usage in all communication activities

EXAMPLE   After specific instruction and practice, the teacher studies applications in student writing. Excellent examples of sentence variation are brought to the attention of the class. Students who do not attempt to vary sentences are reminded of the possibility. Grading is based on the actual use, in writing and speaking, not on results of drills.

The basic method described here is subject to much variation.[21] Even direct instruction in sentence structure may be presented through modifications of this method. The teacher may select areas of emphasis, use student sentences for analyses, base diagnosis on previous writing, provide instruction only for those with obvious needs, and follow through by later presenting for analysis occasional sentences taken from the students' own papers. The method is appropriate for a series of brief lessons or drills spread over several days, as well as for two or three hours of intensive study. Some teachers prefer to introduce instruction of this type after each writing or speaking activity, with brief lessons and individualized drills developed according to needs identified by analyzing student writing and speaking. Others devote the short intervals between units to the concentrated study of usage, although infrequent concentration tends to be less effective than brief, frequent practice. A few teachers like to "take time out for repairs" whenever needs so indicate, and they do not hesitate to substitute instruction and practice in language skill for other activities whenever they and their classes agree. Whatever the exact combination of procedures, the teacher will want the instruction to grow from and contribute to the actual communication activities of the class.

The Textbook Problem

Teachers attempting to improve their present programs to incorporate new approaches must consider ways of utilizing presently available language texts. Some of these books confuse the teaching of grammar and usage, stress only one or two dimensions of usage (usually of a single, standard variety), and often rely on a deductive, rigidly sequential approach. Although such books are improving, most teachers will find that they might better rely on their own pattern of organization for teaching. Lists of sentences and some of the exercises included in available textbooks can be used with appropriate intro-

---

[21] Further illustrations of this approach are presented in the plan, "Establishing a Usage Habit Within a Unit," pages 707–11.

duction and will often save preparation time. Thus material in the conventional textbook can be used in such ways as the following:

As source material in comparing elements within sentences
Students are asked to find signal words that introduce adverbial clauses in a group of sentences.
As source material in comparing sentence patterns
The teacher introduces a basic sentence pattern, then asks students to find additional sentences of this pattern in a list printed in the textbook.
As the basis for oral usage drill
The teacher divides the class into pairs or small groups to complete drills that require students to select appropriate from inappropriate usages in a sentence context—for example, He did his work (good) (well). As each student reads a sentence aloud and selects what he believes to be the appropriate form, his companion indicates agreement or disagreement. Disputed usages are referred to the teacher.
As the basis for individual drill
The teacher maintains a series of duplicated one-page explanations of recurring problems, such as those concerned with parallel construction or sentence fragments. Accompanying each corrected composition returned to a student is an explanatory sheet reviewing the problem in sentence structure with which the student has had difficulty. Each sheet refers to appropriate drills in the language book, which the student must complete. Thus students in any class may be assigned different kinds of exercises at the same time. (Copies of explanatory sheets prepared for one occasion are saved by the teacher for future use.)
As material for reviewing capitalization, punctuation, and the conventions of language usage
Classes or groups needing to review the uses of capitalization in designating the titles of particular persons or the use of commas separating items in a series are assigned appropriate explanations and exercises.
As source material for diagnostic exercises and tests
The teacher uses a list of twenty-five sentences as the basis for assessing the ability of students to identify similar structural elements. For example, students may be asked to underline all words or groups of words used as *running* is used in "I believe that running is good exercise."

These are only a few of the ways in which teachers, trying to develop a meaningful program for their students, may adapt the material of current textbooks. The exercises are used to reinforce principles after students are led initially to recognize concrete examples of these principles in their own use of language.

What Research Says

Effective instruction is more likely to result when the classroom approaches are similar to those tested by research. In teaching both usage and sentence structure, teachers can use the following tested procedures: approach instruction positively; emphasize a thought approach; use diagnostic procedures, including self-diagnosis; use the laboratory method whenever possible.

APPROACH INSTRUCTION POSITIVELY   Effective instruction focuses upon strength rather than weakness. The teacher directs the attention of students to models of good writing, whether the distillation of thought in an offering by a student or the compression in a sentence by Sean O'Faolain. The teacher also encourages students by praise so they will recognize their own achievement and will strive for even greater accomplishment. Recognizing that most individuals work to sustain real growth but become discouraged when they see little improvement, the teacher tries honestly to build positive attitudes.

EMPHASIZE A THOUGHT APPROACH   Instruction emphasizing errors in sentence structure as problems in the thinking processes, rather than as subjects for grammatical analysis, produces improvement in writing, according to a study by Ellen Frogner.[22] Her research indicates that learning occurs through the thought method and a grammar method but that the former produces greater improvement in sentence structure and a longer retention of the abilities involved. For students of superior intelligence, the methods were found to be about equal in effect, although the thought method was more economical of time; for students of average intelligence, the thought approach clearly resulted in greater learnings. In this approach, "Running to the rescue, the fire burned me" becomes a problem in communication rather than an exercise in recognizing a dangling participial phrase, with the key test being whether the sentence conveys meanings intended by the speaker. Similarly, instruction on coordination and subordination may be introduced without reference to grammatical terminology if the teacher wishes.

This approach emphasizes thinking through each idea. This method can be introduced in a number of ways. A study by Silvy Kraus reveals that significant gains in student learning were obtained through three variations of the approach: by presenting instruction in sentence structure in logical sequence, with appropriate sentence exercises but no related writing; by presenting instruction in the same predetermined order but assigning a weekly theme as well; by including instruction in a unit on literature and introducing it as needed in relation to specific problems in student composition.[23] All approaches were effective, but the results achieved by relating instruction to actual writing problems were achieved in only *one-third of the time.* The first method required thirty hours of instruction; the second, twenty-four; the unit based on lessons required only ten. Kraus describes the sequence for a typical unit-based lesson as follows:

[22] Ellen Frogner, "Grammar Approach Versus a Thought Approach," *English Journal,* Vol. 28, No. 7 (September 1939); also reported in *School Review,* Vol. 47, No. 9 (November 1939).

[23] Silvy Kraus, "A Comparison of Three Methods of Teaching Sentence Structure," *English Journal,* Vol. 46, No. 5 (May 1957).

Reading a particularly effective student paper which deals with content of the unit. Discussion of ideas presented and of the effectiveness of the composition. Discussion of basic errors found in sentences taken from student papers.

Division of class into groups to work on problems in sentence structure according to needs demonstrated in the compositions.[24]

All three of the over-all approaches tested by Kraus used the thought approach and showed the importance of discussing structure in relation to the ideas being presented. Under each method, too, provision was made for individual differences, with a student excused from group and individual assignments if he had demonstrated mastery of the concept.

USE DIAGNOSTIC PROCEDURES   Most theories of learning and almost all research in language indicate that effectiveness is increased when instruction is based on the needs of individuals. The pretest-teach-retest approach is one that has been thoroughly proved, especially when students recognize the instruction needed and the teacher avoids unnecessary drill. Since the task of improving language usage is complex and difficult even when not considered in relation to the limited time available for instruction, teachers do well to distinguish items that are essential from those that are desirable but unnecessary. Several ways of doing this are described in the Suggested Learning Experiences at the end of this chapter.

USE THE LABORATORY METHOD   A completely individualized program in which many students are writing while others are completing exercises or working with the teacher seems visionary in today's large classrooms, yet research repeatedly shows the effectiveness of such a program. Particularly in the high school and the junior college has this laboratory approach been shown to result in permanent gain. Normally the method involves working on drills and writing papers according to individual need, with the teacher making himself available for conferences with individuals and groups. Much varied practice in writing is offered; indeed, this may account for the demonstrated effectiveness of the approach. Comparisons favor the laboratory method over organizations involving extensive workbook drills, weekly themes, and classroom sessions in which instruction is presented to the total group.

Teachers who are unable to organize their classes in this manner may still utilize the approach. They can avoid the assignment of endless practice for students who demonstrate reasonable mastery of a form. Such individuals may be set to writing or reading while instruction is presented to other pupils. More group teaching may be provided, so that students can obtain help without distracting the attention of the entire class. Finally, teachers can provide for individual writing and drill to the greatest extent possible.

If selectivity is the crux in organizing the content of the program in grammar and usage, certainly application is the clue to determining the

[24] *Ibid.,* p. 280.

method of learning. The problem in teaching is to organize instruction so it will be related to the communication of young people. The approaches discussed here lead the teacher in this direction.

SUGGESTED LEARNING EXPERIENCES

Research and experience have long demonstrated the futility of attempting to improve the written and oral usage of students through reliance only on fragmentary and isolated lessons on English grammar. The learning experiences suggested in the following pages will prove effective only if they are introduced in relation to the writing and speaking of students. Because these experiences stress inductive approaches, they can perhaps be most skillfully incorporated in class work during moments devoted to formulating concepts concerning the ways students use language in spoken and written communication.

TO PROVIDE EXPERIENCES IN USING ORAL LANGUAGE
TO FACILITATE DEVELOPMENT OF EFFECTIVE AND VARIED PATTERNS OF USAGE

► *Arrange the classroom to facilitate oral communication of ideas*

1. Permanently arrange portable classroom furniture in an open circle or, if the size of student groups makes this impossible, arrange for half of the class to face the other half. Such arrangements will at least encourage students to speak to one another. Where desks are permanently bolted to the floor, arrange to have students grouped in pairs so individuals can converse. The physical arrangement of most classrooms is far from perfect, but teachers who understand the significance of intergroup communication in improving the use of language will continue to press for large classrooms, portable furniture, seminar rooms, tape recorders, phonographs, and classroom work areas.

2. Plan seating so students do not regularly and permanently sit near individuals in their own social group who may be presumed to speak approximately the same dialect. Provide opportunities for young people from different dialect groups to converse informally about topics, ideas, and problems related to their interests.

3. Encourage informal conversation and discussion whenever possible, especially between young people in different dialect groups. Small group discussions, team projects, informal play-reading and poetry-reading sessions, student-led seminars, role playing and improvised drama—these approaches help, within the limits of reasonable classroom decorum, to provide young people with many experiences in discussion. Remember that no one can improve and extend his use of language in a regimented, silent classroom.

► *Practice adapting oral language to the situation*

Provide speaking activities affording young people an opportunity to adapt their oral language to different kinds of situations. Teachers may ask mature secondary students to reflect on how they used language after the experience is completed, perhaps by replaying fragments of the conversation on a tape recorder. With younger students and those experiencing difficulty in modifying their language behavior, the varied experiences themselves may be sufficient. The following kinds of situations, intended to be illustrative rather than complete, are of the kind that call for varied uses of language and are not always within each student's own experience.

Goal-directed activity in small groups Creating a four-minute film to illuminate an idea; for example, the principle of balance in esthetic expression, the tension of an athletic contest.

Talking with the elderly Asking a group of students to interview retired long-time residents in the neighborhood, perhaps to ascertain how the area has changed (while reading a book like *How Green Was My Valley*). What questions to ask? How to put the questions? How to begin a conversation?

Being interviewed Arranging with a local employer to conduct several mock interviews before the class or arranging to send a group seeking positions to an actual job interview and recording what is said.

Communicating over the telephone or radio Arranging a two-way tele-lecture or radio discussion of a problem common to both groups of students. When groups have substantially different patterns of usage, the value of such an experience is enhanced. Notice the limits of language when the two groups do not know one another.

Conversations with young people from another school Arranging with a teacher from another school to bring groups together, preferably in an informal situation to discuss common matters of interest. Such plans can be relatively simple and involve meetings of boys and girls working on a similar project or unit, or rather elaborate, such as inviting a group of children from the city to visit a suburban or rural school for a day or two.

Questioning a specialist Inviting to the classroom an adult who has a unique specialty or vocation interesting to pupils and related to other classwork. Discuss in advance how such a visitor should be questioned, the purpose of the questioning, and the kind of questions that are appropriate.

▶ *Introduce experiences in listening*
   and responding to language other than one's own

1. In tracked comprehensive schools, which tend to group young people with similar language habits, or in schools with a relatively homogeneous population, seek opportunities for pupils to converse informally with young people who speak a different English dialect. Occasional intra-class projects may help; so may visits to other schools. An exchange student or teacher from England, Canada, or some other region of the United States may be invited to meet with the class.

2. From time to time read aloud to the class an interesting selection that introduces young people to patterns of language different from their own. Occasional informal periods devoted to the reading of poetry by students to students can also be productive. Try to introduce such readings in the most informal settings possible —the school court or lawn, a school lounge (if available), the library (if not rigidly formal and restrictive). Divide pupils into groups. Let them choose and listen. Avoid any suggestion of the rigidity of memorization or formal oral reading.

3. Use tape recorders to provide first-hand experiences in speaking and listening. Ask one pupil to speak briefly into a recorder, perhaps situated in a special carrel; ask another to listen to what his classmate has said and respond to what he hears. Failing to arouse sufficient interest in an issue or idea to elicit fluent speech, the

teacher may ask some pupils to read brief written papers and others to respond to the ideas in the papers.

4. Plan a weekend workshop at a local conference ground for pupils with similar interests. Such a workshop might be organized like similar events for teachers, with general lectures or panels, study groups, related films, outside consultants, and so on. If possible, try to involve young people from more than one school or area in the groups. Among the emphases that might be especially appropriate for English students at such workshops: some aspect of creative writing, with a poet or novelist participating; Shakespeare, with a university scholar as consultant; alienation of youth as reflected in contemporary literature; film study, supported by the viewing of selected motion pictures; a dimension of drama involving active participation, with specialists from the theater participating. Such activities may also be introduced as continuing after-school activities but are unlikely to achieve the same degree of impact as an overnight conference at some location removed from home and school.

TO ACHIEVE VARIETY IN EXPRESSION

▶ *Study variations in the writing of others*

1. Compare two translations of a single passage as evidence of the varying effects that may be achieved in expressing identical ideas in English. While studying *Cyrano de Bergerac,* by Edmund Rostand, for example, consider such an example as the following:

> Why you might have said—
> Oh, a great many things! Mon dieu, why waste
> Your opportunity? For example, thus:—
> *Aggressive:* I, sir, if that nose were mine,
> I'd have it amputated—on the spot!
> *Friendly:* How do you drink with such a nose?
> You ought to have a cup made especially.
> *Descriptive:* It is a rock—a crag—a cape
> A cape?—Say rather, a peninsula!
>
> TRANSLATION BY BRIAN HOOKER

> One might make, oh, my Lord, many
> Remarks, on the whole, by varying the tone,
> For example. Listen:
> *Aggressive:* Sir, if I had such a nose, I should
> have it amputated at once!
> *Friendly:* It must dip into your cup;
> In order to drink you must have a goblet
> made for you!
> *Descriptive:* It is a rock! It is a peak!
> It is a cape! What did I say? A cape?
> It is a peninsula!
>
> TRANSLATION BY HELEN B. DOLE

2. Ask each student to select a passage of prose he particularly admires. For practice, ask him to imitate the sentence patterns in an original paragraph of his own.

3. Urge students to have special sections of their notebooks in which they copy interesting sentences from their reading and paste sentences clipped from magazines and newspapers. Ask students to classify their findings according to the basic sentence patterns.

4. After studying introductory adverbial clauses, students may be asked to write without punctuation three sentences using such clauses. Then have class members exchange papers and correct and punctuate each other's sentences. Exercises of this type require a twofold analysis of original sentences, since students not only create examples but must analyze them.

▶ *Practice compressing ideas*

1. Help students express ideas in different ways, such as by writing a single sentence to capture the basic thought of the following description:

> The title of a film, "Snow White," was listed on the theater marquee. A small candy counter was situated at a newsstand next to the theater. A woman in a brown suit was dragging a small child and stopped to make a purchase at the candy counter. She then dragged the child to the ticket office, purchased a ticket, and entered the theater.

2. Analyze the variations found in sentences written by students to demonstrate ways of subordinating ideas.

3. Stress at every opportunity the value of compression and economy. La Rochefoucauld stated, "True eloquence consists in saying all that is necessary and nothing but what is necessary." Place the quotation on the chalkboard. Drive the point home whenever possible. Encourage students to reduce long statements by asking class members to summarize discussions, to restate the plot of a story in a single sentence, or to compress a printed paragraph into a few original words and expressions.

4. Flash student papers on a screen with the overhead projector. Direct attention not only to sentences to be rewritten but to examples of effective expression.

▶ *Practice achieving variety in expression*

1. Provide exercises in which students combine two or more ideas. For example, ask students to list six events that happened to them over a weekend. Then involve them in writing original statements to illustrate the following: relating two ideas by using a word like *and* or *but,* relating two ideas by using a word like *however* or *then,* relating two ideas by using a word like *since* or *although.*

2. Ask students to achieve variety in expression by including examples of the following in their paragraphs: quotations; questions; inverted sentence order; introductory sentence starting with adverb, prepositional phrase, or participial phrase; appositives, "free" noun or adjective clusters such as Francis Christensen recommends in his generative sentence models (see page 375).

3. When introducing the analysis of sentences by average students, encourage individuals to use their own sentences as examples. Ask them to select a particular kind—for instance, a sentence in which inverted word order is used. In some cases teachers mark appropriate sentences in the compositions of each pupil and follow the return of papers with a lesson in grammatical analysis.

▶ *Practice transformational sentence combining drills*

John C. Mellon, in an important recent study,[25] reported that seventh-grade children improved significantly in their writing as a result of weekly exercises in sentence combining, whether or not such activity was related to instruction in grammar. Basing his weekly exercises on the basic transformations identified by a transformational-generative grammar, but always emphasizing the process, not the grammatical principle, Mellon devised such inductive drills as the following:

1. *Something* seemed to suggest *something.*
   Bill finished his lessons in less than an hour.
   He had received special help from another student.
   CORRECT STUDENT RESPONSE   The fact that Bill finished his lesson in less than an hour seemed to suggest that he had received special help from another student.

2. In her letter Mrs. Browning demonstrates *something.*
   So much feeling may be conveyed by a few words.
   CORRECT STUDENT RESPONSE   In her letter Mrs. Browning demonstrates how much feeling may be conveyed by a few words.

TO PROVIDE EFFECTIVE PRACTICE IN USAGE

▶ *Relate instruction to students' writing and speaking*

1. Plan for some compositions to be written in class so that instruction may be presented to students at the time when they will recognize the need and have opportunity for practice. Write on the chalkboard any sentences on which an individual requires help. During the final ten minutes of the period, correct these sentences with the entire class.

2. Introduce pre-correction periods as a regular activity before papers are passed to the teacher. Before collecting the first composition assigned after a lesson on sentence structure, ask students to scan their papers especially for glaring errors of a particular type. Some teachers ask students to attach to their papers a statement that they have engaged in pre-correction.[26] Others give students check sheets, such as the following, that may be attached to compositions before papers are passed to the teacher.

SAMPLE CHECK SHEET (GRADES 7–8)

I have checked my paper for the following items
_____ appropriate form, penmanship, margins, neatness
_____ spelling
_____ end punctuation
_____ fragments
_____ run-together sentences
Signed _____

[25] John C. Mellon, *Transformational Sentence-Combining, A Method for Enhancing the Development of Syntactic Fluency in English Composition,* Cooperative Research Project No. 5-8418 (Cambridge, Mass.: Harvard Univ. Press, 1966) multilithed. A critique of this study points out the dangers inherent in overemphasizing such activity. (Cf. Francis Christensen, "The Problem of Defining a Mature Style," *English Journal,* Vol. 57, No. 4 (April 1968), pp. 572–79.

[26] See the discussion of pre-correction in Chapter Eight, "Written Expression," pages 345–46.

3. Encourage alertness to inappropriate oral usage. Some teachers regularly ask students to identify the two or three errors they find most common in their own speech. Special practice may be introduced to eliminate problems that seem to be widespread.

▶ *Provide oral practice*

1. Plan oral drills on appropriate forms—for example, follow instruction aimed at establishing "This isn't a pumpkin" as more appropriate than "This ain't," with five unison readings of the desired usage.

2. In junior high, plan simple oral games or exercises. For example, to concentrate on eliminating *ain't* or the double negative, schedule five minutes of drill in which different individuals attempt to "guess" an object selected by a class and various students respond with the appropriate usage form:

QUESTION	Is it a yo-yo?
ANSWER	No, it isn't a yo-yo.
QUESTION	Is it a bloodhound?
ANSWER	No, it isn't a bloodhound.
QUESTION	Is it a spaceship?
ANSWER	No, it isn't a spaceship.

Most teachers find that games of this type result in learning by younger pupils when the purpose is clear, when students understand the appropriate form being emphasized, and when the drill is continued for only a few minutes.[27]

3. Follow the drill involving the choice of correct and incorrect forms by oral repetition of the correct responses. Through this method ask the students first to distinguish the correct forms in such sentences as:

(Him and me) (He and I) went to the show.

Then ask them to write each correct sentence five times and to recite the correct form in a unison reading. Here again effectiveness is increased when the forms being stressed are clearly those pupils recognize as causing them difficulty. For example, an appropriate time for such a drill is after a lesson in which pupils have had an opportunity to check their compositions and have agreed on the usage items on which they need help.

4. Use an oral drill requiring students to indicate whether sentences read aloud by the teacher conform to appropriate usage. Usually ten sentences are presented, all concerning the same problem of usage. Five of the sentences are correct; the other five are incorrect versions of them. After preliminary explanation of the error and the appropriate form, ask students to fold their papers in half vertically and number from 1 to 5 on the first lines of the left side, from 6 to 10 on the identical lines of the right. With each student placing only the left side of his paper before him, read five sentences aloud, being careful not to betray by voice or expression which ones are right and which are wrong. If the sentence sounds correct to the student, he is to place an s sign after the appropriate number on his paper; if it sounds incorrect, he is to place an NS. After the first five sentences have been read,

[27] Many suggestions for oral exercises of this type are to be found in Marjorie Burrows, *Good English Through Practice* (New York: Holt, Rinehart & Winston, 1956).

ask the student to turn over his paper so that only the right side shows. This time, the teacher reads the corresponding five sentences, presenting whichever form was not used earlier. The following ten sentences might be read aloud to illustrate the problems of compound subjects and objects.

1. Evelyn felt very upset about David and me.
2. Mick wouldn't speak to Barbara and me.
3. Tessie and me forgot about going.
4. My aunt and I are going to the park.
5. The swimmer said he'd give my sister and I a lesson.

6. Evelyn felt very upset about David and I.
7. Mick wouldn't speak to Barbara and I.
8. Tessie and I forgot about going.
9. My aunt and me are going to the park.
10. The swimmer said he'd give my sister and me a lesson.

Already on the board are the numbers from 1 to 10, and when the sentences have been pronounced, the teacher writes the key: s = standard, ns = nonstandard.

1. s   6. ns
2. s   7. ns
3. ns   8. s
4. s   9. ns
5. ns   10. s

Since the first five sentences parallel the second five—one of each pair presenting the correct form and the other the incorrect—students are able to see at a glance the usages they understand. When they understand, parallel items are correctly marked; when they do not understand, parallel items are incorrectly marked; when they are confused or uncertain, only one of a pair is correctly marked. After correcting the papers and discussing the forms, conclude the drill by asking the group to recite in unison the five correct sentences. For this purpose, the sentences may be repeated after the teacher or copied on the board.

5. Encourage students to read their compositions orally for the purpose of noting awkward constructions. Occasionally divide the class into pairs or into groups for this purpose. Students with severe writing problems sometimes will recognize poor sentences more quickly by listening to their papers read by another person—preferably the teacher.

6. Teacher readings of sentences containing problems in faulty reference are often enjoyed by students. Such examples as the following may often be found in student compositions:

After picking up the baby, Margaret placed a bottle in her mouth and walked to the crib.

One neighbor, meeting another, complained that his beagle puppies were playing on his lawn among his shrubs, and that they were nearly ruined, and he had better look after them.

7. Encourage pupils to conduct oral drills by the coach and pupil method. Divide the class into pairs. One member of each pair repeats sentences aloud, while the other keeps a record indicating which are standard and which nonstandard. When the first student finishes the drill, the roles are exchanged.

► *Utilize brief, varied usage drills*

Use the following check list as a guide in planning instruction.

A CHECKLIST FOR VARYING DRILL IN ENGLISH USAGE

Kind of drill	*Examples*
writing original sentences	As an exercise in punctuating conversation, students write jokes using dialog.
varying sentences	The teacher writes five sentences in the simple past tense (I went). Each student expresses past time in at least two other ways (I was going, I have gone, and so on).
adding examples	After studying the formation of the past tense with irregular verbs, each student writes five additional examples, such as: I *ring* today, and I *rang* yesterday; I *rise* today, and I *rose* yesterday.
correcting sentences written by students	Students pass original sentences to a neighbor, who rewrites, punctuates, or checks as directed.
choosing correct form	Students are asked to select the appropriate form in such sentences as: I gave it to (he) (him).
completing a statement	Students are asked to complete a sentence: Yesterday Tillie (use form of "to sing") to me.
replacing a word	Students substitute ten other words for *better* in the following sentence: She is better than I am.
correcting errors	Students rewrite sentence or paragraph marked incorrect.
written repetition	Students are asked to write five sentences using correct forms, such as statements including adverbial modifiers.
dictation	Students copy sentences or paragraphs dictated by the teacher. (Particularly useful spelling and punctuation drill.)
proofreading	Students correct and change a paragraph that is presented without punctuation and capitalization.
changing forms	Students are asked to reword such statements as the following to use plural subjects: The mouse runs in the house. The girl doesn't want to go. I witness the phenomenon.
oral drill	See suggestions advanced on pages 124–25 of this chapter.

TO APPROACH LANGUAGE INSTRUCTION POSITIVELY

► *Praise effective expression by students*

1. In evaluating panel discussion, respond to the ways in which ideas are presented, particularly if a statement deserves special comment. Similarly, in classroom discussion, react to concepts presented succinctly and well by commenting, for example, "Will you say that again, Roland? Notice how forcefully his idea is

stated." Without being insincere or overly obvious, find opportunities for commenting on the oral expression of students.

2. Encourage students to develop in their notebooks sections called "Ideas Worth Remembering Expressed by Class Members." Whenever a particularly interesting idea is presented by a student, ask the others to add the sentence to their lists.

3. Share with the class sentences, words, and phrases from the written work of students. One teacher culled an entire set of compositions to list a dozen well-turned phrases. Similar lists may be made of apt descriptive terms, original images, compressed ideas, or unusual sentence patterns. From an analysis of compositions, develop a bulletin board display.

4. In correcting papers, respond to the ideas presented—whether by challenging, extending, or agreeing—and react to the way in which these ideas are expressed. The more specific the comments, the more helpful. "I like your use of colorful verbs" conveys more than the enigmatic "good," as do reactions to the effectiveness of the parallelism, the nature of the sentence structure, and the clarity of the idea.[28]

▶ *Emphasize important ideas with entertaining arguments*

Whenever possible, utilize opportunities for stressing appropriate language. Use graphic examples to be found in literature or current affairs. Shaw's *Pygmalion*, for example, suggests some valid arguments for increasing our command of English, as do the lyrics of the song, "Why Can't the English?" from *My Fair Lady*. Introduce Victor Borge's humorous recording on punctuation to underscore the importance of separating ideas.

TO USE DIAGNOSTIC PROCEDURES INCLUDING SELF-DIAGNOSIS

▶ *Construct diagnostic tests*

When responsible for a list of usage items to be presented or reviewed, attempt to ascertain the students' prior understandings by constructing a special diagnostic test. If students demonstrate ability to recognize complete sentences, detect run-togethers, or classify individual words in the way desired, proceed to an analysis of language on a more advanced level. If the diagnostic test identifies fifteen students needing definite instruction in any one area, plan group assignments. Usually pretesting reveals a few individuals so deficient they will require special help. Some may be found to be extremely proficient; assign these advanced studies. Diagnosis of this type offers a way of identifying able and gifted pupils who become bored and resentful when faced with repetitious drills on skills they have long since mastered.

1. A comprehensive diagnostic test may be given early in the year. The teacher selects items that will test the basic understandings—sentence, subject and predicate, main and subordinate clauses, capitalization and punctuation—whatever is to be emphasized.

A second test can be administered at the end of the year.

2. In some classes a comprehensive test may be impractical; teachers may prefer to test items separately. The following tests will serve as examples.

Usage

Subject and Predicate

A. Underline the simple subject with one line and the predicate with two lines.

    1. The Martians rushed into the street.

[28] For additional suggestions on correcting student papers, see Chapter Eight, "Written Expression," pages 343–46.

2. In the park grew beautiful marshmallow trees.

3. Has your brother purchased a new sports car?

. . .

B. Underline the appropriate standard form and copy it on the line in the left-hand margin.

_____ 1. I heard you (was, were) at the bowling alley.

_____ 2. He (don't, doesn't) plan to study engineering at college.

. . .

Pronouns

Underline the appropriate standard form and write it on the line.

_____ 1. The aviator sent my brother and (he, him) on an errand.

_____ 2. (Us, We) girls will go to college in three years.

_____ 3. The girls met mother and (they, them) at the station.

_____ 4. The teacher assigned (us, we) boys detention.

. . .

Verbs

Fill in the blank with the appropriate standard form of the verb in parentheses. Indicate some form of past time in every sentence. Read aloud whenever you find doing so will help you.

(know)   1. The student _____ the answer to every question.

(sing)   2. The robins _____ early this morning.

(wear)   3. The rear tires had _____ well.

. . .

Note Reread your answers to this question to see that every verb is in some form of past time, not in the present.

Modifiers

Underline the appropriate standard form and write it on the line.

_____ 1. He went down the freeway (quicker, more quickly) than his pal in the foreign sports car.

_____ 2. The patient is not so (well, good) as he was yesterday. (applies to health)

. . .

(This test is to be administered orally by the teacher. The pupil follows the printed sentences with his eyes as the teacher reads each one aloud.)

Put a *C* in front of all sentences that sound appropriate to you. If the sentence uses a nonstandard form, underline the nonstandard expression and indicate the change on the line in front of the sentence.

EXAMPLE

His	That book is his'n.
C	That book is his.
omit *of*	He jumped off *of* the plane in his parachute.

_____ 1. We could of done better if we had tried.

_____ 2. We gave the child a orange.

_____ 3. If he's wrong, it don't matter what he says.

_____ 4. The leprechauns sang the song and then left.

. . .

▶ *Collect information on usage habits*

Record information on specific usage problems observed in the speech and writing of students. Use a single card for each student and enter information as on the following sample:

SUGGESTED TEACHER RECORD FOR ANALYSIS

name *David Whitford*	oral usage
fragment ✝✝✝✝ //	*"could of"* 2/30, 4/5 5/15 *"can't never"* 4/5
run-together sentence ////	
dangling modifier /	
misplaced modifier ///	
reference /	
parallelism	
agreement ✝✝✝✝	
spelling ✝✝✝✝ //	
punctuation ✝✝✝✝ ✝✝✝✝ ///	

▶ *Ask students to record errors*

Often teachers encourage pupils to maintain the records, possibly by developing a cumulative file of all written work with a covering tally sheet on which the record is maintained, as in the Individual Record shown on pages 130–31. Approaches of this kind encourage self-evaluation, which can result in a heightened readiness for drill and instruction. Much of the value of this type of analysis emanates from such motivation. Teachers find that students who identify their own problems—even through such a simple activity as examining papers—tend to better understand the goals of instruction and to question the purpose of instruction less.

► *Analyze needs with students*

1. Periodically ask students to review recent compositions kept in a permanent classroom file and to report the kinds of writing problems occurring most frequently in their papers.

2. With seventh- or eighth-graders construct a Usage Traffic Signal chart based on results of a diagnostic test (see page 132). Introduce the procedure early in the year, when planning the semester's work. If separate sections of the test deal with basic problems—such as case forms of pronouns, agreement of pronoun and antecedent, agreement of verb with subject, forms of irregular verbs, and choice of verb forms—then a chart like the one illustrated here may be constructed. Allow students to choose pseudonyms to avoid broadcasting information on their proficiencies to the entire class. During a study period, ask students individually to color their own sections; place the chart at a rear table to preserve the mystery of the pseudonyms. Although the standards vary for each situation, a student with no more than one nonstandard usage in a single area may color the appropriate square green (for "Go"), one with three or four errors may use yellow ("Proceed with Caution"), whereas more than four nonstandard usages may result in the use of red ("Stop!"). Once all scores are recorded, the teacher and students may examine the chart to find:

> *Areas where the total class needs instruction*   These appear as almost solid red vertical lines, as the Case Forms and Irregular Verbs on the sample.
>
> *Areas where segments of the class need instruction*   These are divided between green and the other two colors.

INDIVIDUAL

Paper	*Problems*			
	Spelling	*Punctuation*	*Reference*	*Agreement*
9/18 Essay	//	///		/
9/26 Story	///	/		
9/29 Paragraph	//	//		
10/4 "My Favorite Sport"	///			/

Individuals who need special instruction   These are represented by solid red
horizontal lines, as in numbers 1 and 5 on the sample.

Individuals who might be assigned advanced work   Student 6 on the sample should be excused from lessons planned for the remainder of the class.

Often a parallel form of the test is presented at the end of the school year so students may see their improvement.

▶ *Analyze recorded conversation*

Divide the class into small groups and assign a topic for each group to discuss.
Use questions that will appeal to students so that their language will flow easily.
Limit each conversation to ten minutes and record it in the rear of the room while
other students are reading. Enter the conversation only to question diffident participants. Use the recorded conversations for the following kinds of analysis:

For diagnosis of special needs   Try to identify students with problems in
fluency as well as in grammatical usage. Then observe the language of these
students during later in-class and out-of-class situations.

As the basis for conferences with parents   Play the recordings during parent
conferences and encourage parental cooperation in improving the student's
usage at home.

As a basis for assessing growth in oral language   Record one conversation
in September, another at the end of the year. Use a comparison of the
two as one way of estimating growth.

TO PROVIDE FOR INDIVIDUAL PRACTICE

Develop over a period of time a file of mimeographed drill sheets dealing with
various usage items. Periodically, devote time to completing such drills with each
exercise assigned according to individual need.

RECORD

Problems				
Parallelism	*Misplaced Modifier*	*Dangling Modifier*	*Run-Together Sentence*	*Fragment*
	/			/ / / /
		/		⊁⊬⊬⊬
				/ /
/				/

USAGE TRAFFIC SIGNALS					
Student	Pn. case	Pn. ag.	Verb-sub ag.	Verb irreg.	Verb tense
1	Red	Red	Red	Red	Red
2	Red	Red	Yellow	Red	Yellow
3	Red	Yellow	Yellow	Red	Red
4	Red	Red	Green	Red	Red
5	Red	Red	Red	Red	Red
6	Green	Green	Green	Green	Green
7	Red	Red	Yellow	Green	Yellow
8	Red	Yellow	Red	Red	Green
9	Red	Yellow	Green	Red	Red

Green	Go	0-1 Problem
Yellow	Caution	2-3 Problems
Red	Stop	4 or more Problems

When each student has an individual copy of a handbook, assign drills needed for improving papers. Those students who reveal only limited understanding of the sentence may be referred to an appropriate exercise; others may study lessons on punctuation or variety in sentence structure. Ask individuals to file the completed drills with their corrected papers.

Some teachers identify two or three individuals with unusual problems in writing and ask each to write a paragraph a day for several weeks.

To increase individual awareness of the problems involved in communicating ideas, tape record a reading of a paper exactly as written by a student. Ask the writer to listen carefully to the recorded material before the paper is returned for correction. A similar, less dramatic procedure involves having a paper typed exactly as it is written and returning it to the student for correction. Often problems that the writer initially failed to see become clear through such methods.

SELECTED READINGS

BRITTON, JAMES (ed.). *Talking and Writing.* London: Methuen, 1967. A useful British book describing the relationship of informal speech and the uses of language.

HOGAN, ROBERT F. (ed.). *The English Language in the School Program.* Champaign, Ill.: NCTE, 1966. This collection of essays includes eight articles on teaching English usage.

JOOS, MARTIN. *The Five Clocks.* New York: Harcourt, Brace & World, 1967. A scholarly discussion of the varieties of English usage.

LOBAN, WALTER. *Language Ability: Grades Seven, Eight, and Nine.* Office of Education, U.S. Department of Health, Education, and Welfare; Washington, D.C.: U.S. Govt. Printing Office, 1966.

————. *Problems in Oral English.* NCTE Research Report No. 5. Champaign, Ill.: NCTE, 1966. Report on a twelve-year developmental study of language growth, which indicates clearly that not the ability to analyze sentences but the ability to achieve flexibility and variety within known sentence patterns is the real measure of proficiency with language.

LYNCH, JAMES J., and EVANS, BERTRAND. *High School English Textbooks: A Critical Examination.* Boston: Little, Brown, 1963. Although their study is based on textbooks available around 1960, the authors raise considerations in Part 2 that should be considered in using any language textbook.

MARCKWARDT, ALBERT H. *Linguistics and the Teaching of English.* Bloomington, Ind.: Indiana Univ. Press, 1966, pp. 27–65. A readable exposition of a point of view by a leading American linguist.

MOFFETT, JAMES. *A Student-Centered Language Arts Curriculum, Grades K–13.* Boston: Houghton Mifflin, 1968. Practical suggestions for language experiences involving pupil interaction at all levels of instruction.

POOLEY, ROBERT C. *Teaching the English Language in Wisconsin.* Experimental edition. Madison: Dept. of Public Instruction, 1967. A practical guide for language programs developed for the Wisconsin Curriculum Study Center in English.

————. *Teaching English Usage.* New York: Appleton-Century-Crofts, 1949. A standard reference.

QUIRK, RANDOLPH. *The Use of English.* Rev. ed. New York: St. Martin's Press, 1964. A major British linguist discusses the uses of English.

STEWART, WILLIAM A. (ed.). *Non-Standard Speech and the Teaching of English.* Washington, D.C.: Center for Applied Linguistics, 1964. Provides a discussion of problems involved in teaching students with nonstandard dialects.

FOUR
LOGICAL THINKING

It cannot be said too often that no one can give the
learner his concepts. If he is to have them at all he
must construct them out of his own experiences.

BROWNELL AND HENDRICKSON [1]

PERSPECTIVE

"The central purpose of education," states the Educational Policies Commission, "is learning how to think," and thinking in our culture largely means
learning to think through language.[2] Students need help in learning the steps
and skills involved in logical thinking and the ways to use reason in disciplin-
ing emotion through language. Unchecked and unevaluated emotional responses offer no reliable guide for behavior. Research, as well as experience,
has demonstrated that the planned study of methods of reasoning clearly
contributes to the ability to make sound judgments and form intelligent
conclusions.[3] The findings of research in perception and social psychology
seem to demonstrate that the way an individual thinks determines in some
measure what he thinks and how he acts. Such relationships have been
observed both in individuals who lean toward rigid, authoritarian patterns
and in those who are far more complex and flexible.

This chapter is concerned with the structure and methods of rational and
orderly thought processes in relation to the dynamics of language and nature
of language considered in the previous chapters. The unique role of emotion
and feeling in imaginative thinking is presented in the chapter that follows.
Together, these five chapters present the framework underlying the use of

[1] W. A. Brownell and Gordon Hendrickson, "How Children Learn Information, Concepts,
and Generalization," in Forty-Ninth Yearbook, National Society for the Study of Education, Part 1, *Learning and Instruction,* ed. by G. Lester Anderson (Chicago: Univ. of
Chicago Press, 1950), p. 112.

[2] Educational Policies Commission, *The Central Purpose of Education* (Washington, D.C.:
National Education Association, 1961).

[3] For example, as one indication of the effectiveness of direct study, R. L. Lyman reported
that twelfth-grade students who had received detailed instruction in reasoning during
the eleventh year were clearly superior in detecting sound and unsound arguments to
those who had received no instruction. R. L. Lyman, "How High School Seniors Explain
Common Errors in Reasoning," *English Journal,* Vol. 12, No. 5 (May 1923), pp. 293–305.

language and are thus fundamental to all phases of the total English program.

Whether we can actually distinguish separate processes in the thinking of individuals or whether processes are intricately interrelated and an inseparable part of the totality of the person is a problem about which researchers are not yet in agreement.[4] For the purpose of planning instruction, however, teachers find classifications to be helpful. Categorizing thinking processes, even if somewhat arbitrary, aids in considering the basic problems involved in improving thinking. This chapter discusses three kinds of thinking important in English—concept formation, problem solving, and judgment making.

Concept Formation

We begin to organize facts as soon as we perceive them. We sort and sift basic information, bringing order to a multitude of impressions, observations, and associations. An adolescent's first impression of a large high school is vague and generalized as he considers three floors, one hundred rooms, and a few distinguishing characteristics. Later he begins to identify separate impressions—the office suites, the industrial arts center, the English department, the areas reserved for recreation. His general impression is gradually refined as he classifies his observations. In similar ways, each of us develops concepts by differentiating and integrating ideas and impressions. To understand the role of the teacher in helping students organize and evaluate their ideas, we must understand how concepts develop; how such forces as bias, selectivity, and emotion affect the process; and how both inductive and deductive methods may be used in the classroom.

UNDERSTANDING HOW CONCEPTS DEVELOP

Concepts emerge through a gradual and sequential process that varies with person and situation. This is not to say that concepts are developed through a fixed, logical series of steps that can be presented to students as a formula for logical thinking. The process is complex and subject to much variation; yet always it tends in the same direction—from the specific to the general, from hunches evolved out of similarities in past experience to generalizations that prove useful in assimilating impressions obtained in future experience.

One's conception of form in language grows from perceptions early in life. "It is . . . easy to forget that a student's earliest experience with form and pattern in his study of English is in the language itself. In fact, long before a child ever comes to school he has begun to grasp the sense of form and

---

[4] E. A. Peel in *The Pupil's Thinking* (London: Olbourne, 1965), leans toward the interrelated approach. David H. Russell, in *Children's Thinking* (Boston: Ginn, 1956), offers a typology. For an interesting discussion of the research on this problem, see Russell Stauffer (ed.), *Cultivating Higher Thought Processes* (Champaign, Ill.: NCTE, 1967).

pattern which is necessary in using our complex communication system." [5]
So writes a committee headed by literary critic Northrop Frye, noting how
these early concepts become expanded and enlarged. The forming of concepts
involves a continual grouping and regrouping of one's ideas—a reorganization
influenced not only by new facts and new experiences but by ingenuity and
imagination in seeing new relationships. Each of us must recognize that his
concepts, based on fairly restricted experience, are subject to limitations;
since more complete information may force modification, never can we say
we know everything about anything.

For children in school, planned learning of certain concepts may extend
over several years as crude, undifferentiated initial responses become gradually
more refined and full of meaning. This is the crucial characteristic of Jerome
Bruner's "spiral" curriculum. Basic ideas introduced through simple illustrations at lower grade levels are reintroduced and expanded at regular intervals
later.[6] Thus a seventh-grader's relatively simple conception of a paragraph
as a loosely related group of sentences becomes modified throughout his
years of instruction in English as he reads and analyzes many paragraphs,
discovers a method of organization within each paragraph, and considers the
relationship of the paragraph to the over-all organization of the essay or
theme. Undoubtedly, the ultimate development of such understanding will
vary with the abilities, experiences, and motivations of the learner, and with
the nature of his instruction. In general, the basic role of the teacher at any
level is to encourage students to formulate their own generalizations rather
than to present the final generalization as a verbalization to be memorized.
In attempting to develop concepts, the teacher bears in mind three important
considerations: the impact of prior experience, the gradual nature of conceptual growth, and the need for selectivity in identifying concepts to be
taught.

An extensive background of experience serves as the basis on which
generalizations are built. Some students are fortunate enough to have had
many broadening opportunities—travel, reading, observation of many dimensions of life. Less privileged youngsters have only meager backgrounds on
which to draw. For such children, often those from low socio-economic
environment, the teacher continually struggles to develop a basic background
for understanding. Carefully planned experiences—both real and vicarious—
directly related to the ideas being discussed, will facilitate the formulation
of concepts. Motion pictures, recordings, excursions, and reading offer possible
approaches. Ruth Strickland has noted even the contributions that teacher
readings of literature can make to extending the linguistic experience of
disadvantaged children. For such children literature alleviates the poverty
of what Basil Bernstein calls the "restrictive" language of inner-city groups

[5] Northrop Frye (ed.), *Design for Learning* (Toronto: Univ. of Toronto Press, 1962), p. 46.
[6] Jerome Bruner, *The Process of Education* (Cambridge, Mass.: Harvard Univ. Press,
1960).

and introduces children to the rich vocabulary and syntax of more "elaborative" language.[7]

Such expansion of experience can take many forms. For example, the North Carolina Advancement School developed a highly successful unit emphasizing sensory experiences for disadvantaged eighth-grade boys. Listening to the sounds of the sea and the sounds of the city led to attempts to describe personal reactions through language. Responding to Leonard Bernstein's music from *West Side Story* prompted attempts to express reactions through interpretive dance. Viewing films on contemporary social problems—*On the Waterfront* and *The Quiet One*—awakened sensitivity to the brutalities of modern life. As the boys became engaged in responding to different kinds of experience with a high degree of impact, they used language in new ways to express deep personal feelings and they gradually developed new concepts concerning the nature of human responses.

Not all concepts emerge automatically, of course, even out of a rich background of experience. Some must be deliberately introduced. Planning many varied classroom experiences tends to deepen understanding. Even ideas that seem to emerge from a moment of insight or illumination almost always have been preceded by a period of mulling over or conscious study. In developing important generalizations, most students profit from repeated opportunities to think ideas through in different situations. For example, in attempting to increase understanding of the complete sentence, some teachers introduce several brief activities—analysis of student errors in writing, practice in rewriting sentences, oral and written drills. Continued emphasis on the same basic principle through different types of experience tends to be more effective than either repeating a similar type of exercise or extending the length of a single activity.[8] The interrelationship of purpose, drill, and economy of learning leads teachers away from lengthy, mechanistic drill periods, deadening to the student's zest for learning, toward briefer and more frequent drills and experiences with clearly defined purposes.

Selectivity, also, is important in identifying concepts for emphasis. Children learn thousands of ideas, in school and out. Recognition that every concept cannot be taught demands the selection of a few for emphasis. For example, in a single work of literature, such as *Julius Caesar*, the teacher emphasizes a few of the major themes or ideas rather than all those possible, letting the basic purposes of instruction control the selection. In most studies of *Julius Caesar*, for example, understanding Brutus' personal dilemma is more important than acquiring general ideas about the power struggle in ancient Rome.

Often teachers wish to structure learning situations sufficiently to en-

[7] Ruth Strickland, "The Contributions of Structural Linguistics to the Teaching of Reading, Writing, and Grammar in the Elementary School," *Bulletin School of Education Indiana University*, Vol. 40, No. 1 (1964), pp. 1–44.

[8] See Percival Symonds, "Practice Versus Grammar in the Learning of Correct Usage," *Journal of Educational Psychology*, Vol. 22, No. 2 (February 1931), pp. 81–95.

courage the development of a particular idea. In teaching *Johnny Tremain,* for example, a teacher will encourage young readers to view the novel in part as an expression of an adolescent boy's experiences in developing maturity of judgment. Insight into Johnny's development as a person will occur only if the reader considers the nature of the boy at different moments in the story and the forces that bring about changes in his outlook and behavior. A teacher who encourages students to construct their own generalizations can provide basic guidance through a sequence of discussion questions. The first phase of the discussion may be limited to a consideration of the narrative, since readers must understand *what* happens in a novel before they consider *how* and *why* things happen. Once basic understandings are clarified, the teacher encourages some tentative interpretations of the meaning of events. Ultimately he asks students to detect relationships between various passages. Thus, through a carefully planned series of thinking tasks, the student's understanding of the novel is deepened and extended. The various levels of analysis of a novel are suggested in the accompanying chart, which deals with the behavior of Johnny Tremain.[9]

A pattern such as that presented in the chart would develop gradually over several related discussion periods rather than during any single hour. Continually, the teacher would assist students in gathering, organizing, and relating facts. Although the amount of class time spent discussing the narrative would vary with the abilities of students and the difficulty of material, in each class some opportunity should be provided for such processes of interpretation and generalization. The same approach might be applied, of course, to actual rather than fictional situations.

Studying the reliability of our impressions

The sources of our concepts require classroom study. How we react depends upon what we perceive as truth; since no two persons perceive a situation in exactly the same way, no two will have exactly the same reaction. In constructing concepts, we select and organize our impressions in terms of a point of view that depends largely on our earlier experiences and on our purposes at the moment. Difficulties frequently result when ideas or action are based upon incomplete or misinterpreted evidence. No information is so persistent and compelling as that obtained first hand; yet even personal experience offers no guarantee of truth. Students who understand the following three concepts will recognize the necessity for weighing impressions carefully: purpose controls selectivity of observations; bias may color interpretation; recall may involve sharpening and leveling.

The orientation of any individual affects what he selects as significant. Men with differing values rarely look at objects in similar ways. In his history of

---

[9] For a further discussion of methods to use in structured discussions, see Chapter Seven, "Oral Language," pages 295–302.

THE DEVELOPMENT OF CONCEPTS THROUGH DISCUSSION

LEVEL 1 GRASPING THE NARRATIVE	LEVEL 2 INTERPRETING THE FACTS
Basic question What happened?	*Basic questions* What does this mean? How and why did it happen?

Sample incidents

EARLY

Johnny displays scorn and sarcasm in his treatment of Dove and Dusty at the silversmith's shop.	Johnny's actions reveal pride, a sense of superiority, and a lack of tolerance for those who try hard but are limited in ability.

LATER

Through friendship with Rab, Johnny learns to think before speaking ("to count ten"). Johnny gives Cilla time to apologize when she soaks him with water.	Johnny is learning to be patient and tolerant and is developing some conception of the feelings of other people.

CONCLUDING

He reacts negatively to the rigid rank-and-file relationship between the British officer and the private.	
Johnny is so worried about Rab, Cilla, and the cause of freedom, that the discovery of his own birthright leaves him unmoved.	Johnny forgets himself in his concern for other people.

LEVEL 3   GENERALIZATION ABOUT THE WHOLE

Basic question   If the interpretation of incidents is valid, what does this reveal about the purpose of the entire novel?

Student-formulated generalization   *Johnny Tremain* is a book that reveals how a selfish, arrogant boy learns consideration of other people.

---

art, André Malraux observes that each succeeding culture has placed new interpretations on the beauties of primitive art, and he comments, "We prefer Lagash Statues without their heads, and Khmer Buddhas without their bodies, and Assyrian wild animals isolated from their contexts. Accidents impair and Time transforms, but it is we who choose." [10]

Just as cultures vary, so do individuals. A motion picture is viewed differently by a critic, a member of the audience, and an actor appearing in the film. The three reactions may be illustrated by such statements as "The mood is sustained," "The film left me breathless," and "I was better in *Cool Hand Luke*." An individual attempting to base a judgment on one of these comments must understand the peculiar orientation of the speaker. The critic's analysis

[10] André Malraux, *The Voices of Silence* (Garden City, N.Y.: Doubleday, 1953), p. 67.

would excite those who value thoughtfully executed films; the viewer's would tempt those who wish a "breathless" experience; quite possibly the actor's might discourage attendance.

By considering the diverse motivations of individuals (see Chapter One), we can teach how purposes influence perception. Illustrations are found in every community. Pupils react positively or negatively to the rebellious behavior of young protest groups depending upon whether the behavior threatens or supports their previous point of view toward such groups and their motivation. Purpose leads individuals to interpret impressions differently. A strong desire to see a flying saucer or a celebrated sea serpent may well lead one observer to attach significance to phenomena that would be overlooked by another. Teachers find many opportunities for introducing a discussion of selectivity in perception.[11]

Bias, too, may color interpretation. Almost all of us claim to recognize the insidious effect of prejudice in shaping the views of other people. Fewer of us allow for the operation of such affective influences in our own thinking. During the past two decades, the noteworthy efforts of many individuals and groups both inside and outside the schools have resulted in heightening our awareness of the ways in which prejudices influence thought and action. Some intellectual understanding of the effects of prejudice is necessary to the improvement of individual thinking; it does not insure, however, that the individual will be alert to controlling his own emotional biases. Although efforts to destroy false concepts and stereotypes, which erect barriers between various social and racial groups, are essential, this work must be supported by preparing students to handle the effects of emotional bias in less inclusive, everyday situations.

Students seldom recognize that every strong loyalty or attitude may operate as a prejudice capable of blocking clear thinking. Some loyalties are important —loyalty to family, to friends, to country. These are cohesive forces, binding individuals together for the common good and serving a necessary and important function. Deep feeling surrounds every basic loyalty, however, and deep feeling sometimes creates a bias that prevents a person from thinking objectively. An active proponent of a political or social movement does not bring the same understanding to an outside action threatening the success of the cause as does a student who is not a member. Either one may be biased. Adolescents who are themselves unskilled in social amenities may be keenly sensitive to the feelings of such literary characters as Stephen, the ungainly protagonist of "Clodhopper." The result of such deep involvement is worthwhile if it enables the reader to understand a character more fully. If not balanced by rational consideration of all observable factors, however, such emotional involvement may result in misinterpretation. Some adolescents identify so completely with the boy that they do not attempt to understand the attitudes of those who surround him. Continual study of the dimensions

[11] A number are suggested in Chapter One, "Language as Dynamic Process."

of emotional bias is necessary to prepare students to handle emotionally charged issues.

Furthermore, memory of events may not be accurate. The further a report is removed from the time of occurrence, the greater the possibility of distortion. We remember more accurately our actions of yesterday than those of a month ago. Our natural tendency to forget details is only one facet of a transformation involving shifts in emphasis and changes in point of view. Most of us have had the experience of relating the same incident on repeated occasions. Perhaps we describe a visit to Disneyland. Our first presentation may be colored with detail—a twenty-minute gem. Later we find we can compress the report without losing effectiveness. We condense; we eliminate; we drop details which no longer seem important. After repeated presentations we find we can present the "same" information in less than ten minutes. Actually we have not presented the same ideas at all. Many changes are consciously made; others, unintentionally. In reconsidering a particular event, we tend to modify our perspective. Minor observations may be sharpened to major proportions; others may be leveled. These tendencies, differing among individuals and not necessarily undesirable in their effect, are encouraged by the responses of listeners. A passing comment on the cleanliness of Disneyland, which interests one group, may on subsequent occasions be restructured as a major conclusion to capitalize on its audience appeal; a telling observation on the characteristics of the park's patrons may be de-emphasized or eliminated if it fails to arouse comment. Sometimes we so modify our views that we completely shift our focus.

Understanding possible effects of sharpening and leveling helps students evaluate the comments of others. Occasionally a segment of a complete event may be so overemphasized as to distort the entire perspective. Thus an individual disturbed by the questionable refereeing of a crucial play in a football game may in time recall little about the game except "sloppy officiating," even though only one of forty decisions was questioned. Occasionally, rumors are unintentionally created, as when careless words seem to convey the unjustified impression of a causal relationship between an industrial accident and the presence nearby of a group of laborers or businessmen. Students should be encouraged to exercise particular care in evaluating reports that may be harmful to other individuals and groups. A first step in improving accuracy is to lead students to examine the reliability of their own perceptions and the perceptions of their friends.

Studying the ways of reasoning

Beyond guiding the formation of students' concepts and providing for the study of the reliability of sources, the teacher has an obligation to provide for the study of the processes through which concepts are formed. In most secondary classes, such an approach calls less for a disciplined analysis of the principles of logic than for careful attention to crucial problems involved in using deductive and inductive processes of reasoning.

INDUCTIVE AND DEDUCTIVE THINKING   Thus far the emphasis in this chapter has been on inductive thinking—the formulation of concepts or generalizations based on many examples or facts. Beginning at a concrete level, this approach minimizes the danger of verbalization—the rote acceptance of abstract ideas without an understanding of their basic meanings. Most students will assimilate generalizations developed from many examples.

Deductive reasoning—the application of concepts to specific facts and situations—is a process that becomes increasingly important as we mature and extend our experiences. Much of our knowledge is acquired deductively as we apply learned concepts to new situations; for example, we assume we understand the difficulties involved in providing shelter in Antarctic regions because of our prior reading and our personal experience with problems resulting from snow and ice in other situations. Much learning in our classrooms is of this nature. The use of teaching procedures that encourage students to apply ideas tends to be less time consuming than building concepts inductively, but is perhaps less vivid and less thorough.

Sustained thinking is neither purely deductive nor purely inductive but involves a combination of the two approaches. In searching for the answers to a single problem, we almost always shift back and forth. At the same moment that we identify the theme of a short story through inductively relating key episodes, we also test the validity of concepts deductively against our own perception of truth. Seldom do we use one or the other exclusively. Teachers rely on both approaches in the classroom.[12] They aid students in evolving concepts and then encourage students to apply them. The maturity of the learner and the nature of the learning task determine the approach. Many understandings may be taught in either way, as in the following example:

> *Desired student understanding*   Newspapers differ in their treatment of news, in their degree of objectivity, in the extent of their coverage.
>
> *Deductive approach*   The class discusses an article asserting that newspapers vary considerably in the treatment of news. The article may be read by the teacher or assigned to be read in a textbook. Following the discussion students find illustrations of the generalizations discussed. Several representative newspapers are brought to class and compared.
>
> *Inductive approach*   Front pages of many different newspapers for a single date are examined by the students in class. During the discussion period that follows, the students compare observations and develop tentative generalizations regarding the similarities and differences. Because generalizing from specific instances can lead to dangerous simplification, the teacher gives students a home

---

[12] In a recent study Geraldine La Rocque suggests that deductive approaches are sometimes more effective than inductive. Here again results vary with the content, the purpose of instruction, the materials, and the teacher. See *The Effectiveness of the Inductive and Deductive Method of Teaching Figurative Language to 8th Grade Students*, doctoral dissertation, Stanford University, 1965.

assignment to analyze more than one newspaper in the light of generalizations developed by the total class. Thus students are encouraged to test and further modify their observations.

Regardless of which method is introduced, genuine learning will result only if students do the reasoning. No one can do this for them. The teacher's role is to guide and assist the process. One of the important ways in which the teacher can be of assistance is to help students recognize and avoid faulty and misleading thought processes that prevent the development of sound concepts. In secondary classrooms, instruction may well be concerned with three recurring flaws: oversimplifying, avoiding issues, and assuming false relationships.

OVERSIMPLIFYING   The searching analysis of fact—the heart of sound reasoning—does not come easily. In our impatience for answers we sometimes accept quick and easy generalizations as carefully substantiated conclusions, even when a thorough examination of available evidence would lead us to modify our thinking. This is one mistake which Bernard Shaw's Henry Higgins made in regard to Eliza Doolittle. Higgins' initial assumption that the mere acquisition of upper-class manners and mores will be sufficient to make Eliza happy overlooks both her personal feelings and her future position in society. To help students avoid conclusions based on incomplete data and recognize these errors in the reasoning of others, we may focus on three common forms of oversimplification.

Sweeping generalizations occur when individuals attempt to reason on the basis of inadequate data. Obviously such statements as "Children are no longer being taught any discipline" and "Teen-agers are wild drivers" involve overstatement of the facts. Such observations tend to be reported by individuals who advance conclusions after considering one or two cases. By failing to qualify such generalizations, a speaker or writer applies his conclusions to "all children" or "all teen-agers." Possibly he does so because he is not conversant with all the facts; he may mislead himself as well as the persons with whom he is attempting to communicate. Seldom, indeed, may such inclusive observations be applied to all members of a group. Students need to learn that general statements of this type often correspond to truth only when modified by such terms as *some, many, few,* or *sometimes.* Unqualified statements that seem to have universal application should be examined critically.

The *either-or fallacy* in thinking occurs when an individual reduces to a clear-cut dichotomy an argument that will admit other possibilities. For example, the statement "Either Bob or Mary is right" is sound reasoning only if we have examined and discarded the possibility that both may be right or both wrong, or that there are other alternatives. We must particularly guard against reducing to extremes our consideration of a problem involving many points of view. The reference to "both sides of the question" is often a signal heralding the possibility that an oversimplified presentation will be introduced.

Formula explanations—clichés and stereotypes—are pat judgments and conclusions. They hamper sound reasoning when individuals apply them to particular situations without thinking through the available evidence. Often they are evoked by superficial similarities between the immediate problem and the commonly accepted explanation. Here again the thinker attempts to generalize on the basis of inadequate data. Dubious behavior by the son of a disreputable father dismissed with the pronouncement, "Like father, like son"; a child's delinquency interpreted as being the result of an unhappy home, with no further attempt to examine the situation for other explanations; an "emotional block" offered to explain failure in spelling—such explanations are sometimes adequate but certainly not always. To immature minds such concepts seem acceptable because they are familiar.

Oversimplification is common in the thinking of immature persons. Students should not be reprimanded for each sweeping generalization, either-or fallacy, or stereotyped argument; rather they should be led to examine the complexity of each problem and the reasons why their thinking was faulty.

AVOIDING THE PROBLEM   Individuals utilize many ways of evading direct consideration of specific issues. A speaker or writer who wishes to avoid committing himself may evade answering by commenting on the nature of the problem rather than the issue itself—for example, "It's a serious situation" or "It's a very difficult problem." A pupil who neglects to submit a theme may claim that the assignment is of no value because "it's all mixed up." Sincere or not, such a student offers no real support for his argument, but simply restates his opinion in different words. In attempting to overcome any tendency to avoid issues, high school students may well concentrate on three recurring fallacies.

Begging the question occurs whenever a speaker or writer assumes a conclusion that requires proof. The statement of the student mentioned above is no less a case of question-begging than such obvious reliance on unproved assumptions as "Everyone of course agrees that . . ." and "No one who has studied the problem would doubt that . . ." A special form of question-begging is circular reasoning, in which two statements are used reciprocally to prove each other—for instance: "The boys at South High are delinquents; you know they must be trouble makers because they go to that terrible school." Circular reasoning, like other forms of question-begging, is a way of avoiding the central issue.

Basing argumentation on personalities or on personal qualifications rather than on fact is a familiar occurrence in school discussion. The boy who says that he is voting for Pearl because he "can't stand" Adele, Pearl's opponent, is merely circumventing any real consideration of the factors that give rise to his decision. Similarly, when John, told by Mary that he could improve his oral report if he would speak from notes rather than from a complete manuscript, replies, "You did that yourself," or "Practice what you preach," he is responding in terms of personalities rather than of ideas. Similar illustrations may be observed in many classroom discussions.

Extending and exaggerating are more difficult to eliminate than the other fallacies discussed here because students do not easily recognize gross misinterpretation as a way of avoiding a problem. For example, as a suggestion for increasing participation in extracurricular activities, a student suggests lowering the cost of admission to athletic events. Rather than consider the proposal fully, an opponent of the idea responds, "In other words you want to give tickets away." Clearly the second speaker's purpose is to represent the idea as extreme and unworthy of consideration. "From the way you talked one would think . . ." and "If you carried that line of reasoning to its conclusion . . ." are other phrases that sometimes introduce attempts to evade objective consideration by extending a statement to a point that is untenable.

Not always, of course, must the exploration of a complex problem terminate in a clearcut resolution. Students need to learn that the process of investigation may well end by demonstrating the inconclusiveness of available evidence. For example, a consideration of the roots of racial disorder in our cities could honestly end with the suspension of judgment concerning basic causes and still be a valuable explication of a major social problem. In directing students' attention to the dangers inherent in avoiding the issue in argument, teachers must avoid giving the erroneous impression that generalized conclusions are always possible. Modern rhetoricians tend to stress writing as an act of discovery, an act of uncovering new truths, rather than a process of demonstrating the validity of received truths.[13] The consideration in the classroom of ways of exploring problems needs to steer a sound course between the Scylla of question begging and the Charybdis of fixed conclusions.

ASSUMING FALSE RELATIONSHIPS   Questionable generalizations will sometimes result when individuals assume relationships without thoroughly examining the data. Consider the following:

A. Because this is the author's latest book, it is his best.
B. Because John plays baseball, he's a good sport.
C. Because two subjects are equally difficult, they are of equal importance to the learner.

Statement A is based on an assumed causal relationship between the writing experience of an author and the quality of his work, an assumption that does not always correspond with known facts. Statement B tends to equate sportsmanship with participation in a single sport—certainly a conception based on inadequate evidence. Statement C assumes that two objects that are similar in one respect remain similar in others—a fallacious assumption of the kind we must guard against particularly in reasoning by analogy. The think-

---

[13] See, especially, the discussion of invention in Robert Gorrell (ed.), *Rhetoric: Theories for Application* (Champaign, Ill.: NCTE, 1967).

ing that produces such generalizations results from a failure to identify and examine all dimensions of the relationships involved. Having noted certain connections between objects or events, we often suspect the existence of a particular relationship. Sound thinkers conceive of such inferences as hypotheses requiring verification rather than as proved generalizations. Students need to learn to reason with discrimination and care, suspending final judgment until all the evidence has been examined, organized, and evaluated.

Since unreliable and misleading methods of thinking result only in spurious conclusions, an important step in improving the student's ability to form sound judgments is to help him examine his present thinking—the reliability both of his impressions and of his methods of thought. Such examination, particularly if it occurs more or less continuously throughout the secondary school years, will heighten the student's awareness of the need to refine thought processes.

Perceiving the cruciality of relationships

Basic in all learning is the ability to relate ideas; such ability is of particular significance in the English class, where students sometimes have difficulty in linking the verbal learning of the classroom to the experiences of outside life. The perception of relationships—involved in both induction and deduction—is essential if the student is to see the bearing that concepts developed in the English class may have on personal behavior.

Some students see little value in poetry. Others wonder why they must read about "all the dead people" in *Julius Caesar*. Some find *Our Town* to be "hopelessly dated." Readers react to literature in this manner when they see little connection between the book and the experience of life itself. Unless they do perceive an essential relationship between the two, literature becomes for them a study apart from experience—an unimportant exercise, a time-filler easily forgotten. The problem of improving students' ability to relate their vicarious experiences in literature to the real experiences of life is an important aspect of our over-all program for encouraging individuals to examine all available data.

As it is with literature, so it is with other aspects of the English program. Ninth-graders may see no connection between propaganda techniques in examples presented for analysis by the teacher and the "big sell" used by advertisers on their favorite "pop" music program. Seventh-grade students may need help in perceiving the relationship between a class discussion on the reasons people have hobbies and their own interest in collecting stamps or mounting botanical specimens. Such generalizations are the durable factor in learning.

The most important general method of helping students organize their experiences is the unit approach in planning instruction. A unit is a sequence of related classroom activities organized around a central core of content and extended over a period of time. Suggestions for this type of planning are presented in "Program and Plan," and several illustrative units are included at the ends of the various sections of this book. In any unit, the reading, writing, and oral activities are organized for a unified impact on the student, and each new experience is developed from work previously introduced. Students are continually asked to sift their multiple impressions of class activities in terms of the unifying topic. They are forced to compare and contrast, to relate new ideas to those already known, and to apply the ideas in writing and discussion. The learner gains breadth and depth of understanding, as well as experience in perceiving relationships.

Students will form concepts with or without guidance from others. By helping them with the processes involved in this type of thinking, the teacher is more likely to find their generalizations to be sound, logical, and grounded in fact.

Problem Solving and Methods of Inquiry

Problem solving is a special form of logical thinking, one that individuals use in attempting to overcome obstacles in the way of definite objectives. It is the specificity of the direction, rather than the processes themselves, that distinguishes problem solving from concept forming. This kind of thinking aims at achieving a particular goal. In recent years educators have designated classroom methods that stress the identification and resolution of problems or questions as "inquiry training" or the "discovery method." [14] Confronted with a question demanding consideration, we direct our energies to the achievement of a reasonable solution. Whether it is a question of determining action or developing a theoretical understanding, we engage in a sequence of thinking activities that lead us from an identification of the problem to what seems a satisfactory solution. Thus many of the processes of reasoning discussed previously in this chapter are used in problem solving and inquiry approaches.

Throughout the years of schooling, teachers aid students in facing present concerns and prepare them for facing concerns they will meet in the future. The two responsibilities cannot be separated. Students must learn to deal with the concerns of the present if they are to acquire the self-confidence and the methods of inquiry and reasoning needed for attacking later problems. Fear of failure and other emotional pressures frequently interfere with these processes. Most teachers can supply from their own experience examples of the ways in which anxiety affects the performance of individuals in speaking situations and in examinations. By providing successful experiences in problem solving in the classroom, we encourage growth of confidence and proficiency in the skills necessary for the successful formulation of solutions.

In the English classroom, the tasks that face students may either involve action (discovering how to locate a library book) or understanding (discovering why "The Fall of the House of Usher" has such a frightening impact

[14] P. W. Bridgman, "Scientific Method," *Teaching Scientist* (December 1949), p. 23.

when one first reads it). Whether either kind of task emerges as a problem to students or as a way of solving problems depends on the nature of the learning situation. The teacher organizes instruction so the student will acquire or modify his behavior, but the pupil learns this behavior only if he needs it to accomplish some purpose of his own. Thus, before he learns how to locate a library book, he wants to find a particular title; before he studies the effect of the short story on himself, he feels its impact and then the desire to unlock the puzzle of how Poe achieves the effect. In both situations, a specific desire leads to learning—a skill on the one hand, a knowledge of the writer's craft on the other. In either case, the teacher, in addition to improving processes of problem solving, must encourage students to establish goals that bring about the learning of desired patterns of behavior. This means that the teacher's primary goal and that of the student will often differ; but the student, to accomplish his own goal—the acquisition of a library book—must first accomplish the teacher's—perfecting certain locational skills.

The nature of the problem and the situation in which it is to be faced affect the learner's solutions. Difficult tasks far beyond an individual's capacity tend to provoke aimless trial and error rather than systematic analysis. For example, assigning the preparation of a panel to students who have had no prior experience with this form of organized discussion will almost always result in confusion. Similarly, teachers would not ask junior high students to consider such mature problems as the choices that Sir Thomas More had to make between religious ideals and political responsibility, although problems involving the same conflicts have meaning for young adolescents if related to the values of the peer group. Better than problems faced by adults only are questions like, "Should boys who violate school regulations be permitted to participate in athletics?" Issues must be real and immediate to the learner if the experience is to prepare him for more difficult situations later.

The physical, experiential, and emotional condition of the learner will also influence his solutions. A learner who is overly tired, must work in cramped space, feels insecure, or is tortured by self-doubt and fear of failure is seldom one who will venture many imaginative solutions. Productive methods of inquiry require a fresh, alert, self-confident student who finds materials available and adequate space in which to work. The conditions of time under which he works will often shape his willingness to begin and his ultimate success or failure. In addition to necessary work space and adequate resources —for example, books, typewriters, library tools, graphic materials—individuals need reasonable time. Teachers must recognize the limitations imposed by the rigid time restrictions in most classrooms. For example, projects involving extended inquiry by groups of students into complex and difficult problems will not seem reasonable to the learner unless adequate class time is provided for research, study, and discussion. Too often library research or panel presentation or dramatization results in failure because we do not allow time for careful preparation. Students who have had bitter experience with such failure may well be wary of undertaking a new project unless they see how and when it can be accomplished. Any plan for extensive reliance on inquiry methods in longer units of instruction must allow sufficient time.

Social factors also influence students' abilities in problem solving. Research indicates that groups of students often produce better results than do individuals working alone.[15] A higher level of aspiration is set by the group than by the individual even though more time tends to be required for solution. Undoubtedly some of the superiority of the group approach may be attributed to the opportunities provided in the social situation for the analysis, discussion, and consideration of many potential solutions. The nature of the task should determine whether the teacher wishes to encourage group or individual thinking. The group approach seems to be most appropriate when problems require the expression of various points of view or the consideration of many experiences—such as the identification of the complex causes of the alienation of youth. The citizens of a free society solve problems individually and in groups. The school needs to provide experience in both approaches.

Judgment Making

In the play, *Teahouse of the August Moon,* Captain Fisby is forced to choose between building the teahouse requested by the Okinawan villagers and building the pentagon-shaped schoolhouse required by American military planners. Fisby's assigned task is to teach the Tobiki villagers to be democratic and self-supporting. Through his experiences with Sakini the captain has learned a great deal about the nature of Okinawans and the way in which they live. He must draw upon these ideas in making his decision—a task that involves comparing, discriminating, and weighing evidence in choosing between alternatives. Fisby's behavior illustrates important differences between the processes of judgmental thinking and the processes involved in other kinds of reasoning. In developing his ideas regarding Okinawans (concept formation), and in considering how to accomplish democratization of the village (problem solving), Fisby engages in reasoning that is essentially *productive.* However, in choosing between the teahouse and the schoolhouse (making a judgment), his action is *decisive* by nature. The processes involve somewhat different considerations.

Judgments are used in forming concepts and in solving problems, of course; for this reason, it is important to distinguish those aspects of judgmental thinking that need to be studied separately. Individuals make three types of judgments: conceptual judgments in perceiving and organizing facts and ideas, judgments regarding hypotheses in considering alternative solutions to problems, and value judgments in determining preference for objects, ideas, and courses of action. The first two types are essential to productive thinking and involve the sublimation of emotional considerations to the demands of logical necessity. Value judgments, however, involve the determination of qualitative

[15] David H. Russell, *Children's Thinking* (Boston: Ginn, 1956), pp. 266–69.

distinctions and therefore tap the feelings. Hence, a real problem in making sound judgments of this type is the control rather than the suppression of emotion. For this reason, value judgments merit consideration as a separate form of thinking.

To understand what can and what cannot be taught to students in a classroom, teachers need to consider how children and young people learn the values on which their judgments are based. In a real sense each person is both developing his values and being guided by them as he makes his decisions. Choices tend to be determined by beliefs an individual thinks important; yet not until one makes a choice and tests that choice in action do values become operational. The complexity of this interrelationship needs to be recognized by teachers. So too does the fact that all elements in a culture may influence what one learns to prize. Awareness of how values develop over a long period of time out of the totality of a person's experience emphasizes that only carefully planned, cumulative instruction in judgmental thinking, extending over the six secondary years, is likely to have a substantial effect.

Value development proceeds from the simple to the complex, from the specific to the general. Children first learn to observe simple rules of conduct, later to relate individual action to their total ethical behavior. Ultimately they become aware of some of the problems and dilemmas of life involving clashes in ethical values.

Value development proceeds from the external to the internal. In childhood, choices of conduct are often determined by parental injunction, school regulation, or neighborhood mores. Later, individuals substitute internal regulation for the external control—a self-enforced code of behavior for the external reward and punishment.

Orientation in decision making moves from the present to the future. Children consider each decision in terms of immediate satisfaction; mature thinkers, in terms of the implications of actions. Until an individual begins to base judgments on larger ideals, such as honesty, justice, and love, he is guided by egocentric pleasure-pain appeals.

Values are learned from models. Through emulation, imitation, and identification, youth acquires his ethical point of view. These identifications may be with parents, members of the peer group, teachers, athletic and entertainment heroes, or even characters in fiction and biography.

Thus, the ability to make sound value judgments develops slowly, and it is best developed through actual conduct. Not until students have opportunity to consider decisions in concrete situations do they make substantial progress. To be sure, the most disturbing choices faced by adolescents occur out of school; the classroom seldom offers direct opportunities to help them with their most basic problems. Yet, the school can guide students in wrestling with problems of certain kinds, can introduce in the literature program the directed study of values held by other people, can offer analysis and discussion of decisions young people face. In every term, students should have some opportunity, within the limits of the curriculum, to choose among alternatives;

the choice must be real, not one the student has reason to suspect has already been determined. The unit "Meeting a Crisis" suggests possible approaches. Many additional suggestions are offered in Chapter Thirteen.

In making decisions, individuals try to achieve a balance between internal and external demands. Our personal wishes, needs, and ideals must be balanced against facts and realities over which we have no control. For example, in judging the worth of a classroom procedure, teachers weigh their own attitudes toward the method—the satisfactions they obtain and their enjoyment in using the approach—against objective considerations—the learning of pupils, the resources available, the various other procedures they know. The extent to which we permit personal feelings to influence us varies with each task. In evaluating methodology, we are guided largely by a dispassionate appraisal of the learning situation because we know our choice affects many individuals; in selecting books for personal reading, we follow our own preferences.

The identification of our personal preferences and desires is the first step in controlling them. In making the judgments involved in selecting clothing to wear, or in choosing motion pictures to attend, we base decisions largely on our feelings at the moment. More frequently, however, our wishes are balanced against outside demands. We need to be aware of our personal feelings, even as we consider other matters.

Any decision has both antecedents and consequences; behavior does not occur in a vacuum. Students must learn to consider the ways in which present action may influence future events. They need to recognize also their responsibility for the consequences of their decisions. As Muriel Crosby has noted, the inability to forecast the probabilities of the future, the lack of understanding of causal relationships, is particularly characteristic of some disadvantaged children.[16] Prediction of the results of behavior is not always easy. In making judgments such as those involved in choosing between college preparatory, commercial, or vocational courses of study, many secondary students recognize the importance of their decision. However, in a decision involving less obvious consequences, such as considering whether to accept a position on the school paper, individuals may overlook many factors—time, obligation to the school, conflict with other activities, learning that may be required. Often predictions of behavior will be inaccurate, since each particular situation presents its own problem. However, continued experience in balancing internal and external demands as one estimates probable and possible outcomes encourages wiser decisions.

Individuals make mature decisions based on all perceivable considerations only after much thoughtful experience in judging. However, participation in decision making is no guarantee of growth. Adolescents are faced daily with decisions outside the classroom, yet often fail to learn from their activity. To

[16] Muriel Crosby, *An Adventure in Human Relations: The Wilmington Story* (Chicago: Follett, 1964).

encourage growth the teacher must plan appropriate experiences in judging. But these become productive, thoughtful experiences only when the processes of reasoning are later analyzed and considered. Thus the role of the teacher involves organizing both the experience and the follow-through.

As students identify with characters and become involved in situations, their emotional response is intensified. Under such conditions they can learn to weigh both internal and external considerations. Teachers generally find that involvement is likely to occur when the decision situations emanate from experiences that seem important and real to adolescents. Certainly seventh-grade students cannot comprehend emotionally the dilemma facing Hamlet, and they would lack sympathy with the Dane's philosophical orientation even if they could understand it. However, such students respond strongly to Tom Sawyer's skirmishes with Aunt Polly, or to a local conflict between a group of adolescents and community shopkeepers, since problems involving conflicts with adult authority are central in the developmental experiences of this age group.

Decision situations that induce strong student empathies may be introduced by displaying pictures of adolescents facing recognizable dilemmas, by reading appropriate cuttings from stories, by presenting short films designed to confront young people with choices, by describing verbally a problem that will admit solution by role playing.[17] In addition, the choices that students face in planning class activities will frequently provide opportunities for analysis. Once the problem is introduced, the students may be led to examine each decision by applying the questions discussed earlier: What are my personal feelings in the matter? What are the possible consequences? How will the decision affect others?

The same questions may also be applied to the decisions of characters in literature. Because literature deals with the impact of experience on the individual, it offers unique source material for studying the ways people think. Analysis of the thinking processes used by literary characters and study of the ways in which their decisions affect subsequent behavior may well sharpen students' insight into the varied dimensions of decision making.

> Literature provides illustrations of individuals who base their decisions only on their emotions. "I Can't Breathe" offers a humorous portrait of a girl completely lacking in objectivity.
> Literature shows how judgments affect other people. *A Man for All Seasons* and *Galileo* illuminate the impact of an individual's personal resolve on members of his family.

[17] These procedures are discussed in detail elsewhere in this book. For use of the picture stimulus, see "Written Expression," page 354; for the unfinished story technique and role playing, "Imaginative Thinking," pages 193–94. R. N. Pemberton-Billing and J. D. Clegg, *Teaching Drama* (London: Univ. of London Press, 1965), is a recent British book on creative drama in the English class and contains valuable suggestions. See also Fanny and George Shaftel, *Role Playing for Social Values* (Englewood Cliffs, N.J.: Prentice-Hall, 1967).

Literature provides experiences in evaluating difficult decisions involving conflicts in loyalties. In *Loneliness of the Long Distance Runner* the traditions of class clash with the bold egalitarian strivings of a new generation.

Discussion of examples from literature gains in effectiveness when the teacher encourages students to relate examples from their own experiences. Thus the analysis of complex decisions in the Sillitoe novel may be followed by such questions as "How would you have reacted?" or "What different results might a different decision have provoked?" "At what time in your own lives have you been faced with similar conflicts in loyalties?" Such questions tend to increase student involvement.

A study of value judgments may help students become aware of the complex nature of their own values. Recognizing the influence of personal codes on behavior can help students clarify their thinking concerning important decisions they must make. Such understanding may relieve the doubts and anxieties felt by many adolescents who discover that their desires sometimes conflict with their beliefs. It almost certainly will make them more able to interpret human behavior, both their own and that of others. Continuing appraisal, through carefully planned classroom experiences, of the ways his own values and those of characters from literature affect decisions should convince a student that the life he builds depends not only upon the values he selects but upon the volition he brings to bear in making them function in practice.

The control of emotion by reason, which has been discussed in this chapter, does not embrace the total spectrum of thought. To concept formation, problem solving, and judgmental thinking, we would add at the least the processes of numerical reasoning and imaginative thinking.

The methods discussed here for teaching students to formulate sound conclusions have three general characteristics.

The approaches provide directed experience in forming conclusions about present problems, coupled with a provision for intellectual assessment of processes used to achieve these ends.

The problems selected for consideration are appropriate to the maturity of the learner and are capable of eliciting his involvement.

The approaches provide experience and instruction in different kinds of thinking—in forming concepts, solving problems, and making judgments.

Classroom procedures sharing these characteristics will help the learner improve his ability to think logically. As an individual and as a member of a group, the citizen of a free society constantly makes choices that affect others as well as himself. This is his right as well as his responsibility. The teacher in this society must prepare each citizen to make such decisions as soundly and wisely as possible. This is the teacher's obligation and his opportunity. And the teacher of English deals with language, the medium through which most decisions are made.

Do teachers overstate the importance of the task, if they, like Gilbert Highet, see this search for sound conclusions as one of the "strongest and most permanent forces in human affairs"? In assessing Plato's reliance on reasoning, Highet writes:

> Ask the questions. Examine the answers. Go on discussing until the reason is satisfied with the result. As you think by yourself, all alone, you should converse with Reason almost as though Reason were another person, with claims to respect at least equal to your own. When you argue with someone else, the argument should not be a fight between you two, but a hunt after Reason, in which you both join, helping each other to detect and capture the truth you both desire.[18]

THE TEACHING PROBLEM

ORGANIZING INSTRUCTION

Clearly the program of instruction in thinking outlined in this chapter envisions the planning of curricular offerings extending over several years. Improvement in any skill occurs only after repeated practice. Continual stress on sound reasoning, supported by brief, frequent lessons, tends to be more effective than reliance on infrequent, intensive study. Teachers will want to consider ways of incorporating in lessons learning experiences such as those described in this chapter as well as ways of insuring a sustained sequential program throughout the secondary school years.

Certainly the principle of readiness applies here as elsewhere in the English program. Learning experiences are most effectively introduced at times when students make particular errors and can be led to recognize a need for learning. For example, the sharp polarization of student attitudes toward accepting or rejecting Jerry, the orphan boy of "A Mother in Mannville," has been used to introduce a class to the analysis of dangers involved in either-or thinking; similarly, for individuals who fail to support or qualify broad sweeping statements in their compositions, some teachers provide the necessary class or group instruction. Often special correction symbols are used to direct attention to such errors; brief personal comments written by the teacher are even more effective. The opportunities to relate instruction to need are many. Most units of instruction require students to form concepts, solve problems, or make judgments, and thus provide opportunity for instruction as well as for practice.

How do we assure continuity in learning over the years? The problem is not an easy one. Ultimately it depends on each teacher's accurate assessment

[18] Gilbert Highet, *The Art of Teaching* (New York: Knopf, 1950); in the paperback edition (New York: Knopf Vintage, 1954), this quotation appears on pp. 163–64.

of the needs of the learner and the teacher's ability to build on what has gone before. From the primary level on, teachers can direct students' attention both to flaws in reasoning and to methods of thinking that lead to sound conclusions. Probably at each level a few items may be emphasized; perhaps the following, in grade 9: either-or thinking, sweeping generalizations resulting from failure to qualify ideas, seeing relationships—the difference between comparing and contrasting.

Given a few such items for emphasis with a particular class, the teacher may observe student behavior in writing and speech and plan suitable learning experiences. Thus the problem for the teacher is to find for each desired learning a teachable moment in the classroom. Because individuals continually rely on their impressions of fact, and because they of necessity use the methods of thinking discussed in this chapter in formulating conclusions, the task of capitalizing on readiness and motivation in teaching the skills of thinking is less arduous than it first appears.

SUGGESTED LEARNING EXPERIENCES

Here as elsewhere in this book learning experiences are suggested to illustrate the principles and procedures that are discussed. These activities result in effective learning only when introduced at appropriate times. Many of them require more extensive preparation and follow-through than can be discussed here. Illustrations of some ways in which specific learning experiences may be integrated within longer units of instruction are developed in the illustrative units presented at the end of each section of the book.

TO RECOGNIZE HOW PURPOSE CONTROLS THE SELECTIVITY OF OBSERVATIONS

▶ *Analyze situations from different points of view*

1. Present to the class a brief film involving controversial behavior, such as the "fishhook" sequence from the film *Captains Courageous*. In this episode the spoiled boy, Harvey, ties knots in a fisherman's line to make certain that his friend Manual will catch the most fish. Manual wins a bet by catching the most fish but discovers the boy's duplicity and throws his catch overboard in anger.

Before showing the film, divide the class into three groups and ask each to view the incident from the viewpoint of one of the characters—Manual, Harvey, or the rival fisherman. Ask each student to describe the events that have the greatest impact on the person whose role he is assuming.

2. In reading a book such as *To Kill a Mockingbird*, in which point of view is an important feature, not only discuss how different episodes would be reported by different characters but offer students the opportunity of rewriting passages from a different perspective.

3. Ask students to analyze the possible motives of persons in newspaper stories. Particularly useful are stories in which individuals are reporting on events they have witnessed, for example—Woman Sees Wild Animal in Patio, Pilot Describes Flying Saucer, Tourist Reports Sea Serpent at Loch Ness. In considering motives and the

possible points of view of such individuals, ask students such questions as, "What impressions would this person stress?" "Which would he be likely to overlook?"

▶ *Study the impact of experience on purpose*

Gather twenty-five or thirty small objects in a paper carton. Include miscellaneous items, such as pencils and erasers, toy trinkets, several fruits, eight or ten cooking utensils—cookie cutter, baking dish, grater—and eight or ten small tools—pliers, screwdriver, chisel. Introduce the activity as an exercise in observation and show the contents for about sixty seconds to the class at two separate times. After the first showing, ask the students to write the names of as many *objects* as possible; after the second trial, ask them to write the names of as many *tools* as possible. Then lead the class in a discussion aimed at explaining differences in the two lists that have been compiled. The following guide suggests principles that may be developed:

PROBABLE RESULT	POSSIBLE EXPLANATIONS
Students list more objects on the second trial.	The specific task of looking for tools aids individuals in organizing observations.
Boys list more tools than girls.	Familiarity with objects affects speed and accuracy.
	Greater familiarity with objects enables boys to recognize tools quickly. To test this generalization, class might refer to results on the first trial to determine whether girls listed more cooking utensils than did the boys.
	Memory of the first experience may aid in the second.

TO DISCOVER HOW BIAS COLORS INTERPRETATION

▶ *Analyze the prejudices of students*

1. Display a number of portraits clipped from news magazines. The personages should be unnamed but should include many types of individuals—criminals, humanitarians, statesmen, and so on. Ask students to describe the kind of behavior they would expect to be characteristic of each person depicted. Then compare their predictions with a report of the known behavior of each person. In the ensuing discussion, lead students to see that in relating character to physical appearance they are merely reflecting their emotional biases and that sound judgments of character must rest on more objective information.

2. Ask for three volunteers to report independently on a controversial speech or discussion to be broadcast on television or radio. Ask each student to summarize what is said and to describe the apparent purposes of the speaker. Arrange for each to report separately so he will be uninfluenced by the other summaries. Lead the class in an examination of differences in the reports. Frequently these are great enough to suggest that each reporter listened to a separate broadcast. A teacher who suspects that the differences will be great may wish to record the program so that it is available for reference. The success of this activity depends on the degree of the students' involvement in the issues being discussed. Adolescent problems are particularly appropriate subjects.

3. Write the following quotations on the chalkboard of an eleventh-grade classroom:

"To be prepared for war is one of the most effective means of preserving the peace."

"Labor is prior to, and independent of, capital. Capital is only the fruit of labor and could never have existed if labor had not first existed."

". . . governments are instituted among men deriving their powers from the consent of the governed. . . . Whenever any government becomes destructive to these ends, it is the right of people to alter or abolish it."

"The workingmen are the basis of all government, for the plain reason that they are the most numerous."

Then ask each student to select the author of each statement from the following list of names:

Thomas Jefferson	Joseph Stalin
Fidel Castro	George Washington
John F. Kennedy	Abraham Lincoln
Karl Marx	

When student choices are tabulated, many statements will be attributed to Castro, Marx, or Stalin. Then reveal the actual authorship: Washington, First Annual Address, 1790; Lincoln, Speech, Cincinnati, 1861; Jefferson, Declaration of Independence, 1776; Lincoln, First Annual Message to Congress, 1861.

In the discussion that follows, lead students in an examination of the reasons the quotations are incorrectly attributed. Ultimately most students will see that they are guided by personal feelings, attributing ideas that seem questionable to disliked personalities. Then consider the implications of the finding for life situations, including illustrations of the ways in which an individual's emotional impressions —whether of fellow students, politicians, or television personalties—influence his willingness to accept or reject rumors or stories.

▶ *Analyze propaganda techniques used by others* [19]

Guide mature students in the critical analyses of selected statements designed to influence the reader's thinking by capitalizing on his biases. False appeals and specious arguments provide excellent materials for such exercises.

Sample paragraphs from a letter that was widely distributed in a bitter election campaign illustrate one type of available material. Here the references to particular individuals have been eliminated, but the type of material will be recognizable. The kinds of questions that aid in directing student thinking are suggested by the study problems that follow.

ILLUSTRATIVE PARAGRAPHS FROM A PRINTED LETTER

While We Pray the Enemy Plots Our Destruction

Dear Christian American Friends:

(1) This letter contains vital information which you cannot afford to miss—in fact, this may turn out to be the most important warning and the most practical information you have ever received through the mail.

(2) On November 3, John Jones let the cat out of the bag. He lifted the

[19] Other examples are to be found in "Language as Dynamic Process," pages 46–55.

curtain and gave us a peek behind the scenes. Said Jones: "If the opposition wins this election, the other nations of the world will look to Russia for leadership. Following a brief administration, by the opposition party, America will go Communist."

(3) *The hidden hand which has directed the black political magic* for the past several years is now reaching for the jugular vein of our Party. Rats that have deserted the sinking ship are now creeping into the Party, hoping that they can rule or ruin the coming Congress.

(4) *You are to be congratulated* on being a part of this crusade which did much to help bring about the recent election victory. We endorsed 187 candidates for Congress and the Senate. Nearly 170 were victorious. In scores, yes, almost hundreds of political campaigns, my name and the name of the cause you and I represent became issues. Practical politicians who only a few months ago thought my endorsement to be the "kiss of death" discovered that the support of us Nationalists brought victory. In state after state literally millions of circulars were put out by the enemy. In practically every one of these cases our man was victorious.

ILLUSTRATIVE STUDY QUESTIONS BASED ON THE MATERIAL

Salutation   What favorable connotation would the reader of this letter be expected to supply for "Christian"? For "American"? Does linking these two words carry the implication of excluding any group of Americans who are not Christians? What group in particular might be so intended here? Is this implication favorable or unfavorable to this group? What is the implication of "friends"?

Paragraph 1   What in this paragraph is intended to lead the reader to adopt a favorable attitude toward what will follow in the letter? Is such an attitude justified?

Paragraph 2   Does the secrecy implied in the expressions "Let the cat out of the bag," "lifted the curtain," and "a peek behind the scenes" seem to be a secrecy concealing a pleasant surprise or a sinister, undesirable situation? What makes you think so?

Paragraph 3   In what ways is this paragraph related to the statement attributed to Jones? Whose is the "hidden hand"? What does the writer seem to mean by "black political magic"? What emotional attitude seems to be induced by the foregoing expressions? By the phrase "the jugular vein of our Party"? Does the writer supply evidence to enable you to identify the "rats"? Is the implication that this desertion and creeping is participated in by many or by a few? What would be the significance in either case?

Paragraph 4   What is likely to be the effect of the first sentence upon the uncritical reader? Why? What affective value is provided by the word "crusade"? The implied argument is that since "we" endorsed nearly 170 candidates who were elected, the endorsement was therefore a cause of their winning. Is the argument sound? If not, where is its weakness? What is the implication of the expression "practical politicians"? If the reader of the letter deems himself a practical politician, what effect might this phrase and this sentence have upon him? Make a list of the connotations that "Nationalist" has for you. Are all these connotations favorable to the attitude of the writer of this letter? What is the emotional value of "the enemy"? What are the implications of this word in contrast to those of, say, "the opposition"?

The teacher can follow such detailed analyses of selected individual paragraphs by asking students to assess the over-all contentions and purposes of the author (or sponsoring organization) in the total letter. Individual students who are proficient in such analysis may be urged to locate similar examples of persuasion, which they can analyze in a class presentation.

TO PERCEIVE HOW SHARPENING AND LEVELING INFLUENCE RECALL

▶ *Urge students to study their own retellings*

1. Ask students to write brief summaries of the narrative immediately after reading a short story such as Payne's "Prelude." This is the story of a troubled romance between a high school sorority girl and an unkempt boy from an immigrant family. In the story the heroine is forced several times to endure taunts from her snobbish friends and is ultimately faced with a choice between material and human values. One week after reading ask students to summarize the story a second time without the aid of review. Request a third summary three or four weeks after the initial reading. Then return the three papers to the students. By analyzing carefully chosen examples from student papers, the class will see how modification and distortion occur when events are recalled over a period of time. Appropriate selections for such an activity are those that elicit many dimensions of response. "Prelude," for example, will be recalled by some as a pleasant love story of a rich girl and poor boy, by others as a bitter, driving denunciation of high school sororities.

2. Ask four or five volunteers to leave the room in preparation for an experiment in recall. Then display a large photograph showing a dramatic situation involving several figures. The effectiveness of this activity is increased when the photographic situation is sufficiently ambiguous to require rather extensive comment and interpretation. The picture should suggest a conflict without specifying its exact nature. Illustrations depicting adults and adolescents in apparent disagreement are particularly effective in high school classes. Ask one class member to describe the situation in the photograph to one of the volunteers who returns to the room. Neither the student describing the situation nor the listener who has returned is able to view the photograph, yet the two students should be so situated that the photograph remains discernible to remaining class members. Each of the volunteers is asked to return individually. After listening to a description of the situation, he repeats the description to the next returnee. Since the picture remains visible to the class, the students are later able to discuss the examples of sharpening and leveling that occur.[20]

TO IMPROVE INDUCTIVE AND DEDUCTIVE REASONING

▼ *Study ways of classifying data*

1. Ask the students to "learn" the following nonsense words written on the blackboard:

shro	sigg	sid
sorr	shum	simm
seg	sunpt	shig

[20] An interesting psychological experiment of this type is reported in Gordon Allport and Leo Postman, *The Psychology of Rumor* (New York: Holt, Rinehart & Winston, 1948), pp. 63–74. James I. Brown has also described a similar classroom project in "Dealing with Bias as Readers and Listeners," *Exercise Exchange*, Vol. 5, No. 1 (October 1957), pp. 9, 10.

After a moment examine the various ways in which individuals attempt to impose order on the nonsense syllables. How many pronounce the words in attempting to find a phonetic pattern? How many examine structural clues? Alphabetical sequence?

The exercise shows students how individuals strive for order even in nonsense material. It also illustrates how data may be classified in various kinds of categories.

2. If students have difficulty in organizing, present a series of items such as the following, to be grouped in two or more categories:

> automobile, washing machine, train, dishwasher,
> orlon, wool, airplane, cotton, electric range

Increasingly difficult exercises of this type may be introduced in preparation for writing activities. A class may be encouraged to list all possible facts and ideas concerning a general topic before attempting to categorize them. For example, in developing ideas for a composition on the topic "The Impact of Science Fiction on the Imaginations of Teen-Agers," a class may suggest varied items: nightmares, television programs and motion pictures, changed reading habits, belief in the supernatural, increased interest in scientific facts, curiosity regarding the unknown. With teacher guidance, each item may then be grouped either as a potential cause of, as a possible result of, or as unrelated to the increased adolescent reading of science-fiction material. This activity requires students to perceive levels of abstraction ranging from the simple and concrete to the complex and universal.

► *Stress similarities and differences in generalizing*

1. Ask students to group the following occupations into two or more categories:

> laborer, farmer, businessman, mechanic, waitress,
> white collar worker, politician, policeman, secretary,
> real-estate broker, lemon grower, bulldozer operator,
> stevedore, electrician, insurance salesman

For each category, discuss with students both the unifying characteristic and the differences overlooked.

2. Analyze with students the effect of categorization implied in such statements as those below. What similarities are stressed? In what ways are the statements misleading?

> Sportsmen enjoy basketball, track, fishing, hunting, and ping pong.
> Almost everyone laughs at cartoons, jokes, comedy situations on television, clowns, and the antics of young children.
> If you enjoyed reading *A Tale of Two Cities*, you will enjoy *Henry Esmond*, *Northwest Passage*, and *Decision at Trafalgar*.

► *Recognize the importance of "open-mindedness" in reasoning*

1. To illustrate how our understanding of words is extended through the processes of analysis and synthesis, ask students to explore and define the meaning of nonsense words used in several contexts.[21] Example: *zupu*

---

[21] Examples of this kind have been used in an interesting study of the development of children's understanding of verbal symbols. See Heinz Werner and Edith Kaplan, *The Acquisition of Word Meanings* (Evanston, Ill.: Child Development Publications, 1952). Other classroom uses of this method are illustrated in the unit "Power Over Language" and "Reading."

I was sick because the sea was *zupu* today.

His skin felt *zupu* because he had not shaved.

The *zupu* diamond was sent to the stone cutter.

He had had little education and his language seemed simple and *zupu*.

The students talked so much they gave the substitute teacher a *zupu* time.

2. Discuss in a simple way the importance of thinking in terms of degrees. Consider the impossibility of determining the extent to which individuals possess such traits as the following:

beauty-ugliness	honesty-dishonesty
superiority-inferiority	goodness-badness

Discuss the imperfect nature of generalizations concerning the behavior of individuals and the use of such qualifiers as *often, sometimes, seldom, seems to, tends to,* and *appears to be.*

▶ *Compare inductive and deductive methods*

Ask students to develop arguments to prove such generalizations as the following:

Schools should operate on a twelve-month basis.

Television has a beneficial effect on viewers.

The rates for baby sitting should be increased.

Ask half of the class to develop one idea inductively and the remaining students to do this deductively. Selected paragraphs may then be analyzed for logical development. Experiences of this type require students to utilize and compare the two basic approaches.

TO EXAMINE OVERSIMPLIFICATIONS IN OUR OWN REASONING

▶ *Study oversimplifications in the discussion of students*

Tape record a panel of students discussing an issue about which they feel strongly, such as problems involved in raising the minimum grades required for participation in extracurricular activities, in establishing a ten o'clock curfew for adolescents, or in abolishing political action groups in the school. Play the recording and ask the class to analyze the arguments of individuals to discover oversimplified statements. Do not hesitate to interrupt the playback at appropriate times to highlight illustrations. A discussion of this type furnishes excellent material for such an analysis.

▶ *Identify common forms of oversimplification*

1. Present students with a list of clichés and assumptions such as those below. Urge them to add to the list. Ask students to change, modify, or rewrite the statements to make each express an idea they would be willing to defend.

Long ear lobes are a sign of aristocracy.

Individuals with red hair have quick tempers.

A stitch in time saves nine.

Italians make good opera singers.

Women live longer than men.

An apple a day keeps the doctor away.

In the final review, students point up the flaws in reasoning involved in each statement as originally expressed.

2. Ask students to examine statements such as the following to determine whether each may be considered as (a) never true, (b) always true, (c) sometimes true, (d) of uncertain truth (insufficient data to determine).

> High school students are interested in science.
> Football is played in the fall.
> The first Monday in September is Labor Day.
> A young child who is spoiled is seldom successful in school.
> Rapid readers remember little of what they read.
> Drag racing will keep boys out of trouble.
> Women can shed ten pounds in thirty-six hours on a diet of yogurt and fresh pineapple.

Plan a discussion of the students' answers to develop an understanding of the importance of basing generalizations on adequate data.

Both of these activities begin with concrete statements that students are asked to examine. The choice of examples will determine whether the exercise will concentrate on various manifestations of a single problem—for example, using stereotypes—or will deal with many kinds of oversimplification. Many teachers introduce exercises of this type after the need for such concentrated study is revealed by repeated problems in the students' writing and speech.

TO DETECT METHODS OF EVADING CONSIDERATION OF AN ISSUE

▶ *Study the evasions of others*

1. Sections in magazines and newspapers that reprint letters to the editor are a fertile source of illustrative material. Examine a letter such as the following with a class:

> Dear Editor:
>
> There can be no doubt that John A. was wrong when he wrote that trash books do not cause delinquency. These so-called magazines have increased tremendously during the last few years and so has our juvenile problem. Either John A. has no children or he doesn't know how they spend their time. From the way he reasons he would permit young minds to read anything.
> Sincerely,
> Mrs. G.

A few key questions aid students in analyzing such letters: Why was the letter written? What is the central thought? What evidence is offered to support this proposition? Such examples may well be used to introduce study of the problem or to clinch the students' understanding.

2. Encourage students to bring to class interesting examples of evasion. Develop a special bulletin board to illustrate the methods people use to avoid answering questions. Ask students to examine the reasoning and to identify the particular error involved in such examples as the following:

> "I don't know what's wrong with Mary at school. All her grades seem to be low. She got a C in Algebra and a B— in English. Her only explanation is that she gets as good grades as her friends. They don't seem to teach self-discipline in schools any more."

Man   "Do men attach as much significance to manners as they once did?"
Woman   "Well, I didn't see you offering your bus seat to any elderly ladies."

TO DISTINGUISH SOUND RELATIONSHIPS FROM THOSE FALSE OR MISLEADING

▶ *Examine relationships between ideas*

1. Ask students to indicate which of the supporting statements are unrelated to the argument in such propositions as the following:

> Ara Parseghian is a great coach.
>   a. His teams won many games.
>   b. He developed many plays.
>   c. He coached at Notre Dame.
> Beagles make excellent pets.
>   a. They are gentle with children.
>   b. They are becoming increasingly popular.
>   c. They respond well to obedience training.
> "Hello, Dolly" is a wonderful song.
>   a. It was written by Jerry Herman.
>   b. Its melody seems fresh and lilting.
>   c. The lyrics seem to express the feeling of the music.

2. Ask students to consider whether the relationship between such paired statements as the following may be considered to be (a) perfect, (b) pronounced, (c) slight, (d) unrelated, or (e) unknown.

> the color of the hen; the color of its eggs
> the height of children; the height of parents
> the fullness of the moon; the height of the tide
> the weight of the green vegetables eaten; the curliness of one's hair
> the price of automobiles; the price of wheat
> school grades in English; school grades in geometry

3. Provide a list of statements such as the following and ask students to indicate whether the reasoning is sound or unsound. Discuss with students the reasons for their decision.

> John claimed that Knute Rockne was a more original coach than either Frank Leahy or Ara Parseghian because he was the first great Notre Dame coach.
> *Sound* or *Unsound?*   Reason: _____
> A person should vote Democratic because it is the party of such great modern leaders as Franklin D. Roosevelt and John F. Kennedy.
> *Sound* or *Unsound?*   Reason: _____
> John's high grade on the test was the inevitable result of his command of the subject and his long hours of work.
> *Sound* or *Unsound?*   Reason: _____
> Our neighbors the Joneses must be wealthy because they can afford two cars.
> *Sound* or *Unsound?*   Reason: _____

▶ *Practice drawing sound relationships*

At a time when the class is considering how to develop ideas, ask students to identify several possible hypotheses that might be developed from sets of data like the following:

The consumption of carbonated beverages has increased since 1918.

The average height of fifteen-year-old boys appears to have increased during the past thirty years.

Mental institutions are more crowded today than after the First World War.

The population has increased considerably during the past thirty years.

What causal relationships are suggested? How many are tenable?

Jack is a sophomore in high school. During the past year Jack
    has read many new books.
    bought a TV set which he watches nightly.
    has become friendly with a boy who is an amateur taxidermist.
    joined a school club for nature study.
    has had a new science teacher.

Which of these would logically explain the improvement in Jack's grades in science?

Clearly many possible hypotheses would be instantly rejected as unreasonable, yet even extreme examples may reveal to some students how spurious relationships may become accepted as truth.

TO IMPROVE ABILITY TO SEE RELATIONSHIPS

► *See parallels in life and literature*

Begin with familiar experiences in introducing the study of literature. On a breezy spring day discuss the sounds and rhythms of the wind before introducing "Who Has Seen the Wind?" and "The Wind Has Such a Rainy Sound." Share common experiences of embarrassment and awkwardness in social situations before reading "Clodhopper."

In these learning experiences students are required to identify points of contact between the literature and experiences in the world today. The first exercise involves recognizing possible similarities in motive and situation. The second requires identification of parallel feelings and emotion.

► *See differences in literature and life*

1. Provide opportunities for an objective appraisal of teen-age literature dealing with delinquent behavior. Not all stories concerning adolescents present valid and realistic portrayals. Swayed by a tendency to identify with youthful heroes and moved emotionally by contrived patterns of suspense, many adolescents fail to test incidents in their reading against their own daily experience. Organize a panel of students to report on representations of behavior in books of such varying quality as *Hot Rod, Street Rod, The Dark Adventure, Blackboard Jungle, In Cold Blood, The Amboy Dukes.* Provide panel members with such thought questions as the following:

Study the portrayal of the leading figures in the book. To what extent are these figures presented as representative of most adolescents? To what extent are they presented as unique?

What reasons are suggested to explain the behavior of adolescents in this story?

To what extent do your own friends act in this way?

To what extent are their motives similar?

What other evidence can you find to show that boys and girls act this way? Do you conclude that this book presents a fair portrait of adolescents today? Why or why not?

2. Organize similar panels to evaluate motion picture and television performances. In such an experience students are required to identify the basic assumptions concerning adolescent behavior that seem to underlie the author's point of view and then to test these assumptions against the reality around them.

▶ *Compare the treatment of common themes in several selections*

1. The comparison of literary selections aids students to see that similar ideas may be expressed in many different ways. For example, choose a pair of selections for class study. Normally one selection would be studied intensively, the second being read more quickly for comparative purposes. Some interesting pairings:

Colman's *Classmates by Request;* Sterling's *Mary Jane*
Gipson's *Old Yeller;* Rawlings' *The Yearling*
Saroyan's *The Human Comedy;* Wilder's *Our Town*
Eliot's *Silas Marner;* Steinbeck's *The Pearl*
Cather's *My Antonia;* Buck's *The Good Earth*
Shakespeare's *King Lear;* Hardy's *Return of the Native*
Shakespeare's *Macbeth;* Dostoyevsky's *Crime and Punishment*

2. When students have been reading related individual titles, ask them to compare the treatment of a topic through discussion in small groups. For example, ask tenth-grade readers of books on family life to analyze the various methods used by characters in making decisions. Each student is to analyze selected situations in the book he has finished and compare his findings with ideas presented by others.

TO IMPROVE SKILL IN PROBLEM SOLVING

▶ *Develop a "questioning" attitude*

A spirit of inquiry encouraging the exploration of ideas helps individuals identify problems of personal concern. Restricted to subject matter prescribed by the textbook, a student will seldom develop initiative in identifying tasks of his own, nor will he share the excitement of finding new problems through the study of language and literature. Undoubtedly the use of multiple learning materials and the extension of learning beyond the classroom through the discriminating use of excursions, audio-visual aids, and guest speakers will broaden the student's horizons. So also will a classroom atmosphere that encourages class members to raise issues and questions. Some teachers use planned approaches such as the following in encouraging students to identify problems and to phrase questions.

1. Divide the class into several small groups for a brief discussion period. Ask the students in each group to raise questions or problems concerning the content being studied by the class or the methods that are being used in learning. Ask each group to propose one problem for consideration by the entire class. Teachers who introduce such periods frequently find them a helpful way of encouraging students to consider the purposes underlying learning.

2. During the introductory phase of a unit, ask students to formulate questions to answer through reading and study. For example, after a class has decided to

study the use of humor in literature, ask each individual to list questions concerning humor in which he is particularly interested. Discussion of these personal lists culminates in the formulation of a series of objectives for the entire class.

▶ *Relate new information to what has been learned before*

Success in coping with major problems depends largely upon an individual's mastery of basic skills and his ability to apply the knowledge he has previously learned. A boy applying for a job in a strange section of the city relies on his ability to read directions in reporting for an interview. A mature reader of George Stewart's *The Years of the City* must summon his prior understandings about the Greek city-state; so must an adolescent about Cortez in reading Shellabarger's *Captain From Castille*. In a real sense all classroom learnings tend to prepare students for the problems they face in the future. Yet individuals must still be taught ways of drawing upon the knowledge they possess in tackling the problems of the present. Teachers use such approaches as these:

1. Present to the class a topic for composition on which many students may reasonably be expected to have some background of information or experience—"The Fun of Large Groups" for the junior high school years, "Man's Dependence on Nature" or "Some Influences of Television on Adolescents" for older students. Many students do not believe they possess sufficient information to write on such topics. Show them that by asking appropriate questions that tap their storehouse of knowledge—Who? What? When? Where? Why?—they may list many facts, impressions, and ideas related to the topic and later organize these ideas in writing.

2. Plan class work over the year so that each new unit of work will be related to earlier classroom experiences. For example, seventh-grade students who have studied characteristics of world folklore through reading books about Robin Hood, King Arthur, and stories from the Arabian Nights will draw upon this experience in a subsequent analysis of American folklore heroes. Similarly, *Julius Caesar* was used as a year's culminating study for tenth-grade students who had completed separate units on poetry, language and the mass media, the theme "The Nature of Truth," and the topic "Lost Worlds and Modern Problems." Analysis of the tragedy involved concepts that had been considered in all four units. Students were forced to re-evaluate many of these ideas.

▶ *Learn methods and habits of thinking conducive to exploring hypotheses*

In exploring and testing possible solutions to problems, individuals must learn to suspend final judgment, to consider willingly all conceivable solutions, to predict probable results of alternative courses of action, to withhold final decisions until the consequences of actions have been examined. Faulty anticipation of outcomes is, of course, a frequent source of error in thinking, yet realistic methods of appraisal come primarily through experience in predicting. An "if-then" approach to the examination of a problem—"if" the proposed solution is assumed, "then" what are the consequences?—encourages an attitude that seems conducive to a realistic analysis of hypotheses. Such a point of view may be nurtured in school if teachers provide many genuine experiences in problem solving and occasionally analyze with students the dangers of snap judgments and easy solutions. Such experiences as the following may suggest methods:

1. With teacher guidance the class examines the processes of thinking used by literary characters in solving problems. Caddie Woodlawn's thorough analysis of the possible consequences of voting to return to England is an excellent example of "if-then" thinking. So, also, is Ronny Perry's consideration of how to gain acceptance at school in *All-American.* Conversely, in *Operation A.B.C.,* Tom Roerdan's attempt to avoid school tests for fear of revealing an inability to read offers a clear, if exaggerated, illustration of an inadequate solution accepted by an individual who fails to consider the consequences of his action.

2. Provide frequent opportunities for groups and individuals to plan classroom action. Following the reading of Morrow's *On to Oregon,* for example, an eighth-grade class may be organized into groups for work on projects related to their reading on westward expansion. Ask each group to develop a presentation for the entire class. Whether the project involves creating a bulletin board, preparing a dramatization, explaining a model, or arranging for several illustrated talks, the groups are faced with a practical problem. Before determining action, they must consider the time allowed for planning, the resources available, and the extent to which the class audience must be prepared for the presentation. For students with little experience in self-directed activity, the teacher arranges for special guidance. Specific suggestions for directing group work are contained in Chapter Seven, "Oral Language."

TO REFINE SKILL IN MAKING JUDGMENTS

► *Establish the basis for judging*

1. By establishing standards for classroom behavior with the students and by evaluating progress in terms of these criteria, the teacher is able to demonstrate the importance of definite and realistic bases for evaluation. For example, ask a class to decide upon aims and goals for group work early in a semester, then evaluate subsequent group activity in terms of these standards—through discussion, individual rating, selected student observers, and periodic review and reassessment of the selected criteria. Determine whether the standards should be lowered or upgraded.

2. Study the judgments of motion picture, literary, and television critics. Practice in judging is the only really effective method of encouraging students to develop discrimination in evaluating novels, motion pictures, and television programs; however, students do benefit from examining analyses written by experienced critics. One method that has proved useful in developing criteria for book reviews involves clipping professional reviews from such periodicals as *Saturday Review, Harper's,* the *Atlantic, The New York Review of Books,* and *The New York Times Book Review.* Allow students thirty minutes to study and exchange the printed reviews. Then ask the class to note characteristics that seem to be common to many reviews. In the discussion that follows, help students identify the basic elements of a well-written review—selection of an idea from the book that can be developed as an essay, expansion of the idea with reference to the point of view of the reviewer, and the conclusion.

3. Present to students such a list of decisions as the following. For each situation ask students to identify the factors that must be considered with respect to personal preferences, consequences of the decision, its probable effect on other people.

a sixteen-year-old boy wondering whether to purchase an automobile on time
    payments

the father of a twelve-year-old girl wondering whether to vote for or against
    a proposed ten o'clock curfew for adolescents

a family trying to decide whether to vacation in the mountains, at the sea-
    shore, or in a large city

the manager of an office selecting a receptionist

a high school student deciding whether to enroll in public speaking, drama, or
    journalism

This exercise requires students to identify elements affecting each decision and to
predict the probable results of each choice.

4. Mount on a bulletin board six illustrations of men and women who appear
to be successful in different endeavors. Include, perhaps, a football player, a military leader, an actress, a nurse, a statesman, and a mountain climber. The pictures
should be large enough to be seen by all students. Ask each student to select the
one of the six whom he considers to be the most successful and to write a paragraph
explaining his choice. In the discussion that follows, develop an understanding of
the various dimensions of success and the extent to which the judgments of students are based on different criteria.

► *Improve objectivity in making inferences*

Ask students to write brief paragraphs describing the type of individual suggested by each of the following groups of adjectives:

        shy, reticent, quiet, precise, insecure, perceptive
        vital, chic, sporting, beguiling, talkative, poised
        dangerous, sharp, quick-witted, energetic, shrewd, sly

Compare student descriptions. Examine with the class the extent to which inferences are based on emotional as well as logical factors.

► *Evaluate authorities*

1. Ask students to evaluate carefully whether they would accept the authority
of each of the following individuals on the topics indicated:

        an international party hostess, on international affairs
        a world traveler, on color photography
        a tennis player, on tennis balls
        an opera singer, on television programing
        a motion picture star, on hair tonic

Follow this discussion by asking class members to suggest possible authorities on
whom they would rely in obtaining information on such topics as the following:

        modern warfare   Air Force general
                           senator
                           Secretary of Defense
        hydroplane races *Sports Illustrated*
                           president of a motor company
                           hydroplane pilot

2. Ask students to select from a list of names on the chalkboard those persons
whom they consider to be reliable authorities in the following three fields: nuclear

energy, American baseball, contemporary fashion. List real-life examples of people with such occupations as:

leader in industry	humanitarian
designer of hats	manager of a baseball team
motion picture star	owner of a local women's store
administrator of a nuclear project	sports writer
Secretary of Defense	dress designer
physics laboratory assistant	pitcher
President of the United States	army general
physicist	

3. Provide experiences in choosing between authorities. Present students with a request for certain specific kinds of information (List A). Ask them to select from List B the authorities whom they would consult in obtaining the necessary facts.

LIST A INFORMATION DESIRED	LIST B POSSIBLE SOURCES OF INFORMATION
State parking and speeding regulations for automobiles	Local nurseryman
	Interested neighbor
Directions on how to repair a leaky faucet	Plumber's handbook
	Classified advertisements of a newspaper
Information on the best location for planting camellias and rhododendrons	*Encyclopaedia Britannica*
	Popular Gardening magazine
	State motor vehicle code
Suggested procedures in planning a wedding reception	Judge of a local court
	Etiquette book published in 1935
	Writer of a newspaper column designed to answer questions on personal problems
	Etiquette book published in 1970
	Society section of a newspaper

4. Ask students to consider the biases of authorities by evaluating a series of statements on a selected topic. Ask each individual to estimate the degree of bias in such statements as the following by rating the speaker's degree of objectivity on a five-point scale. Ask students to note the reasons for each rating.

JUDGING POSSIBLE BIAS

Directions to students   How much confidence would you place in each of the following statements? Indicate your opinion concerning the possible bias of each speaker by rating each statement on a five-point scale ranging from *Objective* to *Extreme bias.* Then write your reasons for the rating. In considering the speaker's qualifications, think not only about his knowledge of the subject but his possible motivation for making the statement.

1. "This is certainly one of the greatest comedies that Hollywood has produced and one that no one can afford to miss."   (motion picture editor of a leading news service, at the Hollywood première)

1	2	3	4	5
Objective				Extreme bias

Reasons: _____

2. "Certainly no one can resist the gay new comedy from Twentieth-Century-Fox. It is a merry romp calculated to dispel all gloom, and Katherine Drew has never looked lovelier." (movie critic, writing in a monthly motion picture [fan] magazine)

3. "This offers further evidence that Hollywood films are successful only when they fail to come to grips with ideas." (Broadway drama critic, New York paper)

4. "I accept only roles that my fans will enjoy, and this, I am sure, is my best." (star, making a personal appearance with the film)

5. "Some may object to the film's searching and intimate portrayal of middle-class marriage, but most will recognize the serious social criticism intended." (executive producer, at a press interview before release of the film)

6. "I guarantee that this is one of the most compelling films which we have shown in two-and-a-half years." (printed advertisement attributed to manager of local theater)

7. "The stars do their utmost with stilted dialog and inept direction and they do manage to make the affair moderately diverting, but those who have expected the ultimate in screen comedies will be sorely disappointed." (local newspaper critic, after the film opens)

▶ *Weigh evidence and varied points of view*

1. Students need much experience in weighing different points of view. Ask tenth-grade students who have selected biographies for individual reading to assess the objectivity of the authors involved. With guidance lead the class to study the effect on biographical writing of the author's point of view, his particular interests, his selection and organization of incident. Then ask each student to obtain basic facts regarding the life of the individual about whom he is reading, to locate and read at least one or two interpretive articles on the person in addition to the longer book, and to compare the accounts.

When students are being introduced to the problem of evaluating the objectivity of biographers, some teachers prefer to plan some common study for the entire class. For example, students might compare the eulogistic description of Louis Pasteur by his son-in-law, Vallery-Radot,[22] with the severely critical account of the scientist by Paul DeKruif. These contrasting points of view might later be compared with that of the motion picture *The Story of Louis Pasteur*.

2. Provide exercises for juniors and seniors that require the analysis of printed materials prepared for specific propaganda purposes. Sometimes materials published by special groups within the United States are useful. Documents published for English readers by foreign countries are of special interest since these reveal unusual points of view toward American readers. With mature readers in some school situations, teachers find that propaganda materials released by communist countries provoke thoughtful analysis.

In asking students to analyze such documents, prepare a special guide that includes such pointed questions as the following:

[22] René Vallery-Radot, *The Life of Pasteur* (New York: Doubleday, 1923).

Judging from the contents of the issue, what kinds of events and ideas seem most important? Political? Cultural? Athletic? Industrial? Military? What gives you this impression? What factors may explain this selection by the editors?

What is the dominant impression that the publication seems to convey? How is this reflected in choice of articles? In illustrations? In headlines?

Select any single article you believe would have been rewritten or eliminated if the paper had been prepared for domestic reading and explain why.

The purpose of the program described in this chapter is to teach students to think clearly in spite of their irrational feelings and thoughts. By analyzing the thinking of students and by teaching them ways of forming concepts, solving problems, and making judgments, we strive to improve their understanding of the conclusions of others and their ability to form sound conclusions of their own. Ultimately then, the basic test of the program is to be found in the maturity of the students' grasp of the skills and arts of the language and in the soundness of their values.

SELECTED READINGS

ALLPORT, GORDON, and POSTMAN, LEO. *The Psychology of Rumor.* New York: Holt, Rinehart & Winston, 1947. An interesting report of experiments with adults, children, and youth. Teachers will appreciate the suggested exercises. Chapter 10 presents some interesting examples of rumors, which may be used with secondary students. A "Guide for the Analysis of Rumor" is also included.

BLOOM, BENJAMIN S. (ed.). *Taxonomy of Educational Objectives, Handbook I: Cognitive Domain.* London: Longmans, Green, 1956. Helps identify concrete objectives of the acquisition of knowledge and the attainment of intellectual skill. Of particular use in teaching are some of the test questions suggested to measure such complex skills as synthesizing, making judgments based on external and internal evidence, and seeing relationships.

BRUNER, JEROME S., GOODNOW, JACQUELINE J., and AUSTIN, GEORGE. *A Study of Thinking.* New York: Wiley, 1956. Contains a thorough analysis of the psychological aspects of thinking, including some treatment of language and categorization.

HAYAKAWA, S. I. *Language in Thought and Action.* 2d ed. New York: Harcourt, Brace & World, 1964. This well-known volume not only contains an analysis of language and thought but suggests many activities that can be used in secondary schools.

PEEL, E. A. *The Pupil's Thinking.* London: Osbourne, 1960. An impressive analysis of the strategies of thinking related to adolescent growth patterns.

RUSSELL, DAVID H. *Children's Thinking.* Boston: Ginn, 1956. A readable compilation of research bearing on the thinking of youth. Teachers will be especially interested in chapters 12 and 13, which deal with the improvement of thinking.

SALOMON, LOUIS B. *Semantics and Common Sense.* New York: Holt, Rinehart & Winston, 1966. A useful college textbook dealing with the clear expression of thought.

STAUFFER, RUSSELL (ed.). *Cultivating Higher Thought Processes.* Champaign, Ill.: NCTE, 1964. A bulletin containing a series of articles summarizing research in children's thinking.

FIVE

IMAGINATIVE THINKING

> . . . the real crisis in the life of our society is the crisis of the
> life of the imagination. . . . we need to come alive again, to
> recover the virility of the imagination on which all earlier civiliza-
> tions have been based. . . . It is principally by the process of
> education that the flaw can be healed.
>
> ARCHIBALD MACLEISH [1]

PERSPECTIVE

John Stuart Mill's father believed in the value of mental tasks for his son. At the age of three, the child began his study of Greek. By the time he was eight, he had read numerous books on government as well as Plato and Xenophon in the original. So that his education might assume a "more serious phase," he studied arithmetic at night until fully prepared for higher mathematics. When he was twelve, a more advanced stage was added to his instruction—logic. He read through the *Organon*.

At this point, the father judged that his son's education had begun in earnest. Mr. Mill had an immense distrust of feelings and emotions. Most children were annoyingly addicted to outbursts of enthusiasm and petulance, but now logic could fortify reason, pruning away any remnants of childish weakness. And, indeed, Mr. Mill appeared to be right. His son continued to devote his mind to logical thought day and night, suppressing any tendencies toward feeling—until he was twenty.

One rainy November evening, the youth looked up from his books, aware of an intense gloom and mental depression. Sensibly, he went to bed, assuming that a good night's sleep would fortify his logical determination to eliminate this unfortunate melancholy. Sleep apparently was no solution, for the next day he collapsed completely. Up until this point he had been increasing his control of logic; now logic, along with consuming his feelings and emotions, had apparently lost its power.

Throughout that winter the young Mill remained in a trance of listless melancholy. His entire personality was in a process of revolt and transformation, but not until spring was there a sign indicating a break in his apathy.

[1] Archibald MacLeish, "The Poet and the Press," *Atlantic*, Vol. 203, No. 3 (March 1959), p. 46.

While reading about a boy who performed an act of kindness, John suddenly shook with violent emotion and tears flowed down his cheeks. During the next month he groped painfully toward equilibrium, turning to the poetry of Wordsworth and the music of Weber. From these beginnings he reached out to other romantic poets, Shelley and Goethe, and to lighthearted people around him. And by 1831, when Carlyle met him, Mill was no longer merely a logical machine; he was a slender youth "with earnestly smiling eyes, modest, remarkably gifted with precision of utterance; enthusiastic yet lucid, calm." He was ready to write his famous essay *On Liberty*.[2]

Balancing Reason and Imagination

For their students, teachers of English endeavor to achieve by less dramatic means this balance of lucidity and enthusiasm. Educational efforts to develop a bare intellectuality are doomed to failure because by nature men are emotional as well as intellectual. The study of English concerns more than systematic thinking. Although the importance of logic and analysis as educational imperatives should not be minimized, students' feelings and imaginations must also find frequent expression lest the classroom become a grim intellectual gymnasium. Too heavy an emphasis upon logical thought to the exclusion of imagination and inspiration eliminates the zest and satisfaction of learning.

NO SHARP DISTINCTION BETWEEN IMAGINATION AND REASON   Reason and imagination are not, however, two distinct kinds of thinking; sometimes they are conveniently symbolized as two ends of a continuum. Dominating one end is logic, with its realistic problem solving and its objective appraisal of the actual world. At the other end? Imagination, reverie, and intuition—all those forms of mental activity nourished by man's internal needs and impulses. Thinking shifts rapidly back and forth along the scale, never completely realistic, never completely imaginative. The mature individual maintains a delicate balance, emphasizing according to the situation the requirements of outer reality or the inner needs of his personality. The danger, always, is to lose equilibrium. Evidently John Stuart Mill moved perilously close to an inhuman world devoid of feeling. Schumann, Nietzsche, Nijinsky—to choose three examples—apparently upset the balance in the other direction, disregarding the demands of objective reality. The scientist uses both kinds of thinking, often simultaneously. Systematic thinking is so often interfused with imagination that even a presentation of these powers as opposite ends of a continuum (as in this chapter) risks false interpretations.

In this chapter, we urge the case for a balance that includes the imagina-

[2] This account of John Stuart Mill's breakdown and recuperation is drawn from his *Autobiography* (New York: Columbia Univ. Press, 1924), and from Emery E. Neff's *Carlyle and Mill* (New York: Octagon Press, 1964).

tion. Obviously, an intense classroom preoccupation with pixies and leprechauns would press all but the most docile adolescents into justified revolt and disenchantment. Nor do we advocate that instruction in English imitate the cold harsh logic of stern figures like John Stuart Mill's father. Respect for the whole nature of man, not for intellect alone, not for feeling alone, becomes the equilibrium the English teacher must skillfully maintain.

A DEFINITION OF IMAGINATION   What is this imagination, this brand of thinking so often claimed as a basis necessary for appreciation and creative expression, so often confused with the fantastic and unusual? Imagination is a mental activity that—because it is relatively free from realistic demands—enables one to summon up images, feelings, memories, sensations, intuitions. Because of this freedom from immediate practicality, the imaginative thinker can rearrange and recombine these mosaics of association to create both delightful and useful relationships. The essential ingredient is the creative synthesis, the new whole made by combining elements experienced separately. These elements may be conscious or unconscious; in fact, it is the access to the unconscious that gives special power to the imagination.

But if the mental activity in imagination is freer, bolder, less dependent than logic upon demonstrable proofs, it is not irresponsible fantasy. Between imaginative and systematic thought no radical distinction exists; both are a part of imaginative intelligence, a single entity. Reason, says George Santayana, is itself a method of imaginative thought, and the only valid distinction between imagination and understanding is a pragmatic one. Constructs of the imagination that prove useful in daily affairs or the work of the world are called the ideas of understanding; others, less useful in predicting the future or directing one's daily life are called imagination.[3]

The importance of the imagination may be demonstrated by returning to our emphasis upon its power to synthesize diverse elements. Among the qualities the imagination can balance or reconcile, Coleridge lists "a more than usual state of emotion with more than usual order; judgment ever awake and steady self-possession with enthusiasm and feeling profound or vehement." He ascribes to imagination "the power of reducing multitude into unity of effect and modifying a series of thoughts by some one predominant thought or feeling."[4] This balance, this equilibrium, draws into action more of the human personality than does most thinking. Whether scientists, poets, or ordinary human beings, we find that the imagination opens our minds to more expansive perceptions. Whenever we see more fully, not through a single response, but coherently and simultaneously through many responses, we are experiencing imaginative insight. Such insight is the mark of wisdom, not a garnish or frivolous decoration.

[3] This concept of the unity of imaginative and systematic thought is based upon the ideas of Santayana. See George Santayana, *Dominations and Powers* (New York: Scribner's, 1951), p. 463.

[4] These quotations are taken from Coleridge's *Biographia Literaria,* chapters XIV and XV.

The imagination is no trivial plaything of the dilettante. Imagination is vital to the housewife, who must make leftovers palatable, to the carpenter, who must envision spaces and stresses, and to the teacher, who must devise ways to make wisdom prevail. Add to the list: the driver in city traffic, the diplomat, the young man seeking a job. To some degree, everyone must think like the poets, and the poets themselves have recognized that their subjective art is not truly divorced from reality:

> We are the music makers,
> And we are the dreamers of dreams,
>
>   . . .
>
> Yet we are the movers and shakers
> Of the world forever, it seems.[5]

Moreover, the scientist must be as imaginative as the poet. Of the physicist Michael Faraday we read: ". . . Faraday's first great characteristic was his trust in facts, and his second his imagination. . . . Only, it is important to remember, these two characteristics were not separate and distinct. . . . It was because in Faraday they were held together in vital tension that he became so potent an instrument of research into Nature's secrets." [6] In all the most important acts of life, in all vocations, imagination marks the difference between success and mediocrity. "Imagination," said Einstein, "it is more powerful than knowledge."

The Language of Imagination

Man is a rational being, but it is not prudent to forget that his consciousness includes emotional and volitional spheres. Feeling and will, like reason, also require expression. Yet language is an inadequate medium for expressing the whole nature of man. Language

> merely names certain vaguely and crudely conceived states, but fails miserably in any attempt to convey the ever-moving patterns, the ambivalences and intricacies of inner experience. . . . If we say that we understand someone else's feeling in a certain matter, we mean that we understand why he should be sad or happy, excited or indifferent, in a general way; that we can see due cause for his attitude. We do not mean that we have insight into the actual flow and balance of his feel'ngs. . . . Language is quite inadequate to articulate such a conception.[7]

Thus Susanne K. Langer sums up the limitations of language for expressing feeling.

[5] Arthur William Edgar O'Shaughnessy.

[6] Havelock Ellis, *The Dance of Life* (New York: Grosset & Dunlap, 1956), pp. 123–25. Ellis quotes John Tyndall, Faraday's friend and fellow worker.

[7] Susanne K. Langer, *Philosophy in a New Key: A Study in the Symbolism of Reason, Rite and Art* (New York: New American Library, 1948), p. 92. In other passages, Langer expresses her respect for the power of language.

To be sure, emphasis, tone of voice, and other forms of vocal coloring do contribute some feeling quality to what a speaker seeks to convey, but they do so uncertainly. In writing, even with the help of italics, underlining, and exclamation points, feeling is difficult to express. Consequently man has developed, and is still developing, ways to express his feelings, ways to flash awareness of inner states of mind from one person to another: art, symbol, and ritual. Of these, the way that most concerns teachers of English is literature.

Literature, like all the arts, uses special ways to evoke experience in others. True, literature uses words, but careful examination reveals that the language of literature is not the language of everyday use. Although anchored to the grammar of ordinary language, literature seeks to express realms of experience inaccessible to that ordinary language and does so more often by symbolism than by logical statement. Lyric poetry is the purest example of the way literature accomplishes this evocation of the full response—emotional, volitional, and rational. Listen to Yeats: "Poetry bids us touch and taste and hear and see the world, and shrink from all that is of the brain only, from all that is not a fountain jetting from the entire hopes, memories, and sensations of the body." Poetry expresses more of the poet than does ordinary language; poetry invigorates more of the total human response than do the forms of everyday language. The aim of lyric poems like Herrick's "To Daffodils" and Housman's "Loveliest of Trees" is certainly not to bring us horticultural information about daffodils or cherry trees. The poets are expressing their feelings about the transience of beauty and the brevity of man's life and are seeking to evoke in us these same feelings. If their symbols are successful, there occurs a flash of insight, stirring our entire consciousness—rational, emotional, volitional, and whatever else is still hidden from psychology and philosophy.

How much poetry and imagination are akin can be understood by referring to the definition of *imagination:* summoning up images, feelings, memories, sensations, and intuitions . . . enthusiasm and feeling profound or vehement . . . modifying a series of thoughts by some one predominant thought or feeling. Yet the imagination is more than poetry, just as the mind of man is more than brain. The mind of man is more than either reason or feeling. It is art and science; it is conscience, morality, religion. It is music and poetry as well as chemistry and homemaking. Whenever *thinking* is used in this book, this entire range of man's consciousness is intended.

Some Approaches to Imaginative Thinking

Methods used to foster imaginative insight need to be closely fitted to an accepted definition of imagination. The definition used in this chapter yields five approaches as a teaching guide for those seeking to extend the range of classroom thinking. The order here is based upon a progressively increasing admixture of logic: flexibility and fluidity of thought—the opposite of rigidity; vitality, but a controlled vitality—the opposite of apathy; insight, a notable bias toward searching for implications—the opposite of obtuseness, of superficial and unwary acceptance of appearances; synthesis, the fusion of varied elements by some unifying design—the opposite of randomness; understanding, an intellectual grasp of the nature and importance of the imagination—the opposite of ignorance concerning its nature and function.

TOWARD FLEXIBILITY, AWAY FROM RIGIDITY   There are many occasions when teachers want to encourage pupils to be original, to observe freshly, and to strike out in new directions. The fluent thinking underlying such creativity appears in all studies of the imagination. As a result of his research, Frank Barron says of imaginative persons, "They have exceptionally broad and flexible awareness of themselves. The self is strongest when it can regress (admit primitive fantasies, naive ideas, tabooed impulses into consciousness and behavior), and yet return to a high degree of rationality and self-criticism." [8] Not only for notably creative pupils but for everyone in the classroom, the teacher contributes to the health of the mind by fostering a disposition to break occasionally with habit and to express feelings. The purpose is not to produce emotional misfits and exhibitionists; a balance of perspective will prevent such excesses. A release from stultifying grooves of thought and a wholehearted response to life contribute to the supple mentality that was lacking in young John Stuart Mill.

TOWARD VITALITY, AWAY FROM APATHY   Wherever imagination appears—in good conversation, in scientific discovery, in decorating a home—vitality is essential and contagious. In a classroom, this energy radiates most forcefully from the teacher himself. Important also are the connections students see between what they are studying and life beyond the school. Other elements are a classroom climate of mutual respect, clear awareness of aims, alternations of serious effort and relaxing pleasures, and times when the teacher introduces some element of surprise, challenge, or humor.

Creative people, it has often been noticed, have an exceptional fund of physical and mental energy. Note, for instance, a description of high school students during the act of creation: "writing accompanied by elation, by an almost unnatural feeling of well-being; fatigue disappears; enormous quantities of labor can be accomplished; one can work for hours without a demand for rest, or even for food or sleep. Young people know all about this characteristic of the vital energy. . . ." [9] Recent research also reinforces this description. Donald W. MacKinnon depicts the creative person as having access to more of his intelligence, as being more discerning, more observant, more alert, more able to concentrate attention readily and to shift it appro-

[8] Frank Barron, "The Psychology of Imagination," *Scientific American,* Vol. 199, No. 3 (September 1958), p. 164.
[9] Hughes Mearns, *Creative Youth* (New York: Doubleday, 1925).

priately, more fluent in scanning thoughts. He is one who does not characteristically suppress or repress, but rather expresses.[10]

But vitality alone is never enough. This phase of imaginative insight
must be conceived as an ordered vitality, dominated either by a significant
goal or a drive toward form and order. This search for order is one of the
links between imaginative thinking and rational thinking. There is no sharp
division between the powers of imagination and the powers of rationality.

TOWARD SYNTHESIS, AWAY FROM RANDOMNESS   When a pupil is drawing upon
imagination, he is more than usually alert and in control of his thought.
Under the power of a heightened understanding, an extended mental horizon,
he is able, through use of energy and insight, to impose patterns on what
might otherwise be a jumble of confused ideas and impulses. The patterns
vary enormously, for structures are as diverse as the universe itself—the
metaphors and symbols of the poet, the constants and variables of the
physicist. They, like the musician working with the chaos of sound, impose
order on a variety of elements that would otherwise be random and meaningless. Witness this evocation of fireworks from the creative writing of a high
school boy:

> *Rockets*
>
> A genie's arm, all sleeved in gold
> Was thrust across the sky. Behold
> How from his smoking palm there falls
> A silent chime of colored balls.[11]

The same boy, watching acrobats, jaunty and glib at the end of their act,
wonders if they've really comprehended that "They've tickled Death along
his bony rib." In both poems, unlike elements are related through a sudden
flash of imaginative insight.

Perhaps one of the most interesting findings of recent research is the
evidence that imaginative persons like the challenge of disorder. Barron's
subjects, both artists and scientists, preferred paintings and figures that to
the unimaginative viewer might appear unbalanced and disordered, and they
expressed an aversion for things that were simple and too obviously sym-
metrical. The illustration on page 179 underlines some of the differences
between creative persons and others selected at random. Barron relates these
findings to synthesis, pointing out that

> Behind this inclination to like and to construct what is not too simply ordered
> there appears to be a very strong need to achieve the most difficult and far-
> reaching ordering. When confronted, for instance, with the Rorschach inkblot test,
> original individuals insist to a most uncommon degree upon giving an interpre-

[10] Donald W. MacKinnon, "Identifying the Effective Teacher," *California Journal for
Instructional Improvement*, Vol. 1, No. 1 (October 1958), pp. 12, 13.
[11] From "Fireworks" by Tom Prideaux, from Mearns, *Creative Youth*. Reprinted by permission of Hughes Mearns.

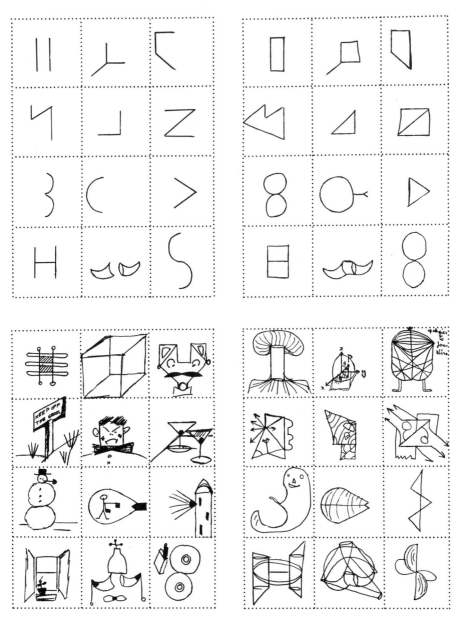

Drawing-Completion Test, devised by Kate Franck. Figures to be completed are at top left; a typical response at top right. Bottom sections show drawings by creative individuals. Reprinted from Scientific American *(September 1958), by permission of the Institute of Personality Assessment and Research, and of S. S. Dunn, Assistant Director, Australian Council for Educational Research.*

tation of the blot which takes account of all details in one comprehensive, synthe-sizing image.[12]

Barron sees the most imaginative persons as those who can live with com-plexity because they have confidence they can meet the challenge of confusion by finding the order that lies behind it. To resolve their discomfort by find-ing simple solutions is a temptation they resist. Thus they refuse to achieve order at the cost of excluding evidence; they realize to reject any evidence precludes the satisfaction of attaining a larger perspective and more appro-priate judgments.

Synthesis, then, is part of the search for order that must be imposed upon flexibility and vitality if these traits of the imagination are not to be distractions to effective thinking. The order, however, must be appropriate to the material, taking all of it into account. Simple solutions for complex problems, mechanical structures for supple or human situations—these will fall short of the true order imagination requires.

TOWARD INSIGHT, AWAY FROM OBTUSENESS   Flexibility, vitality, and synthesis combine to make possible the mental behavior called insight. *In*-sight is mental vision, *seeing into* the true inner nature of things. Sudden, gradual, or partial, there are different degrees of insight, varying with persons and situations. Even children can discover the essential principle in one situation and through insight transpose it to others.

Adult insight in chemistry, poetry, or mathematics requires the same ability to see into a situation, to understand it as a whole. Insight merges reason and imagination so firmly that one can readily understand that reason is itself a method of imaginative thought. Turned toward structures and proc-esses in the outer physical world insightful thinking is called reason. Turned toward the inner feelings and desires of man himself, insightful thinking is called imagination. Both are part of the same psychic energy welling up in all human beings. Joined together, they become the way of thinking of the poet and the scientist—and of all thinkers in all times and places.

The imagination is like an X-ray, penetrating surfaces, exploring the reality behind deceptive outer appearances. Imaginative insight becomes one of man's ways to strive toward deeper interpretations, for what appears on the surface does not always correspond to the truths available to the imagi-nation. Here is the ancient riddle of shadow and substance. Teachers seek not only to make their pupils aware of this complexity of truth, but also to foster a disposition to recognize implications, to look for interpretations, and to feel at home with symbols. It is true that native ability limits the degree of insight each individual may reach, but almost everyone has the potential of more than he uses.

TOWARD UNDERSTANDING, AWAY FROM IGNORANCE   Should students become consciously aware of the main features of imaginative insight? A thin line

[12] Barron, p. 155.

exists between ignorance about the imagination and vague, inaccurate use of the term. Instruction will remain ineffective unless the student gains a clear awareness of what is at stake. For senior high school classes, we can go beyond the evoking of imaginative reactions; we can design lessons intended to identify the dimensions of imagination, to fix firmly in each student's mind some of its salient features. In addition to the four approaches to imagination already presented—flexibility, vitality, insight, and synthesis—we add this fifth approach of understanding, an intellectual grasp of the nature and function of the imagination.

Back of this viewpoint lies the principle that goals and purposes must be clearly understood by the learner, not only with respect to the significant details of performance but also with respect to the broad pattern of response. Students should be fully aware of the importance of imaginative insight; they should recognize its key qualities and characteristics so that success will not be merely accidental and therefore infrequent.

Commenting on his father's plan of education, which systematically eliminated emotion from thinking, John Stuart Mill wrote in his *Autobiography:* "I was left stranded at the commencement of my voyage with a well-equipped ship and a rudder, but no sail; without any real desire for the ends which I had been so carefully fitted out to work for. . . ." The methods of teaching described in this chapter are based on a conception of imaginative thinking as a necessary balance for logical thinking. Without the full range of human thought, pupils in school can also be stranded without sails, without guidance toward clear thinking, appreciation of beauty, and lives of awareness.

THE TEACHING PROBLEM

ORGANIZING INSTRUCTION

Although not expecting their efforts to eventuate in perfection, English teachers can help pupils think more clearly, communicate more effectively, and feel more intensely. Suggested Learning Experiences like those at the close of this or the previous chapter have little or no effect if presented as isolated exercises. However, as part of a total classroom climate where expression replaces repression of thought and feeling, these suggested experiences can extend the range of thinking for most pupils.

Much depends upon the classroom climate. Insecurity can induce rigidity of thought, stifling the expression of feelings and the production of new ideas. Young people have an immense amount of plasticity; if not too insecure, they can break with routine more easily than adults and can envisage new alternatives, thus becoming more hospitable to originality. The stubborn and inescapable truth is that adolescents in urban, technological cultures like ours have every reason to be insecure and therefore vulnerable to the dulling impact of peer group conformity. Schools can do much to encourage pupils to observe freshly, to think fluently, and to strike out readily in new directions of promise. Schools can foster the disposition to break with useless habits and to express feelings and emotions—all part of a release from stultifying grooves of thought. However, these goals require teachers who encourage, through their methods and their attitudes, the expression of feelings as well as ideas. Such expression withers in authoritarian, disorderly, or apathetic situations.

A climate of sincerity and friendliness encourages pupils to become imaginative and creative, to respect each individual, to be secure enough to value and enjoy variations of opinion and personality. One study of two groups of subjects shows that a threatening situation for one group increased the members' rigidity of thinking and reduced their powers of abstract thought.[13] For most people strong fears and anxieties have an adverse effect on imaginative or creative production. A number of other studies describe the inflexible personality, notable for unimaginative and stereotyped thought, as related to considerable anxiety, conflict, and fear of ambiguity.[14] The teacher whose warmth of personality is guided by sound thinking provides both the model and the situation for an increase of imaginative insight among his pupils.

USING THE INSIGHTS OF RESEARCH   In recent years, creativity and the imagination have received marked attention in American, Canadian, and British education, for in all three nations there has been a revolt against a narrowly cognitive emphasis in education. Thus the terms *divergent thinking* and *convergent thinking*, used often in the writings of J. P. Guilford, have become familiar to most of us: convergent thinking, more restrictive, setting the learner to finding the one prescribed answer or solution to a problem; divergent thinking, more creative, setting the learner to generating new relationships and new information.

Among the increasing number of reports from research, one by R. S. Crutchfield and M. V. Covington focuses upon improving creative skills and strategies.[15] These two psychologists found that pupils who received instruction

---

[13] Ernst B. Beier, "The Effect of Induced Anxiety on Flexibility of Intellectual Functioning," *Psychological Monographs*, Vol. 65, No. 9 (1951), pp. 1–19.

[14] Else Frenkel-Brunswik, "Interrelationships Between Perception and Personality: A Symposium; Part I, Intolerance of Ambiguity as an Emotional and Perceptual Personality Variable," *Journal of Personality*, Vol. 18, No. 1 (September 1949), pp. 109, 130–34; Sidney Siegel, "Certain Determinants and Correlates of Authoritarianism," *Genetic Psychology Monographs*, Vol. 49 (May 1954), pp. 187–229.

[15] See, for example, J. P. Guilford, "Creative Thinking and Problem Solving," *Education Digest*, Vol. 24 (1964), pp. 29–31; M. V. Covington, and R. S. Crutchfield, "Experiments in the Use of Programmed Instruction for the Facilitation of Creative Problem Solving," *Programmed Instruction*, Vol. 4, No. 4 (January 1965), pp. 3–5.

in imaginative thinking performed significantly better on problem-solving tasks than control groups without such instruction. Five months later, the experimental group still retained its advantage. Boys and girls showed equal ability, and for subjects of different intelligence levels, the amount of growth was substantially the same. The Productive Thinking Program,[16] a result of this research, is aimed at upper grade pupils and consists of sixteen lesson booklets, each of which features a detective-like mystery the pupils attempt to solve. As the pupils work on these mysteries, they learn about and practice various aspects of productive thinking: how to think of new ideas, especially imaginative and unusual ones; how to look at a problem in fresh and original ways; how to defer judgment and keep an open mind; how to look at problems from many differing viewpoints. Creativity and innovation are woven into the fabric of these lessons, which can be used in the junior high school as well as in grade 6.

Other reports from research (see the reports listed in the bibliography at the close of this chapter) list the characteristics of creative, imaginative persons: open to experience, intuitive, spontaneous, flexible, complex in outlook, independent, having greater capacity than most people to tolerate conflicting values and dispositions within the self, not distinguished for high grades in high school or college, not strongly motivated to achieve in situations demanding conforming behavior, finding theoretical and esthetic ways of thinking enjoyable, revealing an awareness both of the inner self and the outer world, inclined to give expression to most aspects of inner experience.

One research psychologist[17] contends that increased esthetic sensitivity, self-awareness, and imaginativeness are more likely to be encouraged by a study of the arts, humanities, courses in literature, history, poetry, and the drama than by professional training in creativity. He also includes among his recommendations study of the psychology of personality and the sociology of ideas. "In such areas of human experience the student most easily can be brought to an awareness of the meaning and uses of analogy, simile, and metaphor, or the symbolic equivalents of varied experience, the delights and possibilities in imaginative play, and the place of human experience in the cosmic scheme."[18] Thus literature becomes important in a classroom organized to encourage creativity.

LITERATURE: THE TEACHER'S FINEST RESOURCE   For fostering imaginative thinking, the English teacher's best resource is literature. Using both rational and imaginative thought, both referential and emotive language, literature requires a full range of human response. Literature requires a reader to be wide awake and lifts him toward the fullness of his powers as a human being. It promotes

---

[16] M. V. Covington, R. S. Crutchfield, and L. B. Davies, *The Productive Thinking Program,* Series One: General Problem Solving (Berkeley, Calif.: Brazelton Printing Co., 1966).

[17] Donald W. MacKinnon, "Education for Creativity: A Modern Myth?" *Education for Creativity* (Univ. of California, Berkeley: Center for Research and Development in Higher Education, 1967).

[18] *Ibid.,* p. 17.

in him an equilibrium, a harmony that diminishes petty, narrow concerns, replacing them with a refreshing, resonant awareness of being alive.

Instruction in literature inevitably concerns itself with language, but the enterprise, both for teacher and for pupil, must primarily be one of delight and wonder. Whenever analysis of language becomes tiresome, the danger of blight is imminent. "You may take the noblest poetry in the world, and, if you stumble through it at a snail's pace, it collapses from a work of art into a rubbish heap." [19] To avoid this collapse, pupil inquiry and discovery must dominate teacher lecturing and telling. The whole range of human powers—thought, feeling, purpose, and imagination—must be called into play by awareness of the language in a literary selection, but awareness of metaphor, irony, perfect word choice or whatever must be as delightful to pupils as the sound of music to those who love it. Indeed, sensitive response to intricate organizations of feeling, sensation, and imagery in minds more subtle and powerful than our own does expand our powers of imagination. A coldly analytical mind never experiences the requisite jubilant mood of excited discovery.

THE TOTAL PROGRAM IN ENGLISH CONTRIBUTES TO IMAGINATIVE THINKING   Literature may be the teacher's foremost resource for encouraging imaginative thinking, but the rest of the English program is scarcely less valuable. To use oral language effectively, to write with power, to listen creatively—these, too, give scope to the life of the imagination. Instruction in them need not invariably be aimed directly toward imaginative insight, which often is incidental—but never accidental.

Incidental teaching should not be confused with accidental teaching. Incidental instruction of a concept or relationship rises naturally from a teacher's philosophy and his over-all design for teaching. A clear understanding of the ends of instruction helps the teacher foresee opportunities for incidental teaching and also helps him recognize those he has not foreseen. The teachable moment cannot always be predetermined; typically it must be seized whenever it presents itself, and the right conditions for emphasizing imaginative thinking will occur in many different activities.

Emerson believed that imagination was not the talent of some men but the health of every man. The teacher who conceives of imaginative thought as a pervasive influence in the entire classroom is more likely to conduct a healthy, pleasant program with learning at its optimum.

SUGGESTED LEARNING EXPERIENCES

Difficult goals in English cannot be won in a single semester or year. However, most pupils can improve in their ability to think imaginatively, and teachers who are patient may count on satisfying pupil growth over a period of six years in the secondary school.

[19] Alfred North Whitehead, "The Place of the Classics in Education," *The Aims of Education* (New York: New American Library, 1929), p. 76.

However practical any of the following suggestions may be, the teacher must be able to invent from them still more appropriate and flexibly applicable classroom procedures. Specific suggestions, no matter how valid, do not of themselves insure imaginative thinking. For such instruction, a sound theoretical position remains the only source of effective method.

TO EXPRESS MOODS AND FEELINGS

▶ *Use music to motivate writing*

Because most music evokes emotional responses, it can enhance or support teaching for imagination. One method uses a musical background for writing. The teacher may announce the plan in advance,[20] or on the day of the writing, say something like this: "Today, we are going to try something different. I am going to play some music. While I play the record for the first time, don't write; just listen, and try to feel the music. What mood does it express? What ideas and images cross your mind? Then when I start the record a second time, begin writing. Write whatever seems appropriate, whatever the music makes you feel. The music may suggest a story or a poem; it may merely indicate a scene or a mood you will try to capture in words; it may toss up some idea you will want to develop logically. Whatever you offer, long or short, I will accept. The only requirement is that it be your sincere product in response to the music."

Play the record several times if necessary, and then allow the writing to continue without music. Too much repetition may dull the response or irritate some pupils.[21]

Unfamiliar music, not too apparent in style, succeeds better in stimulating the imagination than a composition like Rimski-Korsakov's "Flight of the Bumblebee." Because famous compositions like "Clair de Lune" elicit ready-made associations from many pupils, they should be avoided. For a short recording, a composition like "Fêtes" by Debussy evokes a wide variety of reactions. Longer but equally stimulating recordings can be selected from among the works of Ravel, Satie, and Holst. Each teacher will experiment with various musical backgrounds and will select music with his particular class in mind.

▶ *Display nonrepresentational art*

A variation to the method of writing to music adds or substitutes a single painting in color, preferably something abstract or nonrepresentational—reproductions of paintings by artists like Tanguy and Miro, because they do not limit or direct the pupils' imagination and interpretive abilities as much as representational works.

What writing does one get? A variety of results: many stream-of-consciousness products; occasional poems; prose tinged with the dreamlike quality of "Kubla Khan"; some stories; and some compositional dough that fails to rise. Obviously the method is not designed for teaching logical organization or encouraging simple straightforward writing. However, its general success in eliciting some writing, particularly from students who have previously been somewhat reluctant to write, warrants its use several times each year.

[20] Advance planning with the class, with committees, or with student chairmen pays dividends in classroom management and effective learning. For more explicit discussion of this topic, see page 688 in "Program and Plan."

[21] For an account of the use of music to exercise student's imaginative thinking, see Harold P. Simonson, "Music as an Approach to Poetry," *English Journal*, Vol. 43, No. 1 (January 1954).

▶ *Relate reading to form and color*

To stimulate interpretation, two teachers [22] used finger painting, encouraging students to express in color and pattern their personal reactions to one of several poems. When they were finished, each student wrote an interpretation of his painting. Before these papers were read, the paintings, identified only by the titles of the poems represented, were placed along the chalkboard in front of the class. Attempting to select the most appropriate representations required an intensive and profitable examination of the poems themselves.

From these first steps, the two teachers proceeded to lessons on symbolism and the use of symbols in four dramas. Once again, the students finger painted their reactions, this time expressing definite symbols through color and pattern. In addition to releasing student response to literature the method provided nonverbal pupils with a means of expressing imaginative reactions to their reading.

▶ *Discuss feelings through the medium of literature*

Adolescents' problems are often too personal for open discussion. In groping fashion, young people look for wisdom on many problems about which they feel deeply: the dangers of daydreaming, how to stand against or conform to the ways of their age groups, the consequences of making choices. An open discussion of these problems, using characters in literature, often elicits an expression of feelings that would otherwise be too personal were the adolescent himself the topic of discussion. Try reading aloud a story like "Not Wanted," or the essay "Mary White." In advance of reading, pose one or two questions, alerting students to certain insights the story provides and offering a springboard for the discussion to follow. Sometimes the teacher leads the discussion; at other times, individuals, pairs, or panels of students direct it.

TO INCREASE FLUENT THINKING

▶ *Pose novel problems to be solved*

Borrow some of the methods used in the research that examined the creative thinking abilities of Army Air Cadets.[23] Although developed for application to science, engineering, and invention, these methods may easily be transferred to the English class. Learning, whether by air cadets or adolescents, is more than storing bits of knowledge, and the process of reorganizing and integrating requires more than mere accretion. The methods described here can help to promote flexibility with words and ideas, one aspect of imaginative learning.

1. Ask pupils to list as fast as they can all the uses they can think of for an ordinary brick (or bricks). The average student will list such items as making a wall, a path, or a doorstop, outlining a garden border, supporting a sagging floor. More imaginative students will think of a weight to hold down papers, a wedge to place behind a car wheel on a slope, an item in a still-life composition for an artist-painter, a base for a lamp, a weight to place on the head for practicing erect walking, and the like. Let pupils score their papers twice, once for number of items and

[22] James R. Squire and Merritt Beckerman, "The Release of Expression," *English Journal*, Vol. 39, No. 3 (March 1950).
[23] Robert C. Wilson, J. P. Guilford, Paul R. Christenson, Donald J. Lewis, "A Factor-Analysis Study of Creative Thinking Abilities," *Psychometrika*, Vol. 19, No. 4 (December 1954).

once for number of categories, such as a building material; a weight of some kind; a support of some kind; uses by volume, thickness, or abrasive quality; an unusual use. Grant extra points for unusual uses that are not unreasonable.

The first time the students try this exercise, many will not fully use their imaginations. After the exercise is completed and results are compared, they will usually be eager to try again. Other items to use: a burro, aluminum, glass, tar, a wheelbarrow, string, a pine tree, a sheet of typewriter paper.

2. Within a time limit, have pupils list as many things or actions they can think of that are impossible to do: drive a car to the top of Mount Everest; listen to Chopin playing his "Fantasie Impromptu."

3. Let students separate words run together in continuous discourse. For this activity, the teacher needs to duplicate relatively difficult passages, running them completely together, the words as well as the sentences. The students place light pencil lines between the words, heavy or colored lines between the sentences. When completed, individuals volunteer to read the passages aloud. The passages, about five to eight sentences long, should cover content varying from science to literature, from description to narration. After the first few trials, time limits may be set in order to encourage fluency rather than slow, deliberate solutions. *Caution* Explain the time limit so that it is not a threatening element in the lesson.

4. Try a consequences test. Let pupils list the immediate or remote and far-reaching consequences of certain hypothetical changes in the world—everyone becomes deaf; each year the world grows warmer as the sun slowly approaches; large numbers of people begin to live more than two hundred years; space travel becomes common; a scientist discovers a harmless chemical that dispels feelings of anger and aggression in human beings; the laws of chance cease to operate; everyone grows two feet taller; Brazil finds a way to raise the average I.Q. of its people fifty points.

5. Present synonyms. Let pupils write several synonyms for each of ten words such as *jolly, cheap, dull,* and others suitable to the age and ability of the class members.

6. Ask pupils to suggest two improvements for each of several social institutions: school, courts, labor unions, large corporations, small businesses.

▶ *Try a judicious use of brainstorming*

Brainstorming is a method of searching for solutions to problems. Its modern promoter [24] calls it "creative collaboration by groups." When the technique is used in business organizations, a number of people are brought together to use their brains to storm, in commando fashion, some objective in the world of ideas. Certain rules are understood and followed. Judicial judgment is initially ruled out. Criticism of ideas must be withheld until later. *Combination and improvement are sought.* In addition to contributing ideas of their own, participants should suggest how ideas of others can be turned into *better* ideas; or how two or more ideas can be joined into still another idea.[25]

In the English classroom, students and teacher may choose some problem such as these, which were used in one school: How can we have more speeches and group discussions without giving up time needed for literature and writing? What could be done to reduce the criticism that this school is too much dominated by

[24] Alex F. Osborn, *Applied Imagination* (New York: Scribner's, 1953).
[25] *Ibid.,* pp. 300–01.

student cliques? Groups of six pupils, including one student-secretary, pour out their ideas as rapidly as they can within a fixed time limit. The secretaries then meet to organize a presentation to the class. From this presentation, the best solutions are distilled, and the class evaluates both the solutions and the value of the brainstorming session.

▶ *Create a shift in perspective*

1. Describe a new or different kind of world, one in which many of the customs and normal events taken for granted in our world have shifted. For instance, one teacher describes the setting for *The Machine Stops* by E. M. Forster, a world of the future in which everyone lives in underground chambers beautifully lighted and perfectly tended by a universal world machine. Taking this particular pattern, students describe an hour of life in such a situation or work out some problems such as the kinds of television programs such people would prefer, the books such people would like to read, or how governing would be accomplished.

This exercise may be followed by one in which groups of students deal with a world that is continuously rainy or a world turned completely dry or one growing colder every year. Within the framework of these unfamiliar patterns, each group of students is to envisage the new alternatives that emerge with the shift in perception. For instance, a group imagining a world growing increasingly colder will realize that ships would cease crossing oceans, people would be driven to live underground, means of heating and of keeping warm would become crucial, resort cities with famous bathing beaches would lose their advantage. After working out these possibilities, each group tells some of the interesting shifts and changes it envisions.

2. A similar approach might be called "Utopias." The teacher describes some of the famous utopias: More's *Utopia*, Plato's *Republic*, Bacon's *New Atlantis*, Butler's *Erewhon*, Bellamy's *Looking Backward*. After discussing the meaning of utopias, students—either individually or in groups—are set to the problem of describing facets of life in a utopia of their own. In one junior high school, students worked in groups, each group drawing a map of an imaginary island and selecting a name for it. Girls described the fashions in this utopia; boys described the sports, the forms of adventure; groups devised plans for government, education, and crime control.

After such exercises, the teacher may pose for his pupils less spectacular but more exacting shifts in perspective: living in another country, in another income or racial group, or in another climate. Looking at issues from the point of view of a parent, a teacher, a small child, or a member of the opposite sex can be illuminating and challenging.

▶ *Use squiggle stories in junior high school*

Ask each child to draw three squiggles—random lines—at the top of a sheet of paper. Students then exchange papers, each one to complete the squiggle lines in such a way as to create a reasonable drawing. As soon as the drawing is completed, a story is to be written about the illustration. Students "should be reminded that in a story: (a) something must happen, (b) it must happen in sequence, and (c) it should have a definite ending or a punch line." [26]

[26] Robert C. Wilson, "Creativity," Chapter 6, p. 123, in Fifty-Seventh Yearbook, National Society for the Study of Education, Part II, *Education for the Gifted* (Chicago: Univ. of Chicago Press, 1958).

TO PROJECT THE FAMILIAR INTO IMAGINARY SITUATIONS

▶ *Predict how characters in literature might react in new situations*

To extend story situations pupils must draw upon their imaginations as well as upon what they know about a character. The solutions to imaginary literary situations impose problems of seeing relationships between new situations and behavior established by an author. Here are several ways teachers have set such challenges.

1. The teacher reads or describes the imaginary dinner conversation of historical personalities in books like Landor's *Imaginary Conversations* or Van Loon's *Lives*. Students "invite" three literary or historical characters to a dinner or some suitable event and write or dramatize their conversation. In a junior high school class, pupils may imagine the boys from *Roosevelt Grady, Little Britches,* and *North Fork* enrolling in the same class at school. Informal dramatic skits planned in advance may serve as the vehicle for expression.

2. Another extension of this idea in grade 11 might be a discussion of pioneer experiences by characters in *Let the Hurricane Roar, The Way West,* and *Giants in the Earth.* This approach offers a variation from other forms of reporting individual reading.

3. Students describe the impressions of a book character on an imaginary visit to their school. What classes, clubs, and activities would provide the greatest interest for tomboys like Kate (*The Good Master*) and Caddie Woodlawn? For Ralph (*Man of the Family*) and Jade Snow Wong (*Fifth Chinese Daughter*)? Groups of pupils may discuss these matters and report their consensus to the class.

4. Interested students write additional entries in Anne Frank's *Diary of a Young Girl* or extend the personal journal presented in Ring Lardner's story "I Can't Breathe." At their best, such assignments achieve not only logical prediction of behavior but also maintenance of tone, mood, and style.

5. Junior high school students who have read stories about boys and girls of other lands pretend they are on shipboard or at an international airport like Shannon or Honolulu. Meeting on their way back from the countries represented in their books, they reminisce about their travel experiences, incidents adapted from books they have just read.

These skits succeed best if groups of three pupils present them. Once the books have been completed, one planning session on the part of the trios can produce genuinely imaginative and entertaining skits for the rest of the class.

6. After a short story, a play, or a novel, plan a class exercise entitled "Grasp of Human Conduct." By setting before pupils the problem of how a certain character might behave in a situation not present in the literary selection, the teacher focuses attention on interpreting human behavior. The following is related to a group of short stories just completed by a tenth-grade class:

SAMPLE FROM GRASP OF HUMAN CONDUCT EXERCISE

To the pupil Each of the following items concerns one of the more important characters in the short stories you have read. Each item also contains the description of a situation that is not in any of the stories. After each situation described, five courses of action are listed. On the basis of your acquaintance with the character, you are asked to check the course of action the character would most probably follow. Remember, do not check what *you* would do in the situation described or what you think the character *should* do. Rather, consider all the evidence of the story and bring it to bear upon the problem: How would this character probably conduct himself in this situation? Then place a check in front of that course of action that *best* describes what you think the character would do.

1. CHARACTER   Jerry, in "A Mother in Mannville" by Marjorie Kinnan Rawlings.

   SITUATION   During a baseball game on a vacant lot in a nearby town, one of the players bats a ball through the window of a convertible passing by the lot. Jerry is playing left field at the time and is not the boy who batted the ball. The boys run away.

   COURSES OF ACTION

   Jerry runs away with the other players.

   Jerry pretends he was merely walking by and saunters down the street.

   Jerry runs away with the other players but tries to persuade them to go back in a body and face the consequences. They won't go back so Jerry gives in to the majority opinion.

   Jerry goes to meet the angry car owner. He offers to work out his share of the blame.

   Jerry stands paralyzed with fear, unable to run or even think what is best for him to do.

2. [Other characters and situations from other stories]

Teachers using this method avoid rigid adherence to so-called right answers. The teacher willingly acknowledges that human beings do not always act consistently. However, in the light of Jerry's behavior in the story, which answer does seem most logical? The stimulus to class discussion justifies the use of such an instrument, even if no scores are recorded for evaluation purposes. Disagreements will lead to rewarding class discussion. Sometimes the teacher may test students' alertness by creating a set of "answers" no one of which could possibly be correct. Either before or after such an incident, the teacher and students might agree that whenever answers appear inadequate, students may write in one of their own.

▶ *Transpose the familiar into myths, fantasies, and tall tales*

After reading such myths as the account of Phaethon or Pandora, students write myths of the modern world, transposing familiar events into fantasy and wonder tales. Variations of this method include the use of tall tales—such as those about Paul Bunyan, Mike Fink, Davy Crockett, Miss Pickerel, or Mary Poppins. Indian legends represent other materials that might be used; Norse, Irish, Finnish, and Oriental mythologies have seldom been fully exploited in American schools. In some classes modern fantasies like James Thurber's *The Thirteen Clocks* and *Many Moons* will stimulate imaginative writing, as will Antoine de St. Exupéry's *The Little Prince* and Agnes Smith's *An Edge of the Forest*.

▶ *Use literature with parallel and contrasting elements*

The use of parallels and contrasts in literature offers many adaptations and extensions. The attitudes of Homer, of *The Human Comedy,* and Pip of *Great Ex-*

pectations can be compared and contrasted; the ways two boys learn to accept responsibility can be seen in *Captains Courageous* and *Black Boy*.[27] Nor does the parallel always need to be linked to content. An aspect of form, for instance, may interest teachers presenting the short story as a type. Or the emphasis on form may represent the culmination of a planned program of literary parallels increasing in difficulty. The illustration to be used here directs attention to an author's tone, but the methods described are applicable to a wide range of literature.

For adolescents exploring the dimensions of literature, Saki's tone—tart, bracing, antiseptic—is frequently a new kind of reading experience. One high school teacher begins a study of tone with "Blue Jays" by Mark Twain and a single story by Saki, either "The Open Window" or "The Lumber Room." She first places brief samples on the board. For instance, this quatrain with its definite tone of wry protest:

A-tomic Ache

My confidence in terra firma
Now I find in error
O Science, rest! I daily feel less
Firma and more terra.[28]

At this point the teacher defines tone and asks, "How do we detect the poet's tone?" Next she reads "Blue Jays" aloud, asking students to watch for its indirect comment on the comic ways of the human family.

The teacher then assigns the Saki story as a trial of the students' insight into tone. The student must be alert and imaginative enough to read between the lines. Almost everything that is really important is deliberately left for the reader to supply.

In a subsequent lesson the parallel might be theme, point of view, or setting. Benét's short story "By the Waters of Babylon" makes an unusually effective thematic parallel with Emily Dickinson's poem "Tell the Truth but Tell It Slant."

▶ *Dramatize selected stories*

In stories where characters represent many points of view, one effective approach may be called the "Jigsaw Puzzle." One student is designated to interrogate or interview seven other students, each of whom represents a character in the story. The interrogator questions each character in order to elicit his version of the incident.[29] In each case the character interviewed is to present the matter exactly from his own point of view within whatever limitations the story imposes. For instance, in Saki's "The Open Window," Framton Nuttel tells his version with complete conviction that the niece was truthful, the aunt addled by her tragedy, and the state of his own nerves such that he might have been overwhelmed by the power of suggestion. The aunt presents her uncomplimentary interpretation of Mr. Nuttel, unaware of the

---

[27] See also page 201. Methods drawing upon parallels in content are further described in Chapter Six, "Literature: Basic Approaches." An excellent account of using novels for comparisons and contrast is David M. Litsey, "Comparative Study of Novels," *English Journal*, Vol. 48, No. 3 (March 1959), pp. 149–51.

[28] Donald S. Klopp, in *English Journal*, Vol. 40, No. 1 (January 1951), p. 11. Reprinted by permission. A cluster of selections featuring the lighter touch of humor—the dry, urbane, and witty poetry of Phyllis McGinley or Richard Armour—also makes a good introduction to tone.

[29] See "Language as Dynamic Process," pages 20–21, for a principle of language covering this example of individuals reacting to what may seem to be the same stimuli, reconstructing highly personal and unique experiences.

extent to which her niece had influenced Nuttel's behavior. The husband and two brothers appear as a trio and briefly contribute their picture of the situation. If some timid or less able student is to be given a minor part, the cyclist can contribute his amazing and brief encounter with Mr. Nuttel. The final witness is the niece who is persuaded by the interviewer, after some preliminary dissimulations, to tell the whole truth—to solve the jigsaw puzzle. Teachers familiar with the noted Japanese movie *Rashomon* will recognize the source of this method.

Except for written questions to which the interrogator may refer, students should avoid any scripts or memorization of their roles. Impromptu and creative dialogue, based upon exceptionally careful reading and interpretation of the story, succeed best.

TO EVOKE FEELING

▶ *Make time for writing poetry*

Under favorable conditions, many adolescents will convert an amazing amount of energy into writing poetry. Teachers whose classes respond to this activity often begin by presenting poems written by young writers, poems from sources like *Scholastic* magazine or from such books as *Creative Power*. While reading a number of these for enjoyment and appreciation, the teacher directs attention to their rhythms, diction, or freshness of observation. From this point on, teachers often follow the general features of the method Hughes Mearns described in *Creative Power*. Essentially, these features include:

> soliciting verses already written—often brought from private hiding places— and a cautious use of these for informal personal instruction, leading students to see why the feeling of the poet did or did not become the feeling of the reader

> an encouraging teacher who does not prescribe or even suggest subject matter or form but who does emphasize the danger of imitation and the importance of original, personal thought (Mearns says he drives pupils back upon themselves, drives them to search within: "I can't tell you what you should write about because I don't know what you know. What sort of experience have you been having? What do you think about most of the time?")

> much sharing and enjoyment of published poetry and prose, favorite selections chosen by individuals rather than prescribed in a single text (for instance, students bring to class poems they like and read them to one another as a preface to spontaneous, informal discussion; they form literary societies and carry on programs; they present programs of "Favorites—So Far")

> an emphasis on sincerity of expression, on respect for every opinion, no matter how naive it may appear to the instructor

> teacher alertness for sincere expressions of imaginative insight—sometimes only a word or a phrase; whenever it appears, praise from the teacher and also from classmates

> the spur of an attractive and regular publication for the best creative writing

Finally, one should note that some pupils in Mearns' classes were content to read poetry rather than write it. Others, writing without scaling any heights of expression, felt supported by the assurance that attempts to express imaginative insight would be respected but not received with insincere flattery.

Teachers using these methods place emphasis on originality and insight. They praise apt comparisons, flexible thinking, fresh insights, new ways of viewing experience. One chalk board or bulletin board may be devoted to Felicitous Phrases and Voluntary Verses, and another to Flat Fulminations and Stale Stereotypes. On the latter, students place clippings illustrating clichés, tired slang, overworked words, and similar hackneyed expressions.

TO INCREASE EXPRESSIVENESS

▶ *Try role playing*

1. If students have never used role playing in previous schooling, explain the technique somewhat in this fashion:

> In role playing you become another person; you try to imagine how that person would walk, talk, and think. In other words, you become that other person insofar as you can with the knowledge you have about him. Role playing is not a rehearsed play; some pre-planning is necessary so the main outlines of the action are blocked out and members taking part are sure of the roles they are playing, but you plan and play the story without memorizing lines or actions. Invent the conversation and divide the main story into a series of scenes. Determine where you will begin and what episodes you will feature; then make a study of the characters.

In a class studying *Boy on Horseback* by Lincoln Steffens, the students decided to enact scenes to show the kind of person Lincoln Steffens was and how he matured. The setting for the first scene was an English classroom before the bell rings. Steffens comes in and talks with some of his friends. (Clues to what they might discuss can be found in the chapter "Preparing for College," where Steffens talks about his interests.) Then the instructor in the story calls the class to order and gives an assignment without much point—for instance, writing a paragraph with three compound sentences, one complex, and two simple. As the book implies, "students" in the drama should all start writing without hesitation, but the boy playing the role of Steffens should question the assignment with an inquiry such as, "What is the reason for the paragraph?"

2. Role playing need not always be based on reading. The teacher may describe situations in which teen-agers find themselves at cross purposes with adults. For instance, the teacher outlines a situation such as this. A girl has just been asked for a date by a boy she likes very much. Because of poor marks on her last report card, her parents have restricted all dating. Students block out action for the father, mother, a grandmother in the home, an older brother or sister, and the girl herself, revealing how the problem is resolved. Those who take adult parts are instructed to do their best to see the situation through the eyes of the adults.

At first, role playing does not always move along smoothly; but students improve each time they repeat a scene, gaining poise and new ideas for action or dialogue. After most scenes they should stop for criticism and suggestions. First the players themselves should have an opportunity to make suggestions for improvement; then everyone should offer advice. Sometimes it is wise to change several players and try the scene again. The teacher should watch to see whether or not the characters are reacting to one another. The main purpose—to see facts and feelings from a new orientation by stepping into someone else's shoes—should bring about a deeper imaginative involvement of the student actors.

► *Act out thumbnail dramas*

1. For slow learning high school students, one teacher writes brief dramatic skits, using only three thousand basic English words and a limited number of characters. The pupils, most of them poor readers, act as they read the parts in their "Walk-on Rehearsal Book." [30] Through this method they have an opportunity for reading and speech experience, a starting point for discussing problems familiar to them, and an activity that is notable for dispelling apathy. "Shining Up the Car," reprinted here, is typical of the method.[31]

SHINING UP THE CAR

TIME   One Friday afternoon.

PLACE   BOB's backyard.

CHARACTERS   JACK and BOB, two high school boys.

BOB *is busy washing his father's car.* JACK *enters.*

JACK   Hi, Bob.

BOB (*surly*)   Hi, yourself.

JACK   What you doing?

BOB   Just playing nursemaid to Dad's old car. Just giving the old crate a shampoo and a shoe shine.

JACK   Thought you washed the car last week.

BOB   Right. And the week before. And the week before that. And the week before the week before—

JACK   Hold it. Evidently this must be a weekly job.

BOB   Some detective, the way you figure things out.

JACK   You don't need to get sore about it.

BOB   No? That's what you think!

JACK   Say listen! I didn't come over to pick a fight.

BOB   Well, see to it that you don't then.

JACK   But I'm not. I mean I didn't.

BOB   Didn't what?

JACK   Didn't come over to pick a fight.

BOB   What did you come over for? Nobody asked you.

JACK   I came over for two things. First, I came to see what you were doing.

BOB   So you came over to see what I was doing? Well, I hope you can see that I am washing, cleaning, and polishing my Dad's car. A job I have to do every Friday afternoon after school.

JACK   Well, what's the idea?

BOB   Because my Dad is trying to sell this old wreck.

JACK   You mean—

BOB   Yes, I mean that my polishing job has to make this car look like what it isn't.

JACK   No one can do that.

BOB   Oh, yes, I can!

JACK   You must be joking. Why, that looks like a pretty good car.

[30] Effie A. Hult, "The Walk-on Rehearsal Book" (mimeographed), Oakland Public Schools, Oakland, California. Used in special education and English workshop classes for retarded readers at the senior high school level.

[31] From "The Walk-on Rehearsal Book," by Effie A. Hult; reprinted by permission.

BOB   Shows how little you know about a car. Why, every time we take it out, it ends up in a garage.

JACK   Kidding, aren't you?

BOB   Says you! Say, I know this car inside out. I've taken it apart and put it together a dozen times.

JACK   It's really bad, is it? The car's really in a bad condition?

BOB   I'd hate to see one in a worse condition.

JACK   I'm surprised.

BOB   Yah, you would be. You don't know a thing about cars.

JACK   But I do now. And thanks for telling me. Thanks a lot!

BOB   Say! What's it to you?

JACK   Because my Dad was figuring on buying that car. But I'll pass the word along. So long. (*Exits*)

BOB   Hey, you! Hey, Jack! Come back here!

The first step in any economical learning, establishing a goal, should be followed by attempts to execute the skill or behavior pattern. The students' goal in such skits is to perform successfully, entertaining and instructing their audience. The skills to be improved should be written on the chalkboard or copied in the students' notebooks—often both. In these short skits, slow learning pupils need to estimate the success of their performances by referring often to these skills, for example, to read without hesitation or to read with an imparting tone or to use gestures and facial expressions corresponding to the meaning of the words. In the light of this evaluation, they are to adapt their behavior in subsequent trials with the same or new skits.

2. Once the method has been established, students can be drawn to more imaginative efforts such as creating their own skits. This can be followed by a series of skits developing a single theme, for example, "It is easier to be wise for other people than for oneself." A coherent and continued serial in which the same main characters reappear once a week for a semester or longer holds the interest of classes regardless of age level or ability. It also gives scope for increasing expressiveness, an important element of imaginative growth.

TO COMPLETE PARTIAL DESIGNS

Some natural law of closure apparently links our human sense of form to the predictable orbits of the planets, to the underlying orderliness of nature. This human need to close gaps in structural systems can be employed in teaching imaginative insight.

▶ *Extend moods and explanations from clues*

1. Some poems present only hints or fragments of meaning. Students often enjoy speculating on the implications of poems like "The Listeners" by Walter de la Mare and "The Skater of Ghost Lake" by William Rose Benét. Others that incompletely etch in their mysterious stories are "Childe Roland to the Dark Tower Came" by Robert Browning, "O What Is That Sound?" by W. H. Auden, and "The Erl King" by Goethe.

2. Some stories provide clues but do not interpret them for the reader. For junior high pupils, use such stories as "Boy in the Dark" and "A Mother in Mann-

ville." For senior high pupils, use "By the Waters of Babylon," "The Lottery," and "The Dragon." In all five, the reader must make leaps of imagination in order to interpret the clues provided by the authors. Whether poem or story, the selection may be read silently, followed by a second oral reading. Occasionally arouse good discussion by suggesting an interpretation obviously off balance or willfully one-sided.

▶ *Construct meaning from incomplete and unusual situations*

Duplicate or place on the chalkboard several ambiguous story openings. Students are to develop written interpretations related to one of these, in keeping with some single mood or effect. Praise writing that maintains the most consistency of effect. In one classroom, the teacher used these four curious beginnings and left a fifth space on the chalkboard to be filled by the best additional contribution chosen from among several volunteered by class members. On the following day each pupil chose one from among the five story openings. Anyone who wished was permitted to substitute an opening of his own.

> Gerry stopped his car, waiting for the elegant red convertible to draw up alongside. At the wheel sat one of the ugliest old crones he had ever seen. Her thin gray hair was blown about her wrinkled face, and she held toward him something resembling a small palm tree—except that it was bluish and withered.
>
> In the trees at the city's edge the American girl suddenly felt oddly depressed. "What," she thought, "am I doing in Portugal? Why did I leave the festival? What do I expect to find in this ruined temple by the olive grove?"
>
> Diane looked at the odd figures decorating the walls of her playmate's room. Suddenly her eye rested on one grotesque animal. Did its eyes move just as she glanced toward it?
>
> Looking out through the curiously shaped window, the passenger saw stars, the moon, and earth far below. To the left, in the strange twilight, he viewed what seemed to be a meadow and on it were moving sad-faced beings half horse, half human. "These," someone said, "are the ones who have been condemned to spend eternity on this distant, insignificant star."
>
> (Additional provocative opener chosen from among any volunteered by class members.)

In accordance with the age and background of his pupils, each teacher will modify such suggested openings. At the junior high level, pupils respond better to incidents similar to their reading interests. Boys usually prefer rugged adventures in situations that imply action in sports or pioneering; girls often like fantasy, mystery, mild adventure, horse stories, and love stories.

▶ *Devise insightful titles*

1. Duplicate poems, omitting their titles. Ask students to create titles to bind the varied elements of the poem into a single unified and imaginative essence. With junior high school pupils, relatively simple but unfamiliar poems like "Past and Present" by Thomas Hood and "Reflections Dental" by Phyllis McGinley are suitable. For older pupils, poems by Robert Frost, Emily Dickinson, and E. E. Cummings serve particularly well. Occasionally one may use a brief poem with a considerable admixture of ambiguity, for instance—Yeats' "The Song of Wandering Aengus." The purpose is to stimulate students to integrate diverse elements through combining, recombining, and reconciling.

2. Other variations of this method depend upon the teacher's presentation of art reproductions—film slides of such modern painters as Rouault and Picasso—and synopses of novels such as may be found in any book review source. Effective also are short stories such as those found in *Literary Cavalcade* and cartoons with their captions removed. As in selecting titles for the poems, the method depends upon listing some of the titles the students submit and then, with their help, selecting the best title indicated by the elements offered by the painter, writer, or cartoonist.

Drawing by Carl Rose; Copyright © 1943 The New Yorker Magazine, Inc.

"Is this seat taken?"

HUMOR AND IMAGINATION ARE CLOSELY ALLIED

This cartoon was a favorite in a class where the teacher had pasted each of 35 cartoons on one side of a cardboard sheet and its caption on the reverse side. The pupils created captions or explanations for each cartoon without looking at the caption pasted on the reverse.

► *Talk extemporaneously on partially sketched topics*

Extemporaneous oral talks require the student to impose order swiftly on the various parts of his experience. Select somewhat unusual or challenging topics and place them on slips of paper for a class secretary or chairman to distribute. Each topic has the initial parts of an outline, indicating the direction in which the talk should be developed. For instance a talk on teen-age driving may be partially designed from the viewpoint of an adult such as a highway patrolman or an insurance agent. Whoever draws the slip must complete the design in the same vein. One student is given three minutes to order his thoughts—usually out in the hallway. As he enters the room to speak, the pupil chairman gives another slip of paper to the next speaker who, in turn, retires to the hallway, preparing his material while the first speaker talks before the class. A committee—or those who have finished—assumes responsibility for evaluating the presentations, using some set of standards agreed upon in advance. Some topics that require a fusion of imagination, knowledge, and insight are listed here:

> If you were a citizen of Alaska, a teacher in this school, a shrimp fisherman in the Louisiana bayous, the editor of a large city newspaper, a visitor from another planet (possibilities here are endless, limited only by the teacher's awareness of those his class can handle), what thoughts might you have as you returned home in the evening?
>
> If you were the parent of a teen-ager who was running wild, what would you do?
>
> How would you improve assemblies in our school?
>
> What will students in the year 2075 study in high school?

▶ *Create a story from multiple authorship*

For slow learning or younger pupils, teachers may build a story by a process of accretion. Using a tape recorder, the teacher tells the opening passage of a story with a pronounced mood of mystery or humor. Each volunteer thereafter adds several sentences or a paragraph to this beginning. The tape is stopped until someone volunteers; usually time is needed for plotting the next surge of action or description, and penciled notes are required for smooth delivery. Several tapes may be produced and reviewed for consistency of mood, unity of characterization, and coherent story line. The students should be aware that they are completing a partial design and that the skill required is consistency.

TO PERCEIVE THE RELATIONSHIP OF PARTS IN AN ORGANIZED STRUCTURE

▶ *Present two versions of the same poem or story*

1. A teacher may read aloud a story or selection and offer two conclusions, the original and one that is not true to the author's development of the story or selection. "The Streets of Memphis" from Richard Wright's *Black Boy* [32] is typical of selections that succeed with either junior or senior high pupils. In the original version, the boy's mother locks him out until he defends himself against the bullies who torment him. A spoiled version, distorting the author's intent, has her relent and open the door.

2. Another variation of this method is the comparison of two versions in different literary forms, such as the original story, "The Man Who Liked Dickens" by Evelyn Waugh and the television adaptation. [33]

---

[32] This selection is available in *Coping,* one of the series of paperbacks called *Gateway English, a Literature and Language Arts Program,* published by Macmillan (1966).

[33] Robert Tallman's TV adaptation of "The Man Who Liked Dickens" appeared in *Literary Cavalcade,* Vol. 6, No. 7 (April 1954). The original story, titled "À Côté de Chez Todd," appeared in Evelyn Waugh, *A Handful of Dust* (Boston: Little, Brown, 1934); paperback (New York: Dell, 1959). It is also available in *Survival,* ed. by James R. Squire (New York: Scholastic, 1960).

► *Locate missing parts in a harmonious design*

Present literary, musical, or pictorial experiences from which some significant part has been deleted. For instance from a poem like "Annabel Lee" or "Ode to the West Wind" some portion is omitted and the abridged version presented either as a listening or a reading experience, the student's problem being to locate the flaw and to suggest the nature of what is needed for a harmonious whole. The method may be applied also to prose, architecture, and to all the graphic arts. By splicing tapes, the same method may be applied to music.

For junior high pupils or in the initial stages with older pupils, the deletions should be quite obvious and damaging to the proportion of the work of art, for example—the entire final stanzas of "High Flight" or "Annabel Lee," or the necessary resolution of a significant phrase in *Eine Kleine Nachtmusik*. Although the English teacher will, of course, emphasize literary forms, he will find a variety of art forms useful in establishing the concept of proportion and wholeness in artistic design.

TO GAIN MORE AWARENESS OF INSIGHT

► *Place thought-provoking questions on the chalkboard*

For a period of time, keep questions like the following before the pupils. Numerous classroom situations and occasions will arise for discussing one or more of these ingredients of insight:

Do you jump to conclusions?

Do you look for implications? Do you read between the lines? Do you look for the reality behind the symbol, the seed beneath the husk?

Are you suspicious of easy formulas, stereotypes, simple solutions, and single causation? Do you know what these are? Can you illustrate each with an example?

Do you keep in a fluid state all the clues to solving a puzzling problem? Do you let your mind hover over a matter before making an important decision?

Do you recognize the reality of facts but use your imagination to penetrate beneath them and to project your thoughts beyond them in your search for creative answers to problems?

► *Feature lack of insight in its comic aspects*

1. On a bulletin board, display posters illustrating lack of insight. Students may be familiar with posters depicting Dilbert, an obtuse person who wrestles at the edge of swimming pools, swims in deep water without knowing a variety of strokes, and dives before checking the depth of the water. Dilbert posters may not be available, but students will enjoy drawing others to take their place and to illustrate other situations. Sunday comic sections provide many examples.

2. Let gifted and interested pupils prepare film strips showing the amusing consequences of failure to see beneath the surface. For example, depict the naive customer at the used-car lot of Giveaway Givins, who "loses his shirt on every sale."

3. Use political cartoons, brief news anecdotes, and *New Yorker* drawings.

TO SEE BEYOND THE OBVIOUS

► *Use fables and parables*

Some students are often hesitant to interpret, to look beneath the surface. Establish the attitude that it is better to have soared occasionally to the wrong implications than never to have soared at all. In fables as in swimming, one must plunge in if learning is ever to take place. Merely to know what happens in most worthwhile stories is to wade in the shallows.

1. Begin with simple exercises. Have students tell—or read to them—Aesop's fable of the fox and the grapes. They will easily grasp the point that it is intended to be more than an account of some animals and grapes. Press them to describe real-life situations, somewhat in detail, in which the sour-grapes attitude shows itself.

2. Next, present a more unfamiliar fable such as the following:

> A pig ate his fill of acorns under an oak tree and then started to root around the tree. A crow remarked, "You should not do this. If you lay bare the roots, the tree will wither and die." "Let it die," replied the pig. "Who cares as long as there are acorns?"

The teacher should be prepared to offer several examples of shortsighted wastefulness if pupils cannot do so. Students who offer implications that are off center or inapplicable should not be discouraged by teacher or classmates. However, assessment of the best illustrations is entirely justifiable and even necessary if growth in seeing imaginative relationships is to occur.

3. From fables, move on to parables, usually somewhat more complex. Use Buddha's parable, Returning Love for Hatred,[34] and some of the Christian, Jewish, and Moslem parables. Once the students understand the requirements of the assignment, meaningful generalization and application may be used with more difficult materials. Encourage, also, fluidity of thought, urging as many applications as possible to a variety of situations. If more responses are forthcoming than can be handled by oral recitation, direct pupils to use some form of abbeviation or private shorthand to record their applications. Then close the lesson by asking each student to write the best application from among those he recorded. Some of the most imaginative and pertinent should be read to the class. (A committee of students to select these can often save the teacher's time for other work.)

4. If the students fare well on this exercise, scale even more difficult heights. Use aphorisms such as these from Eric Hoffer: [35]

> "Rudeness is the weak man's imitation of strength."
> "Fear and freedom are mutually exclusive."

or maxims like these from La Rochefoucauld:

> "Hypocrisy is the homage that vice pays to virtue."
> "Greater virtues are needed to bear good fortune than bad."

Poor Richard's Almanack, Will Rogers' homely wisdom, Thomas Jefferson's *Decalogue*, the sayings of Confucius, and the aphorisms from the Old Norse sagas will furnish further tightly coiled meanings for students to unravel. A pleasant variation: place students in groups, giving all the same maxim to unfold through application; each group then vies with the others to produce the greatest number of apt illustrations, the teacher or a committee acting as judges.

[34] "Parable of Returning Love for Hatred" by Gautama Buddha, reprinted in Luella B. Cook *et al.* (eds.), *The World Through Literature* (New York: Harcourt, Brace & World, 1949), pp. 82–84.

[35] Eric Hoffer, *The Passionate State of Mind* (New York: Harper & Row, 1955).

5. Gifted pupils may continue this course by using *Animal Farm, The Prophet,* or *Fables for Our Time.* All of these offer stimulation for developing an interpretive bent of mind. Multi-leveled, and therefore suited to similar enrichment of meaning, are many children's stories, such as *Charlotte's Web, The Mousewife,* and *The Story of Ferdinand.* Use modern African literature for cross cultural interpretive challenges. *The Strong Breed* by Wole Soyinka is a suitable drama for such a purpose.

▶ *Use "Letter to a Fan"*

For slower classes and for younger pupils who find difficulty in penetrating beyond the literal meaning of literary selections, Howard Pease's "Letter to a Fan" [36] is exceptionally helpful. In his response to the student who had read all but two of his books, Pease asks what it means to read more than the surface elements of a story and then charts the way for many pupils who are unaccustomed to looking beneath the surface events of a story for its theme, symbols, and human values.

▶ *Use poems and stories in parallel*

Another method of helping pupils see beyond the obvious uses short stories or poems with parallel themes. For instance, Robert Frost's "Dust of Snow" and Sara Teasdale's "Wood Song" both assert nature's power to dispel a mood of bitterness. A boy's relation to his parents is the theme of a cluster of very teachable short stories:

> "My Father Is an Educated Man" by Jesse Stuart
> "Mama and Nels" (from *Mama's Bank Account*) by Kathryn Forbes
> "The Duke's Children" by Frank O'Connor
> "The Snob" by Morley Callaghan
> "The Pheasant Hunter" by William Saroyan

In reading and discussing parallel short selections like these, students can discover the value of going beyond what happens in a story. Although many classes will require as the first step a retelling of what happened, they can be taught to take further steps: to analyze and generalize about the motives and behavior of the characters, to seek the theme of the writer, and to note values determining the choices and attitudes of the characters. Gifted students will handle the method of parallel selections with more intensity than other students, but even very slow pupils can relate a brief story like "The Snob" to "Mama and Nels." Here is a method emphasizing relationships rather than simple classification.

▶ *Devote time to reflection*

1. Some teachers provide time for thinking through a topic before discussion. They write a question on the board; then they ask the students to think about the question and to make notes of their thoughts. After four or five minutes, the discussion is opened with the help of some reliable student. This procedure may be varied on different days. Sometimes pupils write for five minutes on a topic, then develop an oral discussion on the same topic. Other times, written reaction will conclude a ten-minute oral discussion. Here is an example of one topic used successfully: when asked the secret of his inventiveness, Thomas Alva Edison replied,

[36] Howard Pease, "How to Read Fiction," in *They Will Read Literature*, A Portfolio of Tested Secondary School Procedures (Champaign, Ill.: NCTE, 1955).

"I listen from within." What opportunities are there in our English class for "listening from within"?

2. Occasionally a topic is placed on the board for silent reflection not to be followed by any talking or writing whatsoever. To be sure, the teacher does not know the student is thinking, but this method often proves extremely effective. For it, teachers use more personal topics than those used for discussion. To illustrate the method, some topics for thought and meditation used with the novel *Silas Marner* are listed here. Teachers will vary the topics according to their purposes and the material they are studying.

TOPICS FOR REFLECTION FOLLOWED BY DISCUSSION, WRITING, OR BOTH

Some people are born lucky; others never have any good happen to them. True or false? Apply your answer to Dunstan, Godfrey, or Silas.

Some choices in life stunt our growth; others help us to grow.

"No man is an island entire unto itself." What connection does this quotation have with this story?

TOPICS FOR REFLECTION FOLLOWED BY NO DISCUSSION

Does selfishness carry its own punishment? Is this true in *Silas Marner?* Is this true in real life?

The need for love and affection is not limited to characters in novels.

Avoid an excess of moralizing on these matters. Students often reject adult preachments if the points are too heavily emphasized.

► *Study metaphor to illuminate relationships*

When a man's heart is compared to a shriveled, sour apple, the adolescent reader, if he is not to be puzzled, must respond with an interpretive turn of mind. Figurative language may be collected by students as an assignment. Each pupil is to search for three imaginative comparisons, copying each on a card. Groups or committees may select the most striking examples for publication in the school paper or for a bulletin board devoted to imaginative writing.[37] One class liked these:

"A lanky boy whose bolts needed tightening." [38]

"He was at that awkward age when he could walk through empty rooms and knock over furniture."

TO DEVELOP A DEFINITION OF IMAGINATION

► *Use an inductive method of defining imagination*

1. Place on the chalkboard several contrasts between imaginative and unimaginative statements:

The helicopter came toward us.

The helicopter descended upon us like an infuriated palm tree.

That assembly program showed very little planning.

That assembly program was about as carefully planned as a hiccup.

---

[37] Ways of developing skill with figurative language are described further on page 464 in Chapter Ten, pages 525–26 in Chapter Eleven, and pages 398–400 in the discussion on vocabulary in Chapter Nine.

[38] From Charles Brooks, *English Spring* (New York: Harcourt, Brace & World, 1932).

After beginning with these simple contrasts, lead the discussion to several more complex examples of imagination:

> Isak Dinesen (Karen Blixen) uses the king's letter to ease the pain in the crushed leg of the African workman. ("The King's Letter")
> Tom Sawyer induces the other boys to help him whitewash the fence.
> Huck Finn outwits the Duke and the Dauphin.

Newspaper clippings or magazine articles relating original or insightful behavior are also useful.

2. Using such examples as these as starters, encourage pupils to tell about other imaginative events, actions, or language, such as creating new recipes, tools, fashions, architecture, laws. After sufficient examples have been described, ask pupils to help in developing a definition for imagination. At first many of them will say "Imagination is when . . . ," continuing to give concrete examples. Do not criticize this at first. Say, "Good! But let's not have any more *examples.*" Point out the need for generalizing from the specific examples. Try to shape the students' contribution toward Coleridge's definition of imagination (see page 174), helping them to discriminate between the *fantastic* and the *imaginative.* For a follow-up assignment, ask rows or groups of students to bring to class examples of

> insightful comparisons in language
> expression of profound feeling or enthusiasm admirably controlled
> multiplicity or diversity brought into order through some unifying or predominant thought or feeling
> originality of action in some situation
> remarkable insight into some situation or some other person's feelings or problems
> creative inventions or actions

The situations described in this assignment may be either actual or fictional.

3. All pupils can profit by a discussion of the difference between appropriate uses of the imagination and inappropriate escape into fantasy. The world of fantasy reaches out to many and the means of escape into it are often learned too easily. Certain poems and stories, useful for discussing this concept, should be known to all teachers:

> *For junior high*
> "Stolen Day" by Sherwood Anderson
> "That's What Happened to Me" by Michael Fessier
> *For senior high*
> "Paul's Case" by Willa Cather
> "Mrs. Ketting and Clark Gable" by Ann Chidester
> "Petit, the Poet" by Edgar Lee Masters
> "Miniver Cheevy" by Edwin Arlington Robinson

► *Use a deductive method of understanding imagination*

Here the teacher reverses the process described above and starts with a definition of imagination. After furnishing some examples himself, the teacher asks the students to supply further examples, both in class and as a home assignment. For example, a student might tell how he successfully used a board that was too short in a woodshop project. This might be an opportune time to recommend certain books for recreational reading, books that stress imagination—*Engineers' Dreams; Jules Verne, the Biography of an Imagination; Kon-Tiki; 20,000 Leagues Under the Sea; The Bright Design.* These books help many boys, especially, to understand that imagination is not exclusively connected with poetry and fantasy.

TO DISCRIMINATE BETWEEN STALE AND FRESH EXPRESSION

▶ *Act out clichés*

Have pairs of students dramatize the idea of an expert on clichés who takes the witness stand and testifies in the following manner: [39]

Q. Where do you live?

A. Any old place I hang my hat is home sweet home to me.

Q. What is . . . your occupation?

A. Well, after burning the midnight oil at an institution of higher learning, I was for a time a tiller of the soil; then I went down to the sea in ships. I have been a guardian of the law, a poet at heart, a prominent club man . . . and—

Q. And you expect to live to—

A. A ripe old age.

Q. What do you thank?

A. My lucky stars . . .

Students may work in pairs to collect overworked phrases and present brief question-and-answer skits before the class. Before the exercise is concluded, devote some time searching for fresh and original ways to express the ideas the clichés represent. Make the point that one of the elements of imagination is seeing new relationships, finding new insight into similarities between unlike elements. Seeing the world in a fresh and original manner rather than through the eyes of others underlies imaginative thinking.

▶ *Substitute fresh comparisons for tired language*

1. The teacher may write hackneyed descriptions like the following:

> It was Dina, a vivid girl with lips like cherries and eyes like stars. (This may be continued for several more sentences.)

Students are to write or locate a description of a girl—a description they nominate for merit on the basis of originality and power to evoke genuine imagery. Subsequent exercises may be descriptions of people, actions, scenes in nature, storms, or fires.

2. Another approach uses duplicated hackneyed comparisons with a space beneath each for more imaginative solutions. Here are a few examples. The teacher or a committee of perceptive students can expand the list.

pretty as a picture	working like a beaver
brown as a berry	dumb as an ox
fit as a fiddle	dead as a doornail
dying to meet someone	poor as a churchmouse

[39] Frank Sullivan, "The Cliché Expert Takes the Stand," *New Yorker* (August 31, 1935).

Before completing each of these lessons, direct student attention to their bearing upon an understanding of the function and purpose of imagination. One avoids prefabricated phrases only through the vitality and creative flexibility of the imagination.

TO EXAMINE THE CREATION OF IMAGES

▶ *Give pupils training in visualizing*

During instruction in literature, the teacher may stop to discuss the pictures evoked by a passage. After volunteers have described their images, he relates his own as vividly as possible. What elements do they have in common? Why? How do they differ? Why? Thus, while stressing the importance of visualization in arriving at meaning, he underlines the fact that the same words will produce in no two individuals exactly the same mental picture since no two ever have identical experiences. Such lessons should begin in the junior high school with relatively easy and impelling selections. At each grade level thereafter, teachers plan some training in visualizing,[40] saving for this purpose passages like the descriptions of Africa in Dinesen's *Out of Africa.* Junior high pupils respond well to passages in books of the Gateway English series: *Coping, Who Am I,* and *A Family Is a Way of Feeling.*

Whether in junior high or senior high, the teacher reads the sentences aloud while the students close their eyes and visualize their responses; then they list what they actually see, making quick pencil jottings. Important at this point is the distinction between what a pupil actually visualizes and what he adds as he describes his thoughts. Discussion of these delayed images and of the variety of images among class members should raise a number of questions: How do words—mere guttural sounds or marks on paper—give us meanings? Why do we not all receive identical images? Do some of us have more complete—or more highly colored—images than others?

▶ *Consider sensory imagery of all kinds*

Play short unfamiliar melodies on the phonograph. Ask students to hold the melody in their inner ear to determine whether or not they have a memory for sound images. Can they repeat the sound memory by whistling the melody? Experiment with odors like geranium, lavender, camphor, peppermint, and orange. Do the same with images of touch—velvet, silk, stone, concrete, metal foil—and taste.[41] Much of the reporting will, of necessity, be subjective. Nevertheless, students become interested in sensory imagery and sensory memory, and the interest enlivens oral discussion. Blindfold tests with sight, sound, odor, touch, and taste will show

[40] In the senior high school, the teacher will want to make clear that in reading the nature of the material and the reader's purpose will affect the extent to which one lingers over a passage, seeking clear images. Many times a reader purposely prefers vague imagery. Such a discussion might easily relate to the reading of Bacon's essay "Of Books."

[41] The teacher need not furnish these odors, touches, and tastes. An individual or a committee from among the students can attend to this. Moreover, because this is a study of sensory *imagery,* the actual presence of all the materials is not always desirable. Pupils may imagine and describe these images without the presence of the physical stimuli.

that human beings have developed sight and hearing much more fully than they have the other senses. Light up the imagination through the five senses. Spur the imagination by giving it abundant data with which to work.

SELECTED READINGS

BOOKS

GETZELS, J. W., and JACKSON, P. W. *Creativity and Intelligence: Explorations with Gifted Students.* New York: Wiley, 1962. This book reports research on students from sixth through twelfth grades. The central purpose was to differentiate pupils who were potentially creative from those who were of high intelligence potential. Two groups were selected, those scoring in the top 20 per cent of creativity but not in the top 20 per cent of the intelligence scores and those scoring in the top 20 per cent of the intelligence scores but not the top 20 per cent of creativity scores. The creative pupils, less popular with teachers than the highly intelligent, were not teacher-oriented. For the high intelligence group, there was a high correlation between qualities preferred for oneself and also believed favored by teachers, but for the creative pupils this correlation was negative. The creative pupils wrote stories with more unexpected endings, playfulness, incongruities, violence, and humor; they were less conventionally success-oriented than the high intelligence group and chose more uncommon careers; they also tended to be less respectful of conventional attitudes.

LANGER, SUSANNE K. *Philosophy in a New Key: A Study in the Symbolism of Reason, Rite and Art.* 3d ed. Cambridge, Mass.: Harvard Univ. Press, 1957. Also in a paperback edition: New York: New American Library, 1948. Langer rejects the theory that reason and imagination are two distinct kinds of thinking. To link insight and intuition to unreason and irrationalism is to fail to see that logic and imaginative insight are only two related ways to truth. Chapter 4 deals with the language of discourse and the language of the feelings.

LOWES, JOHN LIVINGSTON. *The Road to Xanadu.* Boston: Houghton Mifflin, 1930. Also in a paperback edition: New York: Knopf Vintage, 1959. Creative synthesis, says Lowes, is the symbolic road on which the imagination voyages through chaos, reducing it to clarity and order.

MC KELLAR, PETER. *Imagination and Thinking.* New York: Basic Books, 1957. The author analyzes the psychological bases of thinking, imagination, creativity, and originality. Originality consists in connection, rearrangement, and fusion of perceptions in a new way. Conditions for creativity include a suitable and worthwhile field for its exercise. The most profitable fields are those leading to the refinement and extension of ideas; a critical attitude also is favorable to creativity. A period of incubation, involving inactivity or a change of activity is also conducive to creativity.

MEARNS, HUGHES. *Creative Power—The Education of Youth in the Creative Arts.* 2nd rev. ed. New York: Dover, 1958. Primarily concerned with creative writing, this book has been listed by the NEA as one of the twenty foremost books in education in recent years.

RICHARDS, I. A. *Principles of Literary Criticism.* New York: Harcourt, Brace & World, 1924. Also in a paperback edition; New York: Harcourt Harvest, 1961. Richards defines the imagination in Chapter 32.

SANTAYANA, GEORGE. *The Sense of Beauty: Being the Outlines of Aesthetic Theory.* New ed. New York: Scribner's, 1936. This book is concerned with the origin of esthetic values and their relation to other aspects of life. Santayana examines the thought that animates both art and science and discusses the uses of imagination.

————. *The Life of Reason, or, The Phases of Human Progress: Reason in Art.* Rev. ed. New York: Scribner's, 1954. Santayana said that he intended this book to be a history of the human imagination. In it, he recognizes the element of imagination in science and relates it to art as part of the human activity called reason.

VINACKE, W. EDGAR. *The Psychology of Thinking.* New York: McGraw-Hill, 1952. The author includes chapters on the imagination, autistic thinking, and creative thinking. This is a sound, insightful book based upon research.

WALSH, WILLIAM. *The Use of Imagination.* New York: Barnes & Noble, 1960. The active analysis of language, especially in the writings of those whose minds are more subtle, complex, and powerful than our own, should be the central aim of education. This would involve, especially in literature, more than the intellect. The whole concourse of mental powers—thought, feeling, purpose, and imagination— would be called into play. Walsh describes an education such as F. R. Leavis has epitomized: "A discipline of thought that is at the same time a discipline in scrupulous sensitiveness of response to intricate organizations of feeling, sensation, and imagery."

ARTICLES AND PAMPHLETS

BARRON, FRANK. "The Psychology of Imagination." *Scientific American.* Vol. 199, No. 3 (September 1958).

————. "The Disposition Toward Originality." *Journal of Abnormal and Social Psychology.* Vol. 51, No. 3 (November 1955).

DE MILLE, R. "The Creativity Boom." *Teachers' College Record,* Vol. 65 (December 1963), pp. 199–209. Three discernible components of creative productivity—temperament, motivation, and intellect—are discussed. Intellectual abilities tend to be associated with creativity (although not highly correlated) at all levels. The author also discusses the development of creativity in the classroom.

GOLANN, S. E. "Psychological Study of Creativity." *Psychological Bulletin,* No. 60 (November 1963), pp. 548–65. This review of the literature covers four areas of emphasis: the use of products as criteria for creativity, the creative process itself, the devising of measures of creativity (and the relationship of intelligence to creativity), and personality.

GUILFORD, J. P. "Creativity." *American Psychologist.* Vol. 5, No. 9 (September 1950), pp. 444–54.

HEIST, PAUL (ed.). *Education for Creativity.* Center for Research and Development in Higher Education, Univ. of California, Berkeley, 1967. This pamphlet provides the reader with an excellent summary of research into creativity, bringing him up to date on recent developments. One conclusion: creative people do not always exhibit unusual academic ability, and unconventional, creative minds are discouraged, often, long before the college years.

HOLLAND, J. L. "Creative and Academic Performance Among Talented Adolescents." *Journal of Educational Psychology.* Vol. 52, No. 3 (1961), pp. 136–47. The relationships among criteria of academic and creative performance and other variables were studied in a sampling of talented adolescents. The results showed that creative performance at the high school level occurs more frequently among students who are independent, intellectual, expressive, asocial, and consciously original and who have high aspirations for future achievement. Students who are persevering, sociable, and responsible and whose parents hold somewhat authoritarian attitudes and values are more frequently academic achievers.

LEVY, N. J. "Notes on the Creative Process and the Creative Person." *Psychiatric Quarterly*. Vol. 35 (1961), pp. 66–77., This article reviews twenty-one references on creativity. The creative potential exists in varying degrees in everyone. Psychological studies reveal that creative people often seek and live with tension and conflict and are more in contact with the unconscious than are other people. The creative potential is directly related to the periods of psychic freedom a person experiences. Each individual responds to the creative urge in his own way.

TORRANCE, E. P. "Must Creative Development Be Left to Chance?" *Gifted Child Quarterly*. Vol. 6, No. 2 (1962), pp. 41–44. Certain teaching techniques increase original thinking. Evidence links decline in creativity to a low value placed on adventurousness and curiosity and a high value placed on promptness and competitiveness.

EVALUATION:

LANGUAGE, THOUGHT, AND FEELING

THE POWER TO EVALUATE

Everyone agrees that evaluation deeply influences teaching, learning, and the curriculum. If evaluation concentrates upon narrow specifics, then narrow specifics are what pupils learn, what teachers teach. If evaluation stresses a broader profile of characteristics and attainments, such as creative thinking or problem solving, then pupils and teachers will emphasize those attainments. Inevitably the curriculum shrinks or expands to the boundaries of evaluation. In anything so crucial, it is important to distinguish evaluation from testing and measurement.

Tests and measurements concentrate on specific, well-defined skills. They have their niche, but what can be tested or measured is by no means the same as what is important to teach. Paper and pencil testing has a highly limited scope; it serves to measure knowledge of spelling and punctuation but fails to cope with power over the spoken word, appreciation of literature, and appropriateness of written style. In comparison with other kinds of evidence, paper and pencil tests must be firmly assigned a relatively unimportant position.

True evaluation includes all desired competencies, not just a few. It concerns the really significant changes in pupil behavior, changes that are major objectives of teaching. Thus evaluation is much more comprehensive than testing or measurement; it is a continuous process, descriptive as well as quantitative, a comprehensive gathering of evidence on the attainment of significant objectives.

Most published tests measure a startlingly narrow range of the English curriculum. There are those who contend that the forms used in aptitude and achievement tests are actually prejudicial to original and creative thinking.[1] Certainly the standardized tests now used measure what is easy to measure rather than what is important. Although increasingly sophisticated instruments are becoming available, most published tests do little with power over the spoken word; reading is usually confined to vocabulary and para-

---

[1] See, for example, B. Hoffman, "The Tyranny of Multiple-Choice Tests," *Harper's*, Vol. 222 (March 1961), pp. 37–44.

graph comprehension; and written "composition" is limited to spelling, usage, and recognizing paragraphs in writing prepared by someone else. The ability to organize one's own ideas and consciously shape them for a clearly defined audience is seldom a part of such tests. Whether or not a student has developed an enduring interest and mature taste in literature is not measured by the narrow scope of most tests. Yet in many schools where these tests are given, teaching is geared to the nature of such tests, and the curriculum shrinks to the boundaries of limited testing. Schools often become so concerned with achievement in one limited dimension—spelling, for example—that negative results are produced in more important dimensions.

To reduce the curriculum in language to such mechanics as spelling, punctuation, grammar, and capitalization is a dangerous oversimplification. These are not the true fundamentals of language. Teachers should be concerned with good habits not only in details but in the larger adaptations, which are much more important. A perspective that begins with recognizing errors, rather than with a more complete picture of the desired accomplishment, seldom reaches the important aspects of ability, such as interest, pleasure in doing or using, clear organization, purpose, and other large integrating patterns of performance.

It is crucial, also, to decide whether to evaluate progress or achievement. Young teachers often have difficulty in assigning grades because they do not distinguish adequately between measurement of progress and measurement of degree to which students meet certain standards, relative or absolute. The measurement of progress requires a pretest-post-test model of evaluation allowing individual assessment of a student over a given time period. Standards require a scale on which to measure the degree to which students perform.[2]

Methods of appraisal should almost always be devised by teachers actually working with pupils, and in some of the procedures the pupil should participate in rating himself. Major attention needs to be placed upon the individual pupil's development—from his competency at the beginning of a school year to his competency at the close of the year. Achievement must be viewed in relation to each pupil's progressively growing powers so that evaluation includes the process of development as well as the end product.

EVALUATING LANGUAGE AS DYNAMIC PROCESS

As a basis for evaluating language as dynamic process, the English teacher may help the student determine whether he has understood the concepts he has studied and whether he can make use of the knowledge and understandings gained.

EVALUATING UNDERSTANDING   Requiring the student to apply a principle to an unfamiliar situation helps him determine whether he understands the im-

[2] J. T. Shaplin, "Practice in Teaching," *Harvard Educational Review*, Vol. 31 (Winter 1961).

plications of any concept. The following writing assignment evaluates not only knowledge of specific and general purpose in using language but also understanding of relationships between purpose and the motives of speaker and listener:

> Select an occasion when someone tried to persuade you to do something you did not wish to do. Analyze the motives of the speaker as you interpreted them and your own for finally agreeing or refusing. Analyze the appeals used. Can you give reasons why the speaker thought they might be successful? Can you think of others that might have been more persuasive? Why? Looking back on the experience, how accurately do you think you judged it at the time?

EVALUATING PERFORMANCE   The ultimate goal of English instruction is skillful performance that makes use of the knowledge and understandings gained— changes in attitudes and behavior extending beyond the classroom. Obviously the individual's approach to this goal cannot be evaluated accurately. Performance can be tested fragmentarily, usually when the student's attention has been directed toward specific ideas and skills; results of these show what he can do when he tries. His typical behavior cannot be so easily assessed. Here self and peer appraisal supplements the teacher's observation. Although never completely objective, all three are important. Self-evaluation, stressed throughout this book, forces the student to consider his own behavior, his typical reaction under most circumstances; it gives him practice in applying the form of assessment he will utilize most consistently all his life.

In all areas of English instruction, the teacher can observe whether the student is beginning to form desirable habits based upon understandings of language as process.

> In the incidental teaching when attention is focused on the skills of reading, listening, writing, or speaking, does the student notice the emotional tone of words? Is he alert to the effectiveness of metaphorical language? Does he discriminate between fact and judgment? Do the number and variety of examples the student, on his own initiative, finds for the bulletin board indicate he is cultivating awareness of the way language works?

Occasional self-checks on performance help students realize the importance of remaining alert to the dynamic qualities of language. Items for two such lists are suggested below. The first is appropriate for intermediate stages of instruction; the second has been used with mature students who have had considerable experience in studying language as process. Unless used for diagnosis, such checklists should, of course, contain only concepts being developed with a class.

REACTIONS TO COMMUNICATIONS

Indicate the response most accurately describing your habitual reactions. This check is not to secure evidence for grading, but to help you probe your thinking; the reasons are more important than the answers.

Am I more likely   *Yes   No   Sometimes*
   to agree with statements of a person I like rather
   than with those of one I dislike?
Reason _____
   to doubt ideas I want to believe rather than
   those I do not want to believe?
Reason _____

REACTIONS TO IMPLICATIONS OF THE DYNAMIC QUALITY OF LANGUAGE

In answering the following questions, write the letter corresponding to the response most accurately describing your habitual performance: (a) always, (b) usually, (c) sometimes, (d) never.

When I use language either as sender or receiver, do I try
   _____ to determine the user's purpose?
   _____ to notice the appeals used?
   _____ to detect the feeling suggested?
   _____ to consider the possible sources of the information?
   _____ to compare alleged facts with others I believe to be valid?
   _____ to consider, in determining the accuracy of the communication, the
         possible bias of sender and receiver?

EVALUATING THE NATURE OF LANGUAGE

The nature of language should be evaluated primarily with respect to the knowledge acquired by pupils and to changes in their attitudes toward English. Improvement in actual use of language does not directly relate to the study of linguistic history, linguistic geography, and the structure of English. Consequently, methods of evaluating student *performance* in language are presented in other sections—oral expression, written expression, usage and sentence structure.

EVALUATING KNOWLEDGE   Students may be asked to classify lists of words according to the languages from which they are borrowed, to indicate key features of the major American dialect areas, or to apply specific transformations to English sentences. What is tested will be determined by what is taught. Because of the examples explored in any study of language, students can easily fail to grasp important generalizations. Thus, it seems important that examinations stress key generalizations rather than details. More important than being able to identify specific Anglo-Saxon words is knowing the general nature of the contribution from Old English; more important than recalling minute distinctions among dialects is understanding how and why these distinctions emerge. If students understand English grammar, they should be able to use it in analyzing and generating sentences. Even so, if understanding the system of English grammar is the major goal, assessment should concentrate on essential understandings (basic patterns, distinction of deep and surface structure, key transformations) rather than on minute details.

EVALUATING CHANGES IN ATTITUDE   An important goal in studying the nature of language is the development of insightful attitudes toward the variety and complexity of the language. Some teachers obtain an indication of possible changes in student attitudes by asking students before and after study to indicate whether they agree or disagree with or are undecided about such statements as the following:

1. It is possible to identify a clear standard of good English used by educated speakers in all areas of the United States.
2. Slovenly speech habits are characteristic of uneducated people.
3. You can tell the quality of a man from the English he uses.

If class study has been successful, attitudes should shift toward recognizing the complexity of linguistic variation.

Less direct methods of revealing student attitudes are also useful on occasion. For example, by asking students to comment freely on the language used by a speaker in a dialect recording, teachers can estimate the extent to which students have developed an awareness of particular dialect features, whether they still see dialect as a barrier to expression, whether they continue to regard dialect as unique and amusing or have begun to develop reasonable tolerance and understanding.

Probably the most impressive indication of growth is the extent to which students display an increasing awareness of language. Do they raise more questions about the origin of English words after their study of linguistic history? Are they more skillful and more sophisticated in using the dictionary? Are they alert to identifying illustrations of ideas studied in class as they read the daily newspaper or watch television? Do they bring pertinent clippings for the bulletin board? Awareness of the richness and variety of the English language is an important goal of the language program, but our success in approaching the goal can be estimated only against the quickened and continued interest of young people.

EVALUATING USAGE AND SENTENCE STRUCTURE

Ultimately the test of a sound program in usage is found in the writing and speech of students. Other forms of evaluation are secondary to such evidence of achievement. There is a place for objective measurement, but that place must be seen within a total perspective.

Nor is knowledge of technical grammar tested to any appreciable degree on college entrance examinations throughout the country, though such examinations are frequently cited to justify the teaching and testing of grammatical principles. Colleges and universities are interested in students' command and use of English. A study of 142 placement tests reveals that only about 2 per cent of the items on college tests deal with problems in grammar, such as the identification of parts of speech, clauses, and phrases.[3] Eighty-six per cent of the tests include no items on technical grammar. Almost 80 per cent of the items measure actual *use* of grammatical forms along with spelling and punctuation. Where it is economically possible, institutions recognize the need for evaluating the writing of applicants and use an essay examination as either all or part of the test. Clearly the colleges believe that the emphasis in evaluation should be placed on ability to use English.

An understanding of the structure of English is an important goal of programs of general education, but it is a goal largely unrelated to a student's ability to speak and write. Teachers must recognize that tests assessing only the student's knowledge of certain English structures, rather than ability to write and speak, are not in themselves valid and sufficient measures of the effectiveness of a total program. Both use and knowledge must be tested in any complete assessment.

The ways of evaluation are many. Some of the more widely used are described in the next section.

Assess application of instruction to writing and speaking

RELY ON CONFERENCES   Personal conferences are helpful, particularly when based on a sequence of several papers. The teacher and student together can identify apparent strengths, determine weaknesses, and plan a program of study. Try planning such conferences at least at the end of every marking period. Many teachers schedule conferences during study interludes when the remainder of the class is occupied.

MAINTAIN WRITING FOLDERS   Permanent files of written work completed over a period of several months are perhaps the best possible source for evaluation. Include tests as well as hurriedly written papers and those composed with care at home. Suggestions for organizing such folders are presented in Chapter Eight, "Written Expression."

SPONSOR SCHOOL-WIDE ESSAY EXAMINATION   Provide for assessing abilities throughout a school on a once-a-year basis by introducing an essay examination for all classes. Standards for evaluation are best established and applied by a committee of English teachers. Ask members of the English department to exchange papers for grading, with each essay read by at least two teachers.

ASSESS RECORDED SAMPLES OF STUDENT SPEECH   Recorded samples of the conversation of individual students may be analyzed independently by the teacher

[3] David M. Litsey, "Trends in College Placement Tests in Freshman English," *English Journal*, Vol. 40, No. 5 (May 1956), pp. 250–56.

or in a conference with students. Save recorded specimens taken early in the year to compare with later samples of speech. The recording of student speech has been used as one way of illustrating for parents the importance of sound language habits.[4]

Provide for objective measurement of particular skills

EVALUATE CONTINUOUSLY WITH DIAGNOSTIC PROCEDURES Recognize that diagnosis and evaluation are two sides of the same coin. The procedures for diagnosing language needs suggested early in Chapter Two, when repeated after a period of time, provide an excellent basis for evaluation.

CONSTRUCT TESTS TO MEASURE APPLICATIONS OF SPECIFIC LEARNINGS Test the kinds of understandings and practices that have been stressed. Some possible kinds of questions are the following: [5]

> Use a phrase or a clause to do the job of the single-word modifier in each of the following sentences:
>> The *bright* boy sat before us.
>> She walked *carefully* across the field.
>
> From the following sets of statements, select the sentence that does not fit the sentence pattern that the other three do. Rewrite the sentence to fit the pattern.
>> Percy and Cedric fought each other.
>> After going to bed, she read her book.
>> Lady Fizzle wrote a sarcastic letter.
>> Kevin talked without asking **permission.**

MAKE JUDICIOUS USE OF PRINTED TESTS Standardized tests provide national norms with which achievements of particular groups may be compared. When the limitations of the tests are recognized, most teachers find their occasional use helpful. However, printed objective tests cannot and do not measure the students' ability to speak or write. Most deal with ability to select appropriate forms or usages, a related skill. In addition, some older tests include sections based on traditional schoolroom grammar, which demand of students a definitional knowledge largely repudiated by recent research in language. In evaluating growth in the use of language, teachers need to select and use tests or sections of tests that measure the important skills that have been stressed in the classroom and to avoid those tests or sections of tests that deal with other skills. Among the widely used printed tests are the following:

Cooperative English Tests Grades 9–12, 13–14. Various forms are available. English usage is tested on the first of three sections; Parts II and III test spelling and vocabulary. Norms are given from grade 7 through college.

---

[4] Elizabeth J. Drake and Jessie V. Enevoldsen, "Solving the Problem of Correct Usage," *Elementary English*, Vol. 35, No. 2 (February 1958), pp. 101–03.

[5] Many other ideas for specific test questions are presented by Robert C. Pooley in *Teaching English Grammar* (New York: Appleton-Century-Crofts, 1957), pp. 184–202.

(Cooperative Test Division, Educational Testing Service, Princeton, N.J., 1960.)

Iowa Tests of Educational Development No. 3, Correctness and Appropriateness of Expression. Grades 9–12. Objective tests present samples of writing and require students to make appropriate changes. May be used as a self-scoring device. Senior high school. (Science Research Associates, Chicago, Ill., 1942–61.)

Essentials of English Tests Revised edition. Grades 7–13. Widely used for diagnosis as well as evaluation. Three forms available. Objective test of 157 items covers spelling, grammatical usage, word usage, sentence structure, punctuation, and capitalization. (Educational Publishers, Inc., Minneapolis, Minn., 1939–61.)

Sequential Tests of Educational Progress Writing Tests. Promising new test with two forms available for levels 4–6, 7–9, 10–12, and college. Uses forced choice method in making students choose the most effective usages and variations. Tests ability to express ideas logically, to organize, to write appropriate language, and to use conventions of language. (Cooperative Test Division, Educational Testing Service, Princeton, N.J., 1956–63.)

Stanford Achievement Tests Spelling and Language. Advanced tests, grades 7–9. Paragraph meaning, language usage, and spelling. (World Book Co., Chicago, Ill., 1941–64.)

EVALUATING LOGICAL THINKING

How does one evaluate growth in the ability to formulate sound conclusions? Ultimately the real test is to be found only in the learners' ability to cope successfully with increasingly mature decisions, concepts, and problems. Too seldom, however, do teachers have the opportunity to see the ultimate fruits of classroom endeavor. Rather, most teachers rely on evaluating growth toward goals established for a manageable period of time—a lesson, a unit, a semester, or a year.

If lesson and unit goals are identified in terms of specific student behaviors, the task of evaluation is relatively clear. Thus, if improvement of ability to see relationships between two literary selections is an objective, the teacher can provide no better way of determining the effectiveness of the learning than by introducing a comparison of two poems or stories that will require students to use their newly developed skills. Similarly, if the elimination of prejudice and bias from students' thinking has received attention, an effective way of approaching evaluation is to examine individual ability to cope in speech or writing with an issue highly charged with emotional bias. Whatever the specific method, the focus will be on assessing a behavior of the learner, not on his acquisition of factual knowledge. Here we are concerned with the refinement of thinking processes that lead to sound conclusions, so we evaluate in terms of process.

To assess long-range goals—those for a semester, a year, sometimes even for an extended unit—teachers find it helpful to have a touchstone against which individual progress may be assessed. Both standardized tests and informal methods have been used to obtain a general assessment of student abilities.

For teachers who like to compare student abilities with clearly defined norms, two standardized instruments are available:

Logical Reasoning Test General Education Series, Grades 10–12. Ten series of test questions requiring judgment and reasoning developed by the Evaluation Staff of the American Education Fellowship, formerly Progressive Education Association. (Cooperative Test Division, Educational Testing Service, Princeton, N.J., 1939–50.)

A Test of Critical Thinking Grades 7–9. Test yields seven scores on qualities: inquiry, openmindedness, ability to relate concepts. May be reproduced. (Mary and Hugh Wood, Eugene: Univ. of Oregon Press, 1951.)

Except for special research purposes, formal instruments of this kind are seldom used more than every two years or so. Like most standardized tests, these are as helpful in diagnosing needs as in assessing growth.

Most teachers find they must rely in part or totally on informal teacher-made tests of student growth. Here the test-teach-retest method may be used over long intervals of time. By collecting evidence of students' abilities early in a year, the teacher later has a touchstone to which he can refer. Many of the learning experiences described in this chapter may be introduced in September, then repeated in modified form in June. By comparing results on two similar exercises, themes, or even recorded discussions, the teacher gains insight into the changes that have occurred in student thinking. Often, too, the students may make their own assessments of growth by comparing their processes and procedures after receiving instruction with those on which they relied before. Often a cumulative file of sample papers and exercises for each student will be of continual use.

EVALUATING IMAGINATIVE THINKING

Evaluation of imaginative thinking cannot be precise. However, checklists and rating scales should be used. Also helpful are collected samples of student creative production and anecdotal records of students' imaginative behavior. The following procedures have been chosen for their feasibility as well as their value.

SELF-INVENTORY FOR PUPILS These self-questionnaires may be signed or anonymous. Although in the latter case they cannot be used for grading pupils, they do assist the teacher and pupils in reviewing instruction and in planning future emphases. The following questions might be typical of such an inventory.

1. Do you use original comparisons in your speech and writing?
   EXAMPLES   The chandelier was like a silvery fountain stopped by an enchantment. Architecture is frozen music.
2. Do you sometimes imagine and foresee what will happen if you take a certain course of action? If so, give an example.
3. Do you often see a relation between two stories, or two poems, or any two selections? If so, give an example.
4. Can you appreciate a story by a writer whose outlook on life is quite different from yours? If so, give an example.

[*Continue with progressively more difficult items.*]

16. Can you feel yourself into a character well enough to interpret that character in dramatics? If so, name a character you could play.
17. Have you ever written a poem or story expressing something you felt quite deeply?

PUPIL SELF-RATING SCALE: IMAGINATIVE INSIGHT   When a scale such as the following is used at intervals throughout a semester, the pupil will become increasingly aware of the situations in which such items occur. Repetition of any evaluation instrument converts it into a reminder, reinforcing the aims of instruction.

EXAMPLES OF IMAGINATIVE INSIGHT	ALMOST ALWAYS	USUALLY	SOME-TIMES	NEVER
1. When I read a story I try to see more than what happens. I look for its theme or its deeper meanings.				
2. I avoid making snap decisions; I let my thoughts hover for a while before settling important matters.				
3. I can *interpret* the meaning of fables and tales like "The Fox and the Grapes."				

[*Continue with progressively more difficult items.*]

11. I avoid clichés and other forms of overused language. *Examples* as luck would have it; the happy pair; heart-to-heart talk.				
12. In most of the things I do at home or at school, I try to be inventive and to see new ways of doing things. Give one or more examples.				

GUESS-WHO QUESTIONNAIRE   This type of appraisal, first developed in research with adolescents,[6] is now used frequently in teaching. Present students with statements describing varying personalities and ask them to designate the

[6] Carolyn M. Tryon, "Evaluations of Adolescent Personality by Adolescents," *Monographs of the Society for Research in Child Development*, Vol. 4, No. 4 (Washington, D.C., National Research Council, 1939).

names of fellow students who best fit these descriptions. (None of the descriptions should be derogatory.) With slow students, the teacher may read aloud and comment on each item.

GUESS-WHO QUESTIONNAIRE ON IMAGINATIVE INSIGHT

Read each question. Each will describe an individual. Whenever you think of someone in this class for whom the description is suitable, write his name in the blank. You may write the names of more than one person in the blank. You may write a person's name as many times as the description fits that person. You may leave any item blank if you feel no one in our class fits this description. Try to be as fair as possible. Do not sign your own name or list yourself [optional].

1. This person has many good ideas in some specialty like art or industrial arts or creative writing. He (or she) does new, original work and does not imitate any other person's work.

2. This person is almost always enthusiastic and full of good ideas. This person has more interesting ideas in an hour than most people have in a week.

3. This person is remarkably able to understand other people and to see why they act the way they do. If this person were an author, his (or her) books would show great insight into the thoughts and feelings of the characters.

[*Continue with progressively more difficult items.*]

11. This person is not stiff or stubborn in his thinking and acting. He (or she) is quick to see through a situation, can change when wrong, and does not find it difficult to "take in" a situation. This person is quick to see when there is more than one side to an argument.

CASTING CHARACTERS   A variation of the "guess-who" method is the following:

Suppose your class was going to produce some plays. Next to the description of each character, write the names of classmates you think best suited for each part. You may choose the same classmate more than once. If you think of several classmates for any part, write each of them down. Do *not* consider acting ability.

1. Some one who is tremendously alive—full of energy and enthusiasm but never confused. This person *controls* his (or her) energy and enthusiasm.

[*Continue with similar descriptions related to imagination.*]

12. Someone who figures out the best way to do difficult things. Someone who is resourceful enough to imagine ways to get things done when no one else can think of what to do.

Although these "guess-who" methods are by no means precise instruments of evaluation, they often draw upon areas of pupil experience to which the teacher does not have access and supplement measures such as those that follow.

COLLECTION OF SAMPLES   Samples of imaginative writing, creative oral productions on tape, and notations about extra-class creativity in stage designing, woodworking, musical composition, new recipes for cooking, projects in agriculture, and many other areas of human imaginative activity may be kept or recorded by students and reviewed by teachers. In the final analysis, these may be the most effective evidence that the school is encouraging and fostering imaginative thinking.

TEACHER CHECKLIST   Checklists like this one should be used two or three times each term rather than just once.

TEACHER CHECKLIST: IMAGINATIVE INSIGHT

Behavior to be observed	*Names of students*

Insightful about other people, socially sensitive

Flexible and fluid in thought; no evidence of rigidity or
  stereotypes in thinking; adaptable but not vacillating

Interpretive; has a bent toward seeing beneath the surfaces of situations

Uses imaginative language; figurative and original language often evident

Inventive in some special area (such as woodworking, sewing, class leadership)

Writes creatively, notably with imaginative qualities

Uses appreciational skills in reading literature; responds to implication, mood, and style

Evaluation continued on p. 411.

UNIT:

POWER OVER LANGUAGE

A WORD ABOUT UNITS

"Power Over Language" is the first of several illustrative units in this book. Units are means of organizing instruction, strategies for teaching and learning. They are a way of bringing together selected aims, ideas, and learning activities, centering them upon some unifying feature such as a theme, a topic, a genre, a single literary work. The term *unit* indicates the generic meaning of these curriculum mosaics—a combining; a joining to produce unity, integrity, and a sense of wholeness. The aims, ideas, and learning activities of a unit must be capable of being combined logically and effectively.

A unit rests ultimately upon a set of basic concepts contributing to and deriving from the fundamentals of a subject, a discipline. The concepts represent the essential knowledge all students should master; determine the selection of all aims, attitudes, appreciations, and skills to be taught; serve as a practical check against irrelevancy or superficiality; dominate the content, learning, materials, and activities of the unit.

There are various kinds of units and various ways of organizing these structural elements of the English curriculum. The most common types are:

a single literary work or plot
> *Macbeth* (See pages 600–08.)
> *The Silent Don* (comprising *And Quiet Flows the Don* and *The Don Flows Home to the Sea*), by Nobel Prize winner, Mikhail Sholokhov
> the Electra story: *Electra* by Sophocles, *Electra* by Euripides, *Mourning Becomes Electra* by Eugene O'Neill

a single author
> Mark Twain
> Isak Dinesen

a literary type or genre
> lyric poetry
> the pastoral
> science fiction
> tall tales and fantasy (junior high school)
> satire (senior high school)

a theme
> "Meeting a Crisis" (See pages 426–34.)
> Who Am I? (one of the units in the Gateway English Series)

The Individual and the Group—typical of a great many units on the individual: Man Against Society, Man Against Himself, Man Against Nature

The Loss of Innocence—typical of many units dealing with the abrasive experiences of growing up in technological societies; sometimes called The Rites of Passage, Growing Up, and What Is Maturity? Materials like *Catcher in the Rye, Huckleberry Finn, Member of the Wedding, A Separate Peace* are used.

"The Consequences of Character" (See pages 659–75.) Note that this unit does not *begin* with a theme; it *achieves* unity from an inception of diversity.

Feelings Are Facts

The Dimensions of Success

Lack of Integrity: *All My Sons, The Little Foxes, Winterset*

a topic

"Power Over Language" (See pages 223–40.)

Justice (one of the units in the Euclid series of teaching units)

Boys and Girls of Other Lands (junior high school)

The Fearful, Strange, and Irrational (senior high school)

Thematic and topical units cannot always be distinguished by their titles, but through examination one discovers that thematic units focus sharply on some concept. For instance, a thematic unit entitled *The Art of Living* might feature Socrates' idea that the unexamined life is not worth living. Thematic units usually deal with the individual, thus having a humanities emphasis. Topical units such as *The Clash of Cultures* and *The Rise of the Anti-Hero* are more frequently oriented to social and anthropological concerns that also provide valid content in English.

In both thematic and topical units, all genres and types of literature are used if their content is relevant to the theme or topic. Literary form and appreciation are not neglected; indeed, they should be taught as needed. However, the content is central. Form is featured in units based upon literary types or genres, even though the study of content is their ultimate purpose. All the various kinds of units are merely different strategies for accomplishing the purposes of English instruction. In all of them, the elements of English—language, composition, literature, thinking, reading, speaking, viewing, and listening—are integrated. Although thematic and topical units lend themselves somewhat more directly to providing for individual abilities among students (different materials can be used, according to the pupil's ability, provided that all the selections focus upon the central theme), even the study of a single work like *Macbeth* can provide for differing abilities. (See pages 606–07.)

Effective unit design reflects an awareness that learning is dynamic, that skills, concepts, and appreciations all develop together. The unit, properly understood, is a strategy for evoking understanding rather than mere recall. There are many ways to organize units—none sacred. In this book, the units begin with a statement of aims and major concepts. Since these must come alive in actual experiences for learners, the next sections deal with launching, developing, and culminating the unit. At the close are suggestions for evaluating the success of instruction and resources for both students and teacher.

Readers interested in the theoretical and precise exploration of unit creation will find a valuable source in Hilda Taba's thorough discussion.[1] They should also consult "A Concept Centered Curriculum, Concepts of Man: A Curriculum for Average Students," bulletin number three of the Euclid Units, as well as all of the Euclid Teaching Units.[2] Another helpful discussion of the unit method, including an illustrative unit on "Back Country America," may be found in *The English Language Arts in the Secondary School*.[3] The Gateway English Series of units, designed for disadvantaged learners, has already been recommended but deserves to be placed with these other recommendations.

POWER OVER LANGUAGE

This is a *resource unit*. It contains ten times as many suggestions as any teacher will wish to use. From these the teacher chooses, shapes, and adds the materials and activities that will constitute his *teaching unit* suited to his particular pupils and their needs. Within the teaching unit, the teacher develops his daily and weekly lesson plans.

A UNIT FOR GRADE SEVEN

Overview   At some point in his life, the educated person stops taking language for granted and becomes aware of it as a marvelous and fascinating phenomenon. The seventh grade is not too early for pupils to become aware of the importance and some of the most significant features of language, which, if understood, make possible increased power over it. This unit is designed to provide seventh-graders with experiences in standing off to take such a look at language. At the close of this unit, when they start to use language unself-consciously again, they should have the basis for greater effectiveness and precision in handling both thought and communication.

All human beings exhibit a fascination with language. Units dealing with language that are less obviously structured than the one described here have proved successful with even the most difficult and disadvantaged classes.[4]

Aims

A unit is intended to produce specific learnings. Out of many possibilities, the aims listed here have been chosen as most basic and attainable for beginners as

[1] Hilda Taba, *Curriculum Development, Theory and Practice*, Chapter 20, "Development of a Teaching-Learning Unit" (New York: Harcourt, Brace & World, 1962), pp. 343–79.
[2] Euclid Teaching Units, Project Upgrade, School District of Aiken County, P. O. Drawer 771, Aiken, South Carolina, 29801.
[3] *The English Language Arts in the Secondary School*, Chapter 4, "Building Instructional Units" (Champaign, Ill.: NCTE, 1956), pp. 67–121.
[4] See, for instance, Herbert Kohl's description of language study in a Harlem school, "Children Writing: The Story of an Experiment," *The New York Review of Books* (November 17, 1966), pp. 26–32; and David Holbrook's book about teaching British children in the lower streams of the secondary school, *English for the Rejected* (Cambridge, England: Cambridge Univ. Press, 1964).

immature as the typical seventh-grade pupil. For gifted pupils, the unit may be enriched and deepened. For slow learning pupils, the unit may be kept simple, crucial activities being repeated often enough to establish only the first two aims listed here. All pupils, whatever their native ability, can profit from a sharper awareness of language as an instrument of thought and communication. Aims are:

1. to become more aware of the importance of language to individuals and to the peoples of the world
2. to realize that human worth is not determined by the language or variation of that language a person uses
3. to note the purposes for which language is used (This will include abuses of language as well as the range of respected and commendable purposes.)
4. to observe how the English language operates: *through words*—how they get their meanings, how they work with other words, the interest that may be found in them; *through statements*—their functions and relationships

Time plan

This unit should last no longer than three weeks. For most seventh-grade pupils examining language *as language* for the first time, a longer period of study could dissipate their initial enthusiasm. However, many of the aims and activities suggested here deserve to be drawn into the curriculum at later periods throughout the year. For instance, the activities for vocabulary building and those showing how words and statements operate are suitable for use in many other units and for individual daily assignments not incorporated into any unit. Inasmuch as power over language is the English teacher's concern throughout the year, this particular unit may be viewed as an intensified effort to feature attitudes and concepts to be reinforced later in many ways and in many situations. For instance, even though the concept of freedom from linguistic snobbery is presented in this unit, a teacher will wish to maintain the pupils' attempts to rise above narrow provincialism. To eradicate suspicion and ridicule of those using a differing language will require more than a single lesson. Thus "Power Over Language," as a teaching unit, may be said to last for three weeks, yet it is only a preliminary focus on content intended to recur throughout the entire secondary-school period.

Launching the unit

Considering the nature of seventh-grade pupils, the teacher will no doubt wish to open the unit with some activity designed to catch pupil interest immediately. The activities listed in this section are intended to contribute to an interest in words and how words acquire their meanings. The teacher and pupils, planning together, may choose one, two, or all of these suggested activities or others similar in nature. Through them the teacher will seek to initiate an interest in language as a whole, an awareness of its importance, and curiosity as to how one might progress to greater power in using language.

▶ *Home assignment: animal intelligence*

Observe some animal—a pet dog, a cat, or some other animal. Try to decide at what points animals reach the limits of their intelligence in understanding vocal sounds. Then answer two questions, writing about one paragraph for each:

What can animals do with vocal sounds?
What can animals not do with vocal sounds?

Be ready to discuss in class: Can animals think, remember, foresee, understand cause and effect?

► *How words come into the language*

The teacher begins by asking pupils to list words that are new this year. Next they list words that were new during the last ten years.

> Since 1960 what words have come into the language and why? Do any words ever drop out? Why? What conclusion can be drawn about language? It is changing, at least in regard to words. Perhaps the deeper structure remains the same? Or does it? Do you suppose pronunciations change?
>
> Coin some mouth-filling words after examining and laughing at Alastair Reid's ideas for new words in *Ounce, Dice, Trice* (16).[5]

► *Records, films, newspapers*

1. The teacher may pass around the class a recent foreign newspaper, magazine, or comic book. Particularly interesting are contemporary publications in Japanese, Russian, or Tagalog (Philippines) with their pictures, comics, and advertising.

2. Play part of a recording of Chaucer's *Canterbury Tales* read in Middle English (17). Help students realize that their present language may someday sound and look as strange. (If the record is not available, pass around a copy of Chaucer in the original.)

3. Show a short film in which a foreign language is used.

4. Use the film *The English Language: Story of Its Development* (18).

► *Home assignment: silence is golden . . . and difficult*

Each pupil is to attempt, from the dismissal of school until the next class hour, to speak as little as possible, holding all talk to an absolute minimum. What difficulties arise? How does one feel not using language? How do other people react? Did anything notable or amusing occur as a result of such unusual behavior for a seventh-grade pupil? What situations arose that made speech absolutely necessary? (During the discussion of these points the teacher is alert for any misuses of the past tense in all verbs used, making notes for future reference but not, at the time, correcting misuses. The improvement of usage in past tense is suggested as a special aim during this unit.)

► *Building an interest in words and language lore*

The teacher begins by calling attention to the odd fact that most words beginning with *sn* are unpleasant (*snap, snort, snicker*) and goes from there to a consideration of thin measly words, fat sober words, and beautiful-sounding words like *golden, luminous, anemone, trombone,* and *murmuring.* Charlton and Helen Laird (3) and Eloise Lambert (4) offer excellent help in developing an interest in words and their books may be used for assignments. Books by Frieda Radke (6), Alfred E. Holt (2), and Ward S. Miller (5) are equally helpful and should be used as the basis of a series of lessons. Particularly amusing to seventh-grade pupils are

---

[5] Most of the units in this book conclude with a list of resources for the pupil. The figures in parentheses following a title refer to the numbers in this list, which gives full bibliographical data as well as information about where to obtain supplementary materials.

the books of Alastair Reid (16), Marcia Brown (8), Norton Juster (12), Eve Merriam (14), and Charles W. Ferguson (9).

▶ *Films and filmstrips*

The following films and filmstrips, and others similar to them, may be used to develop an interest in words and how they operate:

1. *Build Your Vocabulary* (19), a film demonstrating methods of vocabulary building
2. *Adventures in Words* (20), a series of four filmstrips
3. *Words from Many Countries* (21), a filmstrip dealing with word origins and word derivations.

▶ *Class discussion*

What could we study about language that would be worthwhile for us to know? The teacher lists the pupils' suggestions on the chalkboard. He asks students to group together those that are similar. If some of the important aims of this unit are not suggested by the pupils, he may ask leading questions to induce some pupils to suggest necessary concepts to be woven into the design of this unit. The purpose of this activity: to draw the pupils into the over-all planning of the unit and at the same time to focus their suggestions in the direction of significant aims the teacher envisions for the unit.

Developing the unit

No teacher could carry out all the suggested activities and contain this unit within the three weeks' time limit. These suggested activities are all designed to develop the aims of the unit, but each teacher will select those that appeal to him as most appropriate for his classes according to the relative emphasis he places upon the aims previously stated or the aims as modified for a particular class.

▶ *A world without language*

Ask the pupils to imagine a world in which men and women live without the use of language. After several suggestions have been made, read aloud to the class "A World Without Language," chapter one in *The Tree of Language* (3). Let this selection serve a double purpose: to point up the importance of language and to introduce the book, which is to be used throughout the unit. Conclude by having students try to express ideas without words. Give each individual such sentences as these:

> Danger: sharp curve ahead.
> Young people in the seventh grade begin to realize how interesting language is.
> Don't scratch the chalkboard with your fingernail.
> The next day we tied our flatboat to a small island off the east bank of the Mississippi River.

▶ *Oral reports*

Individual pupils may report on the following interesting matters of communication:

scout signs and signalling
Braille
language of the deaf
Morse Code
international communication among
    aviators of different countries
slang
road signs (a good report for a
    slow pupil)
history of writing

strange alphabets: Arabic, Chinese,
    Russian, Egyptian hieroglyphics
Basque: the mystery language
history of the English language
shorthand
musical notation
symbols in mathematics
artificial languages such as
    Esperanto, Walapuk, and ITO
ballet notation (labanotation)

BALLET STUDY

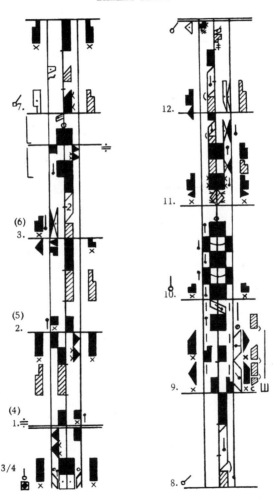

By Regina Lucia. From "Escola de Ballet Dmitri" Niteroi, Brazil. Reprinted by permission of Dance Notation Bureau, Inc., Center for Movement Research & Analysis, 8 East 12th Street, New York, N.Y. 10003.

► *The uses and importance of language*

How many uses of language have you noticed today?

What are some of the purposes for which the peoples of the world use language?

These questions may seem very simple at first, but they are the means of drawing pupils to look at language, its various uses, and its importance. Ask other questions, such as:

> How does language help us to be kind and thoughtful to other people?
>
> How do we use language to make people feel welcome and to express other courtesies?
>
> To what evil or unworthy purposes do some people put language? Illustrate.
>
> Do we use language in thinking? Give examples.
>
> Do representatives of nations use language to bluff one another? For instance?
>
> List all the ways you can recall having used language for the past day or two.
>
> > *Examples* to ask questions, to tease my brother, to persuade my father, to sing while I washed my sweater.
>
> What television programs have you viewed? Besides using language yourself through speech or writing, what reading or listening have you done?
>
> Summarize: Language is important because . . .

► *The abuses of language*

Initiate this activity by alternately reading aloud and telling the incident from *Huckleberry Finn* in which the bogus Duke and King attempt to swindle money from three orphaned girls (chapters 24 to 30). Extend the class discussion to a consideration of some abuses and misuses of language: gossip, slander, libel, perjury, plagiarism, name calling and smear words, and verbalism (using words without knowing their meanings). For seventh-grade pupils, most of these words will be new and will need definition. In some cases, demonstrations help to fix the meaning. For instance, two students may present reports on the early life of Mark Twain, one version to be an uncomprehending reproduction of the material in an encyclopedia (verbalism), the other to be a lively report in the student's own words, in which he shows clearly by an imparting tone of voice and proper emphases that he understands every word he uses.

► *The importance of accuracy and truth in the use of language*

The teacher forms the class into five or six teams of pupils. Each team is to have the same number of players, numbered one, two, three, and so on. The teacher has all number-one players come to his desk to view a somewhat complicated picture. Each number-one player then returns to his group and quietly explains the picture as precisely as he can to player number two on his team. Number two, in turn, explains the picture to player number three. This continues until the final member of the team has received the information. He then jots down what he is going to say and comes before the class to give a description of the picture. The class notes the variations in the presentations of the final members of the teams. Then the teacher holds up the picture for everyone to view and to discuss. Consideration may be given to the problems in the relay wherein language misunderstandings occurred. This game may then be played again, with an attempt at improved precision in the use of language.

One thought-provoking variation of the game—and one that may result in much valuable discussion—can be introduced by a plot between the teacher and one pupil. Without the knowledge of the others, this one pupil deliberately distorts the information. Members of his team will be puzzled as to what has caused them to reach a final description so different from those of the other teams. When the teacher and pupil divulge their duplicity, the occasion has arrived for generalizing about the social importance of integrity in language. Further discussion should explore the seriousness of perjury in courts, the reliability of witnesses, the problems of advertising and propaganda, and the reasons people distort the truth.

▶ *Home assignment: skillful uses of language*

Each pupil is to copy a passage from a book, magazine, newspaper column, or from wherever he chooses. The passage, to exemplify skillful use of language, may be notable for its beauty of phrasing, for its precision, economy, or any other virtue the pupil may wish to feature. A few students may be skillful enough to copy spoken language from a television program, and such contributions if faithfully recorded should also be encouraged. In class the students may read and discuss their choices in groups of five. The best choices from each group are presented to the class, along with comment on the qualities deserving special note.

▶ *How words get their meanings*

Play the game "Substitute." The teacher begins the game by asking students to guess what is meant by the strange new word *gleb* in the following sentences. Students should number from 1 to 10, writing down at each number a guess as to the meaning.

1. There are many different kinds of *glebs* in the world.
2. A *gleb* does not care for music; neither does it dislike music.
3. A *gleb* needs water, but it does not need steak or ice cream.
4. Some *glebs* require a great deal of water; a few *glebs* can go without water for long periods of time.
5. *Glebs* like sunshine, but they do not like snow.
6. We have a *gleb* in this room.
7. *Glebs* are usually colored green.
8. A *gleb* really belongs out of doors, but people often bring *glebs* inside.
9. Sometimes *glebs* do not grow very well, especially if one does not water them.
10. The *gleb* in our room has a red flower.[6]

The game should begin with contexts that are broad and vague. Each sentence, ideally, should sharpen the focus of meaning so that the last sentence occurs in a context making possible success for almost everyone. (It is interesting to note that for some pupils early incorrect guesses often become obstacles to identification as new information appears in subsequent sentences.) The immediate purpose of the game is to determine as early as possible the meaning of the coined word that has been substituted for a word regularly established in the language.

Occasionally, the teacher should employ a word from another language in order to show students that what may sound strange to them has a meaning to other people. For instance, *toalill* (pronounced *tō′ a lĭl*), an Estonian term for house plant,

---

[6] For a note on research employing this method, and suggestions for other classroom applications of it, see Chapter Four, pages 160–61, and Chapter Nine, pages 403–04.

might be used instead of *gleb* in an exercise such as the one above. The ultimate instructional purpose of the game is to lead students to consider how the sounds they call "words" achieve their meanings by association. If they understand the principle of association easily, the teacher may also wish to point out how the principle of reinforcement is added to association. If we use a word correctly, other people respond appropriately; thus our association of sound and meaning is reinforced by the reactions of others.

After the teacher has demonstrated the game, students who understand the ground rules may prepare similar sets of ten sentences for trial with their fellow pupils. The teacher follows the experience by helping the students to generalize from their experience and by extending the principles in four new ways:

1. He asks the students how they learned to associate meaning with words like *jet, nimble, reveille, Brazil,* and new words they have learned recently. What new words have the pupils recently learned in science? In other courses in school? How did they acquire them?

2. He teaches a new word in as many ways as possible, using derivation, root, experiences with the word, dictionary definition, examples in context. In one Wisconsin school, for instance, a mango was purchased as a part of school supplies; the students felt it, smelled it, peeled it, cut it into pieces, and tasted it. They looked it up in the dictionary and the teacher furnished examples of the word's use in literature and other writing. All words are not as concrete as *mango;* yet for words like *incubation, jovial,* and *fickle* an imaginative teacher will turn up a variety of approaches.

3. He reads two passages, one about familiar matters and one about experiences highly unfamiliar to the class. The students are asked to generalize: What happens to our thoughts as we listen to the two passages?

4. He asks questions: What happens to the language of people who leave their own countries and migrate to another country where they must speak a new language? Why do they lose their facility with their native tongue? Do they lose their native language completely? Have any students parents or grandparents or neighbors whom they can interview on this matter?

► *How words can sometimes lose their meanings*

1. To demonstrate that the sound is not the reality, ask the pupils to choose some word. *Pickle, cucumber, participate, capacity,* or *rugged* are excellent choices to offer. Each pupil quietly repeats the word over and over enough times to hear the sound as a strange noise rather than a meaningful word. Many of the students will have the curious experience of stripping the sound almost completely of its meaning.

2. Ask which word in each of these pairs is harder to "un-mean"? Why?

    father *or* atom
    mother *or* fantasy
    home *or* Ceylon
    dog *or* puma

► *Why we do not understand foreign languages*

1. Place on the board this Finnish sentence:

    Temekello on tehtu kullasta.

Why don't we understand this sentence? Then place on the board the translation of the same sentence:

The watch is made of gold.

Why do we understand these words? The teacher must, of course, press beyond the superficial answer that we are not Finnish-speaking people. What is meant by "to learn a language"? What is the best way to learn a foreign language?

2. Summarize these four activities by helping students generalize. Words gain their meanings by the experiences we have with them. We associate meaning with words, but the word, in and of itself, has no meaning. The word is merely a strange sound, or mark—but a strange sound that becomes familiar and meaningful to those who use it in any language family, in any language system. *Temekello* means *watch* to five million people who call their native land "Suomi." We call it "Finland."

▶ *Using appropriate language*

The teacher presents the concept that people who speak differently from us should not be ridiculed, that a man's worth is not measured by the way he speaks his language. Anecdotes and illustrations will help clinch these points.

The teacher follows this by introducing the idea of varieties of usage and illustrating the realities of community pressure for conventional usage, for example— Why would we be surprised if the President of the United States, in a television broadcast, said, "We ain't gonna let no gol-durned furriners hog-tie us"? Pupils can present impromptu skits in which applicants being interviewed for desirable positions are disappointed in their ambitions because of insensitivity to the prevailing conventions of usage.

To avoid the scattering of attention that follows too many language considerations, the teacher should next choose a single element of usage and focus attention on its relation to accepted conventions in language. (For this unit, we have suggested attention to the appropriate use of past tense.[7])

▶ *Jabberwocky sentences and the basic sentence patterns*

1. The teacher reads or presents "Jabberwocky" by Lewis Carroll and asks the students to help him create a few jabberwocky sentences on the chalkboard. He follows this with an explanation of simple subject and predicate. With the students' help, he expands sentences from "skeleton" form, with the student suggesting ways to build up the sentence:

alligator   ate
The *alligator ate* the scientist.
The bright green *alligator* with the sorrowful eyes *ate* with relish the rotund
    scientist who had fallen asleep on the river bank.

These extended sentences may be plotted out on the chalkboard. After each extension, the modifying words may be erased, leaving again only the simple subject and predicate to be amplified in some new way, for example:

The tender-hearted lavender Martian *alligator ate,* as daintily as possible, the
    artichokes brought to him each day by Miss Pickerel, the eccentric tourist
    from Earth.

[7] A complete description of how this might be carried out is presented on pages 709–10.

2. Next, have each student write a brief anecdote using only nouns and verbs. Have some of these read aloud; despite the restriction, the sentences should communicate. Point out that subjects and predicates are the necessary elements of communication in most writing and speaking.

3. When the concepts of subject and predicate are firmly established, the teacher next presents jabberwocky sentences for analysis:

> The saleb tringes tributhed on the flust.
> Arthusta was emfressed by the bibblement.

First let students practice reading sentences aloud, noticing how the pattern invites certain intonations although no specific meaning is conveyed; then guide them to note the natural clues within the sentences, such as the groupings of words and the specific signal words and word endings; from these activities draw some useful conclusions about the way English sentences operate.

4. Conclude by presenting models of the four most common patterns of the English sentence:

> *Pattern I*   John eats.
> *Pattern II*   John eats onions.
> *Pattern III*   Onions are roots.
> *Pattern IV*   Onions are good.

After giving several examples, ask pupils to use each pattern in devising sentences to be given orally. When all four patterns have been sufficiently illustrated, pupils may write several sentences imitating each. The purpose here is to introduce the concept of common patterns of the English sentence.

Technical terminology identifying different kinds of complements need not be given.

A final test of comprehension might be one in which students write jabberwocky sentences to illustrate each pattern, for example:

> *Pattern I*   The shruftsa blumps griggled for their reetsnup.
> *Pattern II*   The kulshind, gargy and stooble, treeped his snipar.
> *Pattern III*   The eertsin was a blik goober.
> *Pattern IV*   An eborsch is neeby ruggy.

The teacher should help students use real words for the linking verbs as well as for determiners, prepositions, and pronouns.

To supplement this activity, suitable drills from available texts may be used with superior classes. However, sentences that include expletives, inverted word order, or understood subjects should be omitted. These tend to confuse the pupils and should be introduced at some other time or in a later grade.

▶ *Explorations in other languages*

1. The pupils may read the sections on language families in Franklin Folsom's *The Language Book* (1). The teacher then helps them read very simple materials, such as fables, brief parables, jokes, or paragraph anecdotes in French, Spanish, German, Portuguese, Chinese, Russian, and Latin, or as many of these as possible. The purpose is not to teach the foreign language but to help pupils explore, in a preliminary manner, each of the major languages studied in schools.

2. Teachers find that if pupils learn only a few common expressions, such as the words for *good morning, I thank you,* and *good-by,* they begin to take an interest in the foreign tongue. Interesting features may be pointed out as the teacher

wishes, for example—the Spanish say *"dar* un paseo," but is it any stranger to *give* a walk than to *take* a walk? Word order, also, is different in various languages; adjectives, for instance, come after the noun in French and Spanish but before the noun in English and German. Some languages identify all nouns as masculine, feminine, or neuter. Germans must remember that *horse* is neuter, Spaniards that *sacrifice* is masculine, Frenchmen that *venison* is feminine. For *rhubarb, atom, brick* and all the other nouns, these people must remember a classification that, fortunately, speakers of English do not use in their system.

The teacher may present as many of these linguistic contrasts as will hold the interest of the pupils. He may even present the need for an international language, along with examples of Esperanto, Basic English, ITO, Walapuk, and Pidgin English. Several of the books recommended as supplementary materials for this unit contain excellent discussions and may be assigned for reading. See especially Laird and Laird (3).

3. The teacher may conclude this exploration of other languages in a number of interesting ways. The pupils may be formed into committees or pairs to investigate languages spoken and read in homes represented in the school; to get information on languages taught in high schools to which they will go; to visit the library to find what newspapers, magazines, and books in other languages are available; to read in books and encyclopedias about the languages of the world and how widely used each language is; to make a language map of the world; to invite language teachers to come to class to describe their languages; to invite people who use other forms of communication—such as Morse Code, Braille, sign language—to visit the class.

Teach the class a few words English has adopted from other languages, such as the following:

FRENCH WORDS AND EXPRESSIONS USED IN ENGLISH

à la mode	de luxe	naïve
au revoir	élite	nom de plume
bon voyage	ensemble	rendez-vous
chic	faux pas	repartee
coiffure	fiancé(e)	R.S.V.P. (*Répondez s'il vous plaît*)
coup d'état	finesse	sabotage
débris	gourmet	tête à tête

ENGLISH WORDS DERIVED DIRECTLY OR INDIRECTLY FROM SPANISH

adobe	burro	coyote	loco	patio
avocado	bronco	calaboose	lasso	pronto
adios	canyon	flamingo	lariat	rodeo
alfalfa	cinch	hoosegow	mustang	savvy
barbecue	corral	hombre	mosquito	vamoose

Individual pupils may also interview students or adults who have come to the United States from other countries. What language difficulties do they recall? What sounds, words, and ways of expression were or are difficult for them?

Examine the preface in 41 languages in *English Through Pictures* (7).

Pupils may interview social studies teachers on the topic of language. How has history been influenced by the existence of so many languages? In closed societies with rigid class structure, what part does language play in keeping people in their class? In open societies such as are now developing in some parts of the world, what part does language have in educating people?

► *Semantics* [8]

The teacher aims at these insights:

A word may have several meanings.
Word meanings are affected by experience, time, and context.
Words are not mechanical parts like sections of an erector set; rather they are
  like notes of music affected by their surroundings.
A statement may have diverse meanings.

1. *Problem*   To show how the same word may have more than one meaning and
depend upon its "neighbors" (context) or the occasion when it is used. Ask students to use, in as many different meanings as possible, words like these:

run, slip, rich, box, date, table, break, glasses, crop

Play guess-the-word for a few minutes several days in a row. A student says, "I am
thinking of a word of four letters, beginning with *d;* it can be eaten, it is a way to
keep track of time, and some boys ask girls for them." Or, "I am thinking of a word
beginning with *c;* some people carry one when they ride horseback; farmers gather
them; a chicken has one; sheep do it to a grazing ground."

2. *Problem*   To realize that word meaning, a product of experience, differs with
each individual. Tell the story of the six blind men and the elephant, or the story of
the fifth-grade girl who read her older brother's world history book and gained the
impression that the French Revolution wrote insulting letters to the American Revolution. ("The French Revolution corresponded roughly with the American Revolution.") Discuss with students how words fool us because we have varying associations with them. Show the film *Do Words Ever Fool You?*

Or discuss how one might explain a term such as "squeeze play" or "bunt"
to a Hindu visitor to the school, who is not acquainted with sports or American
customs.

3. *Problem*   To become more aware of the fact that the word is not the thing.
Ask students to write a short paragraph telling why they think a rocket is called a
"rocket" or a puzzle a "puzzle." In the discussion following, point up the fact that
no necessary connection exists between the word and what it represents. Compare
with other symbolism that may seem more concrete: Could red indicate "go" just as
well as "stop"? What do people in other countries call "rocket" and "puzzle"?

4. *Problem*   To appreciate the fact that in the course of time many words change
their meanings. Explain to students how these words have changed.

	FROM	TO
boor	peasant	rude, ill-bred person
knave	boy	rascal
villain	serf	scoundrel
queen	wife, woman	king's wife

Ask if *juvenile, teen-ager,* and *adolescent* seem to be changing.

5. *Problem*   To see how situations change the meaning of statements. Ask the
pupils to imagine varied situations in which the following statements might have
different meanings:

[8] The teacher will find many useful suggestions on this topic in Chapter One, "Language as
Dynamic Process."

Isn't he a sweet child?

Everyone noticed Mrs. Doolste's Easter hat.

We have come to scalp you.

You must trust me.

Her oral report was quite remarkable.

6. *Problem*   To discriminate among various classifications of statements. What is the difference between these two sentences?

Dover is the capital of Delaware.   (fact)

Dover is the most interesting of all the state capitals.   (opinion)

In similar fashion, present the pupils with pairs of statements that are literal and metaphorical, general and specific, abstract and concrete, formal and informal, in terms of usage. Ask: What value can come to us from noticing these distinctions in language?

7. *Problem*   To see how sentences depend upon context for meaning. Present several sentences alone and then in context. Examples:

Sentence   The powder had to be used carefully.   (face powder? dynamite? tooth powder?)

Sentence in context   On this journey, Livingston's life depended upon the game he was able to shoot. Also, in the jungle, he had to travel as lightly as possible. *The powder had to be used carefully.* The guns, alone, were heavy enough.

Sentence   He was blind.

Sentence in context   Brownie's first memory was of his mother's furry body and of his five squirming, hungry, helpless brothers and sisters. He weighed about a pound. *He was blind.* He could not walk, and he could not stand. He looked more like a rat than a dog.

After a few illustrations the teacher may set students to searching in books for particularly good examples.

The lesson may be concluded by dictating several sentences capable of various interpretations. The students compose paragraphs containing the sentences and then compare versions to see how much the sentences vary in meaning from one context to another. Here are several sentences for such an exercise:

It opened once again.

"We can't even eat him now," she wailed.

They took their time about the licking.

The lady patted him on the head.

► *The distinction between human worth and language*

The teacher may place on the chalkboard these two phrases:

people who are well educated

people with little education

He then asks: Which group is more likely to respect rather than make fun of the differences in English as it is spoken in Australia, Britain, Scotland, Canada, and the United States? As it varies in our own country from New England to the South, the Midwest, Texas, and Hawaii? As it varies in the use of social dialect? (Tapes and records may be played.) The teacher may then read aloud from the writings of Mark Twain to present the goodness of heart of such characters as Huck Finn, Aunt

Polly, and Jim, all of whom use nonconventional patterns of the English language. Tapes and recordings of Scottish, Australian, Cockney, Pidgin, Cajun, and other ways of speaking English may be played.[9]

Culminating experiences

1. Select an effective speaker or actor, on television or in real life, to observe. The pupils are to note, insofar as possible, the qualities the effective speaker manifests. If a telecast or kinescope can be watched during class time by teacher and pupils together, the lesson will be even more convincing. The teacher should help pupils see some of the important attributes of a good speaker:

> usage that does not distract the attention of the listener
> clear enunciation and articulation
> ability to cleave to the point without too much qualification, modification, and random associations
> moderation in speed of speech—neither too slow nor too rapid; variation in rate and volume
> vitality—involvement; energy of speech
> sincerity that makes the words come more easily
> poise from inner security and confidence
> a resonant voice, varied in pitch, characterized by an imparting tone
> a stable personality, free from timidity, self-depreciation, contentiousness, egocentrism

Discuss how one may gain these attributes and improve upon them. Would the students add any more to these? Which ones do they consider the most important?

2. Plan a program for another class, an assembly, or a public meeting; it might be called "The Miracle of Language." Let groups and individuals prepare dramatizations, recitations, and tableaux. Use recordings and film slides. Have an announcer open the program, provide spoken commentary and continuity, and close the program. Ideas for the program should evolve from the aims of the unit. A brief list of suggestions for such a program follows:

> A double reading: A student reads some passage twice, first in a garbled manner and with many inaccurate and misplaced words, second in a clear and lucid version.
> One student argues a point with fallacious reasoning. Three other students point out the fallacies.
> Contests in which students find definitions in dictionaries, find suitable substitutes for trite expressions, answer questions over important points taught during the unit.
> Dramatizations of situations in which language is used for thinking, for being considerate of others, for communicating important messages or ideas.
> Some of the best oral reports listed on page 227 of this unit.
> Brief talks on "What I Want to Remember from this Unit."
> *Who Makes Words?* (film) (22)
> *Documents of America, George Washington's Farewell Address* (record, NCTE, Number EAD–4)

[9] Evelyn Gott, "Teaching Dialects in the Junior High School," *English Journal,* Vol. 53, No. 5 (May 1964).

Evaluation

The most important results of this unit concern attitudes and choices of behavior; these do not lend themselves easily or fully to paper and pencil tests. The development of an interest in studying a foreign language, increased reading skill in relating words and statements to their contexts, wiser judgment of human worth regardless of the use of language, increased effectiveness in oral communication—these are some of the important outcomes that may operate in situations beyond the teacher's province. However, although the complete scope of evaluation is not possible, the teacher should gather as much evidence as is available. The following suggestions are offered with the restrictions of evaluation fully acknowledged.

▶ *List of learnings and a paragraph of recommendation*

Ask the pupils to list the most important new learnings they have gained from this unit. After making the list, the students are to write a paragraph (or, if they are gifted pupils, several paragraphs) recommending improvements and changes in the unit before it is taught again to the next class. The teacher then assesses the extent to which the important concepts of the unit have been grasped by the pupils.

▶ *Checklist of attitudes*

Ask pupils to check anonymously lists such as the following, perhaps by drawing stick figures in the appropriate columns. Student committees may collect the lists, tally the answers, and present the findings to the class and the teacher for a discussion on the strengths of the unit and ways to improve it.

MY POINT OF VIEW

	Where I stand		
The view	TRUE OF ME	SOMETIMES TRUE OF ME	NOT TRUE OF ME
As a result of this unit, I am less likely to dislike a person who speaks with an accent different from mine.			
As a result of this unit, I have some definite plans for ways I can improve my speaking in everyday communication. For example_____			
As a result of this unit, I am now paying more attention to the "neighbors" of words in the reading I do outside the English class.			
As a result of this unit, I am paying more attention to the "neighbors" of sentences in the reading I do outside the English class.			

[The teacher tries to assess the ten most important attitudes or concepts he hoped to establish during the unit.]

▶ *Completion test*

Items such as the following will give approximate samples of the extent to which some of the aims of this unit have been accomplished.

WHAT I HAVE LEARNED

1. I can give examples of the differences between statements of opinion and statements of fact:
     Opinion_____
     Fact_____
2. Telling lies under oath is called_____
3. Three effective ways that good talkers hold their listeners' attention are
     a.
     b.
     c.
4. The *context* of a word or a statement is_____
5. Three ways I can improve my use of written language are
     a.
     b.
     c.
6. One way English and Spanish are unlike is_____
7. In one paragraph, explain why telling lies under oath (see question 2, above) is considered such a serious crime by the courts.

▶ *Conventional use of past tense*

The real test of effectiveness in this skill may be determined by observing the pupils' use of past tense in their everyday speech and in their writing for other classes as well as for English. However, some testing may be used to determine whether or not fewer errors appear than occurred previous to instruction. Oral tests, in which the pupils listen to the teacher read a series of sentences, some standard and some nonstandard, will furnish better insight into this problem than do paper and pencil tests. As the teacher reads each sentence, the pupils mark S (for standard) or NS (for nonstandard) after the number corresponding to the sentence the teacher is reading aloud. See pages 124–25 for a full description of this method.

MATERIALS AND RESOURCES FOR STUDENTS

For the purpose of this unit, the teacher should have available in the classroom several copies of some of the following books or of similar books recently published. Books dealing with language are appearing more and more frequently on publishers' lists.

1. Folsom, Franklin. *The Language Book.* New York: Grosset & Dunlap, 1963.
2. Holt, Alfred E. *Phrase and Word Origins.* New York: Dover, 1962.
3. Laird, Charlton and Helen. *The Tree of Language.* Cleveland: World, 1957.
4. Lambert, Eloise. *Our Language.* New York: Lothrop, Lee & Shepard, 1955.
5. Miller, Ward S. *Word Wealth Junior.* New York: Holt, Rinehart & Winston, 1960.
6. Radke, Frieda. *Word Resources.* New York: Odyssey Press, 1955.

7. Richards, I. A., and Gibson, Christine. *Spanish Through Pictures*. New York: Washington Square Press, 1950; *French Through Pictures*. New York: Washington Square Press, 1960; and *English Through Pictures*. New York: Pocket Books, 1952.

SUPPLEMENTARY BOOKS

8. Brown, Marcia. *Peter Piper's Alphabet*. New York: Scribner's, 1959.
9. Ferguson, Charles W. *The Abecedarian Book*. Boston: Little, Brown, 1964.
10. Funk, Charles Earle. *A Hog on Ice and Other Curious Expressions*. New York: Harper & Row, 1948.
11. Jacobs, Frank. *Alvin Steadfast on Vernacular Island*. New York: Dial Press, 1965.
12. Juster, Norton. *The Phantom Tollbooth*. New York: Random House, 1965.
13. Kay, Helen. *How Smart Are Animals?* New York: Basic Books, 1962.
14. Merriam, Eve. *It Doesn't Always Have to Rhyme*. New York: Atheneum, 1965.
15. O'Neill, Mary. *Words, Words, Words*. New York: Doubleday, 1966.
16. Reid, Alastair. *Ounce, Dice, Trice*. Boston: Little, Brown, 1959.

RECORDINGS, FILMS, AND FILMSTRIPS

For complete addresses of suppliers of films and recordings, see the bibliography on pages 729–59.

17. Chaucer selections from the *Canterbury Tales*. Numerous recordings are available in Middle English.
18. *The English Language: Story of Its Development*   film, Coronet Films
19. *Build Your Vocabulary*   film, Coronet Films
20. *Adventures in Words*   filmstrip series, Long Filmslide Service
21. *Words from Many Countries*   Test-Film Division, McGraw-Hill
22. *Who Makes Words?*   film, Coronet Films

MATERIALS AND RESOURCES FOR TEACHERS

BOLINGER, DWIGHT L. "The Life and Death of Words." *Reader and Writer*. Ed. by Harrison Hayford and Howard Vincent. Boston: Houghton Mifflin, 1954, pp. 435–45.

BOMBAUGH, C. C. *Oddities and Curiosities of Words and Literature*. New York: Dover, 1961.

LAIRD, CHARLTON. *The Miracle of Language*. Cleveland: World, 1953. Also in a paperback edition: New York: Fawcett, 1957.

LAMB, MARION. *Word Studies*. Burlingame, Calif.: South-Western Publishing Co., 1963.

MATHEWS, MITFORD. *American Words*. Cleveland: World, 1959.

NCTE. *Ideas for Teaching English, Successful Practices in the Junior High School*, section on vocabulary. Champaign, Ill.: NCTE, 1966.

MELCHIOR, THOMAS E. "A Language Unit in the Junior High School." *English Journal*. Vol. 56, No. 6 (September 1967), pp. 858–62. This article offers many excellent ideas for classroom activity. The unit illustrates the newer emphasis upon "language as content" or "the miracle of language" now developing in the English curriculum.

SMITH, DORA V. *Communication, The Miracle of Shared Living.* New York: Macmillan, 1955.

WEEKLY, ERNEST. *The Romance of Words.* New York: Dover Publications, 1961.

ZAHNER, LOUIS. "The Teaching of Language." *English Journal.* Vol. 44, No. 7 (November 1955), pp. 443–45, 458.

———. "What Kinds of Language Teaching." in Edward J. Gordon and Edward S. Noyes, eds., *Essays on the Teaching of English.* New York: Appleton-Century-Crofts, 1960.

TWO

UNDERSTANDING AND COMMUNICATION

SIX

LISTENING AND VIEWING

*The spoken word belongs half to him who speaks,
and half to him who hears.*

FRENCH PROVERB

PERSPECTIVE

Listening is the communication skill used most often in daily living; in all face-to-face discourse—social, business, professional—the ability to listen with appropriate response is a valuable asset. Recognition of the part listening plays in the development of each individual and in the transmission of culture points up its social and historical significance. Realization of its role in the dissemination of ideas and values makes critical listening important for all. The necessary skills and behavioral attitudes should receive attention in the classroom. A realistic program can be built on two understandings: listening is a complex process demanding specific attitudes and skills; television is an influential medium affecting the entire society and individuals within that society, even those who spend little time with it.

Certain attitudes and practices are basic to effective listening. The following summary served as a classroom poster in one school's crusade to improve the audience for assembly speakers.

GENERAL HABITS OF THE GOOD LISTENER

In every listening situation
    he knows why he is listening.
    he tries to avoid distractions.
    he looks at the speaker.
    he concentrates, adapting to the speaker's rate.
    he is willing to share responsibility with the speaker.
In regard to the communication he tries
    to determine the speaker's purpose.
    to remember important points.
    to note reasons for illustrations and examples.
    to understand fully before he judges.
In his evaluation he tries
    to relate the speaker's points to his own experience and interests.
    to determine why he agrees or disagrees.

Although these characteristics were chosen as necessary for the listener in formal situations, they are equally desirable for participants in the give and take of everyday business and social intercourse.

The Listening Process

The listening process is manifestly complex. It requires a high degree of concentration not only to perceive the relationships among facts, ideas, opinions, and illustrations, but also to detect all the nuances of language that denote tone and feeling. The process has three aspects: comprehending, interpreting, evaluating.

COMPREHENDING LITERAL MEANING Competence in listening requires the ability to direct attention first to literal meaning. What exactly do the words say? What is the fundamental meaning that anyone who understands the language will grasp? Comprehending the literal presents three problems:

> understanding the precise meaning of each assertion
> following the sequence of ideas
> sensing relationships: determining the central idea; distinguishing between the main and supporting ideas; perceiving the relation of each part to the others and to the whole; recognizing the scheme of organization

INTERPRETING THE COMMUNICATION Understanding language as dynamic process makes us aware that almost any communication is subject to various interpretations. The same words may assume widely divergent meanings for different persons. Aware that everyone's viewpoint is colored by his particular experience, we try for objectivity as we attempt to identify the speaker's field of perception. What does his use of language seem to indicate about him? What is his real purpose? In interpreting we try to

> discern the connotative force of words
>> distinguish emotionally-toned from reportorial words
>> determine the level of abstraction
> recognize type of statement
>> differentiate between factual and judgmental statements
>> perceive the degree of bias in judgments
>> sense the relative importance of the general versus the concrete
>> notice extension of meaning through the use of figurative language
> arrive at total meaning
>> recognize underlying assumptions
>> realize implied meanings
>> make generalizations warranted by information and arguments
>> identify the speaker's purpose as revealed by his attitude toward his subject and his audience.

EVALUATING THE COMMUNICATION   An honest evaluation demands an inquiring attitude concerning the worth of the communication, an attempt to discover the reality behind the language. Agreement or disagreement is not enough. Aware of his own bias, the listener uses his powers of critical analysis to make a rational appraisal. Recognition of the fact that often this can be only tentative, since he is not in a position to know all the facts, is an important aspect in learning to think objectively. So, too, is awareness of the need for checking, to the limits of available resources, the reliability and possible bias of the speaker.

The competent listener does not consider these aspects consecutive steps, for they take place, in part, concurrently, and one influences others. Purposeful listening is often hard work: it demands concentrating to avoid loss of meaning that may well be irretrievable; it demands assimilating the significance of many stimuli at almost the same time. These requirements make the mastery of this means of intake worthy of anyone's mettle.

The Effect of Emotion on Judgment

Listening for information, the concern of this chapter, is essentially a logical process. However, in situations where the information is crucial, what we hear and how we interpret what we think we have heard are almost never governed wholly by reason, for we bring to the current experience the weight of our past, with its emotional load of self-interest and bias. Emotion, if we are able to evaluate it in our own thinking and in that of others, does not necessarily prevent our arriving at valid conclusions. We can all recall speakers whose restrained emotion enhanced an argument based on indisputable facts; we can recall others whose emotional involvement seemed to foster total disregard for reality and logic. When listening is reinforced by the visual, we must be constantly aware that pictures can generate emotion and thus have tremendous persuasive potential. Even when a cameraman's purpose is not to persuade but to make a picture that will sell, even when the only purpose of those selecting pictures for a television broadcast is to prepare an effective program, the persuasive effect is there. "A picture is worth a thousand words" contains a psychological truth and television demonstrates it repeatedly.

THE INFLUENCE OF TELEVISION

Inherent in all media of communication is the capacity for wielding considerable power. The nature of each medium determines the type and size of audience it can create and therefore the kind and amount of influence it can exercise. The age of print lasted for centuries. Although its public continually expanded, it remained selective and small by today's standards. The influence of newspapers was overt and localized; the majority of the people were conscious of the power of the press only when it was exerted in specific instances concerned with particular issues or personalities. The adjustments to change required of those living in this age were slow and gradual, sharply contrasting with the immediate adaptability demanded of today's adults, propelled abruptly as we have been into the era of electronic communication.

Radio was at first considered more likely to succeed as a gadget for hobbyists than as an instrument useful to society. Even after earphones were no longer necessary—some time after 1924—listening did not begin to be popular until radio writers learned how to write for the ear. Radio acquired stature as a newscaster in the period from 1933 to 1945. External events made the public eager for news, and radio met their demands. It not only established an effective style and format for newscasts; it provided commentators to interpret daily events. Important as radio is in its own right, in the development of communication it is significant mainly as the bridge between print and television.

The power of television lies in its immediacy, its intimacy, and its persuasiveness, its ability to mold a vast and diverse audience into cohesive form. We shall consider television as medium, as shaper of environment, and as newscaster.

TELEVISION AS MEDIUM   Among those who have written about the media of communication, Marshall McLuhan has made one of the most distinctive contributions. Over the last decade he has made an intensive study of media in relation to historical change. His basic conclusion: a radical change in the dominant medium of communication is the primary initiating force behind *human* change. Two of his recent books are *Gutenberg Galaxy,* showing how the invention of movable type shaped Western culture, and its sequel, *Understanding Media: The Extensions of Man,* showing how television is shaping the culture of today.[1] The first book was more widely accepted, probably because it is easier to examine the past than to predict the future. McLuhan's conclusions stir controversy but cannot be lightly dismissed.

The tone and style of *Understanding Media* irritate some readers. Probably this was McLuhan's intention. Impatient with educators slow to accept the aid he thinks electronics can give, he has assumed the role of gadfly to the teaching profession. He alienates many by the comprehensive influence he accords television, for the aspects of experience he thinks shaped by it are legion. But irritation should not blind us to his significant insights nor tempt us to turn his deductions into hard generalizations. Nor should rejection of some of his themes prevent us from accepting others. For example, even if we cannot grant television the influence he claims, our common sense applied to our observations over the last few years should convince us it is a force to be reckoned with. McLuhan has turned attention previously directed to aspects of the message to the medium itself. We think he has something im-

[1] Marshall McLuhan, *Gutenberg Galaxy* (Toronto: Univ. of Toronto Press, 1962); *Understanding Media: The Extensions of Man* (New York: McGraw-Hill, 1964).

portant to say to teachers. Three ideas from his writings will help students understand medium as distinct from message.

"All media are sense-extensions." All significant and radical inventions, from wheel to spaceship, have extended man's powers. All media have increased the power of his senses. One of the earliest in the electric age, the telephone, widened the range of voice and ear. Radio magnified this range, multiplying the number of persons and locations as well as increasing the distance the voice could reach; because it encouraged visualization, it made listening more enjoyable and effective. Electronics created the instant age, making all news current and universally available; television, because it stimulates multisensory perceptions—aural, kinetic, visual—increases the viewer's pleasure.

"The content of a new medium is the preceding one." All media inherit an established environment and public. Each, because it is new, imitates the one that preceded it. Each medium tries to find the most effective mode of operating. This mode, when found, will in its turn affect the environment because it will create a new public. The first television newscasts were primarily listening experiences; they followed the pattern set by radio, adopting some of its sound effects; they differed from radio only in that one could watch the speaker. The industry soon learned, however, that to compete with the established media a more stimulating format had to be devised—hence, a period of experimentation with news related by several reporters in different areas, a few items illustrated by pictures. Today, pictures dominate newscasts and television seems to be satisfied with the audience the camera has created. Concerted effort by those who do not automatically accept television's output is needed to convince the industry that it is not meeting the needs of viewers.

"The medium is the message." As different media appeared, they either changed the environment (radio) or created a new one (television); the consequences of that change are more important than the messages transmitted. McLuhan does not imply that messages are unimportant. For example, the consequence of the fact that today millions know a little about a multitude of complex situations and problems is far more significant than the sum of their information. Technology, social conditions, and the nature of man—all interrelated—bring changes that affect the physical environment, but the attitude of the public toward these changes shapes the social environment. Television did not create our problems; it merely revealed their magnitude and urgency. Our reaction to this knowledge produced the harsh climate we have today.

McLuhan grants the communication medium a more basic and far-reaching influence than the preceding explanation may suggest. He believes it changes man's perception of experience and the manner in which he thinks: type fostered the linear, structured—introduction, development, conclusion—message; television, by using repetition, juxtaposition, overlap, and disjunction, fosters bits-and-pieces communication requiring the recipient to put it together. Thus the printed page encourages sequential thinking; television, configurate. It is easy to recognize a degree of truth in this observation, for it is supported by the difference we know exists between written and oral language—a difference our experience with printed material and broadcasts substantiates. It is difficult to forsee a time when both kinds of thinking will not be important.

Marshall McLuhan has embraced this trying age and all its works. Among the many voices of doom he sounds an optimistic note. If we cannot respond with enthusiasm, we can at least respond thoughtfully. His view is bewilderingly comprehensive, however, for he takes the whole cultural sphere as his province. McLuhan predicts a revolution of the mind comparable to those we have experienced in science and technology, one that will enable man to live in greater harmony with the two.

TELEVISION AS SHAPER OF ENVIRONMENT   Of the many terms used to describe our society, *frustrated* and *confused* occur frequently and seem most accurate. Confusion is not the basic cause of our frustrations, but it contributes to them and intensifies their emotional effect. In another troubling time President Lincoln said, "If we only knew where we were and whither we were tending, how much easier it would be." Today a considerable number of the world's people know where we are: we are enmeshed in a materialistic civilization, the result of the long reign of technology, the nature of which is to make things, with no concern for the human purpose; that is the message the medium is flashing to all able and willing to understand. Until recently we were tending not so much toward physical extermination but toward what some observers think would be an equally great catastrophe—the destruction of qualities that make us human. That trend is in the process of being reversed.

Our fear of physical destruction is not so great as it was twenty years ago only because the possibility of total annihilation was universally acknowledged and the wisest among us sought—and still seek—to lessen the possibility and to direct the potential of the atom toward humane ends. The fact that we were confining ourselves in a technological labyrinth that was becoming more and more unmanageable was not revealed so suddenly and dramatically: before the advent of television, it was only hinted at by sensitive observers of the social scene—a few columnists but more often those in the creative arts.

Archibald MacLeish, writing of our frustrated society, calls the take-over by electronics, its usurpation of the hitherto human role in shaping civilization, "a sort of technological coup d'état." [2] If it seems we have been slow in grasping what was happening, we forget that transcontinental television was not inaugurated until 1951, that sets in sufficient number to make a noticeable impact on society were not available until almost the end of the 1950's. If we remember the climate of the early 1960's, we know that the difference between then and now represents a change comparable to that once marked by centuries.

As the realization grows that the cause of our most crucial problems lies not in the machinations of evil men but in a past that cannot be eradicated, some fear our frustration will increase. It may temporarily. But just as not know-

[2] Archibald MacLeish, "The Great American Frustration," *Saturday Review*, Vol. 51, No. 28 (July 13, 1968), pp. 13–16.

ing encourages euphoria, so knowing without understanding breeds mental and emotional distress, increasing the feeling of helplessness. Knowledge of the cause of our problems must be accompanied by the understanding that the advance of technology was inevitable. Its cause is in the nature of man—his intellectual curiosity, his desire to know what seems unknowable, his determination to conquer what remains unconquered. At this point in history, we must be persuaded to admit that the cause of our predicament is a *what* not a *who*. We have willingly accepted technology's gifts with no thought of harmful side effects. We have danced, and now the piper is demanding his pay.

Even in a past seemingly simple in retrospect, when confronted with contradictory evidence, one found it difficult to determine the truth. Today when most problems are presented as crucial and most conflicts as crises, we can scarcely establish priorities for our personal worries. People catapulted into the electronic era, knowing too little about too many complexities, have a right to be confused. However, the right to remain in confusion, doing nothing more profitable than seeking a scapegoat for what has happened and trying to find a miracle worker to solve our problems overnight, has just about expired.

MacLeish places the Industrial Revolution as the start of the machine's encroachment on man's prerogatives. We need not go back so far to find evidence that the advance of science and technology was inevitable:

> Turn to "Important Inventions and Discoveries" in *The World Almanac*. Consider those since 1878, when the first commercial telephone exchange was opened. Why did President Hayes not stop the march of progress then and there? Where would we, armed with the dubious wisdom of hindsight, have stopped it if we could? Can we pick a date where we would be willing to forego the creature comforts and scientific benefits that later inventions and discoveries have given us?

Although men cannot control events, men can direct their consequences—and always have. Honest men have never disagreed greatly about the nation's goals; they have differed about ways to attain them.

The total picture, therefore, is not so dark as specific events may lead us to believe. We are not robots; the information stored on computers must be interpreted by men. The communication medium can present evidence, but interpretation of the evidence must come from a human source. It almost seems that configurate thinking has revealed the enormity of our predicament but that we have been unable to apply the cold, logical, sequential thinking needed to see its causes and possible remedies in the proper perspective.

The repetition of such remarks as "no simple answer," "cannot be done quickly," "long-range program," although often obvious truth, irritates those who interpret them as evasion. Our society resembles an individual who, over a long period, has accumulated fifty pounds of excess flesh and after a week of rigorous dieting is angry because only two pounds have disappeared. Helping the public understand is not only a long-range program, it is a continuing one and will be necessary long after those now under thirty have left the scene.

There are only two groups in a position to undertake such a program: teachers and the television personnel concerned with news. Neither can do it if they are not convinced that it needs to be done and that it is part of their job.

If the public can accept the fact that their mental attitude is the natural result of shock—the like of which no previous people has experienced—they may in time be willing to concede that those trying to solve our problems have experienced the same shock and that to expect them never to "fumble" contradicts common sense. Our conspicuous failures should not blind us to the evidence seeming to indicate we are now on the right road and have advanced farther than was thought possible only ten years ago. This evidence also shows that American ideals are not necessarily incompatible with a technological culture, that a technology directed by these ideals can help us more quickly attain our goals.

We are convinced the greatest danger confronting us is our inability to face our lack of comprehension. It is not coincidence that the expression *credibility gap* gained currency in this decade. Whoever coined it described a symptom of the disease, not the disease itself. Adding to the tendency toward incredulity in this incredible age is the fact that the dedicated viewer daily collects snippets of information about events taking place in all parts of the globe. The danger lies in his believing that because he has seen he understands—or should be able to understand—the significance of the parts in the total picture. The mind does not easily tolerate confusion. Automatically we strive to make sense out of what we see and hear; when we cannot, emotion is likely to take over: thinking we know all when we know only part, we are annoyed by the stupidity of those who disagree; or realizing we do not know enough, we are irritated by the malice of those who we suspect know but selfishly withhold the information.

"The great mass of modern man," writes Walter Lippmann, "are not at home in the world they are making." One of the greatest aids to improving the present world is a well-informed public, or at least one that knows when it knows and when it does not. Of all gaps that plague us, the understanding gap is most basic and underlies all others—for example, the gulf that separates the layman's understanding of the ramifications of problems from the understanding of experts who have been called in to solve them; the gulf that separates arriving at an ideal solution on paper and implementing it in a way to please all who are affected.

A majority of the public cannot be expected to understand the extent to which one complex problem impinges upon another of equal complexity. It does seem reasonable, however, to expect right-thinking persons to know when they understand and when they do not, when they must speak and when they must keep quiet because they have nothing to contribute. Now and in the foreseeable future, our major problems will have to be solved by groups of those who seem most likely to find the best answers. They can be helped by a sufficiently informed public as eager to assume their responsibilities as they are to claim their rights.

It is encouraging to know that some in our society believe the consequences of events can be directed and have begun to translate that belief into action. When the majority can bring themselves to believe, the social climate will become more invigorating. MacLeish, crediting the idea to scientists, suggests it is time we recognized the childishness of our attitude toward science and technology: it is time we stopped asking where *they* are taking *us* and began asking how *we* can manage *them* so they will help us achieve *our* purposes— "our purposes, that is to say, as men."

TELEVISION AS NEWSCASTER   Broadcasting information falls into two main categories: documentaries and news. Television has had notable success with the first. Documentaries—analytical, historical, cultural—are almost consistently excellent. The less formal programs appealing to certain groups are well done. Care, experimentation, and a desire to meet the public interest account for the skill television has acquired in these areas. It is time it directed its talents toward developing a more effective way of broadcasting news.

Over the last five years polls have shown that a majority of people prefer to get their news from television; the same polls indicate that few read magazines reporting and interpreting news. Although news items are briefly presented throughout the day, the newscast strategically scheduled during the dinner hour is each network's *pièce de résistance*. Of the many hours of daily broadcasting, this is the one that has over 100 million viewers. If the majority are to be as well informed as it is within the power of television to inform them, this is the hour it must be done. Thus, the reason for suggesting that students investigate newscasts is not to promote interest in current events; it is solely to make them aware of what obligation rests on those granted a license to broadcast news, how the journalistic code interprets this obligation, and to what extent television is meeting its responsibility.

In the beginning, broadcasters had to fight publishers for the right to carry the news. When television gained the privilege, it placed itself in the journalistic tradition where advertisements are never allowed on the front page, where responsibilities of reporter and editor are separate and defined according to a code journalists themselves have devised: to report the hard core of news—good and bad—clearly, objectively, and in sufficient detail to be understandable; to interpret the news, showing the relationship among events; to present a coherent picture of the important segments of news; to make any predictions they think logical. This code has not always been followed, but when its spirit is flagrantly violated, members of the profession and of the public are disturbed.

Time modifies tradition, and conditions have forced modifications on television, as yet a young medium. The always present pressure of the deadline is intensified by the unwieldy bulk of news, the widely scattered locations to be covered, the vast complexity of many events. The cost in energy and dollars of preparing newscasts is astronomical. None of this, however, excuses television's handling of the news. According to the Federal Communications Act, a network is granted its license to serve "the public interest, convenience, and necessity." In this critical time, turning the serious business of reporting and interpreting news into a high-powered, insistently promoted, popularity contest does not serve the public interest.

The first newscasts were presented at the producer's cost as a public service. Today they are big show business. Each network has its star system and promotes its stable of stars with all the ingenuity at its command. Competition is uncompromising, not only at the top but at many of the lower levels. Some of those once known as distinguished journalists are now known only as television celebrities. One would scarcely dare criticize "the freedom of the press" if several of these men had not expressed dissatisfaction with their change in status as well as with the effect television is having on journalism.

Newscasts follow this pattern. The anchor man reports a few items and introduces on-the-spot reporters who use pictures and "interviews"—a question or two asked of one participating in the event. The occasional ten-minute item with pictures chosen and arranged to illumine the spoken content shows how effective these techniques can be in the hands of an expert. Too often, however, events seem to be featured because they lend themselves to dramatic pictures. Today's conflict is no doubt newsworthy, but if visually it cannot be distinguished from yesterday's, the viewer needs not more pictures but trenchant comment.

Television's indiscriminate use of pictures and interviews wastes time, makes too many items seem equally important, eliminates events that cannot be caught by the camera. Thus it presents a blurred and unbalanced view; all that is likely to remain in the memory of those who use this source exclusively are events, startling or dramatic in themselves, and the impression that not much is right with the world.

Television has held the mirror up to our culture. It has let the world see the material benefits technology has given us; it has shown they are unequally distributed. This knowledge has contributed to the divisiveness evident in our society. Because of its size and the different physical and social conditions prevailing in its regions, the United States has always been made up of many diverse groups with diverse opinions. Before television, few groups knew much about the others. Many persons had their first contact with other groups on television newscasts. Some, partially because it is all the evidence they have, judge entire groups by the image a few members have created on television. This is illogical, but when we do not understand and are at the same time under stress, logic has little chance to take command.

This is the first time in our history it has been necessary for everyone to understand the medium of communication, to realize its tremendous power to influence the social environment—a power that a lethargic public could allow to become dictatorial. If the people believe strongly enough that change in any aspect of programing is essential, they can change it. The greatest hope for effecting desirable change lies with the students now in our classrooms. So we return to our basic theme: the only groups in a position to maintain a continuing educational program—information and interpretation—that will reach the majority of our society are teachers, especially on the secondary level, and those concerned with broadcasting the news.

THE TEACHING PROBLEM

Some students do not realize how complicated the listening process is and may think it requires no effort. They should be given enough experience in the classroom to convince them that listening, if it is to be accurate and critical, demands as much skill and as much emotional control as any other facet of communication.

Teaching the Listening Process

ROLE OF LISTENING   In most classes on the secondary level, student needs are most logically and economically met in the areas of the curriculum where listening must always be an integral part of the total experience. In each area, the usual classroom activities offer the most effective springboard for helping students acquire listening skills. Thus the integrated program, recommended throughout this book, stresses the importance of listening in developing appreciation of literature, especially drama and poetry; in acquiring command of oral language; in preparing for written composition; in testing the clarity and style of one's own writing. The majority of students may require no more understanding and practice than that gained through experiences in which listening plays a necessary, though supporting, role.

In some classes, however, listening must substitute for reading. Often used in heterogeneous groups to provide a common background, aural experiences are imperative with pupils of strictly limited ability. Here information needed by all must be given by the teacher, often aided by visual stimuli. Teachers of such classes must rely on oral presentations to give first-hand experience with literary works otherwise denied to all but competent readers. The skills and behavioral attitudes for effective listening are essential for pupils who will probably never become sufficiently proficient readers to seek the written word as a source of information and enjoyment.

A LESSON IN LISTENING   Each teaching-listening experience has three steps. Dictated by common sense, they represent no more than the experienced teacher has employed until they have become automatic: preparation, to stress the purpose and nature of what is to come; presentation, to allow students to concentrate on the points emphasized; follow-up, to evaluate results and, when necessary, discover reasons for lack of success.

Consider an illustration applicable to all classes, even the most brilliant—the giving of assignments. The inexperienced teacher soon learns that if his attitude is casual and his performance haphazard, students respond in like manner. He can save time and prevent students' floundering if he prepares each assignment conscientiously and takes care to present it in sufficient detail. Requiring a section of the student's notebook to be reserved for assignments underlines their importance.

Before asking students to copy an assignment, the teacher discusses it, doing one or more of many things—explaining unfamiliar terminology, connecting the purpose of the assignment with former learnings, suggesting methods of procedure, and so on. After it has been explained and copied, time for questions is in order. Allowing for idiosyncracies of students, the teacher uses the number and type of questions to test the effectiveness of his preparation.

The same basic procedure, telescoped or amplified as the situation demands, is essential for all teaching-listening experiences. For example, the teacher selects a short story with a particular group in mind. How should it be introduced to arouse interest? What information is needed to make it comprehensible when heard once? Should this be a listening experience only or can listening be combined with silent reading? (The composition of the class decides.) If the story must be read, should it be presented in its entirety or in segments? If the latter, what segments? Why? After students have heard the story, what questions about its content and its form will highlight its salient qualities? In short, each experience requires preparation and follow-up; considering each offering in relation to the students for whom it is intended will provide answers to the questions the teacher must ask himself.

Classroom experience and the findings of research indicate that the requisite skills and attitudes for effective listening can be acquired. Since indiscriminate listening leaves one vulnerable to misinformation and to subtle attacks upon opinions and values, teachers serve both individuals and society by helping students become more competent listeners.

Investigating Television as Medium

All teachers should understand the tremendous influence of television. They should try to make most students at least partially aware of what it has done and what it can do. If teachers become convinced such instruction is necessary, then curriculum planners will proceed as they have done in other areas. Moreover, those designing curricula have an invaluable aid in the videotape recorder. These recorders are already being placed in some educational centers, making it possible for teachers to build libraries to meet community needs. Tapes may be made that permit students to compare effective and ineffective reporting, to see the distinction between reports and editorial comment, to evaluate what pictures contribute, and so on. Since emphasis is on the medium and the way it works rather than on the message, items need not be current. But if such tapes are to become available, they must be requested by teachers who plan to use them.

However, for the present we are thinking in terms of emphasis, rather than radical change in content or method. Any idea a teacher thinks vitally important influences his teaching, even if he does not articulate it in the classroom. If our most capable students are eventually to realize the power of television to change environment, the idea must be planted by teachers who think it significant, teachers who will not begin with "this is the way our environment is and television has been instrumental in making it so." Understanding must come over a period of time through evidence the student has been led to discover for himself. That kind of instruction can begin as soon as the teacher thinks it should.

ORGANIZING INSTRUCTION

As society changes the curriculum changes, both in method and in content. Each new emphasis is initiated by individual teachers who recognize a need and experiment in their own classes, trying to find a way to meet this need. Some of our readers undoubtedly pioneered in group work. Many can recall a time when developing listening skills was not a part of the curriculum. Television, as both medium and message, has had such a powerful effect on our society that it can no longer be ignored in the classroom. The way a teacher organizes listening instruction depends primarily on the way he organizes the content that requires listening's support. Creating understanding of television's effect on environment is not yet recognized as the responsibility of teachers. However, any teacher eager to explore the extent of that responsibility will now find areas in the curriculum where aspects of both television and our society can be emphasized.

SUGGESTED LEARNING EXPERIENCES

Teachers on the secondary level feature listening in its own right only when curriculum offerings fail to meet a need. The one aspect of listening where more students are likely to need additional help is in understanding the complexity of the process. The majority of the suggestions in this section are most appropriate when attention centers on either written or oral communication.

TO RECOGNIZE LISTENING IS COMPLEX

▶ *Realize the many elements that make oral communication effective*

The Columbia Records *I Can Hear It Now* series of recordings of Edward R. Murrow's broadcasts of 1933–45 furnishes a mine of material. The total playing time is nine minutes; portions of each band may be replayed as many times as necessary to isolate the particular element being considered.[3]

1. After an appropriate introduction giving the information necessary to set the scene, play the recording. Write on the board the names of the speakers as they speak. In the discussion following, let students bring out as many facts, in sequence, as they can recall, checking each other for accuracy.

Discuss the feelings evoked by the different speakers. Ask students who have definite feelings to try to determine how they were aroused, telling them they will have an opportunity, during a replaying, to check the accuracy of their analysis.

Consider the total effect of the communications as selected and arranged by the editors. The feeling is one of excitement. What causes it? Students may mention only the obvious: sound effects, change of pace, climactic nature of the content. Then replay the recording, asking a few individuals to check points that aroused controversy. Divide the rest into groups, each to watch for one aspect the class has mentioned as contributing to the feeling and to jot down specific examples.

Follow with discussion. In considering the climactic nature of the content, the teacher may wish to emphasize selection of material as a problem affecting both speakers and writers. Students are impressed by the fact that the editors, after listening to over five hundred hours of old broadcasts, selected one hundred hours to be retaped. From this they chose the forty-five minutes of *I Can Hear It Now.* The following has served as a skeletal guide for such a discussion.

> What principle of selection in the chronologically arranged events strengthens the unity?
> How does each event contribute to the climax of the total sequence?

2. In the next replaying, students might turn their attention to the contribution that choice of words, dramatization of events, and repetition of phrases make to the total effect. The teacher asks appropriate questions to point out the means the narrator uses to bring the listener "into" the event:

> use of words that call up visual and auditory images and evoke a mood
> description of specific events, with repetition of the phrases *Where were you?* and *If you were* (What different purpose does each series of phrases serve?)

3. Other replayings can be used to highlight further elements of this particular communication, for example:

> effect of length of sentences and phrases on both pace and mood
> effect of balanced sentences and phrases
> examples of sarcasm, determination, exuberance, etc.
> contrast in accents: Willkie's (Midwestern), Roosevelt's (Eastern), Churchill's (English), Murrow's (shall we say cultivated American?)
> effectiveness of variety—pause, force, inflection, change of rate—in securing emphasis

[3] We searched without success for a more recent example that would illustrate so many aspects of language and communication with so few words. Teachers seeking examples of reporting by one with an unusual command of the English language and a genuine sense of communication will find them in *In Search of Light: The Broadcasts of Edward R. Murrow, 1938–1961*, ed. by Edward Bliss, Jr. (New York: Knopf, 1967).

It is not implied that all these things should be done with all classes or with any class all at one time. The recording has served as the basis for a listening experience as many as six times over a period of three days without exhausting its possibilities. Some classes have asked to have other segments of the recording played several times, without intervening comment, to see how many different aspects of the communication they can discover for themselves. The teacher does just enough to convince students of the need for listening alertly if they wish to evaluate accurately any complex communication.

▶ *Realize that purposeful listening demands the ability to visualize*

1. To show that visualization is necessary to alert listening, the teacher may use any appropriate band of *I Can Hear It Now* with which students are unfamiliar. After the necessary explanation, play the recording; answer any questions that may arise. Then divide the class into groups, each one to concentrate, as the record is played again, on a different speaker and the lines that introduce him.

Ask students to describe what they visualized as they listened. Take the contributions of each group separately, comparing the images of one member with those of another. Discuss possible reasons why they differ in vividness (habitual visualization) and in kind (individuality of experience). If all members of any one group retain no images, or only irrelevant ones, help them determine the reasons. Lack of concentration? Content too foreign to interests? Too few concrete suggestions from the language?

2. To stress the need for visualization in reading, ask students to listen to a selection written to be printed, one characterized by the use of specific examples expressed in vivid language, such as "This Land and Flag," an editorial from the *New York Times*.[4] Compare the images that the same words evoke in different persons. References to California will probably be more meaningful to children in the West; historical allusions, to those interested in history, and so on. How do images aroused by the same example differ? Why?

3. Often a student who retains particularly vivid images from one example misses what immediately follows. Why? When does such an omission matter? If ten examples are given, is it necessary to remember all? Would such omissions be as likely to occur if a student were reading the editorial silently? Why? Such a discussion can underline these facts:

> Visualization, the calling up of bits of mosaic lodged in the memory, is governed by individual experience.
>
> The more closely related the experiences of two listeners are, the more similar are the images evoked in them by the language.
>
> The need for relating the new to that already known is essentially the same in listening and in reading.
>
> In reading, we can stop to savor and reflect; in listening, we must keep up with the speaker lest we miss a point necessary to the total meaning.

▶ *Develop awareness of the significance of tone in communication*

Listening experiences in which voice quality and intonation are of particular importance offer opportunities to introduce students to the nuances of language tone. They can easily recognize the part *vocal* tone plays in meaning; this understanding

[4] Reprinted in William R. Wood *et al.*, *Fact and Opinion* (Boston: Heath, 1945), p. 10.

can be used to help them form the concept that language itself, whether used in speaking or in writing, has its own distinctive tone.

1. Start simply. In a brief discussion, feature the difference between statements and questions. What in vocal tone tells the listener which is which? Is the difference always evident in the structure of the sentence? Discuss the meaning of "We'll see you Sunday" and "We'll see you Sunday?" What causes the difference? Discuss the significance of tone in training animals and in a baby's accurate interpretation of mood and intonation.

2. Experiments with a single sentence will help students discover how logical meaning changes as different words are stressed. For example: "I think he is a good workman."

> I (but others may not)
> think (but I'm not sure)
> he (but I don't know about his partner)
> is (he is proficient right now)
> good (but not outstanding)
> workman (I know nothing about him as a person)

Ask students to compose and be prepared to read aloud a sentence conveying several different meanings through emphasis on different words. In the follow-up, let them work in groups, interpreting meaning as conveyed by vocal tones.

3. Help students experiment with a single sentence to discover how emotional overtones are conveyed by the voice; use an example like the following:

> Mary discovers that Bob has asked Sally to the school dance. Pretend you are Mary; imagine several total contexts in which the remark "Bob has asked Sally to the dance" might be made. Repeat the sentence, trying to show several different attitudes toward Bob, Sally, the event, and yourself.
>
> *Approval tinged with relief*   I thought I'd never get him to ask her.
> *Disapproval tinged with scornful amusement*   Bob will have a time for himself with stumbling Sal.
> *Gloating triumph*   I knew I could swing it!
> *Joy, excitement*   Sally and I with two big wheels!
> *Anger*   That square! How can Bob fall for her flattery?
> *Regret, disappointment*   If I'd kept my mouth shut, he'd have asked me.

Ask each student to compose a sentence appropriate for several contexts and have him be prepared to say it in each context, conveying a different attitude each time. The discussion growing out of such assignments can lead students to see that vocal tone is an important aspect of oral communication.

4. Explore language tone in commercials. Ask students to listen for those with an obvious language tone; the following will serve as examples.

> What do we want for those we love best? Don't we all want the good things of life? Take home a case of Wonder Brew.
> Because she walks in beauty, because she is the essence of spring, give her Dainty Razor.
> No other deodorant contains XYZ.
> Chemists have worked for years to bring you Bradley's Roach Bomb.

Ask students to find two examples of tone in commercials: one to which they respond favorably; the other, unfavorably. They are to analyze each and to be ready to justify their choices.

5. Contrast different attitudes toward the same subject to help students appreciate the importance of tone in literary works. Comparison of Richard Armour's light verses with the news items that inspired them makes a good beginning. Read the news item and determine its tone; then read the verses, noting how the tone changes. *Light Armour* contains examples suitable for classroom presentation.

TO DEVELOP SIMPLE COMPREHENSION AND ORGANIZATIONAL SKILLS

▶ *Listen to remember particular items*

1. Conversation on the simplest level requires remembering names and items for conversational leads. In communities where members of the class do not know each other, ask students either to introduce themselves or to work in pairs and introduce each other; after a dozen introductions, call on volunteers to name in order all who have been introduced. Where students know each other, ask each to answer roll call with an interesting fact. The next day, let volunteers recount as many items as they can remember, giving the name of each contributor.

2. Selecting what to remember is important in both conversation and discussion. When using oral reports in connection with any phase of the work, ask the reporter to prepare a listening test for the class. Evaluate the test; did the reporter select the points for testing wisely or did he expect listeners to remember unimportant details? Vary the procedure by delaying the test until the day after the report. If students have difficulty recalling items, explore the reasons. Does the fault lie with the reporter, the listener, or with the questions asked?

▶ *Listen to improve vocabulary*

1. Before reading a selection or playing a recording, list on the board words that are likely to be unfamiliar. Ask students to determine their meaning from the context. Check with a dictionary when necessary.

2. As they listen, ask students to list all unfamiliar words. Let volunteers consult the dictionary for alternate meanings. Reread the selection, asking students to determine which meaning best fits the context.

3. Open class for a week with a sentence containing a word whose meaning can be determined from context, for example: He put off the job from day to day but finally had to pay the penalty for his procrastination. Ask one volunteer a day to prepare a similar sentence. Add words to personal vocabulary lists.

▶ *Listen to follow sequence of ideas*

1. For practice in remembering steps in a process, use short talks or "how-to" paragraphs read aloud. Accustom students to being asked to recall main points of a speech in order of presentation.

2. To help students recognize conversational leads and provide continuity, ask for volunteers—one each for as many groups as the size of the class demands. Each volunteer prepares to relate an event he thinks will interest the class.[5] As he speaks to his group, each member jots down ideas that could be introduced into a conver-

[5] See the descriptions of role playing on page 193.

sation on the subject. These may be no more than a question; they may have only a tenuous connection with the matter at hand, so long as an introductory remark can make the connection clear. After the narrator has finished, each member tells how one of his ideas could be introduced.

After this trial run, repeat with a second group of volunteers. In each group, after the prepared talk has been given, students converse, introducing their remarks into the conversation as smoothly as possible.

3. For further practice in conversational listening, play the game "That Reminds Me." Ask students to prepare to tell an anecdote and to decide possible ways of introducing it into a conversation. Place students in small groups, one member starting the conversation. The problem—to bridge the gap between contributions—demands careful listening.

▶ *Listen to determine the main idea*

Read a short news item; ask students to write appropriate headlines. Read a longer news item; have students summarize it as a news flash. Plan a series of listening experiences based on paragraphs developed by different methods—specific details, examples, comparison and contrast. Ask students to devise appropriate titles.

▶ *Sense relationships in aural contexts*

Initially, examples are read by the teacher; later, volunteers may prepare and read original material illustrating the principle involved. Two minutes daily for a week shows pupils they can train themselves to concentrate. Start simply; read only once; recognition of relationships will be instantaneous if pupils are listening.

1. *Among items in a list*   Ask students to detect irrelevancies among items belonging for the most part in the same category: sparrows, thrushes, wrens, robins, nightingales, tigers, eagles. Gradually increase the length of the lists and the number of irrelevant items. Other categories: flowers, trees, fish, sports, vocations, professions, parts of an automobile.

To help students recognize coordination and subordination of items, read a list of specifics. Include a general term applicable to all; for example, substitute *birds* for *tigers* in the above list. Gradually build the list to three or four categories with several items under each.

2. *Between clauses*   Read complex sentences to the class, omitting the conjunctions; let students supply those that show appropriate relationships: He could not go (until, before, although) he had bought his ticket.

3. *Between sentences in a passage*   Ask students to supply the connecting links:

The Lord is my Shepherd: (therefore) I shall not want. (for, because) He maketh me to lie down in green pastures; (and) He leadeth me beside the still waters.

4. *Between paragraphs*   The secretary lists on the board all transitional phrases the class can name—*in the second place, on the other hand, finally, in contrast*—as well as devices such as repetition of key words and phrases. The teacher helps students group those denoting time, cause, contrast, and so on, and discusses the use of such devices by speakers and writers as aids in directing thinking. Then he reads a passage in which students are to note these aids.

► *Distinguish main ideas from subordinate*

1. Before reading a passage to students, say, "The author makes these two points." State them. Ask students as they listen to determine the central idea the points develop. Reread, asking students to listen for the support of each of the two points. After practice with such specific aids, students may be asked to determine the main points without help.

2. Prepare a jumbled list of ideas, facts, and illustrations used by an author. Read aloud the selection from which the list is derived. Then give the list to students, asking them to separate the main ideas from the subordinate, placing the latter under correct headings and arranging points in logical order. This procedure may be used several times, the material becoming gradually more difficult.

► *Predict conclusions and recognize conventional patterns of organization*

1. Occasionally have student speakers stop before the conclusion; ask listeners to predict a logical conclusion. Analyze reasons for success or failure. Do the same with recordings.

2. Introduce articles employing different methods of organization—chronology, series, analysis-solution—so students will become familiar with those in common use. Ask students to determine the patterns of assembly speeches. Compare plans, trying to determine reasons for discrepancies. Was the speaker or the listener at fault? Was a plan discernible? Did the listener try to fit the speech to a formula the speaker did not use?

► *Learn to devise a structure for different forms of presentation*

Since speakers frequently do not use conventional patterns of organization, experiences with both structured and unstructured presentations should be provided for the capable student. Thus, in listening to lectures, speeches, and discussions, the student will realize he must decide early whether outlining or note taking is the more appropriate method for getting down the speaker's ideas.

1. In presenting outlining,[6] use well-organized material of increasing difficulty. Give students supporting points; let them supply main ideas. Give them main headings and the number of subpoints under each; let them fill in the support. Give the skeleton form (correct lettering and numbering) that the speech follows; let students fill in both main and subpoints. After sufficient practice with these methods, let the student make the outline without help; start again with simple material and move to the more complex.

2. Material lends itself better to note taking if the organization is not immediately apparent. Although students planning on college will undoubtedly have to take notes, relatively little can be taught about note taking. Teachers can spend time to greater advantage trying to teach the student to think clearly, so that he is able to take useful notes, whatever the material. Everyone must devise his own system, but teachers can give a few pointers and spend a limited amount of time in practice. Through discussion, bring out the following points:

[6] "Oral Language" suggests that students learn the principles governing outlining more easily by devising plans for their own short talks and by evaluating the plans evident in the talks of their classmates. Such practice increases ability to determine the design in longer and more complicated material.

Note taking calls into play all the techniques learned about organization—discovering speaker's purpose, main points, and so on.

Competent note-takers

strive for accuracy and brevity

concentrate on careful listening and alert reaction, rather than on writing

try different methods, adapting to the material (They jot down words to suggest key ideas, and fill in after the speech.)

reflect upon notes as soon as possible to clinch ideas and help later recall

make up their own scheme of abbreviating

For practice material select interviews, discussions, question-and-answer periods after panels. First, use material that allows students to be told the general plan the discussion is to follow—for example, recordings and loosely structured magazine articles. Then, use material where students receive no advanced help, such as radio and television panels and debates.

3. The listener in both formal and informal situations must structure the idea for himself. The better organized the speaker, the more completely does he convey the design the idea has for him. However, the worth of the communication to the listener depends upon the structure of the idea he himself evolves; this structure may or may not agree with the speaker's. For example, speaker and listener may disagree on the relevance or the relationship the parts have to each other or to the whole. Comparisons of the various structures students make of the same presentation will show the direct dependence of evaluation on the way the listener "sees the design" of the central idea. What reasons might a speaker have for deliberately trying to confuse with a blurred design? [7] Discussion can stress the fact that one who wishes to use language with integrity must structure his communication so as to give it meaning and stability.

TO DEVELOP THE ABILITY TO EVALUATE A COMMUNICATION

Much of the information upon which we base opinions and decide upon action comes to us through the aural sense. Help students develop alertness to irrelevance and contradictions within the communication.

► *Use sentences*

Read a list of sentences, asking students to mark a numbered list with + if the sentence makes sense, zero if it does not. In a group of sentences whose meaning is instantly clear, include one or two that are ambiguous, contrary to experience, or ludicrous because of malapropisms or faulty constructions:

The father told his son that he would have to leave.

We walked toward the setting sun, our long shadows bobbing before us.

He greeted me with an angry epitaph.

Driving due west from Chicago, you can reach New York in two days.

Swimming around the bend, the land came in sight.

He told me an antidotal story that made me roar with laughter.

I don't care for anesthetic dancing.

In the distance I heard the crack of a rifle; I ducked as a bullet whizzed past my ear.

[7] See "Logical Thinking," pages 156–59.

In exercises such as this, do not warn students to look for discrepancies. Most of the above are so obvious they can be spotted immediately if the listener is alert. The activity is helpful in pointing up the need for accuracy in listening, the role of past experience in interpreting what we think we hear, and man's need for meaning and wish to impose order on chaos.

▶ *Use paragraphs*

Take any well-written paragraph with a clearly stated topic sentence; insert a sentence connected with the topic but irrelevant to the aspect being developed. Ask students first to listen for the topic sentence. As they listen a second time, they check to see whether each sentence is pertinent.

▶ *Use outlines*

Tell the class you will read a skeletal outline for a speech; the first sentence will state the central idea; all those that follow will represent supporting points.[8] Read the central idea sentence. Then give this direction: "Listen to each sentence as I read; if you think that when adequately developed into a paragraph it will lend support to the statement that governs the speech, mark plus; if not, mark zero." Then read each supporting sentence slowly, giving a few seconds for reflection:

> I enjoy watching television.
>> I find several programs consistently entertaining.
>> I especially like the sportscasts.
>> Repetition of the same advertisements becomes boring.
>> Many old movies are shown.
> Our assemblies should be improved.
>> Often speakers cannot be heard.
>> The talent assembly was the best of the year.
>> We should have more student performers.
>> I didn't like the talk on science.
> C_____ is the best school in this vicinity.
>> It has an excellent basketball team.
>> Its building is modern.
>> Its classrooms have the latest equipment.

One outline is sufficient for a lesson. The exercise can be used repeatedly, the problems becoming more complex. At this point students should not be concerned with the truth or falsity of the statements; neither should they confuse proof with support. They should decide whether the supporting statements are coordinate; which, if any, should be deleted; and which, if any, could be revised to support the argument. For each governing statement, they should consider what method of development is required. For example, the key word in the third outline is *best*; hence none of the statements is pertinent since support demands comparisons. Let volunteers prepare similar listening tests.

▶ *Learn a formula for quick evaluations*

1. Isolate a few basic essentials:

Find the main idea.
Discard the irrelevant.

[8] Compare with speech plans in "Oral Language," pages 273–76, 314–16.

Determine whether the purpose is mainly to inform or to persuade.

Determine whether assertions are mainly factual or judgmental.

Such streamlining of an intricate process cannot insure correct appraisal, but the habit of concentrating on a few essentials does give a basis for approaching accuracy on the spur of the moment.

2. Practice evaluating by formula. Evaluate student talks in groups, talks before the class, speeches in assemblies, and communications received by radio and television.

3. Evaluate personal communications. Give students a week to select a segment of one particular conversation to evaluate. They meet in groups, trying to appraise the strengths and weaknesses of the formula as an instrument for quick evaluation. Class discussion synthesizes results.

TO DISCOVER HOW TELEVISION USES NEWS TIME

▶ *View the national networks' evening broadcasts*

1. Ask three committees, one for each major network, to view for a week, determining the approximate amount of time spent on advertisements, pictures, other news items, editorials. As they report findings, discuss contrasting purposes of reporting and editorializing. Tell them that not until 1967 were reporters allowed the editorial privilege. Why not before? Why now?

2. Discuss possible purposes of pictures: Clarity? Interest? Emphasis? What are possible reasons for illustrating one item instead of another? Compare the ways newscasts and newspapers give importance to what they want to emphasize. If emphasis is not made with discretion what is the result?

3. Ask volunteers from each committee to compare the evening newscast—choice of items and depth of coverage—with the front page of the morning paper. Do back pages report events the well-informed need to know? Are the pictures on television more or less enlightening than the details on the front page? Why?

4. Ask volunteers to compare a week's television coverage with that found in a weekly news magazine. Discuss ways some persons habitually use to keep better informed. Why is it difficult? Important?

▶ *Cultivate awareness of two aspects of newscasting*

Read to the class "The Missing Dimension" by R. L. Shayon (*Saturday Review*, April 27, 1968, page 52). Even though events referred to may be long past, the situation may remain substantially the same. Using two loosely related events occurring simultaneously, Shayon shows how television covers one well but neglects the other. Discuss why this happens. Ask students for other examples.

TO DISCOVER POSSIBLE IMPACT OF TELEVISION ON POLITICS

▶ *Recognize definite changes*

1. Discuss the type of nominating convention that existed throughout most of our history. Students may know the connotation of "dark horse," "smoke-filled rooms," "nomination by entrenched party leaders." Has television forced a change? If so, is it for better or worse? Why?

2. Discuss the style of oratory thought appropriate for politicians before television. Why is it no longer effective? Discuss the power of television to reveal more

than the words say. Is this an advantage or not for the electorate? For the candidate? When one says X lost because of "too much exposure" what is he really saying? "Too little exposure"?

► *Consider two opposing opinions*

"Some observers claim TV is producing a more alert and better-informed electorate; others, that it is reducing our politics to a mixture of high-pressure salesmanship and beauty contests," according to Arthur Schlesinger, Jr. Can you give evidence to support either view? Where do you think the truth lies? Is choice ever influenced by "beauty"? Substitute a word that you think more nearly fits what the observer complains of. In general how does television help a voter decide? Give specific examples.

► *Consider relative effectiveness of the means available to candidates*

1. Discuss with students the probable effectiveness of face-to-face debates, seperate conferences before the same newsmen who ask the same questions of each candidate, individual speeches, spot announcements. Which is likely to appeal to most viewers?

2. A reporter, considering a television debate he had witnessed between two aspirants for the presidential nomination, remarked, "Whether or not a president can debate effectively is irrelevant. What he has to do is to know how to listen." Evaluate the soundness of this judgment. What does the thinking behind it overlook? What qualities desirable or undesirable for a president might be revealed by a debate that would not be revealed in any other way?

TO INVESTIGATE PROGRAMS SUPPLEMENTING THE NEWS

Those restating and clarifying the "social dilemma and political pickle" qualify.

► *Compare different types of interview*

1. Compare *Meet the Press, Face the Nation,* and *Issues and Answers* with "talk shows" as to purpose and possibility of opinions' being allowed to pass as facts. Stress the importance of being aware of the communication situation in getting information.

2. Investigate the value of face-to-face serious conversations between two persons —for example, *Firing Line* and *Dissenters* on NET. When compared with interviews like the three previously mentioned, which type is more likely to furnish the better example of mind meeting and responding to mind, progression toward a definite conclusion? Why?

3. Describe the communication situations in each of the three types of interview. What factors make the context different?

► *Investigate documentaries*

This is one type of program likely to be excellent. Ask students who have seen one of interest to give the subjects. Discuss briefly how documentaries differ from newscasts.

1. Ask the initiated to act as scouts to discover a documentary that the rest of the class might like to see. Encourage those who seem interested to view it. Tell them you will later discuss with them the following: purpose and point of view; evidence of research; choice of details and sub-incidents; progression; central point of

the whole. Let the class listen to the discussion only if you think it might interest more students in this type of program.

2. Ask a committee to survey programs of local stations and keep a list of documentaries posted. Do not neglect NET, if available, but only rarely recommend a program lasting longer than one hour.

3. Help students select a school problem to serve as the basis for a documentary. If equipment is available, make a short film. Even if this is impossible, planning the direction and steps for such a program is a good way to generate discussion.

▶ *Consider the commentator's role*

The teacher needs to know the current policy of each network concerning editorials within the evening broadcasts.

1. Ask three volunteers to cover the NBC, ABC, and CBS evening newscasts for a week and to decide what the editorial policy of each seems to be. Distinguish between national and regional editorials.

2. Tape record or ask a student to record a series of editorials from the network that seems to offer the greatest number of national interest. (These will run 3 to 4 minutes each and will pinpoint an aspect of a larger problem.) Study the editorials to determine how they differ from a news item; their continuity, if any; their cumulative effect, if any. Discuss the part commentators should play today. Are they fulfilling this role? Give reasons for opinion.

3. If a class or individuals can be interested in such programs on NET as *News in Perspective, Washington Week in Review, NET Journal,* they can very quickly learn the importance of commentators; some may find these programs interesting enough to view regularly. Teachers should also recommend programs concerned with minority groups, usually combining fact and comment, found on the commercial stations and NET. Programs focusing on members of these groups as persons rather than a group with a problem are now appearing frequently.

TO STRESS THE IMPORTANCE OF BOTH MEDIUM AND MESSAGE

▶ *Discuss the meaning of these quotations*

In 1942, E. B. White wrote, "We shall stand or fall by television—of that I am quite sure." In 1967 he wrote, "television should address itself to the ideal of excellence, not to the idea of acceptability." What does he mean by "stand or fall"? "Ideal of excellence" versus "idea of acceptability"? Give examples to illustrate each.

▶ *Discuss comments on contemporary culture*

1. Read to the class "The Conquest of Violence" by Norman Cousins. After considering the editorial (*Saturday Review,* June 22, 1968), discuss selected lines—for example, "tragedy of a world that somehow became one before it became whole"; "all men, whatever their faces or moods, rub together in a way that makes for limitless upheaval or promise." How did the world become one before it became whole? Why does Cousins say, "upheaval *or* promise"? What promise? Can it be upheaval *and* promise? If so, how can the promise be fulfilled? What is our responsibility?

2. Organize a panel based on "Must We Rewrite the Constitution to Control Technology?" Wilbur H. Ferry (*Saturday Review,* March 2, 1968, pp. 50–54). Ask several students to read the article, present the ideas, lead a discussion.

3. Ask students to suggest recordings making significant observations—for ex-

ample, "7 O'Clock News/Silent Night" in the Simon and Garfunkel album *Parsley, Sage, Rosemary and Thyme* (Columbia Stereo CS 9363) makes a powerful comment on our society.

▶ *To continue focusing on the impact of culture*

Obviously, in the majority of classes it would be futile to try to lead students to make the broad and deep connection between the medium and society that McLuhan makes. However, in many classes it should be possible to lead them to minor conclusions pointing in that direction. Students know more about their society than they think they do. Since newscasts are scheduled at the dinner hour, many must be at least vaguely familiar with them. There is no reason why we cannot foster a more accurate understanding of medium and society with no reference—or only casual ones—to the relationship between them. We can trust future experience to help students make a significant connection.

Creating an understanding of our society is essentially an exercise in critical thinking. We suggest a procedure that has long been effective in providing practice in recognizing blocks to straight thinking: analysis of selected statements through brief discussions before regular classwork begins. If the effect is to be cumulative, discussions must occur with a degree of regularity—perhaps once a week. Such a procedure is encouraging because the need for discussion gradually becomes less. Quick recognition becomes sort of a game. For content, we suggest the source that has always proved prolific, varied, and readily accessible: columnists, those who seriously analyze events and those who satirize human aspects of both major and minor happenings; news items; cartoons; jokes where the humor lies in recognizing a universal human characteristic. One who reads a daily paper and a few magazines does not have to hunt for material; it is thrust upon him.

These examples show the range of comments. At first they must be presented in more detail than will be necessary later.

> *Ninth-graders*   A travel columnist reported that someone who spent the summer in Rome heard his hotel clerk say, "The Americans are the most impatient people in the world." Why would a columnist think this worth reporting? On what probable evidence did the clerk base his remark? Narrow the clerk's generalization to a statement more compatible with the probable evidence. Is impatience a typically American characteristic? Is there any reason why we should be more impatient than citizens of other countries? Give evidence for opinion.
>
> *Capable seniors*   Here is a quotation from a magazine article: "It is evident that electronics has given man a considerable degree of control over his environment; it is not so evident that man at the same time increased the potential of electronics to control him." Over a period of time, students could bring in examples to confirm or deny the latter half of the statement. When interest begins to lag, a tentative conclusion can be drawn from the evidence.

Teachers who want to help students develop understandings about their environment can do so without encroaching on time ordinarily devoted to other subjects. For classes, groups, or individuals, this topic will serve as well as any other—if not better—to motivate oral and written composition. It lends itself particularly to imaginative writing. Since our interest is not in technology but in the effect of a technological culture on humanity, the subject is especially appropriate for classes in English.

SELECTED READINGS

BOOKS

FARRELL, EDMUND J. *English, Education, and the Electronic Revolution.* Champaign, Ill.: NCTE, 1967. Provides a background for understanding this revolution, one in which humanists have high stakes.

MC LUHAN, MARSHALL. "Environment as Programmed Happening" in Walter J. Ong, ed., *Knowledge and the Future of Man.* New York: Holt, Rinehart & Winston, 1968, pp. 113–24. This essay and others in this stimulating collection discuss the impact of contemporary culture on the perceptions and learning of man.

WITTY, PAUL. *Studies in Listening.* Champaign, Ill.: NCTE, 1959. This monograph, with reprints of several articles from *Elementary English,* reviews and interprets experimental studies on listening as a way of learning and gives many suggestions for teaching.

ARTICLES

CULKIN, JOHN M. "A Schoolman's Guide to Marshall McLuhan." *Saturday Review.* Vol. 50, No. 11 (March 18, 1967), p. 51, and KOSTELANETZ, RICHARD. "Marshall McLuhan." *Commonweal.* Vol. 85, No. 3 (January 20, 1967), p. 420. These two articles are recommended especially to readers who have not read *Understanding Media.* Briefly, clearly, objectively, Culkin and Kostelanetz react to McLuhan's major ideas.

MAC NEIL, ROBERT. "The News on TV and How It Is Unmade." *Harper's Magazine.* Vol. 237, No. 1421 (October 1968), pp. 72–80. An illuminating account of the effect of television on journalism and newscasting by one who works within the industry.

NILES, OLIVE S., and EARLY, MARGARET J. "Listening." *Journal of Education.* Boston University, Vol. 138, No. 3 (December 1955). Brief discussion of listening skills with suggestions for teaching and a selected list of source material.

RUSSELL, DAVID H. "A Conspectus of Recent Research on Listening Abilities." *Elementary English.* Vol. 41, No. 3 (March 1964), pp. 262–67.

WITTY, PAUL. "A 1964 Study of TV: Comparison and Comments." *Elementary English.* Vol. 42, No. 2 (February 1965), pp. 134–41.

SEVEN

ORAL LANGUAGE

*Let your speech be always with grace, seasoned with salt
that ye may know how ye ought to answer every man.*

COLOSSIANS 4 : 6

PERSPECTIVE

Writers from Solomon's day to the present have testified to the power of the spoken word; dictators have paid their tribute by attempting its suppression. In man's development of Western civilization, speech has been an important tool; today it is a significant instrument in making possible the cooperative activity necessary in the complex society this civilization has created.

One who attempts to teach students to speak effectively must have a deep respect for the force that can be unleashed by those who use this power skillfully. He knows that the right of free speech implies the obligation both to use language with integrity and to discriminate among the many voices clamoring for attention. The teacher himself must have savored the pleasure that comes from the ability to say exactly what he means, to express the appropriate thought or feeling with telling effect. For only one who understands the complexity of communication appreciates the difficulties—intellectual, emotional, and technical—that confront his students.

Constantly, the teacher of oral communication must be deeply aware of speech as a form of human behavior—significant behavior because it reveals the speaker to his public. Instinctively, we have always known the power of speech to reveal; too infrequently have we considered that silence too can tell things about us. Until recently concern for the fact that our speech might betray us was not thought of as "the desire to project a favorable image," but that is what it is called today. Television has made a vast public conscious of how much more than words even a brief "exposure" may convey. Almost nowhere in the communication context does the wish to protect oneself weigh more heavily than with young people in the classroom. We each have an ideal self-image, inextricably bound to our sense of personal dignity. Even though we may know beyond doubt that our self-image flatters us, one who does not treat that image with respect blocks communication. This is the reason we stress so insistently the need for creating a climate where the student feels secure enough to express himself freely. Many things are necessary in order to help students learn to use oral language with honesty and vigor, but the proper environment is the *sine qua non.*

In daily life the context of oral communication is usually the give and take of conversation; only occasionally is it the speaker-audience situation. In planning learning experiences, teachers use both contexts. To insure the most practice for the greatest number, they use discussion to develop skills needed for informal speaking; they use small groups as the setting for prepared talks demonstrating the principles underlying effective speech. All procedures suggested in this chapter are variants of these two methods. Both place the reluctant pupil in a situation where he can operate more successfully; both allow all students to perform according to their respective abilities; both save time and permit integration with other areas of English. Since similar principles govern effectiveness in discussion and in more formal speaking, skill in one reinforces skill in the other. Thus, using a combination of the two approaches, the teacher can provide sufficient practice to help students speak better in the many informal situations of daily living.

The Social Situation

Oral communication takes place in many different kinds of situations, each with its own particular aura. The pervading atmosphere may be genial or strained, favorable or antagonistic, but language is used for saying something to someone—and for valid reasons. When the exchange is between two persons, either what is said or the way it is said may inject a discordant or harmonious overtone; so too may the entrance of a third individual. The social situations in life resemble what the dramatist calls *scenes.* Even a one-act play with only two characters is made up of numerous scenes, the atmosphere changing as disclosures made by one or the other bring relief or create tension. The climate in which oral communication takes place has direct bearing on its effectiveness, and each participant has a stake in creating that climate.

Communicate means literally *to give to another as a partaker.* All communication requires a sender, a receiver, and something shared. With speech, the relationship of the three is immediate and apparent; every social situation must have a speaker, a listener, and spoken language—the medium of exchange between the two. Control of this medium is equally important to both speaker and listener, for speech can serve either as a bridge or as a barrier between ourselves and others. Our command of language, with all that phrase implies,[1] determines in part how well we can function in the various social situations, no two identical, of which we are a part. This emphasis on communication rather than on language in isolation pervades all instruction in English.

THE CLIMATE   A flexible situation where participants are relaxed and self-confident is essential for effective communication. Thus, maintenance of a

[1] See Chapter One, "Language as Dynamic Process."

classroom climate conducive to learning is nowhere more important than in the teaching of oral skills. The desire and the ability to use language honestly takes root only when conditions are favorable; they will not flourish unless carefully nurtured over a long period of time. In the main it is the teacher's attitude toward himself, toward others, and toward ideas that determines whether he can create an environment to stimulate growth. If the student feels that the subject being discussed strikes at the heart of his world, if he knows that any opinion he can support will be treated with respect, if he is assured of an interested response, he will learn to speak. Even the slow and inarticulate student has demonstrated repeatedly that, given subjects on his own level and interested listeners, he can learn to discuss with enthusiasm and a fair degree of skill. He is reluctant only when he has no desire to communicate or is beyond his depth—and who isn't?

The teacher can create a favorable atmosphere by providing a classroom where students know they can say what they think; where it is not only their right but their duty to have opinions and to defend them; where the ideas will not, however, be accepted automatically but will be examined impartially and critically. Yet, even such an atmosphere will fail its purpose unless the teacher starts with content at the level of the interests and abilities of his students. In the beginning they should be asked to discuss only matters of particular concern to them—the only ideas about which they can be expected to have convictions that merit defense.

Although introduced by topics sure to challenge response, the oral program does not stop there. The teacher begins gradually and consistently to broaden the base of the content, attempting to widen and deepen the interests and to increase the abilities. In this way he can help young people develop the characteristics that seem desirable for those who are to realize their potential in the kind of society to which they belong.

What qualities do we hope the oral skills program will foster in students? The reader will probably not quarrel with the characteristics selected as desirable. His response is more likely to be, "Sounds fine! Now tell me *how!*" As he well knows, no tricks or gimmicks will perform this miracle. The habit of using language with integrity is formed, if at all, over a long period of time as students practice principles of effective communication in environments that build confidence and stress the responsibility for straight thinking and honest communication. Nor does honest communication imply saying what one thinks in any way one pleases; the effect on the listener has to be considered; no instruction and no skill are required if the purpose is to antagonize. This chapter is concerned with a program that gives emphasis both to honesty in the use of language and to skills necessary to make that honesty function.

THE SPEAKER   Speech and personality are related. Over two thousand years ago Aristotle in his *Rhetoric* extolled the persuasive power of the "man of honesty" in contrast to the man of "sharp argument." Today too we select *integrity* as the basic requirement for the speaker; we must be convinced he speaks the truth as he sees it. We require a degree of *authority*, a certainty that in the limited field of the moment he knows what he is talking about. We want him to show a healthy respect both for himself and for others, admitting their rights to their own opinions but not relinquishing his own unless convinced of his error. We are likely to admire the man with *courage,* one who will not curry favor by evading unpleasant truths that must be stated to clarify the issue; one who, with unfailing good humor and tact, voices honest opinions he knows are unpopular with the majority. We expect *vitality,* that the speaker's manner will convey his belief that he is saying something of importance to himself and his listener. Lastly, we want *intelligibility,* evidence that the speaker realizes his obligation to make his ideas comprehensible, to hew to the line of his argument with directness and economy of words. Students can be helped to develop these qualities in classrooms where they deal with increasingly complex problems in an atmosphere that encourages tactful and critical appraisal of independent thought and expression.

THE LISTENER   The listener needs the same qualities as the speaker. He is equally important; without him there would be no communication. Even when he is in a situation where he cannot interrupt with questions and where his rebuttal must be silent, his mind is active, accepting this fact, rejecting that conclusion. He shows his vitality by remaining alert; his integrity, by weighing honestly opinions at variance with his own; his authority, by marshaling facts to confirm or refute and by following the line of argument to detect sound or fallacious reasoning. He shows his respect for himself and others by quiet admission that the question may have more facets than he had anticipated and by an earnest effort to relate the new facts to his previous understanding of the problem; his courage, by changing his opinion when the evidence seems conclusive. In all this he is using his ability for intelligent expression as an aid to straight thinking, for the two are inseparable. The listener is neither a complacent sponge ready to absorb heedlessly everything he hears; nor is he a stone wall, bristling with preconceived notions, automatically rejecting ideas without giving them a chance to penetrate. He never plays a passive part; his is the role of active collaborator.[2]

THE SPEECH   In the ordinary affairs of life most oral communication is brief, fragmentary, and impromptu. These qualities are evident in conversation where the speaker, with no time for specific preparation, must determine quickly the relevancy of his remarks to the context. Knowing the complexity both of language and of man forces the realization that effective speaking on all occasions is impossible even for the most brilliant. Human nature is limited.

   The most adept speaker, although he may possess unusual natural ability, has not acquired his great skill by chance. Usually he is a man of lively curiosity and varied interests. His expertness in speech is based upon a store

---

[2] For suggestions for teaching listening, see Chapter Six.

of information and upon discriminating judgment of human beings. Although he may never have enrolled in a speech course, somehow he has learned to speak by speaking; he has done a lot of it and he has been doing it a long time. He has developed certain characteristics of mind and has made certain methods of procedure more or less habitual. His expert control is a mark of his maturity.

Being realistic, we cannot expect a high degree of competence from all those enrolled in our English classes. We can, however, give the student specific methods for attacking the problems of oral communication; if the principles and practices are sound, those motivated to perfect the skill can, over the six-year period, acquire a reasonable degree of effectiveness in the use of oral language.

The Communication

An effective communication—whether a long speech or a contribution to a conversation—has certain characteristics. The speaker has an idea important to him and, he hopes, important to the listener. This idea, whether expressed in one sentence or in many, is ordered in intelligible form. Automatically, the competent speaker uses and the listener expects the patterns inherent in the language. However, a well-ordered idea is not yet communication. If thoughts and feelings are to be shared, the listener's needs and the skills of expression assume importance. The gifted but inarticulate employee with an idea the head of the firm would welcome; the learned specialist, world famous but unable to hold an expectant audience—these are individuals equipped with ideas and probably able to organize them but lacking the power to communicate. These factors of communication, as they pertain to the classroom, are considered in the following sections: selecting material, organizing material, communicating ideas.

SELECTING MATERIAL

The student is often convinced he has nothing worthwhile to say. Sent forth on his own to try to find material—something with the dignity and importance the classroom seems to demand—he will go directly to a magazine, or worse yet to an encyclopedia and come back with a poorly digested, pallid imitation of the original. Reports based solely on library research have their place, but the teacher cannot depend upon them to develop oral skill—certainly not with beginners. Unless the reporter is proficient in speaking, his attention will be on content rather than on communicating ideas. Students, within the storehouses of their own experience, have a wealth of subjects on which they can speak; they need help in selecting suitable ones. The teacher must let them know he is not necessarily expecting from them accounts of world shaking events or opinions on international problems. The things he likes to hear from them concern themselves—what they have done, what they would like to do, what pleases them, what annoys them, what frightens them; in short, what they know, think, and feel about this, that, and the other as it impinges upon their lives.

GENERAL SOURCES OF MATERIAL   Most pupils can be taught to make brief, carefully prepared speeches. However, such learning should operate as a means to a larger end; the ultimate aim is to acquire attitudes and skills that will make communication effective in the impromptu situations of most daily speaking. On such occasions, as well as on those allowing preparation for an organized speech, the material comes from the same general sources—thinking, listening, observation, personal experience, and reading. One characteristic of the expert speaker is his awareness of the worth of all experience as possible grist for the conversational mill. In finding topics suitable for classroom work, the teacher helps students tap those sources, helps them realize that all facets of both direct and vicarious experience furnish the raw material one adapts to one's own purpose in using language.

MATERIAL FOR THE CLASSROOM   One cannot learn to speak effectively without some writing; precision in diction and in organizing ideas demands the use of pencil and paper. One cannot generate and clarify ideas if he depends solely on direct experience; he must read. Conversely, discussion aids both writing and comprehension. Thus, the teacher is being realistic and economical in directing learning when he fuses these activities in the classroom. The literature studied and the books for individual reading offer many ideas to challenge students; both are indispensable for teaching oral skills. In addition, students should have a chance to explore problems of vital concern that they themselves choose. These three sources furnish ample material to teach both the skills needed for orderly discussion and the techniques required for organized speech.

ORGANIZING MATERIAL

The principles of organizing material are the same whether one is taking part in a discussion or a conversation, preparing a speech, or writing expository prose. Identical for the novice and for the expert, they are controlled by three basic rules: make assertions capable of development; support adequately assertions made; create an over-all design by arranging assertions in a meaningful pattern.[3] In informal communication, although no one individual makes the over-all pattern, his sensitivity to its need helps him contribute to it.

---

[3] Students understand the need to apply these rules in organizing a speech; they require help in perceiving the relevancy of all, and especially of the third, to discussion and conversation.

Repetitions, irrelevancies, and belated references to points already covered cannot be avoided. Ideas do not come straight-jacketed and with military precision; too close adherence to any pattern dampens spontaneity and restricts the flow of thought. However, sensitivity to order, an aim of most classroom instruction, is a characteristic both of the good conversationalist and the effective platform speaker. In conversation, as in more formal types of oral communication, all three principles apply.

MAKING ASSERTIONS   Before we are ready to make a statement we intend to support, we have to be sure the scope of the topic is narrow enough to be covered in the time at our disposal. For the student in the ordinary English class this always means a small area, whether he is to speak for a minute in discussion or longer before a group. Situations in daily life—interviews, committee meetings, sustained conversations—demand the same directness and economy. The give-and-take of informal communication implies that the speaker states a fact or expresses a point of view to which he expects a response; if challenged, he should be ready to give evidence—cite events, incidents, reasons—to win the listener's acceptance. Moreover, anyone aware of the nature of communication is sensitive to the danger of monopolizing, to the need for giving everyone a chance to speak. Practice in making significant statements capable of support in a short time prepares the student for much of the oral communication he uses in daily life.

SUPPORTING ASSERTIONS   The student tends to rely too heavily on generalizations, on bald statements of opinion, often confused in his mind with fact. He must learn that support is needed for assertions in any form of communication. He can see the need for amplification most easily in speech, where the listener must keep pace with the speaker; where an idea, to be understood, accepted, and remembered, must be built up with the specific. The support of single assertions is the most useful aspect of organization to teach all pupils. Indeed, it is the only one possible with those strictly limited in the capacity for sensing more complex relationships.

The necessity for concreteness in developing statements, for helping the listener visualize, is an important idea for pupils to assimilate. Therefore, the use of illustrations and examples to amplify ideas should receive considerable stress. The more capable students, however, should attempt to secure variety in the kinds of material used for support; most of the problems they themselves select to explore demand the ability to discriminate between facts and alleged facts; between sound, unbiased authority and incompetent or prejudiced opinion.[4] Using different kinds of material—facts, illustrations, testimony—in their own communications teaches students the difficulties involved in assessing each and the contribution each can make to the total context.

The accomplished speaker is discriminating; he seeks to vary his material,

[4] See Chapter One, pages 25–26, and Chapter Four, pages 156–58.

using just enough of each kind to accomplish his purpose—facts to give substance, illustrations to enliven, and testimony to add emphasis.

CREATING THE DESIGN To create an over-all design, the speaker must arrange assertions in a meaningful pattern. The ability to see correct relationships among ideas underlies all forms of purposeful communication and of sustained thought.[5] Because a speech appears to the student less tangible than an essay, he is likely to accept the need for a preliminary outline as more imperative here than in his written compositions. In preparing for oral work he has an opportunity to practice outlining step by step, eventually persuading himself of its usefulness in both speaking and listening. This knowledge can then be applied to his writing and reading.

Building the outline for a speech is somewhat similar to building the framework for a house. First, the central idea sentence (CIS),[6] the foundation that defines the form and the limits, is constructed. After that come the topic sentences (TS), the skeleton framework for the entire structure. Finally, the sub-topic sentences (STS), the details of each section, are fashioned. The completed design of a speech and that of a house are similar, for both have a psychological as well as a logical aspect. Logically, the plan of each shows the relation of parts to each other and that of each to the whole. Psychologically, both take into account that the finished product is being designed for human beings whose particular needs and interests must be considered. Therefore, the best plans are made by speakers or achitects who, aware of the demands of the material and of the persons for whom the structure is intended, create both logical and psychological designs.

Although pupils have had experience with outlining in elementary school, they must receive instruction throughout the secondary-school years as well. As thinking grows more complex, outlining becomes more difficult. Each outline presents a fresh problem in the organization of thought. The form—the conventions of numbering and lettering—can be reviewed in very little time. The student needs to know, first, that the visual outline is made to help the memory after the reasoning process has determined the logical relationship of ideas, hence the form is important because it shows these relationships quickly. Numbers and letters are guideposts and should be placed so they can be seen at a glance. If cluttered with words above and below, they are no more use to the reader than are traffic signs obscured by weeds to the motorist. Secondly, the student needs to know that an outline, made for any one of many purposes, is always as brief as is consistent with usefulness; it contains a great deal in a little space. In short, the student should see the outline primarily as an exercise

[5] See "Teaching a thinking skill within a unit," pages 703–07.

[6] These names are arbitrarily assigned to the statements representing the three steps to be recommended in teaching the plan for a speech: The central idea sentence (CIS) controls the organization of the entire speech; the topic sentences (TS) state the main ideas used to support CIS; the sub-topic sentences (STS) are statements of the facts, illustrations, testimony, used to amplify the topic sentence. The teacher will use whatever terminology will aid the student.

in thinking and after that as a succinct and helpful recording of the thought.

After students understand the principles governing organization, learning experiences should consist of making written plans for most prepared talks. The plan then becomes not an isolated activity but a means of organizing thought for a definite objective—effective speech.

COMMUNICATING IDEAS

The aspects of expression previously discussed are concerned with preparation—having something to say and organizing it to have meaning for the listener. The ideas still have to be communicated. The teacher can aid the student best by placing him in a situation in which he feels reasonably secure; by letting him know that the aim is not to make a perfect speech each time but to gradually acquire skills to improve his control in all social situations; by helping him realize that the ultimate objective of this instruction is to develop a command of language enabling him to speak effectively without specific preparation—to use language on those many occasions when he is called upon to answer questions, give directions, engage in the informal talk so much a part of daily living.

EXTEMPORE METHOD OF DELIVERY The extempore method of delivery—a method where content and order of ideas have been prepared but the words and sentence patterns come "out of the time"—gives the best practice for impromptu speaking. Speaking extemporaneously, one may or may not use notes; that too depends upon circumstances. If at all possible, it is better from the very beginning to accustom the student to speaking without this prop, for sooner or later it has to be removed. If the teacher maintains the right atmosphere and gives time for adequate preparation of a limited idea, notes should not be needed.

QUALITIES OF DELIVERY What qualities of delivery should be stressed? In the beginning with most classes they should be nontechnical and minimal. Since he can acquire skill only by speaking, the first objective is to get the student to like to speak; once that is accomplished, it is comparatively easy to guide him in attaining higher standards. If attention is kept mainly on content, suggestions for improvement in delivery can be postponed. Examples of good practices should, however, be pointed out. Young people might well concentrate on these desirable traits: audibility, intelligibility, directness, and vitality. A simple guide helps both listener and speaker:

Can the speaker be easily understood?
  Does he use the necessary volume?
  Does he enunciate clearly?
Can his speech be easily followed?
  Is his plan apparent?
  Does he omit extraneous details?

Is his manner direct?
Does he meet the eyes of the listener?
Does he seem to be talking with the audience?
Does he seem straightforward and sincere?
Does he show vitality?
Does his voice have sufficient energy?
Does he seem to think what he is saying is important both to him and to his listener?

Only after the student has gained a degree of assurance—and sometimes not even then—should his attention be called in private conference to distracting mannerisms of body, voice, and expression. Moreover, many nervous habits disappear as soon as the speaker is sure of himself. When progress is discernible, additional objectives may be added.

Practice in finding, organizing, and communicating ideas for specific purposes should help the student gain confidence. But even more, it helps him acquire skills preparing him for those informal social situations where his only allies are his general background of information, his knowledge of human nature, and his habitual ways with language.

Discussion

The oral skills program stresses *communication* and therefore *consecutive* discourse. In daily classroom discourse the teacher should distinguish sharply between the oral quiz and discussion. In the first the student speaks not because he wishes to communicate but because he must present evidence that he remembers items the teacher already knows. His contributions consist for the most part of disconnected words, phrases, or sentences. In discussion, ideas are important, and the participant has a chance to develop those he favors and to challenge those he thinks untenable. His information and opinions do not drop into a void, but elicit response. Even though in large classes lack of time prevents a single participant's making lengthy remarks, he should in any well-conducted discussion see the unity and development of the whole. The oral quiz has its place in the classroom, but both teacher and student should see its purpose as other than the promotion of oral skill.

DISCUSSION DEFINED   Continued experience throughout the secondary-school years should help students see discussion for what it is—a learning device through which everyone contributes a little and where each learns from all. They should see it, first, as a means of thinking together to bring out the facts, the possible interpretations, and the different points of view on any particular question; second, as a process of reasoning to determine what tentative conclusions can be drawn from these facts and judgments.

Discussion is not a debate where the speaker sets out to prove he is right and those who disagree with him are wrong. It in no way resembles a lecture or a monologue. It is not quibbling over facts; they can be verified. It is not the bald statement of opinions without support. The aim of discussion is not always to find an answer; it may be merely to explore the various aspects of a topic. Often, however, the purpose is to find a solution to a problem or to reach a decision affecting all members. Although the result may not be entirely satisfactory to anyone, and some may completely disapprove, consideration of the issues as a preliminary to formulating plans for group action is the recognized mode of operation for free men in a free society.

ROLE OF DISCUSSION LEADER   A discussion is an experience in group thinking. If it is to accomplish its purpose, the leader must assume a twofold responsibility: to help the participants explore the implications of the content and to conduct this exploration so the result will represent the best thinking of the entire group. If students are to learn the requisite skills, they must be concerned with more than tacit acceptance of the conclusions reached; they must be aware of the procedure used and play their individual parts in making that procedure effective. In leading, the teacher strives for both interplay of ideas and involvement of as many contributors as possible—throwing opinions of one participant to another for reaction, calling for summaries at strategic points, tactfully halting one disposed to talk too long, encouraging the reluctant with appropriate questions. In evaluating discussions, he calls attention to procedures demonstrated. Thus he helps students understand that both process and product are important, that both logical and psychological aspects are significant.

TRANSFER OF SKILLS   The principles of effective speaking can perhaps best be taught through short talks prepared individually. Teachers must then help students see that the same rules apply to discussion; after students have learned the importance of the controlling sentence in their own speeches, let them determine a governing sentence for a discussion just completed; after they have studied support of assertions, ask them for examples of statements that have been adequately developed. Before starting a discussion, briefly review the concepts taught through individual speeches and suggest that students try to put them into practice. In evaluating, try to draw from the class ways individuals have used effective speech, whether in selection of content, awareness of organization, or clear and forceful presentation.

The similarity between discussion and conversation may not be apparent to pupils. The teacher should help them realize that skills of oral communication can serve them in places other than the classroom. Questions similar to the following may act as springboards for discussions emphasizing the desirability of capitalizing on abilities being developed. Has anyone used an illustration to amplify a point made in conversation? Heard a statement which the speaker when challenged could not support? A conversation where misunderstanding arose because of imprecise use of language? Do you know anyone who refuses to stick to the point? Anyone who bores a listener with unimportant details? In some such way, teachers can keep re-emphasizing the idea that the same principles underlie effectiveness in formal and informal speech.

The Group Process

Today the interdependence of men demands that each person participate in many groups; productive participation requires of him the ability to work with those groups of which he is a member as well as to accept the coexistence of others to which he does not belong. Experience in the English classroom can aid him in developing the necessary insights and skills. On the first day of almost any class the student finds himself in a large group; he may be associated with one of several cliques or sub-groups; he may be completely isolated. One of the teacher's first tasks is to weld the class into something resembling solidarity—necessary both for morale and for learning. With widely heterogeneous classes this welding process can rarely be accomplished except through the formation of many small units within the class as a whole, the personnel of each group periodically changing. Thus, the teacher can make it possible for the contribution of each student to be recognized, for him to be accepted as a participating member of the class. Through group efforts, as students learn the content of the course, they can improve the skills needed for working in any social group.

FROM THE STUDENT'S VIEWPOINT   Most students recognize the desirability of becoming more adept in group participation. Some, highly grade-conscious, may at first be fearful their contributions will not receive due credit; they will be reassured if they understand that individual learning is still the focus, although accomplished through group effort. During adolescence, a time of confusion and ambivalence, the student is trying to learn his role both as an individual and as a group member; peer approval is probably more important now than at any other period of his life. Classroom experience can help him find himself as he gains skill in working with others; consideration of divergent viewpoints can deepen his understanding of those whose backgrounds differ from his own. Thus, he becomes more aware of the social significance of the group process. He knows or can learn that most of the world's problems, if they reach solution, are solved around the conference table—the importance of the committee work of congressional leaders, the significance, in settling labor disputes, of discussion among representatives of various factions. The realization that he is learning skills to use not only in the classroom but in life convinces him of the practicality of learning better ways of working with others.

FROM THE TEACHER'S VIEWPOINT   The advantages for the teacher in using the group method are far-reaching in their import. Since each member can contribute according to his capacity, this type of instruction allows teachers to take care of particular interests and needs, to accept the student as he is and to help him progress at his own rate toward his potential goals. Moreover, the interaction of minds, one of the salient characteristics of group work, provides a stimulation that can be gained in no other way.[7] Above all, because this plan creates a situation comparable to those met in life, it lends itself to many of the objectives in education. Working in small groups, the more capable need not adjust his pace to the less competent; the slowest, the most diffident, the most inarticulate, can be placed in an environment where he can be taught to function. Group work gives experiences in leading and following; it affords opportunities to think through problems under peer and teacher guidance; it furnishes small, realistic audiences for the student's attempts at expression, where he may learn to evaluate his own opinions and those of others. Teachers who use the group method find it pays big dividends.

Helping young people acquire oral skills asks from the teacher a hard head and a soft heart. In an atmosphere of free inquiry where students know they can say what they think but realize their opinions require support; where they recognize that proficiency demands practice over a long period of time; where both speaker and listener accept responsibility for making communication effective—in such an atmosphere the individual can develop both the habit of using language honestly and the skills for using it effectively.

THE TEACHING PROBLEM

Because oral communication is so frequent, because it pervades everyday experience, a multitude of situations exist for teaching. This very multiplicity presents both an opportunity and a problem: an opportunity, because as soon as students understand the purpose of instruction, most see the desirability of becoming more adept in handling a tool they use so widely; a problem, because a program must be devised to encourage transfer of attitudes and skills developed in the classroom to the varied social situations the individual encounters daily.

ORGANIZING INSTRUCTION

In organizing instruction, the teacher asks himself questions similar to these: What problems can be anticipated? What content is appropriate? What particular skills are to be emphasized? What methods will produce the best results? These questions are not discrete, nor can the suggested answers be;

[7] See the discussion of the learning process in John Dixon, *Growth through English* (Reading, Eng.: National Association for the Teaching of English, 1967), pp. 44–70.

all interact with one another. However, problems of organizing instruction are considered in the following sections: establishing a climate to promote growth; broadening the content base; emphasizing principles of effective speaking; using discussion; using group process.

Establishing A Climate to Promote Growth

Several basic problems, inherent in the nature of oral communication and thus pertaining to a climate conducive to the development of appropriate attitudes and skills, require initial consideration.

FINDING THE NECESSARY TIME   Students cannot learn to speak without speaking; if the skills of this week are to build on those of last, practice must be continual. Thus, if the teacher is dedicated to a program stressing individual speeches to which the whole class listens, he is defeated before he starts. Time is not available to build the necessary attitudes and skills in this way. We have suggested two time-saving methods—discussion and group work. The teacher has to convince himself he can provide instruction enabling pupils to speak better if he places them in situations where they can gain confidence; although he divides his time as best he can, he does not have to listen to every speech and every group discussion.

Using the course content as the major source of material also saves time. For instance, ideas gleaned from the study of several short stories can provide practice in applying the principles of effective speaking if process, as well as content, is emphasized in discussion. Likewise, skills demanded for making a speech plan can be used in writing if students are helped to effect the transfer. Integration of all areas of instruction, helping students see the unity and relationship among the various aspects of the English program, not only promotes learning but is economical of classroom time.

PROVIDING PRACTICE FOR ALL   In apportioning time to give the most practice to the greatest number, the teacher considers the problems of both the glib and the unwilling. Instruction stressing improvement through genuinely motivated communication—in contrast to aimless talk—is basic to solving the problems of each. The excessively vocal must learn what communication means; he must be taught to channel his fluency—a real asset—for conciseness and pertinence; he must recognize that for him cultivating responsiveness as a listener may be more important than speaking upon every question.

The shy and unwilling presents a greater problem. The teacher tries to discover the reasons for his attitude. Undoubtedly, individuals differ in degree of articulateness and in the pleasure they derive from conversation; however, all have the need to communicate. If placed in situations where this need can be satisfied, they will acquire the necessary skills. The seeming aversion to speech in the classroom cuts across all levels of maturity and intelligence.

Fear of exposure is one cause; the individual may have been conditioned in classrooms giving sole importance to the right answer and to correct usage. Reluctance may be induced by a feeling of superiority, often unconscious; the situation may seem so purposeless as to make meditation more profitable than attempts to contribute. Placing those inclined to talk too much and those forever silent in situations where they have the desire and opportunity for honest communication is crucial. Use of discussion in small groups offers a partial solution; allowing students some voice in selecting content helps; finally, the correction of mistaken ideas concerning purposes of the program and methods of evaluating improvement and thus of determining grades promotes a climate conducive to growth.

EXPLAINING PURPOSE AND SCOPE   Failure to recognize the purpose and scope of the oral skills program partially accounts for the attitude of those unconvinced of its value. The first weeks of any English course—when needs are diagnosed, goals explored, and standards agreed upon—provide opportunity to promote desirable understandings. The student is likely to equate speech as taught in the classroom with that of the accomplished speaker addressing an audience. Perhaps he has been in classes where the only oral work considered grade-worthy consisted of reports based on research and given for extra credit. Unaware of any objective except expertness in "public" speaking, he may reject the program because he cannot see himself as a platform speaker.

One of the first discussions in any school year might well be concerned with leading students to realize that one major purpose of oral communication is to help the individual exercise a degree of control in the social situation. What follows is a skeletal plan for such a discussion, with irrelevancies and digressions omitted.[8] Although many discussions result in tentative or alternate conclusions, here the teacher has decided beforehand what the result is to be, but only because it seems so obvious as to be inescapable. Even with only one conclusion possible, helping students think through the steps increases their understanding of the problem and prepares for acceptance of the inevitability of the conclusion.

In this abridged version, the minor ideas leading to the major conclusion are italicized. As each is reached, it may be written on the board. This teaching device helps students see that each discussion has purpose and pattern.

A discussion leading to an understanding of the purpose and scope of the oral skills program might go something like this:

How have you used speech recently?

Talking with friends, shopping, meeting in committees, explaining to the repairman what's wrong with the TV, talking with my family around the dinner table, asking my father for an increased allowance, planning a party, asking for a date

[8] Other examples of discussion sequence are given in this book. See pages 139, 296–97.

How have you used writing?

Note to a friend, letter to my aunt, list for the laundry, assignment in English

Which do most people use more, writing or speaking?

Speaking.

Yes, most people speak more than they write. This has always been true. There are many things we don't know about the origins of language, but one thing scholars agree upon is that it appeared first in its spoken form and existed in only that form for centuries. Today *spoken language is the most widespread form.*

In telling how you used speech, no one mentioned a type of experience I've had many times—speaking before a group. Has no one had that experience? Is it so uncommon?

Yes and no. It depends upon the person, his situation, and his work.

Certainly, by far *the greatest part of our speaking takes place in informal situations.* But even if you're sure you'll never stand before a group and speak, is there anything we can learn from practice of more formal speaking that might help us use speech effectively even on informal occasions? What are some of the things you'd like your speech to tell about you?

That I'm not afraid, that I know what I'm talking about, that I can make people understand, that I'm a person worth knowing, that I'm able to express my own opinion

Is it enough just to express your opinion? Don't you have to do more than that? What if your listener differs? What do you do then?

Tell him why I think the way I do.

You've mentioned self-confidence, poise, clarity and effectiveness of the statement, impression on the listener, support of an idea. . . . Are these much different from the characteristics of an effective speaker and speech on more formal occasions?

No, *similar principles underlie effective use of language in both formal and informal situations.*

All the speech occasions we've mentioned have concerned more than one person, as they always do. In other words they're social. What elements do we find in every social situation?

Speaker, listener.

Isn't there another, equally important? How do speaker and listener get together, if they ever do?

By speech.

We can agree that *any social situation has three elements: speaker, speech, and listener.* This is true whether the communication is formal or informal; speech is the instrument that allows sender and receiver to understand each other. In attempted communication does understanding always result? Have you ever asked directions for reaching a certain place, received them, and then found you couldn't follow them? What was wrong?

The speaker did not know or did not explain clearly; the listener did not listen carefully or did not interpret correctly.

Yes, the fault may lie with either or both. When language creates confusion—when you can't follow directions—speech does not accomplish its purpose. Besides confusion, what other unpleasant effects can language have?

It can irritate, antagonize, arouse contempt, make a person unsure of himself.

Then we could say, couldn't we, that *speech may either bring persons closer together or drive them farther apart?* If two persons in any situation really want to establish satisfactory contact, what must each do? For instance, I'm giving an assignment, you're talking to a friend. What must each of us do?

The speaker considers the listener, presents ideas clearly, watches the reaction, adds additional explanation when necessary; the listener remains alert, tries to understand, responds actively.

We'll come back to this point often during the semester. Now let's leave it and see if we can pin down the speaker's purpose a little more exactly. What were you trying to do on those occasions you gave as examples of speech used recently?

To get the TV fixed, to make the date, to enjoy our friends, to persuade my father.

In every social situation there is something we are trying to do. Let's try to find a general statement that will cover all purposes of speech on all occasions. Help me fill in this sentence: The purpose of speech is to help us _____ the social situation. We're looking for verbs now. Suggest some. We'll find out what they mean and which is more exact.

Dominate, control, govern, adapt to, change, adjust to, withdraw from.

We might want to do any one of these on some particular occasion, but have we any words here that include some of the others?

Control, adapt to.

If we qualify "control" and use instead "exercise a certain degree of control," would that help? What is the difference in the connotation of the two terms? For now, let's accept *the purpose of speech is to help us exercise a degree of control in the social situation.* You check all the work we do in speech against this purpose; if later we find it doesn't fit, we'll change it.

In the above illustration, the teacher definitely tried to direct the thinking toward one certain conclusion. However, the framework given is not the discussion, which would never proceed with such clockwork precision; it would not be a discussion if it did. A teacher's integrity demands that he drive for one certain decision only when no other seems possible. Presumably, he would not lead such a discussion if he did not think the conclusion broad enough to include all forms of oral communication and, therefore, any specific example a student could give. If he had encountered any unforeseen evidence that did not fit, he would have had no choice but to qualify his preconceived conclusion. A procedure that brings out all phases of a topic and admits objections and counter arguments, even if it leads to one inevitable result, is an expression of a democratic principle. It is the duty of the teacher to lead students through the thinking that will convince them of its inevitability.

ESTABLISHING BASES FOR GRADING   A second misunderstanding arises because in many classrooms progress is evaluated mainly on ability to write and to pass tests proving knowledge. Thus when a student returns after absence and is moved to ask if he has missed anything, he is not disparaging the teacher's ability to maintain a scintillating classroom. What he really wants to know is whether there has been a written assignment, now represented by a blank space after his name in the record book. Grades may not represent a worthy motive for learning. However, they do indicate to both learner and teacher— and to parents, colleges, and employers—an estimate of individual accomplishment. They cannot be ignored; while the teacher avoids using them as incentives, they are facts that must be faced. Students in each particular classroom have a right to know on what bases the grades for the course will be determined. Because of the fluid nature of oral communication, the need for understanding is perhaps greater here than in other areas of English instruction.

Understanding the general purpose of oral communication will prepare students for the many aspects needing emphasis. As each is singled out for instruction, practice, and evaluation, the student comes to realize that his grade depends, not upon his ability to make a finished speech each time, but upon how well he has met specific requirements. In order to help pupils appreciate the firm basis for grading, the teacher should assure them that first assignments will be concerned with only one or two principles—for immature pupils, audibility, or conversational tone, or meeting the eyes of the listener. He must then give them a chance to use these skills in speaking and help them evaluate the results. He should let them know that skill in speech is cumulative, that they will be given time to consolidate their gains.

FUSING WITH TOTAL PROGRAM   In fusing the oral experiences with other phases of instruction, the teacher fits method to content. In general, either problems chosen by students or ideas emerging from books read individually offer the most practical material for teaching the principles governing effective speech and for providing practice for their application in small groups: the content here is largely individual and thus lends itself to short talks. Ideas from the literature studied and synthesis of experiences with either the selected problems or personal reading furnish material for class discussions: here a mutuality of experience supports the give and take of informal communication. No arbitrary division is intended; each teacher experiments to find the methods most suitable for teaching the course content with a particular class.

The teacher also considers the timing of oral work, usually trying to combine speaking with reading and writing so that one experience flows naturally into another. Thus reading may provide ideas for discussion, which in turn gives incentive for writing. The illustrative units furnish many examples. However, when it seems desirable, oral work can be inserted without interrupting the continuity of other curricular activities; the teacher uses a split schedule. By careful planning, he can devote portions of several class hours to experiences stressing oral skills, the rest of the time being spent on other aspects of instruction. Several days at the beginning of the year, when teacher and students are exploring the potential of the course, or short interludes at the completion of units offer other possibilities for brief instruction and practice. Oral communication is so much a part of life that opportunities to help students develop the necessary skills present themselves continually.

Broadening the Content Base

Although ideas emerging from various facets of the curriculum are the chief source of material for the oral program, students should also have a chance to discuss problems that concern them personally. In many classes teachers can approach this aspect of oral work directly. In others, however, it is often unwise to begin by asking outright what subjects merit discussion. Suspecting a snare presaging dire things to come, some will deny interest in anything. An oblique approach helps counteract this difficulty. Teachers, taking a tip from the pollsters, have found an indirect way to discover what students feel deeply about. The following example will show how one teacher of an eleventh-grade class used an opinion poll to find suitable topics and to introduce the techniques of discussion with the aid of group work.

AN OPINION POLL   From his observation of the class and from his knowledge of problems that were disturbing faculty and students, although often for different reasons, the teacher made up a list of provocative statements similar to the following:

OPINION POLL

Directions If you strongly agree with the statement, circle SA; agree, A; are undecided, U; disagree, D; strongly disagree, SD.

1. Students usually do better work in school when there   SA   A   U   D   SD
   is close relationship between parents and teachers.
2. Too few students in this school have an opportunity   SA   A   U   D   SD
   to participate in student government.
3. High school clubs encourage segregation.   SA   A   U   D   SD
4. Students should have a part in determining regulations SA   A   U   D   SD
   governing student conduct.
5. This class should be so organized that homework   SA   A   U   D   SD
   would be unnecessary.
6. School parties and dances are so closely supervised   SA   A   U   D   SD
   that many students are unwilling to attend.

The teacher introduced the subject by saying he knew certain problems connected with school affairs seemed of concern to many. Thus he was temporarily assuming the role of Mr. Gallup to determine how the class as a whole felt about them. As in all such surveys the identity of the participant was unimportant; no names were to be signed. He gave no hint that the exercise was more than a slight detour to satisfy the curiosity of an eccentric instructor.

The returns seemed to indicate many of these controversial questions were of vital concern to students. Probably because the community was being agitated by some parents who wanted an increase of homework, this topic provoked the most decided reactions. The students, however, were disinclined to make any concessions to unreasonable adults; over two-thirds said they believed the class should be conducted so that no homework would be necessary.

When the class arrived the next day, they found the statement concerning homework on the board with a tabulation of the opinions expressed; fifteen strongly agreed; ten agreed; eleven disagreed; no one was undecided. The teacher said that since this was a question affecting all of them, it had better be discussed; that although he could make no promises, he would consider seriously any conclusions reached by the class. Accordingly, he was dividing them into groups for the purpose of discussion.

Bringing his knowledge of his students to bear, he had previously determined the personnel of the groups, placing, as he thought, two dissident members in each. Before taking their places the students were asked to jot down reasons for their opinion, not to hand in but to use to help group thinking. The written reports from the secretaries were to indicate the number advocating each point of view and the reasons accepted as valid support. They were allowed ten minutes. Wishing to leave the student free to express himself honestly without fear of incrimination, the teacher ignored the discussions, a procedure that cannot often be employed with group work.

As was to be expected, the reports were similar; all indicated that the students had difficulty finding support for their opinions. Substantiation for both viewpoints was based on lack of time, but with a difference. Those favoring homework did so because there was not time in class to complete assignments; those opposing, because there was not time outside of class.

Both opinions seemed to have a basis in fact. Previous estimates of the average time per day spent outside the classroom in preparing for English ranged from two who spent none to three who spent over an hour and a half. The teacher's records showed that about one-fourth of the students were employed in part-time jobs, about one-half were carrying heavy academic loads, about one-third were active in the extracurricular program; a few could be placed in all three categories.

Taking into consideration the caliber of his students and trying to anticipate objections, the teacher prepared carefully for the next day's discussion. His purpose was twofold: to devise a practical plan for accomplishing the essential aims of the course and to lead students to see their responsibility for facing facts honestly. The problem seemed to revolve around the following questions: To what extent are the reasons given for the opinions valid? What do we need to know before we can come to a decision that will affect the group? Where can we get additional information?

The teacher wished students to realize the demands imposed by the course, the necessity for considering their own problems as individuals, the need for evaluating their study habits and for budgeting their time. He therefore attempted to find the questions and examples that would help him direct the thinking along lines logically and psychologically sound—facts he hoped would lead to the conclusion that everyone, in school or out, faced the responsibility of planning for himself a realistic program.

The next day he began by reviewing quickly the aims of the course and what had been accomplished to date. He then read a news item in which a representative of a labor union, currently negotiating for certain benefits, tried to justify the demands. The reliability of the writer as an authority was briefly discussed, the class deciding that he could be accepted only with reservations because bias had to be suspected. Most of the students were, of course, well aware where such an admission was leading.

After these preliminaries, the teacher proceeded with the discussion, selecting questions from the following, when and if they seemed pertinent:

Previous assignments

Have they been excessive? Suggestions for curtailment?

Should a teacher always give identical assignments for all students? Why?

What type of work for English do you prefer to do in class? Outside?

What are the advantages of long-term assignments? Difficulties?

Study habits

According to your own estimates, the amount of time spent in preparation for this class varies widely. How do you account for this?

Is it possible for two students, equally intelligent, to spend the same amount of time and produce results of different quality? Reasons?

What are some of the characteristics of a study period if the time is to be spent profitably?

Does the time that you reported spending on English represent that much time in concentrated effort?

How many of you know specific ways that you could improve your study habits?

Budgeting time

How many are taking subjects that require less preparation time than English? More? How many feel that their general schedule is too heavy?

How do you apportion your time among several assignments? Let's say you have problems to work and turn in for mathematics and a story to read for English. You think the two should take an hour; you have only half that time. How do you proceed?

Some people with charge accounts at several stores, finding at the end of the month they can't take care of all of them, pay a little on each in order to maintain credit. What do you think of this plan? Is there any similarity between maintaining credit at the store and at school?

You may have read articles that express alarm at the credit situation in the country as a whole. Some writers seem to think that too many people, buying on time, contract debts they will never be able to pay. Suppose for the moment this is true. Why do you think people become so involved? Is it unavoidable? Under what circumstances?

In planning your schedule, do you have any responsibility for seeing that it is one you can handle?

SUMMARY OF TENTATIVE CONCLUSIONS

Preparation for final discussion

Magazines have devoted quite a bit of space recently to the question of home-work. Would some of you be willing to consult the *Reader's Guide,* look up an article, and report on it?

Do any of you know someone whose opinion on homework—reasonable amount of time, system, and so on—might be worth having? A teacher who is able to organize his course so that all the work can be done in class? A student who has a good plan? How about getting the opinion of your counselor? Parents? Do you know anyone in no way connected with the school—a business or professional man—you could consult?

Assignment This time next week we'll finish discussing this problem and see if we can come to some sound conclusions. We'll hear reports from volunteers; there will also be time for other information anyone else may find either from reading or interviewing.

As a result of the final discussion, the teacher and students arrived at the following conclusions:

Two hours a week was not an excessive amount of time to devote to home-work for English.

Long-term assignments would help, especially if some system of intermediate checking were devised to insure that work was progressing at an acceptable rate.

The most desirable type of homework was that connected with reading and individual projects.

There should be two types of assignments—one required of all, the other where the student had some choice.

Although, most assuredly, not all students will comply with regulations set up in this way, the fact that they have followed the argument step by step makes them more ready to accede to demands that have seemed reasonable to the majority.

The entire experience required little class time; it showed that many kinds of learning may take place concurrently. In less than three periods the teacher had given all a chance to talk, both in group and class discussion, had helped them face and think through a problem of vital concern, had made provision for volunteers to interview, to read, and to report the results; he had, without mentioning oral skills, laid the foundation upon which a sound program for developing oral skills could be built.

Furthermore, the poll seemed to indicate that other subjects on the list might be worth investigating. The results of the poll were, therefore, given to a student committee to discover which of the five remaining topics had aroused most vigorous response. Their report follows:

Topic	SA	A	U	D	SD
1	0	0	0	20	16
2	10	5	9	2	10
3	12	10	2	2	10
4	14	3	0	11	8
6	0	6	20	10	0

Through class discussion, the first topic was immediately discarded. The other four seemed to have something in common. With some rewording and organization, the teacher and class arrived at the following plan. If students could make their own regulations what would they suggest should be done about (1) securing wider participation in student government, (2) putting membership and activities of clubs on a more democratic basis, (3) planning parties and dances to appeal to greater numbers? The class was divided into three groups, each to investigate one aspect of the problem. The procedure followed was substantially the same as in the preceding experience. The discussion resulted in an editorial written by a student committee and published in the school paper. However, the greatest benefit probably derived from the fact that these young people were able to consider all phases of the problem and both participants and nonparticipants in school activities had a chance to see themselves through the eyes of the other.

A SIMPLE QUESTIONNAIRE   The above plan can be used in many junior high classes; even seventh-graders who have had similar experiences in elementary school may be capable of the sustained attention such procedures demand; however, many immature pupils are not. For these, a simpler form of questionnaire with fewer follow-up activities is suggested.

Directions   Check the proper column; do not sign your name. Have you recently discussed with any member of your family or any of your friends

                                                Yes   *No*

1. Grades you've received in school subjects?
2. Your choice of friends?
3. Time you have to be in at night?
4. Choice of or time spent on television programs?
5. Number and selection of movies you are permitted?
6. Length of your telephone conversations?
7. The books you are reading?
8. Comic books?
9. Time spent on homework?
10. Your allowance?

Follow-up   Suppose 4 and 6 are answered affirmatively by a majority of pupils; discussion can be provoked by either of two methods: role playing or demonstration.

Role playing is a term applied to an extemporaneous dramatization of a social situation involving conflict, with an attempt to suggest a solution.[9] It differs from similar dramatizations made from stories children have read in that here the plot is not ready made; the situation delineates a problem students face and for which they try to find alternative answers. Scripts are not written; a general plan of presentation is agreed upon—the main ideas, the role of each character, the direction the dialogue will take, and so on. After the general plan is agreed upon, lines are spoken impromptu.

Television Students are asked to suggest difficulties that may arise over privileges, types of program, and so on. The one they select to dramatize may be similar to one of these:

Three children with different interests, each wanting priority with the TV, discuss their respective claims.

Four parents discuss crime programs, giving different points of view regarding the effect on young people.

Several students evaluate different kinds of programs, assessing their value as entertainment.

The same situation is used by several groups and the solutions compared. The discussion of the various interpretations of the problem is often the most significant part of the experience, pointing up, as it may, examples of straight thinking, tact, and thoughtful consideration of opposing viewpoints.

In preparing for role playing, the participants should answer such questions as: What is the attitude of each character? What are the reasons for this attitude? What action follows logically from this attitude? What are the effects of the action on the other characters? What changes are to occur as the dramatization unfolds? How are these changes to be brought about?

For the first experience in role playing it is well for the teacher to lead the class through the preliminaries—helping pupils define the problem, selecting the situation to be used, analyzing possible attitudes and action—and then to accept volunteers for the performance.

Sometimes the facets of a subject lend themselves to individual demonstrations. Pupils working in pairs give their versions of both the correct and incorrect procedure:

Telephone List on the board as many examples as students can give of different uses they have made of the telephone. With pertinent questions draw out others that are common. The list might look something like this:

chatting with a friend
taking a message
sending a telegram
placing an emergency call—ambulance, fire department, police
making a complaint about a mistake in delivery
ordering several items from a department store
asking information about planes, trains, and buses

[9] See also Chapter Five, "Imaginative Thinking," page 193.

accepting an invitation
declining an invitation
asking for release of party line in order to make a call

Both the demonstrations and the discussions that follow can emphasize the desirability for clarity, brevity, and courtesy in the use of the telephone.

The use of some kind of poll offers a quick and effective way of discovering some topics of concern to students. Followed by instruction and by practice in applying the principles of effective speaking, such devices provide a basis for extending interests as well as developing attitudes and skills.

Emphasizing Principles of Effective Speaking

In selecting principles of effective speaking to emphasize, the teacher remembers he is trying to develop attitudes toward speaking and habitual methods of procedure. Instruction and practice may focus now on one aspect of content, organization, or delivery, and now on another; thus skills are gradually built.

GRAPHIC PRESENTATION OF SEQUENCE   As instruction in oral communication proceeds, graphic presentation can help students concentrate in practice on the various principles studied. They may keep in their notebooks a chart listing each emphasis as it is introduced. Items may first be recorded in their own words; as standards are periodically reviewed, teacher and pupils may reword and reorganize. The completed chart for any class will represent only those aspects of effective speech students have had an opportunity to practice. The one below offers a sample of the beginning of such a chart for a class with little previous instruction. Each of the three horizontal blocks represents the focus for a single assignment. In addition, the individual should try each time to apply all the principles previously listed. Thus in the review speech no new idea would be injected, giving time for synthesis of various skills.

SEQUENCE OF EMPHASES

Content	Organization	Delivery
interesting to speaker		easily heard easily understood
	beginning that interests conclusion that clinches idea	
controlled by purpose	governed by a central idea	eye contact with listeners conversational tone

Review speech, demonstrating application of all principles studied

The suggested sequence of emphases—indicated by horizontal blocks—is not intended to dictate an arbitrary order. Since sequence depends upon the experience and the maturity of the class, the order cannot be determined far in advance. Above all it must be flexible, starting with simple objectives students may be expected to achieve in a few attempts and continuing with others added one or, occasionally, two at a time. The teacher proceeds slowly; time is not lost, even if no new principle is introduced, because each repetition builds confidence, which in turn aids in the development of skills. After the teacher has drawn from students what they believe to be the characteristics of effective speaking, the class can decide what to strive for first. With some students, attaining only a few elementary goals may be enough to expect even after six years' practice. With others, each assignment may emphasize several objectives. Even with the capable, however, skill is acquired gradually. Many brief speeches, each concentrating on one or two points, produce better results than a few longer ones trying to incorporate everything.

ADDITIONAL OBJECTIVES   The chart below suggests further objectives, some of which certainly should be added for many classes or suggested for individuals at the teacher's discretion.

CONTENT	ORGANIZATION	DELIVERY
interesting to listener	ideas pertinent	straightforward, seems sincere
few abstractions, many concretions	support adequate	authoritative without being overly aggressive
variety in material— facts, illustrations, testimony	sequence planned to maintain interest	paced to make comprehension easy
material from several sources	transitions clear	posture that does not call attention to itself
facts accurate	use of devices to begin and end other than statement and restatement of central idea sentence	with vitality
evidence of originality		free from distracting mannerisms
		precise and vivid language

If the teacher keeps in mind that the second chart lists some objectives suitable only for the mature and gifted, he will avoid pushing pupils to the point of discouragement. If students continue to want to speak, skills can be developed.

TEACHING THE SPEECH PLAN   In the beginning, even ultimately for many pupils, three steps (I, A, 1) in the outline for the main part of the speech are enough to teach. If the student learns to apply these, he can later learn to deal with more complex material, for the principle is the same. If he cannot understand three-part relationships, it confuses him to be allowed to run the gamut of lettering and numbering denoting intricate points and sub-points; the complex outline should be reserved for the clear thinker working with complicated material. Moreover, three steps should be sufficient for the oral work most students may be asked to do in the English class.

What type of outline is most useful in teaching oral communication? Since the purpose is to help the student form the habit of perceiving exact relationships, the sentence outline is most effective. Only this form permits teachers to determine quickly whether the writer is precise in his thinking; the individual conference time demanded for all other types prohibits their use. It is immediately apparent that it is impractical to try to teach this difficult form to the pupil who still has trouble recognizing a sentence; teachers should spend all their efforts in helping him learn to support single assertions.

Even competent students resist making speech plans in sentence form, their chief contention being that it takes too long to write ideas as statements.[10] However, it is the thinking, not the writing, that takes the time. They are also prone to believe they know what they want to say but cannot write it. Such a conclusion betrays spurious thinking. Writing gives training in exactness, and repeated practice in ordering one's ideas in a form another can follow fosters clarity of thought and precision of statement. If the student can gain facility in the thinking that even three steps in the sentence outline demands, he has acquired a valuable tool, which becomes more useful as thinking and communication grow more complex.

The beginning and the ending of the prepared talk are difficult for the inexperienced; therefore the student should formulate his introduction and conclusion rather carefully. Because first impressions are likely to either quicken or deaden interest, the first sentence is important. The experienced speaker gets into the main part of his speech as rapidly as the occasion permits, avoiding apologies and details that seem to discredit the listener's intelligence. The ending is equally significant, for it must, by drawing the threads together, leave the listeners with a sense of completeness. The speaker avoids inserting new ideas, drawing out his material, giving repeated warnings of closing. Although a long speech may require recapitulation of the points covered, a general statement clinching the central idea is sufficient for the short talk.

The student, after becoming proficient in building both introduction and conclusion around the restatement of the central idea, may experiment with other types. If pressure of time makes such experimentation impractical, variations can be tried in the writing experiences, for problems of speaker and writer are similar. A series of questions, a pointed anecdote, a vivid description of an apt situation arouse interest and help lead into the development of speech or essay. A quotation, a word picture strong in sensory appeal, an impressive illustration—anything epitomizing the central idea—make effective conclusions.

---

[10] The topical outline is usually sufficient for expository writing, since student and teacher can examine the thinking in the complete communication as it assumes permanent form on paper.

Using Discussion

Several major problems in using discussion to teach content and develop skills will be considered: preparing to lead, starting effectively, arriving at conclusions democratically, securing variety through different patterns.

PREPARING TO LEAD

Guiding group thinking through discussion requires understanding of the implications of content and insight into characteristics of group members.

CONSIDERING CONTENT   Significant questions in a significant order are essential if students are to think their way through content to logical conclusions. No activity requires more careful preparation on the part of the teacher. In considering the implications of content, he must decide: What ultimate conclusions are logical? What minor conclusions build to these? What questions will help students think through each step? If the issues are identified correctly, the success of any discussion depends mainly upon the questions that guide thinking—questions that bring out the facts and probe the reasoning based on those facts.[11] Failure to ask the right questions results, after a period of perhaps enjoyable but aimless conversation, in the more capable students or the teacher telling the class what the facts seem to indicate. Such a failure is serious, for it defeats the main purpose of discussion.

How does the teacher find the right questions? It is not easy. Even when he thinks he has found them, students fail to oblige with the anticipated answers. However, most of the difficulty seems to arise from two closely allied errors: asking, too soon, questions that require an abstract rather than a concrete answer; attempting to skip links in the chain of reasoning. Both these mistakes in strategy force students to take steps for which they are not ready. Conscientious preparation on the teacher's part, which, in framing questions, takes into account the students' experience, will help eliminate both errors.

CONSIDERING GROUP MEMBERS   Since the aim is to involve as many students as possible without detriment to the discussion, the teacher in directing questions gives some thought to the abilities of individuals. Usually the *what*, and sometimes the *how*, questions laying the groundwork for each minor conclusion, can be answered by the less able. If the brilliant and vocal are allowed to volunteer this information, no contributions are left for those incapable of abstract thinking. This is not to say the pace should be slowed to accommodate the inarticulate. Teachers have, however, helped the student overcome reluctance in various ways. They have advocated to individuals the wisdom of mak-

[11] See pages 288–89 for illustration.

ing remarks early before fear has a chance to take hold. During preliminary study periods they have given time for specific preparation—handing to a pupil a copy of the opening question and telling him he will be called upon first; asking him to listen to initial points and to be ready to give the first summary; letting him select some phase of the topic he feels ready to discuss. Discouraging raised hands until discussion grows controversial and always when others are speaking helps create an atmosphere more favorable to participation. In short, considering the strengths and weaknesses of group members can insure more fruitful discussion.

STARTING EFFECTIVELY

Sometimes the beginning of a discussion moves so slowly that most of the allotted time is spent in preliminary skirmishes. Even when students are in possession of the facts, they may not be able to marshal them quickly. Time is lost and interest wanes as participants grope their way, trying to interpret questions, searching for pertinent evidence. Often a short period spent in preparation with pointed direction to stimulate thinking serves to get the discussion moving fast and purposefully.

USING PRELIMINARY GROUPS   A brief warming-up session in small groups, with questions to be used later for the entire class, gives students a chance to mobilize their thinking. Such preparatory work bolsters the confidence of the timid, who may be more ready to voice ideas they know have some support; other students whose deductions have been challenged are likely to be eager to prove their thinking correct. Illustrations of preparation for discussions with different purposes and for different levels follow.

Suppose a class of widely varying abilities has read "The Necklace," by Guy de Maupassant. The reader will recall the story of Madame Loisel, who loses a diamond necklace borrowed from a friend, finds a replica to replace it, works all her life to repay the debt incurred by the substitution—only to learn in the end that the lost jewels were paste. In the discussion the teacher's purpose is to lead the class to discover how the author reveals the total meaning by the skillful arrangement of incidents built around particular characters. The teacher prepares questions similar to those here to point the way to the concepts the author develops:

> What do we learn of the character of Mme. Loisel and of her husband from what the author tells us about their actions?
> What, from their respective thoughts?
> What courses of action were open to Mme. Loisel when she discovered the loss of the jewels? Was the course chosen consistent with her character? Explain.
> Would the outcome of the story have been changed if the jewels had been real? Would there have been irony in the story even if Mme. Loisel had never discovered the jewels were paste? Why does the author make the jewels paste? Consider our study of symbolism.

The teacher divides the class into groups, giving each one of the questions, assigning the third and fourth to the most capable students. In large classes two groups may be given the same problem. In the class discussion, he uses the same questions; to clinch the ideas developed and to point up the alternative meanings, he uses this quotation: "How little a thing is needed for us to be lost or saved." What "little thing" is Mme. Loisel referring to? Does the author think she has been lost by a "little" thing?

With less mature students who have read Corey Ford's "Snake Dance," the teacher's purpose might be to explore the relationship that exists between the problems presented in stories and those we meet in life. This story tells of a boy who, for what he considers the best of reasons, deceives his parents; instead of attending college as they expect, he has taken a job as a soda fountain clerk. In the preliminary work, each group may be given all the questions.

> What did the boy's parents want?
> Has the boy given up all chance of fulfilling the ambition his parents have for him?
> Is it believable that the boy will be able to deceive his parents long? Why or why not?
> What was the boy's reason for the deception?
> What will happen if it is discovered? What effect do you think it will have on his mother? On his father? Could the discovery cause the very damage the boy has been trying to avoid?
> Can you from your reading or from experience suggest other incidents where people have been forced to choose between what they consider two evils?

In the class discussion that follows, the motivation of the three characters can be clarified, the arguments for and against the deception weighed, and perhaps the conclusion reached that finding a totally satisfactory answer to important questions is seldom easy.

USING DIRECTED STUDY   A variation of this method may be used without recourse to group work. The teacher may list on the board questions representing the major steps planned for the discussion, and give each row of students a different question. Students are to jot down evidence to support a definite answer. After the study period the discussion proceeds as planned, the students who worked on a certain question being given the first chance at answering. This plan offers an advantage to the more capable and to those well prepared; it throws the laggards on their own resources. The effect is salutary, for students must not come to rely upon group work to save them from the penalty of faulty preparation.

Another method allows students to compose their own questions for the literature studied. Suppose all have read five chapters of a novel. The class may be divided into five groups for a study period; each individual, working on one assigned chapter, prepares two questions that touch upon the salient points. These questions are then given to a capable member of the group; he is allowed time to select two to guide him in leading the class in discussion.

After the five chapters have been examined in this fashion, the teacher takes over as leader, calling attention to important aspects of the story that may have been overlooked, clarifying the ideas that this segment of the novel presents.

Not all classes nor all discussions require the impetus of preliminary work. To lend variety to the program and to tailor the oral procedures to the needs and abilities of the students, the teacher will experiment with different methods.

ARRIVING AT CONCLUSIONS DEMOCRATICALLY

Occasionally, disapproval is voiced of carefully planned and guided discussions on the grounds that they invite the authoritarian approach. Such critics seem to misunderstand the function of the teacher-leader. A leader, from lack of either integrity or perceptiveness, might drive for a predetermined conclusion that ignored the facts and their implications as well as the sensibilities and intelligence of group members; a teacher cannot. Presumably, he is wiser than his students; he has prepared more carefully than they; he is interested in teaching them how to think, not what to think. Admittedly, all these assumptions may be false in any particular instance. However, if they are true, the teacher in preparing has considered the merits of all possible inferences and has taken pains through his questions to see that the facts pointing to these conclusions are given fair play. He is morally obligated not to reveal his own opinion until the implications of the evidence and of all viewpoints have been taken into account. His aim is to guide individuals to think for themselves rather than to spend their energies trying to guess what he wants. The time has long passed—indeed it probably never existed—when secondary-school pupils looked upon teachers as founts of infallibility. Continued experiences similar to those described below may convince students the teacher sees one aspect of his job as concerned with teaching thinking rather than with providing answers.

AVOIDING PAT RESPONSES   The film *Right or Wrong?*, often used at the junior high level, presents the case of a boy under pressure to give information about an act of vandalism he has witnessed. He can exonerate himself by telling what he knows, but the price of immunity is distasteful. The last scene shows his distress as he realizes that the deadline for his decision is fast approaching. What would you do? Any honest adult will probably have to admit that he is not absolutely sure what he would do. However, as the pupil watches the incident unfold he is likely to suspect a none too subtle attempt to underline a moral lesson. He may be willing to voice acceptance of approved attitudes—vandalism is wrong, everyone should aid the police—and finish the distasteful matter with dispatch. Obviously, the right-thinking citizen is on the side of law and order. If the purpose in showing the film is to extract this admission from the class, the enterprise seems hardly worth while.

The film certainly does not suggest any pat answer; it does provide material for a stimulating discussion. The basic problem does not concern juveniles nor their delinquency, but the recognized truth that all of us, often through our own lack of foresight, find ourselves enmeshed in circumstances where whatever decision we make will not please us. The roots of any problem and of the way any individual attempts to solve it go back, sometimes far back, in time.

The discussion, therefore, will be more fruitful if it centers upon the universality of the problem—the necessity of considering the consequences of behavior, the inevitability of being forced sooner or later to assume responsibility for one's own actions. It should leave the student with sharpened awareness that painful decisions are not confined to the young nor to a life of crime but are the lot of all human beings. The question as to what the boy in the film should do can be left to each individual to ponder.

PERMITTING ALTERNATE CONCLUSIONS   In interpreting levels of literary works, the teacher has another opportunity to show students he is not always sure of the answer. He can let individuals draw conclusions differing from his own. After students have presented their evidence, he can suggest some they have overlooked, but he cannot force a conclusion their experience is not ready to accept. "The Necklace" will again serve as an example. The immature student, inclined toward romanticism, will interpret the shock of the ending as the author's way of forcing the realization that the woman has been betrayed by chance. Apparently that is Madame Loisel's interpretation, as she thinks of the little thing by which one may be lost or saved. The mature reader may interpret the story more realistically; he may think the author uses *little thing* ironically. Evidence at the beginning of the story shows that this woman's whole life is guided by selfish and materialistic values; one might conclude that if she had not been betrayed by the loss of the necklace, something equally foolish would have produced the same result. The author does not state his theme; he lets the reader make up his own mind. After all the evidence has been presented, the teacher must accord his pupils the same privilege. They will take it anyway; conclusions cannot be forced. Only varied experiences with literature will lead students to interpret facts below the level of the obvious.

Not all discussions are as strictly guided as those used as illustrations in this chapter. Sometimes the teacher's purpose may be to stimulate a group of seemingly inarticulate pupils or to explore the possibilities of some topic preparatory to more intensive study; thus a definite order would be too restrictive. However, too many discussions without logical sequence are likely to frustrate the intellectually able and convince them that to the teacher *discussion* and *random talk* are synonymous. If the student is aware of the purpose of each discussion, he can recognize the relation of form to content.

SECURING VARIETY THROUGH DIFFERENT PATTERNS

Useful as discussion is as a way to learning, too much repetition of the same pattern blunts its effectiveness. Teachers, in planning with students the oral program for a year—or a semester—vary the approach.

THE ROUND TABLE   The round table, which the preceding examples illustrate, is probably the most satisfying way for a group to consider problems. As the name suggests, it refers to a number of persons seated or conceived to be seated around a table for the purpose of discussion. At its best, this arrangement permits each member to speak several times, thus fostering informal exchange of ideas and interaction of thinking; ideally it resembles stimulating conversation. Although limited time and large numbers do not allow every student to contribute orally, nevertheless class discussions follow the round-table pattern. To meet the problems posed by the far from ideal classroom situation, teachers supplement class discussions with those of small groups. Although for most occasions the round table may be preferable, panels and symposiums, both highly adaptable to student interest and need, also have their place in the classroom.

THE PANEL   The panel, similar in some respects to the round table, is composed of a chairman and from two to six members, who sit before an audience and discuss a question. In preparation, the issues are decided and the manner of presentation planned. No set speeches are made; the exchange is informal, no one talking much more than a minute at a time. The chairman steers the discussion according to the outline agreed upon by the members. Usually about half the time should be reserved for audience participation. Occasionally, a listener may ask for clarification or make a suggestion before the panel has finished. As a rule, this is postponed until the chairman makes a brief summary and invites comments. The panel, characterized by flexibility and spontaneity and thus requiring some degree of ability in impromptu thinking and speaking, is difficult for the less confident; it should be tried first with students not easily daunted by such demands. The chairman's job is particularly difficult, since he must fit the pieces into the over-all design. Sometimes the teacher is the only person competent to act in this capacity, as, for example, in discussions of several books with which no one student can be expected to be familiar. However, as often as it can be done without harm to either content or class, a student assumes the role.

THE SYMPOSIUM   The symposium, like the panel, consists of a chairman and several members. Here, however, speeches are prepared; presentation is more formal, adhering to a preconceived plan. The subject chosen will suggest different ways in which the responsibility for its exploration may be divided. Sometimes it is more effective if the speakers represent divergent points of view; at others, each may give a certain aspect of the topic. In any case, the purpose is the same as that of the panel—to provoke discussion. Therefore, information must be given, issues clarified, pertinent questions raised. Then the audience, under leadership of the chairman, takes part. Since the speakers are presumably experts on the subject, the symposium lends itself to class-room experiences where intensive research is necessary and can be delegated to a few. However, the more knowledge the class has acquired on the subject, the more stimulating is the discussion likely to be.

These various approaches to discussion have been used to good effect on both radio and television. Over the years such discussions have aroused and sustained nation-wide interest in important questions. Today, transmission by satellite allows producers of *Meet the Press* and similar programs to bring together participants far distant from each other. Representing varied and ideological backgrounds, presenting contrasting viewpoints, they offer a broader base for considering world problems. They also provide a platform for examining bias—one's own and that of the speakers. Investigation of worth-while programs should be suggested to students with special interests. At times, groups may volunteer to listen and to report to the class.

Books from the guided reading program provide an abundance of material for panels and symposiums:

> Several mature students who have read biographies might comprise a teacher-led panel built upon criteria devised by a committee for judging the medium, such as the following, the product of a class of eleventh-graders: (1) Is the biography historically accurate in that it depicts the individual in relation to his times? (2) Does it present not a type but a human being, showing the gradations of human character? (3) Does the author bring both incidents and characters to life? To include all students, the class discussion might center on how well the criteria for judging biographies apply to the evaluation of works of fiction being read.
>
> Any grouping of stories—pioneer, teen-age, adventure, sports—with student-chosen or teacher-suggested items for comparison can be used. When several have read the same book, either panel or symposium makes a satisfying manner of presentation.
>
> Problems in which students have evinced interest [12] can be handled as a series of panels or symposiums prepared by groups who plan the attack, do the necessary research, design the arguments, and select members to represent them as speakers.
>
> Any topic that adds informational spice to other class work may be used in the same way. A group of ninth-grade pupils attempted to trace similarities in ideas in the folklore of widely separated locales as a contribution to the class study of folk literature. Seventh-graders, combining story telling with appropriate background material, entertained with American tall tales from Davy Crockett to Superman.

The variations to which either the panel or the symposium lends itself are numerous.

[12] See pages 289–90.

Material for discussion, whatever the type and however initiated, abounds in any well-integrated English course. Teacher and students may pick and choose; the problem is really one of elimination.

Using Group Process

Group work within the classroom is a common activity for elementary-school children; in addition, many pupils have had such practice in youth organizations. In planning work for secondary-school students, the teacher will build on this experience. Even those who have had little previous practice can learn with guidance to work effectively in small units within the class.

GUIDELINES FOR THE TEACHER

FORMING THE GROUPS   The teacher's purpose will guide him in deciding upon the personnel of groups. Those that are to be maintained over a period of some weeks are usually composed of students of somewhat similar needs, interests, or abilities; groups may be formed for those who need to learn certain points of grammar or usage, for those seeking to eliminate particular errors in sentence structure, for those whose reading skills are below par for the class. They may be made up of students interested in preparing a bulletin board, in presenting a play or a panel, in studying a literary work. For such long-term activities, the size of the group may be comparatively large; more often than not it is led by the teacher while the rest of the students are quietly engaged with individual work.[13]

However, dividing the entire class into small units to work at the same time on identical or similar problems is also advantageous. This is especially true in teaching oral communication. These groups meet only for a few times, occasionally only once. Student-led, they should be limited to no more than six members. Here the purpose is to aid the handling of any of the day's activities—to warm up for class discussion, to provide a small audience for those reading poetry, to give the student a chance to secure face to face response for his original work.

The teacher may use almost any plan he wishes in selecting those to make up each group. His choice, even though the result of much thought, should at first seem casual, the make-up of groups changing frequently to give each student a chance to work with as many different individuals as possible. Often planned heterogeneity in group formation during the early weeks will contribute substantially to the socialization of the class. Until he is sure of his students, the teacher will proceed cautiously, trying to place individuals where they can function most easily. He is usually careful to separate those who seem antagonistic to each other; to place special friends together only when

---

[13] See also the units "Meeting a Crisis," pages 426–34; "The Consequences of Character," pages 659–75.

he thinks it will help rather than hinder; to divide both the shy and the talk-ative among the groups; to include in each at least one person who shows potentialities for leadership. Even if pupils have had experience with group work in elementary school or in preceding classes, the teacher cannot take skill for granted. Behavior may change with different environment and with different group personnel; each class needs a period of orientation.

After students have developed some skill in working together, a less careful selection of groups may be possible. Students may be grouped alphabetically or according to their position in the room. Even placing the very slowest, as if by accident, all in one group often brings out unexpected initiative. Occasion-ally, pupils may form their own groups. If they know of the plan in advance, it can be put into effect without commotion and waste of time. Experimenta-tion will point the way to many effective groupings.

DOMINATING THE PHYSICAL SET-UP   Unquestionably, movable furniture and extra space are desirable in group teaching; however, it is a mistake to think them essential. The method has been used successfully in overcrowded rooms with narrow aisles and with seats screwed inexorably to the floor. To make listening easy and to avoid bothering others, groups should be as compact as

A CLASSROOM WITH 48 SEATS AND 48 PUPILS

(FRONT)

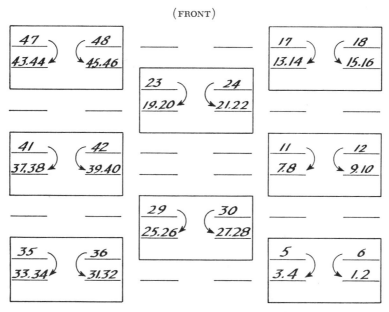

Each block of four seats will take care of six pupils, leaving sufficient space between groups so that one need not disturb the other. For teacher-led dis-cussions, nine seats in any corner of the room will accommodate eighteen students, over one-third of the class; this leaves nine vacant desks to provide insulation for those working on their own. Teachers have made the groups even more compact by using stools placed in the aisles.

possible. Since the time to be spent in such formation is short, participants will not be unduly uncomfortable even when sitting two in a seat. Because the question of suitable arrangement in crowded space has been asked so often by prospective teachers, the diagram on page 303—showing how a room filled to capacity may be used for this type of work—is included, even at the risk of being overly explicit.

PLANNING INCREASINGLY COMPLEX EXPERIENCES Realizing he is trying to teach skills demanding a degree of intellectual and emotional maturity, the teacher will be careful not to push students into experiences for which they are not prepared. Initially, he plans simple tasks with the help of the class, moving slowly, avoiding problems that invite conflict. He starts with very short meetings of no more than ten minutes, perhaps only five. In order to discourage dilatory practices, he errs on the side of allowing too little time rather than too much. Alert to evidence indicating he may have misjudged the readiness of students, he is prepared to turn to a more formal type of activity at the first sign of possible disintegration of groups. Any flagrant disregard of standards,[14] even if only on the part of a few, should mark an end of group work for the day. He avoids being influenced by the pleas of those who have been working conscientiously; the method has to work for all groups or not at all. At this point the teacher can rarely be too strict. He is careful, however, not to make writing or reading sound like a punishment for disorder. He may tell the class calmly that since this does not seem to be a good day for group work, it will be postponed, as there are many other things to do. Since this obvious truth promises a second trial, it usually satisfies a class. If he has laid the groundwork carefully, he can expect help from the students in making the method work next time. Most young people enjoy working together and often bring their disapproval to bear on those who find self-discipline difficult.

Gradually, as students become more adept, the tasks become more difficult, and the time spent in groups becomes longer. It is impossible to give definite rules; necessarily, the complexity of the problem and the time allowed for its solution depend upon the level of maturity the teacher has been able to achieve with any particular class. The progression is through teacher-led activities toward those in which the student assumes more and more initiative; different classes and different individuals move forward at different rates. If a series of problems of carefully graduated difficulty is dealt with and if the standards of procedure are observed, three or four sessions should reveal the potentialities inherent in the method.

GUIDELINES FOR STUDENTS

Since students possess the salient facts, the teacher may use the inductive method in introducing group work. He, therefore, prepares questions to lead

[14] See pages 306–07.

students to heightened awareness of the importance of the small group meeting in conducting everyday affairs, to fuller understanding of the nature of guided discussion and of the standards governing its effectiveness.

INTRODUCING THE GROUP PROCESS Any day the teacher wishes to introduce the group process to a class, he will have no difficulty finding current examples to illustrate its extensive use. With some classes, a reference to a previous discussion of a school problem is the best approach. Teachers have used such varied topics as ways of securing wider student participation in assemblies, the possibility of providing music during lunch hour, the responsibility for keeping halls and classrooms neat, the prevention of vandalism on Halloween, conduct worthy of a sportsmanship award. The practice in many schools of publicizing the results of such class discussions by a report to a school-wide committee, an editorial for the school paper, a letter to the principal, or items on a central bulletin board emphasizes for students the significance of their own contribution. If a class is fortunate enough to be familiar with similar procedures, reference to such experiences will stress the importance of any group to the whole and will show pupils the practicality of using small group discussions as a help in arriving at class decisions.

With more mature students, a community, national, or international event may provide greater incentive. The morning paper will furnish material. Teachers have used such current happenings as negotiations to settle a steel strike, a youth conference in the national capital, a meeting of the Security Council of the United Nations, a protest by a youth group, a national conference of scientists meeting near by. Since the purpose of the discussion is not, for example, to help settle the strike but to understand the procedure used in trying to bring it to a satisfactory conclusion, the selection of such a topic does not presuppose any great amount of technical knowledge on the part of either students or teacher.

ANTICIPATING DIFFICULTIES Before even the simplest type of group work is launched, it may be helpful for students to consider the difficulties they may encounter. Any guided discussion tries to arrive at the approximate truth through consideration of various points of view; it may attempt to reconcile divergent opinions in order to bring about desired action. Therefore, one can be sure of meeting disagreement and conflict; he can expect his opponents to cling as tenaciously to their opinions as he does to his own. What must he do then if he wants to work effectively with others? Is it enough to believe he is right? How does he handle opposition? Of what significance are his own mood and motives? Those of the rest of the group? Of what importance are tone of voice and choice of words? Consideration of the obvious truths that living with others has already taught students leads to the conclusion that sensitivity to the total situation, tact, and patience are needed if one is to develop group skills. Such a conclusion sets the stage for understanding the role of participants and for devising standards for the group work to follow.

UNDERSTANDING ROLE OF PARTICIPANTS   Since results of discussion should represent the best thinking of the group and not merely that of the brilliant or the vocal, the most significant concept for students to assimilate is that all participants are important. This will follow logically if class members agree on the desirability of everyone's learning to exercise a degree of control in the social situation.[15] Students, familiar with most of the roles of group members, may list the duties of each. Tell students that one of the aims of group work is that each person should try many roles and that for a time these roles will be given to volunteers. When the personnel of groups changes often, it is a waste of time to allow students to go through the process of election. The chairman, impartial to individuals and to ideas, coordinates the efforts of all by maintaining an atmosphere conducive to participation, by keeping the discussion on the question, and by asking for a summary whenever necessary. He calls for clarification of facts and tries to help the group reconcile conflicting opinions. But all this should not be left to him; the rest should realize he is neither a disciplinarian nor an authority; he is a leader. Every member, alert to his own responsibilities, should be willing to assume any of these tasks when it seems necessary. The secretary keeps an account of the arguments given and the tentative conclusions reached; if a written report is required, he takes care of it. His notes assist the reporter in preparing an oral résumé of the results. At times, in mature groups, when it seems desirable to focus more directly on process, an observer may be added. He takes no part in the discussion; his job is to discover and to report specific practices that have facilitated or obstructed the performance. It is important that his report concern these and not personalities.[16] All participants try to state their views briefly so all may have a chance to ask for amplification of obscure points, to consider the evidence objectively, to think for themselves.

All these requirements cannot be gleaned from students; therefore, take only what the class thinks essential as a guide for the first group meetings. Others, discovered as the work progresses, can be added. Try to leave the class with one idea—if each fulfills his role, the resulting interaction of minds insures cooperative group thinking.[17]

SETTING STANDARDS   In guiding students in setting standards, the teacher should first draw from them the difficulties they see in their particular situation—restricted space, nearness to other classes, necessity for six or seven groups working at the same time. He may show students a chart giving the best seating arrangement he has been able to devise, calling attention to the compactness of groups and his attempt to separate one from the other. Why?

---

[15] See pages 282–84.

[16] To develop oral skills students must constantly keep in mind that communication is a two-way process; it can be aided or hindered by both logical and psychological factors. Reports of observations—a suitable task for gifted students in the beginning and later for the less gifted—can be used to lead students to generalize on the nature of communication and on practices that foster its effectiveness.

[17] See, in Bert Strauss and Frances Strauss, *New Ways to Better Meetings* (New York: Viking, 1951), "Salvaging Problem Members," pp. 64–75, and "The Group Learns to Produce," pp. 76–83.

He will probably assure them in the beginning he will give exact directions and an exact time limit for the completion of the work. Again, why? A series of questions will result in a set of simple standards suitable for beginners working on simple tasks: What must you know before you get into groups? How can forty persons move into and out of groups without disturbing classes under us or next door? When you are in a group what is your responsibility if the method is to work? What is the teacher's responsibility?

Make the necessary preparation This would usually mean doing the assignment; for impromptu groups it may mean only being familiar with the directions, assuming a cooperative attitude.

Get into groups quickly and quietly Before the class separates into groups, every student should know with whom he is to work and in what part of the room.

Follow the directions given Directions must be specific; if they are not very simple, they should be written. They may be placed on the board if all are engaged on the same problem; if not, the chairman of each group may be given a copy.

Ask for help just as soon as needed The teacher moves from group to group, giving what help he can; he is careful not to let the more aggressive students monopolize his attention.

Keep the work within the group That each group must work without disturbing other groups cannot be overemphasized. Whispering can be as distracting as noise; help students see that talking in a low conversational tone is best.

Be willing to contribute Willingness to express one's own views, to consider those of others, to ask pertinent questions, to allow everyone to speak, is a minimum requirement.

Return to seats quietly and quickly In the interests of control, work should usually be planned so that students assemble as a class before dismissal. Too, an immediate discussion of the work undertaken by the groups is often helpful.

The standards may be copied in the pupil's notebook where he can refer to them in evaluating his own work. Although other requirements may be added, these usually refer to the material rather than to methods of procedure. These simple standards give enough emphasis on *process* to serve the purpose with most classes.

Teachers adept in using groups within a class find the method, since it permits the student to function at his ability level, conducive both to the improvement of morale and to the promotion of learning.

In organizing instruction, the teacher tries to plan a program economical of classroom time, designed to motivate individuals of varying interests and abilities. Central to such a program is helping students realize that the acquired skills will serve them in the demands of everyday life.

SUGGESTED LEARNING EXPERIENCES

For purpose of emphasis, skills required for responsive and critical listening and those needed for effective speaking have been discussed separately in this book. In practice such division is unrealistic. The teacher, in planning the oral skills program, will consider the two as a unit, selecting from each chapter those experiences most meaningful for particular students at any particular time. Too, since all communication has much in common, he will realize that many of the suggestions for oral and written communication are interchangeable; one can be used to supplement the other.

TO ACQUIRE SKILLS FOR INFORMAL COMMUNICATION

▶ *Develop awareness of all experience as the source of material for talks, discussions, and conversations*

1. Discuss the reasons professional writers and speakers carry notebooks to jot down observations.

2. Encourage students to collect brief, interesting items that may be useful in oral work—anecdotes, jokes, quotations, vivid comparisons, startling facts. Ask each to contribute an item a week to a class file of ideas.

▶ *Discover some qualities of effective conversation*

Discuss in small groups quotations concerning various aspects of conversation: [18]

> I don't like to talk much with people who always agree with me. It is amusing to coquette with an echo for a little while, but one soon tires of it.
> CARLYLE

> Never hold anyone by the button in order to be heard out; for if people are unwilling to hear you, you had better hold your tongue than hold them.
> CHESTERFIELD

> It is wonderful that so many shall entertain those with whom they converse by giving them a history of their pains and aches.   STEELE

> For good or ill your conversation is your advertisement. Every time you open your mouth, you let men look into your mind.   BARTON

> The tongue is only three inches long, yet it can kill a man six feet high.
> JAPANESE PROVERB

> Know how to listen and you will profit even from those who talk badly.
> PLUTARCH

> It is good to rub and polish your brain against others.   MONTAIGNE

> As we must render an account of every idle word, so we must of our idle silence.   AMBROSE

> Not only to say the right thing in the right place, but far more difficult, to leave unsaid the wrong thing at the tempting moment.   SALA

> Those who have finished by making all others think with them have usually been those who began by daring to think for themselves.   COLTON

Ask members of each group to interpret the author's meaning, to decide to what extent they agree, to give examples from experience to support their opinions; summarize the conclusions through class discussion.

▶ *Recognize that school situations demand oral skill*

1. Talk over with students the importance of making classroom visitors feel welcome; let different students assume the role of host or hostess, greeting these visitors, supplying them with books, explaining the work being done. Ask the most outgoing students to take responsibility for making new students feel at home.

[18] These quotations, reprinted with the permission of the publisher, are taken from *The New Dictionary of Thoughts* (New York: Standard, 1954).

2. Use social events such as open houses, father-son dinners, teas for parents as occasions for review of simple forms of introduction. Discourage any practice that smacks of formula and rigidity. Since the aim is always to put those who do not know each other at ease, explain the importance of giving a conversational lead to the two introduced. Students will be less self-conscious if asked to devise leads for fictional characters—for example, let them decide what one statement about Tom Sawyer or David Copperfield would best serve as a lead in introducing him to a boy his own age, to a girl, to an adult.

▶ *Practice conversational skills in interviews*

Ask each student to hand in one subject he enjoys discussing with his friends and upon which he feels reasonably well informed. Divide the class into groups, each to select the person with the subject most interesting to them; later other group members are to interview him. Ask each interviewer to prepare questions to ask the speaker and to select, from his own information on the subject, items he might be able to introduce to enliven the conversation.

On the following day, groups meet and conduct the interviews; one member acts as observer. Observers report to the class, noting the general tone, examples of good transitions, tactful questioning, extent of participation, and the like. Teacher and class compile a list of characteristics marking the good conversationalist.

▶ *Welcome opportunities to practice impromptu speaking*

1. Help students briefly review the concepts of controlling idea, support, and clinching sentence. Limit impromptu speaking to one or two paragraphs. Speakers should aim at poise, directness, clarity, clear-cut organization. It is too much to expect adequate support.

2. Give students a formula: start with the controlling sentence; support with an illustration or not more than two detailed facts; restate the controlling sentence to clinch the idea.

3. Provide time for practice. Let each volunteer draw one item from the idea file to use as the basis for a talk. Occasionally arrange for a few spare minutes; ask if anyone within the last week has observed or read anything he'd like to tell the class. Give him a minute to organize before he speaks impromptu. Or, let not more than six students practice impromptu speaking in a group. Each member can announce a topic and call on another for a one-paragraph talk.

TO SELECT CONTENT

▶ *Find out what is likely to interest*

1. Give students a week to notice subjects being discussed in other classes, at home, among their friends, in newspapers and magazines, on radio and television. Ask them to hand in a brief list of those they find most stimulating; to star those profitable for class work. Duplicate the list of starred topics and give a copy to each student; ask him to make a first, second, and third choice. After a student committee has tabulated results, discuss with class and make selections for a tentative program.

2. Use an opinion poll to discover problems (see page 286).

▶ *See relationships among topics*

If several have chosen aspects of medicine and a few science, they may be willing to combine, selecting such topics as implications of the Hippocratic oath, recent scientific discoveries applicable to the medical field, possibility of using atomic energy in medicine, quackery in the name of medicine. One ninth-grade class, combining topics handed in by several members, arranged programs under these topics: Moments to Remember, Moments to Forget, I Wish Parents Wouldn't, My Parents Wish I Would, I Would Like to Know Why.

▶ *Consider appropriate ways of presenting ideas*

Discuss how interest of listeners, number of speakers, nature of the subject matter may affect the method of presentation. Tentatively select subjects that might be better presented in prepared talks to small groups, to the class by panelists, through general class discussion, and so on. This procedure is applicable to any class and usually nets more ideas than can be used for oral work in any one semester, since the literature studied and the books read in the guided reading program will furnish many more. The initial selection of subjects, however, should not be considered final. As interests expand, some topics may be discarded and others added.

TO WIDEN AND DEEPEN INTERESTS

▶ *Exchange recommendations for reading*

1. Ask each of the more capable students to assume responsibility for reading one certain magazine a month and for recommending its best article to others; post the list in the library or in the classroom; arrange time for those who have read the same article to discuss it.

2. Have a class committee accept students' recommendations of books worth reading; keep such a list posted on the bulletin board; when several have read the same book, plan a group discussion or a presentation for the class.

▶ *Form the habit of collecting conversational bait*

1. Encourage individuals to clip from newspapers and magazines short items of wide appeal; place these on a table in the rear of the room where students who finish work early may browse. If there is no space for a table, the material may be kept in large envelopes and made available to those who want it.

2. Let volunteers who maintain personal files meet occasionally in a small group for ten minutes to give one member a chance to start a conversation that will allow introduction of ideas suggested in his file.

▶ *Become an expert on several subjects*

It has been said that the good conversationalist knows a little about many things and a lot about a few. Using students' original lists of topics, encourage individuals to become authorities in one or two areas that interest them. Then arrange for a series of interviews called "The Expert Speaks."

TO LEARN TO CONSIDER RECIPIENTS IN COMMUNICATIONS

▶ *Study the significance of impersonal questions as means of starting conversations*

1. Introduce by discussion: Why impersonal? Why questions? Why questions requiring more than one-word answers? Since openers grow out of particular situations, ask students to consider the English classroom on this particular day and to suggest questions that might serve to start conversations.

2. Each student lists on a card three ideas he enjoys talking about; students exchange cards. Working in pairs, each composes several questions suitable for starting conversations on topics suggested by the other; they agree on one example to be reported to the class; the class evaluates these according to the criteria set.

▶ *Plan a communication to interest one particular person*

Each student writes on a slip of paper his name and a topic. Students exchange slips; each is to write for the other a composition on the given topic that will arouse and hold interest. The two read their papers to each other; the listener decides whether or not the purpose has been accomplished and determines reasons for the writer's success or failure.

Teacher and students explore means successful writers have used, trying to discern similarities that may indicate some things likely to create interest—suspense, conflict, unusual details, strange facts, humor, illustrations, colorful language.

TO LEARN THAT IDEAS FORM THE CORE OF COMMUNICATION

▶ *Recognize ideas capable of development*

Ask students to decide which sentence in each of the pairs below expresses an idea the speaker might prefer "to leave with his listeners."

> We started for Yellowstone early in the morning.
> Our Yellowstone trip had several highlights.
>
> Our class officers will meet after school.
> After school our class officers will meet to transact important business.
>
> Madame Defarge spent a lot of time knitting.
> Madame Defarge's knitting proved to be more than an innocent pastime.
>
> After Caesar's death Antony addressed the mob.
> Antony showed his knowledge of mob psychology in his speech over Caesar's body.
>
> I just finished reading *Manchild in the Promised Land*.
> *Manchild in the Promised Land* is a disturbing story.

This exercise should take very little time, as the controlling sentences are easy to recognize. The difficulty will come later when the student tries to construct a plan for a talk controlled by one sentence. If a student selects the first one of any pair, ask how he would develop it; for example, I just finished reading *Manchild in the Promised Land*. If his purpose is to tell something unusual about the finish of the book, he can compose a better sentence. Let him try.

▶ *Construct sentences expressing a point of view capable of development*

Ask students to write a sentence that could be developed into a one-paragraph talk and to exchange with his neighbor, who is to write a brief statement as to what he would expect from a communication so controlled. Move about the room, trying to discover examples that deserve the attention of the class. After the papers are returned to the owners, hold a brief discussion to correct misunderstandings. Even though all students may not have written satisfactory sentences, it is better not to belabor the point at this time. Since it is central to organization, it will recur repeatedly in later work.

TO LEARN TO SUPPORT ASSERTIONS

▶ *Learn to support with illustrations*

1. Read a short anecdote, parable, or joke. Ask students to construct sentences that it might be used to support. Discuss.

2. Duplicate several of the less well-known fables of Aesop, omitting the moral. Give each student a copy of one. Have him write a controlling sentence. Divide the class into groups according to the fable read; ask each group to select the best sentence and to choose one member to read the fable to the class, concluding with the sentence chosen.

3. Ask each student to choose a favorite anecdote or joke, compose a controlling sentence, and prepare as a short talk to be given to a group.

4. Read Kipling's "If." Let each student select one statement from it as a controlling sentence, support it by a factual or fictional detailed example, and prepare a short talk.

5. Ask each student to select a proverb or aphorism—a penny saved is a penny earned; one man's meat is another man's poison—to support it with one specific example developed in detail, to restate the proverb in other words to clinch the idea, and to prepare to give the paragraph orally.

6. Ask students to develop a general statement by three concise specific examples. Write a paragraph to be handed in after being read in a group. *Follow-up* Ask each group to select one or two examples, vividly worded, to read to the class, giving the statement each supports.

7. Suggest an assignment based on books from the guided program. Use as a controlling sentence an opinion you have formed concerning a character in the book you are reading. Support with three specific examples briefly stated. Conclude with a sentence that will clinch the idea in the minds of your listeners: "(Character) in (title) by (author) shows great bravery," or "is too perfect to be credible," or "overcomes many obstacles," or "meets defeat through his own fault." Prepare a short talk.

For the follow-up, students meet in groups to give talks; after each member speaks, questions like these are considered:

> Was there a controlling sentence, either stated or implied?
> Were illustrations well chosen? Brief? Did they give enough information to be meaningful?
> Did the conclusion clinch the idea?

The group chooses one member to give his talk before the class.

8. Take general statements applicable to work previously studied for either oral or written work. Use statements like:

> *Treasure Island* provides many exciting moments.
> Ellison in *The Invisible Man* makes the misunderstanding between black and white Americans comprehensible to the reader.
> The short stories studied represent many different locales; present various problems; help us understand human nature.

► *Learn to support with facts*

1. To help students become aware of the use of facts in differing kinds of contexts, ask them to do the following:

> Select an article from the daily paper or from a weekly news magazine. List the facts; give the sentence they are used to support.
>
> Choose an editorial; state its proposition in one sentence; list the facts given. Does the writer use any other type of supporting material?
>
> Write a sentence that will give the reader an impression of the setting for the book being read. List the facts the author gives in creating this impression.
>
> Choose a fictional character. What details does the author give to help the reader visualize him? Summarize the general effect in one sentence.

2. Ask students to prepare a one-paragraph talk, supporting a controlling sentence by facts. Let them make their own choices but suggest some easy subjects: explanation of how something is made, description of a pet, the rules for playing some game, the reasons for a person's being featured in the news.

3. Give students a week to become aware of interesting facts that come to their attention. Then ask them to select the most unusual; give them a minute to prepare; take the reports as rapidly as possible. After all facts are given, ask the class to select two or three of the most stimulating. Discuss their value in a talk where the information would be pertinent.

► *Learn to support with testimony*

1. To call attention to the different purposes for which testimony is used, suggest that students do the following:

> Find an ad that uses testimony. Is it convincing? Give reasons.
>
> Select a news item that contains a quotation; read the quotation, stating the idea it supports.
>
> Select a current happening that has aroused conflicting comments; clip or compose statements representing different viewpoints; discuss in groups.

2. The following experience is suggested only for able students; however, it has proved successful in grades from 8 through 12.

> *Assignment* Choose the most interesting character in the book you are reading. Consider the facts given about him from the point of view of a lawyer who has accepted this person as a client. Imagine you are defending him on a specific charge. (If you prefer, you may act as prosecutor.) What other characters would you subpoena as witnesses? Has the author given any explanation that would make his testimony desirable? Present the evidence you think would acquit (or convict) the defendant of the charge made against him.

If two students have read the same book, they may like to take opposite sides, presenting the evidence for and against. Another variation allows a class, after study of a short story, novel, or play, to dramatize an imaginary courtroom situation dealing with one of the characters. In giving such an assignment, the teacher can illustrate with examples suggested by the literature studied:

> You are defending Aunt Polly as a suitable guardian for Tom Sawyer.

Antony is charged with willfully inciting a mob to violence. You are prosecuting attorney.

You are defending Lady Macbeth as an accessory to murder.

You are prosecuting Barsad for perjury.

You are defending Miss Pross on a charge of manslaughter.

▶ *Learn to support by combining the three types of material*

1. Let students work in groups of six to select a subject for which they are to find the three types of material, two members to bring in each particular type. Since the research problem should not be formidable, the teacher suggests easy topics and calls the first group meeting a few days in advance of the follow-up.

Follow-up The groups meet, compose controlling sentences for which they have support, disregarding irrelevant material; one member reports to the class. (The problem of interesting but nonpertinent material at times troubles all speakers—and writers. Students should learn there are only two choices—elimination and reorganization to permit inclusion. Class and teacher can often suggest a change in the controlling sentence that makes such items apt.)

2. Ask each student to make a statement concerning the book he is reading and to prepare to support it with the three types of material. For example: (Author) in (title) gives a picture of intrigue in eighteenth-century England; fails to provide sufficient motivation for behavior; tells a hilarious story; develops suspense; has created unforgettable characters.

TO LEARN THE PRELIMINARIES TO SPEECH PLANNING

▶ *Break down a broad subject into logical parts*

Take an easy subject to which all can contribute as it is worked out on the board —for example, Union High School.

    I. Academic education
   II. Vocational education
 III. Social education
 IV. Physical education
      A. Class work
      B. Intramural sports
      C. Interscholastic sports
         1. Basketball
         2. Baseball
         3. Track
         4. Football
            a. Team
            b. Coaching system
            c. Season's program
               (1) Upsets
               (2) Next game

This process is not always necessary; some minds leap automatically through several steps at once. Younger or slower students, however, may profit by following the procedure with several topics; with some pupils it is necessary to start with a much narrower one—for example, football.

► *Decide upon a point of view*

1. Consider the effect of the speaker's interest. In a talk on the next football game what might be the viewpoint of the business manager? The coach? A member of the rally committee? A member of the team? One interested in the fine points of the game? One interested only in being a member of the crowd? Help students formulate assertions capable of development and expressing different viewpoints:

> You should enjoy our next football game.
> We have a good chance of winning our next game.
> The team needs your support at the next game.
> Our next game will be a colorful spectacle.
> We face stiff competition in our next game.
> Our next game is the most important one of the season.
> Certain changes are promised for our next game.

Any of these assertions could serve as the controlling sentence of a short talk; it may or may not appear in the talk itself, but both speaker and listener should be aware of it. If the communication has unity, they will be.

2. Study the implications of the controlling sentence. Discuss questions similar to the following: What development does each suggest? Can one be used to support another? Is there any one that does not take the listener into account? What possible concerns of listeners are stressed? Which appeals would be most likely to move *you?* Help students see that the controlling sentence converts a topic into an idea suggested by the topic; this important concept—ideas, not topics, govern the communication—needs continued emphasis.

TO LEARN HOW TO MAKE A SPEECH PLAN

► *Reduce outlining to a three-step formula*

> Construct a central idea sentence (CIS) asserting an idea that expresses your point of view toward the subject.
> Construct topic sentences (TS) that, when developed, will support CIS.
> Construct sub-topic sentences (STS), to be amplified by facts, illustrations, testimony, to support each topic sentence.

Use hypothetical material that, having no restrictions, allows attention to psychological as well as logical aspects of communication.

1. Review the first step (CIS). If students have been supporting assertions in their oral work, they will have many examples of appropriate central idea sentences to offer. Let the class select assertions formulated on a topic studied in preliminary work—in this case, the next football game.

2. Learn the second step by formulating topic sentences (A, B, . . .) to support the central idea sentences selected. Two examples devised by one class follow:

> CIS: You should enjoy our next football game.
> A. It will be a colorful spectacle.
> B. It is the most important one of the season.
> C. We have a good chance of winning.
> CIS: Certain changes are promised for our next football game.
> A. Jim Smith will be tried out as quarterback.
> B. Reports of a new play have the fans guessing.

3. Learn the third step—the construction of sub-topic sentences (1, 2, . . .) to support the topic sentences—using one of the partially developed examples and identical procedure. After the class has selected the plan to be completed, the secretary writes the skeletal plan on the board. Let the class think of facts, examples, or testimony that may be used to amplify the topic sentences. Give students time to select items and to compose sentences; then the class chooses those seeming to offer the most interesting development, deciding on the arrangement likely to hold the attention of listeners; the secretary inserts the sentences in the plan:

> CIS: Certain changes are promised for our next football game.
> A. Jim Smith will be tried out as quarterback.
>   1. Jim's track performance last spring caught the coach's eye.
>   2. In practice Jim has shown keen understanding of football strategy.
> B. Reports of a new play have the fans guessing.
>   1. Some predict a new aerial offense.
>   2. Others foresee a different blocking arrangement.

Such a plan emphasizes both logical and psychological aspects of communication. The proper relationship of the various statements has been indicated, and the nature of the audience has been taken into account. The planners have assumed that the majority will be interested in something affecting their school; they have made use of at least one of the basic wants—the desire for new experiences. In ordering this material they have placed the stronger point last, trying to develop suspense through climactic arrangement. They have attempted to devise a psycho-logic structure.

▶ *Try a simple plan*

1. Help the intellectually limited compose assertions that express a personal point of view. Even a factual talk given by a seventh-grader governed by "there are three steps in making a kite" presumes he is familiar with the procedure and has determined it has three aspects; he is not merely reporting on an article he has read.

2. Use topics rather than sentences in developing the idea. Ask pupils to think of one adage that experience has taught them contains a kernel of truth; let the class choose one for development. List on the board, in the order given, illustrations and details volunteered by pupils. Experiment with different groupings, combining some items and eliminating others. Help students compose topical headlines for major groups; consider advantages of different sequences, agreeing on one to be used. Then arrange in outline form, using pupils' own words; this should result in the proper relationship of ideas, although the language usually needs revision. Leave the original outline on the board for later comparisons; help students rewrite coordinate ideas in parallel constructions.

The procedures demonstrated for class teaching are intended to show ways of attacking the problem initially; group and individual teaching must be continual as pupils make plans for actual talks they are to give.

TO LEARN TO GIVE AND TO TAKE CRITICISM

The ability to criticize tactfully and honestly is important in the classroom, but especially so in daily living; it smooths the relationships between parent and child, husband and wife, employer and employee. Every human being has to accept, and probably feels inclined to give, his share. The classroom offers no better occasion for practice than in experiences concerned with the improvement of oral skills.

► *Learn the purpose and meaning of criticism*

Study remarks sometimes made in discussing classroom speeches. Give students a list of statements; these should illustrate the completely adverse and the completely favorable, the concrete and the general, tactful and aggressive tone, acceptance and rejection of responsibility for listening.

> He has a good voice.
> He made three mistakes in grammar.
> He said, "_____"; that's not true.
> You said, "_____"; I wonder if that's always true?
> Your beginning story made us want to listen, but when you began to talk about _____, I became confused.
> You just mixed me all up.
> He should have told us why _____ is so wonderful if he expects us to believe him.
> You chose an interesting subject and had good material, but you hesitated so often I found it hard to follow.
> I was bored.
> It was a wonderful speech.
> He kept looking out the window and he mumbled and kept shifting around, but it was a good speech.
> Mr. J., will you explain *come* again. I'm not sure he used it correctly.
> That's the best speech I've heard him give.
> I noticed an improvement over his last speech. This time he looked at us more and had a better conclusion, but he needs to keep working on directness.
> I'd like to know what makes you think . . . ?

Ask students, assuming the statements true, which ones they would most willingly accept as criticisms of their own speeches, and to divide the statements into two groups, the most helpful and the least, and to then check those in the first group that they think most constructive. Give to a committee to tally.

Before presenting the results to the class, return the papers to the owners; ask them to try to discover the basis on which they made the division and then to determine why they checked the items they did. Through discussion—"When *you* make a speech what do you want to know about it?"—lead students to see that the purpose of classroom criticism is to help the one receiving it to improve and that criticism implies evaluation—the judging of strengths as well as weaknesses. (This might be the time for a brief lesson on language—connotation and denotation, tone.)

► *Develop constructive attitudes toward criticism*

1. As the sender, keep in mind the purpose—to help someone else improve. Establish a formula: greatest strengths; greatest weakness; specific suggestions for overcoming weakness. Remember that the way criticism is given is as significant as what is said.

2. As the receiver, keep in mind the purpose—to improve. Try to receive graciously. Try to weigh impartially, keeping attention on what is said, disregarding

favorable or unfavorable opinion of the critic or the way he has expressed himself.

Developing the skill of giving apt and helpful criticisms and the habit of subordinating the personal element in those received demands from students the utmost in communication skill—ability to listen accurately, to fashion a communication that will accomplish a particular purpose with a particular listener, to interpret rationally statements that may seem highly personal and critical in a situation likely to be emotionally charged. Students know, but perhaps should be reminded, that no adult ever consistently maintains this ideal. The mature person does, however, strive for these skills in communication. Teachers who have worked with students trying to develop healthy attitudes toward criticism find such experiences contribute much to the oral skills program.

SELECTED READINGS

BOOKS

BENNETT, ROBERT A. *Speech in the English Classroom.* Champaign, Ill.: NCTE, 1961. A portfolio presenting reprints of professional articles.

GRAMBS, JEAN D., IVERSON, WILLIAM J., and PATTERSON, FRANKLIN K. *Modern Methods in Secondary Education.* Rev. ed. New York: Dryden Press, 1958, pp. 229–52. Suggestions for handling groups in the classroom.

JENKINSON, EDWARD, ed. *Teacher's Guide to High School Speech.* Indianapolis, Ind.: State Department of Public Instruction, 1966. This publication of the English Curriculum Center at Indiana University offers help in teaching speech, dramatics, and broadcasting.

LEE, IRVING. *How to Talk with People.* New York: Harper & Row, 1952. A discussion of the understandings and practices necessary for effective communication.

MC BURNEY, JAMES H., and HANCE, KENNETH G. *Discussion in Human Affairs.* New York: Harper & Row, 1950. A presentation primarily for college students but valuable for teachers interested in deeper understanding of the principles governing discussion and the techniques of leadership.

MOFFETT, JAMES. *A Student-Centered Curriculum in the Language Arts, K–13.* Boston: Houghton-Mifflin, 1968. Imaginative suggestions for enlivening class work through role playing, creative dramatics, and group discussion are presented throughout this useful textbook.

PARRISH, LOUISE, and WASKIN, YVONNE. *Teacher-Pupil Planning.* New York: Harper & Row, 1958. A brief account with many specific examples designed to help teachers plan instruction with pupils and to work with groups within the class.

SQUIRE, JAMES R., and APPLEBEE, ROGER K. *A Study of the Teaching of English in Selected British High Schools* (Cooperative Research Project 6–1849). Washington, D.C.: United States Office of Education, 1968, pp. 225–82. This publication describes in detail the ways in which oral language and classroom dramatics form the basis of English teaching in selected British schools.

WILKINSON, ANDREW. *Spoken English.* Reading, Eng.: National Association for the Teaching of English, 1965. (Available from NCTE) Discusses the importance of group interaction, providing interesting illustrations from British classrooms.

EIGHT

WRITTEN EXPRESSION

> *The very nature of writing indicates it must be learned through actual experience in putting words together to express one's own meaning. One does not learn how to create a sentence by adding or subtracting words and punctuation marks in a sentence someone else has created. Composing a paragraph or an essay is a closely knit operation, and playing with the pieces will not substitute for making the whole.*
>
> LOU LA BRANT [1]

PERSPECTIVE

To write clearly, students must think clearly. To write competently, they must think competently. To write with power and imagination, they must think with power and imagination: think/write write/think—these processes cannot be disjoined. When a student has learned to write better he has learned to think better. This is a law. There is no way around, only through.

The Nature of Writing

In writing as in gardening, placing vigorous roots in fertile soil is more important than pruning foliage. Too much emphasis on spelling or punctuation —especially in perfunctory writing—undermines the aims of instruction. Distracted from the heart of the matter, the learner is led to focus on subsidiary features. The truly fundamental aspects of communication have already been presented in the opening chapters of this book. Those chapters view power over language as dependent upon disciplined reason, creative imagination, and an awareness of how language works. To write effectively, students must grapple with their own feelings and thoughts, and the more aware they are of language in relation to audience and purpose, the more readily will they impose order on their expression.

[1] Commission on the English Curriculum, *The English Language Arts in the Secondary School*, NCTE Curriculum Series, Vol. 3 (New York: Appleton-Century-Crofts, 1956), p. 297.

But, one might ask, does writing really differ in any fundamental way from speaking? Since the foundations of teaching writing and speaking converge on the point of effective thinking, why not emphasize speech in almost all lessons on expression? Even without the evidence of research, we realize most human beings talk far more than they write. Why not grant that power over the spoken word is of paramount importance? Why teach anything about writing, other than spelling, capitalization, and punctuation?

The answer is clear. Writing, whenever human beings resort to it, usually conveys crucial meanings in situations where sender and receiver are separated. Love letters, applications for jobs, communication between scattered families and friends—these, like most writing, relate deeply to the needs of human beings. Furthermore, the act of writing, by virtue of its permanence and especially its separation from the reader, demands much more careful attention than speech. In his daily talk, a speaker can easily modify his presentation, shift to a new approach, elaborate points that appear to mystify his listener. In writing, where the receiver of thought is absent during the writing and the creator absent during the reading, such spontaneous modification of communication is impossible. Unless sentences as well as paragraphs reveal a sure grasp of concepts and their relationships, a reader may become either confused or disinterested. Thus, the two considerations of cruciality and separation of the communicants explain why expression cannot be taught solely through speaking. Properly taught, writing becomes a valuable way to clarify thought, a way placing a high premium upon precision and clarity, and therefore a significant part of the curriculum for all pupils.

Writing is clarification of thought and feeling. Through writing, one comes to know more fully what has heretofore been incomplete or confused. A writer explores his own thinking, struggles to discriminate among the various feelings and concepts swirling about in his mind, uses words on paper to control and find the most fruitful relationships among his ideas. Because writing is one of the ways of *coming to know,* it is also one of the ways of becoming an educated person.

Speaking and writing necessarily share many elements. Any effective communication—whether a speech, a paragraph, or an essay—has certain characteristics. The speaker/writer has an idea important to him, and, he hopes, important to the listener/reader whom he has in mind. This idea, whether expressed in few sentences or in many, is ordered and intelligible. Moreover, the principles of organizing are the same whether one is taking part in a discussion or a conversation, preparing a speech, or writing expository prose. For either the novice or the expert, the expression is controlled by certain basic processes:

searching for an idea capable of development within a limited time or space
arranging, clarifying, and developing details and assertions that support or test the idea
restating the idea, arriving at an over-all design that relates details or assertions to one central meaning

Because speaking and writing have much in common, many learning experiences suggested in Chapters Seven and Eight—"Oral Language" and "Written Expression"—are interchangeable; only slight adaptation in material or method is needed to make them suitable for teaching either speaking or writing. The integrated program stressed throughout this book recommends that speaking and writing be taught so that students will see their parallelism and thus be helped in transferring to one area skills gained in the other. Having something to say, a desire to say it, a plan, and someone to whom to express it are as important in learning to write as in learning to speak. Finding and clarifying one's own ideas and arranging these ideas for an audience are the determinants of effectiveness in both modes of expression.

RHETORIC WITH A NEW LOOK *Rhetoric,* a chastened word now climbing back to respectability after a long period of disfavor, is the art of composing effectively and responsibly whether in speech or in writing. It is the effective use of language to communicate genuine feeling and sound ideas.[2] Originally part of the medieval trivium along with grammar and logic, rhetoric later came to be regarded as a set of clever devices for persuading. More recently *rhetoric* has been reunited with standards of intellectual honesty and responsibility. Today a rhetorician assumes that arguing merely to overcome an opponent and expressing false feeling are signs of immaturity or insecurity. What is important in modern rhetoric is the sincere struggle—spoken or written —to distinguish shoddy from sound, trivial from significant, and to communicate these distinctions effectively. Composing in speech or writing is not just a clever set of tricks, but instead is an important means of ordering experience, of discovering ideas and rendering them more precise. It is intimately related to thought itself.

Thus, rhetoric deals with form organically linked to meaning and purpose. It also includes open admission of opposing views and careful concern for logic and reason. Rhetoric today means almost the opposite of the extrinsic ornamentation—the false brilliance once inserted into speeches in order to impress and sway audiences.

Just as new systems of grammar have developed in recent years, so too have new visions of rhetoric. One of these, based upon a careful examination of contemporary writers, has been proposed by Francis Christensen. The foundation of this generative rhetoric ("one that will generate ideas") views the main clause of most sentences merely as a base on which meaning will rise; in effective writing both the noun and the verb clusters of the main clause will usually be kept short: "The main clause exhausts the mere fact

[2] An exceptionally helpful discussion of rhetoric may be found in Wayne C. Booth, "The Rhetorical Stance," *Toward a New Rhetoric* (Champaign, Ill.: NCTE, 1963), pp. 1–7. Booth defines rhetoric as the art of finding and employing the most effective means of persuasion on any subject, considered independently of intellectual mastery of that subject. To him, what is essential in teaching rhetoric is the maintenance of a balance among three elements: the available arguments about the subject itself, the audience, and the voice (the implied character) of the speaker or writer.

of the idea; logically there is nothing more to say." [3] What is important is added by sentence modifiers. For instance, in these two sentences all the addition, all the generation of ideas, occurs in the italicized modifiers of the main clause:

> He shook his hands, *a quick shake, fingers down, like a pianist.*
>
> SINCLAIR LEWIS

> She came among them behind the man, *gaunt in the gray, shapeless garment and the sunbonnet, wearing stained canvas gymnasium shoes.*
>
> WILLIAM FAULKNER

These sentences, quoted from materials of the Nebraska Curriculum Development Center,[4] illustrate the cumulative sentence, in which "the additions stay with the same idea, probing its bearings and implications, exemplifying it or seeking an analogy or metaphor for it or reducing it to details. Thus the mere form of the sentence generates ideas." [5]

In this generative rhetoric, other features include:

the *direction* of the added sentence modifiers (Do they point ahead or back to what they modify? In the two examples above, the modifiers point back to *shook* and *she*, but modifiers can and often do precede the words they modify.)

the levels of abstractness or concreteness of the main clause in relation to the same quality in its modifiers

the texture—the density and variety of the modification

the paragraph as a sequence of structurally related sentences, structurally related in that they have a subordinate or parallel relationship to other sentences in the paragraph

a topic sentence that usually occurs first but may occur elsewhere in the paragraph (Some paragraphs have no topic sentence; it must be inferred.)

In general, this new rhetoric presents a shift away from a heavy emphasis upon subordinate clauses and periodic sentences. Instead, we find an increasing emergence of noun, verb, and adjective clusters used in cumulative sentences.

KEYSTONES OF COMMUNICATION   The three keystones of effective communication—whether oral or written—are clear thinking, the desire to communicate, and the skills needed to make communication effective. Instruction in writing, it follows, must emphasize the effective organization and expression of thoughts and feelings for others. Such an emphasis places mechanics and conventions where they properly belong—as means to an end, not as ends in themselves.

---

[3] Francis Christensen, "A Generative Rhetoric of the Sentence," *Toward a New Rhetoric* (Champaign, Ill.; NCTE, 1963), p. 18.

[4] "The Rhetoric of Short Units of the Sentence," *A Curriculum for English,* Student Packet (Lincoln: Univ. of Nebraska, Nebraska Curriculum Development Center, 1965), pp. 29–30.

[5] Francis Christensen, *op. cit.,* p. 27.

Whenever methods of teaching writing are wisely chosen, the learner will feel a concern for his reader. Since unconventional spelling and punctuation distract a reader's attention from the ideas a writer seeks to communicate, he strives to avoid them. Nevertheless, careful organization of significant thoughts and feelings should remain uppermost in his mind. Dull, lifeless prose, no matter how perfect the spelling or punctuation, is even more to be feared than genuine thought and feeling written without a proper attention to the conventions. If the three keystones of communication are firmly placed in classroom instruction, neither extreme needs to prevail.

Ferment of Ideas

The futility of methods that neglect the learner's own thought and feeling cannot be overstressed. "Persons who have read little and thought less will find the writing of an acceptable essay somewhat beyond their powers. But those who have learned to recognize the meaning and significance of personal experience will have the material out of which an acceptable essay may be constructed." [6] What teachers do in advance of writing to help students develop thought and feeling often proves as valuable as instruction about the actual composing or perfecting of the manuscript. Instruction in writing can never ignore Henry Seidel Canby's dictum: "Writing is like pulling the trigger of a gun; if you are not loaded, nothing happens."

Ideas for writing, just as for speaking, come from all experience. Students observe the world around them and through their five senses take in the raw materials by which thought is stimulated. Because they are human, they are curious, develop interests, read books, view television, brood, and day-dream. They have feelings and emotions: humor, sympathy, and anger need outlets; attitudes, antipathies, and affinities require exploration, understanding, and expression. Like all adolescents, they have needs: to accept their size, shape, and sex; to grow toward emotional independence; to make choices in their encounters with other people and with the values in their culture. In the preceding chapter, we stressed the necessity of a classroom atmosphere where students know they can say what they honestly think but where ideas will be examined impartially and critically. In that chapter, we said the teacher should start with content at the level of the interests and abilities of his students. In the beginning they communicate best matters of particular concern to them. Through the impact of literature and discussion these concerns extend and deepen. The teacher who is growing, both in his mastery of his subject and in his understanding of adolescents, devises many ways to re-lease this vitality of thought necessary to good writing.

[6] Report of the Board of Admissions and Relations with Schools, C. W. Jones, Chairman (Berkeley, Calif.: Univ. of California, April 8, 1958).

Facets of Composing

The teacher of writing is indeed concerned with the ferment of feelings and ideas, for he knows if he neglects vitality of thought, expression falters or withers away completely. But he is equally concerned with helping pupils harness this vitality to prevent aimless and incoherent overflow. The goals of instruction in composing are to teach pupils how to make an over-all design suitable for the content, how to present this content in a form that will catch and hold the attention of the reader.

CREATING A DESIGN   In the world of nature men harness rivers, steam, and electricity to good use; in the human world they applaud the control and form of a superb musician, a ballet troupe, a basketball team. Students' writing, humble though it may be, must acknowledge this universal necessity to impose pattern on thought, form on content, order on vitality. If pupils are to write, they must first release the forces of thinking and feeling, but they must not be left like the sorcerer's apprentice, lacking the wisdom and skill to impose order on those forces.

Consciousness of form is one of the notable abilities of good writers. At Michigan State University, A. M. Barch and R. L. Wright studied the characteristics of good and poor writers among freshmen students and reported some remarkable contrasts.[7] The good writer worries about organization, about not having anything to say, about not being specific, about having no clear-cut purpose in his writing, and about not being direct and to the point. But the poor writer worries about none of these things. Rather, he is concerned about spelling, about vocabulary, about alignment in handwriting, about all sorts of mechanical matters. Moreover, poor writers, unlike the good, are unable to recognize effective writing.

To many adolescents, the importance of form presents itself most clearly in team sports, dancing, and popular music. The concept of order as one of the most significant elements in everything from a parking lot to a religious service has not occurred to them any more than it has to most adults. Consequently the value of design and form cannot be assumed; it must be consciously featured. For many students, exposition, with its inherent requirements of logical organization and clear presentation, contributes most directly to this growing awareness of form in writing. However, exposition is not the only means of teaching precision and ordering of ideas. Sometimes the best writing students do is highly personal. Thus the subtler evocative forms of poetry and imaginative prose should not be neglected, for pupils also perceive experience through these fairly complex patterns and balances.

USING AN INDIVIDUAL STYLE   Adolescents observe style in clothing, in automobiles, and in dancing. They are interested not only in fashions but also in

[7] A. M. Barch and R. L. Wright, "The Background of Good and Poor Writers," *Journal of Communication*, Vol. 7, No. 4 (Winter 1957).

the characteristic appearance or manner of the things that fascinate them. Style commands their attention because it is related to something they care about. Style in writing must also be founded upon genuine interest. Instruction is futile when pupils have no intensity of living, no depth of feeling or thinking they wish to share through writing. Even when the teacher has provided for this fundamental motivation, instruction in style will still be far from easy. To let meaning choose the words rather than the opposite is never simple; there is, indeed, a tyranny of words, particularly of stereotyped phrases, clichés, and imprecise expressions. Developing a personal style requires honesty and much effort. The most realistic goal for the majority of pupils may be clarity, smoothness, and sincerity of expression. Those genuinely interested in learning to write may achieve at least the beginning of an individual style. But the ability to recognize a distinctive style in others and to attain it oneself is a product of maturity; it comes only with wider reading and more practice in writing than the secondary school years offer.

OBSERVING THE CONVENTIONS Why do teachers want students to observe the conventions of language? Certainly not because these matters are important ends in themselves. But teachers do see language as a window opening to the view beyond. Like window glass, language should be as inconspicuous as possible, permitting the communication to reach reader or listener without distracting his attention from the idea by the manner in which it is expressed.[8]

Whether expressing the logic of reason or the patterns of imagination, thought and feeling deserve to be presented effectively. A genuine desire to communicate his ideas prompts a writer to seek a design appropriate for the content, to search for the exact word and the most felicitous arrangement, to observe the conventions the reader expects. Design, style, conventionality— the writer considers all three as he plans how to best present his ideas.

Instruction in Expository Writing

The following discussion, with the learning experiences suggested later in support of the ideas expressed here, is based on these beliefs:

A series of short compositions serves the purposes of learning much better than a single long theme.

For some pupils, the ability to write a well-developed paragraph will be the ultimate goal; certainly, in junior high this is a sufficient challenge for the average pupil.

The long research paper is inappropriate to the secondary school and wasteful of time needed for more fundamental kinds of writing. The skills needed for constructing the long research paper can be learned and more readily checked in a short paper.

[8] There are, of course, stylized uses of language that are exceptions to the principle stated here.

Expository writing—whether a composition of some length or a single paragraph—requires disciplined thought; thus instruction in the necessary skills provides an opportunity to teach clear, systematic expression.

To achieve some progression in a maze so intricate, the teacher should consider with students three stages of composing that guide experienced writers: exploring the topic, making an effective plan, perfecting the presentation. These features of composing characterize the writing of all expository prose—whatever its length. However, to clarify the differences in teaching the short composition and the paragraph, each is discussed separately. The same desirable attitudes toward communication may be fostered by continued emphasis on either form. The following discussion focuses in turn on teaching the short composition, teaching the paragraph, and developing attitudes.

TEACHING THE SHORT COMPOSITION

A good expository composition implies a writer able to perceive parallelism, subordination, and order of importance among ideas, and a writer able to develop ideas adequately. We recommend the ability to write effective paragraphs as a realistic goal for the average junior high pupil, not because we think he should never attempt something longer, but because frequent concern with a limited idea allows the teacher over a period of time to help pupils acquire sentence-sense and to achieve some degree of sentence-control—both important objectives at this level. For the average senior high school pupil, however, the short composition of several paragraphs provides the best opportunity for effective instruction.

As teacher and class explore the facets of a topic, informal discussion plays the first significant role.

> The teacher questions the pupils, the pupils question the teacher, and the pupils question one another. The purpose is not to provide the indolent with material that is ready to use, but to give everyone enough of a basis to enable him to do thinking of his own. In the lower grades, the exercise is frequently nothing more than questions and answers designed to reveal the accuracy with which observations have been made; but in the higher grades it assumes the character of an interesting round-table discussion.[9]

The teacher maintains a flexible situation, for his purpose is to stimulate thinking: to show the problems that must be considered before one begins to write. In a demonstration, he helps the class search for ideas about the topic, leading them to see that even the simplest topic has various aspects, each possible as the focus of a composition, that some topics must be discarded because they cannot be adequately developed in the allotted time. When several suitable ideas have been selected, he helps the pupils translate each into an assertion that will express a certain point of view and thus

[9] Rollo Walter Brown, *How the French Boy Learns to Write* (Champaign, Ill.: NCTE, 1965), p. 76.

govern the scope of the writing.[10] He leads a discussion on one or more of the assertions, encouraging the class to contribute ideas, facts, and illustrations that might be used in support and to consider the kind of readers to whom this facet of the topic might appeal. In short, he leads students through the thinking a competent writer undertakes in making the decisions necessary before he begins to compose—the thinking the student must undertake in exploring a topic of his own choice, whether he plans to write a long composition or a paragraph.

Although the same principles—limiting a topic, considering the point of view of the writer and the intended readers, finding adequate support, arranging ideas in the best order—apply to the organization of both the short composition and the paragraph, the plans for the two differ. Here we consider first the short composition with a number of paragraphs.

MAKING A TENTATIVE PLAN   The plan the experienced writer makes before beginning to write resembles a hasty sketch rather than a complete map. In exploring his chosen topic, he comes up with a variety of ideas—probable, possible, questionable. He works fast, jotting these down as they occur but making no special effort to weigh their value. Usually from these ideas he can formulate a central idea sentence; sometimes, however, he can assemble only concepts, facts, and feelings about the subject. This does not delay him, for he knows he can coil back into his controlling sentence later. The one thing he does not do is waste time dredging for more material or trying to make a perfect plan. He knows that writing will generate further ideas, that it will help him clarify and evaluate his thinking.

No pupil is expected to make a detailed, logical outline and then follow it exactly as he writes. Even the professional writer rarely finds this procedure effective. It is important to realize how crude the first plan is likely to be— a tentative statement of the central idea, a few rapidly written phrases to be later translated into supporting topic sentences, a provisional order, possibly a title or an idea for an introduction or conclusion. This preliminary outline will be revised during the actual writing; at this early stage it is only a beginning, a place marker.[11]

[10] Teachers will find helpful Walker Gibson's kinescope *The Speaking Voice and the Teaching of Composition*. Through "role" and "voice" Gibson examines the method of defining oneself in composition and shows the implications of "the speaking voice." The kinescope is available from the Commission on English, 687 Boylston Street, Boston, Mass. 02116.

[11] The organization of exposition is the same whether the composition is written or oral. We suggest different plans for each; because of the contrasting situations in which each is presented, each serves a different purpose in learning. The perfected sentence plan is recommended for extemporaneous speech because it discourages the habit of writing out and memorizing speeches, giving the pupil a logical, easily remembered format to sustain him in times of stress, and because it is the most efficient way for a teacher to help the pupil check his logic. With written exposition, it is impractical to require writing topic sentences in advance, because one can be certain only of the form they should take as one composes; here teachers use the rough draft in helping the pupil examine, clarify, and evaluate his thinking. See Chapter Seven, "Oral Language," pages 273–76, 314–16.

Young writers should be helped to develop a healthy respect for the completed rough draft. Many pupils, when things are not going smoothly, have formed the habit of discarding what they have written and starting over. Sometimes this must be done, but too many false starts waste time better spent on capturing ideas—even if expressed crudely and incompletely—and establishing some sort of continuity to serve as a basis for testing logic and aiding revision. Competent writers usually double or triple space their first draft; they may leave trouble-spots unfinished, returning to them later for final decisions. A completed draft—whether for a single paragraph or for several structurally connected paragraphs—allows the writer to see more clearly the whole, the separate parts, and their mutual relationships.

A composition longer than one paragraph requires a controlling sentence and supporting topic sentences that must be submitted to the tests of reason. Is there any overlapping among the subordinate ideas? Does each hold up logically? Is each capable of being developed as genuine support? Or does the writer, as he exposes relationships, find reason to change or modify his viewpoint? If so, he returns to his central idea sentence to revise it. Essentially what the pupil is learning is an attitude: composing is exploring and coming to know; it is not thought fully developed in advance. Ideas take form as they are written; assertions and their relationships hold up or fold up.[12]

Having satisfied himself that his skeletal plan is logical, the writer next considers the development of each paragraph, first as a unit, then in relation to the others. Does the composition as a whole show evidence of these three qualities of effective writing?

> *unity*   excluding the irrelevant and extraneous; sticking to the purpose and furthering it
>
> *coherence*   guiding the reader from one stage of the subject to the next so he sees clearly the relationships and encounters no abrupt leaps and confusing gaps
>
> *emphasis*   bringing out those central elements deserving to be featured and subordinating those merely supportive or illustrative

Later the writer will be guided by these same principles in revising his sentences and their arrangement.

PERFECTING THE PRESENTATION   The experienced writer, sure of a logical plan and the effective development of his topic, next concentrates on the style and tone of his composition. Both, of course, have been considered from the beginning, but now these matters are lifted to a special phase of attention. Even though he has made many language decisions, his clearer sense of

---

[12] Emphasis on always having a topic sentence and always following prescribed methods of development can be overdone. It does, however, help the writer to think logically. Students who do not need this practice should be allowed freedom to design their own patterns. Materials demonstrating other approaches are now being developed at such experimental centers as the Curriculum Study Center in English, Northwestern University (Wallace Douglas, Director).

purpose and audience may necessitate additional changes. In this stage of composing, he is concerned mainly with improving his diction and sentence patterns. Lastly, he proofreads his manuscript to see that no careless errors have crept in.

Although these stages of development present an over-all sequence of composing, the actual process never advances so regularly, step by step. Composing alternates dynamically between the production of thought and the structuring of thought. Conceiving, capturing, ordering, and reordering ideas are elements of a process that moves like a rising tide—with forward surges, recedings, cross-currents, and counter-currents, followed by renewed surges toward dominion over the elusive thought. And even as the raw material is written down, the thought-stuff alters: the act of writing modifies or transforms it, requires almost immediate reorganization of what has scarcely been put upon paper. Equally for beginner and for experienced writer, composing is a struggle to spark ideas and to seize them in patterns that clarify, that expose their relationships. T. S. Eliot called it "a raid on the inarticulate."

The satisfaction of the professional writer—or of one genuinely interested in learning to write—comes from achieving gratifying results. Although moments of pleasure, even excitement, lighten the frustrations encountered in the process of composing, rarely does one who makes his living by writing think it fun; it is mostly hard work.

TEACHING THE PARAGRAPH

For some pupils, acquiring the ability to write well-developed expository paragraphs will be a sufficient achievement. However, all pupils—even those undaunted by the thought of more time-consuming writing—need help in making their paragraphs effective. Here, although one is dealing with a single topic sentence and its support, there is the same struggle to capture, focus, and express an idea.

PLANNING THE STRUCTURE   When one writes a single paragraph, an outline is not useful; instead a simple design—direct comparison, analogy, supporting detail—clearly manifested in the predication of the topic sentence, is the major consideration. The student can be led to realize that the verb he has applied to his subject in making his assertion determines how his idea will be developed. For instance, one teacher working with total class groups confronted this particular need for instruction in two very different classes:

GRADE NINE

Cosmonauts belong to the same class of heroes as Columbus and Magellan.

Space exploration gives us a new hero unlike those of the past.

Cosmonauts, final actors in a series of daring decisions, deserve only a small part of the fame they receive.

Glorifying cosmonauts dramatizes man's curiosity and his search for truth.

These topic sentences were developed on the chalkboard by a class of very able ninth-grade pupils in a working-class neighborhood. At this point the teacher is helping the pupils consider the kind of support each predication indicates. The first predication necessitates a *comparison* design, the second a strategy of *contrast*. The third topic sentence emphasizes conditional statements and judgments about what is *deserved*. *Dramatizes* is the key word to the last sentence, and two human characteristics are to limit the dramatizing.

GRADE EIGHT

Most men really want to be hoboes.
Hoboes and tramps like to be that way.
If you have no aim in life, you are a tramp.
Hoboes have lost their ambition.

These topic sentences were developed, only after difficulty and effort, by a low ability eighth-grade class in the same school. The sentences are not ideally phrased, exact, or polished, but the teacher decided that to lose interest through further sentence refinement would be a greater hazard than to settle for the four topic sentences as they appear here. Earlier sentences had been banal (All the boys in this class are bums) or uniformly definitional (Hoboes are drifters).

In these lessons, after asking pupils to choose two of the four topic sentences, the teacher used the chalkboard and group composition to illustrate the process of paragraph development.

At the beginning the teacher furnishes much help—suggestions, discussion, topic sentences, chalkboard paragraphs; there are stages of independence in learning to write. Gradually, however, the student assumes more responsibility.

In the learning experience described above, the teacher's target was to show young writers how to choose a predication deliberately and wisely and then to stay with that choice.[13] For instance, "Most men really want to be hoboes" may call for illustrations of constraint and discontent in organized life contrasted with the wanderer's freedom; emphasis will be on the basic difficulty of conforming to social existence, the advantages sought in rejecting it.

Instruction can help the pupil recognize some of the common methods of organizing paragraphs: instances and examples, comparison and contrast, repetition with variation, cause and effect. All the ways are too numerous to list, but the study of lively models and guided classroom experiences in writing can familiarize pupils with a few of the most frequently used. However, the teacher must use restraint; too much emphasis on specific methods of organization usually does more harm than good. Even experienced writers do not say, "Now I will develop this paragraph by a series of contrasts," and then do so forthwith. Organization, inherent in the predication

---

[13] At another stage, the teacher will show how modification of the subject limits and controls the topic. For instance:

The TV addict _____.
The teen-age TV addict _____.
The teen-age TV addict who wants to regain his sanity _____.

of the topic sentence and the modification of the subject, is not imposed from without. A pupil can learn to see, however, that although he is developing his paragraph through a series of illustrations, one or two of his sentences, devoted perhaps to contrast or definition, fit rather awkwardly.

PREPARING THE FINAL DRAFT   Perfecting the presentation of either paragraph or composition could cover many aspects of writing, but wise teachers refrain from attempting too much at one time. Professional writers have reported writing many versions of troublesome passages before obtaining satisfying results. We do not expect such dedication in most of our pupils. Nor does the young writer, though he has the will, know the way. What he needs is encouragement and a task offering a chance of some success.

Although the following suggestion aims at some progression, it is obviously imprecise as to order and classification. Moreover, the meaning of the terms in reference to learners is not absolute; each item may represent various degrees of achievement. Only the teacher who knows his pupils can decide which aspects of improvement should be attempted.

for the least able   sentence-sense, effective beginning and ending, unity, proof-reading

for the majority   some or all of these: use of concrete and precise words, vivid verbs; elimination of ambiguity; coherence and emphasis, transitions; streamlining unwieldy sentences by paring away unnecessary words, especially colorless adverbs and adjectives; avoiding the "which- and that-mires" by scrutinizing subordinate clauses to see how many "that's" and "which's" can be removed without marring clarity; variety of sentence pattern, of paragraph design

for some classes and individuals   over a long period of time and many compositions, instruction about clichés and jargon; pretentiousness of big words when small ones are clearer; danger of mixing levels of usage; need for consistent figures of speech

Teachers experienced in helping pupils will recognize these items as reminders, aspects of composing that at times need emphasis. Each teacher makes his own choice and determines the order of priority.

The final step in improving one's writing places emphasis on diction, sentences and their arrangement, transition from one idea to the next. Here the linkage between written and spoken language can be used effectively. Pupils should be encouraged to develop an "inner ear": they should form the habit of testing the sense, the clarity, the smoothness, of what they have written by listening to the way it sounds. This device, especially when teacher-directed to various aspects of the composition, makes young writers more aware of ambiguities and awkward expressions; it helps them avoid monotony of word-choice and sentence-pattern. Teachers may foster the habit in different ways:

allowing class time, before compositions are handed in, for each to reread his own in a quiet voice

providing an audience by placing students in small groups or in pairs to read
their compositions

encouraging each pupil to read into a tape recorder and then to listen to his own
voice as he follows his written form

One critic, discussing Willa Cather's style, concludes, "She meets the
ultimate test; her work reads well aloud." Out of context, this single criterion
for judging prose style may seem an over-simplification, but all the critic is
saying is that an effective style sounds right; it does not call attention to
itself, distracting the reader from the content. In judging the style and tone
of their own work, many writers find the ear a more reliable guide than the
eye.

DEVELOPING ATTITUDES

What counts most in the writing-instruction program is helping pupils develop
realistic attitudes. They must accept the fact that more than one draft is
standard procedure. They must come to realize that composing a paragraph,
whether it is to stand alone or become part of a composition, is a dynamic
procedure, not an execution by formula; for most pupils and indeed for most
adults this requires much rewriting, erasing, marking word clusters with arrows
to indicate new placements, jotting words and phrases in the margin—ideas
captured as they surface to the writer's mind. Because it is very human for
young writers to be lured by side issues and fortuitous associations, they need
to be reminded often to cleave to the direction set by the predication of their
topic sentences.

A second attitude to be fostered is the realization that composing ideas
in words is a valuable experience in improving and clarifying one's own
thinking and feeling. Through composition we come to terms with experience;
we explore and express our inner world; and in some measure we more fully
realize our own identity. Both pupil and teacher must come to appreciate
the value of composition as fidelity to experience, or the gains will not be
sustained and in fact never even realized. This attitude of respect for the
process of thinking, feeling, and expressing, this realization that composing
is searching for and finding relationships and making them clear to ourselves
as well as to someone else, is all important; it must be presented forcefully
by the teacher at frequent intervals; it must be discussed fully and assimilated
by the pupils over a long period of time.

A third attitude concerns style. At the heart of style is integrity of thought:
a genuine concern for letting meaning dominate the language. And the
meaning must be what the writer really means, an expression of his authentic
self. Integrity of thought and expression is fortified by respect for one's own
feelings and ideas and a desire to present them in a way to gain an appropriate
response from the reader. The teacher's sincere reaction to the pupil's composition most effectively supports the belief that good writing is important.

The communicative process is complex, for language may act as a barrier as well as a bridge. An effective communication, whether written or oral, requires more than a command of basic skills. The writer or speaker, besides having a desire to secure the appropriate response, must have respect for himself and his own ideas; he must accord his reader or listener the same privilege.

Thus, helping pupils gain skill in composing is a long and gradual process. No single year will ever accomplish the task, and each teacher needs to sense his role in each pupil's stage of development. Helping pupils learn to write simple and clear prose takes all of twelve years, including kindergarten where an effective beginning in using ideas can be initiated.

Instruction in Imaginative Writing

Imaginative writing based upon personal feeling and experience deserves a significant position in the English curriculum. Words are a means of putting order into our inner world—not just the outer world most frequently emphasized in expository writing. Helping pupils use language to express all experience is necessarily the aim of English instruction, and the teacher who includes personal writing finds many of the proficiencies sought through exposition fostered even more powerfully through highly personal narration and description. All writing is exposition; too sharp a division between modes is self-defeating. In a time when the claims of practicality lack their former urgency, concern about the creative processes of writers is one of the emerging interests of those who teach composition. Most of this scholarship has not yet been developed sufficiently to guide high school instruction, but teachers as well as some classes and some individual pupils might like to use a textbook such as *Writers on Writing* by William West.

DEFINITION   By imaginative writing, we mean writing of the kind the *Oxford English Dictionary* defines as "literature," writing that makes "a claim to distinction on the grounds of beauty of form or emotional effect." The terms *creative, personal,* or *literary* are sometimes used to distinguish imaginative from expository writing, but exposition, too, is often creative, personal, or literary, and many arguments circle about these terms. In this book, *imaginative,* contrasting with writing for practical purposes, is applied to the composition of those who find pleasure in expressing personal thoughts and feelings in forms literary writers employ.

Even though it is often the product of prolonged effort, imaginative writing seems more like quicksilver than conscious arrangement of logical thought. Certainly the unconscious enters into these acts of creating much more pervasively than it does in expository writing. Robert Frost described the surprise of "remembering something I didn't know I knew. . . . There is a glad recognition of the long lost and the rest follows. Step by step the wonder of unexpected supply keeps growing. The impressions most useful to my purpose seem always those I was unaware of and so made no note of at the time when taken . . ." [14] But however spontaneous the result may seem, imaginative writing, like the expository, still requires appropriate design if either writer or reader is to realize the full import of the expression.

CLIMATE   Helping adolescents find the best organization and form for their imaginative writing requires even more sensitivity to the purpose of the writer than does such help with expository writing. The delicate imagery, the unconscious freight of emotions, move mysteriously but not always successfully toward form. Often the teacher cannot suggest solutions without interfering with the inner process. As Hughes Mearns suggests repeatedly in *Creative Power*,[15] the teacher can really be helpful only by providing a climate of encouragement and sincere, tactful criticism based on the apparent purpose of each creation.

All pupils will not respond to such opportunity. Even so, imaginative writing should not be reserved for the gifted few; all students deserve an opportunity to try writing in which they strive to capture experiences and moods for their own sakes. Teachers who introduce imaginative writing are often surprised at how much satisfaction and learning occur for certain pupils, hitherto quite mute and unresponsive to other parts of the English curriculum. In both the United States and Great Britain reports of methods used with disadvantaged pupils have been impressive. In *Teaching the Unteachable*,[16] Herbert Kohl describes his instruction of resistant pupils in Harlem, and in *English for the Rejected*,[17] David Holbrook presents his similar instruction with lower stream pupils in England. The introduction to Kohl's pamphlet makes clear what is central to both teachers' ways of helping their pupils:

> If we are to make real progress in improving student writing, the first lesson we have to learn is this: A student will only be concerned with his own use of language, will only care about its effectiveness, and therefore try to judge its effectiveness—and therefore be able to improve its effectiveness—when he is talking to an audience, not just one that allows him to say what he wants as he wants, but one that takes him and his ideas seriously. . . . It is the effort to use words well, to say what he wants to say, to people whom he trusts, and wants to reach and move, that alone will teach a young person to use words better. No doubt, given this starting point, some technical advice and help may at times be useful; but we must begin from here or we will make no progress at all.[18]

The classroom climate, which includes the teacher's attitude toward his pupils, is crucial to any plans for encouraging personal and imaginative writing.

[14] Quoted by Lawrence Thompson in *Fire and Ice: the Art and Thought of Robert Frost* (New York: Holt, Rinehart & Winston, 1942), p. 31.
[15] Hughes Mearns, *Creative Power* (New York: Dover, 1958).
[16] Herbert Kohl, *Teaching the Unteachable* (New York: New York Review of Books, 1967).
[17] David Holbrook, *English for the Rejected* (London: Cambridge Univ. Press, 1961).
[18] John Holt in Kohl, *op. cit.*, pp. 8, 9.

PRACTICES ENCOURAGING IMAGINATIVE WRITING Imaginative writing succeeds best in classrooms where emphasis is on generating ideas and determining the best design for them. A background of discussion and shared experience should usually precede writing. The essential feature of the classroom becomes a climate of encouragement and of sincere reaction to whatever is written. To secure such conditions, the teacher discusses the importance of sincerity and tact in reacting to imaginative writing, explaining that the "audience" may be the entire class, a group within the class, or an individual who might be either the teacher or a fellow classmate. Approaches teachers have used successfully are presented here for consideration by those wishing to organize similar classroom situations.

Encourage accurate description; place before pupils some object such as autumn leaves, contemporary sculpture, or a piece of gnarled and twisted driftwood; have pupils first describe the object with accurate and logical expression. Finally, ask them to describe the object imaginatively and creatively, seeing it in some new way.

Experiment with several verse forms, including free verse, and encourage groups of interested pupils to extend their experimentation to other verse forms. The Japanese verse forms *hokku* and *tanka* sometimes serve effectively for developing creativity beyond the limerick, quatrain, and cinquain.

Occasionally plan for a group composition, sometimes in prose and a few times in free verse; group composition often proves successful in junior and senior high school classes with many slow learners.

Write plays, dialogs, and pantomimes for junior high puppet shows, for graduation exercises, and for assemblies. Vary the situations and the audience for imaginative writing; write for children, age mates, adults, so that a wide range of situations and audiences may be experienced.

Often, junior high pupils with creative writing interests like to use puns and malapropisms; they also like to parody juvenile books in series such as the Tom Swift and Nancy Drew titles; they like to surprise readers with unexpected endings, "the thrill that was really a dream, the dear feminine friend who turns out to be a boat, the terrible danger that proved to be merely a cat in the attic." [19]

Discuss the earliest memories one can summon up from childhood. Early memories are often strongly related to sensory experiences. After sharing some of these, including, perhaps, one from the teacher, the class writes on the topic "A Vivid Memory from My Early Childhood."

Use some of the methods described earlier in Chapter Five, "Imaginative Thinking"; see pages 184–206.

Have a desk drawer where contributions may be placed at any time. Urge pupils to bring creative writing they have finished at home; criticize it honestly in terms of its apparent purpose.

[19] Commission on the English Curriculum, *The English Language Arts in the Secondary School*, NCTE Curriculum Series, Vol. 3 (New York: Appleton-Century-Crofts, 1956), p. 309.

Form creative writing clubs and permit students to present literary writing in lieu of regular assignments. In some schools the writing club can be made a regular part of the class work.

Keep a file of the students' best imaginative writing; read from it occasionally, without indicating the student-author; ask various classes to list positive points to be copied down by a student-secretary; return these notes to the author.

Encourage individuals to keep journals with daily entries; from these journals they may draw ideas for literary writing to submit instead of expository composition assignments.

Nominate outstanding students for the NCTE Achievement Awards program, which is based mainly upon compositions written by the student. Information about these awards is printed and available from the National Council of Teachers of English.

Without building hopes too high, encourage many pupils to submit materials for contests in the *Atlantic, Scholastic,* and other magazines.

Suggest to local school and community clubs that they offer prizes at some stated time for the best literary writing presented annually.

To honor writers of merit, place their creations along with their pictures in the school showcase.

Let an art class read several superior creations and illustrate them in linoleum block, water color, and oil.

Publish a collection of students' best literary writings; the publication may be as humble as a collection of typewritten sheets, covered with a simple paper cover on which an appealing title is lettered; it may be a looseleaf scrapbook, covered with a brightly colored oil cloth on which has been imposed a decal design and a stenciled title. On good paper of various colors, the selections should be copied by the authors or typed by a good typist. If the teacher shows genuine enthusiasm, tells other classes about the collection uses models from it, and places it on a special table in the library, the contributors will be gratified and the next publication will include a larger number of contributors. These collections of writing may be kept from year to year to serve as initiators for further literary writing.

Does imaginative writing have real value for all pupils? We believe so. Surely something more than mere skill in composing must justify the time and energy given to any writing, expository or creative; some crucial, long-term values should result from so much effort. The Dartmouth Seminar of British, Canadian, and American teachers of English agreed that by writing, pupils "learn how to order and shape their experience, thereby learning more about life and themselves." [20] Precision of thought and the attitude of integrity, of taking a stand and saying truly what one means or feels are attainments in composition that should carry over to oral discussions and to response in the literature class. They should transfer to other classes and to action beyond the school, and they should be as valuable for nonacademic

[20] Herbert J. Muller, *The Uses of English* (New York: Holt, Rinehart & Winston, 1967), p. 98.

pupils as for the college-bound. This kind of writing experience should radiate to the learners' thinking and feeling long after the doors of the school have closed behind them.

THE TEACHING PROBLEM

ORGANIZING INSTRUCTION

In a commendable desire to insure adequate attention to writing, teachers have sometimes allocated a semester or several days a week to composition. The disadvantages in this method, which implies separation from the other arts of language and from the stimulation of ideas in the rest of the curriculum, almost always undermine the alluring promise and simplicity of such an organization. A better plan proves to be an integrated English program, emphasizing writing throughout all six years of the secondary school. Such a plan, combining writing with discussion, reading, literature, and other school subjects, engenders a vitality composition cannot achieve as an isolated activity. It is based on a principle of economy of energy. The teacher uses one activity to motivate another rather than starting each activity anew.

Establishing Basic Understandings

Certain basic understandings help teachers plan instruction in written expression. First of all, what pupils write about should have a broad base; possibilities for content should be viewed as little less than everything in the world, all of life, all that the imagination and curiosity of youth can conceive. Secondly, the program in writing should distinguish between ideas and topics; in this sense, ideas are attitudes or points of view toward a topic or subject. Thirdly, provisions for genuine communication must never be neglected; students should write for someone they want to persuade, entertain, inform, or convince. As often as possible, their reader should be someone interested in the ideas expressed, not merely a proofreader detecting mistakes.

CONTENT WITH BROAD BASE   Writing succeeds best in the classroom when it is part of a larger concern with significant ideas, no matter whether they begin in the English class, elsewhere in the school, or in life beyond the school. Writing may be related to the total English program in a number of ways. For example, during unit instruction the incubation and motivation of thought is reinforced by all the language arts. Even more frequently writing draws its vitality from the study of literature. Writing and literature complement each other so naturally that their mutual reinforcement is one of the arguments for integrating the elements of English. The culminating activity for the unit on *Macbeth* (pages 600–08), an organized essay, is a clear example. Insofar as the teacher is alert to relationships between English and other subjects in the school, writing may also originate in shop, homemaking, school sports, social studies, and science. Nor should the world beyond the school, especially the local community, be neglected. The more comprehensive the content in English, the more opportunities the pupil has for writing. In the main, instruction should frequently interrelate the arts of language as they are interrelated in life beyond the classroom.

None of what has been said is intended to dismiss the value of pausing in a unit or a study of short stories in order to give direct attention to skills needed in writing. A teacher may indeed pause to identify or to teach an important segment of the whole without destroying that whole, much as a coach stops a basketball practice game to inspect or improve a faulty technique. It is precisely at this point that the integrated program reveals its advantages, for any skill—physical, mechanical, or conceptual—acquires more significance and clarity when learned in relation to some more comprehensive purpose.

But the entire policy for student writing need not reflect such integration. No one kind of organization should be used exclusively, and it is entirely possible to use the benefits of synthesis without excluding special separate lessons in composition. A number of such lessons appear in the Suggested Learning Experiences later in this chapter. Conditions do vary and require modified teaching designs. English teachers learn to be flexible, using many approaches but favoring those that, like integration, sustain a principle of economy.

CONCERN FOR IDEAS   This book stresses throughout a concern for ideas. In writing, this means students cannot be expected to talk or write effectively about vast topics. They should be helped to see how an idea about a topic must be the base for their communication. For this idea, they must have a point of view, an attitude toward the topic, and a clear predication of their topic sentence. Applying this to writing, one teacher makes a clear distinction between a topic and the controlled development of an idea. His distinction is illustrated in two sets of titles.[21]

TOPICS	IDEAS
Hamlet	Hamlet's conduct in the scene with his mother shows him to be mad.
Hamlet's Conduct	
Hamlet's Conduct in the Scene with His Mother	Hamlet's conduct in the scene with his mother shows him to be sane.
Hobbies	Raising pigs is the best way I know to make money and have fun at the same time.
My Hobby—Raising Prize Pigs	

[21] Bertrand Evans, "Writing and Composing," *English Journal*, Vol. 48, No. 1 (January 1959).

Initially, this teacher suggests, supplying pupils with ideas may be a stepping-stone to genuine composition. Because this implies using someone else's ideas, the instruction should move quickly to providing only the frame of an idea—for example, Hamlet's conduct in the scene with his mother shows him to be _____. The final achievement is to help a pupil comprehend the importance of restraining his impulse to write until he has evolved an idea of his own to dominate his selection of content. Then he will truly compose what he writes.

Beginning writers usually feel they must tell everything. The "interesting experience" one teacher wryly describes is all too familiar. It

> starts off as the alarm rings at 5:30, proceeds through the breakfast details, the trip in the car, the first night, the stops at filling stations, the luncheon menus, until at last we get to the race for the shore on a storm-swept lake, only to find that a sentence or two has carried us through the climax, and we are lunching and filling-stationing our own way home again, "where we arrived at 6:35, having had a very interesting and thrilling experience." [22]

Whether in personal narrative or exposition of ideas, most pupils need planned instruction in learning to select what they present in terms of purpose and audience. They must find a controlling idea around which to construct the total design.

WRITING TO COMMUNICATE   As often as possible, students should write for someone who is to receive their ideas. There are many ways to organize instruction by this basic principle of communication. Arrangements may be made for pupils to write to others of their own age in various parts of the United States and the world. Just before Christmas many teachers present the form and spirit of thank-you letters. When a pupil is away from school for any bereavement or illness, students write letters of condolence, or get-well notes. Toward the close of school the teacher presents the letter of application in relation to summer jobs. Friendly letters may be studied at any time during the year, first drafts being written in class in order to receive suggestions and corrections, provided the student wants the teacher to read them. Special recognition might be given for letters neatly copied and brought to class in stamped envelopes ready for mailing. Whatever the arrangement, it is essential that pupils have experiences in writing to someone other than the English teacher.

However, the principle of communication does not always require such lifelike situations. Any teacher instructing at least two classes of approximately the same grade level may organize plans to accommodate a pupil's desire to express something for someone his own age. In the following paragraphs one such plan is described in detail.

The first step is to explain that students in each class will write a composition to be read and evaluated by members of the other class. The teacher

---

[22] Eric W. Johnson, "Stimulating and Improving Writing in the Junior High School," *English Journal,* Vol. 47, No. 2 (February 1958).

points out the importance of evaluating the composition and not the student. For this reason each student is to choose an alias, a *nom de plume.* Only one person, someone selected by the class or already elected as class secretary, is to have a complete list of the names of the students and the aliases chosen. Not even the teacher will know whose compositions will have at the top such names as Jet Pilot, Methuselah, or Butterflop.

Next the students suggest topics that might interest the other class. These topics are placed on the chalkboard. Students and teacher discuss them, selecting four or five. The teacher then takes one of the topics and conducts a lesson on how it might be limited, reminding students of such important matters as effective beginning, development of the main body of the composition, and effective conclusion. Any conventions or mechanics in which the class has been weak may receive attention before students are set to writing their rough drafts. Meanwhile the other class is following the same procedure.

During the writing period, the teacher moves about the room, willing to answer any questions but not reading the compositions. After the rough drafts have been polished and copied, the student secretary gathers the papers, none of them identified except by the alias. When compositions have been completed in both classes, the student secretaries exchange them and the evaluation process begins.

Each student receives a composition from the other class. (If there are not enough compositions to go around, two students may work together on a single composition. If there are too many compositions, some able student may be allotted two.) He reads it several times, carefully and thoughtfully. When he has completed his study, he writes his own comments about it. The teacher has listed on the chalkboard points one should look for in good compositions. It is important to stress the positive, for few schoolroom sights are more unpleasant than a group of adolescents inflamed with the fever of the chase, hunting for mistakes in spelling and punctuation. The teacher must lift their sights to more significant aspects, such as the author's intention and whether or not he has successfully carried it out.

Next, the students move into groups of five. Now each student reads aloud the composition he has drawn and the comments he has written. The other members of the group discuss each paper, adding any comments they wish; the person in charge of the paper acts as secretary, making note of these contributions. Each person, in turn, follows the same procedure until all compositions have been read.

Each group chooses the best composition, or in some cases the best two, and these are read to the class. Comments from class and teacher are now added to each of these excellent papers. In many cases the student who has drawn such a composition writes as much as the original writer, viewing this as an opportunity for further writing experience. This attitude can be established if the teacher talks over the purposes of written composition and the value of experience in writing material to be read by someone else. In this case the original owner of the paper is going to be extremely interested in reading all the comments.

Now the class affixes some kind of symbol—a star or a decorative seal—indicating that the five or six papers just read have been selected as the best. The papers are then returned to the authors. In each class the students whose papers were selected by their peer group are honored by having their real names divulged. Their compositions are read aloud, and the virtues and qualities they have exemplified are noted and praised as goals to be emulated.[23]

If the teacher has no group with whom to exchange compositions, the plan may be used with a class taught by another. In the group reading of compositions, there is excellent opportunity for comparing and contrasting points of view on writing; students may learn from one another. For those whose papers are chosen, there is some small degree of honor, and this gives the teacher an opportunity to set up models for others to follow. Sometimes good papers are drawn by poor readers, but this disadvantage is offset to some degree by the fact that each paper must be read aloud to a wider group, and the individual reader's opinion is supplemented by the opinions of four or five other students. Certainly not the least of considerations is the fact that the teacher carries on instruction but, for this one composition, does absolutely no reading.

Note that this method gives the teacher many excellent opportunities to teach the qualities of good writing. The method may be adapted to any level from grades 7 to 12; it may be used successfully several times a semester. It has been presented here as an illustration of how a teacher may use the principles of communication—having something worthwhile to express, a desire to express it, and someone to whom the pupil wants to communicate it. Then, and only then, can there exist effective instruction in how to express ideas.

Organizing Efficient Routines

Because instruction in writing involves such diverse and complex strategies, a teacher must develop a system to care for all the details of filing, checking, and conference time. Foremost in importance is a folder for each pupil, in which are kept all his compositions, other written work, lists of spelling errors, and pertinent duplicated material—everything listed cumulatively on a table of contents. A *student* writing chairman, working in collaboration with his teacher, may be responsible for filing and distributing the folders. This perma-

---

[23] In some instances, the teacher himself has written a composition, also using a pseudonym. If the teacher does write, everybody is on his mettle to read carefully the composition he has drawn—for who knows—he may have the teacher's composition. It is considered fair in such a situation for the teacher to write a single composition to be used in both classes, and for him to have some conspirator in still another class who does the job of copying the teacher's composition twice so no one will know the handwriting.

nent file, invaluable to both pupil and teacher, determines the agenda for many pupil-teacher conferences.

HOLDING CONFERENCES Conferences with pupils may be planned for times when the class is writing or studying. If the teacher writes on the board two lists of students he wishes to see and if on either side of his desk he places a chair, no time will be wasted. As the teacher finishes with one student he turns to the other while the one who is through goes to the board, erases his name, and quietly notifies the next pupil on the list. Teachers using this method do not write on the pupils' papers. Instead each pupil, as soon as he returns to his seat, records the teacher's evaluation—both positive and negative —clips the evaluation to his composition, and files it in his folder.

During some periods when students are writing, a teacher may remain at his desk to confer with individuals on the organization of their writing. During this time the teacher will give no assistance on such matters as spelling, punctuation, and usage. Students receive help only on the improvement of paragraphs or the design of their total composition, including unity, coherence, emphasis, style, and tone. On the "Consultation Board"—a chalkboard clearly in view of all students—is a column where may be written the names of individuals who either are requested to consult with the teacher or who wish to do so. Also on the Consultation Board questions and admonitions like these appear:

CONFERENCE COMMENTS

Remember Today's conferences are to help you with the organization of your writing. Do not ask for help on spelling, punctuation, or usage.

Questions on organization Is the beginning right for your topic? Does it catch the reader's attention? Did you plan it or just start? Are there any confusing gaps, abrupt jumps that will leave the reader behind? Are the most important points given the position of greatest emphasis? Or the greatest length? Are the other parts treated in proportion to their importance?

Whenever the conferences concern papers longer than a single paragraph, teachers can work more effectively if students have underlined the topic sentence in each paragraph containing one. Students should also have jotted down questions and matters about which they seek help.

SETTING STANDARDS If they are to encourage high-quality work from their classes, teachers must establish high standards. From the beginning of the school year, they must make clear that only papers meeting reasonable criteria of neatness, legibility, and content are to be accepted. Papers not meeting these requirements may be returned for rewriting. The exact standards will of course vary with the age and maturity of the students. However, any tendency in September to overlook standards stressed during the previous June only encourages slovenly work. Like children pressing for certainty on the limits permitted them, many pupils will try out a new teacher—passing in something less than presentable if they believe it will be accepted. The recurring human tendency to test limits often manifests itself in the composition program.

Among the special questions students will want answered with respect to standards for composition are the following: Is there a routine heading? Margin? Form? (Some junior high school teachers post model papers on the bulletin board or display larger than life size models as reminders.) Which papers must be written in ink? Is typing acceptable? Under what conditions will papers be returned unread? For each of these, the teacher will want to establish a policy.

Evaluating compositions by the method of a double grade offers another way to establish standards for individuals who have special problems with the conventions of expression. Some teachers use this device only with students who produce and develop ideas more skillfully than they present them. At the senior high school level, the more able learners respond quickly to the challenge of low scores on such mechanical skills.

USING STUDENT HELP   Often a rotating team is used to assist with routines. One teacher [24] recommends a secretary to keep a complete class log and assignment book that may be read on any day review seems desirable. Absentees, with their inevitable question "Did I miss anything?" are referred to the secretary and his class log. Paper monitors assume responsibility for collecting homework and distributing supplies and materials. Such assistants often have responsibility for a table or a single row of seats. They are particularly helpful when the class is meeting in groups and materials are difficult to distribute. Some teachers prefer not to introduce too formal a structure and rely upon appointed or elected student assistants for many projects.

Reading and Judging Compositions

All who are seriously concerned about the teaching of writing in our schools realize that finding time to read compositions and to help learners with their difficulties is the English teacher's greatest frustration. In desperate but futile efforts teachers sometimes resort to cram courses for seniors planning to go on to college. Yet proficiency in writing, developing as it does over a long period of time, requires skilled instruction from primary school through high school. Furthermore, the pupils who do not go to college also benefit from that most important contribution of sustained instruction in composition: the clarification of thinking and feeling.

Yet until English teachers are assigned work loads commensurate with the

[24] Grace Daly Maertins, "Organizing the Class," *English Journal,* Vol. 47, No. 7 (October 1958), p. 416. This article, with its suggestions concerning the solution of problems of classroom management, is recommended to beginning teachers.

task they have been set, they must contrive to do the best they can under the circumstances. The conscientious English teacher, if he fulfilled present expectations, would read enough pupil papers each week to equal *War and Peace* and would write enough incisive comments to rival the length of *Gone with the Wind*. One possible solution may be a year with special composition emphasis—perhaps grade 8 or 9—with the number of English teachers doubled and classes reduced by half. This would not imply a decrease in composition at other grade levels, for sequence and cumulative learning are crucial to composition learning. Another partial solution may be realignment of priorities. Recent research shows that frequent writing, even with teachers' comments, is not particularly helpful. This realization may shift emphasis to genuine motivation and oral discussion as preparation for writing—a concern for the total writing process, including audience, voice, and especially the thought preceding the writing.[25]

CLARIFYING PURPOSE OF CORRECTION   The teacher's purpose is not so much to improve a particular composition as to help pupils become more self-critical so that their writing ability may improve. Thus he needs to consider whether the long hours he spends reading and commenting upon compositions yield sufficient returns. For instance, the meticulous marking of every error has been rejected by almost everyone who has studied the problem; on the other hand, research confirms the fact that comments emphasizing aspects of thinking and writing are helpful.

Stress upon clarity of thought, upon stylistic elements independent of grammar, upon sentence structure, has proved to be effective with junior high pupils.[26] At the college level, research indicates the importance of a wealth of ideas, a discussion of those ideas, and the instructor's concern for effective organization and presentation.[27] One committee studying substandard writing among undergraduates reports these findings: difficulties of organization and structure are predominant; proficiency in the technique of grammatical usage

---

[25] Lois V. Arnold, "Writer's Cramp and Eyestrain—Are They Paying Off?" *English Journal,* Vol. 53, No. 1, January 1964. Recent research showing that frequent writing practice does not in itself improve writing is summarized in *Rationale for a Sampler of Practices in Teaching Junior and Senior High School English* (Champaign, Ill.: NCTE, 1966). In the National Study of High School English Programs, James R. Squire and Roger K. Applebee reported most teachers overestimating what can be accomplished through correction and underestimating what may be accomplished through instruction before writing. See *High School English Instruction Today* (New York: Appleton-Century-Crofts, 1968).

[26] Irvin O. Ash, "An Experimental Evaluation of the Stylistic Approach in Teaching Written Composition in the Junior High School," *Journal of Experimental Education,* Vol. 4, No. 1 (September 1935).

[27] J. D. Clark, "A Four-year Study of Freshman English," *English Journal* (college edition), Vol. 24, No. 5 (May 1935); Roy C. Maize, "A Study of Two Methods of Teaching English to Retarded College Freshmen," unpublished doctoral dissertation, Purdue University, 1952; summarized in *Review of Educational Research,* Vol. 25, No. 2 (April 1955).

seems to accompany general ability to organize material logically.[28] All these studies and many others point to the value of stressing the rhetorical aspects of thought and judgment rather than the mechanical problems of habit and rule.

USING TIME-SAVERS   In view of the problem of time, what methods do English teachers use in order to cope with the paper load? What short cuts and strategies within the limits of integrity help to alleviate an almost impossible burden? Experienced teachers know that time well spent in oral discussion to prepare for writing is eventually time saved:

> by establishing understanding of the purpose of an assignment—what students may learn, what the teacher anticipates as a finished product
> by sparking ideas, securing motivation, clarifying thinking

Besides making oral discussion an integral part of teaching composition, teachers use other practices to save time:

> waiting until students have three compositions in their folders and then asking them to turn in for grading the one they think best
> using the *nom de plume* method described on pages 339–41
> using lay readers
> recording comments on tapes or discs

Any one of these devices, properly used, can save time without impairing instruction.

USING PRE-CORRECTION   The most effective teacher protection, however, is planned pre-correction—a method insuring definite proofreading before the teacher ever sees the finished manuscript. Pre-correction procedures, even under utopian conditions, would be sound pedagogy; in a crowded school day, they become a necessity. Two class periods, usually on successive days, are required.

During the first period the teacher moves about answering student questions, making suggestions to individuals, and advising those whose composition problems he remembers from previous assignments. Fifteen minutes before the end of the class period, he goes to the board and writes a series of questions. For example:

> Are there any words in my composition that may be misspelled? If there are, I should draw a circle around each one, and check it in the dictionary tonight.
> Have I any awkward sentences reflecting muddy thinking? (EXAMPLE   My greatest ambition is to be a nurse which I have had from when I was a child.) Can I revise any of my sentences to reflect clearer thinking?
> Have I used any run-on sentences? (EXAMPLE   The car came to an abrupt

<hr>

[28] Committee on University Prose Standards, University of California, Berkeley, in "Report of the Committee on Educational Policy" (October 29, 1957), and "Proposed Report of the Committee on University Prose Standards" (September 1951).

stop, in it was a stout woman and a great many children.) This is sometimes called "the baby blunder." To check, read your sentences aloud.[29]

The teacher may place on the board as many questions as the students will assimilate, but experience suggests it is better to focus on a few problems each time rather than to scatter efforts on a great many. Those composition difficulties that have appeared most often in earlier compositions should be emphasized, and as different problems of writing come to the forefront, the questions should vary.

As soon as the questions have been listed on the board, the students should stop writing, and together with the teacher, read the questions and search their rough drafts for the problem involved in each. Unless time for this scrutiny is provided in class, some will not bother to use this help. After applying the questions to their manuscripts, students are asked to complete and polish these rough drafts at home; they are reminded to bring materials for copying the final draft in class the next day.

At the beginning of the second class period, the teacher mentions briefly the purpose of neatness and the elements of attractive appearance in a manuscript. As the class begins copying the final draft, the teacher writes on the board a new set of questions such as the following:

> Have I remembered to use question marks and periods in places requiring them?
> Have I discovered any colorless verbs or nouns in my rough draft and replaced them with more vivid or precise words?

After students have had an opportunity to copy their manuscripts, to check for points covered by the questions, and to obtain the teacher's help on special problems, a final oral reading check is made. All pupils need to establish this habit of looking back over their writing and of hearing it as it sounds in the mind of a reader.[30] To develop this inner ear, each pupil now reads aloud his own composition in a quiet voice. Such a practice assures a product in which many careless errors will be caught by the writer.

Ideally, writing should be taught in situations providing maximum opportunity for individual instruction. Although such situations are frequently impossible, the method of pre-correction described here enables a teacher to instruct the group and at the same time to talk with many individuals. Both groups and individuals receive help at the time learning is most likely to occur. Problems in usage, mechanics, and form can be anticipated, thus making it possible for the teacher to read the compositions later with attention focused on larger considerations—organization, tone, good taste, precision of thought, and other qualities of effective writing. Even for this, there will not be enough time.

---

[29] For a longer list suitable to grades 11 and 12, see the one used by Henry Fitts, Winchester, Mass., High School, in *English Journal*, Vol. 48, No. 1 (January 1959), p. 39.
[30] Anyone who has ever reread a personal letter is aware of the manner in which careless errors find their way into written symbols—words are omitted, or are written twice in a row, diction needs improvement, or *come* has been set down for *comes*.

Summary: Principles Underlying Effective Instruction in Composition

The bases for effective instruction in composition may now be summarized.

Imaginative writing provides experience in expressing and ordering both ideas and experiences and does so in highly personal ways; it contributes significantly to the pupils' over-all development in writing.

Pupils must write with a genuine sense of communication; they must have something to say, someone to say it to, and a desire to say it; only then can a teacher help them organize and express it.

Pupils must grapple with their own ideas and feelings, consciously shaping them toward effective communication; verbalizing principles and studying models are not sufficient by themselves.

The help students receive in generating, organizing, and expressing ideas before and during the actual process of composing is more important than the help they receive after writing.

In exposition, pupils need to be taught that a controlling idea is needed for composing; thinking and writing cannot be separated.

Practice in actual writing, usually limited to short compositions and aimed at specific problems of achievement, surpasses other plans in effecting pupil achievement.

Teachers should plan for a progression in the attainment of specific skills of composition; this progression should encompass all the grades of the secondary school.

Evaluation of student writing and all revision should extend beyond a concern for mechanical correctness; the heart of the matter is clarity, forcefulness, and vitality of expression.

The best organization of instruction relates composition to the rest of the English curriculum, to other school subjects and activities, and to pupil concerns beyond the school.

The complexity and difficulty of teaching writing require careful planning of routines, filing, conferences, and reading of compositions.

SUGGESTED LEARNING EXPERIENCES

The following suggestions are intended to start readers on ideas of their own. In teaching pupils to write, there is need for unlimited ingenuity; the ideas presented here, practical ways to carry out the principles that have just been presented, are by no means the only ways to proceed.

In their present form, these suggestions cannot carry with them all the richness of context they would have in an actual classroom. More frequently than not, lessons like these would constitute elements of some larger plan—important adjuncts to literary study, mosaics in a unit, parts of the strategy for team teaching, or preparation for a film. For instance, the first suggestion actually grew out of a unit in which pupils read and discussed literary selections about characters whose choices revealed their values. Many of the other ideas presented here developed from some previous activity and evolved into further lessons not included in the description. Occasions for writing may, of course, be separately motivated, but the larger curriculum plan provides momentum that ought not to be neglected.

TO AWAKEN INTELLECTUAL CURIOSITY

▶ *Consider the bases for making choices*

1. All literature, from *Call It Courage* in grade 7 to *A Separate Peace* in grade 12, contains situations involving problems of conduct and choices among values. For instance, discuss and write about "Legal and Moral Justice" after reading *Billy Budd, The Winslow Boy, Antigone,* or "In the Train" by Frank O'Connor. Posing such problems almost invariably starts the ferment of thought, the lively discussion, that must precede writing. For instance, the discussions may be related to problems such as "What Price Advancement?" "The Individual Versus the Group," and "The Idea of the Hero."

2. Some teachers may wish to compare their students' value choices with those of other adolescents. One composition, "The Person I Would Like to Be Like," has been rather widely used in research. Robert J. Havighurst's directions for assigning this essay ask for the age, character, appearance, occupation, and recreations of the ideal person; results are reported for a variety of communities as well as social and age groups.[31] As a variation, pupils may write on the topic, "A Person I Would Not Like to Be Like."

3. Pictures can stimulate discussion. Mounted on cardboard with a series of thought-provoking questions pasted beneath them or on the reverse side, such pictures become the bases of numerous compositions. Over a period of years, an excellent file of picture stimulators, tested and winnowed by use, can be accumulated. In the file, also, should be clippings, headlines, poems, and quotations, all of which may be used to stimulate ideas for writing that emphasizes choices.

▶ *Consider codes of living*

Duplicate a list of sayings and mottoes that reflect various outlooks—from ruthlessness to unselfish altruism—and have the class check reactions anonymously. The sheet will look like this:

NOTHING BUT THE TRUTH

Read each statement carefully and thoughtfully. Then, after each statement, check the response with which you honestly and actually agree. There are no right or wrong answers. Do not sign your name. Write comments if you wish.

1. In this world it's every man for himself and the devil take the hindmost. You can't be too thoughtful of others or you will lose out yourself.

Strongly agree _____   Undecided _____   Strongly disagree _____

Agree _____   Disagree _____

Comment if you wish: _____

---

[31] Robert J. Havighurst and Hilda Taba, *Adolescent Character and Personality* (N.Y., Wiley, 1948); Robert J. Havighurst, M. Z. Robinson, and M. Dorr, "The Development of the Ideal Self in Childhood and Adolescence," *Journal of Educational Research,* Vol. 40, No. 4 (December 1946).

For the rest of the items, provide the same response framework. Other items that might be included: do unto others as you would have them do unto you; do unto others as they would do unto you, only do it to them first; fools are made for wise men's profit; self-respect is possible only to those who do not stoop to take advantage of others; if everyone admitted the truth, we would discover that everyone is looking out for himself and for a "big deal"; honesty is the best policy; he who does not live somewhat for others does not fully live himself; the race is to the swift; I am my brother's keeper. Add others, as desired.

Because he represents an adult authority symbol in our society, the teacher may wish partly to dissociate himself from the exercise by having a small committee of students pass out the sheets, collect them after the class has completed them, and tally the results. The committee then reports back to teacher and class, leading a discussion open to all class members. The teacher will merely help pupils select a basis for limiting their ideas and an opening for writing their reactions.

If a more complete development is desired, the teacher may include selected materials from literature and carry out a brief project called "The Choices We Make." For this purpose copies of suitable stories, biographies, and other selections are placed on a reserve table in the library or classroom. Some selections used successfully with high school students are listed here, but each teacher may have favorites of his own.

SHORT STORIES	ONE-ACT PLAYS
"I Can't Breathe," Ring Lardner "Success Story," James Gould Cozzens	*Two Crooks and a Lady,* Eugene Pillot
"Too Late to Lie," Donald MacKenzie	*Confessional,* Percival Wilde
"The Snob," Morley Callaghan	*Finders Keepers,* George Kelly

From class discussions of self-interest versus good will there should develop enough tension of ideas to motivate writing. Of course the teacher should avoid condemning self-interest unless he wants a flood of idealistic thoughts, few of them completely sincere. One does well to make clear that honest conviction is preferable to perfunctory moralizing; otherwise these lessons may produce a crop of saints as short-lived as New Year's resolutions.

▶ *Envision unfamiliar modes of living*

Assign the topic "If I were _____." The main features the teacher would present in helping pupils with such a composition are:

OCCUPATIONS	RACES	NATIONALITIES	RELIGIONS
policeman	Caucasian	Japanese	Islam
housewife and mother	Oriental	German	Buddhism
teacher	Negro	Arab	Christianity
union leader	Indian	Hindu	Judaism
nurse	Polynesian	Mexican	
businessman			
stenographer			
truck driver			

Ideas for development My point of view would be _____. My loyalties or dislikes would be _____.

Components of "If I were" The circle graph depicts rather freely some of the possible components of such a composition.

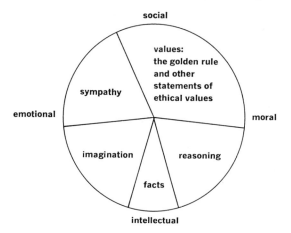

When successful, this composition may contribute to some of these desirable purposes of education: more precise observation, better understanding, more objectivity, expansion of imaginative feeling, diminished ethnocentricity, and increased sensitivity to other people.

▶ *Present two opposing points of view*

1. For either junior or senior high pupils, tension of ideas can be created by presenting two sides of a question. Usually, issues at stake should relate to the interests characteristic of the age group. For instance, the following lesson succeeded with a number of junior high school classes. The teacher duplicated the materials, passed them out, and read them aloud. A brief discussion, moderated by the teacher, was followed by writing.

> *General instructions* Opinions differ as to the intelligence of animals. In the paragraphs that follow, two former students have indicated their ideas on the wisdom of dogs. Read the paragraphs carefully. After you have given thought to the matter, may we hear your viewpoint?

> *One point of view* Dogs are wiser than we think. They can foretell what is to come and they can sense the death of a beloved master, even when he is far away. A dog who was sent home from Europe by a sailor intuitively recognized his master's wife. An American dog at a concert sat through "God Save the King" but rose on all fours and stood with quiet dignity for "The Star-Spangled Banner." Some dogs do not like to see their masters drink and will get up quietly and leave the room after the second or third cocktail. Dogs are far more knowing than the average person believes them to be.

> *Another point of view* Popular misconceptions about dogs would fill a volume. People like to credit dogs with high intelligence and out of affection often go beyond the truth in telling about their dogs. If dogs were so faithful, wise, and skilled at detecting villains, there would be one stationed at the door of every store to intercept shoplifters; they would bark at robbers, forgers, and other felons. Although they are intelligent animals, dogs are far less knowing than the average person believes them to be.

2. Editorials and letters to the editor in local and school newspapers provide a good source of materials for similar exercises.

▶ *Discuss the nature of evil*

For classes with many gifted and thoughtful pupils, discussion may center on problems of a more difficult order. The nature of evil, for instance, is a topic with universal interest. What is evil, how do religions and philosophies explain it, and how does a young person come to terms with it as he leaves the cloistered security of childhood? Such questions, a challenge to the keenest minds in any class, interest any thoughtful adolescent. Concrete illustrations may be drawn from local news and current events of the international scene. Literature, especially, will awaken thoughts on this topic.

▶ *Explore puzzling issues*

Excellent discussion leading to writing often develops from topics that puzzle young people. Even if some topics prove too complex for simple answers, the discussion can reveal why some of the puzzles exist and why teachers and other adults have not provided clear-cut answers. In one tenth-grade class, the pupils listed twenty-three items on the chalkboard. A few examples follow, phrased in the pupils' own words:

I'D LIKE TO KNOW

How can people actually believe we came from monkeys? If we did, why are there any monkeys left today and why can't we watch the apes on earth turning into human beings?

Just what is Communism? What makes some Americans become Communists, and are they real Communists or do they just take a different attitude?

Is the age for getting a driver's license going to be raised, and if so why should all teen-agers suffer just because some are careless?

Although such questions include considerations that must be handled with care, they furnish valuable opportunities for reasoning and imaginative thinking, both in the preliminary discussion of the question and in the subsequent written compositions. Class discussion often reveals that questions are inaccurately phrased or beg the real issue. After a preliminary inspection of all the questions, the teacher might ask pupils to select two or three topics they consider particularly promising for writing. After these have been chosen, each student spends the next few days learning everything he can about one of the chosen topics, trying to discover any differing points of view, trying to assess dispassionately the ultimate problems behind each question.[32] Whenever the pupils show enough readiness of ideas, the lesson may be transferred from discussion to writing.

▶ *Exploit local history*

One class invited to school old settlers who remembered the community's early days. The students recorded on tapes all the memories the older people offered, and

---

[32] If the topics appear to involve controversial material, the teacher should not evade the issues. He can discuss the matter with his principal or the parents' association in advance, explaining what he is seeking to do and requesting their approval for genuinely educational procedures.

from the tape recordings mimeographed *Wagon on the Trail,* a series of writings based on the reminiscences.

► *Serialize topics suitable for several compositions*

Seventh-grade students in one school wrote a continued story about a truck driver named Matt. Their writing began when a young teamster came to school at the teacher's invitation to explain his work and tell some of his adventures. The students liked him and readily followed the teacher's suggestion that they write about him. Their writing became a continued series that eventually grew into a class book called *Matt's Miles.* About once every three weeks the students wrote another set of stories. From each set, a superior episode was chosen for the class book. The pupils learned a great deal about the world of labor, unions, and the national economy.

► *Take advantage of nearby building construction*

Teachers have often turned to advantage the construction of new buildings in the vicinity of the school—usually new schools or additions to the existing one. Pupils keep records of construction progress and write about the multiple aspects of building: engineering principles, bulldozers and construction equipment, the building trades unions, esthetic design, use of color, landscaping, and building materials. Modern building construction provides enough possibilities to interest every pupil, including any boys who classify English as a subject designed especially for girls. Here is an example of intellectual curiosity and increased powers of observation combining and reinforcing each other as bases to stimulate writing.

► *Use a time machine*

Students are often intrigued by H. G. Wells' idea of a time machine for traveling backward and forward in history. The teacher may choose some year of the past such as 1295, when Marco Polo returned to Venice, and prepare several illustrative paragraphs to serve as stimulators for discussion and models for writing. For samples of the future, the teacher may read aloud "The Main in Asbestos" by Stephen Leacock or portions of E. M. Forster's "The Machine Stops." In discussing the models, the teacher will need to recommend that students avoid an unimaginative imitation. The basic idea, however, is excellent for stimulating response.

► *Relate composition to film and to all literature studied*

Writing should most frequently draw its vitality from the study of literature, whether film or book. Wherever literature is successfully taught, motivation for writing emerges as an integral part of the discussion and response. Aware that finding and developing entirely new topics for composition consumes time, teachers take advantage of this fortunate parsimony of effort.

The compositions need not always be critical opinions of the literature read or films viewed. There are a number of approaches combining writing with literature: associations the literature elicits; explanations of some event or reference in the film or selection; interpretations; evaluations or critical appraisals; imitations of the author's style; parodies, which often require a deep understanding of the original work.

TO EXTEND AND SHARPEN OBSERVATION

▶ *Feature the five senses in descriptive observations*

1. Assign or plan with students a description in which students use words to make a reader hear, feel, taste, smell, and see. Emphasize the use of effective verbs rather than adjectives. Where adjectives are used, recommend those that refer to one of the five senses: pungent smell of orange peel; salty crispness of bacon; snarling rasp of machinery in a sawmill. If duplicated, part of the assignment might read like this:

> Choose one of the following and describe the subject as exactly as possible. Ideally you should write immediately after having had the sensory experience. These are only suggestions. If you wish, choose an equally useful experience of your own.
>
> the feel of a baseball snugly caught in a mitt, a bat firmly striking a baseball, a fabric such as satin or velvet; the feel of a baby's cheek, of a baby chicken
>
> the take-off of a jet plane
>
> a builder's crane lifting a heavy object
>
> a bulldozer in action
>
> the smells and sounds of a shop class
>
> the noon rush of students down the stairs to the lunchroom (Does it remind you of something else?)
>
> the sight of a parade or school carnival from a high window (Does it look like something other than what it is?)
>
> the smell of burning leaves, roasting coffee, or tar on a hot summer day
>
> the sound of a high wind, noises at night, or band practice in the music room
>
> the world seen through gently falling snow or heavy fog
>
> a perfect dive (What did it look like? How did it feel?)
>
> the sight of moving traffic from a hilltop or a plane (Does it look like something else?)
>
> the taste of olives, toasted marshmallows, onions, strawberries, or peanuts

2. Like the scientist, the skilled writer has developed his powers of observation. Students who have completed one of the descriptions above could improve their writing through careful, exact observation and the practice of recording such observation in concise language. They might try some of these exercises in observation as a follow-up to the first assignment:

> Students visit the shops at school or observe machinery in operation during an excursion to a factory. They record observations and compare the results.
>
> Students draw a plan of some friend's house, listing colors, furniture, and arrangements. They take the plan with them on their next visit, as a check-up, and report their degree of success in a written statement to the teacher.
>
> At home, students watch a dog, squirrel, or bird for ten or fifteen minutes. To this study they should bring both a sharpened alertness in observing everything that would escape the attention of most persons and an inquiring mind in connection with what they observe.

At Christmas, the class divides into groups to describe the sights, sounds, smells, and tastes peculiar to the season, each group specializing in one sense, the final product a class composition.

A committee gathers an assortment of objects into a large bag: spark plug, velvet cloth, cellophane-tape dispenser, flour sifter, hose nozzle, chore boy, plastic toy, other relatively unfamiliar objects. Each student reaches into the bag, selects one object, attempts to familiarize himself with that object through the sensation of touch. Then he writes a description of the object in terms of the sense of touch—textures, shapes, thermal qualities. Descriptions can be read to the class, and other pupils may guess what object is being described.

A committee arranges on small paper plates or sponges a slice of lemon peel, geranium leaf, vanilla beans, fresh chewing gum, turpentine, witch hazel, coffee, moth balls, crushed lavender, and similar odoriferous things. Everyone shuts his eyes. Members of the committee carry the plates from student to student. They also distribute a score pad to be used by each student after he has identified or described the odors. Discuss the results.

Prepare similar tests for taste and hearing.

Note that our language contains more words for seeing and tasting than for smelling, hearing, or kinesthetic feeling. If dogs had a language, which sense would command the most words? Encourage a gifted or interested pupil to report on the language of smell that permeates the biography of Flush, Elizabeth Barrett Browning's spaniel.[33]

Select some person outside the class to pay an unexpected visit. Let him carry a number of different objects as well as speak and act in some surprising manner. After he has gone, have students write an account of his surprise appearance and actions.

At home have students observe, describe, and compare two processes— such as a dog and a cat drinking.

▶ Describe someone you know

Let pupils choose one of the following situations:

A friend, relative, classmate, or acquaintance has disappeared and the authorities enlist your aid in writing a description.

You are traveling for the first time to Vancouver or San Francisco and will be met at the airport by a relative who has never seen you before. Write a letter describing yourself and the clothing you will wear so there will be no possibility of not being recognized.[34]

▶ Use photographs to emphasize careful scrutiny

Training in observation is the focus of a paperback entitled *Stop, Look, and Write!* by Hart Day Leavitt and David A. Sohn. Subtitled "Effective Writing Through Pictures," the book includes more than one hundred dramatic photographs, as well as teaching help on comparison, contrast, emphasis, and point of view. Many pictures appeal to other sense impressions as well as to sight.

[33] Virginia Woolf, *Flush* (New York: Harcourt, Brace & World, 1933).
[34] Suggested by Frank Whitehead in *The Disappearing Dais* (Champaign, Ill.: NCTE, 1968), p. 165.

▶ *Present models illustrating sensory perception*

1. Effective models of writing featuring sensory appeal may be identified in literary selections studied or read aloud while students listen in order to note down outstandingly effective words and phrases. In such a case the models should be read several times. In the first rendition the students listen for the over-all meaning; in the others they listen to select certain words or phrases. Two that have proved effective are reprinted here.

MODERN MUSIC

At that moment, everybody began clapping. The conductor, a tall foreign-looking chap with a shock of grey hair that stood out all around his head, had arrived at his little railed-in platform and was giving the audience a series of short jerky bows. He gave two little taps. All the players brought their instruments up and looked at him. He slowly raised his arms, then brought them down sharply and the concert began.

First all the violins made a shivery sort of noise that you could feel travelling up and down your spine. Some of the clarinets and bassoons squeaked and gibbered a little, and the brass instruments made a few unpleasant remarks. Then all the violins went rushing up and up, and when they got to the top, the stout man at the back hit a gong, the two men near him attacked their drums. . . . The noise was terrible, shattering: . . . walls of houses were falling in; ships were going down; ten thousand people were screaming with toothache; steam hammers were breaking loose; whole warehouses of oilcloth were being stormed and the oilcloth all torn into shreds; and there were railway accidents innumerable. Then suddenly the noise stopped; one of the clarinets, all by itself, went slithering and gurgling; the violins began their shivery sound again and at last shivered away into silence. The conductor dropped his arms to his side. Nearly everybody clapped.[35]

EARLIEST MEMORY

I was five. Already I had known the drowsy scent of red peonies in a hot corner of the garden, the friendly smell of cool apples. Taste I knew, too—the puckery, restraining taste of forbidden chokeberries, the taste of sulphur and molasses, lingering and powdery long after it should have gone. And the yellow of a floor was to me never so yellow as a great ball of dandelions which my father had once made for me and which he rolled to and fro, hither and yon, across the clipped green grass.[36]

2. To vary this method, teachers sometimes present pupils with a version pared to its least evocative paraphrase. Students are to take a skeleton such as the following, develop it more fully, and finally compare their own work with the original. For example, the first paragraph in the model just above can be reduced to a version like this:

[35] John Boynton Priestley, *Angel Pavement* (New York: Harper & Row, 1930), pp. 234 ff. Other passages following this one may also be used. They include further descriptions of contemporary music and of Brahms' *First Symphony*.
[36] Mary Ellen Chase, "A Kitchen Parnassus," from *The Golden Asse and Other Essays* (New York: Holt, Rinehart & Winston, 1929), p. 111. The passage following this is also an excellent model.

Already I had known the smell of flowers in the garden and of apples. Taste I knew, too, the taste of chokeberries and the taste of sulphur and molasses. The floor paint was not as yellow as some flowers.

TO EXPLORE FEELINGS

▶ *Relate amusing incidents of everyday living*

All pupils have some comic anecdotes worth sharing. In order to elicit some of these in writing, the teacher may read aloud some droll account of everyday living such as "Mama and Uncle Elizabeth" from *Mama's Bank Account,* "The First Prom Is the Hardest" from *We Shook the Family Tree,* or "The Slom Season" in Selma Lagerlöf's *Marbacka.*[37] Because all story writing demands rather a stern effort from students, a teacher may wish to let this project represent more than a single composition. The story may be planned so that it falls into several parts, each representing a single composition, each part to be turned in over a period of time. For the first assignment, only the first segment is to be completed.

▶ *Describe an act of generosity*

A written activity that has succeeded for a number of teachers requires initially an act of generosity on the part of the pupils. Each is to do or give something without expectation of money or acknowledgment in return. Students have carried out such individual projects as cleaning the house, baby-sitting, visiting some sick or aged person, helping a brother or sister with lessons, making something as a gift to please someone, washing the car. The written account is usually divided into three parts: what was done, how it was received, and how the giver felt about his experience in generosity.[38]

▶ *Probe feelings about school*

In "Five Ripe Pears," [39] William Saroyan tells of being punished in the first grade. He had brought to school five ripe and beautiful pears; taking them from a tree along the way, he had not realized he was stealing. His wryly amusing account will evoke students' memories of schoolday troubles. Such topics as "The Best Thing That Ever Happened to Me in School" and "The Teacher I Remember Best from Grade School" set pupils to considering positive characteristics of schooling and teachers. Students should avoid identifying individuals.

▶ *Use picture strip stories*

For slow students the teacher may draw and duplicate a series of five pictures, simple and cartoon-like in nature, illustrating an incident that has recently caused deep feelings among the pupils—for example, an April Fool prank, a happy picnic or party. The students then complete the series by drawing balloons to the mouths of the characters and writing in what each person said. After this, they may be in-

---

[37] Or "The Seventeen Cats," also from *Marbacka;* see also "The Marseillaise," from her *Memories of My Childhood* (Garden City, N.Y.: Doubleday, 1934). Some other examples of everyday comedy are "The Apricot Tree" from *The Human Comedy* by William Saroyan, as well as many of his short stories; and the chapter on the shopping expedition from Shirley Jackson's *Life Among the Savages.*
[38] Edyth W. Hadley, Youngstown, Ohio, describes such a lesson in "Techniques in Teaching High School Students to Listen," *English Journal,* Vol. 40, No. 7 (September 1951).
[39] From his book *Inhale and Exhale* (New York: Random House, 1936).

terested in writing more "comic book" stories, in which they draw the pictures and write stories to go with the pictures. After several of these lessons, the teacher assigns an explanatory paragraph to be placed under each picture series, thus leading these slow learners to a more conventional type of composition.

▶ *Offer free choices*

Offer some occasions when pupils choose the writing they will do, when their compositions will not be graded: "You need not even put your name on them, but I or a student committee will look them over and read some to the entire class." A committee of students draws up five areas of ideas to serve as an impetus for the first writing section. One committee adopted the following procedure: five boxes, in which the students could place themes, were placed at the rear of the room. The boxes were labeled:

I APPRECIATE   I SHUDDER ABOUT   I HATE   I HOPE   I WONDER WHY

Pupils placed finished compositions in one of these boxes; the committee chose compositions for oral presentation.[40]

▶ *Choose from several suggestions*

The following suggestions to be placed on the blackboard represent a list from which pupils may choose one subject they prefer to develop. Each title has been selected for its relation to the affective side of pupils' lives. Discussion groups in advance of writing stimulate many ideas.

Controlling My Temper	The Sorrows of a Bashful Person
The Pleasures of Being Alone	Sometimes I Worry About _____
The Pleasures of Being with People	I Am Happiest When _____
A Day I'd Like to Live over Again	Things That Bother Me
The Meanest Thing I Ever Did	When I Am Older

TO INCREASE ABILITY TO INTERPRET

▶ *Present models with a range of interpretiveness*

From a set of compositions select four ranging from exceptionally interpretive to cryptic. From these delete the names and with masking tape arrange the compositions on the front chalkboard. Beside each one write comments showing how selection of details, illustrations, and word choice add expressiveness to writing. During study times invite individuals to go forward to read compositions and comments. For a variation of this method choose a model, from student writing or from literature, and pare it to a Spartan lack of expressiveness. The original and the "skeleton" are then duplicated and compared for effectiveness.

▶ *Write biographies and autobiographies*

One teacher assigns a composition called "To Every Man His Boswell." The students draw names and write the biography of the person whose name they draw. In other schools an autobiography at about the ninth or tenth grade is the major writing project of the year. Subtitles within such autobiographies may include "Important Firsts," "Turning Points," "My Happiest Memories," and "Important Deci-

[40] Idea for grade seven, *Teaching Speaking and Writing in Wisconsin* (Madison, Wis.: Dept. of Public Instruction, January 1966), p. 75.

sions." The value of detail and example in such material, where a pupil draws on his own experience, is sometimes easier to demonstrate than in more impersonal writing.

▶ *Tell a whopper*

Students enjoy reading tall tales about Paul Bunyan, Pecos Bill, and Baron Munchausen. After reading and discussion each student fabricates his own tall tale, using some event in his own experience as the nub for uninhibited expansion.

▶ *Expand "personals"*

Clip items from the personal column of any newspaper and let pupils choose one from a large number. "Personals" are almost always capable of varied interpretations. If several pupils expand the same item, the less imaginative may come to see what possibilities of interpretation exist in a few words such as these:

> T. M. Kept appointment, Cougar Cafe. Displayed token at table; so may I apply for renewal? D. F.
> Reba, be at big tree, Lime Drive, noon, same day as before. Important information. J. F.

Sometimes grouping three or four pupils together to write an expansion permits the less imaginative in each group to observe how others set about expanding a "skeleton."

▶ *Base compositions on relationships*

After the pupils have read several short stories, place a series of quotations on the chalkboard: for example, the unexamined life is not worth living; every man takes the limits of his own field of vision for the limits of the world; skill is stronger than strength; luck is infatuated with the efficient; sweet are the uses of adversity. Not all the quotations need be pertinent to the stories; in fact, some should not. Make sure there are relationships between the stories and some but not all of the quotations placed on the chalkboard.

Through class discussion, develop the meanings of the quotations and their relevance or irrelevance to some of the stories. Add some new quotations and have the pupils write a paragraph discussing the relationship between one quotation and the literature.

▶ *Develop the suggestions from kinescopes*

The Commission on English in Appendix C of *Freedom and Discipline in English* provides a list of kinescopes made available for teacher use.[41] "Invention and Topics; or, Where to Look for Something to Say" makes clear that a good composition assignment gives a student something to make a discovery about.

▶ *Interview imaginary persons*

The students write their imaginary interviews with a character in a novel, or a person of the historical past. Preliminary discussion of the possibilities will lift the level of thought that goes into such a composition.

---

[41] Write Commission on English, College Entrance Examination Board, Publications Order Office, Box 592, Princeton, N.J. 08540.

TO CONNECT WRITING WITH PERSONAL NEEDS AND INTERESTS

► *Compile a youth guide*

Two classes list for one another some of the major problems they believe today's youth must encounter. The lists are exchanged and used for class discussion. Usually this discussion is led by the teacher; sifting the problems and organizing them requires leadership in seeing relationships and placing items in proper categories. When the listing is completed, the most important teen-age problems are chosen for compositions that will represent the best advice distilled from class discussion. Thus, the students in each class select several problems listed by the other class. In suggesting how the problems might be handled or solved they bring to bear upon each the best wisdom they can offer. The essays may be polished and, after being read by the class raising the problems, bound for the library or for the teacher to use as models next semester.

► *Rate and discuss handicaps*

To motivate writing, one teacher asks his students to list twelve handicaps, rating them in two different ways: first, as deterrents to success in school life, and second, as deterrents to success after school. Handicaps typically listed are lack of poise in social situations, poor looks, unattractive home, poor health, poor speaking ability, and lack of money. This topic usually proves deeply interesting and almost always motivates intense discussion leading to equally intense writing.

► *Suggest topics for speculation*

    If I could have three wishes come true
    I want my husband (or wife) to be _____
    Three cars I would never own: from bad to worse
    Tomorrow as I would like to spend it
    A day I would like to live over again
    What I expect of my teen-age son (or daughter) (Assume you are a parent.)
    The advantages of not being well adjusted

► *Begin the year with an exchange letter between students and teacher*

Some teachers open each school year by addressing a letter to each student, explaining that he does not know the student and has not consulted previous teachers or any records. He will consult records later; now he prefers to form his own individual impression of each student. In order to help in forming this impression the student is requested to write a letter in which he tells something about himself as an individual and as a student of English. First of all what are his interests, likes, and dislikes? What are his plans and hopes for the years after high school? Next, how has he fared in English up to this point? Has he been a successful student? A good or weak reader? What of writing? Speaking? Skills such as spelling? What difficulties has the student had and how does he account for those difficulties? What especially should be chosen for improvement during the coming year? How can the teacher be of the greatest assistance?

These letters, it is explained, will remain confidential and will never be placed in the files of the school. They will, however, be kept in the individual folders of the students and at the close of the semester, the teacher and the student will examine them to see whether or not the student's plans and requests for help have received attention. Teachers who use this approach find that students respond very favorably. In addition to learning something about the characteristics of the students, the teacher gathers information on how well they write, organize their ideas, and use conventions of spelling, punctuation, and capitalization. Thus the letter is diagnostic in multiple ways.

▶ *Let pupils research the year of their birth*

The experience of hunting for books, magazines, and (if available) newpapers dealing with the year of one's birth is highly motivating. Most pupils are curious about what was happening during the time period of their birth. Some students will even carry out intensive research into the day of their birth. Others like the idea of researching the years of their parents' births or that of some favorite relative, sending the finished composition as a gift. Subsequently students may be led to select some year that intrigues them and write up the major events of that year. For this last topic, tell them about and read a passage from Bernard De Voto's *The Year of Decision: 1846. Time* magazine has been publishing special books of the year to cover at least the past thirty years—enough to document the lives of any adolescents now in school.

▶ *Keep daily journals and vignettes*

Many teachers plan some writing for fifteen minutes each day, usually diaries or paragraphs of personal reflection and comment. From these vignettes the pupils copy out the best of their entries for a weekly or bi-weekly assignment. In one class the results were stored in the student's manila folders. Any amount was acceptable, one sentence or twenty, as long as the student wrote something every day. On Fridays, students received their folders and copied a selection from the previous week's writing. Only this portion of the writing was read and evaluated. The project started slowly. Some students, disliking English, were appalled at the prospect of daily writing. "What'll I write about?" they complained. Class discussions provided some suggestions; quiet students wrote out attitudes they would not discuss aloud; other students wrote stories, adding an episode a day; others kept diary-like records of their experiences and changing points of view. For a while the teacher wrote on the board each day five provocative ideas. Later he wrote only one and students supplied the other four. These ideas often helped pupils find content for their writing.

TO WRITE FOR PRACTICAL AND IMMEDIATE USES

In order to persuade students of the importance of writing and the value the world places on it, teachers often use evidence from the business world. Some firms employ personnel officers who confer with teachers on the writing skills they seek in new employees. Students may also interview adults on the values and uses of writing and report these interviews to the class. Finally, the range of financial rewards and the deeper satisfactions successful writers enjoy should be occasionally emphasized as well as the amazing variety of occupations open to those skilled in writing.

▶ *Correspond with youth abroad*

The experience of writing to young people, whether at home or abroad, transcends mere considerations of letter form. Although students should realize their letters become models for those learning our language, they should be even more aware of how their letters' content and tone reflect political ideals and a particular way of life. Some of the agencies where teachers may enroll pupils for foreign correspondence are:

> International Students Society, P.O. Box 239, Hillsboro, Oregon 97123
>
> Swedish Central Committee for International Exchange Between Schools, Skolgränd 2, Stockholm SV, Sweden
>
> Student Letter Exchange, Waseca, Minnesota. Names of foreign students who write in English will be furnished.
>
> For letter exchange entirely in English, the Executive Secretary, International Friendship League, 40 Mount Vernon Street, Boston, Massachusetts, provides names and addresses.
>
> For information on the International Albums Program, write local Red Cross chapters. School and classroom groups enrolled in the Junior Red Cross in the United States now correspond with similar groups in sixty countries.
>
> Letters Abroad, 18 East 60th Street, New York, New York 10022, serves students aged fifteen and older.

▶ Send letters to age mates

One junior high school class in Minneapolis wanted to correspond with other American youngsters living in communities different from their own. They chose three towns whose names intrigued them: Horse Heaven, Washington; Cody, Wyoming; and Osceoles, Arkansas. They wrote a letter to the eighth-grade teacher in each of these three communities asking whether or not that teacher would be willing to furnish names of students who wanted to correspond. After these letters to the three teachers had been composed in rough draft, they were examined by the entire class for proper tone and completeness of information. The teacher helped plan appropriate letter form, and once such conventions had been reviewed, the final versions were neatly written and mailed.

Horse Heaven proved to be a small rural school with only three eighth-graders, but the other two towns furnished larger numbers of correspondents, and the teachers in all three schools saw value in the project. The result was that for a year the Minneapolis students corresponded with students in the other three communities. The individual writers told about themselves, their schools, families, and communities, receiving in return similar letters to be shared with the rest of the class. These became the basis for lessons, not only on letter form, but on writing in general. So many Minneapolis students became intrigued by the Horse Heaven Hills, the Rattlesnake Hills, and Lost Horse Plateau in south central Washington that letters were finally dispatched to several eighth-grade teachers in larger towns located near those exciting geographical place names. Other pupils, however, retained their allegiance to Cody and Osceoles.

▶ Keep class minutes

In some schools, minutes are kept for every class meeting, and most class hours begin with a reading of the minutes from the previous day. For many pupils this provides a sense of continuity and direction. Confused often by the multiplicity of assignments and activities in many different subject matters, they find in the minutes a sense of security. Rotating responsibility for keeping and reading the previous day's minutes provides everybody in the class with an opportunity to do some useful writing. The minutes, kept in a looseleaf notebook, include all assignments, in order to help students who are absent. Some pupils keep class logs that include also their personal reactions.

▶ *Write for publication*

1. On public controversies pupils may be helped to write letters that exhibit rational and sensible thought. The best of these are sent to the local or nearest newspaper's letters-to-the-editor column.

2. Occasional news sheets or collections of creative writing prepared by the class can be duplicated and distributed in the school.

▶ *Write for other courses*

Occasionally the English classroom should become a writing laboratory for papers required in other courses such as social studies, homemaking, science, and journalism.

▶ *Write self-evaluations at marking periods*

In many schools an impressively functional exercise is the self-evaluation students write just before grades are to be made out. These compositions aid teachers in assigning grades and in some schools they are attached to the pupils' reports and sent home. A copy should certainly be filed in the pupil's writing folder. Usually these evaluations are titled, "What I Have Learned This Marking Period." Duplicate or outline on the chalkboard the major goals of instruction during the period of time in question, discuss these goals, and remind the students of some ways they have worked toward them.

▶ *Enter writing contests, both local and national*

Service groups and other clubs in the local community sponsor writing contests, and many of these offer excellent opportunities for students to write for a genuine purpose.[42] In cases where past contest titles have been considered too broad or vague, teachers have met in advance with representatives of the sponsoring groups. Almost always teachers have found these men and women only too anxious to phrase topics that will contribute to both instruction in writing and the intent of the sponsoring organization. Contests are offered also by *Seventeen, Literary Cavalcade,* and other national magazines.

▶ *Write letters of appreciation*

Write to authors or illustrators of favorite recent books. Do not ask questions or request a reply.

TO FOCUS ON THE PARAGRAPH

▶ *Build a paragraph in class*

To teach how details relate to the topic sentence, ask the class to suggest a topic sentence that can be developed by the use of detail—for example, the mem-

---

[42] The National Association of Secondary School Principals, 1201 Sixteenth Street, N.W., Washington, D.C. 20006, publishes every year (usually in September) in its magazine *The Bulletin* an "Approved List of National Contests and Activities for the Year ——." This organization maintains a committee that has studied contests of all kinds for over two decades.

bers of the band were tuning up; girls need a course in shop; a baby sitter does more than sit. Have a student write the sentence on the chalkboard. Class members contribute statements using details to develop the topic sentence. The secretary records appropriate details on the chalkboard. The class then evaluates the relevance of each suggested detail, giving reasons. With the assorted accepted details in full view on the board, each student writes his version of the paragraph, including the topic idea and arranging the sentences in a logical order.

▶ *Present strong and weak models*

1. Not all models should be adult. There is among teachers an increasing concern that reliance on rhetorics based exclusively on adult writing is not helpful to the majority of immature writers. Although we do not yet have rhetorics based upon pupil writing, we can encourage more study of models selected from our own pupils' writing. In many schools—certainly in some where disadvantaged pupils attend —a book like *From the Ashes: Voices of Watts,* edited by Budd Schulberg, would provide models to tie in with the increasing emphasis on imaginative writing.

2. Duplicate examples of paragraphs that ramble from their unifying topic or fail to support a topic with sufficient detail. These models are often effective means of identifying the crucial features of strong and weak paragraphs.

3. Some teachers like a variation of the above method, the selection of several superior paragraphs on topics appealing to students. Each superior paragraph is matched with a version the teacher has distorted. The two passages are duplicated, or shown with an opaque projector. The students read the two versions, tell which is the better and why they think so. This method of spoiled versions, because it shifts the role of explanation from teacher to pupil, proves to be a highly effective method of instruction.

4. Some teachers type the sentences of paragraphs on separate slips of paper, jumble them, and put them in envelopes. The pupils take the envelopes and assemble the paragraphs in the best order. Such exercises can be helpful, but eventually the learnings involved must be proved in the pupil's actual experience of composing his own ideas into a unified paragraph.

▶ *Learn to write different kinds of paragraphs*

From class texts, assign a different paragraph to be read by each individual in the class. The problem: to determine what each paragraph does.[43] Through class discussion formulate the awareness that writing can be classified as narration, description, exposition, and argumentation, or a combination of these types. List these major classifications across the chalkboard. Be sure students understand the purpose of each of these kinds of writing. Fill in some methods by which paragraphs in each kind of writing may be developed, but guide pupils away from any stress on nomenclature as an end in itself.

NARRATION	DESCRIPTION	EXPOSITION	ARGUMENTATION
Details in time order	Details grouped by location	Definition	Reasons for
	Details grouped for emotional effect	Details	Reasons against
		Examples	
		Comparison and contrast	

[43] For this method and others that follow in this section, the authors are indebted to the English teachers of George Washington High School, San Francisco.

Read one or two sample paragraphs. Have the class decide into which classification each one fits and what method of development is used. (Some good paragraphs will not fit easily into a single category.) Have students read aloud paragraphs of their own, afterwards checking them against the chart.

Encourage students to use variety of paragraph development in compositions.

TO PLAN LONGER COMPOSITIONS

▶ *Help students narrow a specific subject*

On the board draw three columns, headed *Subjects, Topics,* and *Central idea sentences.* Explain that a subject, the largest of the three concepts, can be handled in a book. Obtain from volunteers suggestions for subjects: Today's Youth; The United Nations; The Problems of Minority Groups. Have each student who makes an acceptable suggestion write it on the board in the subject column and then reduce it from a subject to a topic—for example, Fads of Teen-agers; Pitfalls of the U.N. Organization; Housing Restrictions in a Democratic Society.

Explain that the central idea sentence (CIS) governing the organization is the phase of the "topic" selected for the essay. Obtain from students suggestions for central idea sentences derived from the topics now written in column two. These sentences are then written in their appropriate places in the third column.

> In adopting fads, teen-agers find some of the security they seek.
> From the beginning of the United Nations the power to veto has been a hindrance to the successful functioning of this organization.
> The widely publicized _____ case was a clear-cut instance of selfishness and prejudice.

Now that the columns have been filled out, discussion follows. Questions are asked; ideas are exchanged. The teacher makes certain the class grasps the necessity for narrowing a subject, selecting a point of view, and addressing the writing to a definite reader or audience.[44]

Each member of the class now prepares his own chart, filling in new subjects, topics, and central idea sentences. If one of the topics on his chart pleases a student sufficiently, it may be used for his next essay.

One teacher begins this lesson on narrowing a subject by asking, "If your home was burning and you could carry from it only three things, what would you choose?" After discussing the bases of such choices, he asks, "What if you could carry out only one thing?" Finally he draws from the students the analogy of selecting for a purpose in composition.

▶ *Conduct pupils through a complete experience in composing*

Students quite naturally find difficulty in applying generalizations like "be coherent" or "maintain unity of thought." But their learning is reasonably rapid whenever teachers actually show them how to grapple with their own ideas and how to arrange them effectively. The obstacle, however, to such desirable instruction is the sheer impossibility of penetrating the thoughts—or half-formed thoughts—of more than one pupil at a time. To solve this difficulty in large classes, teachers sometimes use one effective strategy. They select a topic of interest to as many pupils as pos-

[44] Compare this with the same problem in "Oral Communication," pages 314–16. Correlation of similar skills in speaking and writing reinforce the learning of skills.

sible and conduct the entire class through the steps of composing an essay on that topic. In his description of this method, Joseph C. Blumenthal used the topic of military training for every boy.[45] With younger pupils, the question of extending the American school year to twelve months is nearly always successful; in fact, on this issue student involvement is deep at any grade level.

After selecting the topic, the teacher makes an assignment. Each pupil is to write two single-sentence arguments, each one on a separate card or half-sheet of paper. For instance, here are two arguments opposing the twelve-month school year:

1	2
Parents with several children in school could not plan vacations that would include the whole family.	Children need rest and change if they are not to weary of school.

Two arguments are much better than one; the teacher is seeking a variety of points for the composing about to be carried out in class, and a greater diversity appears among the students' second arguments than among their first.

Next the students read their arguments aloud and the teacher helps them find general headings for the various points. Blumenthal's students, for instance, found that all their arguments against military training would fit under one or another of such headings as "Ineffectiveness" and "International Distrust."

These general headings are then written horizontally across the chalkboard and the students place their cards, or slips of paper, on the chalk ledge beneath the appropriate headings. The pack of cards for each general heading is then assigned to a committee, which reduces the arguments by eliminating duplicate ideas. The committee is to design the best possible order for the arguments that remain and to prepare reasons for the order they select. Now the committee writes a paragraph (the arguments in the sequence they have chosen) for their general heading on the chalkboard. One special committee, or the class as a whole, turns its attention to the best sequence for the general headings, learning that there is no one right way but several equally good ways. "The important point is that we present our ideas according to a plan, not in the hit or miss way in which they march through our minds." [46] The plan chosen should take into account the impression or conclusion the writer wants to leave in the mind of a particular reader or group of readers. The total method is an example of how a teacher does more than merely assign writing. Most students, if they are to improve their writing, need to be taught how they may do so.

► *Summarize the essentials of an impressive model*

From a magazine or nonfiction book choose a well-organized selection on a topic of interest to adolescents. Ask students to read it and submit a brief summary. Have several read aloud. Probably all will be incomplete in one way or another. Refer to the article; have students select the main idea. Have a member of the class con-

[45] Joseph C. Blumenthal, "Without Form and Void, A Device for Teaching Organization in Expository Writing," *English Journal,* Vol. 35, No. 7 (September 1946).
[46] *Ibid.,* p. 379.

struct an outline on the board based on topic ideas suggested by the class. Leave space under each.

Have students point out subordinate ideas and documentation for each of the sections. Help students see the close-knit thought that characterizes good organization and ask how they can transfer what they have learned.

TO FEATURE EFFECTIVE BEGINNINGS AND ENDINGS

▶ *Use advertising to illustrate beginnings and endings*

Almost all successful magazine ads have effective, eye-catching beginnings and skillful closes. Variety shows on television illustrate the same principle. Beginnings and endings may be unusual camera shots or some skillful arrangement of acts, but inasmuch as they do illustrate the universal importance of an appropriate beginning and close, the principles may be transferred and applied to writing.

▶ *Write with the pupils*

Several times each semester organize some compelling topic on the chalkboard, writing out with pupil suggestions the first two paragraphs, thinking out loud as the composing progresses. Students need more than completed models; they need the learning that can come only through observing the process and realizing the thoughts and considerations accompanying that process. After the teacher has demonstrated the initial paragraphs, students and teacher may complete the composition individually as a basis for discussing their strategies and the reasons for them. The first time a teacher carries out such a demonstration, he may prefer a topic he has considered in advance, but eventually he will find more challenge—and be more effective—with topics requiring him to organize from absolute zero.

▶ *Feature clear thinking and planning*

After a lesson on planning has been taught and students have written some longer papers, choose two for illustration. Have their authors copy on the board the introductory and concluding paragraphs of the essays. The class is asked to speculate on what should logically be found in the paragraphs of development. The two authors will then write their other topic sentences on the board and read the missing paragraphs. The class decides whether the body of the essay fulfills the promise of the introduction and accomplishes what the conclusion says it has accomplished. The class should check to make sure that no new ideas are introduced in the final paragraph.

TO IMPROVE TRANSITIONS

▶ *Teach transitional words and phrases*

1. To teach students the necessity of using accurate transitional devices as "bridges" in their writing, the teacher may read aloud a sample of writing overusing *and* as a connective and a sample of writing using no connectives at all. Ask the class to determine what is wrong with each of the two pieces of writing. Have the class contribute some useful substitutes for *and*. Keep the suggested words on a side board. Write on the front board the types of transition words with examples of each. If pupils develop the list themselves, the exercise will be far more effective.

> words referring back to something or somebody already mentioned (the personal and demonstrative pronouns): he, she, it, this, that, these, those

words of time: meanwhile, afterward, soon, later, eventually, at this moment

words of number: first, second, in the first place

words continuing the same line of thought: also, furthermore, moreover, like-wise, besides, similarly, for example, in fact, for instance

words introducing contrasting thoughts: but, then, nevertheless, still, how-ever, yet, on the other hand, on the contrary

words stating degrees of certainty: certainly, undoubtedly, presumably, in-deed, perhaps, possibly, probably, anyhow, anyway, in all probability, in all likelihood, at all events

words of consequence or result: therefore, consequently, accordingly, hence, then, thus, as a result, so

2. Choosing a composition from his own folder, each student may underline every transitional word he has used and indicate by an *x* the place where one could have been used to advantage.

TO INDUCE BETTER SUBORDINATION

► *Teach the value of subordination*

1. Use sentences appropriate to the level of the class. For young students, for ex-ample, put on the board sentences such as the following:

Buck was a big dog. He lived on an estate. There was a gardener on the estate. He needed money. One day he stole Buck. He sold Buck to some men. These men were going to Alaska.

Have the students read these aloud and offer suggestions for improving them.

2. For a period of time, ten minutes a day spent on revising a single sentence written on the board will achieve results.

► *Use précis writing*

Précis, presented briefly in the pupil's own words, summarize the main ideas of longer materials. They can help students analyze writing for its essential ideas. Through exercises like the following, pupils can learn how shearing off illustration and repetition helps to extract the essential thought of a passage. They also experi-ence the necessity of subordination.

DIFFERING VIEWPOINTS

Opinions differ on the possibility of space travel to other planets. In the two selections that follow, the writers have given their respective ideas on the subject. Read the selections carefully and follow the directions below. (Here the teacher would offer two selections with differing viewpoints on the possibility of space travel.)

Write a well-constructed paragraph in which you explain one of the view-points.

Write a paragraph (or two) in which you set forth your own reaction to the ideas in these two selections.

► *Require students to write economically*

Of some composition topic the teacher says, "You may choose one hundred and fifty words to spend. Who can get the most for his one hundred fifty?" This method gives the teacher an opportunity to emphasize appositives, various kinds of phrases, subordination, and unity of paragraph construction. Learning to use appositives and phrases will be stressed, of course, rather than merely learning to identify them in some drill book.

TO BECOME INTERESTED IN DESIGN

▶ *Compile booklets of student writing*

1. Some schools publish mimeographed booklets of student writing selected for class study. Committees of teachers, sometimes augmented by student members, choose good and weak models of paragraphs for a booklet, deleting the names of those whose paragraphs are presented. Longer compositions, when collected into such booklets, also become valuable aids to instruction. Although composition textbooks available on the market contain models for such purposes, homemade booklets have two special advantages—the vitality deriving from the students' awareness that these compositions were written in their own school and the teachers' familiarity with materials they have personally selected and arranged for instruction.

2. Many colleges and universities publish statements on the quality of writing they seek, for students who continue their education beyond high school. Included in these statements are samples of student prose, varying in quality, along with analyses of the strengths and weaknesses of the samples. Such publications may be used to advantage in many senior high school classes, not only for college-bound students, but for all who need to think and write more clearly. The method when used most effectively begins with reading and discussing the samples, followed by a study of the comments of the college instructors. Typical of these aids is Indiana's "Standards for Written English in Grade 9." [47]

▶ *Use the opaque projector and the overhead projector*

Opaque and overhead projectors make it possible for an entire class to view a student's composition while the teacher and pupils point out positive qualities: a student has organized his material well, has made good transitions, has established a definite point of view. It is much easier to talk about arranging ideas in the order of magnitude if an actual composition is thrown on the screen or wall before the students. (For the overhead projector, a student can copy the compositions onto the transparency.)

TO ESTABLISH STANDARDS

▶ *Agree upon a set of error taboos*

Early in the school term, the students list conventions and mechanics they know so well that only carelessness could account for mistakes. Because students are often overzealous and optimistic about their good intentions, the teacher will need to prevent this initial list from growing too long. Once agreed upon, the list should be posted conspicuously for a period of time; additions should be made as new learnings occur; and copies should later be duplicated for all composition folders. Many groups have an agreement that whenever the teacher notes one of these

---

[47] *Indiana English Leaflet,* Vol. 4, No. 4 (June 1962). Lois M. Grose, Dorothy Miller, and Erwin Steinberg, *Suggestions for Evaluating Junior High School Writing,* Pittsburgh Association of English Teachers of Western Pennsylvania, 1963. Both publications and others are available from NCTE, Champaign, Ill.

errors he may, without further reading, return the paper to the student.[48] One teacher has actually purchased a rubber stamp with the word *TABOO*. Whenever one of the standards on the list is violated, the teacher merely stamps the composition *TABOO* and returns it ungraded to the student.

▶ *Place reminders on the chalkboard*

At the time of writing, the teacher lists examples, both right and wrong, for items that have troubled many pupils in the previous composition. For instance, in an eighth grade, a reminder like this might be helpful:

> Subjects and predicates agree even though a phrase comes between them.
> The *sails* (of the boat) *wave* in the breeze.
> The *hands* (of the clock) *jump* forward.
> *One* (of the boys) *is going.*

The teacher reviews the material on the board before the students start to write. Some teachers use ditto sheets of common problems in writing. The class checks these before turning in writing.

▶ *Have a round-up day*

The teacher, under this plan, reads papers only for content, paying no attention whatsoever to problems of spelling, punctuation, capitalization, and sentence construction. After each student has written five compositions, the teacher arranges at his side five or six able students, either from his class or from some student-helper club formed for this purpose. The students bring their folders and present their last five compositions to the teacher and his aides, who place check marks by errors and circle misspelled words. Checked papers are returned to their owners, who tabulate the marks, usually on a duplicated sheet provided for this purpose:

DIFFICULTIES	COMPOSITION NUMBER				
	1	*2*	*3*	*4*	*5*
capitalization					
commas in a series					
run-on sentences					
sentence fragments					
clear handwriting					

> List the words you have misspelled; indicate with red pencil the correct spelling at the point of difficulty.

Each student aide, carefully prepared in advance, looks for a single type of problem, one he has just thoroughly reviewed in a handbook. These aides become specialists on commas in a series, or run-on sentences, or whatever problem they are prepared to note. In some schools, older pupils receive points toward honors for such assistance with the younger pupils. Through their help the teacher can reach many students in a short time. As the pupil finishes with each of the five or six student aides, he is to study his errors, tabulate them, and then consult with the teacher about steps to take toward improving his control of conventional usage.

---

[48] Some teachers avoid using a red pencil for noting errors. Anything in red always praises effective or appropriate writing.

▶ *Rewrite some compositions*

Parents sometimes ask whether compositions, after being corrected, should be rewritten by the students. Explain that a flexible approach may provide a better solution. Sometimes it is helpful to require that a set of compositions be corrected and returned in perfect form. Other times, however, such a requirement could be unwise. Students often feel the writing they have finished is cold; they have lost interest in that particular composition. Rewriting under such circumstances would be of dubious value. A wise teacher merely notes the kinds of difficulties in that set of compositions and prepares to teach better solutions just before the next writing assignment. If compositions are filed in personal folders, these errors may also be pointed out in conferences, or students may tally their particular problems.

When compositions are to be corrected—not entirely rewritten—the following technique may be used. Errors marked are to be corrected on the back of the preceding page in sentences numbered to correspond with the error marked (see page 371).

▶ *Establish school-wide standards for written work*

Some schools establish basic standards for written English, standards that are applied in all departments. Each fall the principal of one high school distributes to all students a bulletin that includes the following points:

> The ability to use English effectively in both oral and written communication is an essential skill, in school and out.
> Consequently, our teachers in every department require students to adhere to a few simple English standards in oral and written work.
> (A statement of standards, the form to be used in all papers, and words to be spelled correctly may be included.)

▶ *Use checklists—and use them regularly*

Provide students with checklists to be turned in, properly marked, with each composition. By regularly using checklists the students become progressively more alert to the items involved and reflect this alertness in their writing. The example offered here is for senior high or for advanced junior high classes.

> *Check off each item as you examine your paper.*
> ____ 1. Has the opening paragraph definite points to be developed?
> ____ 2. Has each paragraph a topic sentence? (Occasional deviation from this standard is possible and acceptable but such deviation should be the intended exception, not the rule.)
> ____ 3. Is each paragraph completely developed and unified?
> ____ 4. Are there bridge words between the sentences within the paragraph wherever such words would be appropriate?
> ____ 5. Does the closing paragraph embody the subject of the preceding paragraphs? (There must be no new points introduced here.)
> ____ 6. Does the closing paragraph conclude with a strong clinching sentence?
> ____ 7. Is there a run-on sentence or sentence fragment anywhere in the theme?
> ____ 8. Is there a definite, unmistakable antecedent for every pronoun used?

On the river he noticed
a large rock on an
island that was in
the middle. As they
came closer Steve felt
sure their island held
the secret. His greatest
ambition which he had
had from when he
was a boy was to
find some buried
treasure. He learned;
forward eagerly as
we are steered the launch
toward a sandy beach.
As soon as the boat
landed he leaped out
and rushed to the
granite rock. Toward
its base he found a
runic carvings and just

ambiguous
What was in the middle? the rock or the island?

① *awkward*

③ *tense*

① On the river, he noticed a
large rock on the middle of
an island.

② Ever since boyhood his
greatest ambition had been
to find some buried treasure.

③ As soon as the boat
landed he leaped out and
rushed to the granite rock.

Checklists like this may be varied from one part of the semester to another or from one class to another, depending upon the most crucial needs of instruction. Items such as the above may be replaced by items dealing with punctuation, capitalization, letter form, or whatever the teacher wishes to emphasize.

TO ACQUIRE AN EFFECTIVE STYLE

► *Direct attention to the art of writing*

1. Encourage students to become interested in the art of writing. Give brief dictation once every two weeks from some writer on the art of writing. Discuss and explain the ideas, and make the dictation the basis for supplementary study.

2. Have students jot down in their notebooks samples of writing that impress them as particularly forceful and effective. Have a round-up of these ideas and quotations.

3. Offer varied and frequent experiences with words. Use the vocabulary suggestions presented on pages 398–401 in Chapter Nine, "Reading." Encourage pupils to purchase and use a pocket thesaurus.

4. Read many prose passages aloud, having the students listen for the rhythms of the English sentence, musical quality, pleasing balances of sentence structure.

► *Identify style and forceful expression*

1. Select a paragraph from any effective pupil writer and substitute weak verbs; delete from it as many modifiers as possible, leaving a bare core. Present mimeographed copies of the denuded passage for reconstruction by the class. Through class discussion establish the need for the exact or vivid word and the striking metaphor. Point out the pitfalls of wordiness and flowery adjectives. From class suggestions work out the first sentence or two on the chalkboard. Give time for students to comment on both good and poor suggestions. Read several of the finished student paragraphs anonymously and discuss. Then read the original passage, not as perfection but as one solution.

2. For variations of this technique, try adding excess words, shifting the sequence of ideas, and omitting transitions in the prepared copy.

► *Study the impact of audience upon writing*

Pupils are assigned a topic to be written twice: once for reading by a group of fifth-grade pupils in the local school district; once for reading by a group of adults or pupils older than the class members. Before delivering the compositions to the readers, analyze the differences in strategy, diction, and style in some of them.

Good topics: recommendation of a TV program, the promise and problem of science in the age of automation, the latest exploit in space travel, how to gain an acceptance of going to the dentist, good books for children.

► *Use helpful "commandments"*

To help students, whether in junior or senior high school, the teacher proclaims a "Helpful Commandment": no word is to be repeated within an interval of ten sentences. Certain justifiable exceptions such as *the* and *a* and forms of *to be* will not count, of course.[49]

---

[49] The intentional use of repetition for a valid purpose is not, of course, to be ignored. When students are more aware of style, the teacher may present this side of the coin.

With many pupils, other "Helpful Commandments" prove effective: none of the following words is to be used in this composition: nice, pretty, interesting, good; no prepositional phrases are to be used in this composition; *be* and *have* in any form are not to be used.

▶ *Present two versions of the same passage*

Begin a discussion of style by playing two or three versions of the same song or melody. Many students are experts on the musical style of popular singers and orchestras. Then choose some author, notable for his style. Hemingway is particularly effective because he supports classroom work on selecting vigorous verbs to replace adjectives. Read passages from his short story "Big Two-Hearted River" and discuss the style with students. Tell the students that when Hemingway was a young man learning to write, he gave his manuscripts to older and more famous writers who returned them with most of the adjectives crossed out. Put two passages on the board, or read, dictate, or duplicate them. Ask pupils which version they consider better:

AN ESCAPE

I ducked down, pushed between two men, and ran for the river, my head down. I tripped at the edge and went in with a splash. The water was very cold and I stayed under as long as I could. I could feel the current swirl me and I stayed under until I thought I could never come up.[50]

I rapidly pushed two big gruff, burly men away from me and ran between them like a very fast streak to the swiftly flowing and icy water of the river. When I was in, I was soon able to feel the chilling, awful cold, but I remained patiently beneath the murky and icy pitch black cold water. The rapid, running current brought me down the swiftly flowing stream where I was under until my paining, bursting lungs told me to come to the dangerous top surface for some rapid, life-giving fresh air which made me realize how good life was and how good it was to be alive and kicking.

If any students claim they prefer the second version, do not force them to recant. Indicate that the first represents Hemingway's style; probably the author would say the second description distracts the reader's mind from the action and the speed with which the escape took place. Students may be taught *about* an author's style without being told they must prefer it.

▶ *Build the cumulative sentence*

Place on the chalkboard a base sentence like this one.

The boy played his guitar, _____.

Work through with pupils the kinds of sentence modifiers that will add to the base clause. With this and other sentences, demonstrate the importance of keeping the main, or base, clause simple. The base clauses' subjects, objects, and complements, overloaded with modifiers, can be read aloud to demonstrate how awkward such additions may prove to be. Emphasize especially the free noun cluster, the non-

---

[50] In Malcolm Cowley, ed., *The Portable Hemingway* (New York: Viking Press, 1944), p. 309.

restrictive appositive, the verbid clauses and absolutes that Francis Christensen calls "free modifiers." [51]

▶ *Stress sentence variety*

Keep model sentence types on the chalkboard—cumulative sentences, compound sentences, complex sentences containing *who* and *which* clauses, sentences beginning with prepositional or adverbial phrases, sentences containing appositives, sentences with verb first, subject last. Show the possibilities of sentence variety.

TO LEARN CONVENTIONAL LETTER FORMS

▶ *Teach letter form as fashion*

1. On the day when personal letter writing is to be introduced, discuss changing styles in clothing: men wear or do not wear suit vests; boys change their haircuts; derbies and straw hats go out of fashion; clothes patterned on the Beatles characterized the early 1960's; the Nehru look and African dress, the late 1960's; in the 1970's. . . . What will be the new look in the 1980's? Fashions in architecture also change, as do the designs of cars, airplanes, and television sets. What is popular in music in one decade appears old-fashioned to another.

What then is fashionable in letter writing? The teacher reads aloud to his classes some samples of formal style in letters from the eighteenth and nineteenth centuries. Next he asks what is fashionable in letter writing today. In friendly letters how does a writer usually begin? What punctuation does he use for the salutation? What tone and manner characterize most friendly letters? Are there differences in these matters between letters to friends, letters of condolence, thank-you letters, and invitations?

Attention to the formalities of invitations and situations students will not encounter for many years should be avoided. Students may be referred to library books on letter writing and etiquette which will be available if ever they encounter such situations. The main emphasis should be upon the typical kinds of letters students are writing or may soon be writing. Friendly letters, thank-you letters—taught just before Christmas holidays—and expressions of sympathy and condolence are probably their main needs.

2. Save forty or fifty business letters, or ask students to bring in letters. All these are placed in a folder. On the day business letters are introduced pass out one or several letters to each student. Then ask what is the present style in business letters. What kind of headings do most of these use? Is there an inside address? How many students find a comma after the salutation? How many find nothing at all? How many find a colon? How many find a semi-colon? How many find something else? When it is established that at least 90 per cent of the business letters use a colon after the salutation, this point requires no further teaching. Are paragraphs indented or not? How many find a comma after the complimentary close? The advantage of this method is that students devise their own rules from the actual practices of business firms. This impresses pupils and proves a painless way to teach business letter form. Instead of being told what is convention, pupils tell the teacher what they find to be acceptable practice.

3. Discuss whether or not the new tape casettes, with cartridges so easy to mail,

[51] Francis Christensen, "The Problem of Defining a Mature Style." *English Journal,* Vol. 57, No. 4 (April 1968), pp. 572–79.

will soon replace most personal and business letter writing. Or will it become fashionable to use long distance telephoning?

Composition should encompass the expression of both reason and imagination. There should be no sharp distinction between the powers of imagination and powers of intelligence or understanding. Santayana concludes that reason is itself a method of imaginative thought and that the figments of the imagination are created by the same faculty that enables man to grasp the systematic relation of things in time and space, and to recognize their dependence upon one another. But whether imaginative or systematic, thought is necessary for reputable written expression. Of this final principle we may truly say, "There is no way around, only through."

SELECTED READINGS

BOOKS

BRADDOCK, RICHARD, LLOYD-JONES, RICHARD, and SCHOER, LOWELL. *Research in Written Composition.* Champaign, Ill.: NCTE, 1963. According to the authors, "The conclusion can be stated in strong and unqualified terms: the teaching of formal grammar has a negligible or, because it usually displaces some instruction and practice in actual composition, even a harmful effect on the improvement of writing." The authors review past research and present five studies, one of which (British) again finds the study of grammar to have a negligible or even a relatively harmful effect on the correctness of pupils' writing.

BROWN, ROLLO WALTER. *How the French Boy Learns to Write.* Champaign, Ill.: NCTE, 1965. Although Brown realizes Americans must work out their own problems and should not blindly adopt methods used in France, he does believe French boys write with sharper accuracy of thought and more intelligent freedom than American boys of the same age. Certainly the importance of full oral discussion in advance of writing comes through clearly. A reprinting of an important classic originally published in 1915.

COMMISSION ON ENGLISH. *Freedom and Discipline in English.* New York: College Entrance Examination Board, 1965. Teachers need to make clear that correctness, important as it is in one sense, does not touch the heart of the matter. The serious faults are obscurity, ambiguity, and incompleteness. The section on composition concerns the preparation of pupils continuing on to college, but much of its help pertains to all instruction in writing.

CHRISTENSEN, FRANCIS. *Notes Toward a New Rhetoric.* New York: Harper & Row, 1967. This paperback explains more completely the ideas on pages 321–22 of this textbook.

GORRELL, ROBERT (ed.). *Rhetoric: Some Theories for Application.* Champaign, Ill.: NCTE, 1967. This monograph contains a series of papers treating various aspects of rhetoric that have pertinence in the schools.

GUTH, HANS P. *English Today and Tomorrow.* Englewood Cliffs, N.J.: Prentice-Hall, 1964. The chapter on rhetoric makes clear that language is a vehicle for the expression not merely of ideas but of sensations, feelings, and attitudes. Effective patterns of organization are not applied from the outside but are inherent in the material.

HOLBROOK, DAVID. *Children's Writing, A Sampler for Student Teachers.* London: Cambridge Univ. Press, 1967. A lively collection of written work by elementary and secondary pupils in British schools with commentary by a British specialist on the creative process.

————. *English for the Rejected.* London: Cambridge Univ. Press, 1964. This account of teaching in the "low stream" of the British schools is a searching consideration of slow learners, their nature and needs, their written responses to surroundings.

MOFFETT, JAMES. *Teaching the Universe of Discourse.* Boston: Houghton-Mifflin, 1968. Moffett presents a challenging and specific theory of discourse, applying it to classroom instruction.

KITZHABER, ALBERT R. *Themes, Theories, and Therapy.* New York: McGraw-Hill, 1963. Although this book discusses (often caustically) the teaching of writing in college, it is applicable to secondary-school instruction. Chapter 3, which deals with "panaceas," includes: "It has long been known that the study of school grammar has little or no perceptible effect on the student's ability to write good prose. It may or may not help him to write more correctly, but correctness is only the absence of error, a negative virtue, important but by no means synonymous with quality in writing."

ARTICLES AND PAMPHLETS

CHRISTENSEN, FRANCIS. "Notes Toward a New Rhetoric." *College English.* Vol. 25, No. 1 (October 1963), pp. 7–18; and "A Generative Rhetoric of the Paragraph." *College Composition and Communication.* Vol. 16, No. 3 (October 1965), pp. 144–56. These two articles, in addition to those already suggested in the present chapter of this book, develop the major ideas of a new rhetoric, which suggest that in the twentieth century writers are shifting from the complex to the cumulative sentence and away from the eighteenth-century acceptance of authority and precise control of form.

JEWETT, ARNO and BISH, CLARENCE E. *Improving English Composition.* Washington, D.C.: National Education Association, 1965. Practical and basic suggestions derived from a series of pilot experimental centers.

JOHNSON, ERIC W. "Stimulating and Improving Writing in the Junior High School." *English Journal.* Vol. 47, No. 2 (February 1958). The highly specific suggestions here are useful in senior high as well as in junior high school. Johnson uses one of his five English periods each week as an independent reading and conference period when students come prepared to read silently or to confer with him about their writing.

MILES, JOSEPHINE. "Essay as Reason." *Educational Leadership.* Vol. 19, No. 5 (February 1962). The first help the teacher can give the student is to make him see whether the predication he has chosen to apply to the subject is really supportable by what he knows or can discover. Secondly, the teacher sees whether the student has arranged the elements of support in the order and connection best for his purposes.

ORWELL, GEORGE. "Politics and the English Language." *A Collection of Essays.* Garden City, N.Y.: Doubleday Anchor Books, 1953. Orwell criticizes vagueness and incompetence in writing; sloppy writing that avoids clarity of meaning by "gumming together long strips of words" consisting of stale images, prefabricated phrases, and needless repetitions. He concludes with six elementary rules for writing.

ROSENSON, JULIUS. "An Oral Approach to Sentence Sense." *English Journal.* Vol. 42, No. 7 (October 1958). Students learn to recognize complete sentences through oral practice with juncture patterns.

SLEDD, JAMES. "On Not Teaching English Usage." *English Journal.* Vol. 54, No. 8 (November 1965). Sledd believes teachers' besetting sins are aloofness from the students' real concerns and unreasoned insistence on their own interests and their own standards. Teachers do more harm than good by insisting that pupils write only about literature. One paper a student writes because he wants to write it is worth a dozen he writes to satisfy a teacher.

NINE

READING

PERSPECTIVE

"You are barking at print," says the British teacher when school children fail
to understand the words they call out, often with glib perfection. As teachers
in all nations realize, reading is infinitely more than sounding out words.
Reading with comprehension is indeed a very elaborate procedure, involving
a balance of many elements in a passage and their organization in the proper
relation to each other.

As in all the arts of language, reading depends on an intricate network
of perception and learning. Nevertheless, human beings persist in an understandable but hopeless yearning to find simple solutions for complex language problems. Adults no longer pluck daisy petals to determine fortunes
in love, but they often transfer their petal-plucking simplification to new
problems. No machine, no book of instruction, no simple three- or five-step
technique will ever provide the infallible recipe for teaching reading. Yet
sometimes people continue to seek an easy formula; they rest their hopes on a
reform of phonics in the second grade, a new machine for the junior high
school, or the Schartz-Metterklume method for the low Z group in grade 10.
We are all very human; long after childhood we still pluck at petals.

No panaceas are offered in this book. Some pupils find all language situations difficult; neither threats of hell nor hopes of paradise will enable them
to read beyond the limits of their capacity. Money, materials, and classes small
enough for individual assistance could improve many inadequate situations,
but our classrooms are not located in Utopia. The methods presented here
will, therefore, avoid formulas and golden visions from the New Jerusalem.
However, when the quest for simple answers is abandoned, many reading
problems do yield to instruction.

[1] Edward L. Thorndike, "Reading as Reasoning," *Journal of Educational Psychology*, Vol.
8, No. 6 (June 1917), p. 329.

Improving Comprehension

In this chapter we are mainly concerned with ways to help pupils make literal meaning from straightforward prose passages. This level of comprehension precedes any independent voyages to the realms of gold. Poor readers may take some stimulating literary excursions with a teacher-pilot at the helm. They may even venture a few short trial runs by themselves, but any sustained solo voyages leading to a lasting association with literature must wait apprenticeship in reading comprehension. It is this apprenticeship with which we are concerned here.

DEMAND FOR MEANING   Throughout time and in all places, people have read either for enlightenment or enjoyment—often for both at the same time. Whatever the purpose, the skills necessary for comprehension are basic. To understand, to grasp with the mind—this is the ultimate goal of all reading improvement. The precise meanings of words, the relations among words in sentences, and the hierarchies of main ideas in a total structure of prose or poetry must all be balanced. Yet none of these skills flourish unless the learner's volition is operating. Without a demand for meaning on the part of the learner, a teacher's efforts are wasted and the pupil's skill is not increased. How the will to understand drives people to read better than they usually do has been described by Mortimer J. Adler:

> When they are in love and are reading a love letter, they read for all they are worth. They read every word three ways; they read between the lines and in the margins; they read the whole in terms of the parts, and each part in terms of the whole; they grow sensitive to context and ambiguity, to insinuation and implication; they perceive the color of words, the odor of phrases, and the weight of sentences. They may even take the punctuation into account. Then, if never before or after, they read.[2]

Fortunately or unfortunately, the materials for improving reading in the schools cannot be a series of love letters, but the principle is clear. When strong purpose with its attendant desire to understand is part of an instructional situation, learning almost certainly occurs; when indifference or perfunctory efforts predominate, learning is meager. When they sense a purpose in their reading and want very much to accomplish that purpose, learners select more readily the meanings that hold the key to understanding. To increase reading skill, therefore, teachers plan many reading experiences appealing to the pupil's interests and needs.[3] Such reading is intended to bring about an efficient fusion of reading skills, a fusion occurring most dramatically when

[2] Mortimer J. Adler, *How to Read a Book* (New York: Simon & Schuster, 1940), p. 14.
[3] A teacher need not underestimate the capacities of youth; students can be stretched toward the thoughts and experiences of maturity. However, ignoring the needs and interests of adolescents can be as unwise as determining subject matter solely on the basis of their present interests. See Chapter Ten, "Literature: Basic Approaches."

a reader's demand for meaning is so intense he can scarcely wait to read the next paragraph or turn the next page. Thus, in reading, the comprehension problem centers on students' determination to receive the writer's communication. Everything teachers can do to create a demand for meaning will increase learning efficiency.

TWO PILLARS OF COMPREHENSION   Beyond the critical factor of motivation, comprehending communication—written or spoken—requires two basic skills. Students themselves may be led to see that understanding the words and perceiving their patterns of relationship are the two main pillars upon which comprehension rests. These fundamentals, discussed at length in the preceding chapter on listening, will not be elaborated here. Reading and listening, both instruments of intake, necessarily have elements in common. (The reader will note, too, that many of the learning experiences suggested in these two complementary chapters are interchangeable; only slight adaption in material or method is needed to make them suitable for teaching either listening or reading.) The integrated program stressed throughout this textbook indicates that reading and listening should be so taught that students will see their parallelism and thus be helped in transferring to one area skills gained in the other. Whether in listening or reading, understanding words and their relationships are the pillars of comprehension. Sometimes the pillars are subdivided.

The first—perception of words—may be thought of as cracking the code; the reader must recognize and be able to sound out the words before he can derive any meaning from them. However, to stop there is only to bark at print. The second pillar requires higher levels of thinking—comprehension of ideas, reaction to ideas, integration of ideas. Both pillars are necessary for reading with comprehension.[4]

REMEDIAL AND DEVELOPMENTAL READING   Facts are stubborn, and the facts of individual differences in reading need to be faced. Inasmuch as grade placement is on the basis of pupils' chronological age, the spread of reading ability in the secondary school will be very great—and superior instruction in the elementary school will only increase the spread. It is unlikely that schools will ever be organized on the basis of reading level; if they were, the startling spread of chronological age would cause educational problems even more serious than those resulting from age grouping. To accept the facts of human linguistic variability, seeking to bring each individual up to his maximum performance, is the only sensible solution. Teaching each individual to read in accordance with his maximum capacity is called *developmental reading*. Teachers distinguish it from *remedial reading*, a term reserved for the help given pupils whose skill is clearly below the level their mental ability indicates

[4] William S. Gray, *On Their Own in Reading* (Chicago: Scott, Foresman, 1960), pp. 10–12. See also Helen M. Robinson's later development of Gray's four aspects, in *Reading: Seventy-five Years of Progress* (Chicago: Univ. of Chicago Press, 1966).

they should be able to reach. This is a highly important distinction; when it is observed, schools do not place students of low native ability in remedial classes and then expect miracles. Remedial reading is for pupils whose handicaps can be remedied. Developmental reading is for all other pupils—brilliant, average, or dull—who need help with the skills required for reading at their individual stage of development.

LITERATURE AN ADDED DIMENSION   The more subtle challenges of literature lie beyond the fundamental skills of comprehending simple prose structures. Like all the fine arts, literature uses special ways to evoke experience in others. By particular uses and arrangements of words, it seeks to express realms of experience inaccessible to ordinary language. Such uses of language account for much of the distress unskilled readers experience when they try to comprehend literature as if it were a series of matter-of-fact statements. Without training and imagination they cannot understand the special language of literature nor enter the domain it charts. The special skills required in reading literature are discussed elsewhere in this book.[5] Here we wish only to make the point that basic comprehension rests upon two pillars—understanding words and perceiving correct relationships; that on such basic comprehension are built the deeper insights and keener perceptions that literature demands.

Problems Unique to Reading

As in listening, comprehension in reading depends upon knowing the literal meanings of words in various contexts. Like the listener, the reader must also be able to distinguish between the main idea and supporting ideas and to perceive the relation of each part to the others and of each to the whole. Beyond lie even more complex kinds of thinking—grasping the significance of what is heard or read and judging its value, for example. However, five problems specifically related to reading rather than to listening can be identified.

ADAPTING RATE TO PURPOSE AND CONTENT   Speed, the first of these problems, is a variable the reader can control, whereas the listener cannot. To improve reading speed, the best approach proves to be indirect, through improving comprehension. Except for a few able students who have fallen into habits of undue slowness, emphasis upon speed itself should usually be avoided.

Both natural and artificial methods have been used to improve rate and comprehension of reading, and a considerable amount of controversy continues to surround their use. Natural methods depend upon helping pupils through materials that reflect their interests and through heightened awareness of simple ways to increase speed; in the process the learner competes

---

[5] See Chapter Ten, Chapter Eleven, and the units "Macbeth" and "The Consequences of Character."

with himself. Mechanical methods depend upon external means. They include tachistoscopes, films, accelerators, the Controlled Reader, the Language Master, and other devices.[6] Mechanical aids frequently do prove to be temporary levers for motivating improvement; this is particularly true for boys with a deep interest in mechanisms. But two reservations about machines occur to many teachers: their expense scarcely seems justified when more books are needed in a school; and even more serious, they tend to oversimplify, in the pupils' minds, the real task of reading. Hope that some external force such as a machine will solve the internal need for volition is futile. Nothing will ever replace the will to understand. A simple card, held by the reader, covering each line as he completes it, is often better than any machine.

Competent readers adapt their speed and depth of attention to the nature of the material and their purpose in reading, whereas poor readers take in everything at the same rate and with the same exactitude or lack of it.[7] Teachers should, therefore, guide students to vary concentration and speed in relation to definite purposes and the nature of the content.

RECOGNIZING PRINTED WORDS   Many of the weakest readers compensate for poor word recognition by avoiding reading and by increasing their dependence upon speech. Usually they need help in all the elementary skills of word recognition: phonics, word structure, and contextual cues. They usually need help both in recognizing clusters of words that meaningfully go together in oral intonation and in using punctuation clues. Focusing and drill are needed for these elementary skills, but the drill cannot be long separated from concern with meaning in selections that compel the pupil's interest, or the gains will quickly erode. As in special attention to other language skills, exercises in reading must as soon as possible be fitted back into meaningful reading that engages the mind and the will.

LINKING READING TO REALITY   Some pupils tend to read as if words had no connection with reality, as if symbols were names without meanings. In the secondary school, this verbalism often increases with the pressures to read more and to read faster. Methods to counteract verbalism depend very much upon the teacher and his perspective. A judicious use of textbooks, rather than a determination to devour them, often helps. Showing pupils how to make applications and grasp implications is another way to improve the

---

[6] The Controlled Reader is a product of Educational Developmental Laboratories, Huntington, N.Y. This machine presents reading materials of all levels of difficulty and regulates the speed with which the materials appear before the individual reader. The Language Master is made by Bell and Howell Company, Chicago. Each printed card contains a strip of magnetic recording tape on which the printed words are recorded. When these strips are passed over the sound track, the audio presentation reinforces the visual form of the words. The teacher can type and record his own cards or he can purchase cards on which the words and recording are already prepared.

[7] Paul Blommers and E. F. Lindquist, "Rate of Comprehension of Reading: Its Measurement and Its Relation to Comprehension," *Journal of Educational Psychology*, Vol. 35, No. 8 (November 1944).

VIRGIL PARTCH

Courtesy True, The Man's Magazine

comprehension level of most readers. Beyond all specific methods, however, lies the crucial matter of classroom climate; when a pupil feels absolutely free to say, "I'm sorry, but I just don't understand this," verbalism has little hope of surviving. That pupil and his classmates are developing reading consciences.

IMPROVING ORAL READING   Silent reading has necessarily received so much attention that some teachers have begun to ask, "Should we do anything about oral reading? Does it slow down a pupil's rate of reading?" The answers are not difficult. Of course teachers should do something about oral reading. The emphasis on silent comprehension, crucial though it is to much learning, was never intended to eliminate oral reading. Learning to read aloud competently can contribute substantially to comprehension in silent reading, for through oral reading the learner can develop an "inner ear." He can become aware of the emphasis of italics, the tone of printed conversations, nuances of style, modifications of a main idea, and interpolation of subsidiary related elements.[8]

LOCATING INFORMATION IN BOOKS AND LIBRARIES   The skills of using books and libraries are often included in reading instruction. Any assumption that most students will naturally absorb this kind of knowledge is unwarranted. Often the librarian will provide the actual lessons. The teacher will cooperate, planning the periods in the library and reinforcing the lessons with filmstrips, movies, and continued practice.[9] For most pupils, the important knowledge to be gained is how titles are arranged in the card catalog; how books are

[8] For an extensive discussion of oral reading, see "Literature: Drama and Poetry," pages 492–98, 509–14.
[9] For a practical guide to library lessons, see Jessie Boyd, Leo B. Baisden, Carolyn Mott, and Gertrude Memmler, *Books, Libraries, and You*, 3rd ed. (New York: Scribner's, 1965).

arranged on the shelves; and how dictionaries, encyclopedias, and any reference books in the library may be found and used.

Whenever a textbook is introduced in a classroom, the teacher has an opportunity to show how skilled readers take advantage of its organization. From time to time, the student needs to be reminded of the function and usefulness of the title page, foreword, table of contents, chapter headings, glossary, and index. The teacher should also point out the help to be gained from format—significance of italics, different sizes of type to indicate parallelism and subordination, use of boldface, and so on.

Because each is based on comprehending and interpreting language, reading and listening have much in common. Because the mediums that transmit the messages differ, certain ways of teaching these two facets of communication differ.

THE TEACHING PROBLEM

No effective program in reading can begin without a knowledge of student needs in reading. Nor can any program produce results if hasty or impromptu action mars the plans. At least a year in advance, survey testing and diagnosis need to be started, preferably by administrative action of the school rather than by one teacher working alone. Such an appraisal of the situation yields certain important clarifications.

Four kinds of readers will be identified: average readers of average ability, reading approximately at their grade level; accelerated readers, usually of average or better ability, reading above grade level; retarded readers of average or better ability, reading below grade level; poor readers of less than average ability, doing the best they can.

The tests and diagnoses show which students may be handled in the regular classes and which ones should be given special instruction, if at all possible. Details about such tests and diagnoses will be described more fully later in this chapter.

This classification of readers points in turn to a benefit in counseling pupils and their parents. Since reading cannot be viewed in isolation but must be related to native ability, intelligence must be considered in the reading program. Because true native ability is very difficult to determine, several tests are better than one, and caution in their interpretation is necessary, particularly with pupils from the least favored socio-economic backgrounds. However, if a low intelligence quotient is found in combination with poor reading ability, that knowledge helps the school to guide pupil and parents.[10] A child

---

[10] Reading comprehension and reading rate have been shown to be positively correlated both with verbal and nonverbal intelligence in the research of Dean S. Hage and James B. Stroud, who tested 800 ninth-grade students. "Reading Proficiency and Intelligence Scores, Verbal and Non-verbal," *Journal of Educational Research*, Vol. 52, No. 7 (March 1959).

who does not have this one kind of ability—verbal ability—undoubtedly does have other kinds; without verbal ability, however, he is unlikely to find high school easy or college possible, and his plans for the future should take such factors into account. This point of view accepts the broader definition of intelligence that Allison Davis proposes in *Social Class Influences on Learning*,[11] but does not minimize the importance of language power in secondary and higher education.

Finally, such testing and diagnosis will reveal that pupils at any single level of the secondary-school range from very low to exceptionally high reading ability. Human variation being what it is, a grade spread of six or seven years—sometimes even more—should surprise only the naive. Elementary-school instruction cannot prevail over native ability nor completely nullify home background. Furthermore, as children become older, individual differences become even greater, as a result of the increase in range of mental age and individuals' interaction with their unique environments. With these kinds of knowledge about students' needs in reading, a program to meet each local situation is entirely possible.

ORGANIZING INSTRUCTION

Reading programs vary according to the size of the school and the curriculum offered. No single plan of organization can be offered as a perfect universal model, but the most desirable is one in which the entire school system provides instruction in reading skills for all pupils from kindergarten to grade 12. In many situations, however, the English teacher may be thrown upon his own resources. Organizing classroom instruction to improve reading will center, for him, around two problems: maintaining a flexible learning situation and diagnosing students' needs.

Maintaining a Flexible Learning Situation

Whether or not an all-school program exists, the English teacher will find that a departure from an exclusively formal organization is one of the more effective steps toward improving reading in his own classroom. By reducing the amount of single-text recitation and increasing the amount of time for guided study and individual conferences, a teacher can often turn a tide of mounting reading difficulties. He can, within limits of time and library facilities, help not only poor readers but average and capable ones as well. With a variety of reading materials ranging from easy to difficult, he can improve

---

[11] Allison Davis, *Social Class Influences on Learning* (Cambridge, Mass.: Harvard Univ. Press, 1955). If a student's cumulative record shows a decreasing IQ, he may come from a culturally deprived home and be able to learn to read much better than present IQ indicates.

the reading of all pupils, seeking to help each individual reach his maximum reading capacity.

Such an increase in flexibility of method and materials does not, of course, imply complete rejection of similar content for all pupils. What is needed is a modification, not a revolution, in classroom strategy. A better balance among the ways of instruction frees the teacher to work with pupils who most need help in reading—some of them stumbling, others so gifted they lose interest under confining routines.

USING MULTIPLE MATERIALS   Under such circumstances the teacher may use differentiated materials to advantage. For instance, one eighth-grade class was formed into groups to read about youngsters whose experiences led them to mature responsibilities: *Little Britches* for average readers, *Captains Courageous* for superior readers, *Smuggler's Island* for poor readers, *National Velvet* and *Mountain Laurel* for girls who disliked boys' books. Five pupils not identified with any group read individually books like *Boy on Horseback,* books whose content also related to the general theme of responsibility. Seniors, having completed *Lilies of the Field,* extended their reading to thirty-five different novels, dramas, and biographies, all bearing on the same theme of human dignity and ranging from easy to difficult. Through sharing this extended reading, the students applied the general concepts of responsibility and dignity to many particular incidents, and in turn new generalizations were related back to each individual's reading.

USING THE UNIT METHOD   The unit method offers one effective solution to many problems of pupil variation. It need not be used exclusively throughout an entire school year, but its advantages as a way of integrating content and providing for individual differences recommend it as a frequent approach. In the junior high, units may be topical and quite broad: "Boys and Girls of Other Lands," "Wagons Westward," "Myths and Legends." In the senior high, the units should usually be more sharply centered: "The Meaning of Courage," "The Dimensions of Success," "Man Against Society." When instruction is organized topically or thematically, the teacher is able to guide slower students to reading less demanding than the books used by more able pupils, but still related to the over-all design. For examples of this individualization of reading through unit instruction, see the unit "The Consequences of Character," in this book.

GROUPING ACCORDING TO ABILITY   Another plan allowing for individual differences groups students according to reading ability. Ability grouping is one of the unsettled issues of American education. If English classes number twenty-five pupils or less, a teacher can adapt the curriculum to any reasonable spread of reading ability. However, as soon as classes increase beyond twenty-five, many teachers prefer ability grouping, not because of any illusion that students will be markedly similar, but rather because time-consuming extreme cases of reading ability and disability need not be handled in the same class. Any reduction in the spread of reading ability helps somewhat in planning for all pupils.

Within a single class, grouping by reading ability is entirely possible. Reading-ability grouping should be only one method of grouping, and frequent changes in group membership provide variation within that method. Students with meager language facility need to realize the teacher is as sincerely gratified over their limited progress as he is over more rapid progress in other groups.

DIFFERENTIATING ASSIGNMENTS   Not always does a teacher have time to design lessons and units providing for such a variety of materials—nor should all instruction be differentiated to such a degree. It is often possible to provide for a range of reading abilities within the frame of a common assignment. Just as the works of Shakespeare and Mark Twain elicit various levels of understanding, so also can many reading assignments. Students with reflective powers and superior reading ability may be challenged with more difficult problems while poor readers may at the same time be set to less complicated questions. In one class, the teacher assigned a story about a boy and his prize steer. At the close of the story, the book included seven questions for study. Before assigning the story for silent reading in the classroom, the teacher told his students they would read better if they would concentrate on some one problem in the story. Consequently, there were to be three groups in the class; each group would be alert to a single problem. On the board the teacher wrote:

> *Q group*   arrangements of events in the story. Keep track of the order in which the events happen; answer questions 1, 4, and 7.
> *R group*   understanding characters. Be able to explain why the father and sister think and act as they do; answer questions 3, 6, and 7.
> *S group*   main character. How does the author make Johnny seem a real person? Answer questions 2, 5, and 7.

As the pupils began their silent reading, the teacher moved quickly down the aisles writing *Q, R,* or *S* lightly in pencil on the margins of their books. In general, he assigned to the *Q* group pupils whose reading abilities were poor; the best readers received *R* assignments and the average, *S* classifications. After the reading period, the answers were discussed orally, each group contributing to the questions suited to its powers and all grappling with the important seventh question, which concerned a relationship between the story and life beyond the story.

USING STUDENT HELPERS   Occasionally, insightful and able readers may help other pupils in the class. The teacher makes the same classroom reading assignment for everyone, but as soon as each of the selected helpers completes the assignment, he receives from the teacher a set of duplicated study questions and sets up shop in a designated corner of the room. As other students complete the assignment, the teacher sends them to join one of these skilled readers, trying to match personalities for good working solidarity. Poor readers are placed with the best possible student teachers. Each group is to probe the selection with the help of the study questions and the group leader. Fifteen minutes before the close of the period the teacher asks the entire class to discuss or write on several questions selected from the study guides. If this method is not overused, there is no danger of exploiting superior readers and they, as well as those they help, profit from the experience.

USING PROGRAMED LEARNING   Programed lessons in reading can be valuable or worthless depending upon the quality of insight behind their creation. Characteristically, the programs are presented in book form through a series of frames, steps by which the learner is led to focus his attention. At his own rate, the individual pupil proceeds step by step in the learning task and cannot go on to more difficult material until he has mastered all the sequential steps for comprehension or application. At each step in the learning process he is given immediate knowledge of results so he will not continue in confusion.

In programed learning, both the answer and the process leading to it are deemed important. Because the sequences of the learning experience are determined by the steps, teachers need to examine programs carefully to be certain an increasingly integrated organization of responses and concepts is presented. Such superior programing is rare, but the possibility of creative new materials impels us to watch all developing programs.

Many schools have used programed reading materials like the *Sullivan Remedial Reading Program* [12] and *Lessons for Self-Instruction in Basic Skills.*[13] It is generally agreed that such programs succeed if teachers do not expect them to accomplish all the instruction in reading. For the pupils the monotony of filling in frames must be offset and diminished by spacing the days spent on the program, by including listening to tapes while following the printed page, by reading aloud into tape recorders and replaying the tape while watching the print, by games, by individualized reading, and by dramatics.[14]

Not all programs depend upon frames in books. The attempt to develop machines responsive to the learner's needs continues to challenge educational engineering. The Talking Typewriter, a device now being used in some schools, locks in such a manner that the learner can type only those words

[12] M. W. Sullivan, *Remedial Reading Program*, Series 1 through 5, Behavioral Research Laboratories, Box 577, Palo Alto, California. This program includes high-interest, low-vocabulary readers coordinated with the series, tapes, and placement examinations.
[13] California Test Bureau, Del Monte Research Park, Monterey, California.
[14] For instance, use simple game boards similar to that used in Monopoly. Each square contains a word; to claim their advances, pupils must say each word in an appropriate sentence; occasional traps require them to repeat all words they have covered to that point or else return to the starting line.

that correctly answer questions on the screen before him.[15] A taped program includes a voice that gives directions to the learner and records his spoken answers. The Talking Typewriter, expensive and housed in an insulated booth, is not yet suited to large-scale instruction but is symbolic of the American desire to devise and use machines. It represents the first of many machines that undoubtedly will become flexible and effective in the next decade.

These various patterns of flexibility can accommodate activities such as those presented in the Suggested Learning Experiences that follow. A teacher may select for emphasis several reading skills most needed by the least able readers. In the course of assignments, unit instruction, or group work, the teacher may stress any one of these skills, presenting them only to those who need them and relating them to the larger concerns of reading, whether within school or without. The process is always one of weaving back and forth between the larger whole—the activity, unit, or lesson—and the specific skill on which the pupils' attention is to be temporarily focused. A teacher should not be fearful of stopping the larger activity to improve the skill, a process much like stopping orchestra practice long enough to concentrate on some special aspect, such as a key change.

In selecting skills for emphasis, the teacher is fortunate if his school has studied the reading problem and has developed a guide to the skills to be emphasized throughout each of the six years of secondary education. When such a guide is not available, he must select those skills that appear to have the highest priority for his class.

Diagnosing Students' Needs

In order to organize instruction competently, the teacher needs to know the reading difficulties existing in his classes. In some classes, pupil reading ability may vary widely, but other classes may present completely different pictures: three very slow readers—third-grade level, at best—in the midst of thirty-two average and good readers in a small school with no other class in which to place them; five gifted and nine poor readers in a class supposedly average and grouped homogeneously; thirty-nine pupils of fairly uniform reading ability. How is the teacher to know what the true situation is? Before sailing off in what may be a wrong direction, he must chart the course.

In schools where standardized reading or achievement testing programs exist, cumulative folders provide reasonably valuable data. If there are no records or if they tell nothing about reading, the teacher will need to plan some strategy for survey and appraisal. Therefore three aspects of diagnosis will be considered here: survey testing; retesting to determine even more

[15] The Talking Typewriter, Responsive Environment Corporation, 200 Sylvan Avenue, Englewood Cliffs, New Jersey 07632.

precisely the level of reading for some individuals; and testing to locate particular disabilities.

SURVEY TESTING If the school budget permits, reading achievement tests should be purchased. In selecting these, a teacher new to such testing will wish to consult someone with experience—someone in his school, in the county schools office, or in the state department of education. Local situations vary in this respect; larger schools have guidance personnel whose training includes test selection, whereas smaller schools must depend upon the teacher's knowledge or his contacts with someone whose advice is sound. If there is time to examine a number of survey reading tests, making the final choice will be a valuable learning experience for the teacher.[16]

Standardized reading tests tell nothing about a pupil's interest in reading or his disposition to read outside the classroom, nor do they measure all the critical and appreciational skills needed for reading literature. But when administered carefully and interpreted sensibly, these objective measuring instruments do improve upon rough estimates, and their norms provide comparisons with larger numbers of pupils throughout the nation. However, it is well to remember that national norms do not provide all the answers one wishes. Pupils in a slum area cannot expect to equal the performance of those in favored socio-economic circumstances; a wealthy suburb may be above the national mean without occupying the position its pupils should and could reach.[17] Because national norms are not the best guides, many school systems keep their own local norms on these standardized tests. Recorded over a period of several years, such norms enable a teacher to know how his pupils perform in relation to the local junior or senior high school population.

The teacher may prefer—or lacking funds, find it necessary—to gauge the reading situation through informal testing. Drawing materials from reading planned for his English course, he constructs questions over the paragraphs selected for this purpose. Even though they provide no comparison with norms established for large groups of pupils, informal tests of this kind are useful.

Whether survey testing is standardized or home made, the secondary-school teacher will usually find pupils ranging from very low to exceptionally high reading ability. Numerous surveys of reading in all parts of the country repeat the same spread of achievement and lead to the same conclusion: pupils need to improve their skills of reading at their own level of development and at their own rate. The evidence also shows that students whose survey tests place them at the same grade level still vary widely in the nature of their reading difficulties. Although the teacher may not have time to retest and

---

[16] See page 424 for further help in locating standardized reading tests.
[17] A new trend in test norms: standardized norms for city pupils, another set of norms for suburban children, as in the *Gates-MacGinitie Reading Tests.* New York: Teachers College Press, Columbia Univ., 1969.

diagnose more than a few students in each class, the survey testing will help him choose those in need of further study.

RETESTING INDIVIDUALS   In a further analysis of the reasons a student reads poorly, the student's cooperation should be elicited. He should know what is being attempted, but it is enough that he realize the teacher is trying to establish the level of difficulty he can handle best. For many a student, it is discouraging to be told he is reading at the fourth-grade level, which connotes small children. He is not yet secure enough to handle such information, nor does he know, as the teacher does, that the average reading level of adults falls somewhere between seventh- and ninth-grade levels and that the unfortunate classification of reading abilities by school year grades has occasioned a vast amount of confusion. Fortunately, many of the newer materials are not labeled as to grade level. To improve the pupil's attitude and to avoid unnecessary threats to his self-respect, the teacher should explain the importance of diagnosis. "If you went to a doctor for a health examination, you would not try to mislead him by holding ice in your mouth just before he took your temperature. Here in class I will often try to locate sore spots in your educational anatomy. You will want to help me find them so I can prescribe the right remedies for you."

Once again, having to devise one's own means of individual retesting need be no occasion for regret. The familiarity gained from developing such materials has distinct advantages; insights, hunches, and certainties occur that might be bypassed by more regulated procedures. For instance, the teacher may plan an assignment to occupy most members of the class while he works in one part of the room with readers who have measured low in the survey testing program. For them he selects materials with the grade level of reading difficulty already established. The teacher locates the level at which the pupil reads comfortably with genuine comprehension. To do this it is best to use several selections, including some at grade levels above and below the level located.

Where materials designed specifically for testing are not available, the pupils' level of ability can be determined through the use of short selections in basic and supplementary readers from the elementary schools. Teachers, having no access to elementary readers or fearing adverse reactions from pupils who might surmise the source of the material, use short books for which the reading level is known. *The Sea Hunt* and *Treasure Under the Sea*, for instance, are books in the Deep-Sea Adventure Series with a second-grade level of difficulty. Other titles in the same or similar series may be selected for third-, fourth-, and higher grade levels.

Whatever materials are used, the teacher asks the pupil to read until his frustration or loss of comprehension is apparent. If the pupil is reading aloud, the teacher asks questions at the close of each selection to determine whether the pupil is comprehending or merely "barking at print." If he is reading silently, the questioning may, of course, be either oral or written. The number

SHORT DIAGNOSTIC GUIDE

Name _____ Date _____

	No problem	*Problem*	*Comment*

Word attack and analysis
  Context clues
  Vowels and vowel combinations
  Consonants
  Blending
  Guessing
  Use of syllables
  Letter names and sounds
  Prefixes, suffixes, roots
  Sight vocabulary

Reading habits
  Reverses words; repeats, substitutes,
    or omits words; becomes confused
  Reverses letters, confuses, substitutes,
    or omits letters
  Does not think of whole sentence
    meaning (voice betrays "word calling")
  Cannot handle three-syllable words
  Does not isolate and recognize units of
    thought; does not use punctuation
  Vocalizes, moves lips, during silent
    reading
  Reads too fast for comprehension
  Very slow rate

Eye problems
  Finger pointing or head movements
  Loses place
  Is there a recent test showing normal
    vision?

Voice problems
  Speech defects
  Enunciation
  Voice control

Hearing
  If audiometer testing is not available,
    try speaking to pupil in a low voice.

Indication of emotional difficulties
  or poor social adjustment

Intelligence Quotients [18]

---

[18] Several are better than one. Scores on the *Wechsler Intelligence Scale for Children* (WISC) and the Stanford-Binet Scale, Form L-M, are particularly helpful.

of selections used, the number of occasions the student is tested, and the extent of questioning depend upon the teacher's time and the number of pupils he feels he can help.

All such diagnoses should be tentative. Obviously, the teacher would like to bring to bear upon the problems as much information as possible. However, under the pressure of time, this ideal can be only approximated; what we have described is practicable rather than complete.

LOCATING PARTICULAR DISABILITIES Locating the specific reading difficulties underlying poor reading ability involves additional diagnosis. Once again, the English teacher must frequently proceed on his own initiative, without expert help or elaborate apparatus. If such is the situation, he will be wise to select only a few pupils, presumably those in greatest need of help, and begin a search for their particular problems. Using materials similar to those described above, he must provide some means of recording his observations.

Some teachers have found check sheets like the Short Diagnostic Guide, which is based on oral and silent reading sessions, both feasible and helpful. They interview informally each pupil chosen for diagnosis and ask him to read aloud and then to read silently. As he reads, they fill out this sheet to the best of their ability. When the reading can be taped, repeated listening has revealed weaknesses not noticed in the initial observation. Later, on the basis of what has been gleaned from several diagnostic sessions, the teacher makes tentative plans for helping the pupil. These check sheets show that poor reading is almost always a result of multiple causes. Single causation and simple solutions, apparently, have nothing to do with reading.

For a thorough diagnosis in schools where money is available, the *Diagnostic Reading Tests* [19] (see page 424) may be recommended. Teachers interested in improving their informal diagnoses of individual reading might ask their schools to purchase several of these diagnostic tests for evaluative trial. On the basis of this tentative use, a teacher can decide whether or not these aids are feasible for his purposes. Also useful are the *Diagnostic Reading Scales* [20] by George Spache. They provide a complete picture of an individual's reading problems, locating three levels of the pupil's reading performance: instructional level, independent level, and potential level.

Diagnostic tests are necessarily elaborate and time-consuming. Because of this, a teacher may decide on administering them to only those pupils showing the greatest motivation. For others who appear to read very poorly a simpler kind of test can be administered easily and will reveal mastery of primary phonics. This is the *Kottmeyer Diagnostic Spelling Test,* which also can be used for phonic diagnosis.[21] Ideally the Kottmeyer test should be

[19] Committee on Diagnostic Reading Tests, Inc., Mountain Home, North Carolina 25758.
[20] California Test Bureau, Del Monte Research Park, Monterey, California (1963).
[21] See William Kottmeyer, *Teacher's Guide for Remedial Reading* (St. Louis: Webster, 1959), pp. 87–90.

supplemented by a diagnostic test such as the *Stanford Diagnostic Reading Test* or the *Reading Capacity Test.*[22]

Because a single session may be deceptive, a teacher should plan diagnosis for a series of occasions. The child's physical condition or mood on any one day may be responsible for an erroneous impression. Spreading diagnostic sessions over a period of time not only results in more accurate data but avoids discouraging pupils at the beginning of the school year by making them feel less competent than they are.

Although the methods described here lack the thoroughness of ideal diagnosis, they will help teachers locate the reading levels and problems of pupils in distress. Skill to do will come with doing, and if a little knowledge is a dangerous thing, the teacher can comfort himself with T. H. Huxley's reaction, "Where is the man who has so much knowledge as to be out of danger?"

Reading in All Subjects

English teachers need to be wary of the assumption that improvement of reading is the sole responsibility of the English department. The issue is not one of saving time and effort for English teachers but rather one of placing reading instruction where it will be most effective. The nature of reading content heavily influences the way students must read; thus, the various reading skills require different emphases in different subjects. From research we know that competent readers learn readily to adjust their rate of reading to varied levels of difficulty and that in certain fields like science and mathematics, students who slow down and read carefully are higher achievers than those who do not.[23] Specific reading instruction in each subject is therefore essential if students are to adapt reading skills to the requirements of different subject disciplines.

Organizing a school-wide reading program is a complex strategy. In approaching the problem, English teachers must be tactful; it is easy to antagonize busy instructors of science or homemaking by seeming to imply that they are not fulfilling all their responsibilities. However, when signs of interest are noted, colleagues may be encouraged to consider what might be done about the reading problem. For instance, teachers of English may recommend that all teachers check their textbooks for vocabulary not included in the first 5,000 words of the Thorndike and Lorge list of words classified according to frequency of use.[24] A *dart* in home economics is very different

---

[22] By Bjorn Karlson, Richard Madden, and Eric F. Gardner, *Stanford Diagnostic Reading Test* (New York: Harcourt, Brace & World, 1966); Donald Durrell and Helen Blair Sullivan, *Reading Capacity Test* (New York: Harcourt, Brace & World, 1967).

[23] Blommers and Lindquist, *op. cit.;* Eva Bond, *Reading and Ninth-Grade Achievement,* Teachers' College Contributions to Education, No. 756 (New York: Columbia Univ. Press, 1938), pp. x, 62.

[24] E. L. Thorndike and I. Lorge, *The Teacher's Word Book of 30,000 Words* (New York: Teachers' College Bureau of Publications, Columbia University, 1944).

from a *dart* in physical education; simple words like *source* and *correspond* trouble many readers in history; *bisect* and *integer* often remain vague in the minds of pupils having difficulty in mathematics. Teachers who take time to establish vocabulary pertinent to their own subject fields reap a harvest of greater satisfaction and pupil achievement.[25]

In-service education enrolling one or more teachers from different departments has some advantages; involvement of the entire staff secures even better results. Some secondary schools have featured reading instruction in meetings and bulletins, with many applications to classroom instruction and evaluation. Some of these programs have lasted for a year, others even longer. Librarians have often aided teachers in encouraging students to extend their reading in special subject fields: *The Wonderful World of Mathematics* might be recommended by the teacher of general mathematics; *Lou Gehrig, A Quiet Hero,* by the coach; and *No Other White Men,* a carefully documented account of American history for some interested eighth-grade pupil.

Where the entire faculty is not yet ready for a school-wide reading program, English teachers may sometimes take the initiative in discussing the matter with administrators. In one district, the administrators of the secondary schools organized a series of meetings devoted to reading. At the first session, one teacher discussed reading in the content fields and passed out this statement:

EVERY TEACHER TEACHES READING

You are already teaching reading

if you teach your students how to use the textbooks in your class by discussing the title, the table of contents, the subject headings, and the index. Do you do this?

if you assign an article or a section in a book and give a certain number of guide questions to direct the students' understanding of the subject matter content. Do you do this?

if you show by your assignments when you expect the students to skim, scan, analyze, or read for details. Do you do this?

if you use the study part of the hour to analyze levels of pupil reading ability, to locate slow learners and those having difficulty understanding the meaning. Do you do this?

if you select textbooks that are not too difficult for most of the students in your class. Do you do this?

if you ask students to select the important from the unimportant. Do you do this?

if you encourage students to read about your subject for their leisure time reading. Do you do this?

The following year all secondary teachers in this district considered the reading problem in a series of meetings. Lists of reading skills and teaching methods for each subject were developed.

---

[25] Hemphill Reid, "Improving Linguistic Ability as a Factor in Solving Problems in Algebra," in Kansas Studies in Education Series, *Abstracts of Doctoral Dissertations in Education,* Vol. 2, No. 6 (Lawrence, Kansas: Univ. of Kansas Publications, 1941).

There are many ways to help all teachers realize how the reading problem transcends instruction in English. Whatever can be done to widen the base of concern about reading will improve the quality of the total instructional program.

Reading in Special Classes

Slow learners reading as well as they can be expected to read, reluctant readers linking reading to all that is repulsive about schools, retarded readers whose inadequate skills do not match their good native ability—not infrequently the reading problem becomes more than an individual teacher can solve. Some strategy, more direct than classroom modification, is demanded. What are the possibilities of remedial classes? Electives designed for developmental or recreational reading? Reading laboratories for a variety of problem readers? English teachers cannot be expected to provide the services of reading specialists, but often in curriculum development they are expected to play a major role in deciding school policy on special classes in reading.

Unless special reading classes are part of a coherent plan for the entire school, they seldom succeed. Unless they have status with students, their success is almost always doubtful. They are most likely to justify their existence whenever their addition to the curriculum has not been ill-conceived or hasty. If they are considered dumping grounds for problem pupils or slow learners, the strategy fails. If, after a semester or a year of drill, the "remedied" pupils return to inflexible classroom situations like those that contributed heavily to their reading misfortunes, the strategy fails. The value of special reading classes can usually be determined by the answer to a single question: Do the students in these classes view them as an opportunity or a cross to be borne?

Most poor readers require, before anything else, a primary revision in attitude. Defeated and discouraged, they have learned to protect their egos by adopting ingenious substitutes for reading or attitudes of indifference. Not infrequently they insist they do not need to read. Every outwardly defiant nonreader needs the support of a teacher who believes in his ability to acquire reasonable reading competence, a teacher who is sincerely willing to help him. However, priority lists of patients are often necessary, based on considerations of greatest need and greatest response to therapy. Like one of Dickens' characters, the teacher who accomplishes anything in reading must have affection beaming in one eye and calculation shining out of the other.

READING LABORATORY   For students who can profit from remedial instruction, one approach is a reading laboratory, a room fitted with a number of varied practice areas:

> on one table, a tape recorder with tapes of easy to read books that the pupils can follow with their eyes as they listen (This linkage of the eye and ear is especially important.)

present in abundance, copies of *Scope*,[26] *Hot Rod*,[27] *Reader's Digest Skill Builders*, vocabulary books like *Word Wealth*,[28] and up-to-date booklets on vocations

on the teacher's desk, a copy of *Fare for the Reluctant Reader*,[29] *Book Bait*,[30] *Hooked on Books* and *Hooked on Books: Program and Proof*,[31] and to assist him in this book-bait angling, a classroom library of at least 100 appealing books with colorful covers—ranging from the simple *River Ranch* to *The Pearl* (Paperbacks are especially necessary.)

at another table, many word games, phrase cards, phonic wheels, and sight-word cards

at another table, boxes of selections varied in difficulty with keys to the comprehension questions

in several booths Controlled Readers and materials for them

Within this realm, the teacher moves about from groups to individuals, helping them carry out plans organized at the beginning of the period. On some days the entire class works together on skills needed in common; on others, individuals and groups work on the specific skills they need. On some days the teacher reads aloud or plays a tape while the pupils follow with their eyes; on others, every pupil reads a different book chosen from the voluntary reading library. With small classes and careful budgeting of each class period so everyone knows what he is to accomplish, a reading teacher can usually salvage most of the pupils who attend for a single half year.

Where the causes are not primarily emotional or physical, techniques and methods must be adapted from the primary grades. The pupils will dictate short simple stories about matters close to their interests, stories the special teacher will type as the basis for each pupil's reading. These "experience stories" need to be supplemented by the use of sight-phrase cards, picture-word games, and basic-sight cards. Word recognition through phonics must be added to sight recognition and meaningful association with experience.

The only students who belong in these reading classes, however, are those whose reading skill is markedly below teachers' estimates of their native intelligence. Customarily, the reading ability is two or more years behind estimated native ability. Such students—and only such students—are capable of being "remedied"; the term *remedial* is misused when applied to classes for students of low mental ability who are probably already standing on tiptoe in reading achievement. To press and harass students who are reading as best they can, albeit not at their chronological grade level, is to raise false hopes for child, home, and other teachers.

[26] *Scope Magazine,* Scholastic Corporation, 33 W. 42nd St., New York, N.Y. 10036.

[27] *Hot Rod Magazine,* Petersen Publishing Co., 5959 Hollywood Blvd., Los Angeles, Calif. 90028.

[28] Ward S. Miller, *Word Wealth* (New York: Holt, Rinehart & Winston, 1958).

[29] Anita Dunn, *et al., Fare for the Reluctant Reader* (Albany: State Univ. of New York, 1966).

[30] Elinor Walker, ed., *Book Bait* (Chicago: American Library Association, 1966).

[31] Daniel N. Fader and Morton Shaevitz, *Hooked on Books* (New York: Berkeley, 1966). Daniel N. Fader and Elton B. McNeil, *Hooked on Books: Program and Proof* (New York: Berkeley, 1968).

Recognizing that reading and thinking cannot be separated, the teacher of English does not expect infallible recipes to improve comprehension. As best he can, he selects classroom activities, similar to those suggested here, in the light of what is known about learning. A teacher must place theoretical concerns central in his viewpoint; rather than blindly accepting techniques, he must create procedures consistent with his own philosophy and theories of learning. He must assess procedures such as are recommended here, adopt and adapt those he approves, and devise more of his own.

TO IMPROVE VOCABULARY

An English writer, discussing the schools of Britain, regrets that many teachers do not realize that words are of less importance than ideas, that a stock of words is of little value unless one knows how to use them.

> Yet the practice still exists among teachers of aiming at the enlargement of vocabulary by means of formal exercises, as though such enlargement were in itself of value. It is the mind that needs enlargement. The enrichment and illumination of experience by observation and discussion is a surer way to the genuine enlargement of vocabulary than can be secured by concentration on formal exercises in the correct use of words the need for which is not personally felt.[32]

The following suggestions for vocabulary development are intended to encourage interesting excursions into *thought*. They accept the plausible truth that remembering the meaning of a word like *mango* is more likely to last if one has picked and eaten a mango, and that similar forces are involved in comprehending such concepts as *bland* and *stolid*. Successful vocabulary study—growth that is retained—rests ultimately on enlargement of experience.

▶ *Extend vocabulary lessons over an entire term*

Spaced vocabulary discussions, recurring throughout the school year, succeed better than concentrated attack. The ultimate aim, to develop an interest in words, becomes firmly fixed only if the teacher himself is intrigued by language and words. Vocabulary discussions often arise spontaneously: "He was hurt to the quick." Now, where is the quick? "She was left in the lurch." What an odd expression! Where do you suppose the lurch is? How could such an expression have originated? What do you mean, he was in the pink of condition? Can you say a word over and over until you divest it of all meaning? Thinking only of its sound, say *shrub* or *cellar door* until you begin to hear it as it must sound to a Dane or Samoan hearing English for the first time. (Frenchmen have been known to say that *cellar door* has a charming sound.) Ideally, every teacher should have the poet's combination of exuberance and exactitude with words. But even if he is not a Keats or a Tennyson, a teacher interested in language may still acquire enough zest to interrupt planned instruction with many an interesting spontaneous excursion.

[32] A. F. Watts, *The Language and Mental Development of Children* (Boston: Heath, 1947), p. 58.

▶ *Urge a balance between using context and dictionary*

Point out that one of the purposes of vocabulary study is to acquire flexibility in the approach used in acquiring new words. One important way competent readers learn a word is by context.[33] Make clear the importance of balance: learning all words by context is certain to promote sloppiness and fuzziness; likewise resorting to the dictionary for every unfamiliar word is as foolish as it is time-consuming.

▶ *Vary the approach*

Listed here are a few of the many facets of word study, all deserving exploration during the school year. They should be distributed over a semester or year rather than grouped as a single unit. Sometimes they may be related to an assignment or a reading lesson, or the teacher may introduce one of them for special focus in its own right. Brief but pleasant, they often serve to fill in the extra ten minutes at the close of some class hour or to take the chill off Monday morning before settling down to the major plans of the week. The ideas suggested here might be used as teacher reminders. During the course of a semester, a teacher could check off each as it is used, adding others not listed here, making certain of interest and variety.

> *Interesting word origins*   Give students a list like the following, only longer, and commend those who find the origin of the greatest number: curfew, tantalize, tawdry, bedlam, sardonic, sinister.
>
> *Malapropisms*   The bride's guardian gave her a costly torso. He took two cigars from his cuspidor and gave one to me. They went to Mexico to photograph a total collapse of the sun.
>
> *Words with multiple meanings*   moor, run, slip, bank, crop
>
> *Word structure*   prefixes, roots, and suffixes related to words frequently used: portage, porter, report, import, deport, export, portmanteau; or to words whose spelling will be made easier, such as *accommodate*
>
> *Words whose meanings have shifted*   villain, knave, silly
>
> *Place names*   Begin with George Stewart's *Names on the Land* [34] and extend to your own locality and state.
>
> *Subject matter words*   Group students according to interests and have them report on the meanings and origins of interesting words in subject matter fields: republic, soviet, fascist, and isolationist in social studies; similar words in chemistry, astronomy, mathematics, biology, shop, and homemaking.
>
> *Connotation and denotation*   The meaning of winter to a Hawaiian, to an Alaskan; the association of names for cars (Riviera, Impala), housing developments (Oak Manor), fabrics (Allure), motels (The Townhouse). Why do we buy perfume called "Evening in Paris" rather than "Evening in Junction Village"? Do we prefer Royal de luxe Viennese Hapsburger to ground dead cow? Golden Diplomat Pudding to bread pudding?
>
> *Snarl words and purr words*   My wife is stubborn but I am firm of will? She is skinny or slim or svelte? [35]

[33] Constance McCullough, "Learning to Use Context Clues," *Elementary English Review*, Vol. 20, No. 4 (April 1943).

[34] George Stewart, *Names on the Land* (Boston: Houghton Mifflin, 1958).

[35] S. I. Hayakawa, *Language in Thought and Action*, 2nd ed. (New York: Harcourt, Brace & World, 1964), contains many other examples like this one and countless ideas for use in studying words.

Language and prejudice   The use of names intended to hurt or belittle other groups: kraut, kike, wop, greaser, chink, jap, spic, nigger, bohunk, honkey, whitey, WASP.

Idioms   Be on hand. See a thing through. Try your hand at this.

Games   For instance, this game of homonyms: supply the correct sets of homonyms for these definitions:

1. no; cry of a horse   (nay, neigh)
2. guided; a metal   (led, lead)
3. female sheep; evergreen tree   (ewe, yew)

Word sources   words deriving from Arabic like sherbet, zero, algebra, almanac; words from music: rhapsody, oboe, concerto, symphony; words from the sea: scuttlebutt, bosun, gunwale; words from mythology: jovial, martial, echo, cereal, plutocrat, atlas, Wednesday

Abstract and concrete words   courage, democracy, scarlet tanager

Word immigrants   List words in English borrowed from other languages; make a world word map.

Imaginative comparisons   Begin with common usage like iron will, shadowing a suspect, a bitter disappointment; next consider more imaginative comparisons like "The snows of moonlight came drifting on the town." Concentrate on the aptness of comparison, not on terminology. Continue on to other imaginative, fresh comparisons.

Synonyms, antonyms, heteronyms, and homonyms   Stress not only the likenesses but also the differences in synonyms. In what contexts would *ominous, sinister,* and *portentous* be appropriate?

Crossword puzzles   Students can be taught to devise these.

Onomatopoeic words   murmur, tinkle, growl, whisper, rattle, click

Words not common in speech but often encountered in reading   stolid, bland, alacrity, myriads, resplendent

Slang, its use and misuse

► *Use films*

Many films feature the uses and values of a superior vocabulary. Some of these might be made part of the year's plan for conquering the English language: *Build Your Vocabulary, Do Words Ever Fool You? Words: Their Origin, Use, and Spelling.*

► *Replace colorless verbs*

Write on the chalkboard sentences like the following:

The gang of boys *went* down to the lake to swim.
The strange man *walked* across the street.

Ask students to find replacements for the verbs. For *went,* more vigorous verbs like *dashed, sprinted, raced,* or *streaked* might be suggested. Students may think of *ambled, lurched, strolled, dawdled, sauntered, trudged,* and *shuffled* to replace *walked.* Junior high pupils should volunteer to imitate these various ways of walking, noting contrasts and similarities.

► *Plan an experience to develop new concepts and therefore new vocabulary*

1. If the class can visit any unusual place—a naval ship, a tannery, or a museum of science and industry—the excursion may become a base for "enlarging the mind"

through new concepts to be discussed afterwards. The teacher should, of course, prepare students for the experience, helping them identify these new concepts and discover words to express them. This "growing edge" expands most rapidly and permanently when students consciously realize they are to be alert to certain features of the forthcoming excursion.

2. The same advantages and the same principles of method apply to any planned use of television, films, and recordings.

► *Use direct instruction and specific practice*

1. None of the emphasis on motivation, experience, or spontaneity is intended to diminish respect for planned lessons in vocabulary study. Books like the following may be used effectively in planned vocabulary study:

> Lee C. Deighton, *Vocabulary Development in the Classroom* (New York: Teachers' College, Columbia University, 1959).
> Margaret S. Ernst, *More About Words* (New York: Knopf, 1951).
> Charles E. Funk, *Thereby Hangs a Tale* (New York: Harper & Row, 1950).
> Frieda Radke, *Word Resources* (New York: Odyssey, 1955).
> Joseph T. Shipley, *A Dictionary of Word Origins* (New York: Teachers' College, Columbia University, 1959).

There are other good textbooks, not listed here. A vocabulary textbook imaginative and well organized can be a most useful adjunct to the teacher's aims, saving valuable time for other planning.

2. Many teachers devise programs to encourage individual pupil vocabulary lists. They help pupils set up forms for recording new words encountered in reading. As they read, the pupils check unfamiliar or vaguely understood words. They then copy each word and enough of its context to make possible a suitable dictionary definition. For instance, the opening page of one student's notebooks might read like this:

> Words I Have Subjugated (I have vanquished, drubbed, surmounted, and gained ascendancy over these words.)
> from "The Heathen," by Jack London
> *stolid* "The natives fell into a condition of dumb, *stolid* fear." dull, impassive, showing no emotion
> *dissipate* "The hurricane will *dissipate* the . . . horde (of sharks)." scatter, disperse

Student diligence in persisting with these vocabulary lists may be considerably bolstered by teachers who inspect the lists, commend them, and use the inspection as one element in grading pupil effort. If these individual vocabulary lists are to succeed, the teacher must help students initiate the project and establish the form. Students do not always understand the importance of including the context, and they may also need instruction featuring sound judgment in selecting appropriate dictionary definitions. Although such matters seem obvious to adults, many students have not yet reached this level of sophistication. At some point they must learn that words do not have a single, push-button meaning. *Dissipate*, in the preceding exercise, is a good example of this versatility in words; the dictionary definition *squander* will not suffice. Ask students why it is wise to avoid learning words in isolation. Although they will not know the psychology of learning or Thorndike's

Law of Meaningfulness, some of them may be able to explain that we learn the meanings of new words by associating experience with them.

TO SEE RELATIONSHIPS

Vocabulary growth alone will not solve the reading problem. Even though the teacher has clearly underscored the fact that word meanings vary with context, many students still hope to read sentences and paragraphs as if they were constructed like parts of a toy erector set. But language, subtle and resilient, eludes such rigid molds. Reading requires accurate recognition of words; it also necessitates fusing words into larger patterns of related thought. As Thorndike has pointed out, such processes of thought require selecting, repressing, emphasizing, and organizing. Comprehension demands a dynamic balance of all the elements in a passage.

▶ *Emphasize relationships of words within sentences and passages*

1. Have someone play a familiar melody on the piano or other instrument, deliberately ignoring the musical phrasing. Every note is played as if it were completely unrelated to all the others. The teacher, or a selected student, then performs a parallel mechanical reading of a passage in a book available to everyone. Reading aloud, the performer ignores punctuation, makes no attempt to group words by cadence or meaning, and avoids all such aids as stress on key words and contrast for qualifying or parenthetical elements. The demonstration concludes with meaningful performances of both the music and the prose passage. Class discussion, followed by practice, both oral and silent, completes the sequence. Such exercises need to be pointed toward the reading to be done in English, in other courses, and in adult life. The teacher chooses prose in which the content is relatively appealing to the majority, and he also asks, "Where now and in adult life will you use these skills?"

2. Place on the chalkboard sentences similar to this model:

Yes, we're going to the bowling alley however
                                 if
                                 nevertheless
                                 after
                                 although
                                 and
                                 but

Discussion and completion of the sentences should illuminate one of the ways relationships are expressed.

3. In sentences prepared by the teacher practice inserting the missing transition words, finding the word that spoils a sentence, finding the phrase or clause that is out of place in a sentence, and finding the sentence that is out of place in a paragraph.

4. For slow learning classes, prepare a study guide stating the essential meaning of passages in selections being read by the class. Knowing in advance the general import of the passage, poor readers often show more confidence in reading aloud the segment when they locate it. An example, for an eighth-grade class:

Find the passages that show:
Bertie was uncertain of himself.

Bertie was *not* a thin boy—far from it!
Bertie liked Marcia Dale better than Hyacinth.

By having pupils read aloud the passage they locate, the teacher may emphasize careful reading and call attention to the weight of various words and the relationships among them.

5. In the junior high school, research has shown, typical comprehension difficulties arise from failure to see relationships—failure, for instance, to see parts of sentences against the total context.[36] Eighth-grade pupils have a tendency to disregard or misconstrue certain parts of the sentence, such as the initial phrase in "*Aside from the fireplace,* the candle was the chief source of light." Many of them also consider the reading process as merely verbalizing words regardless of meaning. Methods such as we have described are intended to help such pupils rise above the mechanical concept of reading, to see reading as reasoning, and to make vocabulary growth a permanent gain.

In teaching sentence relationships, the teacher may sometimes stop in the reading of a selection to analyze its sentences and paragraphs. What is the significance of this word or this phrase to the meaning of this passage? Is there any plan by which this paragraph has been put together? Does any sentence express the topic of the paragraph? Which sentences supply examples? Which add significant details? What word is likely to mislead the reader if he does not take into account the rest of the sentence? What inappropriate association might the reader bring to this phrase if he is not alert? These occasional halts to stress thoughtful reading can be highly effective. Particularly is this true when these analyses are means to understanding selections in which the students' interest is wholehearted. The effectiveness of direct methods like those described above depends upon motivation. Unless a student sees the value of what he is doing, unless his will is involved, the impact of all such instruction is negligible. The teacher must often ask, "Why are we doing this, class? Who can remind us?"

► *Encourage flexibility of interpretation*

Let the teacher ask himself, "Am I doing anything to encourage that suppleness of mind, that freedom from rigid response, which counts for so much in reading skill? What can I do to help these students become impressed with the enormous importance of a tentative hovering above all the elements in a sentence or paragraph, of modifying and shifting perspective in a highly complex equilibrium of all the forces involved in a passage?"

One effective method, developed by Heinz Werner and Edith Kaplan,[37] interests students because they first view it as a game. However, its value transcends this initial appeal, and through the technique of artificial words a teacher may demonstrate to students the need for an alert and resilient response to all reading. The teacher presents students with sets of six or more sentences, each one containing

[36] J. C. Dewey, "A Case Study of Reading Comprehension Difficulties in American History," *University of Iowa Studies in Education III*, Vol. 10, No. 1 (1935).

[37] Heinz Werner and Edith Kaplan, "Development of Word Meaning Through Verbal Context: An Experimental Study," *Journal of Psychology*, Vol. 29, No. 2 (April 1950); and *The Acquisition of Word Meanings* (Evanston, Ill.: Child Development Publications, 1952). The exercise described here is adapted from this research. See the unit "Power Over Language," page 229, and Chapter Four, page 167, for other suggestions for classroom use of this method.

the same artificial word and each one contributing an additional clue to correct interpretation.

> By seven, the light was *soldeving.*
> The older it gets, the sooner it will begin to *soldeve.*
> We felt unsafe because the road seemed to *soldeve* into the foggy dimness.
> People like a bright flower better than one that is *soldeved.*
> Putting the dress on the sunny lawn made the color of the cloth *soldeve.*
> "Old soldiers never die, they just *soldeve* away."

Each teacher will develop his own collection suited to concepts within his pupils' range of understanding. He will soon discover that some pupils fix upon a certain meaning—such as *bad* or *dawning* in the first sentence above—and then cling tenaciously to that concept despite all the evidence, in subsequent sentences, that *bad* or *dawning* is erroneous. These pupils need to become less desperately "certain." Often they need help in becoming more secure, both in the classroom and in all their school experiences. Through such help they may become readers who can reason and adapt, who do not expect language to perform like mechanical player-pianos.

▶ *Keep individual charts of improvement in comprehension*

Although slow learners respond especially well to this method, most human beings show a pleasure in charting their own progress on any skill. The charts, kept in individual notebooks or folders, may represent the per cent of comprehension questions answered correctly on a series of reading materials. Whatever variations may characterize the method, the one essential is the integrity of the comprehension questions. They must measure understanding of *significant* content and the relation of parts of a passage to each other and to the whole. Both students and teacher should discuss frequently what is important to notice and remember in a given selection and how the selection is organized. Very often the comprehension questions should measure pupil ability to correlate several parts of a reading selection or to see how a writer's purpose leads him to include or exclude certain things.

▶ *Distinguish between main and supporting ideas in paragraphs*

1. Whereas successful readers effortlessly recognize degrees of potency in words and sentences, others read as if every word were of equal importance. For the latter, instruction in differential "loading" is necessary. The teacher may demonstrate by reading passages aloud twice—the first time in a tone that grants equal significance to every word and sentence; the second time, overemphasizing the difference between major and subordinate elements. After such a demonstration, the practice must be transferred to the students, and the lesson may conclude with their own generalizations written on the chalkboard.

2. Choose from an assignment or unit a passage in which the author has effectively subordinated some ideas to others. Rewrite the passage, blurring the distinctions between important and subordinate elements. An effective way to do this is to change subordinate clauses into main clauses; shift principal ideas into phrases or dependent clauses; flatten emphasis through coordination rather than subordination. Present both passages for discussion and evaluation. Focus on this question: Which passage does the better job of emphasizing important ideas?

3. From current classroom reading, select well-constructed paragraphs exemplify-

ing the use of topic sentences. The sentences are then rearranged indiscriminately, and senior typists prepare them for class use. Students rehabilitate the "deranged paragraphs." Retention of specific lessons like this will, however, be slight unless the lesson is linked to something larger—reading that has interest or significance for the learner.

▶ Employ the SQ3R method

Some students like the security of a definite technique, such as the SQ3R method: [38] Survey the material, Question the material, Read, Recite, and Review. There is a memory-sticking rhythm to the abbreviation, and if pupils do not view the five steps as an easy and infallible formula for solving reading difficulties, the behaviors fostered by the method can be beneficial. Using several kinds of material, the teacher demonstrates how to emphasize relationships. Students often need help in seeing that *why* is often a more important question than *what, when,* or *who.*

▶ Compose headlines for newspaper clippings

From newspapers or magazines, clip short articles requiring no more space than an ordinary sheet of typing paper. Remove the headlines and paste each one on one side of cardboard or colored art paper; paste the article itself on the other side. When enough clippings are available for the entire class, pass out the sets, requesting students not to read the headlines on the reverse side. Each student studies his article with a view to composing a headline emphasizing the main ideas. After the student headlines have been completed, the cards may be turned over for a period of class discussion. Some of the articles are read aloud to determine whether the student or the original headline editor most nearly approximates an ideal statement of the article's essence. For a variation of this method, assign pairs or groups of students to work on a single article. Through comparison of ideas, students often modify their own partial grasp of the article's structure and central significance.

▶ Summarize passages requiring close reading

Discuss Schopenhauer's maxim, "Do not read, *think!*" After writing it on the board, choose a passage in a selection students are about to read. Show how the total passage influences the relations among its parts and how the parts contribute to the whole. For similar intensive analysis assign other passages in which important things are said compactly and in well-organized form. After practice with short passages, assign a longer selection. Various methods of summarizing the longer selection may be used:

> expressing the theme of a story in one sentence
> writing a précis of nonfiction
> finding examples to support generalizations the teacher presents
> finding generalizations for examples the teacher presents

TO ADAPT READING METHODS TO PURPOSE AND CONTENT

Students often understand an analogy between reading and driving an automobile. The same engine—general reading ability—travels the highways of mathematics, poetry, homemaking, and science, but the driver shifts gears and changes speeds

---

[38] For a comprehensive discussion of this method by its originator, see Francis P. Robinson, *Effective Study* (New York: Harper & Row, 1946), pp. 13–41.

according to the terrain. The nature of the material one reads affects the speed and concentration with which he proceeds; so, too, does his purpose in reading. Science, mathematics, and poetry cannot be read like *Yea! Wildcats!* To skilled readers, these elementary points are obvious. Not so to the average adult reader, nor to most pupils. In the English class alone, pupils encounter many kinds of reading; in the school at large and beyond the school they meet an even greater variety.

▶ *Demonstrate how to read selections of varying difficulty*

Ask two girls to bring to class the mirrors from their purses. While the others watch, the two sit at the teacher's desk. While one is reading, the other, placing her mirror in a position to reflect the reader's eyes, reports her observations to the class. She notes that eye movements are by no means a smooth flowing process; rather they are a series of stop-and-go movements with occasional reversals to the left. Teacher and students ponder and discuss these points:

> the value of an eye-span that takes in as many words as possible at a single glance—provided the words are understood
>
> the importance of reading by phrases and word groups rather than word-by-word—provided the word groups are comprehended
>
> the importance of the stop (or fixation) in the stop-and-go movement of the eyes, when the mind takes in as much as can be comprehended
>
> the futility of trying to increase reading power through eye-movement exercises, eye movements being efficient or inefficient in relation to understanding
>
> the crucial significance of what takes place between eye and brain, not between page and eye, indicating that ways to improve comprehension are more important than ways to improve speed
>
> the importance of the reader's will to understand as a basis for increasing comprehension during the moment of fixation

Next, list on the chalkboard the titles and page numbers of four selections in the literature anthology, typically, an uncomplicated short story, some nonfiction with closely packed meaning, a light humorous poem, and a more difficult poem with inverted sentences, some symbolism, and effective but unusual imagery. Using the complete poems and only portions of the prose, read each selection aloud, then ask pupils to help analyze the thought processes necessary for comprehension. Stress the importance of clarifying one's purpose in reading. At the close of the lesson, place on the wall a prepared placard to remain there for several weeks:

LEARN TO SHIFT GEARS IN READING. YOUR OWN PURPOSE IN READING
AND THE DIFFICULTY OF THE MATERIAL SHOULD AFFECT HOW YOU READ

With senior high classes, assign or read aloud Bacon's essay "Of Studies" on the day the placard is to be taken down. The class gives examples to illustrate that "some books are to be tasted, others to be swallowed, and some few to be chewed and digested." Then remove the placard from its place of prominence, saying, "You cannot always have this advice before you. I hope I have taught you well enough to make such a crutch unnecessary."

This method may be converted to use with younger pupils. After the use of mirrors and the discussion that follows, demonstrate with suitable content the adjustment to purpose and the nature of the material. The placard, too, may be used,

In Square Span,	which you are now reading,	each unit is read	as a whole,	not as separate words.	Notice how easily
these units are visualized.	The eyes are permitted	to focus quite naturally,	not strained by lines	of narrow print.	Fewer shifts
at the end of lines	result in fewer	interruptions of thought.	Also, thought groups		are seen in word groups,
making for speedier comprehension	and longer memory.				
The ideal size	for a standard reading unit	in Square Span	has not been accurately determined.	For example,	units which are
two, three, or even four	lines in depth	might be used.	A critic	has suggested	Square Span may be	the "Model-T"	of future reading power.

Square Span: A drastic, but imaginative rearrangement of the traditional presentation of printed words. Do you think your eyes would function better this way than moving like a weaver's shuttle along one line, then another?

Devised by Robert B. Andrews, reprinted from *The Texas Outlook*. Copyright 1949 by The Reader's Digest Association, Inc.

but instead of all of Bacon's essay, only the famous quotation is presented and discussed as an occasion for the removal of the placard.

► *Skim material for main ideas*

1. This lesson should be used for a practical purpose. For instance, when a class is searching for materials to use in a unit or project, the teacher demonstrates this skill, using some textbook or book the class has in common. Pointers for skimming should be copied in the students' notebooks and several trial runs with classroom material should occur before the class adjourns to the magazine table or the library.

2. Prepare paragraphs into which irrelevant sentences have been inserted. Students search the paragraphs to cross out the nonessential elements. The lesson should conclude with a discussion of what has been learned and how it can be applied to all reading.

TO RELATE READING TO INTERESTS AND NEEDS

A teacher can grant a position of importance to individual reading. Instead of calling it "outside reading" or "recreational reading" or "free reading"—terms indicating that teacher and school consider such activity peripheral—he labels it Guided Individual Reading or Voluntary Reading and uses it effectively as a fundamental part of the developmental reading program. To share this reading the teacher chooses methods such as are suggested here and, in more detail, on pages 472–77 in Chapter Ten, on teaching literature.

► *Let students recommend books to each other*

1. Some teachers use file boxes, in which pupils place cards for favorite books. The usual content of such cards: title, author, and a recommending statement that avoids divulging the crucial developments of fiction. The students sign their names and over a period of several years a substantial and useful file accumulates. The best of these cards may be organized into mimeographed reading lists or booklets to be used in both library and classroom.

2. Assign to a class a sum, allotted from the library budget, for purchasing ten books. Let students set up committees to review books, choose among the best not yet in the library, and prepare a list for purchase.

TO LINK READING AND REALITY

At some time in his career, almost every teacher has cringed as some pupil has read verbatim a report copied from an encyclopedia, revealing by his presentation that he comprehends not at all the sentences and words he is uttering. The problem of an empty verbalism persists in all education. The fundamental problem rests upon the curriculum and the reasonableness of the school's expectations for each individual child; but there are also specific actions a teacher may take to point up the necessity of a demand for meaning in all reading. Such suggestions as the following may be incorporated into individual lessons and unit activities.

► *Apply generalizations to the students' reading*

By urging pupils to name people, actions, and circumstances to illustrate generalizations, the teacher indicates his interest in helping students see relationships between words and their referents in reality. Instruction may include many exercises like the following:

APPLYING IDEAS

Directions   As a means of indicating that you understand their meaning and significance, apply the following ideas from Saint Exupéry's essay to your own life:

Men's words wear out and lose their meaning. With what words or phrases does the author illustrate his point? With what words associated with school life can you match them? How might the term *school spirit* run the danger of losing its meaning?

There is but one means of building that something more vast than oneself: the free gift; the gift that demands nothing in exchange. What in the selection itself was "that something"? Where in school life is it exemplified? What would the "free gift" be in the study of the arts? science? literature? Wherein does the student who works for marks miss the joy to which the author refers?

TO IMPROVE ORAL READING

► *Read aloud to small children*

Pupils work in groups, practicing reading children's stories like *Charlotte's Web*, *Madeline's Rescue*, and *Millions of Cats*. When the group pronounces a member ready, a student representative of the class arranges with the teacher of an appropriate elementary-school group and the secondary-school reader makes his debut as a reader to youngsters. Wherever this has been carried out, the results have been encouraging and well worth the careful arrangements.

Poor readers used as tutors for younger readers have improved both themselves and their young charges.

▶ *Use tape recorders and records*

1. Let pupils tape and listen to playbacks of their oral reading. As an assignment each pupil should make recommendations for his own improvement. Although the teacher will not have time to listen to each tape, he may identify in advance some of the main speech problems as a guide to self-criticism: lack of the variation of voice needed for an imparting tone, word-swallowing, pauses at inappropriate places, failure to keep the eye and mind slightly ahead of the voice.

2. Pupils take turns at taping a passage describing some character in a book such as *Light in the Forest, Roosevelt Grady, Adam of the Road*, avoiding any obvious clues to the character's name. Each pupil tapes and erases until he is satisfied with his own rendition. The total tape becomes a pleasant literary guessing game for some later period, even for subsequent classes.

This chapter began by stating that no simple formula will ever be discovered for improving reading comprehension. Reading, like all the arts of language, can never be improved apart from the energizing and maturing of the intellect in all its functions; the intellect can never be fully separated from imagination, feeling, and volition. In "Language, Thought, and Feeling," we emphasized precise thought and controlled feeling as dynamic processes. Understanding and receiving communication, the focus of the chapters in this section, also depend upon more than mechanical abilities. Nothing less than effective logical and imaginative thought will lead to clarity and power in what might at first examination seem to be a mechanical skill. Reading is, indeed, an elaborate process involving "a weighing of each of many elements in a sentence, their organization in the proper relations one to another, the selection of certain of their connotations and the rejection of others, and the cooperation of many forces to determine final response." [39]

SELECTED READINGS

BOOKS

BOND, GUY L., and TINKER, MILES A. *Reading Difficulties: Their Diagnosis and Correction*. 2nd ed. New York: Appleton-Century-Crofts, 1967.

COHN, STELLA M., and COHN, JACK. *Teaching the Retarded Reader*. New York: Odyssey Press, 1968. This book summarizes the New York City experience with problem readers during the past decade. It includes graded book lists.

HARRIS, A. J. *How to Increase Reading Ability*. 4th ed. London: Longmans, Green, 1961. This book has long been considered one of the most useful of aids to secondary-school teachers seeking help.

[39] Thorndike, *op. cit.*, p. 329.

KARLIN, ROBERT. *Teaching Reading in High School*. Indianapolis: Bobbs-Merrill, 1964. Karlin presents in careful detail what needs to be done for all kinds of readers in junior and senior high school. The first section of the book relates psychology and reading with notable skill.

ROSWELL, FLORENCE, and NATCHEZ, GLADYS. *Reading Disability: Diagnosis and Treatment*. New York: Basic Books, 1964. This book provides advice on diagnosing reading difficulties.

STAIGER, RALPH, and SOHN, DAVID A. (eds.). *New Directions in Reading*. New York: Bantam Books, 1967. Prepared under the auspices of the International Reading Association, this collection of articles includes answers to many reading questions that puzzle secondary-school teachers. Sections of particular interest are "The Speed Reading Controversy" and "Reading for Culturally Disadvantaged Youth."

ARTICLES AND PAMPHLETS

CARRILLO, LAWRENCE. *Reading Institute Extension Service*. Chicago: Science Research Associates. This service, at 259 East Erie St., Chicago, Illinois 60611, is composed of a series of eight units that cover all the phases of secondary-school reading. They are sensible and useful for any school system wanting practical guidance on improving the reading situation.

LEICHTY, V. E. "How Slowly Do They Read?" *English Journal*. Vol. 45, No. 5 (May 1956). Leichty believes that the teacher should emphasize careful reading. Through discussing meaning and worrying less about speed and quantity of reading, the teacher makes his greatest contribution to the pupils.

MCCULLOUGH, CONSTANCE M. "What Does Research Reveal About Practices in Teaching Reading?" In *Teaching Reading: Selected Materials*. Edited by Walter B. Barbe. New York: Oxford Univ. Press, 1965. This article considers the implications of research for developing vocabulary, comprehension, speed, tastes and appreciations, and means of evaluating. The article is notable for its temperate applications of research and its balancing good sense.

NILES, OLIVE S. "Systemwide In-Service Programs in Reading." *The Reading Teacher*. Vol. 19, No. 6 (March 1966), pp. 424–28. Dr. Niles, a director of reading, kindergarten through grade 12 in the Springfield, Massachusetts, schools, presents the full range of possibilities for increasing the reading sophistication of all teachers and administrators. This is a sensible and comprehensive plan.

ROBINSON, H. ALAN (ed.). *Reading: Seventy-five Years of Progress*. Chicago: Univ. of Chicago Press, 1968. The proceedings of the twenty-ninth conference on reading at the University of Chicago. This volume relates research and theory to classroom application.

EVALUATION:

EVALUATING ORAL LANGUAGE: LISTENING AND SPEAKING

To place oral language in its proper position, the most effective action a school can take is to plan local classroom evaluation of speaking and listening as a unit. Methods of appraisal should usually be devised with particular students in mind; they should eventually include all competencies the teacher thinks appropriate for any certain class. Major attention to the individual pupil's development—the improvement he makes from the beginning of a semester to the end—is especially important with oral language because it is so closely tied with self-image and personality.

If the student thinks of classroom speech as communication, understands the purpose of instruction, is given time for practice of individual principles, and is helped to evaluate progress, the plan of organizing instruction suggested in Chapter Seven makes sense to him. In a small way it helps him discriminate between learning as a goal and fulfilling a series of assignments with his accomplishment identical to the total of the individual grades assigned. The final grade is unlikely to be any more subjective than grades in other areas of learning where retention of factual information is not the sole aim.

The individual speech

The problem of tactfully and helpfully handling impromptu evaluations of speeches worries the inexperienced teacher. However, with any new class even the skilled teacher feels his way. Before individual evaluations start, usually a period of work passes with comment only on the most elementary principles involved. Therefore, the first evaluations, used primarily for teaching, will be designed for the class as a whole. Such a procedure allows the teacher to set an impersonal tone with no appraisal of individual work. He does this by his casual acceptance of speaking as a common daily experience, by focusing upon specific examples of effective communication, by emphasizing content first and, only after that, form and delivery. Thus he begins to build acceptable standards. Eventually, some students will want to know how they are progressing. This is the time to begin appraisal of individual performances.

Much of the teaching in reference to particular oral skills is accomplished by impromptu evaluations given before the class. The situation is often emotionally charged. It is necessary, therefore, for the teacher to establish a flexible

411

guide for his remarks. A good evaluation has three characteristics: it provides motivation; it is concerned only with immediate and essential problems; and it is specific enough to help the pupil with the next step.

An evaluation should convince the student that he has already shown potential and that he is capable of doing the next assignment. The order in which points are given is important. The student must first know that his current offering has had some merit; only after he has been told in what way he has succeeded will he be receptive to adverse comment. Once the strengths have been pointed out, the student may be told of one weakness he should try to overcome first. In making suggestions for improvement, the teacher tries to fit the task to the individual. For one, he may pick a fault difficult to correct; for another, something comparatively easy. He gives concrete ways for attacking these weaknesses.

Evaluations should stress only the essential; they should be as concise as possible. The student can be hampered rather than helped when attention is called to trivial faults that are almost automatically eliminated when he gains more confidence. The class should realize the teacher knows that acquiring any skill takes time. The teacher does not begin with a list of requirements only a professional could meet.

Since the aim of the oral skills program is never perfection in any one endeavor but an over-all record of improvement, every assignment should stress a principle of effective speaking needing to be taught or retaught: not the vague, "Tell us something interesting you did over the weekend," but "Give one opinion you've formed about a character in the book you are reading; furnish enough evidence in support so we may decide whether your opinion is justified." In fulfilling each assignment, the student tries to exemplify not only the new principle but, whenever possible, the ones previously discussed. The evaluation, therefore, after brief mention of ways the speech has illustrated familiar concepts, centers on the current problem. This practice is effective because it provides for a brief review and directs attention to only one new point. Such a procedure, consistently followed, emphasizes the cumulative nature of any skills program.

If the class is to profit from the work of each individual, and if the student himself is to work purposefully, the approach to evaluation must be positive and the comments specific enough to point the way in preparing future work. For example:

> To the student who speaks too fast: "Next time, try to think of your speech as a succession of ideas; pause between them to give us a chance to digest each one and get ready for the next."
>
> To call attention to a good introduction: "You caught our interest immediately by a reference to an experience we have all shared."
>
> To one seemingly unprepared: "After you've thought through your next speech, make out a list of key words to aid your memory as you practice."

Such generalities as "good," "interesting," "excellent voice" give very little enlightenment or help. Specific advice gives the student direction for his next attempt and makes all more aware that purposeful speaking is governed by well-defined principles.

It is important too that the teacher remember advice previously given to each student. Keeping for each class member a card on which appraisals are noted will help both teacher and student evaluate progress.

If the evaluation leaves the student convinced he has strengths upon which he can rely, if he feels the next step is within his capabilities, if he knows exactly what to work for next, teaching has been good. These three requirements, stated here in reference to the speech before the class—a small portion of the oral skill program—are pertinent to evaluating all oral language.

Discussion

To help students recognize the dual purpose of discussion, evaluations should direct attention to both process and product. At first this can be done informally with the teacher guiding the class in appraisal. When some degree of skill has been attained, individual evaluations should be made. Students need to be reassured that pertinence, not quantity of talk, is what counts; that often attentive listening is the most helpful contribution to make. Especially, they need to know that grades are recorded not for each discussion but for several; thus sufficient evidence will be accumulated to assess values more accurately.

Since in discussion the teacher is trying to give students practice both in purposeful speaking and in the use of group skills, any evaluation will necessarily be based on the principles governing both. A simple rating sheet serves the purpose for beginners.

CHECKLIST FOR SELF-RATING AS A SPEAKER

Number of discussions included in rating _____
Content   Were my facts correct? My opinions supported?
Organization   Were my comments immediately clear? Concise? Pertinent?
Delivery   Did I speak so all could hear? Enunciate clearly? Was my tone courteous?
My chief contributions have been _____

The following brief check list was prepared by a tenth-grade class. The teacher first asked each pupil to list practices of listeners that aided him as he spoke as well as those that hindered. These lists were given to a committee, which summarized the responses for the class. Then teacher and students prepared the guide.

CHECKLIST FOR SELF-RATING AS A LISTENER

I can help a speaker by   *Yes*   *No*

Appearing interested: Do I
   look at him as he speaks?
   try to attend even if the subject seems dull?
   avoid distracting movements?
   refrain from comments and questions until he has finished?
Reacting intelligently to his ideas: Do I
   try to accept ideas on their own value rather than on
     personality of the speaker?
   try to consider impartially statements I'd like to believe
     and those I'd like to reject?
Evaluating honestly: Do I try to
   help the speaker rather than impress with my cleverness?
   comment on strengths as well as matters needing im-
     provement?
   make my remarks concise and specific?
   maintain an impersonal tone?
I notice the following improvements in my ability to evaluate: _____

The value of using rating sheets lies in their repetition. The reiteration of desirable qualities serves as a guide not only as the pupil evaluates his past performance but also as he prepares for performances to come.

Using various means to evaluate lends interest, provides different viewpoints, and involves more students in this important aspect of learning. Teachers have found the following methods effective. Before the discussion, pair students, each to write an informal evaluation of the other.[1] After the discussion, give students five minutes to analyze the performance of the one who has contributed most. It is good teaching to discuss the papers, selecting the two or three persons most often chosen and evaluating their contributions. This should be done without identification of the individuals. The specifics given will stress the qualities of good participation—the aim of such an activity.

Assign students to act as observers, each to note a different aspect. This is ideal work for those who contribute little orally. They may be asked to find examples of questions that helped clarify an issue, information that supported or refuted a point made by another, logical or faulty reasoning. They may note when and how digressions arose, how the discussion was brought back into focus, the extent and quality of participation. The use of such an evaluation method implies some degree of skill and confidence on the part of students. The teacher should, of course, add the items gradually, starting with only one and asking several pupils to act as observers. To the extent suggested here, it is suitable only for the mature and capable.

Ask several students to observe the discussion and to pool their finding for a general evaluation.

Whatever form the evaluation of discussion takes, it should be specific; it

---

[1] Such an assignment presupposes that students have had instruction in giving and receiving criticism. See pages 316–18.

should be concerned with only the most pressing problems; it should leave students confident of the progress they have made and of their ability to take the next step.

Group experiences

Evaluating the group process has much in common with evaluating discussion. Here, too, both process and product are essential; the teacher provides frequent means for evaluating both.

The group process can be evaluated as formally or as informally as the situation warrants and can be done in a variety of ways. Perhaps if the results have exceeded the teacher's hopes, a general discussion will be sufficient to elicit reasons why certain groups have been able to accomplish more than others; to highlight practices that have helped, disregarding for the time those that have hindered. To make it as easy as possible for individuals who find it difficult to speak, the teacher can call attention to examples of attentive listening, to an instance when the right question helped clarify the issue.

Suppose, however, that the teacher discovers he has expected too much from this first venture. Then his task is to discover something, however small, that augurs well for the future, to enlarge upon it, to review the steps that should have been taken. Were the directions clear? Did the group have the necessary facts? Did the leader understand his duties? The teacher assumes a share of the blame. This may be the time to ask the student to make a simple written evaluation of his own participation. He may be asked to mention his own contribution only and to think of one thing he might have done to insure smoother operation. If a more complete evaluation seems desirable, the teacher can review the standards and ask for a comment in reference to each item. Sometimes it is well for the teacher to tell the class he too is writing an evaluation of his own performance. The very act of writing down first impressions sometimes has a wholesome effect on both students and teacher. Self-evaluation is not a magic wand either for adolescents or adults; it carries no guarantee of immediate transformations. However, it has so often demonstrated its effectiveness that it is well worth trying.

A rating sheet based upon the objectives previously agreed upon often helps each group diagnose its own difficulties and evaluate its own accomplishments. The same holds true for the individual. The first two forms may prove useful with beginners.

GROUP'S SELF-RATING

Purpose: _____
1. Did we get to work promptly?
2. Did we stick to the point?
3. Did we work quietly?
4. Did all contribute?
5. Did we ask for help as soon as it was needed?
What did we accomplish? _____

Such a reaction sheet, filled out by the group, serves as impetus for a class evaluation that re-emphasizes the purpose of the experience and the means used for its accomplishment.

BEGINNER'S CHECKLIST FOR SELF-RATING

Subject: _____

1. Had I prepared sufficiently?
2. Did I follow directions?
3. Did I make the best use of my time?
4. Did I work without disturbing other groups?
5. My chief contribution to my group was _____

After several meetings let students draw names to rate one other member.

EVALUATION OF A GROUP MEMBER

1. What was his chief contribution?
2. What factor should he first try to improve?
3. Evaluation by _____

With an experienced group, a more complete rating is possible. In making up a form, select only the items in which instruction has been given and ask the student to select several aspects of his performance to evaluate in a brief essay.

CHECKLIST FOR SELF-RATING BY MORE MATURE STUDENTS

1. Did I assume the responsibility the group wished?
2. Did I listen alertly?
3. Did I willingly express my own point of view?
4. Did I try to understand the viewpoint of others?
5. Did I attempt to assess the strengths and weaknesses of all opinions expressed?
6. Did I encourage those who seemed reluctant to speak?
7. Did I help the chairman maintain a friendly, businesslike atmosphere? Keep the discussion moving purposefully?
8. Did I subordinate by own wishes to further the aim of the group?
9. My greatest contribution to the group was _____

Focusing on the evaluation of process can, of course, be overdone. It is useful, at first, as a teaching device to emphasize standards. When students become more adept, it may be needed only rarely.

In one respect, evaluation of the product of a group does not differ from that of the same work done by an individual. The result, weighed against the purpose, is judged by the completeness with which that purpose has been fulfilled. Has the subject been adequately handled? Has a possible solution that accords with the facts been offered? Have the results been presented in an intelligible form? In assigning a grade, we may run into difficulties. Some teachers believe the product of each group should be assessed and all members should receive the same grade. We have not found this practice successful. The conscientious student, working with laggards or absentees, justly resents being penalized. Group stimulation often produces amazing results from those who lack initiative to produce on their own, but it is unrealistic to expect this always. We know which pupils we find hard to motivate; we should not demand from students what we are unable to do ourselves. It is wiser and fairer to grade on an individual basis.

Groups require continual guidance if they are to work at maximum capacity. Therefore, it is not difficult, as we move from one to another, to be aware of those who produce and those who do not. It is always wise to discuss the method of grading with a class and never more essential than here, where the student is likely to think the situation so nebulous as to defy accurate appraisal. Constant supervision while work is in progress—private hints to the dilatory as well as judicious praise for the conscientious, suggestions that those who have achieved certain proficiencies devote themselves to more fruitful experiences—will disabuse the student of the idea that the individual performance is being submerged in the general.

We can avoid possible recriminations by periodically letting the student know where he stands. The task is neither arduous nor time-consuming. After several group meetings, the teacher may tell the class he wants them to know the grades recorded for individuals. He wants everyone to be sure of the basis on which evaluations have been made. Therefore, he is asking each to assess his own work and decide what grade he thinks he deserves. The sole purpose is that teacher and student understand each other before it is too late to do anything about it; if there are discrepancies in ratings, individual conferences will be arranged. Then he passes out dated slips of paper on which students are to record the grades they believe they deserve. The next day he returns the slips with his estimate; he asks for signatures and collects the slips to be filed. He then plans a study hour so that he will have time to talk with individuals. Usually there are not many; for the most part, students are fair judges of their own performances. Those who underestimate themselves need encouragement; those who value their work too highly need to face the facts.

Such periodic reports on progress will prepare the student for the final assessment from which there is no recourse. A dated and signed record of evaluations of his group skills should be included in the student's folder of written work. The essential thing here, as in all grading, is that the student know the teacher is keeping a record that is available to him and that his final grade is not determined by the whim of the moment.

EVALUATING WRITTEN EXPRESSION

In written expression, as in the other arts of language, the least critical factors are the easiest to appraise. Many standardized tests are available for measuring a pupil's ability to proofread for errors in usage, capitalization, spelling, and punctuation. But power over language, power more dependent upon thought than upon rules, does not lend itself so easily to objective testing procedures.

The really significant evidence, as always, concerns the effectiveness of the pupil's thought and changes in attitudes toward writing. Most of all, teachers want to know if the pupil takes more interest in writing, is less reluctant to revise, and is expressing his thoughts and feelings with more clarity and originality than before instruction. The aims of teaching expression through writing include the habit of clear, orderly thinking about matters within the learner's own experience and the power to organize and express thought and feeling effectively for others. For appraising such significant aims evidence can usually be found in only one place—the pupil's composition folder with its accumulation of writing saved over a period of time. The care and pride with which the pupil has kept his folder can be estimated. Has he saved all his papers? Are they carefully arranged? Are there revisions and practice drills and vocabulary improvement lists? Do the compositions actually exemplify growth in clear, orderly thinking? Is there a decrease in hasty generalizations, prejudice, and narrowness of sympathy and understanding? Do the later compositions avoid the errors and problems of the earlier ones? No better evidence of growth in written expression is likely to be located.

Some of the ways to evaluate written expression, garnered from many classrooms, are presented here.

REPEAT THE SAME CHECK SHEETS AT REGULAR INTERVALS   At the time of examining student folders, the teacher can help himself and the pupil by using a check sheet listing the items most important to examine in the folder. These check sheets include columns for both pupil and teacher to indicate degree of success. A portion of such a check sheet might look like this:

WRITTEN EXPRESSION—PUPIL-TEACHER CHECK SHEET

Directions to the student   These ten scales can help bring out more definitely some of the important learning you should gain from the writing we are doing this semester. For each item, rate yourself on a scale from 1 to 5. Number 1 is low and is described by the words at the left-hand side of the scale. Number 5 is high and is described by the words at the right-hand side of the scale. Numbers 2, 3, and 4 represent degrees between high and low, with 3 about average. For each of the ten scales, circle the number you honestly think describes your present ability.

Scale 1. Organization of material

Rambles; shows no plan or direction; thoughts just spill out as they occur; paragraphs not unified around a single idea.

Plans what is written; controls ideas and the order in which they occur; logical paragraphs built around one idea.

Student rating	1	2	3	4	5
Teacher rating	1	2	3	4	5

Scale 2. Effective sentences

All sentences put together the same way and of about the same length. Some sentences awkward or incomplete. Sometimes two sentences are run together with only a comma between.

Sentences varied and flexible in length. No instances of fragments, comma blunders, or long confused sentences.

Student rating	1	2	3	4	5
Teacher rating	1	2	3	4	5

Scale 3. Originality of thought

Tends to repeat ideas of others; does not think for himself; uses overworked words and phrases; afraid to be different from the crowd.

Thinks through to a position of his own; avoids thoughts and language that have been overworked; originates ideas of his own; independent thinker.

Student rating	1	2	3	4	5
Teacher rating	1	2	3	4	5

Scales 4 to 10, not shown here, may deal with spelling, handwriting, effective openings and conclusions, or whatever aspects of composition the teacher wishes to emphasize. Perhaps the most important point to make about such a check sheet concerns repetition. If the check sheet is used a number of times, the students begin to be more conscious of the scales in relation to their writing. Such lists serve more than the purposes of evaluation; they actually prove to be teaching devices, identifying desirable qualities and serving as levers to improve writing.

USE GRAPHIC CHARTS TO IDENTIFY PROBLEMS   Teachers often puzzle about the papers of students whose ideas are impressive but whose written expression does not measure up to their ideas. To encourage such students—and these are often above-average individuals—some teachers use double grades; others use graphic devices in evaluating each theme. Below are reproductions of three stamps used for grading themes.

Ideas	
Organization	
Mechanics	
Appearance	
Grade	

Content	
Organization	
Reasoning	
Style	
Mechanics	
Grade	

Subject _____	Style _____	
Originality _____	Mechanics _____	
Organization _____	Appearance _____	
	Grade _____	

Some teachers do not place any grades on papers before the students have had an opportunity to revise their compositions. As one of these teachers points out, "No one wants to return to the scene of the accident."

USE IDEAFORM PAPER   The National Council of Teachers of English prints a special composition paper prepared by the members of their High School Section Committee with the advice of teachers of college composition courses. On the back of each sheet are spaces for the teacher to comment on the ideas or content of the pupil's writing and a place to check such items as organization, spelling, and sentence structure.

APPLY EVALUATION FORMS   Forms like the following may be duplicated. This example features structure rather than originality, but in some classes this may be exactly what is needed. Forms such as these may always be altered to fit the aims of special situations. Junior high students require simplified variations of the forms shown here.

Is the purpose suited to the interests of the reader?

1	2	3	4	5	6	7
Minor degree of interest.		Probably of interest to most people.			Worthwhile purpose; provokes considerable interest.	

Is there a unifying idea?

1	2	3	4	5	6	7
Paper leaves no single impression.		Attempted, but subordinate ideas detract.			One idea dominates the paper.	

Do the details build up and make clear the purpose?

1	2	3	4	5	6	7
Details chosen with little regard to purpose.		Majority of details clarify purpose.			All details chosen to build up purpose.	

Is irrelevant material omitted?

1	2	3	4	5	6	7
Many unnecessary points.		Some wandering from the point.			No effort needed to follow; smooth transitions.	

Are mechanics acceptable for pupils' level of maturity?

1	2	3	4	5	6	7
Mechanics seriously interfere with attempt to read paper.		Average number of minor errors.			Almost perfect mechanically.	

Forms such as these may be modified by the aims a teacher emphasizes. For students whom the teacher judges to be in need of heightened powers of observation and an increased awareness of the values in all experience, the last three items of the chart directly above might be replaced by others more pertinent to imaginative or descriptive writing. Similarly, in the form that follows, originality of ideas might be deemed important enough—in certain classes or during certain periods of instruction—to replace organization as described in the present form.

Scale for Characterizing Student Themes

I. Organization [2]

1	2	3 4	5
A. Plan not evident on careful first reading.	Plan evident but lacking in logic or suitability to the subject.	A definite and suitable plan, clear throughout.	
B. Useless introduction and summary.	Simple and direct beginning and ending.	Attractive and effective beginning and ending.	
C. Two or more cases of lack of continuity between paragraphs.	Two or more cases of mechanical or awkward transitions.	Logical and unobtrusive continuity.	
D. Emphasis lost by obvious errors of proportion or position.	Adequate but not skillful use of proportion and position to secure emphasis.	Effective proportion of main point.	
E. Two or more pseudo-paragraphs, or ineffective paragraph fragments, or paragraphs containing irrelevant material.	Prevailingly simple, clear paragraphs but without adequate development.	Logical and effective paragraphs.	

COMPARE STUDENT ACCOMPLISHMENT   The teacher may compare his own students' works with the published standards of other teachers in such pamphlets as these: *Suggestions for Evaluating Junior High School Writing* (English Teachers of Western Pennsylvania); *Evaluating Ninth Grade Themes* (Illinois English Bulletin); *Evaluating Student Themes* (University of Wisconsin); *A Guide for Evaluation of High School Student Essays* (California Association of Teachers of English). All these and others, published by the National Council of Teachers of English, are helpful to both teacher and students. Sample student themes illustrate what the teacher hopes for in composition. Students may be led to compile similar sets of student themes, using their own compositions.

[2] The total scale would include presentation, content, and mechanics in addition to organization.

USE PUPIL EVALUATIONS   Read aloud a composition and ask everyone in the class to write a comment. Then collect and read aloud the comments, discussing comments and composition.

TRY SELF-EVALUATION   At regular intervals or just before grading periods, students write self-evaluations that include a statement of errors they have learned to overcome. For the first occasion of such self-evaluation, the students will profit from an example placed on the board. One model, dealing with conventions, read as follows:

> I have learned that I have a tendency to run together two different sentences. For instance, in my first essay I wrote: "I jumped as if I had seen a rattlesnake then I swallowed my tooth." Now I know what I used to do that was wrong. I hurried along without thinking how the sentences would sound if I spoke them. Also I know more about subjects and predicates, and I have finished the three mimeographed exercises on run-on sentences. Also I have deliberately written, as Mr. Jordan suggested, three Horrid Examples of run-on sentences, aware all the time that I was making the mistake. I think this cured me more than anything else.

Such self-evaluation may continue, dealing with other indications of growth: organization, paragraphing, spelling, awareness of loose thinking.

GRADE THE SAME SET OF PAPERS WITH OTHER TEACHERS   Groups of English teachers should read and discuss together the probing and useful ideas in Paul B. Diederich's article "How to Measure Growth in Writing Ability" [3] and Sister Judine's paperback *Guide for Evaluating Student Composition*.[4] Evaluating the compositions of students is always a highly subjective procedure. Teachers' estimates of quality vary markedly, and although it will never be possible to standardize such evaluation, it is almost always a profitable, and sometimes a very chastening, experience for a group of teachers to read the same set of compositions and rate them separately. For a secondary-school teacher, one value of grading papers with several of his collegues lies in the evidence on whether he tends to be an easy, typical, or overly severe grader. Quite often a grading bee of this kind results in a departmental study of the aims of composition and the standards that are reasonable to expect. Inevitably such a study brings about some improvement of instruction and evaluation.

EVALUATING READING COMPREHENSION

In this book, reading comprehension has been stressed; reading speed has received only incidental mention. This has been deliberate, for it is our ex-

---

[3] Paul B. Diederich, "How to Measure Growth in Writing Ability," *English Journal*, Vol. 55, No. 4 (April 1966), pp. 435–49.
[4] Sister Judine, *Guide for Evaluating Student Composition* (Champaign, Ill.: NCTE, 1967).

perience that the public—and many school people as well—place rate of reading in a much higher position of importance than it deserves. Early reading tests used in the schools were so designed that a high correlation between speed and comprehension was inevitable. This artificial result of these early tests led the unwary to conclude that fast readers were necessarily the best readers. We now know that when speed and comprehension are measured in such a way that the scores are not dependent upon each other, the correlation is positive but low.[5] Improvement in comprehension is more important than gains in speed.

If the primary aim of reading instruction is effective comprehension, those who evaluate such instruction will choose means suited to this aim. This implies that where standardized commercial tests are used for testing before and after a semester or year of instruction, the test used should feature comprehension of paragraphs, or even longer selections, rather than word recognition or sentence understanding. The directions and questions for the comprehension section of a test deserve scrutiny also. Sometimes the diction is so difficult that the test becomes an intelligence-vocabulary test before the reader ever arrives at any trial of his comprehension.

Many teachers consider the present commerical tests helpful but limited. These teachers, convinced that their home-made evaluation creates no more pitfalls than commercial testing, plan their own battery of appraisal. They record scores on comprehension questions for a series of reading selections on which broad time limits have been set. Usually these selections are spaced over a period of three or four weeks toward the close of the semester, and they represent the kind of material the teacher considers important for his students to understand. In addition to such evidence, these teachers also include in their evaluation some or all of the following kinds of appraisal:

1. Questionnaires and self-inventories that deal with attitudes, interests, and behavior.

> I am doing better in reading my assignments for other classes now. True ____
> Uncertain ____ Not so ____
> This past week, I have been reading _____
> I would read more if _____
> The reason I read better now is that I have learned _____
> My biggest problem in reading seems to be _____

Such inventories and questionnaires require judicious interpretation, but at least they throw more light on the reading problem than do mere low scores on a standardized test.

2. Progress charts and graphs kept by students and teacher. These may be growth charts such as those provided in the SRA *Reading Laboratory*. They may be home-made charts based on the answers to comprehension questions or teacher-devised questions for materials in local textbooks.

---

[5] Paul Blommers and E. F. Lindquist, "Rate of Comprehension of Reading: Its Measurement and Its Relation to Comprehension," *Journal of Educational Psychology*, Vol. 35, No. 8 (November 1944), pp. 449–73.

3. Self-appraisal by students, who evaluate their own reading by writing answers to such questions as these: How have I improved in reading? What have I learned that helps me to comprehend better? What can I do to improve my comprehension?

4. Case studies, diaries, or anecdotal records kept by teachers or counselors. In most schools, of course, it is not feasible to do this for more than a few crucial cases.

Good discussions of the various commercial tests and their values may be found in *Remedial Reading*,[6] and *How to Increase Reading Ability*.[7] Oscar K. Buros' *Mental Measurements Yearbook* [8] reviews the tests a teacher may wish to examine.

The following table presents tests used and gains recorded by two schools evaluating instruction in reading through such testing:

SCHOOL	NATURE AND DURATION OF INSTRUCTION	TEST USED	AMOUNT OF GAIN
Mexico High School, Mexico, Mo.	Reading instruction integrated with English; regular English classes; no homogeneous grouping; instruction aimed at improving vocabulary, word attack, and comprehension, speed; duration of one year	*Cooperative Reading Comprehension Test,* C1; *Diagnostic Reading Tests,* Section IV, Word Attack, Part 2, Silent	As mean percentile score gains: vocabulary 5.0, word attack 15.5, comprehension 7.0
Cole Junior High School, Denver, Colo.	Small reading groups; duration of one year	Nelson Silent Reading; Stanford Reading Test	2 to 2½ years in reading grade level for all except lowest IQ's, who had gains of about 1½ years

A limitation of all such reports: information about the pupils' retention of reading growth is seldom available. Do the subjects remain at the higher level or is their encouraging gain only a temporary result of their recent instruction? *After another year's lapse of regular school work, do they still retain the advantage gained?* Eventually, evaluation of reading progress must include evi-

---

[6] Maurice D. Woolf and Jeanne A. Woolf, *Remedial Reading* (New York: McGraw-Hill, 1957), pp. 85–87.

[7] Albert J. Harris, *How to Increase Reading Ability* (London: Longmans, Green, 1961).

[8] Oscar K. Buros, *Sixth Mental Measurements Yearbook* (Highland Park, N.J.: Gryphon, 1965). Buros covers all commercially available tests and all measurement books published in English-speaking countries. The reviews by well-qualified experts are informative, evaluative, and thought provoking.

dence on retention, and schools should plan to carry out repeated measures over a fairly long period of time.

The use of the mean or median to indicate progress is another limitation, for it obscures the changes in individual pupils. Some may regress, others progress, and yet the mean improves. Test-harried teachers, for instance, learn to raise a mean score by working intensively with pupils who are just below the mean on the first test. A chart of the scores of individual pupils tells more about real gains than does the rise in mean score for the group.

Like most evaluations in the arts of language, appraisal of improved reading skill ultimately rests upon a broad base. Genuine evidence of success must take into account important but complex results like these:

> the average number of books and other materials drawn from the school library—figured on a per pupil basis in order to avoid increase due merely to school population growth
>
> accurate evidence that the proportional number of students dropping out of school is declining
>
> improved average achievement of pupils on the same or similar test materials over a period of years

Standardized reading tests are useful but limited. Teachers will do well to use such tests when money for them is available. But the best evidence will always be students who read eagerly and comprehend what they are reading. Students voluntarily checking out books from libraries, students buying books they actually read—these actions diminish all other forms of appraisal. Some circumstantial evidence is very strong. When a tree bears apples, we can be quite certain it is a fruit tree.

(Evaluation continued, page 552.)

UNIT:

MEETING A CRISIS

Overview: Life is characterized by a series of crises, some great and some small. Whether they seem tragic or trivial to the observer, to the protagonist they assume importance because of his emotional involvement. How we react in a crisis depends at times upon the state of our physical health, but always upon our mental and emotional maturity. Our degree of maturity, in turn, depends upon the extent to which our experience has accustomed us to examine the possible courses of action, to predict the probable consequences of each, and to exert volition to follow the course that seems wisest.

Because the short story "attempts to reach some point of vantage, some glowing center of action from which the past and future will be equally visible," [1] and because it exists in sufficient quantities on all levels of difficulty, this literary form is featured in this unit suggested for classes where reading ability ranges from average to low. Because in the short story interest is centered on one individual in a crucial moment of his life, the less able readers can identify the problem, examine the motivation for the decision, and determine whether the outcome seems inevitable; the more highly endowed can gain subtler appreciations of this literary form.

This unit, depending as it does upon a single copy of a selection, or at most only a few, is suitable for the teacher who finds himself without enough sets of material for an entire class. At times, to give unity to the experience, the teacher may read a selection aloud; at other times, a few students may present plays and panels; the short poems may be made available to all by using a projector. The major portion of the time is spent on individual reading and the learning experiences growing out of this reading.

Aims

Understandings: Recognizing that literature presents problems with universal implications admitting of no one simple solution; sharpening awareness of the influence

---

[1] Frank O'Connor, "And It's a Lonely, Personal Art," in Francis Brown, ed., *Highlights of Modern Literature* (New York: New American Library, 1954), p. 77.

426

of habitual patterns of thinking and of belief in values in determining decisions made in moments of crisis.

Skills: Improving ability to recognize similarities and contrasts among various literary works; gaining skill in supporting a general statement with specific examples; improving ability to make pertinent contributions in discussion.

Appreciations: Developing sensitivity to the intellectual and emotional impact of literary works; extending imagination to apply concepts to various situations; sensing the irony underlying situations in literature and in life.

Time plan

Five weeks is the maximum time suggested for the unit. By eliminating some of the introductory experiences or by limiting the time for individual reading, the class may complete the unit in three to four weeks.

Launching the unit

To arouse interest in some of the concepts to be developed—comparison of themes in literature, application of ideas in literature to life—introduce some of the following experiences and activities.

▶ *Explore the differences between one who tries to think objectively and one whose habit of indulging in unrealistic daydreams clouds his perception*

1. "Gold Mounted Guns," by F. R. Buckley (1).[2] In order to help a boy make an important decision, the sheriff forces him to put himself in the place of the persons he has wronged. Have you ever tried to understand another by attempting to look at his problem from his point of view? What difficulties did you encounter?

2. "Mrs. Ketting and Clark Gable," by Ann Chidester (11). Mrs. Ketting, a confirmed dreamer, finds it impossible to face reality. Find in the story the evidence that proves Mrs. Ketting has been a dreamer for years; show why the choice she made was the only logical one within the framework of the story.

3. "The Road Not Taken," by Robert Frost (18). The decisions we make along the way make "all the difference." Discuss the use of symbolism. Discuss the roads open to the protagonists in the two stories just mentioned; what in the situations and in the characters themselves accounts for the choice each made?

4. "Miniver Cheevy," by Edwin Arlington Robinson (9). An ironical portrait of another dreamer who avoids facing reality, and "Death and General Putnam," by Arthur Guiterman (15). An imaginative recreation of events in the life of Putnam shows why the General was able to meet death gallantly. Compare the ideas and characters in these two poems with those in the two stories. Compare the short story and the poem as media for presenting characters and ideas.

Suggestions for writing: Write of a wise or unwise decision you have made; give the reasons that made you decide as you did and the effect of the decision on yourself and others. Or, write of a daydream as it persists in the mind of an imaginary character; tell how this dream might affect his action.

---

[2] The numbers in parentheses refer to anthologies that contain the stories mentioned; titles and full bibliographical data are given in the list of resources at the end of the unit.

► *Explore blocks to clear thinking and wise action engendered by tradition, culture, and environment; discover the conflicts likely to occur when a person is not sure which of his values are most important*

1. "England to America," by Margaret Prescott Montague (1). "Lord, but English people are funny." Elicit from the class examples of preconceived notions hampering judgment.

2. "The Enemy," by Pearl Buck (12). A Japanese couple, born in Japan but educated in America, find the two cultures in conflict when a decision is to be made. Discuss the possibility of conflict for the individual even within a nation such as ours, where different segments of the population have different values arising from various traditions, cultural strains, and environments.

3. *Confessional,* by Percival Wilde (13). A crisis helps the members of a family see themselves and each other as they really are, not as they thought themselves to be. Discuss confusion of values as a deterrent of wise choice.

4. "Mending Wall," by Robert Frost (18). We sometimes substitute clichés for thinking. Discuss with students some of the factors that influence the formation of personal values.

5. "The Unfamiliar," by Richard Connell (19). The people of Crosby Corners discover that courage has more than one dimension.

Suggestions for writing: Investigate some value you think helps guide your behavior, trying to discover what has led you to think this value important. Or, write of one specific instance where your belief in a certain value guided, or failed to guide, your action. Describe your feelings, both as you tried to decide and as you considered the results of your action.

► *Compare the decision of a real person with that of a fictional character*

1. "Daniel Webster," by John F. Kennedy (16). Webster is forced to choose between personal political advantage and his responsibility to the nation.

2. *Dust of the Road,* by Kenneth Sawyer Goodman (13). Using the symbolism of Judas Iscariot, the playwright portrays the remorse of the protagonists plagued by an unwise decision.

Suggestions for writing: Choose a decision made by a character in a book you have read or in a selection studied in class; explain the considerations weighed in making it and its effect. Or, compare a decision you have made with one made by a fictional character, showing similarities and differences in the motivation for the decision and in its results.

Developing the unit

PHASE I: TEACHER-PUPIL PLANNING

Purpose: To help pupils understand the conditions under which they will be working; determine a focus for the unit; develop a guide that will direct the reader's attention to the values to be considered; and agree upon a plan for recommending stories, for both inclusion in the unit and for recreational reading. Before planning the unit, the pupils should know that the number of copies of each selection is limited, and that while it is desirable that several read the same story, a copy may not be available at the time the reader wishes it; therefore, while waiting, he should substitute another selection.

Reviewing concepts: Ask students to copy in their notebooks O'Connor's statement concerning the short story (quoted in the "Overview" of the unit, page 426). Divide the class into three groups, giving each group one of the following assignments:

> Examine the stories studied thus far and determine how successful the authors have been in choosing and developing an action that suggests both the past and the probable future of the protagonist.
>
> Review the ideas concerning human behavior brought out in the discussions of the selections studied.
>
> Write a definition of irony as it is exemplified in the illustrations we have found in our reading (this for the top group).

Devising study guide and title: Place students in groups to use the discussion of material already read as a guide in devising questions applicable to the stories that students will select for individual reading, and then to use the questions in finding a title for the unit.

Teacher and pupils select the best questions from each group to formulate a guide for studying stories to be read in the unit. The following was made in one class:

STUDY GUIDE

1. In what conflict is the character involved?
2. What is the crisis? Could it have been prevented? If so, how?
3. Does this same crisis or a similar one occur often in life? Give examples.
4. Does the person meet the crisis successfully? Why or why not?
5. What hints do we have in his character and background that might explain the decision he makes?
6. Can you think of similar situations in which this person might be forced to make an important decision? What values would probably guide his decision?

The class then agrees upon an appropriate title for the unit. The class using the above study guide selected "Meeting a Crisis"; other classes, having devised slightly different guides have chosen "Moment of Decision," "The Best Choice," and "Conflict in Values."

Planning mechanical details: To insure that the class will run smoothly and that time will not be wasted, the teacher needs to do the following:

1. Be able to suggest the first story for each to read. Therefore, the volumes in the room library must contain stories presenting problems of varying complexity—some important to girls, others important to boys, and some important to both girls and boys. They must also offer various levels of reading difficulty. (The list of titles given at the end of the unit meets these requirements, but each teacher must compile his own from the material available and with a particular class in mind.)

2. Help students decide how to record information about stories they read that are not included in the unit. (Students, after the initial story, select the ones they wish to read; therefore, some means must be found to acknowledge reading which, because of the pressure of time or the story's failure to illustrate the theme of the unit, cannot be included.) Some classes have agreed to compile a list, with titles briefly annotated, to be posted in the library: "Recommended

for Students by Students." Others have prepared lists that the teacher might use in other units or might suggest as reading for individuals. (The reader can record the information on 3 x 5 cards; the compilation can be taken care of by volunteer groups.)

3. Provide means for informing the class of recommended stories and for segregating the volumes containing those stories. A bulletin board can be kept, where the one making the initial recommendation places a 3 x 5 card with title, author, volume, and his name. Anyone who reads the story adds his name. Students use the cards in finding suggestions for reading; the teacher, in forming groups for discussion. Or, perhaps the class can designate a shelf to which volumes containing recommended stories are returned; if the shelf is empty, the student knows he is to try to find "another first."

4. Provide a means of keeping the books circulating without waste of time. Allow students to sign up for stories they wish to read as soon as a copy is available. Give the responsibility for handling reservations to one or more of the faster readers, who can pass quietly around the room, discover the present reader, and arrange with him to pass it next to the one for whom it is reserved.

PHASE II: EXPERIENCES GROWING OUT OF READING

Discussion: Review the standards for discussion—the need for listening carefully to be able to make pertinent contributions, to evaluate support of generalizations, to summarize and synthesize; and the need for speaking clearly and to the point. After all pupils have read at least two stories, form groups of those who have read the same story or ones that can be related; meet with each group, while other students continue reading, helping individuals to relate the concepts and judge the skill of the author. Or, conduct a class discussion on the ideas and characters, exploring similarities and contrasts in the examples given.

Alternate between class and group discussions. Permit several students who wish to discuss a story to do so without supervision. Whenever possible, meet with a group who have read some of the more difficult stories to discuss the less obvious aspects of the author's technique.

Panels: Encourage the better readers to select stories not discussed to present to the class in the form of a panel, which will point up likenesses and differences. For one such presentation the following stories were chosen:

> "The Snob," by Morley Callaghan (5)
> "Split Cherry Tree," by Jesse Stuart (9)
> "The Piece of String," by Guy de Maupassant (7)
> "Freshman Fullback," by Ralph D. Paine (10)
> "Her First Ball," by Katherine Mansfield (17)

Expository writing: The purpose of this writing is to help students learn to support by the use of specific examples. These assignments will need to be repeated more than once, if not for the entire class, at least for individuals. For each type of assignment, work out an example with the class on the board. For the first assignment given below, use a story studied in the introduction of the unit, letting the class suggest several topic sentences before one is selected. For the second assignment, which is much more difficult, follow the same procedure; this time give the class several topic sentences from which to choose. After a choice has been made, accept examples from any stories individuals have read, helping students select salient details and secure precision of statement.[3] Assignments:

> Use a statement about a character, a setting, a story, or the like, as a topic sentence; develop a paragraph with one detailed example.[4]

> Using a general statement as a topic sentence, develop a paragraph by a series of three specific examples, each briefly stated.

> Write an essay defining *crisis* (substitute any term used in the discussion of the stories—conflict, universality, motivation of action, foreshadowing, irony); illustrate by two or three specific examples, each constituting one paragraph.

> The same as the preceding assignment, except that the development is to be in two paragraphs, one giving a detailed example and the other a series with each item concisely stated.[5]

Imaginative writing: The purpose here is to extend the imagination by applying concepts presented in literature to life situations. Assignments:

> Considering the implications of "The Road Not Taken," show how the life of any one of the characters in the stories we have read might have been different if he had taken another road; consider the changes necessary in his sense of values to have made the choice of another road possible.

> Select any character you have read about during this unit and place him in an imaginary crisis; show what you think he would do in such a situation.

Culminating experiences

Relating literature to life: Ask students to find, in newspapers, accounts of persons in moments of crisis. Let the class select the situation that seems to present the most complex problem and help students relate this to the concepts that have been developed. While one class was working on this unit, the story of a man who was attacked and beaten by a group of hoodlums appeared in the local papers; those who witnessed the scene were reported to have acted in the following ways: one stood and watched; one went to the help of the man and was severely beaten; one called the police; many ran away.[6] This episode was selected by the class and the following plan was devised by teacher and students, sparked by the question: What probable interpretations can be made to explain the reaction of the witnesses?

The students handed in questions to be used in guiding discussion; from these, with additions by the teacher, the following guide was devised:

DISCUSSION GUIDE

What was the probable motivation for each of these actions?
What kind of person might react in each of these ways?

---

[3] See "Program and Plan," pages 706–07.

[4] This may be all the slowest students can master; if so, the assignments from this point should be differentiated—for example, such individuals can move to the third assignment without achieving competence in the skills necessary for the second.

[5] Accounts of seemingly senseless acts of violence appear so frequently in the news media that teachers should have no difficulty finding a current example. Considering reasons for such actions is now more important than ever. Elinor Wylie's "Village Mystery" could be used to spark the discussion (21).

Who made the "wisest" decision? Why?
With which one are you most in sympathy?
With which one are you least in sympathy?
Do you think any of the persons you have read about in this unit would react as
    any of these spectators did in this situation?
Do you know anyone who might have a reaction similar to any of these?
Why is the public disturbed by such occurrences?

Students were given the guide and time to come to their own conclusions before being placed in groups for discussion; each group, having considered the
questions, selected one member to represent them in a round-table discussion in
which the teacher acted as leader.

Synthesizing ideas: Organize a series of student panels to review the various
aspects of the short story that have been covered in the essay assignments. Each
panel member illustrates the particular concept with an example taken from one
of the stories he has read. The series should be represented by as many stories as
possible, with few or no duplications.

Expository writing: In preparation for writing, help students compare the traits
of characters who seem to have met crises successfully with the characteristics of
those who apparently failed. Any similarities and contrasts? Usually students find a
sufficient number of clear-cut examples to show that many who were successful had
the following characteristics; in like manner, those who failed lacked these attributes:

> They were able to exercise self-control.
> They were able to forego a selfish advantage when the welfare of others was
> in question.
> They were able to discount immediate advantage for future benefits.

Ask students to explain maturity and to develop their ideas with examples taken
from literature and from personal experience.

Imaginative writing: Select either "Lucinda Matlock" (9) or "George Gray" (9)
by Edgar Lee Masters; show how one of the characters you have read about might
develop into such a person as is described in the poem. Write a poem that might
be used as an epitaph for one of the characters studied.

Evaluation

OF INDIVIDUAL GROWTH

The teacher has evidence, gained from the discussions and from the writing, upon
which to base an estimate of individual growth. The student may:

> examine his folder of written work to determine what improvement he has
> made.
> review his oral work and check progress in oral skills; a form, such as those
> suggested on pages 413 and 416, including only those items pertinent to
> the teaching in the unit, can be used as a guide.
> list the most important insights he has gained concerning one, several, or all
> of the following:
> > motivation of behavior
> > need for considering consequences of decisions

universality of certain problems and ideas

values that energize the personality versus those that enervate

Write a paper criticizing the adequacy of the following guide for use in making important decisions:

What is the principle by which I justify this course of action?

Will this action ultimately tend to bring about what I believe to be most worth while?

OF THE PLAN OF THE UNIT

Teacher and pupils may evaluate the unit as a whole to decide which experiences should be retained and which should be modified or eliminated if the unit is to be taught to another class; and to determine, on the basis of progress made, some of the learning experiences that should receive priority in the immediate future.

A FEW TITLES

1. "Five Minute Girl," Mary H. Bradley (1). Judy discovers that the price for saving face comes high.
2. "The Fifty-first Dragon," Heywood Broun (8). Self-confidence is gained in many ways.
3. "Four Men and a Box," Leslie G. Barnard (4). Only the promise of a clever man brought these four men safely out of the jungle.
4. "Snake Dance," Corey Ford (5). Jerry tries to play the game, but not on the football field.
5. "Prelude to Reunion," Oliver La Farge (5). Pride betrays a young college student into making a pledge he will have difficulty keeping.
6. "The Quiet Man," Maurice Walsh (2). A man of peace wins a moral and physical victory.
7. "Barn Burning," William Faulkner (2). Sarty learns that the time has come when he must think for himself.
8. "Prelude," Albert Halper (3). Prejudice and vandalism invade the rights of the individual.
9. "Bred in the Bone," Elsie Singmaster (6). A wife's decision brings about an event she is trying to avoid.
10. "Every Man for Himself," Robert Zacks (4). Jimmy faces the last test to qualify him for membership in the submarine crew.
11. "Traffic Incident," Edward Doherty (5). Grampa Jerry finally gets a traffic ticket that can't be fixed.
12. "One Throw," W. C. Heinz (4). Manari considers throwing the game in order to get even with the manager.
13. "Molly Morgan," John Steinbeck (2). Molly avoids discovering the truth because she prefers keeping her illusions.
14. "Pilot's Choice," Hunt Miller (4). Brady has to decide whether to risk the lives of his crew in a desperate attempt to effect a rescue.
15. "The Cub," Lois D. Kleihauer (4). A boy in his victory learns one of life's truths—a poignant discovery.
16. "The Last Lesson," Alphonse Daudet (14). The last lesson is an emotional experience for teacher, pupils, and townspeople.

17. "The Scapegoat," Paul Laurence Dunbar (20). Mr. Ashbury plans a revenge.
18. "We're the Only Colored People Here," Gwendolyn Brooks (20). Maud Martha, and Paul venture into unfamiliar territory.

MATERIALS AND RESOURCES FOR STUDENTS

1. *Great American Short Stories: O. Henry Memorial Award, 1919–1934.* Garden City, N.Y.: Doubleday, 1935.
2. Jennings, Frank G., and Calitri, Charles J. (eds.). *Stories.* New York: Harcourt, Brace & World, 1957.
3. Daly, Maureen (ed.). *My Favorite Stories.* New York: Dodd, Mead, 1949.
4. Berger, Eric (ed.). *Best Short Stories.* New York: Tab Books, 1958.
5. Wood, William R., and Husband, John D. (eds.). *Short Stories as You Like Them.* New York: Harcourt, Brace & World, 1940.
6. Singmaster, Elsie. *Bred in the Bone and Other Stories.* Boston: Houghton Mifflin, 1925.
7. Inglis, Rewey Belle, and Stewart, William K. (eds.). *Adventures in World Literature.* New York: Harcourt, Brace & World, 1936.
8. Lass, Abraham Harold, and Horowitz, Arnold (eds.). *Stories for Youth.* New York: Harper & Row, 1950.
9. Inglis, Rewey Belle *et al.* (eds.). *Adventures in American Literature.* New York: Harcourt, Brace & World, 1941.
10. Mikels, Rosa Mary (ed.). *Short Stories for English Classes.* New York: Scribner's, 1926.
11. Brickell, Herschel (ed.). *Prize Stories, 1950.* Garden City, N.Y.: Doubleday, 1950.
12. Cook, Luella B. *et al.* (eds.). *The World Through Literature.* New York: Harcourt, Brace & World, 1949.
13. Goldstone, George (ed.). *One Act Plays.* Boston: Allyn & Bacon, 1926.
14. Kielty, Bernadine (ed.). *A Treasury of Great Stories.* New York: Simon & Schuster, 1947.
15. Guiterman, Arthur. *Death and General Putnam.* New York: Dutton, 1935.
16. Kennedy, John F. *Profiles in Courage.* New York: Harper & Row, 1956; New York: Pocket Books, 1957.
17. Burnett, Whit (ed.). *Time to Be Young.* Philadelphia: Lippincott, 1945.
18. Untermeyer, Louis (ed.). *Robert Frost's Poems.* New York: Pocket Books, 1953.
19. Cook, Luella B., Miller, Jr., H. A., and Loban, Walter (eds.). *Adventures in Appreciation.* 3rd ed. New York: Harcourt, Brace & World, 1950.
20. Hughes, Langston (ed.). *The Best Short Stories by Negro Writers.* Boston: Little, Brown, 1967.
21. Wylie, Elinor. *Collected Poems.* New York: Knopf, 1963.

Teachers wishing to try a unit similar to this should consider the rich source of inexpensive material—both short stories and poetry—available in paperback editions. The purchase of several copies of each title allows one to remove appropriate stories and poems, staple them individually or by groups in heavy paper covers, and thus promote wider circulation.

APPRECIATION

TEN

LITERATURE:
BASIC APPROACHES

The human values of a particular literary experience are to be determined finally in relation to the needs of individual human beings.

THOMAS CLARK POLLOCK [1]

PERSPECTIVE

Proficiency in comprehending expository writing may be sufficient to insure understanding of a scientific treatise, an article on foreign affairs, or a passage from the encyclopedia, but such proficiency will not guarantee adequacy of response to a poem or a play. A young reader may be able to understand what happens in "The Pied Piper of Hamelin" without feeling "And the grumbling grew to a mighty rumbling; / And out of the houses the rats came tumbling," but to what avail? Older readers who fail to perceive the relationship of form to content in "My Last Duchess" miss much of the subtlety and the impact of the poem. Beyond the rational comprehension of facts and ideas, reading with appreciation demands emotional as well as intellectual perceptiveness—a totality of response in the individual, who must comprehend, interpret, and respond.

Appreciation of literature can result only from reading many books that have a genuine impact on the individual. The teacher's major goal is to guide the selection of books and to help adolescents read literature as human experience—not to teach a fixed number of books, a smattering of biographical data, or a miscellaneous collection of historical fact. Such information may support and extend but can never supplant the reader's perception of experiences communicated by the author. This chapter discusses the significance of literature in the educative process, the kinds of reading material having great impact on young people, and the attitudes and abilities needed for appreciation.

[1] Thomas Clark Pollock, *The Nature of Literature in Relation to Science, Language, and Human Experience* (Princeton, N.J.: Princeton Univ. Press, 1942), p. 203.

436

Literature as an Active Experience

Because literature offers a distillation of human experience, we find in it a significance comparable to that found in life. As an art form, literature achieves unity and order that evoke in the reader an emotional response. But its unique characteristic is the author's attempt to communicate imaginatively his insights concerning individual thought and action—insights into the meaning of experience.

> Other qualities of poetry and prose are important, but insight—the writers' personal view and his ability to see others as he sees himself, from within, his ability to estimate those inner values which cannot be checked by measuring rods, weights, clocks, and thermometers—is the indispensable quality, the distinguishing trait of literature. Literature may offer more than insight, but it cannot offer less, it cannot lack insight without becoming another kind of writing.[2]

The scientist and the social scientist look on life externally; they consider individuals in terms of the group, in relation to measurable truth or to social values. The literary artist searches for truth internally, viewing the human situation in relation to the individual and through the individual. As David Daiches writes:

> Fiction enables us to explore the recesses of man's head and heart with a torch; history allows us only the natural light of day, which does not usually shine into such places. Literature is Man's exploration of man by artificial light, which is better than natural light because we can direct it where we want it.[3]

Thus Winston Churchill lucidly describes the Allied occupation of Italy during World War II in terms of global strategy and social implications, but we need John Hersey to interpret its impact on individuals in books like *A Bell for Adano*. Both ways of looking at life are important; both must be taught to students; but the way of literature is the internal way, and it is in literature and through literature, almost exclusively among secondary-school subjects, that the student learns the humane approach to examining thought and action.

To share the insight of any author, an individual must respond actively as he reads. Emotionally and intellectually he enters the conflict between Huck Finn and his father or identifies with the misery of Richard Wright. Whenever the reader so enters the experience of art, the work may have greater impact on him than does any experience of life. At various times he shares an intensity of feeling, identifies with a diverse personality, looks on life through foreign eyes, becomes involved in a problem situation. It is this creative two-way process—the author attempting to communicate the experience, the reader reaching out to share it—that is the essence of literature.

[2] Henry Alonzo Myers, "Literature, Science, and Democracy," *Pacific Spectator*, Vol. 8, No. 4 (Autumn 1954), p. 337.
[3] David Daiches, *A Study of Literature for Readers and Critics* (Ithaca, N.Y.: Cornell Univ. Press, 1948), p. 24.

Values in Literature

Many perceptions and understandings acquired from primary experience may also be attained through literature. One person discovers the gnawing pains of self-incrimination by being unkind to a friend; another reaches similar insight by sharing the anguish of the unthinking protagonist in Robert Coates' story "The Need" or, if a child, of Maddie in *The Hundred Dresses*. Such experiences do not automatically result from reading, just as they do not automatically occur in life, but they may happen whenever literature touches a reader deeply. In describing what individuals gain from such literary experiences, we emphasize various things. We speak of the power of literature to delight, to humanize, to develop sensitivity—or we in some other way identify important outcomes of the literary experience. Most teachers, however, agree on at least three major goals—self-understanding, imaginative illumination, and a balanced perspective on life. Illustrated here in the reading of young people, these occur no less frequently in adult reading.

Literature can help us understand ourselves. It can reveal the significance of our emotions and actions—and reveal it in many ways. A child sharing the companionship of Charlotte and Wilbur in *Charlotte's Web* may sense for the first time the meaning of loneliness and the obligations of friendship, just as an adolescent may measure his own loyalties against the relationship of Jim Hawkins and Long John Silver in *Treasure Island* or an adult find similar illumination in *War and Peace*. Anne Emery's *Sorority Girl* offers young readers a chance to compare moral and material values in a context fraught with immediacy, just as Salinger's portrait of Holden Caulfield's search for stability offers an illumination of the turbulence of adolescence within a changing society. Through evaluating and sharing different images of life, each reader builds his own sense of values and alters the way he looks on himself and his world.

Some literature exists primarily to stimulate flights of fancy, to delight us with the brilliance of its execution. The whimsical nonsense of *Mary Poppins*, the richness of "The Eve of St. Agnes," the unrelieved suspense of "The Tell-Tale Heart"—such selections offer enjoyment, variety, and escape. We are swept by the adventure of Rogers' Rangers in *Northwest Passage* or the harrowing ordeal of *Boon Island;* we travel the underground railroad of Harriet Tubman in *Railroad to Freedom;* we revel in the eastern splendor of the Arabian Nights. Some readers find pleasure in the rolling cadences of "The Charge of the Light Brigade" or the rhymes of "Jabberwocky," while others delight in the deftly turned phrases of Kenneth Grahame, the economy and control of Joseph Conrad, the imagery of Emily Dickinson. Certainly it is more than a naive pleasure in the obvious for which teachers strive in attempting to develop appreciation. It is rather toward an appetite for different kinds of beauty, toward a heightened perception of artistic excellence, which may be discovered in the most subtle ways, so that a single person may rejoice in many kinds of literary experience.

Literature can give a balanced perspective. Through literature we test life by sharing experiences with many individuals. We feel sympathy and antipathy for persons quite different from ourselves and find more opportunities for choosing among different emotional responses and courses of action than life itself can offer. We may accept or reject the compassion of Peggotty in *David Copperfield,* the pride of Mary Lou Wingate in defying Northern soldiers in *John Brown's Body,* or the self-centeredness of Becky Sharp. In doing this we comprehend the needs of personalities quite different from our own. By evaluating different modes of conduct we deepen and extend our consciousness of the richness of life.

Through literature we can achieve freedom from the penalties and restrictions of singularity. Suspending our own values, we look at life through the eyes of Jane Austen, Mark Twain, or Henry James. The bitterness of Thomas Hardy forces us to consider life in ways we normally might reject, as do the romanticism of Emily Brontë, the controlled realism of Edith Wharton, and the frightening insights of James Baldwin.

This capacity of literature to permeate thought and emotion makes possible its ultimate impact. Some books shape our thinking slowly and subtly; some influence it not at all. A few selections affect us momentarily during critical periods in our life while others serve as continuing sources of influence.

Selecting Literature for Adolescents

What literature will provide significant experiences for adolescents? Not necessarily the same books that provide literary experiences for adults. Goethe's *Faust,* for example, is a great book; its profound analysis of good and evil offers insight to mature readers, regardless of time, place, condition, or philosophical orientation. But *Faust* is not a great book for most immature readers, who lack points of contact with the ideological struggle between Mephistopheles and Faust. For many, *The Bridge of San Luis Rey* or *Our Town* are better literary experiences, even though these works may fail the supreme tests of quality. In reacting to genuine but less demanding literary selections in terms of his peculiar personal experiences, the adolescent may learn how to read literature so that ultimately he can respond to the challenge of Goethe, Melville, and other great authors, whereas the direct classroom imposition of difficult selections like *Faust* may result in no reading experience at all. Indeed permanent damage to the reader's attitude may result if teachers disregard the level of maturity and experience of adolescents. For example, Annis Duff relates clearly how her daughter, even though nourished on a rich diet of books at home, responded to Coleridge in the eighth grade:

> We were made very much aware of a situation that developed at school when a young teacher, still not accustomed to the temperament of boys and girls at this age, undertook a detailed study of "The Rime of the Ancient Mariner." Simply read through as the wonderful adventure of a ghostly ship and its crew, it would probably have been well liked. But discussion of its mystical and meta-

physical aspects went against the grain because it was neither understandable nor interesting to eighth-graders, and they refused to take it seriously. . . . It was a wise man who said, "There are poems whose fineness and delicacy are of such a character that in forcing them prematurely on the attention one runs the risk of rendering them permanently distasteful, or vulgarizing them by incongruous association." (W. J. Alexander in the Preface to *Shorter Poems*) . . .

Six years after this dreary little eighth-grade episode a group of our daughter's classmates were talking about their work in English literature in college. When one of them spoke of reading "The Ancient Mariner" there was the immediate question, "How did you like it this time?" The girl hesitated before answering, and then said quite seriously, "I really tried to like it because the others thought it was so wonderful. But I still kept feeling upset the way I did when Mr. T. talked about guilt and penance and all that . . . ."[4]

Does this suggest then that all classics be eliminated from our program in literature? Not at all. Testimony from teachers and evidence from research indicate clearly that many major works continue to transmit meaning to the young.[5] *Macbeth, Julius Caesar,* and *Silas Marner* are today the only longer works taught in a majority of public schools,[6] no doubt because they continue to be well received, but students respond to many other works of distinction. Shakespeare, Steinbeck, Hemingway, Dickens, and Hardy were recently identified as favorite authors by one large group of twelfth-graders; the same students urged that books like *Lord of the Flies, 1984, Crime and Punishment, The Scarlet Letter, War and Peace, Grapes of Wrath,* and *Return of the Native* be added to the school curriculum.[7]

Any book offering genuine insight into the significance of human thought and action can provide a literary experience. Much writing for and about adolescence, like *Seventeenth Summer* or *Old Yeller,* will strike a reader with telling impact only during a brief interval in his life. But although they lack the universality of major writing, these stories can offer the youth a moment of insight into his own world as only literature can. From such active participation in a literary experience, mature appreciations may grow. The girl who this year responds to Maureen Daly may next year discover Charlotte Brontë and later Willa Cather and Jane Austen. Such growth occurs slowly over a long period of time, but there is a close affinity between the girl who perceives meaning in Maureen Daly's work and the adult who turns to Jane Austen for insight into human relationships.

[4] Annis Duff, *Longer Flight* (New York: Viking, 1955), pp. 113–15. Teachers of English will be interested in this warm, book-length discussion of family reading experiences.

[5] See Helen M. Robinson, "What Research Says to the Teacher of Reading: Reading Interest," *Reading Teacher,* Vol. 8, No. 6 (March 1955), pp. 173–77; Phyllis Lenner, *The Proof of the Pudding* (New York: John Day Co., 1957); George W. Norvell, *The Reading Interests of Young People* (Boston: Heath, 1950).

[6] Scarvia Anderson, "Between the Grimms and *The Group;* Literature in American High Schools" (Princeton, N.J.: Educational Testing Service, 1964).

[7] James R. Squire and Roger Applebee, *A Study of English Programs in Selected High Schools Which Consistently Educate Outstanding Students in English,* Cooperative Research Report No. 1994 (Urbana, Ill.: Univ. of Illinois Press, 1966), pp. 167–70.

Modern classics for young people as well as standard selections from the literary canon deserve a place in the program. In 1967 the National Council of Teachers of English reported that its members had listed the following as the best books for young people published during the past twenty-five years. Titles that appear in more than one category were suggested by different groups of respondents.

OUTSTANDING BOOKS FOR ADOLESCENTS

Johnny Tremain, Esther Forbes
Diary of a Young Girl, Anne Frank
A Separate Peace, John Knowles
Catcher in the Rye, J. D. Salinger
To Kill a Mockingbird, Harper Lee
Lord of the Flies, William Golding
Light in the Forest, Conrad Richter
Swiftwater, Paul Annixter
The Old Man and the Sea, Ernest Hemingway
Wrinkle in Time, Madeleine L'Engle

OUTSTANDING ADULT BOOKS FOR YOUNG ADULTS

FICTION AND NONFICTION

Catcher in the Rye, J. D. Salinger
Lord of the Flies, William Golding
A Separate Peace, John Knowles
The Old Man and the Sea, Ernest Hemingway
To Kill a Mockingbird, Harper Lee
Profiles in Courage, John F. Kennedy
The Pearl, John Steinbeck
Cry, the Beloved Country, Alan Paton
Kon-Tiki, Thor Heyerdahl
Diary of a Young Girl, Anne Frank

DRAMA

Death of a Salesman, Arthur Miller
The Glass Menagerie, Tennessee Williams
The Crucible, Arthur Miller
A Man for All Seasons, Robert Bolt
A Raisin in the Sun, Lorraine Hansberry
The Miracle Worker, William Gibson

POETRY

"Fern Hill," Dylan Thomas
"Do Not Go Gentle into That Good Night," Dylan Thomas
"Auto Wreck," Karl Shapiro
"Elegy for a Dead Soldier," Karl Shapiro

The role of the teacher of literature is clear: to help young people find meaning and experience in literary works; to help them develop appreciation for literary form. He can lead students to see parallels between the greed of Silas Marner's world and that apparent today, between the fear of the unknown expressed by Henry Fleming in *The Red Badge of Courage* and the adolescent's own ambivalence before uncertainty. He can also help them see how the artistry of George Eliot and Stephen Crane creates the impact of the literary experiences. Helping readers relate literature to life is one responsibility of the teacher, but such interaction is possible only if the elements of a book actually touch elements in the reader's experience. Helping students understand how an author achieves artistic unity is another of the teacher's responsibilities, but such understanding builds slowly, requiring experience with literary works varying in degrees of excellence. Appreciation of both content and form can be fostered; it cannot be imposed by royal edict.

Students can learn more easily to recognize universality of subject matter than to savor niceties of style; naturally their first reaction is to characters and the story. This interaction between book and reader may not always be favorable. Parallels that stir unpleasant relationships can sometimes cause books to be rejected. Anxieties awakened by Murray Heyert's "The New Kid" may prevent identification by a boy experiencing problems in group acceptance. When aware of potential problems, teachers can plan appropriate introductory activities. For example, Jessamyn West's story "The Hat," from *Cress Delahanty*, deals with an adolescent girl's attempt to impress a boyfriend. Boy readers are sometimes made uncomfortable by Cress' antics, and their reactions can block free discussion. One imaginative teacher assigned for reading at the same time "That's What Happened to Me," a story in which a boy wished to impress his peers, and read aloud another short story in which a boy wishes to impress a girl, "I'm A Fool." The resulting discussion focused on the desire to impress others. By relating the problem of Cress Delahanty to a widely experienced human need, the teacher made it possible for most readers to respond to the literary experience.

In selecting literature, teachers avoid yielding to the ephemeral and the meaningless. Not all books written for adolescents attempt to communicate genuine experience. Not all are stylistically acceptable. Many—too many—are trite, contrived commercial ventures feeding on stereotyped preconceptions existing in the adolescent's mind. In selecting literature, teachers will want to encourage the reading of the best books to which immature readers can respond. Realistically, teachers recognize that the level of quality will not always be as high as desired and that here as elsewhere in the program they can raise the student's level of response only through sound and organized guidance. Exercising such guidance requires that the teacher provide a balanced literature program. Appropriate reading in all genres should be part of each pupil's experience.[8]

In determining the actual reading interests of their students, most teachers find it helpful to examine a few studies of reading preference.[9] Who can say whether the continued popularity of animal themes among readers in grades 7 and 8 is a reflection of a widespread concern for pets or an indirect expression of the thirteen-year-old's desire to assume the responsibility of caring for a dependent? Who is certain that the world of *Great Expectations* is not closer to some boys than the America of Gregor Felson or Stephen Meader? Certainly teachers must be careful to examine the reactions of each individual and to interpret them in relation to his total behavior.

Undoubtedly consideration of taste and propriety must also affect the selection of all reading materials. Can we not discourage the reading of brutal, sordid exploitations of human misery, yet urge students seeking "strong" fare to consider *Cry, the Beloved Country* or *Lord of the Flies*—books with "earthy" qualities that possess other values, such as authenticity of character and concern for human dignity?

Ultimately the improvement of taste must start with the students' level of appreciation. This necessarily demands that young readers be taught to evaluate and reject both saccharine portraits of an artificial, adolescent world as well as the synthetic drug-store potboilers. Over a period of time the immature reader can learn to distinguish between genuine and contrived experiences. The teacher's job is to find the level of active response and then to build upon it and extend it.

Skills and Attitudes Needed for Reading with Appreciation

Skills involved in literary analysis must be taught, but the way the reader approaches a selection is important, too. Certainly critical reading of literature can occur only if the reader is skilled in interpreting both the form and the content of a literary selection. Beyond the basic competence of comprehension, students must acquire advanced skills in reading that enable them to explore the full richness of literature. A recent national study of teaching practices found that few secondary-school teachers distinguish clearly between teaching the text and teaching how to read the text as preparation for additional literary experiences.[10] Among the more important abilities to be developed

---

[8] James Lynch and Bertrand Evans report widespread neglect of the essay in *High School English Textbooks; A Critical Appraisal* (Boston: Little, Brown, 1963).

[9] Some of the more interesting studies of reading preferences are listed at the end of this chapter.

[10] James R. Squire, "Evaluating High School English Programs," *North Central Association Quarterly*, Vol. 40, No. 3 (Winter 1966), pp. 247–54.

are those involved in seeing relationships between form and content, in perceiving the development of character, theme, symbol, and in detecting the multiplicity of meaning. Young readers need these skills to understand the over-all impact of a selection and to read literature more fully on their own. Thus instruction needs to emphasize the use of each skill in understanding a complete selection, rather than the development of the skill in isolation.

Moreover, teachers need to remember that basic sensitivity to literary form develops over the six years of secondary school. Most skills are acquired slowly, at different times, and in relation to many diverse selections. Most of the important skills fall into three categories:

> those needed to perceive the beauty in form that closely parallels content: the author's selection of media; his uses of rhythm and balance; the interrelationship of setting, tone, and point of view
>
> those needed to perceive development: the structure of the narrative, the logic of the characterization, the relationship of incident and theme
>
> those needed to explore meanings below the surface: the basic theme, the connotative effect of words, the use of imagery, the signs and symbols, the satire and irony, the underlying myth or archetype

Procedures for teaching the several skills are described in detail in the Suggested Learning Experiences presented later in this chapter.

Young readers also need to overcome many immature kinds of responses that interfere with their ability to interpret literature. Anxious to encourage factual comprehension or stylistic understanding, teachers can place too restrictive an emphasis on the literary selection itself and too little on the way in which literature is best approached—on *how* the reader looks at and responds to a story or a poem, rather than on the poem itself. Indeed the way in which a reader learns to approach a romance like *Ivanhoe* and the attitudes he takes away from reading it will have a more lasting influence on his appreciation of literature than will the specific understandings derived from the Scott opus.

To emphasize ways of approaching literature that produce intelligent and appreciative reactions, teachers focus on improving the processes each individual undergoes in responding to a poem, play, or work of fiction, rather than on the development of knowledge about a single work or on the refinement of discrete reading skills. In doing this, teachers become, at least momentarily, less interested in teaching "The Sire de Maletroit's Door" or in increasing the student's ability to detect rising and falling action than in considering the over-all methods the younger reader employs in approaching, responding to, and evaluating any literary work. Among the more helpful attitudes to be cultivated are responding with genuineness, suspending judgment, weighing evidence objectively, searching for several meanings, and fusing intellectual and emotional reactions.[11]

---

[11] This analysis is based on a study of adolescent response to reading. See James R. Squire, *The Response of Adolescents to Literature* (Champaign, Ill.: NCTE, 1964).

REACTING WITH GENUINENESS   Real appreciation develops only through h̶
We need to think for ourselves, even if our judgment is not always the b̶
We reject or accept, like or dislike, are scornful or enthusiastic about a poem̶
a character, or a passage because of the effect produced on us as we read.
Many subtleties of idea and image will escape us until we become keenly
attuned to the complexities of fine writing, yet if literature is ever to work
its magic, we must learn to be honest with ourselves. If a young reader finds
pleasure in the poems of Emily Dickinson, well and good; if not—if he finds
pleasure only in "Casey at the Bat"—let teachers accept him at this level and
try to help him find pleasure in other kinds of poetry. Too often adolescents
seem to mistrust their own feelings and ideas and substitute instead the
pronouncements of their teachers or the standards of their peers.

Teachers expect and welcome a range of response to any selection, but
need to avoid placing too high a premium on enjoyment and place more on
understanding. "Isn't this a great poem?" should be less the question for a
class than "What is the poet attempting to say? How does he say it? What
effect does the poem have on you?" Once students find that they are required
neither to wax eloquent over every selection nor to reflect standard literary
judgments, they become more willing to express and analyze their basic
feelings.

Genuineness in response can be encouraged or discouraged through such
approaches to instruction as the following:

CLASSROOM APPROACHES THAT TEND TO STULTIFY GENUINENESS	CLASSROOM APPROACHES THAT ENCOURAGE GENUINENESS
Offering students prejudgments on a selection before reading and urging them to find out why the selection is "good"	Evaluating a selection with students after it is read and understood
Making students feel that there is only one acceptable response to a selection	Accepting a range of responses to any selection, providing that these do not conflict with verifiable facts
Overemphasizing the externals surrounding literature, such as the author, the period in which he lived	Emphasizing the literary experience— what a selection says or what it does to the reader

SUSPENDING JUDGMENT   Mature readers approach interpretation with a spirit
of tentativeness and delay final judgment until they search for possible
meanings throughout a selection. Most of us learn through experience that
real understanding develops slowly and that people and situations are not
always what they initially appear to be. Young people must discover that in
the well-constructed story the inexplicable behavior of persons like Miss
Haversham or Rochester ultimately becomes clarified; more important perhaps, they discover that at times characters who may initially seem clear-cut
and understandable—Mrs. Penn in "The Revolt of Mother," Mattic in *Ethan
Frome*—are later revealed to possess unsuspected complexity.

:hers do to help students develop tentativeness in interpre-
they may teach students how meaning is discovered—that
:r, for example, readers examine an individual's statements
ll as what others say about him. To understand the necessity
)n, students need only study a selection in which a charac-
himself departs radically from the views of others as, for
's in "A Mother in Mannville." In such cases the reader is
he basic nature of the person.

Certainly young readers can be encouraged to withhold final judgments
regarding elements other than characterization, such as the symbolic meaning
or the basic intent of the author. Usually these cannot be determined completely until the total selection is weighed. In the secondary school, much of
the danger of rash, thoughtless prejudgment occurs in assessing characters,
since it is with respect to people that many students tend to jump to conclusions.

WEIGHING EVIDENCE OBJECTIVELY   Readers have been known to react so negatively to the indiscriminate enthusiasm of the girl in "I Can't Breathe" that
they miss the humor of the story; others, enraged by the adolescents who
call Stephen clodhopper in Sara Addington's story, view the selection primarily
as one depicting injustice and snobbery rather than compassion and understanding. Indeed, a sympathetic identification with Stephen may prevent
understanding the actions of the girl in the story. Still other readers respond
so favorably or unfavorably to the theme or the imagery in poems like "To
an Athlete Dying Young" or "Richard Cory" that they accept, reject, or
misinterpret because of their strong emotions. With such a statement as "He
must have been crazy to shoot himself with all his money," they dismiss
"Richard Cory" without seeing the irony implicit in the poem. Boundlessly
optimistic in viewing the future, few young people will express anything
except sympathy for the death of a young athlete and either overlook or
repudiate Housman's solace in seeing the "man" pass before the "name." Thus,
emotional predispositions often color reactions to literature and block sound
perception and interpretation.

Insisting that students substantiate their judgments encourages them to
weigh impressions and evidence. If a reader wishes to deny that Housman
finds solace in the death of a youthful hero, let him find documentation and
let the teacher and other students be alert to point out ideas and images that
cannot be reconciled with such interpretation. Many situations and motives
arouse strong feelings, and unless the incidents are studied carefully, readers
may accept only their initial emotional reactions.

SEARCHING FOR SEVERAL MEANINGS   Young readers need to learn ways of
exploring the complexity of literature. Skill in detecting irony, satire, and

symbolism contributes to the perceptiveness of readers, but the development of a basic orientation that fosters this searching attitude extends beyond the acquisition of specific skills. What is to be encouraged is an interest in detecting nuances and an appreciation for richness and complexity.

FUSING INTELLECTUAL AND EMOTIONAL REACTIONS Any successful attempt to improve response to literature recognizes the importance of emotional as well as rational reactions. To a considerable degree, the reader relies on his emotions as a guide in entering the literary experience, or else he does not respond actively and vitally. However, the analytical study of literature is a valuable and necessary supplement to emotional experience and one that often follows it. Jarred by the impact of a Poe story, a reader may try to discover how the effect is achieved. Individuals can sympathize with Amelia in *Vanity Fair* without consciously analyzing their feelings, yet a study of passages to which they react may clarify and even heighten their understanding and appreciation. There is strength in responding to the emotional impact of the whole as well as in relying on a detailed textual analysis of the parts; to help pupils acquire both habits, teachers avoid overstressing either.

There is only one sure way for students to learn to appreciate literature and that is by reading. The teacher's responsibility is to encourage wide reading throughout secondary-school years and to supplement this effort by instructing students in how to read literature. In teaching any selection, however, the teacher does well to remember that it will be an attitude toward reading—toward Shakespeare, toward poetry, toward "The Rime of the Ancient Mariner"—that the pupil will retain long after he has forgotten the particular lesson.

THE TEACHING PROBLEM

ORGANIZING INSTRUCTION

Certainly there is no royal road to the organization of significant classroom experiences in literature. Beyond recognizing that instruction in literature, as in the skills of communication, is most effective when organized by units of instruction, teachers find different kinds of arrangements to be appropriate at different times. Many units are based on literature, since poems, essays, stories, and the like provide content for discussion and writing. Within each unit, important reading experiences may be introduced for individuals and groups as well as for the total class. Thus several problems in planning must be considered.

Approaches to Teaching Literature

The sound approaches to teaching are those emphasizing literary experiences rather than the facts surrounding literary works. Ultimately the teacher's basic competence is more likely to determine his effectiveness than any method of organization; yet certain kinds of units appear to be appropriate for particular groups.

THEMATIC AND TOPICAL ARRANGEMENT Thematic or topical units deal with values, ideas, and human experiences. To compare the treatment of similar ideas, readers direct their attention to the content of literature in such thematic units as "In Sight of Maturity" (*Johnny Tremain, The Yearling, Swiftwater*); "Justice" (*Mutiny on the Bounty, Les Misérables, The Caine Mutiny*); "The Meaning of Love" (*Romeo and Juliet, Cyrano de Bergerac,* "The Eve of St. Agnes"). In well-organized thematic units, the central experiences with which each selection deals are closely associated with the unifying theme.

Topical units also provide opportunities for contrasting similar selections, although usually on a much broader basis. Such topics as "The Pioneers Move West," "Survival," and "Meeting Successful People" are of interest to younger adolescents and offer a framework for relating diverse literary pieces, but clearly the organization here is less intimately related to the central ideas expressed in the selections than in most thematic units. Whereas the themes usually illuminate universal human experiences, the topics tend to be general categories for grouping related ideas. For example, *The Yearling* reveals certain patterns of family life in depicting the Baxter family's struggle for existence in the Florida interior and has sometimes been taught in units on "Family Life" or "Back Country America"; yet the novel is basically a study of Jody's struggle to assume adult responsibility. When introducing such a selection to illuminate a topic, teachers can see that readers perceive the unique experiences of the story before introducing the elements related to the general topic being studied. Topical units are often introduced during the junior high school years when wide reading of many books is characteristic of the student-reader.

ARRANGEMENTS BY TYPE AND BY LITERARY GENRE Units based on any form can encourage development of concepts of genre. All adolescents need some direct assistance in learning to respond to poetry, drama, and the essay, and many require help with difficult problems in interpreting fiction. However, the skills and insights needed for reading any genre can often be considered within the context of a different kind of unit. What is more important than the over-all framework in which class study is organized is that the approach to each selection focus on the unique form, ideas, and experiences communicated.

THE STUDY OF A SINGLE TEXT   Major works of literature offer such a rich
tapestry of interwoven images, themes, and experiences that they are difficult
to study within a thematic, topical, or typological unit. During each school
year, many teachers provide for the common study of at least one longer text
that seems to possess significance for most adolescents in the class. Certain
works, such as *Johnny Tremain* and *Lord of the Flies,* are often taught in
separate two- or three-week units, as are such standard literary fare as
Macbeth, Julius Caesar, and *My Antonia.* Intensive concentration on a single
work permits the study of many interrelated ideas and formal characteristics
in terms of the unified purpose of an entire selection.

ARRANGEMENTS OVEREMPHASIZING EXTERNALS   Approaches that enable the
teacher to place primary emphasis on the critical reading of the selections
themselves provide the most compelling literary experience.[12] Through the
considered use of almost any approach, an intelligent teacher may direct
continuous attention to the experiences conveyed by literature and to the ways
in which literature conveys these experiences. The exploration of ideas and
of literary method may be confined to works written during a single literary
period or even by one author. However, too often units stressing historical
background or lives of authors degenerate into little more than factual surveys
of incidents and social settings more appropriate to the social science classroom
than to the English class. The necessary background information to support
the study of a given selection can be presented even in units focusing on
ideas and literary experiences. The necessary literary considerations must be
part of reading in units focused on historical or social periods. But concentrating primarily on biographical detail—such as using *Huckleberry Finn* to
advance a study of the life of Mark Twain rather than to illuminate understanding of human dignity and freedom—misdirects the focus of the reader.
Such emphases seldom encourage growth in appreciation and tend, according
to one professor of English, not "to teach what literature is about, but only
about literature—or perhaps we should say, around literature." [13]

ARRANGEMENTS STRESSING HUMANITIES   During recent years, schools have been
introducing courses and programs in the humanities, emphasizing the relationship of literature to other forms of art. Many such programs are arranged
chronologically or by major cultural periods. Others attempt to provide an
introductory esthetic education by studying related principles of creative
endeavor in art, architecture, film, music, and literature. Whatever the organization, a perception of literature as human and esthetic experience is unlikely

---

[12] Dwight Burton found that concentration on themes resulted in as great a measured
growth in literary appreciation as did instruction that emphasized style. Dwight Burton,
"An Experiment in Teaching Fiction," *English Journal,* Vol. 42, No. 1 (January 1953),
pp. 16–20.

[13] James J. Lynch, "The English Teacher's Greatest Resource," *English Journal,* Vol. 45,
No. 10 (October 1956), pp. 388–94.

to emerge if study focuses on ideas about literature and the humanities rather than on the literary experience itself. Relating literature to other art forms may lead young people to fresh perceptions concerning the nature of esthetic experience, but many of the newer humanities courses, in their emphasis on the external history and characteristics of culture, represent one more evasion of genuine literary study.

ARRANGEMENTS STRESSING LITERATURE OF PARTICULAR GROUPS AND COUNTRIES
Recently some teachers have sought special opportunities for young people to read widely in literatures not well represented in conventional school anthologies. Thus, a two-week study of African literature in English might offer some insight into the place of literature in an emerging culture through works like Chinua Achebe's *Things Fall Apart*.[14] Similarly, literary selections written by American Negroes are sometimes studied intensively for a period of time. In organizing instruction in this way, teachers need to clarify their fundamental purpose, lest literature be taught only for its social implications.[15]

Teaching Literature to the Entire Class

Selecting worthwhile literature for presentation to any class of pupils poses such a major challenge that some teachers advocate meeting the problem through the almost exclusive use of group and individual reading. Each of these procedures is considered later in this chapter. While both offer sound and manageable ways of providing for individuals, in most classrooms students need to share a few common literary selections. Such unifying experiences provide an underlying core of ideas—a point of contact between the intellectually able and the intellectually limited—on which a subsequent program of guided group and individual reading may be based. Such common study also permits the teacher to provide the intensive help students need when confronted with difficult selection. Few would claim, for example, that any but the very superior pupils be encouraged to read Shakespeare without careful classroom assistance from the teacher, or even that the very superior are ready for such independent reading until after a carefully planned program of instruction. Teachers can organize classrooms to present special lessons to groups of students, but some direct instruction is usually presented through common class activity.

[14] An excellent introduction to non-Western literature is presented by Francis Shoemaker in "New Dimensions for World Cultures," *The Record*, Vol. 919, No. 7 (April 1968), pp. 685–98.

[15] For guidance in selecting literature written by and about black Americans, see Charlemae Rollins, ed., *We Build Together* (Champaign, Ill.: NCTE, 1967), and Barbara Dodds, *Negro Literature for High School Students* (Champaign, Ill.: NCTE, 1968). Also, Abraham Chapman, *The Negro in American Literature* (Stevens Point, Wis.: Wisconsin Council of Teachers of English, 1966). Available from NCTE. The Dodds book includes a unit taught in the Detroit public schools.

Not all plays and novels elicit responses with various dimensions of meaning. Many difficult, reflective selections, like *Hamlet, Moby Dick,* and *The Scarlet Letter,* must properly be reserved for mature readers, since in both content and form they possess obstacles that discourage any but the most persistent youngsters. Other worthwhile selections, however, captivate both the gifted and the slow and involve many readers within a single classroom. Some junior high school readers, for example, react only to the adventurous narrative of *Johnny Tremain,* while others recognize the symbolic association of Johnny's physical handicap with his warped and restricted outlook on life; a few, perhaps, grasp the intimate parallel between the boy's growth toward maturity and the colonies' struggle for independence. All students read the book with profit, but at different levels of meaning.

Certainly provision needs to be made for some teacher-directed study of books that interest the least able and yet tax the gifted. Probably one or two classics, either standard or modern, should be introduced in most classes—perhaps one novel and, beyond the ninth grade, one long play in addition to numerous short selections. Certain familiar works continue to be taught successfully. For example, *Macbeth, Tom Sawyer,* and *Our Town* are taught to entire classes; in contrast some teachers reserve such selections as *Lord Jim* and *The Mayor of Casterbridge* for special groups. The identification of the specific books to be taught to heterogeneous classes and those to be assigned only to special groups is a task that requires both understanding of literature and understanding of the students to whom the literature is to be taught.

FREEDOM TO READ   The response of today's students to the vigorous, realistic fiction produced by American writers of the twentieth century frequently creates problems with book selection. Surely no student should read in school a book that he must hide from his parents at home, but teachers of English who pride themselves on introducing young people to the American cultural heritage must see that the realistic fiction of the past sixty years is one of America's great contributions to the world of letters. A school-wide policy for the selection and use of literary works is mandatory in today's schools.[16] Teachers must ever be ready to defend the works they choose for class study, but in the face of parental opposition, they should permit substitute choices. If a parent prefers that his son not read *Catcher in the Rye* or *Intruder in the Dust,* substitute *A Separate Peace* or *To Kill a Mockingbird.* But do not penalize other students in the class. A sound school policy that all teachers understand and a willingness to discuss problems openly with parents does much to reduce the possibility that problems will arise.

APPROACHING INDIVIDUAL SELECTIONS   The classroom approach to be used in studying any selection must depend in large measure on the work itself. During the past few decades, distinct schools of literary criticism have re-

[16] A widely used procedure for handling complaints is discussed in Edward Gordon, ed., *The Student's Right to Read* (Champaign, Ill.: NCTE, 1962).

vealed values in psychological, sociological, formalist, mythic, and archetypal approaches. Each approach has contributed to our understanding of literature, and each can assist young people in unlocking the experience that a particular work has to offer. Human motivation, so prominent in psychological approaches, seems singularly important in reading such plays as *The Glass Menagerie;* some emphasis on literature and society is important in reading books like *The Great Gatsby* or *The Grapes of Wrath,* which can best be understood against the cultural scene; formalist approaches, concerned largely with the esthetic structure of a selection and the intrinsic relationship of parts to whole, are valuable in studying much poetry. The power of collective and communal myth provides some works with an enduring, inner spirit that gives their form vitality. Critics may argue over the validity of various approaches in criticism, but the wise teacher, concerned not only with the work but with the response of the student to the work, will utilize any combination of approaches to illuminate the nature of a particular selection for student readers.[17]

PROVIDING VARIATION WHEN TEACHING A SINGLE SELECTION   Much can be done to provide for individual differences, even in teaching a single selection to a total group. In leading a discussion, teachers can ask questions that encourage students to respond at various levels of interpretation. Basic factual problems can be directed to students responding only to the narrative; others will seem ready to consider the meaning of the action and events; a few may be able to assess form in relation to content or to delve into the basic significance of a selection. Since teachers usually ask some factual, some interpretational, and some critical questions in the study of each literary work, they can see that each member of the class has opportunity to make a contribution.[18]

Students require differing amounts of teacher help in reading any selection. Some teachers circulate casually around the room during reading periods to provide needed guidance. Others meet with four or five students while the remainder of the class is occupied. Thus, in directing a study of *Great Expectations,* the teacher would provide for periodic discussions by the entire class—probably emphasizing the significance of Pip's changing attitude toward the social scene—and supplemental discussions with slower readers or absentees. Usually these special meetings stress understandings of the narrative as a

---

[17] Two useful books that discuss modern critical approaches to literature are Wilfred L. Guerin *et al., A Handbook of Critical Approaches to Literature* (New York: Harper & Row, 1966); Wilbur S. Scott, *Five Approaches of Literary Criticism* (New York: Macmillan, 1963).

[18] Edward J. Gordon believes we have five levels of questioning to consider: (1) to remember a fact, (2) to prove a generalization that someone else has made, (3) to make one's own generalization, (4) to generalize from the book to its application in life, and (5) to carry over the generalization into one's own behavior. Edward J. Gordon, "Levels of Teaching and Testing," *English Journal,* Vol. 44, No. 1 (September 1955). An important discussion of this method is also included in the introduction to Muriel Crosby, ed., *Reading Ladders for Human Relations,* 4th ed. (Washington, D.C.: American Council on Education, 1964).

supplement to the interpretational emphases developed with the total class. The more able readers, who complete the novel well before their fellows, could participate in all class activities but might be encouraged to read other books by Dickens or books with similar themes.

Some teachers find success in teaching a single work to four or five groups functioning at different levels of learning. For example, the teacher plans a series of discussion meetings to follow the reading of specific segments of *The Red Badge of Courage.* The first six students to finish reading the first assignment meet with the teacher for discussion, while others continue to read; the next group to finish the first section meets with the teacher during a subsequent class hour; the slowest students, who require specialized help, make up the final group to consider each reading assignment. Despite similar content, each discussion varies. Such a plan permits individual guidance, yet provides common reference for the class so that discussion, panels, audiovisual and other total class experiences may be introduced in relation to the novel.

Teacher-planned abridgments, condensations, and summaries are useful and appropriate in certain classrooms.[19] Long and difficult descriptions or explanatory passages discourage some youthful readers in such books as *Treasure Island* or *Silas Marner.* Often slow-moving content may be condensed and presented by the teacher to encourage reluctant readers to move forward to more compelling chapters. When, after several days of study, a teacher finds some students falling behind the remainder of the class, he may summarize the important events prior to a particular reading assignment and then encourage slow readers to continue from that point. This must be done judiciously, of course, for certain new dangers accompany the method. Some teachers ask the more able students who have read ahead to prepare summaries or even informal dramatizations of the chapters that may be difficult for some to read. Unlike printed adaptations, such condensations and summaries are made by a particular teacher with the needs of a special student group in mind.

These suggestions have dealt with ways of organizing instruction with a heterogeneous group so that the single selection may be read by all. For the most part the longer works, the novel and play, should be read rapidly rather than painstakingly. A class cannot analyze the structure of a work and perceive the significance of individual episodes until they have the opportunity to grasp the whole. Thus detailed analysis of any scene or chapter from a longer work is fruitless until total reading is completed. Seldom also do stu-

---

[19] These should be distinguished from the adapted or completely rewritten "classics," which offer the shell of a literary work without the essential content. To study a version of *Gulliver's Travels* rewritten for fourth-level readers is merely another, more objectionable, way of teaching about literature rather than teaching literature itself. Curiously, such adaptations are sometimes defended as presenting cultural experiences for the slow reader, yet few of the volumes contain anything but the names, events, and most obvious narrational features of the original book. Fortunately, the supply of genuine books for slow readers is increasing, and teachers need no longer accept these ill-conceived substitutes.

dents retain interest in a single work for more than three or four weeks. When
a longer period is allowed for reading, many fail to see the whole as a unified
presentation. The students should grasp the story first and with reasonable
rapidity; then scheduled rereadings, careful analyses, and some intensive study
can follow.

PRESENTING LITERATURE ORALLY   Many common experiences in literature may
be introduced through oral readings by the teacher. Slow learners often respond to the emotional appeal of verse, particularly when it is presented in a
dramatic oral interpretation. When students possess scripts so that they can
follow the reading, their understanding usually increases. Informal dramatization of a Shakespeare play in the classroom may bring Shakespeare to life
for some students. Similarly, short stories that tax beyond endurance the
silent reading abilities of some individuals can be made understandable when
read aloud by the teacher. For example, a ninth-grader reading at fourth-
grade level, who finds "By the Waters of Babylon" an almost insuperable
obstacle as home reading, may listen enthralled as a teacher presents the
story. Such readings provide opportunity for all students in the class to share
and discuss a common selection.[20]

Directing Group Reading

The use of multiple materials and grouping procedures offers a manageable
way of providing for the diversities that face teachers in large classes. Before
selecting literature and organizing group activity, teachers do well to identify
situations in which they plan to teach literature to groups as well as those in
which they intend to provide for student reading and sharing while offering
only general guidance. Both require sound and careful planning, but they serve
differing purposes.

PROVIDING GENERAL GUIDANCE   Many books can be profitably discussed and
analyzed by students without immediate assistance from the teacher. Often
group reading assignments of this type develop during a unit of instruction,
such as when class members choose the most interesting of three or four
topics during a unit called "Lost Worlds." Following the common study of a
few selections to provide a basic core of ideas, students, with teacher help,
select several interesting areas for group reading and study: the destruction
of civilizations of the past, imaginary worlds of the future, distant worlds of
the present. In each of these groups, students may read and share ideas
gleaned from such titles as the following:

[20] Two useful books to assist in oral presentation are Robert Beloof et al., The Oral Study
of Literature (New York: Random House, 1966); Don Geiger, The Sound, Sense, and
Performance of Literature (Chicago: Scott Foresman, 1963).

ANCIENT CIVILIZATIONS	DISTANT LANDS	IMAGINARY WORLDS
Last Days of Pompeii	Kon-Tiki	Earth Abides
Aku-Aku	People of the Deer	Animal Farm
Scrolls from the Dead Sea	Conquest of Everest	The Time Machine
	Annapurna	Lost Horizon
Incas, People of the Sun	Kabloona	A Connecticut Yankee in
Lost Cities and Vanished		King Arthur's Court
Civilizations		The Machine Stops

When the reading is completed, each group meets to discuss insights gained and to plan a presentation or report to the entire class. Some reports stress basic ideas through an organized panel—for example, a discussion of the motivation of men in primitive societies; other groups find dramatic or graphic presentation to be effective. The teacher's role in such activity is essentially that of consultant; having assisted in the planning and in selection of books, he remains in the background ready to assist as needed.

A similar kind of situation occurs when students select titles rather than topics for reading. For example, during a seventh-grade unit called "Animals in Literature," pupils are asked to choose among *Silver Chief, Incredible Journey, National Velvet,* and *Lassie Come Home.* Units on biography may involve the study of five or six different persons by separate groups. Opportunities for such experiences may be found in almost any unit.

Occasionally teachers prefer not to organize the discussion sections until much of the reading is completed. In such cases, a teacher brings into the classroom trays of fifty or sixty anthologies of short stories and, specifying little more than a minimum assignment, permits students to choose and read a number of selections. Sometimes thirty or so may be specially recommended. After several days the rapid readers perhaps have completed seven or eight stories, while slower readers have read only one or two. The stories most frequently read, and thus of the greatest interest to the class, serve as the content for discussion. The unit "Meeting a Crisis" illustrates this procedure.

TEACHING BY GROUPS   Special considerations are involved when instruction is necessary because the literature being read by groups is unusually difficult or challenging. Some teachers successfully organize class periods so as to meet separately with each group for twenty or twenty-five minutes every two or three days. For example, groups may be taught various plays over a three-week period. The more able readers study *Galileo;* intermediate groups read *The Admirable Crichton* or *A Man for All Seasons;* the slowest readers, studying *The Miracle Worker,* may require much teacher help to understand even the basic situations developed in Gibson's play. Often class work can be organized to permit independent group meetings led by the teacher, as illustrated in the unit "The Consequences of Character." In rooms provided with adjoining conference cubicles, meetings can be scheduled away from the class; otherwise a corner of the room may be utilized. In any event, students must be provided with ample study and reading materials before the teacher attempts to meet separately with a group. To facilitate such small group discussions and to aid reading, teachers prepare students with guides in advance of each meeting so that individuals will be prepared to raise questions and issues. This plan has been adapted in such ways as the following:

> Teaching four novels: *Les Misérables, The Good Earth, Turmoil,* and *The Count of Monte Cristo* were read by diverse groups and students were encouraged to search for points of contact between the novels.[21]

> Teaching four short stories: Separate group discussions were used with Joyce's "Araby," Cather's "Paul Case," Daly's "Sixteen," and Fessier's "That's What Happened to Me." [22]

> Teaching various types of literature within an over-all topical or thematic framework: During a unit called "The American Dream," one group of students examined dreams of liberty (Benét, Baldwin, Whitman), while others read selections concerned with economic development (Steinbeck, Poole, Sinclair), with social equality, and so on. Some groups require more help than others, since the subtlety and implications of difficult selections undoubtedly escape students without expert guidance.

Teachers also can provide instruction for groups while the remainder of the class is working on regular assignments. This method is often used in providing for gifted individuals within the heterogeneous class. While most students are completing the reading of *Medea,* for example, a few advanced readers meet with the teacher to discuss "The Lottery," a story with overtones similar to those of classical tragedy. Or, in the seventh grade, some children are excused from the assigned reading of poems and stories on family situations for a special study of the ways in which patterns of family life differ in various countries around the world. At appropriate times such groups meet with the teacher as well as separately.

GUIDING INDIVIDUAL READING   Wide independent reading contributes to the development of both skill and appreciation. Through intensive reading the child learns to apply the skills of comprehension and word analysis in many kinds of situations. Through wide reading he explores interests and ideas and learns how to choose those that satisfy his own peculiar needs; he discovers and builds touchstones and standards against which he is able to evaluate selections. As Helen C. White says, "It is quite true that wide reading can often be aimless without critical direction and reflection, but it is no less true that critical reflection without wide reading can be a very sterile thing." [23] A sound

---

[21] See detailed description in Margaret Ryan, "Achieving Unity with Diversity," *English Journal,* Vol. 40, No. 10 (November 1951), pp. 547–52.

[22] See description in James R. Squire, "Individualizing the Teaching of Literature," *English Journal,* Vol. 45, No. 9 (September 1956), pp. 314–19. Also, see various suggestions in Arno Jewett, ed., *English for the Academically Talented* (Washington, D.C.: National Education Association, 1960).

[23] Helen C. White, *Changing Styles in Literary Studies* (Cambridge, England: Cambridge Univ. Press, 1963), p. 22.

individual reading program offers solid support for the entire curriculum in reading and literature.

The values of wide reading are not achieved unless careful guidance is provided. The observations of experienced teachers and the results of careful research indicate that unguided reading results in little change in student behavior. Without assistance, many adolescents remain at a fixed level of interest [24]—a boy who enjoys mysteries may read nothing else, a girl who responds to one adventure of a series heroine may devote six months to thirty similar books. In the large classes they face, teachers need somehow to develop more appropriate ways of assisting individuals.

Many teachers reserve regular times for individual reading—for example, every Tuesday or twenty minutes on Monday and on Friday may be reserved for such activity. On these occasions students bring volumes from outside or plan to read a book from the classroom collection. Some teachers reject the rigidity of fixed reading periods but attempt to reserve an equivalent amount of time each week, depending on a flexible schedule. Others report that slower readers respond to daily reading periods, ten to fifteen minutes in length. When books are available in the classroom, such students can enjoy unassigned reading during the opening minutes of every class hour. For some groups such regularized activity aids in establishing a quiet, studious atmosphere.

Classroom book collections are helpful in offering teachers an indirect way of guiding reading choices and of increasing interest in books. One recent national conference of English department chairmen recommended collections of 500 titles in every classroom.[25] With a balanced collection of books available, students often turn to reading when they finish other activities. Some teachers change the selections every few weeks to maintain continual interest; many obtain books on long-term loan from public, county, or school libraries. Some classes might respond favorably to reading stories and poems by Negro writers for a three- or four-week period. Most of the selections should not be overly demanding, since students will be reading on their own.

Fixed lists of books from which individuals are asked to make their own selections have been criticized in recent years, but it is the rigidity with which such lists are used rather than the list itself that is to be avoided. Those intended primarily to suggest titles that can be supplemented by individual arrangement prove helpful and offer a convenient way of organizing reading guidance in large classes. Often teacher and class together may prepare a list of appropriate titles, or the teacher may suggest ten or twelve books that previous groups have enjoyed. Students may also search for interesting selections in standard annotated bibliographies, such as *Books for You* or *Your Reading*, the continually revised booklets prepared by the National Council of Teachers of English. Any procedures that encourage reading varied and challenging titles are appropriate in the classroom.

[24] See Bertha Handlan, "The Fallacy of Free Reading as an Approach to Appreciating," *English Journal*, Vol. 35, No. 4 (April 1946), pp. 182–88.

[25] Robert LaCampagne, ed., *High School Departments of English: Their Organization, Administration, and Supervision* (Champaign, Ill.: NCTE, 1965).

PROVISIONS FOR SHARING When individuals become really excited about a book, they want to discuss it, and out of such sharing may emerge a clarification of the experiences and value of the reading itself. The standardized book report, whether submitted orally, on a mimeographed form, or as a two-page composition in which separate paragraphs are devoted to the plot, theme, character, and the most interesting episode, certainly does little to quicken interest.[26] Most students would read less, not more, if faced continually with the unpleasant task of standardizing their responses on a form, and the endless procession of five-minute formal talks is enough to deaden any spark in all but the most lively groups. Informal grouping of students within a single class encourages greater student participation, results in more animation and interest, and provides for practice in oral communication. Each student is asked to discuss a particular book in a smaller group, and the most interesting presentations are repeated for the class.

More and more, teachers are attempting to bring outside reading inside, to relate the guided reading to the unit in progress. Opportunities for such experiences occur not only in planned situations but spontaneously as the students are able to contribute incidents and ideas from their reading during class discussion of many topics. In considering attitudes toward racial minorities, for example, some use illustrations from *Durango Street* while others tell of the realities of race in the music circles depicted in *Jazz Country*. The extension of a unit to embrace the guided reading program thus affords adolescents an opportunity of deepening and extending understanding developed through class discussion.

The approaches used in the classroom will reflect the purposes of instruction. If literature is taught as human experience, procedures compatible with this goal will be selected. If the varied tastes and abilities of students are considered, provision will be made for individuals and groups. Most teachers will seek a balance among the various activities.

SUGGESTED LEARNING EXPERIENCES

The program in literature envisioned in these pages can be accomplished only through carefully selected learning experiences. Most teachers prefer to create their own lessons with the needs of particular pupils in mind; for them the section that follows will serve as a source of suggested classroom activity to which they may turn for ideas. They will know that any particular activity should be introduced only when it is related to the other work of the class, to the ultimate goals of instruction, and to the unique purposes of the learners.

[26] Traditionally, directions for book reports ask students to write separate sentences on the author, the title, the main characters, the setting, and the most interesting incident. These widely accepted directions for a written book report encourage students to violate basic principles of organization by asking for separate paragraphs or sentences on six or eight different items. More often the student should select and develop a controlling idea in relation to the book he has read.

▶ *Relate literature to personal experiences*

1. Try to stress parallels between literary selections and the lives of young readers by asking appropriate questions in discussions and writing assignments. For example, *Ginger Pye* includes a vivid sequence on how the loss of a pet affects boys and girls. Seventh-grade readers may be asked to discuss or write about the topic "When I Lost a Dog." In making such an assignment, recognize the uniqueness of each individual experience. Not all children in a class will have had the experience. These students may write on "How It Feels to Lose a Gift," or perhaps on some completely different experience.

2. Follow a reading of "Descent into the Maelstrom" or a similar imaginative selection by asking each student to sketch "Things I Have Imagined." When chalk or charcoal is used, little time is required for sketching, and most of the hour can be reserved for follow-up activities. Ask students to write brief paragraphs describing their pictures. In the seventh grade try asking students to sketch "What Makes Me Mad" after reading about Jancsi's exasperation with cousin Kate in *The Good Master*. Activities of this type encourage readers to respond to the feelings of characters or to react to the emotional overtones of a selection.

3. Walter Van Tilburg Clark's story "The Portable Phonograph" portrays a Debussy nocturne and a rusty phonograph as the final remnants of Western culture following a devastating world conflict. While the impact of the story is still fresh in the minds of class members, the teacher may ask students to listen imaginatively to "Nuages" in an attempt to recapture the thoughts of characters listening to the nocturne under the conditions described by Clark.

▶ *Create puppet plays and other dramatizations*

Junior high school students enjoy producing puppet plays based on stories they have read. To minimize the effort involved in puppet construction, some teachers keep stock puppets available for students to redecorate, or teach students to use paper-bag puppets or shadow plays. More elaborate presentations may involve experience in reading, writing, constructing, rehearsing, and revising a play, as when seventh-graders prepare a puppet dramatization of *Jungle Book* for a school assembly. Experiences in dramatization are most fruitful when students have examined the characters and literary situations with care and attempt to reproduce these faithfully. A number of valuable ideas are suggested in *Drama: What Is Happening*, by James Moffett.[27]

▶ *Compare the form of diverse selections*

Try contrasting such different stories as "The Gift of the Magi," "Araby," and "The Great Stone Face." Note that all three stories are built upon surprise endings. Compare the purpose and effect of the revelation and the extent to which each is foreshadowed. Consider how a change in selection and organization of incident, in the nature of characterization, in setting or atmosphere would affect each story. Through discussion fill in at the chalkboard such a chart as the following:

[27] Available from NCTE, 508 South Sixth Street, Champaign, Illinois 61820.

STORY	PURPOSE OF ENDING	IF ENDING HAD DIFFERED
"The Gift of the Magi"	Supplies ironical twist to plot, underscoring theme of selfless love.	Would not have altered characterization or theme, but story would have seemed flat and maudlin.
"The Great Stone Face"	Supplies essential insight into theme of story.	Theme would have been altered; parallelism of the separate episodes concerning general, statesman, poet, and Ernest, and their relationship to the life span of man, would have been affected.
"Araby"	Supplies insight into the nature of character.	Would destroy purpose of a story, which exists primarily for this moment of insight into character.

▶ *Direct attention to the author's selection and use of his media*

1. Discuss the principles of significant inclusion and significant omission. Why are certain purposes best achieved through the use of particular images, incidents, and literary forms? Questions like the following can be considered as different works of art are introduced:

> Would "Loveliest of Trees" be more effective as an extended personal essay? Discuss reasons for the lack of stage setting in *Our Town*.
>
> What is the purpose of a narrator in a short story? To what extent is the device used to encourage the reader to suspend disbelief in Poe's "The Fall of the House of Usher"? How does the use of a narrator increase the dramatic irony of Browning's "Soliloquy of the Spanish Cloister"? Would the impact of Ring Lardner's "Haircut" differ if the story were told in the familiar third person?

2. Compare and contrast the diction of authors or of the same author in attempting to achieve diverse effects in two or more selections. Ask gifted students, for example, to compare the diction and tone of Shirley Jackson in "The Lottery" and in her delightful character portrait of an errant kindergartner, "Charles."

3. The reading of parodies often points up the most telling characteristics of an author. Some students may follow their reading of parodies of such widely copied rhythms as those in "Hiawatha" or "The Raven" by writing their own spoofs. Less well known, but eminently usable, are John Steinbeck's parody of "Murders in the Rue Morgue" and "The Tell-Tale Heart" in "The Affair at 7, Rue de M——," and the parody of *Macbeth* and other Shakespearean plays in Richard Armour's *Twisted Tales from Shakespeare*.[28]

4. After reading and studying intensively the prose styles of several authors, classes may be interested in considering how the selections would fare in the hands of diverse authors. What would Poe do with Hawthorne's "Ethan Brand"? How

[28] Teachers along with their students will also enjoy Armour's parody of study questions that often accompany textbook editions of the play, for example, "Continue and bring to an interesting conclusion Lady Macbeth's unfinished poem: 'The Thane of Fife had a wife. . . .' "

would Hawthorne introduce symbols of evil into Ring Lardner's "Haircut"? Would Lardner have handled "A Municipal Report" as did O. Henry? Some students may even want to try rewriting stories in the manner of another author.

TO DEVELOP SKILL IN PERCEIVING NARRATIVE AND CHARACTERIZATION

▶ *Explore the structural development of a fictional selection*

Select a relatively direct yet carefully constructed story, such as Wilbur Daniel Steele's "Footfalls," and review with students the basic structural elements: exposition, conflict, rising and falling action, climax, moment of revelation, denouement. A linear outline such as the following may help students perceive the directness of narrative development:

| | DEVELOPMENT OF | | | |
| EXPOSITION | CONFLICT | CLIMAX | REVELATION | DENOUEMENT |

Characterization of Boaz Negro; his attitude toward his son *Events of the evening, aural clues; the fire; long wait; changes in Boaz Negro* *Boaz' moment of revenge* *Discovery of identity of the murderer* *Resulting changes in Boaz Negro*

Once students grasp the basic pattern of narrational organization, show how authors achieve special effects by departing from the normal pattern, as in the following:

Frank Stockton, "The Lady or the Tiger?"; story purposely ends at moment of climax (the choice).

| SITUATION | DEVELOPMENT OF PLOT | CLIMAX |

Walter C. Brown, "The Puzzle-Knot"; story introduces basic conflict before exposition so as to maintain suspense.

| CHAM TAI'S PROBLEM | EXPOSITION AND DEVELOPMENT | CLIMAX | DENOUEMENT |

Robert Coates, "The Need" which consists of a series of self-contained episodes, each of which includes rising and falling action. Meaning and total impact result only from the accumulated insights developed through all episodes.

► *Encourage students to record significant impressions*

Introduce aids that enable students to record the significant details suggesting themes in characterization, plot development, or situation.

1. The systematic recording by students of their impressions of Martin Arrowsmith's problems, attitudes, and concerns helps them to summarize the novel and to be aware of the changes in Arrowsmith's perception. A table such as the following may be filled in by students in their notebooks:

PERIODS OF ARROWSMITH'S LIFE	MAJOR INFLUENCES	DETAILS TO BE REMEMBERED
adolescence	Dr. Vickerson	Gift of microscope; early interest in science
college and university days	Dr. Gottlieb; Leora	Gottlieb's interest in Martin; his scorn for Martin's first attempts at research; Martin's desire to be a "genius"
rural doctor in the Dakotas	Death of Leora's baby; death of Novak child; Dr. Winter	Dissatisfaction with country life; loss of yearning for research as "sanctuary"
public health work	Dr. Pickerbaugh's insincerity; Angus Dauer	Incidents involving public relations; emphasis on the practical
McGurk Institute	Dr. Gottlieb; Dr. Tubbs	Concern for "reputation"; the "great" experiment that seemed too late
St. Hubert Island	Leora's death; Joyce	Problems of maintaining scientific detachment during epidemic
McGurk Institute	Director Holabird	Joyce's dedication to material values
Research, Vermont	Terry Wickett	Martin's realization he is just "beginning work"

In reviewing responses of students to each episode, the teacher is able to build on differences of opinion so as to develop a real understanding of the conflict within Martin Arrowsmith. Use of such a chart should ultimately make clear to a reader Martin's continuing search for truth, his singleness of purpose, and his lack of strength to face the world alone, as well as Lewis' use of scientific research as a symbol for truth.

2. Ask students to record in their notebooks significant quotations revealing some facet of character. When a number of such revelations have been identified concerning the protagonist in a drama or a novel, a review of the items will aid students to see changes in such characters as Pip in *Great Expectations,* John in *Go Tell It on the Mountain,* or Eustacia Vye in *The Return of the Native* (see a similar approach used in teaching *Macbeth,* pages 600–08).

► *Use outlines to guide the reading of difficult selections*

Even mature readers benefit from using an outline as a guide through the narrative labyrinth of *War and Peace* or the rhetorical tapestry of *Areopagitica.* Similar aids to understanding can direct younger readers to important purposes of the author and to shifts in point of view that otherwise might pass unnoticed.

1. Some outlines may be little more than informal notations concerning a poem, placed on the chalkboard to guide students' reading in class. For example, such notations as the following may serve to aid juniors or seniors studying Tennyson's "Ulysses."

lines 1–5	Ulysses contemplates his present circumstances.
lines 6–18	He explores the significance of past travels.
lines 19–24	He generalizes on the nature of life and experience.
lines 24–32	He pledges to continue his life of activity.
lines 33–42	He bequeaths his throne to his son.
lines 43–49	He considers his ships and his mariners.
lines 50–70	He reaffirms his desire to search until the last.

2. Outlines of longer selections can be detailed or can direct students to consideration of important incidents and relationships, as in the following sample developed for ninth-grade readers of *David Copperfield.*

    I. The early boyhood of David Copperfield
       A. the contrast in David's relationship to Peggotty and to his mother
       B. the circumstances of family life at Peggotty's
       C. changes wrought at home by Murdstone
       D. the impact of Salem House on David
       E. changes in Murdstone's treatment of David following his mother's death

▶ *Use adjective checklists in developing understanding of characters*

Present checklists of adjectives that require the responder to identify the most salient characteristics of a fictional personality; disagreements often form the basis of stimulating discussion. Some teachers ask students to rate a character on an adjective checklist after reading only a portion of a long work and then to file the list for future use. Days later, when the reading of the work has been completed, students are asked to rate the characters again. A comparison of the checklists may emphasize several important understandings: the ways in which characterization develops, the dangers of judging behavior on ambiguous clues. Imagine a rating of Becky Sharp based on only the first fifty pages of *Vanity Fair.* Following are two illustrations of adjective checklists:

1. *Junior high school* The following descriptive terms have been applied to Johnny Tremain. Indicate those you consider to be his desirable qualities by marking plus (+); mark those that seem negative with a minus (−); for characteristics that seem neither positive nor negative, mark zero (0); draw a line through any words that do not seem to apply. After reviewing your judgments, describe a passage from the novel that reveals both admirable and regrettable characteristics of the boy.

____ awkward	____ deliberate	____ mischievous
____ aloof	____ energetic	____ masculine
____ ambitious	____ honest	____ methodical
____ changeable	____ intelligent	____ opinionated
____ conventional	____ insensitive	____ obliging
____ courageous	____ ingenious	____ (etc.)

2. *Senior high school* Check on the following lists each of the adjectives you believe applies to Antonia. Then for each adjective checked, try to indicate at least one incident or statement in Willa Cather's novel to support your judgment.

____ contented	____ diffident	____ resourceful
____ changeable	____ efficient	____ simple
____ courageous	____ energetic	____ steady
____ coarse	____ patient	____ shrewd
____ conventional	____ practical	____ vital
____ cautious	____ reliable	____ sensitive

TO DEVELOP SKILL IN EXPLORING MEANINGS THAT LIE BELOW THE SURFACE OF LITERATURE

▶ *Consider how meanings are revealed through theme, plot, and characterization*

1. After junior high school students have read such books as *Swiftwater, Julie's Heritage,* or any equally good selections that will stand careful analysis, read aloud Howard Pease's "Letter to a Fan." [29] Apply Pease's concept of levels of meanings to the book that has been read.

2. Compare three short stories in which plot, theme, and characterization receive different degrees of emphasis. "The Most Dangerous Game" is primarily a story of suspense in which plot is of paramount significance; "The Dead Dog" exists largely for its revelation of character; theme is of major significance in "A Success Story." Such a selection as "Leiningen Versus the Ants" may be introduced to illustrate the harmonious balance achieved when the emphasis on plot in a tale of suspense is strengthened by careful and necessary characterization of a protagonist and by the over-all unity achieved through an underlying theme.

▶ *Consider the use of metaphorical language*

1. The teacher may introduce students to the expression of ideas through figurative language by directing attention to terms used in informal speech and writing:

> hot rod
> an idea that is "far out" or "on cloud nine"
> like a granite wall at left tackle
> going over the hill
> peaches and cream complexion

What is the literal meaning of each statement? What are possible meanings? What elements are being compared?

2. Select obvious examples in introducing students to the use of figures of speech, such as "There is no frigate like a book." Ask students to consider possible implications. In what way does Emily Dickinson see books and frigates as similar? What is her emphasis? Ultimately, introduce students to the more subtle uses of figurative language including selections that may be considered an extended metaphor, such as "The Chambered Nautilus" or "The Physicists."

[29] Howard Pease, "How to Read Fiction," in *They Will Read Literature, A Portfolio of Tested Secondary School Procedures* (Champaign, Ill.: NCTE, 1955).

► *Consider the use of signs and symbols*

1. Direct students' attention to obvious uses of symbolism in the titles of books, poems, motion pictures, and plays—"A Man Can Stand Up" (in *Johnny Tremain*), *The Corn Is Green, Long Day's Journey into Night, To Kill a Mockingbird, A Raisin in the Sun, Lord of the Flies.*

2. Discuss familiar signs and symbols that are important in communicating ideas in everyday life—legends on maps, road signs, the symbols of various holidays, symbols and signs used in advertising. A student group may enjoy preparing a bulletin board display.

3. Compare uses of different symbols to convey similar ideas. To Heinrich Heine, "The Lorelei" expressed the same hypnotic pull toward beauty and escapism that is expressed in the song "Bali Hai."

4. Compare the crumbling statue of "Ozymandias" as a symbol of the futility of faith placed in material values with vivid photographs of ruins resulting from air raids during recent world conflicts.

5. Read with students a story that strikes the reader as bizarre and wildly implausible if the meaning is accepted literally. An excellent example for secondary-school students is "The Bound Man," Ilse Aïchinger's description of the beauty and meaning an individual can discover in living within the confinement of binding ropes and of the unwanted sympathy his constriction arouses. Although interested in the initial image, students soon find they must grope for many implied meanings. To aid in their search, divide the class into four or five groups and ask each to consider the thoughts suggested in the following representative quotations:

> "In that he remained entirely within the limits set by his rope, he was free of it—it did not confine him, but gave him wings and endowed his leaps and jumps with purpose."
>
> "The antics [of others to release him] amused the bound man, because he could have freed himself if he had wanted to, whenever he liked, but perhaps he wanted to learn a few new jumps first."
>
> "He felt a slight elation at having lost the fatal advantage of free limbs which causes men to be worsted."

During the teacher-led discussion that follows, the presentations from each group may be examined and analyzed. The use of groups to analyze such selections is particularly helpful if the purpose is to identify a multiplicity of possible meanings. However, students need to learn that any potential interpretation cannot conflict with facts and details presented in the story.

► *Consider the uses of satire and irony*

1. Students may be introduced to obvious uses of irony in casual conversation and in the dialog of stories and plays. Frequently the ironical intentions are made clear when readers consider the tone of the speaker. How would these lines be spoken by Antony: "For Brutus is an honorable man"?

2. Introduce more advanced readers to the irony implicit in such situations as the following:

> the choice of pigs (not dogs, cats, horses) as central in the society of *Animal Farm*

the butler possessing major resources for survival and emerging as the true
leader of the island society in *The Admirable Crichton*

the humane, sentimental attitudes of the gambler and the dance hall hostess
in "The Outcasts of Poker Flat"

the nobleman Pierre receiving his greatest lesson from the peasant Platon
Karataev in *War and Peace*

Social satire is involved in many of the ironical situations suggested above. Once
students are sensitive to the meanings of such selections as *The Admirable Crichton,*
consider the possible intentions of the authors. For what purpose would Barrie
wish to show Crichton as the peer of British social leaders? Questions of this type
may lead students to see that true satire usually reflects a desire to influence change.

3. Introduce the better readers to some memorable contemporary satirical
writing: *Animal Farm, Point of No Return, Babbitt.* Encourage individuals to report
good examples of satire to be found in political cartoons, comics, and newspaper
editorials.

TO DEVELOP ATTITUDES THAT ENCOURAGE READING WITH APPRECIATION

▶ *Read and interpret with students*

The most helpful approaches usually involve the teacher's reading with students
and interpreting literary selections. An oral reading by the teacher that the students
follow in their books permits the teacher to demonstrate how a mature reader approaches a selection. Unlike an oral interpretation designed primarily as a listening
experience, these readings by the teacher may be interrupted momentarily after
key words and passages to give students an opportunity to consider meanings and
effects. Help with challenging selections should be offered at the time of reading,
not only at the end of reading, so that the student learns how to discover the significance of clues on which sound interpretations are based. Is it surprising that we
discover many problems in the ways in which young readers approach literature
when most of our help is offered only after reading is completed?

▶ *Study responses to separate segments of stories*

Divide such a story as "The Bet" into several segments to be studied independently. After reading each segment, ask class members to share their feelings and
ideas about the situations and characters. The analysis of the early passages may be
reconsidered after reading the story is completed. Why were some readers able
to predict behavior? How did others go wrong? A comparison of such responses
offers a rich source of information on how individuals respond.

Occasionally reactions may be written and compared; on other occasions, the
teacher may lead students in an informal discussion of possible meanings. Such
specific events as the changes in the kind of books requested by the prisoner during
his fifteen years internment—or changes reflecting materialistic, spiritual, and philosophical concerns—will evoke various comments. Some will grasp Chekhov's apparent
intent from the beginning, while others hazard wild, implausible guesses, indicating
that they have not yet learned to test for possibility. Sometimes the teacher may
wish to approach a discussion of a segment of a story by referring to the interpretation of a single reader. For example, the following reaction to the exposition of
"The Bet" has been read to students:

I think that the lawyer will be sent to prison where he decides that he's been tricked. He will dig his way out with his hands. Incognito he will establish a business firm and ruin the banker financially before he reveals himself.

After listening to the reaction, the students consider whether any elements in the exposition of "The Bet" justify such a romantic, melodramatic solution to the conflict, whether such behavior is consistent with the character of the lawyer, indeed whether an individual who finds it so easy to ruin the banker would subject himself to fifteen years imprisonment to gain great wealth. Such an analysis leads to an explanation of the situation as presented in the story:

> *the banker*   compulsive (offers bet); lacks understanding of behavior; superior (feeling of power)
>
> *the lawyer*   avaricious (desire for gain); intellectual (intellectual bet)
>
> *situation*   detailed delineation of character and incident, despite improbable nature of event

At any level of instruction, such guided experience in analyzing literature permits the teacher to overcome barriers to sound interpretation and to develop the favorable attitudes discussed earlier in this section. Literary selections that reveal meaning only gradually through a carefully plotted series of ambiguous clues and symbols are appropriate for such class activities.

▶ *Begin with the reader's initial response*

Ask students to write their impressions immediately after reading selections like Saroyan's "Locomotive 38" (junior high) or a poem like "My Last Duchess" (senior high). The papers may then be set aside as the class studies the selections intensively. After meanings are clarified through analysis, compare the final judgments with initial impressions to point up the importance of searching for a plurality of meanings.

TO TEACH A SELECTION TO THE ENTIRE CLASS

▶ *Prepare students for reading a work of literature*

Recognize the importance of readiness. Develop interest before passing out new books, by using varied approaches: bulletin board displays, previewing excerpts read aloud by the teacher, listening to tape recorded dramatizations of scenes prepared by another class, relating the new work to reading that has been completed. Try to prepare students in advance for special obstacles in reading, such as the unfamiliar names in the Arabian Nights or the dialectal terms in *The Yearling* or in much of Mark Twain's writing. Recognize that presentation of the background material before reading is the teacher's responsibility and that student research, as on the French Revolution during the time of *A Tale of Two Cities*, better evolves after the reading. Usually the background students need before beginning a selection may be presented in less than a full class period. Short reports by students can be introduced at appropriate times during the reading of the book. For example, a description of the guillotine comes better while the class is discussing the executions in the Dickens novel than before the group begins the book.

▶ *Encourage rapid reading of longer works*

1. To help encourage rapid reading, divide a novel into four or five long segments (fifty pages or more) to be read by certain dates. Preparatory to each dis-

cussion, present a few leading questions or ideas related to the reading to help students organize their thinking. Individuals can thus be encouraged to consider a selection in terms of major conflicts and patterns rather than specific details, as sometimes occurs when discussion is planned on a chapter-by-chapter approach.

2. Encourage students to read as rapidly as they wish by providing a generous portion of class time for silent reading. Help students make a start on the book by reading the first chapters aloud. Especially in classes with many mediocre readers, such a beginning is wise.

3. Consider keeping an accurate estimate of each student's progress in reading by a Chapter Record. It is often better to ask a student to keep this record than for the teacher to keep it himself. Not only does this save time, but individual pupils, if they are reading slowly, may be more likely to report accurately to one of their trusted peers. For this record, each pupil has a pseudonym, and the chart is marked each day by the chosen recorder. When the daily lines have been drawn, the recorder shows the chart to the teacher so he can gauge how far to carry the discussion. A few students will have read beyond most, and some pupils will be considerably behind the others. Experience with this chart has been favorable in many classes. A typical chart:

DAILY PROGRESS CHART: SIXTH-HOUR CLASS

Chapters

Alias	I	II	III	IV	V	VI	VII	VIII	IX
Sunny									
Butterflop									
Jet Pilot									
Methuselah									
Rusty									

Teachers who realize that a closer control on the reading would be in the best interests of a particular class may easily keep a chart like this for themselves, using actual names. Their students report progress daily during the reading part of the hour. The names and reading positions of individuals should not be made public, however. Such publicity tends to embarrass the slow reader and sometimes mars the faster reader with a taint of smugness. Sometimes, too, such publicity promotes a race to finish the book among some students, and their reading is superficial. The advantage of this approach is that it encourages students to read rapidly but at their own rates.

▶ *Provide aids to assist comprehension*

1. Keep a list of basic information on the board, along with some identifying phrase or sentence. As the reading progresses, add to the list. In a class without an assigned room, have the pupils keep these and similar records in their notebooks. For *Silas Marner*, such cues as the following are useful:

Place Raveloe, a village in central England

Time About 1810–12, during the Napoleonic Wars and the Industrial Revolution

Characters Silas Marner, a lonely weaver; Jem Rodney, a mole catcher (Add characters as the plot progresses.)

2. Occasionally introduce some regularized task permitting students to organize their reactions to the book. For example, after each discussion ask students to summarize in notebooks the major generalizations that have been drawn. Similarly, ask students to record important ideas the class discovers in a play or novel. Some teachers prepare a general outline or series of questions to guide the reading of difficult selections and ask individuals to think about or even to write answers to questions after reading designated sections of longer works. The following study questions were used in teaching the first nine chapters of *The Human Comedy*.[30]

THEME OF DISCUSSION   "THE EXPERIENCE OF DEATH"

1. *Ulysses*
   Relate the incident in which Ulysses first confronts death.
   Does he understand what death means?
   Does the thought disturb him? How does he react?

2. *Homer*
   Relate the incident in which Homer brings news of death to another. (Chapter 5)
   What do you know about Mrs. Sandoval?
   How did Homer feel about delivering the telegram?
   What was the author's comment? ("This woman was not to hear of murder in the world and feel it in herself." Chapter title, "You go your way, I'll go mine.")
   How does Homer relate the incident to his mother when he returns home? Has the incident affected him?

3. *Mrs. Macauley*
   How does Mrs. Macauley react to Ulysses' question concerning his father?
   How does she explain "life" to him?
   How does Mrs. Macauley react to Homer's feeling?
   Mrs. Macauley comments upon "loneliness." What does she say? Does what she says make sense to you? Is loneliness a part of growing up? What is the meaning of change?

3. Slower readers profit from activities that direct attention to the meaning of specific events. Study outlines, such as the following for *Les Misérables*, are helpful because they tend to stimulate active response by utilizing a comparative approach to generalizing:

Direction   For each point select at least two incidents that illustrate the attitude of the character.

	Valjean	*Javert*
Attitude toward fellow man	1	1
	2	2
Attitude toward the law	1	1
	2	2
Attitude toward human justice	1	1
	2	2

[30] Adapted from a plan by Jean Gringle Pirner, formerly of Las Lomas High School, Walnut Creek, California.

Answers to such study questions would of course be reviewed in teacher-led discussions so that misunderstandings could be clarified.

TO DIRECT GROUP READINGS

▶ *Develop group assignments within larger units*

1. Following the reading and study of *Our Town,* ask students to select four basic quotations or key ideas as themes for further study. Organize groups around the basic ideas and plan with the students a series of appropriate readings with each group ultimately required to report back to the class on the points of view examined. Such themes and suggested reading as the following were chosen by one class:

> "We don't have time to look at one another."
> *The Human Comedy, Death of a Salesman, Arrowsmith, Catcher in the Rye, The Autobiography of Malcolm X.*
> "Do any human beings ever realize life while they live it?"
> Helen Keller, *The Story of My Life;* biography of Albert Schweitzer; poetry of Emily Dickinson; Dag Hammerskjöld, *Markings*

2. Ask students in an advanced class to study various interpretations of a single theme, such as the theme of love. Form separate interest groups to pursue the analysis in such selections as "Tristan and Iseult," *Cyrano de Bergerac, Liliom, Jane Eyre, Ethan Frome, Romeo and Juliet.*

▶ *Provide for special groups of gifted or slow students within the heterogeneous class*

1. Provide opportunities for individuals and groups to listen to recorded literature. During a study of the conflict between the individual and society, a group of gifted students in the twelfth grade may listen to the Siobhan McKenna recording of *Saint Joan.* In a similar manner, slow readers unable to pursue at length the reading of legends may be permitted to hear recordings. In the seventh grade, one teacher planned a series of experiences in listening to story-telling records for eight able learners who did not need the special instruction on spelling designed for the other twenty-five students. Although group listening assignments of this type are easily arranged when a soundproof listening room adjoins the classroom, teachers also find that earphones may be attached to a phonograph to permit individuals and groups to listen to recordings without disturbing other class members.[31]

2. Ask mature students to conduct special research projects related to the ideas being discussed. For example, during an eighth-grade analysis of humor in literature (slapstick, farce, folk humor, incongruity), five students planned a special investigation into the kinds of humor preferred by junior high school students. The group developed a special questionnaire, presented it to selected seventh- and ninth-grade groups, analyzed the results, and prepared a report for the class and for the school paper.

3. Urge rapid readers to survey contemporary literature, possibly by reading and reporting on current best-selling fiction and nonfiction. A report of recommended reading may be prepared for the school newspaper or posted in the library on a special bulletin board. Similarly, one or two able students might review the opening

---

[31] For suggestions, see Morris Schreiber, ed., *An Annotated List of Recordings in the Language Arts* (Champaign, Ill.: NCTE, 1964).

performance of a play at local theaters. Some managers provide complimentary admission for student reviewers.

TO STIMULATE INTEREST IN LESS FREQUENTLY STUDIED LITERARY FORMS

▶ *Encourage the reading of essays*

1. Utilize the same basic method of analysis followed in reading fiction and drama, insuring that pupils understand the author's thesis before they attempt to assess its validity. Recognize that in much essay writing the organization and flow of the argument will require separate attention.

2. Study the general style of selected essays, perhaps deriving broad categories of classification such as those used by Walker Gibson in *Tough, Sweet, and Stuffy.*[32] Encourage young people to read widely in essay collections of their own choice and classify each selection as tough, sweet, or stuffy in style.

3. Analyze an essay like James Baldwin's "Many Thousands Gone" for what it reveals about the mind of the author, the sharpness of his observation, his vision of the human condition, his concern with personal and social realities. Follow by reading selections by diverse essayists (James Reston, George Orwell, James Thurber, E. B. White) and ask pupils to discuss their impression of the personality of each writer.

4. Build a classroom collection of arresting, well written essays by modern columnists with appeal to young people. The film criticism of Pauline Kael, the scientific humanism of Loren Eisley, the social commentary of Dwight MacDonald, or the political observations of James Reston can be clipped from many popular periodicals. Vary regularly scheduled periods of independent reading by occasionally urging pupils to read selections from the essay collection to identify outstanding examples of differing tone, method of organization, and arresting ideas worth class consideration.

5. See suggestions for teaching the essay offered by James Knapton and Bertrand Evans in *Teaching a Literature-Centered English Program* (New York: Random House, 1967).

▶ *Encourage the reading of biography*

1. Preface the independent reading of selected biographies by classroom discussion of the qualities of excellence in biographical writing: fidelity to truth, skill in organizing and dramatizing the subject, insight into individual behavior. Such points may be made by comparing and contrasting several short biographical sketches depicting the same personality from different points of view.

2. Encourage pupils to distinguish between several forms of biographical writing: scholarly biographies; documentary biographies that attempt primarily to catalog facts; popular biographies that often contain the free interpretation of fiction; biographical novels; modern documentary novels based on fact, such as *Hiroshima* by John Hersey; and historical novels.

3. Ask pupils reading a popular biography to select one major incident in the life of the subject and to do library research to unearth as many details concerning the incident as possible. Basing their observation on the event as they found it to be, the pupils should then be asked to study the treatment of the incident in the

[32] Walker Gibson, *Tough, Sweet, and Stuffy* (Bloomington, Ind.: Indiana Univ. Press, 1967).

biography to identify any liberties taken with the subject, the omission of any significant details, any elements heightened to serve the biographer's purpose.

4. Read aloud selected passages from mature biographies that may seem inappropriate for reading by the total class, such as *Nigger* by Dick Gregory or *The Autobiography of Malcolm X*. Use such readings to stimulate writing or discussion.

5. Encourage a student committee to prepare a special library or room display of biographies dealing with the men and women most admired by the student body. To prepare the display, the committee may have to conduct an opinion survey. When the display is completed, encourage every pupil to read one of the listed books.

6. Use the suggestions for teaching biography as an esthetic form contained in Paul Murray Kendall, *The Art of Biography* (New York: Norton, 1965).

TO PROVIDE GUIDANCE FOR INDIVIDUAL READING

▶ *Encourage pupils to prepare book lists and plan displays*

1. Ask committees of gifted pupils to review current books and suggest titles to be purchased for the school library.

2. Toward the end of a year encourage students to list books recommended for future classes. A seventh-grade group may select "Ten Books Too Good for Seventh-Graders to Miss."

3. Organize a special weekly book club. One junior high teacher provided for three students to be selected to prepare a bulletin board display, which included their photographs, their favorite books, and special recommendations.

▶ *Organize "literary sampler" periods*

1. Introduce students to books that have been added to classroom and school libraries. Show the books, read selected passages, permit children to examine the books. When such "sampler" periods are followed by reading periods, many pupils will seize the opportunity to begin reading the stories that have been presented.

2. Try introducing junior high pupils to new books through playing "musical books." Place a variety of unfamiliar books on tables throughout the room. Have a phonograph available. Urge children to skim through a book until the music stops, then exchange the book for another. Permit three or four minutes for each skimming and four or five exchanges as a maximum. At the end of the experience, divide students into small groups and ask each individual to describe the most interesting book that he has seen. Permit individuals to "sign out" books immediately after this activity. Some teachers find this approach to be helpful in motivating reluctant readers.

▶ *Refer to similar titles*

Capitalize on the current reading preferences by referring pupils to similar books. For some popular books teachers have developed such recommendations as the following:

> If you liked *King of the Wind*, you'll enjoy *Silver Chief, Lassie Come Home,* and *National Velvet*.
> If you enjoyed *Strawberry Girl*, try *Blue Willow, Sensible Kate, The Wonderful Year*, and *Understood Betsy*.

Recommendations of this type may be dittoed and passed to individual readers or displayed on bulletin boards.

► *Write papers comparing books*

Encourage an advanced student to select a topic that interests him, to read several books on the subject, and to write a paper presenting insights gleaned through such reading. Teachers have used such topics as the following: "The Solace of Religion," "The Impact of War on the Individual," "Responses to the Sea," "The Face of Evil."

► *Encourage graphic displays*

1. Charts and other graphic displays interest students and direct attention to stories and books. Children respond well to a pocket chart where each child has a pocket in which he files a separate card for each book read, including a brief review that may be examined by others.

2. Some pupils enjoy designing illustrated book jackets for the stories they have read. "Reviews" may be written on the leaf of each jacket.

3. Encourage the reading and reporting of stories of Western adventure by developing a Western mural. For each story read, a student may add an appropriate symbol to the mural (cactus, horse, tombstone) on which is written the title and author of the selection and a one-sentence summary of the story.

4. A gallery of characters from books read during the semester sometimes serves as a bulletin board display in the classes of one teacher. Students are asked to keep notebooks in which word pictures of characters are written, sometimes accompanied by sketches. Late in the semester the class gallery is displayed.

► *Provide for the sharing of reactions to books*

1. Where all pupils have read similar types of books (animal stories, adventure books), divide the class into groups and ask each to answer specially prepared questions. For example, seventh-grade students may be asked to list the various things characters find amusing in their books (possibly as a part of a larger study of humor) or the problems people have in communicating with each other, such as misunderstandings and inadequate means of communication.

2. Encourage pupils to read aloud brief, interesting excerpts. Preparation is necessary for such oral interpretations. Some teachers arrange for readings to be presented informally in small groups with the best reading from each group selected for presentation to the entire class.

3. Arrange occasional panel discussions by pupils who are reading similar books or even the same title. For example, seventh-graders reading *Patricia Crosses Town*, *The Empty Schoolhouse*, *The Swimming Pool*, *Skid*, and *Hurricane: Story of a Friendship* might discuss the problems that black children encounter in establishing personal relationships in various social settings.

4. Dramatics appeal to certain pupils who enjoy formal experiences in acting out scenes from books. Junior high students will often respond well to the dramatic situation of the book trial, in which a defendant is accused of reading a dull book. Bailiff, prosecuting attorney, and judge add to the effectiveness, and some students are hard pressed to convince a student jury of three members that they are not guilty as charged.

► *Organize individual reading records*

1. A cumulative reading record maintained throughout school years offers information valuable in studying the development of taste and should be maintained

SUGGESTED MODEL JUNIOR HIGH SCHOOL BOOK LADDER

BOOKS TO USE IN GUIDING INDIVIDUAL READING

STEP I

(Books with only a few elements of appeal)

Juvenile series such as Nancy Drew, Tom Swift, comics, Bomba the Jungle Boy, the Hardy Boys, potboilers from newsstands.

(Many of your pupils will be at this stage when you begin to offer individual reading guidance.)

STEP II

Going on Sixteen Betty Cavanna
Anchor Man Jesse Jackson
Bulldozer Stephen Meader
A Date for Diane Elizabeth Headley
Flaming Arrow Carl Moon
Henry Huggins Beverly Cleary
Northend Wildcats C. B. Davis
Red Horse Hill Stephen Meader
Silver Chief books Jack O'Brien
Smuggler's Island Clarissa Abia Kneeland
Sue Barton books Helen Boylston
The Tattooed Man Howard Pease
Toby Tyler James Otis
Young Razzle John Tunis
The Raft Robert Trumbull
On to Oregon Honore Morrow
The Black Stallion books Walter Farley
Ready or Not Mary Stolz
Durango Street Frank Bonham

STEP III

Blue Willow Doris Gates
Caddie Woodlawn Carol R. Brink
Call It Courage Armstrong Sperry
Cress Delahanty Jessamyn West
Homer Price Robert McCloskey
My Friend Flicka Mary O'Hara
Little Britches Ralph Moody
Little Vic Doris Gates
Little Women Louisa May Alcott
No Other White Men Julia Davis
Otto of the Silver Hand Howard Pyle
Smoky Will James
Thunderbolt House Howard Pease
America's Paul Revere Esther Forbes
Old Yeller Fred Gipson
Swiftwater Paul Annixter
Shane Jack Shaefer
Adam of the Road Elizabeth J. Gray
Jazz Country Nat Hentoff
When the Legends Die Hal Borland

STEP IV

(Books with many elements of appeal)

And Now Miguel Michael Krumgold
A Boy on Horseback Lincoln Steffens
David Copperfield Charles Dickens
Huckleberry Finn Mark Twain
Johnny Tremain Esther Forbes
The Light in the Forest Conrad Richter
Men of Iron Howard Pyle
National Velvet Enid Bagnold
The Prince and the Pauper Mark Twain
The Secret of the Andes Ann N. Clark
The Three Musketeers Alexander Dumas
Tom Sawyer Mark Twain
Treasure Island Robert Louis Stevenson
The Witch of Blackbird Pond Elizabeth G. Speare
The Witchcraft of Salem Village Shirley Jackson
The Yearling Marjorie Kinnan Rawlings
The Good Master Kate Seredy
Abe Lincoln Grows Up Carl Sandburg
Island of the Blue Dolphins Scott O'Dell
Goodby, My Lady James Street
An Edge of the Forest Agnes Smith

SUGGESTED MODEL SENIOR HIGH SCHOOL BOOK LADDER

BOOKS TO USE IN GUIDING INDIVIDUAL READING

STEP I

(Books with only a few elements of appeal)

Zane Grey, Edgar Rice Burroughs, Ian Fleming, comics

(Many of your pupils will be at this stage when you begin to offer reading guidance.)

STEP II

Adventures of Sherlock Holmes Arthur Conan Doyle
Back to Treasure Island Harold A. Calahan
Call of the Wild Jack London
Escape on Skis Arthur Stapp
I Married Adventure Osa Johnson
A Lantern in Her Hand Bess Aldrich
The Raft Robert Trumbull
Seventeenth Summer Maureen Daly
Smoky Will James
To Have and to Hold Mary Johnston
20,000 Leagues Under the Sea Jules Verne
Banner in the Sky James Ramsey Ullman
Two and the Town H. G. Felsen
Lilies of the Field William E. Barrett

STEP III

Arrowsmith Sinclair Lewis
Bridges at Toko-ri James Michener
Cress Delahanty Jessamyn West
Let the Hurricane Roar Rose W. Lane
Mutiny on the Bounty Charles Nordhoff and James N. Hall
Northwest Passage Kenneth Roberts
Showboat Edna Ferber
Winter Wheat Mildred Walker
The Yearling Marjorie Kinnan Rawlings
The Loon Feather Iola Fuller
Ishi in Two Worlds Theodora Kroeber
To Kill a Mockingbird Harper Lee
A Separate Peace John Knowles
The Pearl John Steinbeck
Catcher in the Rye J. D. Salinger
A Single Pebble John Hersey
On the Beach Nevil Shute

STEP IV

(Books with many elements of appeal)

The Prophet Kahlil Gibran
The Bridge of San Luis Rey Thornton Wilder
Giants in the Earth Ole E. Rolvaag
The Good Earth Pearl Buck
How Green Was My Valley Richard Llewellyn
Huckleberry Finn Mark Twain
Les Misérables Victor Hugo
My Antonia Willa Cather
The Old Man and the Sea Ernest Hemingway
Return of the Native Thomas Hardy
Ring of the Löwenskolds Selma Lagerlöf
The Scarlet Letter Nathaniel Hawthorne
Vanity Fair William Thackeray
The Secret Sharer Joseph Conrad
Lord of the Flies William Golding
Cry, the Beloved Country Alan Paton
Sons and Lovers D. H. Lawrence

whenever possible. Commercially printed records are available,[33] some school systems design their own folders.

2. Many junior high teachers encourage students to maintain pie charts of their reading in their notebooks. The circle is divided into sections for various kinds of literature—adventure stories, poetry, science books, and so on. When a pupil finishes reading a book, he pastes a star in the appropriate section and writes a brief summary of the book in his notebook. A glance at this chart shows the individual and the teacher whether he is reading many types of literature or is concentrating on only one or two types.[34]

▶ *Use the book ladder approach in guiding individual reading*

Both teachers and pupils develop a sense of direction and focus in the independent reading program if they sense progression in quality and maturity of the books selected. Many teachers develop reading ladders like those on pages 474–75 to give young people some understanding of qualitative differences among books.

▶ *Utilize available resources for selecting books*

Maintain, in the library, the department center, or the classroom, a collection of annotated books useful in suggesting titles for individual reading. Many of the titles are useful with students, too. New lists are constantly appearing but among the more basic are:

> Ralph Perkins, *Book Selection Media*, rev. ed. (Champaign, Ill.: NCTE, 1967). An annotated index to book lists.
>
> Charles B. Willard, ed., *Your Reading* (New York: Bantam Books, 1966). Junior high school list.
>
> Richard S. Alm, ed., *Books for You* (New York: Washington Square Press, 1964).
>
> Edward Lueders, ed., *Books in Literature and The Fine Arts* (New York: Washington Square Press, 1962).
>
> G. Robert Carlsen, *Books and the Teen Age Reader* (New York: Bantam Books, 1967).
>
> Daniel N. Fader and Elton B. McNeil, *Hooked on Books: Program and Proof* (New York: Berkeley, 1968).
>
> Robert O'Neal, *Teacher's Guide to World Literature for the High School* (Champaign, Ill.: NCTE, 1966).
>
> Charlemae Rollins, ed., *We Build Together* (Champaign, Ill.: NCTE, 1967). Books by and about American Negroes.
>
> Barbara Dodd, *Negro Literature for High School Students* (Champaign, Ill.: NCTE, 1968).

This chapter has suggested three important goals of the literature program —self-understanding, imaginative insight, and a balanced perspective. The suggested methods for organizing class, group, and individual instruction or for teaching important attitudes and abilities contribute to the attainment of

[33] One is published by the National Council of Teachers of English, 508 South Sixth St., Champaign, Illinois.

[34] Printed pie charts are available as "My Reading Design," from the *News Journal*, North Manchester, Indiana.

these ends. Only when teachers actually think through the underlying rationale of programs in literature can they really hope to plan a sequence of reading experiences to foster the development of permanent appreciations. Providing materials for individual reading that satisfy only the momentary interests of students is no more sufficient for a total program than is relying on intensive, detailed analysis of a few mature classics, which are often closer to the teacher than to the students. Programs can have significance for both today and tomorrow only if young readers are continuously able to gain from their experiences the real values literature has to offer—insights concerning themselves and their peers, imaginative release, and a rich and ever widening perspective on life.

SELECTED READINGS

ON TEACHING LITERATURE

BURTON, DWIGHT. *Literature Study in the High School.* Rev. ed. New York: Holt, Rinehart & Winston, 1964. A recent general reference on literature for adolescents that contains many helpful teaching suggestions.

CARLSEN, G. ROBERT. *Books and the Teen-Age Reader.* New York: Bantam Books, 1967. Excellent discussion of literature written for adolescents, with annotated bibliographies.

COMMISSION ON LITERATURE. *Freedom and Discipline in English.* New York: College Entrance Examination Board, 1965. A sound discussion of intensive, classroom approaches for the able student.

CROSBY, MURIEL (ed.). *Reading Ladders for Human Relations.* 4th ed. Washington, D.C.: American Council on Education, 1964. The introduction to this excellent, annotated list of books presents many suggestions for leading discussion in the classroom.

DUNNING, STEPHEN. *Teaching Literature to Adolescents—Poetry.* Chicago: Scott, Foresman, 1966. A fresh and invigorating approach to the teaching of poetry.

GORDON, EDWARD J., and NOYES, EDWARD S. (eds.). *Essays on the Teacher of English.* New York: Appleton-Century-Crofts, 1960. Especially valuable for essays on teaching *Huckleberry Finn, Silas Marner,* "The Rime of the Ancient Mariner," and *Julius Caesar,* this volume also contains help on organizing individual reading.

LEARY, LEWIS (ed.). *The Teacher and American Literature.* Champaign, Ill.: NCTE, 1965. Provides a summary of recent scholarship and curricular implications on various dimensions of American literature.

MURPHY, GERALDINE. *The Study of Literature in High School.* Waltham, Mass.: Blaisdell, 1968. Blends scholarly and critical points of view on fiction, poetry, and drama with practical applications for teaching academic pupils.

ROSENBLATT, LOUISE. *Literature as Exploration.* Rev. ed. New York: Noble and Noble, 1968. Offers valuable insights into ways of increasing the contacts between book and reader, of providing for experiences in literature rather than information about literature.

RYAN, MARGARET. *Teaching the Novel in Paperback.* New York: Macmillan, 1963. Supporting the idea that appreciation of this genre can be fostered only if pupils study novels they can respond to actively as they read, the textbook suggests a sequence of fourteen with study guides; discussion of novelist's craft, with specific examples, presents aspects of form characteristic of all fiction.

SQUIRE, JAMES R. (ed.). *Response to Literature.* Champaign, Ill.: NCTE, 1968. Papers and recommendations from Dartmouth seminar concerning teaching of literature.

————, and APPLEBEE, ROGER K. *High School English Instruction Today.* New York: Appleton-Century-Crofts, 1968. This report of a national study of outstanding high school English programs presents recommendations on both the teaching and testing of literature and reports on the reading of 16,000 adolescents.

STAFFORD, WILLIAM. *Friends to This Ground.* Champaign, Ill.: NCTE, 1967. A statement prepared by the Commission on Literature concerning literary study in our culture today.

ON THE READING PREFERENCES OF ADOLESCENTS

BERNSTEIN, MARGERY R. "Relationship Between Interest and Reading Comprehension." *Journal of Educational Research.* Vol. 49, No. 4 (December 1955). Demonstrates the relationship between interest and understanding.

CARLSEN, G. ROBERT. "Behind Reading Interest." *English Journal.* Vol. 43, No. 1 (January 1954), pp. 7–12. Suggests some of the motivations for the preferences expressed by individuals.

JEWETT, ARNO. "What Does Research Tell About the Reading Interests of Junior High Pupils?" *Improving Reading in the Junior High School.* Education Office Bulletin No. 10. Washington, D.C.: Dept. of Health, Education, and Welfare, 1957. Summary of Research on the interests of early adolescents.

MECKEL, HENRY C. "Research in Composition and Literature." In Nathaniel Gage, ed., *Handbook of Research in Teaching.* Chicago: Rand McNally, 1963, pp. 992–97. Summarizes recent research on studies of interest and response.

ROBINSON, HELEN M. "What Research Says to the Teacher of Reading: Reading Interest." *The Reading Teacher.* Vol. 8, No. 6 (March 1955), pp. 173–77. A nontechnical summary of implications for classroom teaching.

SIMPSON, ROY H., and SEARLES, ANTHONY. "Best and Least Liked Stories in the Junior High School." *The English Journal.* Vol. 54, No. 2 (February 1965), pp. 108–11. A study of the response of 4,250 adolescents to 862 short stories, with an analysis of the 77 least-liked and best-liked selections.

ELEVEN

LITERATURE: DRAMA AND POETRY

Magic may be real enough, the magic of word or an act, grafted upon the invisible influences that course through the material world.

GEORGE SANTAYANA [1]

Although drama and poetry have much in common with other types of literature, each calls for facets of appreciation not necessarily required of other forms. Both are concise, suggesting much more than they say; both are written to be heard. Thus in presenting either a play or a poem, the teacher relies primarily on an oral approach. This chapter will be concerned with the teaching problems arising from the fact that both drama and poetry convey meaning and feeling more by implication than by statement, that both gain much from competent oral presentation. The two forms will be discussed separately.

PERSPECTIVE: DRAMA

To read dramatic literature with emotional response, one must be able to sense quickly the possible implications of the dialog, to visualize both the setting and the speaker, to hear the shades of meaning and feeling, as they would be revealed if heard in the theater. The novelist permits a more leisurely manner of interpretation; the playwright depends upon the reader to interpret multidimensionally as he reads.

As with all literature, the study of drama has both immediate and long-range objectives. The immediate aim is to help the student appreciate one play as a record of human experience presented in a unique literary form. The purpose of reading many plays over a period of six years is to help him develop his capacity for appreciating dramatic literature so he will select it

[1] George Santayana, *The Realm of Spirit* (New York: Scribner's, 1940), p. 283.

479

more wisely on television, screen, and stage and thus find richer delight in what he does select. A quickening of perception and a refinement of discrimination for this type of literature is particularly important because so many of our students will give more time to the spoken word in the mass media than to reading. The cultural heritage, significant social concepts, and values for personal living may reach them through film and television, even though plays in printed form may appeal to only a comparatively small percentage of any population.

Everyone is interested in a story. Drama, like fiction, tells a story but in its own distinctive way. Children in elementary school read stories for themselves; they have had some experience in reading dialog. In teaching drama, one builds upon this foundation. A reader accustomed to the narrative style of fiction needs additional skills if he is to develop appreciation for the dramatic form. The student acquires such skills through a sequential program, which includes the study of plays over the six secondary-school years. Because each tells a story, fiction and drama have some things in common; it is the manner in which the story is told that makes reading a play frustrating for the inexperienced reader. An understanding of the nature of drama as manifested in the play underlies the planning of instruction in all aspects of the dramatic form.

Nature of Drama

The word *drama* signifies action. Action, originating in some human or superhuman will and moving toward the accomplishment of a purpose, is a necessary ingredient of drama. It forms the framework of any play. Within this framework the playwright depicts his basic idea, which gives the play its roots in life. Creating characters and providing them with dialog to evoke emotional response, he weaves the total fabric of the dramatic illusion.

A COLLABORATIVE ART FORM While writers of other literary forms rely entirely on their own imaginative efforts, the playwright is essentially a collaborator. True, "the stirring of the idea; the gradual feeding out of information; the shock and countershock of circumstances; the flow of action; the interruption of action; the moments of allusion to earlier events; the preparation of surprise, dread, or delight—all that is the author's and his alone." [2] Nonetheless, whether writing for the stage, movies, or television, he must consider the possibilities and limitations of his production medium; he must take into account the part others will play in bringing his play to life. [3] He depends upon designers to fashion, not backdrops, nor pictures, nor costumes, but an image—an image

[2] Thornton Wilder, "Some Thoughts on Playwriting," in Augusto Centano, ed., *The Intent of the Artist* (Princeton, N.J.: Princeton Univ. Press, 1941), p. 95.
[3] For similarities and contrasts among the media see "The Popular Arts," pages 538–39; in this chapter we are concerned primarily with writers for the theater.

creating an environment in which action and character will have their being. He looks to the actors to convey by voice and body the nuances of meaning and feeling. He relies upon the director to fuse the various elements of light and shade, sight and sound, repose and movement, which evoke the complete dramatic experience. Is it any wonder that many students find the silent reading of a play baffling? To substitute one's own imagination for that of playwright, designers, actors, and director requires long experience with the complexities of the dramatic form.

THE TIME ELEMENT   Both the external and the internal time elements of drama contrast with those of fiction. With no restrictions on length, the novelist can pile up details allowing gradual assimilation of meaning; by entering the minds of his characters as they explore the byways of memory or go forward in anticipation into the future, he can take as much time as he needs to portray events long past or to reveal the hope or dread of what may come. The dramatist can do none of these things; the more rigid time limits of his medium permit revelation only by vivid etching or by brief allusion; brevity demands action and dialog fraught with implication and suggestion.

The internal element of time in drama assumes even greater significance than does the external. Although any story is forward-moving, fiction moves toward the present but concerns itself with what is past; its events have already happened; we know they have because one who knows has said so. In contrast, drama achieves the semblance of reality through the immediate responses of human beings to situations as they occur; we believe because we see these events happening before us. Drama looks toward the future; "it deals essentially with commitments and consequences." [4] The dramatist must so order his material as to give the illusion of life unfolding before us; the past and the future must be explicit in the present. Drama takes place, as Wilder has said, "in a perpetually present time." Within this present, pregnant both with a past that has created the situation and with a future containing the seeds of the past, the tensions of drama are created.

When a play is seen on the stage, the audience has the aid of the playwright's collaborators to summon intellectual and emotional response. Seeing events as they happen, feeling the surges of emotion, sensing the ebb and flow of the action, absorbing implications from voice and gesture—all induce spontaneous reaction. Oral presentation of plays in the classroom offers a poor substitute for the vitality of the theater. Silent reading does even less. However, oral reading by the teacher, opportunities to listen to recordings, re-creation of scenes through classroom productions, can release the imagination and attune ear and voice to shades of meaning and feeling. The study of dramatic literature, with comparisons and contrasts of plays seen by students on stage, screen, and television, can quicken discernment of the subtleties of the dramatic form.

[4] Susanne K. Langer, *Feeling and Form* (New York: Scribner's, 1953), p. 307.

The Structural Elements of a Play

Young people gain appreciation of drama through the study of examples—a sequence of plays illuminating dramatic literature as an art form—and through continual evaluation of those available on stage, screen, and television. Although advanced students in drama may be interested in the details of play construction, students in English classes may well be concerned with only a few aspects—setting, conflict, theme, language. Appreciation of these factors will give a basis for deeper understanding and keener discrimination applicable to all literature presented in play form.

SETTING   On the stage a play begins with the opening of the curtain, whether or not lines are spoken. No important conversation takes place in the first few minutes. The audience needs time to become familiar with the scene, so that, the details having been assimilated, the impression may sink below the conscious, serving its purpose as background for what is to come. For the reader the same is true; with the details of setting, the author has provided the environment for his characters and their story. If, as in much modern experimental theater, the setting is extended to involve the audience, and actors mingle with onlookers, perceiving the narrowing of stage distance is particularly important in understanding the author's purpose.

If the reader is to follow the essential movements of characters, the need for visualizing the setting—the physical surroundings in which overt action is to take place—is apparent. More important, such visualization helps establish the mood and meaning the scene is intended to convey. In what colors do we see it? Is any particular emphasis given to angled lines? To curved? To horizontal? To vertical? Does it suggest the familiar? The exotic? Does it express joy? Sadness? Strife? Foreboding? Is the light bright and gay? Shadowy and somber? Calm and soothing? Angry and disturbing? What is the total impression?

Skilled playwrights rigorously follow the rule that an audience should see nothing extraneous, that everything should have its purpose. Therefore, the reader must be alert to the clues given in the setting. We can expect the scene to do more than fix the physical limits of action; it will reflect something of the inner life of the play—at some times, suggesting very simple things and at others, ideas grasped by only the most perceptive. Even seventh-graders see the significance of these details describing the interior of a log hut in the Antarctic, in *The Brink of Silence:*

> No windows, an oil stove burning, packing boxes serving as chairs and cupboard, a pile of battered books and magazines.

The teacher may have to direct attention to *battered* to elicit the fact that the men have been there some time.

Experienced readers have learned that a certain type of scene—hotel lobby, bus station—provides a logical reason for the brief appearance of many characters. Thus the setting for *Rhinoceros,* unchanged throughout the play, encourages the assumption that the idea to be dramatized affects the whole town:

> Square in a small provincial town . . . entrance to grocer shop, to cafe . . . cafe terrace set with tables and chairs.

The importance of the theme is also stressed by the fact that some characters are unnamed except as waitress, logician, and so on. Perceptive readers recognize the symbolism in these details of the setting for *Death of a Salesman:*

> The salesman's house—a "fragile-seeming home" hemmed in by "a solid vault of apartment houses"; "the blue light of the sky" falling on the house, "an angry glow of orange" on the surrounding area. "An air of the dream clings to the place"—the skeletal house, "partially transparent, the roof-line one-dimensional."

Pertinent details of settings noticed by students in movies and on television can serve as a bridge to the more difficult art of sensing clues on the printed page.

CONFLICT   Conflict, an essential of dramatic action, is based upon an issue—something the protagonist wants to attain or avoid. Around this issue the contest is waged. Because of the conciseness of the one-act play, the elements of structure are more easily comprehended by junior high pupils through this medium than through other literary forms. In a play the struggle is starkly etched; the close reading demanded increases awareness of the series of crises making up the action. Thus young people discover concrete examples of steps in a particular conflict as a particular person meets a sequence of minor triumphs or defeats; they recognize the factors working for him and those hindering him; they realize why he wins or fails. Continued study of short plays builds, more or less unconsciously, understanding of the significance of the play form without the need of technical terminology.

THEME   Theme is strictly idea—the idea that gives the play its roots in life, the idea that pervades and gives universality to the action. It is the overriding truth behind the story, the comment the author wishes to make on human values and human experience. Any number of plays may be concerned primarily with greed, each with a different theme determined by the attitude the writer takes toward his subject. Occasionally, lines from the play may state the theme to the reader's satisfaction—"That is all of wisdom, the wearing of crowns before the eyes of life," from *The Slave with Two Faces.* At times the title gives specific direction—*You Can't Take It with You, They Knew What They Wanted.* More often it stirs the imagination by suggesting a clue to tie events to the underlying idea—*The Green Pastures, Journey's End, The Little Foxes.* In any case, the playwright trusts his theme to be revealed by the unity of his dramatic design. What does the play, always greater than the sum of its parts, say about human beings and their struggles to achieve their aspirations?

LANGUAGE   Action may be basic to the play, but it is with language, giving substance and spirit to the action, that the dramatic spell is created. Whether a line alludes to the past, foreshadows the future, advances action, exposes feelings, highlights facets of character, clarifies motives—whether it is understatement, exaggeration, or evasion—the words are primarily evocative rather than descriptive; they must be if the audience—or the reader—is to be aware of each instant as it passes. The playwright, as he shapes his ideas and delineates action, tries to hear the words as his audience will hear them, to picture the images that may come to mind. Story and theme are essential, but it is the language that reveals the subtleties of both.

From the qualities that belong to drama as distinct from other literary forms, the teacher derives the principles for organizing instruction to build basic understandings and to foster appreciation.

THE TEACHING PROBLEM

The nature of drama determines the core of the teaching problem: helping students visualize, read for implications rather than for description or statement, hear the words as the character would speak them, see the play as a whole. These problems concern the teacher as he plans instruction in dramatic literature.

ORGANIZING INSTRUCTION

In planning for any class, the teacher first tries to learn as much as possible about the previous experience of his students. While those teaching a play in junior high school can safely assume that knowledge of this literary form is slight, even here some students will read better than others; some will have participated in plays both within the classroom and without; some will have acquired a degree of discrimination in selecting motion pictures and television programs. A brief survey covering their experiences with plays presented in the different media—experiences pupils have found meaningful—will give some indication of the level of sophistication of individuals and of the group. Thus enlightened, the teacher may make plans for instruction. Instruction in any class takes into account the learning experiences desirable during the secondary school years. Therefore, the following discussion will suggest guide lines for four major concerns of an over-all program—content, the study of an individual play, oral interpretation, and teaching Shakespearean drama.

Content

In the English class, experiences with drama should center on the experience and interpretation of dramatic literature. Types of play, history of drama, lives of actors, Shakespeare's life and times, the latest news of television personalities—all such peripheral information should remain peripheral. It can too easily substitute for the real thing—the play itself.

The guide lines for a six-year program will take into account the nature of drama and the difficulties entailed in understanding and interpreting this literary form. Probably all English teachers would agree that one goal should be the appreciation of those Shakespearean plays appropriate for inclusion in the secondary-school curriculum. Such appreciation requires a long apprenticeship with simpler forms—one-act plays for seventh- and eighth-graders, a three-act modern play for the ninth grade, and Shakespeare reserved for senior high students.[5] With a thorough grounding in the complexities of drama in its simplest forms, the student has a basis for acquiring the reading skills necessary for Shakespearean plays—skills upon which to build genuine appreciation.

Helping students of widely varying abilities attain desirable objectives requires three groupings of material, each demanding progressively more initiative and skill on the part of the student: at least one play to be studied by the class, plays on different levels of difficulty to be studied by groups, plays to be read by individuals. The first can serve as the main vehicle for teaching the necessary skills; students can then apply what they have learned to similar problems encountered in group and individual work.

The following grouping of plays (see pages 486–87) is not fixed, any one in different circumstances being suitable for different purposes. At some times an entire class may profit from the study of *Winterset;* at other times, only five or six students; at still others, only one. The list is not intended to be exhaustive; it contains only some of the plays used successfully with junior and senior high school students. Each teacher will have his own favorites. The labeling of difficulty represents personal opinion.[6]

After the class has studied one play, the teacher can provide further experience through group and individual work. In suggesting plays for groups, he will be guided not only by the caliber of the students but by the time he can give to each group. Student opinion should have weight in selecting plays for group study; letting students choose the play encourages reading on the part of individuals and insures better group morale. Buying ten copies of four different plays rather than forty copies of one play makes some choice possible. If individual reading of plays is started at the same time, students will be occupied while the teacher is busy with groups. School and public librarians, dedicated to the promotion of lifelong reading habits, will help in making available the resources at their command. A classroom library is an invaluable

[5] For gifted and able pupils, this sequence may be telescoped into less time.
[6] An asterisk indicates plays that are suitable for junior high school students.

LEAST DIFFICULT

Life with Father Howard Lindsay
  and Russell Crouse
Ah, Wilderness! Eugene O'Neill
The Far Off Hills Lennox Robinson
The Ivory Door A. A. Milne
I Remember Mama John Van Druten
The King and I Richard Rodgers
  and Oscar Hammerstein II
The Miracle Worker William Gibson
Our Town Thornton Wilder
Purlie Victorious Ossie Davis
Sunrise at Campobello Dore Schary

SHORT PLAYS

The Brink of Silence Esther Galbraith
Dust of the Road Kenneth Sawyer
  Goodman

The Eldest Edna Ferber
Exchange Althea Thurston
The Fifteenth Candle Rachel Field
Finders Keepers George Kelly
The Finger of God Percival Wilde
The Man Who Married a Dumb Wife
  Anatole France
Romancers (Act I) Edmond Rostand
Sham Frank G. Tompkins
The Slave with Two Faces Mary
  Carolyn Davies
Spreading the News Lady Gregory
The Valiant Holworthy Hall and
  Robert Middlemas
The Will James M. Barrie
The Wonder Hat Kenneth Sawyer
  Goodman and Ben Hecht

aid. Once initiated into the techniques of seeing with the inner eye and listening with the inner ear, many young people, reluctant to embark on a long novel, have found plays a less formidable venture. Lured, at first, by drama's comparative brevity and its rapid development of action through conversation, many have come to realize the pleasure such reading can bring.

THEATER OF THE ABSURD   In extending dramatic experience, some teachers may consider plays of the Absurd theater. A brief description of how such plays differ from the traditional may be helpful. Because of its presentation on television, *Waiting for Godot* is perhaps most widely known; we have it in mind in making the following statements. In general, however, a combination of the following qualities in any play marks it as belonging to the theater of the Absurd:

protagonist   Extreme neurotic, what psychiatrists call the "borderline personality."
his situation   When one resembling this type (Hamlet) appears in the classical or traditional play, he is placed *within* an established relationship; in the Absurd he is *outside.*
conflict   Between his intense desire to form a satisfying relationship and his intense fear that if he does he will destroy his own identity.
theme   Statement about such problems as isolation, loneliness, confusion between reality and illusion, despair, difficulty of communicating.
dialog   For the most part, repetitious and monotonous; humor, inserted for relief, is likely to make a sensitive audience uncomfortable since it comes from the situation, which is not funny.

form   Although the playwright structures his material, his structure is not easily
      discernible; thus the content may seem amorphous to one knowing only plays
      in traditional form.
resolution   None.

With such a protagonist in such a predicament, traditional treatment would
be impossible. Critics have accused playwrights of the Absurd of saying life
has no meaning. They do not say that. Precisely because the writer thinks life
does have meaning, he finds those searching for meaning with little hope of
finding it a worthy subject for drama.

We have enough evidence to know that plays of the Absurd are not
acceptable fare to many adults, even inveterate play-goers. We think such
plays unsuitable for the majority of our students. We say this not because
young people might find the theme depressing and the problem hard to
understand, but because the endless talk, getting nowhere, might bore them.

Undoubtedly, some "honors" classes and other sophisticated groups and
individuals may be curious. They should have a chance to investigate this
segment of the theater. *Rhinoceros* makes a good introduction. While significant aspects of this play are absurd, the play itself is not part of the theater
of the Absurd. It should be suitable for many classes. At times it might be
followed by class or group or individual study of a play of the Absurd. Com-
parsion can make the distinction between the two types clear. For selected
students one play representing the theater of the Absurd should provide an
extension of the dramatic experience.

The Study of an Individual Play

If the class has had very little experience with dramatic literature, a play will
require special attention; better learning results if teaching is so planned to
provide the needed instruction for this literary form. The study of a play
usually begins with an initial reading accomplished as quickly as the difficulty
of the material permits; this first reading is then reinforced by discussing and
rereading key lines and scenes to delineate the design of the action and the
idea that controls it; oral presentation of scenes follows—always desirable, it
is essential for those inexperienced in reading plays. If recordings are available, listening to skilled actors present the play makes a stimulating finale for
the total experience.

FIRST READING   The first reading stresses visualization and clues to deeper
meaning in setting, lines, and action. As far as time allows, students should
hear the play read aloud, at first by the teacher and the more capable readers.
The teacher may read the first scene as the class follows the text. After the
opening scenes have filled in the background and clarified the initial situation,
the teacher may ask for volunteers, selecting only those he knows will give

an adequate reading. If the scenes to be read orally the next day are announced, interested students may select characters and, through individual oral practice, prepare for reading. Those who cannot be taught quickly to read aloud should not be forced to at this time, since they distract others from the flow of the action. However, after instruction in oral interpretation, all should have a chance to read parts suited to their abilities.

Walt Whitman once said, "I seek less to display any theme or thought and more to bring you into the atmosphere of the theme or thought—there to pursue your own flight." The playwright strives in similar fashion. The teacher, as intermediary for author and reader, tries to bring students into the atmosphere of the play. Thus it is almost always essential to start a play with oral reading of the opening scenes. Suppose the play chosen for study is *Death of a Salesman*. The shadowy setting establishes the mood for the entrance of the salesman with his heavy packs.

THE SETTING

What is the effect of seeing the salesman's home as skeletal? What different impression would a firmly built structure give?

Why not have the salesman return when the room is lighted or when the sun is shining?

Why are the tall buildings so close? Why not have their tops showing in the distance?

Why the contrasting blue and orange light?

THE SALESMAN'S ENTRANCE

What do we learn from the lines of his body even before we see him clearly? How do you think he would walk?

What hint does the author give the actor to suggest the weight of the packs? Can you feel that weight?

The first few pages of the opening scene, a conversation between the salesman Willy Loman and his wife Linda give background information and present the immediate situation. The reader learns that Loman, a man of sixty, lives in his own New York home, paid for by a lifetime of work. For years he has been the New England representative of a Manhattan firm, traveling back and forth by automobile. He has two sons; before leaving on his selling trip, he has quarreled with the thirty-four-year-old Biff, who has recently returned home. The father is worried because his son's plans for his life work have always been erratic and ineffectual. Loman has turned back without completing his business because he finds himself blacking out and the car repeatedly leaving the road. He plans to ask for a transfer to the New York office and to have another talk with Biff. These are the facts; the implications in the way the author has ordered his lines are left for the reader to discover.

The purpose of questions so early in the play is to stimulate thinking and feeling, to underline the need for close reading, not to find categorical answers. Initial questions probe for meanings, as yet only vaguely suggested, to be clarified as the play unfolds.

Assured by her husband that "nothing has happened," Linda still asks, "You didn't smash the car, did you?" Why not, "Did you smash the car?" How do the connotations differ?

Willy boasts of his early record with the company. Why is this significant? Why does he say he is vital to New England?

What is the purpose of Willy's line, "some people accomplish something"?

Willy says Biff is a lazy bum; later he contradicts himself. Why does the author have this happen? Which does Willy believe? Does he know? Why does he reminisce about Biff's early days? When has he been touched by nostalgia before? Is it significant these two instances occur so early in the play?

Linda seems at present an almost neutral character; her lines with the exception of "life is a casting off" are unrealistic, almost glib. Is she shallow? Dull-witted? Or has she been forced to bolster her husband's belief in himself so often her response has become automatic?

For most classes analysis of the first few scenes of any play is necessary. The same procedure is suggested for the entire short play read by immature students. With the more competent, working on longer plays, particular scenes can be examined and a study guide provided for the portions of the play they will read as assignments. Class discussions can insure understandings. Careful reading and penetrating analysis of the lines make form, structure, and total meaning more apparent.

SECOND READING   The first reading of any play promotes understanding of certain human beings and their story. As the class reviews key lines and scenes, they come to realize with what economy the author has depicted his characters and built the action—the lines, written to reveal the individual's attitudes and values, his deep-seated fears and hopes; the action, created to portray situations showing him as a particular kind of person confronted with particular problems. The significance of details in the setting—the skeletal home, the angry orange light that intrudes, the harsh actuality of the encroaching buildings—has also become apparent. Now the reader realizes that none of the opening lines have been thrown away; they fill in background, but in a way to suggest Loman's dilemma. His nostalgia for the days when he envisioned material success—the only kind that had seemed important—becomes poignant as the dream contrasts with the reality. So too does the father's fear that his son's life will repeat the pattern. The significance of Willy's rejection of Linda's belief that "life is a casting off" is now clear. His life-long refusal to cast off his illusions prepares us for his final inability to accept the truth about his son and himself.

This compression of both lines and action essential to drama helps students recognize the basic structure. As Loman relives events in his past, the commitments he has made, with their attendant consequences, delineate the steps in the conflict. The forces working for and against him, as well as the deciding agent, which has been present in the play from the beginning, become evident. All these can be stated in broader terms as the reader realizes they exist under different guises in all lives. The accompanying table, using well-known plays, illustrates how the elements of a particular dramatic conflict reveal their universality when translated into general terms.

CONFLICT IN DRAMA

	Issue	*Forces*	*Deciding agent*
Death of a Sales-man	Loman wants to continue to believe in his success.	His illusions versus reality.	Recognizing he can no longer face reality.
The Bishop's Candlesticks	The Bishop wants to give Jean Valjean a chance for rehabilitation.	Jean's attempt to secure his freedom versus the attitude of society toward convicts.	The wisdom and humanity of the Bishop.
The Ivory Door	Perivale wants to discover the truth behind the door.	An inquiring mind versus superstition.	Perivale's courage.
Elizabeth the Queen	Elizabeth wants to keep her throne and Essex.	Elizabeth's pride and ambition versus Essex's pride and ambition.	Essex's objective appraisal of the situation.
The Little Foxes	Regina wants to possess the wealth at any cost.	Regina's greed versus her husband's efforts to protect himself.	Regina's ruthlessness.

Perception of the elements of conflict in their universal aspects leads to an understanding of the idea or theme the drama exemplifies. The teacher, not belaboring the point nor insisting upon acceptance of any one statement, should try to help even young pupils recognize the idea that so stirred the author that he tried to translate it into the concrete situations that make up the play. The beginning teacher is at times distressed because he cannot root out the heresy that theme and moral are synonymous. May it not mean only that readers have had too little experience to see the difference? Granted, the purpose of art is not to teach a lesson; however, its subject is humanity in all aspects; if the immature reader thinks the lesson he gains epitomizes the author's meaning, the play still has had impact. Ability to recognize a theme consistent with the total context comes only after varied experiences with literature and with life.

THIRD READING   Ideally, the study of a play should end with the oral presentation of key scenes. Presumably, unless the class is composed of students experienced in the play form or the teacher has assumed most of the presentation himself, oral interpretation up to this time has been negligible. Most classes need instruction in translating printed symbols into vocal sounds conveying meaning and feeling. However, all classes, since they now understand the design of the play, should be able to select the scenes that will give an audience the highlights of the drama. In fact, this selection is a test of their understanding of the play as a whole. Insofar as time allows, teachers plan some oral interpretation as the final experience with any play the class studies.

Oral Interpretation

The classroom presentation of plays is essentially a reading and listening experience. While children may benefit from the impetus that costumes and props give if appropriate, usually such paraphernalia, hastily collected and oddly assorted, serve only to defeat the real purpose—participation in an imaginative experience. Even stage movement, unless adequate rehearsal time has been allowed, can be a detriment. Students, seated at a table before the class, can effectively convey the meaning and spirit of a play through voice and facial expression. Time allowed for preparation can be more profitably spent in working on interpretation of lines and character portrayal, with students continually changing their roles from listener to reader. Helping students present a play in the classroom falls naturally into two parts: teaching interpretation and preparing a shortened version for oral presentation.

TEACHING INTERPRETATION

Since time for teaching oral interpretation in the English class is limited, the teacher, after the play has been studied, can develop skill in both appreciative listening and oral presentation by concentrating on a few scenes. A play need not be on the level of sophistication of *Death of a Salesman* to illustrate the nature of drama as a distinct form. Even the simplest play can do this; even the briefest scene in a play presents many problems for beginners. Suppose, for example, a junior high class has studied *The Bishop's Candlesticks*, the Norman McKinnel dramatization of the well-known incident from *Les Misérables*. Two short scenes—the opening one between Persomé and the maid and a later one between the Bishop and the convict—may serve as material for intensive instruction and practice. They give both boys and girls a chance to participate, and they present problems found in any dramatic scene: portraying characters, interpreting lines, projecting total meaning.

PORTRAYING CHARACTERS By appropriate questions the teacher will review what the play has revealed about the characters. *The Bishop's Candlesticks* has two problems of balance as related to characterization. The emotional opening scene can easily be overdone, with a portrayal of Persomé as a shrew—a concept the total play does not support. Understanding the play as a whole brings into proper focus the incident in which she discovers the silver salt cellars have been sold. They mean more than pieces of silver to her; they symbolize all the refinement of living she and her brother once enjoyed. The Bishop's attitude toward her reveals much; he recognizes in her a fundamental kindness her speeches belie. The key to a sympathetic interpretation of her character in the opening scene lies in all the facts the play has disclosed.

The second problem concerns the relationship between the Bishop and Jean Valjean. Reading the melodramatic and volatile lines given the convict with all stops out will disturb the harmony of the play, which must be dominated by the quiet strength of the Bishop. Thoughtful interpretation of the characters as delineated by the author avoids striking a discordant note and throwing the play off balance. Young people can learn much about oral presentation, as well as more about the drama itself, by reading and listening to various interpretations of these two scenes. In like manner, with scenes chosen from any other play, students, listening to voice quality, intonation, and suggestion of feeling, can decide who best preserves the delicate balance between too little and too much, who best conveys the inner spirit of the character as conceived by the playwright.

INTERPRETING LINES Instead of reading and rereading any scene from any play, center attention on individual lines. All students should have an opportunity to read; all can judge the quality of the performance. Although students focus on what the lines are intended to convey, the teacher may feel that some technical knowledge concerning interpretation is helpful.

Logical meaning is conveyed by phrasing and emphasis. No fixed rules can be given for either; both are vocal expressions of mental activity on the part of the reader. Through phrasing—the division of a passage into thought groups —the reader helps the listener focus on the sequence of ideas; through emphasis—the highlighting of significant words and phrases and the subordination of others—he points up relationships and thus reveals total meaning. Phrasing sometimes causes difficulty because the thought groups the interpreter must use do not coincide with the marks of punctuation, which are guides to the meaning but highly fallible guides for the voice. Beginners tend to pause at every mark of punctuation and nowhere else; the experienced reader knows that such pauses, as in the following, are not always necessary: "Not yet, madam . . ." "Ah! You thought . . ." and that often pauses, at times so slight as to be almost imperceptible, are essential where no punctuation is indicated: "But you had no right/to do so// without asking me." When problems in phrasing arise, let students compare several readings to determine which gives the sense. Almost never is there only one right way.

All forms of emphasis—force, duration, pause, change of pitch—are inherent in the normal pattern of intelligible speech, for the most part learned by imitation and employed unconsciously. However, the student needs help in transferring to the words and thoughts of another a technique he has heretofore used automatically. Expressive speech is marked by variety. Any form of emphasis may be overused—duration, for example, by the affected "gusher" —but force, the most obtrusive, is perhaps the worst offender with the beginning reader.[7] Let students try different ways of stressing words to bring out meaning. Thinking of what the lines say will result in variety without the need of technical terms. Continued attention to careful listening will enable students to select the interpretation that conveys the total meaning, yet avoids monotony and unpleasant vocal quality.

In teaching a minimum of interpretation, the teacher has a chance to show some of the distinctions between oral and written language. The latter, a symbol of the former, is inadequate for indicating to the reader how lines should be spoken. For instance, unless given to an overly precise person, such expressions as "it is rude" and "that is no reason" usually should be translated into conversational idiom—"it's rude" and "that's no reason." Expressions showing states of mind or feeling—"ahem" and "ha! ha!"—are hints for interpretation, not lines to be read. Though obvious to the competent reader, these helps for reading need to be recognized by the inexperienced for what they are. Practice in transferring the printed symbols to the vocal calls attention to an important aspect of language.

Conveying emotion presents for some students a difficult problem; they may not be able to project themselves into the feeling of the character. For instance, in the opening scene described above, Persomé moves from irritation to horrified amazement, to sorrow tinged with fear. The student who reads the scene too matter-of-factly may be helped by questions to aid her either to recall occasions when she felt the same emotion or to conjure up imaginary ones. What makes you irritable? How do you act? How do you think you sound? If questions do not bring results, it is often worthwhile with beginners to turn aside from the play momentarily and allow a few minutes' practice on another sentence, first to convey the meaning pleasantly, then in an irritable manner: "I'm sorry, but you can't borrow my sweater; I'm going to wear it myself." However, too much time should not be spent on such devices; the real problem may be inhibition. Thus, repeated unsuccessful trials bring only embarrassment and make future attempts less likely to succeed. The teacher needs a light touch in teaching interpretation and must be guided by the belief that frequent brief attempts are likely to secure better reading than prolonged sessions that aim at acceptable standards for all.

PROJECTING TOTAL MEANING   After practice in interpreting lines, students are ready to attempt the projection of the scene as a unit. Any scene selected will have its own aspect of the conflict and its own crisis, however minor in reference to the total play. Through reading the scene and through discussion, students will discover that the main considerations concern tempo and climax. With beginners, maintaining proper tempo is largely a matter of forming the habit of picking up cues. Interpretation has taken care of tempo

---

[7] The "Suggested Learning Experiences," pages 256–58, in Chapter Six, are pertinent here.

within speeches. Young people have difficulty learning that each speech, even if it is to be spoken slowly, must follow immediately the one that precedes. Speeches that interrupt present a nice problem, since the first word must be spoken almost simultaneously with the last word of the previous speaker:

> Madam said I was not to chatter, so I thought—
> Ah! You thought!

The matter of timing, crucial in all drama, deserves special attention in practice; whatever the prevailing tempo of a play, the flow of action is lost unless readers are capable of conveying the feeling of continual onward movement.

The crisis of any scene must be viewed in relation to the total play. For instance, the opening scene of *The Bishop's Candlesticks* builds steadily from the beginning to the end with two minor peaks between. It cannot be read on as high an emotional level as the lines in isolation might seem to suggest. Such a reading would destroy the effectiveness of later events and disturb the balance of the play. Other scenes from other plays will present similar but different problems. Each scene, from whatever play, must be considered not only for its internal unity but in its relation to the play as a whole.

The two plays discussed—*Death of a Salesman*, appropriate for twelfth grade, and *The Bishop's Candlesticks*, suitable for seventh grade—are examples, nothing more. They demonstrate that certain problems are characteristic of all drama; the procedures suggested are applicable to all plays. Any play requires close study; any play needs oral presentation to bring it to life. Continued attempts to interpret lines and to portray characters, continued experience in trying to judge the effectiveness of classroom presentations, establish a basis for discrimination in listening, in viewing, and in reading dramatic literature.

PRESENTING THE ORAL VERSION

The limited time for teaching interpretation is the reason for having inexperienced readers present a few scenes rather than the entire play. A sequence of brief scenes is likely to provide a more satisfying experience for both performers and listeners.

PREPARING THE SCRIPT The preparation of a script may progress in some such manner as is described here. A time limit, rigidly adhered to, should be agreed upon—perhaps no more than fifteen minutes for the one-act and thirty minutes for the long play. Through a total class experience in preparing a script the teacher can smooth the way for similar procedures students will later undertake on their own initiative.

The scenes selected should represent some of the highlights in the play. They may include one of exposition, one presenting a minor crisis or the major climax, one illustrating some salient characteristic of the play—its humor, its dramatic power, the vivid portrayal of a character. The literary work itself determines the choice. It is well to ask each student to review the play and to select the scenes he thinks will give the fullest understanding to a listener unfamiliar with the play. After advocates present their arguments for including certain scenes, the class may make the final decision, keeping within the over-all time limit.

Since the presentation should be clear to listeners who do not know the play, the class must plan narrative to connect the scenes. This activity, as well as the arguments advanced for the selection of the scenes, shows how well students understand the play. The secretary may list on the board items individuals think should be used to introduce each scene. After the class eliminates all but the essential points, a volunteer or a committee may write the narrative. This writing is an exercise in compression and discrimination; with clarity and brevity the narrators try to preserve as far as possible the style and the spirit of the play.

Stage directions within the chosen scenes are kept to a minimum. Only descriptions of significant movement and of pantomime the listener must visualize in order to understand the lines should be included.

REHEARSING AND CASTING   Each scene may first be read by volunteers, and the reading should be followed by discussion to bring out the problems it poses. Then various interpretations of difficult lines and ways of suggesting attitudes and feelings deserve attention. After this preliminary work, the class may choose two casts for each scene; practice for this assignment does not require group meetings, although interested students often arrange for rehearsals on their own time. The following day, after listening to both presentations of all scenes, the class selects one cast, a narrator, and someone to read the stage directions for the final performance. Since all have had a chance to read during the preliminary work, teachers should not feel obligated to use as many students as possible for this final reading. When one person portrays the same character throughout, a more convincing performance is possible.

PRESENTING THE FINAL READING   The final presentation furnishes testing ground for the skills and appreciations acquired by both listeners and readers. A tape recording will be invaluable in checking evidence to substantiate critical judgment and in permitting the reader to determine whether his spoken lines sound as he had hoped they would.

One cannot expect a professional performance from young people; one can, however, accustom both readers and listeners to center attention on the play rather than on the performers. Some discussion of the support one actor gives another in preserving the unity of plays seen on television will stress similar needs in the classroom. All readers, even those with only a few lines, should follow the script closely. Thus, avoiding distractions, students are better able to maintain tempo and mood to the limit of their potential.

In the kind of presentation recommended here, the part of the narrator is particularly significant; without him, the production would lack unity. He requircs as much skill as do the actors. His reading should be as vital as he can make it; it carries the action forward as definitely as do the scenes. A play can be spoiled as a play by a single line as effectively as by many. Teachers should help all performers realize that every part is important.

The person reading stage directions describes the setting, making it as simple or as dramatic as the details warrant. He reads the directions within the scenes quickly and matter-of-factly, subordinating them to the sweep of the action.

Those who are not reading do not follow the text; they listen to enjoy, to appreciate, to evaluate.

Obviously, students differ in the natural equipment they bring to the arts of listening and interpreting. However, intensive instruction based on a limited amount of material, with ample opportunity for all to take part and with the less able learning from the more talented, provides a foundation upon which each can build according to his interests and native endowment.

EXTENDING INTERPRETIVE EXPERIENCE Further experience in interpretation can come from plays studied by groups and from those selected for individual reading. After a group has studied a play, it may follow the procedure suggested above—select a few scenes, prepare the necessary narrative, and give the shortened version of the play as a round-table reading before the class. Often teachers find ways to use these presentations outside their own classrooms: *An Enemy of the People* or *A Raisin in the Sun* for a class in social problems; *State of the Union* for a group studying United States history; *Abe Lincoln in Illinois* for an invitational assembly; an eighth-grade reading for seventh- and eighth-graders taking English at the same hour; a presentation by advanced students for a tenth-grade class. When two classes are studying the same play, exchange of oral readings forms the basis for interesting comparisons. If a recording has been made, these tapes can be used without disrupting school schedules in any class where the teacher thinks the material suitable. In fact, the opportunities for providing further oral experiences are so abundant a teacher can use only a few of those offered.

Teachers may encourage competent oral readers to present brief passages from the individual plays read. The selection, one that can be adequately handled by a single reader, should furnish the key to one of the essential factors of the play. If the student selects a scene, it will require an introduction; if he selects several brief excerpts, connecting commentary is necessary. In any case, he avoids telling the story; instead, the selection should represent an exercise in discriminating judgment. The student should ask himself what one impression of the play does he want to give? What passages will best express it? He may decide to stress lines presenting a decision affecting central action, depicting the resolution of the conflict, showing a character's philosophy, reflecting the theme. These individual presentations may be given in small groups, with listeners selecting those that best accomplish the purpose each reader has set for himself. Those chosen can later be given before the class.

The study and oral interpretation of drama by the class as a whole can arouse the interest of the student and help him acquire some of the skills needed for appreciation. Group and individual experience in reading and interpreting plays provides the necessary time and impetus for him to explore on his own—an exploration essential if he is ever to enjoy reading plays for himself or to become a more responsive and discriminating participant in those he sees presented.

Teaching Shakespearean Drama

Shakespeare wrote his plays to be acted, to be seen, to be heard. The ideal way to develop appreciation for them would be to have pupils study them in the classroom and then see them performed by professional actors. But this utopian dream is far from reality. We can, however, approach a Shakespearean play as living theater, not as an academic chore. Stripped of his language and verse, Shakespeare is not Shakespeare. Since one of the English teacher's aims is to inculcate in as many students as possible a respect for the beauty and power of their own language, we should use the most perfect vehicle in the curriculum to disclose that beauty and power. Students should visualize the action, hear the lines read, see the play unfold. They do not need a mimeographed synopsis of the story to mediate between them and the playwright; they do need the vitality, the insight, and the expressive voice of the teacher.

PRESENTING THE PLAY ORALLY Few secondary-school students are prepared to read Shakespeare silently on their own. The problems posed by the poetic form with its inverted word order and figurative language, the archaic expressions, the convention of the soliloquy, the multiplicity of characters and scenes, the absence of description of setting and of stage directions—all these often evoke negative attitudes even in superior students who, with diligent attention to footnotes, may ultimately fathom the essential meanings. The answer to the challenge that resistance to *Julius Caesar* or *Macbeth* creates is not the elimination of Shakespeare from the curriculum but rather the provision of more assistance to students when difficulties occur as they read. Oral reading by the teacher as students follow in their books is likely to spark more understanding and enthusiasm than will lengthy home reading assignments. Such a reading can convey both the essential conflict of the play and the power of the language. Moreover, the teacher can stop after an important scene or a moving speech to encourage the necessary understanding and reflection. Most plays can be read aloud in this manner in seven or eight class hours, with intensive analysis postponed until students have grasped the drama as a whole. Assignments requiring the rereading of scenes out of class or calling for exploration of passages in writing may be given to supplement the oral reading.[8]

[8] See the unit "Macbeth," pages 605–06.

This suggestion for oral presentation is not a plea for the teacher to out-herod Herod. Reading is not acting; it is the mere suggestion of meaning and feeling to bring life to the printed page. Anyone who understands a play can learn to read it aloud acceptably; a little private practice does wonders. Then, too, so few Shakespearean plays are taught on the secondary-school level that it is not an impossible task for a teacher to learn to read them aloud. Occasionally class members will volunteer to read; such interest should be encouraged, but unless the teacher knows the reading will be competent, he is wise to reserve for himself the major lines carrying the meaning of the play. It is important at this point to distinguish the basic difference between teaching students how to read Shakespeare and providing experiences in oral interpretation. Students' readings are perhaps best rehearsed and presented after the play has been read and understood.

SUPPLYING NECESSARY INFORMATION Consideration of background material should be limited, particularly before the plays are read. An understanding of the political turmoil in eleventh-century Scotland, inviting invasion by foreign powers, is necessary to the reading of *Macbeth;* some conception of economic and political conditions in ancient Rome, to *Julius Caesar;* for *Henry IV, Part I,* a cursory grasp of the circumstances that brought Henry to the throne: the help the Percys gave him in deposing Richard II, the contrasts between Henry and Richard as young men. Such information is necessary but can be quickly supplied by the teacher. He can fill in further background as the reading proceeds. He needs to resist the temptation to plan extended research projects on the history of the times, on the Globe theater, on the Elizabethan Age; to refrain from assignments on the introduction, no matter how delightfully written. Shakespeare should speak for himself—and as soon as possible. After a play has been read, if student interest remains high, supplementary reports on pertinent topics may well be encouraged.

Another help teachers can give concerns the names of characters and their relationships, particularly when genealogies are mingled and confused. A few minutes with the help of the chalkboard will show how near and yet how far Macbeth was from becoming king legally, will explain why Duncan favors him over Banquo. Sometimes it is wise to suggest that students direct attention initially to motives and actions of only a selected group of characters: Caesar, Brutus, Antony, and Cassius in *Julius Caesar;* Henry, the Percys, Hal, and Falstaff in *Henry IV.* Such suggestions may prevent conscientious but confused adolescents from becoming overly apprehensive and yet offer direction for basic understandings, which can be broadened as the play is read.

STIMULATING IMAGINATIVE RESPONSE Begin the study of any Shakespearean play with enthusiasm and some device to spark the imagination.[9] For instance, the day before introducing *Julius Caesar,* place some large printed headlines

[9] For the use of music to introduce a play, see "Macbeth," pages 603–04.

on the board. Done in color, they should get every student's attention as soon as he enters the room:

Patriots Combine Against Dictator
Assassins Attack Noble Leader
Plot Involves Trusted Officials
Chaos Reigns in City

The headlines should not reveal time, locale, or whether the attack was successful. Ask students to look them over carefully to see just what is revealed, to suggest to what event and to what country they might apply. After students have discussed possible times and places, ask if there is any contradiction in the headlines; they will spot the first and second as being opposite in point of view. Practice of such slanting can be referred to later as the play is read. Then tell students these headlines never appeared, not because the events did not happen, but because newspapers had not yet come into being; supply the year 44 B.C. After establishing that the place was Rome and the attack upon Caesar, begin the introductory material for the play. With students so familiar with the curriculum they know *Julius Caesar* is next on the docket, such a device may not prove a very good guessing game. However, the discussion should stress in some way the timeliness of the themes they will discover as they read the play.

PLANNING SPECIFIC TASKS   Planning specific tasks that point out significant lines and passages will aid in directing attention to the meaning of the play. Such exercises as the following have been used as assignments to help students examine action and character in *Julius Caesar:*

After reading the first scene, find the lines that show:
Pompey had formerly been as popular as Caesar
Not all Romans were ready to renounce Pompey
Caesar's growing power was considered dangerous
After reading Act I, examine the different points of view toward Brutus reflected in the following quotations:

I am not gamesome. I do lack some part
Of that quick spirit that is in Antony.
                                        BRUTUS (Scene 2)

Well Brutus, thou art noble; yet, I see,
Thy honorable metal may be wrought
From that it is disposed. . . .
                                        CASSIUS (Scene 2)

Oh, he sits high in all the people's hearts;
And that which would appear offense in us
His countenance, like richest alchemy,
Will change to virtue and to worthiness.
                                        CASCA (Scene 3)

What picture of this man seems to be emerging? Application of this principle is illustrated on different levels of sophistication in the *Macbeth* unit at the end of this part.

USING INSTRUCTIONAL AIDS Instructional aids of various kinds prove particularly valuable in teaching Shakespearean drama. Motion pictures with sound—film adaptations and kinescopes of television presentations—provide a provocative experience, stimulating worthwhile discussions. The many recordings of plays usually taught on the secondary level are perhaps of greatest assistance; used either in part or in their entirety, they may serve various purposes. They offer a novel approach to character study; for instance, the student may consider which reading of Macbeth's plotting of Duncan's murder most nearly coincides with his own impression. Anthony Quayle's? Alec Guinness'? What differences are apparent in the Hamlet soliloquies recorded by Laurence Olivier, John Gielgud, Richard Burton, and Maurice Evans? An evaluation of varying interpretations encourages the reader to reassess his own point of view. Invaluable as a finale is a recording of the full play, allowing listeners to sense the flow of action and to savor the beauty and power of the language. Helpful as these aids are, they are nevertheless supplemental; students derive the greatest satisfaction from a professional reading of a difficult play only after previous study has prepared for its appreciation.

A six-year curriculum, beginning with the study and oral interpretation of simple plays, continuing with those of gradually increasing difficulty, and culminating with the more challenging modern as well as Shakespearean drama, provides a program that can develop appreciation for literature and for plays presented by the various media.

SUGGESTED LEARNING EXPERIENCES

Classroom experiences to increase understanding and appreciation of drama are concerned with plays students read and see. Thus, the following merely suggest ways of emphasizing various aspects of such understandings and appreciations after a play has been studied by the class and while students continue reading individually and in groups.

TO LEARN TO INTERPRET CLUES IN THE SETTING

▶ *Realize setting may convey both facts and feelings*

1. The following descriptions show some of the facts and feelings settings can suggest. Read these aloud, and ask students to visualize the scene as they listen to the facts, then to determine what the facts seem to imply about the nature of the play. What do the paired settings have in common? How do they differ in implication?

A foreign, medieval setting contrasts with a modern. Why do the facts in the second carry strong psychological overtones?

Two Blind Men and a Donkey   A public square; to left, an inn with the sign of The Green Dragon, to right, the shadowy arch of a monumental gate. Stone bench under a little shrine; in background, a glimpse of tortuous streets and protruding gables.

Dead End   A city street ending in wharf over river. To left, a high terrace and white iron gate leading to the back of exclusive apartments. Hugging the terrace and filing up the street, a series of squalid tenement houses.

A season is used either to symbolize an idea or only to create a mood. The first setting is for a short play with almost no dramatic tension; characterization rather than plot is emphasized: What kind of characters, what type of events, is the reader led to expect? The second setting occurs at the end of a long play. Cyrano knows he is dying; he relives the frustrations of his life.

Uncle Jimmy   By the steps grow flowering almond and bleeding heart. Trellis covered with blooming wisteria; at the back, lilac bushes in a riot of bloom.

Cyrano de Bergerac   All the foliage is red, yellow, and brown; heap of dead leaves under every tree. Leaves are drifting down.

The next pair presents two contrasts: natural elements and type of setting, realistic versus fanciful. The first, opening a long play, is the scene of Mary's arrival in Scotland to become queen; her entire reign will be a time of stormy intrigue. The other is the setting for a harlequinade; the formality of the scene points up the set pattern this type of play follows; the deliberate exaggeration individualizes the play—an amusing satire.

Mary of Scotland   The half-sheltered corner of a pier; sleety windy night. Tall piles in background and planks underfoot shine black and icy with their coating of freezing rain. Two iron-capped guards.

The Wonder Hat   A park by moonlight; formal fountain. Backdrop represents a night sky with an abnormally large yellow moon.

2. Introduce plays for group and individual study by reading descriptions of settings and asking students to predict something of the nature of the play.

3. Place in groups students who have individually read different plays; ask each to give details of setting and determine how well the group can interpret the clues.

TO LEARN TO DRAW IMPLICATIONS FROM LINES

▶ *Realize single lines and passages may serve several purposes*

Ask students to find lines combining two or more of these purposes:

referring to a significant event of the past
foreshadowing the future
revealing a character trait of the speaker
showing the speaker's opinion of another's character
helping create mood
showing an attempt of the speaker to evade the issue
showing an attempt of the speaker to conceal his thoughts or feelings
showing the speaker's attempt to persuade by appeal to another's needs or
  weaknesses.

▶ *Select evidence to support conclusions*

After the play is well started, ask students to begin collecting evidence for a final writing assignment requiring quotations from the play in support of conclusions. As they read, students should copy, either on cards or in their notebooks, references pertinent to the problem they are investigating. Give them a choice of purpose:

Show the gradual development of a principal character: show how the author has developed the character of one of the principal personalities of the play; for each stage of development, supply evidence.

Explain the role of a minor character: select a minor character; show why he is necessary to the play.

Show mood as conveyed by lines: analyze the mood of the play, giving examples of lines that help to change or intensify it.

Reconcile conflicting evidence: select a character whose actions often contradict his words or whose words and actions are at variance with what is said about him; justify your opinion of him by reconciling the conflicting evidence.

TO DEVELOP AWARENESS OF CONFLICT AS BASIC TO DRAMA

▶ *Realize that life has its dramatic moments*

1. Ask students to clip a news item describing a conflict between individuals or groups—something that might serve as the basis for a scene in a play—and to determine the issue and the opposing forces. If it is resolved, what is the deciding agent? Let students consider the problem in groups; later use class discussion to clarify controversial points.

2. As a basis for writing, ask students to think of a conflict in which they have been involved, to decide upon the separate factors in that conflict, and to list them in specific terms, and then to write a few paragraphs conveying to the reader the clash of purposes and the final resolution.

▶ *Recognize the fundamental factors of conflict in screen plays*

1. Ask students to determine the factors of the conflict in one motion picture or one television play they have enjoyed. Divide the class into groups, where each member is to report briefly on issue, opposing forces, and deciding agent; conduct a class discussion for the purpose of answering questions the groups have not settled to their satisfaction.

2. Use the same material and the same groups to explore these questions: Do all the plays follow the same formula or do some stand out as being different from the others? If they are very similar, in what do the likenesses consist? If one is different, what makes it so? Take the reports from each group; then conduct a discussion leading the class to see the amount of repetition and of original touches in the plays students have viewed.

TO BECOME MORE AWARE OF THE IDEA THE ACTION ILLUSTRATES

▶ *Realize that every dramatic story has a unifying idea*

Show a short biographical film—*The Great Heart* or *The Story of Dr. Carver;* in such biographies author and director through selection and arrangement have ordered the events to sustain interest; analyze with students the conflict and the idea depicted. Give the class fifteen minutes to write as many specific conflicts as they can think of which might be used by a playwright in developing the same idea; conduct a discussion in which the class is helped to see that the same theme may be delineated in many different conflicts; devise a definition of theme.

► *Recognize that ideas governing conflict differ in significance*

Have students hand in the title and time length of one motion picture or television performance they have seen; ask them to state in one sentence the idea unifying the events in the story. Give the papers to a committee to list the themes; use the list as the basis for a discussion of ideas being depicted in the mass media: Do some seem more basic than others? Do basic ideas predominate? If so, why? If not, why not? How much repetition appears? What are some ideas which seem to interest many, if we can use these presentations as criteria? Can we? Why or why not?

TO RECOGNIZE THE ADVANTAGES OF PLANNED VIEWING

► *Be aware of television programs you would like to see*

During the last few years, many plays and dramatizations of fiction offered as specials on television have been excellent; programs on educational channels have become more varied. Selected viewing, therefore, is now an important means of reinforcing classroom teaching. Instruction can be planned in advance, for networks give publicity to programs in preparation. Sometimes the offering is appropriate for classroom study; even without such study, brief attention to a coming performance can give some direction and encourage viewing.[10] For example, suppose a dramatic presentation of *Spoon River Anthology* is to appear. In classes where it is appropriate, a portion of a period allows a teacher to explain the plan of the anthology, to illustrate by reading one or more poems and discussing them briefly. After students have seen the production, further discussion may be desirable. The amount of thought and money now being spent in an effort to provide worthwhile programs behooves us to keep ourselves informed of offerings in this medium. Notes of appreciation to networks and sponsors will encourage more of the best.

► *Keep informed about community plays*

1. Encourage interested students to act as a committee to keep the class informed about planned productions; little theater groups and nearby colleges will be glad to furnish students with information about plays young people may enjoy.

2. Allow students who see productions to substitute reviews for other writing assignments; these reviews should be concerned with the unified impression of the total play, or its lack. What contributed? What detracted? Attention should be given to setting, character portrayal, the building of the action, the theme, and the language. Regular play-goers can learn to discriminate between faulty writing and faulty portrayal.

---

[10] We except Shakespeare. His plays are difficult for young people to follow on television unless they have more familiarity with them than can be gained through brief discussion. It seems wiser to recommend them only to selected individuals and to classes who have studied the play.

TO EVALUATE PERSONAL TELEVISION VIEWING

▶ *Determine the character of plays habitually viewed*

1. Ask each student, for a period of two or three weeks, to keep in his notebook a chart similar to that on page 491, listing the plays he has seen and the time limit of each; call these in each week to gain information for planning follow-up experience; at the end of the period ask the student to use his chart to write an evaluation of the time spent in terms of value received. What similarities does he find among the plays selected? Does the total viewing represent a variety or do most of his selections follow the same pattern? Is there variety among his choices in subject matter or does the total lean heavily toward one type—Westerns, mysteries, serials of family life?

2. Plan a discussion based on characters portrayed in the plays. In preparation the student is to select two characters—one who seemed true to life, another who did not. For each he is to present evidence for his opinion. In the discussion the secretary may briefly list on the board the evidence given for each type. Then help the class organize the material, drawing up a list of practices that make for stereotyping of either situation or character, then those that make character and situation believable. Encourage students in their television viewing to look for credible characters in credible situations; tell them the subject will come up again.

▶ *Develop standards for selective viewing*

Ask individuals, using their charts and evaluations, to list the qualities that made some of these plays worth watching and to add other factors they think should be included in their ideal play. Using only what students suggest, help them organize tentative standards as a guide. The teacher should make it clear he is not interested in the quality of the play selected; he is concerned with the evidence produced in support of their judgment guided by criteria they themselves have set.

Taste for the best on television is acquired slowly. Like appreciation for any art form, it does not come from paying lip service to external standards; it grows from within through experiences in which one weighs the merits of the superior and the inferior. Teachers can encourage comparisons, but one must see the contrasts for himself. This takes time. A developmental program through which students learn to appreciate better plays as they present them in the classroom offers the most promise for improvement of taste.

PERSPECTIVE: POETRY

If any province of literature requires response from the whole nature of man, that province is poetry. "Poetry bids us touch and taste and hear and see the world, and shrink from all that is of the brain only. . . ." [11] All literature shares this potential of invigorating the entire personality; poetry, when it

---

[11] William Butler Yeats, in his famous dictum, is asking for a more complete definition of the mind than that given by logic. To the analytical intellect, Yeats adds the powers of imaginative thinking.

succeeds, merely does so more completely. Because the paramount characteristic of poetry is its power to dispel dullness and confusion, methods of using poetry with adolescents should emphasize delight and vitality.

On one level, teachers define the objectives of studying poetry in an operational way: to help pupils find genuine pleasure in reading poetry, to extend their ideas of what poetry is and what it can do for them, to help them understand the special language of poetry. But on a deeper level, teachers know that poetry, more than any other kind of literature, can make pupils more aware of being alive. If it succeeds, poetry lifts those who respond to it above the petty or narrow concerns that consume the lives of dull, unimaginative people. Poetry stabilizes one's whole experience—thoughts, feelings, and sensations. These deeper harmonies represent the goal of all efforts to help pupils respond to poetry. What teachers really aim at, then, is a heightened sensitivity to experience, a sensitivity so pleasant and rewarding that pupils will continue, beyond the class, to seek more of this form of literature.

Like all other arts, poetry can be enjoyed by those who do not have a scholarly knowledge of its formal qualities. However, the enjoyment is greatly increased by knowledge, and teachers, especially, need this trained awareness. They need not know all the poet's craft; but to appreciate it, they must cultivate sensitivity to the connotation of words, to figurative language, and to the artistic use of sound. They need to understand how imagery, symbols, and the entire tonal pattern serve communication.

Poetry, like music, is written to be heard. With both art forms the printed page is meaningless to the untutored unless brought to life by voice or instrument. Only after much experience can the reader of either medium hear the musical pattern without the production of actual sound. To arouse his interest, the student must hear poems read often and hear them read well; to nourish a gradually maturing taste for poetry, he must be able to read it for himself.

In the poetic form, the teacher has almost unlimited resources for reaching students of diverse interests and abilities. More than any other literary type, because of its brevity and its many-faceted appeal, poetry offers in one sitting the direct impact of a literary experience that can be encompassed by each student to the limit of his own potential. Because of the many short poems with something for almost everyone—ranging, perhaps, from simple enjoyment of melody or story to full appreciation of the poet's art—this literary form is particularly suitable for all types of classes.

In the study of poetry, both sense and sound are important. Although the two combine to form an artistic whole, we shall consider them separately here as the language and the music of poetry.

The Language of Poetry

Poetry exists in the language of imaginative insight. Through its language, poetry so sharpens our senses and freshens our awareness that we understand, almost intuitively, what would otherwise be impossible to express. Through images and metaphor, closely allied with the symbols he creates, the poet attains the rich suggestiveness of his language, evoking the most subtle emotions.

IMAGERY   Just as no reader can give a completely rational description of his personal re-creation of the vision the poet communicates, no poet can explain the creative ferment that brings forth a great poem. However, poets who have tried to make the creative process comprehensible to the layman all agree that it is a blending, through the writer's image-making faculty, of his intellectual, emotional, and sensuous experiences; thus, he arouses imagination, enabling each reader to fuse what he himself has known and felt and thought. The poet, perceiving relationships between things essentially unlike, clarifies or intensifies for the reader different aspects of life and, in so doing, evokes for him a completely new experience.

Imagery vivifies sensory impressions for the reader or the listener. The poem helps him see, hear, touch, taste, and feel. In "A Wanderer's Song" we hear "The clucking, sucking of the sea about the rusty hulls." In "The Eve of St. Agnes" we almost taste the "lucent syrops, tinct with cinnamon"; we feel the cold—so bitter the Beadsman fears "the sculptured dead . . . may ache in icy hoods and mails." Thus, the right word, vivid and alive, summons up sensations lying fallow in the memory. The reader, surrendering to the power of the poetic language, vitalizes the feeling the poet attempts to convey. He savors the language freighted with rich associative value. Through the images, fully realized, he recaptures moments of his past; he sees "the gray dawn breaking," hears "the sea-gulls crying," feels "the wheel's kick" under his hand, the wind "like a whetted knife" across his face. In some such way he arouses within himself "the first fine careless rapture" which quickened the poet's spirit and brought the words to life.

If the student is to re-create the sensory impressions as he reads, the teacher must help him cultivate a sharpened awareness of this aspect of poetic language. A teacher may begin by showing how the poet selects words to evoke associations and, thus, to control the reader's mood and to direct his expectations. One teacher asks why the perfume maker labels his product "Evening in Paris" rather than "Evening in Brooklyn." [12] Another asks why Poe chooses a raven and opens his poem with these lines:

> Once upon a midnight dreary, while I pondered, weak and weary,
> Over many a quaint and curious volume of forgotten lore

Why not a crow arriving at high noon just as Poe was stirring up a tasty snack of pork and beans?

This single feature of poetic language should be presented in a simple situation, where the concept is obvious and encumbered with few or no side

[12] Edward J. Gordon, "Teaching Students to Read Verse" in *They Will Read Literature, A Portfolio of Tested Secondary School Procedures* (Champaign, Ill.: NCTE, 1955).

issues. Thus it is possible to demonstrate quickly one way the language of poetry draws upon the vast resources of the imagination, how the poet, by selecting, releases the enormous force of a few words. Once the concept is clear, students watch for the poet's intention in a number of poems: in junior high, poems like Masefield's "Sea Fever" and Coffin's "Hound on the Church Porch"; in senior high, poems like "Chicago" and "The Eve of St. Agnes."

METAPHOR AND SYMBOL   Metaphor, in which we include all figurative language, is the most crucial of all the concepts needed for reading poetry. Here one comes most nearly to the heart of poetic language. The value in teaching most students to discriminate among the various figures of speech is highly dubious. Instead the typical boy or girl must come to see, through many examples, how any apt comparison of two disparate and logically unrelated things flashes meanings from poem to reader, meanings that long paragraphs of exhausting explanation becloud as often as they illumine. Our delight at the sudden insight and our awe at this daring leap of the imagination ranging over time and space give metaphor a central place in the language of poetry.

Metaphor, with its accompanying image, is nothing strange to the student; continually he thinks and speaks in figurative language, commonplace for the most part. It is the function of the poet to discover metaphors that release feeling and meaning. They may be as simple and straightforward as the likening of one concrete thing to another, or the concrete to the abstract, or the abstract to the concrete; they may be infinitely more subtle, woven into the texture of the poem to unify the theme. Teachers present this concept inductively, beginning with the metaphor our everyday language uses to communicate ideas sharply or vividly.[13] Students can illustrate with the slang currently in favor.

Symbols may be viewed as part of metaphor. Teachers begin with easy symbols: the stars and stripes, Santa Claus, the grim reaper, the dove of peace, the cornucopia, the school colors. Next they note the cross of Christianity, the wheel of Buddhism. Inductively the students build a definition: a symbol is a representation of something else—often something difficult to explain. The final step is to note how words can represent concrete symbols and convey a wealth of meaning.

When the concept of the ramifications of metaphor begins to take shape for pupils, the teacher turns to poetry.

O Captain! my Captain! our fearful trip is done,
The ship has weathered every rack, the prize we sought is won . . .

With older students he may turn to life as a "dome of many-coloured glass," to the climbing of birches as a symbol of human aspiration, to the Moving Finger that writes,

[13] Chapter One, page 23, stresses the importance of helping students see metaphor not as a device used by poets but as an integral feature of language development.

and having writ,
Moves on: nor all your Piety nor Wit
Shall lure it back to cancel half a Line,
Nor all your Tears wash out a Word of it.

As students unlock a poem like Robert Frost's "Birches" or Shelley's "Ode to the West Wind," they learn the power of symbols to represent complicated thoughts, to create the enormous force of a few words.

The Music of Poetry

If the study of poetry is not to be an exclusively intellectual pursuit, the student must be taught both to listen appreciatively to poems and to read them aloud for himself. In the beginning, he should have contact with much poetry where the listening experience is complete and satisfying in itself—where all the study necessary can be done in class under the direction of the teacher. Later, after instruction in oral reading, he can provide worthwhile listening experiences for others.

Much of the charm of poetry comes from the patterns of sound devised by the poet to intensify the images and thus to heighten emotion and vitalize meaning. Therefore, ear training plays a tremendously important part in helping students develop appreciation. Through purposeful listening, they can sense the significance of the rhythmical language, woven inextricably into the total meaning as the servant of thought and feeling. The first step in making them active participants is to involve them emotionally in any given poem. In the junior high grades, poems like "High Flight" and "To Satch" usually succeed; in the senior high, such poems as "The Bugle Song" and "When I Was One-and-Twenty." The next step is to shift the pupils to reading poetry aloud for the pleasure of themselves and others. The rest of this chapter is primarily a guide to the accomplishment of this all-important aim.

Coleridge defined poetry as "the best words in the best order." The words of a poem—every one the best the author can devise—largely determine the tone color. The best order, varied by repetitions and omissions, accented by rhyme, determines the rhythmical pattern. Appreciation of tone color and rhythm, each an integral part of meaning, makes for greater enjoyment of poetry.

TONE COLOR

The poet in selecting the best words for his purpose is swayed by their tone color, the evocative power of their sound. He knows that, quite apart from their intellectual and emotional content, the sounds of certain words can affect feeling. That much of this power may stem from associative ideas does not alter the fact that even nonsense syllables can evoke a mood, convey meaning.

It is well to begin casually with the words themselves—perhaps with *brillig* and the *slithy toves* and the *whiffling, galumphing* Jabberwock. We may ask students to think of the many *-ump* words giving a notion of heaviness and clumsiness: clump, dump, plump, stump, hump, bump, lump, rump. We look for lines of poetry where successful sound words exist. We may read Elinor Wylie's "Pretty Words," which suggests certain categories, and ask students to add others. We may read and note in the shivery "Daniel Webster's Horses" the repetition of consonants

> Rattling the trees
> Clicking like skeletons'
> Elbows and knees.

and play Saint-Saëns' "Danse Macabre" to see how music suggests similar effects. In some such way we attempt to show how poetic language appeals to the ear as well as to the mind.

Although the poet frequently uses rhyme, alliteration, assonance, onomatopoeia, such devices usually account for only a small proportion of the words that create the musical pattern of his poem. The tonal quality of every syllable is part of the total fabric of sound, just as each pigment selected by the painter is an essential element of the finished picture. Both artists can run the gamut of color from the light and gay to the dark and somber.

The tone color of a word is analogous to the timbre of a musical instrument, easy to recognize, at least in its broad distinctions. Although the listener may never have heard the oboe and is unable to identify the instrument producing the music, he cannot fail to sense the difference in the characteristic quality of its tone and that of the violin—a difference that derives from the variance in the physical make-up of the two instruments. In like manner, qualities in the sounds of words come from their construction, from the juxtaposition of the vowel and consonantal elements that compose them.

VARIOUS TONAL VALUES The music of the voice is carried, for the most part, by the vowels—the more open the sound, the more sonorous the quality. The range extends from the long *o*, leading all others in tonal depth, through the other long vowels and those of intermediate length, diminishing to the light quality that characterizes all the short vowel sounds. Consonants, too, although their chief function is to provide the stops, differ in tonal value—some, such as *l, m, n,* being noticeably softer and more flowing than the breathy or guttural sounds of *g, j, k.* Thus we notice that the open vowels and liquid consonants give depth and dignity to

> Roll on, thou deep and dark blue ocean, roll

that the succession of short, bright sounds lends brilliance and grace to

> How they tinkle, tinkle, tinkle,
> In the icy air of night.

that the doubling of hard consonants produces the harsh tonal quality of

> Listen to the quack horns, slack and clacking!

An appreciation of tone color helps the student develop an interest in the sound of words, an important quality in the magic the poet casts.

TONAL QUALITIES COMPARED   Students have learned to appreciate the differing tonal qualities of words with the help of such a record as Benjamin Britten's *The Young Person's Guide to the Orchestra,* designed to help the listener distinguish the different musical instruments.

Examine with junior high pupils the contrast in tonal values of the first two stanzas of "The Highwayman" by Alfred Noyes. The brooding, liquid melody of the first, characterized by full-bodied tones, sets the eerie mood; the quickening excitement of the second, with its short, crisp sounds, presents the glitter and dash of the swashbuckling highwayman. Substitute *maroon* for *claret, throat* for *chin;* accent the last syllable of *forehead* and give *breeches* the long *e* sound—both pronunciations acceptable according to some dictionaries—and notice the different effect. Then play the record, asking students to select the instrument that best represents the tonal quality of each stanza. Invariably, the majority pick the poignant timbre of the cello to establish the haunting mood of the first and the brilliant, agile notes of the trumpet to express the lively, staccato quality of the second.

One such experience shows the student that the poet chooses words for the tone color appropriate to the emotion in much the same way that the symphonic composer writes his music for the instrument that will best transmit the feeling the music intends.

RHYTHM

To teach rhythm, the teacher can again use music. He may play excerpts from a Virginia reel, "Bolero," "Ritual Fire Dance," "The Swan," a march, a dirge, a waltz, a polka. The selections are not identified; instead the students are asked to suggest suitable titles or appropriate associations. The application to poetry is never difficult; poets, too, avail themselves of this same powerful device for influencing the listener's imagination. However, as students read "The Highwayman" in junior high school or, in later years, "General William Booth Enters into Heaven," they note that rhythm in poetry cannot be so pronounced as in music. It must blend with the ideas; it must not intrude.

The teacher may use different rhythm patterns to show how a poem suggests speed and excitement or evokes peace and tranquillity. He may intersperse the reading of poems with questions about the place of rhythm in life: in typing letters, sawing logs, good style in swimming and tennis, work songs, waves of the ocean, the seasons—and the latest popular dance forms. He may read poems representing a variety of rhythms, usually starting with the obvious rhythms imitating physical movements and gradually introducing the more subtle uses of rhythm in poetry.

VARIATIONS   Attention to repetition and to the omission of sounds and words helps students understand the poet's practice of establishing a basic rhythm from which he is free to depart and to return. The teacher reads several ballads, noting their refrains intended for audience participation. Some pupils know this method from group experiences around camp fires. On a more complicated level, students discover the ironic importance Sandburg grants to the three lines he repeats so often in "Four Preludes on Playthings of the Wind." Once again music can demonstrate how composers repeat phrases or set a pattern of rhythm only to vary it with syncopation or silent "breaks" to increase the listener's pleasure. Just as musicians, to hold their listeners, must avoid a metronomic regularity, so must poets.

RHYME AS A FACTOR   While all poems have rhythm, many also have rhyme. Here, since recurrence of similar sounds at regular intervals delineates the pattern more sharply, the difficulty in maintaining the correct degree of intimacy between sound and sense is accentuated. The tendency to use force on the rhyming syllables and to end each line with a downward inflection, followed by a pause, is often characteristic of the beginner. Such a reading usually distorts both rhythm and meaning. How can we teach the student to give the rhyme its just due and no more, to allow the listener to hear echo and re-echo, not as something important in itself, but as one of the devices used to integrate sounds with rhythm and meaning, thus binding all elements into a unified whole? Here the principle of sustaining tone and of blending one with another becomes important. Understanding a clearly observable phenomenon of language—the fact that some syllables can easily be prolonged while others cannot—lays the foundation for intelligent practice.

PROLONGATION OF SOUNDS   The long vowel sounds (ā, ō) can be sustained almost indefinitely; the intermediate (â, ô), somewhat; the short (ă, ĕ), almost not at all. Consonants show the same variation. They differ greatly in the degree of decisiveness with which they can terminate the vowel sounds. For example, b, d, p, and t are short, dying as soon as they are uttered; it is, consequently, difficult and usually inappropriate to prolong such words as pop and tidbit. On the other hand, l, m, n, ng, and w, being comparatively long, permit words like full, calm, moon, hung, now to be prolonged at will. The poet, although he cannot arbitrarily assign a definite time length to one word in comparison with others, as the conventions of musical notation permit the composer to do, nevertheless works on the same principle. One reading music knows that ♩ is equal in duration to ♫ or ♬; one reading poetry must be just as alert to the less exact suggestions of the poet, who through the combination of meaning and sounds in any word, phrase, or sentence also indicates a time value relative to the whole.

BLENDING OF TONE Any tone that can be sustained can be blended imperceptibly with the one following. The poet, probably for the most part unconsciously, makes use of this characteristic of language. In his ordering of clipped and prolonged syllables, he might be compared to one who writes for the piano. The composer may exploit either the vibrating or the nonvibrating qualities of his instrument. In the former case, the notes, sustained and blended by the pedal, produce a singing tone; in the latter, where the sound dies as soon as the finger is lifted from the key, a crisper, more brittle effect results. The poet, in building his melodic and rhythmic patterns, exploits the characteristics of the sounds of words in the same way. Three illustrations, using lines with problems of increasing complexity, will clarify for the pupil the principle of sustaining and blending sounds.

Rhyme causes almost no problem in maintaining rhythm in those occasional passages where each line expresses one complete and distinct thought, as in these lines by Wordsworth:

> Ne'er saw I, never felt, a calm so deep!
> The river glideth at his own sweet will;
> Dear God! the very houses seem asleep;
> And all that mighty heart is lying still!

Here the reader need not resist the temptation of the downward inflection and the marked pause at the end of each line, since both are in keeping with rhythm and meaning. His only problem is to show how the poet uses rhyme to help bind the elements of sound into an integral pattern. He does this by slightly prolonging the rhyming syllables, thus insuring the echo of *deep* with *sleep* and *will* with *still*. The tones lingering in the air emphasize the melody as do the vibrations of recurring notes from a musical instrument.

The last stanza of Bourdillon's simple lyric "The Night Has a Thousand Eyes" furnishes examples of the other two problems: lines containing separate but closely related ideas and lines that are an integral part of those following.

> The mind has a thousand eyes,
>   And the heart but one;
> Yet the light of a whole life dies
>   When love is done.

In the above stanza, the first two lines, representing two closely related but separate ideas, present a problem slightly more complex than do the lines from Wordsworth. As in the Wordsworth passage, a gradual downward inflection on the last word will denote the completeness of the first thought; prolongation of the tone will take care of the rhyme. Here, however, proper blending of the lines becomes important. The pause is briefer, and "eyes and the heart" is treated almost as if it were a word of four syllables, with the first and last sustained and the second and third pronounced rapidly. The run-on line is still more difficult to read. However, the blending is practically the same here as in the previous example, although more pronounced—almost an elision. This necessary mingling of tone is effected by sustaining the rhyming syllable with no noticeable inflection and by making the break between it and the next imperceptible. Again, think of "dies when love" as one word with a clipped second syllable.

Understanding these simple principles has proved helpful to the student in learning to make the pattern of sound a subordinate but integral part of the thought and feeling. Of course, these principles of interpretation must be taught to reinforce the meaning behind the words. If the poem is fully understood by the reader, most of the interpretive problems are solved, and such matters as blending and inflection are readily learned as means to an end.

THE TEACHING PROBLEM

ORGANIZING INSTRUCTION

Dependent as it is upon the artistry and enthusiasm of the teacher, successful instruction in poetry will vary considerably with each individual instructor. Some teachers prefer to arrange a sustained period of poetry with one day reinforcing the next. Others like several brief and separate samplings, teaching a few poems each time, with intervals for other activities, before entering into much more extensive development. Some teachers draw poetry into thematic units, stopping to examine aspects of form as each poem is studied and then fitting the total experiences of the poem into the larger theme of the unit. This textbook will recommend a number of short lessons devoted solely to poetry, but some teachers may find this unsatisfactory. Obviously, planning how poetry will be taught is a very personal matter, depending upon the personality of the teacher, the particular class, and the plans for the rest of the English course. Because of these considerations, this section will emphasize practices that stimulate interest in poetry and touch only lightly upon the organization of instruction, seeking to remain as free as possible from any prescription or dogma.

Similarly in presenting poetry to adolescents, because our purpose is to develop genuine appreciation, prescription and dogma prove equally blighting to the pupils. An inductive approach, especially in the beginning, turns out to be the best strategy for assuring that whatever standards pupils gain will be their own rather than the teacher's imposed judgments. Pupils must put together their own experience of what they feel and think about a poem. For a long time now, we have had the warning I. A. Richards sounded in *Practical Criticism:* even graduate honors students in universities do not know what to do with a new poem when they have never developed their own responses to literature.[14] On pages 570–99 we present a model for the inductive approach

[14] I. A. Richards, *Practical Criticism* (New York: Harcourt, Brace & World, 1961).

for grades 7 through 10, using actual poems to illustrate how teachers may help younger pupils in knowing what they really enjoy and why.

The need for balance in teaching students to read poetry cannot be over-emphasized. One who hopes to establish poetry merely by reading builds on quicksand. Equally dangerous is the so-called scholarly approach, in which close analysis belabors each poem as if it were an intellectual puzzle. The teacher walks a razor's edge, in danger always of leaning too far in either direction. But there are ways to maintain a positive poise. First, the teacher must be genuinely appreciative of student response; he should welcome reactions and suggestions, no matter how banal. Startling and naive levels of appreciation make clear to him where he must start with the learner. Second, he must teach the language and music of poetry without forcing these considerations into a central position. Content or some other basis of relationship may frequently decide the organization: "Not Exactly Serious," "Freedom's Ferment," "Poems by Youth"—these groupings may hold a central position in the pupils' attention. Within such clusters, the formal elements of appreciation may make their appearance. Even so, the teacher moves cautiously, stressing only one aspect of poetic form at a time, holding the others in check until another propitious moment. Perhaps symbols can be handled best during a unit on "The Dimensions of Courage," when the class reads "Mother to Son," by Langston Hughes:

> Life for me ain't been no crystal stair.
> It's had tacks in it,
> And splinters,

Perhaps imagery may very well be presented during "Poems with a Touch of a Shiver." However these aspects of form may be woven into the course, a restrained teaching of form in relation to content supports rather than weakens the pleasure of poetry. Reading poetry solely for what it says is to miss the route to discovering what it actually does say.

In planning lessons for adolescents, the teacher should not be lured to his college anthologies to find something he has learned to like. Eighth-grade pupils, for instance, are not adults; because of their emotional immaturity, they will respond better to "The Highwayman" than to *The Waste Land*. James Thrall Soby, who is commended in the *Saturday Review* for his taste in art, admits he received his first impetus to enjoyment from a print of a colorful, yet ordinary, picture bought from an itinerant salesman. Taste for the best in poetry often springs from such humble beginnings.

Lovers of poetry agree that, although it requires close, careful reading, it should be taught with a light hand. The purpose of the first presentation of a poem is not to exhaust its possibilities but to whet the appetite for more. When, under the teacher's direction or of his own accord, the student returns to a poem, he begins to see that great poetry reveals its power only after many rereadings. Poetry works its magic, if at all, in small doses over a period of time.

Although for most classes it is better to focus on the various aspects of poetic form one at a time, pupils should realize that any poem has more than one simple feature. A poem should always be presented as a poem—a work of art—letting the class sense it as an entity, each student taking what his experience permits. After the class has enjoyed it in this way, the teacher may through questioning bring out one of its most salient characteristics as poetry. As soon as the various aspects have been taught, students can learn to fuse these separate qualities. However brief or lengthy the discussion, with short poems the teacher should allow time for a rereading. From the beginning, students should realize that analysis of poetry is a means to an end. The poem itself deserves the final word.

The teacher, attempting to stimulate interest in any literary form, tries many avenues of approach. Because of its conciseness and its suitability as basis for a listening experience, poetry lends itself to various modes of presentation. Through this variety teachers are often able to involve students by one method when another has failed. The following recommendations, distilled from classroom experience, are intended to support and nourish interest in poetry.

Read Many Poems Incidentally

Keep on your desk a file of typed copies of poems—not to be used as part of a unit or as a lesson illustrating an aspect of poetry, but merely some you enjoy reading and think students may like. Ready at hand, these suggest occasions for poetry that might otherwise be overlooked. Once the practice of reading from this file is started, invite students to add to your collection. The star of one teacher's file is an illustrated copy of James Weldon Johnson's "Creation," prepared by a senior class as their favorite. A close second is Sandburg's "Primer Lesson," given by a boy in apology for a pert remark.

Choose high or low moments of the school year as opportunities to read poetry aloud. On the morning of a heavy snow read Wylie's "Velvet Shoes" or Frost's "Stopping by Woods on a Snowy Evening." When spring fever strikes, try Richard Le Gallienne's "I Meant to Do My Work Today." After an assembly or film has left everyone in an exalted mood, "Taught Me Purple" or "I Had No Time to Hate" may be appropriate. Concern with local intergroup disturbances might stimulate the reading of a poem celebrating the black American's pride in his heritage and his long struggle for freedom, such as James McCall's "The New Negro." On a day of jangled nerves, limericks or the verse of Ogden Nash may contribute a needed laugh.

Read poems not only for special occasions but when a disrupted program causes unavoidable delay or when scheduled work is finished sooner than expected. If only one student asks to borrow the copy of the poem or takes down the name of the author because he is interested in reading more, the time has not been wasted. Watching the reactions of the class, noting what poems are asked for repeatedly, helps determine the level on which the next unit of instruction in poetry may begin.

Accommodate Diverse Personalities

Granting that some aspects of poetry should be taught to all and that some poems should be read in common, teachers plan other ways to take into account the variety of temperaments and interests among their students.

A poetry collection prepared for future classes; a booklet to which each student contributes one of his favorite poems; days on which everyone brings a poem he likes and reads it aloud to a group, a few of the best-liked to be selected for class enjoyment; mimeographed lists of topics and themes with several titles listed under each and many spaces for addition by students who locate suitable poems from a wide selection of books and magazines; occasional recitals by groups or individuals reading poems centered on one theme —all these are ways of accommodating varieties of pupil response to poetry.

Although a few classes may benefit from a thorough investigation of the techniques of versification and the variety of forms employed by poets, usually only a limited number of individuals in the regular English class react favorably to such complete study. For this group, a knowledge of the mechanics of verse not only may be fascinating in itself but may be helpful to those seriously interested in trying to write poetry. Usually the teacher asks for volunteer committees to investigate and report to the entire class. These committees choose poems to present, as examples of stress patterns and verse, forms with which the class has had no contact. Since such work is voluntary and appeals only to a small group, students are not held responsible for the information.

Since poems, or even respectable verse, cannot be written on order, attempts to write in metrical form should also be voluntary. However, some students gain a more secure basis for appreciation of the poet's craft by trying their hand at writing limericks or parodies, the easiest forms for the beginner. Ask each student to compose only the first line of a limerick; let the class pick the line they prefer to work with as, under the teacher's guidance, they write the rest of the limerick together. Testing the merits of alternate lines suggested by individuals results in a certain nontechnical understanding of some of the simpler elements of meter and rhyme. Volunteers may then compose limericks starting with a line suggested by the teacher or students. The following written by a tenth-grade girl acted as a spur for some students to extend their efforts to other forms of verse.

> There once was a student at Tech.
> Desirous of saving her neck,
> She walked on her knees,
> All teachers to please
> And now she's a physical wreck.

Reproductions of paintings aid in sparking the imagination; they occasionally inspire poems, but more often flashes of metaphor and rhythmic lines. Teachers use this approach as a stimulus for brief writing periods, asking students to jot down vivid words and phrases descriptive of what the picture makes them see or feel. To some, nothing will come; to others, only the trite; but a few will respond with the germ of a poetic idea. The teacher takes contributions from volunteers, considering alternate phrases, sometimes letting the class decide whether the light or serious line is more in tune with the mood. The intensity and vitality of El Greco's "View of Toledo," with its threatening movement and awesome gloom, has released expression in some; the tranquillity of "The Wheat Field" by Jacob van Ruisdael has moved others to creative reflection; the shimmering iridescence of the drifting cloud shapes and elusive light of Monet's "Argenteuil Bridge, 1874" has secured a fanciful response from still others.

Moments of crisis can also be moments of involvement and great learning, as the following examples show. Visiting Americans have described the moving poetry written by boys at the Royal High School in Edinburgh, Scotland, on the morning following the Aberfam mining disaster in Wales that took the lives of scores of children.[15] Schoolchildren in Washington, D.C., poured their emotional reaction to the assassination of Dr. Martin Luther King, Jr., into some remarkably sensitive verse.[16]

This type of work does not lend itself to probing; images and illuminating fragments come spontaneously or not at all. Hence, brief, frequent exposures are best. A few apt expressions each time, a few students inspired to extend the experience to voluntary writing, make the activity worthwhile. The results need not be used as a basis for grading.

Many students like to defend their choices of the best. A teacher may learn something of his success in teaching poetry, and may be guided somewhat in selecting poems to be taught again, by an activity similar to the following. At the end of the semester, list most of the poems that have been taught. Ask each student to select from the list the three poems he thinks should unquestionably be taught to incoming classes, giving brief reasons for his choice. A variation is to ask for the first poem to be dropped from the course. If there is considerable agreement, try to discover the reason. Does it lie in the poem or in the way it was presented?

Another approach can be repeated as often as seems profitable. Write several different versions of one line (from a stanza of an unfamiliar poem)— one line with clumsy rhythm, one changing the prevailing mood, one substituting a trite for an apt metaphor, one replacing simple language with pretentious. Write the original and the alternates on the board. (With some classes, start with only one substitution.) Read the stanza aloud, each time with a different line; ask students to pick the best. Discuss each of the re-

---

[15] James R. Squire and Roger K. Applebee, *A Study of the Teaching of English in Selected British Schools.* Washington, D.C.: U.S. Office of Education, 1968 (pp. 167–68).
[16] *Children of Cardoza Tell It Like It Is.* Washington, D.C. Public Schools, 1968.

written versions, trying to draw from students how each detracts from the poem. What makes the rhythm intrude? Does word choice or rhythm or both disturb the mood? Why does the rejected metaphor lack communicative power? How does the connotation of the poet's words differ from that of those substituted? After the discussion, read the entire poem.

Another effective technique is called the Connoisseur's Choice or the Spoiled Version. Based on principles of contrast and comparison, it offers the student two versions of a poem—one authentic and one spurious. In deciding which of the two versions he prefers and the reasons for his decision, the student must consider the relationship of parts to the whole. Here, for instance, the method is applied to the rockets stanza from Tom Prideaux's "Fireworks." [17]

A genie's arm all sleeved in gold,	A ghost's hand, we were told,
Was thrust across the sky. Behold	Was put into our view. Behold
How from his smoking palm there falls	How from his big fist there drops
A silent chime of colored balls.	A hundred red chimney tops.

When the teacher first introduces this method, he will find it best, as in the example above, to present one version so obviously and grossly spoiled that almost everyone in the class can detect the differences in quality. As students become skilled at critical reading, the differences may be more subtle. Working with unfamiliar passages, students will discover and put into words the concepts the teacher wants them to learn. This shift from passive to active learning stimulates their full response.[18]

Teachers who use this method frequently include some pairs of equally unworthy versions for the same "poem"; this practice has the merit of keeping students on their mettle. Once they have become aware that a defensible choice requires thinking, that it does not permit settling into comfortable routines, students bring more alertness to the exercise and to similar succeeding exercises.

Use Different Stimuli

Guest readers have an impact so beneficial that their appearance should be staged several times each semester. However, they should be carefully selected; frail or eccentric personalities can easily harm the cause of poetry. Community poets and representatives of speech and English departments of nearby colleges have served as impetus to enjoyment in many high school classes. Perhaps the most successful guests are those only a little older than the listeners:

[17] From "Fireworks" by Tom Prideaux, from Hughes Mearns, *Creative Youth.* Reprinted by permission of Hughes Mearns.

[18] Some teachers have reservations about presenting to their students distortions of fine literature. They prefer to use this method with poems of lesser merit or to prepare two versions for poems of their own devising. They believe the latter course prevents any danger of permanently fixing unpleasant associations with fine poetry.

a recent graduate; two upper class boys and a girl, seated at a table before the ninth grade, reading "The Listeners," "Lone Dog," and "The Pied Piper of Hamelin"; or a similar trio of seniors before the eleventh grade, reading poems of more delicately balanced imagery—Sarett's "Wind in the Pine," stanzas from "The Rubáiyát," "The Death of the Hired Man." Records make it possible to have as guests, at the teacher's and pupils' own convenience, the poets themselves or skilled actors reading the poets' lines.

When poetry is read aloud, the listeners should frequently have the printed words before them, the meaning reaching the mind by way of eye and ear. As they hear repeated performances of poems they like, most pupils will discover that their need for visual support disappears.

Students may also prepare their favorite poems and read them aloud in small groups. Then each group selects a poem read effectively; all members of each group search for a musical recording that will provide the perfect background for a reading of the chosen poem: "Pomp and Circumstance," "Finlandia," or "Largo" from *Xerxes* for Kipling's "Recessional"; something by Debussy for "La Belle Dame sans Merci"; an instrumental version of "Nobody Knows the Trouble I've Seen" for "We Have Been Believers" by Margaret Walker. These are actual choices; another class may find more suitable correspondences. The following day, with the help of several boys as technicians, the six or seven effective poems are read aloud before the class while the musical recordings are played quietly in the background.

One of the English teacher's best allies is the tape recorder. The first time anyone hears his own voice, amazement and ego-deflation result. However, a supportive teacher can convert the disappointment into an incentive for deeper study and for more oral practice. The second recording almost invariably shows commendable improvement, arising from more thorough understanding and better voice control. One of the most satisfying projects for an English department is the building of a collection, either on tape or records, of students' readings, not only of poetry but of other literary forms.

Experiment with Choral Reading

Although students enjoy hearing teachers read, as soon as possible they should begin reading for each other. Choral speaking will help bridge the gap between interested listener and solo reader. Here, where attention centers on the group rather than the individual, the reluctant participant can submerge himself until he gains confidence. Adapting his voice to the tempo and rhythm decided upon through general discussion, at first he may effect control only through imitation, but ear and voice are being subconsciously trained. Soon he should be willing to read bit parts, until gradually he loses the fear of his own voice. Then he is ready for individual readings, at first for small groups, perhaps later before the class.

The reluctance of beginning teachers to attempt the choral approach to the study of poetry may be due in part to the fact that much of the writing on the subject has been directed to those preparing choirs for public performance. Consult these books, by all means, but remember that the English teacher's aim is to foster an appreciation of poetry through accustoming ear and voice to respond to the nuances of poetic language. Begin casually, emphasizing only the need for pleasant voice quality and crisp enunciation to bring out the meaning. Have sections of the class listen at first, to point up the complementary aspects of reading and listening. Soon students learn to listen to themselves in practice; finally, they learn that if, after sufficient practice, attention during the reading is focused on the meaning, the poetic elements will usually take care of themselves. The English teacher need not fear the technicalities of choral speaking. Moved by the desire to infect his students with his own enjoyment of poetry, all he needs is willingness to experiment.

In teaching students who have had little experience in interpretation, the teacher starts with a poem that will disclose some of its values quickly. Knowing that the response to pronounced rhythm is universal and that stories have wide appeal, he usually selects a poem that exemplifies either one or both of these characteristics. Perhaps he may decide to use "Columbus" by Joaquin Miller, since the meaning is apparent upon the first reading and the verses themselves may be familiar to the students. At this point, such foreknowledge is a help rather than a hindrance; the simple problems in listening and in interpretation offered by this poem can lay the foundation for more complicated work to come later. Problems concerning mood, characterization, tempo, and climax—almost always aspects of any narrative poem—can be studied within these five stanzas.

The following steps are suggested as a method of procedure. Although the method here is applied to "Columbus," it can be adapted to any suitable poem. The teacher reads the poem to give a unified first impression.

First four lines Purpose? (To establish a mood of loneliness.) How achieved? (Long vowels and sounds capable of prolongation produce a slow moving, mournful sounding line.) The teacher suggests reading the lines together, trying to convey the feeling; groups of students take turns listening. (Even the slowest tempo should never drag. Work for a light attack on each syllable.) Repeat several times until voices convey both the mood and the flowing rhythm.

Characters Notice contrast between the two characters, which must be shown through voice; a mere suggestion is sufficient. Let students decide on the voices which best suggest the quality. (Probably the deeper, fuller voice will better convey the determination and strength of the Admiral.) Select several readers for each part.

Climax The excitement and suspense of the story moves from the feeling of loneliness, through mounting anxiety, to the deep fear of the mad sea, and finally to the joy at sighting land. Let the selected readers take just the lines of the mate and the Admiral, trying to intensify the feeling with each question and answer. Select two boys to read the parts.

Tempo The tempo increases, although some lines offer contrast ("They sailed. They sailed" suggests the hopelessness of the quest), until the beginning of the last stanza, where it slows to suggest the darkest hour but picks up again when land is sighted. Readers, like musicians, often retard the last phrases of a poem to prepare listeners for the end.

Casting (one possibility) Boys for Admiral and mate; girl for narrator who takes straightforward lines such as "The good mate said." All girls for "The words leapt like a leaping sword." One girl for the first three lines of the fifth stanza. Four groups (all but characters and narrator), starting with one group and adding the others one at a time, for the line "A light! A light! A light! A light!"

Reading Work for clear tone, crisp utterance, maintaining mood and rhythm.

Since first attempts at choral reading can be expected to lack the niceties the rendition of great poetry requires, a story in verse, which cannot be spoiled by mass attack, makes a good beginning.

While the arrangement for choral speaking of some poems seems inherent in their patterns, many lend themselves to a variety of effective readings. Students can make valuable suggestions; in reaching agreement, they deepen their understanding of poetic principles. As they try both appropriate and inappropriate versions, they become more sensitive to the close relationship between form and meaning. The following, all used successfully with secondary-school students, will suggest others to the teacher. (The asterisks mark poems that have been used with junior high students.)

POEMS WITH REFRAIN

* "The Pirate Don Durk of Dowdee"   Mildred P. Meigs
* "Jesse James"   William Rose Benét
* "Macavity, the Mystery Cat"   T. S. Eliot

POEMS WITH DIALOG OR ANTIPHONAL PASSAGES

* "Who Has Seen the Wind?"   Christina Rossetti
"Invocation," from *John Brown's Body*   Stephen Vincent Benét
* "The Raggle Taggle Gypsies"   Old Ballad
* "Sir Patrick Spens"   Old Ballad
* "The Song of the Mad Prince"   Walter de la Mare

POEMS EFFECTIVE IN VARIOUS ARRANGEMENTS

* "April Rain Song"   Langston Hughes
* "African Dance"   Langston Hughes
* "Jazz Fantasia"   Carl Sandburg
"Three Kings"   James P. Vaughn
"Brown Baby"   Oscar Brown, Jr.

POEMS FOR SMALL GROUPS

Poetry of great delicacy or of intense feeling sometimes can be read effectively only by small groups; many lyrics, of course, are suitable only for solo reading.

"Holidays" Rod McKuen
"Four Preludes on Playthings of the Wind" Carl Sandburg
"The Freedom of the Moon" Robert Frost
"To His Father" Robinson Jeffers
"The Express" Stephen Spender
"If There Be Sorrow" Mari Evans

In the list, both selections and categories are suggestions only. Perhaps the greatest values come when students find poems they like and then decide upon appropriate arrangements. Therefore, a corner for poetry anthologies, reserved for browsing, is almost indispensable. A weekly-changing bulletin board, "Poems I Like," with selections made by students, is another source for both individual and group work. Since we cannot all like the same poems and since we know that even great favorites are not companionable for all moods, presenting a range wide in interest appeal is necessary if poetry is to offer stimulation for all.

Encourage Memorization

In every reasonable way, memorization should be fostered, for phrases of beauty and the concepts they embody live on into adult life. Use praise and your own example. Keep a corner of the chalkboard for brief poems students might find worth memorizing; do not comment; see how many take the bait. Occasionally set aside a portion of a period for those who wish to "read" poems from memory. External pressures such as grades or requirements are a hindrance. Will there, then, be students who will avoid memorization? Assuredly. But better none at all than that done under duress. Certainly, nothing kills a poem more quickly for the listener than to be forced to endure a halting, glassy-eyed reading of lines meant to soar and lilt. There seems no good reason for the student to perform publicly—certainly not until he has made the memorized lines his own—and that takes time.

Suggest ways others have found helpful in committing lines to memory. The best methods stress the gradual, unforced aspects of the process, the concentration on meaning rather than on words, the re-creation of the sensory images each time the lines are repeated. Give volunteers instructions like these:

Copy material in notebooks where it is readily accessible.
Memorize the sequence of ideas or images.
Read over several times a day so that memorization comes naturally.
Avoid memorizing one line at a time; the relation of parts to the whole proves the best basis for memory work.
Concentrate in each reading not on memorization but on bringing out thought and feeling; vivify the images; hear the lines.
Keep your copy before you, using it less and less, until the poem "says itself."

Help volunteers establish some standards for their expenditure of time. Over the years Robert Frost and Emily Dickinson wear better than Edgar Guest and Robert Service. However, each must find this out for himself. Continue to point out notable passages and poems worthy of memorization, but leave the final choice to the student. Undoubtedly, he will select some that seem of little value, but this tendency should not worry the teacher unduly. Like many popular tunes, which run in one's head to the point of exasperation, commonplace lines soon pall for one who is becoming sensitized to the language and feeling inherent in great poetry; before long he will find others of greater worth to replace the trite. In this way he acquires discrimination—one of the most important values to be derived from memorization.

SUGGESTED LEARNING EXPERIENCES

These suggestions should serve merely as ideas that teachers may alter and modify into activities suited to their own artistry of instruction. In general, the learning experiences presented here have been chosen because they illustrate basic principles of teaching poetry: the importance of balancing both enjoyment and analysis; the acknowledgment that taste, highly personal, develops slowly; and the importance, the inescapable importance, of appreciating form and the pattern of sound as an integral part of meaning.

TO LEARN TO LISTEN TO A POEM

▶ *Listen for the story*

Start with something that requires no analysis for at least superficial appreciation, an exciting narrative with vigorous rhythm. Before reading, give sufficient explanation to make the poem easily understood. Browning's "How They Brought the Good News from Ghent to Aix" might be introduced like this:

A horse, Roland, is the hero of this poem, which tells the story of three riders —Dirck, Joris, and the speaker—who are sent with a message from Ghent, in Belgium, to Aix, in West Prussia. The poet describes the ride but does not tell us what the good news is. We do sense the urgency of the message.

The fact that the message is sent by riders indicates what about the time of the story? There are several words that further suggest the medieval, foreign atmosphere—*postern, askance, aye and anon, burgesses.* Meaning?

Notice how the poet shows the passage of time—moonset, twilight, cock's crow—and the progress of the ride by giving the Belgian towns through which they pass—Lockeren, Boom, Düffield . . . Dalhem.

Listen to the way the author suggests the headlong, breathless speed, the echoing hoofbeats of the galloping horses.

Finally, read the poem aloud.

▶ *Examine the rhythm*

1. Reread the first two lines to show how the short, hard syllables suggest the sound and the speed of the plunging hoofbeats.

2. Let volunteers try reading them to emphasize the need for crisp, clear-cut articulation, the fact that to maintain the rhythm in poetry every syllable counts.

3. Let volunteers, trying to maintain the tempo, read some of the lines describing the passage through the towns.

► *Discover some of the characteristics of poetry*

1. Poetry suggests more than it tells. Is it effective to leave the details of the message to the reader's imagination? Why, or why not?

2. Poetry is not concerned with factual material. The poet mentions the names of real towns. Does this mean the story recounts an actual event? What then is the author's purpose (to tell an exciting story, to commemorate a heroic act)?

3. The rhythm the poet selects is an important factor in conveying the emotional charge.

► *Listen again to enjoy the way tempo, rhythm, and story are integrated*

Other narrative poems suitable for an initial experience are "The Highwayman," "Ballad of East and West," "Lord Randal," "King Robert of Sicily," "Danny Deever," and "Lepanto."

TO APPRECIATE SENSUOUS IMAGERY

► *Notice appeals in specific poems*

1. Read poems composed mainly of images:
   "To ———" ("Music, when soft voices die"), Percy Bysshe Shelley. In eight lines, the poet presents three images—music, odor of violets, rose leaves—each appealing to a different sense.
   "Cargoes," John Masefield. In each of the three stanzas we have a picture of a different era, from ancient times to the present.
   "A Birthday," Christina Rossetti. Two stanzas composed primarily of images—the first, a series of comparisons; the second, a list of exotic images appealing to sight.

2. After a browsing period, ask students to respond to roll call by reading lines containing one image.

► *Consider the effectiveness of imagery*

1. Reread any of the poems used before. Consider reasons for the imagery and its effectiveness. Of what value is compression in the Masefield poem? Does the extravagance of the Rossetti images help or hinder the desired response?

2. Encourage volunteers to try making a familiar object vivid through comparisons that create an image—a deserted house, a football, a schoolroom desk.

TO RESPOND TO METAPHORICAL LANGUAGE

► *Notice the difference between the imaginative and the trite*

Ask students to substitute trite expressions for the poet's metaphorical language. Coleridge, in "The Rime of the Ancient Mariner," describes phenomena of nature we all recognize and portrays emotions we have all felt—but in images that vivify such experiences for us.

WE MIGHT SAY	COLERIDGE SAYS
a broiling sun	"All in a hot and copper sky, The bloody Sun, at noon, Right up above the mast did stand, No bigger than the Moon."
dying of thirst	"And every tongue, through utter drought, Was withered at the root; We could not speak, no more than if We had been choked with soot."
scared to death	"Fear at my heart, as at a cup, My lifeblood seemed to sip"

▶ *Sense the symbolism unifying metaphorical elements*

1. Read poems where the same symbol signifies different things: "Fog" and "Wind Is A Cat"

2. Read poems where different symbols are used for the same purpose: "Lincoln, the Man of the People" and "O, Captain, My Captain!"

3. Read poems with fairly obvious symbols:

"Blow, Blow, Thou Winter Wind" (the sharp bite of the wind: ingratitude)
"Barter," "Dream Pedlary" attainment of spiritual values in terms of the market place)
"How Can One Ever Be Sure" (tangled hair: confused thinking)
"Loveliest of Trees," "To Daffodils," "The Falling Star," and "Unlost" (cherry blossoms, daffodils, a star, a candle flame: fleeting quality of life and beauty)
"Nature" (Nature's discipline: a mother's discipline)

4. Read poems where the use of symbolism is more subtle:

"November Night" and "Warning" (falling leaves, flight of a moth: death)
"The Tyger" (brute force and fascinating beauty of the tiger: evil; the lamb: good)

Through the use of imagery, metaphor, symbol, and choice of language, the poet synthesizes his experiences and opens up new worlds for those who have learned to appreciate his art.

TO STUDY THE EFFECT OF TONE COLOR

▶ *Discover how words gain tone color*

1. Compare music and poetry (see page 511).

2. Investigate the effect created by different combinations of vowel and consonant sounds (see pages 511–12). Divide the class into two groups for five minutes; students in one group are to write words that lend themselves to prolongation; those in the other group write words difficult to prolong. Call on students to respond quickly with several words they have listed, demonstrating the characteristic orally. Then give a few minutes for each student to write a line, using words from his list. Consider those volunteered, noting different effects. Finally, discuss association of meaning as contributing to tone color.

► *Discover how poets use tonal values to help convey total meaning*

1. Read "The Old Song." Compare the two stanzas, noticing how within an unchanged rhythm different tempos and moods are created. Lead students in a unison reading.

2. Study Poe's "Eldorado." Notice how tempo changes with mood. Discover how the poet effects this change.

3. Study "The Patriot." Ideas in opening lines usually describe a gay scene. How does the poet achieve the opposite effect?

TO RESPOND TO DIFFERENT RHYTHMS

► *Read poems where the reason for the rhythm is obvious*

Walking
   carefree   "Tewkesbury Road," John Masefield
   mournful   "Marching Pines," Lew Sarett
   desperately monotonous   "Boots," Rudyard Kipling

Riding
   "Cavalier Tunes," Robert Browning
   "Charge of the Light Brigade," Alfred, Lord Tennyson
   "Sweetwater Range," Lew Sarett

Rocking
   "Sweet and Low," Alfred, Lord Tennyson
   "Lullaby," Christina Rossetti

The Sea
   "Break, Break, Break," Alfred, Lord Tennyson
   "Neptune's Steeds," William Crittendon

The River
   "Song of the Chattahoochee," Sidney Lanier
   "How the Waters Come Down at Lodore," Robert Southey

► *Read poems where the reason for the rhythm is more subtle*

Inner Strength
   "Invictus," William E. Henley
   "Requiem," Robert Louis Stevenson

Tranquillity
   "It Is a Beauteous Evening, Calm and Free," William Wordsworth
   "Composed upon Westminster Bridge," William Wordsworth

Delicacy
   "Silver," Walter de la Mare
   "To a Snowflake," Francis Thompson

TO LEARN TO READ POEMS ORALLY

► *Re-create the images as you read*

In order to experience the emotional impact and to heighten it for his listener, the reader must vivify, as he reads, the sensations conjured up by the words of the poet. Help the student who reads a line too matter-of-factly to gain the correct emotion by asking appropriate questions to stimulate his imagination.

> Roll on, thou deep and dark blue ocean, roll!
> Ten thousand fleets sweep over thee in vain.

As you try to get the feeling that Byron intends, what are you thinking of? Is the scene you visualize wholly imaginary or do you recall a specific experience? Where are you? On the shore? On a ship? How would you differentiate the sound of waves against a beach from the sound of those against a ship? Can you feel the spray on your face? Taste the salt? What colors do you see in the water? Is the sun shining? Is the sky overcast? Are there threatening clouds? Can you possibly visualize ten thousand fleets? If not, why does the poet use this expression?

Such questions help students realize that if the poet is to have a chance to work his magic, both listener and reader must take an active part.

▶ Learn to stress rhythm rather than meter

Understanding the intricacies of metrical form is unnecessary for reading poetry. Even with no knowledge of scansion, the inexperienced reader often finds it difficult not to capitulate to the insistence of the metric beat.

1. Demonstrate for students, using a few lines of poetry. Read first, stressing the accented syllables to produce a jerky, sing-song rhythm.

> *Dárk brown* is the *ríver,*
>
> *Gólden* is the *sánd.*
>
> It *flóws alóng foréver,*
>
> With *trées* on *éither hánd.*

Read again, combining inflection and slight prolongation of sound on the italicized words to produce a smooth-flowing rhythm. Let students decide which best suggests Stevenson's river; let them try to determine what caused the two different effects. Then lead students in a unison reading to accustom ear and voice to rhythm reinforcing meaning.

2. Explain the difference between meter and rhythm. Meter, a convention of prosody, exists on the printed page; rhythm exists in the reader. A product of thought and emotion, it results from the tension set up between meaning and meter.

3. Stress the necessity for concentrating on meaning while reading. These rough diagrams have helped students understand the problems a reader faces:

What is one who reads like this doing?

Overemphasizing meter.

One who reads like this?

——————   ——————

——————

Completely disregarding the sound pattern, probably giving a prosy, matter-of-fact reading.

One who reads like this?

Trying to make rhythm reinforce meaning.

▶ *Practice making the sound pattern reinforce meaning*

Nursery rhymes, with their regular meter and simple rhyme, make excellent material for practice. Ask students to select one, to practice reading it, to prepare to read in groups. After work in groups, let students record their readings. Have the class listen to recordings to select examples of readings in which the sound pattern supports meaning.

Even this much attention to rhyme and rhythm should result in enough acceptable readings to serve as motivation for better interpretations of poems to be studied later. Since the problem recurs, students will have further opportunities for practice. Skill in stressing rhythm to bring out total meaning develops slowly.

Poetry, appealing to our imagination by using language in a special way, sharpens our senses and thoughts so that we see the world around us with heightened perception. Like all literature, poetry lifts us to a new equilibrium; if it is truly appreciated, it makes us more aware of life. It "stabs us broad awake." That is the ultimate justification for teaching poetry to adolescents.

SELECTED READINGS

DRAMA: BOOKS

A Guide to Play Selection. 2nd ed. New York: Appleton-Century-Crofts, 1958. An NCTE publication, this is a description of full-length, one-act, and television plays, a list of anthologies with the plays contained in each, and a list of references on various aspects of play production.

AGGERTT, OTIS J., and BOWEN, ELBERT R. *Communicative Reading.* New York: Macmillan, 1956. A discussion of the principles underlying interpretive reading, with suggestions for the oral reading of prose, poetry, and drama.

BARNES, DOUGLAS (ed.). *Drama in the English Classroom.* Champaign, Ill.: NCTE 1968. In September 1966, the Anglo-American seminar on the teaching of English was held at Dartmouth College. These papers present the ideas emerging from the drama section.

CENTANO, AUGUSTO (ed.). *The Intent of the Artist.* Princeton, N.J.: Princeton Univ. Press, 1941. Thornton Wilder, in "Some Notes on Playwriting," describes the nature of drama seen from the playwright's point of view.

LANGER, SUSANNE K. *Feeling and Form.* New York: Scribner's, 1953. "The Dramatic Illusion" is a brilliant discussion of drama as a distinct art form.

MOFFETT, JAMES. *Drama: What Is Happening.* Champaign, Ill.: NCTE 1967. Moffett's belief that a dramatic pedagogy is superior to the expository pedagogy that has long been maintained puts the entire English curriculum into new perspective. Teachers who know the appeal of stage drama for young people should consider the extension of drama and dramatic techniques suggested in this important book.

TRAVERSI, D. A. *An Approach to Shakespeare.* 2nd ed. Garden City, N.Y.: Doubleday Anchor, 1956. An analysis of Shakespeare's development as a playwright, with stimulating evidence to show how his maturing experience is reflected in his language and in his poetry.

WEBSTER, MARGARET. *Shakespeare Without Tears.* New York: Fawcett, 1957. Background material concerning Shakespeare and his theater, with comments on many of his plays.

ARTICLES

COEN, FRANK. "Teaching the Drama." *English Journal.* Vol. 56, No. 8 (November 1967), pp. 1136–39. Using *Six Great Modern Plays* (New York: Dell, 1956), Coen helps students develop objective criteria to support esthetic judgment.

LEARY, BARBARA BUCKETT. "The Stage and Discovery: Allegorical Plays for Junior High School." *English Journal.* Vol. 57, No. 3 (March 1968), pp. 345–49. Makes a good case for literary bonuses, basic theater arts, large casts. Outlines in detail production scheme of play. Annotated bibliography.

MEADOWS, ROBERT. "Get Smart: Let TV Work for You." *English Journal.* Vol. 56, No. 1 (January 1967), pp. 121–24. A plan to involve students critically—in observation, script writing, production, evaluation.

RASKIN, GERALD. "On Teaching Drama." In Edward B. Jenkinson and Jane Stouder Hawley, *On Teaching Literature.* Bloomington, Ind.: Indiana Univ. Press, 1967, pp. 106–34. Discusses form and convention; provides detailed analysis of *Death of a Salesman* and *A School for Scandal.*

POETRY: BOOKS

DREW, ELIZABETH. *Poetry, a Modern Guide to Its Understanding and Enjoyment.* New York: Dell, 1959. The author writes with wisdom and depth of insight. She keeps a clear balance between meaning and form, not losing sight of either one in her enthusiasm for the other.

DUNNING, STEPHEN. *Teaching Literature to Adolescents: Poetry.* Glenview, Ill.: Scott, Foresman, 1966. Stimulating presentation by Dunning, aided by two poets, Robert Francis and Philip Booth, who discuss their poems.

GEIGER, DON. *The Sound, Sense, and Performance of Literature.* Chicago: Scott, Foresman, 1963. Geiger develops the thesis that oral interpretation is an important aspect of literary study, illuminating the qualities and values of specific texts for both interpreter and listener. His discussion and examples focus on poetry, but the ideas presented are also applicable to other literary forms.

GROSSER, MAURICE. *The Painter's Eye.* New York: New American Library (Mentor), 1963. Grosser discusses the interplay of technique and subject matter, using copious examples. Concerned with visual art, he gives the reader an understanding of various problems confronting the painter. It is interesting to compare these with those encountered by artists who work with words.

HENDERSON, HAROLD G. *Haiku in English.* New York: Japan Society of New York, 1965. For those wishing help in teaching this popular but complex form. (Available from NCTE.)

MAC LEISH, ARCHBALD. *Poetry and Experience.* Boston: Houghton Mifflin, 1961. Developing a few basic concepts through discussion of great poems, the author presents a sensitive and stimulating introduction to the appreciation of poetry, showing what it is and how it gains its emotive power.

RICHARDS, I. A. *Practical Criticism.* New York: Harcourt, Brace & World, 1961. This reports Richards' famed experiment with students at Cambridge. He presented them with poems of assorted merit, not revealing the authors. The students commented upon the poems as best they could, and with complete anonymity returned their comments to Richards.

WALTER, NINA WILLIS. *Let Them Write Poetry.* New York: Holt, Rinehart & Winston, 1962. A handbook for teachers wishing to use the writing of pupils as a springboard to appreciation.

ARTICLES AND PAMPHLETS

HYNDMAN, ROGER (ed.). *Modern Poetry in the Classroom.* Champaign, Ill.: NCTE, 1965. Articles by English teachers on how to teach selected poems.

PETITT, DOROTHY (ed.). *Poetry in the Classroom.* Champaign, Ill.: NCTE, 1966. A collection of articles on teaching poetry.

SIMONSON, HAROLD. "Music as an Approach to Poetry." *English Journal.* Vol. 43, No. 1 (January 1954), pp. 19–23. Music as a useful approach to poetry has been emphasized in this textbook. This article offers further ideas.

SMITH, JAMES STEEL. "Some Poetry Is Popular—But Why?" *English Journal.* Vol. 46, No. 3 (March 1957), pp. 129–39. This article is an unflinching and hard-headed examination of the kind of poetry that is genuinely popular, poetry that "gives in monotonously repetitious and elementary forms a set of platitudes so general and bland they almost lack meaning." Teachers should read this article, uncomfortable though it may be to our egos.

What to Say About a Poem. Champaign, Ill.: NCTE, 1965. This is a collection of articles from Josephine Miles, Laurence Perrine, and W. K. Wimsatt, Jr.

TWELVE

THE POPULAR ARTS

> *There is a great deal that is mediocre, repetitious, and patronizing in television or the movies. Yet in closing their eyes to the significant contributions of the mass media, the detractors encourage the very banality they purport to despise.*
>
> DAVID MANNING WHITE [1]

PERSPECTIVE

In contemporary culture, listening and viewing are clearly the most popular means of receiving communication. This recognition neither minimizes the value of reading and the permanence of the printed word nor ignores the fleeting nature of much that appears in the movies and on television. Rather it admits that Americans devote far more time to these media than they spend with books, magazines, and newspapers. Since the communication of ideas is a major instructional concern, teachers of English cannot ignore the impact on modern minds of these carriers of idea and image.

The twentieth-century revolution in communication has been beneficial. Children scarcely leave swaddling clothes before they are transported visually and aurally to other times and places. The vicarious extension of experience surely contributes to growth in listening and speaking vocabularies. Then, too, at their best movies and television bring us the most eloquent expressions of humanity—the music of Mozart and Beethoven, the writings of Chekhov and Shaw. More than 20 million Americans witnessed *Romeo and Juliet* on motion picture screens; an estimated 50 million people saw the television première of *Richard III*. Film makes possible transmitting Laurence Olivier's National Theatre production of *Othello* to viewers throughout the world. Certainly the popular arts increase the common experiences of Americans. Teachers of English can do much to increase understanding and appreciation of these massive instruments of communication.

The term *popular art* is applied here to all mass entertainment—not solely to television and motion pictures, but also, insofar as they offer forms of art,

---

[1] David Manning White, "Mass Culture in America: Another Point of View," in Bernard Rosenberg and D. M. White, eds., *Mass Culture* (New York: Free Press, 1957), p. 16.

532

to recordings, periodicals, radio, and newspapers. Our need to educate students to examine critically the media as conveyors of information is discussed elsewhere in this book.[2] This chapter is concerned not with improving skills in viewing and listening but with ways of increasing understanding of the popular arts and of upgrading student tastes.

No clear-cut dichotomy need be established between popular art and other kinds of art for the purposes of teaching; they must be considered together. Our job in the classroom is to teach students to understand and to respond thoughtfully. To move students from uncritical assimilation to careful discrimination requires no major upheaval in curriculum. This is a continuing task for teachers of English, not one to be accomplished in a single three-week unit or assigned capriciously to the elective program. The values and understandings that support intelligent reactions to television and screen are similar to those needed for intelligent reactions to literature. Yet if a transfer of habits from reading to viewing is really to take place, appreciations and skills must be taught so that students can see their applications. Clearly this calls for the serious study of such art forms in the classroom. A complete program involves a threefold approach—the analysis of the popular arts as commentary on contemporary culture, a study of the conditions under which these arts are created, and the analysis of the forms in which they are expressed.

Popular Art and Contemporary Culture

Popular art both reflects and influences the society from which it emerges. Interaction between popular expression and culture is always difficult to assess, especially in a society like ours in which rapidity of change creates an uncertain perspective. Yet if students are to consider seriously the ideas presented through the media, they must understand something about the context from which these ideas flow. A minimal program will consider the popular arts as commentary on contemporary culture, as products of important industries, and as responsible instruments of expression in our society.

CONTEMPORARY IDEAS AND ATTITUDES In popular art are expressed the responses of serious artists to the problems, values, and conflicts of our world. Carefully attuned to the nuances of contemporary opinion, these arts are quick to reflect ideas prevalent in our culture. Whether indeed television and the movies are more instrumental in shaping and molding opinion than in reflecting changes caused by other factors is a problem that may well be studied carefully. The facts indicate, however, that when Americans feel deeply patriotic convictions, such as during years of war, the media attempt to communicate stirring human experiences in which love of country is weighed against other loyalties; when Americans are disturbed by intergroup relations

---

[2] See Chapter One, pages 24–37; Chapter Four, pages 156–59; Chapter Six, pages 243–52.

within the democratic scene, scenario writers address themselves to such problems.

On a deeper level, there are those who contend that a historical revolution is occurring, that the communications media are radically transforming the way man actually experiences his world. Marshall McLuhan thinks each age is molded by its form of communication.[3] From Gutenberg to the present, man has been influenced by print, a form of communication giving dominance to the visual sense, to linear, connected, continuous communication, to reading and thinking in isolation, to privacy and individualism. Before Gutenberg, in the pre-print age, men were predominantly tribal; and their sense of hearing determined their responses. In an electronic age of television and high-speed space communication, time and privacy begin to disappear; the senses of hearing and touch regain their full importance; and television contributes to a revival of all the senses. According to this view, the generations reared on television will move toward mass culture and a tribal existence involving all the senses. Tribalism widens the gap between the present generation and their teachers. Furthermore the life styles of the young do show signs of an increasing indifference to any social register of old families and wealth and more concern about group feeling than about logical meaning. The force of this argument can be felt when one considers the impact of television on public response to civil rights strife and to modern reporting of war on the scene.

ECONOMIC CONDITIONS AND THE ARTS   To react intelligently to motion pictures or television, one must understand certain economic forces that shape these purveyors of popular culture. The amount of class time devoted to such matters should be limited, however. Just as the study of facts about literature —literary history, biographical data, and the like—must be carefully introduced only to support the student's ability to read with appreciation, so the consideration of facts about mass communication needs to be intelligently limited to the significant few that really help him understand. Too often units on television or the movies stress extended studies of motion picture history or of the mechanics of television production, rather than analysis of communication through the media. Student attention can be restricted to a limited number of understandings. Economic dependence on vast audiences, continuing experimentation and discoveries in electronics, widespread concern for regulating and controlling the instruments of communication—such developments influence even obscure judgments of broadcasters and writers. In the classroom, such considerations may best be introduced gradually, in relation to the analysis of special broadcasts or current problems, rather than as subjects for special study.

The popular arts are sensitive to the nuances of social opinion. Indeed, so

[3] Marshall McLuhan, *The Medium Is the Message* (New York: Bantam Books, 1967). See also Chapter Six, pages 245–49.

readily do the industries respond and appeal to mass interests that they are often accused of cretinizing tastes. In striving for vast audiences they seem to perpetuate the superficialities of our culture. Yet it is important that students do not think of producers of the popular arts as linked in a giant conspiracy to undermine the mores of Americans. Rather they should understand that broadcasters and film-makers, economically dependent on vast audiences, attempt to create a product that mirrors prevailing attitudes and interests. For instance, broadcasts often skirt controversial issues; for economic reasons many industries that create or sponsor popular art fear offending any recognizable segment of our society, whether war veterans, taxicab drivers, or even dog lovers. Evidence of this is found in attempts of broadcasters or film-makers to avoid scrupulously any situations or characters that could offend a particular racial or national group. Only attitudes widely supported by popular opinion are safe.

Inevitably the result of any attempt to placate a vast audience is a substitution of the comfortable for the unsettling, the bland for the meaty, the trivial for the thoughtful. Not all expression in these media is compromised, but much reliance on the stereotyped situation and the stock figure can be so explained. Indeed those few broadcasters and film-makers who brave prevailing public attitudes often tend either to be subjected to harsh criticism or to be virtually ignored. The latter, of course, can result in economic strangulation through low ratings or box-office failure.

The commercial world influences the selectivity of the media in other ways. Pervasive, but certainly unplanned, is the consistent point of view toward American life depicted through so many of the media and the closeness of this image to that held by the business world. Cleanly scrubbed children, modern homes out of *Better Homes and Gardens*, fashionable mothers, two-car families—this is the picture of the American family too often created. A stereotyped portrait of the American black man has long been perpetrated in stage, screen, and television; yet rising public indignation over the struggle of the Negro for justice in our society led the Columbia Broadcasting System in 1968 to explode the myths in its celebrated television series "On Black America." Observers have noted the inadequate coverage of American labor as well as the failure of the media to sustain serious criticism of the business community itself.[4] However great this selectivity may be, it seems born less from deliberate motives than from compatible points of view. The popular arts are products of the business world. The producers and directors—often the writers too—are willing participants at the market place and share many commercial values. To distinguish the audiences for films of different kinds and thus gain greater flexibility, the American motion picture industry recently inaugurated a public rating system to indicate those offerings suitable for general family groups and

---

[4] See Educational Policies Commission, *Mass Communication and Education* (Washington, D.C.: National Educational Association and American Association of School Administrators, 1958), pp. 26–27.

those to be restricted to adult viewing. Students might well be asked to examine the purposes underlying such classifications. As distinct from the popular folk art of many past cultures, one of the distinguishing features of contemporary popular art is that it emerges from great commercial enterprises.

THE EFFECT OF THE AUDIENCE Students can be led to see, too, that the vivid, outspoken commentary on the values of our society often found on the contemporary stage is not the result of accident. Writing for a minority audience and seldom subject to the extreme pressures of popular taste, except in creating major musicals, which demand return of an investment of several hundred thousand dollars, the dramatist is comparatively free to examine explosive issues. Interesting changes have occurred in motion pictures as television established itself as the major media catering to popular taste. Influenced by an economic need for audiences even larger than those that sustain motion pictures, television tends to be less venturesome and "offensive" than the other media.

SOCIAL RESPONSIBILITIES OF THE MEDIA Understanding the influence of economic factors is not enough; students also need to consider the function of the media in our society. What are the responsibilities of television broadcasters for informing the public about contemporary affairs? Should film-makers be permitted unlimited freedom of expression and choice of subject matter —even in films distributed in foreign countries? What methods of censorship, if any, should be adopted? Is freedom of broadcasting guaranteed by the First Amendment, much as freedom of the press—even though the stations are licensed by the Federal Communications Commission and agree to operate in the public interest? Or must we forge new definitions of freedom and restriction because of the potential power of these media? Such controversial questions need careful consideration. They are not easy to answer in the classroom, because society itself has still to resolve them. In studying such problems, students may form intelligent opinions by weighing many points of view.

Varied Forms of Popular Art

Just as intelligent analysis of poetic form contributes to understanding what the poet says, so the study of form in television and films can deepen appreciation of popular art. The analysis need not be detailed; some understandings developed during the study of dramatic literature apply equally to these methods of expression. In the dramas presented on the screen or broadcast over air waves, characters are created, conflicts developed, scenes and settings created to convey particular moods. Form in literature is often compared to mood, unity, or climax in the popular media of entertainment. Thus teachers almost automatically develop student awareness of similarities and contrasts between literary works and the offerings of the popular arts. In addition, some special study of the better plays written for these media may be introduced. Selected viewing of original television dramas and the reading of a good motion picture script, together with frequent listening to recorded plays, are resources for the direct study of drama as presented in several media. The table (see pages 538 and 539) summarizes a few differences that may be considered.

If students understand some factors influencing various art forms, their ability to evaluate different kinds of presentation will be heightened. For example, the problem of selectivity is common to all media. The poet selects sounds and images; the novelist, particular incidents and a point of view; the dramatist, key scenes and moments of revelation. The organization of the selected images and impressions contributes to the ongoing rhythm of a work and to its over-all unity. Such problems affect the screen and television writer in surprising ways. Selection and arrangement of scenes are as important as they are on the stage. Moreover, the way in which incidents are presented visually must be considered. Should the camera shoot from a distance or close up? Should the lens focus on a significant object, revealing its import immediately to the viewer—as on the dusty, dirt-filled corners of an untidy boarding house—or should the nature of the scene be referred to through dialog or merely suggested by the background as the camera concentrates on the actions of the central characters? In the movies, a total scene may be presented; on television the size of the picture limits the presentation to a fragmentary suggestion. In this, the media are entirely different.

Physical restrictions in each medium also influence the form and content of presentations. Obviously radio relies on sound; the vastness of the motion picture screen makes possible visual spectacles that cannot be reproduced on the stage or on television. Original video presentation seems particularly well adapted for intimate dramas, which demand a close affinity between audience and actor, since the limited size of the picture tube and the easily exhausted patience of the sponsor tend to check any tendency of the playwright to rely on the excesses of spectacle. However, in teaching such distinctions, the teacher must help pupils perceive the differences between drama written especially for video and the many televised motion pictures appearing on home screens.

Other differences are less obvious to the casual observer. The rigid timing of television forces writers to tailor expression to the demands of fixed periods of time—the fifty-minute hour, the twenty-two-minute half-hour, the seventy-five-minute hour and a half. Inevitable results of this rigidity in timing are padding and cutting, the one often resulting in the introduction of extraneous material, the other in loss of continuity. Other practices have also emerged. Concerned with the kind of impressions that appear most effectively on small, home screens, the creators of television drama show interest in plays of character, or at least in intimate, realistic episodes similar to the "slice of life" stories, which reveal a single dimension of character. Certainly the demands of each medium help shape and mold both content and form.

	Theater	*Movies*
unity	Restricted to selected scenes. Much action occurs off stage. Physical limitation in number of settings.	Virtually complete freedom of movement in space and time.
setting	Sharply limited, even with contemporary experimentation involving composite settings that rely on lighting to smooth transitions.	From 150 to 500 separate settings in average film, with perhaps twice as many separate camera shots. Few scenes of long duration.
revelation of meaning	Speech and action of characters convey meaning within the overall setting. Dialog is chief instrument for highlighting meaning.	Greater reliance on movement than on auditory clues, although musical effects are used to advantage. The camera often focuses on key impressions. Most literal of media.
continuity	Division into scenes and acts.	Elaborate methods for photographic transitions between scenes—pans, dissolves, abrupt changes, montages—depending on effect desired.
content	Much variation. Tendency to rely on the impact of a unified effect rather than a series of visual or auditory impressions. Compression within sharply defined time and place.	Much reliance on visual scope; crowds, massive sets, many characters, pageantry, trick effects. Fluidity of time and space plus potential length of feature films make possible treatment of complex subject matter.

THE TEACHING PROBLEM

ORGANIZING INSTRUCTION

Once teachers recognize the importance of studying the popular arts, they face two tasks: planning a program of study and organizing instruction to improve student tastes. Each will be discussed briefly.

THROUGH FOUR MEDIA OF COMMUNICATION

Records and radio	*Television*
Most fluid of all media. Virtually complete freedom of movement in space and time.	Usually restricted in time and setting as is drama, although taped programs gain some of the freedom of movies.
Unlimited number of scenes. Narrator is often used as cohesive force. Setting suggested by dialog or music.	Limited to few scenes unless filmed. Fragmentary, suggestive. Viewer must fill in partial clues. Author must allow for costume changes, restrictions in settings, unless program is taped in advance.
Complete reliance on auditory clues—dialog, narration, music, and sound effects.	Combines attention to movement as in movies with attention to dialog of theater. Selective camera controls direct viewer to significant objects or persons.
Reliance on music in fade-ins and fade-outs between scenes. Because of time restrictions, scenes advanced by suggestion rather than carefully plotted detail.	Combines division into episodes or acts of stage play (allowing for commercial and station breaks) with many visual shifts of the motion picture. Frequency of breaks establishes unique form.
Number of characters usually limited because of audience inability to differentiate voices. Short plays limit characterization; characters more comprehensible types.	Fairly limited subjects. Concentrates on problems of few characters, often emphasizing character revelation in familiar situations and short episodes, not in long continued action. In this limitation can be much strength.

Planning a Program of Study

The same principles of clarity and purpose apply to communication in the popular arts as to communication elsewhere. Teaching programs must recognize the students' need to see the relationship among many ways of expressing ideas.

A unified approach means that teachers plan no separate programs for instruction in the popular arts; rather, experiences will be introduced throughout the six-year program. Three principles can serve as a guide:

> Use the products of popular art in the same way other esthetic expression is used—to motivate, to study, to enrich.

Recognize that a single community of ideas involves all forms of expression; use many avenues of extending breadth and depth of the classroom study of ideas.

Study examples in popular culture of language and thought in operation; use illustrations to illuminate the study of language operation, logical thinking, and emotional thinking.

Extending Interest and Improving Taste

Underlying appreciation of all esthetic expression are basic standards of taste. Although the evaluation of any form of art requires considerable understanding of the medium as well as command of criteria against which to measure the expression, an individual's ability to appreciate and judge seems to develop as part of his over-all outlook on life rather than as a fragmented series of attitudes toward separate fields of endeavor.

The close parallel between the methods of literature and those adopted in the popular arts—the fact, indeed, that modern instruments of communication often fulfill in society a function almost identical with the historical role of literature itself—suggests that to a considerable degree we may build discriminating habits of viewing and listening as we teach students to value and appreciate literature.

In attempting to refine the tastes of pupils in the popular arts, teachers can be modest in their goals. To all Americans the media offer popular, convenient, and inexpensive entertainment. The school cannot possibly confine students' experiences to the few truly significant productions released each year. Much that students choose themselves will be ephemeral, superficial, and unworthy of analysis. The real goal is not to eliminate such trivialities but to extend the range of interests so that individuals will find pleasure and see qualitative distinctions in many kinds of expression. As novelist W. Somerset Maugham wrote:

> I am not so stupid as to mean that all people have such a naturally good taste that they will always prefer what is best to what is of no great value. After all, we none of us do that, and few of us are so delicately constituted that we can put up with nothing but the first rate. I know for my part I can get a great deal of pleasure out of an opera of Puccini's, but it is a different sort of pleasure from that which I can get out of an opera of Mozart's. There are times when I would rather read the stories of Conan Doyle than Tolstoi's *War and Peace*.[5]

APPLYING STANDARDS   Standards developed through the study of literature may be applied to other media of expression, but the fit is not entirely perfect. A group, agreed on the characteristics of a "good" novel, may use their standards to judge a representative film or drama, and the attempt will usually yield some criteria that apply to almost any art form. For example, the work pre-

---

[5] W. Somerset Maugham, in the introduction to *Great Modern Reading* (Garden City, N.Y.: Doubleday, 1943), p. xiii.

sents real insight into human action, rather than a synthetic point of view; the incidents are well selected, truthful, and unbiased; the plot develops logically, with reasonable attention to motivation, characterization, and the demands of probability; meaning is supported and re-emphasized by atmosphere, setting, and symbol. But to such lists must be added certain standards of performance: the acting is convincing; the setting aids in establishing tone, place, mood; the photography supports rather than distracts from the theme of the story.

Thus the class must consider the peculiar demands of each form of expression. The comparative approach is helpful because it can be developed in relation to the total curriculum in literary appreciation. However, teachers using this approach need to avoid suggesting that reading books is *ipso facto* more cultured or more highly valued—or even necessarily "more active"— than viewing television or motion pictures. If the choice is between reading the pap in many magazines or viewing a distinguished film, valid argument clearly supports the cause of the motion picture. What is important is to encourage in students an ability to evaluate as well as appreciate many kinds of presentation.[6]

COMPARING MEDIA   One effective way of helping students apply standards of literary judgment is to encourage them to compare the treatment of a story in different media. For instance, junior high readers find *Johnny Tremain* to be a gripping, humane portrayal of the experiences a young boy faces in assuming adult responsibilities. The struggle of the American colonists forms a rich, reinforcing background, but the novel essentially illuminates the experiences of an individual. Students who compare Forbes' book with the motion picture adaptation find little but superficial resemblances between the two. Gone in the film is the inner struggle of Johnny, the development of his sensitivity to others, the rich personal relationships. Symbols of Johnny's conflict such as the scarred hand remain, but they have been divested of meaning; motivation of character is overlooked. What remains may be a compelling re-enactment of some events of the revolutionary period, but certainly no unified work of art. Opportunities for comparisons are rich with possibilities for teaching. Fortunately not all adaptations are as bland as that of *Johnny Tremain*. Indeed some, like the play *Teahouse of the August Moon,* the motion picture *The Bridge on the River Kwai,* and the light opera *The King and I*, may possess greater clarity, unity, and impact than do the original stories. Others, like the Zeffirelli production of *Romeo and Juliet,* offer such arresting new interpretations that they are worthy of special study.

REVIEWING FILMS AND BROADCASTS   Just as teachers provide for reviews of books, so they can assign reviews of motion pictures, television, and records.

---

[6] Study helps for forthcoming films, broadcasts, recordings, are found in *Media and Methods. The Motion Picture and the Teaching of English* (Champaign, Ill.: NCTE, 1965) and *Movies: Universal Language* by Sister Bede Sullivan, O.B.E. (Notre Dame, Ind.: Fides, 1967) are the best handbooks available.

Some teachers require one review of a film, motion picture, or stage performance during each six- or eight-week grading period. Some class time may be reserved regularly each month for the presentation of oral reviews, and on the slated day students may be divided into small groups for informal sharing of reports. Groups may be organized for each of the popular arts or formed so that television, motion pictures, and records are discussed in each section. Whatever the method, such assignments can encourage thoughtful viewing and provide opportunity for careful assessment.

Before preparing reviews, students may need special instruction. If standards for reviews of books have been discussed in the literature program, the student may be led to discover that the essential principles of good reviewing are similar for books and broadcasts. The particular value of reviews, which communicate information to readers or viewers who have not shared the primary experience, can be illustrated in the writing of professional critics. Different reactions to a single film may be contrasted, and the standards of each reviewer assessed. Such assignments often introduce students to unfamiliar magazines and to many leading newspapers as contrasted with fan magazines.

Sound instruction in the popular arts focuses on understanding the new media and on improving student taste and discrimination. These goals are not achieved through a separately organized program but through the application to the popular arts of understandings and insights developed elsewhere.

SUGGESTED LEARNING EXPERIENCES

Too often the consideration of popular art in the classroom, divorced from the study of language and literature, becomes little more than superficial, unrewarding comment. This eventuality will not occur if teachers insist that each experience be carefully planned in relation to the continuing intellectual interests and needs of the learners. Here as always purposes need to be identified with clarity and learning activity related to previous instruction in skills of thinking. If this happens, the activities suggested on the following pages can be modified by teachers to add depth and breadth to the study of English.

TO STUDY CONTEMPORARY ATTITUDES IN POPULAR ART

▶ *Relate ideas in popular art to ideas in literature*

1. Initiate a discussion of the ethical choices faced by the young business executive in a television drama and of the clash of values in our contemporary business world as reflected in the writing of Sinclair Lewis, John Marquand, Cameron Hawley, and others.

2. Use television productions like *Peter Pan* to interest junior high school students in reading selections treating the youthful desire to evade responsibility, for example, "As Ye Sow, So Shall Ye Reap" by Jesse Stuart, *Goodbye, My Lady* by James Street.

3. Prepare a special book list of titles related to forthcoming broadcasts so that students can follow their viewing with good reading experiences.

4. Collect products of popular arts that someday may be useful in the English classroom. Develop a personal library of tape recordings consisting of five to ten minute "bits," for example, a reading of a poem by May Swenson, a talk on interpretive reading by Charlton Heston, a discussion on the nature of language change between two authorities on linguistics.

► *Extend ideas in literature by referring to other media*

1. After discussing instances of prejudice found in stories like "One Friday Morning" or books like *My Antonia*, study ways in which prejudice against individuals may affect an entire culture, as shown in the historical film *The House of Rothschild*, a depiction of the Jewish banking house during the Napoleonic era.

2. Use the transcription of "When Greek Meets Greek: A Study in Values," an imaginary conversation between Athenian and Spartan youths, in a unit exploring the universal problems resulting from conflicts in cultures. Preparation for listening —or follow-up—may involve reading and discussing such books as *A Bell for Adano*, *The King and I*, and *Teahouse of the August Moon*. (The transcription is one of the programs in the "Ways of Mankind," a series of thirteen discs produced by the National Association of Educational Broadcasters.)

► *Provide intensive study of worthwhile presentations*

1. In courses that include some study of contemporary literature, introduce analyses of provocative current works. Such ideas as the following seem repeatedly illuminated in contemporary art and are of interest to student groups: the effects of any breakdown in communication in the modern world; the irony of individual loneliness within large, complex industrial cities; the survival of human values in the holocaust of atomic war; the power of ideals in shaping human action.

2. Important contemporary broadcasts and films that achieve a considerable degree of artistic integrity deserve analysis on their own merits. Outstanding offerings of each season, or classic productions like *Loneliness of the Long-Distance Runner* and *The Seventh Seal*, which are often reshown on television and in theaters, may be analyzed with students for the theme, the development, and resolution of the conflict. The content of each offering may be considered in determining the grade level of the classes in which it should be discussed. However, many films and broadcasts provide excellent viewing for seventh- and eighth-grade students, even though a few are best reserved for senior high school students.

3. Study with students a recording of Kurt Weill's one-act folk opera *Down in the Valley*. Show how the artist has expanded the simple situation implied in the folk tune into a strong, unified conflict. Encourage students to emulate Weill by selecting a similar situation in another folk song and expanding it to short story length.

► *Prepare students for worthwhile experiences in viewing and reacting*

When an important dramatic event is scheduled—whether on the stage, on television, or in the motion picture theater—prepare students for viewing either by a brief teacher "preview" of the work or, on occasion, by a thorough study. Brief lessons are particularly important in preparing for viewing works posing problems in comprehension. Immature, unprepared adolescents will seldom attempt to derive much meaning from Shakespearean productions, or from performances of plays like *High Tor*, *The Corn Is Green*, *Cyrano de Bergerac*, or *Rhinoceros*.

TO UNDERSTAND SOCIAL AND ECONOMIC CONDITIONS AFFECTING POPULAR ART

▶ *Study how the mass audience affects communication*

1. Examine selected films or broadcasts adapted from another medium. Consider the apparent reasons for changes in racial or religious identification of a character in a film adaptation of a novel or a stage play, or the basic "refinements" in narrative that are designed to bring about "acceptable" denouements. Read selections from contemporary articles that discuss these compromises. Perhaps some student would be interested in reporting on Lillian Ross' *Picture*,[7] which describes the mutilation of the filmed version of *The Red Badge of Courage* when producers attempted to "redo" Crane's story in terms of their image of popular taste. Follow this report with an examination of a superior adaptation such as *A Man for All Seasons*, to illustrate how differences in each medium necessitate changes in form, some of which can add to a drama's effectiveness.

2. Examine the broadcasting industry's attempts to appeal to different interests at different times of the day. Compare the programs presented on television and radio during the following hours: before 3 P.M.; 3 P.M. to 7 P.M.; 7 P.M. to 10 P.M.; and after 10 P.M. Even more startling differences may be seen by comparing broadcasts on Saturday and Sunday afternoons. This activity has been used with both junior and senior high school groups.

Extend the study to a consideration of popular magazines and motion pictures. Encourage students to study the more subtle differences—the social class of the heroes, the conception of family life presented through illustration or setting, the nature of the advertising and what it suggests about the advertiser's conception of his audience.

A few gifted students may be encouraged to select a magazine and study a number of issues to determine the topics and values presented. Alert students will perceive important distinctions between such magazines as *Life, Good Housekeeping, Reader's Digest, True Confessions*, and *Ebony*.

3. Ask students to select a continuous three-hour period during the day or evening and to classify all television or radio broadcasts available during the interval according to the nature of their appeal. For each program, ask students to indicate the over-all purpose, the possible reasons for listening, the audience for whom it is intended. A comparison of the findings will reveal the nature of audiences responding to these media at different times as well as the nature of the broadcasts prepared for limited groups.

▶ *Study the effects of financial conditions*

1. Write on the chalkboard the following average costs:
    $3 million to $5 million to start a magazine
    $1.3 million for a Grade A motion picture
    up to $100,000 recurring costs for thirty minutes of television time [8]
    $10 billion spent by advertisers in the popular arts during one year [9]

---

[7] Lillian Ross, *Picture* (New York: Holt, Rinehart & Winston, 1952).

[8] These figures are reported in Wilbur Schramm, *Responsibility in Mass Communication* (New York: Harper & Row, 1957), p. 270. Similar figures, increasing yearly with the rising inflation of the American economy, are obtainable in occasional reports in weekly news magazines.

[9] 1956. See Bradford Smith, *Why We Behave Like Americans* (Philadelphia: Lippincott, 1957), p. 238. Inflation will also increase these figures.

Ask students to suggest how such figures help to explain the shortage of creative ideas in these industries.

2. Circulate copies of *Variety* and *Billboard* newspapers in a junior or senior high class. Direct attention to the ways in which products of the popular art industries are assessed—motion pictures in terms of gross income, television by audience ratings, records according to sales. Ask a group to draw conclusions concerning the nature of the industry.

3. Ask a group of mature students to prepare a panel discussion on the ways in which advertising affects presentation in the media. In preparation for the panel, require students to read "What We Read, See, and Hear" by Harry Overstreet, a chapter in *The Mature Mind*.[10]

▶ *Analyze evidence of introspection and self-criticism*

1. Read aloud interesting excerpts from articles that satirize aspects of the popular arts. Ask students to explain the basis of humor. For example, use the following statements from *Punch:* [11]

> TV does not change the adult fundamentally. Seven out of ten people recover almost completely when no longer exposed to television. . . .
>
> Four out of ten suffer only slightly from channel sickness, and a relatively insignificant proportion of viewers go gaga. . . .
>
> At first TV causes adults to read less, but after a time the consumption of print is more than made good by increased perusal of *TV Times.*

2. Read aloud the following satirical stanza by Phyllis McGinley.[12] Discuss the poet's purpose. Appoint a volunteer to locate Miss McGinley's complete poem, which is part of the series called "The Jaundiced Viewer." Encourage others to write stanzas of their own. Eighth-, ninth-, and tenth-graders have enjoyed this activity.

Reflections Dental

How pure, how beautiful, how fine
Do teeth on television shine!
No flutist flutes, no dancer twirls,
But comes equipped with matching pearls.
Gleeful announcers are all born
With sets like rows of hybrid corn.

▶ *Weigh the responsibilities of the popular arts*

Assign individual reports or panel discussion on one or more of the following topics. Information of this kind is included in trade journals, in almanacs devoted to the various industries, in occasional articles in current periodicals.

> *The Influence of Audience Rating Systems* To what extent are these methods of determining popularity valid and desirable?
>
> *The Impact of Advertising on Broadcasting* The cost of television commercials; programing influences; the desirability of pay-as-you-go television;

[10] Harry A. Overstreet, *The Mature Mind* (New York: Norton, 1949).
[11] *Punch*, Vol. 235, No. 6176 (December 24, 1958), p. 819.
[12] From "The Love Letters of Phyllis McGinley" by Phyllis McGinley. Copyright 1953 by Phyllis McGinley. Originally appeared in *The New Yorker*. Reprinted by permission of The Viking Press, Inc.

methods of financing used in other countries, for example, England, Canada, Sweden.

The Influence of the Federal Communications Commission Its purpose, authority, regulatory and licensing power. Write to the Superintendent of Documents, Washington, D.C., for the pamphlet *Rules of the Federal Communications Commission.*

Regulation of the Mass Media Evidence of their influence on morality. Voluntary and involuntary censorship, such as the motion picture code, state controls, the Legion of Decency.

Responsibilities of the Media to Provide for Minority Tastes Provisions made for children, for various cultural groups.

Program Awards The selection of "bests," their purpose and meaning.

The Production of Films and Broadcasts The function and contribution of various individuals—writer, director, actor, producer, editor, cameraman.

The Ten Biggest "Box-office" Films of All Time Why were they popular? What do these films suggest about popular taste? Compare with the ten best sellers.

TO UNDERSTAND THE FORMS OF POPULAR ART

▶ *Compare treatment in diverse media*

Ask students to analyze the treatment of a work in several media. A study of superior adaptations—Brainerd Duffield's television drama based on "The Lottery"; Howard Estabrook's scenario for *The Human Comedy*—directs attention of students less to the mutilation of a work of art than to the differences that arise when a selection is presented well in two media. Similar comparisons have been made between *Anna and the King of Siam* and *The King and I; Cry, the Beloved Country* and *Lost in the Stars; Mama's Bank Account* and *I Remember Mama.* "The Photographer," an exquisite depiction of the photography of Edward Weston, demonstrates the problem of selectivity in any visual medium.

▶ *Provide study of the film as art*

Use television screenings of old motion pictures as source material for studying historical development of motion pictures. At intervals throughout the semester ask students to watch such performers as John Barrymore, Greta Garbo, Katharine Hepburn, Rudolph Valentino, and others, or such distinguished American and foreign films as *Chushingura, Shoeshine, Raisin in the Sun, The Seventh Seal,* and *In the Heat of the Night.* Run contemporary films for a study of the art of the film. See the bibliography at the close of this chapter for aids to studying the film as art.

▶ *Make some films*

Use whatever camera equipment is available to you and your pupils. Eight-mm. cameras and a tape recorder will do even if you do not have synchronizers and tapes fitted to expensive cameras. Plunge in and create some films of your own, letting the students prepare outline scripts, experiment with ideas for transitions for the use of music and sound effects. Help the pupils transcend merely playing with a new toy in order to create something inventive or ingenious, even if it lacks the polish of commercial film.

Portable videotape recorders are another possibility for home-made treatments of film art.

Have the students write to Kodak Teen-age Movie Awards, Eastman Kodak Company, 343 State Street, Rochester, New York 14650, for information about its teen-age movie awards given each year. Kodak's pamphlet *Tested Tips on How to Make a Prize-Winning Movie* is helpful.

TO EXTEND STUDENT INTERESTS IN POPULAR ARTS

▶ *Survey prevailing interests*

1. Use a questionnaire to survey prevailing attitudes and tastes. Ask students to answer such questions as:

> What are your three favorite television programs?
> What are the three best motion pictures you have seen?
> Approximately how many hours a day do you spend watching television? On weekdays? _____ On weekends?_____
> On the following list, place a plus before the type of television and radio programs you prefer. Place a minus before the types you dislike. ____news ____western ____variety ____comedy ____mystery ____sports ____drama ____dance music

There are decided implications, of course, in the differences between ninth-graders who prefer only western films and those who choose sophisticated drama, and certainly only rough distinctions can be identified through this method. The approach offers a superficial, but sometimes helpful, portrait of the level of interests of an entire group, with little accompanying insight into the reasons for the expressed preferences or the personal evaluation of students. However, tabulations of the preferences can occasionally be used as a springboard to a more considered study of the mass media.

2. Use a "listening log." For a single week ask students to record on individual charts the amount of time they spend in viewing or listening to different kinds of programs. This approach has been used at both junior and senior high school levels.

SUGGESTED LOG FOR RECORDING TIME SPENT VIEWING AND LISTENING

Hours

	1	2	3	4	5	6	7	8	9	10
Program types										
Serials										
Westerns										
Mystery										
Music										
Comedy										

Striking contrasts in the number of hours spent in viewing programs of different types may startle some adolescents into reassessing their own uses of leisure time.

▶ *Direct attention to worthwhile, overlooked offerings*

1. With junior high school classes, survey the kinds of television offerings that are not widely viewed. Using their own expression of preferences as a starting point,

one group identified the following categories: children's programs, serials, drama, crime-mystery, westerns, situation comedy, quiz programs, popular music, variety, sports, news, panel discussions, miscellaneous. Use a bulletin board to indicate the outstanding program in each classification and those considered mediocre. Before agreeing on a qualitative rating for each broadcast, review with students some criteria for evaluating each kind of offering.

2. Spotlight special offerings. When, through reviews, magazines, or special announcements, advance information is obtained on broadcasts or motion pictures of extraordinary merit or interest, share the information with classes. Often young people can be directed to the unusual, which otherwise would be ignored, such as the presentation of a Bernard Shaw play on television or an outstanding foreign film in a local theater. One junior high school class appointed a voluntary committee to construct a weekly graphic display on the "TV Program of the Week." The students studied scheduled offerings, agreed on the most promising, and posted appropriate clippings and photographs. A similar project can be instituted for the "Film of the Month."

3. Try reserving regular times in class for previewing the programs with students.

▶ *Plan individual projects requiring special study*

1. After classifying a list of the ten most popular television programs according to audience ratings, ask a student to locate in magazine files a report on the ten most popular radio programs of the 1930's. Compare the type of programs on both lists (mystery, western, quiz) and consider the probable reasons why popular taste has changed so little that broadcasters can rely on the same basic formulas. The list of most popular programs may also be compared with lists of highly rated motion pictures.

2. Increase students' awareness of the limited range and questionable quality of much of the content of the popular arts by encouraging interested groups of volunteers to analyze the treatment of particular subjects on television or in motion pictures. For example, in a unit on biography, study the treatment of heroes. By checking on the weekly reviews in news magazines, students may obtain data on the subjects of biographical films during the preceding year. An analysis of programing schedules for television will yield comparable data. The great emphasis on athletes and entertainers in the popular arts may be compared with the greater range of subjects in recent biographical writing by checking findings against a year's list of nonfiction best sellers.

3. For a special project, possibly included in a longer unit, ask a student to select one of the popular arts, to review recent developments in the area, and to report on current trends. In addition to motion pictures and television, include among possible topics the dance, contemporary music, the popular book, the modern stage.

4. Survey with students the entertainment offerings of a community. Often the activity is introduced in relation to the study of the community in social studies, sometimes as early as the seventh grade. Provide for evaluating the quality of each by using the survey to prepare an annotated list of entertainments or examples of popular art that should not be missed by visitors from foreign countries. Consider:

> motion picture theaters   (types, offerings)
> theatrical events   (commercial, repertory, community theater)
> broadcasting centers   (television, radio)

art exhibits; musical events; museums

film festivals

libraries   (permanent collections, exhibits)

community centers   (recreation departments, art stores, centers for certain
   ethnic groups)

college and university events

TO DEVELOP STANDARDS OF JUDGMENT

▶ *Provide experiences in judging*

1. During the annual discussion each spring of potential "Oscar" and "Emmy"
award winners, encourage students to nominate and vote for their own best program and pictures. Individuals may wish to present brief statements supporting
the choice of a particular documentary or public service program and will thus need
to identify appropriate criteria for judging.

2. Urge students to write letters commending broadcasters for outstanding productions that do not elicit widespread popular support. Ask them to request that
special kinds of programs be considered. Serious letters of this type require that
writers think through their own attitudes and values.

3. When possible, assign to committees the task of recommending records for
classroom purchase or for school use. The group may select available albums (poetry
recordings, recorded drama) preview, survey educational needs, and make recommendations to the school.

4. Some junior high school classes enjoy producing "fan" magazines. With guidance such projects can be productive if magazines include thoughtful reviews of
current productions, critical comments on the nature of broadcasting or motion picture production, and basic information on the function of the media in our society.

▶ *Evaluate the judgments of others*

1. Introduce students to Russell Lynes' charts depicting the changes in highbrow, middlebrow, and lowbrow tastes during the past 100 years.[13] Construct with
students a similar chart on the tastes of "highbrow," "lowbrow," and "middlebrow"
adolescents with respect to motion pictures, television, radio, and library materials.
Most students will identify a range in taste in the appeal of television programs and
motion pictures from shoddy horror movies created for adolescents to serious works
of art.

2. Ask a mature student to select a recent motion picture that he admires and
to locate at least three reviews of the film. Then ask the student to write a composition summarizing the critics' attitudes toward the film and including his own as well.

3. Read criticism of radio serials derived from the content analysis by Rudolf
Arnheim.[14] Ask students to study serials currently on television to see if the criticisms
still apply.

[13] Russell Lynes, "The Tastemakers" (New York: Harper & Row, 1954), pp. 326–27.
[14] Rudolf Arnheim, "The World of the Daytime Serial," in Daniel Katz, ed., *Public
Opinion and Propaganda* (New York: Dryden, 1954).

SELECTED READINGS

BOOKS

BEDE SULLIVAN, SISTER. *Movies: Universal Language.* Notre Dame, Ind.: Fides, 1968. A structured approach to the study of film. Chapter three distinguishes the film from other art forms. The book concludes with a description of how students learn to shoot their own movies.

BLUESTONE, GEORGE. *Novels Into Film.* Berkeley, Calif.: Univ. of California Press, 1961. The author analyzes what is appropriate to books and to films, using such book-to-film pairs as *Wuthering Heights, The Ox-Bow Incident,* and other works of literature often taught in secondary schools.

KAEL, PAULINE. *Kiss Kiss Bang Bang.* Boston: Little, Brown, 1968. Pauline Kael's reviews of motion pictures transcend her skilled dissection of plot, directing, acting, and photography. She sifts genuineness from falseness and relates these insights to our civilization. Her writing is vivid and her comments, whether on mass culture, juvenile delinquency, or the shifting codes of love, compel the reader's full attention.

SHERIDAN, MARION, *et al. The Motion Picture and the Teaching of English.* Champaign, Ill.: NCTE, 1965. This guide for teachers of English offers practical classroom suggestions.

SKORNIA, HARRY J. *Television and Society.* New York: McGraw-Hill, 1964. As information transmittal becomes instantaneous and vast numbers of people view the same entertainment, television makes its impact on our society. This book is less subjective than those by Marshall McLuhan.

TAYLOR, CALVIN W., and WILLIAMS, FRANK E. (eds.). *Instructional Media and Creativity.* New York: Wiley, 1966. The proceedings of a conference on creativity are reported in this book. The papers presented explore ways to improve creativity through media. For instance, one idea is the development of media to present the mystery of things: birth, the universe, hypnotism, insight, and intuition.

ARTICLES AND PAMPHLETS

Audiovisual Instruction. This magazine is published ten times a year, September through May by the Department of Audiovisual Instruction, National Education Association, 1201 Sixteenth Street, N.W., Washington, D.C. 20036.

AV Communication Review. This is a more scholarly journal than *Audiovisual Instruction,* but nevertheless it contains numerous articles of practical value to teachers. It is published by the Department of Audiovisual Instruction, National Education Association, 1201 Sixteenth Street, N.W., Washington, D.C. 20036.

FARRELL, EDMUND J. *English, Education, and the Electronic Revolution.* Champaign, Ill.: NCTE, 1967. This pamphlet seeks to alert humanists to the revolution now occurring and to encourage their participation in guiding its direction.

GLENNON, MICHAEL L. "Small Groups and Short Films." *English Journal.* Vol. 57, No. 5 (May 1968), pp. 641–45. This articles lists the films that were successful in an eleventh-grade film study. It is a good guide for a school embarking upon the study of media.

MALLERY, DAVID. *The School and the Art of the Motion Picture*. Boston: National Association of Independent Schools, 1964. Beginners in classroom film-use consider this one of the most helpful readings.

MANCHEL, FRANK. "Film Images of the Negro." *Media and Methods*. Vol. 3, No. 8 (April 1967), pp. 19–23. This useful article is typical of the varied kinds of information available in this magazine, published nine times a year (September through May) by Media and Methods Institute, 124 East 40th Street, New York, N.Y. 10016.

ONG, WALTER J. "Wired for Sound: Teaching, Communications, and Technological Culture." *College English*. Vol. 21, No. 5 (February 1960), pp. 245–51. An arresting analysis of what the shift to an oral culture may mean to teachers.

POSTMAN, NEIL. *Television and the Teaching of English*. New York: Appleton-Century-Crofts, 1961. A helpful report by the committee on the study of television of the National Council of Teachers of English.

STEWART, DAVID C. *Film Study in Higher Education*. Washington, D.C.: American Council on Education, 1966. Reporting on a conference on film study in the colleges, this monograph offers secondary teachers useful course outlines and information on archives, film societies, and distributors.

Teaching with Video Tape. Published by Minnesota Mining and Manufacturing Company, St. Paul, Minnesota. Video tape has become an important part of educational television, and its possibilities for school use are described without objectionable advertising in this publication by a company commercially interested in the development of education.

EVALUATION:
APPRECIATION

LITERATURE: BASIC APPROACHES

The kind of evaluation a teacher uses has a strong influence on what pupils learn. From tests, quizzes, and similar instruments the student can perceive whether his teacher is concerned with the depths or the superficialities of literature. If his teacher urges individual voluntary reading but does nothing to evaluate growth in personal taste, the pupil will soon learn not to expend his energies on voluntary reading. Or, if a teacher asks pupils to apply what they have learned about poems or short stories to new poems or unfamiliar short stories, the pupils will learn how to transfer what they have learned to new situations. In literature the ultimate purpose of instruction is not to insure familiarity with a certain canon. Rather, the pupil is to learn to enjoy and appreciate literature so that he can deal on his own with literature never discussed in class. Repeating what the teacher has illuminated about a certain selection encourages dependent, immature responses. Evaluation of literature should frequently be based upon selections the pupils have never seen before.

Suggestions are offered here for evaluating growth in four important areas: ability to interpret behavior; sensitivity to form and style; grasp of idea and theme; growth of personal tastes.

Evaluate ability to interpret behavior

1. A simple but effective way of assessing the reader's grasp of characterization is to present an examination in which the student is asked to identify the subjects of several rather precise descriptions of persons written by the author. Such an approach becomes little more than a prosaic exercise in recall if the cameo descriptions offer anything less than vivid etchings of personality. In studying accomplished novelists one can use these tests to direct attention to important elements of characterization. The following exercise was planned for readers of *Pride and Prejudice*.

MATCHING TEST ON CHARACTERIZATION IN PRIDE AND PREJUDICE

____There was a mixture of sweetness and archness in
her manner which made it difficult for her to affront
anybody. . . . She had hardly a good feature in her
face . . . [but] it was rendered uncommonly intelligent by the beautiful expression of her dark eyes.

____She was a tall, large woman, with strongly marked
features, which might once have been handsome. Her
air was not conciliating. She was not rendered formidable by silence; but whatever she said was spoken in
so authoritative a tone, as marked her self-importance.

____[She was said to be] exceedingly proud; but . . .
she was only exceedingly shy . . . there was sense and
good humor in her face and her manners were perfectly
unassuming and gentle.

____She was a woman of mean understanding, little
information, and uncertain temper.

____[She] was a stout, well-grown girl of fifteen, with
a fine complexion and good-humored countenance. . . .
She had high animal spirits, and a sort of natural self-
consciousness, which [had] increased into assurance.

1. Mrs. Bennet
2. Jane Bennet
3. Elizabeth Bennet
4. Mary Bennet
5. Catherine Bennet
6. Lydia Bennet
7. Carolyn Bingley
8. Georgiana Darcy
9. Lady Catherine
   de Bourgh
10. Mrs. Gardiner
11. Charlotte Lucas
12. Mrs. Phillips

2. Present a series of quotations or descriptions of incidents that reveal
character; have students arrange them in chronological order and then interpret the meaning. For example, only a student who understands the progression of Macbeth's downfall can rearrange series of quotations as suggested
on page 608.

3. Ask students to predict the behavior of a literary character in a new
situation. The discussions that follow tests of this type may be among the most
stimulating in any classroom. Having thought through (or felt through) the
reactions of characters, students will be ready to express divergent views,
many of which will add spice to the analysis. The teacher will of course accept
all reasonable explanations and through studying the comments obtain an
estimate of each reader's perception and understanding of the character.

4. An opinion poll can be used to survey the reactions of individuals to
characters and events in a short story as well as to indicate the intensity of
each response. In the opinion poll the reader is asked to react to a series of
statements on a five-point scale, indicating which of the positions most closely
represents his own.

_____ Strongly agree (SA)
_____ Agree (A)
_____ Uncertain (U)
_____ Disagree (D)
_____ Strongly disagree (SD)

Explanation box

(In this space, the
student gives the rea-
son for his opinion.)

Statements like the following were presented after a reading of "The Snob."

> 1. John Harcourt did not recognize his father in the store because he thought the meeting would embarrass the father.
> 2. John was angry at Grace because he recognized that she was a snob.

The positive wording of incorrect or undesirable responses, such as in the second sentence, helps to identify unthoughtful readers who accept John's rationalization of his behavior. (Adequacy of the response recorded in such opinion polls depends both on the individual's perceptiveness while reading and on his analysis of each statement.) Most teachers consider such exercises to be learning experiences and plan directed discussion once student answers have been collected.

5. Assign questions requiring readers to evaluate particular characters or selections in terms of questions like the following:

> Do people really act the way _____ does?
> Can we detect the motivation for _____'s actions?
> Is _____ only a stereotype? Does the author rely on common clichés concerning behavior? [1]

Students may be asked to examine such questions in assigned compositions, group or panel discussions, or teacher-led class discussions. Some teachers rely on comparisons in which students are asked to compare superficially drawn and multidimensional characters. For example, junior high school students may contrast the development of the city boy in Stephen Meader's *Red Horse Hill* with the portrayal of Jody in *The Yearling*. Older readers could compare some of the portraits of women drawn against the soil: O-Lan in *The Good Earth*, Beret in *Giants in the Earth*, Caroline in *Let the Hurricane Roar*, Leslie in *Giant*.

Evaluate sensitivity to form and style

Able students easily learn to memorize definitions or to pluck figures of speech from sentences and stanzas supplied by the teacher. Fewer perhaps become sensitive to hearing, feeling, and responding to the beauties of the author's craft. Evaluating sensitivity to form may encourage readers to be a bit more responsive to the emotional effects of fine writing.

1. Readers may try to identify the effect the author is attempting to achieve. Adolescents will experience difficulty in answering such questions if they have had little instruction in this area. Such tests resemble classroom experiences in which students select appropriate musical accompaniment for the oral reading of a poem or discuss the color imagery to use in reproducing a work of literature in graphic media—approaches mentioned earlier in this

---

[1] Some excellent questions for such exercises are to be found in G. R. Carlsen's "The Dimensions of Literature," *English Journal*, Vol. 41, No. 4 (April 1952), pp. 179–86.

book. In this example, a group of tenth-graders was asked to distinguish the mood suggested by a series of paragraphs from *Oliver Twist*.

SUGGESTED TEST OF ABILITY TO DETECT MOOD

Directions In the left column are listed passages from the novel in which Dickens attempted to convey a certain mood or atmosphere. Select from the list of terms at the right the number of the word that best describes the pervading mood of each paragraph. If a passage should suggest two moods, select only the more appropriate term.

____ The chilly mist rolled along the ground like a dense cloud. The grass was wet. The damp breath of an unwholesome wind went languidly by, with a hollow moaning.	1. peacefulness 2. hatred 3. coldness
____ An unfinished coffin on black trestles, which stood in the middle of the shop, looked gloomy and deathlike. Against the walls were ranged, in regular array, a row of boards cut into the same shape, looking like high-shouldered ghosts with hands in their pockets.	4. dimness 5. loneliness 6. fear 7. eerieness 8. filthiness
____ It was a dark, quiet night. The stars seemed, to the boy's eyes, farther from the earth than he had ever seen them before. There was no wind, and the somber shadows thrown by the trees upon the ground were deathly still.	

2. Try testing responses to language by asking advanced readers to distinguish fresh from faded styles. The opinion-poll approach can be used and students asked to judge twelve to fifteen selected sentences, rating each on a five-point scale ranging from highly effective or vivid to ineffective or colorless. Once initial ratings are made, students may be asked to select the word that best justifies each of their reactions (trite, vivid, awkward, pretentious, rhythmical).

Justification

____ The sidewalk flower stands exuding such clouds of heavy perfume that their owners should be arrested for fragrancy.

——— The traveler on his happy journey, as his foot springs from the deep turf and strikes the pebbles gaily over the edge of the mountain road, sees with a glance of delight the clusters of nut-brown cottages that nestle among those sloping orchards, and glow beneath the boughs of the pines.

____ The tiny white pebbles of the clean pathway swept down to the azure lake, which, when it was full, seemed to glisten like sparkling crystal, and when empty, revealed the mud and muck of the shore.

For groups of older students, complete paragraphs may be substituted for the sentences and more complete justifications required.

3. Follow some of the leads of research in devising "measures" of ability to visualize—a skill found to be related to general appreciative factors in at least

two studies.[2] After reading *My Antonia,* for example, students may be given thirty minutes to describe those situations they most clearly recall. The teacher may study the papers to identify the readers who recall events with the greatest and least degrees of vividness.

Evaluate grasp of idea and theme

1. Teachers need to assess students' understanding of the purpose of a selection as distinct from comprehension of the narrative. Many teachers examine students through questions requiring interpretation and generalized thinking on the part of the reader as in the following examples:

> In "Leiningen Versus the Ants," Stephenson is attempting to say that:
> a. dauntless courage will always win against insuperable odds.
> b. flashes of inspiration will frequently save lost causes.
> c. man will always overcome brute force by using his power to reason.
>
> I believe that statement ＿＿ best expresses the theme of the story because . . .
> To what extent are the ideas in the two poems "Mother to Son" and "Nancy Hanks" similar? Compare the two in a paragraph.

2. A difficult assignment—which may seem ridiculously obvious to the untutored—involves asking students to summarize the significance of a short story in one sentence. This assignment requires compression of ideas. A review of sentence summaries written over a period of several weeks offers important insights into each student's growth in perceptiveness. As reading, discussion, and writing of sentence summaries continues, students can be led to see that the essential elements of many selections are not to be found in plot alone.

3. To offer immediate information on the reader's responses to a selection— to character, situation, incident, even style—follow the reading of a story with a request that individuals complete such open statements as the following, based on "Reflections of Luanne":

> I think that this story . . .
> Luanne . . .
> The thing that interested me most was . . .
> I did not understand . . .
> I think that Janet Buck . .
> This story is about . . .

If such responses are to have any meaning, students must write freely and recognize that there are no perfect answers. Such an exercise should not be considered more than a sampling of opinion. The responses may reveal aspects of a selection that are best understood as well as those misinterpreted. Often the reactions will suggest important instructional needs.

[2] Earl Forman, "An Instrument to Evaluate the Literary Appreciation of Adolescents," unpublished doctoral dissertation, University of Illinois, 1951; Henry C. Meckel, "An Exploratory Study of Responses of Adolescent Pupils to Situations in a Novel," unpublished doctoral dissertation, University of Chicago, 1946.

4. Unstructured free responses are useful after the reading of a selection that has a particularly strong impact. Before any attempt is made at discussion, urge students to write their first thoughts, or to describe how the story impresses them, or whatever occurs to them about the people, the plot, or the ideas. These responses present teachers with material that can be analyzed for clues to each reader's personal reactions. On occasion, special methods of content analysis may be applied. For example, some teachers try checking the elements mentioned by each student in his free response against a list of elements to which sensitive and mature readers (at the age level of students) may be expected to react. For example, the free responses of eighth- or ninth-graders to "The Restless Ones" could be checked against the following hoped-for reactions:

ITEMS INVOLVING CONTENT

Jerry's unwillingness to assume responsibility for his actions

Jerry's restlessness being caused by a lack of personal resource as much as by the shortage of avocational opportunities

pending military induction as a factor contributing to the boy's failure to consider the future

comic books and motion pictures being possible causes of delinquent behavior

Jerry's demand to be accepted as an adult conflicting with his unwillingness to assume adult responsibilities

ITEMS INVOLVING FORM

inadequacy of character motivation (Do comic books really affect youngsters in this way?)

questionable realism of the dialog (awkward wording, clumsy slang expressions)

contrived nature of the situation (use of flashback technique and boy's misconception concerning death of storekeeper to maintain suspense)

use of common stereotypes (comics, movies, and television as a cause of delinquency; military induction as a cause; the use of "blind" parents who see their son as a problem only after the crime is committed)

use of fresh and original elements (ironical use of juvenile authorities to arrest the boy, thus adding to his resentment toward adults; paradox implied in use of seemingly childish behavior—crying—as a sign of newly found maturity)

These approaches to studying responses to literature do not offer numerical scores that can be accepted as precise and valid measures but do suggest ways of gaining some understanding of the complex emotional and intellectual experiences of literary response.

Evaluate growth in personal taste

CONSIDER OVER-ALL GROWTH Since the program in literary appreciation is intended to refine personal taste and discrimination, an accurate gauge of accomplishment may be found in records of individual reading. Teachers must remember, of course, that appreciations change gradually over long periods of time and that seldom can they expect to bring about important and permanent shifts in perception during a single semester or school year. On occasion, all teachers enjoy working with an adolescent who suddenly discovers a literature he has not known existed—a girl whose first acquaintance with modern drama results in the reading of fifteen or twenty plays, the students who become excessively interested in the Civil War, or who so enjoy *The Fellowship of the Ring* that they must read all other Tolkien novels. Such impressive splurges are heady experiences in the reading careers of gifted pupils, but they tend unfortunately to be rather rare. More often teachers see trends and tendencies develop over many semesters.

MAINTAIN READING RECORDS   Most teachers attempt to maintain some kind of reading record. To measure growth in personal taste, cumulative information maintained over several years and passed from teacher to teacher offers invaluable data. For example, such cumulative records reveal whether an individual's experiences with first rate literature has been confined only to selections studied or assigned in the classroom.

PLAN INDIVIDUAL CONFERENCES   Teachers concerned with what a student sees in his reading know that the mere recording of book titles offers little information. They often schedule regular reading conferences, each fortnight or month depending on the teaching loads, and attempt to record on individual cards the ideas discussed, the books mentioned, the insights gleaned. Such a form as the following has been used:

SAMPLE RECORD OF READING CONFERENCE

Name of student _____   Grade 8

Date	Books read	New titles suggested	Comment
9/28	Lassie Come Home Silver Chief	National Velvet Call of the Wild	Interest in animal stories continued from seventh grade. Concerned largely with plot, suspense. Discussed plausibility of Lassie's return—what made it seem realistic.
10/20	Return of Silver Chief	Call of the Wild	He noted absence of theme in *Silver Chief*, inferiority of the book to *Lassie* in this respect. Some interest in Alaska and primitive areas.
11/16	Call of the Wild White Fang	Biography of Jack London	Very interested in London. Discussed humanization of animals. Noted foreshadowing of London in building suspense—possible application of classroom study of foreshadowing in O. Henry.

USE SELF-EVALUATION   Teachers may ask students to complete the following evaluation form at the end of each semester. The questions vary, of course, with the aims of the teacher and would be very different for grades 7, 8, and 9. Reproduced here are possible questions and answers for a boy in a tenth-grade class:

SUMMARY OF VOLUNTARY READING

Name _____ English _____ Date _____

An evaluation of your voluntary reading program should show that you have improved during the second semester in the reading that you select for yourself. Check below those ways in which you feel you have benefited from this program. Below each section that you check, write in the names of three books that have helped you reach that goal.

√ 1. I enjoy reading several different types of books: biography, drama, poetry, history.

Anna and the King of Siam, Black Like Me, Story of the F.B.I., Modern Architecture

√ 2. I enjoy reading books with varied geographical backgrounds.

The Ugly American (Vietnam), *Anna and the King of Siam* (Thailand), *Diary of a Nightmare* (Germany), *A Night of Watching* (Denmark)

√ 3. I enjoy reading books whose stories take place in various historical periods.

Anna and the King of Siam, Autobiography of Ben Franklin, A Night of Watching

___ 4. I have reached the point where I can read a long book of 500 or more pages.

√ 5. I have read at least one book that has influenced my life (my conduct, or my thinking, or helped me solve a problem).

Black Like Me, Modern Architecture, The Ugly American

√ 6. "My Reading Design" shows that I have read books in twelve sections (list one title in each section).[3]

The Wooden Horse, You Only Live Twice, Huckleberry Finn, Modern Architecture, Hot Rod, Lou Gehrig: Iron Horse of Baseball, Inside Story of the F.B.I., We Die Alone, Drums, Black Like Me, Anna and the King of Siam, Autobiography of Ben Franklin

√ 7. I like the book whose title appears below the least of those I've read in the second semester.

Captains Courageous

√ 8. I like the book whose title appears below the best of those I've read in the second semester.

The Story of Willie Mays

√ 9. How do you account for the difference in your opinion of the books in 7 and 8?

In *Captains Courageous* the setting was the same and the different events didn't vary enough. In *The Story of Willie Mays* something new was always coming up and some events were entirely different. The things that happened were laughable and worth reading for me because I play baseball myself.

[3] Section refers to categories agreed upon by teacher and students, such categories as historical fiction, social problems, biography.

___√___ 10. Do you like to read books about grownups and their problems? If so, name one or two such books.

Yes. *Black Like Me, Anna and the King of Siam*

PREPARE EXAMINATIONS THAT MEASURE APPRECIATIVE ABILITIES   Some teachers include questions that assess student abilities to interpret as well as to comprehend. For example, some teachers prepare three-part tests for students. Part one of the test, the "C" section, consists of rather obvious factual questions. Students who complete only this portion receive grades no higher than "C." Sections "B" and "A" deal with interpretive questions. To receive higher grades, students must complete all sections of the test satisfactorily. The following sample questions, taken from an examination on *Abe Lincoln in Illinois,* show the range in difficulty: [4]

SAMPLE THREE-PART TEST FOR ABE LINCOLN IN ILLINOIS

This is a kind of test designed to show not only your knowledge of the facts connected with the play we have just read but to reveal your skill in interpreting what you read and your ability to relate a literary experience to the life about you.

C Section

1. In what village and state does the play open?
2. Why did the professional politicians want Lincoln?
3. What political party asked him to run?
4. Which of these words best characterizes the Whig party: conservative, radical?

B Section

Choose one of the following and write specifically and fully about it.

1. What did each of the following scenes contribute to your knowledge of Lincoln's character?

scene 1   the grammar lesson with Mentor Graham
scene 2   Lincoln invited to run for assembly
scene 3   Lincoln after Ann's death

2. The following is the text of the prayer for Seth's son, ill of swamp fever in a covered wagon. Sherwood says in his notes that "The prayer which Lincoln gives for a sick boy is, in effect, a prayer for the survival of the United States of America." Show in your discussion how this prayer could take on that meaning.

[Here is reproduced the prayer from the play.]

3. Here are five statements by Lincoln recording his gradual change in attitude toward slavery. Arrange them by numbering them from 1 to 5, from the most conservative position to the most radical.

_____ "And as to slavery, I'm sick and tired of all this righteous talk about it. When you know more about law, you'll know that those property rights you mentioned are guaranteed by the constitution. And if the Union can't stand on the Constitution, then let it fall."

_____ "This government cannot endure permanently, half slave and half free."

[4] Prepared by Lucille Hildinger, Wichita, Kansas.

____ "That Freeman's League is a pack of hell-roaring fanatics. Talk reason to them and they scorn you for a mealy-mouth."

____ "It's made me feel that I've got to do something, to keep you and your kind in the United States of America."

____ "I am opposed to slavery. But I'm even more opposed to going to war."

A Section

Abe Lincoln in Illinois is a play dealing with pioneer life and the development of one of our national heroes who lived over a hundred years ago. The external action of the play seems remote but the inner life of the people, the motives that drove them toward happiness or tragedy are the same that affect our lives today. Has this play helped you to understand some type of human behavior or to feel differently toward it in any way? Consider the following questions carefully. Choose one and write a discussion of 150 to 200 words.

1. Do you know a Clary boys' gang who, in trying to impress others, show only their own crudities? On school occasions have you ever observed any East High Clary boys who make spectacles of themselves as successfully as the Clarys did in Scene 2? [The short questions are merely prompters.]

2. Lincoln apparently always hated slavery; his determination to do something about it took years to develop. Have you, on a much smaller scale, found belief in a principle difficult to translate into action? Have we, as a school, had any experience of this kind? Does cheating come in here? Is there racial prejudice in this class?

3. Do you know people like Mary Todd Lincoln? Are they driven by some ambition? Do they drive others? Are they satisfied when they get what they want or have they destroyed part of their happiness in reaching their goal? Is there something of Mary Todd in the teen-agers who throw over old friends for new?

USE THE FORCED-CHOICE APPROACH   A different approach to evaluating growth in personal taste is suggested by the test of contemporary literature developed by Dora V. Smith.[5] In this test, students are asked to identify familiar adolescent books of inferior and superior quality. Half of the eighty questions on such tests deal with worthwhile literature for younger readers, books like *Johnny Tremain* and *Caddie Woodlawn*. The other half concerns books of inferior quality like the Nancy Drew mystery stories. The items are arranged so that superior and inferior titles are scrambled. For example, the following items might be included on such a test:

> *The Lance of Kanana* is a story of (1) a south sea shipping vessel's encounter with whales; (2) a famous weapon handed down for three generations; (3) an African boy hunter; (4) a native of India; (5) a boy who gave his life for Arabia.
> *The Blackboard Jungle* is a story about (1) hobos in a shanty town; (2) the growth of an American industry; (3) incidents in a vocational high school in New York City; (4) the life of students in Africa.

As Smith has suggested, teachers should prepare such forms for their own classes using popular contemporary titles appealing to a range of tastes—from

[5] Dora V. Smith, "Test of Contemporary Reading" (Minneapolis: Univ. of Minnesota, College of Education, 1936).

Mickey Spillane and the corner newsstand potboilers to good standard adventure fiction like *Shane* or superior books for students in the age group, such as *The Bridges of Toko-ri* and *The White Stag.*

USE A PLOT COMPLETION TEST   Some years ago a special plot completion test was developed by Sara Roody. This test presents ten plot situations. Students are asked to choose the probable ending to the situation from the five which are given. For example, here is plot 3: [6]

> Donald was a bright, intelligent boy with high ideals of honor. His scholastic rating was very important to him. One day in a ten-weeks' examination in English he came to a question that called for detailed information about the *Atlantic Monthly,* including the name of the editor. Though he did not remember the name, he had a copy of the magazine in his desk. Since the boy in front of him was tall, Donald was able to open his desk and look at the magazine without being observed by the teacher. He did so. The next day, ashamed of having cheated, he told the teacher, whom he knew to be a fair-minded person. What do you think happened?
>
> Read the endings that are listed below, keeping in mind the facts of the case, the personality of the boy, and that of his teacher. Then number the endings in the order of their probability.
>
> a. The teacher told the class what happened and gave Donald a zero on his examination. Since that test was counted as one third of his ten-weeks' average he received a failing grade on his report card. "Let this be a lesson to all of you," said the teacher.
>
> b. The teacher said, "Thank you for telling me. I reward you for your honesty. I will give you full credit for all the answers on your paper, including the one that you copied." Donald received the highest grade in the class.
>
> c. The teacher told no one else, but gave Donald another set of questions to answer. He made a high score.
>
> d. Donald did not copy the answer from the magazine. He left a blank space on his paper.
>
> e. The teacher allowed Donald to take another examination. The questions were more difficult for him than those on the original test. Though he did well, his grade was somewhat lower than his score on the first test.

Although the complete test is not presently available, the sample item suggests an approach individual teachers may use in their own classes. A similar instrument has been developed by Burton.[7] Somewhat similar in part are the tests of literary discernment and the literary preference questionnaire developed by the curriculum study center at Carnegie Institute of Technology.[8]

[6] Reprinted with permission of Sara Roody, Nyack High School, Nyack, N.Y.

[7] Dwight Burton, *Literature Study in the High School,* rev. ed. (New York: Holt, Rinehart & Winston, 1964), pp. 143–56.

[8] Erwin R. Steinberg and others, *Sample Selections from a Senior High School Curriculum in English for Able College-Bound Students* (Pittsburgh: Carnegie Institute of Technology, 1967), pp. 87–102.

Standardized instruments for measuring appreciation

In addition to devices introduced in the classroom for instructional and evaluative purposes, teachers occasionally wish to use printed measures of general growth in appreciation rather than instruments designed to concentrate on specific abilities. Among the more interesting printed tests are these:

Herbert A. Carroll, *Prose Appreciation Test* (Minneapolis: Educational Test Bureau, 1931). Graded tests for various secondary levels, requiring students to discriminate the quality of prose selections.

Tests of literary appreciation evolved in an eight-year study, reported in Eugene R. Smith and Ralph Tyler, *Appraising and Recording Student Progress* (New York: Harper & Row, 1942).

E. F. Lindquist and Julia Pederson, *Ability to Interpret Literary Materials,* Test 7 of the Iowa Tests of Educational Development, Grades 9–12 (Chicago: Science Research Associates, 1942–61). Contains literary materials and related multiple-choice questions.

DRAMA

Development of appreciation for the play form, both on printed page and on stage and screen, is the ultimate goal in teaching dramatic literature. Such growth cannot be charted semester by semester with mathematical accuracy. The teacher does, however, have several methods of appraisal—some precise, others tenuous but practical enough to be useful.

Evaluating understandings

Understandings are comparatively easy to evaluate. For instance, it is possible to determine with a certain degree of exactness how much students have learned concerning the various aspects of the structure of drama.

INTERPRETING CLUES FROM SETTINGS Give students mimeographed copies listing the details of settings of several unfamiliar plays—largely factual details for immature pupils and those with psychological overtones for the more advanced. Ask them to determine what atmosphere the playwright seems trying to create; what kind of play they would expect from such a setting.

READING FOR IMPLICATIONS Give students a copy of the opening scene of an unfamiliar play. Ask them to select and explain lines that seem to suggest more than they say. (Students cannot be expected to infer exact meanings; they can recognize lines that hint at things of the past, portend the future, and so on.)

ANALYZING CONFLICTS AND DETERMINING THEMES   Show a short dramatic film, as suggested on pages 503–04. Follow with a brief test, asking students to determine the issue, the opposing forces, and the deciding agent and then to state the idea exemplified by the action. Such devices give sufficiently exact information for judging understandings of the structural elements of drama.

Evaluating oral reading

Progress made in the skills of oral interpretation is more difficult to appraise precisely. In addition to the continual assessing and reassessing as students present scenes in groups and before the class, a final evaluation benefits individuals, although it should not weigh too heavily in determining grades. Much depends upon the time the teacher has been able to give for instruction and upon the personal temperament and endowment of the student. All pupils, though, should be able to learn to maintain tempo and, if not to convey the spirit of play and characters adequately, at least to do nothing to detract from it. A comparison of tape recordings of brief scenes, one made at the beginning and another at the end, will supplement the teacher's observation and provide a means for students to note the gains they have made in ability to convey meaning and feeling through vocal expression. A written self-evaluation, comparing the two readings, usually reveals the student's attitude toward the experience and his feelings about its worth for him; it gives material for a personal conference in those cases where one seems necessary.

Evaluating appreciation

Appreciation can be gauged only indirectly. Does the student voluntarily select plays for individual reading? If so, what does he choose? Do his comments as they arise spontaneously in class discussion show he likes the better plays appearing on television? Do writing assignments asking for comparisons of films he has seen show he is developing standards for judging? Not precise, to be sure, such observations do give some indication of growth.

Many teachers give students a list of various learning experiences presented during a semester or year and ask them to rate them anonymously, placing first in order those from which they have received the most benefit. This furnishes material for fruitful discussion as students review the course. Reasons for choice or rejection give the teacher insight as to whether the study of plays has approximated its desired objectives, and direction in planning for future classes.

A procedure similar to the following gives some help in judging the impact of instruction on the growth of appreciation. Early in the semester ask students to write a paragraph:

>The best television play I've seen recently is _____. I choose it as the best because . . .

Long enough after completing the study of plays so it will have no direct connection to dramatic literature, repeat the assignment, asking for an additional paragraph:

>The worst television play I've seen recently is _____. I choose it as the worst because . . .

The reasons given in each case will be more significant than the choice of play.

When this same assignment is repeated once a year, with student folders being passed from one teacher to the next, the sequence of choices with the supporting opinions provides basis for evaluation of growth in appreciation. For any improvement shown, the English teacher can assume only part of the credit. Appreciation for the best in any art form grows slowly and many factors contribute to its development.

POETRY

Successful teachers enjoy poetry, avoid the monotony of a single approach, and emphasize inductive teaching. Similarly, evaluation should be alive, varied, and probing. Here are some suggestions.

READING POEMS ALOUD The teacher may present students with several poems to be studied individually and recorded on tape. Poems similar to each other may be used before and after studying poetry—for example, two similar poems by the same author. The tape recordings will help considerably to reveal whether or not the students have made progress in interpreting poetry.

BEHAVIOR OF STUDENTS Students who begin to read more poetry, who want to write poetry, who choose poetry for voluntary projects, who list poetry on their individual reading lists, who purchase recordings of poetry and share them at school—all are giving the teacher some basis for evaluating the impact of his instruction. He must, of course, avoid wishful thinking and biased observation.

RATING BY STUDENTS Teachers may ask pupils to rate, anonymously, the topics studied during a semester. If poetry is consistently ranked at the bottom of students' preferences and judgments of worth, the teacher should review his procedures.

SELECTING THE MISSING LINES From the four choices offered them, students are to write in the lines that are omitted and explain the bases of their choice. Example:

MOONLIGHT [9]

My father hated moonlight,   He was an old frontiersman,
And pulled the curtains down   And on their deadly raids,
Each time the snows of moonlight   Comanches rode by moonlight
Came drifting on the town.   In stealthy cavalcades;

And took the settlers' horses,
Or left a trail of red—

_____

_____

Choices for last two lines:

(1)   (2)
And stole the settler's harness   The women cowered in the darkness
While they were fast abed.   And shivered at each new tread.
(3)   (4)
He came to love the darkness,   The curtains like women's tresses
And hate the moon, he said.   Symbolized my father's dread.

Unwary pupils, lured by the word *symbolized*, will often choose 4; students who have
gained little will continue to choose 1 or 2.

IDENTIFYING SYMBOLS   From a group of poems studied, the teacher may use a
matching test to discover whether or not pupils comprehended the symbols
used. Example:

Directions   How are the following symbols used? What, in other words, does
each one stand for? On the line at the left place the number of the phrase that
correctly identifies the meaning of each symbol.

____ a broken sword   1. the joys of childhood
____ the moon   2. death
____ old swimmin' hole   3. the land of heart's desire
____ Sherwood Forest   4. the leader of a nation
____ Eldorado   5. modern man's power
____ captain of a ship   6. wonder and romance
____ the Elf-King   7. man's eternal quest for adventure
                                 8. the will to win in spite of odds
                                 9. man's source of strength
                                 10. life's challenge to youth

IDENTIFYING THEMES   It is usually more important to be able to match poems
with their themes than poems with authors, metrical feet, or literary movement. Example:

A. "The Elf-King"
B. "The Broncho That Would Not Be Broken"

[9] "Moonlight," from *Flute in the Distance* by Berta Hart Nance. (Dallas: Kaleidograph
Press, 1935.) Reprinted by permission.

C. "Lee"
D. "Little Giffen"
E. "Old Christmas Morning"

Directions On the line at the left place the letter of the poem referred to in the following brief descriptions of the underlying theme:

_____ 1. the invincible hero, great even in defeat
_____ 2. a proud spirit that would not be subdued

Another method: present a thematic poem, omitting title and author. Have pupils choose an appropriate title for the poem.

THE POPULAR ARTS

Increasing discrimination in reading, in viewing, and in listening to the popular arts is the ultimate goal of instruction. The success can be judged only by seeking the answer to three basic questions:

Do students seem to understand the popular arts better?
Do they seem to be extending their interests in the media?
Do they seem to be developing and applying standards of critical judgment?

Many learning experiences described in Chapter Twelve will help teachers assess growth in discrimination. For example, analyses of programs written in September may be compared with analyses written in May as a way of evaluating changes in response occurring during the school year. Diagnosis and evaluation are two sides of the same coin; both occur continuously. Thus parallel forms of any surveys or questionnaires may be used by teachers who desire concrete evidence of growth. Teachers also rely on less formal ways of noting changes in behavior. They observe students who increasingly see parallels between the art of the classroom and the art outside. They study the contributions made in impromptu discussion, the compositions, the reading of students, for evidence that individuals are learning to draw ideas from many sources.

Specific procedures for evaluating growth in understanding and appreciation can be grouped into four categories.

COMPARE QUALITATIVE RESPONSES Obtain qualitative responses to programs and motion pictures to help in understanding individual points of view. Ask students to complete open statements about two or three television broadcasts or motion pictures each individual feels have been the most engrossing or have had the greatest impact on him during the previous month or semester. Such statements as the following might be used:

I remember that . . .
It made me feel . . .
I would like . . .
They should change . . .

Such completed statements offer insight into the causes underlying student preferences as well as occasional information on the adequacy of the responses. Individuals who seem to respond only to narrative and suspense may well profit from some study of characterization; those who fail to discriminate beyond "feeling good" or "feeling bad" may be helped to discriminate different shades of "good" and "bad" emotion. When responses are obtained early in the year and again later, teachers have a basis for assessing the impact of instruction and changes in the reactions of individuals.

REPEAT INTEREST SURVEYS   Questionnaire surveys of student interests may be repeated, or new listening logs may be maintained late in a semester. (See suggested forms on page 547.) By comparing responses obtained during the final weeks of a term with those reported earlier, students, with or without teacher help, may examine whether they have extended their viewing interests.

USE CHECKLISTS TO EVALUATE THE RANGE OF COMMENTS   Assess student awareness of standards for evaluating offerings in the popular arts by maintaining a checklist of elements studied, against which student critiques may be compared. For example, in a ninth-grade class the following aspects of dramatic art may receive some attention:

ELEMENTS OF CONTENT	ELEMENTS OF PRODUCTION
relation of plot and theme	photography
foreshadowing	pacing
characterization	adequacy of acting

Ask students to review motion pictures or television broadcasts. Examine the reviews to determine whether students indicate an awareness of the elements that have been studied.

ENCOURAGE SELF-ASSESSMENT AT THE END OF THE YEAR   Ask students to review their own viewing-listening habits in a special questionnaire that requires individuals to consider extension of interests in a number of areas. The method may be used with a class at any grade level, although questions will vary depending on the maturity of the students. Questions like the following are especially appropriate:

I have increased my understanding of three kinds of television programs during the semester. (Mention each of the three and explain the change in your attitude.)

I listened to at least one program containing a discussion of an important problem that I had not considered before. (Please describe.)

I viewed at least three dramas emphasizing characterization. (Please list titles and describe.)

I viewed at least one program dealing with a problem similar to one about which I have been reading. (Mention the program, the problem, and the reading.)

Continuing evaluation is an integral part of teaching and learning; it keeps teacher and students informed of what has been accomplished as well as what remains to be achieved.

PLAN:

TEACHING POETRY
INDUCTIVELY

I. A. Richards' discovery that his college honors students could not react confidently to a poem without knowing who wrote it convinced teachers that the scholarly approach did not have the effect they had hoped. The discovery, however, did not tempt them to swing to the opposite extreme; it served as impetus for research on response to all forms of literature. The research continues today. The findings reiterate this principle: although young people need direction in developing appreciation, it must be the kind that helps them examine specific examples of literary forms in reference to themselves and their understanding of the world.[1] If an adolescent is to like a poem for its own sake this year and is to be able next year to discard it for one he likes better, he must come to each poem without preconceived ideas. This plan for presenting poetry is directed toward that ideal.

The discussion is based on ideas given in Chapter Eleven and is designed to be used with that chapter; it offers poems a teacher may wish to add to his collection and a guide for developing desirable concepts and skills. It presents a specific and extended example of an idea from that chapter: poetry requires careful reading but must be taught with a light hand.

The junior high years are exploratory; for many young people the period of exploration extends throughout the tenth grade and beyond. Certainly this is true of experiences with poetry. We have long known we could not help our students develop discriminating taste in fiction if we relied entirely upon the intensive study of a few selected works; it is even more unlikely we can help them appreciate poetry if each semester we consistently depend upon a few great poems taught to exhaustion. With fiction, the guided reading program has helped solve the problem; with poetry, a guided listening program will serve the same end.

If students entering the seventh grade profess to like poetry, usually they mean they like to listen to poems that tell a story or have a touch of humor or make an agreeable statement in metered rhythm and regular rhyme. The wise teacher, facing an unknown class, starts with what he thinks students will like. Over the formative years, young people should hear and discuss—and

---

[1] Alan C. Purves with Victoria Rippere, "Elements of Writing About a Literary Work: A Study of Response to Literature" (Champaign, Ill.: NCTE, 1967), pp. 60–63.

eventually read for themselves—a vast number of poems, varying in difficulty, quality, and kind.

The same principles guide the inductive approach to teaching, whatever the literary genre. Inductive teaching of poetry is first letting students discover what they can in a poem, rather than telling them what they must find and pointing out proof it is there. It is next examining these discoveries—accepting statements pupils make, considering the implications, asking for evidence to support the implications. Finally, it is helping the class draw a conclusion in line with the evidence. Attention centers on the poem; the teacher's purpose is to encourage students to respond fully and honestly.

This description may create the impression that inductive teaching will work with precision if only one can learn the skill. The truth is that unadulterated inductive teaching, effective for a considerable portion of an hour, is rare indeed. In our own thinking we constantly veer from inductive reasoning to deductive; one aids the other. The belief that the inductive method will work under all conditions and for as long at one time as the teacher wishes is largely responsible for the frustration of those who discover it will not work for them. Our observation of those trying to use the method convinces us that it is ineffective in situations where teachers are guided by two ideas—valid ideas that always seem to impress the inexperienced teacher deeply. "You must not tell; you must extract." This seems to imply there will always be something worth extracting; if it takes an hour to bring it to light, so be it. "Students should be allowed to express any opinion they wish." In classes where many are eager to speak, it is easy to disregard the other half of this injunction: "They should be asked to supply evidence in support."

The principles underlying the inductive approach to teaching are sound. They are the teacher's over-all guide; he puts them into practice whenever they are appropriate. But it is equally important to remember that a lesson focusing on the inductive does not exclude occasional leading questions or an occasional switch to the deductive. This procedure is sometimes the only recourse a teacher has to prevent students' sinking into a verbal bog or, if they are already mired, getting them out. This viewpoint removes the inexperienced teacher's fear of the inductive method, which we interpret as fear of intruding on the student's domain. If the teacher knows that his first attempts, although only partly inductive, are respectable, he will learn more quickly how to use the method effectively.

The teacher must choose the poems to be presented to any particular class. The search for suitable ones never ends. No anthology, no group of anthologies, can be all things for all time to all teachers—or to all students. Each teacher and each student must make his own. For both teacher and student such an anthology must be flexible in form—a file or loose-leaf notebook—for it is constantly changing, some poems being discarded and others added. Thus, it is possible a reader may find few poems in these pages to suit his purpose, but he will realize that the guide the poems illustrate is applicable to any poems he may select.

In choosing the poems, we had two requirements: brevity and adaptability. Even if lack of space had not prevented including long poems, we would have rejected them, for this is only part of the poetry program—the part based primarily on listening. Here the short poem is best.[2] In a limited amount of time, it can be introduced, read by the teacher, briefly commented upon by students, re-read, and dismissed with a clear conscience. If the teacher follows this procedure, he will be less tempted to point out; he will accept the fact that all possible discoveries about the poem need not be made at one time. Most of the poems here are short enough to be written on the chalkboard or shown on the screen and copied in notebooks if such a procedure seems desirable.

Since our target covers a wide range, we wanted the examples to represent an area equally broad, with poems adaptable to different purposes and to different levels of maturity and experience. Clearly, a few of them will be offered only to the most mature adolescents; others are simple enough for seventh graders to understand. However, it should be possible, in the right circumstances, to present the majority to several grade levels. Many can be used in various ways, requiring different time limits. Some poems, used in a particular instance—perhaps to fill an odd moment or to introduce a more difficult poem— need little more than a listening ear; yet, under different circumstances, these same poems may require more time because they need to be carefully examined.

We are writing for teachers; therefore, sections are arranged in what seems the most logical order for developing the concepts intended to serve as a teaching guide. There is no logic to the order of the poems; they are numbered consecutively only for reference. Since each provides a complete literary experience, the majority could have been used as illustrations in sections other than those in which they appear. Their placement intends neither to restrict their use nor to indicate an order for teaching.

The following statements about poets, readers, and teachers are personal opinions. We encourage the reader to supply his own if's and but's.

THE POET'S JOB

Poets, discussing their work, have thrown some light on the creative process, while admitting it cannot be satisfactorily explained. Granted, the process is elusive; the product is not. Poems stand still to be examined, and the examination of a sufficient number reveals what poets consider their job to be:

> the poem has a job to do . . . with pain and difficulty [poets] are attempting to understand, clarify, and make articulate the dark [obscure] processes of human life.[3]

[2] Many narrative poems, longer than those printed here, are particularly appropriate for listening; in introducing poetry to some classes, the narrative may serve best.
[3] Thomas Blackburn, *The Price of an Eye* (New York: Morrow, 1961), pp. 9–10.

Each poem, therefore, presents an experience through which the poet communicates his insights concerning some aspect of life. Familiarity with many poems by different authors shows that poets have in common not only this purpose but also two basic ways of accomplishing it. Consequently, we can expect most poems to have three facets: the experience

1. implies a comment on some aspect of the human situation—*statement;*
2. uses imagery, often comparing something not perceptible to the senses to something that is—*metaphor;*
3. organizes language to produce a pattern of sound, rhythm, and movement that fuses thought and emotion—*musical pattern.*

These three generalizations are basic to poetry; they provide a framework accommodating almost any detail one would want to teach; they suggest concepts that students, while noting exceptions, can assimilate inductively and eventually formulate. They do not, however, apply to everything written in verse, nor do they explicitly cover everything that can be said about an individual poem. Although each facet of a poem may be examined separately, the three are not independent; they exist in reference to each other within a particular context. Poems on any subject could be used to illustrate the individual facets, but it seems more appropriate here to listen to poets who have concerned themselves more or less specifically with each of the three.

The human situation

We live in two worlds: the world perceptible to the senses; the inner world, essentially psychological. Both are important to the poet, but the inner world of thought and feeling is his chief concern. Faulkner, speaking of the complexities and contradictions of life, once said that the mere fact of having been created human commits one to the responsibility of living up to his humanity. Poets continually remind us of this obligation.

Christopher Morley contrasts the impression created by an Irish wolfhound with that made by some who come to look and judge.

1

AT THE DOG SHOW

Long and gray and gaunt he lies,
A Lincoln among dogs; his eyes,
Deep and clear of sight, appraise
The meaningless and shuffling ways
Of human folk that stop and stare.
One witless woman, seeing there
How tired, how contemptuous
He is of all the smell and fuss,
Asks him, "Poor fellow, are you sick?"

Yea, sick and weary to the quick
Of heat and noise from dawn to dark.

He will not even stoop to bark
His protest, like the lesser bred.

Would he might know, one gazer read
The wistful longing in his face,
The thirst for wind and open space
And stretch of limb to him begrudged.

There came a little, dapper, fat
And bustling man, with cane and spat
And pearl-gray vest and derby hat—
Such were the judger and the judged!

What statement does the poem make? Evidence for opinion? Select examples of slanted language. Investigate the rhyme scheme. Notice the variation in stanza form and rhyme in relation to stanza. Is there an idea here applicable beyond the bounds of the incident presented? If so, what? How universal is its application? If it is not universal, why isn't it?

Ezra Pound makes a general statement with no support; he leaves it to his readers to imagine specific examples of behavior that might lead them to the same conclusion.

2   **MEDITATIO**

When I carefully consider the curious habits of dogs
I am compelled to conclude
That man is the superior animal.

When I consider the curious habits of man
I confess, my friend, I am puzzled.

Statement? Specific examples? What may Pound be trying to communicate through his title, which is Latin so simple that no knowledge of the language is necessary in order to translate it correctly? "Meditation" would not be distinctive enough to make an impression. Pound seems to be saying, "This seemingly simple poem is not really simple; it is worthy of your meditation."

When they first hear "Meditatio," students unfamiliar with free verse do not think much of it as a poem. However, it has been used successfully with seventh-graders; its meaning is immediately clear, and they have no difficulty in finding examples to illustrate its statement. Given a few minutes to compare it with a short, familiar poem in traditional form, they can state in their own words the obvious points of difference: no regular meter, no rhyme, lines of uneven length. With very little help they can discern the poem's pronounced rhythm and definite pattern. Hearing the first line read several times enables them to sense the rhythm; a brief explanation shows that English is an accented language and that prose and speech and free verse have rhythm. This poem uses the rhythm of conversation. The poet writing free verse takes as much care to order his lines in a rhythmical flow appropriate for the idea expressed as does the poet writing metered verse.

Long before they reach junior high school, children have been using the sentence in its various patterns. Without the use of technical terminology, they can be helped to see that the second sentence of the poem repeats the pattern of the first, but with logical omissions and with variation. Probably in other poems they have noticed the use of repetition of words, phrases, initial consonant sounds and can appreciate how much these techniques contribute here to the rhythm and to the over-all sound pattern.

A brief consideration of points of similarity between this poem and one in traditional form will show their differences are peripheral rather than basic. Students then can make up their own definition of free verse.

Through the use of details, W. H. Auden points out some fundamental distinctions between man and particular elements in his environment.

3

THEIR LONELY BETTERS

And rustling flowers for some third party waited
To say which pairs if any should get mated.

As I listened from a beach-chair in the shade
To all the noises that my garden made,
It seemed to me only proper that words
Should be withheld from vegetables and birds.

A robin with no Christian name ran through
The Robin-Anthem which was all he knew.

No one of them was capable of lying,
There was not one that knew that it was dying
Or could have with a rhythm or a rhyme
Assumed responsibility for time.

Let them leave language to their lonely betters
Who count some days and long for certain letters;
We, too, make noises when we laugh and weep,
Words are for those with promises to keep.

What experiences does Auden say belong exclusively to man? On what basis does he seem to make his selections? Does the poem build to a climax? If so, how? What is the significance of the title? Give reasons for your opinions.

Robert Frost presents an experience of one conscious of his responsibilities.

4

STOPPING BY WOODS ON A SNOWY EVENING

Whose woods these are I think I know.
His house is in the village though;

He will not see me stopping here
To watch his woods fill up with snow.

My little horse must think it queer
To stop without a farmhouse near
Between the woods and frozen lake
The darkest evening of the year.

He gives his harness bells a shake
To ask if there is some mistake.
The only other sound's the sweep
Of easy wind and downy flake.

The woods are lovely, dark and deep,
But I have promises to keep,
And miles to go before I sleep,
And miles to go before I sleep.

In what sense is poem 4 more specific than poem 3? Less specific? Does its statement have universal application? Why?

The function of metaphor

Discursive language, used to make statements that can be verified, fails the poet mainly concerned with the subjective experience—attitudes, feelings, intuitions—of man. The poet relies upon metaphor. In order to illumine an aspect of the subjective world, he projects an idea onto an element in our objective world; he clarifies something we cannot see or taste or touch by showing its resemblance to something that is perceivable to our senses:

And as imagination bodies forth
The forms of things unknown, the poet's pen
Turns them to shapes, and gives to airy nothing
A local habitation and a name.[4]

Often we do not see what we look at or at best observe only the most obvious aspect of things. The poet, more perceptive than we, his imagination more alive and more disciplined, sees in an object more than its outward appearance.

Elizabeth Coatsworth recalls an experience showing how acute perception and an active imagination heighten the pleasure of the observer.

5   **TO THINK**

To think I once saw grocery shops
With but a casual eye
And fingered figs and apricots
As one who came to buy.

[4] Shakespeare, *A Midsummer Night's Dream*, Act V, Scene 1, lines 14–17.

To think I never dreamed of how
Bananas sway in rain,
And often looked at oranges,
Yet never thought of Spain.

And in those wasted days I saw
No sails above the tea,
For grocery shops were grocery shops
Not hemispheres to me.

Elinor Wylie uses extended metaphor to help us understand the nature of imagination.

6   THE FALCON

Why should my sleepy heart be taught
To whistle mocking-bird replies?
This is another bird you've caught,
Soft-feathered, with a falcon's eyes.

The bird Imagination,
That flies so far, that dies so soon;
Her wings are coloured like the sun,
Her breast is coloured like the moon.

Weave her a chain of silver twist,
And a little hood of scarlet wool,
And let her perch upon your wrist,
And tell her she is beautiful.

Is the poet addressing herself, the reader, or both? Why do you think so? Why *sleepy* heart? *Whistle? Mocking-bird* replies? Why the contrast in line 4? What likenesses between a falcon and imagination are stated or implied? Why does Elinor Wylie think imagination should be pampered? Does she think it should be allowed to run wild? How can you tell?

Mark Van Doren eulogizes the accomplishment of mind and imagination disciplined and made articulate.

7   THE STORY-TELLER

He talked, and as he talked
Wallpaper came alive;
Suddenly ghosts walked,
And four doors were five;

Calendars ran backward,
And maps had mouths;
Ships went tackward
In a great drowse;

Trains climbed trees,
And soon dripped down
Like honey of bees
On a cold brick town.

He had wakened a worm
In the world's brain,
And nothing stood firm
Until day again.

Before reading, the teacher may give the meaning of *went tackward* (changed course); *drowse* (doze); otherwise, explanations to satisfy the literal-minded should be avoided. One can determine the comment the poem makes without being able to explain each image. Why does Van Doren think story-tellers are important? Would the history of this art form support him? Why or why not?

The musical pattern

Although the poet must be a keen observer, although he needs deep insight into the heart and mind of man, only through language can he communicate his vision. The image he has chosen to connect man's two worlds can function effectively only through the right words composing the right sounds, movements, and rhythms to fuse thought and emotion.

Stephen Spender speaks of the power of the word.

8   **WORD**

The word bites like a fish.
Shall I throw it back free
Arrowing to that sea
Where thoughts lash tail and fin?
Or shall I put it in
To rhyme upon a dish?

Does the poem's comment apply only to poets or to all who use language? Why? Explain the last two lines to accord with your answer. Can you select a word chosen for both connotation and sound? A line whose movement helps you visualize the movement described? What do you notice about the sound when you compare lines 3 and 4? How does Spender secure this effect?

Carl Sandburg's "Primer Lesson" might serve to pave the way for poem 8 in certain classes.

9   **PRIMER LESSON**

Look out how you use proud words.
When you let proud words go, it is not easy to call them back.
They wear long boots, hard boots; they walk off proud; they can't hear you
    calling—
Look out how you use proud words.

Robert Louis Stevenson considers the long-continued effect the poet often hopes for.

10   BRIGHT IS THE RING OF WORDS

> Bright is the ring of words
> When the right man rings them,
> Fair the fall of songs
> When the singer sings them.
> Still they are carolled and said—
> On wings they are carried—
> After the singer is dead
> And the maker buried.

Is any characteristic of poetry praised by Stevenson exemplified in his own poem? Discuss the first four lines. What qualities must a poem have if it is to survive? Can you name any poems you think pass this test? Why do they pass?

The authorship of certain passages in Shakespeare has been questioned by those who say that one who wrote such great poetry could not be guilty of the pedestrian passages they are able to cull from his work. Poets, however, know creativity is marked by peaks and valleys. One writer characterizes the travail of the poet as a time of waiting for all his powers to be in conjunction at the peak—a time when the poet seems to be the instrument of the poem.

Archibald MacLeish describes such an experience.

11   WORDS IN TIME

> Bewildered with the broken tongue
> Of wakened angels in our sleep—
> Then, lost the music that was sung
> And lost the light time cannot keep!
>
> There is a moment when we lie
> Bewildered, wakened out of sleep,
> When light and sound and all reply:
> That moment time must tame and keep.
>
> That moment, like a flight of birds
> Flung from the branches where they sleep,
> The poet with a beat of words
> Flings into time for time to keep.

How would you characterize the rhythm and rhyme? Select the words in the first stanza showing the nature of the poet's first encounter with his vision. Why both *light* and *music*? *Bewildered* is used twice. How do the reasons for bewilderment differ? Discuss the dual application of *beat*, line 11. (Beat of wings/beat of words.) Notice the repetition of cadences, for example, at the ends of lines in stanza 3. Besides the meaning of *time* in our everyday speech, the word is also used to describe the general movement of a musical composition with reference to its rhythm, metrical structure, and tempo. The word is used in the poem four times. Define its meaning in each instance. What does it mean in the title?

In determining what should be said about a poem, the teacher keeps in mind the three focal points: statement, metaphor, musical pattern. However, he avoids falling into a routine; he does not feel obliged to mention all three with every poem nor to discuss exhaustively the aspect he intends to emphasize. Above all, he is willing to let a poem go, although he knows there is much more that could be said.

At times, the teacher may ask for the statement, without preliminary questions. This probably will be the procedure in poems 2, 5, 11. Sometimes details must be considered first, as in poems 6 and 12. Often in discussing a rather complex poem, the teacher reads stanzas and passages more than once because students need to hear them and because the practice helps subordinate discussion to the poem itself. He develops understanding of the function of metaphor and musical pattern gradually, connecting each example with content. When appropriate, either because of similarity or contrast, he suggests the current example be compared with another from a previous poem. Occasionally he reviews, asking students to recall illustrations of a particular facet of poetry, helping them generalize about the purpose the illustrations serve.

In every instance the poem, not the discussion, holds center-stage. After attention has been focused on the parts, the student's last impression should be of the poem as an experience complete in itself. He listens as the teacher reads it again.

THE READER'S RESPONSIBILITY

The reader's responsibility to a poem is to understand it. All poems have a literal meaning; some have only that; some have more. The student should learn to distinguish between what the poem says and what he may be tempted to read into it. Certainly, a quality of poetry is to suggest more than it states: Robert Frost once said, "I'm glad if you find ulteriority in my poems"; but, on the other hand, he was impatient with readers who sought assurance that extensions they had made in interpreting certain of his poems were what he had intended. Scholars have differed about the meaning of complex poetry; but in the comparatively simple poems we offer to young people, if clues are carefully noted, there should be substantial agreement among readers on the literal meaning as well an on the "ulteriority."

By examining a sufficient number of poems with students, we can help them understand that certain inferences and extensions are necessary, certain others are possible but unnecessary; still others are impossible because they distort meaning.[5] It is a reader's privilege to take from a poem whatever serves his purpose; it is his responsibility to know where the poem stops and at what

[5] For a helpful discussion, using specific illustrations, see Josephine Miles, "Reading Poems," *English Journal*, Vol. 52, No. 3 (March 1963), pp. 157–64; and Vol. 52, No. 4 (April 1963), pp. 243–46.

point he begins to write his own. We can start in the seventh grade to develop understandings and skills to insure more accurate reading. The following discussion stresses three aspects of this problem: considering the point of view, interpreting clues, acquiring realistic expectations.

Considering the point of view

Awareness of the implications of the author's viewpoint is an important factor in determining meaning, for the attitude a writer takes toward his subject and his readers affects both content and tone. The poet, choosing a segment of experience, gives it uniqueness and vitality not because the idea is new but because the way he presents it is.

Amy Lowell presents contrasting viewpoints in

12   POINTS OF VIEW

> Youth cocks his hat and rides up the street.
> Age cocks his eye only to see it.
>
> Youth puts his horse at a five-barred gate.
> Age chuckles grimly and sits down to wait.
>
> Youth limps by with a broken-kneed horse.
> Age through the shutters, mutters, "Of course."
>
> Youth curses Fate for his splitting head.
> Age lights the candle and hobbles to bed.

Two points of view are dramatized, but a third is present also, for the poet discloses her own. Does she try to persuade you that one viewpoint is preferable to the other? Or is she objective, saying, "This is the truth; take it or leave it"? What do her choice of incident and manner of presenting it reveal about her attitude toward her subject and readers? Is the statement the poem makes universally true? Why or why not? Usually in a poem the tempo of the lines corresponds with the idea expressed. In each couplet, which line moves more slowly? Why? When a poet wishes to slow the pace, he either adds more syllables or chooses and arranges words that require more time to articulate clearly. In couplets 1 and 3, the lines have the same number of syllables. Compare *hat and rides* and *eye only*. How would substituting *just* for *only* affect the pace? Notice the effect of *through . . . shutters, mutters* (line 6) on the tempo.

Phyllis McGinley reveals two points of view.

13   THE ANGRY MAN

> The other day I chanced to meet
> An angry man upon the street—
> A man of wrath, a man of war,

A man who truculently bore
Over his shoulder like a lance,
A banner labeled "Tolerance."

And when I asked him why he strode
Thus scowling down the human road,
Scowling, he answered, "I am he
Who champions total liberty—
Intolerance being, ma'am, a state
No tolerant man can tolerate."

"When I meet rogues," he cried, "who choose
To cherish oppositional views,
Lady, like this, and in this manner,
I lay about me with my banner
Till they cry mercy, ma'am." His blows
Rained proudly on prospective foes.

Fearful, I turned and left him there
Still muttering, as he thrashed the air,
"Let the Intolerant beware!"

What point of view does the poet want you to accept? How can you tell? Select words that carry unpleasant connotations. How do variants of *tolerate* affect both meaning and musical pattern? Discuss the irony of a person's thinking he believes one thing when his actions, without his realizing it, contradict what he says. What comparison is suggested by *banner* borne *like a lance?* Does this comparison and the use to which the banner is put heighten the irony?

Satire is used by writers of both prose and poetry to make fun of human foibles and frailties. The ability to recognize satirical intent is important in determining point of view. To make plain his purpose is satirical, a writer often uses exaggeration as Colin Francis does.

14   TONY O

Over the bleak and barren snow
A voice there came a calling;
"Where are you going to, Tony O!
Where are you going this morning?"

"I am going where there are rivers of wine,
The mountains bread and honey;
There Kings and Queens do mind the swine,
And the poor have all the money."

What details place this incident in a remote time and place? Where is this place? Why might a satirist think remoteness desirable? What human frailty does the poet make fun of? The last line sounds somewhat paradoxical. Can you see any reason for the idea being so stated? Satire ranges from the gentle and amused to the bitter and scornful. How would you characterize it here? A critic of television commercials has said that many try to lull our minds in order to lure us into some never-never land. Can you give examples of some that appear to do this? Do these fantasies bear any resemblance to Tony O's?

A BACKWARD GLANCE   Poems 12–14 based on specific incident; someone other than the poet in the leading role; primary appeal to intellect. In poems 12 and 14, poet as observer, maintaining his distance from the action; presentation objective. In poem 13, poet as participant; presentation slanted to influence opinion.

The next poem, by Langston Hughes, differs from poems 12–14 in that it is based on a situation rather than on an incident; the poet, speaking for himself and others in a similar predicament, is the protagonist; he shows emotion and intends to arouse emotion in his reader.

15   WATER-FRONT STREETS

> The spring is not so beautiful there—
>   But dream ships sail away
> To where the spring is wondrous rare
>   And life is gay.
>
> The spring is not so beautiful there—
>   But lads put out to sea
> Who carry beauties in their hearts
>   And dreams, like me.

If you heard water-front streets mentioned, what picture would probably come to mind? How would it differ from that evoked by bay-view streets? You will notice that there are no words in the poem with unpleasant connotations. What is the effect of having experience presented in terms of the dream? Of using pleasant but nebulous imagery to emphasize an unattractive situation? Reread the poem often enough to let students become familiar with the musical pattern. Lines 1 and 5 are flowing, broken by a downbeat at the end; lines 2, 3, 6, 7 are melodious, with a slightly brighter tone; lines 4 and 8 are slow, with a pause and falling cadence. Students should hear the thuds with which the last lines in each stanza fall. Ask them to select lines with similar melody. Why does the melody change? What technique does Hughes use to effect change? Help students see that emotion is evoked by the tension of subtle contrasts in the way the concept is presented and in the musical pattern, both of which are in conflict with what the majority of the words taken out of context have conditioned us to expect. If students are likely to recognize the author's name, withhold it until the poem has been examined. Students should not think of this as a "Negro" poem or a poem about those who live in undesirable locations. The truth it presents is universal. What might water-front streets represent? Why spring rather than another season? Why such vague imagery?

Tone is an integral part of point of view. It is hard to define but easy to recognize in speech. In the next two poems Carolyn Hall (poem 16) and Robert Frost (poem 17) use the same symbol for human aspiration; because they have different viewpoints, they make different statements, and the tone of one differs greatly from that of the other.

16   FIREFLIES

> Little lamps of the dusk,
>   You fly low and gold
> When the summer evening
>   Starts to unfold.
> So that all the insects,
>   Now, before you pass,
> Will have light to see by,
>   Undressing in the grass.
>
> But when the night has flowered,
>   Little lamps agleam,
> You fly over tree-tops,
>   Following a dream.
> Men wonder from their windows
>   That a firefly goes so far—
> They do not know your longing
>   To be a shooting star.

17   FIREFLIES IN THE GARDEN

> Here come real stars to fill the upper skies,
> And here on earth come emulating flies,
> That though they never equal stars in size,
> (And they were never really stars at heart)
> Achieve at times a very star-like start.
> Only, of course, they can't sustain the part.

Let students listen to both poems before discussing either. (To allow them to make up their minds solely on the evidence of the poem, teachers may withhold the names of authors, whose reputation is likely to be known to students.) Compare the two as to statement: *over tree-tops* and *in the garden; goes so far* and *star-like start.* Compare the cadence of these phrases: How does it affect tone? Does the fact that poem 16 uses personification and apostrophe and poem 17 uses the third person have any effect on tone? That Robert Frost mentions fireflies only in the title, using *emulating flies* in the poem? How does the connotation of *emulating* differ from that of *imitating*?

If tone is a concept new to students, consider its significance in reference to both speaking and writing (pages 256–58). List on the chalkboard adjectives that might be used to describe tone: gentle, melodious, dry, blunt, soft, vigorous, dispassionate, wistful, emotional, sympathetic. Avoid words that may have negative connotations. Ask students to select words best describing the tone of each poem or to substitute others they think more appropriate.

A BACKWARD GLANCE   Tone is a factor in any poem. Spend some time in determining the tone of other poems studied. For instance, compare tone in poems 1 and 2 and in poems 1 and 12.

After reading the following poem by Theodore Roethke, give students a few minutes on their own to determine its tone.

18   THE SLOTH

In moving-slow he has no Peer.
You ask him something in his Ear,
He thinks about it for a Year;

And, then, before he says a Word
There, upside down (unlike a Bird),
He will assume that you have Heard—

A most Ex-as-per-at-ing Lug.
But should you call his manner Smug,
He'll sigh and give his Branch a Hug;

Then off again to Sleep he goes,
Still swaying gently by his Toes,
And you just *know* he knows he knows.

The poet's attitude toward his reader and its influence on the point of view and consequently on the tone is probably revealed most clearly in poems giving advice. This advice may be offered in a straightforward manner (poems 19 and 20) or presented in camouflaged form (poems 21 and 22). Young people, in their relationships with adults, are familiar with both approaches. The direct approach may vary from the gentle cajolery of Victor Hugo (poem 19) to the blunt command of Hamlin Garland (poem 20).

19   BE LIKE THE BIRD

Be like the bird, who
Halting in his flight
On limb too slight
Feels it give way beneath him,
Yet sings
Knowing he has wings.

20   DO YOU FEAR THE WIND?

Do you fear the force of the wind,
The slash of the rain?
Go face them and fight them,
Be savage again.
Go hungry and cold like the wolf,
   Go wade like the crane:
The palms of your hands will thicken,
The skin of your cheek will tan;
You'll grow ragged and weary and swarthy,
   But you'll walk like a man!

William Carlos Williams' advice is similar to Garland's but more subtly expressed. He does not bring the reader into the poem; he pretends his discovery applies only to himself.

21   THE MANOEUVRE

I saw the two starlings
coming in toward the wires.
But at the last,
just before alighting, they
turned in the air together
and landed backwards!
that's what got me—to
face into the wind's teeth.

Aesop's fables, written in Greek prose, have been translated into many languages. They have been derided by some and admired by others for the same reason, the moral; still others have been content just to enjoy the anecdotes. Of all those who have followed in the Aesopian tradition, Jean de La Fontaine (1621–95) is the most notable. His fables, written in French verse, have challenged several translators. Marianne Moore has preserved the charm, humor, satire, and flexible verse of the original.

22   THE GRASSHOPPER AND THE ANT

Until fall, a grasshopper
Chose to chirr;
With starvation as foe
When northeasters would blow,
And not even a gnat's residue
Or caterpillar's to chew,
She chirred a recurrent chant
Of want beside an ant,
Begging it to rescue her
With some seeds it could spare
Till the following year's fell.

"By August you shall have them all,
Interest and principal."
Share one's seeds? Now what is worse
For any ant to do?
Ours asked, "When fair, what brought you through?"
—"I sang for those who might pass by chance—
Night and day. Please do not be repelled."
—Sang? A delight when some one has excelled.
A singer! Excellent. Now dance."

Ask students to determine the statement: if *should* appears, help them see the poem does not make such a direct comment. In what does the satire consist? Characterize the humor. Is it genial, arrogant, whimsical, sarcastic, bitter?

After discussing the poem as fully as the situation warrants and rereading it, ask a student, who has previously agreed upon the assignment, to read the Aesop fable. Its moral is "It is best to prepare for the days of necessity." Discuss the disadvantages in fiction or poetry of the author's specifically stating a moral. How does he restrict the implications of his work?

A BACKWARD GLANCE   Poems 19–22 are placed at the end of this section because viewpoint and its effect on tone are fairly obvious. These poems or others similar to them can clarify and clinch ideas about point of view that have been emerging from the study of poems that may be more complex. Necessarily, in inductive teaching, examples—in this case poems—stand out with satisfactory completeness, while the ideas generated by the examples remain somewhat fragmentary and unfocused. The teacher, by judicious review, is in a position to help students pull together the various strands concerning this aspect of poetry study and so formulate the necessary concepts.

Interpreting clues

Each poem provides an opportunity for stressing the need to use all clues in order to arrive at accurate meaning. However, it is often enlightening to show what distortions may occur or what subtleties may be lost if a clue is overlooked.

Present Nym Wales' poem without title or date.

23   JAPAN IN CHINA

A frog jumped
into an old pond
and made a magnificent ripple,
then all was quiet
and the butterflies came again.

MARCH 2, 1940

Even seventh-graders will get an approximate meaning and will be able to give examples to illustrate, but probably none of the examples will account for *old*. Give the omitted clues, emphasizing the significance of 1940. Students can now see the significance of *old*.

Present Langston Hughes' poem without mentioning its title or author.

24   EVIL

Looks like what drives me crazy
Don't have no effect on you—
But I'm gonna keep on at it
Till it drives you crazy, too

Use the same procedure as with poem 23. At least some of the examples will represent annoyances rather than evils. When students are given the title and learn the author is a Negro, they will realize what *it* refers to.

At first glance the next title may seem unimaginative; however, when we return to it after reading the poem, we discover William Carlos Williams is telling us his poem is a metaphor: the pace and rhythm of cat and poem, the tension of the cat's muscles and the poem's lines, the appearance of the poem on the page—all delineate the imaginative comparison the poem suggests.

25   POEM

As the cat
climbed over
the top of

the jamcloset
first the right
forefoot

carefully
then the hind
stepped down

into the pit of
the empty
flowerpot

Many of the preceding poems can be presented solely as a listening experience; this one must be seen as it appears on the page, as well as heard. Why no punctuation? At what line does the tempo quicken? Why? How? How, in addition to the words, does Williams give a sense of completion to the poem?

Poets often take as much care in devising a title that will create the effect they want as they do with the poem itself. John Updike belongs to this group. If you knew nothing about his work and came upon a poem entitled *The*

Stunt Flyer, what image might come to mind? What kind of poem would you expect? What emotion do you think it would evoke?

26   THE STUNT FLYER

I come into my dim bedroom
innocently and my baby
is lying in her crib face-down;
just a hemisphere of the half-bald head
shows, and the bare feet, uncovered
the small feet crossed at the ankles
like a dancer doing easily
a difficult step—or,
more exactly, like a cherub
planing through Heaven,
cruising at a middle altitude
through the cumulus of the tumbled covers,
which disclose the feet crossed
at the ankles à la small boys who,
exaulting in their mastery of bicycles,
lift their hands from the handle bars
to demonstrate how easy gliding is.

No matter what a reader's expectations, as he becomes involved in the poem, he is likely to forget them. Thus, after reading, the title comes as a delightful twist—similar to the surprise ending of a story. The title not only unifies the images but also adds to the humor. Select some examples of precise diction. How would you describe the tone?

Some poems can be appreciated fully only if the reader is familiar with other poems. Seventh-graders with no knowledge of poem 27 by Robert Browning can enjoy poem 28 by Edith Sitwell. In some classes where poem 28 is to be presented, teachers can give students the additional pleasure of recognizing an allusion by presenting poem 27 first.

27   SONG FROM PIPPA PASSES

The year's at the spring,
The day's at the morn;
Morning's at seven;
The hillside's dew-pearled;
The lark's on the wing;
The snail's on the thorn;
God's in his heaven—
All's right with the world.

28   MADAM MOUSE TROTS

Madam Mouse trots,
Gray in the black night:

Madam Mouse trots:
Furred is the light.
The elephant-trunks
Trumpet from the sea . . . .
Gray in the black night
The mouse trots free.
Hoarse as a dog's bark
The heavy leaves are furled . . . .
The cat's in his cradle,
All's well with the world!

Consider repetition, consonance, unusual imagery. Edith Sitwell has said she likes to experiment with unusual images appealing to different senses. *Elephant-trunks/trumpet* and *Hoarse . . . furled* appeal to sound and touch. *Rough* seems the simplest word to describe both. What we visualize is probably the mouse enveloped by sounds a human being might find unpleasant but making no impression on Madam because dogs and elephants are not her arch-enemies. What is the effect of the incongruous linking of *madam* and *trots?* What does each of the two words contribute to the imagery? The sound and rhythm patterns are too intricate to be considered in detail with all classes, but students should hear the poem often enough to sense its music.

To reinforce the importance of interpreting all clues, the teacher may, after presenting several poems emphasizing the point, allow students to check their progress. If the class is unfamiliar with "Evil" (poem 24) the teacher writes the title and the poem on the board, gives the students a few minutes to jot down one specific statement to describe the idea of the poem. At the end of the time allowed, he tells the class the poem was written by Langston Hughes and then gives time for each student to consider the statement he has written. Is it appropriate? If not, why not? What important clue has been overlooked? This is a difficult test that many adults might fail, but its purpose is not for grading but only to dramatize an idea. It is important that students realize that no reader, given only the clues they had to begin with, could exactly pinpoint the meaning of the poem.

Acquiring realistic expectations

Sophisticated poetry readers are aware that recognizing the form—sonnet, ballade—in which a poem is cast gives some indication of what to expect. Young people, without identifying forms, can enjoy a poem for what it says and the way it says it. They should, however, know that some poems—admittedly, the minority among those called great—are purely descriptive. The poet selects an animal, object, phenomenon from man's environment and bids us look at it. His purpose is to call attention to its beauty, magic, wonder. He gives no hint of what the experience should mean to us other than that we should be aware of the world around us.

Eleanor Farjeon's poem is descriptive, helping us see and hear an example of a natural process.

29   **THE TIDE IN THE RIVER**

> The tide in the river,
> The tide in the river,
> The tide in the river runs deep.
>
> I saw a shiver
> Pass over the river
> As the tide turned in its sleep.

Why are repetition, the chosen rhythm, the exact rhyme, appropriate for the subject matter? Why are lines 3 and 6 longer than the others? Why is *turned* significant to both meaning and movement? Without using technical terms, help students see how the repetition of consonant sounds (*s, v*), dissonance (here, juxtaposing related but not identical vowel sounds—*tide, in*), and assonance (repetition of similar vowel sounds—*in . . . river*) form part of the musical pattern.

The following poem is descriptive; the reader gets the feeling that Robert F. Tristam Coffin thinks his picture sufficiently significant in its own right.

30   **THUNDER POOLS**

> Now the sudden shower's done,
> A new world and a deeper one
> Is lying under every tree,
> Small blue cousins of the sea.
>
> Made of water from on high,
> These pools of unearthly dye
> Show the elm tree's arching crown
> And the white clouds upside down.
>
> Such pools are not pools to wade,
> It would make the feet afraid
> To walk through such a lovely wonder
> Poured from the hogsheads of the thunder.

Consider picture-making phrases and suggested comparisons.

In contrast, Wallace Stevens' examples seem less important to him than does the idea they illustrate; with a list such as his a sensitive reader almost automatically adds a few of his own. There's no temptation to do this with the detailed picture given in poem 30. Whether these observations are correct or not, poem 31 is not a descriptive poem. Stevens suggests what the imagery means to him—enjoyment of little things—and so by implication what he would like it to mean to us.

31 BOWL

> For what emperor
> Was this bowl of earth designed?
> Here are more things
> Than on any bowl of the Sungs,
> Even the rarest:
> Vines that take
> The various obscurities of the moon,
> Approaching rain,
> And leaves that would be loose upon the wind;
> Pears on pointed trees,
> The dresses of women,
> Oxen . . .
> I never tire
> To think of this.

Why does Stevens use *this* instead of *these* in the last line? Would *these* have changed the meaning of the poem? If so, how? What is the grammatical reference of *this?*

The first poem in the next three pairs is descriptive; in the second poem, the poet uses a similar environmental element to make a comment on human life and human values.

Compare Christina Rossetti's purpose in poem 32 with that of A. E. Housman in poem 33.

32 OH, FAIR TO SEE

> Oh, fair to see
> Bloom-laden cherry tree
> Arrayed in sunny white:
> An April day's delight,
> Oh, fair to see!
>
> Oh, fair to see
> Fruit-laden cherry tree,
> With balls of shining red
> Decking a leafy head,
> Oh, fair to see!

33 LOVELIEST OF TREES

> Loveliest of trees, the cherry now
> Is hung with bloom along the bough,
> And stands about the woodland ride
> Wearing white for Eastertide.
>
> Now, of my threescore years and ten,
> Twenty will not come again,

And take from seventy springs a score,
It only leaves me fifty more.

And since to look at things in bloom
Fifty springs are little room,
About the woodlands I will go
To see the cherry hung with snow.

Compare Mark Van Doren's description of a natural phenomenon in poem 34 with the use Sandburg makes of it in poem 35.

34   FORMER BARN LOT

Once there was a fence here,
    And the grass came and tried,
Leaning from the pasture,
    To get inside.

But colt feet trampled it,
    Turning it brown;
Until the farmer moved
    And the fence fell down.

Then any bird saw,
    Under the wire,
Grass nibbling inward
    Like green fire.

35   GRASS

Pile the bodies high at Austerlitz and Waterloo.
Shovel them under and let me work—
    I am the grass; I cover all.

And pile them high at Gettysburg
And pile them high at Ypres and Verdun.
Shovel them under and let me work.
Two years, ten years, and passengers ask the conductor;
      What place is this?
      Where are we now?

    I am the grass.
    Let me work.

Compare William Butler Yeats' Minnaloushe with T. S. Eliot's Macavity.

36   THE CAT AND THE MOON

The cat went here and there
And the moon spun round like a top,

And the nearest kin of the moon,
The creeping cat, looked up.
Black Minnaloushe stared at the moon,
For, wander and wail as he would,
The pure cold light of the sky
Troubled his animal blood.
Minnaloushe runs in the grass
Lifting his delicate feet.
Do you dance, Minnaloushe, do you dance?
When two close kindred meet,
What better than call a dance?
Maybe the moon will learn,
Tired of that courtly fashion,
A new dance turn.
Minnaloushe creeps through the grass
From moonlit place to place.
The sacred moon overhead
Has taken a new phase.
Does Minnaloushe know that his pupils
Will pass from change to change,
And that from round to crescent,
From crescent to round they range?
Minnaloushe creeps through the grass
Alone, important and wise,
And lifts to the changing moon
His changing eyes.

37   MACAVITY: THE MYSTERY CAT

Macavity's a Mystery Cat: he's called the Hidden Paw—
For he's the master criminal who can defy the Law.
He's the bafflement of Scotland Yard, the Flying Squad's despair:
For when they reach the scene of crime—*Macavity's not there!*

    Macavity, Macavity, there's no one like Macavity,
He's broken every human law, he breaks the law of gravity.
His powers of levitation would make a fakir stare.
And when you reach the scene of crime—*Macavity's not there!*
You may seek him in the basement, you may look up in the air—
But I tell you once and once again, *Macavity's not there!*

    Macavity's a ginger cat, he's very tall and thin;
You would know him if you saw him, for his eyes are sunken in.
His brow is deeply lined with thought, his head is highly domed;
His coat is dusty from neglect, his whiskers are uncombed.
He sways his head from side to side, with movements like a snake;
And when you think he's half asleep, he's always wide awake.

Macavity, Macavity, there's no one like Macavity.
For he's a fiend in feline shape, a monster of depravity.
You may meet him in a by-street, you may see him in the square—
But when a crime's discovered, then *Macavity's not there!*

He's outwardly respectable. (They say he cheats at cards.)
And his footprints are not found in any file of Scotland Yard's.
And when the larder's looted, or the jewel-case is rifled,
Or when the milk is missing, or another Peke's been stifled,
Or the greenhouse glass is broken, and the trellis past repair—
Ay, there's the wonder of the thing! *Macavity's not there!*

And when the Foreign Office find a Treaty's gone astray,
Or the Admiralty lose some plans and drawings by the way,
There may be a scrap of paper in the hall or on the stair—
But it's useless to investigate—*Macavity's not there!*
And when the loss has been disclosed, the Secret Service say:
"It *must* have been Macavity!"—but he's a mile away.
You'll be sure to find him resting, or a-licking of his thumbs,
Or engaged in doing complicated long division sums.

Macavity, Macavity, there's no one like Macavity,
There never was a Cat of such deceitfulness and suavity.
He always has an alibi, and one or two to spare:
At whatever time the deed took place—MACAVITY WASN'T THERE!
And they say that all the Cats whose wicked deeds are widely known
(I might mention Mungojerrie, I might mention Griddlebone)
Are nothing more than agents for the Cat who all the time
Just controls their operations: the Napoleon of Crime!

Compare the two poems as to sound and music-pattern. In each case show how the pattern fits the content. Could you interchange the names of the cats without violating the integrity of the poems? Why or why not?

If the teacher, using poems similar to those reprinted here, has been developing the concepts suggested, it may be time to test the results of his labors. Students may be given copies of poem 38 (Amy Lowell), poem 39 (Edwin Arlington Robinson), and poem 40 (Emily Dickinson [6]). They should listen to them as they are read. Then they may set to work finding likenesses and differences among the three. They should be able to compare imagery, musical patterns, and statements to determine whether each poem is descriptive or not.

38   NIGHT CLOUDS

The white mares of the moon rush along the sky
Beating their glass hoofs upon the glass heavens;
The white mares of the moon are all standing on their hind legs
Pawing at the green porcelain doors of the remote heavens.

[6] Only seven of Emily Dickinson's poems had been published before her death in 1886. Among her manuscripts were found many without titles, among them this poem about the sun.

Fly, mares!
Strain your utmost,
Scatter the milky dust of stars,
Or the tiger sun will leap upon you and destroy you
With one lick of his vermilion tongue.

39   DARK HILLS

Dark hills at evening in the west,
Where sunset hovers like a sound
Of golden horns that sang to rest
Old bones of warriors under ground,
Far now from all the bannered ways
Where flash the legions of the sun,
You fade—as if the last of days
Were fading, and all wars were done.

40   BLAZING IN GOLD AND QUENCHING IN PURPLE

Blazing in Gold and quenching in Purple
Leaping like Leopards to the Sky
Then at the feet of the old Horizon
Laying her spotted Face to die
Stooping as low as the Otter's Window
Touching the Roof and tinting the Barn
Kissing her Bonnet to the Meadow
And the Juggler of Day is gone

The teacher's purpose in presenting descriptive poems is not to help students apply the right label, but to prevent their searching for something that is not always there. We should discourage the idea that all poems have a deeply hidden meaning. Certainly we should discourage a search for symbolism. Anyone reading poem 40 and knowing that the implications of the swift passage of time preoccupy poets may for a moment suspect a deeper-than-surface meaning. Since Emily Dickinson gives time a beginning and an end, may she not be using the day as a symbol? Familiarity with the bulk of her poetry indicates she is not; but, more important, there is no evidence in the poem itself to indicate it means other than what it says. Poem 40 can stand as a poem on its literal meaning—a vivid, fast-moving description of a day in the life of the sun.

It is probably wiser to allow young people to consider symbolism a part of metaphor. However, if the teacher thinks students should be able to distinguish between the two, there is a simple test. In metaphor, comparison between things essentially dissimilar is indicated; in symbolism, it is not. In poem 6, Elinor Wylie tells us her falcon stands for imagination; in poem 42, she does not say what she intends the hunt to mean. When the literal meaning of a poem is clear, as it is in poem 42, and yet the imagery suggests no counterpart in the outer world, we assume the poet is using symbolism.

THE TEACHER'S CHOICE

Not the least of the pleasure for the teacher in presenting poetry is the freedom it gives for experimenting. In no other literary form is there so much and such varied material. Moreover, each experience is brief. If one chooses unwisely, a ten-minute disaster can be endured by both teacher and students. Of course, a long series of such failures results in frustration and rebellion; but teachers, too, learn from experience. The best judge of poems for a particular group is the teacher who is to present them. He must, however, look at each from the viewpoint of one considerably younger than he.

Anyone who habitually reads poetry cannot help but be impressed by the number of recurring subjects: love, death, war, man's anxieties caused by pressures of time and his mortality, nostalgic regret for youth and other magical moments that defy recapture. Many memorable poems have been written on these subjects. One collecting material for his teaching-anthology finds many such experiences, simply presented. He is reluctant to pass them by. Yet experienced teachers know that, with occasional exceptions, they must reject them. It is not that the poems present truths too harsh for the sensibilities of the young nor that the pessimistic outlook may prove depressing; youth is likely to be as tough and resilient as age. Teachers reject them because they know their students have not lived long enough to experience the emotional impact the poems deserve, that a steady diet of such fare defeats the purpose in presenting poetry.

Compare two poems with related themes: youth—even students who could not logically explain particular lines—responds emotionally to Wade Oliver's eager, high-spirited, approach to life, conveyed through bright imagery, lively rhythm, rapid movement.

41   WHO'LL RIDE WITH ME?

> Who'll ride with me in the gypsy weather,
> (Youth held lightly is Youth held fast!)
> Light and light as a white owl's feather,
> Till we win to the world's last edge at last?
>
> Who'll ride with me to the ultimate faring,
> (Dream held sorely is dream held long!)
> Till the winds are knives in the teeth of our daring,
> And the last, lone star is a thin-spun song?
>
> For what is youth but a coin to squander,
> (Youth spent lightly is age deferred!)
> And what is Dream but a voice out yonder,
> And what is Life but a flying bird?

This poem communicates the excitement of one who looks upon life as adventure. Even those unable to define all its terms know what ride the poet means; they share his emotional experience as he anticipates the journey. Too much questioning of details would spoil this poem. It is one that, like youth, can be held lightly—and then let go.

Now consider another poem on the same subject but from a different point of view. Elinor Wylie celebrates the persistent search, the affirmation of life in all its aspects.

42   MADMAN'S SONG

Better to see your cheek grown hollow,
Better to see your temple worn,
Than to forget to follow, follow,
After the sound of the silver horn.

Better to bind your brow with willow
And follow, follow until you die,
Than to sleep with your head on a golden pillow
Nor lift it up as the hunt goes by.

Better to see your cheek grown sallow
And your hair grown grey, so soon, so soon,
Than to forget to hallo, hallo,
After the milk-white hounds of the moon.

Normally, tenth-graders would enjoy the sound and rhythmical pattern if they listened to this poem. They could explain each line: as far as diction is concerned, poem 42 is less difficult than poem 41; the ideas are as easy to grasp. Students would recognize the symbolism. In a superficial way, young people know life takes its toll, but their response will be of the mind only. They are too far away from the hollow cheek and the gray hair to react with feeling. It is not inconceivable that some may suspect the silver horn and the golden pillow are not all that incompatible. Discussion can help students master intellectual content, but no amount of explanation can substitute for experience they have not had time to acquire. Poems similar to poem 42 fail to evoke the appropriate emotional response from immature students and thus fail as poetry.

As a matter of conviction, the experienced teacher selects poems he thinks will appeal to his students—poems within the range of their intellectual and emotional capacity. We have suggested that, as we present such poems, we help students develop certain concepts concerning the nature of poetry, certain approaches applicable to all poetry. In considering an unfamiliar and complex poem, the sophisticated reader comes armed with specific knowledge and techniques. He is aware that:

a poem has three important facets: statement, metaphor, musical pattern
some poems require inferences and extensions beyond the literal
some poems permit inferences and extensions but, since they are unnecessary,
    their application is personal and not universal

some poems do not admit extension because it distorts the meaning
with every poem it is essential to consider the implications of point of view
    and to interpret all clues the poet has provided.

As our readers know, we are not implying that tenth-graders will become sophisticated readers of poetry, no matter what poems have been presented and what method has been used. However, if the majority have not found at least a few that they like, something is wrong with either the poems or the way we have presented them. We disagree with those who think young people are prejudiced against poetry; the teacher who starts with this assumption starts with a handicap.

In a classroom containing many anthologies, the student should be allowed, but not pressured, to browse; he should be encouraged, but not required, to make his own collection of favorites. If he is really gaining an appreciation for poetry, some poems that at first seem insightful will later be dropped. Discarding what has become useless indicates growth.

What we suggest is that, in addition to presenting poems—meaningful now but perhaps not for ever—we at the same time develop concepts concerning poetry and foster attitudes toward reading poetry that will never have to be discarded. If the student can see basic relationships among the poems he likes, if he has a guide to help him understand others, he has been placed on the right road. How far he travels along that road is a personal matter he will decide for himself.

Although we have illustrated the inductive method of teaching with poems suitable for grades 7 through 10, the method is just as effective on higher levels. The student who enters the eleventh grade with the background suggested here should be able to handle poems of greater complexity than would otherwise have been possible. When he leaves the secondary-school classroom, he can—should he care to do so—continue under his own power.

UNIT:

MACBETH

Overview Every curriculum has elements of requirement and elements of free choice. This unit is offered as an example of the former. Designed for a class of students ranging in ability from average to gifted, it is largely teacher-planned and teacher-directed. Because of the nature of the class—individuals sensitive to appreciation on different levels—and because of the teacher's purpose—to help students re-create a dramatic and a literary experience—individual projects are disregarded so that attention can be centered solely on the play. Students are not asked to read in advance; assignments are concerned with explorations to probe the depths of actions and lines already heard in context. Thus the necessary compression of time helps students sense the headlong rush of the action and feel the tensions the play creates. Although not as broadly based as the other units in this textbook, the individual experiences—reading, listening, speaking, and writing—achieve unity through the literary work. However, no teaching time is spent on any skill but reading.

Appreciation for form can be enhanced by the study of *Macbeth*—one of those desirable models Thornton Wilder might recommend for youth.[1] More than any drama widely studied at the secondary-school level, it gives students a chance to experience what is meant by "suspense of form—the incompleteness of a known completion." [2] This suspense, occurring not because of the reader's eagerness to discover what will happen next but because of the artistic structure in which the playwright has cast his work, creates a tension between the past and the future meeting in the present and conveys a sense of destiny. This suspense of form, rather than suspenseful development of plot or characters, accounts for the pleasure derived from repeated readings of this literary work.

[1] See page 652.
[2] Charles Morgan, "The Dramatic Illusion," quoted by Susanne K. Langer, *Feeling and Form* (New York: Scribner's, 1953), p. 309.

600

Aims

Understandings   To perceive the development of the major theme; to recognize how minor concepts support major concepts.

Skills   To discover the implications of lines; to develop awareness of dramatic reasons for action; to comprehend the subtleties in the revelation of character.

Appreciations   To respond to Shakespeare's poetry—its rhythm and imagery; to sharpen sensitivity to the contribution made by symbolism; to sense the force of the dramatic irony underlying the play; to heighten awareness of form in relation to content.

Time plan   Three weeks.

Form in relation to content

Appreciation of the esthetic form—its degree depending upon the sensitivity of the reader—is first absorbed subconsciously as the play is quickly read; the discussions following the reading can help students discover how the author has ordered his material to create the total effect.

TWO PERFECTLY INTEGRATED ELEMENTS   These are initiated by the murder of a king and move simultaneously toward an inevitable conclusion: the destruction of harmonious order within a state; the disintegration of two human beings—the murderers.

ECONOMY AND LOGIC OF THE SEQUENCE OF EVENTS   Sequence is presented in three stages and directed toward a destined end. The beginning to Duncan's murder shows an established society with a good king surrounded by his loyal subjects, among them the able Macbeth, each contributing to the welfare of all; but the disorder to come is foreshadowed in the opening scene—"Fair is foul and foul is fair"—and in the discontinuity of Macbeth's speeches as soon as he actually conceives the murder.

The scenes from Duncan's death to the senseless murder of Macduff's family show the change that takes place both in a society and in an individual when disorder replaces harmony.

The final scenes show the disintegration of the two murderers as well as the restoration of harmony within the kingdom by the reinstatement of the gracious Malcolm (Act IV, scene 3, establishes his character) with the help of another good king, Edward of England.

The controversial Porter scene is not primarily a humorous interlude for audience relief, but an integral part of the play's design, heightening tension because it contrasts with the preceding world of darkness and hallucination and represents the reality the two murderers must immediately face.

SYMBOLISM   *Planting*   signifying growth, the healthy aspects of life, the future: a symbol of fertility and fruition as it pertains to Duncan, changing to one of sterility and decay in the lines of Macbeth, and returning to its original significance as used by Malcolm in the last speech of the play.

Darkness   the atmosphere of the play relieved only twice, once in the beginning when Duncan approaches Macbeth's castle and again at the end when the kingship is restored to Malcolm; between is the darkness of evil.

Masking   symbolizing the disguises assumed to hide from oneself and others, a complex interweaving of many strands—inappropriate garments, borrowed robes, drunken hope as a dress, a giant's robe stolen by a dwarf; the innocence of the flower concealing the serpent, the eye winking at what the hand does, darkness as a protective covering for crime, the smoke of hell concealing the wound from the knife. This imagery is used in the beginning in a sense complimentary to Macbeth; then for the greater part of the play, to represent his desire to mask his evil from himself and others; and finally, contemptuously by Malcolm's followers in referring to Macbeth as one unfit to wear kingly robes.

The Babe   symbolizing both the unpredictable future and the compassionate qualities in man that make him human; children appearing again and again throughout the play in various guises—as characters, metaphors, and symbols; highlighting the irony of Macbeth's attempts to control a future he believes the witches already know in order to establish a dynasty—a desire that makes him human. These symbols, often combined in a single passage, are closely interwoven in the fabric of the drama.

LANGUAGE   Its discriminating rhythms and images reflect the repose or inner conflict of the different characters.

The elements of form may be discussed briefly with students during the initial reading and synthesized in reviewing passages after the play has been read. Such preparation will make the artistic unity of the whole more understandable as the class finally listens to a recording of the play.

Concepts

Major   the disintegration of a state by the evils resulting from the overthrow of a lawful order; Duncan, Malcolm, and Edward as symbols of that order.

Supporting   the disintegration of the human personality by the disruption of inner order and harmony, which is delineated in the story of two human beings, Macbeth and Lady Macbeth.

The conflict of good and evil forces, universal in its implications—the witches symbolizing the projection of evil already existing in the human heart.

Contrast in the *immediate reactions* of Banquo and Macbeth to the meeting with the witches:

Banquo, concerned with externals, questions the evidence of his senses: "Were such things here . . . ?"

Macbeth is interested in what has been said: ". . . tell me more. . . . Speak, I charge you."

Contrast in the *moral predisposition* of each:

Banquo thinks of the witches as an evil influence:

> What, can the Devil speak true?
>
>   But 'tis strange.
>   And oftentimes, to win us to our harm,

The instruments of darkness tell us truths,
Win us with honest trifles, to betray 's
In deepest consequence.

Macbeth is psychologically and morally ready for the evil suggestion:

why do I yield to that suggestion
Whose horrid image doth unfix my hair
And make my seated heart knock at my ribs,
Against the use of nature?

If chance will have me king, why
chance will crown me,
Without my stir.

Each time Macbeth meets the witches, he seeks not help, but assurance of success. At no time does he blame the witches or Lady Macbeth for his crimes; implicit in his every line is his belief that he acts of his own volition.

Complementary natures of Macbeth and his wife form the perfect instrument for the embodiment of the conflict that Shakespeare envisioned.

Macbeth, physically brave   shown consistently, from the first report of him in Act I to his last words to Macduff; *hypersensitive and imaginative:* the majority of his lines are the poetry of a disturbed imagination, heaping one image upon another (Act II, scene 2, lines 36–40, contain six images for sleep); always more concerned with what might happen than with things as they are:

Present fears
Are less than horrible imaginings.

Lady Macbeth, practical   quick to "catch the nearest way"; when awake, nothing impresses her but immediate facts as she sees them; most of her lines are sharp and incisive, without the imaginative concepts that Shakespeare gives to Macbeth; *lacking in foresight and reflective powers:* ". . . we'll not fail."

Who dares receive it other,
As we shall make our griefs and clamor roar
Upon his death?

the attempt and not the deed
Confounds us.

Shrewd: understanding her husband's nature, she hurries him along without giving him time to retreat, showing him his own arguments against the crime are really arguments for it.

Launching the unit

Sensing the predominant mood   Sometime before the study of *Macbeth* begins, students, as motivation for impressionistic writing, may listen to the Richard Strauss tone poem "Macbeth" while it is unidentified; although responses will vary, the mood communicated by the music is so intense that the words *war, conflict, struggle, storm, fear,* will be found in most of the papers. On the day texts of *Macbeth* are given out, several student papers—impressions invoked by the Strauss work—may be read to the class and the title of the music given; then students are told that one critic has described Shakespeare's *Macbeth* as a "tempest set to music";

the class discusses the criticism in reference to the feeling conveyed by the tone poem.

Understanding the background To avoid stopping as the play is being read, the teacher sees that the class has the following information:

approximate time of Macbeth's reign (1040–58) ending shortly before the Norman invasion

the relationship between Duncan and Macbeth—to show that Macbeth's hopes of eventually becoming king were not without foundation

unrest in Scotland—the revolt, the invasion—with the names of the king's generals and the opposing forces written on the board

two attitudes—toward war and toward witches—which have substantially changed since Shakespeare's day

Developing the unit: First reading of the play

Aims to help students understand the action, expressed in terms of human beings and a story; see and hear each scene as theater; appreciate the gradual development of character; recognize individual images and symbols and thus prepare for their cumulative force as the play unfolds; and respond intellectually and emotionally to the poetry.

General plan reading aloud of entire play by teacher and those students willing to give time for practice; discussion of each scene after reading; and writing of brief papers designed to probe the thinking and to spark imagination.

▶ *Analyzing Act I*

The analysis of Act I calls attention to concepts the play develops, poses some of the questions students should consider as they read, suggests a procedure for conducting the first reading of the four remaining acts. Lack of space prevents giving an analysis of the entire play; teachers will find that both Cleanth Brooks and D. A. Traversi, referred to at the end of the unit, give valuable help on interpretation.

SCENE 1 If you were staging this scene, how would you set it? What colors? What lighting? Listen to the sound of the lines. What movement would you suggest to actors to help an audience see what it hears? What is the purpose of the scene? What is the meaning of "Fair is foul, and foul is fair"? (The purpose of such a question is to direct attention to a salient point; a definitive answer cannot be given until the play has been read.)

SCENE 2 What do we learn of Macbeth and Banquo from the report of the battle? How is Macbeth to be rewarded for his support of the king? Why is he marked for honor when Banquo apparently conducted himself with equal ability and loyalty? Logical reason? Dramatic reason?

SCENE 3 Notice the difference in the language used by the witches when speaking among themselves and when speaking to Macbeth. Dramatic reason? (Among themselves the witches speak as women of the lowest class, for that was the class to which they were thought to belong; to Macbeth they speak in the lofty tones and cryptic utterances commonly associated with oracles. One purpose, an element of the dramatic irony underlying the play, is to confuse Macbeth, making fair things seem foul, and foul things fair. This purpose is not clearly stated until Act III, scene 5, lines 26–33.)

Macbeth in his first line uses *fair* and *foul* to describe the day, apparently referring to the outcome of the battle and to the weather, respectively. Dramatic reason? What is the significance of the effect of the witches' prophecy upon Banquo as compared with its effect upon Macbeth? What is the dramatic purpose of Macbeth's being made thane of Cawdor at this particular time? (To establish his belief in the power of the witches as supernatural beings.)

Consider the symbolism: lines 86 and 118 (these references to children are not symbolic, but should be pointed out as indicating Macbeth's concern, not yet obsessive, for the future); lines 108–09 and 144–46 (because they belong to the wearer, the clothes are not ill-fitting here, in contrast to most of the garment metaphors appearing later); lines 58–59 (planting as a symbol of the unpredictability of the future is introduced here).

SCENE 4   What is the dramatic purpose of Duncan's naming Malcolm his successor at this time? Notice examples of dramatic irony: lines 11–21, lines 54–58. Consider the symbols of planting, lines 28–33, and of masking, lines 50–53.

SCENE 5   How does Lady Macbeth characterize her husband? (Examine the validity of this characterization as the play proceeds, finally determining to what extent her description of her husband fits herself.) What is the meaning of Lady Macbeth's line, "I feel now the future in the instant"? (Later, determine how much of the future she was really aware of.) Another example of the masking metaphor occurs in lines 52–56.

SCENE 6   Notice the example of dramatic irony in the lyrical description of the castle, contrasting with the scene of horror that preceded. Contrast Lady Macbeth's greeting to Duncan—its formality, stilted phrasing, emphasis on duty—with the warmth of Duncan's remarks. Notice how Shakespeare indicates Lady Macbeth's feelings by the labored rhythm of the lines.

SCENE 7   Compare the sense of values, methods of thinking of Macbeth and Lady Macbeth. She does not foresee the consequences of the king's murder; he does, but hopes to avoid them. Notice how each uses the same facts to arrive at different conclusions. Is either more logical than the other? Is either more sensitive to the feelings of others? Analyze this scene for evidence of their somewhat complementary natures.

What is the significance of lines 51–54? Throughout this scene Lady Macbeth, as she has promised, gives an exhibition of her skill in chastising with the valor of her tongue; notice the range of the appeals by which she attempts to move her husband to act.

The symbol is further developed: the child, signifying both the humanity of man and his insurance for the future, lines 21–25 and 54–59; variants of the masking imagery, lines 32–35, lines 35–38, and lines 81–82.

▶ *Writing*

As the reading of the play progresses, students may be asked to write briefly on selected topics that probe their thinking concerning the implications of lines and scenes significant to concepts being developed. Illustrations from the first two acts will serve as examples.

Act I   (1) What impression have you formed of Lady Macbeth? (The obvious one at this time is that she is a fiend, but later developments may suggest a woman, consciously steeling herself to commit an act against nature.) (2) "There is no way to partition off the continuum of time; the future is implicit in the present." [3] Explain. Do you agree with this statement? Do you think Macbeth would? Discuss in reference to his speech in scene 7, lines 1–28.

Act II (1) Does Lady Macbeth really faint or only pretend to? (If she is a fiend, the faint may be pretense; however, the murder of the guards is evidently a surprise to her, the first evidence that she has unleashed a power she cannot control. The shock of knowing the king's murder is not the end but the beginning may well have caused her to faint.) (2) In scene 2, lines 73 and 74, Macbeth says, "Wake Duncan with thy knocking! I would thou could'st!" Is the wish sincere? Consider in relation to his character as portrayed thus far. (3) If you were staging the play, would you use a real dagger in scene 1, lines 33–49? Give reasons.

▶ *Audio-visual activities*

After the reading of each act, it is helpful to have students listen to some of the key speeches (not the entire act) spoken by accomplished actors; the recording with Maurice Evans and Judith Anderson, still available in some schools, is ideal for this purpose; unfortunately, it is no longer on the market; selections from the Old Vic recording might be used the same way.

After the first reading of the play, some teachers use the film *Shakespeare's Theater,* which suggests a method of staging the last act of *Macbeth.*

Second reading of the play

Purpose   to help students understand the interrelation of the various elements that make up the whole.

Procedure   using the section "Form in Relation to Content" as a guide, the teacher reads significant but *brief* passages to illustrate the interweaving of the various elements in each act; if this is to serve its purpose, it must be done quickly without belaboring points and with no effort to make every student see the significance of each.

Culminating experiences

▶ *Synthesis*

1. *Group work*   In preparation for the final discussion, the class may be divided into six committees, each to review the evidence concerning one aspect of the play. Necessarily, since the various aspects are well integrated, the evidence of one overlaps that of the others.

The Witches: symbolic role in the play; the prophecies and the manner of their fulfillment.

Macbeth: the course of his crimes; his impelling motives; his increasing tension.

Lady Macbeth: her intellectual processes in regard to the crimes to which she is accessory; the development of her emotional experiences.

The "Fair is foul, and foul is fair" theme: passages where it is stated, implied, illustrated.

[3] Cleanth Brooks, *The Well Wrought Urn* (New York: Harcourt, Brace & World, 1947), p. 2.

Symbolism: use of babes on various levels—as characters, symbols, and elements of metaphor. The garment and masking symbolism—from Macbeth's initial impulse to reject "borrowed robes" to Angus' description of him in the last act as a "dwarfish thief" trying to wear a "giant's robes." The plant symbolism, reflecting the development of the play—from the early references to seeds and planting, symbolic of the fertility surrounding Duncan, to Macbeth's lament that his life "is fall'n into the sear, the yellow leaf."

Dramatic irony: during the reading, the Oedipus myth may be discussed in relation to similarities and contrasts with *Macbeth;* Oedipus struggled to overcome a fate that had already been decided; Macbeth, although he believed the witches possessed "more than mortal knowledge," tried to impose a plan on the future, contrary to that which they had predicted.

2. *Discussions* Led by the teacher, the final discussion should attempt to integrate the evidence of these various elements into a unified whole.

► *Writing*

In writing the final essay, students may be allowed to choose any one of the following topics.

The Prophecies A factual account of the substance of the prophecies and of the manner of their fulfillment.

Ideal Partners in Crime An analysis of the complementary natures of Macbeth and Lady Macbeth, supported by specific examples.

Dramatic Irony Critics have compared the structure of dramatic irony underlying *Macbeth* with that of the Oedipus myth. Discuss dramatic irony as it operates in each case, noting the similarities and contrasts in the two situations.

Symbolism as an Integrating Force Select any one of the series of symbols that run throughout the play—masking, seeds and planting, the babe; explain its contribution to the drama; give specific examples.

► *Final reading*

The students follow in their books as they listen to the Old Vic recording of the play.

► *Listening and viewing*

Shakespeare has proved popular on television; his plays will continue to appear; at least two versions of *Macbeth* have been shown. Available now is a powerful and moving recording: three records; an impressive and well-balanced supporting cast, Stanley Holloway as Porter; Anthony Quayle and Gwen F. Davies in leading roles. (Shakespeare Recording Society. Caedmon, 505 Eighth Ave., New York, N.Y. 10018.)

Evaluation

Appreciations Genuine appreciation of the play as a dramatic and literary experience cannot be evaluated exactly; the teacher has to depend upon observations of personal reactions.

Skills and understandings The teacher has class discussions, the short papers written as the reading progresses, and the final essay, which may be used for purposes of evaluation.

Brief key quotations, listed in scrambled order, to be arranged in proper sequence, prove useful in testing some of the more subtle understandings of the development of the drama; for each, a short explanation of the significance of the sequence the student selects should be required. Quotations that could be used are lines from Macbeth's speeches showing his mental and emotional states as his affairs grow progressively worse, or lines containing symbols—especially the masking and planting metaphors—which change in their application as events in the play change.

Aftermath

After the completion of the unit, the students may enjoy hearing one of their number read James Thurber's essay, "The Macbeth Murder Mystery."

RESOURCES FOR TEACHERS

BROOKS, CLEANTH. *The Well Wrought Urn.* New York: Harcourt, Brace & World, 1947. See especially Chapter 2, "The Naked Babe and the Cloak of Manliness."

HALIO, JAY L. (ed.). *Approaches to Macbeth.* Belmont, Calif.: Wadsworth Publishing Co., 1966. This anthology of criticism concerning *Macbeth* presents diverse points of view and study questions.

ORNSTEIN, ROBERT. *Shakespeare in the Classroom.* Urbana, Ill.: Educational Illustrators, 1960. Available from National Council of Teachers of English.

THURBER, JAMES. *My World and Welcome to It.* New York: Harcourt, Brace & World, 1942.

TRAVERSI, D. A. *An Approach to Shakespeare.* Garden City, N.Y.: Doubleday Anchor, 1956. See especially pp. 150–81.

WEBSTER, MARGARET. *Shakespeare Without Tears.* New York: Fawcett, 1957. See especially Chapter 10, "The Tragic Essence."

UNIT:

HUMANITIES FOR THE SEVENTIES: PERMANENCE AND CHANGE

A RESOURCE UNIT FOR GRADE ELEVEN OR TWELVE

Overview The humanities have value and pleasure for all pupils and they are especially for those who will not continue their education in college. The plan suggested here is intended for juniors or seniors, many of whom are not academic in their talents or interests. Like all adolescents, however, they respond to beauty, and they puzzle about experience.

The present plan starts with whatever may be the class's latest enthusiasm in music, film, dance, fashions, or television and gradually consolidates its activities around the unifying theme of "Permanence and Change." All the arts and contemporary history are drawn upon in this resource unit, but the humanities most emphasized are poetry, film, and drama. To feature Socrates' idea that the unexamined life is not worth living, the unit asks four questions about American life and culture:

Where have we been?
Where are we? What seems good and solid to us in the 1970's?
Where are we going?
In spite of change, what persists?

It is of the greatest importance that the teacher enjoy this unit as much as the students do. Although the teacher will have his aims clearly in mind, he should not be troubled if he cannot know in advance all the routes he will follow. He and the students will explore together; he will learn much from the students just as they will learn much from him. Insofar as possible, the teacher will ask questions and search with the students, rather than tell or generalize for them. Throughout the unit the teacher must remind himself of Robert Louis Stevenson's admonition: "To miss Joy is to miss All."

To teach a unit like this requires a teacher with some daring, zest, and experience. Furthermore, time is needed to collect in advance some of the necessary materials. (Pupils will furnish many more if the plan appeals to them.) Administrators and department chairmen also need to share in the initial design long before the plan is carried out. However, any teacher—especially one without experience—may work toward the total plan by starting

609

with small parts of it the first year, refining and combining until the full-scale operation is feasible a second or third year.

Teachers using a unit such as this will have their own ideas, literary selections, and film choices and will very likely prefer their own to those recommended here. Indeed such modification to suit individual teachers and schools is desirable. The plan as suggested here should never be considered fixed: it has been designed to accommodate new ideas and new materials. "Permanence and Change" should be measured in part by ideas and materials students contribute and in part by the spontaneous associations and ideas sparked daily in the teacher's mind. This plan is not a museum specimen, brittle and dry; it is a set of living materials or a set of materials waiting to be brought to life.

Materials required

To make this plan come alive it is essential that many materials not often associated with past programs in English be available. Records, films, and tapes of modern jazz and poetry need to be budgeted for and ordered in advance. Television programs, art reproductions, slides, and cameras must be planned for and used. The teacher should be willing to experiment boldly with new materials and to vary the use of those suggested here.

Aims

Understandings The arts are meant to be enjoyed and to deepen one's capacity for responding to experience: man needs purpose; man seeks change within stability; man seeks order; beauty is a form of order; the best order is not stale or dead; it is living vital order.

Skills To express feelings and ideas in honest, clear language; to recognize rhythm, unity, and planned variation in more than one art form.

Appreciations To realize that taste in the arts depends upon choice; choices should be both sincere and examined; to enjoy beauty in designs that leave room for freedom—yet not so much freedom that the over-all designs break down; to begin an awareness of the distinction between stale, dead forms of expression and dynamic, living forms.

Time plan Flexible. Five or six weeks are recommended.

Launching the plan

Although the teacher will have a conceptual map in his mind, a map of the territory ultimately to be covered, he need not know all the opening trails. First, the students must begin with their world. The teacher seeks to learn what his students enjoy and respond to. If they can verbalize why they like it, good, but if they cannot, he does not press them to analysis at this stage. Some of but not all the following suggestions may be usable. Each teacher will think of others.

On the first day, have the classroom flamboyantly decorated with contemporary material: Pop Art, *Hot Rod Magazine,* the designs of Marimekko or other textile designers; large pictures of customized cars, standard automobile and jet plane designs; posters for movies; designs for record jackets; speed boats and sailboats in miniature or photograph; blown-up photographs of students and familiar local events; illustrations from magazines of clothing fashions and hair-styling; absurdities such as a photograph of Merit Oppenheim's fur-lined teacup and spoon or Salvador Dali's painting of watches dripping over a table ("The Persistence of Memory"); the Marina Towers in Chicago; reproductions by Picasso, de Chirico, Jackson Pollack, Klee, Miró; pictures of innovative new theaters, factories, school buildings, and libraries; photography, shop work, paintings, sculptures, and poems already executed by class members (no matter how crude, the latter are imperative). Class members who have previously been planning with the teacher and decorating the room are playing records—whatever is currently popular—as the rest of the students enter the room on the first day.[1]

The teacher need not be in any hurry, but at an appropriate time, when several records have been enjoyed, he may begin questioning, asking: "What's in fashion? What's out of fashion now (in music, television programs, actors, popular singers, fads, fashions)? What do you enjoy?"

Show pictures, demonstrate, or describe with the help of students the fads of previous years and of the present.

> *Games and amusements*   mahjong, canasta, monopoly, dating by computers, hula hoops, dance marathons, flagpole sitting, surfing, guitar-playing, skateboards
> *Dances*   waltz, fox trot, Charleston, Lindy, mambo, jitterbug, rock and roll dances, the latest
> *Language*   teen slang; expressions from the 1920's: O, you kid!, 23 skidoo!, vamp. For the 1930's through the 1960's several pupils can do advance research by looking up stories about young people in magazines on file in libraries and by asking parents to recall slang of their youth.
> *Television programs*   *Mod Squad, Laugh In, Batman,* currently popular ones.
> *Comics*   whatever they are reading
> *Movies*   (discussion, not viewing) mystery, horror, spy, gangster, musical comedy, teen-age beach and surfing pictures
> *Art*   pop, kinesthetic, psychedelic, folk art, other recent developments

Use advertising (such as "You're in the Pepsi Generation!") to show the appeal to being "in." Discuss: Why do people prefer being "in"? Who determines what is in fashion? Who isn't "in"? Are there any not "in" because they do not choose to be? Do any slang words stabilize and last? What people have won fame because the world came to them rather than because they tried to please or to be popular?

Greta Garbo
Billie Holiday
Robert Frost

---

[1] "Taste, when it is spontaneous, always begins with the senses. Children and savages, as we are so often told, delight in bright and variegated colors. . . . Such simplicity is not the absence of taste but the beginning of it. . . . When sincerity is lost, and a snobbish ambition is substituted, bad taste comes in." George Santayana, *The Sense of Beauty* (New York: Dover, 1955), p. 79.

Some leaders of the Third World movement may qualify for this list. Teachers should be alert to include them.

Play records of Greta Garbo and Billie Holiday.[2] Distribute and read aloud copies of Frost's poem "The Road Not Taken." Discuss its possible meaning in relation to Frost and the others who also took the road less traveled. What is meant by the term the "lonely crowd"? Continue with one or more poems such as the following to extend this theme:

> "Bluebeard" by Edna St. Vincent Millay
> "The Room" by C. Day Lewis

These poems deal with the need for privacy and selfhood and the need to resist pressure and exploitation by others.

Concluding questions: Is there a need to be "in"? Is there also a need to be authentically one's own self, not a face in the lonely crowd? Do you know this conflict? (This is an excellent topic for composition, either creative personal expression or exposition. The problem of "What's 'in'? What's 'out'?" is indigenous to a fluid society.)

On the following day, move the discussion to "Change." Begin with fashion in clothing, illustrating men's and women's fashions of the period 1920 to the present. Show pictures or slides of cars and planes, from the earliest models down to the present. Students can help to prepare and carry out this lesson. Conclude: Does everything change? Will we look old-fashioned some day when some teacher shows pictures of us? In some classes, this entire lesson could be prepared and presented by individuals and committees of pupils.

Continue the attention to change:

Architecture

Painting

Hair styles

Music styles   Play hit songs associated with leading performers and band leaders from 1920 to the present—Rudy Vallee, Paul Whiteman, Harry James, Elvis Presley, the Beatles, Joan Baez.[3] Some have a lasting quality: play recordings by Billie Holiday and Louis Armstrong.

Cinema celebrities   Valentino to the present, Mary Pickford to the present. To illustrate lasting quality, play sections of *Garbo,* a recording of scenes from her movies.

Conclude: Many fads and celebrities disappear but some last. Why?

Read passages from a book about teen-agers. Many magazine articles and books deal with the new nonaristocratic youth culture emerging in all urban Western nations as well as in Japan. The teacher need not read whole chapters or articles. Excerpts to discuss and to lead into writing are sufficient. For instance, the title selection from *The Kandy-Kolored Tangerine-Flake Streamline Baby* by Tom Wolfe will elicit enough response for a full class hour.

---

[2] Sources of recordings as well as all other book and film titles will be found in the list of materials and resources at the end of the unit.

[3] *I Like Jazz,* a Columbia recording, is useful in presenting a selection of old songs, ranging from "Maple Leaf Rag" to the contemporary artistry of Dave Brubeck. Victor Vintage, RCA Victor LPV-558 is a recent album featuring early jazz.

Developing the plan

The suggestions so far have been presented as a means of launching this study of humanities. Those that follow are chosen as possibilities for accomplishing the understandings, skills, and appreciations. Inasmuch as this is a resource unit, the teacher will find here more suggestions than he could possibly use. He will, for his own teaching unit, need to select from these suggestions, add some of his own, and organize them into his own plan.

As the teacher helps students develop these suggestions—or any others he and his students devise—he should remember that the humanities are concerned with feeling as well as knowing. Young people will often be concerned with emotion and personal response.

▶ *Permanence and change*

This discussion may be initiated and sustained by either a teacher or a student leader (or leaders). Fullness of meaning for permanence needs to be assured. Either on the chalkboard or through discussion, use examples such as permanent wave, permanent and temporary jobs, a permanent injury, permanent chairman, a passing fad, a transient worker.

Discuss planned obsolescence: automobiles, refrigerators, fashions for young people. What advantages do youth-aimed industries gain from change? What risks do they face? Who determines the youth market? Compare advertising aimed at youth with advertising aimed at adults. Try requesting that a particular recording be played on a local disc jockey show. Note the effect on weekly ratings.

Can change be too rapid? Does anyone ever weary of keeping up with what is the latest? Are there recordings or styles or dances you do not wish to relinquish?

How do you complete these two unfinished statements? (The answers may be in the form of writing and can be developed into paragraphs. The adjectives in parentheses are not provided for the pupils.)

Too much rapid change produces people who are (restless, uncertain, discontented) but flexible.

Too much permanence produces people who are (bored, dull, complacent, unimaginative) but stable.

Concluding questions: Are balance and equilibrium good answers to the issue of permanence and change?

▶ *Unity and variety*

What do we mean by *unity plus variety* in a featured number of an ice skating follies show? In architecture? In dancing?

Listen for what is central or unifying and what is embroidery or variation in two musical numbers, "Mack the Knife" and "La Cumparsita." The Kurt Weill jazz, for instance, provides variety and generates a powerful sense of increasing excitement through upward harmonic shifts whereas in "La Cumparsita," a giddy, volatile subsidiary melody seems always striving either to escape or to come into the foreground permanently, yet the dominant tango melody continually triumphs and controls in a delightful and satisfying manner.

These two musical compositions have been used successfully. Teachers and pupils may have other choices. The purpose is to illustrate the power of an esthetic principle: unity combined with variety; permanence linked with change. At the close of the lesson, students should be helped to transfer this esthetic principle to other art forms.

Suggestions:

> pictures of custom-made, foreign, and domestic cars
> dance number in a musical comedy
> film clip of a dance team
> live demonstration of dancing by students in the school
> folk songs, "Greensleeves," similar ballads
> recent folk rock
> reproduction of a painting
> film clips of basketball, football, rugby, soccer
> full-page magazine advertisements
> structure of a television variety show
> film clip of a ballet
> poems such as "The Raven" by Poe and "We Real Cool" by Gwendolyn Brooks
> pictures of household objects, tools, and industrial design
> architecture: models or pictures, actual visits
> interiors in homes
> public parks and landscaped gardens
> kinesthetic sculpture

► *What is beautiful? What is ugly?*

Committees prepare and present examples of what they consider beauty in the following:

Design   cars, planes, furniture, clothing, hair styling, tableware, textiles, ceramics, guns, boats, hardware tools, dishes, industrial design, architecture, landscaping (including Japanese), interior decoration, kitchens, highways and roads

Landscapes   (colored stills, slides)

Painting   (colored reproductions)

Movement   surfing, diving, rowing, playing basketball, swimming, ice skating, skiing, dancing, tumbling, running (Is there beauty in batting a ball? Catching a ball snugly in a mitt?)

Nature   ferns, flowers, rocks, butterflies, autumn colors, snowscapes

Is everybody interested in beauty? The teacher elicits classroom discussion relating beauty to permanence and change. Beauty is important to everyone, part of everything important enough for us to care about—not just mountains and trees and flowers but also jet planes and science and dancing. Everything that means anything to us is bound up with beauty.

Sometimes students ask, "Isn't it silly to study about beauty? That's for artists and people like that, isn't it?" The teacher welcomes such questions and, in turn, questions the students along the lines sketched in the following paragraphs.[4]

---

[4] The first time, the teacher may need to furnish some of the answers, but as the unit is repeated, the teacher can draw most of the answers from the pupils. The inductive method requires more time, but the results are, most teachers believe, more pervasive and lasting.

How would you feel if someone said you were homely, that your nose was too long or your feet too big?

What is it you enjoy when you watch a good basketball game? **Or** a skilled diver? Why not save your admiration for a belly-flop? Remember that diving sequence in the film clip (the marvelous coordination of bodily movement to achieve its purpose)? We said that was a beautiful dive. Why?

Did you see any beauty in the movement of those sailboats? **The rowers in** the small boats? The basketball players? The ice skaters? The swimmers in **the race?** What pleases you, gives you delight in such movements?

Some words you used to describe diving, rowing, swimming, skating may **give** us a clue for looking beneath the surface on this matter of beauty. You said a skater or a basketball team shows good *form,* that a diver has good *balance,* that a rowing team has *rhythm.* Do you ever sway or clap to music? Why? Do you feel the music more fully? Why?

When you apply these important terms to anything that gives you deep lasting pleasure and delight, you'll find they usually add up to the idea of *order*—the opposite of imbalance, irregularity, and confusion.

We might list some opposites like this. All these words are necessary to understanding what beauty is:

formed	patterned	designed	arranged	neat
unformed	unpatterned	undesigned	unarranged, disarranged	messy, sloppy
balance	equilibrium	proportion	order	
imbalance	disequilibrium	disproportion	disorder	
symmetrical	centered	regular	rhythmical	
asymmetrical	uncentered, lopsided	irregular	nonrhythmical, sporadic	

Can there be too much order? Do you ever like disorder? Do you agree with Francis Bacon, who wrote, "There is no excellent beauty that hath not some strangeness in the proportion,"? (Essay 43, "Of Beauty")

Now can you think of some examples of order?

music (In music what is put in order?)
department store, supermarket
a game or sport (What happens if there are no rules?)
flower arrangement (Notice pleasing asymmetry.)
traffic control at an airport

Can you think of examples of disorder?

messy room
dancers or musicians who do not maintain the rhythm
someone singing off key and out of rhythm in a chorus
traffic jam

Show one or both of the following short films, which lack classical continuity: *Very Nice, Very Nice; Free Fall.* Admit that the films probably evoke feeling and are intriguing, but note also their lack of unity and familiar order. What is your reaction to them? Play some electronic music or John Cage's "Aria with Fontana Mix." What do you make of them?

Do you think confusion and mess can influence the lives of people who spend considerable time in the midst of disorder? What about too much order? Does it influence living? How? Are order and disorder related to the rapidity or slowness of change?

Is there order and balance and rhythm in nature (day-night, sunrise-sunset, the seasons, the rising and falling tides)? Have you thought of your heart beat, your breathing, waking-sleeping, planting-harvesting? Have you ever seen the beauty of the orderly symmetry of a snowflake under a magnifying glass? Do any of these relate to permanence and change?

Show slides presenting sights like the following. Can you see any order or balance or rhythm in these?

starch grain (swollen, breaks to smaller units in concentric layers)
cross-section of human bone
butterfly wing
sea coral (distributes its branches evenly, no big holes, no overcrowding)
nerve cell of our brain (similar to sea coral)
dragonfly wing

Try to elicit from the class members such generalizations as these: The rhythms and patterns in nature are the end products of processes taking place through movement and change over a period of time. Consider the following:

the slow growth of the rings of a tree
a comb of beeswax to hold honey
the development of a nautilus sea shell

Each of these represents a time-stream of processes that has taken form. They have a rhythm of growth and development adding up to balance, symmetry, proportion —order—and like in rhythmical diving, skating, music, and poetry, there are no useless, purposeless movements and parts. Whenever we say something is beautiful, we usually find it has an order similar to what we discover in the world and perhaps the universe. If we "stop" nature's movement by looking at a frame of a moving picture, we can see the arrested process as a fountain having become a chandelier of motionless water, fireworks having become a flower.

Show the film *Donald Duck in Mathemagic Land* to clinch effectively these ideas about order and beauty, permanence of form, and the transience of disorganized, formless things. Ask pupils to summarize what they have learned. For example:

Beauty is not just a useless luxury to be hidden in art museums. Beauty is in all life. Without it, we become confused and bewildered. To understand beauty we must see it as the expression of living order.

But there is something more, something very important. If there is too much order the beauty is lost. Something goes dead when there is complete order and regularity. We all like a little variation. Asymmetry can be beautiful. To keep life in anything there must be surprise.

play dull jazz and vibrant jazz; also, some Calypso songs to note how monotony is cleverly evaded
consider dangers and possibilities of modern architecture
read sing-song verse and some powerful free verse

The *pearly nautilus sea shell lengthens* or *grows at a fixed ratio.*

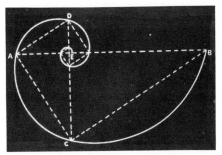

The *logarithmic curve of mathematics lengthens at a similar fixed ratio.*

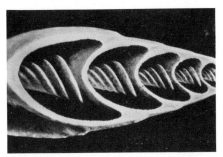

What *we admire as beauty in the achieved form is the product of an orderly development.*

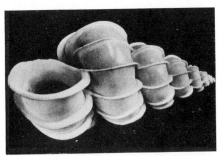

Form *is the precipitate of the underlying dynamics of growth.*

A *medusa jellyfish: symmetry, unity, variety.*

Twelfth *century Japanese scroll: asymmetry with a rhythmic repetition of lines slanting from lower left to upper right.*

SCIENCE, MATHEMATICS, AND ART TELL A SIMILAR STORY

Beauty is harmony, balance, variety within unity, freedom within order.

ACKNOWLEDGEMENTS: Photograph at top left courtesy of "DuPont-Better Living." Center photographs from A. Ehrhardt, *Muscheln und Schnecken* (Hamburg: H. Ellerman, 1941). Photograph at bottom left from E. H. Haeckel, *Kunstformen der Natur*, 1904. Photograph at bottom right from K. Toda, *Japanese Scroll Painting*, 1935. Reprinted by permission of the publisher, The University of Chicago Press.

consider   television programs: some full of stock responses and formula routines, others innovative and imaginative

Beauty is design leaving room for freedom—but not so much freedom that the overall design breaks down. Similarly, we need a balance of permanence and change. Life and art need dynamic equilibrium, not dead perfection.

▶ *Beauty and ethics*

Does beauty extend beyond what we see and hear? Are order and proportion needed in our lives? What do we mean when we say:

"It was an ugly thing to do." "It was a beautiful thing to do."

Discuss the fusion of esthetic and ethical values by using or assigning a television drama in which vicious and destructive behavior can be seen as discord and disorder and harmonious living represents equilibrium and proportion. A biographical account of a living person can accomplish the same purpose or prove a further illustration. *The Little Foxes,* a drama by Lillian Hellman, shows ugly, vicious behavior. Biographies of Martin Luther King, Jr., and Malcolm X show growing order and purpose in their lives.

▶ *Where have we been in American life and culture?*

Read *Only Yesterday* by Frederick Lewis Allen to examine change. Use chapter 1, "Prelude: May, 1919," as an introduction with the class:

What daily life was like just after the war: clothes, news, sports, cost of living, automobiles, business conditions, bull market of 1919, parades, jazz, drinks, books, movies, theater—and what was still to come.

Assign pupil groups responsibility for chapters 2 through 13 (chapter 13 deals with the 1929 stock market crash). Assign to the whole class chapter 14, "Aftermath: 1930–31."

Ask a committee to read *The Pop Makers* by Carolyn Silver, an examination of British rock and roll, then to comment on the impact of "the Liverpool sound" on American popular music.

Read and listen to the recording of *Death of a Salesman* by Arthur Miller [5] to build the concept of man's need for purpose and order.

These plays are suggested for individual or group reading:

Teahouse of the August Moon, John Patrick
The Miracle Worker, William Gibson
A Raisin in the Sun, Lorraine Hansberry
Rhinoceros, Eugene Ionesco (Refer back to the need to stand against the crowd.)

Whenever possible, groups should present scenes informally, reading or improvising the parts rather than memorizing them.

▶ *Musical drama:* West Side Story

The purpose of considering *West Side Story* is to look at urban man's need for order and to see how hate and aimlessness create disorder. The complete text is in a paperback published by Pocket Books. A recording of the major songs and dances is available from Columbia Records, OS-2001. See Ann C. Farnell's complete

[5] See pages 489–90 for teaching suggestions.

teaching unit outline for *West Side Story* on pages 79–97 in *Hooked on Books* by Daniel Fader and Morton Shaevitz. The teacher may wish to read aloud some of Pauline Kael's criticism of the movie (pages 127–33 in *I Lost It at the Movies*).

▶ *Film*

View and discuss one or several of these films to illuminate the concept of permanence and change and to show the individual resisting the pressures and exploitation of others.

The Loneliness of the Long-Distance Runner
On the Waterfront
Rebel Without a Cause
Lonely Boy

For example, in presenting *The Loneliness of the Long-Distance Runner*,[6] do not moralize or lecture. Let the pupils discuss. They will, in their own way, bring out:

Colin's search for self (Ask: Is knowing one's self and one's values a task appropriate to our study of the humanities? Does Colin change? Is anything in his life permanent?)
Colin's rejection of the middle-class values surrounding him

Offer instruction subtly, delicately, mostly through questions about symbols, transitions, contrasts, ironies, foreshadowings, selection of incident. The dialect will require some advance preparation. Ask: Does the film offer anything constructive to replace the false values it attacks? What should change in Colin's world?

Compare the film with the long short story, *The Loneliness of the Long-Distance Runner* by Alan Sillitoe (New York: Knopf, 1960). Have the school's drama class read the story aloud to your class or tape portions of the story in advance of your use. The film radically alters the character of Colin, making him a champion of social justice, a gentle and sensitive hero. The incidents in the film that achieve this alteration may be noted and discussed. Do they improve or distort the story?

▶ *Discussions*

Where are we now? Where are we going? How do we cope with change? What is lasting? Some of these discussions should be taped:

A. Heroes
  1. What is a hero? A villain? A scoundrel? A phony? Who is to be admired and why?
  2. Which heroes and heroines in youth culture are real? Phony?
B. Science
  1. How has science affected life in our times? (urbanization, speed, dislocation of family, community)
  2. What is at the basic purpose of scientific efforts? (to improve human existence and man's understanding and control of nature)
  3. Could we do without science? How is it related to change?

[6] This film is available from Continental Distributors, 241 East 34th St., New York, N.Y. 10016. A helpful discussion of the movie and the book from which it was adapted is "How the Long-Distance Runner Throws the Race" in *I Lost It at the Movies* by Pauline Kael (pages 230–35). Teaching the movie is discussed in Sister M. Amanda Ely, O.P., "The Loneliness of the Long-Distance Runner: First Film Fare," *English Journal*, Vol. 56, No. 1 (January 1967), pp. 41–44.

4. What are some changes to come? (moving sidewalks, jitney helicopters, world weather control, underwater living, wrist television sets)

C. Youth and change

1. The ferment of youth is perennial.
2. Eventually every generation finds equilibrium, stabilizes.
   a. But individuals can lose their way, live wasted lives.
   b. A few individuals achieve in new ways.
3. In our time the search for self and authenticity is difficult, especially in urban life.
   a. The rites of passage from childhood to adulthood are neither easy nor clearly identified in urban, technological societies.
   b. People feel dwarfed in big cities; they are "faces in the lonely crowd."
4. Values and outlooks are changing rapidly. We seem to be in a transition period of history. Once we glorified work and thrift. What takes their place in a world of automation?
5. There are permanent truths: one who lives without giving and receiving love becomes warped; one cannot be prodigal of health and potential without paying for it.

We will have to learn to adapt to continual change as a way of life. We will have to learn to be flexible. We will have to regard education as a lifelong process. By 1980, it is estimated, 50 per cent of the work force will be employed on jobs not even in existence now. The majority of these jobs are not yet even in our imaginations.

▶ *Writing*

Any of the discussions in this unit can be converted into occasions for writing to be shared in class, with other classes, with other schools.

▶ *Reports*

Have a student tell the class about John Kennedy's *Tommy Steele, The Facts About a Teenage Idol and an "Inside" Picture of Show Business* (London: Souvenir Press, 1958). Excerpts from this book can be read to show how the taste-makers exploit youth.

Students can prepare readings of "Poetry of Our World," using poems such as these with their comment on permanence and change:

poems written by class members
"Twentieth Century Songs," Elsa Gidlow
"We Real Cool," Gwendolyn Brooks
"Dirge: 1-2-3," Kenneth Fearing
"A Brook in the City," Robert Frost
"Hawaiian Hilltop," Genevieve Taggard
selections from *The People, Yes,* Carl Sandburg

▶ *Television*

Choose a committee of students (or a series of committees) to keep the class informed in advance of important programs. Both oral announcements and bulletin board information should be used. A special bulletin board display of pictorial material may be prepared for special programs.

Several popular dramatic serials or programs may be compared for good and weak points of characterization, credibility of plot, lack of forward movement and the logic of solutions and resolutions. Obtain video tapes of some television programs. At least once in a semester some television program will merit special preparation in advance and discussion after the event. Very likely some television drama will best contribute to a humanities focus on permanence and change.

▶ *Television idols and recordings*

Play some of the latest popular records. Ask, "Are records played because young people like them or do young people like them because they keep hearing them?" Discuss this quotation:

> Any thinking person knows that the teenage idols are largely the creation of self-seeking wire-pullers with little principle and less artistic discernment. Of course the stock excuse is that the kids get what they ask for. That's nonsense. The truth is that the teenagers don't really know what they want until they get it.[7]

Follow this with a composition on one of these topics:

> The Record (Television Program) I Like Better Than Any Other and Why I Like It
> Am I Developing a Personal Taste, One That Represents Me, Not Just a Conditioned Response?

▶ *Drama*

If a local community theater is producing a suitable play, ask the theater group to make two opening night tickets available to student reviewers. Post or print the reviews. Make arrangements to encourage other pupils to attend.

Culminating experiences

Prepare "Only Today," a class project depicting the pupils and their world. Place it (bound) in the school library for future students. Include poems, drawings, stories, photography, essays, jokes, epigrams, satire, lists of preferences in music, art, literature, amusements, sports, movies, television. View it as a real find, a source document to be discovered by the Frederick Lewis Allen of the year 2000.

▶ *Make a tape with slides*

This could illustrate permanence and change in the local community.

▶ *Make some films*

Using 8-mm. cameras such as are used for home movies (plus sound on a tape recorder),[8] students should make movies of their own. Plan on fifty feet of shooting, using one-third of the footage. Splicing equipment can be bought for home movies. More elaborate equipment is emerging. Use it by all means if it is available to you.

One class filmed examples of the regimentation and aridity of mass civilization, using as a base W. H. Auden's poem "The Shield of Achilles." In another school

---

[7] Vic Lewis in *Melody Maker* (November 1958). *Melody Maker* is a British magazine.
[8] Or 16-mm. film with sprocketed tape synchronized with the film. However, 16-mm. film equipment and processing are still very expensive.

where groups competed, the winning film, "Ghetto," highly inventive in technique, dealt with the problems of suburban, close-minded affluence versus inner-city deterioration. The films were technically rough, but in an age abounding with spoofs, thoroughly honest.[9] The film made in this particular humanities unit might feature permanence and change.

► *Predict 1984*

Use short stories, poems, novels, dramas, essays, films: *Rhinoceros, Fahrenheit 451* (novel and film), *The Machine Stops, 1984* (novel and film), *2001: A Space Odyssey,* "By the Waters of Babylon," "The Portable Phonograph." Individual pupils or groups read or see these and tape a group discussion, their reaction to these predictions of future regimentation or eventual loss of social controls.

► *Looking ahead*

If this brief view of the humanities has been successful, pupils will want to discuss how they are to extend their interest beyond school, to continue enjoying and learning on their own for the rest of their lives. Use class time for an overview of music, literature, and art. Work out some charts and lists by themes such as

MAN'S SEARCH FOR

a deity	truth
freedom	social order
beauty	a good life

Note historical periods: primitive, classical Greek, Roman, Renaissance, Sung, Ming, and so forth.

Play some Mozart, Beethoven, Bartók, and Gershwin; read aloud excerpts from Tolstoy, Ibsen, Steinbeck, and poems by Emily Dickinson; play some recordings of poetry in a foreign language.

Introduce some non-Western humanities: music from India and Japan, Hiroshige and Hokusai prints, African sculpture, Polynesian myths, Persian miniatures and *The Rubáiyát,* Soviet poetry in translation.

List sources for future use, such as libraries, educational television, adult education centers. Draw upon some of the Encyclopaedia Britannica films (*The Humanities: What They Are and What They Do; Chartres Cathedral*).

Conclude with some guiding ideas: the proper study of mankind is man; the humanities will not help you make a better living, but they can help you live better; the unexamined life is not worth living.

Evaluating the plan

Have the teacher and pupils enjoyed this unit?

Have the pupils expressed themselves honestly and often and in a variety of ways and situations? Have they examined some important values rather fully and made their own evaluations?

Do their taped discussions and written products show a deeper understanding of change?

[9] Rev. J. Paul Carrico, C.S.C., "Matter and Meaning of Motion Pictures," *English Journal,* Vol. 56, No. 1 (January 1967), pp. 23–37.

Can they apply the esthetic principles to new objects of art they have not studied?
Is the project "Only Today" close to the best product they can produce?

MATERIALS FOR THE TEACHER

CARRICO, REV. J. PAUL. "Matter and Meaning of Motion Pictures." *English Journal.* Vol. 56, No. 1 (January 1967), pp. 23–37.

KAEL, PAULINE. *I Lost It at the Movies.* New York: Bantam Books, 1966.

———. *Kiss Kiss Bang Bang.* Boston: Little, Brown, 1968.

WALKER, JERRY L. "Bach, Rembrandt, Milton, and Those Other Cats," *English Journal.* Vol. 57, No. 5 (May 1968), pp. 631–36.

WOLFE, TOM. *The Kandy-Kolored Tangerine-Flake Streamline Baby.* New York: Farrar, Straus & Giroux, 1966.

Chapter Thirteen, "Discovery of Values" (pp. 628–58), in this book will be useful to those using this unit.

MATERIALS FOR CLASSROOM DEVELOPMENT OF THE UNIT

NONFICTION

ALLEN, FREDERICK LEWIS. *Only Yesterday.* New York: Harper & Row, 1931.

CLAYTON, EDWARD. *Martin Luther King,* Englewood Cliffs, N.J.: Prentice-Hall, 1967.

KENNEDY, JOHN. *Tommy Steele: The Facts About a Teenage Idol and an "Inside" Picture of Show Business.* London: Souvenir Press, 1958.

MALCOLM X. *The Autobiography of Malcolm X.* New York: Grove Press, 1965.

SILVER, CAROLYN. *The Pop Makers.* New York: Scholastic Books, 1967.

RECORDS

Garbo. No. E-4201. MGM Records, 1350 Avenue of the Americas, New York, N.Y. 10019.

Greensleeves. Sung by Susan Reed. No. 116. Elektra Records, 1855 Broadway, New York, N.Y. 10023.

I Like Jazz. LP 36081. Columbia Records, 51 West 52nd Street, New York, N.Y. 10019.

John Cage: Aria with Fontana Mix. No. 58003. Time Records, 1290 Avenue of the Americas, New York, N.Y. 10019.

"La Cumparsita," *In the Latin Flavor.* Arthur Fiedler and the Boston Pops Orchestra. Victor LM 2041. Radio Corporation of America, Record Division, 155 East 24th Street, New York, N.Y. 10010.

"Mack the Knife" (Moritat). *Kurt Weill in Berlin.* Angel Stereo S 35727. Angel Records, Capitol Records, Inc., 1750 North Vine, Hollywood, Calif. 90028.

"Travelin' Light." *Lady Sings the Blues.* Billie Holiday. Verve 8099. MGM Records, 1350 Avenue of the Americas, New York, N.Y. 10019.

West Side Story. OS 2001. Columbia Record Club, 51 West 52nd Street, New York, N.Y. 10019.

P O E M S

AUDEN, W. H. "The Shield of Achilles." *The Shield of Achilles.* New York: Random House, 1955.

BROOKS, GWENDOLYN. "We Real Cool." *Selected Poems.* New York: Harper & Row, 1961.

FROST, ROBERT. "A Brook in a City." "The Road Not Taken." *Complete Poems of Robert Frost.* New York: Holt, Rinehart & Winston, 1958.

FEARING, KENNETH. "Dirge: 1-2-3." In *American Poetry.* Ed. by Karl Shapiro. New York: T. Y. Crowell, 1960.

GIDLOW, ELSA. "Twentieth Century Songs." In Charles W. Cooper, *Preface to Poetry.* New York: Harcourt, Brace & World, 1946.

LEWIS, C. DAY. "The Room." In *Poet's Choice.* Ed. by Paul Engle and Joseph Langland. New York: Dell, 1966.

MILLAY, EDNA ST. VINCENT. "Bluebeard." *Collected Poems: Edna St. Vincent Millay.* New York: Harper & Row, 1956.

POE, EDGAR ALLAN. "The Raven." In *100 Story Poems.* Ed. by Elinor Parker. New York: T. Y. Crowell, 1951.

Rubáiyát of Omar Khayyám. Ed. by Edward Fitzgerald. Cranbury, N.J.: A. S. Barnes, 1965.

SANDBURG, CARL. *The People, Yes.* In *The Complete Poems.* New York: Harcourt, Brace & World, 1950.

TAGGARD, GENEVIEVE. "Hawaiian Hilltop." In *Poems for a Machine Age.* Ed. by Horace J. McNeil. New York: McGraw-Hill, 1941.

D R A M A

GIBSON, WILLIAM. *The Miracle Worker.* New York: Knopf, 1957.

HANSBERRY, LORRAINE. *A Raisin in the Sun.* New York: Random House, 1959.

HELLMAN, LILLIAN. *The Little Foxes.* In *Six Modern American Plays.* Ed. by Allen G. Halline. New York: Modern Library, 1951.

IONESCO, EUGENE. *Rhinoceros.* New York: Holt, Rinehart & Winston, 1961.

MILLER, ARTHUR. *The Death of a Salesman.* New York: Viking, 1949.

PATRICK, JOHN. *Teahouse of the August Moon.* New York: Putnam, 1954.

N O V E L

BRADBURY, RAY. *Fahrenheit 451.* New York: Simon & Schuster, 1967.

ORWELL, GEORGE. *1984.* New York: New American Library, 1954.

S H O R T   S T O R I E S

BENÉT, STEPHEN VINCENT. "By the Waters of Babylon." In *People in Literature.* Ed. by Luella B. Cook *et al.* New York: Harcourt, Brace & World, 1957.

CLARK, WALTER VAN TILBURG. "The Portable Phonograph." In *People in Literature.* Ed. by Luella B. Cook *et al.* New York: Harcourt, Brace & World, 1957.

FORSTER, E. M. "The Machine Stops." In *Modern Short Stories.* Ed. by Leonard S. Brown. New York: Harcourt, Brace & World, 1937.

F I L M S

A Raisin in the Sun. Audio Film Center, 10 Fiske Avenue, Mount Vernon, N.Y. 10550.

Chartres Cathedral. Encyclopaedia Britannica Films, 5625 Hollywood Boulevard, Hollywood, Calif. 90028.

Donald Duck in Mathemagic Land. Walt Disney Productions, 2400 West Alameda, Burbank, Calif. 91506.

Free Fall. Contemporary Films, 267 West 25th Street, New York, N.Y. 10001.

The Humanities: What They Are and What They Do. Encyclopaedia Britannica Films, 5625 Hollywood Boulevard, Hollywood, Calif. 90028.

The Loneliness of the Long-Distance Runner. Continental 16, Distributors, 241 East 34th Street, New York, N.Y. 10016.

Lonely Boy. New York University Film Library, Washington Square, New York, N.Y. 10003.

On the Waterfront. Audio Film Center, 405 Clement, San Francisco, Calif. 94118.

Rebel Without a Cause. Seven Arts Films, 200 Park Avenue, New York, N.Y. 10017.

Very Nice, Very Nice. Contemporary Films, 267 West 25th Street, New York, N.Y. 10001.

THIRTEEN

DISCOVERY
OF VALUES

Excellent performance is a blend of talent and motive, of ability fused with zeal. Aptitude without aspiration is lifeless and inert.

And that is only part of the story. When ability is brought to life by aspiration, there is the further question of the ends to which these gifts are applied. We do not wish to nurture the man of great talent and evil purpose. Not only does high performance take place in a context of values and purpose but if it is to be worth fostering, the values and purpose must be worthy of our allegiance.

THE PURSUIT OF EXCELLENCE [1]

PERSPECTIVE

All life is a search for meaning, a continuing struggle to impose reason and order on the fragmented moments of experience. The wisdom of the choices made determines to what degree the search will be satisfying and the striving productive. Edgar Lee Masters uses a boat with a furled sail, at rest in a harbor, to symbolize the life of one who, through fear of disillusionment, refused to grapple with the challenge of the unpredictable. George Gray, the subject of Masters' portrait, realizes too late that if life is to have meaning, one must

> . . . lift the sail
> And catch the winds of destiny
> Wherever they drive the boat.
> To put meaning in one's life may end in madness,
> But life without meaning is the torture
> Of restlessness and vague desire—
> It is a boat longing for the sea and yet afraid.[2]

---

[1] Rockefeller Brothers Fund, Inc., *The Pursuit of Excellence: Education and the Future of America* (Garden City, N.Y.: Doubleday, 1958), p. 45.
[2] Edgar Lee Masters, *Spoon River Anthology* (New York: Macmillan, 1931), p. 65.

At the opposite extreme, Masters presents a woman whose lifted sails caught the winds of destiny—a woman who for over ninety years reached out to life with understanding and purpose. Lucinda Matlock accepted the eternal tension between the forces that sustain life and those that destroy as the price one pays for being human. Decrying flabbiness and discontent, she leaves as her legacy a statement epitomizing her faith and courage: "It takes life to love Life." [3]

Little more than half a century separates us from the world Lucinda Matlock knew. During that short time technological advancement has had an impact on our culture that could scarcely have been envisioned fifty years ago. Changes have been great, and there is no reason to believe that change will not continue. One thing, however, remains constant—man's deep-seated struggle to develop values that will guide him toward self-realization. In a "Seminar of Basic Ideas" concerning the purposes of education, Viktor Frankel of the medical faculty of the University of Vienna selects man's search for meaning as the truest expression of the state of being human. He suggests that each individual, although he may begin by questioning life, must eventually realize that "it is he who is being questioned—questioned by life. It is he who has to answer—by answering life." He commends the wisdom contained in Nietzsche's words "He who knows a Why of living surmounts almost every How" as an appropriate motto for all education. [4]

What the student accepts as the whys of living serves as the foundation for his values, which, in turn, determine the choices he will make. Making intelligent choices involves almost everything of importance in the education of young people in a free society, for decision-making implies not only the ability to select wisely among many competing interests but also acceptance of personal responsibility for the choices made. In any time or place, adherence to one's code, with its inevitable conflicts, requires conviction and stamina. The youth of Lucinda Matlock's generation were at least spared the confusion of trying to determine what their culture prized. In the relatively stable life of that day, there seems to have been fairly general agreement as to what was worthwhile. In contrast, young people in contemporary America are confronted by a bewildering array of conflicting values, each sanctioned by various segments of society. "The principal causes of our adolescents' difficulty," Margaret Mead concludes, after contrasting our young people with Samoan youth and their serene way of life, "are the presence of conflicting standards and the belief that every individual should make his or her own choice." [5] If we agree with her we must conclude that our schools should grant more attention to the considerations underlying wise decisions and to the significance of choice as the inevitable consequence of freedom.

In our culture, with its ever accelerating change, the role of the English teacher in helping students develop values has become more difficult than in

---

[3] *Ibid.*, p. 229.
[4] *Saturday Review*, Vol. 41, No. 37 (September 13, 1958), p. 20.
[5] Margaret Mead, *Coming of Age in Samoa* (New York: New American Library, 1949), p. 154.

the past but basically has remained unchanged. For those of us who teach language and literature, the decision to deal with values is by no means a new urgency.[6] Our subject matter has always led us to a concern with both the ethical and the esthetic aspects of life. Literature cannot be taught apart from the morality of humanity; speaking and writing unrelated to truth can become twisted and debased, a threat to the very basis of communication. Nor is it a mere quirk of legalistic minds that perjury is so seriously regarded in the courts. The need for sincerity and integrity in everyday use of language, the power of literature to illuminate choices among values—we have always accepted these as basic in the teaching of English. Cultural change has only made more apparent the importance of the liberal arts.

In the pressures resulting from society's concern with the need for helping youth acquire values, we must maintain our balance. Literature, unlike propaganda, is not intended to secure immediate, practical results. It is not a poultice to be applied to weaknesses in moral perception. Between *Macbeth* and *Mein Kampf* a difference exists, and that difference is immense. The precarious harmony of any work of art is a balanced structure of innumerable tensions, qualities, and relationships. To view literature as a formula for moral action is to mistake its nature and to miss its rewards. However, because it can enlarge our awareness of values and refine our discrimination among values, literature is a force of tremendous potential for education. Literature can disclose for the reader wider and deeper perceptions and organizations of experience. Literature can lift the reader above the petty and narrow concerns that consume his time. No one who has appreciated a play by Shakespeare or a poem by Li Po is left unchanged. To whatever extent a good life is dependent upon discrimination among the values in experience, literature can contribute to the liberal education our civilization seeks for as many human beings as possible.

The point of view throughout this book has been directed toward the discovery of values. The over-all aim has been to suggest ways to help the pupil build a solid core of integrity that will resist attrition in the pressures of everyday existence. Implicit in the underlying philosophy is the belief that "comfort" is unsatisfying as a final goal, that the zest of living comes from the struggle— the pursuit of values the individual considers worth while. Therefore, the ideals our students choose are important, for without durable values the learner will always fall short of true power with language and literature. But on one point there must be no doubt: we cannot teach values, although students learn them in our classrooms. They learn them from our attitudes and actions, which derive from our own beliefs about what shall receive priority in our teaching. They learn them through experiences planned with the long-range aim of stimulating

[6] For a discussion of the relation of literature to moral attitudes, the authors recommend Louise M. Rosenblatt, *Literature as Exploration*, Revised edition (New York: Noble and Noble, 1968). For a discussion of the role of the English teacher in a changing society, see Committee on National Interest, *The National Interest and the Teaching of English* (Champaign, Ill.: NCTE, 1961).

and guiding individuals in self-discipline and in self-development. Hence the emphasis throughout this book on the necessity for helping the student set standards for achievement and for behavior, for making self-evaluation an integral part of learning, for developing understanding of the resources of literature and the power of language—both of which lead to the discovery of values.

Although for the purpose of emphasis, two aspects of personal values—the ethical and the esthetic—are discussed separately in this chapter, in reality they are inextricably fused. Moral and esthetic values have an identical foundation; the good and the beautiful, traced to their ultimate considerations, dissolve into a single principle—the law of harmony. Vicious and destructive behavior may be viewed as discord and productive living as harmony. In *Spoon River Anthology*, George Gray's withdrawal from life strikes a discord because it destroys his human potential; Lucinda Matlock's acceptance of all that life offers creates a harmony that makes living an adventure. We are concerned here with choices wise men and women make in their search for harmonious lives.

Understandings Concerning Values

A value represents the essence of experiences the race has found to be worth while. Over the centuries, man, guided by the forces of instinct and intelligence, has moved toward the humanitarian ideal. The student, in the disciplined forms of literature, discovers the same forces at work; here, he finds bared the restless, searching human spirit. The literary artist, highlighting now one aspect of experience and now another, is concerned with the mystery of man. Cries Stephen Dedalus in pledging himself to art: "Welcome, O life! I go to encounter for the millionth time the reality of experience and to forge in the smithy of my soul the uncreated conscience of my race." [7] Literature, embracing as it does the accumulated conscience of the race, provides a medium that allows the student to grapple on his own level with the ideas and values that have guided man in his long struggle from the cave toward the light.

Whether or not a teacher should help any particular group formulate principles concerned with values must remain at the discretion of that teacher. Certainly he will not do so unless the concepts can be arrived at inductively, until he has helped students examine motivation for behavior in many concrete situations, and until he has helped them probe their thinking concerning some of the beliefs they think they hold. All this presupposes a mature class. It presupposes students who have formed opinions of the worth of many ideals, who have discovered some of the difficulties in determining the basis for beliefs and in making those beliefs function in action. Granted these con-

[7] James Joyce, *Portrait of the Artist as a Young Man* (New York: Modern Library, 1928), p. 299.

ditions, two understandings may help students become more realistic in assessing problems concerned with values: values are guides, not prescriptions, for conduct; values are a balance of rational thought and controlled emotion.

VALUES AS GUIDES

A value merely points the way, directs the course. Although we have the experience of humanity to guide us, we have no chart that all may follow. We can see similarities among the ideals chosen by men and women of both fact and fiction in building harmonious lives. But each individual must choose his own ideals, for it is to his own life that he must give meaning.

PRINCIPLES GUIDE ACTION   Students can more readily comprehend the function of a guiding principle if they see it impersonally in historical perspective. An example, of which they are at least dimly aware, is the manner in which through the years the United States has tried to implement the belief, first stated in 1776, that "all men are endowed by their Creator with certain inalienable rights." Recalling with a class some of the steps we as a nation have taken to insure any one of our personal rights will help young people appreciate how a value acts as a guide toward any goal.

> In the classroom the necessity for redefinition of values has been highlighted by means of a discussion on the right to vote, initiated by citing the case of Susan B. Anthony, who was arrested for voting in the presidential election of 1872.
> The Fourteenth Amendment (1868) stated, "All persons born or naturalized in the United States and subject to the jurisdiction thereof are citizens. . . ." The Fifteenth Amendment (1870) stated, "The right of the citizens of the United States to vote shall not be denied or abridged . . . on account of race, color, or previous condition of servitude." On what grounds could Miss Anthony be tried, found guilty, and fined one hundred dollars (a fine that was never paid)?
> Call attention to the fact that *men* of the Declaration of Independence has been translated to *persons* in the amendments. What meaning did Miss Anthony give to these two words? What did those who arrested her think they meant?
> Not until 1920, when the Nineteenth Amendment gave women the right to vote, was Miss Anthony's interpretation of these words accepted.
> The last decades have witnessed the continuation of this struggle as minority groups have sought and gained specific confirmation of their legal rights. But having one's legal rights reaffirmed is not enough. Legalism must lead to the attainment of social and economic rights. Society's efforts are now being directed toward that end.

Critics of our culture say, with truth, that in the United States discrimination against individuals and groups has always existed. But when they cite examples as being indicative of the failure of democracy, they are confusing democratic ideals with the democratic process, which is often prolonged and cumbersome. The evolution of our rights, based on belief in the worth of the individual, has been slow; gradually the definition of these rights has become more precise as official documents have defined what enables men to maintain their dignity. Those who blame democracy for tolerating discrimination fail to recognize the gap that always exists between ideals and attainment. Margaret Mead in answer to one such critic stresses the need of "recognizing that in the tension between ideals and practice which must fall behind those ideals, lies the dynamic of American democracy—that the whole point of hitching one's wagon to a star lies in the tension on the rope." [8]

VALUES PROVIDE DIRECTION   The tension on the rope serves as well for the individual as it does for the nation. Belief in a certain value will pull him in the direction he thinks will help him attain it; the more firmly rooted the belief, the more forceful the pull and the greater his chance of approaching his ideal. But it is approximation only, never complete realization. Those who profess faith in the perfectibility of man speak in relative terms—they believe that inherent in man is the urge and the capacity for moving toward perfection. The student should understand that it is the pursuit of worthwhile values, not their perfect attainment, that will characterize his efforts; that intermediate successes keep him on the right road but that the ultimate goal will always lie ahead. For, as Alfred North Whitehead says, "When ideals have sunk to the level of practice, the result is stagnation." [9]

Understanding the progress his nation has made toward the ideal first stated nearly two centuries ago helps the student realize that a value acts as a guide, not as a prescription, for conduct; it makes him aware of the relationships ideals bear to practice; it helps him see values as flexible in operation, continually tested in specific situations, constantly reassessed and redefined in the light of greater knowledge and widening experience. As with a people, so with the individual: his values are guides providing direction but giving no formula for conduct. Each person must determine for himself what behavior at any particular time is consistent with the belief he professes, what line of action will help him approximate his goals.

> What constitutes kindness in any particular instance? To allow a friend to copy from one's paper in a test? To allow a friend to use one's name in obtaining parental permission to remain out later than usual when one is not involved in the situation? Was Jerry in "The Snake Dance" being kind, as he thought, in deceiving his parents?
>
> What constitutes loyalty to friend or duty? Does loyalty to Tom Brown, a member of my club demand I vote for him in the school election, even though I think his opponent better qualified for the job? Has Javert in *Les Misérables* become so emotionally involved in his sense of duty to his job that his pursuit of Jean Valjean has become an obsession?

[8] Margaret Mead, *New Lives for Old* (New York: Morrow, 1956), p. 158.
[9] Alfred North Whitehead, *The Aims of Education* (New York: New American Library, 1949), p. 40.

VALUES AS A BALANCE OF THOUGHT AND EMOTION

Personal values are the result of an individual's reflective experience, in both its intellectual and its emotional aspects. Both elements—they are rarely separable—must correspond to the reality to which they refer. That is, if there is no thinking or only confused thinking, if there is too little or too much emotion, a value lacks the force needed to make it a guide for action. Thus, we try not only to determine a reason for the importance of any ideal we hold but also to become alert to the complexities of its application as a guide to behavior. We try to develop discrimination in our emotional involvement with any value.

A perfect balance of rational thought and controlled emotion is impossible to maintain; its approximation is a mark of maturity. In trying to achieve equilibrium, everyone has difficulty. Understanding the ways thought and emotion operate in developing values will prepare the student for some of the complexities involved in making important choices.

WHEN EMOTION RULES   The first sense of values is acquired in an emotionally toned, either-or world; the child is taught by verbal commands and exhortations to conform to the demands of his immediate environment. His world is small, his choices limited. Reactions of adults quickly inform him that one type of conduct wins approval, its opposite disapproval. His conflicts arise not in determining the right course of action but in summoning volition to obey the dictates of the person he wishes to please. Failure brings discomfort, even a sense of guilt. When he begins to reason, to ask why, he is met with either circular reasoning ("That's the way nice little boys act," "We want you to grow up to be a good man") or appeals to external pressures ("When you go to school, you'll have to behave," "No one will want to play with you if you're going to lose your temper"). Thus, first values, never the product of reasoning, carry an emotional load, vestiges of which remain throughout life.

Such an orientation makes it difficult to eradicate the idea that all choices are between the good and the bad, each easily identifiable. Gradually one learns that each situation may present its own problem; that values are sometimes in conflict; that many choices are concerned with several "goods," each desirable in its own right, or with several "evils," making a completely satisfactory course of action impossible. Individual progress toward belief in and understanding of a multi-valued world is slow and painful.

The child, learning rules of conduct by rote, accepts the words without the necessary experiential basis to give the language meaning; consequently, the abstract statement becomes for him the reality. The formula, embedded in his emotions, admits of no question until further experience subjects the value to the searchlight of reason, reinforcing, modifying, or negating it. For example, as the child's world enlarges, he may notice that others win popularity by methods he has been taught are unacceptable. Then his conflicts begin as he tries to square teaching with practice. What adolescent, unless he has been wisely and continually guided in examining the basis for his values, has not at times been shocked to discover that a principle he has long accepted as valid—and which of course may well be—has no roots in his thinking, only in his emotions?

After viewing such a film as *Right or Wrong*, or reading such a story as "Bill's Little Girl," students may be asked to write on a topic similar to the following: Tell of a decision you were forced to make between two courses of action which seemed either almost equally desirable or almost equally distasteful; what was the compelling factor leading you to decide as you did?

WHEN INTELLECT RULES   As adults we sometimes encounter the problem in reverse. Our first contact with statements of democratic values probably occurs in the elementary school when we memorize portions of the Declaration of Independence. "All men are created equal . . . ." Each time we hear the words we may respond to the moving language; we may even experience a vague feeling of pride in the nobility of our political heritage. Almost automatically we have accepted the values as our own, but rarely do we think of them in reference to our own conduct. When we are first conscious of meeting the test in action, we may discover we have fooled ourselves. What we have is not a value but an intellectualized concept that lacks the emotional involvement needed to give it vitality.

Admittedly, stating a value may be verbalization only—that is, it may lack either the reasoned acceptance or the emotional involvement sufficient to commit one to action; it may lack both. Must we then conclude that because verbalisms sometimes betray us, students should never be helped to formulate the principles underlying a series of experiences planned to stress certain values? Certainly not. Understanding the relationship between the concrete and the abstract is as desirable in studying values as in developing concepts in science. We must, however, lead students to see that the formulation of a personal code is important only if it influences conduct. We cannot doubt that our national ideals have had such influence. Nor can we doubt that our privileges as individuals would have been curtailed if more autocratic principles had been selected to guide the nation. Admittedly, the expressed ideals are not incorporated into the behavior of every citizen. However, their acceptance in individual thinking means they are part of the nation's thinking; their violation nags at the nation's conscience. The danger lies not in putting our beliefs about values into words but in deceiving ourselves by thinking that the language and the values are synonymous.

The Slave with Two Faces illustrates how the verbalization of a value may be accepted as the reality. This symbolic play contrasts the attitudes of two girls toward life. The firm belief that a person should show no fear guides the conduct of one girl. Her companion, verbally accepting what the other has "taught" her, discovers that the ideal lacks the necessary roots in her thinking and in her emotions to serve as a guide for action when the test comes.

Continued and varied approaches are necessary in the consideration of ethical values; but fundamental to the effectiveness of both content and method is the maintenance of a climate encouraging growth. Admittedly, the search for standards to give meaning to life is an important part of the education of the adolescent, but the school is only one factor in his environment and experiences in the English classroom only one aspect of the school. The educational problem is at heart the problem of helping young people select from their culture all constructive values, all striving for wholeness, and of helping them subdue or convert the tendencies that are destructive, negative, wasteful, and smugly complacent. The learning experiences within the English classroom may be placed in the balance that is tending toward this aim. The clear-sightedness and the integrity of the teacher will be the significant factor in this dynamics of forces. Not always will the teacher succeed, but success comes often enough to justify the effort.

Ethical Values

To deal with moral concepts and values requires tact and wisdom. Does it need to be said that a heavy-handed frontal attack does more harm than good? That literature converted into a group of homilies to illustrate goodness loses its power as literature? We assume wiser readers than this. We also assume readers who realize that literature cannot be sharply separated from consideration of ethics any more than it can be divorced from an awareness of beauty. We assume readers who know that both written and oral communication reflect the man himself and that "no amount of practice in composition courses will draw anything but a cheap style out of a cheap person." [10]

We need no prescriptive maxims in our study of values in the classroom. All we need is awareness of the experience of the human race. Any belief that man is manipulated solely by his environment or by a blind fate contradicts the inner consciousness of the healthy segments of humanity. Any mode of thought that reduces man to the status either of a machine or of an animal, any mode of conduct that uses man as a means to an end, is an affront to his essential dignity. The literature we teach offers numerous studies of harmony— Cather's Neighbor Rosicky, Eliot's Dolly Winthrop, Dickens' Joe Gargery— and discord—Macbeth and his wife, Huck Finn's father, Madame Defarge. Literature gives an illumination to the study of values, which prescriptive maxims lack. So too do the methods we use to teach literature and the ways we devise to help students gain power over language.

A student may gain some of his most valuable insights into the meaning of "respect for the individual" through six years practice in the form, not necessarily the content, of discussion. Here as teacher and pupils practice the courtesies of disagreement, the student can acquire the attitude of welcoming opposition to his own ideas, a sense of responsibility for expressing minority

[10] Howard Mumford Jones, *American Humanism* (New York: Harper & Row, 1957), p. 91.

opinions, a realization that he can preserve his integrity while at the same time maintaining respect for the person whose values he cannot accept.

After students have had some experience with discussion techniques, a teacher may stimulate thinking by giving out copies of questions, for reflection only:

> Has opposition to one of your pet ideas ever given you fresh insights that caused you to modify your opinions?
>
> Is there anyone you know whose values differ greatly from your own but who, nevertheless, commands your respect?
>
> Can you remember any time when your integrity forced you to voice an objection or to support an opinion although it would have been safer and more pleasant to keep still?

Occasions when students may be allowed some choice occur often in our classrooms. Through a sequence of experiences similar to the following, students, practicing decision-making over a six-year period, can assimilate the ideas that freedom has limitations, that it carries its own responsibility, that a degree of freedom is possible for all only when controversial issues are settled in disciplined ways:

> Recently, a student teacher of thirty-five eighth-graders helped them plan a mural that was to culminate a unit on poetry. From the preparatory work for the mural to its completion, the principle of choice operated. These young people were being involved in consideration of ethical and esthetic values without, of course, being burdened with the distinction—without, in fact, hearing *value* mentioned.
>
> Early in the planning they saw that choice has practical limitations, that the size of a mural is dictated by the spaces available; that, in turn, size and placement bear a relationship to the number and the size of the illustrations. They preserved their right of dissent while they saw personal choices subjected to the will of the majority, as poems and symbols sponsored by different individuals were eliminated.
>
> They considered esthetic values as they decided what effect the color of the walls would have on the color scheme chosen for the mural, as they evaluated rough over-all sketches submitted by volunteers, as they weighed the significance of symbols to choose the one best expressing the literary experience, and as they reluctantly eliminated poems whose essence would be distorted by visual representation.
>
> Finally, they considered ethical problems as the teacher helped them choose the type of contribution each could make. Patiently, with skillful questions on the day of final choice, the teacher led the class to see the difficulties and requirements of each type of work—abilities needed, probable amount of time demanded, necessity for working as an individual or as one of a group, the inevitable deadlines. Wisely, she postponed decisions to give students time to determine what they had to offer and how much time they were willing to give. Setting the class to work, she provided time for conferences with those asking for guidance. The choice was important to all, for it was personal and irrevocable; each student realized his obligation to complete the work he chose as his contribution.

To understand both what we can and what we cannot expect to do with our students, we need to consider how young people discover values. Many elements in one's background and environment assume significance—home, friends, church, school, community, all aspects of the culture of which one is a part. Influences in one area may fortify or nullify those in another. Thus classroom experiences must, if they are to have any effect, generate cumulative force over the six secondary-school years. Commendable traits cannot be implanted directly in another person; personal values are built slowly over a long period of time out of the totality of individual experience.

Our purpose is to teach students the considerations involved in making wise choices, not to teach them the choices that must be made. Translated into terms for the classroom, our purpose is to give students continued experience in appraising the effect of different beliefs on conduct and the influence of habitual conduct on the destiny an individual creates for himself. Our purpose, if understandings are to bear fruit in behavior, is to place the student as often as possible in situations where he is allowed to make his own decisions and where he must assume responsibility for the choices he makes. Such a program throughout the six secondary-school years, although it cannot insure volition, does provide the necessary practice and understandings. It takes much traveling in "goodly states and kingdoms" to discover for oneself even a few of the whys of living.

SELECTING VALUES FOR EMPHASIS

If we keep in mind just what we can do in helping students discover values, we may be less reluctant to come to grips with the problem in the classroom. We realize that the emphasis on free choice within the American culture militates against imposing, even if we would or could, any particular values; we realize too that the condition of freedom itself offers the most compelling argument for education for choice. Yet even in our society, which encourages wide deviation in thought, we find a certain community of belief and, especially, widespread approval of the values inherent in democratic practices. During recent years we have seen several important statements of values that might be emphasized during twelve years of public schooling:

> Humanist values in American culture: knowledge, creativity, experimentation, man as the measure of things, the intelligent ordering of life as based on knowledge, sense of responsibility to self and others, living as an essentially cooperative venture.[11]

> American ideals: human rights and freedoms, equality of opportunity, social responsibility, and discipline.[12]

[11] H. Otto Dahlke, *Values in Culture and Classroom* (New York: Harper & Row, 1958), p. 66.

[12] James C. Stone, "A Curriculum for American Ideals," unpublished doctoral dissertation, 1949, a contribution to the American Ideals Project of Stanford University, Palo Alto, Calif.

Moral and spiritual values in the public schools: human personality, moral responsibility, institutions as the servants of man, common consent, devotion to truth, respect for excellence, moral equality, brotherhood, the pursuit of happiness, spiritual enrichment.[13]

The above statements have much in common; they illustrate the extent of agreement possible in our society. On the other hand, we have available a growing body of literature demonstrating that such ideals are only imperfectly communicated in many schools.[14] Statements dealing with the dislocation of educational programs, including pedagogical summaries like Fantini's and Weinstein's or personal observations like Kozol's, will help teachers better relate the general values to the social and ethical imperatives of their pupils in changing urban schools. All such statements, whether designating goals desired for all or calling attention to the fact that the approach to these goals is inadequately implemented, give direction but are too general for specific application to the classroom. That they are stated in general terms merely underlines the necessity for each school to translate them into specifics applicable to its own pupils.

How can such broadly stated ideals be used as guides for learning experiences? Ideally, the teaching staff in each school should determine the focus for instruction in terms of students' needs. In one school where many members of different racial and cultural backgrounds enter the seventh grade, *North Fork*, a novel by Doris Gates in which a boy finds himself a member of a minority group in an American Indian community, is read by all students. Indian-Caucasian relations present no problem in this particular school; thus, the study of such a work provides a not too specific but yet pertinent experience designed to increase understandings among those of divergent backgrounds. *North Fork* is for pupils of this age a good literary experience. Moreover, the issues and concepts implicit in the novel point up and reinforce basic values needed at this time by these seventh-graders. Thus, as pupils consider the difficulties likely to be encountered by minorities in any group, the broadly stated ideal "respect for the individual" is translated into concrete terms of particular cogency.

In school situations where racial conflicts are pervasive, some teachers are able to foster greater understanding by encouraging students to read and discuss appropriate titles dealing specifically with the search for justice and for group identity—*Take a Giant Step, Manchild in the Promised Land, To Kill a Mockingbird.* How direct the approach can be in discussing conflicts in which whole communities are emotionally involved will depend upon the maturity of the pupils and upon personal relationships within the school. Each school can select content that, while fostering insights necessary for its students at par-

---

[13] Developed by the Educational Policies Commission of the National Education Association, Washington, D.C. (1951).

[14] Mario D. Fantini and Gerald Weinstein, *The Disadvantaged: Challenge to Education* (New York: Harper & Row, 1968), and Jonathan Kozol, *Death at an Early Age* (New York: Houghton Mifflin, 1967).

ticular times, will still provide a well-rounded experience with literature and communication.

INFLUENCE OF THE CURRICULUM   However, too much must not be expected from the teaching of a single book or a single unit. Selection of content for such a specific purpose would represent only one phase of instruction and in no sense should such emphasis dominate the curriculum. The way in which values are discovered and the multitude of choices offered in our culture preclude such restriction.

Teachers of English desiring to develop a systematic approach to encourage the discovery of values might first choose broad areas for emphasis, then be alert for ways to permit the recognition and appreciation of values to take their appropriate place within the context of literature and communication. A systematic approach will assist the teacher in choosing content. The values needed by students might well be the determining reason for selecting *Great Expectations* instead of *Wuthering Heights,* or for directing written expression to an honest exploration of the difficulties involved in avoiding self-deception or in practicing disciplined ways of settling difficulties. Students themselves provide a guide by their concern with significant values involved in the problems they select to investigate. Both the content and the way instruction is organized contribute to the climate of the classroom and provide the setting for the discovery of values through the study of language and literature.

INFLUENCE OF THE TEACHER   The design of any curriculum represents only a few choices among the multiplicity offered; so too does that of any course within that curriculum. Both present guidelines toward goals the planners think desirable; both direct attention to the general needs of adolescents. Within each classroom, however, the teacher is the motivating force; daily he makes his own choices with particular students in mind. Through his selection of content and method, he emphasizes values. He does so as he reveals his own values in actions reflecting his conviction—or lack of it—about the importance of using language honestly and recognizing the worth of literature in helping man endure and prevail.

FOCUSING ON VALUES

In providing learning experiences, the content selected by the teacher and the methods used will influence the effectiveness of attempts to help students discover values.

THE COMPARATIVE APPROACH   Teaching two or more selections having parallel themes or points of view often proves an effective way for later discussion of ethical values. For instance, "The Bishop's Candlesticks" by Victor Hugo and "The Rat Trap" by Selma Lagerlöf deal with the redeeming influence of true charity. In the French story, Jean Valjean is influenced by a priest who believes in the moral worth of each individual; in the Swedish story, a tramp is reformed by a girl who treats him as a human being.

Each story is considered on its own merits, the students being led to recognize its ethical and esthetic elements. After each has been taught, the comparable themes are noted. Perhaps after teaching several selections, the teacher asks, "Do you see anything in common between any of these stories?" It is from such questions that the focus on the value—in the case of the two stories cited above, the significance of love in helping a person maintain human dignity—can be established.

SELECTIONS WITH PARALLEL THEMES

family cohesiveness	*The Happy Journey to Trenton and Camden,* Thornton Wilder "The Car," Dorothy Thomas "The Ten-Dollar Bill," Richard T. Gill
unselfish courage	"Granny," André Birabeau "When Hanna Var Eight Yar Old," Katherine Peabody Girling
need for love and affection	"Yours Lovingly," Eugene Courtright "Not Wanted," Jesse Lynch Williams "A Mother in Mannville," Marjorie Kinnan Rawlings
scapegoating and human dignity	"The Horse," Marian Hurd McNeely "The New Kid," Murray Heyert "Prelude," Albert Halper "The Lottery," Shirley Jackson
response to good will	"The Kiskis," May Vontver "The High Hill," Mary Deasy
integrity	"Glory in Bridgeville," William Wise "Most Valuable Player," D. Tracey

Teaching by organizing experiences around topics or themes is only an extension of teaching by parallels.[15] The same challenge to discern similarities and relationships among selections is present. During each school year a few units of instruction, featuring the particular emphasis desired, may be shaped rather directly toward a concern with ethical values. The illustrative unit "Meeting a Crisis" uses in part this approach.

USING THE CLASSICS   When a teacher is dealing with one of the classics, attention to moral values falls into place among consideration of the many other important facets of the literary work. *Macbeth, A Tale of Two Cities, John Brown's Body*—each exhibits a rich composition of many elements. There is always the danger of emphasizing one aspect to the detriment of the others;

---

[15] See page 448 for discussion of this method of organization.

there is likewise the danger of examining parts at such length that the unity of the whole breaks down. As a great philosopher has pointed out,

> Every poem is meant to be read within certain limits of time. The contrasts, and the images, and the transition of moods must correspond with the sway of rhythms in the human spirit. These have their periods, which refuse to be stretched beyond certain limits. You may take the noblest poetry in the world, and, if you stumble through it at a snail's pace, it collapses from a work of art into a rubbish heap.[16]

Whitehead's comment concerning poetry is equally applicable to any literary work; the teacher aims first to help students see it as a whole; he avoids overemphasis on either the ethical or the esthetic values, trusting that later consideration of both will clarify and intensify first impressions.

However, when the first reading has been completed, the classic may be examined from various points of emphasis; one may well be concerned with the ethical values implicit in its context. Both fiction and drama offer note-worthy examples not only of characters who have values in accord with the ultimate order of the universe—Captain Dobbin, Joe Gargery, Cordelia—but also of those whose lack of unity and harmony creates imbalance in their lives —Becky Sharp, Miss Havisham, Goneril and Regan. Within the limits of literature it is possible to study values as they are being developed over a period of time; to see what happens when persons, each governed by fully integrated but conflicting values, impinge upon each other; to understand how a person of soundness and integrity, or one twisted and debased, can influence some lives greatly but have no apparent effect on others: these are all signifi-cant ideas for students. Moreover, since the author through his characters presents various philosophies, many literary works permit the selection of key statements expressing ideas pertinent to life; students can be helped to apply these to their own experience.[17] Thus, the complex texture and rich scope of great literary works, if they are wisely selected for the right students at the right time, have an unparalleled force and vitality in their impact.

USING BIOGRAPHY   For stressing the universal need for a personal code, biography is excellent. The idealism of many adolescents leads them to ad-mire excellence whatever its source. Through study of our own leaders of the past and present, students can become aware of the premium our heritage has always placed on moral values. Enlarging that study to include the lives of men and women of integrity who represent diverse origins and cultures will strengthen the belief that no nation, race, or creed has a monopoly on high courage and spiritual stamina. Noble men of all countries, whether Juárez of Mexico, Gandhi of India, or Nansen of Norway, exemplify the desirable qualities all human beings share. Admirable men of various faiths, whether Schweitzer, Damien, or Tenzing, command respect. Particularly important is the inclusion of respected Americans from various ethnic groups—Malcolm X,

---

[16] Whitehead, *op. cit.*, p. 79.
[17] See "Applying the Ideas," page 408.

John F. Kennedy, Richard Wright, J. Robert Oppenheimer. Stories of the lives of real people have for some pupils at certain times a greater impact than do stories of imaginary characters; for all students, biography is a necessary complement to fiction. Especially is this true in focusing on moral values that flourish regardless of boundary lines.

USING GUIDED READING   Experiences planned in connection with the guided reading program offer opportunities for consideration of problems concerning values.[18] In organizing topics for discussion for readers of many diverse works, teachers can sometimes select rather restrictive questions that will channel attention toward the decisions and judgments that are made. Any question similar to the following offers an appropriate guide for groups of five or six students who have read different titles:

> Select one situation in your book in which a character must make a decision that will affect someone else. How does he act? To what extent does the knowledge that others will be affected influence his decision?
>
> Find an incident in your book in which a person either fails to live up to one of his ideals or fears that he will fail. How does he respond in this situation? Why?
>
> How many examples can be found where a character is confronted by a situation in which two rights are in conflict, making a completely satisfactory solution to a dilemma impossible?

Discussions of this type can lead groups to explore and appraise many different kinds of behavior and the similar and contrasting values that motivate each.

USING PROBLEM SITUATIONS   By presenting problem situations and by encouraging students to make appropriate decisions, teachers can approximate the conditions under which individuals learn through making actual choices. Reactions to such situations can touch adolescents deeply only if problems seem real and responses honest and valid. Such questions as the following are not easily answered:

> If a group project breaks down, what is my personal responsibility? Should I do more than my share even if another shirks?
>
> What is each participant's responsibility to the group? What is his responsibility to himself?
>
> Suppose he disagrees with a decision?
>
> Suppose he is uninterested?
>
> How should the group react to one who is shirking responsibility?

Films, magazine illustrations depicting conflicts, flat pictures such as those in the Focus collection [19]—any of these may elicit sufficient interest to initiate the exploration of a problem through discussion, writing, or role playing.[20]

[18] For discussion of the guided reading program, see pages 456–58 and 655–57.

[19] *Focus on Choices Challenging Youth,* A Discussion Kit, National Conference of Christians and Jews, New York.

[20] See pages 193 and 291 for discussion of role playing.

Once presented, a problem will need clarification. Teachers can encourage students to review what is known about the persons involved, the issues facing them, the prevailing feelings and attitudes. The next step is for students to suggest solutions; much give-and-take occurs when classes are divided into small groups to allow for exchange of opinion and for exploration of the effect of different courses of action. Productive too are assignments requiring each class member to examine the conflicting motives, predict probable outcomes, and select an appropriate solution. Role playing, if students learn to share the feeling of the roles they assume and if reversal of roles allows them to compare the contrasting feelings resulting from differing circumstances, is especially effective with junior high school pupils.

Whatever the form of exploration, the culmination of the experience should represent an evaluation of the solutions considered. In role playing, for example, both the cast and the audience should examine the validity of the different solutions, the effect of each on the attitudes and actions of the characters. Similarly, in following up composition and group discussion assignments, the teacher can provide opportunities for students to share and evaluate ideas; selected papers can be read, or representatives from each group can join an informal panel discussion of the probabilities involved in each situation. Whatever means the evaluation takes, students should have had a chance to see the ramifications of the problem and be left to draw their own conclusions; we must refrain from trying to impose ours.[21] We have to trust to our faith not only in the power of reason but in the capacity of human beings to display, more often than not, the qualities that make them human.

Esthetic Values

Thoreau notes in his *Journal* that the perception of beauty is a moral test. It is true that beauty and morality cannot easily be separated; both are based on the laws of harmony. We may even use the same terms to describe the two: out of context one could not tell whether "it was an ugly thing to do" referred to a violation of an ethical or an esthetic principle. However, just as we may for purposes of emphasis concentrate on the ethical aspects of the art of living, so too, by directing attention to aspects of beauty, we can help students understand some of the principles underlying the esthetic experiences that enrich life. The aim here, therefore, is to suggest a simple framework within which esthetic values may be studied in their own right.

FOCUSING ON AWARENESS AND ORDERLINESS

Few adolescents are indifferent to beauty. Even less than anyone else do they wish to be told that they are homely, that their voices are unpleasant or their

[21] See pages 298–99 for a specific illustration.

"Sea shells, lady?"

Drawing by George Price; Copyright © 1933 The New Yorker Magazine, Inc.

teeth crooked. Like all human beings they respond to music, color, pageantry, dancing; they prefer some kind of law to chaos. The problem is not to initiate an awareness of esthetics but rather to educate their discriminations. Here, the aims of the teacher, quite simply, fall into two parts: to increase awareness and, by clarifying standards, to decrease confusion.

How do teachers include these desirable aims in their teaching? How, aside from transmitting by contagion their own aliveness and balance, do they teach these esthetic considerations to their pupils? In general, one acquires a taste for the best in somewhat the same manner that one establishes habits that foster ethical values. Both develop slowly; both demand discipline of the intellect and the emotions; both require continued evaluations—in experiences of gradually increasing complexity—of models of the excellent contrasted with the inferior. Here, as well as with the ethical, if students are not to confuse verbalizations of acceptable standards with genuine appreciation of the esthetic qualities of life, time must be allowed for internalization and synthesis. Esthetic values cannot be implanted directly in another any more than can the ethical; both are highly personal, growing out of the individual's experience.

Although this entire book is intended to describe the strategy of teachers who exalt vitality and disciplined control of that vitality, this section features a special emphasis on esthetic choices. In the paragraphs that follow, experiences to support the two aims of awareness and orderliness are described.

To be aware, to be vitally alive, is one of the most important of all choices, an essential ingredient of all productive living. It is what Lucinda Matlock had, what George Gray lacked. Erich Fromm, in a context dealing with ethical values, writes, "Man is gifted with reason; he is life being aware of itself." [22] It is this awareness of living that teachers want to help students cultivate as a base for the esthetic values.

In *Our Town*, when Emily determines to return to life for a day, the dead urge her not to choose one of her happiest days. "No," says one. "At least, choose an unimportant day. Choose the least important day of your life. It will be important enough." At the close of that return visit, Emily says, "I didn't realize. So all that was going on and we never noticed. . . . Clocks ticking . . . and Mamma's sunflowers. And food and coffee. And new-ironed dresses and hot baths . . . and sleeping and waking up. Oh, earth, you're too wonderful for anybody to realize you." It is then she asks, "Do any human beings ever realize life while they live it—every, every minute?" And the answer is "No. The saints and the poets, maybe—they do some."

BEAUTY OF THE EVERYDAY   To make students aware, to lead them to realize and respond more fully to the beauty of life as it exists around them, is the first aim of the teacher concerned with esthetic choices. This aim implies a concern first of all with the everyday experiences of life, with freshly ironed dresses and the feel of a baseball smacking snugly into a mitt. Too hasty a preoccupation with Brahms, Dante, or Cézanne can be as disastrous for an adolescent as can a ride on a bicycle for a two-year-old child. The foundation for appreciating art lies first in a heightened awareness of the wonder and beauty of the familiar.

The teacher plans an initial lesson based on one of the many poems celebrating delight in the familiar things of life; depending upon the age and abilities of the pupils, the choice of poems ranges from "Autumn" by Emily Dickinson and "A Vagabond Song" by Bliss Carmen in the seventh grade to passages from *A Stone, A Leaf, A Door* by Thomas Wolfe and "Pied Beauty" by Gerard Manley Hopkins in the senior high school.

The students prepare a list of everyday pleasures they have appreciated; these are grouped into categories—sights, sounds, odors, tastes, physical feelings, emotional satisfactions. Committees representing each category prepare free verse catalogs of pleasures.

Individuals read aloud appropriate passages, such as "I Hear America Singing" by Walt Whitman or the dramatic lines from Emily's celebration of life in the final scene of *Our Town*.

The class concludes the series of lessons by reading "God's World" or parts of "Renascence" by Edna St. Vincent Millay.

Audio-visual materials to support the theme of familiar beauty are numerous:

> *Begone Dull Care*   Color and line take momentary shapes before merging into new forms.
> *Nature's Half Acre*   Time-lapse photography portrays nature's way with birds, plants, and insects.
> *Ansel Adams, Photographer*   Nature studies, insightful portraits, and examples of industrial design reveal the beauty of the everyday aspects of life.

[22] Erich Fromm, *The Art of Loving* (New York: Harper & Row, 1956), p. 8.

And Now Miguel The film on which Joseph Krumgold's Newbery Prize novel for young people is based uses camera techniques that point up esthetic values in familiar things.

BEAUTY IN THE ARTS We can make our students aware of some of the esthetic principles underlying all the arts. At the very least we can help them understand how artists in every medium, stimulated by their environment, select and organize elements of their intellectual and emotional experience to create moments of beauty accessible to all. In addition we can perhaps encourage our more sensitive students to educate their eyes, ears, intellects, and emotions, in order to respond more fully to the vision of experience the artist provides; to cultivate awareness of the arts as a chief means of clarifying and interpreting individual experience.

Discussion arising from the study of Helen Keller's essay "Three Days to See" forms an effective bridge from awareness of the beauty of the everyday to sensitivity to the beauty revealed by the artist.[23] A bulletin board for which students collect material featuring the sculptors and painters mentioned in the essay provides initial stimulus for increasing awareness. An appropriate quotation for the bulletin board taken from the essay might be:

> Artists tell me that for a deep and true appreciation of art one must educate the eye. One must learn through experience to weigh the merits of line, of composition, of form, of color. If I had eyes how happily I would embark upon so fascinating a study! Yet I am told that, to many of you who have eyes to see, the world of art is a dark night, unexplored and unilluminated.[24]

A committee of students interested in the visual arts may agree to keep the display "up to date"—to search for illustrative material, to call attention to local art exhibits and expertly illustrated articles in magazines, and, finally, to preserve the most effective material in a scrapbook to be used with future classes.

To underscore Helen Keller's awareness of beauty and its meaning, permit students to choose one musical recording to which they are to listen as if they are to be struck deaf thereafter; call attention to some esthetic element of the music—its variations in tone color, its appropriate rhythms, its diversity within a pattern, and so on.

Play recordings of poetry or prose read by an expert reader. Good choices are "To Helen" and "The Bells," read by Alexander Scourby, or Ullman's "Behind the Ranges," read by Arnold Moss.

Audio-visual materials that can be used are:

"The Photographer" To emphasize the principle of selectivity.
"Art in Our World" To stress environmental sources of inspiration to artists.
"Art and Motion" To show how artists make use of motion in painting, mobiles, camera techniques.

[23] A recording of this selection and of the poems mentioned is available on *Many Voices* (New York: Harcourt, Brace & World, 1958).
[24] In Walter Loban, Dorothy Holmstrom, and Luella B. Cook, *Adventures in Appreciation* (New York: Harcourt, Brace & World, 1958), p. 389.

"The Rime of the Ancient Mariner" Occasional animation and camera techniques give movement to reproductions of the Doré engravings used to accompany the reading of Coleridge's poem.

Since awareness is based on intellectual curiosity and imaginative insight, both essential for the balanced individual, we need to do all we can to help young people develop these characteristics. J. Christopher Herold, former editor-in-chief of the Stanford University Press, in commenting upon the danger of passivity said, "Without an active imagination there can be no curiosity, no sympathy or love, but only passive acceptance and complacency. And these are the true dangers to our civilization." [25]

The second aim, to decrease confusion by clarifying esthetic standards, is to foster the search for order and harmony that goes on in every life. The universal yearning for a dynamic order partially explains why adolescents like to dance; the fluid movements of the body are patterned; there is the same vitality under control that we recognize in the music of Mozart and in the poetry of Shelley and Pope. This wonder of form inextricably related with meaning is also what the teacher wants students to achieve in a written essay or in a panel discussion; it is what delights all who sincerely enjoy Frost's "Stopping by Woods on a Snowy Evening" or Debussy's "Images."

Absolute chaos is incompatible with life. Upon each fleeting moment in the flux of experience, impulse, habit, or reason imposes some kind of order; automatically, we organize into some coherence and form the multitudinous impressions constantly impinging upon us. The need for order is so insistent that it represents a danger to productive living; one who is to live creatively for himself and for society must maintain a precarious balance between too little and too much order. A highly organized society has its rewards and its penalties. At the one extreme, the individual, either because he is resentful of any conformity or because he is unable to so order his personal experience as to give meaning to his life, may settle for anarchy and confusion; at the other, he may accept a rigid order, often not of his own making, as the ideal pattern. Students need help in developing two concepts concerning the role of order in the art of living: order as necessity and order as controlled vitality.

ORDER AS NECESSITY   Students are aware of the manifestations of order within the school—the requirements for graduation, the scheduling of classes, assignment of rooms, regulations governing behavior in the halls, in assemblies, on the playground. They are also aware of the need for order within each classroom if learning is to take place, although the teacher must help them first recognize and then maintain the balance between too much rigidity and too much flexibility. A school organized to permit students to have a degree of genuine participation in determining some of the regulations that come within their province—they are as wise as are adults in recognizing what that province is—makes a real contribution to the development of the individual. It gives the student the opportunity not only to understand the necessity for order but also to realize that segments of his life are within his own control if he develops the

[25] Quoted by Charles Einstein, San Francisco *Examiner* (May 3, 1959).

necessary wisdom and volition. The English classroom organized to permit some choice within the limits of the curriculum is making a similar contribution. As teachers we have a responsibility to help students discover that the need for order inherent in human nature is manifested in all aspects of living. Using Pope's line "Order is heaven's first law" as a theme, the teacher elicits examples that support the idea; appropriate questions will insure a wide variety of illustrations:

ORDER IN NATURE

movements of the planets, seasons, tides, darkness and light, heart beat, breathing, waking and sleeping, planting and harvesting

MAN-MADE ORDER

dictionary, telephone directory, arrangement of books in a library and of parts of a book

traffic regulations—streets and highways, water and air routes, train and bus schedules

organization of events—track meet, golf tournament, crowds at a football game, preparation for a school dance

business—newspaper, grocery store, cafeteria serving counter

The recording *Rhythms of the World* dramatizes the universality of order.

With an opaque projector the teacher shows pictures of order and disorder in a wide variety of situations: store windows, traffic jams, landscaping, flower arrangement, architecture, advertising, clothing; inclusion of photographs of children abandoned in squalid homes and of the shambles in which certain eccentrics live will be helpful for later emphasis on the relationship of disordered thinking to living. These pictures can be related to an example of disordered writing similar to the following:

"Do you know of any *personal* reason why she
might want to leave home?"

Drawing by George Price; Copyright © 1938 The New Yorker Magazine, Inc.

For a competitive sport, fansy diving is wanna most difficult for a Boy. I have notice lotsa kids shiver when they Get near the bored and he ain't cold on such warm days as we had last summer the sun was so hot that you could scarcely help but *boil* an egg if we hapen to drop it on sidewalk. My sister says that when I dive, I have manage to poise perfectly. You were always in danger of making a flop the diver takes three steps up the Board and then they made a final leap, she says a diver hasta be born with a sense of balance. Not that anyone cares. The water—the French call it *L'eau* and there are some who say aqua *however* Bud who is my pal from Bodal, a town near where they give watermelons *away* free everry Fourth July is the best competer in all kindsa sport, including diving, which is my favarit.

Next the teacher shows several examples of clear, ordered writing, if possible from compositions the students have recently written; he identifies outstanding illustrations of unity, coherence, and planned emphasis. A series of lessons similar to these will help students assimilate the idea that order is a necessity of life, not only for a society but for an individual as well.

The teacher helps students relate outer disorder to inner imbalances that enervate human beings; for this purpose, fictional characters are most useful in furnishing commentary on problems of personal living. Junior high school favorites like *Lou Gehrig, A Quiet Hero,* and mature plays like *Craig's Wife* and *Death of a Salesman* chart the distance between order and confusion in the art of living.

Discussions centering upon the price individuals pay for confused values may grow out of the study of any literary work depicting a character whose lack of inner order creates his failure to find satisfaction in human relations: Many of Ring Lardner's stories—"Haircut," "I Can't Breath," "Travelogue"— feature a character whose penalty for inability to appraise action in terms of standards is the confusion in which he lives.

Literature the students have studied earlier in the year and in previous years, as well as examples from the guided individual reading, should be recalled to support the concept.

In junior high school, *Only Child, Johnny Tremain,* and *Julie's Heritage* are novels suitable for this purpose; Scrooge in *A Christmas Carol,* the bogus duke and king in *Huckleberry Finn,* and the launch thief in *Smugglers' Island* are characters some pupils know and in whose lives the unfortunate results of confused values can be demonstrated.

In senior high, some students may be familiar with the sons of Wang from *The Good Earth,* Eliza Gant from *Look Homeward, Angel,* Willy Loman from *Death of a Salesman,* Alice Adams from the novel of that title, Captain Bligh from *Mutiny on the Bounty,* and Clyde Griffiths from *An American Tragedy.*

In these discussions, the appeal to ethical standards need not be introduced; the uncertainty of lives out of balance, in contrast to those that achieve equilibrium, is sufficient ground for instruction; like lopsidedness in a deformed tree, imbalance in the art of living may be viewed as an esthetic flaw.

An assignment to follow such discussion might be to locate in newspapers and magazines accounts of persons whose failure to make distinctions in the realm of values has plunged them into trouble. One tenth-grade class brought in clippings concerning teen-age groups who crashed parties to which they had not been invited. The students found no difficulty in X-raying the protests of one delinquent who asserted he had a right to protect himself when the father of the young hostess tried to expel the intruders.

With junior high school pupils, films are effective for conveying the values of a well-ordered life; *Make Your Own Decisions* and *Understanding Your Ideals* are two short films dealing with the ingredients of that personal harmony that characterizes self-reliant, psychologically mature individuals.

ORDER AS CONTROLLED VITALITY   Order, to be effective, must be flexible and vital, not mere routine that dulls the senses and deadens response to life.[26] It is this vitality, expanded in striving toward self-fulfillment and controlled by intelligence, that we wish for our students. Although it is in the contemplation of great art that we can most easily recognize an ordering of forces that intensify and clarify experience, we can create such moments in our everyday existence. Irwin Edman, discussing the universality of esthetic principles, writes, "So far from having to do with statues, pictures, and symphonies, art is the name for that whole process of intelligence by which life, understanding its own conditions, turns them to the most interesting and exquisite account." [27] Literature is the most powerful ally of the teacher's own disciplined vitality in helping the student acquire sufficient discrimination among values to use this noblest faculty and thus to turn more and more conditions of life to exquisite account. All literature can in some way enlarge and enrich the idea of the need for a vital order; a few examples:

> *The Scarlet Letter,* a novel showing the restrictions imposed by society and the effect on two persons reacting differently to the impact of those restrictions
>
> "Mending Wall," a poem that presents the dangers of routine patterns of reaction, either due to ignorance or indolence, that evade the need for independent thinking
>
> *Macbeth,* a tragedy depicting the effects of the overthrow of order both on the state and on the human personality

Acquiring discrimination in awareness and in appreciation of the characteristics of a necessary but flexible order requires a series of experiences growing in depth and breadth over a long period of time. A carefully planned program of the six years of secondary school should give students both a basis for evaluating the multi-hued facets of life and a realization of the significance of the esthetic qualities that enrich one committed to the search for harmonious living.

[26] The unit "Humanities for the Seventies," pp. 609–24, illustrates ways of developing this concept in the classroom.
[27] Irwin Edman, *Arts and the Man* (New York: Norton, 1939), p. 10.

FOCUSING ON LITERARY FORM AND LITERARY ARTISTS

The English teacher has an important role to play in directing pupil attention to the critical aspects of esthetic merits in literature, for this is an appreciation few achieve on their own but one that can be cultivated through able instruction. Although critical analysis, concerning itself with gradually deepening complexities, is needed, appreciation is never a wholly conscious process. Also necessary is what Thornton Wilder calls "the admiration of a series of admirable examples—a learning that takes place in the subconscious." And, Wilder adds, "Beware of what you admire when you are young." [28] Appreciation for what is best in literature evolves most surely from a careful developmental program beginning in the first grade with, for example, *East of the Sun and West of the Moon* and building toward *Ethan Frome* in grade 12 or *Victory* in junior college. Through such a program, the teacher identifies and illuminates two important esthetic standards: the concept of form in the literary work and the concept of the integrity of the literary artist.

Students need help to see that all elements of a literary work of art are combined into a design conveying balance and wholeness. This is not a matter solely of technical elements—climax, rhyme, and point of view; it most certainly does not rest primarily upon mechanical identification of narrative devices, sonnet patterns, and figures of speech. It includes recognition of the balancing and unification of human feelings, ideas, and attitudes. Form is the organic relationship of many elements—emotions and ethical values as well as symbols and foreshadowing; teaching these esthetic elements of form requires attention to the harmony of the total artistic structure. The examples below illustrate form in fiction and poetry. [29]

FICTION   Because of the length and complexity of most novels, it is often difficult for students to see the total design; however, even readers inexperienced with this literary form can be taught to recognize some of the esthetic elements. Such recognition, gathering force as different fictional works are studied, finally results in the ability of synthesis—the appreciation of individual factors culminating in an understanding of the logic of the whole. Two novels, the first usually recommended for the tenth grade and the second for the eleventh or twelfth, have been selected for analysis.

SILAS MARNER

The unusual passivity of the central character, comparable, as far as significance to the plot is concerned, to an axis around which the events revolve. Things happen to Silas; he does not make them happen.

[28] Quoted by Ross Parmenter in "Novelist into Playwright," an interview with Thornton Wilder, *Saturday Review*, Vol. 28, No. 7 (June 11, 1938), p. 11.

[29] Answers to questions on "The Necklace" should lead to an understanding of form as it is achieved in this short story; a discussion of form in drama can be found on pages 601–03 in the *Macbeth* unit.

The balancing of various elements around that center:
1. the simple humor of the village characters, contrasting with the deadly seriousness of Silas
2. the gold and the child, each serving a twofold purpose
   a. as a link between the two main groups of characters, because of Dunstan's theft and Godfrey's child
   b. as a symbol of a way of life, one leading to the stunting of the human spirit; the other, to happiness and fulfillment
3. the sincerity and wholesomeness of Dolly Winthrop, contrasting with the hypocrisy of William Dane
4. at a deeper level, the pervasive influence of these two characters as essential links in the account of a human being's gravitation between isolation from mankind and integration into the community of man

Even these few understandings will give students some feeling for literary form on a significant level.

ETHAN FROME

Harmony existing among
1. characters—dignified, inarticulate, repressed
2. setting—grim, barren, bleak
3. events—inexorably tragic

Story
1. told without sentimentality or emotionalism by an observer remote from the actual happenings
2. given body and vitality as details are gleaned gradually from Herman Gow and Mrs. Hale, each revealing an individual interpretation of the events
3. given dramatic compression in recounting events spanning a generation by the use of the flashback technique

Crushing irony of the climax, making the ending unexpectedly dramatic
Unadorned style, as stark and uncompromising as the events it describes

No false notes are struck in this literary work; it is particularly effective for teaching the combination of all esthetic elements into a seemingly inevitable design.

POETRY With poetry, as with other literary forms, an understanding of artistic entity grows slowly, from pleasure in the rhymes of *When We Were Very Young* to deepening appreciation of the complicated tensions and organic structure of the great poems of the English language. We cannot hurry this process in our students, even if we would; we can, however, nurture its growth. We teach poetry on the secondary-school level by a constant use of concrete examples; in the early years we use poems requiring little or no analysis, trusting to the lure of rhythm and rhyme, story and sentiment, to create a desire for more. Starting in the seventh grade, or somewhat later with certain classes, and still working with many individual poems rather than with explanations of the mechanics of poetry, we can begin to help students inductively build the foundations for an appreciation of esthetic form.

For immature pupils, the ballad permits an effective introduction to the study of organic form in poetry. The following procedure has been used successfully with "Lord Randal."

> reading of the poem to the class by the teacher with any discussion necessary to make the details of the ballad clear
> second reading of the poem
> perhaps a comparison of the impact of the ballad with that of a hypothetical news item based on the facts given

The study of organic form presupposes that pupils have at least slight knowledge of some of the individual qualities that characterize poetry—rhythm, rhyme, clarity of image, precision of language; with appropriate questions the teacher will help students discover the artistic structure of the whole:

STORY

A dramatic moment, revealed entirely by dialog, presented in five steps without the customary devices of explanation and transition used in narration.

The transitions effected by form: rhythm, rhyme, repetition; the first four stanzas composed of questions and answers; the last by statements, but with other elements keeping the form consistent with that of the other four.

Compression and precision gained by selectivity and economy of concrete details.

MOVEMENT

Within the stanza, rapid in the first two lines but slowing in the last two; within the whole, not a steadily flowing smoothness but five successive waves as the pause between stanzas provides a slight break in momentum.

SIGNIFICANCE OF VARIATIONS IN THE LAST STANZA

Because the mother has led the reader, almost without his being aware, to make the same series of inferences she herself has made, the finality of statements in contrast to questions gives a sense of completeness. "I'm sick at the heart" replaces "I'm weary wi' hunting." Why sick at the *heart?* The answer is in the poem.

Encouraging speculation on the true love's motive or probing for reasons to explain the mother's ready suspicion is a mistake because it takes us outside the poem.

EMOTIONAL RESPONSE

Evoked by the tension and balance of all elements, emotion mounts gradually from the first seemingly commonplace question to a realization of the hints at tragedy in those that follow; the irony of the situation is made explicit as the young man admits that his spirit as well as his life has been destroyed.

Final reading of the ballad—always necessary after attention has been directed to its parts—give students an opportunity to synthesize intellectual and emotional response and restores the poem to its significance as a literary experience.

Whether a writer may be called a great literary artist depends upon innate qualities enabling him to illuminate aspects of the human condition in a form that makes them universal and enduring. Whether a writer may be called an artist in any degree depends upon his integrity. The study of the artist's integrity profits from negative examples as well as from positive models. The corrupt brightness of much that appears in print, if it is to be seen for what it is, requires the searching ray of light a teacher can provide; the ways in which some authors violate their material in order to spawn situations and manipulate outcomes to attract readers deserve attention. The inconsistencies of these writers are such that they can echo an easy morality about the unimportance of material possessions, yet reward their heroes with unexpected inheritances or their heroines with contrived marriages to wealth. In their books simple causation is substituted for multiple causation, and life's most difficult problems yield to simple formulas. By comparing the excellent with the inferior, teachers can help students appreciate integrity as an indispensable quality of the literary artist.

STUDY THROUGH LITERATURE   Through comparisons of the author's method of expression with that which might have been used by one less skilled and less conscientious,[30] and through demonstrations of consistency among the various elements of a literary work, teachers can help students acquire respect for the integrity of the writer. This quality of genuineness announces itself in freedom from clichés, stock characters, easy generalizations evoking stereotyped responses, nonsensory prose straight-jacketed into conventional metrical patterns—all those devices by which pseudo-literature seeks to contrive stories and poems to entice the reader. The genuine artist, in contrast to those writers whose sole aim is to exploit the shifting demands of the market, seeks to give us the image of life that stirred his imagination, and is uncompromisingly patient and exact in devising the best form to capture this inner world he attempts to shape into artistic expression. The exactness of the descriptions and their use for more than one purpose, the inevitability of action, the relationship among all the elements of the literary work—character determining plot, setting establishing mood, rhythm fortifying meaning, diction evoking the associations required by the content—all this economy of means combines to create the esthetic pleasure we find in literature.

STUDY THROUGH GUIDED READING   However, the desire to choose the writer of integrity in preference to his opposite is not an easy one to foster in a culture where sensationalists rate as favorites among authors. Repeatedly in specific works we can direct attention to instances where integrity is maintained or where it is violated; repeatedly we can demonstrate, compare, and contrast, to the point of exhaustion; but if students themselves do not read widely enough to give an appreciation for the best a chance to develop, the seed falls

[30] For examples see pages 518–19.

on stony ground. It seems fairly obvious that nothing but a developmental program in guided individual reading, where the literature studied is supplemented by intimate acquaintance with books of all kinds, can insure for as many young people as possible not only recognition of the importance of this standard of integrity but also its acceptance as a guide for personal living. Only such a program permits the student to see the relation between the principles of literary art taught in the classroom and their presence or absence in the books and television programs he selects for himself. The nonreading television addict will readily admit that the ease with which the slim young detective surprised by several husky thugs fells them with a series of knock-out punches and finishes the performance slightly disheveled but still intact is incredible. But what of it?

Another aspect of the problem of helping the student make the connection between integrity in art and integrity in life deserves mention; here the ground is treacherous. What of the integrity that excludes from the classroom all portrayals of violence and sordidness except those stamped with classical approval? Of the too rigorous control of books students are allowed to read for "credit"? Charles Calitri, in a discussion of this problem, writes,

> Until we can allow a boy to come to us with *God's Little Acre* saying "Can I read this?" and nod to him, suggesting that his report answer the question, "Why did Caldwell put the word God in the title . . . and what does he say about man's relationship with God?" we must silently suffer the knowledge that he is going to read that book anyway, hidden, on his own, with no chance of guidance and with no opportunity to see past the sordidness and the perversion of the life of the people it depicts.[31]

Is this a plea to provide students with the strongest fare they can take? Certainly not. It is a plea for a realism in the classroom that will enable teachers to help students understand life; it is a plea for the wisdom of discrimination in guiding the reading of the sensitive young girl and of the boy who, at first hand, already knows more about the seamy side of life than his teacher ever wants to learn. Certainly, it is not the business of the English teacher to suggest to adolescents books that parents will be horrified to find their children reading; neither is it his business to ignore the books known to be passing surreptitiously from locker to locker, from desk to desk. Impartial examination of such books with the help of a wise teacher dissipates the lure of the forbidden and lessens the possibility of the young reader's gaining a warped impression. If not all teachers are wise, one can only point out that this dilemma has been raised before:

> If we were to suspend all religious activities until we found the perfect leaders, churches would soon close; if we were to suspend all medical activity until we found perfect doctors, the death rate would rise alarmingly. Complete mastery

[31] Charles Calitri, "Macbeth and the Reluctant Reader," *English Journal*, Vol. 48, No. 5 (May 1959), p. 260.

may well be an idealistic goal of our instruction; happily it has never been a prerequisite to teaching.[32]

In senior high school the dissection of an unworthy novel has been used to establish many important touchstones of good taste. In some communities, the teacher has planned the lessons in advance with parent groups and school administration; in other schools, mature teachers have presented for student organizations dignified reviews of salacious books students are known to be reading. In many classrooms, the problem is handled through individual conferences or through discussion in small groups. Whatever the method chosen, avoidance of sanctimonious horror and assumption of reasonable maturity on the part of students can do much to establish a situation in which principles of esthetic judgment become clearer.

In the junior high school also, where the comic book is much more likely to need the attention of the teacher, direct attack and condemnation will do less good than an examination of the varying quality among the comics. Teachers of seventh-graders have used a study of literary supermen—Hercules, Paul Bunyan, Stormalong—as a springboard for analysis, first, of favorite comic strips and then of favorite television programs. In suggesting books as likely competitors for more stereotyped fare, teachers should remember that:

> Books must be easily accessible in classroom libraries.
>
> Books assume importance when the teacher gives them a central position in the curriculum, providing time for discussing and sharing the enjoyment of reading.
>
> Books must be supplied in sufficient variety to appeal to the interests of the individual reader and satisfy some of the needs that draw children to the comics. For many young children, such books as *Homer Price, Box Car Children, Smugglers' Island, Henry Huggins* have proved effective lures. For slower readers, *The Five Hundred Hats of Bartholomew Cubbins, Mr. Popper's Penguins*, and *Deep Sea Adventure* have been keys to turn the lock.

One eighth-grade class keeps a large scrapbook called "Distinguished Books"; each page is fifty inches high and twenty-five inches wide; at the top of each page is the title of some book enthusiastically recommended by a petition signed by at least five members of the class. Only by petition can a book acquire enough fame to be listed, and each entry must include a review of the book written by the petitioners. After a book has been chosen, each pupil who reads it adds his comment, being careful not to reveal elements later readers should discover. In the course of several years, the pages for such books as *No Other White Men, Ginger Pye, Little Vic*, and *On To Oregon* fill up and become the reading guides for new groups of eighth-graders. The teacher often chooses a superior book like *Call It Courage* and compares it with some weaker title for such esthetics as naturalness of conversation or growth of the main character during the course of the story.

[32] Robert Hogan, "Education for Wise Choice," *California Journal of Secondary Education,* Vol. 33, No. 4 (April 1958), p. 240.

Whatever means the teacher provides for sharing the pleasures of reading—book courts, panels, discussions, written recommendations—if he takes every opportunity to focus attention on such basic esthetic qualities as originality of humor, consistency of character delineation, inevitability of action, use of description to contribute to plot, he will be helping pupils acquire effective standards for judging integrity in literature.

The need for integrity in the writer and for belief in the indestructibility of the qualities that make men human has never been more eloquently stated than by William Faulkner in his speech accepting the Nobel Prize for literature. Expressing his desire to share the acclaim accorded him with "all those who work not for glory and least of all for profit, but to create out of the human spirit something which did not exist before," he contrasts such writers with those who write "not of the heart but of the glands." Teachers have used, with mature classes, these quotations as a theme for a final review of literature, as students recall the literary works they have studied and the books they have read in an effort to illuminate the ideas with specific examples. Testifying to his faith in the nobility inherent in humanity, Faulkner charges the literary artist with the responsibility for helping man nurture the best that is in him:

> I believe that man will not merely endure: he will prevail. He is immortal, not because he alone among creatures has an inexhaustible voice, but because he has a soul, a spirit capable of compassion and sacrifice and endurance. The poet's, the writer's, duty is to write about these things. It is his privilege to help man endure by lifting his heart, by reminding him of the courage and honor and hope and pride and compassion and pity and sacrifice which have been the glory of his past. The poet's voice need not merely be the record of man, it can be one of the props, the pillars to help him endure and prevail.[33]

The essence of the help we can give the student in discovering values, both ethical and esthetic, lies in our ability to create in a six-year program a sequence of learning experiences that may foster integrity in communication and a desire to explore the vast resources of language and literature. We can only trust that such experiences, providing some choice and much evaluation, will make him somewhat wiser in the decisions he makes outside the classroom, where the most crucial tests come. With a faith in the invincibility of the human spirit equal to Faulkner's, we must believe that although the effect of our influence is rarely revealed to us, the help we give may tip the balance away from a life as disillusioned and futile as that of a George Gray toward one marked by the vigor, the fortitude, and the high purpose of a Lucinda Matlock.

[33] Reprinted in *Saturday Review Reader*, Vol. I (New York: Bantam, 1951), p. 68.

UNIT:

THE CONSEQUENCES OF CHARACTER

A UNIT FOR GRADE TWELVE

Overview The study of a long literary work by a class heterogeneous in intellectual and esthetic potential often proves an unrewarding experience for many students. The answer to the problem need not be a single novel aimed at either the best readers or the average; nor need it be a program depending entirely on guided reading to meet individual needs. One solution may be found in teaching several novels to groups of varying ability; another, in the study of a work offering insights on several levels of appreciation. With the latter, however, unless the work is comparatively short, allowing the teacher to present the most difficult parts orally (see the unit on *Macbeth*), appreciation on even the most elementary level proves an unrealistic goal for some students. An incompetent reader may gain from the discussions based on the ideas in the literary work; he misses direct experience with the literature.

This unit illustrates the use of both recommended methods. Conrad's *The Secret Sharer* (others used have been *Ethan Frome* and *The Old Man and the Sea*) offers on the lowest level of awareness the suspense and excitement of plot; it gives capable readers an opportunity to appreciate ramifications of theme and insights into symbolism and irony. The study of different novels in groups allows the student enough intellectual and esthetic stretching to stimulate growth.[1]

Material required

The plan requires three groupings of material: a fictional work long enough to show character development and to increase understandings of novelistic technique; six or seven novels from which the groups may make selections;[2] many novels for

---

[1] See Margaret Ryan, "Achieving Unity with Diversity," *The English Journal*, Vol. 40, No. 10 (December 1951), pp. 547–52. This article describes the method in greater detail, using different material.

[2] When this unit was taught, students chose a novel from a group of six with foreign backgrounds; they eliminated *The Good Earth* and *Cry, the Beloved Country* in favor of Walter Macken's *Rain on the Wind*. Since Macken's novel is now out of print, we have substituted the one that seems most comparable to it in difficulty: *The Good Earth*. In discussing the latter novel, we have kept the original form of the unit, attributing to students decisions we have been forced to make ourselves. Substituting one literary work for another affects only the final synthesis.

individual reading. The guided reading program, always important, is essential here to provide additional materials for the faster readers. A simple diagram helps a class comprehend the organization.

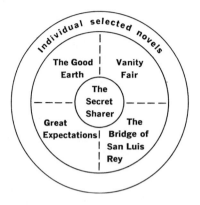

The plan has the following advantages:

It allows the teacher to adapt the learning experiences to the abilities of the students, to provide for the gifted and the less competent.

It allows the teaching of each novel as a distinct experience; therefore, the temptation to distort the literary work to fit a preconceived theme is eliminated.

It can be used even if the teacher decides to omit any unifying ideas in the various novels selected, allowing each group to be concerned with only one novel.

This unit, therefore, is designed to give the teacher help in teaching any form of literature by groups; in preparing a novel for teaching; and in helping students see relationships among literary works of the same genre.

The plan suggested here may sound formidable to the inexperienced teacher; the amount of preparatory work required for teaching one class for a period of four to five weeks may seem unjustifiable. The answer to such objections is simple; the beginning teacher should not attempt it. He should postpone its use until he has had time to experiment with the method—perhaps trying it first with short stories or essays in several classes—and until experience with teaching several novels has provided a backlog of study guides that can be adapted to particular groups within a class. Since the guides are designed to help students discover the values the teacher discerns in the literary work, they may be used with slight change for successive classes. Often, members of English departments in large schools build up a central file of such guides; a single English teacher in a small school can gradually collect his own. Many novels printed as textbooks for high school use include study questions that can be adapted for this purpose. The inexperienced are reminded also that the guided reading program must be well under way before the teacher can be freed to teach several novels concurrently.

Aims

To understand and appreciate a particular novel; to increase awareness of devices used in fiction; to see how the writer's purpose influences form in relation to content.

To realize similarities and contrasts among literary works.

Launching the unit

The Secret Sharer

Purpose   To develop awareness of possible levels of meaning in a literary work; to become more familiar with novelistic techniques

▶ *Reading for the story*

1. A brief introduction by the teacher, stressing Conrad's fascination with the sea and the East as settings for his stories.

2. Reading of approximately first ten pages aloud by the teacher, followed by discussion to insure understanding of setting and initial situation.

3. Silent reading, with the teacher available to answer individual questions as students finish the story.

4. Writing in class the next day on one of these topics:

> Throughout the story the captain links himself with Leggatt, stressing they are both strangers on a ship with which all other crew members are familiar.
>
> Would *The Two Strangers* serve as well for the title as the one Conrad chose? Why or why not?
>
> Who is the protagonist, the captain or Leggatt? Give reasons for your answer.

▶ *Individual study*

1. Divide the class into four groups and the story into four parts of approximately ten pages each. Allow fifteen minutes for students, working individually, to find in the assigned section as many different ways as they can in which the captain identifies himself with Leggatt; to find any instances where the author implies a similarity between the two men that the captain does not mention.

2. Conduct a discussion leading students to see points of comparison.

▶ *Group study*

Divide the class into heterogeneous groups, each to explore the answers to questions similar to these:

1. Explain why the author makes

> the captain see Leggatt first as an indistinct form, then as a man without a head
>
> the fugitive first to appear "as if risen from the bottom of the sea" and at the end disappear into the sea again (Why is the reader not allowed to see him reach land?)
>
> the fugitive come and leave under cover of darkness
>
> the captain provide a sleeping garment rather than a daytime suit
>
> the captain insist Leggatt take his (the captain's) hat

2. Consider these two statements:

> "None whatever" (p. 45) [3]

[3] Page references are to the Signet Classic edition, No. CD4, published by New American Library.

"And suddenly I rejoiced . . . singleness of its purpose." (p. 23)

What literary device do they illustrate? Are they both on the same level of significance? Why or why not?

3. Review the ending:

Why does the reader never learn the name of the captain?

Why was it "a matter of conscience" for the captain to "shave the land as close as possible"? (p. 57) Why did he think Leggatt would be able to understand this feeling? (p. 59)

Why, at the end, is attention centered on the captain and his ship?

4. Compare these thoughts of the captain:

About himself— "Nothing! No one in the world . . . the perfect communion of a seaman with his first command." (p. 61)

About the fugitive— "A free man, a proud swimmer striking out for a new destiny." (p. 61)

► *Final synthesis*

Without trying to provide categorical answers and without making conclusions a matter for testing, the teacher leads the class to discern relationships among plot, possible themes, the irony, and the possible symbols.

► *Final paper*

Choose either subject:

One critic has called *The Secret Sharer* "a powerful *fable* of the *mystery* man must *know* and *master* before he can . . . *save himself from himself.*" [4] Explain, paying particular attention to the italicized words.

If you have changed your mind since writing your paper after the first reading, or if you can more fully substantiate the opinion expressed then, use the subject chosen at that time for your paper.

Developing the unit—the study of novels in groups

► *Choosing the novels*

1. Bring into the classroom sets (ten to fifteen copies) of six or seven novels on different levels of ability; introduce the novels to the class, telling something of the nature of each and its degree of reading difficulty. Tell students that no more than five, preferably four, groups will be formed. (More than five prolong the study unduly—bad for both the class and the novel.)

2. Allow time for students to examine the novels and to make a choice. Place titles on the board, leaving space for students to write their names under each as soon as they have reached a decision. The groups need not be equal in size; often it is worthwhile to teach a difficult novel, or an easy one, even though it is suitable for only a small group. Usually at the end of the hour enough interest in two or three novels warrants forming groups; let those in groups too small to be maintained take other novels overnight and reconsider their decisions.

[4] Morton Zauwen Zabel, *The Portable Conrad* (New York: Viking, 1947), p. 607.

3. Allow students to change. Those with a novel much too difficult offer no problem; they will "not like it" and will change quickly to another. Those with a novel too easy will usually change to one more suitable to their ability if they understand the purpose of the group study and if their first choice is accepted as part of their individual reading. Occasionally as the work progresses, fast readers may wish to join a second group. Such interest should be encouraged.

In one class in which this plan was used, *Vanity Fair* was chosen by the more able students; *The Good Earth*, by a group of less competent readers; *Great Expectations* and *The Bridge of San Luis Rey*, by two more heterogeneous groups. These four novels, as studied in this class, will be used to illustrate the method.

▶ *Preparation of novels for teaching*

In preparing a novel for instruction, the teacher must first decide what values the work offers both as an artistic achievement and as a record of human experience. After such an analysis he then selects the emphases most meaningful to his students, assigning priority to the elements most essential to foster appreciation and including as many others as time and the particular group allow. He calls attention to these points in a study guide to help students discover significant aspects of content and form as they read. Both aspects of preparation—analysis and study guide—will be illustrated. The most difficult of the four novels has been chosen as an example.[5]

Vanity Fair

The subject is the world of well-to-do Britain at the beginning of the nineteenth century—a world seen in terms of specific human relationships among characters placed in concrete social situations.

The central problem concerns marriage and the difficulties of personal relationships in marriage at this time and in this society.

The method is panoramic, in that Thackeray surveys a broad field and does not allow the reader to get inside the characters; the reader knows all about them although he is not directly involved in their feelings. The term *panoramic* misleads if it suggests anything of the documentary or implies that the characters are not important.

PLOT AND DEVELOPMENT OF MAJOR CHARACTERS

Becky and Amelia complement each other—the one, "bad" and active; the other, "good" and passive; their careers parallel each other in contrasting curves of development—Becky's low at the beginning, then gradually rising, but falling again at the end; Amelia's, the opposite.

Becky	*Amelia*
childhood of poverty; despised position at Miss Pinkerton's	protected childhood; apparently idyllic childhood romance with George
disappointment over failure to get Jos to propose; governess at Queen's Crawley	bankruptcy of old Mr. Sedley; break with George enforced by his father

---

[5] Courtesy of Robert Holloway, Cubberley High School, Palo Alto, Calif.

Becky	*Amelia*
marriage and prospect of happiness with a reformed Crawley; failure to effect a reconciliation with Miss Crawley	marriage, and fright at how little she means to George
"affair" with George, Becky's most pointless cruelty	prostration over George's death; slavish devotion to an unrealistic image of the late "saintly" George
living in grand style on "nothing a year"; affair with Lord Steyne	life of self-abnegation in lodgings with her parents and her little boy
descent into a Bohemian life of degradation	loss of son Georgy to old Mr. Osborne
depredations on Jos	return of Jos and Dobbin; reunion with Georgy; re-entry into society
final equivocal re-entry into society as a "reformed" woman	awareness of past selfishness toward Dobbin, marriage

THEMATIC RELATIONSHIPS

PRINCIPAL CHARACTERS

Becky	*Amelia*
In Becky is satirized the vanity of the social climber; for her nothing exists *but* social position.	In Amelia is satirized the vanity of romantic love, for whose practitioners social class and position are at most delightful obstacles to be overcome.
Becky, seldom mistaken about a person's character or motives, always falls prey to her crucial defect of the heart.	Amelia, often fooled about character and motives, is able to redeem the most flagrant errors through her generous sympathy.

Many readers feel that much of the novel's interest stems from the vitality of Becky. Amelia after fifteen years of self-deception certainly cannot be expected to command our unqualified sympathy. Becky wins not our approval but a certain human fellow-feeling; a woman of spirit and intelligence, she rebels openly and consistently against a life of subservience. She uses systematically all the weapons society has reserved for men, plus a few of her own; her way leads to moral degradation. Amelia, "the little parasite," chooses the way approved by society; she is rewarded at the end, but not until even Dobbin sees her as she is.

Thackeray's tone is ambiguous: Is he pronouncing a moral judgment? Does he approve of Amelia? Is he condemning Becky? Or is he presenting two women, both products of their individual temperaments, characters, backgrounds, social environments?

Are the themes of the novel applicable only to the early nineteenth century?

Is the novel primarily, as has been said, "a comedy of manners" or an exploration of human nature?

MINOR CHARACTERS

Through these the author satirizes particular vanities: Jos, person and dress; Miss Crawley, "enlightened" free thinking; George Osborne, "gentlemanly honor"; old Mr. Osborne, dynastic ambition—"family tyrant"; Mr. Sedley, commercial ambition; Dobbin, excessive humility. Thackeray uses minor characters to praise particular virtues: Dobbin, personal loyalty and steadfastness to an ideal; Colonel O'Dowd, faithfulness to duty; Mrs. O'Dowd, kindliness; Miss Briggs, personal loyalty.

POSSIBLE SYMBOLS

Thackeray is not a "symbolic novelist" but passages similar to the following may be suggested as having a significance beyond or aside from the immediate revelation of character or exposition of plot.

The "Dixionary" episode. Spurning this book, Becky not only expresses her resentment of Miss Pinkerton but foreshadows her rejection of life in the subservient position of a woman who must earn her own living.

The frontispiece representing Isaac and Abraham in the family Bible from which old Mr. Osborne strikes his son's name. The symbolism here is ironic—Abraham was reluctantly ready to sacrifice his son to God; Osborne sacrifices George merely to Mammon and his own angry pride (p. 233).[6]

The "great funereal damask pavilion in the vast and dingy state bedroom" which serves as Amelia's bridal chamber—note especially *funereal* (p. 264). The symbolism is again ironic—Amelia had envisioned her love match as a thing of sweetness and light, quite apart from the sordid cares of mankind; however, the weight of commercial motives entering into a marriage contract, even though defied by George, makes itself felt in this image.

The pastoral pictures Amelia paints and tries to sell may be taken as types of the romantic conception of love with which she still deludes herself; the paintings, significantly, are unsalable.

Becky's secret desk in which over the years she hides money from Rawdon may be suggested as a symbol of that inner core of her being, which is never touched and which never participates genuinely in any ennobling human relationship.

HISTORICAL BACKGROUND

The years covering the novel are especially eventful; one might consider them as showing, broadly, a movement toward democracy within nations and self-determination among nations.

▶ *Study guides*

The teacher trusts to a study guide to do some of his teaching for him; these guides, in the method suggested here, are divided into no more than five parts, each part representing a segment of the novel and each used as the basis for one discussion. Since the time the teacher can spend with each group is necessarily

---

[6] Page references are to the Modern Library, college edition, published by Random House (1950).

limited, the guide will include more points than can be discussed. In this way attention is called to significant details requiring little or no explanation but which careless readers might overlook.

Here are four excerpts from the complete study guides covering the four novels chosen by the students. These particular segments have been chosen to show different aspects of the study of any novel.

Vanity Fair

The first, for *Vanity Fair*, is included to show the teacher's attempt to translate his understandings of the values of the novel, as shown in the analysis, into questions that will lead students to discover these values for themselves.

FIRST DISCUSSION: CHAPTERS 1–14

What purposes do you see in the "Dixionary" episode?

Contrast Becky and Amelia in as many ways as possible. What do they have in common?

Although each treats her differently, Becky reacts to Miss Jemina and Miss Pinkerton in the same way. What purpose may the author have in presenting this? What are Becky's reasons for her actions?

Analyze Becky's technique for ingratiating herself with persons she wants to impress. How does this work for and against her?

What were the consequences of Dobbin's victory? Do they seem logical? Why or why not?

Chapter 11 introduces Bute Crawley and his wife. What impression do you get of each?

What seems to be the attitude of Becky and George toward each other? Support your opinion.

Can you find any evidence of irony in Chapter 12? If so, at what or whom is it directed? If not, what is the purpose of the chapter? What does Thackeray mean (p. 112), "This was not . . . time should come." Why use *good* three times in one sentence?

Why were Becky's tears *genuine?* (p. 144)

Be prepared to comment on the following quotations:

"Say a bouquet . . . genteel." (p. 1)
"All the world . . . of his own face." (p. 9)
"Are not there . . . rest of the history?" (p. 49)
"I'm a liberal . . . my own station." (p. 57)
"Whatever Sir Pitt . . . disguise of them." (p. 68)
"there is always such a lady in a coach . . ." (p. 70)
"And, as we bring . . . which politeness admits of." (p. 79)
"and if Harry the Eighth . . . this season?" (p. 81)
"Miss Crawley . . . made her beloved anywhere." (p. 85)
"And it's to this man's son . . . unchristian." (p. 101)
"She's faultless . . . play for it." (p. 117)
"Whenever he met . . . Briton can do." (p. 123)

Notice the references to historical and social background (pp. 8, 52, 61, 82, 111).

The Good Earth

For *The Good Earth* we have selected the third discussion guide. Less competent readers often find the middle section of a novel a crucial point. Therefore, the teacher takes times to review significant points made in previous discussions and to stress details foreshadowing future events.

THIRD DISCUSSION: CHAPTERS 16–22

In clarifying the situations covered by the following questions, the teacher may need to review these points:

the land as a symbol
dependence upon physical elements in the environment
factors accounting for Wang Lung's prosperity
contrasts between life in city and in country
contrasting attitudes of Wang Lung and Olan toward begging and other things
Wang Lung's relationship with his uncle
Wang Lung's attitude toward the House of Hwang

Does Wang Lung or Olan have a better understanding of the other? Evidence?

How does Wang Lung explain the fall of the House of Hwang? What steps does he take to prevent a similar disaster to his family? Why does he later change his plans?

Explain the significance of "Wang Lung was not afraid." (pp. 158, 159) [7] Compare with "Wang Lung was afraid . . . ." (p. 138)

Chapter 19 starts with a series of conditions. Do you agree with the author's premise? Why or why not?

Examine Wang Lung's attempts to justify his actions concerning the jewels and his taking a concubine. What validity has his reasoning? Is this type of thinking common? If so, give examples. At whom or at what is he angry?

What is the effect of the return of the uncle?

Should Wang Lung have been prepared for Olan's resentment of Cuckoo? Why? Is it significant that Olan resents her more than she does Lotus?

Trace the events that weakened Lotus' hold on Wang Lung? Is his change in attitude logical? Why or why not?

"Wang Lung was surprised." (p. 210) Should he have been? Is the reader?

Be prepared to comment on the following quotations:

"and she answered . . . never in her eyes." (p. 139)
"And he was moved . . . did not understand." (p. 141)
"The woman fell silent . . . life has gone." (p. 146)
"And so for the time . . . can be swallowed." (p. 149)
"for the elder . . . from the earth." (p. 158)
"But he flung himself . . . only was frightened." (p. 162)
"But Olan returned . . . spread over the stone." (p. 179)

The next two partial guides prepare for the final discussions of two novels of contrasting patterns. Dickens through novelistic techniques presents a closely woven tapestry in which recurring motifs are important; Wilder depends on a stark undergirding structure to create the basic design of his novel.

[7] Page references are to the Pocket Book edition (1953).

Great Expectations

The following are examples of the devices used to weave plot, characters, and themes into a unified whole.

FINAL DISCUSSION

Developing mystery and suspense
    Pip's fears of what will happen (p. 13) [8]
    the stranger with the file (p. 73)
    the pain Estella was to cause (p. 78)
    Jaggers at Satis House (pp. 78, 79)
    Pip's realization of why he made Biddy a confidant (p. 92)
    Wemmick's telling Pip to notice Jaggers' housekeeper (p. 193)
    Estella's troubling resemblance to someone (p. 228)
    the stranger crouching on the dark staircase (p. 313)

Developing characters and themes
    Pip's feelings of guilt and remorse
        stealing the food (p. 14)
        being ashamed of his home (p. 102)
        providing the iron with which his sister is injured (p. 116)
        rejecting his home and Joe (pp. 139, 311, 404)
        not deserving his wealth (p. 238)
        being responsible for Magwitch's possible capture (p. 328)
        being "misremembered" after death (p. 408)
        intending to desert Magwitch (p. 442)
    Gentlemen and working men—the rich and the poor
        Joe and "his honest old forge"
            contentment with his lot (pp. 67–68, 142)
            explanation to Pip of "common" (p. 67)
            reaction to Miss Havisham (p. 96)
            burning the indenture papers (p. 141)
            pride (pp. 143–44)
            constraint with Pip and his understanding of their relative positions (pp. 214–15)
        Pip and his life of ease
            reference to the rich man and the kingdom of Heaven (p. 141)
            first deference shown him by Trabb and Pumblechook (pp. 145–47)
            Herbert's unrealistic ideas of gaining wealth (pp. 175–76)
            Pip's belief his money was not good for him (p. 261)
            Magwitch's telling Pip that one man's hard work enables another to become a gentleman (p. 307)
            the rich and the poor before the law (pp. 335–36)
            Pip's content with his life at the end (p. 462)
    Pip's need for the security and love parents can give
        Pip's forming his impressions from the engravings on the tombstones (p. 1)
        Pip's rejection of his sister as a suitable parent (p. 59)

[8] Page references are to the Pocket Book edition (1956).

Pip's connecting Magwitch's footsteps with those of his dead sister (p. 302)

Magwitch's claiming him as a son (p. 307)

Pip's rejection of dependence on Magwitch, his preference for a lifetime of work at the forge (p. 328)

Pip's realization that Magwitch is Estella's father (p. 391)

Pip's final understanding and acceptance of Magwitch

Pip's relationship with Joe

Any novelistic devices the teacher thinks important for a particular group would be referred to in appropriate places in the study guide and reviewed after the completion of the novel.

The Bridge of San Luis Rey

The following questions explore the relationship between form and meaning.

FINAL DISCUSSION

Does the use of parallel episodes add or detract from the impact of the novel? Explain.

Analyze the role of the Abbess in the novel—her relation to plot, characters, themes.

Do the five who die have anything in common? Do any of those who remain after the tragedy—Brother Juniper, Don Andres, Alvarado, the Abbess, the Perichole—have anything in common?

Explore the meaning of the comments Wilder makes about:

literature and the readers of literature (p. 15) [9]

the art of biography (pp. 108, 109)

Are these comments particularly relevant to this novel? Why?

Does Wilder directly answer the question the novel poses? If so, what is his answer? If not, why doesn't he? Does he suggest a solution, complete or partial, to the difficulties which cause human beings to ask the same question?

How are the separate stories linked to create a unified design?

▶ Writing

1. As the novel is being read it is essential that reading and clarification through discussion should continue at the fastest pace the group can maintain while at the same time acquiring the necessary understandings; however, some novels are longer or, even if shorter, more difficult than others; individuals within each group will also differ. Therefore, the writing program should be flexible:

The same number of writing assignments need not be given to all groups. Under ordinary circumstances, those reading *The Bridge of San Luis Rey* should finish before other groups do; the teacher and students must decide whether writing or some of the reading and discussion activities suggested will be more profitable.

Writing experiences (suggested by topics from the study guide) should be

[9] Page references are to the Pocket Book edition (1955).

brief; [10] the teacher's purpose is to probe for deeper meanings suggested in the novel, not to teach particular writing skills. Those students who have difficulty maintaining the pace set by the group should not be asked to write.

2. After the reading has been completed, an essay to which students bring all their skill in interpreting the novel, in organizing, and in precise expression serves as a good culminating and evaluative device. Students should have time for preparation (see time schedule) before writing the final draft in class; they should have some choice as to topic—one where understanding developed through the discussions will enable them to do an acceptable job; another that demands insights the discussions may have touched upon but have not fully probed. Examples of both kinds of topics follow.

Vanity Fair

Thackeray says his novel is without a hero. Has it a heroine? If so, who is it? Define *heroine* and substantiate your opinion. If you think the book contains no heroine, why do you think so? What might be the author's purpose in writing a novel without a hero? With neither hero nor heroine?

Conrad, in *The Secret Sharer,* is concerned with an individual's struggle to attain maturity. Does any one of the characters in the Thackeray novel embody the same struggle? If so, who? Explain. If not—since *Vanity Fair* covers a considerable portion of the life span of his characters—why does the author omit such an important aspect of individual human development? Give evidence to support whichever point of view you choose.

The Good Earth

Which seems to you the stronger character, Wang Lung or Olan? Give evidence from the novel to support your opinion. Since your essay will be based on a comparison, you will need to discuss both characters and define what you mean by *stronger*.

We have discussed the three perfectly integrated strands that make up this novel: personal happenings, social scene, development of theme. Select two significant personal events in which different characters have the predominant role. Show how the author in presenting the event has linked it with the two other aspects of the novel.

Great Expectations

You will remember we agreed that *gentleman* used today in a complimentary sense means "a man of fine feelings or instincts—irrespective of social position and training—as shown by his behavior and especially by his generous consideration of others." Select the character in the novel that best exemplifies these qualities; give specific examples to support your choice.

Compare Pip and the captain in *The Secret Sharer* as to the essence of the total experience of each; does Pip in any sense have his Leggatt too? Explain.

The Bridge of San Luis Rey

The major theme of the novel concerns "the justification of the ways of God to man." Is this statement true or false? If true, support your belief with evidence from

[10] See the writing assignments for *Macbeth*, pages 605–06.

the novel; if false, state what you consider the theme to be and provide evidence to support your opinion.

In *The Secret Sharer* the captain says, "I wondered how far I should turn out faithful to that ideal conception of one's own personality every man sets up for himself secretly." Apply this statement to any one of the principal characters of the Wilder novel, showing what the ideal conception is, the obstacles hindering its attainment, and the final degree of success achieved.

▶ *Time schedule*

Each student received a copy of the schedule; another was posted on the bulletin board. The class hour was fifty-five minutes, allowing approximately twenty-five minutes for each discussion. Thus while the teacher was working in one corner of the room with those studying *Vanity Fair*,[11] all others were reading. One student from each group was asked to take care of signing slips, receiving messages—all those "emergencies" likely to interrupt a class.

A glance at the schedule shows the need for thorough understanding of procedural routines before discussions start, a well-established guided reading program with many novels available on various levels, and a class with sufficient experience in assuming responsibility for self-guidance.

MONDAY	TUESDAY	WEDNESDAY	THURSDAY	FRIDAY
Discussion 1 Group 1 * Group 2	Discussion 1 Group 3 Group 4	Reading, discussion, conferences	Discussion 2 Group 1 Group 2	Discussion 2 Group 3 Group 4
Reading, discussion, conferences	Discussion 3 Group 1 Group 2	Discussion 3 Group 3 Group 4	Discussion 4 Group 1 Group 2	Discussion 4 Group 3 Group 4
Reading, conferences discussion	Discussion 5 Group 1 Group 2	Discussion 5 Group 3 Group 4	Study period to prepare for writing	Final writing

* 1. *Vanity Fair*   2. *The Good Earth*   3. *Great Expectations*   4. *The Bridge of San Luis Rey.*

As the schedule indicates, class time should be allowed between some of the discussions; the slower students may need it to complete the assigned reading; others may use it for writing or for student-led discussions on the books in the guided reading program. The teacher also needs the time—usually to confer with absentees, and occasionally to confer with those who may require more help than the discussions give.

▶ *Over-all designs of the four novels*

These diagrams, worked out with each group, were used to show the different basic designs; the bulletin board committee—a volunteer from each group—prepared legends, using illustrations from the novel to make the diagram concrete.

[11] See page 303.

Vanity Fair

The Good Earth

Great Expectations

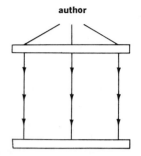

*The Bridge of San
Luis Rey*

*Author at the core
of story observes,
comments, interprets,
stands between
the reader and the
characters.*

*Omniscient author
allows the reader
to "get inside" the
characters and
become involved in
their thoughts and
feelings.*

*Story is told through
the impression
persons and events
make on the
principal character,
allowing the reader
to become involved
to the extent Pip is
involved.*

*Omniscient author
allows his readers
to become involved
with his characters
but works out his
ideas in parallel
episodes, linked
through characters,
events, and themes.*

Culminating experiences

▶ *Ideas and characters*

Student-led groups were asked to select ideas and characters from each novel, using specific criteria. First, each student, in preparation, was to select the three characters most essential to the novel and prepare to defend his choice; to select no more than three important ideas the novel emphasizes, submitting evidence to support his opinion. Then, students met in groups to agree upon characters and ideas and to make a list of both to be handed in. The following were selected: [12]

Vanity Fair
Becky, Amelia, Dobbin
attitude toward social position; effect of social inequalities; position of women

The Good Earth
Wang Lung, Olan, their sons
man's resilience in meeting disaster; position of women; effect of cultural
  change on social conditions and thus on the individual

Great Expectations
Pip, Joe, Estella
child's need for security and wise guidance in becoming a worthy adult; attitude
  of the individual and of society toward wealth and social position; the poor in
  relation to the social institutions of the time

---

[12] The problem in selecting ideas is one of elimination, since all of any importance will
  have been stressed in the discussions; certain characters, too, are inevitable choices, but
  usually the third and sometimes the second demands a rather close look at the novel.

The Bridge of San Luis Rey
The Abbess, the Marquesa, Uncle Pio
desire of human beings to discover whether the events in their lives are part
   of an over-all plan or occur by chance; the need for courage and love in human
   relationships

▶ *Comparison of novels*

Student-led groups were asked to discover similarities and contrasts among the
problems presented in the four literary works.[13] These ideas were selected as significant:

attitude toward wealth and social position (novels 1 and 3)
position of women in different times and cultures (1 and 2)
achieving maturity in stable and changing cultures (2 and 3)
man's resilience in meeting frustration and disaster (2 and 4)
the need for courage and love in human relationships (all four)

These characters were chosen as having something in common:

Amelia, Wang Lung, Pip, the Marquesa
Dobbin, Olan, Joe, the Abbess, Uncle Pio
Becky, Wang Lung's sons, Estella

▶ *Final synthesis*

Students in original groups were to suggest ways of handling the presentations,
their suggestions being given to a committee to devise plans. This committee made
the following decisions:

a series of oral reports, each followed by contributions from the class
two students to compare problems encountered by Pip and Wang Lung's sons
   in attaining maturity, showing how and why they differed
two students to discuss the position of women as shown in *Vanity Fair* and *The
   Good Earth,* giving reasons for similarities and differences
a student from each group to present one example of man's resilience in meeting frustration and disaster, one of the four introducing the subject and drawing conclusions from the examples
a student from each group to give an example of love and loyalty, with similar
   introduction and conclusion
a panel that would consider the characters chosen

The groups met once more to select members to represent them in the final presentations. The time allowed: two periods for the first four, one period for the panel.

For a final assignment, the teacher asked the class to consider all the work
that had been done on the novels and to try to suggest a suitable title for the unit.
All titles growing out of the ideas discussed were immediately rejected as being

---

[13] The teacher planning to use this method should not try to select literary works which
   fit a preconceived theme; the important thing is to have novels which challenge each
   group. The study of each individual work reveals its unique values. Since all are records
   of human experience, they will have points of similarity—sometimes as basic as here; at
   other times, relatively minor—which students can discover for themselves. The probing
   takes place in the study of each work; recognition of likenesses in the various works
   should come spontaneously if it is to be worthwhile.

too limited. Many concerned with character were considered, but most were eliminated because examples from one or more novels seemed to invalidate them. Finally only two remained—"Character Makes the Man" and "The Consequences of Character"; the latter was selected.

Evaluation

Evaluation is continual and ways for evaluating are inherent in the methods suggested for teaching.

▶ *Teacher evaluation*

1. *Through discussion*   Does the student show increasing ability to detect motives in the actions of characters? Is he growing in ability to see relationships among characters? Is he able to connect the events and characters in the novel with those in life? Is he becoming more aware of the methods and devices used by the novelist to create a unified impression?

2. *Through writing*   Does the student always select the "safest" topic for writing, the one for which the discussion has prepared him? If so, does he show understanding of the concepts being developed? Is he at times willing to try the more difficult of the two assignments? If so, does his writing show deepening insights into the literary works? How does his final writing on the group novel compare with that done on *The Secret Sharer?*

3. *Through comparisons with books read individually*   An assignment similar to the following will test the student's understanding of design in the novel:

Keeping in mind the over-all designs of the four group novels, consider others you have read; does any one conform in general to one of the four designs of the novels studied? If so, give title and author; discuss, showing similarities. If not, explain the design of the novel you have selected.

▶ *Student evaluation*

Assignments similar to the following (not to be used for grading) will give the teacher some insight into what students think of content and method:

If such a unit were to be taught to similar classes, should the novel studied by your group be included? Why or why not? From the impression you have gained of other group novels, do you think any one should be omitted? Why or why not?

Do you see any advantages in studying a novel in groups rather than with the entire class? Any disadvantages?

What did you gain, if anything, from the culminating experiences? If you consider your gains slight, why do you think so?

Do you consider *The Secret Sharer* a good novel for high school seniors? Defend your point of view.

Editions of novels

Paperback editions were used for all novels. Inexpensive editions of the many literary works continually appearing on the market allow teachers to experiment with fresh material to supplement, or perhaps eventually replace, that already in the curriculum. Thus, a more flexible program can be maintained. The following editions were used in this unit:

BUCK, PEARL S. *The Good Earth.* New York: Pocket Books, 1953.

CONRAD, JOSEPH. *The Secret Sharer.* New York: New American Library (Signet Classic, CD4), 1957.

DICKENS, CHARLES. *Great Expectations.* New York: Pocket Books, 1956.

THACKERAY, WILLIAM MAKEPEACE. *Vanity Fair.* New York: Random House (Modern Library, College edition), 1950.

WILDER, THORNTON. *The Bridge of San Luis Rey.* New York: Pocket Books, 1955.

PROGRAM AND PLAN

Good planning of many kinds is crucial to good teaching. Without sound planning, instruction is haphazard, and what students learn depends mainly on chance. A basic curriculum pattern for six or twelve years influences many classroom decisions. So too do the requirements of particular courses. Thus, planning work before students arrive is as necessary as adapting plans prepared in advance to the class that appears. Occasional lessons may bear little direct relationship to those that precede or follow. Others are integral steps in a developing unit and can be considered only in relation to over-all objectives. It is not possible, then, to predict the sequence in which every teacher will engage in various planning activities. Consequently, the diverse stages of planning are discussed here in separate sections so they will be accessible to each reader as needed: planning a six-year program, a one-year program, a single unit, and a single lesson.

PLANNING A SIX-YEAR PROGRAM

Through the directed study of significant values and concepts students grow in ability to receive and to communicate ideas. Teachers of English recognize that a value-centered or idea-centered curriculum contains a basic content that prevents the study of language skill from becoming isolated, apathetic, and sterile. The Rockefeller report on education said:

> Education is not just a mechanical process for communication to the young of certain skills and information. It springs from our most deeply rooted convictions. And if it is to have vitality both teachers and students must be infused with the values which shape the system. No inspired and inspiring education can go forward without powerful undergirding by the deepest values of our society.[1]

If the development of values, the development of understandings, and the development of skills are important parallel goals in our English curriculum, through what organizational framework can these be achieved? The pattern varies with school size and organization, but certain characteristics are com-

---

[1] Rockefeller Brothers Fund, Inc., *The Pursuit of Excellence* (Garden City, N.Y.: Doubleday, 1958), p. 49.

mon to many programs. Usually the six-year secondary English curriculum includes a balanced general program for all students during grades 7 through 10, with literary study, some study of language and rhetoric, much reading, and considerable work on basic skills of communication introduced in every classroom. Increasingly in later secondary-school years, however, schools tend to emphasize the study of literature and specialized interests in writing, speech, and dramatics. This basic pattern, illustrated in Chart 1, is fairly common throughout America, although little agreement is to be found concerning titles of courses or grade placement of books, materials, and specific learning experiences. Then, too, some schools require only five years of secondary English, with individuals permitted to substitute electives in drama, journalism, business English, humanities, or creative writing during the junior and senior years.

CHART 1   A POSSIBLE ORGANIZATION OF THE ENGLISH CURRICULUM IN GRADES 7–12

7 8 9 10	11	12
General English	*American literature*	*Special courses*
Balanced program for all literature, language, composition in written and oral dimensions often organized around units of instruction attention throughout to skills involved in thinking, speaking, reading, and listening	Emphasis on American ideals and ideas Continued work on skills as needed	Advanced composition Advanced literary study Major works English, world, modern Humanities (literature, art, music) Drama Journalism Public speaking Creative writing Business English General English for those needing review

Special courses for individuals

1. Corrective reading
2. Individual speech work, sight-saving instruction, and remedial reading instruction
3. Directed reading
4. Independent study
5. Special class for the severely retarded
6. English as a second language

Common variations

1. Block or Common Learnings Programs; English–social studies combinations in grades 7 and 8

2. Some elective courses in grades 7, 8, 9: journalism, drama, directed reading
3. Advanced placement programs in grades 10–12
4. Introducing electives at grade 11 with students permitted to select a specified number of one semester courses focusing on such studies as poetry, the novel, history of language, advanced composition.

GROUPING IN SECONDARY ENGLISH   The requirement that students complete five or six years of English does not necessarily suggest a common standard of achievement for all. Schools have learned to expect great variation of ability in any single group and have attempted to meet the differences in many ways: by providing multiple copies of books and learning materials at varying levels; by sectioning students into average, advanced, and slow learning classes; by organizing "opportunity" classes for those who need special help or reveal special talents. Many teachers prefer to work with homogeneous classes in which an attempt is made to reduce the range of differences in ability; others just as conscientiously believe that the wide variation in student abilities and diversity of student backgrounds contribute to learning by providing important experiences in communication between students from all social and cultural groups. In one recent Anglo-American conference on the teaching of English, the majority of participants recommended homogeneous grouping, at least during the first ten years.[2] For every class the important question to be considered is the educational purpose. On this depends either the wisdom or shortsightedness of both rigid and flexible patterns of sectioning. Different kinds of sectioning may be introduced to achieve special purposes, but almost surely these should include at times a planned heterogeneity that brings together students with many kinds of backgrounds and abilities.[3] As experienced teachers know, a range of differences in the classroom continually poses a challenge to the ingenuity of teachers, regardless of the type of sectioning used.

GRADE LEVEL–AGE LEVEL EMPHASES   Given some underlying framework, many school programs provide for continuity in student learning by designating content, skills, or experiences for emphasis at each age level or grade level. An over-all pattern gives some guarantee of cumulative learning. Moreover, textbooks usually offer only limited help in identifying and establishing

[2] See the report of these discussions in Herbert J. Muller, *The Uses of English* (New York: Holt, Rinehart & Winston, 1967), and John Dixon, *Growth Through English* (London: National Association for the Teaching of English, 1967). Available from NCTE.

[3] Readers familiar with recent sociological studies of education know that rigid sectioning procedures tend to discriminate against students from lower socio-economic groups. See Allison Davis, *Social Class Influences on Learning* (Cambridge, Mass.: Harvard Univ. Press, 1952); Robert Hollingshead, *Elmtown's Youth* (New York: Wiley, 1949); James Coleman and others, *Equal Educational Opportunity* (Washington, D.C.: Superintendent of Public Documents, 1965). Often those who protest against ability grouping do so because they believe that true ability is obscured by our present methods of assessing intellectual power.

continuing goals. Such books are prepared to assist not to control teachers. Only a few years ago James J. Lynch and Bertrand Evans examined several series of secondary-school language textbooks and found most series devoid of any coherent developmental program, full of repetition from grade to grade, and in complete disagreement concerning when, how, and what elements of language study should be introduced.[4] Both the Commission on English of College Entrance Examination Board and the National Study of High School English Programs recommended after careful study that such continuity be achieved by a consensus of teachers of English in every school, not by large district, state, or national groups.[5]

To provide some direction to learning, schools use different approaches. From teaching experience and from the evidence of modern research beginning with Sir Thomas Galton, teachers know that youngsters in a classroom at any grade level will vary considerably in language proficiency no matter how the students are selected. Consequently, the once familiar pattern of basing an instructional program on rigid grade standards has yielded to approaches that neither restrict the advanced nor penalize the slow.

EMPHASIS WITHIN GRADE-LEVEL CYCLES In the Cleveland Heights–University Heights experimental program an attempt is made to identify skills and understandings to be introduced, emphasized, and reinforced at every grade level. The over-all chart (Chart 2) provides teachers with an overview of the total secondary-school curriculum in English and attempts to avoid repetitive teaching.[6]

BLOCKING PARTICULAR UNITS The Curriculum Study Center of the University of Nebraska planned sequential programs in language and composition and in literature and composition by identifying major units for each grade level (Chart 3).[7] The selections each teacher might use within each unit would vary somewhat with the abilities of children in the class, but the basic pattern of study remains constant throughout the six-year program.

IDENTIFYING AN OVER-ALL CONCEPTUAL BASE The curriculum developed at Carnegie Institute of Technology for able college-bound pupils views English as embracing three areas of study: language, literature, and composition or

[4] James J. Lynch and Bertrand Evans, *High School English Textbooks: A Critical Appraisal* (Boston: Little, Brown, 1963), pp. 215–406. See also similar findings of two decades earlier reported by Robert C. Pooley in "Language Arts Survey in Wisconsin Elementary Schools," *Elementary English Review*, Vol. 13, No. 1 (January 1946), pp. 8–14. This issue is discussed in Chapter Three, pages 111–16.

[5] Commission on English, *Freedom and Discipline in English* (New York: College Entrance Examination Board, 1963), p. 42. James R. Squire and Roger K. Applebee, *High School English Instruction Today* (New York: Appleton-Century-Crofts, 1968).

[6] Used by permission of the Cleveland Heights–University Heights Public Schools, Ohio.

[7] From "A Curriculum in English," developed by the Curriculum Study Center, University of Nebraska.

CHART 2   EXAMPLES OF ALLOCATING SKILLS BY GRADE LEVEL:
SKILLS TO BE MASTERED IN ENGLISH IN GRADES 7–12

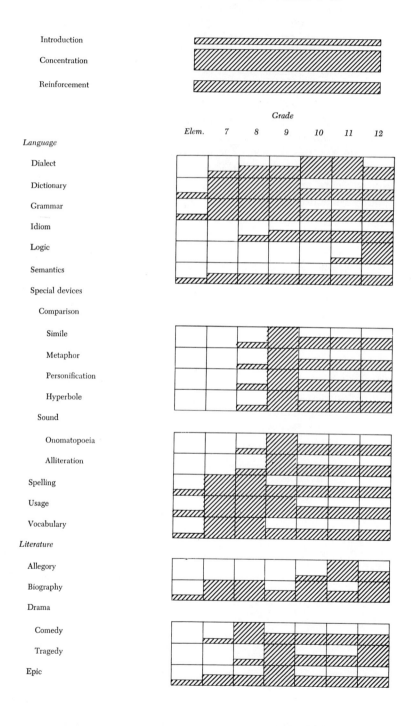

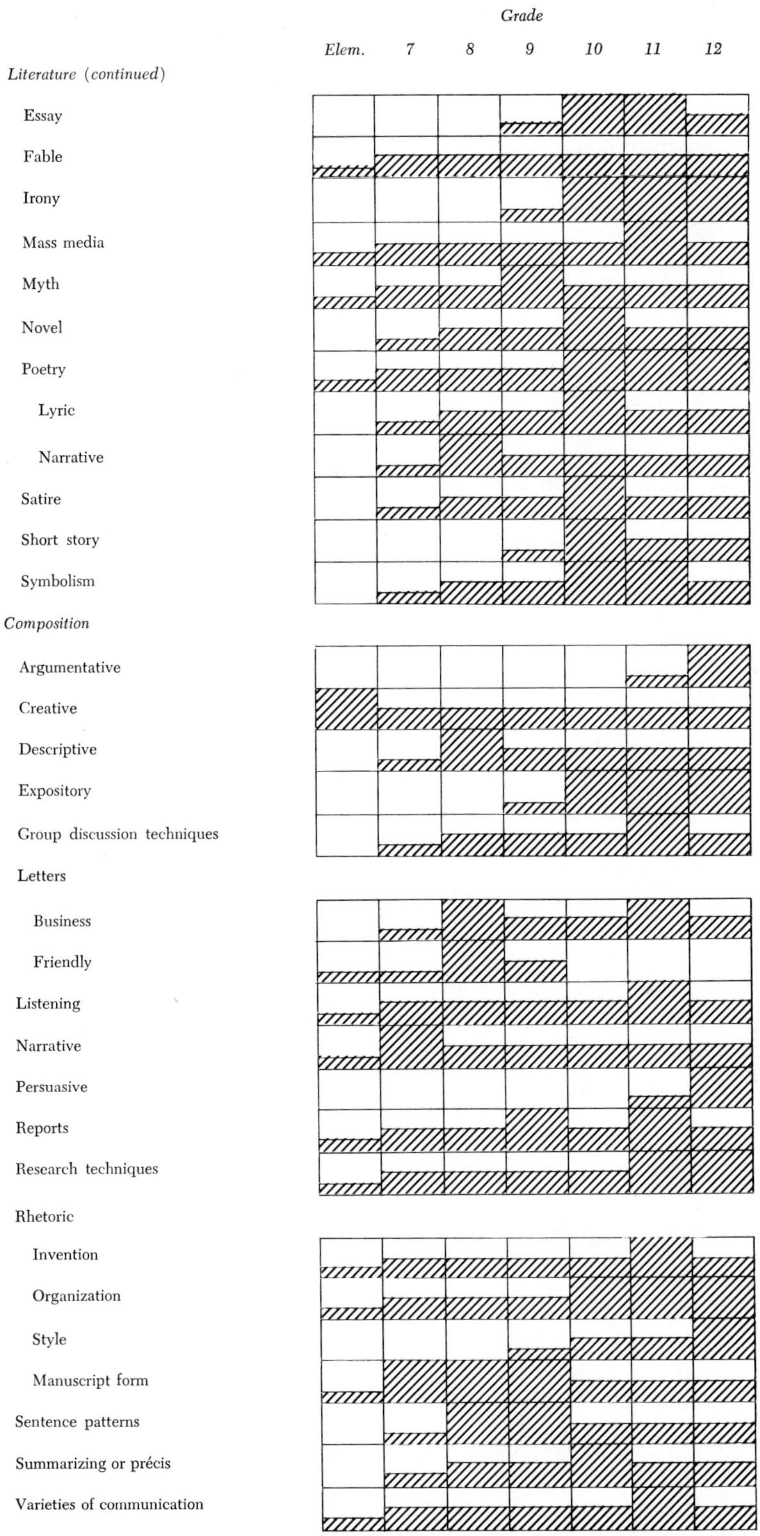

Grade

	Elem.	7	8	9	10	11	12

Literature (continued)

Essay

Fable

Irony

Mass media

Myth

Novel

Poetry

  Lyric

  Narrative

Satire

Short story

Symbolism

Composition

  Argumentative

  Creative

  Descriptive

  Expository

  Group discussion techniques

  Letters

    Business

    Friendly

  Listening

  Narrative

  Persuasive

  Reports

  Research techniques

  Rhetoric

    Invention

    Organization

    Style

    Manuscript form

  Sentence patterns

  Summarizing or précis

  Varieties of communication

CHART 3   ALLOCATING UNITS TO PARTICULAR GRADES

Grade	Language and composition	Literature and composition
7	The Form Classes The Dictionary Spelling	Myths and religious narratives The Making of Stories The Meaning of Stories Religious Story Part 1. Classical Part 2. Hebrew Part 3. Indian Stories of the American West Autobiography
8	History of the English Language Syntax Words and Their Meanings	The Hero Making of Heroes Journal Novel Hero Historical Novel Hero Epic Hero: Beowulf and Roland Heritage of the Frontier
9	Dialect Phonology The Uses of Language Syntax and the Rhetoric of the Sentence	The Kinds Attitude, Tone, Perspective: The Idea of Kinds Satire The Idea of a Play Comedy Epic
10	Rhetoric of the Short Units of the Composition Part 1. Sentence Part 2. Paragraph Rhetoric of the Long Unit of the Composition	Man and Nature, Society, and Moral Law Man's Picture of Nature The Leader and the Group Sin and Loneliness Tragedy
11	Rhetoric	Three Themes in American Civilization Individualism and Nature Sin and Loneliness Satire: American Materialism Conclusion: Individualism and Nature Reconsidered
12	Rhetoric	Forms and Themes in English Literature Shakespearean Tragedy Christian Epic Satire: Restoration and Augustan The Writer as Rebel and Prophet The Writer and the Class System

communication. The directors of this program see the interrelationship of these areas much as three interlocking triangles: [8]

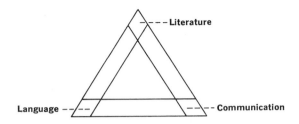

The percentage of class time devoted to each segment of what has become popularly known as the "tripod" curriculum is approximately 56 per cent for literature, 26 per cent for composition, and 18 per cent for language. Literature, then, is the core of this program, but the relationship of the study of language and composition is indicated by the interlocking triangle image. The over-all pattern of the three-year program is based on examination of three underlying concepts in each of the three areas of study, each concept to receive major stress during one of the three years. As can be noted in Chart 4,[9] however, some treatment of each major concept is provided each year.

PROVIDING FOR COMMON AND DIVERSIFIED EXPERIENCES A still different consideration in developing a six-year program involves identifying the instruction all students need in common as well as that possible for the academically advanced or the academically limited. Often this is done with reference to plans for a particular school grade, as in Palo Alto, California, where classes are divided into A and B sections. In eleventh-grade classes in American literature, for instance, thematic emphases are held common for both groups, but certain related sub-themes are taught to particular groups.

Literature selected in relation to the designated themes reflects the abilities of the students. Thus, A-lane students may approach considerations of "Freedom, Individualization, and Acceptance" by reading *Arrowsmith* and *The Scarlet Letter*, B-lane students by reading *The Caine Mutiny* or *The Big Sky*. Like other plans mentioned in this chapter, the Palo Alto approach reflects the attempt of English teachers to provide sound sequence and continuity in learning within the context of the great diversity they continually experience in public school classrooms.

OFFERING UNGRADED ELECTIVES Recently a number of schools have reported considerable success in organizing ungraded high school English programs that

[8] Erwin Steinberg and others, *Sample Selection from a Senior High Curriculum in English for Able College-Bound Students* (Pittsburgh: Carnegie Institute of Technology, 1966), p. 2.
[9] *Ibid.*, pp. 3, 10, 11.

CHART **4**   IDENTIFYING CONTROLLING CONCEPTS IN LITERATURE,
COMPOSITION, AND LANGUAGE

Literature

Grade 10 World Literature	Universal concerns of a man	M ———	L ———
Grade 11 American Literature	U ———	Modification by culture pattern	L ———
Grade 12 English Literature	U ———	M ———	Literary art forms, genres, techniques

Composition

Grade 10	Idea: the writer discovers, isolates, defines his message	M ———	M ———
Grade 11	I ———	Message sent: the writer puts it into language	M ———
Grade 12	I ———	M ———	Message received: the writer modifies it according to the needs of his reader

Language

Grade 10	Structure of the language	S ———	R ———
Grade 11	S ———	Semantics: meaning	R ———
Grade 12	S ———	S ———	Rhetoric: the effective use of language

permit pupils to choose courses from among twenty to thirty separate one-semester offerings. Such programs normally require completion of six or eight courses in English, often specify that at least one semester must be spent on some aspect of composition (Basic Writing, Narrative Writing, Advanced Composition) and perhaps one on some aspect of American literature (The Novel of the Frontier, Modern American Poetry, Contemporary Drama). First-, second-, and third-year pupils may be enrolled in the same class by choice, say, Afro-American Literature, Shakespeare I, or Speech Arts. In addition to such standard one-semester offerings as Early American Literature, The English Language, or British Poets, such programs often permit teachers with special interests to develop rather unique courses; for example, American Folklore, Opera and Literature, The Literature of Alienation. The state of California recently adopted a framework for English programs that calls for a program of "English by Choice" at the upper levels:

> The required English program for the eleventh and twelfth grades should therefore include a variety of courses in literature from among which students may take choices. . . . Every effort should be made by each school to provide as rich a selection as possible of courses combining literature with composition and continuing study of the English language for eleventh and twelfth grade students. . . . The courses proposed should not be construed as "electives" in addition to requirements in English for the eleventh and twelfth grades. They should rather be designated to satisfy the curricular requirements for the final two years of English. . . . Efforts should not be made to emulate the diverse spread of historical and genre courses typically offered in collegiate departments of English.[10]

Schools experimenting with programs of ungraded courses believe that the element of selection encourages greater student responsibility and involvement, that the variety of courses gives each teacher a better chance to teach in an area for which he is particularly well prepared, and that weak courses can be withdrawn and new courses added with little difficulty.

A few schools, such as the Trenton Public Schools in Michigan, have moved one step further into a phase-elective curriculum. A phased curriculum is an ungraded curriculum in which classes are arranged according to the abilities of pupils. At each level, from remedial English to the honors phase, an array of courses is provided for student selection. In Trenton, the twenty-nine courses include offerings in Basic Reading Skills, Mass Media, Modern Literature, Speech, World Literature, Creative Writing, Seminar on Ideas, Humanities, Research Seminar, and Theatre Arts, to mention only a sampling.[11]

PLANNING FOR THE DISADVANTAGED Equality of educational opportunity does not necessarily imply identical English programs for pupils in slums, suburbs, and savannahs. Although the aims are similar for all learners, the content and emphasis in instruction needs modification to accommodate the experiences and sophistication of the learners. *Gateway English,* the program developed at the Project English Center, Hunter College, provides the teacher with lesson plans and related activities based upon the specially tested materials in that project's

[10] *English Language Framework for California Public Schools, Kindergarten through Grade Twelve* (Sacramento, Calif.: California State Department of Education, 1968), pp. 90–91.

[11] *Project Apex,* Trenton Public Schools, 2601 Charlton Road, Trenton, Michigan 48183. Other experimental programs of this kind are described by James R. Squire and Roger Applebee in *High School English Instruction Today* (New York: Appleton-Century-Crofts, 1968), pp. 204–36.

anthologies of readings.[12] The lesson plans present the teaching of language skills as an integrated part of the study of literature. The authors of *Hooked on Books: Program and Proof* [13] asked, "Who are the unreachables? Who are the unteachables? Do they have any reality other than in the blind eyes of the beholder?" Their program was one in which materials were selected to meet the needs of the student rather than the more abstract needs of the subject:

> For example, such extremes of the same language as Shakespeare and the daily newspaper are found to have much in common. In terms of the practical needs of the student, the newspaper takes precedence. Because it begins more nearly where he is, it may prove to be the bridge across which he crawls, stumbles, and finally walks, erect, to where he should be. If he finds Shakespeare at the other end of the bridge, then the simple, inelegant newspaper, magazine or paperback book has become a legitimate and necessary means to attaining a complex, eloquent end.

In their Hooked on Books program, these Michigan innovators saturated the school environment with paperback books, magazines, and newspapers. The contributors to *English and the Disadvantaged* [14] stress an awareness of English as process rather than content, a bold choice of suitable films and books, and a learning model that is mainly inductive. *English for the Rejected,*[15] a British presentation, stresses sympathetic respect for the learner and imaginative-creative emphases, both in the teacher's planning and in the emphasis in the curriculum. The author quotes a pupil in a school where the streams were not called *A, B,* and *C* but *Red, White,* and *Blue:* "We're Blue, sir. Blue. We ain't never gonna be White." The quotation reminds us of recent startling research into the self-fulfilling prophecy. The experimenters chose at random five children in each class of a school and told the teachers these children could be expected to show unusual intellectual gains in the coming year. The children were tested throughout the year, and at the end of the school year they, on the average, had gained four points more in I.Q. than their counterparts did, and in reasoning I.Q. the average gain was seven points more. Other children in the low ability groups who also gained in I.Q. during the year found that their teachers reacted negatively to them.[16] This is worrisome, for it indicates that teachers of a higher socio-economic status expect pupils of a lower socio-economic status to do poorly.

In a remarkable series of personal testimonies, a number of gifted teachers of English have recently reported their success in engaging disadvantaged

---

[12] Marjorie Smiley *et al., Gateway English, A Literature and Language Arts Program* (New York: Macmillan, 1966).

[13] Daniel N. Fader and Elton B. McNeil, *Hooked on Books: Program and Proof* (New York: Berkeley Publishing Corp., 1968).

[14] Edward R. Fagan, ed. *English and the Disadvantaged* (Scranton, Pa.: International Textbook Co., 1967).

[15] David Holbrook, *English for the Rejected* (London: Cambridge Univ. Press, 1964).

[16] Robert Rosenthal and Lenore Jacobson, *Pygmalion in the Classroom* (New York: Holt, Rinehart & Winston, 1968).

students in vital experiences with language and literature through stressing immediate emotional responses.[17] Unlike more traditional teaching that emphasizes cognitive development and the acquisition of knowledge, these new approaches seem to focus on nonrational, sensate experience that can immediately involve young people in classroom activity. Fantini and Weinstein, who describe such approaches as attempts to achieve "a contact curriculum," recently outlined their major characteristics:[18] flexibility rather than rigid uniformity and prescheduling, experience-based rather than symbol-based learning, vertically programmed small-step sequencing of skills rather than horizontally programmed disjointed sequencing, immediate orientation rather than past-and-future orientation, emphasis on social participation (doing) rather than academic preoccupation (knowing), exploration of reality, an equal emphasis on affective and inner content rather than sole emphasis on cognitive, extrinsic concern. Such approaches to curriculum planning actually apply to all learning situations in English, as the discussions of imaginative and rational learning throughout this volume have indicated; but they may be particularly crucial in programs that are seriously coping with the educational malaise of the severely disadvantaged. In no way a repudiation of the more formal approaches to planning discussed elsewhere in this chapter, they suggest how a sensitive and experienced teacher may make the learning of boys and girls who do not readily respond to conventional schoolroom practice more relevant. In many ways the unit "Humanities for the Seventies" suggests some important ways of approaching a contact curriculum.[19]

PROVIDING FOR A BALANCED PROGRAM Schools rely on various ways of assuring a sound balance of learning experiences in English. An intelligent six-year program provides for continuity and balance from grade to grade, yet permits each teacher sufficient flexibility to care for varying interests and needs. Overly rigid requirements penalize the slow student who may learn language at capacity rate and still be far less proficient than his peers; they also penalize the talented who are often restricted by doctrinaire attempts to enforce minimal learnings for all. Teachers of English have learned to expect seventh-graders to arrive from elementary schools with varying capacities and abilities. By the time these students finish six years of secondary English the range of differences should increase. Researcher John Flanagan in a study of able youngsters reported that one-fourth of all ninth-graders are more advanced

[17] Herbert Kohl, Thirty-six Children (New York: New American Library, 1967); Jonathan Kozol, Death at an Early Age (Boston: Houghton Mifflin, 1967); James Herndon, The Way It Spozed to Be (New York: Simon and Schuster, 1968).

[18] Mario D. Fantini and Gerald Weinstein, Toward a Contact Curriculum (New York: Anti-Defamation League of B'nai B'rith, 1968) (315 Lexington Avenue, New York, N.Y. 10016). This readable 55-page monograph, remarkably sensitive to the problems of the urban classroom, impresses us as one of the most helpful new references for teachers in the growing body of professional writing on the education of the disadvantaged.

[19] See pages 609–25.

in learning than a majority of twelfth-graders.[20] Because of the tremendous variation in students' rates of learning, good program planning and good teaching result in an extension rather than a narrowing of differences in achievement. The examples of six-year programs presented here suggest ways of organizing to make such extension possible.

PLANNING FOR ONE YEAR

Just as English departments need over-all curriculum plans to encourage reasonable continuity in instruction, so individual teachers need long-range plans for a semester or a year to set the direction for a class. Some work must be planned in advance, before students arrive; some is best planned with students. But while assessing the needs and interests of particular groups of young people, the teacher must consider each course in relation to the total school program, the community setting, and the resources available. The first task of any teacher is to study the context in which learning will occur.

> *Total school program*
>   Is a course of study or guide available?
>   What is the relation of each class to the total program? To classes that precede and follow?
>   Are there certain concepts or skills to be stressed in the particular class?
> *Resources available in school or school district*
>   What arrangements may be made for use of books, records, and other learning materials?
>   What services are available from librarians? Curriculum supervisors? Department heads? Counselors? Others?
> *Resources in the local community*
>   What special resources are available in community? Libraries? Theaters? Television stations? College or university centers? Others?
>   Are there opportunities for worthwhile field trips pertinent to the course aims? For consultant help? For relating classroom activities to the work world outside?
>   What knowledge about the community will assist in understanding the young people in the classroom?

INVOLVING STUDENTS IN PLANNING   Not until the teacher has met and studied each class can detailed procedures be developed. No two groups are exactly the same; general plans formulated in advance must be adapted to satisfy needs, interests, and abilities of each. With over-all purposes in mind, the teacher considers with students their personal interests and needs for improving communication skills.

The attitudes students bring into the English class may be important determinants of what can and cannot be first attempted. Students' interests may

[20] John Flanagan *et al.*, *Studies of the American High School* (Washington, D.C.: Cooperative Research Division Project 226, U.S. Office of Education, December, 1962).

suggest problems or topics for consideration. Even when faced with a seemingly inflexible course of study, teachers will encourage greater motivation and involvement if students share in planning some activities. Among the useful approaches are the following:

Encouraging students to express personal concerns   The attitudes of students must be considered in selecting reading material and units for study. Compositions written during the opening days, for example, "Why I Hope This Class Will Be Different," or "What Changes I Would Make in Last Year's English Program," offer one way of assessing predispositions. Some teachers meet regularly with a steering committee of students who are elected to represent all class members in such planning. Others give each student an opportunity to express his opinion and to help plan class activities by discussing suggestions in total class or small group sessions.[21]

Giving pupils opportunity to choose   If the literature to be studied or the units to be organized are drawn from a preplanned list, students may be asked to indicate the selections or topics that interest them the most. Choices may be presented within clearly prescribed limits. Thus the teacher explains that the class definitely will study *Abe Lincoln in Illinois, Our Town,* and the popular arts in America, but that the reading for the initial six weeks may be drawn either from the literature of the frontier or the literature of social criticism. Before making a decision, students will need time to investigate the possibilities inherent in each choice.

Involving parents in the planning   Teachers can capitalize on the concern parents express by inviting the mothers and fathers to voice opinions. Junior high school pupils may write letters home explaining the nature of a course and asking for comments. Older students may interview their parents. Sometimes classes may prepare a special questionnaire for parents. From the considered involvement of parents in thinking through the objectives of English with their sons and daughters may emerge greater cooperation between home and school.

DIAGNOSING LANGUAGE NEEDS   In a well-organized classroom, diagnosis and evaluation operate continually, but at the opening of a school year the task requires special attention. Detailed suggestions for assessing needs in particular areas are included in appropriate chapters of this book. Here, however, the discussion concentrates on approaches to use during the initial weeks of school before long-range plans are organized.

A helpful preliminary step is the establishment of individual folders in which data on students may be collected. Some teachers summarize information on note cards; others use large envelopes into which clippings and comments may be dropped. On some occasions students may maintain the folders themselves; on others the teacher will wish to preserve confidential records. Whatever the method, the teacher should do the following:

---

[21] A helpful reference for teachers venturing into cooperative planning for the first time is Louise Parrish and Yvonne Waskin, *Teacher-Pupil Planning* (New York: Harper & Row, 1958). See also John Dixon, *Growth Through English* (London: NATE, 1967).

Begin with the type of activity in which the class is involved. If literature is important, assess students' ability to interpret; if understanding of grammatical generalizations is a goal, plan an appropriate task to check the understandings students already possess.

Be specific in diagnosing language needs. Recognize that the primary purpose of large group surveys is to identify first those individuals who may need special study and help. Later diagnoses permit refinement.

Involve students in appraising their own needs. Remember that self-identification of problems may offer motivation for subsequent learning.

The suggestions for evaluation presented at the end of the major sections of this book may be used for diagnosis and continual appraisal. Teachers interested in certain areas need only consult the appropriate section.

DESIGNING THE PATTERN OF A COURSE   Once the teacher knows the demands of the curriculum, the resources available, and the particular attitudes and needs of his students, he must consider the flow of class activities during the semester or year. Each course must be organized to allow for an intelligent pattern in the study of ideas, for the sustained development of student skills, and for reasonable variety in class activity.

The unifying concept, as the organizing center of study, has many important advantages. It provides for concentration on a few ideas or skills for a period of several weeks. It avoids excessive reliance on day-to-day lessons, which, however carefully designed, can lead only to fragmentary, unrelated learning. Most skills and concepts develop slowly over a period of time. A division of long-range goals into objectives that can be accomplished in a few weeks is necessary; those established for the entire semester or year are so broad they must be limited in order to have a realistic impact on planning. A unit of work usually organizes instruction for several weeks around a core of ideas and pertinent activities and includes instruction in all areas of language. The unit as a means of organization need not be the sole approach to classroom planning, but its value cannot be overstated.

KINDS OF ENGLISH UNITS   A unit may last for a week or for six weeks, depending on the complexity of the learnings. Among the most familiar kinds of units in English, eleven may be readily identified:

1. *thematic*   "Dimensions of Courage," "Alienation and Contemporary Life"
2. *topical*   "Boys and Girls in Faraway Lands," "Life in the Inner City"
3. *typological*   "Great Poetry," "The Contemporary Essay"
4. *project-oriented*   "Producing a Play," "Conducting a Dialect Survey"
5. *rhetorically-oriented*   "The Language of Propaganda," "The Speaker's Voice"
6. *language-centered*   "Discovering Dialects," "The Sounds of English"
7. *problem-oriented*   "Making Choices," "Overcoming Obstacles," "Foreseeing Consequences"
8. *literary problem*   "Point of View," "Tone in Literature"
9. *study based on a single classic*   "Macbeth," "Tom Sawyer"

10. *study of the work of an author or of a group of authors* "Mark Twain," "Six Modern Poets," "Contemporary Afro-American Literature"
11. *response oriented* "Reacting to a Community Crisis," "Sharing Reactions to the Assassination of a Political Leader"

Usually, units are organized around concepts and themes presented through literature or through a common selection of readings. Whatever the basis of organization, opportunities are provided for the study of selected content introduced through significant experiences in thinking, reading, writing, speaking, and listening. Certain units, such as those that are problem-oriented, may feature more writing than reading. Others, such as thematic units, draw more heavily on literature than on other aspects of English. The thematic unit, with its sharper focus on a basic idea, tends to be more suitable for senior high school, whereas the topical unit is clearly appropriate for serving the exploratory function of the junior high school.

VALUES IN UNIT STUDY   The unit approach lifts teacher and students above the restrictions of day-to-day planning so that they see present work in relation to past experiences and future plans. Division of the semester's work into several units, each varying in length, permits the teacher to plan a series of related lessons designed to accomplish goals that can be achieved only over long periods of time, such as those involving the development of complex understandings or the refinement of important skills. Moreover, in well-planned units students become so interested in communicating ideas that attempts to improve the use of language may be introduced at moments when learners are highly motivated. Since all the skills—thinking, reading, speaking, writing, listening—are brought into play in a unit, the student's growth in one area of language development tends to reinforce his command in another. Thus the words he adds to his reading vocabulary during the unit will frequently be used in his speaking and writing.

The unit approach offers the teacher a manageable way of meeting individual needs. With the entire class concerned about certain key ideas, each individual can engage in related tasks within his grasp that permit him to contribute to the thinking of the entire class. Even students reading very easy books may discover interesting insights on a problem, insights not reported by other class members. During a unit, projects and activities usually become increasingly diversified to accommodate the interests and needs of individuals and groups. This diversification frees the teacher from immediate responsibilities to guide the entire class; thus he is able to work with individuals. Illustrations of such procedures are included in units in this book. Finally, a unit lends itself to exploring the relationships among ideas rather than to the less challenging classification of information. All students may profit from this approach to organizing instruction.

BLOCKING OUT A YEAR   One problem teachers and students must consider early in the year is that of blocking out areas of emphasis. Usually the teacher needs to reserve books in advance, to plan unit-related skill lessons, to arrange for films and speakers; hence an over-all framework is necessary.

One tenth-grade teacher blocks out a semester's work for a general class as is shown in Chart 5. He identifies those areas where students are permitted to choose selections and units as well as the areas in which no choice is permitted.

CHART 5   SAMPLE PLAN FOR TENTH-GRADE SEMESTER

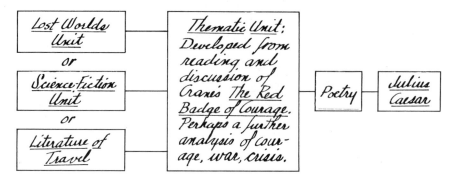

This tenth-grade teacher plans to have the class select and limit one of the initial units. He will then teach the Crane novel to all students, and out of their analysis will come one or two key themes to serve as the focus for subsequent reading and study. Units on "The Meaning of Courage," "Facing Reality," or "How Men React in Crises" are possibilities. Clearly, the teacher is unable to plan all the activities for such a unit in advance. He knows, however, that ultimately the class will study poetry and *Julius Caesar*.

Thus, teachers necessarily plan ahead but they do so only in general terms. The specific activities of each unit—indeed many of the specific readings—may vary depending on the student group. Although in blocking out a semester's work some teachers rely on methods other than the unit approach—on separate long-range programs for teaching vocabulary, spelling, and composition, for example—many find that the organization of learning activities around a unifying problem or idea provides a stimulating and manageable context for language learnings.

ACHIEVING BALANCE IN LONG-RANGE PLANNING   The content of English is so diversified and the goals so numerous that teachers constantly face the danger of overemphasizing one particular aspect of the program. A national study of classroom practices in outstanding high school English programs indicated that more than half of the time in the average program emphasizes literature, a fact that may contribute to the excellence of the programs or reveal areas of neglect. As Chart 6 indicates,[22] the classroom emphases are far more balanced

[22] James R. Squire and Roger K. Applebee, *A Study of English Programs in Selected High Schools Which Consistently Educate Outstanding Students in English,* USOE Cooperative Research Report No. 1994 (Urbana, Ill.: Univ. of Illinois Press, 1966), p. 98.

CHART 6   EMPHASIS IN ENGLISH TEACHING
IN SELECTED HIGH SCHOOL PROGRAMS

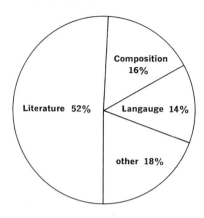

among the other dimensions of English. Most teachers would agree that emphases should vary with the nature and purpose of each class and that programs for nonacademic pupils should probably be less literary than those for the college bound. The following checklist provides a useful frame of reference from which to evaluate a total course.[23]

A CHECKLIST FOR EVALUATING LONG-RANGE PLANNING IN ENGLISH

General

Is the course so planned as to attempt

to provide selected, significant content appropriate to the pupils?

to stimulate both the imagination and the critical thinking of the students?

to integrate the teaching of the four skills—reading, writing, speaking, and listening—so that learning in one reinforces learning in the others?

to explore varied approaches to learning?

to involve students in planning?

Literature

Literary works studied

Is the course planned to include some of the best of both the old and the new? A variety of types—poetry, fiction, drama, essay?

Is the literary work taught so as to preserve its integrity as a work of art, as an ordered presentation of human experiences?

Is the teaching of the literary work correlated with others studied and with the student's experiences with life?

Individual reading

[23] More detailed "Criteria for Evaluating High School English Programs," compiled by Paul H. Jacobs, appeared in the *English Journal,* Vol. 57, No. 9 (December 1968), pp. 1275–96. Reprints are available from NCTE. Also useful as a self-analysis form for teachers or the basis for departmental discussions is *A Sampler of Practices in Teaching English in the Junior and Senior High School* and the accompanying *Rationale for A Sampler of Practices* developed by Anthony Tovatt and others, available from NCTE.

Is this an organized, guided program, with students in the beginning reading books on their own level, but with the teacher attempting to lift that level gradually with specific recommendations of better books?

Is an attempt being made to help the student, through his choice of books, both to deepen his understanding and to widen his horizons?

Is provision made for some discussions of books being read?

Is a cumulative record being kept of books read by each student?

Is this individual reading one of the bases for evaluating the student's work in English?

Oral communication

Are the principles that govern effective speaking and oral interpretation being taught and practiced with standards being built gradually?

Do students and teacher differentiate between discussion and the oral quiz or recitation?

Is the class organized so that most of the individual oral work occurs in small groups rather than in front of the entire class?

Are drama and poetry being approached orally, with students receiving some instruction in the art of oral interpretation?

Listening

Is the teaching of listening an integral part of the classroom experience?

Is the laboratory method—direct teaching through exercises of increasing complexity—used?

Is listening stressed as a necessary complement to all oral work?

Writing

Is there planned progression in the attainment of specific skills? Is the progression planned for all six years?

Is provision made for revision, not only for appropriateness of language, but for greater clarity, forcefulness, and vitality of expression?

Does the teacher provide time and help for pre-correction?

Is a file of each student's papers kept in the room?

Reading

Are the basic comprehension skills given proper emphasis?

Is there a consistent and varied plan for promoting growth in vocabulary skills?

Is there awareness of adapting reading speed to the nature of the material and the purpose of the reader?

Is attention given to depth reading—connotative force of words, metaphorical language, irony, paradox?

Language

Is the program in language organized to develop important understandings about language? Are students being helped to see language, not as a product of grammarians, but as a living, complex organism, to the growth of which all contribute?

Are they aware that

it is always necessary to determine the purpose behind the language?

words change their meaning with context, time, the individual?

statements may be factual, judgmental, normative?

Is grammar taught as the description of a language system?

Is provision made for study of the history, geography, and sociology of language?

Usage

Are individual needs determined by diagnosis and specific items taught only to those who show a need for such instruction?

Is emphasis placed on the student's grappling with his own thought and on the expression of ideas rather than on learning rules, definitions, classifications?

The popular arts

Are motion pictures, television, and radio being studied and wisely used?

by studying important esthetic contributions of these media?

by analyzing the commentary on contemporary life presented in these media?

by using ideas and situations suggested by programs popular with students to motivate writing, speaking, and individual reading?

by correlating suitable programs with the literature being studied?

Are students being helped to develop standards for judging the quality of various types of programs as to their entertainment value? Their artistic worth?

PLANNING A SINGLE UNIT

The kinds of units are many; they vary in the ways they are planned. Those based on a systematic study of content—"Conceptions of Love," for example, in which the class studies in turn chivalric, Renaissance, and romantic ideals—are usually preplanned in detail by the teacher. Those growing out of concerns and problems of students—such as "The Rights and Privileges of Students"—usually develop cooperatively as the work progresses. However planned, effective units emphasize important subject learnings, yet satisfy significant social and emotional needs of young people. Whatever the approach, the planning of any unit involves three fundamental tasks: identifying goals, planning activities to accomplish these, and evaluating the extent of the accomplishment. Once these are clear in the teacher's mind, he is able to choose teaching materials and to determine specific procedures.

The various units used as illustrations in this book may serve as helpful resources. In addition, teachers should become familiar with the many varied and interesting units developed between 1962 and 1967 at curriculum study centers at major universities throughout the country. These materials, usually developed through a collaboration of scholars and teachers, are being made available in a variety of ways. Some are being published commercially, some released by the sponsoring institutions, some disseminated through the information services of the U.S. Office of Education. Inquiries directed to the institution will assist individuals in locating particular items. Among the units of particular interest to secondary-school teachers of English are those prepared at the following institutions: [24]

[24] The development of these curricula and other contemporary trends are described in "The English Curriculum in the Secondary School," *Bulletin of the National Association of Secondary-School Principals*, Vol. 51, No. 318 (April 1967), pp. 1–120, and in Michael Shugrue, *English in a Decade of Change* (New York: Pegasus, 1968). A useful compendium of modern units in language, literature, and composition has been prepared by the Commission on English in *12,000 Students and Their English Teachers* (Princeton, N.J.: College Entrance Examination Board, 1968).

Carnegie-Mellon University, Department of English, Erwin Steinberg and Robert Slack, Directors.

Three-year high school curricula for academically able and less able students.

Florida State University, Department of English Education, Dwight L. Burton, Director.

Varied approaches for teaching English in grades 7, 8, 9.

Hunter College, New York City, Department of Education, Marjorie Smiley, Director.

Topical and thematic units for junior high school pupils in the inner city. These are being published by Macmillan.

Indiana University, Department of English, Edward Jenkinson, Director.

Teaching language, literature, composition, and speech in grades 7–12. Some materials have been published by the Indiana University Press.

Northern Illinois University, Department of English, Andrew Macleish, Director.

Resource units for teaching language in high school.

Northwestern University, Department of English, Wallace Douglas, Director.

Units and materials for teaching composition.

Ohio State University, Department of Education, Frank Zidonis and Donald Bateman, Directors.

Materials for teaching transformational-generative grammar.

Purdue University, Department of English, Arnold Lazarus, Director.

Units for the junior high school focused on the study of single works.

University of Michigan, Department of English, Daniel Fader, Director. A high motivational reading program for unmotivated urban students.

University of Minnesota, College of Education, Stanley B. Kegler, Director.

A six-year series of units dealing with all dimensions of language.

University of Nebraska, Department of English, Paul Olson, Director.

Separate units on language, literature, composition in grades 1–12.

University of Oregon, Department of English, Albert R. Kitzhaber, Director.

A six-year, carefully sequenced series in literature, language (emphasizing transformational grammar), and oral and written composition.

Wisconsin State Department of Education, Robert C. Pooley, Director.

K–12 guides on the teaching of language, literature, and composition.

IDENTIFYING GOALS   Learning objectives are of three types—those involving the concepts and understandings that students are to explore, those involving specific skills to be acquired and refined, and those involving attitudes, appreciations, and similar affective outcomes. The conceptual objectives usually govern the flow of activities, since these are often regarded as the content or subject matter of a unit. For example, if understanding the effect of frustration on the human personality is a conceptual goal, the class will be drawn into an exploration of facets of behavior as revealed in situations of stress; on the other hand, such a content objective as recognizing the chief characteristics of the short-story writing of Hawthorne, Poe, and O. Henry points toward a comparison of fictional selections with an emphasis on literary method. Several kinds of conceptual goals may be identified for a single unit.

Skill objectives usually influence less the organizational design of the unit than the stress within particular lessons. Identification of a few basic skill objectives permits the class to concentrate on a limited number of pressing needs rather than on all aspects of communication. Thus in one unit the class concentrates on certain organizational abilities, such as improving transitions between ideas, and in a later unit, work in other skills is introduced. By concentrating on only a few new learning goals, the students more readily achieve some degree of mastery. Of course, teachers also try to maintain standards by requiring students to use effective, appropriate language at all times.

Attitudes and appreciations are sometimes considered as concomitant learnings rather than as clearly identified goals, yet here particularly teachers need to distinguish between the goals of the students and the goals of the teacher. The teacher may hope to increase a student's inclination to turn to reading as a recreational activity or to improve his attitude toward Shakespeare, yet seldom are such aims explicitly identified by students, nor do they always need to be. The learner is motivated to find information or to solve a problem (conceptual objective) or to develop or improve a particular ability (skill objective). The teacher recognizes, however, that the most permanent learning outcomes of a unit may be affective changes in the student. Perhaps concern for attitudes and appreciations is of greater importance in English than in other curricular areas because of the English teacher's unique responsibility for developing permanent reading habits.

To be of real assistance to the teacher in planning, objectives must be:

concrete, practical, realizable, and suggestive of definite learning experiences—for example, "to be able to write sentences free from the error of misplaced modifiers"

within reasonable grasp during the time available for study—for example, "to distinguish between main and supporting statements," rather than generalized objectives like "to improve reading," a problem for the entire twelve years of education

identified in terms of desired changes in the students' knowledge, behavior, or skills—for example, "to learn certain characteristics of poetry" rather than "to present the characteristics . . . ," an outcome that will be accomplished whether students learn anything or not.

SETTING UNIT GOALS   The extent to which the teacher should preplan the goals of any unit will vary with each situation. Whenever possible, there are important advantages in letting students help to choose specific goals within the over-all framework established by the teacher. The extent of pupil participation will depend, of course, upon the ability and maturity of the students as well as their insight and degree of self-discipline. Teachers have used such methods as the following to engage the class in planning experiences:

WAYS OF INVOLVING PUPILS IN LIMITING CONTENT GOALS

Following a teacher-led class discussion of a general topic, such as problems in family relationships, ask each student to discuss five key problems in written composition. Later they may compare papers in class and select the most persistent or interesting problems for further study.

Ask a student committee to sample opinion concerning the unit theme by preparing an Agree—Uncertain—Disagree questionnaire. In the introduction to a unit on the Dignity of Work, such statements as the following could be included:

A   U   D   1. Individuals who work with their hands (like stevedores and miners) contribute less to society than do most office workers.

A   U   D   2. Line play in a football game is more "play" than "work."

Those statements eliciting the greatest disagreement may form the basis for subsequent study.

Ask the class to elect a steering committee to meet with the teacher during noon hour or before school to develop plans for study.

Record ideas for unit study that emerge from a discussion of reading; for instance, concepts regarding permanence and change from a consideration of *How Green Was My Valley* may be later used as topics for individual or group research.

WAYS OF INVOLVING PUPILS IN LIMITING SKILL OBJECTIVES

Return diagnostic tests or folders of writing to students for analysis. Each student identifies his own areas of need. Skills of concern to all are to be studied by the total class; others, by groups or individuals.

Divide the class into committees to consider oral skills, reading, writing, viewing, and usage. Each committee is charged with the responsibility of identifying standards to guide students in language activities. One group prepares guidelines for written work; another, suggestions for group discussion.

Refrain from introducing specific skill objectives during the initial phase of the unit. However, lessons are introduced later at times when special skills are needed to accomplish goals important to pupils. Thus when individuals become interested in writing letters to obtain information, the teacher presents a lesson on letter writing. In such circumstances, the learner accomplishes the teacher's goal (learning how to write letters) as he satisfies his own (obtaining the desired information by writing a letter).

PLANNING LEARNING ACTIVITIES   At the heart of any unit are activities designed to accomplish the learning goals. Many kinds of experiences are introduced to satisfy the diversity of interests and needs found in thirty or forty boys and girls, some being planned for small groups and individuals and others for the entire class. Since most units involve instruction in language and literature, experiences involving speaking and listening, reading, and writing flow naturally one into the other. The purpose of each activity, however—the relationship between content and skill objectives and the learning experiences—must be continually clear to both teacher and pupils. As an aid in planning, some teachers consider three distinct phases in the development of each unit.

1. *introductory activities,* usually involving the entire class; the purpose is to challenge interest, to establish with students the objectives and scope of the unit,

and to give students an opportunity to suggest activities that help accomplish objectives. Examples:

> After seventh-grade students agree to study a unit on animals, the teacher asks them to list stories they believe will interest others in the class—for example, *Lassie Come Home, Silver Chief.* The students then begin compiling their own individual reading list. Later the teacher and librarian add titles to the list.

> To develop interest in a unit on American literature, a unit planned to involve a study of creative imagination expressed in stories of suspense and fantasy, the teacher begins with a word association test. Students are asked to record the first thoughts that occur to them upon hearing such words as "ballad," "terror," "beauty," "impact," "image," and the like. A discussion of reactions to the words awakens interest in exploring the selections.

2. *developmental activities,* planned for groups and individuals as well as for the total class; the teacher, guiding students from a consideration of the simple to the complex and from the concrete to the abstract, tries to help each student achieve the general goals agreed upon by the group. Examples:

> In a seventh-grade unit students select a folklore hero for intensive study—for example, Captain Stormalong, Pecos Bill, John Henry. Later, groups are organized to share impressions and report findings to the class.

> As part of a study of family relationships, ninth-grade students survey the treatment of families in current periodicals, films, television presentations, and the like. Ultimately, findings are shared concerning popular stereotypes of the American father, mother, kid brother, older sister.

> In reading a Shakespearean play, a class is divided into two guilds of mummers, each with a student master of the guild, master of lighting, master of musical accompaniment. The guilds alternate in acting out scenes as the class progresses through the play. An elaborate method of this kind developed over several decades is used at the Perse School, Cambridge, England, and is described by Christopher Parry in *The Mummery* (London: Chatto and Windus, 1967).

3. *culminating activities,* usually involving the entire class; concepts are clinched and skills reviewed, leaving the class with a sense of unity in the work accomplished. Examples:

> An eighth-grade study of modern communication culminates in the publication of a newspaper. The class elects an editor, an assistant, an editorial steering committee, and others with roles patterned after those observed at a local newspaper—copy writers, rewriters, typesetters, reporters. Each student is required to submit one story for publication.

> After reading and discussing many books and articles on revenge, each eleventh-grade student selects one important idea and writes an essay in which he applies the idea to a related book he has selected from a specially prepared list of readings.

> A junior high school study of great adventures culminates in the preparation of a mural on which each student mounts a figure to represent an adventurer about whom he has been reading. The symbols include a raft (*Kon-Tiki*), a mountain climber (*Conquest of Everest*), Arctic igloos (*Nanook*), jungle figures

CHART 7   BLOCKING A COMMUNICATIONS UNIT FOR JUNIOR HIGH SCHOOL

Week	Reading	Writing	Speaking	Listening
1	Analyze news stories—form, style, leads, headlines.	Reduce wordiness of sentences, phrases. Delete editorializing from sentences, paragraphs. Write news stories. Take notes on class discussion and teacher's suggestions.	Explain reasons for newspaper reading preference. Present digest of day's news. Discuss effectiveness of leads.	Listen to speaker, noting main points and formulating questions. Listen to class discussion and teacher's suggestions, noting main points.
2	Analyze editorials—form, style, leads, headlines. Analyze meaning, purpose of cartoons. Analyze letters to editor. Distinguish between statements of fact and opinion. Analyze newspaper feature, form, headlines. Suggest questions asked by feature reporter.	Summarize theme of editorial in sentence; explain its purpose, organization, effectiveness. Write an editorial suitable for school paper, a letter to editor of school or local paper, a feature story based on interviews.	Present digest of day's news. Discuss editorials, cartoons, letters to editor, ideas for editorials. Interview person of interest. Present interview report.	Listen to class discussion and teacher's suggestions, noting main points. Listen to interview reports and class interviews, noting effectiveness of procedure.

3	Read magazine stories; compare and contrast two newspaper stories. Survey magazine to determine its purpose and appeal. Read two newspaper stories, comparing and contrasting. Analyze newspaper and magazine ads.	Write an ad for one of the media, using qualities to appeal to the audience to which it is directed.	Discuss comparison and contrast of magazine stories with similar purpose. Explain reasons for an ad's effectiveness or lack of effectiveness. Dramatize an original television ad.	Watch movie related to magazines, determining its main points. Listen to class discussion, noting main points. Listen to radio and television ads, noting their ear appeal and emotional effect.
4	Study notebooks, organizing, summarizing, proofreading. Survey a variety of school newspapers for effective ideas.	Prepare class newspaper. Prepare notebooks on unit to submit to teacher. Summarize main ideas of television or radio speech.	Present panel discussions. Give slanted speech. Dramatize class version of program like *Meet the Press*. Discuss principles for censorship. Discuss relative advantages of media.	Listen to class discussion, noting main points; arguments. Formulate questions to news commentators, contrasting tone, word choice, delivery. Listen to radio and television speech; summarize.

(*I Married Adventure*), and many others. In a final discussion, each student interprets his symbol to the class.

A tenth-grade consideration of seeing life from different points of view emerges from the reading of *A Tale of Two Cities*. As a culminating activity, three groups are formed to prepare newspapers reporting the events in France from different points of view—one paper for the revolutionaries, one for the aristocrats, and a third for the onlookers in London. In discussing the problems of writing, the class becomes interested in the problem of bias and perspective.

The ways in which such activities are blocked in advance will vary with each teacher. Some find weekly planning of much assistance, as indicated in Chart 7.[25] Although activities are not specifically labeled as introductory, developmental, and culminating, the necessary progression in student thinking is apparent even in such an abbreviated overview.

EVALUATING GROWTH   Providing for continuous evaluation throughout a unit is as important as measuring cumulative growth at the end of the study. Through the former, teachers assess immediate needs and problems so that they may better plan daily instruction; through the latter, growth and accomplishment over a longer period of time. When unit goals are clearly identified, a teacher may use various ways of measuring progress toward each objective. Methods may be informal, such as in observing behavior in discussion, or may rely on prepared tests and similar instruments. Frequently, pupils can identify their own progress. In considering both continuing and final evaluation within each unit, the teacher must see the relationship among the objective, the methods of achieving it, and the devices to evaluate progress.

LEARNING OBJECTIVE	ACTIVITIES	METHOD OF EVALUATION
Selecting and developing a topic sentence	Dry-run organizational exercise asking students to classify miscellaneous data under the pertinent topics	Evaluation of individuals during work period
	Recognizing topic sentence in selected paragraphs	Brief quiz requiring students to identify sentences
	Developing a topic sentence presented by the teacher	Evaluation of individual papers
	Writing an original paragraph based on a sentence selected by the individual student	Evaluation of papers

CHOOSING LEARNING MATERIALS   Special problems frequently arise in locating textbooks, transparencies, reading materials, audio-visual equipment, graphic supplies, and other learning materials needed in each unit of instruction. In planning any unit, teacher and students must consider the availability of ma-

[25] From *English in the Junior High School* (Boulder, Colo.: Boulder Public Schools, 1967).

terial, just as they consider the time required, the work space, and the other conditions affecting learning. Where library facilities are limited, for example, teachers cannot introduce much diversified reading until they are able to surmount the problem by arranging for the shipment of books from the public library or for the purchase of paperback volumes.

In organizing resource units in advance, many teachers prepare annotated lists of resources, which they use or not, depending on the classroom situation that develops. Over a period of time, teachers are able to build personal files of resources and bibliographies for use in units. Such compilations of related content, purposes, and materials from which the teacher may select are sometimes referred to as resource units in that they provide the raw materials out of which the teacher may create a teaching unit appropriate for his class. The units described in this book suggest ideas for teachers with sparse resources as well as for those who enjoy access to many materials.

TEACHING SKILLS WITHIN A UNIT   Ways of achieving skill objectives within a unit require special attention. Because most units are organized around concepts, teachers sometimes experience difficulty in planning for skill development within a framework of interrelated activities. For these reasons two detailed illustrations of how skills may be taught within a unit are presented here.

As long as teachers perceive the achievement of a skill as an end in itself, they cannot logically present instruction in such a skill within a unit context. Once they see that such competence is a step toward improved communication, they can more easily identify the place of such instruction. Students need specific skills to accomplish particular tasks, and they learn these most effectively when striving to accomplish definite goals. The goals that motivate classroom activities of students are many—to explore career possibilities in the field of atomic energy, to find out why young people act as they do in desegregation controversies, to detect the logic of the symbolism in "Ethan Brand" in preparation for a test. To accomplish any one of these goals, students need certain skills. In a unit the teacher's task is to present the appropriate instruction as closely as possible to the time when students will recognize the need for help; often this means carefully introducing special experiences within each unit to serve as significant settings for this necessary instruction. Clearly, therefore, planning for skill development can neither be left to chance nor be unrelated to the continuing work and interests of the class. Two ways of introducing such specific instructions are given in the following examples.

TEACHING A THINKING SKILL AS AN INTEGRAL PART OF A UNIT

Name of unit   "Meeting a Crisis," a unit for grade 10.[26]

Purposes of unit   To gain insight into motives for human behavior by examining the decisions of individuals, both real and fictional, in moments of crisis; to try

[26] See pages 426–34 for the complete unit design.

to discern, in the light of the information we have concerning their backgrounds, the emotional and thought patterns brought into play when people are presented choices of action.

Specific purposes of writing lessons To support a general statement with specific examples taken from literary contexts and life situations and to develop such a statement in expository writing.

Procedures in teaching the thinking skill This series of exercises was designed to guide the student in his understanding of the skill from the simple to the more complex. In introducing the unit, the teacher assigns the following selections to provide common reading experiences and to introduce, in a sequence desirable for the unit, the analysis of characters in situations of stress.

STORIES	POEMS	PLAYS
1. Gold Mounted Guns	4. Miniver Cheevy	7. Confessional
2. Mrs. Ketting and Clark Gable	5. Mending Wall	8. Dust of the Road
3. The Unfamiliar	6. Death and General Putnam	

▶ *Consider the problem of understanding a particular character*

1. Students choose a character or cluster of characters from one of the assigned selections; they are divided into eight groups, each with a different selection and with all selections represented. For the character chosen students are asked to write the

> facts enabling the reader to understand him
> nature of his problem
> resolution presented
> explanation of the resolution in terms of the character's background

Before beginning the assignment, the class discusses these points: the first three items call for factual information given in the literature; in explaining the resolution, individuals use their own judgment, but in forming opinions they may use only the evidence the author gives.

2. The groups discuss the characters chosen for each selection and decide upon the one whose problem offers the most interest for the total class. After discussion, class and teacher record on the chalkboard the information concerning the chosen characters.[27]

background information	problem	resolution	logic of resolution
1. Will			
Young, bored with his job, believes outlaw's life glamorous and exciting.	To join outlaw's gang when he has a chance or to risk danger by offending with his refusal.	He refuses to join the gang.	Seeing the problem from the viewpoint of those victimized makes him change his mind.

[27] The characters are listed under the same numbers as those of the selections in which the characters appear.

2. Mrs. Ketting

Middle-aged, slovenly, tries to impress people, apes the movie stars, neglects her son, longs for a life of ease without responsibility.	To give up her dream world and become a real mother to her son.	The lure of her own pleasures is irresistible.	The habit, long persisted in, of living in a dream world makes change improbable.

3. People of Crosby Corners

Prejudiced against foreigners, inclined to be contemptuous of what they do not understand; think Velvet Pants, the foreigner, is a coward.	To readjust their estimate of **Velvet** Pants in the light of his later action.	The action of Velvet Pants in a situation in which they themselves had shown fear makes them realize he is not a coward.	Preconceived notions of the inferiority of foreigners required a dramatic concrete example to enable the townspeople to judge an individual foreigner fairly.

4. Miniver Cheevy

Has no job; scorns the commonplace, romanticizes past ages, blames fate for his lack of accomplishment; tries to find solace in drinking.	To face reality.	He continues to evade reality.	The habit has become so deeply ingrained that change is impossible.

5. The neighbor

Believes "Good fences make good neighbors."	To re-examine an opinion that has long been accepted.	He refuses to consider another viewpoint.	Habit of accepting unthinkingly ideas from those we respect.

6. General Putnam

Has lived continually with danger, often close to death.	To face death courageously.	He goes to his death without fear.	Events of his life prepared him to meet death bravely.

7. The family

Worried about their financial situation, anxious to keep up appearances, believing each other's protestations of honesty.	To discover the importance of values to which they give lip service.	The large amount of the bribe leads each to find reasons why it should be accepted.	Never having been so severely tempted, they had not realized that they might be dishonest.

background information	problem	resolution	logic of resolution
8. The man and his wife			
Holding money in trust, they wish to keep it, since their dishonesty will not be detected.	To keep the money or give it to the rightful owner.	They decide to give up the money.	Judas, appearing to them as a tramp, convinces them that the mental anguish likely to accompany betrayal destroys the value of material gain.

▶ *Illustrate flexible methods of selecting examples to support an idea*

1. Students are asked to group the characters, placing in the same group those in any way similar—for example, in type of problem encountered, in motivation for action, in behavioral or thought patterns. Each character may be used as many times as desired.

2. After completing the assignment individually, the class, under the teacher's direction, works out on the chalkboard various categories, such as those that follow. The aim of the teacher in this exercise is to help the students discover the possibility of using the same character to illustrate different concepts, depending upon a writer's emphasis.

Wishful thinking Mrs. Ketting	*Judging from insufficient evidence* People of Crosby Corners Will The neighbor
Misinterpreting evidence The family People of Crosby Corners	*Materialistic values* Mrs. Ketting The family
Rigid thought pattern Miniver Cheevy The neighbor Mrs. Ketting	*Willingness to change* The man and wife People of Crosby Corners Will
Consistent attitude Miniver Cheevy General Putnam Mrs. Ketting	*Failure to judge oneself objectively* The family Mrs. Ketting Miniver Cheevy

▶ *Realize the necessity of a writer's establishing a definite point of view; help students apply the principle—supporting a generalization with examples—to other literary works and to life situations*

1. The teacher asks students to select three examples that may be used to illustrate a general statement. Two are to be from the literature discussed above; the other, either from personal experience or from other stories. Each individual is then to compose a statement to be used as the controlling sentence for an expository essay.

The teacher points out that the purpose of this essay is to explain an idea, and since students are not to recommend a course of conduct, they need to avoid such words as *should* and *ought* in their controlling statements. They may be permitted to use a category already suggested or one of their own.

2. The students, under the teacher's direction, work in groups evaluating the plans for the essays, using the following questions as a guide:

Is there a statement—that is, a sentence, not a topic?

Will the proper development of this statement result in an essay that sets forth and sustains the idea?

Will the illustrations support the controlling statement?

3. After the group work, papers upon which the students cannot agree are given to the teacher for conference with the individual pupil. Each group chooses one model plan to be written on the board. For example:

People sometimes believe what they want to believe.

Mrs. Ketting

Miniver Cheevy

Characters in *The Ivory Door,* a play by A. A. Milne

Failure to secure all the evidence is a common cause of biased thinking.

Will

People of Crosby Corners

The reader who accepts one newspaper as gospel.

▶ *Write an essay from a previously constructed plan*

1. The student is asked to come to class prepared to write the first draft of an essay using the plan he has written.

2. The final draft is written as an outside assignment. The essays are then read in groups where certain ones are selected to be read to the entire class.

▶ *Discover how the material here can be further combined to support a broader concept; learn how ideas developed in each of these short papers may be used as a portion of longer essay*

(In a slow class of immature students this may be omitted.) Representative ideas from the papers are written on the board; similarities and parallels are discussed; the teacher guides the class to group them under representative thesis sentences:

There are various causes for biased thinking.

The evidence may be misinterpreted.

The facts may not all be known.

A person may refuse to admit evidence with which he disagrees.

The support of statements by specific examples receives additional emphasis throughout the unit as writing and discussion demand its use.

ESTABLISHING A USAGE HABIT WITHIN A UNIT

Name of unit "Power Over Language," a unit for the seventh grade.[28]

Purpose of unit To study the nature of communication, to improve understanding of the operation of language.

---

[28] See pages 227–40.

Specific purposes of usage lessons   To use the appropriate form of the past tense in oral and written communication.

Procedure in establishing a usage habit   Early in the unit each student is to observe difficulties others have in communicating with him during a period in which he speaks as little as possible. The experiences are discussed in a lesson called "Silence is golden . . . and difficult."

At the beginning of the school year, long before the unit was introduced, the teacher established a basic plan for language instruction. Ability to use the appropriate tense to convey meaning was only one of several skills slated for emphasis during the seventh year by the scope and sequence guide for the department. Other usages to be mastered were agreement of verb and subject, correct pronoun forms of subject and object.

To diagnose needs   As one way of determining the items on the list needing intensive study, the teacher presented a simple diagnostic word-usage test of the following type:

DIAGNOSTIC WORD-USAGE TEST

Directions   Read the following sentences carefully since many contain errors in word usage. If you think a sentence is incorrect, place a large X before it. After you have finished reading all sentences, rewrite each incorrect sentence so that it is expressed in desirable English. You will find it helpful to read the sentence aloud in a quiet voice.

1. Them was going.
2. He did it.
3. I drunk it all.
4. He brung the lunch.
5. One of the boys goes to the store.

This survey aided the teacher in determining usages causing students few problems and those not understood. The expression of past time, being one of the latter, was scheduled for study during a subsequent unit. However, during the first months of the year, emphasis was placed on the elimination of certain specific problems in student speech and writing, for example, "He don't," "Don't have none."

▶ *Familiarize students with the problem so that they recognize the appropriate forms and the need for instruction and practice*

These three activities are introduced within a single hour and require about twenty-five minutes.

1. The teacher writes on the chalkboard five sentences containing errors in forming past time spoken by individuals during discussions occurring in the past few days.

John seen me but didn't speak.
She brung it to me.
We begun the unit on Monday.
They gived it to me.
I drunk some coke.

The class is asked to substitute desirable forms in each sentence, then to note the similarity of the five problems. To emphasize the major idea, individuals are asked to express the concept of past tense in their own words.

2. The teacher writes five verbs on the board and asks students to write on original sentence using each in describing an event occurring in the present:

is	The teacher *is* talking.
do	I *do* the assignments.
climb	Henry *climbs* out of his seat.
go	I *go* to social studies now.
see	I *see* the problem.

The students exchange papers and rewrite each other's sentences to express the events in past time. A review of the verb forms results in listing appropriate forms of the simple past for each verb.

3. Students open their notebooks to cumulative usage charts maintained since the opening of the semester and used as a way of recalling specific instruction. Here the student enters a record of errors in those items of usage that have been taught. As each item is taught for the first time, he adds a new column and the date. Thereafter he records the frequency of such errors as well as any dates on which supplementary drill has been assigned.

CUMULATIVE USAGE ERROR CHART

How Well Do I Remember?

	9/20	9/26	9/31	10/8	10/15	10/20	11/3*
1. complete sentence	(9/20) ///	(9/26)** ///	/	////	//	//	///
2. beginning capitalization			/	///	/	/	
3. pronoun form —subject			//	/	(10/20)** //		
4. pronoun form —object					////	//	///
5. past tense							///

Dates of returned papers.
**Dates on which additional drill is assigned.*

After "Past Tense" is added to the charts as the most recent usage form studied, the teacher returns the paragraphs written on the previous day and the students record and correct their errors.

▶ *Establish appropriate forms of past tense through brief and varied drill*

During the next few days, the teacher introduces several ten-minute drills on uses of the past tense. These are presented at the beginning of class hours or during interludes between other activities.

1. For oral practice, the teacher divides the class into two teams and writes the following verbs on the chalkboard:

do	begin	have	climb
come	give	bring	drink
is	see		

A student on Team 1 is asked to express a statement in the present tense using one of the verbs; immediately thereafter the corresponding student on the second team repeats the statement as if it had happened the day before. Anyone who falters or uses the wrong form continues for a second or even third round, whereas the others are permitted to sit down. Example:

Student 1   He climbs the tree.
Reply 1   Yesterday he climbed it.   (pupil sits)
Student 2   Mary has many gifts.
Reply 2   Yesterday Mary—uh—had many gifts.   (pupil remains standing)

2. A brief newspaper article related to the unit and describing an event in the present tense is copied on the board. Students are asked to rewrite the article for a monthly news magazine that summarizes recent past events.

3. Students are asked to select the appropriate forms of *climb, drink, begin, bring,* and *give* for ten sentences like these:

John _____ to watch television an hour ago.
He _____ some lunch and I did too.
When I finished, John _____ the stairs.

A review of the sentences clarifies questions concerning appropriate usages, and the practice ends with the teacher leading the group in unison reading of the sentences in an attempt to fix oral usage through sound patterns. Throughout this phase of class work the teacher continually directs attention to effective ways of expressing past time, calling attention to ways used in selections studied in the unit and to usages of students themselves. These reminders are most likely to be effective if they occur just before an activity in the unit when pupils use speaking or writing.

▶ *Provide for individual differences in proficiency by planning assignments for those with particular needs*

1. After three short drills on different days, the teacher introduces a pretest designed to measure progress in using appropriate verb forms. The test involves selecting correct forms in a series of statements like: I (brought) (brung) the helicopter. The exercise is followed by unison reading of the correct sentence.

2. Five individuals who have perfect papers on the test and no difficulties expressing tense in their speaking and writing are excused from subsequent lessons. This procedure is followed regularly for lessons on skills. These individuals continue their activities for the unit "Power Over Language." During writing periods, they sometimes function as special helpers offering assistance to other students. The five meet together to prepare a final test, patterned on the pretest, which they administer later to the class.

3. During study activities in the unit, the teacher presents needed supplementary explanation to four individuals whose scores on the pretest and whose writing reveal continuing confusion about tense. After reviewing the basic principles and discussing several examples, the teacher assigns to these students some special exercises from a language textbook or workbook.

► *Clinch and maintain desirable habits once learning is established*

1. A final test, prepared by the five special students and checked by the teacher, is presented and reviewed as the final class activity dealing with past tense.

2. Before collecting the next set of compositions in the unit, the teacher provides for a fifteen-minute pre-correction period. During this period, the students are asked to read paragraphs aloud in small groups and listen specifically for problems in tense. The class is advised that errors in tense will be weighed heavily in evaluating compositions.

3. The teacher continually notes special problems in uses of the past tense that appear in the writing and speaking of students. Individual problems are discussed in brief conferences held during class study periods. Problems shared by many persons are reviewed with the entire class. Students continue to maintain records of their written errors on the cumulative chart. When a review of the charts, later in the semester, reveals four individuals who still have repeated difficulties in expressing past tense, the teacher arranges for special supplementary instruction in a small group situation.

These two examples illustrate in detail how a series of lessons designed to achieve skill objectives may be incorporated within the context of a unit. The need for careful planning by teachers is emphasized throughout as is the value of much pupil involvement in shaping and evaluating learning. Certainly the planning of class work in units extending over an interval of several weeks gives teachers an opportunity to place in a communication setting a sequence of activities designed to encourage skill development.

PLANNING A SPECIFIC LESSON

If the unit plan provides an over-all guide for maintaining continuity in learning over an interval of several weeks, the individual lesson plan offers the teacher a detailed guide for accomplishing specific learning goals. A lesson may be concluded during a single hour or it may be shorter or longer, the length of any plan being determined by the nature of the learning experience itself. A lesson on a single short story like "To Build a Fire" may require class time on three separate days. On the first, fifteen minutes may be devoted to preparation for reading; on the second, the entire hour to a discussion of the story; ultimately time may be spent on a related writing assignment. On the other hand, a brief lesson dealing with a single language skill may be concluded in thirty minutes.

Individual lessons are usually related through a basic sequence in the overall plan. Thus a unit on the American short story may include separate lessons on ten short stories, one on structure, and perhaps a final cumulative lesson that attempts to draw together all the learning in the unit.

PLOTTING LESSONS How does the teacher plan a sequence of lessons? One effective way is to plan on a weekly basis, with the unit plan offering guidance in continuity and purpose. A weekly schedule for a junior high school class is presented on the following chart. To teach certain reading skills, the teacher has divided the class into three ability sections; the plotting of a weekly schedule assists him in identifying those lessons to plan in detail for each group. This chart does not present the lessons themselves; rather it presents an agenda of lessons, many of which would be developed in great detail.

VARIATION IN LESSONS   Some lessons are routine and require little special attention; others require much teacher preparation. Discussions usually are of the latter type, since teachers must necessarily prepare a series of questions to guide student participation. In the weekly schedule illustrated in the chart, such class hours as the library reading period on Monday and the Friday program presentations depend less on instructional plans prepared specifically for each day than on continuing class standards and routines adopted long before. By organizing classes to rely on sound regularized activity, the teacher, who has little enough time for preparation, may devote his major energies to preparing necessary lessons. The lesson on word attack skills for Group 1, however, and Group 3 study of "Rip Van Winkle" call for plans requiring careful attention. Through advance organization the teacher frees himself to prepare the needed lessons.

CONSIDERING A TOTAL SCHEDULE   Teachers need to devise some way of maintaining a master schedule of preparation for all classes if they are to balance the demands on their time and energies. Carrying as many as five classes, few secondary-school teachers are able to prepare more than two detailed plans for any single day. An intelligent solution to the problem calls for scheduling activities so that those requiring advance planning and much energy and leadership execution are spaced throughout a week. Thus, discussions for period one and period three classes are scheduled on Tuesday when other groups are reading, but on Wednesday when tests are presented during periods one and three, special lessons are presented to other groups. In this manner teachers can provide equitably for all groups.

GUIDE FOR LESSON PLANNING   A helpful lesson plan reveals what is to be accomplished and how. It is a tool to assist the busy teacher. Criteria for evaluating a useful lesson are suggested by the following questions:

> Are learning goals clear and limited to those that can be accomplished during the time interval?
> Are activities planned to lead to the accomplishment of goals?
> Does the plan provide guidance in how teacher and students will move toward accomplishment of goals?
> Is reasonable consideration given to availability of materials?
> Is provision made for variety in learning experiences as needed by the student group?
> At the end of the lesson are important learnings summarized and clinched?
> What provision is made for checking the effectiveness of the lesson?

WEEKLY SCHEDULE FOR JUNIOR HIGH SCHOOL CLASS WORKING ON READING SKILLS

	Group 1 *slow*	*Group 2* *average*	*Group 3* *accelerated*
Monday 50 min.	Class goes to library to exchange individual books, to browse, to review new periodicals, and to read. Teacher uses time for individual conferences to guide reading selections.		
Tuesday 10 min.	Rate of comprehension test, using separate material for each group.		
20 min.	Guided oral reading of story in reader. (T) *	Silent reading to answer questions on chalkboard.	Exercise on context clues.
30 min.	Work on new assignment.	Teacher-guided discussion based on these questions. (T)	Individual reading.
Wednesday 25 min.	Finish Tuesday's assignment. Individual reading.	Work on comprehension assignment made Tuesday.	Review of context clues. Instruction on reading "Rip Van Winkle." Application of context clue skills. (T)
25 min.	Teacher-led discussion and instruction on work-attack skills. (T).	Individual reading.	Silent reading of story.
Thursday 10 min.	Brief skimming drill using same material for all groups.		
20 min.	Direct teacher instruction on vocabulary development for groups 1 and 2. (T)		Complete Wednesday's assignment.
20 min.	Individual reading.	Individual reading.	Preparation for audience reading Friday. (T)
Friday 20 min.	Class meets together listening to prepared audience reading by Group 3.		
20 min.	Informal dramatizations of scenes from reading, Groups 1 and 2.		
10 min.	Writing in notebooks: summary of week's activities.		

* (T) shows where the teacher will be during each interval.

Good lesson plans are more easily seen than described. The following, though not perfect, illustrate different organizational approaches and suggest kinds of planning that may be adapted in many classes. Both are more elaborate than the lesson plans teachers will normally have time to create. However, both are for particularly crucial lessons in the total teaching design, and they do represent English teaching as it should be more often. Careful planning helps to lift teaching to an art.

LESSON ON RESPONSE TO MOOD [29]

Class   Grade 8
Unit   "Responding With Imagination"
Previous activity   Students had been engaged in various speaking and writing experiences in which they had attempted to respond to sensory impressions.
Time   Approximately two hours
Objectives   To develop the desire to write interestingly and descriptively; to increase powers of observation and imagination; to improve effective use of adverbs, adjectives, sensory detail, and the precise word to convey meaning and mood.

COMMENTS	ACTIVITIES
Preparation of the class is important. Here the teacher summarizes what she plans to say.	A. Introduction to experiment in "Mood."
	1. Today we are going to conduct an experiment in which each of you will play a vital part. It is important that each of you listen to directions and follow them carefully if the experiment is to be successful.
Notice the specificity.	2. We are going to listen to a record. While the record is playing, shut your eyes and ask yourself, What does this music make me think of? What words express the mood I feel, or the mood of the record?
	3. After you have listened to the record for five minutes, begin to write on a clean sheet of binder paper—not to be handed in—the words and phrases that come into your mind as you listen to the music.
	(a) At this point, do not worry about spelling, punctuation, sentence structure, or even process.
	(b) Think only of the music and the idea that it brings to mind.
	B. Listening to recording of "Spellbound." Discussion of responses to record.
Here teacher relies on established groupings of students.	1. Listen carefully to the following directions:
	(a) Each chairman is to ask each person in his group to read aloud the responses he made to the record.

[29] Adapted from a plan developed by Mrs. Carol Jensen, formerly of Bancroft Junior High School, San Leandro, Calif.

The activity provides variation from listening and gives all students an opportunity to share ideas.

    (b) The chairman will also ask each to select at least three responses he considers most interesting.

Note that this teacher lists on her plan any item she wishes to emphasize—a sound practice for beginners.

    (c) A recorder should write down five words or phrases that the group selects as the most descriptive, appropriate, and interesting.

    (d) In ten minutes each recorder will be asked to read the responses selected by his group. Remember to talk quietly, to work quickly and efficiently.

Less detailed directions may be appropriate in many classes. This class tended to be difficult to control and the teacher found the reminders to be helpful.

2. Recitation of responses by recorders:
Will the recorder for Group 1 please stand and read so that everyone can hear the responses selected?

3. Each of you has participated in the creation of mood. The record "Spellbound," like beauty, may mean something different to each of us. Whatever it may mean, we must admit that it creates a mood for each of us. That is why music like "Spellbound" is called "mood music."

Teacher tries to pull together and summarize responses. Note that teacher has general conception of ultimate understanding desired although response is to be elicited from students.

    (a) Who can define the word *mood?*
    (b) *Mood* implies a "particular state of mind, especially one affected by emotion—as to be in the mood to work."

C. Moods created in pictures.

Second phase of lesson begins with allusion to earlier writing. This phase may be introduced during a second hour.

1. You all remember the picture shown to you earlier in this unit.
    (a) What was the mood in that picture? (unhappiness)
    (b) What elements created this mood? (expressions, color)

2. Now will each of you choose one word or phrase from the following list which you think best describes the picture I am now holding. (a foggy harbor)

COMMENTS

Here in her planning, teacher attempts to predict student response. However, she must be ready to deal with additional ideas contributed by the class.

ACTIVITIES

(a) mysterious
(b) calm, still, undisturbed, tranquil
(c) gloomy and depressing
(d) death-like

3. How many of you selected mysterious? Why? How many calm, still . . . ? Why? Etc.
4. What elements create mood in this picture?
   (a) stillness, lack of life and motion
   (b) water is still and without a ripple
   (c) the fog lends a hushed quality

D. Moods created in writing.
   1. (Distribute copies of poems.) Follow along with me while I read how two writers give different moods to the same element—fog.
      (a) "It lies cold on the eyeballs and thick in the throat; it is an intangible blanket saturated with the stillness and the heaviness of death."
      (b) Sandburg's "Fog"

Use of printed text as a listening aid reduces distraction and might be desirable here.

   2. Listen and react to the way Poe creates a mood for a knock on the door in this poem, "The Raven." (Play recording of Poe's "The Raven," interpreted by Basil Rathbone.)
      (a) What words set the stage for a knock on the door?
      (b) Midnight dreary, weak, weary, napping, bleak December, dying ember, wrought its ghost. What do these words describe?
         (1) time
         (2) mood of the subject
         (3) activity
         (4) season—time of year
         (5) weather

Again teacher predicts reasonable responses but is prepared to "fish" for exact answers if necessary.

E. Assignment.
   1. Now for the assignment. Tonight you are to describe a knock on the door, too. Create three different moods:
      (a) Write to show it's a desperate fugitive.
      (b) Write to show it's a girl's boyfriend.
      (c) Write to show it's a messenger boy.

Papers will give teacher opportunity to evaluate effectiveness of total lesson.

   2. Listen carefully to the knock on our door. Who wants to try knocking in different ways? (Volunteers.) Pay careful attention to describing. (See C above.)

MATERIALS I PLAN TO USE

A. Recordings
  1. "Spellbound"
  2. Edgar Allan Poe—Basil Rathbone
B. Photograph: Foggy harbor from *Holiday* magazine
C. Copies of poetry anthology
  1. "Fog" (p. 41)
  2. "The Raven" (p. 67)

LESSON ON THE SHORT STORY [30]

Class Grades 11 and 12, advanced group.

Previous assignment The assignment for this lesson, given the preceding day, was as follows. Read "The Fall of the House of Usher" and answer the following questions: (1) How does Poe achieve perfect tone throughout the story? (2) How does he hold you in suspense? (3) How does he achieve a single emotional effect?

Objective To discuss the story and arrive, through questioning, at a complete characterization of Poe's method.

Procedure The use of the following questions to start and guide discussion.

COMMENTS	ACTIVITIES
The teacher has carefully organized this lesson in three parts, and each in turn contributes to the ultimate understandings desired.	A. Questions to draw out the meaning of *perfect tone,* and how it is used:
Teacher attempts to clarify terms and relate them to something familiar to students.	1. The use of the word *how* suggests "by what means" or "with what tools." Therefore, what are the tools Poe uses to achieve perfect tone? First, let us decide what this term means.
	2. What do we mean by "tone of voice," "tone of a musical instrument," and "tone of a poem"? (mood, feeling, atmosphere, spirit, dominant emotion, etc.)
Note specificity. With guidance, students are asked to pick out concrete words. The teacher has previously noted where words occur so that he may aid students if such help is needed.	3. Point out some phrases on the first page that seem to establish the tone. (dull, dark and soundless day, oppressively low, dreary track, melancholy House of Usher, insufferable gloom, bleak walls, decayed trees, utter depression of soul, bitter lapse, hideous dropping, etc.)
	4. Which adjectives in particular seem to describe the tone? (gloomy, oppressive, depressive, sickening of heart, etc.)

[30] Adapted and used with permission of Henry C. Meckel, San Jose State College, San Jose, Calif.

Note that this question suggests a need for summarizing. The teacher would hope to obtain a response similar to the one here.

5. What would you say, then, is Poe's first tool? (choice of words)

6. Read the opening sentence of various paragraphs. Does the author maintain this tone? Is there any change whatever? Do any of the sentences express any other emotion?

Second summary made by students.

7. Therefore, what would you say is another tool by which perfect tone is achieved? (unity)

B. Questions to draw out the meaning of suspense and how it is achieved:

1. What does suspense mean, even outside literary terminology? (concern about what is going to happen next)

2. Pick out some phrases or sentences that arouse your curiosity but leave you in suspense. (but many years had elapsed since our last meeting . . . a mental disorder which oppressed him . . . a very singular summons . . . yet I really knew very little of my friend . . . a barely perceptible fissure . . . a valet of stealthy step . . . an expression of low cunning . . . I must perish in this deplorable folly . . . I dread the events of the future . . . I regarded her with an utter astonishment not mingled with dread; and yet I found it impossible to account for such feelings. That lady, at least while alive, would be seen by me no more.)

3. Which of these seem to point forward to something disastrous?

4. How does Poe deliberately phrase these so as to put a question in your mind?

5. Point out the questions that arise as you read the first paragraph. (Where is the man going and why? Why is anyone living in such a house? What's going on inside? What will happen to the narrator?) Second paragraph. (Why is he going to stay there? Why did Usher send for him? What is his mental disorder?)

Third summary made by students.

6. How would you say, then, that suspense is achieved? (By arousing the reader's curiosity or suspicion by putting questions in his mind and leaving only vague hints as to their answer.)

*Here again note how
identification of concrete
detail and analyses of
detail are used to build
understanding of the de-
sired concept. The teacher
has a sequence of ques-
tions to guide the discussion, and he is able to
call attention to spe-
cific paragraphs in the
selection if students do
not locate these them-
selves.*

C. Questions to draw out the meaning of single emotional effect and how it is achieved:
   1. What emotion is in your mind when you finish
      the story?
   2. Is it mixed with any contrary emotion? For
      instance, fear and horror are difficult to define
      but experience tells us that they are akin; but
      joy (or humor) is obviously their opposite.
   3. Can you find any words, phrases, sentences, or
      paragraphs in the story that do not contribute to
      this emotion?
   4. Can you find any other effect, such as humor,
      philosophy, sympathy, morality, logic, human in-
      terest, love?
   5. What, then, is the object of omitting these?
   6. Would you conclude that unity again is a tool?
   7. What other tools are used? What about tone as
      a tool in achieving single effect?
   8. What does constant suspense do to the total
      effect?
   9. Is the effect stronger at the end if your emotions
      have been allowed to accumulate? Pick out a
      passage that seems to build up, accumulate, or
      lead to a crescendo.
   10. What does the crescendo lead to? Is it the same
       in music? Suppose we call it a *final impact*.
       Does it help to achieve the single effect?
   11. Do you think that Poe devised a plot first and
       strove for effect, or decided upon a certain
       effect and then found a plot that would carry it?
   12. Would you say, then, that the element of plot
       was important?
   13. How about the characters? Is any attempt made
       to acquaint the reader with them?
   14. Is the setting important? In what way? (In
       that it sets the mood but not because it matters
       where the story takes place. The House of Usher
       could be in any country in any gloomy marsh.)
   15. Would you say, then, that subordinating the
       other elements to total effect was a tool?

*This is the understand-
ing toward which the
 ₌er has been lead-
ing the class throughout
the sequence of ques-
tions. In clinching the
idea, he would ask indi-
viduals to summarize.*

The teacher plays the musical selections; such an experience provides variety and helps establish the point.

16. Imagine that you had to choose music as background in a television play of this story. What kind of music would you pick? Would slow and mournful music do? Why not? Does there have to be a note of accumulating excitement or impending disaster? (Compare Grieg's "Ase's Death" with Sibelius' *Finlandia*.)

D. Generalizations (the desired conclusions):

What are the major understandings that lesson is planned to achieve? Clearly every question and every sub-point leads toward these understandings. With less mature groups, the teacher would probably attempt less.

1. Poe's main technique is achieving perfect tone, suspense, and single emotional effect.
2. Perfect tone is achieved by choice of words and by unity, that is, by not allowing any note other than the desired one to enter the piece.
3. Suspense is achieved by arousing curiosity or suspicion and leaving vague hints concerning the outcome. This is accomplished by phrasing in such a way as to leave a question in the reader's mind as to what will happen next.
4. Single emotional effect is achieved by unity, tone, suspense, crescendo, final impact, and subordinating every other element to that of total effect.

The over-all pattern of the English program and the detailed plan of the various segments necessarily complement each other. Both require imagination and vitality on the part of planners. Not all lessons can be as thoroughly developed as the two just presented, nor do curricula like those of Cleveland Heights and Boulder rise spontaneously from a few teachers' meetings. But if instruction is not to be opportunistic, impulsive, and haphazard, if what pupils learn is not to be left to chance, some strategy must be devised to relate means to ends, to reduce to an ordered design the complexity and multiplicity of English teaching.

APPENDIX A

PERIODICALS AND RESOURCE MATERIALS FOR TEACHERS OF SECONDARY-SCHOOL ENGLISH

SELECTED PERIODICALS

Publications of the National Council of Teachers of English, 508 South Sixth St., Champaign, Ill. 61820. NCTE membership includes subscription to one of the following journals:

College Composition and Communication. Official journal of the Conference on College Composition and Communication; quarterly. Many articles on composition and language study are presented. Senior high school teachers will find much that is adaptable to secondary-school classrooms.

College English. Official journal of college section; monthly, October–May. Although contents stress college literature and composition, some articles will interest eleventh- and twelfth-grade teachers.

Elementary English. Official journal of elementary section; monthly, October–May. Contains many discussions of method of interest to junior high school teachers, as well as readable summaries of recent research in English methodology.

English Journal. Official journal of secondary section; monthly, September–May. The most useful single magazine for teachers of English in grades 7 to 12. Contains articles on content and methods, reviews of new teaching materials, information on professional activities. One section, "The Scene," deals with inner city education and technology.

Research in the Teaching of English. Semi-annual journal reporting new research in the teaching of English at all educational levels.

Publications of state English associations

Many state or regional associations, like Illinois, Michigan, Kentucky, Iowa, and New England, publish a regular bulletin, journal, or yearbook. Teachers will find such publications a convenient way of informing themselves on the thinking of fellow teachers, as well as a source of announcements of regional curriculum developments and professional meetings.

Publications dealing with special aspects of English, useful for reference and for teachers working in the areas of concern

Journal of Reading. International Reading Association, Box 695, Newark, Delaware 19711. Articles on recent research in reading and on curriculum projects in reading at the secondary and college levels. Designed to satisfy varying interests at all levels of instruction.

Reading Research Quarterly. International Reading Association, Newark, Delaware. A quarterly presenting reports on recent research in reading and the annual summary of investigations.

The Reading Teacher. Official publication of the International Reading Association, Box 695, Newark, Delaware 19711. Articles, columns, summaries of recent research designed for classroom teachers at elementary and junior high school levels of instruction.

The Speech Teacher. The Speech Association of America, Statler Hilton Hotel, New York, N.Y. 10001. Articles of interest to the teacher of English treat rhetoric, listening, interpretation, classroom drama. Contains useful reviews of new professional books.

Publications that contain material
of special interest to teachers of English

Media and Methods. 134 North 13th St., Philadelphia, Pa. 19107. Monthly discussions of modern media as they affect various dimensions of classroom teaching.

Saturday Review. 25 West 45th St., New York, N.Y. 10036; weekly. Discussions of contemporary events, reviews of books, motion pictures, television, plays, recordings, special issues on books for children and adolescents.

SELECTED CURRICULUM GUIDES IN ENGLISH

The curriculum library of NCTE maintains an up-to-date list of guides selected as outstanding by a national committee. Among those currently listed:

Action in the Language Arts (Grades 7–12). Office of Public Instruction, Orange County, Florida. Presents a philosophy of teaching and covers the areas of listening, speaking, viewing, language, writing, and reading and literature.

Course of Study: Language Arts. (Grades 10, 11, 12). St. Louis Park Public Schools, St. Louis Park, Minnesota. A three-volume series on composition, including language and spelling, developmental reading, speaking and listening, and literature. Also available is the *Modified Language Arts Curriculum* (Grades 10–12) for teaching speech, composition, and literature to slow learners.

Curriculum Guide–English Language Arts–Literature Program K–12. Montgomery County Public Schools, Rockville, Maryland. Includes a twelve-year scope and sequence of skills classified by grade levels and information on general school policies and a general statement on evaluation.

Curriculum Guide for the English Department. (Grades 10–12). Middletown Public Schools, Middletown, New Jersey. Presents both the basic curriculum and electives for senior high school students. Areas covered for several tracks of students are reading, writing, speech, language, drama, and journalism.

Education and Training: Secondary English Curriculum Guide. (Grades 7–12). Directorate, United States Dependent Schools, European Area, APO U.S. Forces 09164 (1965). Bases the English program on the teaching of concepts and relating all phases of instruction within a humanistic framework. Presents detailed suggestions for specific works of literature and activities.

English Language Framework for California Public Schools, Grades K–12. California State Department of Education, Sacramento, California (1968). Presents philosophy, content, and samples of instructional procedures. An excellent bibliography reviews recent professional books and related materials.

English Program: Grades 7–12. Columbus Public Schools, Columbus, Ohio (1965). Includes suggestions for teaching composition, language, literature and reading, and speech.

English 13: Experimental Curriculum Project (Grades 10–12). Fairfield Public Schools, Fairfield, Connecticut (1965). Presents a variety of methods and content for team teaching literature, composition, and language. Designed for below average students.

Language Arts Curriculum Guide. (K–12). Niles Township Public School Districts, Niles, Illinois (1965). A twelve-year guide covering reading and literature and composition. Presents sequences for schools and concepts for each grade level and includes a bibliography for teachers.

Language Arts Guide: Resource Units for Grades 9–12. Lexington Public Schools, Lexington, Massachusetts. Explains what resource units are and how they differ from teaching units. Also included is a series of pamphlets with language, composition, and reading and literature.

Revised Teaching Guide for the Language Arts. (Grades K–12). Oklahoma Curriculum Improvement Commission, Oklahoma State Department of Education, Oklahoma City, Oklahoma. A state guide including a general philosophy and scope and sequence for all areas of English.

Sequential Programs in English for a Restructured Curriculum. (Grades 7–12). Educational Research Council of Greater Cleveland, Cleveland, Ohio (1966). An overview and sequential steps in the development of a "restructured" curriculum in composition, language, and literature.

Thematic Approach to Literature, Language, and Composition: Grades 7, 8, 9. Also, grades 10, 11, 12. Cleveland Heights–University Heights City School District, Cleveland, Ohio (1965). An overview explaining the thematic approach to teaching English and suggestions for methods and sample lesson plans.

12,000 Students and Their English Teachers. Commission on English, College Entrance Examination Board, Box 592, Princeton, N.J. 08540 (1968). Contains tested units in teaching all aspects of English, grades 9–12, emphasizing the curriculum for college bound students.

The Work Oriented Curriculum: Phase IV–Grade 12. Montgomery County Public Schools, Rockville, Maryland (1965). A program for slow learners in English and social studies, integrated around out-of-school work experiences of the students.

GUIDES FOR INSTRUCTION
IN SPECIFIC AREAS OF ENGLISH

Composition

A Compendium of Terms and Usages. Curriculum Office, St. Paul Public Schools, St. Paul, Minnesota (1964). "The primary purpose of this compendium is . . . serving . . . teachers of composition who may want to refer to it on specific points of usage which generally are not included in textbooks or workbooks."

Creative Writing. (Grades K–12). Indianapolis Public Schools, Indianapolis, Indiana (1965). Suggestions and inspirations for the teacher of creative writing.

Freeway to Written Expression. (Grades K–8). Los Altos School District, Los Altos, California (1964). Helpful, specific suggestions for all types of students.

Language Arts Guide: Written Composition (Grades 10, 11, 12). Dade County Public Schools, Miami, Florida (1965). Presents a sequential writing program for written composition.

Language

An English Teacher's Manual of Unit Lessons in Language: Grades 7–12. Granite School District, Salt Lake County, Utah (1964). Contains sequential units in four areas of language study—the dictionary, geographical and social variations, grammar, and the development and history of the English language. Excellent exercises in usage.

Junior High School Curriculum Guide for Social Studies—Language. (Grades 7–9). Department of Education, Alberta, Canada. This province guide correlates social studies and the English language for the junior high level.

Literature and Reading

The Hawaii Semester Elective English Review. (Grades 10–12). University of Hawaii, Honolulu, Hawaii (1965). Describes a new literature-centered curriculum in which the student for a given semester elects one of the six one-semester courses available. The organizational focus is on genres. The student's choice is determined by his emotional and intellectual maturity.

Reading in Florida Secondary Schools. (Grades 7–12). State Department of Education, Tallahassee, Florida. A comprehensive state guide covering planning a program, evaluating and testing, and the relationship between reading and other skills.

Reading in Grades 7–12. The Curriculum Development Council for Southern New Jersey, Glassboro State College, Glassboro, New Jersey (1964). A handbook on reading for secondary-school teachers and administrators.

Reading in the Subject Areas: Grades 7, 8, 9. Board of Education of the City of New York, New York (1963–64). A compilation of reading skills, lessons and additional narrative information in the areas of social studies, science, mathematics, industrial arts, and English.

APPENDIX B

IMPROVING SPELLING

What is the importance of spelling? Acceptable spelling is like all conventions in using language. If a person says, "I ain't got none of them new kinda cameras," other people notice the way he speaks rather than the thought he intends to communicate. Similarly, if a person writes "Happy Ester," the attention of the reader is distracted from the thought itself to the medium of expression. All such distractions interfere with communication and tend to irritate other people. Thus good spelling, like appropriate use of spoken language, becomes not only a measure of one's education but also a measure of his sensitivity to the reactions of other people. To spell accurately is to show consideration for the person who will read what has been written.

The three key words in spelling improvement are *individualize, attack, care.*

Drill is based upon individual lists of spelling difficulty.
The teacher helps each pupil find a method of attacking his difficulties.
The learner develops a spelling conscience.

Identify individual difficulties

By the time pupils are in junior high school, spelling lists identical for all class members are seldom economical. Students vary so much in their spelling difficulties that if progress is to occur, provisions for individualization become imperative. Those who spell competently should be released from many lessons to concentrate on more appropriate learnings. Exceptionally weak spellers need to be grouped together for review of word analysis and lessons in methods of attacking new words. Average spellers should keep lists of their own problem words in their composition folders and work on these during spelling periods. Junior high school pupils enjoy Glen M. Blair's medical analogy. Each pupil is a doctor who has three groups of "patients," or words needing the doctor's care. Some patients are very ill and need frequent attention; others are convalescent, requiring only occasional appointments; the largest number, it is hoped, have been ill but are now hale and hearty, functioning in compositions without the slightest malaise.[1]

To carry out such a method, teachers often have the pupils keep each "patient" on a separate card so that the patient may be transferred from the emergency ward to the infirmary before being released from the hospital. Although such a method is too juvenile for senior high pupils, the same basic principle of individualization needs to operate in the word lists filed in each pupil's writing folder.

EMPHASIZE SPELLING ON COMPOSITION DAYS   Whenever the entire class is writing, whether the subject be a planned composition or an essay test over some period of work, the teacher places reminders about spelling on the chalkboard. For instance, the names of everything on a poster or a magazine cover may be listed and examined before using the picture as stimulus for a composition; baseball words or ice carnival words may be appropriate for other occasions or assignments. During a unit on science fiction, still another list may appear. Often a brief drill on using the dictionary precedes actual writing. At other times the teacher may review the spelling of certain phonetic word families or teach several demons like *separate, necessary,* or *friend,* using colored chalk to call attention to the troublesome spots.

RULES AND DEVICES   Special devices, such as the phrase "Never *believe* a *lie*," should not be overdone lest they become cumbersome. A few of them, such as associating t(*here*) with *here,* or station*e*ry with pap*e*r, may assist a learner with some particularly troublesome word, but too many of these special associations overburden the memory and prove to be inadequate substitutes for an effective method of learning.

Similarly, too many spelling rules will also confuse a learner, especially if there are many exceptions to the rule. Memorizing rules is of no value if one does not understand the principle involved; understanding makes memorization superfluous. Some of the principles that do help many people in spelling are listed here:

> Drop the final *e* before a suffix beginning with a vowel.
> Keep the final *e* before a suffix beginning with a consonant.
> When a word ends in *y* preceded by a consonant, change the *y* to *i* before adding a suffix (unless the suffix begins with *i*).
> Use *i* before *e* except after *c* or when sounded like *a* as in neighbor and weigh.

Teach a method of attack

The difference between good spellers and poor spellers often hinges on an effective method for learning to spell. Good spellers have solved the problem.

[1] Glen M. Blair, *Diagnostic and Remedial Teaching in Secondary Schools* (New York: Macmillan, 1940).

They have a sequence for studying words they want to learn. Poor spellers merely look at a new word helplessly, and when they do try, use hit and miss methods that are ineffective and seldom the same from one time to the next.

Why, then, should everyone not adopt the ideal method of learning used by the best spellers? The answer is easy. Good spellers do not all use the same method. However, almost all of them use some method, and by studying their various ways of learning to spell, each pupil can work out an habitual procedure suited to his own individuality. Among the steps used by good spellers, at least ten are often listed: looking at the word, copying the word, visualizing the word, listening to the pronunciation of the word, pronouncing the word, dividing the word into syllables, saying the letters in sequence, writing the word with large muscle movements (in the air or on a chalkboard) to get the feel of the word, analyzing the difficult places in the word, and using the word in a meaningful sentence. In addition, most competent spellers write their words in a careful, neat fashion. Sloppy, careless handwriting often results in a confused image of the word and uncertainty about its spelling.

Anyone who wants to improve his spelling should seriously consider which combination of the ten steps best suits his learning habits. No one would use all ten, but a combination of those that really assist an individual is all-important. Once the combination has been chosen and after a trial period to test its efficiency, the student should establish this thumb-rule as a regular and habitual method of learning. Probably visualizing the word should be a part of the combination for almost everyone, although oral or kinesthetic cues may claim first place for some pupils.

James A. Fitzgerald, an authority on spelling, has often recommended the method summarized here: [2]

> Understand the use, meaning, and pronunciation of the word.
> Visualize the word.
> Note the spelling of the word.
> Write the word carefully and neatly.
> Check the spelling of the word.
> Use the word as often as possible *in writing*.

This combination of methods may not be best for some individuals, but for many learners these steps, carefully followed, prove to be an effective method of study. By devoting less time to drill and more time to teaching a method of learning, a teacher can improve spelling in most classes.

One teacher provides time for the students to experiment with the various approaches and then, on a day labeled "The Most Significant Day in Our Spelling Year," each pupil writes down the method he has chosen as most suitable to his way of learning. These method testimonials are filed in students' writing folders, and from time to time the teacher asks each one to write a statement beneath his testimonial. These statements are dated and indicate

[2] James A. Fitzgerald, *The Teaching of Spelling* (Milwaukee, Wisc.: Bruce, 1951), p. 38.

whether the student is finding the chosen method appropriate, as evidenced by his degree of improvement in functional spelling situations. This teacher spends much more time studying words and identifying effective ways of attacking words than he does testing words.

Awaken a spelling conscience

Just as there are Sunday Christians, so are there Friday Spellers, persons of limited vision who do not transfer into practice the intention of the ritual. It is the considered opinion of many teachers that little progress in spelling will be made so long as the practice persists of giving grades for spelling drills. If the spelling grade is to foster any carry-over from spelling lessons to application, it must be assigned for actual proficiency in written work. Several times each marking period the teacher should sample his students' papers, both in their writing folders and, if time permits, in written assignments for other courses. Only when pupils really comprehend the importance of applying what they learn will they develop a spelling conscience. To the extent that it is possible, even this use of grades should be replaced by the students' own pride in their spelling skill. Internal pressures such as pride are always more effective than external pressures.

BIBLIOGRAPHY

TITLES, FILMS, FILMSTRIPS, AND RECORDINGS REFERRED TO IN THE TEXT

The following bibliography is included to assist teachers who wish to obtain selections and audio-visual aids mentioned in this book. Whenever possible, references are to publications available in print. Sources likely to be easily accessible to teachers have frequently been used rather than the original publication. Inasmuch as only one source is cited for each title, teachers who wish to look further should consult some of the reference tools listed here.

GENERAL REFERENCE BOOKS

Biography Index, edited by Bea Joseph and Charlotte Warren Squires. N.Y., Wilson, 1953. Quarterly supplements.

Books in Print, edited by Sarah L. Prakken. N.Y., Bowker. Revised yearly.

Essay and General Literature Index, edited by Dorothy Herbert West. N.Y., Wilson, 1960. Supplements issued periodically.

Granger's Index to Poetry, edited by William F. Bernhardt, 5th ed. N.Y., Columbia Univ. Press, 1962.

Index to Children's Poetry: Second Supplement, comp. John E. and Sara W. Brewton. N.Y., Wilson, 1965.

The National Information Center for Educational Media (NICEM), two comprehensive reference books: *Index to 16mm Educational Films* and *Index to 35mm Educational Filmstrips*. In each volume over 14,000 films and filmstrips are cross-indexed under subject-matter headings, alphabetized film descriptions, and producer-distributors. Order from McGraw-Hill Films, 330 West 42nd Street, New York, N.Y. 10036.

Index to Full Length Plays, 1926–1944, by Ruth Gibbons Thomson. Boston, Faxon, 1946.

An Index to One-Act Plays for Stage, Radio, and Television, by Hannah Logasa. 4th supplement. Boston, Faxon, 1958.

Index to Plays in Collections, by John H. Ottemiller. 3d ed., rev. and enl. N.Y., Scarecrow Press, 1957.

Literary History of the United States, edited by Robert E. Spiller *et al.*, rev. ed. N.Y., Macmillan, 1953.

Paperbound Books in Print, edited by Olga S. Weber. N.Y., Bowker. Published monthly.

The Reader's Encyclopedia, edited by William Rose Benét, 2d ed. N.Y., T. Y. Crowell, 1965.

Readers' Guide to Periodical Literature, semimonthly September to June, inclusive; monthly in July and August; cumulated periodically, N.Y.: Wilson.

Short Story Index, compiled by Dorothy E. Cook and Isabel S. Monro. N.Y., Wilson, 1953. Supplements bring this volume up to date.

Twentieth Century Authors: First Supplement, edited by Stanley J. Kunitz. N.Y., Wilson, 1955.

FICTION

PAUL ANNIXTER, *Swiftwater.* N.Y., Wyn, 1950.

VICTOR APPLETON, *Tom Swift and His Great Searchlight;* or *On the Border for Uncle Sam.* N.Y., Grosset & Dunlap, 1912 (part of a series of novels).

RICHARD ARMOUR, *Twisted Tales from Shakespeare.* N.Y., McGraw-Hill, 1957.

ELLIOTT ARNOLD, *A Night of Watching.* N.Y., Scribner's, 1967.

HARRIETTE ARNOW, *The Dollmaker.* N.Y., Macmillan, 1954.

PETER ASBJÖRNSEN and MOE JORGEN, *East of the Sun and West of the Moon.* Eau Claire, Wisc., Cadmus, 1958.

RICHARD and FLORENCE ATWATER, *Mr. Popper's Penguins.* Boston, Little, Brown, 1938.

JANE AUSTEN, *Emma.* N.Y., Grove, 1950.

———, *Pride and Prejudice.* N.Y., Coward, 1953.

ENID BAGNOLD, *National Velvet.* N.Y., Morrow, 1949.

JAMES BALDWIN, *Go Tell It on the Mountain.* N.Y., Grosset & Dunlap, 1953.

DOROTHY BALL, *Hurricane, the Story of a Friendship.* Indianapolis, Bobbs-Merrill, 1964.

EDWIN BALMER and PHILIP WYLIE, *When Worlds Collide.* Phila., Lippincott, 1950.

NANCY BARNES (HELEN S. ADAMS), *The Wonderful Year.* N.Y., Messner, 1946.

WILLIAM E. BARRETT, *Lilies of the Field.* N.Y., Doubleday, 1962.

BETTY BAUM, *Patricia Crosses Town.* N.Y., Knopf, 1965.

J. BÉDIER, *The Romance of Tristan and Iseult,* trans. by H. Belloc. N.Y., Doubleday Anchor, 1953.

EDWARD BELLAMY, *Looking Backward.* N.Y., Harper, 1959.

LUDWIG BEMELMANS, *Madeleine's Rescue.* N.Y., Viking, 1953.

ARNOLD BENNETT, *The Old Wives' Tale.* N.Y., Modern Library, 1935.

FRANK BONHAM, *Durango Street.* N.Y., Dutton, 1965.

HAL BORLAND, *When the Legends Die.* N.Y., Bantam, 1964.

JAMES BOYD, *Drums.* N.Y., Scribner's, 1936.

H. D. BOYLSTON, *Sue Barton, Student Nurse.* Boston, Little, Brown, 1936.

CHARLOTTE BRONTË, *Jane Eyre.* N.Y., Oxford Univ. Press, 1954.

EMILY BRONTË, *Wuthering Heights,* Mark Schorer, ed. N.Y., Rinehart, 1950.

CAROL RYRIE BRINK, *Caddie Woodlawn.* N.Y., Macmillan, 1935.

PEARL BUCK, *The Good Earth.* N.Y., Day, 1949.

E. G. BULWER-LYTTON, *The Last Days of Pompeii.* N.Y., Dodd, Mead, 1946.

SHEILA BURNFORD, *Incredible Journey.* Boston, Little, Brown, 1961.

SAMUEL BUTLER, *Erewhon.* N.Y., Modern Library, 1927.

ERSKINE CALDWELL, *God's Little Acre.* N.Y., Grossett & Dunlap, 1957.

DOROTHY CANFIELD, *Understood Betsy.* N.Y., Holt, 1946.

NATALIE SAVAGE CARLSON, *The Empty Schoolhouse*. N.Y., Harper, 1965.

WILLA CATHER, *My Antonia*. Boston, Houghton Mifflin, 1932.

EDNA WALKER CHANDLER, *Cowboy Andy*. N.Y., Random House, 1959.

FLORENCE CHOATE, *Linda Takes Over*. Phila., Lippincott, 1949.

WALTER VAN TILBURG CLARK, *The Ox-Bow Incident*. N.Y., Random House, 1940.

BEVERLY CLEARY, *Henry Huggins*. N.Y., Morrow, 1950.

ALICE COBB, *The Swimming Pool*. N.Y., Friendship Press, 1957.

HILA COLMAN, *Classmates by Request*. N.Y., Morrow, 1964.

JAMES C. COLEMAN, *The Sea Hunt*. San Francisco, Harr Wagner, 1959.

———, *Treasure Under the Sea*. San Francisco, Harr Wagner, 1959.

———, FRANCES BERRES, FRANK N. HEWETT, and WILLIAM BRISCOE, *Deep Sea Adventure Series*. San Francisco, Harr Wagner, 1959.

JOSEPH CONRAD, *Heart of Darkness*. From *Tales of Land and Sea*. Garden City, N.Y., Doubleday, 1953.

———, *Lord Jim*. N.Y., Rinehart, 1957.

———, *The Secret Sharer*. Garden City, N.Y., Doubleday, 1953.

———, *Victory*. N.Y., Doubleday Anchor, 1953.

STEPHEN CRANE, *The Red Badge of Courage*. N.Y., Modern Library, 1951.

MAUREEN DALY, *Seventeenth Summer*. N.Y., Dodd, Mead, 1948.

CHARLES DICKENS, *David Copperfield*. N.Y., Modern Library, 1950.

———, *A Christmas Carol*. N.Y., Grosset & Dunlap, 1958.

———, *Great Expectations*. N.Y., Rinehart, 1951.

———, *Oliver Twist*. N.Y., Dodd, Mead, 1946.

———, *Pickwick Papers*. N.Y., Coward-McCann, 1955.

———, *A Tale of Two Cities*. N.Y., Harcourt, Brace & World, 1950.

MARGUERITE DICKSON, *Bennett High*. N.Y., Longmans, Green, 1953.

———, *Only Child*. N.Y., Longmans, Green, 1952.

FEODOR DOSTOYEVSKY, *Crime and Punishment*, trans. by Jessie Coulson. N.Y., Oxford Univ. Press, 1953.

THEODORE DREISER, *An American Tragedy*. Cleveland, World, 1925.

ALEXANDRE DUMAS, *The Count of Monte Cristo*. N.Y., McGraw-Hill, 1946.

GEORGE ELIOT, *Silas Marner*. N.Y., Harcourt, Brace & World, 1962.

ANNE EMERY, *Mountain Laurel*. N.Y., Putnam, 1948.

———, *Sorority Girl*. N.Y., Westminster, 1952.

ELIZABETH ENRIGHT, *The Saturdays*. N.Y., Rinehart, 1941.

HELEN WORDEN ERSKINE, *Out of This World*. N.Y., Putnam, 1953.

ELEANOR ESTES, *Ginger Pye*. N.Y., Harcourt, Brace & World, 1951.

———, *The Hundred Dresses*. N.Y., Harcourt, Brace & World, 1944.

———, *The Moffats*. N.Y., Harcourt, Brace & World, 1941.

HENRY GREGOR FELSEN, *Hot Rod*. N.Y., Dutton, 1950.

———, *Street Rod*. N.Y., Random House, 1953.

EDNA FERBER, *Giant*. Garden City, N.Y., Doubleday, 1952.

F. SCOTT FITZGERALD, *The Great Gatsby*. N.Y., Scribner's, 1953.

IAN FLEMING, *You Only Live Twice*. N.Y., Signet Books, New American Library, 1967.

ESTHER FORBES, *Johnny Tremain*. Boston, Houghton Mifflin, 1943.

KATHRYN FORBES, *Mama's Bank Account*. N.Y., Harcourt, Brace & World, 1943.

HENRY WILLARD FRENCH, *The Lance of Kanana*. N.Y., Lothrop, Lee & Shepard, 1932.

WANDA GAG, *Millions of Cats*. N.Y., Coward-McCann, 1939.

DORIS GATES, *Blue Willow*. N.Y., Viking, 1940.

———, *Little Vic*. N.Y., Viking, 1951.

———, *My Brother Mike*. N.Y., Viking, 1948.

———, *North Fork*. N.Y., Viking, 1945.

———, *River Ranch*. N.Y., Viking, 1949.

———, *Sensible Kate*. N.Y., Viking, 1943.

THEODOR GEISEL (DR. SEUSS), *The 500 Hats of Bartholomew Cubbins*. N.Y., Vanguard, 1937.

FRED GIPSON, *Old Yeller*. N.Y., Harper, 1956.

RUMMER GODDEN, *The Mousewife*. N.Y., Viking, 1951.

WILLIAM GOLDING, *Lord of the Flies*. N.Y., Coward, 1962.

OLIVER GOLDSMITH, *The Vicar of Wakefield*. N.Y., Macmillan, 1947.

ELIZABETH JANET GRAY, *Adam of the Road*. N.Y., Viking, 1944.

ALFRED BERTRAM GUTHRIE, *The Way West*. Boston, Houghton Mifflin, 1950.

THOMAS HARDY, *The Mayor of Casterbridge*. N.Y., Harper, 1964.

———, *The Return of the Native*. N.Y., Rinehart, 1950.

NATHANIEL HAWTHORNE, *The House of the Seven Gables*. N.Y., Dodd, Mead, 1950.

———, *The Scarlet Letter*. N.Y., Modern Library, 1950.

THOMAS HEGGEN, *Mr. Roberts*. Boston, Houghton Mifflin, 1946.

ERNEST HEMINGWAY, *The Old Man and the Sea*. N.Y., Scribner's, 1952.

MARGUERITE HENRY, *King of the Wind*. N.Y., Rand McNally, 1948.

NAT HENTOFF, *Jazz Country*. N.Y., Harper, 1965.

JOHN HERSEY, *A Bell for Adano*. N.Y., Knopf, 1944.

JAMES HILTON, *Lost Horizon*. N.Y., Morrow, 1936.

ALICE TISDALE HOBART, *The Peacock Sheds Its Tail*. Indianapolis, Bobbs-Merrill, 1945.

VICTOR HUGO, *Les Misérables*. N.Y., Dodd, Mead, 1925.

WILLIAM BRADFORD HUIE, *The Execution of Private Slovik*. N.Y., New American Library, 1954.

EVAN HUNTER, *Blackboard Jungle*. N.Y., Pocket Books, 1954.

ALDOUS HUXLEY, *Brave New World*. N.Y., Harper, 1946.

JAMES JOYCE, *Portrait of the Artist as a Young Man*. N.Y., New American Library, 1948.

HAROLD KEITH, *Rifles for Watie*. N.Y., T. Y. Crowell, 1957.

CAROLYN KEENE, *Nancy Drew Mystery Series*. N.Y., Grosset & Dunlap, c. 1940–60 (35 books published).

RUDYARD KIPLING, *Captains Courageous*. N.Y., Grosset & Dunlap, 1954.

———, *Jungle Book*. Garden City, N.Y., Doubleday, 1946.

CLARISSA KNEELAND, *Smugglers' Island* or, *The Devil Fires of San Moros*. N.Y., New Voices, 1958.

ERIC M. KNIGHT, *Lassie Come Home*. Phila., Winston, 1940.

JOHN KNOWLES, *A Separate Peace*. N.Y., Bantam Books, 1966.

JOSEPH KRUMGOLD, *And Now Miguel*. N.Y., T. Y. Crowell, 1953.

SELMA LAGERLÖF, *The Ring of the Löwenskölds*. N.Y., Doubleday, 1931.

E. S. LAMPMAN, *Rusty's Space Ship*. Garden City, N.Y., Doubleday, 1957.

WALTER SAVAGE LANDOR, *Imaginary Conversations and Poems*. N.Y., Dutton, 1933.

ROSE WILDER LANE, *Let the Hurricane Roar*. N.Y., Longmans, Green, 1933.

MUNRO LEAF, *The Story of Ferdinand*. N.Y., Viking, 1936.

HARPER LEE, *To Kill a Mockingbird*. N.Y., Popular Library, 1962.

WILLIAM LEDERER and EUGENE BURDICK, *The Ugly American*. N.Y., Norton, 1958.

MADELEINE L'ENGLE, *A Wrinkle in Time*. N.Y., Farrar, Straus & Giroux, 1962.

LOIS LENSKI, *Strawberry Girl*. Phila., Winston, 1932.

SINCLAIR LEWIS, *Arrowsmith*. N.Y., Harcourt, Brace & World, 1925.

———, *Babbitt*. N.Y., Harcourt, Brace & World, 1922.

MINA LEWITON, *The Divided Heart*. N.Y., McKay, 1947.

RICHARD LLEWELLYN, *How Green Was My Valley*. N.Y., Macmillan, 1940.

JACK LONDON, *The Call of the Wild*. N.Y., Arcadia House, 1950.

———, *White Fang*. N.Y., Grosset & Dunlap, 1933.

JOHN P. MARQUAND, *Point of No Return*. Boston, Little, Brown, 1949.

CATHERINE MARSHALL, *Julie's Heritage*. N.Y., David McKay, 1957.

ROBERT MC CLOSKEY, *Homer Price*. N.Y., Viking, 1943.

STEPHEN MEADER, *Down the Big River*. N.Y., Harcourt, Brace & World, 1924.

———, *Red Horse Hill*. N.Y., Harcourt, Brace & World, 1930.

HERMAN MELVILLE, *Billy Budd*. N.Y., Washington Square Press (Simon & Schuster), n.d.

———, *Moby Dick*. N.Y., Grosset & Dunlap, 1956.

JAMES A. MICHENER, *The Bridges of Toko-Ri*. N.Y., Random House, 1953.

RALPH MOODY, *Little Britches*. N.Y., Norton, 1950.

———, *Man of the Family*. N.Y., Norton, 1951.

SIR THOMAS MORE, *Utopia*. N.Y., Heritage Press, 1959.

HONORÉ WILLSIE MORROW, *On to Oregon*. N.Y., Morrow, 1946.

JOHN MUIR, *Stickeen*. Boston, Houghton Mifflin, 1909.

CHARLES B. NORDHOFF and JAMES N. HALL, *Mutiny on the Bounty*. Boston, Little, Brown, 1932.

MARY NORTON, *The Borrowers*. N.Y., Harcourt, Brace & World, 1953.

JACK O'BRIAN, *Return of Silver Chief*. Phila., Winston, 1940.

———, *Silver Chief*. Phila., Winston, 1933.

GEORGE ORWELL, *Animal Farm*. N.Y., New American Library, 1956.

———, *1984*. N.Y., Signet Books, New American Library, 1950.

ALAN PATON, *Cry, the Beloved Country*. N.Y., Scribner's, 1948.

HOWARD PEASE, *The Dark Adventure*. Garden City, N.Y., Doubleday, 1950.

DUDLEY POPE, *Decision at Trafalgar*. Philadelphia, Lippincott, 1960.

MARJORIE KINNAN RAWLINGS, *The Yearling*. N.Y., Scribner's, 1939.

CONRAD RICHTER, *Light in the Forest*. N.Y., Knopf, 1953.

KENNETH ROBERTS, *Boon Island*. Garden City, N.Y., Doubleday, 1956.

———, *Northwest Passage*. Garden City, N.Y., Doubleday, 1937.

OLE E. ROLVAAG, *Giants in the Earth*. N.Y., Harper, 1927.

S. M. RUSSELL, *The Lamp Is Heavy*. Phila., Lippincott, 1950.

ANTOINE DE ST. EXUPÉRY, *The Little Prince*. N.Y., Harcourt, Brace & World, 1943.

J. D. SALINGER, *Catcher in the Rye*. Boston, Little, Brown, 1951.

WILLIAM SAROYAN, *The Human Comedy*. N.Y., Harcourt, Brace & World, 1943.

JACK SCHAEFER, *Shane*. Boston, Houghton Mifflin, 1954.

BUDD SCHULBERG, ed., *From the Ashes: Voices of Watts*. N.Y., New American Library, 1967.

KATE SEREDY, *The Good Master*. N.Y., Viking, 1935.

———, *The White Stag*. N.Y., Viking, 1937.

SAMUEL SHELLABARGER, *Captain from Castille*. Boston, Little, Brown, 1945.

MIKHAIL SHOLOKHOV, *The Silent Don;* Part I: *And Quiet Flows the Don;* Part II: *The Don Flows Home to the Sea.* N.Y., Knopf, 1944.

LOUISA R. SHOTWELL, *Roosevelt Grady.* N.Y., World, 1963.

IRVING SHULMAN, *The Amboy Dukes.* N.Y., Avon, 1946.

HENRYK SIENKIEWICZ, *Quo Vadis?* Boston, Little, Brown, 1943.

ALAN SILLITOE, *The Loneliness of the Long-Distance Runner.* N.Y., Knopf, 1960.

IGNAZIO SILONE, *Bread and Wine.* N.Y., Harper, 1957.

AGNES SMITH, *An Edge of the Forest.* N.Y., Viking, 1959.

ARMSTRONG SPERRY, *Call It Courage.* N.Y., Macmillan, 1940.

———, *Storm Canvas.* Phila., Winston, 1944.

JOHN STEINBECK, *The Pearl.* N.Y., Viking, 1947.

DOROTHY STERLING, *Mary Jane.* N.Y., Doubleday, 1959.

AUGUSTA STEVENSON, *Nancy Hanks: Kentucky Girl.* Indianapolis, Bobbs-Merrill, 1954.

ROBERT LOUIS STEVENSON, *Treasure Island.* Chicago, Rand McNally, 1954.

GEORGE STEWART, *Earth Abides.* N.Y., Random House, 1949.

———, *The Years of the City.* Boston, Houghton Mifflin, 1955.

JAMES STREET, *Goodbye, My Lady.* Phila., Lippincott, 1954.

———, *Tap Roots.* N.Y., Dial, 1942.

JAMES L. SUMMERS, *Operation A.B.C.* Phila., Westminster, 1955.

HILDEGARDE SWIFT, *Railroad to Freedom.* N.Y., Harcourt, Brace & World, 1932.

BOOTH TARKINGTON, *Turmoil.* N.Y., Grosset & Dunlap, 1918.

———, *Alice Adams.* N.Y., Grosset & Dunlap, 1921.

WILLIAM M. THACKERAY, *The History of Henry Esmond.* N.Y., Dodd, Mead, 1945.

———, *Vanity Fair.* N.Y., Modern Library, 1950.

M. W. THOMPSON, *Blueberry Muffin,* N.Y., Longmans, Green, 1942.

JAMES THURBER, *Many Moons.* N.Y., Harcourt, Brace & World, 1943.

———, *Thirteen Clocks.* N.Y., Simon & Schuster, 1950.

J. R. R. TOLKIEN, *The Fellowship of the Ring.* Boston, Houghton Mifflin, 1954.

LEO TOLSTOY, *War and Peace.* N.Y., Grosset & Dunlap, 1956.

PAMELA L. TRAVERS, *Mary Poppins.* N.Y., Harcourt, Brace & World, 1934.

JOHN TUNIS, *All-American.* N.Y., Harcourt, Brace & World, 1952.

———, *Yea! Wildcats!* N.Y., Harcourt, Brace & World, 1944.

MARK TWAIN, *A Connecticut Yankee in King Arthur's Court.* N.Y., Harper, 1943.

———, *Adventures of Huckleberry Finn.* Boston, Houghton Mifflin, 1958 (Riverside edition).

———, *The Adventures of Tom Sawyer.* Phila., Winston, 1952.

JOHN UPDIKE, *Rabbit Run.* N.Y., Knopf, 1960.

HENDRICK W. VAN LOON, *Van Loon's Lives.* N.Y., Simon & Schuster, 1942.

JULES VERNE, *20,000 Leagues Under the Sea.* Chicago, Rand McNally, 1954.

GERTRUDE CHANDLER WARNER, *Box Car Children.* N.Y., Scott, 1950.

H. G. WELLS, *The Time Machine.* N.Y., Berkley, 1957.

JESSAMYN WEST, *Cress Delahanty.* N.Y., Harcourt, Brace & World, 1953.

EDITH WHARTON, *Ethan Frome.* N.Y., Scribner's, 1938.

E. B. WHITE, *Charlotte's Web.* N.Y., Harper, 1952.

WILLIAM LINDSAY WHITE, *Lost Boundaries.* N.Y., Harcourt, Brace & World, 1948.

PHYLLIS WHITNEY, *Willow Hill.* N.Y., McKay, 1947.

KATE DOUGLAS WIGGIN and NORA A. SMITH, eds., *The Arabian Nights, The Best Known Tales.* N.Y., Scribner's, 1933.

THORNTON WILDER, *The Bridge of San Luis Rey*. N.Y., Grosset & Dunlap, 1927.

THOMAS WOLFE, *Look Homeward, Angel*. N.Y., Scribner's, 1929.

HERMAN WOUK, *The Caine Mutiny*. Garden City, N.Y., Doubleday, 1951.

RICHARD WRIGHT, *Black Boy*. N.Y., Harper, 1945.

J. D. WYSS, *Swiss Family Robinson*. Cleveland, World, 1947.

SHORT STORIES

SARA ADDINGTON, "Clodhopper." In Luella B. Cook, Walter Loban, Ruth M. Stauffer, and Robert Freier, eds., *People in Literature*. N.Y., Harcourt, Brace & World, 1957.

AESOP, *The Fables of Aesop*, Walter L. Parker, ed. N.Y., Little and Ives, 1931.

ILSE AICHINGER, "The Bound Man." In Ilse Aichinger, *The Bound Man and Other Stories*. N.Y., Noonday Press, 1956.

HANS CHRISTIAN ANDERSEN, "The Nightingale." In *Six Fairy Tales by the Danish Writer Hans Christian Andersen, Published on the Occasion of the 150th Anniversary of His Birth*. Copenhagen, Det Berlingske Bogtrykkeii, 1955.

———, *Andersen's Fairy Tales*, trans. by Mrs. E. V. Lucas and Mrs. H. B. Paull. N.Y., Grosset & Dunlap, 1937.

SHERWOOD ANDERSON, "I'm a Fool." In Bennett A. Cerf, ed., *Great Modern Short Stories*. N.Y., Modern Library, 1942.

———, "Stolen Day." In Jacob M. Ross, Mary Rives Bowman, and Egbert W. Nieman, eds., *Adventures for Readers*, Book I, Mercury ed. N.Y., Harcourt, Brace & World, 1951.

STEPHEN VINCENT BENÉT, "By the Waters of Babylon." In Luella B. Cook, Walter Loban, Ruth M. Stauffer, and Robert Freier, eds., *People in Literature*. N.Y., Harcourt, Brace & World, 1957.

ANDRÉ BIRABEAU, "Granny." In Luella B. Cook, Walter Loban, Oscar James Campbell, and Ruth M. Stauffer, eds., *The World Through Literature*. N.Y., Harcourt, Brace & World, 1949.

RAY BRADBURY, "The Dragon." In Walter Loban and Rosalind Olmsted, eds., *Adventures in Appreciation*, Laureate edition. N.Y., Harcourt, Brace & World, 1963.

HEYWOOD BROUN, "The Fifty-First Dragon." In Howard Francis Seeley and Margaret Roling, eds., *Recent Stories for Enjoyment*. Morristown, N.J., Silver Burdett, 1937.

WALTER C. BROWN, "The Puzzle Knot." In William R. Wood, ed., *Short Short Stories*. N.Y., Harcourt, Brace & World, 1951.

MORLEY CALLAGHAN, "All the Years of Her Life." In Simon Certner and G. H. Henry, eds., *Short Stories for Our Times*. Boston, Houghton Mifflin, 1950.

———, "The Snob." In Luella B. Cook, Walter Loban, Ruth M. Stauffer, and Robert Freier, eds., *People in Literature*. N.Y., Harcourt, Brace & World, 1957.

WILLA CATHER, "Paul's Case." In Bennett A. Cerf, ed., *Great Modern Short Stories*. N.Y., Modern Library, 1942.

ANTON CHEKHOV, "The Bet." In H. C. Schweikert, ed., *Short Stories*. N.Y., Harcourt, Brace & World, 1934.

ANN CHIDESTER, "Mrs. Ketting and Clark Gable." In Herschel Brickell, ed., *Prize Stories of 1950: The O. Henry Awards*. Garden City, N.Y., Doubleday, 1950.

WALTER VAN TILBURG CLARK, "The Portable Phonograph." In Luella B. Cook, Walter Loban, Ruth M. Stauffer, and Robert Freier, eds., *People in Literature*. N.Y., Harcourt, Brace & World, 1957.

ROBERT COATES, "The Need." In Martha Foley, ed., *The Best American Short Stories, 1953*. Boston, Houghton Mifflin, 1953.

RICHARD CONNELL, "The Most Dangerous Game." In Herbert A. Wise and Phyllis Fraser, eds., *Great Tales of Terror and the Supernatural*. N.Y., Modern Library, 1944.

EUGENIE COURTRIGHT, "Yours Lovingly." In Luella B. Cook, Walter Loban, and Henry H. Miller, Jr., eds., *Adventures in Appreciation*, 3d ed. N.Y., Harcourt, Brace & World, 1949.

JAMES GOULD COZZENS, "Success Story." In William R. Wood, ed., *Short Short Stories*. N.Y., Harcourt, Brace & World, 1951.

MAUREEN DALY, "Sixteen." In R. J. Cadigan, ed., *September to June*. N.Y., Appleton-Century-Crofts, 1942.

MARY DEASY, "The High Hill." In *Harper's* magazine, Vol. 196, No. 1173 (February 1948).

ARTHUR CONAN DOYLE, "The Adventure of the Bruce-Partington Plans." From *The Complete Sherlock Holmes*. Garden City, N.Y., Doubleday, 1936.

WILLIAM FAULKNER, "Barn Burning." In Robert Penn Warren and Albert Erskine, eds., *Short Story Masterpieces*. N.Y., Dell, 1954.

———, "The Bear." From *The Faulkner Reader*. N.Y., Modern Library, 1959.

MICHAEL FESSIER, "That's What Happened to Me." In Walter Loban, Dorothy Holmstrom, and Luella B. Cook, eds., *Adventures in Appreciation*. N.Y., Harcourt, Brace & World, 1958.

COREY FORD, "The Snake Dance." In Frank G. Jennings and Charles J. Calitri, eds., *Stories*. N.Y., Harcourt, Brace & World, 1957.

E. M. FORSTER, "The Machine Stops." From *The Eternal Moment and Other Stories*. N.Y., Harcourt, Brace & World, 1928.

MARY E. WILKINS FREEMAN, "The Revolt of Mother." In Luella B. Cook, Walter Loban, and Susanna Baxter, eds., *Adventures in Appreciation*, Mercury ed. N.Y., Harcourt, Brace & World, 1952.

ZONA GALE, "Bill's Little Girl." In Frank G. Jennings and Charles J. Calitri, eds., *Stories*. N.Y., Harcourt, Brace & World, 1957.

RICHARD T. GILL, "The Ten-Dollar Bill." In Elizabeth C. O'Daly and Egbert W. Nieman, eds., *Adventures for Readers*, Book I. N.Y., Harcourt, Brace & World, 1958.

KATHERINE PEABODY GIRLING, "When Hanna Var Eight Yar Old." In Luella B. Cook, Walter Loban, Ruth M. Stauffer, and Robert Freier, eds., *People in Literature*. N.Y., Harcourt, Brace & World, 1957.

ALBERT HALPER, "Prelude." In Maureen Daly, ed., *My Favorite Stories*. N.Y., Dodd, Mead, 1948.

NATHANIEL HAWTHORNE, "The Great Stone Face" and "Ethan Brand." In *Complete Short Stories of Nathaniel Hawthorne*. Garden City, N.Y., Hanover House, 1959.

ERNEST HEMINGWAY, "Big Two-Hearted River." In Malcolm Cowley, ed., *The Portable Hemingway*. N.Y., Viking, 1944.

———, "A Day's Wait." In Whit Burnett, ed., *Time to Be Young*. Phila., Lippincott, 1945.

MURRAY HEYERT, "The New Kid." In Marian Lovrien, Herbert Potell, and Prudence Bostwick, eds., *Adventures in Living*. N.Y., Harcourt, Brace & World, 1955.

MARJORIE HOLMES, "Reflections of Luanne." In Mary Dirlam, ed., *Hit Parade of Short Stories*. N.Y., Scholastic, 1953.

LANGSTON HUGHES, "One Friday Morning." In Simon Certner and G. H. Henry, eds., *Short Stories for Our Times*. Boston, Houghton Mifflin, 1950.

VICTOR HUGO, "The Bishop's Candlesticks." From *Les Misérables*. N.Y., Norton, 1959.

SHIRLEY JACKSON, "Charles." From *Life Among the Savages*. N.Y., Farrar, Straus & Young, 1953.

————, "The Lottery." From *The Lottery*. N.Y., Farrar, Straus & Young, 1949.

WILLIAM W. JACOBS, "The Monkey's Paw." In Herbert A. Wise and Phyllis Fraser, eds., *Great Tales of Terror and the Supernatural*. N.Y., Modern Library, 1944.

JAMES JOYCE, "Araby." In Charles Neider, ed., *Great Short Stories from the World's Literature*. N.Y., Rinehart, 1950.

MACKINLAY KANTOR, "The Boy in the Dark." In William R. Wood and John D. Husband, eds., *Short Stories as You Like Them*. N.Y., Harcourt, Brace & World, 1940.

SELMA LAGERLÖF, "The Rat Trap." In Walter Loban and Rosalind Olmsted, eds., *Adventure in Appreciation*, Laureate edition. N.Y., Harcourt, Brace & World, 1963.

RING LARDNER, "Haircut." In Bennett A. Cerf, ed., *Great Modern Short Stories*. N.Y., Modern Library, 1942.

————, "I Can't Breathe." In Luella B. Cook, Walter Loban, Ruth M. Stauffer, and Robert Freier, eds., *People in Literature*. N.Y., Harcourt, Brace & World, 1957.

————, "Travelogue." From *Round Up*. N.Y., Scribner's, 1929.

STEPHEN LEACOCK, "The Man in Asbestos." From *The Laugh Parade*. N.Y., Dodd, Mead, 1940.

JACK LONDON, "The Heathen." In Walter Loban, Dorothy Holmstrom, and Luella B. Cook, eds., *Adventures in Appreciation*. N.Y., Harcourt, Brace & World, 1958.

————, "To Build a Fire." In *Best Short Stories of Jack London*. N.Y., Permabooks, 1949.

GEORGE LOVERIDGE, "The Cruise." In *Yale Review*, Vol. 41, No. 1 (Autumn 1951).

DONALD MAC KENZIE, "Too Late to Lie." In *Collier's*, Vol. 126, No. 25 (December 16, 1950).

MARIAN HURD MCNEELY, "The Horse." From *The Way to Glory and Other Stories*. N.Y., Longmans, Green, 1932.

KATHERINE MANSFIELD, "A Cup of Tea." In Harry Shaw and Douglas Bennett, eds., *Reading the Short Story*. N.Y., Harper, 1954.

————, "Miss Brill." In Bennett A. Cerf, ed., *Great Modern Short Stories*. N.Y., Modern Library, 1942.

GUY DE MAUPASSANT, "The Necklace" and "The Piece of String." From *The Great Short Stories of Guy de Maupassant*. N.Y., Pocket Library, 1958.

HONORÉ WILLSIE MORROW, "Child Pioneer." In Jacob M. Ross, Egbert W. Nieman, and Mary Rives Bowman, eds., *Adventures for Readers*, Book I, Mercury ed. N.Y., Harcourt, Brace & World, 1953.

H. H. MUNRO (SAKI), "The Lumber Room." In Luella B. Cook, Walter Loban, and Susanna Baxter, eds., *Adventures in Appreciation*, Mercury ed. N.Y., Harcourt, Brace & World, 1952.

————, "The Open Window." In Walter Loban, Dorothy Holmstrom, and Luella B. Cook, eds., *Adventures in Appreciation*. N.Y., Harcourt, Brace & World, 1958.

FRANK O'CONNOR, "The Duke's Children." From *Domestic Relations*. N.Y., Knopf, 1957.

————, "In the Train." From *Bones of Contention and Other Stories*. N.Y., Macmillan, 1936.

LUCILE VAUGHAN PAYNE, "Prelude." In Bryna Ivens, ed., *The Seventeen Reader.* Phila., Lippincott, 1951.

EDGAR ALLAN POE, "The Cask of Amontillado." In Bernardine Kielty, ed., *A Treasury of Short Stories.* N.Y., Simon & Schuster, 1947.

———, "Descent into the Maelstrom" and "The Tell-Tale Heart." In Philip Van Doren Stern, ed., *Edgar Allan Poe.* N.Y., Viking, 1945.

———, "The Fall of the House of Usher." In Dudley Miles and Robert Pooley, eds., *Literature and Life in America.* Chicago, Scott, Foresman, 1943.

WILLIAM SYDNEY PORTER (O. HENRY), "The Gift of the Magi." In Walter Loban, Luella B. Cook, and Dorothy Holmstrom, eds., *Adventures in Appreciation.* N.Y., Harcourt, Brace & World, 1958.

———, "A Municipal Report." In M. E. Speare, ed., *Short Stories.* N.Y., Pocket Books, 1950.

MARJORIE KINNAN RAWLINGS, "A Mother in Mannville." In Whit Burnett, ed., *Time to Be Young.* Phila., Lippincott, 1945.

J. D. SALINGER, "A Fine Day for Bananafish." From *55 Short Stories from the New Yorker.* (no editor) N.Y., Simon & Schuster, 1949.

WILLIAM SAROYAN, "Five Ripe Pears." From *Inhale and Exhale.* N.Y., Random House, 1936.

———, "Locomotive 38, the Ojibway." In B. A. Heydrick, ed., *Americans All.* N.Y., Harcourt, Brace & World, 1941.

———, "The Pheasant Hunter." From *The Assyrian and Other Stories.* N.Y., Harcourt, Brace & World, 1950.

MARK SCHORER, "The Dead Dog." In William R. Wood, ed., *Short Short Stories.* N.Y., Harcourt, Brace & World, 1951.

WILBUR DANIEL STEELE, "Footfalls." In H. L. Shaw, ed., *Americans One and All.* N.Y., Harper, 1947.

JOHN STEINBECK, "The Affair at 7, Rue de M____." In Walter Loban, Dorothy Holmstrom, and Luella B. Cook, eds., *Adventures in Appreciation.* N.Y., Harcourt, Brace & World, 1958.

CARL STEPHENSON, "Leiningen Versus the Ants." In Walter Loban, Dorothy Holmstrom, and Luella B. Cook, eds., *Adventures in Appreciation.* N.Y., Harcourt, Brace & World, 1958.

ROBERT LOUIS STEVENSON, "The Sire de Maletroit's Door." In Bennett A. Cerf, ed., *Anthology of Famous British Stories.* N.Y., Modern Library, 1952.

FRANK STOCKTON, "The Lady or the Tiger?" In A. G. Day, ed., *Greatest American Short Stories.* N.Y., McGraw-Hill, 1953.

MARTIN STORM, "A Shipment of Mute Fate." In Luella B. Cook, Walter Loban, George W. Norvell, and William A. McCall, eds., *Challenge to Explore.* N.Y., Harcourt, Brace & World, 1941.

JESSE STUART, "As Ye Sow, So Shall Ye Reap." In William R. Wood, ed., *Short Short Stories.* N.Y., Harcourt, Brace & World, 1951.

———, "The Split Cherry Tree." In Albert B. Tibbets, ed., *Youth, Youth, Youth.* N.Y., Watts, 1955.

DOROTHY THOMAS, "The Car." In Luella B. Cook, Walter Loban, Ruth M. Stauffer, and Robert Freier, eds., *People in Literature.* N.Y., Harcourt, Brace & World, 1957.

JAMES THURBER, "The Secret Life of Walter Mitty." In A. G. Day, ed., *Greatest American Short Stories.* N.Y., McGraw-Hill, 1953.

JAMES THURBER, "The Macbeth Murder Mystery." In *My World and Welcome to It.* N.Y., Harcourt, Brace & World, 1942.

D. TRACEY, "Most Valuable Player." In Leo Margulies, ed., *Baseball Round-Up.* N.Y., Cupples & Leon, 1948.

MARK TWAIN, "Blue Jays." (Originally titled "Jim Baker's Blue Jay Yarn.") In Walter Loban, Dorothy Holmstrom, and Luella B. Cook, eds., *Adventures in Appreciation.* N.Y., Harcourt, Brace & World, 1958.

MAY VONTVER, "The Kiskis." In Luella B. Cook, Walter Loban, George W. Norvell, and William A. McCall, eds., *Challenge to Grow.* N.Y., Harcourt, Brace & World, 1947.

L. WALLER (C. S. CODY), "The Restless Ones." In *Collier's,* Vol. 133, No. 3 (February 5, 1954).

HUGH WALPOLE, "The Ruby Glass." From *All Souls' Night.* Garden City, N.Y., Doubleday, Doran, 1933.

JESSAMYN WEST, "The Hat." From *Cress Delahanty.* N.Y., Harcourt, Brace & World, 1953.

JESSE LYNCH WILLIAMS, "Not Wanted." In Luella B. Cook, Walter Loban, George W. Norvell, and William A. McCall, eds., *Challenge to Understand.* N.Y., Harcourt, Brace & World, 1950

WILLIAM WISE, "Glory in Bridgeville." In Herbert Potell, Marian Lovrien, and Prudence Bostwick, eds., *Adventures for Today.* N.Y., Harcourt, Brace & World, 1955.

NONFICTION, BIOGRAPHY, ESSAYS

MORTIMER ADLER and WILLIAM GARMAN, eds., *The Great Ideas—A Syntopicon of Great Books of the Western World.* 2 vols. Chicago, Encyclopaedia Britannica, 1952.

SIR FRANCIS BACON, *Essays and The New Atlantis.* N.Y., Van Nostrand, 1942.

JAMES BALDWIN, "Many Thousands Gone." In *Notes of a Native Son.* Boston, Beacon Press, 1955.

ROBERT BENCHLEY, "Now That You're Tanned—What?" In Egbert W. Nieman and George N. Salt, eds., *Pleasure in Literature.* N.Y., Harcourt, Brace & World, 1949.

CLAUDE BROWN, *Manchild in the Promised Land.* N.Y., New American Library, 1966.

TRUMAN CAPOTE, *In Cold Blood.* N.Y., Random House, 1965.

RACHEL CARSON, *The Sea Around Us.* N.Y., Oxford Univ. Press, 1951.

JULIAN CATE, "A Style-ish Fable." In Walter Loban, Dorothy Holmstrom, and Luella B. Cook, eds., *Adventures in Appreciation.* N.Y., Harcourt, Brace & World, 1958.

C. W. CERAM (KURT W. MAREK), *Gods, Graves, and Scholars.* N.Y., Knopf, 1951.

JULIA ADAMS DAVIS, *No Other White Men.* N.Y., Dutton, 1937.

CLARENCE DAY, *Life with Father,* N.Y., Knopf, 1935.

PAUL DE KRUIF, *Microbe Hunters.* N.Y., Harcourt, Brace & World, 1932.

ISAK DINESEN, *Out of Africa.* N.Y., Modern Library, 1952.

———, "The King's Letter." Part of "Borua-a-Soldani." In *Shadows on the Grass.* N.Y., Random House, 1961.

HILDEGARDE DOLSON, *We Shook the Family Tree.* N.Y., Random House, 1946.

FREDERICK DOUGLASS, *The Life and Times of Frederick Douglass.* N.Y., Pathway Press, 1941.

JOHN H. FLOHERTY, *Inside the F.B.I.* Phila., Lippincott, 1943.

———, *Get That Story: Journalism—Its Lore and Thrills.* Phila., Lippincott, 1952.

ANNE FRANK, *Diary of a Young Girl.* Garden City, N.Y., Doubleday, 1952.

BENJAMIN FRANKLIN, *Autobiography.* Mount Vernon, N.Y., Peter Pauper Press, 1945.

FRANK GRAHAM, *Lou Gehrig, A Quiet Hero.* N.Y., Putnam, 1942.

DICK GREGORY, *Nigger.* N.Y., E. P. Dutton, 1964.

JOHN H. GRIFFIN, *Black Like Me.* Boston, Houghton Mifflin, 1961.

ANNA GERTRUDE HALL, *Nansen.* N.Y., Viking, 1940.

RICHARD HALLIBURTON, *Richard Halliburton's Second Book of Marvels.* N.Y., Bobbs-Merrill, 1938.

DAG HAMMERSKJÖLD, *Markings.* N.Y., Knopf, 1964.

JOHN HERSEY, *Hiroshima.* N.Y., Knopf, 1946.

MAURICE HERZOG, *Annapurna.* N.Y., Dutton, 1952.

THOR HEYERDAHL, *Aku-Aku.* Chicago, Rand McNally, 1953.

————, *Kon-Tiki: Across the Pacific by Raft.* Garden City, N.Y., Garden City Books, 1950.

LANCELOT T. HOGBEN, *The Wonderful World of Mathematics.* Garden City, N.Y., Doubleday, 1955.

DAVID A. HOWARTH, *We Die Alone.* N.Y., Macmillan, 1955.

RICHARD HUBLER, *Lou Gehrig, Iron Horse of Baseball.* Boston, Houghton Mifflin, 1941.

SIR JOHN HUNT, *The Conquest of Everest.* N.Y., Dutton, 1954.

SHIRLEY JACKSON, *Life Among the Savages.* N.Y., Farrar, Straus & Young, 1953.

OSA HELEN JOHNSON, *I Married Adventure.* Phila., Lippincott, 1940.

HELEN KELLER, *The Story of My Life.* Garden City, N.Y., Doubleday, 1954.

————, "Three Days to See." In Robert V. Jameson, ed., *Essays New and Old.* N.Y., Harcourt, Brace & World, 1955.

JOHN F. KENNEDY, *Profiles in Courage.* N.Y., Harper & Row, 1964.

MARTIN LUTHER KING, JR., *Stride Toward Freedom.* N.Y., Harper, 1958.

————, *Why We Can't Wait.* N.Y., New American Library, 1964.

————, *A Martin Luther King Treasury.* Yonkers, N.Y., Negro Heritage Library Series, Educational Heritage, Inc., 1968.

SELMA LAGERLÖF, *Mårbacka.* Garden City, N.Y., Doubleday, 1938.

CHARLES LAMB, "Dissertation upon Roast Pig." In Luella B. Cook, Walter Loban, Oscar James Campbell, and Ruth M. Stauffer, eds., *The World Through Literature.* N.Y., Harcourt, Brace & World, 1949.

MARGARET LANDON, *Anna and the King of Siam.* N.Y., Day, 1944.

HART DAY LEAVITT and DAVID A. SOHN, *Stop, Look, and Write.* N.Y., Bantam, 1964.

WILLY LEY, *Engineers' Dreams.* N.Y., Viking, 1954.

Look's Editors, *The Story of the FBI.* N.Y., Dutton, 1954.

MALCOLM X (with the assistance of Alex Haley), *Autobiography of Malcolm X.* N.Y., Grove, 1966.

JOHN BARTLOW MARTIN, *Why Did They Kill?* N.Y., Ballantine, 1953.

JOHN MILTON, "Areopagitica." In Robert P. Tristram Coffin and Alexander M. Witherspoon, eds., *Seventeenth-Century Prose and Poetry,* 2d ed. N.Y., Harcourt, Brace & World, 1963.

H. A. MORRIS, *Digging in Yucatán.* Garden City, N.Y., Doubleday, 1931.

FARLEY MOWAT, *People of the Deer.* Boston, Little, Brown, 1952.

RUSSELL OWEN, *Conquest of the North and South Poles.* N.Y., Random House, 1952.

PLATO, *The Republic.* Cleveland, World, 1946.

ERNIE PYLE, *Home Country.* N.Y., Sloane, 1947.

ERNIE PYLE, "I Meet Walt Disney." In Egbert W. Nieman and George N. Salt, eds., *Pleasure in Literature*. N.Y., Harcourt, Brace & World, 1949.

WILL ROGERS, *Autobiography*. Boston, Houghton Mifflin, 1949.

ANTOINE DE ST. EXUPÉRY, *Wind, Sand, and Stars*. N.Y., Harcourt, Brace & World, 1943.

———, *Night Flight*. In Edmund Fuller and Blanche Jennings Thompson, eds., *Four Novels for Appreciation*. N.Y., Harcourt, Brace & World, 1960.

CARL SANDBURG, *Abe Lincoln Grows Up*. N.Y., Harcourt, Brace & World, 1928.

MILTON J. SHAPIRO, *The Willie Mays Story*. N.Y., Messner, 1960.

KATHERINE BINNEY SHIPPEN, *The Bright Design*. N.Y., Viking, 1949.

ROBERT SILVERBERG, *Lost Cities and Vanished Civilizations*. Phila., Chilton, 1962.

LINCOLN STEFFENS, *Boy on Horseback*. N.Y., Harcourt, Brace & World, 1935.

———, *The Autobiography of Lincoln Steffens*. N.Y., Harcourt, Brace & World, 1931.

IRVING STONE, *Sailor on Horseback, Biography of Jack London*. Boston, Houghton Mifflin, 1938.

JESSE STUART, "My Father Is an Educated Man." In Luella B. Cook, Walter Loban, and Ruth M. Stauffer, eds., *People in Literature*. N.Y., Harcourt, Brace & World, 1951.

WILLIAM STYRON, *Confessions of Nat Turner*. N.Y., Random House, 1967.

JAMES THURBER, *Fables for Our Time*. N.Y., Harper, 1940.

RENÉ VALLERY-RADOT, *The Life of Louis Pasteur*. N.Y., Knopf, 1958.

V. W. VON HAGEN, *Incas, People of the Sun*. N.Y., World, 1961.

URSULA VON KARDORFF, *Diary of a Nightmare (Berlin 1942–1945)*. N.Y., Day, 1966.

GEORGE H. WALTZ, *Jules Verne, The Biography of an Imagination*. N.Y., Holt, 1943.

WILLIAM WEST, *Writers on Writing*. Boston, Ginn & Co., 1965.

E. B. WHITE, "Afternoon of an American Boy." From *The Second Tree from the Corner*. N.Y., Harper, 1954.

WILLIAM ALLEN WHITE, "Mary White." In Robert J. Cadigan, ed., *September to June*. N.Y., Appleton-Century, 1942.

———, *The Autobiography of William Allen White*. N.Y., Macmillan, 1946.

ERIC ERNEST WILLIAMS, *The Wooden Horse*. N.Y., Harper, 1949.

EDMUND WILSON, *Scrolls from the Dead Sea*. N.Y., Oxford Univ. Press, 1955.

PAUL WITTY, *It's Fun to Find Out* (film-story books). Boston, Heath, 1953.

THOMAS WOLFE, *A Stone, a Leaf, a Door*. N.Y., Scribner's, 1950.

JADE SNOW WONG, *Fifth Chinese Daughter*. N.Y., Harper, 1950.

FRANK LLOYD WRIGHT, *Modern Architecture*. Princeton, N.J., Princeton Univ. Press, 1931.

DRAMA

CHINUA ACHEBE, *Things Fall Apart*. N.Y., McDowell, Obolenski, 1959.

ZOË AKINS, *The Old Maid*. N.Y., Samuel French, 1935.

EDWARD ALBEE, *The American Dream*. N.Y., Coward-McCann, 1961.

MAXWELL ANDERSON, *Elizabeth the Queen, High Tor, Mary of Scotland*, and *Winterset*. In *Eleven Verse Plays, 1920–1939*. N.Y., Harcourt, Brace & World, 1940.

———, *Lost in the Stars*. N.Y., Sloane, 1950.

ANONYMOUS, *Everyman*. In Barrett H. Clark, ed., *World Drama*, Vol. I. N.Y., Appleton-Century, 1933.

ENID BAGNOLD, *The Chalk Garden*. N.Y., Random House, 1956.

JAMES M. BARRIE, *The Admirable Crichton, The Old Lady Shows Her Medals, Peter Pan, The Twelve Pound Look, What Every Woman Knows,* and *The Will.* In *Plays.* N.Y., Scribner's, 1928.

PHILIP BARRY, *Holiday.* In Montrose J. Moses and Joseph Wood Krutch, eds., *Representative American Dramas.* Boston, Little, Brown, 1941.

RUDOLPH BESIER, *The Barretts of Wimpole Street.* In Bennett Cerf and Van H. Cartmell, eds., *Sixteen Famous British Plays.* Garden City, N.Y., Garden City Books, 1942.

ROBERT BOLT, *A Man for All Seasons.* N.Y., Random House, 1962.

BERTOLT BRECHT, *The Caucasian Chalk Circle.* N.Y., Grove, 1966.

————, *Galileo.* N.Y., Grove, 1966.

KAREL CAPEK, *R. U. R.* In John Gassner, ed., *A Treasury of the Theater.* N.Y., Simon & Schuster, 1950.

MARC CONNELLY, *The Green Pastures.* In John Gassner, ed., *A Treasury of the Theater.* N.Y., Simon & Schuster, 1950.

MARY CAROLYN DAVIES, *The Slave with Two Faces.* In Frank Shay and Pierre Loving, eds., *Fifty Contemporary One-Act Plays.* N.Y., Appleton, 1920.

OSSIE DAVIS, *Purlie Victorious.* N.Y., Samuel French, 1965.

HARRY DENKER and RALPH BERKY, *Time Limit.* In *Theatre Arts,* Vol. 41, No. 4 (April 1957).

MATHURIN DONDO, *Two Blind Men and a Donkey.* In Frank Shay, ed., *Appleton Book of Holiday Plays.* N.Y., Appleton, 1930.

MARTIN B. DUBERMAN, *In White America.* Boston, Houghton Mifflin, 1964.

FRIEDRICH DÜRRENMATT, *The Physicists.* N.Y., Grove, 1964.

EURIPIDES, *Electra.* In *Medea and Other Plays.* N.Y., Penguin Classics, 1963.

EDNA FERBER, *The Eldest.* In Luella B. Cook, Walter Loban, Ruth Stauffer, and Robert Freier, eds., *People in Literature.* N.Y., Harcourt, Brace & World, 1957.

WALTER FERRIS, *Death Takes a Holiday.* N.Y., Samuel French, 1930.

RACHEL FIELD, *The Fifteenth Candle.* In Irwin J. Zachar and Rodney A. Kimball, eds., *Plays as Experience.* N.Y., Odyssey, 1944.

LUCILLE FLETCHER, *Sorry, Wrong Number.* In Abraham Lass, E. L. McGill, and Donald Axelrod, eds., *Plays from Radio.* Boston, Houghton Mifflin, 1948.

ANATOLE FRANCE, *The Man Who Married a Dumb Wife.* In Bennett Cerf and Van H. Cartmell, eds., *Thirty Famous One-Act Plays.* N.Y., Modern Library, 1949.

ESTHER GALBRAITH, *The Brink of Silence.* In Milton Smith, ed., *Short Plays of Various Types.* N.Y., Bobbs-Merrill, 1924.

ZONA GALE, *Uncle Jimmy.* In LeRoy Phillips and Theodore Johnson, eds., *Types of Modern Dramatic Composition.* Boston, Ginn, 1927.

JOHN GALSWORTHY, *Justice, Loyalties,* and *The Silver Box.* In *Plays.* N.Y., Scribner's, 1928.

WILLIAM GIBSON, *The Miracle Worker.* N.Y., Knopf, 1957.

SUSAN GLASPELL, *Trifles.* In John Gassner, ed., *Twenty-Five Best Plays of the Modern American Theater.* N.Y., Crown, 1949.

JOHANN WOLFGANG VON GOETHE, *Faust,* Parts 1 and 2. N.Y., Oxford Univ. Press, 1952; *Faust,* Part 1. Baltimore, Penguin, 1958.

WALTER GOLDSCHMIDT and LESTER SINCLAIR, *A Word in Your Ear.* In Margaret Mayorga, ed., *Best Short Plays of 1953–1954.* N.Y., Dodd, Mead, 1954.

OLIVER GOLDSMITH, *She Stoops to Conquer.* In Barrett H. Clark, ed., *World Drama,* Vol. 1. N.Y., Appleton-Century, 1933.

KENNETH SAWYER GOODMAN, *Dust of the Road*. In George A. Goldstone, ed., *One-Act Plays*. Boston, Allyn & Bacon, 1926.

—— and BEN HECHT, *The Wonder Hat*. In Margaret Mayorga, ed., *Representative One-Act Plays by American Authors*. Boston, Little, Brown, 1937.

LADY GREGORY, *Spreading the News*. In George Jean Nathan, ed., *Five Great Modern Irish Plays*. N.Y., Modern Library, 1941.

HOLWORTHY HALL and ROBERT MIDDLEMAS, *The Valiant*. In Bennett Cerf and Van H. Cartmell, eds., *Thirty Famous One-Act Plays*. N.Y., Modern Library, 1949.

LORRAINE HANSBERRY, *The Sign in Sidney Brustein's Window* and *A Raisin in the Sun*. N.Y., New American Library, 1965.

MOSS HART and GEORGE S. KAUFMAN, *You Can't Take It with You*. In Barrett H. Clark and Thomas R. Cook, eds., *Nine Modern American Plays*. N.Y., Appleton-Century-Crofts, 1951.

LILLIAN HELLMAN, *The Little Foxes*. In Allan Gates Halline, ed., *Six Modern American Plays*. N.Y., Modern Library, 1951.

SIDNEY HOWARD, *The Silver Cord*. In Arthur Quinn, ed., *Representative American Plays from 1767 to the Present Day*, 7th ed. N.Y., Appleton-Century-Crofts, 1953.

——, *They Knew What They Wanted*. In John Gassner, ed., *Twenty-Five Best Plays of the Modern American Theater*. N.Y., Crown, 1949.

——, *Yellow Jack*. N.Y., Harcourt, Brace & World, 1939.

LANGSTON HUGHES, *Tambourines to Glory*. In *5 Plays by Langston Hughes*. Bloomington, Ind., Indiana Univ. Press, 1963.

HENRIK IBSEN, *An Enemy of the People*. N.Y., Modern Library, 1945.

EUGÈNE IONESCO, *Rhinoceros*. In *Rhinoceros and Other Plays*. N.Y., Grove Press, 1960.

ROBINSON JEFFERS, *Medea*. In John Gassner, ed., *Best Plays of the Modern American Theater*, 3d series. N.Y., Crown, 1952.

GEORGE KELLY, *Craig's Wife*. In John Gassner, ed., *Twenty-Five Best Plays of the Modern American Theater*. N.Y., Crown, 1949.

——, *Finders Keepers*. In Francis J. Griffith and Joseph Mersand, eds., *Modern One-Act Plays*. N.Y., Harcourt, Brace & World, 1950.

SIDNEY KINGSLEY, *Dead End*. In John Gassner, ed., *Twenty Best Plays of the Modern American Theater*, 1st series. N.Y., Crown, 1939.

EMMET LAVERY, *The Magnificent Yankee*. N.Y., Samuel French, 1946.

JEROME LAURENCE and ROBERT E. LEE, *Inherit the Wind*. In John Gassner, ed., *Best American Plays*, 4th series. N.Y., Crown, 1957.

ALAN J. LERNER and FREDERICK LOWE, *My Fair Lady*. N.Y., Coward, 1968.

HOWARD LINDSAY and RUSSEL CROUSE, *Life with Father*. In John Gassner, ed., *Best Plays of the Modern American Theater*, 2d series. N.Y., Crown, 1947.

——, *State of the Union*. In John Gassner, ed., *Best Plays of the Modern American Theater*, 3d series. N.Y., Crown, 1952.

FEDERICO GARCÍA LORCA, *Blood Wedding*. Trans. by John Garrett Underhill. In E. Bradless Watson and Benfield Pressey, eds., *Contemporary Drama, Fifteen Plays*. N.Y., Scribner's, 1959.

ROBERT LOWELL, *Benito Cereno*. From *The Old Glory*. N.Y., Farrar, Straus & Giroux, 1965.

G. MARTINEZ-SIERRA, *The Cradle Song*. In Bennett Cerf and Van H. Cartmell, eds., *Sixteen Famous European Plays*. Garden City, N.Y., Garden City Books, 1943.

CARSON MC CULLERS, *Member of the Wedding*. N.Y., New Directions, 1951.

NORMAN MC KINNEL, *The Bishop's Candlesticks*. In Esther R. Galbraith, ed., *Plays Without Footlights*. N.Y., Harcourt, Brace & World, 1945.

ARTHUR MILLER, *All My Sons*. In John Gassner, ed., *Best Plays of the Modern American Theater*, 3d series. N.Y., Crown, 1952.

——, *Death of a Salesman*. N.Y., Viking, 1949.

——, *Incident at Vichy*. N.Y., Viking, 1964.

A. A. MILNE, *The Ivory Door*. N.Y., Putnam, 1928.

FERENC MOLNÁR, *Liliom*. In Bennett Cerf and Van H. Cartmell, eds., *Sixteen Famous European Plays*. Garden City, N.Y., Garden City Books, 1943.

EUGENE O'NEILL, *Ah, Wilderness*. In Bennett Cerf and Van H. Cartmell, eds., *Sixteen Famous American Plays*. Garden City, N.Y., Garden City Books, 1941.

——, *Beyond the Horizon*. In Harlan H. Hatcher, ed., *Modern Dramas*. N.Y., Harcourt, Brace & World, 1948.

——, *The Emperor Jones* and *The Great God Brown*. In Saxe Commins, ed., *Nine Plays*. N.Y., Random House, 1954.

——, *Long Day's Journey into Night*. New Haven, Conn., Yale Univ. Press, 1956.

——, *Mourning Becomes Electra*. In *Three Plays of Eugene O'Neill*. N.Y., Vintage Books, Random House.

——, *Where the Cross Is Made*. In Helen Louise Cohen, ed., *More One-Act Plays by Modern Authors*. N.Y., Harcourt, Brace & World, 1927.

LOUIS N. PARKER, *A Minuet*. In Bruce Carpenter, ed., *A Book of Dramas*. N.Y., Prentice-Hall, 1929.

JOHN PATRICK, *The Hasty Heart*. In John Gassner, ed., *Best Plays of the Modern American Theater*, 2d series. N.Y., Crown, 1947.

——, *Teahouse of the August Moon*. N.Y., Putnam, 1954.

JOSEPHINE PRESTON PEABODY, *The Piper*. In Montrose J. Moses and Joseph Wood Krutch, eds., *Representative American Dramas*. Boston, Little, Brown, 1951.

EUGENE PILLOT, *Two Crooks and a Lady*. In Edwin Van B. Knickerbocker, ed., *Short Plays*. N.Y., Holt, 1931.

TERENCE RATTIGAN, *The Winslow Boy*. N.Y., Dramatists Play Service, 1948.

MARY K. REELY, *The Window to the South*. Boston, Walter H. Baker, 1924.

LENNOX ROBINSON, *The Far Off Hills*. In Frank Wadleigh Chandler and Richard Albert Cordell, eds., *Twentieth Century Plays*. N.Y., Nelson, 1939.

EDMOND ROSTAND, *Romancers*. In George R. Coffman, ed., *A Book of Modern Plays*. N.Y., Modern Library, 1925.

——, *Cyrano de Bergerac*. Trans. by Brian Hooker. N.Y., Holt, 1923.

DORE SCHARY, *Sunrise at Campobello*. In Bennett Cerf, ed., *American Plays for Today*. N.Y., Random House, 1961.

WILLIAM SHAKESPEARE, *Hamlet, Henry IV, Julius Caesar, King Lear, Macbeth*, et al. In Thomas Marc Parrot, ed., *Twenty-Three Plays and the Sonnets*. N.Y., Scribner's, 1953.

GEORGE BERNARD SHAW, *Pygmalion*. In *Selected Plays*, Vol. I. N.Y., Dodd, Mead, 1948.

——, *Saint Joan*. In *Selected Plays*, Vol. II. N.Y., Dodd, Mead, 1948.

R. C. SHERIFF, *Journey's End*. In John Gassner, ed., *A Treasury of the Theater*. N.Y., Simon & Schuster, 1950.

ROBERT E. SHERWOOD, *Abe Lincoln in Illinois*. In Barrett H. Clark and William H. Davenport, eds., *Nine Modern American Plays*. N.Y., Appleton-Century-Crofts, 1951.

SOPHOCLES, *Antigone*. In Barrett H. Clark, ed., *World Drama*, Vol. I. N.Y., Appleton-Century, 1933.

———, *Electra*. In *Electra and Other Plays*. N.Y., Penguin Classics, 1953.

WOLE SOYINKA, *The Strong Breed*. In *Five Plays*. N.Y., Oxford Univ. Press, 1968.

JOSEPH STERN and SHELDON HARNICK, *Fiddler on the Roof*. N.Y., Crown, 1964.

TOM STOPPARD, *Rosencrantz and Guildenstern Are Dead*. N.Y., Grove, 1967.

AUGUST STRINDBERG, *The Father*. In John Gassner, ed., *A Treasury of the Theater*. N.Y., Simon & Schuster, 1950.

JOHN MILLINGTON SYNGE, *Riders to the Sea*. In George Jean Nathan, ed., *Five Great Modern Irish Plays*. N.Y., Modern Library, 1941.

BOOTH TARKINGTON, *Beauty and the Jacobin*. In Helen Louise Cohen, ed., *One-Act Plays by Modern Authors*. N.Y., Harcourt, Brace & World, 1934.

ALTHEA THURSTON, *Exchange*. In Roland B. Lewis, ed., *Contemporary One-Act Plays*. N.Y., Scribner's, 1922.

FRANK TOMPKINS, *Sham*. In George A. Goldstone, ed., *One-Act Plays*. Boston, Allyn & Bacon, 1926.

DON TOTHEROH, *The Stolen Prince*. In Francis J. Griffith and Joseph Mersand, eds., *Modern One-Act Plays*. N.Y., Harcourt, Brace & World, 1950.

JOHN VAN DRUTEN, *I Remember Mama*. In John Gassner, ed., *Best Plays of the Modern American Theater*, 2d series. N.Y., Crown, 1947.

SUTTON VANE, *Outward Bound*. In Bennett Cerf and Van H. Cartmell, eds., *Sixteen Famous British Plays*. Garden City, N.Y., Garden City Books, 1942.

CHARLOTTE R. WHITE, *The Wooden Horse*. In Robert Haven Schauffler, ed., *Plays for Our American Holidays*, Vol. IV. N.Y., Dodd, Mead, 1928.

PERCIVAL WILDE, *Confessional*. In George A. Goldstone, ed., *One-Act Plays*. Boston, Allyn & Bacon, 1926.

———, *The Finger of God*. In Frank Shay and Pierre Loving, eds., *Fifty Contemporary One-Act Plays*. N.Y., Appleton, 1920.

———, *Salt for Savor*. In Margaret Mayorga, ed., *Best Short Plays, 1953–1954*. N.Y., Dodd, Mead, 1954.

THORNTON WILDER, *The Happy Journey to Trenton and Camden*. In Francis J. Griffith and Joseph Mersand, eds., *Modern One-Act Plays*. N.Y., Harcourt, Brace & World, 1950.

———, *Our Town*. In John Gassner, ed., *A Treasury of the Theater*. N.Y., Simon & Schuster, 1950.

EMLYN WILLIAMS, *The Corn Is Green*. In Bennett Cerf and Van H. Cartmell, eds., *Sixteen Famous British Plays*. Garden City, N.Y., Garden City Books, 1942.

TENNESSEE WILLIAMS, *The Glass Menagerie*. In John Gassner, ed., *Best Plays of the Modern American Theater*, 2d series. N.Y., Crown, 1947.

POETRY

SAMUEL ALLEN, "To Satch." In Anna Bontempts, ed., *American Negro Poetry*. N.Y., Hill & Wang, 1964.

WILLIAM ALLINGHAM, "A Swing Song." In Alice G. Thorn, ed., *Singing Words*. N.Y., Scribner's, 1941.

ANONYMOUS, "Chevy Chase" and "Sir Patrick Spens." In Delmar Rodabaugh and Agnes L. McCarthy, eds., *Prose and Poetry of England*. Syracuse, N.Y., Singer, 1955.

ANONYMOUS, "Lord Randall." In Edith Sitwell, ed., *The Atlantic Book of British and American Poetry*. Boston, Little, Brown, 1958.

———, "The Raggle Taggle Gypsies." In Herbert Read, ed., *This Way, Delight; a Book of Poetry for the Young*. N.Y., Pantheon Books, 1956.

RICHARD ARMOUR, "Mother Tongue." From *Nights with Armour*. N.Y., McGraw-Hill, 1958.

———, *Light Armour*. N.Y., McGraw-Hill, 1954.

W. H. AUDEN, "O What Is That Sound?" In Walter Loban, Dorothy Holmstrom, and Luella B. Cook, eds., *Adventures in Appreciation*. N.Y., Harcourt, Brace & World, 1958.

KATHERINE LEE BATES, "America, the Beautiful." In Oliphant Gibbons, ed., *A Book of Poems*. N.Y., American Book, 1938.

THOMAS L. BEDDOES, "Dream Pedlary." In Louis Untermeyer, ed., *Yesterday and Today*. N.Y., Harcourt, Brace & World, 1926.

ROSEMARY BENÉT, "Nancy Hanks." In Alexander Woollcott, ed., *As You Were*. N.Y., Viking, 1943.

STEPHEN VINCENT BENÉT, "Invocation." In *John Brown's Body*. N.Y., Rinehart, 1941.

WILLIAM ROSE BENÉT, "Jesse James." In Louis Untermeyer, ed., *A Treasury of Great Poems*. N.Y., Simon & Schuster, 1942.

———, "The Skater of Ghost Lake." In Robert C. Pooley, Irvin C. Poley, Jean Cravens Leyda, and Lillian J. Zellhoefer, eds., *Exploring Life Through Literature*. Chicago, Scott, Foresman, 1957.

WILLIAM BLAKE, "The Tyger." In Dorothy Petitt, ed., *Poems to Enjoy*. N.Y., Macmillan, 1967.

F. W. BOURDILLON, "The Night Has a Thousand Eyes." In Catharine Connell, ed., *Love Poems, Old and New*. N.Y., Random House, 1943.

RUPERT BROOKE, "The Great Lover." In Luella B. Cook, Walter Loban, Oscar James Campbell, and Ruth M. Stauffer, eds., *The World Through Literature*. N.Y., Harcourt, Brace & World, 1949.

OSCAR BROWN, JR., "Brown Baby." In *A Family Is a Way of Feeling*, Gateway English Series. N.Y., Macmillan, 1966.

ROBERT BROWNING, "Cavalier Tunes." In Charles W. Cooper, ed., *Preface to Poetry*. N.Y., Harcourt, Brace & World, 1946.

———, "Childe Roland to the Dark Tower Came" and "Soliloquy of the Spanish Cloister." In Walter Blair and W. K. Chandler, eds., *Approaches to Poetry*. N.Y., Appleton-Century-Crofts, 1953.

———, "How They Brought the Good News from Ghent to Aix" and "The Pied Piper of Hamelin." In P. Edward Ernest, ed., *The Family Album of Favorite Poems*. N.Y., Grosset & Dunlap, 1959.

———, "My Last Duchess." In Rewey Belle Inglis and Josephine Spear, eds., *Adventures in English Literature*. N.Y., Harcourt, Brace & World, 1958.

———, "The Patriot." In Louis Untermeyer, ed., *A Treasury of Great Poems, English and American*. N.Y., Simon & Schuster, 1955.

BLISS CARMAN, "A Vagabond Song." In Louis Untermeyer, ed., *Modern American Poetry*. N.Y., Harcourt, Brace & World, 1942.

LEWIS CARROLL, "Jabberwocky." In Dorothy Petitt, ed., *Poems to Enjoy*. N.Y., Macmillan, 1967.

GILBERT K. CHESTERTON, "Lepanto." In Edward Hodnett, ed., *Poems to Read Aloud.* N.Y., W. W. Norton, 1957.

ELIZABETH COATSWORTH, "Daniel Webster's Horses." In Walter Loban, Dorothy Holmstrom, and Luella B. Cook, eds., *Adventures in Appreciation.* N.Y., Harcourt, Brace & World, 1958.

———, "Swift Things Are Beautiful." In Miriam B. Huber, ed., *Story and Verse for Children.* N.Y., Macmillan, 1940.

ROBERT P. TRISTRAM COFFIN, "Hound on the Church Porch." From *Collected Poems.* N.Y., Macmillan, 1948.

SAMUEL TAYLOR COLERIDGE, "The Rime of the Ancient Mariner." In Louis Untermeyer, ed., *A Treasury of Great Poems.* N.Y., Simon & Schuster, 1942.

NATHALIA CRANE, "The Blind Girl." In Elias Lieberman, ed., *Poems for Enjoyment.* N.Y., Harper, 1931.

ADELAIDE CRAPSEY, "November Night" and "The Warning." In Dorothy Petitt, ed., *Poems to Remember.* N.Y., Macmillan, 1967.

WILLIAM CRITTENDON, "Neptune's Steeds." In Harriet M. Lucas, ed., *Prose and Poetry of Today.* Syracuse, N.Y., Singer, 1941.

WALTER DE LA MARE, "The Listeners." In Luella B. Cook, Walter Loban, Oscar James Campbell, and Ruth M. Stauffer, eds., *The World Through Literature.* N.Y., Harcourt, Brace & World, 1949.

———, "Silver." In Louis Untermeyer, ed., *Modern American and Modern British Poetry,* rev. ed. N.Y., Harcourt, Brace & World, 1955.

———, "The Song of the Mad Prince." In Janet Adam Smith, ed., *The Faber Book of Children's Verse.* London, Faber & Faber, 1953.

EMILY DICKINSON, "Autumn," "I Had No Time to Hate," and "Much Madness Is Divinest Sense." In Mabel Loomis Todd and T. W. Higginson, eds., *Emily Dickinson Poems,* 1st and 2d series. Cleveland, World, 1948.

———, "Tell All the Truth But Tell It Slant," Poem No. 449 in *Bolts of Melody,* N.Y., Harper, 1945.

———, "There Is No Frigate Like a Book." In John Gehlmann and Mary Rives Bowman, eds., *Adventures in American Literature.* N.Y., Harcourt, Brace & World, 1958.

T. S. ELIOT, "Macavity: the Mystery Cat" and "The Waste Land." In *The Complete Poems and Plays of T. S. Eliot.* N.Y., Harcourt, Brace & World, 1952.

RALPH WALDO EMERSON, "Concord Hymn." In Louis Untermeyer, ed., *A Treasury of Great Poems.* N.Y., Simon & Schuster, 1942.

MARI EVANS, "If There Be Sorrow." In Langston Hughes, ed., *New Negro Poets: USA.* Bloomington, Ind., Indiana Univ. Press, 1964.

ANATOLE FRANCE, "A Roman Senator." In Luella B. Cook, Walter Loban, Ruth M. Stauffer, and Robert Freier, eds., *People in Literature.* N.Y., Harcourt, Brace & World, 1957.

ROBERT FROST, "Birches," "Mending Wall," "Stopping by Woods on a Snowy Evening," and "Two Tramps in Mud Time." In Louis Untermeyer, ed., *Modern British and Modern American Poetry,* rev. ed. N.Y., Harcourt, Brace & World, 1955.

———, "The Death of the Hired Man." In Luella B. Cook, Walter Loban, Ruth M. Stauffer, and Robert Freier, eds., *People in Literature.* N.Y., Harcourt, Brace & World, 1957.

———, "Dust of Snow." In Dorothy Petitt, ed., *Poems to Enjoy.* N.Y., Macmillan, 1967.

ROBERT FROST, "The Freedom of the Moon." In Elias Lieberman, ed., *Poems for Enjoyment*. N.Y., Harper, 1931.

ETHEL R. FULLER, "Wind Is a Cat." In Blanche J. Thompson, ed., *More Silver Pennies*. N.Y., Macmillan, 1938.

JOHANN WOLFGANG VON GOETHE, "The Erl King." In Rewey Belle Inglis and William K. Stewart, eds., *Adventures in World Literature*, rev. ed. N.Y., Harcourt, Brace & World, 1958.

THOMAS GRAY, "Elegy Written in a Country Churchyard." In Rewey Belle Inglis and Josephine Spear, eds., *Adventures in English Literature*. N.Y., Harcourt, Brace & World, 1958.

KAHLIL GIBRAN, *The Prophet*. N.Y., Knopf, 1923.

ARTHUR GUITERMAN, "Death and General Putnam." In William Cole, ed., *Poems of Magic and Spells*. N.Y., World, 1960.

HEINRICH HEINE, "The Lorelei." In Luella B. Cook, Walter Loban, Ruth M. Stauffer, and Robert Freier, eds., *People in Literature*. N.Y., Harcourt, Brace & World, 1957.

ROY HELTON, "Old Christmas Morning." In Walter Loban, Dorothy Holmstrom, and Luella B. Cook, eds., *Adventures in Appreciation*. N.Y., Harcourt, Brace & World, 1958.

WILLIAM E. HENLEY, "Invictus." In Louis Untermeyer, ed., *Yesterday and Today*. N.Y., Harcourt, Brace & World, 1926.

ROBERT HERRICK, "To Daffodils." In Louis Untermeyer, ed., *A Treasury of Great Poems*. N.Y., Simon & Schuster, 1942.

OLIVER WENDELL HOLMES, "Ballad of the Oysterman" and "The Deacon's Masterpiece." In Ogden Nash, ed., *The Moon Is Shining Bright as Day; an Anthology of Good-humored Verse*. Phila., Lippincott, 1953.

———, "The Chambered Nautilus." In John Gehlmann and Mary Rives Bowman, eds., *Adventures in American Literature*. N.Y., Harcourt, Brace & World, 1958.

———, "Old Ironsides." In Louis Untermeyer, ed., *Anthology of New England Poets*. N.Y., Random House, 1948.

HOMER, *The Odyssey*. Trans. by Barbara L. Pickard. N.Y., Walck, 1952.

THOMAS HOOD, "Past and Present." In Elizabeth O'Daly and E. W. Nieman, eds., *Adventures for Readers*, Book I. N.Y., Harcourt, Brace & World, 1958.

GERARD MANLEY HOPKINS, "Pied Beauty." In Louis Untermeyer, ed., *A Treasury of Great Poems*. N.Y., Simon & Schuster, 1942.

LADY HORIKAWA, "How Can One E'er Be Sure." In Elias Lieberman, ed., *Poems for Enjoyment*. N.Y., Harper, 1931.

A. E. HOUSMAN, "Loveliest of Trees, the Cherry Now." In Dorothy Petitt, ed., *Poems to Remember*. N.Y., Macmillan, 1967.

———, "To an Athlete Dying Young." In Louis Untermeyer, ed., *A Treasury of Great Poems*. N.Y., Simon & Schuster, 1942.

———, "When I Was One-and-Twenty." In Walter Loban, Dorothy Holmstrom, and Luella B. Cook, eds., *Adventures in Appreciation*. N.Y., Harcourt, Brace & World, 1958.

RICHARD HOVEY, "The Sea Gypsy." In J. N. Hook, Blanche E. Peavey, Miriam H. Thompson, Vesta M. Parsons, and Frank M. Rice, eds., *Literature of Achievement*. Boston, Ginn, 1957.

LANGSTON HUGHES, "African Dance." In Blanche J. Thompson, ed., *More Silver Pennies*. N.Y., Macmillan, 1938.

LANGSTON HUGHES, "April Rain Song." In May Hill Arbuthnot, ed., *Time for Poetry.* Chicago, Scott, Foresman, 1952.

————, "Mother to Son." In Dorothy Petitt, ed., *Poems to Remember.* N.Y., Macmillan, 1967.

EVELYN TOOLEY HUNT, "Taught Me Purple." In *A Family Is a Way of Feeling,* Gateway English Series. N.Y., Macmillan, 1966.

ROBINSON JEFFERS, "To His Father." In Carl Withers, ed., *The Penguin Book of Sonnets.* N.Y., Penguin, 1943.

JAMES WELDON JOHNSON, "The Creation." In Arna Bontemps, ed., *Golden Slippers.* N.Y., Harper, 1941.

JOHN KEATS, "La Belle Dame sans Merci." In Walter Loban and Rosalind A. Olmsted, eds., *Adventures in Appreciation.* N.Y., Harcourt, Brace & World, 1963.

————, "The Eve of St. Agnes." In Luella B. Cook, Walter Loban, Oscar James Campbell, and Ruth M. Stauffer, eds., *The World Through Literature.* N.Y., Harcourt, Brace & World, 1949.

————, "Upon First Looking into Chapman's Homer." In Rewey Belle Inglis and Josephine Spear, eds., *Adventures in English Literature.* N.Y., Harcourt, Brace & World, 1958.

OMAR KHAYYÁM, *The Rubáiyát.* Cranbury, N.J., A. F. Barnes, 1965.

CHARLES KINGSLEY, "The Old Song." In Elias Lieberman, ed., *Poems for Enjoyment.* N.Y., Harper, 1931.

RUDYARD KIPLING, "Ballad of East and West" and "Recessional." In Rewey Belle Inglis and Josephine Spear, eds., *Adventures in English Literature.* N.Y., Harcourt, Brace & World, 1958.

————, "Boots" and "If." In Herbert Potell, Marian Lovrien, and Prudence Bostwick, eds., *Adventures for Today.* N.Y., Harcourt, Brace & World, 1955.

————, "Danny Deever." In Walter Loban, Dorothy Holmstrom, and Luella B. Cook, eds., *Adventures in Appreciation.* N.Y., Harcourt, Brace & World, 1958.

SIDNEY LANIER, "Song of the Chattahoochee." In John Gehlmann and Mary Rives Bowman, eds., *Adventures in American Literature.* N.Y., Harcourt, Brace & World, 1958.

EDWARD LEAR, "The Owl and the Pussy-Cat." In P. Edward Ernest, ed., *The Family Album of Favorite Poems.* N.Y., Grosset & Dunlap, 1959.

RICHARD LE GALLIENNE, "I Meant to Do My Work Today." In Horace J. McNeil, ed., *Poems for a Machine Age.* N.Y., McGraw-Hill, 1941.

VACHEL LINDSAY, "The Bronco That Would Not Be Broken." In Elizabeth C. O'Daly and Egbert W. Nieman, eds., *Adventures for Readers,* Book I. N.Y., Harcourt, Brace & World, 1958.

————, "General William Booth Enters into Heaven." In Louis Untermeyer, ed., *Modern American and Modern British Poetry,* rev. ed. N.Y., Harcourt, Brace & World, 1955.

————, "The Potatoes' Dance" and "The Santa Fe Trail." From *Collected Poems.* N.Y., Macmillan, 1930.

HENRY W. LONGFELLOW, "King Robert of Sicily." In Elinor Parker, ed., *100 Story Poems.* N.Y., T. Y. Crowell, 1951.

————, "Nature." In J. N. Hook, Mildred Foster, Nell M. Robinson, Charles F. Webb, and Miriam H. Thompson, eds., *Literature of America.* Boston, Ginn, 1957.

HENRY W. LONGFELLOW, "Paul Revere's Ride." In Louis Untermeyer, ed., *A Treasury of Great Poems*. N.Y., Simon & Schuster, 1942.

JAMES MC CALL, "The New Negro." In Anna Bontempts, ed., *American Negro Poetry*. N.Y., Hill & Wang, 1964.

PHYLLIS MC GINLEY, "Reflections Dental." In *The Love Letters of Phyllis McGinley*. N.Y., Viking, 1954.

ROD MC KUEN, "Holidays." In Rod McKuen, *Stanyan Street and Other Sorrows*. N.Y., Random House, 1966.

IRENE RUTHERFORD MCLEOD, "Lone Dog." In Horace J. McNeil, ed., *Poems for a Machine Age*. N.Y., McGraw-Hill, 1941.

JOHN GILLESPIE MAGEE, "High Flight." In Olga Perschbacher and Dorothy Wilde, eds., *America Speaking*. Chicago, Scott, Foresman, 1943.

EDWIN MARKHAM, "Lincoln, the Man of the People." In Louis Untermeyer, ed., *Modern American and Modern British Poetry*, mid-century ed. N.Y., Harcourt, Brace & World, 1950.

———, "The Man with the Hoe." In Luella B. Cook, Walter Loban, Ruth M. Stauffer, and Robert Freier, eds., *People in Literature*. N.Y., Harcourt, Brace & World, 1957.

JOHN MASEFIELD, "Cargoes," "Sea Fever," and "A Wanderer's Song." In Louis Untermeyer, ed., *Modern American and Modern British Poetry*, rev. ed. N.Y., Harcourt, Brace & World, 1955.

———, "Tewkesbury Road." In Mary Gould Davis, ed., *The Girl's Book of Verse*. Phila., Lippincott, 1952.

EDGAR LEE MASTERS, "Petit, the Poet." In Louis Untermeyer, ed., *Modern American and Modern British Poetry*, mid-century ed. N.Y., Harcourt, Brace & World, 1950.

———, *Spoon River Anthology*. N.Y., Macmillan, 1931.

MILDRED P. (MERRYMAN) MEIGS, "The Pirate Don Durk of Dowdee." In Helen F. Daringer and A. Eaton, eds., *The Poet's Craft*. N.Y., World, 1935.

EDNA ST. VINCENT MILLAY, "God's World." In John Gehlmann and Mary Rives Bowman, eds., *Adventures in American Literature*. N.Y., Harcourt, Brace & World, 1958.

———, "Justice Denied in Massachusetts." In Louis Untermeyer, ed., *Modern American Poetry*, mid-century ed. N.Y., Harcourt, Brace & World, 1950.

———, "Renascence." In Louis Untermeyer, ed., *Modern American and Modern British Poetry*, rev. ed. N.Y., Harcourt, Brace & World, 1955.

JOAQUIN MILLER, "Columbus." In P. Edward Ernest, ed., *The Family Album of Favorite Poems*. N.Y., Grosset & Dunlap, 1959.

A. A. MILNE, *When We Were Very Young*. N.Y., Dutton, 1924.

ANGELA MORGAN, "Work: A Song of Triumph." In Alice Cooper, ed., *Poems of Today*. Boston, Ginn, 1930.

ALFRED NOYES, "The Barrel Organ." In Louis Untermeyer, ed., *Modern American and Modern British Poetry*, mid-century ed. N.Y., Harcourt, Brace & World, 1950.

———, "The Highwayman." In P. Edward Ernest, ed., *The Family Album of Favorite Poems*. N.Y., Grosset & Dunlap, 1959.

JAMES OPPENHEIM, "The Slave." In Elias Lieberman, ed., *Poems for Enjoyment*. N.Y., Harper, 1931.

BONARO OVERSTREET, "Unlost." From *Hands Laid upon the Wind*. N.Y., Norton, 1955.

EDGAR ALLAN POE, "Annabel Lee." In P. Edward Ernest, ed., *The Family Album of Favorite Poems*. N.Y., Grosset & Dunlap, 1959.

EDGAR ALLAN POE, "El Dorado." In Walter Loban, Dorothy Holmstrom, and Luella B. Cook, eds., *Adventures in Appreciation*. N.Y., Harcourt, Brace & World, 1958.

——, "The Raven." In Elinor Parker, ed., *100 Story Poems*. N.Y., Crowell, 1951.

EDWIN ARLINGTON ROBINSON, "Miniver Cheevy" and "Richard Cory." In Louis Untermeyer, ed., *Modern American and Modern British Poetry*, rev. ed. N.Y., Harcourt, Brace & World, 1955.

CHRISTINA ROSSETTI, "A Birthday." In Rewey Belle Inglis and Josephine Spear, eds., *Adventures in English Literature*. N.Y., Harcourt, Brace & World, 1958.

——, "Lullaby." In Lillian Hollowell, ed., *A Book of Children's Literature*. N.Y., Rinehart, 1950.

——, "Uphill." In Louis Untermeyer, ed., *A Treasury of Great Poems*. N.Y., Simon & Schuster, 1942.

——, "Who Has Seen the Wind?" In Harold H. Wagenheim, Elizabeth Voris Brattig, and Matthew Dolkey, eds., *Our Reading Heritage, Ourselves and Others*. N.Y., Holt, 1956.

——, "The Wind Has Such a Rainy Sound." In May Hill Arbuthnot, ed., *Time for Poetry*. Chicago, Scott, Foresman, 1952.

ARCHIBALD RUTLEDGE, "Lee." In Harriet Lucas and Elizabeth Ansorge, eds., *Prose and Poetry of Today*. Syracuse, N.Y., Leigee, 1941.

CARL SANDBURG, "Chicago." In Oscar Williams, ed., *A Little Treasury of Modern Poetry*. N.Y., Scribner's, 1950.

——, "Fog" and "Four Preludes on Playthings of the Wind." In Luella B. Cook, Walter Loban, Ruth M. Stauffer, and Robert Freier, eds., *People in Literature*. N.Y., Harcourt, Brace & World, 1957.

——, "Jazz Fantasia" and "Primer Lesson." In Dorothy Petitt, ed., *Poems to Enjoy*. N.Y., Macmillan, 1967.

LEW SARETT, "Four Little Foxes." In Adolph Gillis and William Rose Benét, eds., *Poems for Modern Youth*. Boston, Houghton Mifflin, 1938.

——, "Indian Sleep Song," "Marching Pines," "Sweetwater Range," and "Wind in the Pine." In *The Box of God*. N.Y., Holt, 1922.

ALAN SEEGER, "I Have a Rendezvous with Death." In Louis Untermeyer, ed., *Yesterday and Today*. N.Y., Harcourt, Brace & World, 1926.

WILLIAM SHAKESPEARE, "Blow, Blow, Thou Winter Wind." In Rewey Belle Inglis and Josephine Spear, eds., *Adventures in English Literature*. N.Y., Harcourt, Brace & World, 1958.

KARL SHAPIRO, "Auto Wreck" and "Elegy for a Dead Soldier." In John Ciardi, ed., *Mid-Century Poets*. N.Y., Twayne, 1950.

PERCY BYSSHE SHELLEY, "Ode to the West Wind." In Louis Untermeyer, ed., *A Treasury of Great Poems*. N.Y., Simon & Schuster, 1942.

——, "Ozymandias." In Norman C. Stageberg and Wallace C. Anderson, eds., *Poetry as Experience*. N.Y., American Book, 1950.

——, "To Night." In Luella B. Cook, Walter Loban, Oscar James Campbell, and Ruth M. Stauffer, eds., *The World Through Literature*. N.Y., Harcourt, Brace & World, 1949.

——, "To ——." In Elias Lieberman, ed., *Poems for Enjoyment*. N.Y., Harper, 1931.

ROBERT SOUTHEY, "How the Waters Come Down at Lodore." In Luella B. Cook, Walter Loban, Ruth M. Stauffer, and Robert Freier, eds., *People in Literature*. N.Y., Harcourt, Brace & World, 1957.

STEPHEN SPENDER, "The Express." In Oscar Williams, ed., *A Little Treasury of Modern Poetry*. N.Y., Scribner's, 1950.

ROBERT LOUIS STEVENSON, "Requiem." In Walter Loban, Dorothy Holmstrom, and Luella B. Cook, eds., *Adventures in Appreciation*. N.Y., Harcourt, Brace & World, 1958.

———, "Where Go the Boats." In May Hill Arbuthnot, ed., *Time for Poetry*. Chicago, Scott, Foresman, 1952.

———, "The Wind." In Miriam B. Huber, ed., *Story and Verse for Children*. N.Y., Macmillan, 1940.

SARA TEASDALE, "Barter," "The Falling Star," "Stars," "There Will Come Soft Rains," and "Wood Song." From *Collected Poems*. N.Y., Macmillan, 1937.

ALFRED, LORD TENNYSON, "Break, Break, Break," "Bugle Song," and "Ulysses." In Rewey Belle Inglis and Josephine Spear, eds., *Adventures in English Literature*. N.Y., Harcourt, Brace & World, 1958.

———, "The Charge of the Light Brigade." In Egbert W. Nieman and Elizabeth C. O'Daly, eds., *Adventures for Readers*, Book II. N.Y., Harcourt, Brace & World, 1958.

———, *Idylls of the King*. N.Y., Heritage, 1939.

———, "Sweet and Low." In Luella B. Cook, Walter Loban, Oscar James Campbell, and Ruth M. Stauffer, eds., *The World Through Literature*. N.Y., Harcourt, Brace & World, 1949.

ERNEST L. THAYER, "Casey at the Bat." In P. Edward Ernest, ed., *The Family Album of Favorite Poems*. N.Y., Grosset & Dunlap, 1959.

DYLAN THOMAS, "Fern Hill" and "Do Not Go Gentle into That Good Night." In C. Day Lewis and John Herbert Nelson, eds., *Chatto Book of Modern Poetry 1915–1955*. London, Chatto & Windus, 1959.

FRANCIS THOMPSON, "To a Snowflake." In Louis Untermeyer, ed., *Modern American and Modern British Poetry*, rev. ed. N.Y., Harcourt, Brace & World, 1955.

FRANCIS O. TICKNOR, "Little Giffin." In George W. Norvell and Carol Hovious, eds., *Conquest*, Book II. Boston, Heath, 1947.

JAMES P. VAUGHN, "Three Kings." In Langston Hughes, ed., *New Negro Poets: USA*. Bloomington, Ind., Indiana Univ. Press, 1964.

MARGARET WALKER, "We Have Been Believers." In *For My People*. New Haven, Conn., Yale Univ. Press, 1942.

WALT WHITMAN, "Beat! Beat! Drums!" and "I Hear America Singing." In John Gehlmann and Mary Rives Bowman, eds., *Adventures in American Literature*. N.Y., Harcourt, Brace & World, 1958.

———, "O Captain! My Captain!" In Adolph Gillis and William Rose Benét, eds., *Poems for Modern Youth*. Boston, Houghton Mifflin, 1938.

———, "Pioneers! O Pioneers!" In Luella B. Cook, Walter Loban, Tremaine McDowell, eds., *America Through Literature*. N.Y., Harcourt, Brace & World, 1952.

DIXIE WILLSON, "The Mist and All." In Matilda M. Elsea, ed., *Choice Poems for Elementary Grades*. N.Y., Edwards Press, 1944.

WILLIAM WORDSWORTH, "Composed upon Westminster Bridge." In Rewey Belle Inglis and Josephine Spear, eds., *Adventures in English Literature*. N.Y., Harcourt, Brace & World, 1958.

———, "It Is a Beauteous Evening, Calm and Free." In J. N. Hook, Mildred Foster, Nell M. Robinson, and Charles F. Webb, eds., *Literature of England*. Boston, Ginn, 1957.

ELINOR WYLIE, "Pretty Words," "Village Mystery," and "Velvet Shoes." In Elinor Wylie, *Collected Poems*. N.Y., Knopf, 1963.

WILLIAM BUTLER YEATS, "The Song of Wandering Aengus." In Louis Untermeyer, ed., *Modern American and Modern British Poetry*, rev. ed. N.Y., Harcourt, Brace & World, 1955.

ONE NO YOSHIKI, "My Love." In Elias Lieberman, ed., *Poems for Enjoyment*. N.Y., Harper, 1931.

AUDIO-VISUAL MATERIALS
Films and Filmstrips

A.B.C. of Puppetry (B)
And Now Miguel (UWF)
Ansel Adams, Photographer (Daw)
Art and Motion (EBF)
Art in Our World (Darby)
Begone Dull Care (IFB)
Build Your Vocabulary (Cor)
Building Better Paragraphs (Cor)
Captains Courageous (TFC)
The Cinematographer (TFC)
Chushingura (CG)
Do Words Ever Fool You? (Cor)
Driven Westward (TFC)
Due Process of Law Denied (TFC)
Fiddle-De-Dee (IFB)
Four Ways to Drama (UCE)
Getting the World's News (CA)
The Good Loser (Cor)
The Great Heart (TFC)
The House of Rothschild (TFC)
How Green Was My Valley (TFC)
How Honest Are You? (Cor)
How to Judge Facts (Cor)
In the Heat of the Night (UA)
Introduction to Shakespeare (YAF)
Johnny Appleseed (SVE)
The Literature of Freedom (PS)
The Loon's Necklace (EBF)
Macbeth—TV Production (AF)
Magazine Magic (Curtis)
Mahatma Gandhi (EBF)
Make Your Own Decisions (Cor)
Master Will Shakespeare (TFC)
Nature's Half Acre (Disney)
Newspaper Story (EBF)
Nothing But a Man (WCG)

Oliver Wendell Holmes (EBF)
On the Waterfront (AFC)
One Potato, Two Potato (UEX)
The Photographer (UWF)
The Prairie (Barr)
The Public Life of Abraham Lincoln (Nu-Art)
The Quiet One (CF)
Radio, Television, Motion Pictures (YAF)
A Raisin in the Sun (AFC)
Right or Wrong? (Cor)
The Rime of the Ancient Mariner (UCE)
The River (UWF)
Rumor Clinic (ADL)
The Screen Director (TFC)
The Seventh Seal (JF)
Shoe Shine (WCG)
The Story of Dr. Carver (TFC)
The Story of Louis Pasteur (TFC)
The Story That Couldn't Be Printed (TFC)
The Suicide of Society (NET)
The Tell Tale Heart (McGraw-Hill)
Thomas Jefferson (EFC)
Understanding Your Ideals (Cor)
What Do You Think? (CBR)
Words: Their Origin, Use, and Spelling (Long)
Yours Is the Land (EBF)
Understanding Movies (TFC)
Washington Irving (EBF)
Whispers (TFC)
You and Your Newspaper (PS)

The films and filmstrips listed exemplify teaching aids used in specific situations in this textbook. Each year the number of such materials increases so rapidly that even the most selective list soon becomes out of date. The solution to the problem of finding effective audio-visual material lies in the continual search by individuals, each seeking the best for his particular purpose with his particular students. Producers are more than willing to keep interested teachers informed of current releases. For instance, those whose names are on the mailing list of Encyclopaedia Britannica Films have probably received information concerning *An Introduction to the Humanities*. This series of twelve motion pictures in color, each twenty-eight minutes in length, focuses on three historical periods—Modern, Elizabethan, and classical Greek. The four films for each period give scenes from dramatic literature—*Our Town, Hamlet, Oedipus the King*—together with commentary that helps the student appreciate both the cultural heritage of the theater and the timeless universality of the individual dramatic works. The complete series offers a stimulating introduction to the significance of the humanities. This production, made possible by a grant from the Fund for the Advancement of Education, is only one example of the excellent material that is continually being made available for classroom use.

SOURCES

ADL: Anti-Defamation League, 212 Fifth Ave., N.Y., N.Y. 10001.

AF: Association Films, 347 Madison Ave., N.Y., N.Y. 10017.

AFC: Audio Film Center, 406 Clement St., San Francisco, Calif. 94118.

B: Baily Films, Inc., 6509 De Longpre Ave., Hollywood, Calif. 90028.

Barr: Arthur Barr Films, 1265 Bresee Ave., Pasadena, Calif. 91104.

CBR: Canadian Board of Review, 221 Victoria St., Vancouver, B.C.

CG: Cinema Guild, Edward Landberg, 2495 Shattuck Ave., Berkeley, Calif. 94704.

CF: Contemporary Films, 267 West 25th St., N.Y., N.Y. 10001.

Cor: Coronet Films, 65 East South Water St., Chicago, Ill. 60601.

CA: Current Affairs, Films Division, Key Productions, 18 East 41st St., N.Y., N.Y. 10017.

Curtis: Curtis Publishing Co., Philadelphia, Penna. 19105.

Darby: Darby Films, 6509 De Longpre Ave., Hollywood, Calif. 90028.

Daw: Larry Dawson Productions, 611 Howard St., San Francisco, Calif. 94105.

Disney: Walt Disney Productions, 2400 West Alameda, Burbank, Calif. 91506.

EBF: Encyclopaedia Britannica Films, 5625 Hollywood Blvd., Hollywood, Calif. 90028.

IFB: International Film Bureau, 332 South Michigan Ave., Chicago, Ill. 60604.

JF: Janus Films, 24 West 58th St., N.Y., N.Y. 10019.

Long: Long Filmslide Service, 7505 Fairmount Ave., El Cerrito, Calif. 94530.

McGraw-Hill: Text-Film Dept., McGraw-Hill, 330 West 42nd St., N.Y., N.Y. 10036

NET: Net Film Service, Indiana University, Audio-Visual Center, Bloomington, Ind. 47401.

Nu-Art: Nu-Art Films, 112 West 48th St., N.Y., N.Y. 10019.

PS: Popular Science Publishing Co., 355 Lexington Ave., N.Y., N.Y. 10017.

SVE: Society for Visual Education, 1345 Diversey Parkway, Chicago, Ill. 60614.

TFC: Teaching Film Custodians, 25 West 43rd St., N.Y., N.Y. 10036.

UA: United Artists, Hollywood, Calif. 90028.

UWF: United World Films, 105 East 106th St., N.Y., N.Y. 10029.

UCE: University of California Extension, Educational Film Sales, Los Angeles, Calif. 90014.
UEX: University Extension, University of California, Berkeley, Calif. 94720.
WCG: Western Cinema Guild (Brandon Films), 381 Bush St., San Francisco, Calif. 94104.
YAF: Young America Films, McGraw-Hill, 330 West 42nd St., N.Y., N.Y. 10036.

Recordings

Americans Speaking (NCTE)
America Was Promises (Ling)
The American Dream (IDE)
Ase's Death (Columbia AL-35)
The Changing English Language (FW)
The Changing Literary Style (FW)
Danse Macabre (Capitol P-8296)
Down in the Valley (RCA Victor DM 1367)
Eine Kleine Nachtmusik (Columbia MS 6356)
Fêtes (Columbia MS 6271)
Finlandia (Columbia AL-9)
Green Christmas (Capitol 4097)
I Can Hear It Now (Columbia ML 4095, 4261, 4340)
Images (Columbia ML 4979)
In the American Tradition (D:AE)
Macbeth—tone poem (Westminster 18078)
Macbeth—drama, Old Vic (Victor LM 6010)
Many Voices: Six volumes to accompany *Adventures in Literature*, grades 7 to 12 (HBW)
   "Irtnog" by E. B. White, read by Hiram Sherman
   "Three Days to See" by Helen Keller, read by Nancy Wickwire
   "To Helen" and "The Bells" by Edgar Allan Poe, read by Alexander Scourby
   "Behind the Ranges" by James Ramsey Ullman, read by Arnold Moss
Mark Twain Tonight—Holbrook (Columbia OL 5440)
My Fair Lady (Columbia OS2015)
No Man Is an Island (D:AE)
Nuages (Columbia 6271)
Our Changing Language (McGraw-Hill)
Paul Revere (Stud)
Phonetic Punctuation, selection from Caught in the Act by Victor Borge (Columbia CCL646)
Rhythms of the World (FW)
Saint Joan, read by Siobhan McKenna (RCA Victor 6133)
Sorry, Wrong Number, read by Agnes Moorehead (Decca 9062)
Sounds of Chaucer's English (NCTE)
"Spellbound" (Capitol T-456)
Splendid Legend (SG)
Stories to Remember (IDE)
Tales from the Olympian Gods (Decca DA 475)

West Side Story (Columbia OS2001)
When Greek Meets Greek: A Study in Values—thirteen records (NAEB)
A Word in Your Ear (NAEB)
The Young Person's Guide to the Orchestra (Westminster 18372)

SOURCES

ABC: American Book Co., 55 Fifth Ave., N.Y., N.Y. 10003.
Caedmon: Caedmon Records, Inc., 505 Eighth Ave., N.Y., N.Y. 10019.
Carmel: Carmel-by-the-Sea Recording Co., P.O. Box 572, Monterey, Calif. 93940.
D:AE: Decca: Audio Education, 445 Park Ave., N.Y., N.Y. 10022.
FW: Folkways/Scholastic Records, 50 West 44th St., N.Y., N.Y. 10036.
HBW: Harcourt, Brace & World, 757 Third Ave., N.Y., N.Y. 10017.
IDE: Institute for Dramatic Education, 212 Fifth Ave., N.Y., N.Y. 10010.
Ling: Linguaphone Institute, 30 Rockefeller Plaza, N.Y., N.Y. 10020.
McGraw-Hill: McGraw-Hill, 330 West 42nd St., N.Y., N.Y. 10036.
NAEB: National Association of Educational Broadcasters, Suite 1101, 1346 Connecticut Ave. N.W., Washington, D.C. 20036.
NCTE: National Council of Teachers of English, 508 South Sixth St., Champaign, Ill. 61820.
SA: Spoken Arts, Inc., 59 Locust Ave., New Rochelle, N.Y. 10801.
SFC: Scott, Foresman & Co., 1900 E. Lake Ave., Glenview, Ill. 60025.
SG: School Guild-Allied Recording Co., 3232 Greenpoint Ave., Long Island City, N.Y. 11101.
Stud: Studidisc:Audio-Visual Division, Popular Science Publishing Co., 355 Lexington Ave., N.Y., N.Y. 10017.
SW: Spoken Word-Folkways, 117 West 46th St., N.Y., N.Y. 10036.
WBS: World Broadcasting System, 488 Madison Ave., N.Y., N.Y. 10020.

Records with familiar commercial labels may be ordered through regular dealers. The W. Schwann Catalog, 137 Newbury St., Boston, Mass. 02116, lists current releases monthly. NCTE publishes an annotated recording list for teachers of English.

Recordings to Supplement the Study of Literature

DRAMA

MAXWELL ANDERSON, *High Tor*—TV Production (Decca 8272); *Lost in the Stars* (Decca DL 8028)
ANONYMOUS, *Everyman*—Meredith (Caedmon 1031) NCTE
ANTA, Album of Stars—Hayes, Le Gallienne, Gielgud, et al. (Decca DL 9002 and 9009)
STEPHEN VINCENT BENÉT, *John Brown's Body*—Power, Anderson, Massey (Columbia OSL-181)
RUDOLF BESIER, *The Barretts of Wimpole Street*—Cornell, Quayle (Caedmon 1071)
CHRISTOPHER FRY, *The Lady's Not for Burning* (Decca DX-110)
ROBINSON JEFFERS, *Medea*—Anderson (Decca DL 9000)
ARTHUR MILLER, *Death of a Salesman*—Mitchell (Decca DX 102); Discussion by the author of attitudes toward character portrayal, with readings from *Death of a Salesman* and *The Crucible* (SA 704). Excellent recording, also available from Caedmon Recordings.

FERENC MOLNÁR, *Carousel (Liliom)* (Decca 9020)
RICHARD RODGERS and OSCAR HAMMERSTEIN II, *The King and I* (Decca DL 9008)
EDMUND ROSTAND, *Cyrano de Bergerac*—Ferrer (Capitol S-283)
WILLIAM SHAKESPEARE
   "Ages of Man"—Gielgud (Columbia OL 5390)
   As You Like It—Cambridge University, Marlowe Society (London A 4336)
   Hamlet—Gielgud (Victor LM 6007)
   Immortal Scenes and Sonnets—Evans, Redgrave (Decca 9041)
   Julius Caesar—Cambridge University, Marlowe Society (London A 4334)
   Julius Caesar, highlights—Brando, Gielgud, Mason (MGM E 3033)
   A Midsummer Night's Dream—Dublin Gate Theater (SW A5 131-133)
   Othello—Cambridge University, Marlowe Society (London A 4414)
   Romeo and Juliet—Old Vic (RCA Victor LM 2064)
   Soliloquies, *Henry IV* et al.—Rogers (SA 723)
   The Taming of the Shrew—Dublin Gate Theater (SW A-7 151-153)
   Twelfth Night—Dublin Gate Theater (SW A-3 116-118)
GEORGE BERNARD SHAW, *My Fair Lady* (Pygmalion) (Columbia OL 5090)
SOPHOCLES, *Antigone*—McGill University Players (FW 9861); *Oedipus Rex*—Stratford Players (Caedmon 2012)
JOHN MILLINGTON SYNGE, *Riders to the Sea*—Dublin Radio Eireann Players (SA 743)
OSCAR WILDE, *The Importance of Being Earnest*—Gielgud, Evans (Angel 3504-B)

POETRY

America Listens to Literature, to accompany *America Reads,* grades seven to twelve (SFC)
Appreciation of Poetry (NCTE RC-90-1)
Beowulf (NCTE RS-80-2)
Robert Browning—Mason (Caedmon 1048; NCTE) [1]
Lord Byron—Power (Caedmon 1042; NCTE)
Chaucer, "Canterbury Tales" (NCTE RS-80-1)
Lewis Carroll and Edward Lear, "Nonsense Verse"—Lillie, Ritchard, Holloway (Caedmon 1078; NCTE)
John Ciardi, "As If Poems"—Ciardi (FW 978; NCTE)
Samuel Taylor Coleridge—Richardson (Caedmon 1092)
E. E. Cummings—Cummings (Caedmon 1017)
Dante, "The Inferno"—Ciardi (FW FL9871; NCTE)
Early English Ballads—Read (FW FL9881; NCTE)
T. S. Eliot—Eliot (Caedmon 1045; NCTE)
Famous Poems That Tell Great Stories (Decca 9040)
Robert Frost—Frost (Caedmon 1060; NCTE)
Great Themes in Poetry (NCTE RC-90-3)
Hearing Poetry (Caedmon 1021, 1022; NCTE)
John Keats—Richardson (Caedmon 1087; NCTE)
Omar Khayyám, "The Rubáiyát"—Drake (Caedmon 1023; NCTE)
Vachel Lindsay (Caedmon 1041; NCTE)

[1] Double listing indicates that records are available to members at discount from the National Council of Teachers of English; interested teachers should write to NCTE for a current list.

Archibald Macleish—Macleish (Caedmon 1009)
Many Voices; Poetry and Prose (HBW)
Edna St. Vincent Millay—Anderson (Caedmon 1024; NCTE)
Edgar Allan Poe, Poetry and two short stories—Rathbone (Caedmon 1028; NCTE)
Percy Bysshe Shelley—Price (Caedmon 1059; NCTE)
Stephen Spender—Spender (Caedmon 1084)
Dylan Thomas—Thomas (Caedmon 1002, 1018, 1043; NCTE)
Treasury of Modern Poets (Caedmon 2006; NCTE)
Walt Whitman, "Leaves of Grass"—read by Alexander Scourby in Treasury of Walt
   Whitman (Spoken Arts Recordings, Publishers Associates, Box 8160, Universal
   City, Calif. 91608)
William Wordsworth—Hardwicke (Caedmon 1026) NCTE
Worlds of Literature (ABC WL 1, 2, 3)
William Butler Yeats—McKenna, Cusack (Caedmon 1081)

FICTION

Arabian Nights—Melchior (Decca 9013)
Stephen Crane, *Red Badge of Courage*—O'Brien (Caedmon 1040)
Charles Dickens—Williams (London A-4221)
Dickens Duets—Pettingell (SA 741)
Don Quixote—Crocker (FW 9866)
William Faulkner, Author reads from his novels and Nobel Award Speech (Caed-
   mon 1035; NCTE)
Paul Gallico, *The Snow Goose*—Marshall (Decca DL 9066)
Bret Harte, "Outcasts of Poker Flat" and "Luck of Roaring Camp" (FW 9740)
James Hilton, *Lost Horizon*—Colman (Decca 9059)
O. Henry, "Gift of the Magi" (United Artists 4013)
Rudyard Kipling, *Jungle Book*—Karloff (Caedmon 1100)
Plato, "On the Death of Socrates" (FW 9979)
Edgar Allan Poe, "The Pit and the Pendulum"—Highet (NCTE RL-20-3)
Ride with the Sun: Folktales of Many Lands (FW FC 7109)
Robert Louis Stevenson, *Treasure Island* (Mercury MSB 60018)
Stories from Irish Mythology—Susan Porter (Carmel)
Jonathan Swift, *Gulliver's Travels* (Caedmon 1099)
Tales from Ivory Towers: *Caddie Woodlawn, Silver Chief, The Good Master* et al.
   Seven records (WBS)
Mark Twain, *Huckleberry Finn* (Mercury MSB 60021); Stories (Caedmon 1027);
   Tom Sawyer (Mercury MSB 60020)
Jules Verne, *Twenty Thousand Leagues Under the Sea* (Mercury 60026)

Other Producers of Audio-Visual Materials

Audio-visual materials suitable for classroom use are being produced continually.
Teachers may keep themselves informed about current releases by having their names
placed on the mailing lists of the firms already mentioned and of others such as the
following:

Academic Film Co., 516 Fifth Ave., N.Y., N.Y. 10036.
British Information Services, 30 Rockefeller Plaza, N.Y., N.Y. 10020.

Stanley Bowmar Co., 12 Cleveland Place, Valhalla, N.Y. 10595.

Brandon Films, Inc., 200 West 57th St., N.Y., N.Y. 10019.

Churchill-Wexler Films, 801 North Seward St., Los Angeles, Calif. 90038.

Dynamic Films, Inc., 112 West 89th St., N.Y., N.Y. 10024.

Eastin Pictures Co., Putnam Bldg., Davenport, Iowa. 52801.

Enrichment Records, 246 Fifth Ave., N.Y., N.Y. 10001.

Eye Gate House, Inc., 146-01 Archer Ave., Jamaica, N.Y. 11435.

Film Images, Inc., 1860 Broadway, N.Y., N.Y. 10023.

Films of the Nations Distributors, Inc., 62 West 45th St., N.Y., N.Y. 10036.

Filmstrip House, 347 Madison Ave., N.Y., N.Y. 10017.

Ford Motor Co., Film Library, 15 East 53rd St., N.Y., N.Y. 10022.

James A. Fitzpatrick's Travel Pictures, 8624 Sunset Blvd., Hollywood, Calif. 90069.

Fleetwood Films, Inc., 10 Fiske Place, Mount Vernon, N.Y. 10550.

Gateway Productions, Inc., 1859 Powell St., San Francisco, Calif. 94133.

Ideal Pictures, Inc., 58 East South Water St., Chicago, Ill. 60601.

Informative Classroom Pictures Publishers, 31 Ottawa Ave., Grand Rapids, Mich. 49502.

Life Magazine, Inc., Filmstrip Division, 9 Rockefeller Plaza, N.Y., N.Y. 10020.

E. L. Morthole, 8855 Lincolnwood Drive, Evanston, Ill. 60203.

Museum Extension Service, 10 East 43rd St., N.Y., N.Y. 10017.

National Association of Secondary School Principals, 1201 16th St. N.W., Washington, D.C. 20006.

New York Times, School Service Department, 229 West 43rd St., N.Y., N.Y., 10018.

Pictorial Events, 597 Fifth Ave., N.Y., N.Y. 10017.

Training Aids, Inc., 7414 Beverly Blvd., Los Angeles, Calif. 90036.

Trans-World Airlines, Advertising Dept., 380 Madison Ave., N.Y., N.Y. 10017.

Unusual Films, Bob Jones University, Greenville, S.C. 29614.

United States Office of Education, Federal Radio Education Commission, Washington, D.C. 20025.

Yale University Press Film Service, 386 Park Ave. South, N.Y., N.Y. 10016.

INDEX